STREET ATLAS
Staffordshire

www.philips-maps.co.uk

First published in 1995 by

Philip's, a division of
Octopus Publishing Group Ltd
www.octopusbooks.co.uk
2-4 Heron Quays, London E14 4JP
An Hachette Livre UK Company

Third colour edition 2005
Second impression with revisions 2007
STACB

ISBN-10   0-540-08756-4 (spiral)
ISBN-13   978-0-540-08756-3 (spiral)

© Philip's 2007

Ordnance Survey®

This product includes mapping data licensed
from Ordnance Survey® with the permission of
the Controller of Her Majesty's Stationery Office.
© Crown copyright 2007. All rights reserved.
Licence number 100011710.

Printed and bound in Spain
by Cayfosa-Quebecor

Contents

III   **Key to map symbols**

IV   **Key to map pages**

VI   **Route planning**

X   **Administrative and Postcode boundaries**

1   **Street maps** at 3½ inches to 1 mile

282   **Street maps of centres of Hanley, Newcastle-under-Lyme, Longton and Stafford** at 7 inches to 1 mile

286   **Index** of towns and villages

289   **Index** of streets, hospitals, industrial estates, railway stations, schools, shopping centres, universities and places of interest

Digital Data

The exceptionally high-quality mapping found in this atlas is available as digital data in TIFF format, which is easily convertible to other bitmapped (raster) image formats.

The index is also available in digital form as a standard database table. It contains all the details found in the printed index together with the National Grid reference for the map square in which each entry is named.

For further information and to discuss your requirements, please contact james.mann@philips-maps.co.uk

PHILIP'S MAPS

the Gold Standard for drivers

◆ **Philip's street atlases cover every county in England, Wales, Northern Ireland and much of Scotland**

◆ Every named street is shown, including alleys, lanes and walkways

◆ Thousands of additional features marked: stations, public buildings, car parks, places of interest

◆ Route-planning maps to get you close to your destination

◆ Postcodes on the maps and in the index

◆ Widely used by the emergency services, transport companies and local authorities

BEST BUY • BEST BUY
Auto EXPRESS
BEST BUY • BEST BUY

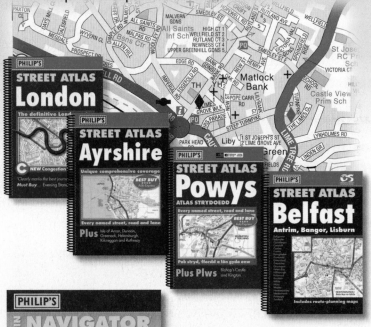

PHILIP'S
STREET ATLAS
London
The definitive Lond
NEW Congestion
'Clearly marks the best journey
Must Buy'... Evening Stan

PHILIP'S
STREET ATLAS
Ayrshire
Unique comprehensive coverage
BEST BUY
Plus Isle of Arran, Dunoon, Greenock, Helensburgh, Kilcreggan and Rothesay

PHILIP'S
STREET ATLAS
Powys
ATLAS STRYDOEDD
Every named street, road and lane
BEST BUY
Pob stryd, ffordd a lôn gyda enw
Plus Plws Bishop's Castle and Kington

PHILIP'S
STREET ATLAS
Belfast
Antrim, Bangor, Lisburn
Includes route-planning maps

PHILIP'S
NAVIGATOR BRITAIN
NAVIGATOR
Britain
New speed camera sites, now with speed limits
30
Major roads named as well as numbered
Thousands of farms, houses, tracks and footpaths
'The ultimate in UK mapping'
The Sunday Times

For national mapping, choose
Philip's Navigator Britain
the most detailed road atlas available of England, Wales and Scotland. Hailed by Auto Express as 'the ultimate road atlas', the atlas shows every road and lane in Britain.

Street atlases currently available

England

Bedfordshire and Luton	Surrey
Berkshire	East Sussex
Birmingham and West Midlands	West Sussex
Bristol and Bath	Tyne and Wear
Buckinghamshire and Milton Keynes	Warwickshire and Coventry
Cambridgeshire and Peterborough	Wiltshire and Swindon
Cheshire	Worcestershire
Cornwall	East Yorkshire Northern Lincolnshire
Cumbria	North Yorkshire
Derbyshire	South Yorkshire
Devon	West Yorkshire
Dorset	
County Durham and Teesside	**Wales**
Essex	Anglesey, Conwy and Gwynedd
North Essex	Cardiff, Swansea and The Valleys
South Essex	Carmarthenshire, Pembrokeshire and Swansea
Gloucestershire and Bristol	Ceredigion and South Gwynedd
Hampshire	Denbighshire, Flintshire, Wrexham
North Hampshire	Herefordshire Monmouthshire
South Hampshire	Powys
Herefordshire Monmouthshire	
Hertfordshire	**Scotland**
Isle of Wight	Aberdeenshire
Kent	Ayrshire
East Kent	Dumfries and Galloway
West Kent	Edinburgh and East Central Scotland
Lancashire	Fife and Tayside
Leicestershire and Rutland	Glasgow and West Central Scotland
Lincolnshire	Inverness and Moray
Liverpool and Merseyside	Lanarkshire
London	Scottish Borders
Greater Manchester	
Norfolk	**Northern Ireland**
Northamptonshire	County Antrim and County Londonderry
Northumberland	County Armagh and County Down
Nottinghamshire	Belfast
Oxfordshire	County Tyrone and County Fermanagh
Shropshire	
Somerset	
Staffordshire	
Suffolk	

Key to map symbols

III

22a	**Motorway** with junction number
	Primary route – dual/single carriageway
	A road – dual/single carriageway
	B road – dual/single carriageway
	Minor road – dual/single carriageway
	Other minor road – dual/single carriageway
	Road under construction
	Tunnel, covered road
	Rural track, private road or narrow road in urban area
	Gate or obstruction to traffic (restrictions may not apply at all times or to all vehicles)
	Path, bridleway, byway open to all traffic, road used as a public path
	Pedestrianised area
DY7	**Postcode boundaries**
	County and unitary authority boundaries
	Railway, tunnel, railway under construction
	Tramway, tramway under construction
	Miniature railway
Walsall	**Railway station**
	Private railway station
South Shields	**Metro station**
	Tram stop, tram stop under construction
	Bus, coach station

	Ambulance station
	Coastguard station
	Fire station
	Police station
	Accident and Emergency entrance to hospital
H	**Hospital**
	Place of worship
i	**Information Centre** (open all year)
	Shopping Centre
P P&R	**Parking, Park and Ride**
PO	**Post Office**
	Camping site, caravan site
	Golf course, picnic site
Prim Sch	**Important buildings, schools, colleges, universities and hospitals**
	Built up area
	Woods
River Medway	**Water name**
	River, weir, stream
	Canal, lock, tunnel
	Water
	Tidal water
Church	**Non-Roman antiquity**
ROMAN FORT	**Roman antiquity**
87 / 237	**Adjoining page indicators and overlap bands** The colour of the arrow and the band indicates the scale of the adjoining or overlapping page (see scales below)

Enlarged mapping only

	Railway or bus station building
	Place of interest
	Parkland

Acad	Academy	Inst	Institute	Recn Gd	Recreation Ground
Allot Gdns	Allotments	Ct	Law Court		
Cemy	Cemetery	L Ctr	Leisure Centre	Resr	Reservoir
C Ctr	Civic Centre	LC	Level Crossing	Ret Pk	Retail Park
CH	Club House	Liby	Library	Sch	School
Coll	College	Mkt	Market	Sh Ctr	Shopping Centre
Crem	Crematorium	Meml	Memorial	TH	Town Hall/House
Ent	Enterprise	Mon	Monument	Trad Est	Trading Estate
Ex H	Exhibition Hall	Mus	Museum	Univ	University
Ind Est	Industrial Estate	Obsy	Observatory	W Twr	Water Tower
IRB Sta	Inshore Rescue Boat Station	Pal	Royal Palace	Wks	Works
		PH	Public House	YH	Youth Hostel

■ The small numbers around the edges of the maps identify the 1 kilometre National Grid lines

■ The dark grey border on the inside edge of some pages indicates that the mapping does not continue onto the adjacent page

The scale of the maps on the pages numbered in blue is 5.52 cm to 1 km • 3½ inches to 1 mile • 1: 18103

0	¼	½	¾	1 mile
0	250 m 500 m	750 m 1 kilometre		

The scale of the maps on pages numbered in red is 11.04 cm to 1 km • 7 inches to 1 mile • 1: 9051

0	220 yards	440 yards	660 yards	½ mile
0	125 m 250 m	375 m ½ kilometre		

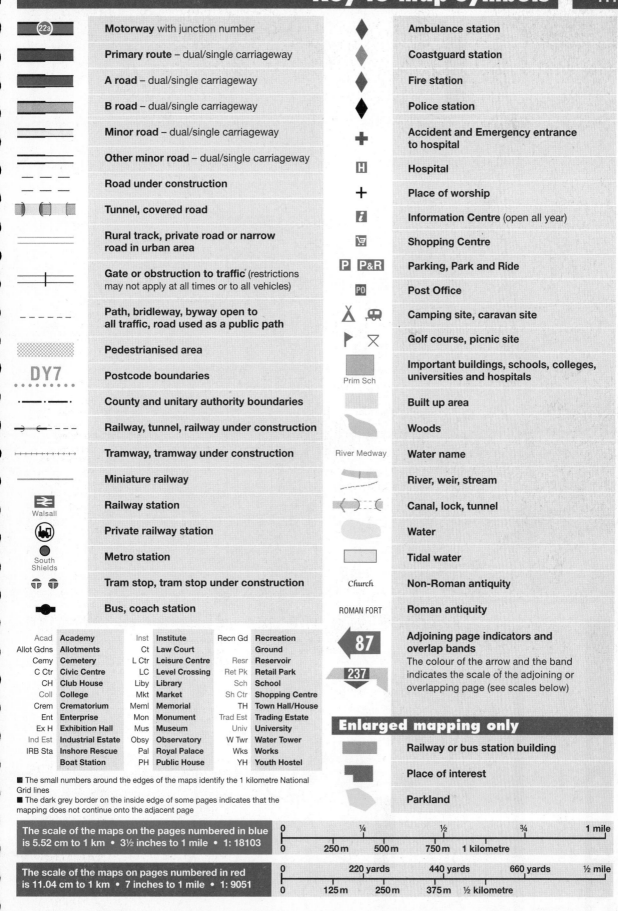

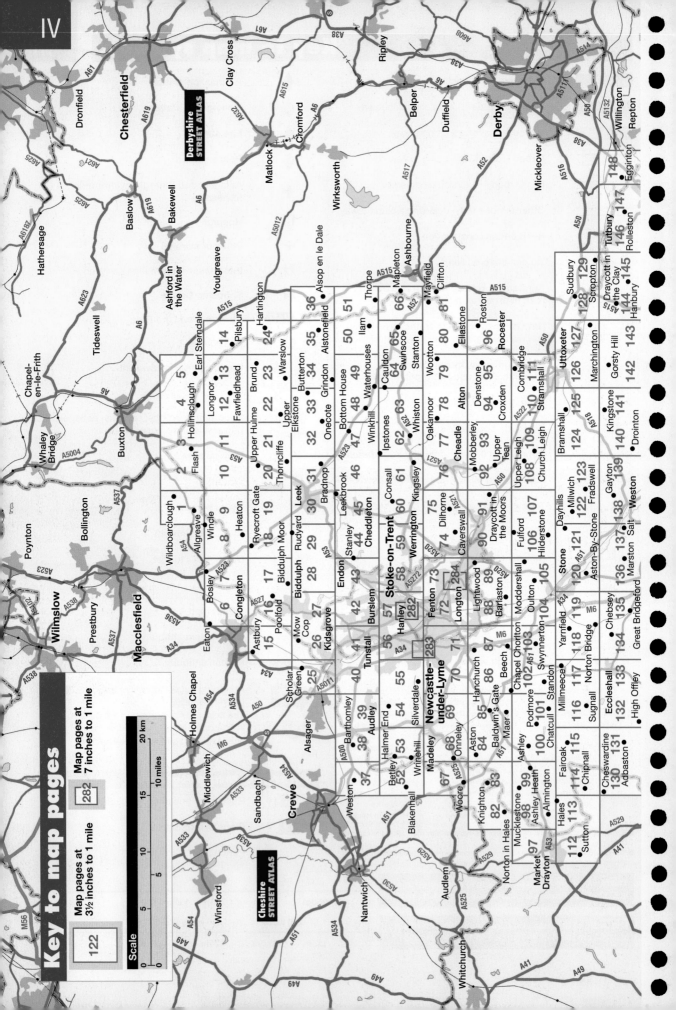

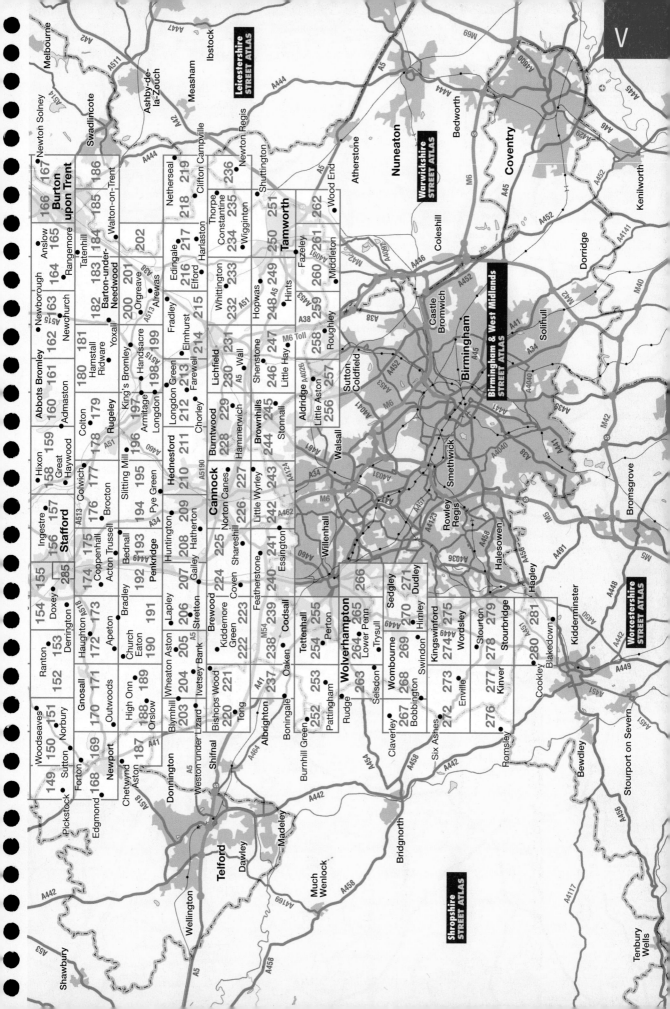

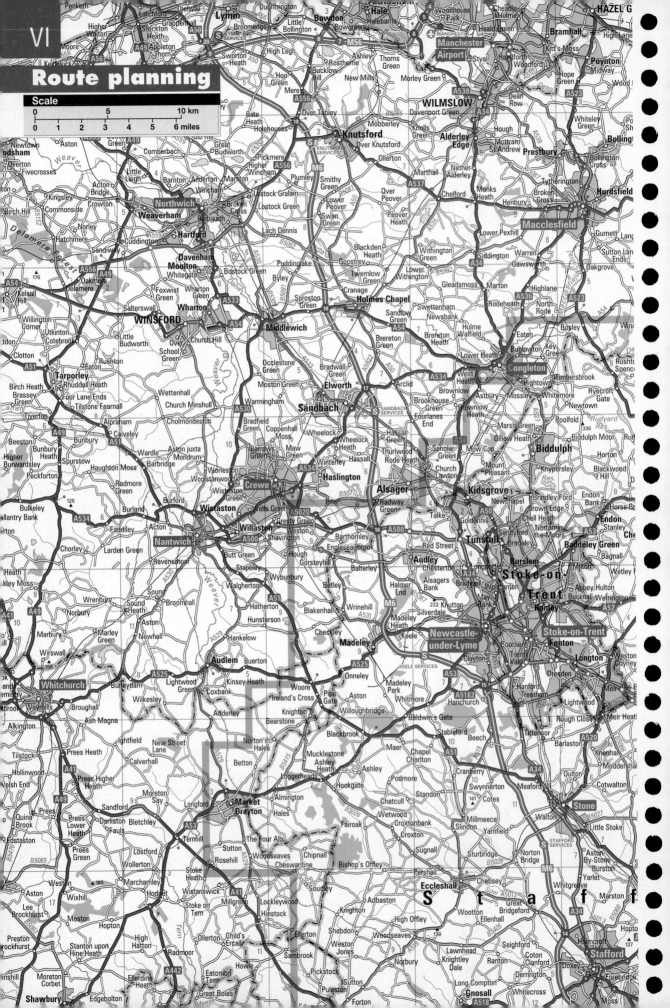

Scale

0   5   10 km

0   1   2   3   4   5   6 miles

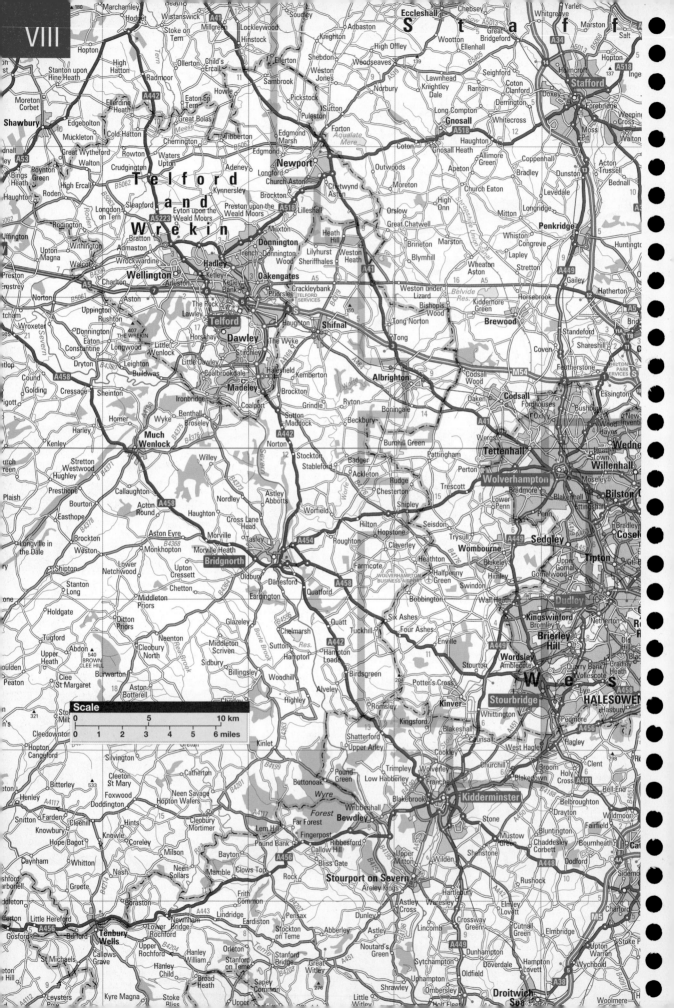

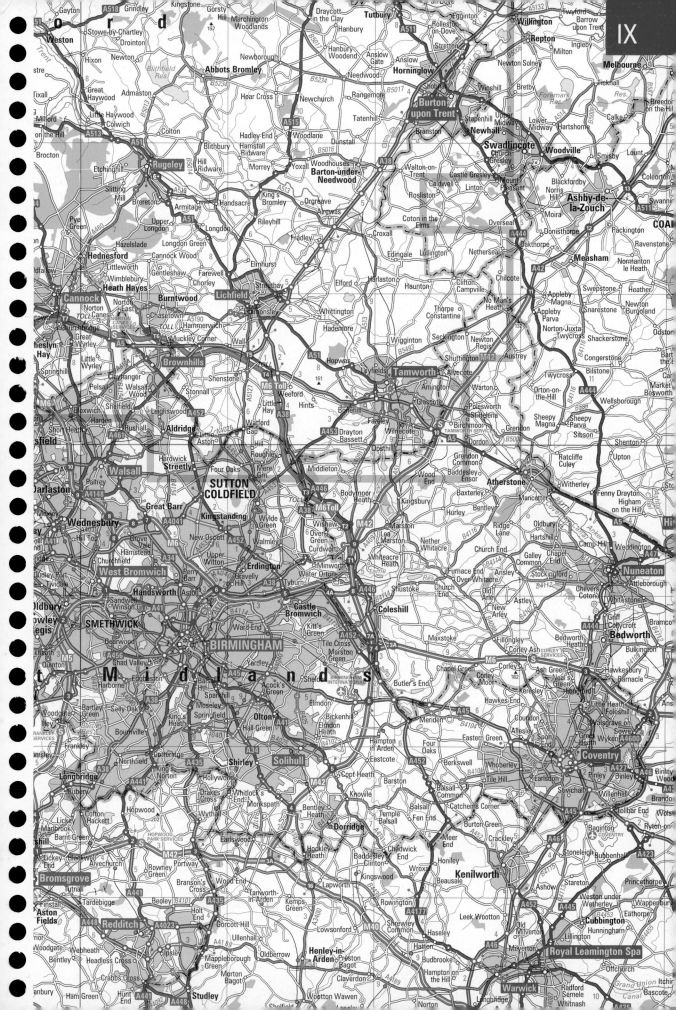

Major administrative and Postcode boundaries

County and unitary authority boundaries

District boundaries

Postcode boundaries

Area covered by this atlas

Scale

0 5 10 15 km

0 5 10 miles

Cheshire

Derbyshire

Shropshire

Telford and Wrekin

Warwickshire

Worcestershire

Sandwell

Dudley

Walsall

Birmingham

City of Wolverhampton

Staffordshire Moorlands

City of Stoke-on-Trent

Newcastle-under-Lyme

Staffordshire

Stafford

East Staffordshire

Cannock Chase

Lichfield

Tamworth

South Staffordshire

SJ SK SO SP

Places: Flash, Wincle, Longnor, Hartington, Warslow, Alstonefield, Biddulph, Leek, Kidsgrove, Weston, Betley, Stoke-on-Trent, Newcastle-under-Lyme, Werrington, Kingsley, Mayfield, Cheddleton, Cheadle, Alton, Woore, Baldwin's Gate, Barlaston, Rocester, Norton in Hales, Ashley, Swynnerton, Church Leigh, Yarnfield, Stone, Uttoxeter, Sudbury, Marchington, Market Drayton, Eccleston, Weston, Abbots Bromley, Tutbury, Egginton, Stafford, Burton upon Trent, Gnosall, Haughton, Brocton, Yoxall, Newport, Rugeley, Longdon, Airewas, Netherseal, Wheaton Aston, Penkridge, Cannock, Fradley, Edingale, Weston under Lizard, Burntwood, Lichfield, Newton Regis, Albrighton, Codsall, Featherstone, Shenstone, Tamworth, Brownhills, Drayton Bassett, Aldridge, Pattingham, Sedgley, Claverley, Wombourne, Kinver, Blakedown

Postcodes: CW12, CW1, CW2, CW5, CW3, SK11, SK17, DE6, ST8, ST13, ST7, ST6, ST9, ST1, ST2, ST10, ST5, ST4, ST3, ST11, ST14, DE6, ST12, ST15, DE65, ST21, ST18, ST16, DE13, DE15, DE14, ST20, TF9, TF10, TF11, ST17, WS15, DE11, WS12, DE12, WS13, B79, WS11, WS7, WS14, WV10, WV9, WS6, WV8, WV11, WS3, WS8, B78, B77, WV7, WS9, WS4, B74, B75, WV6, WV3, WV2, WV4, WV5, DY3, DY1, DY6, WV15, DY7, DY8, DY12, DY11, DY10

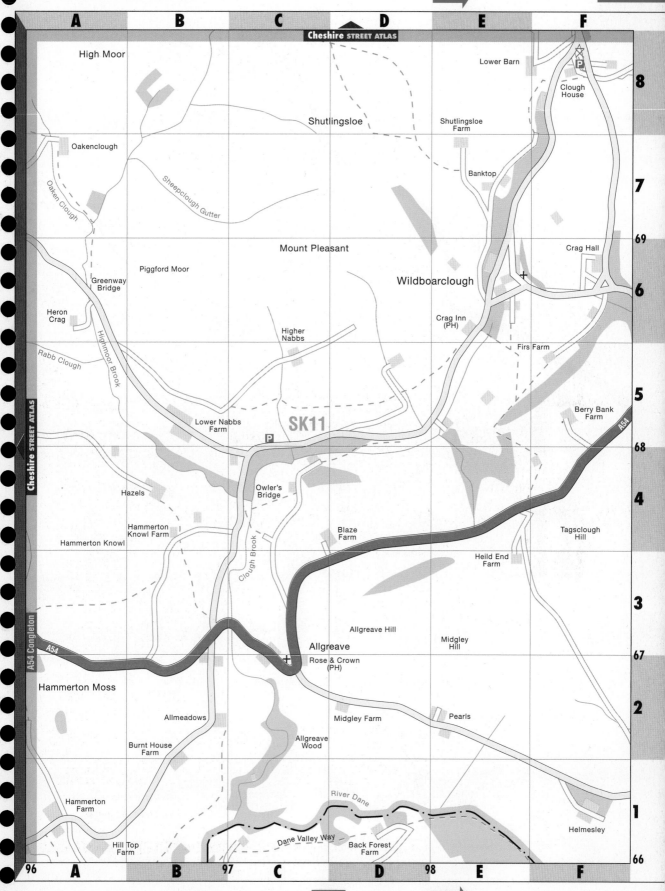

2

Cheshire STREET ATLAS

Cheshire STREET ATLAS

A B C D E F

High Moor

Oakenclough

Oaken Clough

Sheepclough Gutter

Shutlingsloe

Lower Barn

Clough House

Shutlingsloe Farm

Banktop

Mount Pleasant

Crag Hall

Greenway Bridge

Piggford Moor

Wildboarclough

Heron Crag

Rabb Clough

Highmoor Brook

Higher Nabbs

Crag Inn (PH)

Firs Farm

Lower Nabbs Farm

SK11

Berry Bank Farm

A54

Hazels

Owler's Bridge

Clough Brook

Blaze Farm

Heild End Farm

Tagsclough Hill

Hammerton Knowl Farm

Hammerton Knowl

Allgreave Hill

Midgley Hill

A54 Congleton

A54

Allgreave

Rose & Crown (PH)

Hammerton Moss

Allmeadows

Midgley Farm

Pearls

Burnt House Farm

Allgreave Wood

Hammerton Farm

River Dane

Helmesley

Hill Top Farm

Dane Valley Way

Back Forest Farm

8

7

69

6

5

68

4

3

67

2

1

66

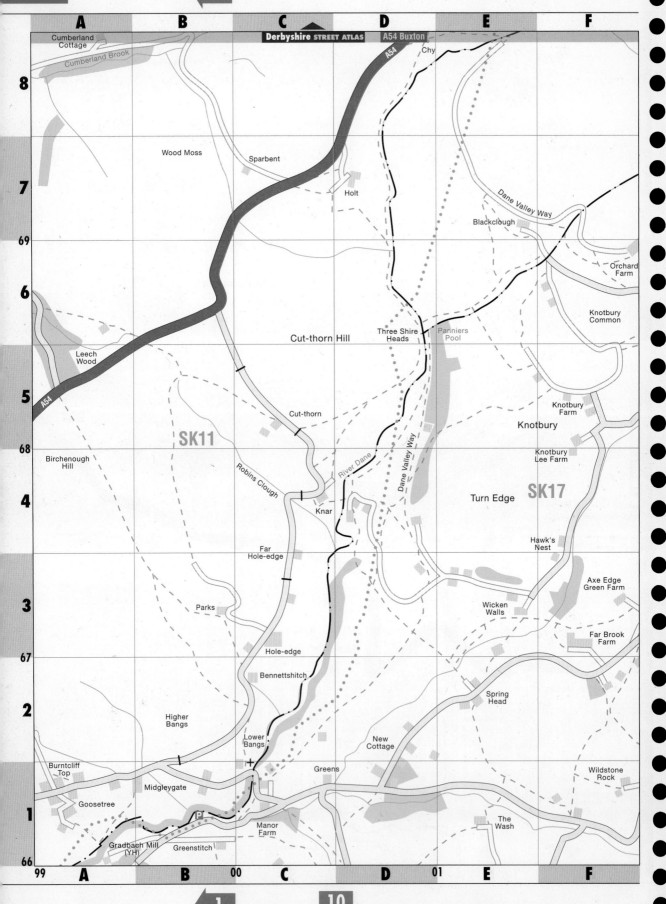

Derbyshire STREET ATLAS

A54 Buxton

A B C D E F

8

7

69

6

5

68

4

3

67

2

1

66

Cumberland Cottage
Cumberland Brook
Wood Moss
Sparbent
Holt
Chy
Dane Valley Way
Blackclough
Orchard Farm
Knotbury Common
Cut-thorn Hill
Three Shire Heads
Panniers Pool
Leech Wood
A54
Cut-thorn
SK11
Knotbury Farm
Knotbury
Robins Clough
Knar
River Dane
Dane Valley Way
Knotbury Lee Farm
Turn Edge
SK17
Birchenough Hill
Far Hole-edge
Hawk's Nest
Axe Edge Green Farm
Parks
Hole-edge
Wicken Walls
Far Brook Farm
Bennettshitch
Spring Head
Higher Bangs
Lower Bangs
New Cottage
Wildstone Rock
Burntcliff Top
Midgleygate
Greens
The Wash
Goosetree
Manor Farm
Gradbach Mill (YH)
Greenstitch

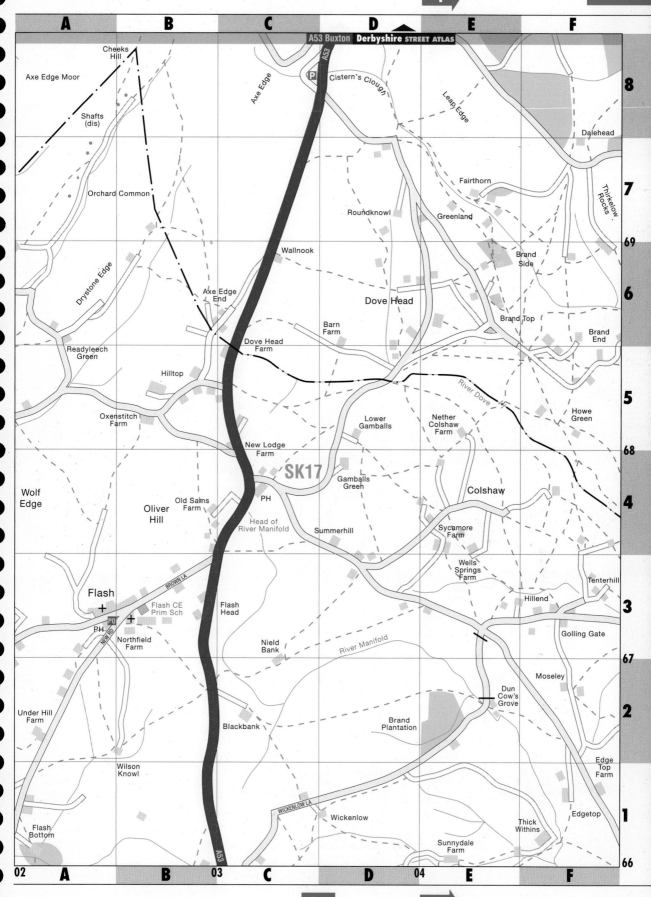

A53 Buxton **Derbyshire** STREET ATLAS

| A | B | C | D | E | F |

Cheeks Hill

Axe Edge Moor

Cistern's Clough

Leap Edge

8

Shafts (dis)

Dalehead

Fairthorn

7

Orchard Common

Roundknowl

Greenland

Thirkelow Rocks

Wallnook

Brand Side

69

Drystone Edge

Axe Edge End

Dove Head

6

Barn Farm

Brand Top

Dove Head Farm

Brand End

Readyleech Green

River Dove

Howe Green

5

Hilltop

Nether Colshaw Farm

Oxenstitch Farm

Lower Gamballs

New Lodge Farm

68

Wolf Edge

SK17

Gamballs Green

Colshaw

4

Oliver Hill

Old Sams Farm

PH

Head of River Manifold

Summerhill

Sycamore Farm

Wells Springs Farm

Tenterhill

BROWN LA

Hillend

3

Flash

Flash CE Prim Sch

Flash Head

Golling Gate

PH

PO

Northfield Farm

NEW RD

Nield Bank

River Manifold

Moseley

67

Under Hill Farm

Dun Cow's Grove

2

Blackbank

Brand Plantation

Edge Top Farm

Wilson Knowl

WICKENLOW LA

Wickenlow

Edgetop

1

Flash Bottom

A53

Thick Withins

Sunnydale Farm

66

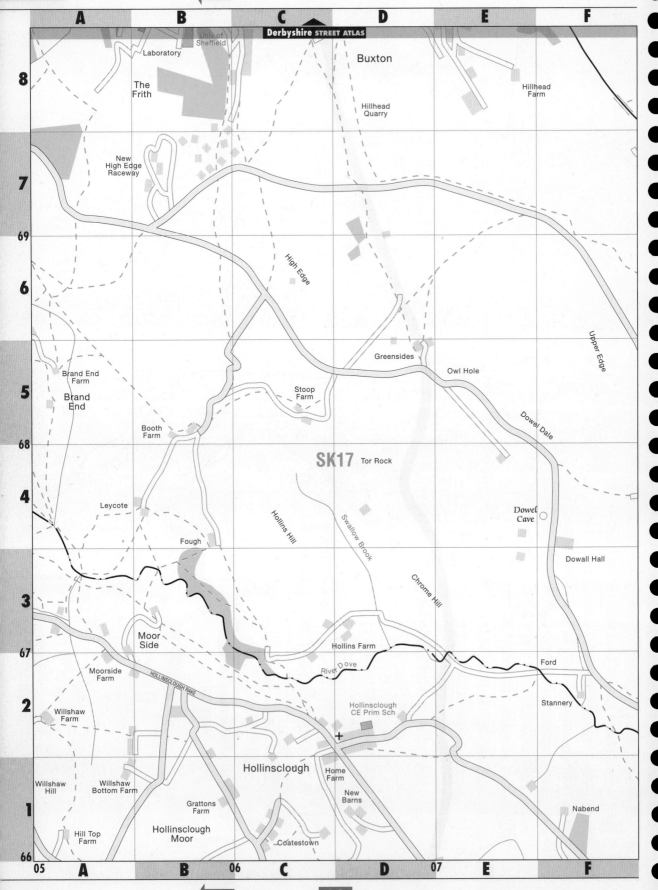

A B C D E F

Derbyshire STREET ATLAS

Univ of Sheffield

Buxton

Laboratory

The Frith

Hillhead Farm

8

Hillhead Quarry

New High Edge Raceway

7

High Edge

69

Upper Edge

6

Greensides

Owl Hole

Brand End Farm

Stoop Farm

Dowel Dale

5

Brand End

Booth Farm

68

SK17 Tor Rock

Leycote

Dowel Cave

4

Hollins Hill

Swallow Brook

Fough

Dowall Hall

Chrome Hill

3

Moor Side

Hollins Farm

67

Moorside Farm

HOLLINSCLOUGH RAKE

River Dove

Ford

Stannery

2

Willshaw Farm

Hollinsclough CE Prim Sch

Willshaw Hill

Hollinsclough

Home Farm

Willshaw Bottom Farm

Grattons Farm

New Barns

Nabend

1

Hollinsclough Moor

Hill Top Farm

Coatestown

66

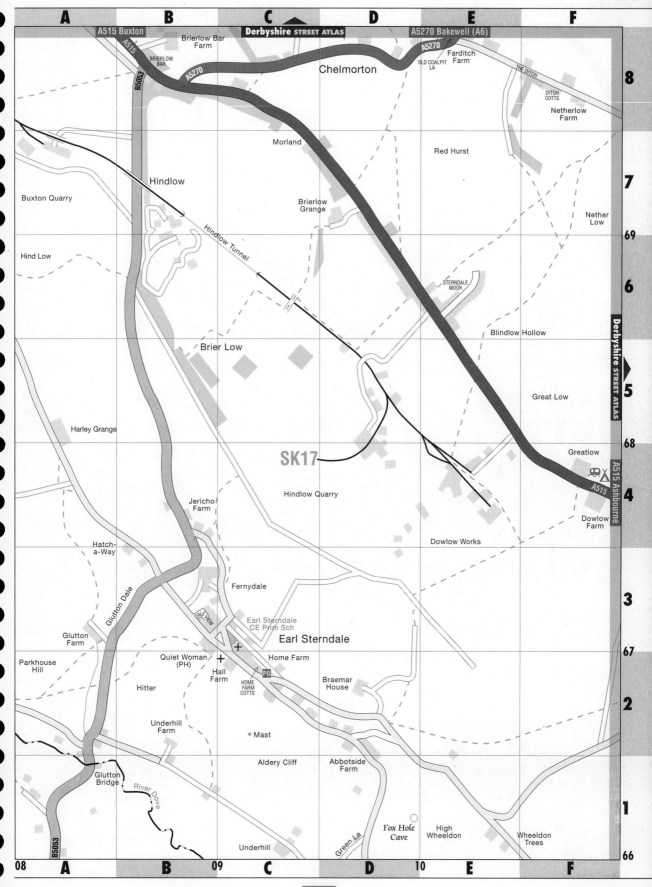

A515 Buxton
A515
B5053
BRIERLOW BAR
A5270
Brierlow Bar Farm
Chelmorton
A5270 Bakewell (A6)
A5270
OLD COALPIT LA
Farditch Farm
THE DITCH
DITCH COTTS
Netherlow Farm

8

Morland
Red Hurst

Hindlow

7

Buxton Quarry
Brierlow Grange
Nether Low

69

Hind Low
Hindlow Tunnel
STERNDALE MOOR

6

Brier Low
Blindlow Hollow

Derbyshire STREET ATLAS

Great Low

5

Harley Grange
Greatlow

68

SK17
A515 Ashbourne
A515

Jericho Farm
Hindlow Quarry
Dowlow Farm

4

Hatch-a-Way
Dowlow Works

Glutton Dale
Fernydale

3

Glutton Farm
DALE VIEW
Earl Sterndale CE Prim Sch
Earl Sterndale

67

Parkhouse Hill
Quiet Woman (PH)
Hall Farm
HOME FARM COTTS
PO
Home Farm
Braemar House

2

Hitter
Underhill Farm
Mast

Aldery Cliff
Abbotside Farm

1

Glutton Bridge
River Dove
Underhill
Green La
Fox Hole Cave
High Wheeldon
Wheeldon Trees

66

B5053

08 A B 09 C D 10 E F

A1
1 LUNE CL
2 DERWENT DR
3 ANNAN CL
4 CORNWALL CL
5 MOSSLEY GARTH CL

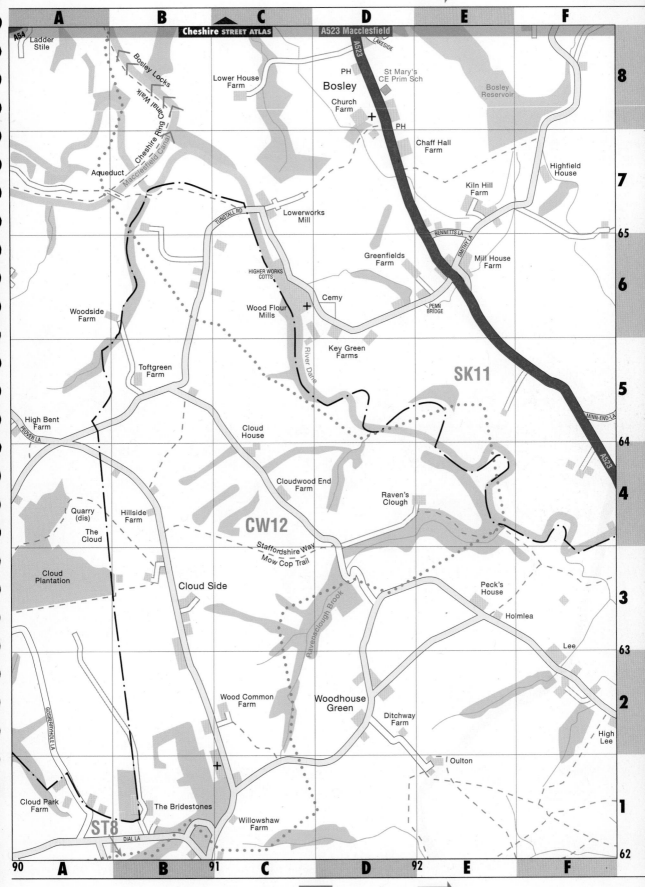

8

A54
Ladder
Stile

Bosley Locks

Cheshire Ring Canal Walk

Macclesfield Canal

A523 Macclesfield

A523

LAKESIDE

PH

St Mary's
CE Prim Sch

Bosley

Bosley
Reservoir

Lower House
Farm

Church
Farm

+

PH

Chaff Hall
Farm

Highfield
House

Aqueduct

Kiln Hill
Farm

BENNETTS LA

SMITHY LA

TUNSTALL RD

Lowerworks
Mill

Greenfields
Farm

Mill House
Farm

HIGHER WORKS
COTTS

Cemy

PENN
BRIDGE

Woodside
Farm

Wood Flour
Mills

+

Key Green
Farms

River Dane

SK11

MINN-END-LA

Toftgreen
Farm

A523

High Bent
Farm

PEDLEY LA

Cloud
House

Cloudwood End
Farm

Raven's
Clough

Peck's
House

Quarry
(dis)

Hillside
Farm

CW12

Staffordshire Way
Mow Cop Trail

Holmlea

The
Cloud

Cloud
Plantation

Cloud Side

Ravensclough Brook

Lee

GOSBERRYHOLE LA

Wood Common
Farm

Woodhouse
Green

Ditchway
Farm

High
Lee

+

Oulton

Cloud Park
Farm

The Bridestones

Willowshaw
Farm

ST8

DIAL LA

17

8

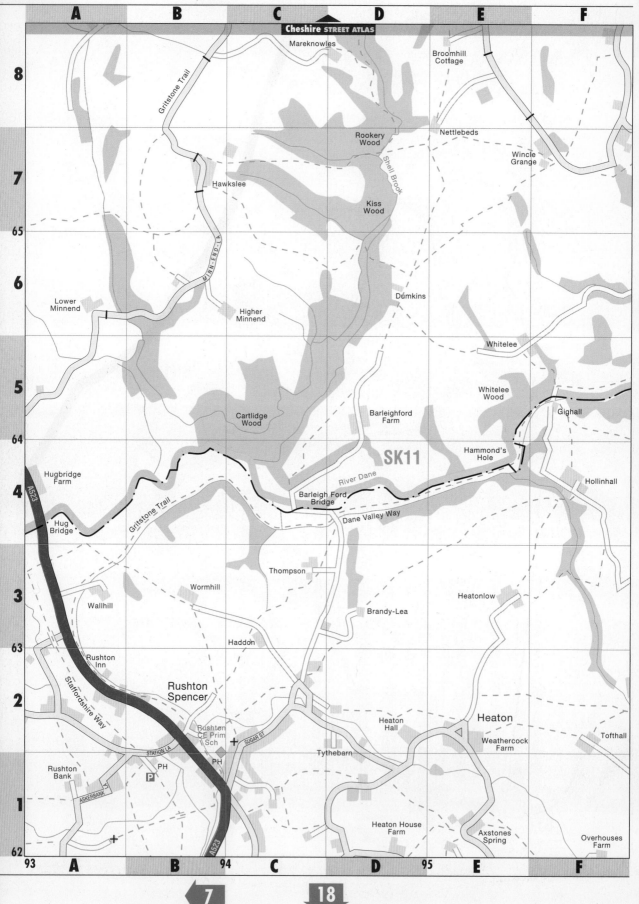

Cheshire STREET ATLAS

A B C D E F

8
7
65
6
5
64
4
3
63
2
1
62

Mareknowles

Broomhill
Cottage

Gritstone Trail

Rookery
Wood

Nettlebeds

Wincle
Grange

Hawkslee

Shell Brook

Kiss
Wood

MINN-END-LA

Lower
Minnend

Dumkins

Higher
Minnend

Whitelee

Whitelee
Wood

Gighall

Cartlidge
Wood

Barleighford
Farm

SK11

Hammond's
Hole

Hollinhall

Hugbridge
Farm

A523

River Dane

Barleigh Ford
Bridge

Gritstone Trail

Hug
Bridge

Dane Valley Way

Thompson

Wormhill

Brandy-Lea

Heatonlow

Wallhill

Haddon

Rushton
Inn

Staffordshire Way

Rushton
Spencer

Rushton
CE Prim
Sch

Heaton
Hall

Heaton

SUGAR ST

Weathercock
Farm

Tofthall

STATION LA

PH

Tythebarn

Rushton
Bank

P

PH

ASKERBANK

Heaton House
Farm

Axstones
Spring

Overhouses
Farm

A523

93 A B 94 C D 95 E F

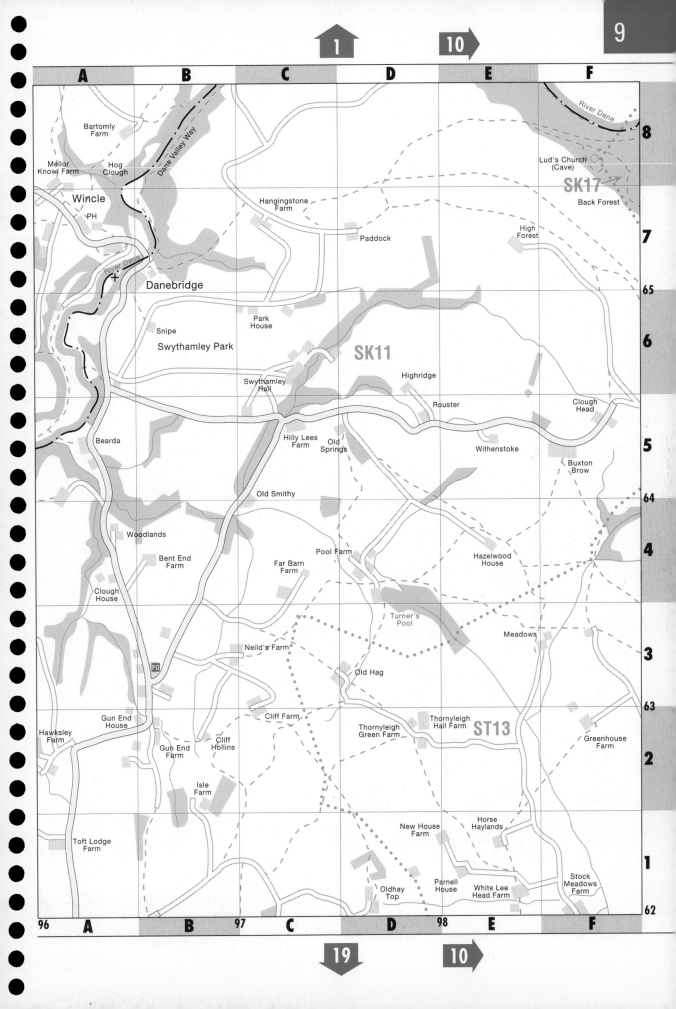

A   B   C   D   E   F

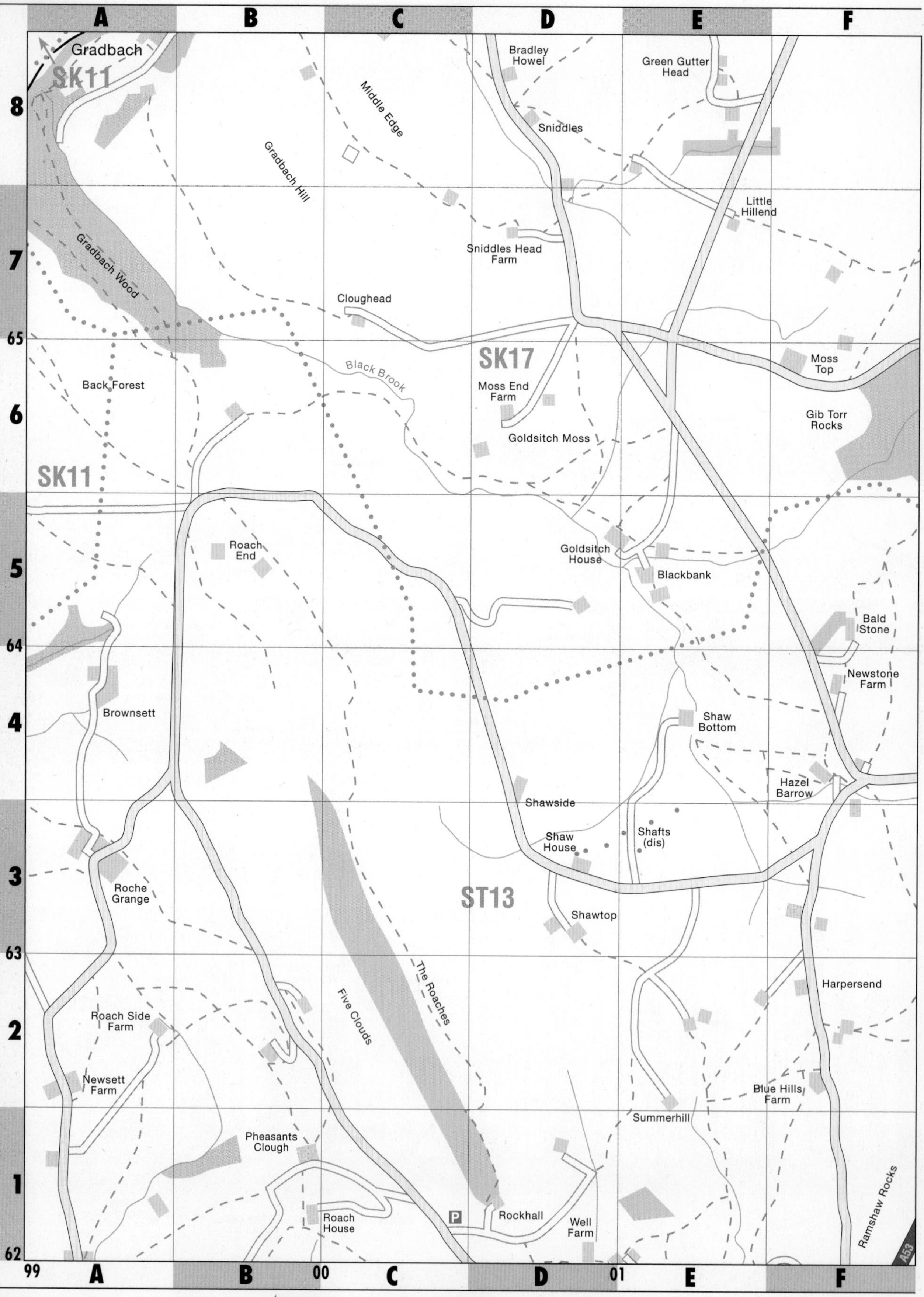

8

Gradbach

SK11

Middle Edge

Bradley Howel

Green Gutter Head

Sniddles

Gradbach Hill

Little Hillend

7

Gradbach Wood

Sniddles Head Farm

65

Cloughead

Black Brook

SK17

Moss Top

Back Forest

Moss End Farm

Gib Torr Rocks

6

SK11

Goldsitch Moss

5

Roach End

Goldsitch House

Blackbank

Bald Stone

64

Newstone Farm

4

Brownsett

Shaw Bottom

Hazel Barrow

Shawside

Shaw House

Shafts (dis)

3

Roche Grange

ST13

Shawtop

Harpersend

63

Five Clouds

The Roaches

2

Roach Side Farm

Newsett Farm

Blue Hills Farm

Summerhill

1

Pheasants Clough

Ramshaw Rocks

Roach House

Rockhall

Well Farm

A53

62

99   A   B   00   C   D   01   E   F

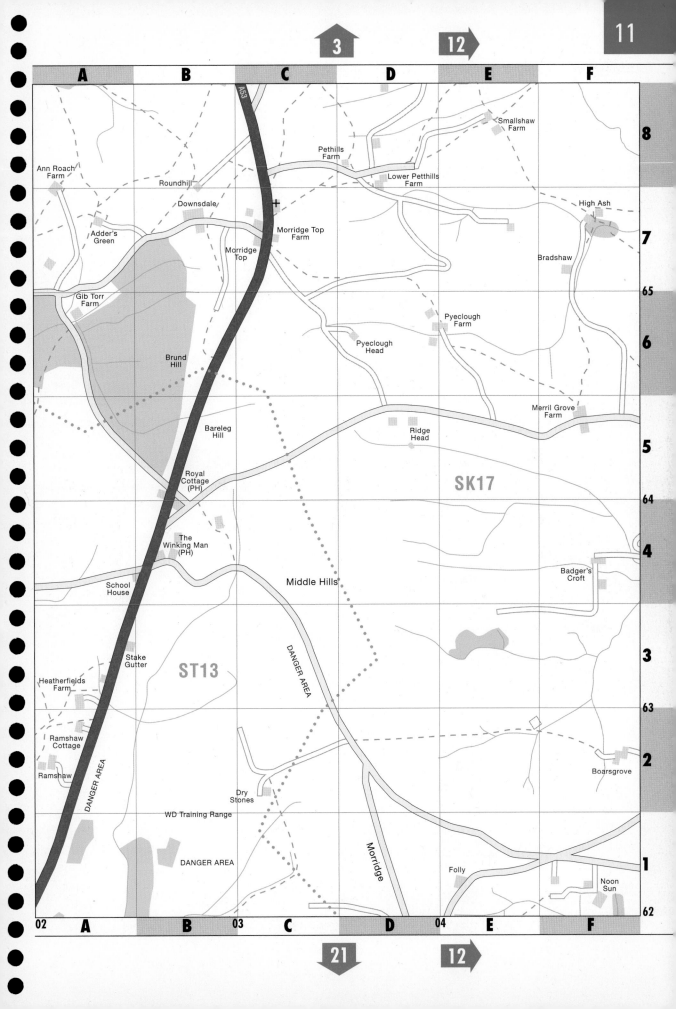

11
4

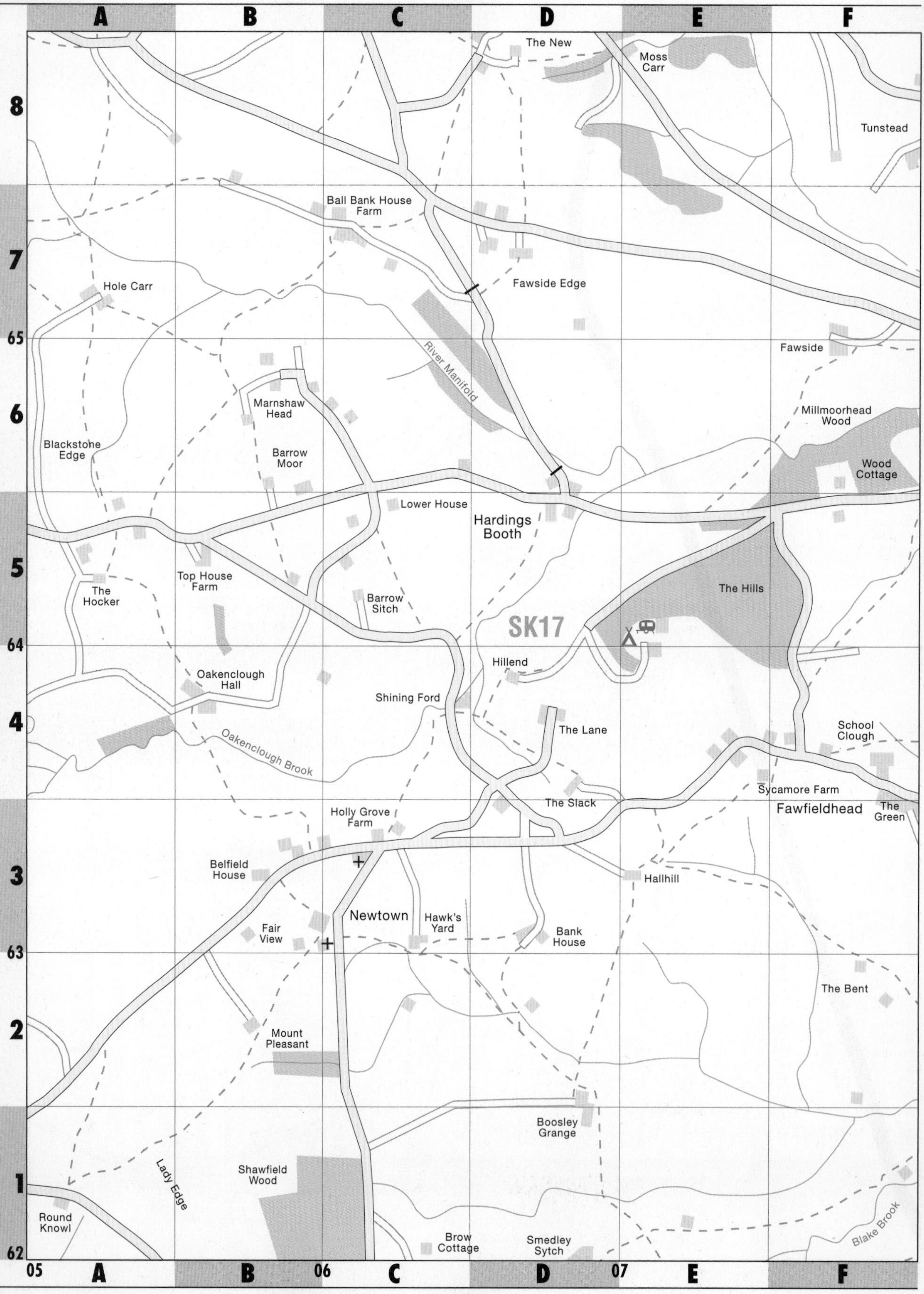

A B C D E F

8
7
65
6
5
64
4
3
63
2
1
62

05 A B 06 C D 07 E F

The New

Moss Carr

Tunstead

Ball Bank House Farm

Hole Carr

Fawside Edge

Fawside

River Manifold

Millmoorhead Wood

Marnshaw Head

Barrow Moor

Wood Cottage

Blackstone Edge

Lower House

Hardings Booth

The Hocker

Top House Farm

Barrow Sitch

The Hills

SK17

Oakenclough Hall

Hillend

Shining Ford

Oakenclough Brook

The Lane

School Clough

Holly Grove Farm

The Slack

Sycamore Farm

Fawfieldhead

The Green

Belfield House

Hallhill

Fair View

Newtown

Hawk's Yard

Bank House

The Bent

Mount Pleasant

Boosley Grange

Lady Edge

Shawfield Wood

Round Knowl

Brow Cottage

Smedley Sytch

Blake Brook

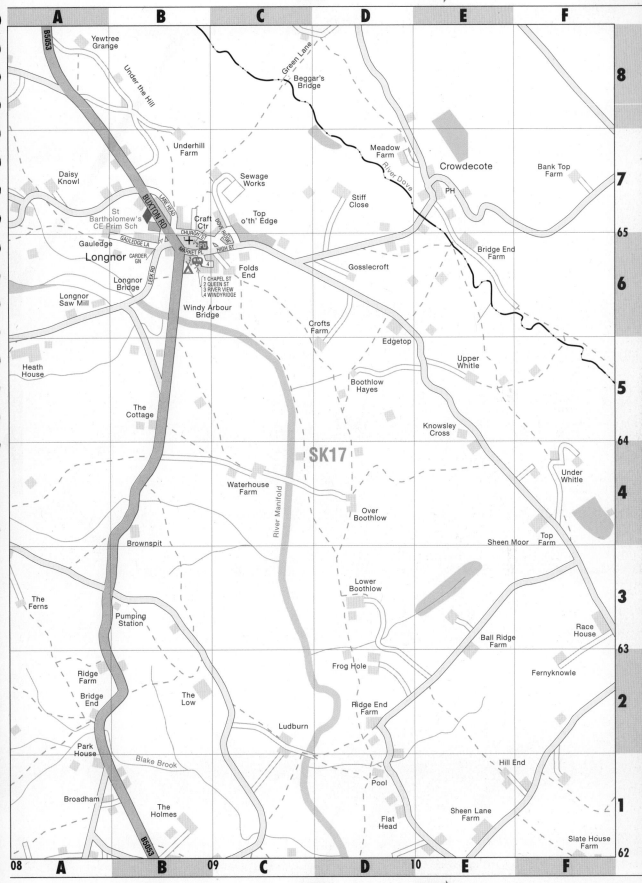

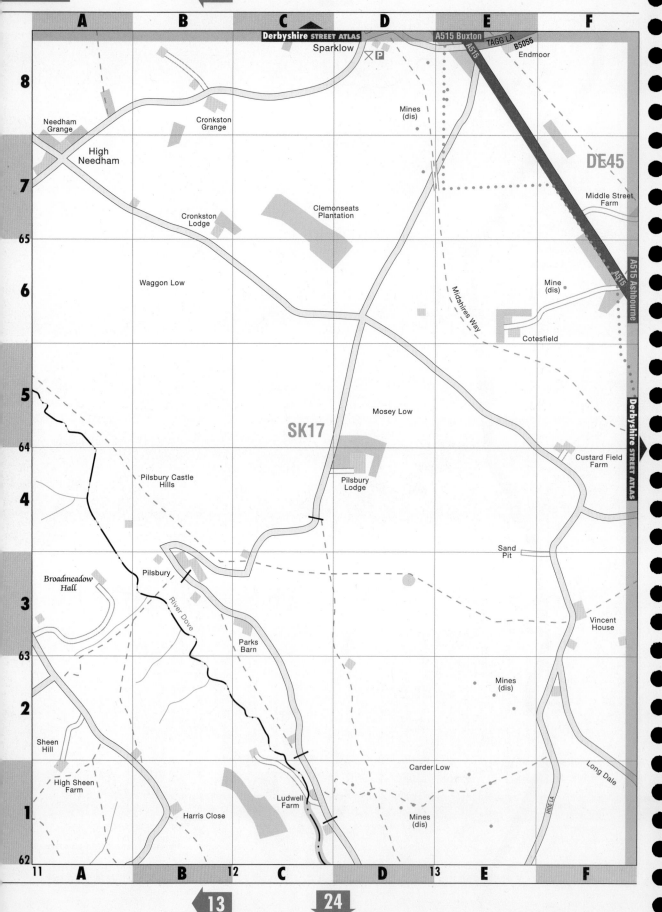

13

	A	B	C	D	E	F

Derbyshire STREET ATLAS

Sparklow

A515 Buxton

TAGG LA

B5055

Endmoor

8

Needham Grange

Cronkston Grange

Mines (dis)

DE45

High Needham

7

Middle Street Farm

Cronkston Lodge

Clemonseats Plantation

65

6

Waggon Low

Mine (dis)

Midshires Way

Cotesfield

A515 Ashbourne

Derbyshire STREET ATLAS

5

Mosey Low

SK17

64

Custard Field Farm

4

Pilsbury Castle Hills

Pilsbury Lodge

Sand Pit

Broadmeadow Hall

Pilsbury

River Dove

3

Vincent House

Parks Barn

63

Mines (dis)

2

Sheen Hill

High Sheen Farm

Carder Low

Long Dale

Harris Close

HIDE LA

1

Ludwell Farm

Mines (dis)

62

13 24

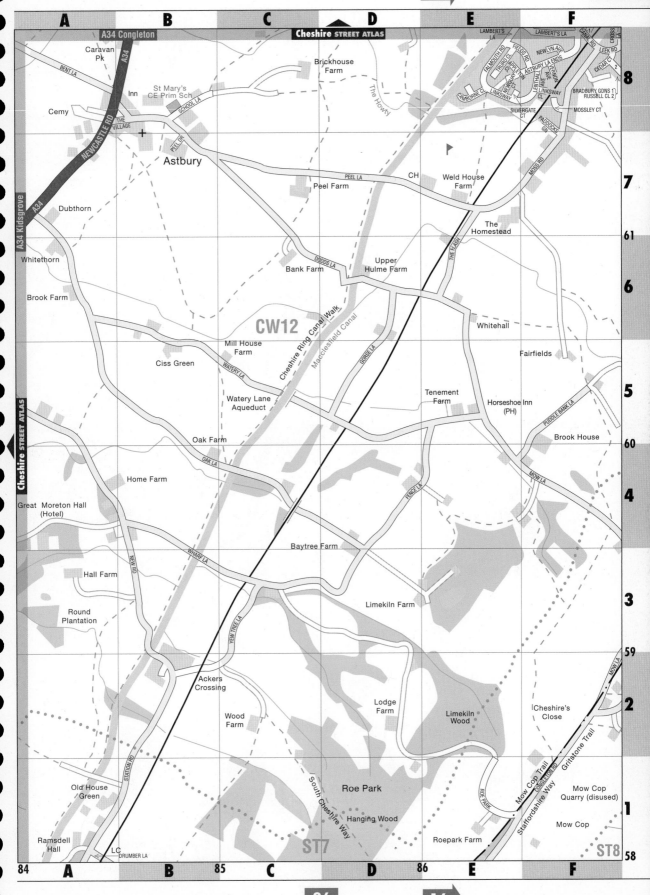

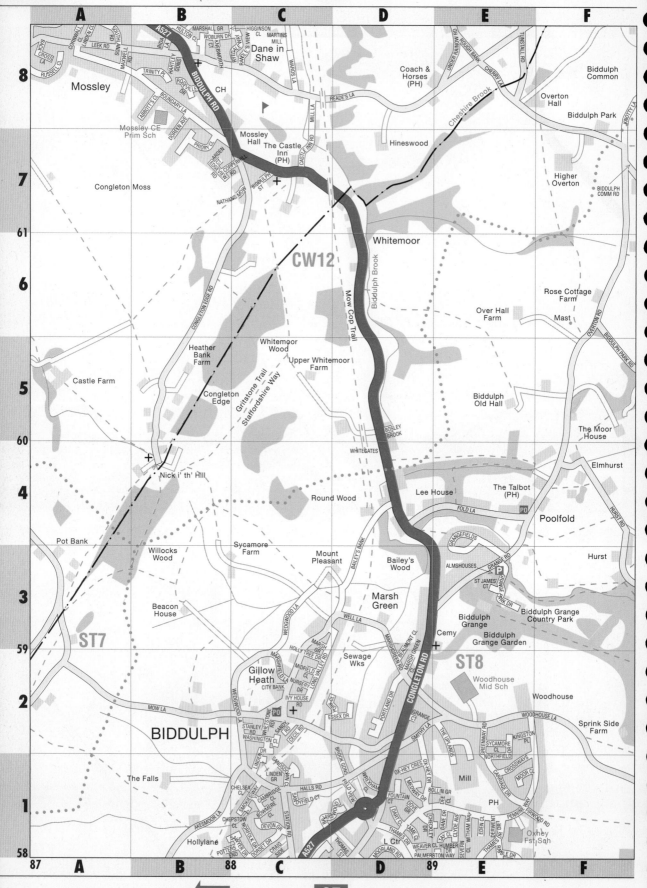

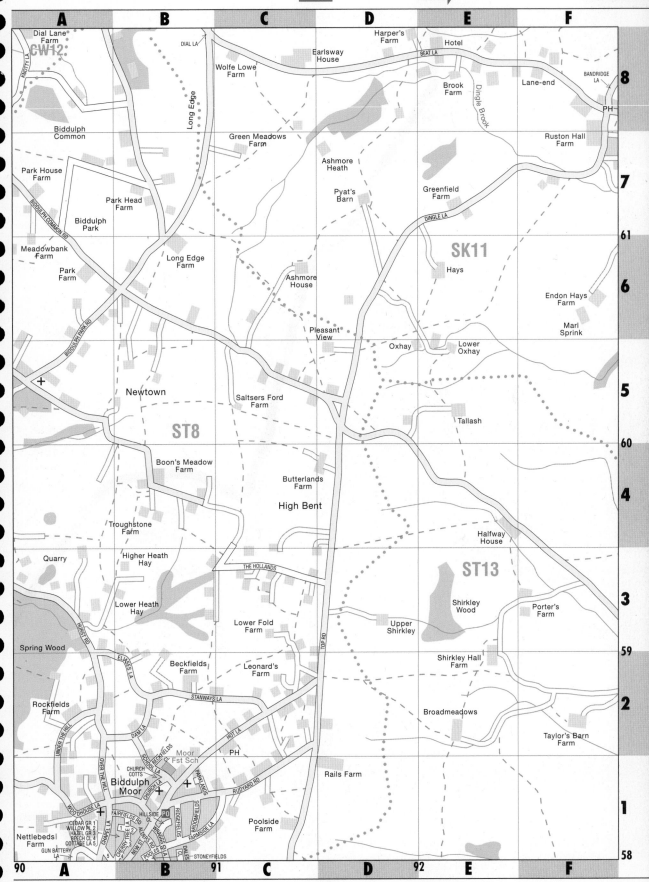

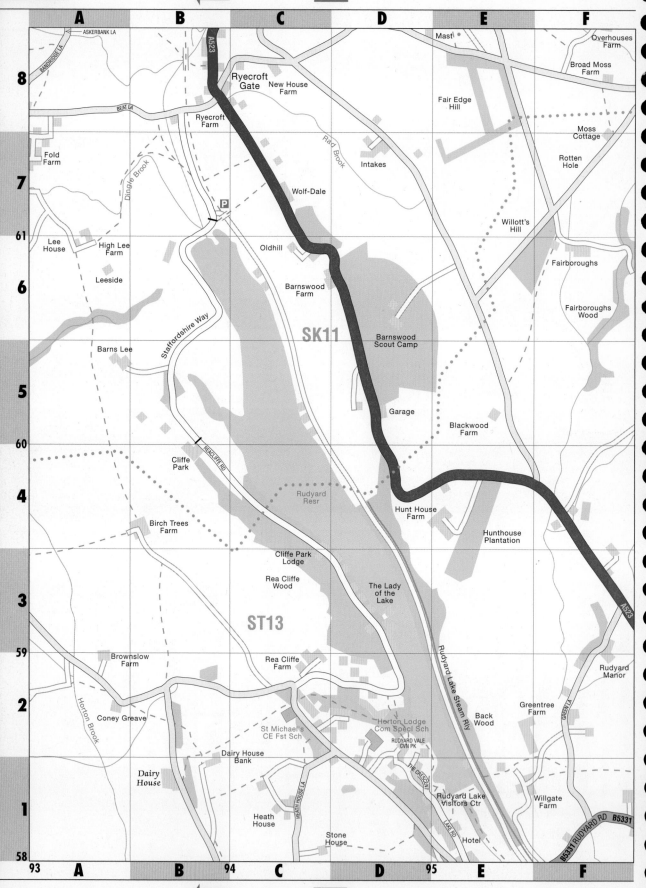

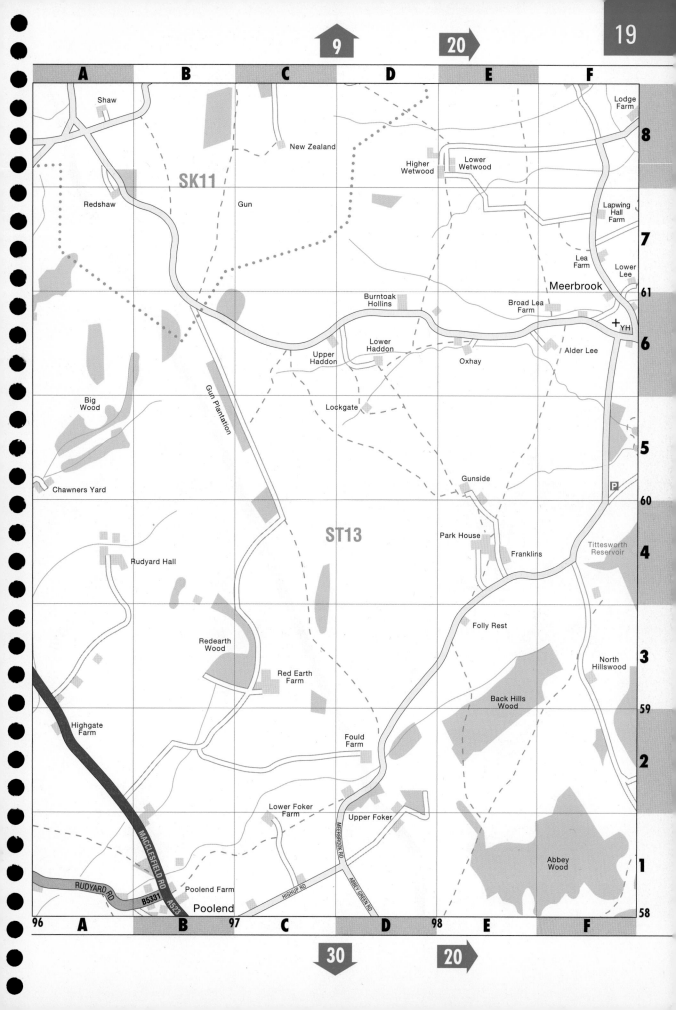

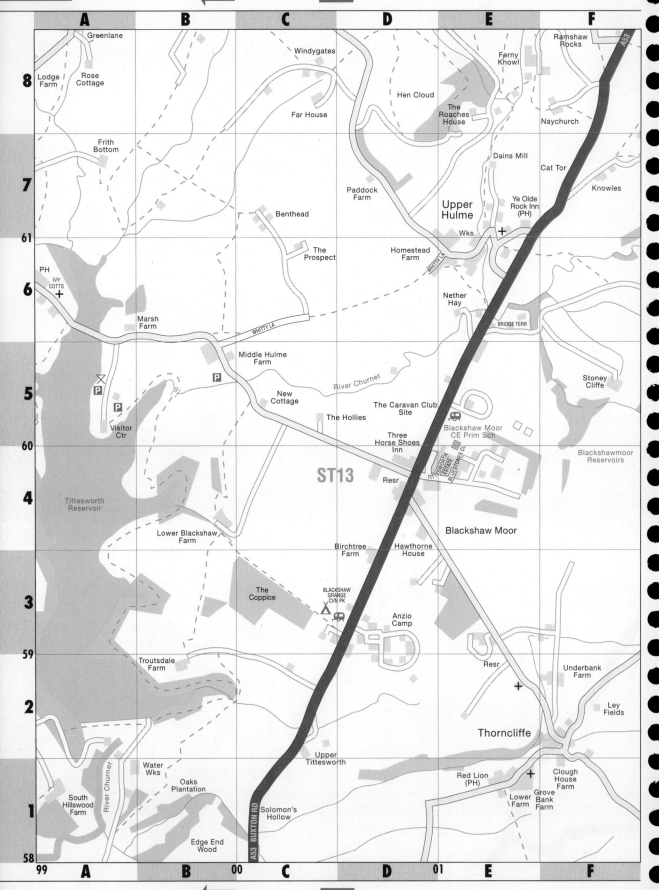

A B C D E F

8 Greenlane
Lodge Farm
Rose Cottage
Windygates
Far House
Hen Cloud
The Roaches House
Ferny Khowl
Ramshaw Rocks
Naychurch

7 Frith Bottom
Paddock Farm
Upper Hulme
Dains Mill
Cat Tor
Knowles

61 Benthead
The Prospect
Homestead Farm
Wks
Ye Olde Rock Inn (PH)

6 PH
IVY COTTS
Marsh Farm
WHITTY LA
Nether Hay
BRIDGE TERR

5 Middle Hulme Farm
New Cottage
The Hollies
River Churnet
The Caravan Club Site
Blackshaw Moor CE Prim Sch
Stoney Cliffe

Visitor Ctr

60 Three Horse Shoes Inn
ST13
Resr
Blackshawmoor Reservoirs

4 Tittesworth Reservoir
Lower Blackshaw Farm
Blackshaw Moor

3 The Coppice
Birchtree Farm
Hawthorne House
BLACKSHAW GRANGE CVN PK
Anzio Camp

59 Troutsdale Farm
Resr
Underbank Farm

2 Thorncliffe
Ley Fields

Water Wks
Oaks Plantation
Upper Tittesworth
Red Lion (PH)
Clough House Farm
Grove Bank Farm

1 South Hillswood Farm
River Churnet
A53 BUXTON RD
Solomon's Hollow
Lower Farm

58 Edge End Wood

99 A B 00 C D 01 E F

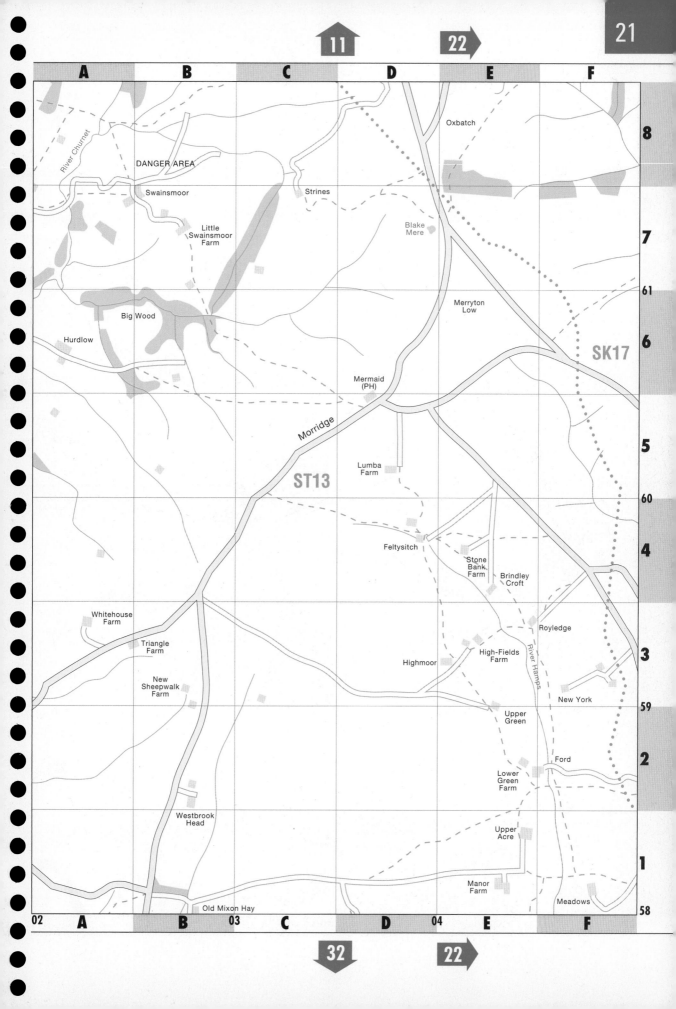

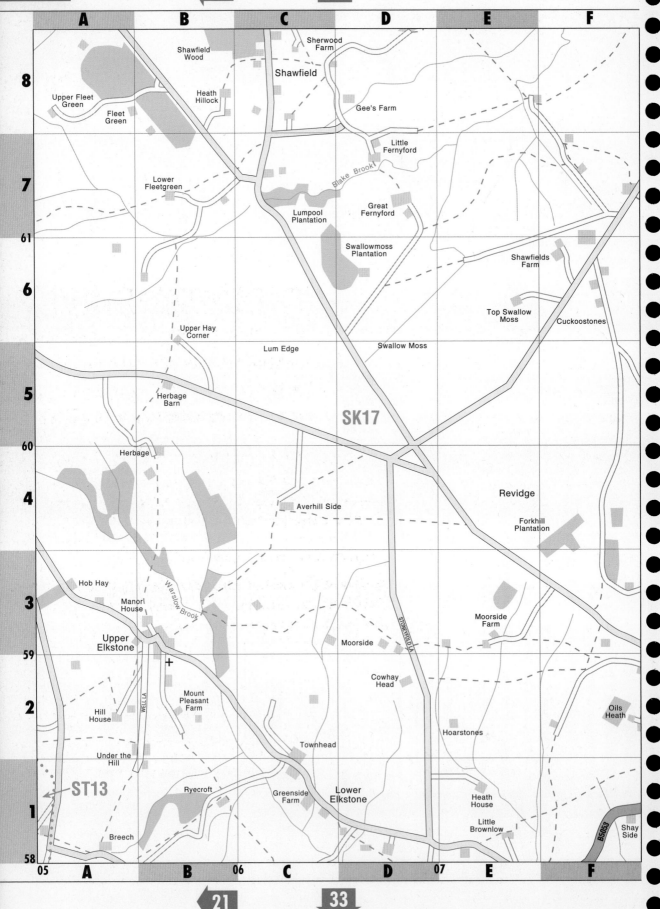

A B C D E F

8
7
61
6
5
60
4
3
59
2
1
58

05 06 07

Upper Fleet Green
Fleet Green
Shawfield Wood
Heath Hillock
Shawfield
Sherwood Farm
Gee's Farm
Little Fernyford
Lower Fleetgreen
Blake Brook
Lumpool Plantation
Great Fernyford
Swallowmoss Plantation
Shawfields Farm
Top Swallow Moss
Cuckoostones
Upper Hay Corner
Lum Edge
Swallow Moss
Herbage Barn
SK17
Herbage
Revidge
Averhill Side
Forkhill Plantation
Hob Hay
Warslow Brook
Manor House
Moorside Farm
STONEY FOLD LA
Upper Elkstone
Moorside
Cowhay Head
WELL LA
Hill House
Mount Pleasant Farm
Oils Heath
Hoarstones
Under the Hill
Townhead
ST13
Ryecroft
Greenside Farm
Lower Elkstone
Heath House
Breech
Little Brownlow
B5053
Shay Side

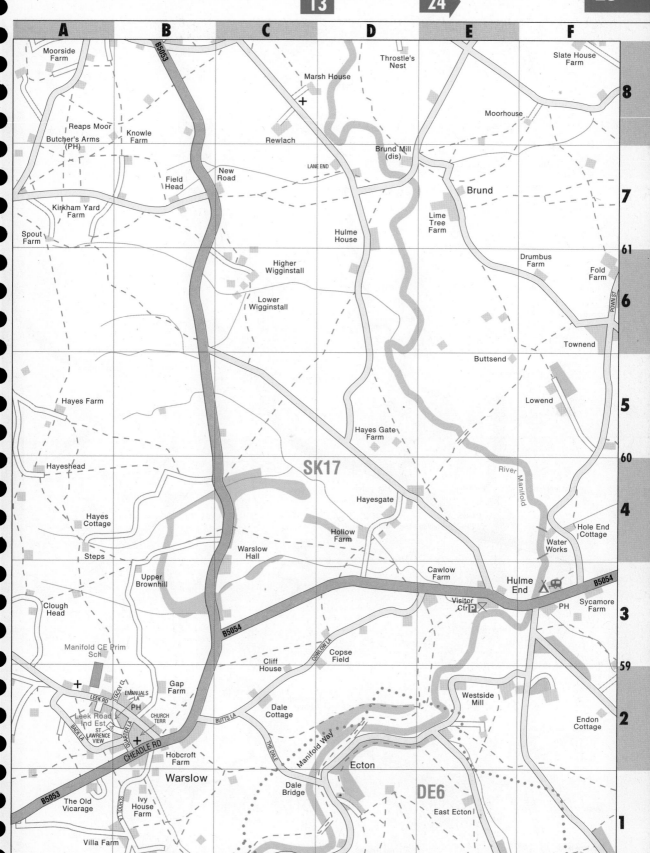

A   B   C   D   E   F

Moorside Farm
Throstle's Nest
Slate House Farm
Marsh House
B5053
Moorhouse
Reaps Moor
Butcher's Arms (PH)
Knowle Farm
Rewlach
Brund Mill (dis)
Brund
LANE END
Field Head
New Road
Lime Tree Farm
Kirkham Yard Farm
Hulme House
Drumbus Farm
Fold Farm
Spout Farm
Higher Wigginstall
POWN ST
Lower Wigginstall
Townend
Buttsend
Lowend
Hayes Farm
Hayes Gate Farm
SK17
River Manifold
Hayeshead
Hayesgate
Hole End Cottage
Hayes Cottage
Hollow Farm
Water Works
Steps
Warslow Hall
Cawlow Farm
Hulme End
B5054
Upper Brownhill
Visitor Ctr P
PH
Sycamore Farm
Clough Head
Manifold CE Prim Sch
COWLOW LA
Copse Field
Westside Mill
Endon Cottage
B5054
Cliff House
LEEK RD
STACEY CL
EMANUALS LA
Gap Farm
PH
CHURCH TERR
BUTTS LA
Dale Cottage
Manifold Way
Leek Road Ind Est
ST LAWRENCE VIEW
BACK LA
QUARTER LA
CHEADLE RD
Hobcroft Farm
THE DALE
Ecton
DE6
Warslow
Dale Bridge
B5053
The Old Vicarage
SCHOOL LA
Ivy House Farm
East Ecton
Villa Farm
ST13

08   A   B   09   C   D   10   E   F   58

61
8
7
6
5
60
4
59
3
2
1

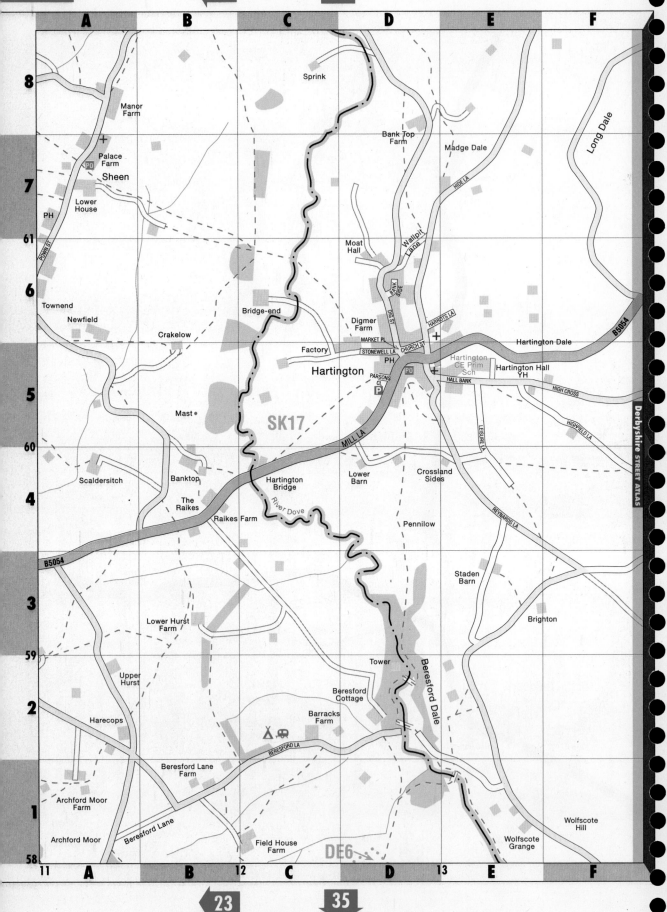

23
14

A   B   C   D   E   F

8   Sprink

Manor
Farm

Bank Top
Farm

Madge Dale

Long Dale

Palace
Farm
PO
Sheen

7

Lower
House

PH

HIDE LA

Wallpit
Lane

61

Moat
Hall

6   Townend

BANK SIDE

DIG ST

Newfield

Bridge-end

Digmer
Farm

HARROTS LA

Hartington Dale

B5054

Crakelow

MARKET PL

Factory

STONEWELL LA

CHURCH ST

PH

Hartington
CE Prim
Sch

Hartington Hall
YH

Hartington

PO

HALL BANK

HIGH CROSS

5

PARSONS
CL

P

LEISURE LA

HIGHFIELD LA

Mast

SK17

MILL LA

60

Lower
Barn

Crossland
Sides

Scaldersitch

Banktop

Hartington
Bridge

River Dove

Pennilow

REYNARDS LA

The
Raikes

4

Raikes Farm

Staden
Barn

B5054

Brighton

3

Lower Hurst
Farm

59   Tower

Beresford Dale

Upper
Hurst

2   Harecops

Beresford
Cottage

Barracks
Farm

BERESFORD LA

Beresford Lane
Farm

Archford Moor
Farm

Wolfscote
Hill

1

Archford Moor

Beresford Lane

Field House
Farm

DE6

Wolfscote
Grange

58

23
35

POWN ST
PH

Derbyshire STREET ATLAS

Cheshire STREET ATLAS

A34 Congleton

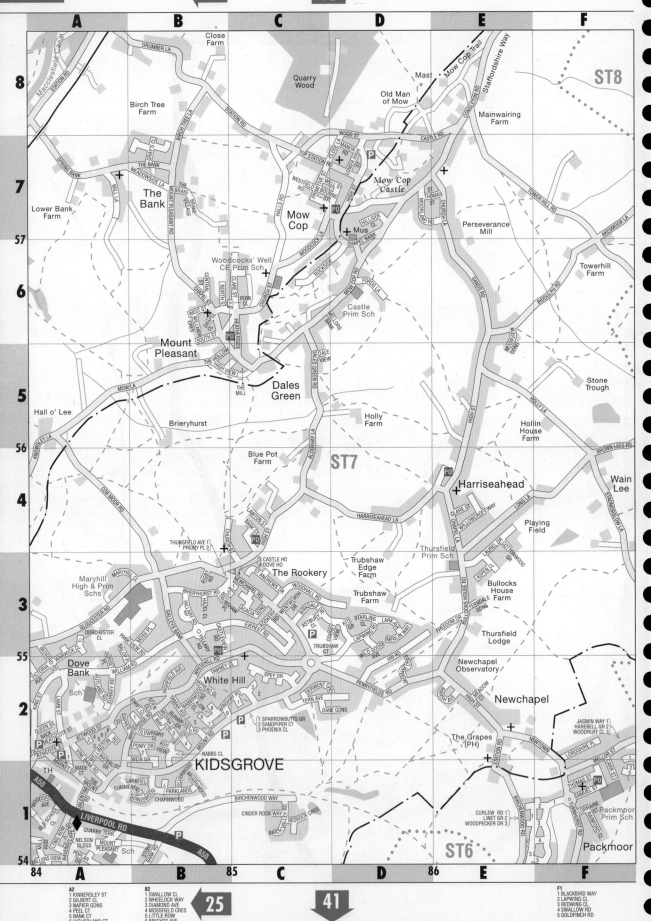

Map labels (read from image):

ST8

Close Farm
Quarry Wood
Mast
Old Man of Mow
Mow Cop Trail
Staffordshire Way
Mainwairing Farm
Castle Rd

Birch Tree Farm
The Bank
Lower Bank Farm
Mow Cop
Mow Cop Castle
Perseverance Mill

Towerhill Farm

Woodcocks' Well CE Prim Sch
Mount Pleasant
Castle Prim Sch

Stone Trough

Dales Green
Brieryhurst
Hall o' Lee
Holly Farm
Hollin House Farm

Blue Pot Farm
ST7
Harriseahead
Wain Lee

Maryhill High & Prim Schs
The Rookery
Trubshaw Edge Farm
Thursfield Prim Sch
Playing Field

Dove Bank
White Hill
Trubshaw Farm
Bullocks House Farm
Thursfield Lodge

Newchapel Observatory
Newchapel

KIDSGROVE
The Grapes (PH)

LIVERPOOL RD
Packmoor Prim Sch
Packmoor
ST6

A2
1 KINNERSLEY ST
2 GILBERT CL
3 NAPIER GDNS
4 PEEL CT
5 BANK CT
6 HIGHERLAND CT
7 WESLEY GDNS
8 VICTORIA CT

B2
1 SWALLOW CL
2 WHEELOCK WAY
3 DIAMOND AVE
4 MOSSFIELD CRES
5 LITTLE ROW
6 BRIGHTS AVE
7 BIRCHES WAY
8 SILVERMINE CL
9 MAGPIE CRES

F1
1 BLACKBIRD WAY
2 LAPWING CL
3 REDWING CL
4 SWALLOW RD
5 GOLDFINCH RD

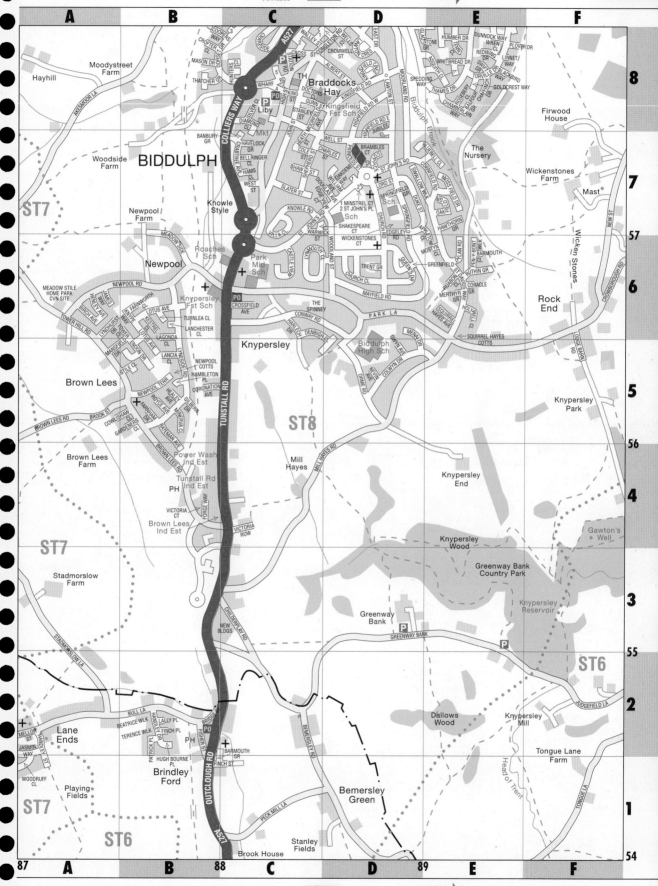

27
17
27
43

ST8
ST13
ST6
ST9

Miriams Farm
New St
Gun Battery La
Cottage La
Stonefields
Wraggs Cl
Davis Cl
Rowan Cl
Trentley Dr
High Cl
Only Wd
Leek La

Robin Hill
Robin Hill

Trent Head Farm
Springbank Farm
Barrage Rd
Moortop
Mast

Three Nooks Farm
Sprinks Farm
Hollins
Catt Hayes Farm
Shutter Shaw Farm
Cliff Wood
Blackwood House

Crowborough
Lask Edge
Top Rd
Lask Edge Rd

Well House Farm
Crowborough Rd
Molehouse
Park House
Damslane

Greenhouse
Chatsworth
The Ashes

Crowborough Farm
Moorfields

Crowborough Wood
Cowall Moor La
White Chimneys
Small Lane
Grange Farm
Blackwood Hill

Cowall Moor
Cowall
Ladymoor Gate
Dalehouse Wood
Park Hayes
Holly Wood

Hollin Wood
Ladymoor La
Ladymoor Farm

Marshes Hill
Lanehead
Holehouse La
Knowles Farm
Little Hollies Farm

Judgefield La
Hodgefield
Hollin House

Tongue La
Coppice Farm
Sands La

Brown Edge Farm
Hill Top
PH
Back La
Hough Hill

Lower Stonehouse
Mast
Top La
Chapel La
Hill Top Cl
Holehouse

Old La
New La
Chapel La
Broad La
Morris House Farm

BOARDMANS BANK 1
CHURCH RD 2
ST ANNE'S VALE 3
St Anne's CE Prim Sch

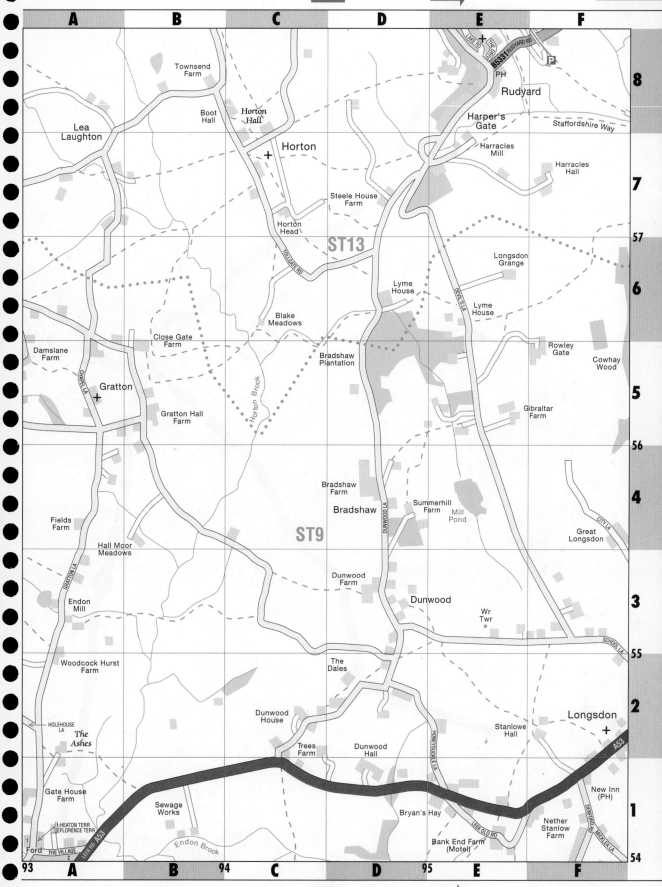

18 30

A B C D E F

8 Rudyard

Townsend Farm

Boot Hall

Horton Hall

Lea Laughton

Harper's Gate

Harracles Mill

Staffordshire Way

Horton

Harracles Hall

7

Steele House Farm

Horton Head

ST13

57

Longsdon Grange

6

Toll Gate Rd

Lyme House

Blake Meadows

Lyme House

Damslane Farm

Close Gate Farm

Bradshaw Plantation

Rowley Gate

Cowhay Wood

Gratton

Horton Brook

5

Gratton Hall Farm

Gibraltar Farm

56

Fields Farm

Bradshaw Farm

4

Bradshaw

Summerhill Farm

Mill Pond

City La

Great Longsdon

ST9

Gratton La

Hall Moor Meadows

Dunwood La

Dunwood Farm

Endon Mill

Dunwood

Wr Twr

3

School La

55

Woodcock Hurst Farm

The Dales

Dunwood House

2

Stanlowe Hall

Longsdon

Holehouse La

The Ashes

Trees Farm

Dunwood Hall

Honeysuckle La

A53

Gate House Farm

Sewage Works

New Inn (PH)

1 Heaton Terr
2 Florence Terr

1

Leek La A53

Bryan's Hay

Leek Old Rd

Nether Stanlow Farm

Denford Rd

Micklea La

Ford

The Village

Endon Brook

Bank End Farm (Motel)

54

93 A B 94 C D 95 E F

44 30

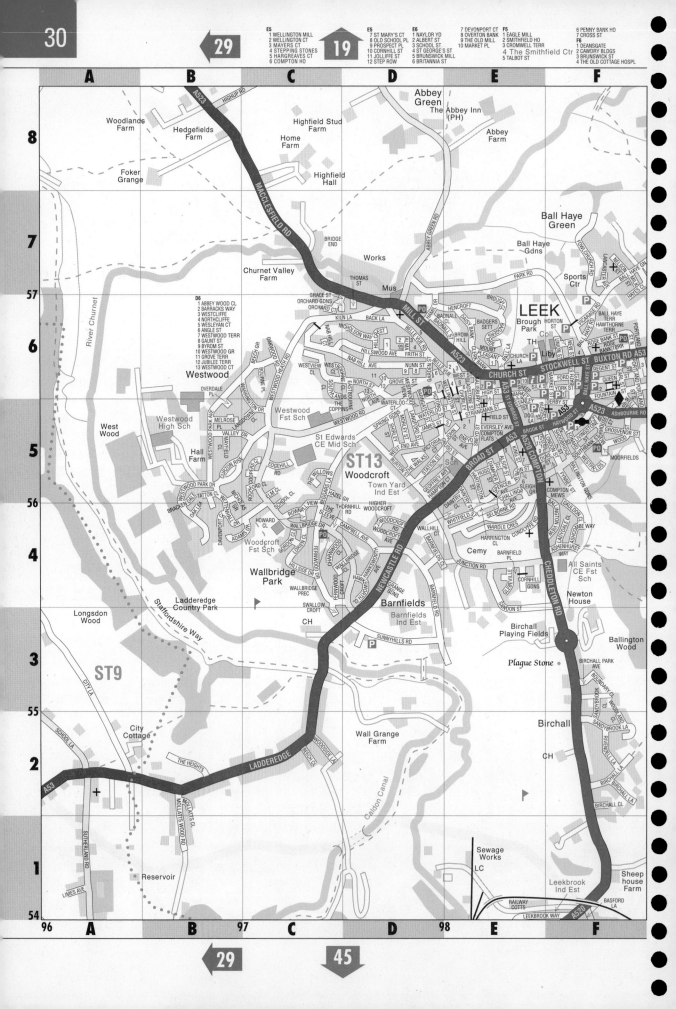

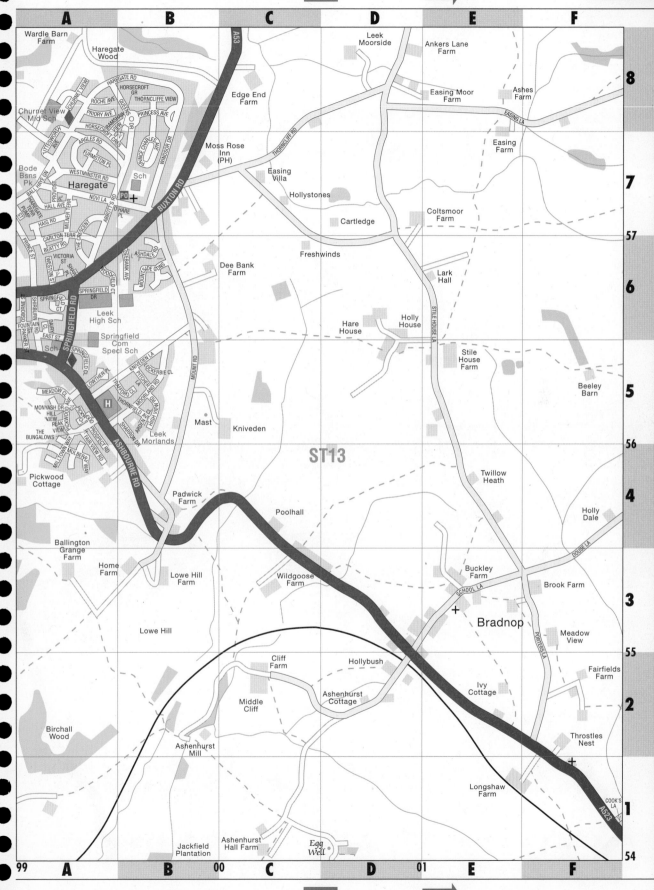

31
21

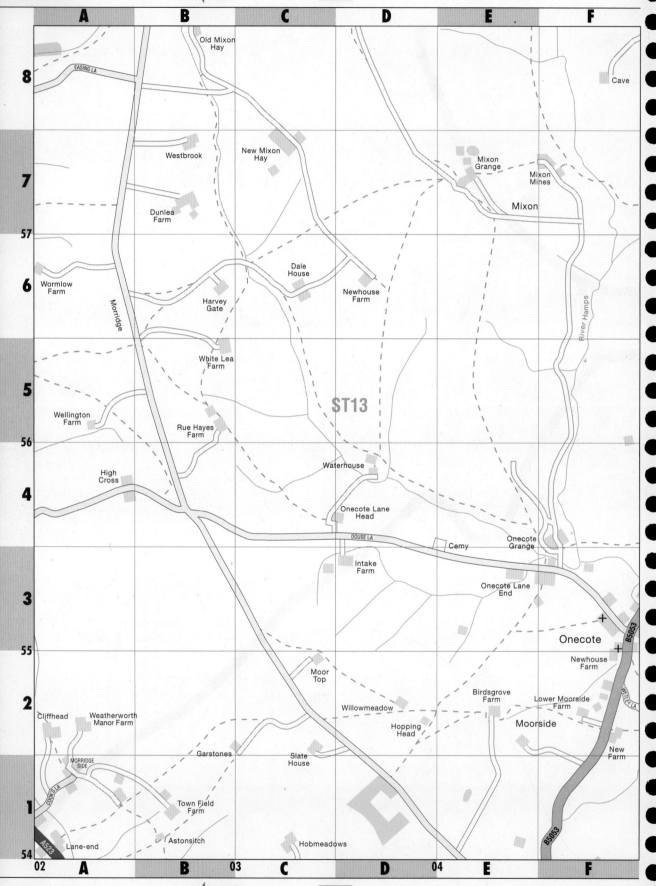

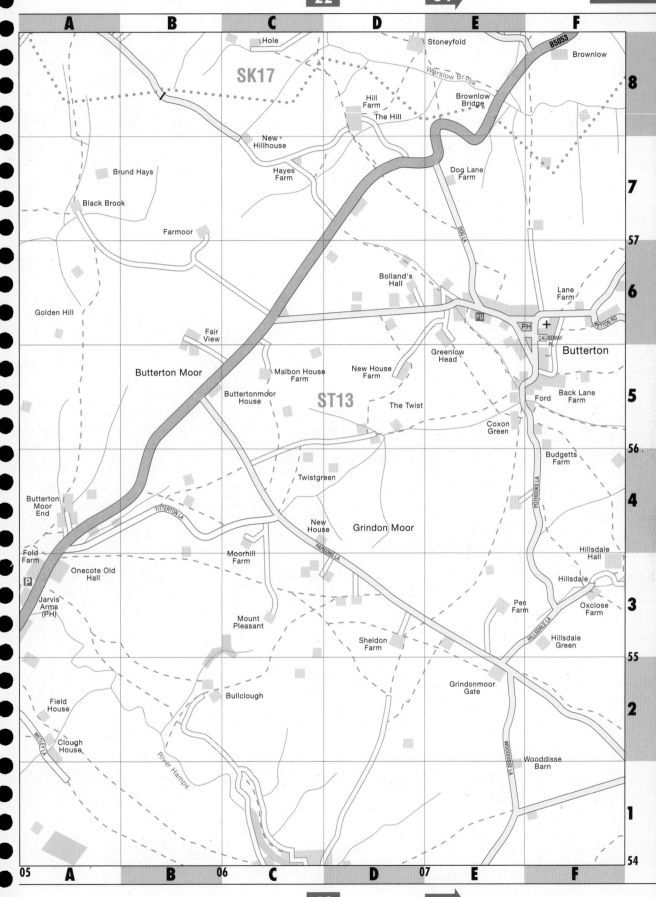

← 33
23 ↑

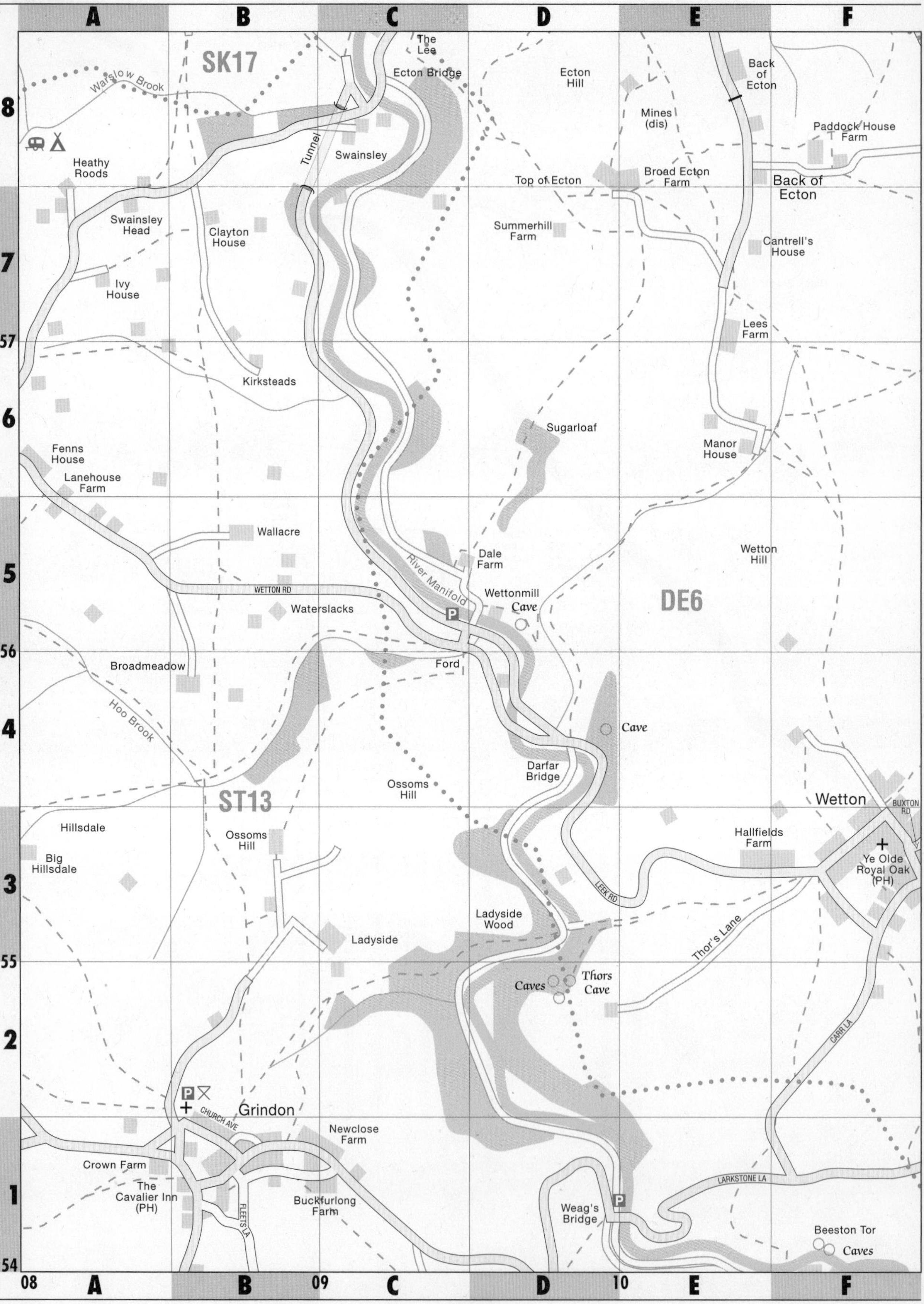

A B C D E F

SK17

8

Warslow Brook
The Lee
Ecton Bridge
Ecton Hill
Back of Ecton
Heathy Roods
Swainsley
Mines (dis)
Paddock House Farm
Top of Ecton
Broad Ecton Farm
Back of Ecton

7

Swainsley Head
Clayton House
Summerhill Farm
Cantrell's House

57

Kirksteads
Ivy House
Lees Farm

6

Fenns House
Sugarloaf
Manor House

Lanehouse Farm
Wallacre
Wetton Hill

5

WETTON RD
River Manifold
Dale Farm
DE6
Waterslacks
Wettonmill
Cave
P

56

Broadmeadow
Ford
Hoo Brook

4

Cave
Darfar Bridge

ST13

Ossoms Hill
Wetton
BUXTON RD

Hillsdale
Ossoms Hill
Hallfields Farm

3

Big Hillsdale
Ye Olde Royal Oak (PH)
Ladyside
Ladyside Wood
Thor's Lane
LEEK RD

55

Caves
Thors Cave

2

Grindon
CARR LA
P

CHURCH AVE

Newclose Farm

1

Crown Farm
The Cavalier Inn (PH)
Buckfurlong Farm
FLEES LA
Weag's Bridge
P
LARKSTONE LA
Beeston Tor
Caves

54

08 A B 09 C D 10 E F

← 33
49 ↓

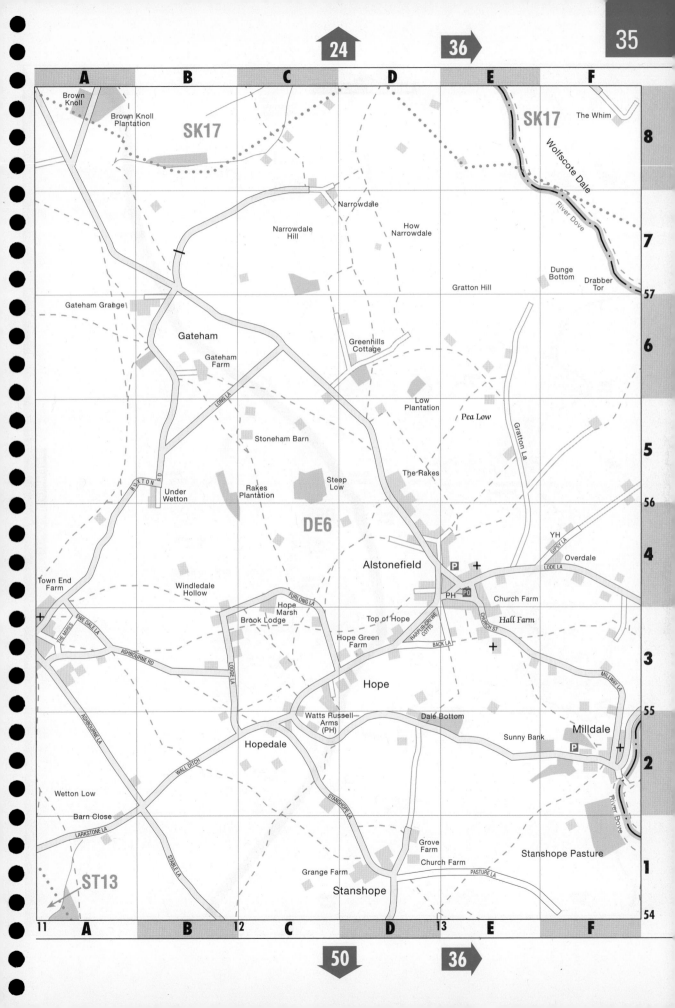

A B C D E F

8

SK17

Brown Knoll

Brown Knoll Plantation

SK17

The Whim

Wolfscote Dale

River Dove

7

Narrowdale

Narrowdale Hill

How Narrowdale

Gratton Hill

Dunge Bottom

Drabber Tor

57

Gateham Grange

Gateham

Gateham Farm

Greenhills Cottage

6

LONG LA

Low Plantation

Pea Low

Gratton La

Stoneham Barn

Steep Low

The Rakes

5

BUXTON RD

Under Wetton

Rakes Plantation

56

DE6

YH

GIPSY LA

Overdale

4

Alstonefield

P

LODE LA

Town End Farm

Windledale Hollow

FURLONG LA

Hope Marsh

PH PO

Church Farm

THE MIRES

EWE DALE LA

Brook Lodge

Top of Hope

HARPUR CREWE COTTS

CHURCH ST

Hall Farm

ASHBOURNE RD

Hope Green Farm

BACK LA

3

LODGE LA

Hope

MILLWAY LA

55

Watts Russell Arms (PH)

Dale Bottom

Sunny Bank

Milldale

ASHBOURNE LA

Hopedale

P

2

WALL DITCH

River Dove

Wetton Low

STANSHOPE LA

Barn Close

Grove Farm

Stanshope Pasture

LARKSTONE LA

Church Farm

1

STABLE LA

ST13

Grange Farm

PASTURE LA

Stanshope

54

A B C D E F

11 12 13

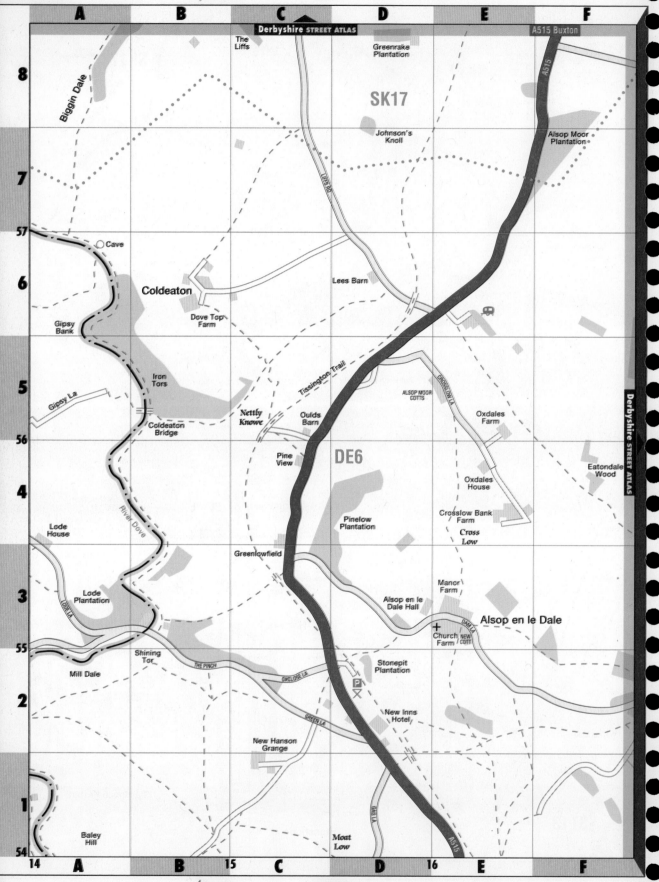

Derbyshire STREET ATLAS

A515 Buxton

A B C D E F

The Liffs

Greenrake Plantation

SK17

Johnson's Knoll

A515

Alsop Moor Plantation

8

7

Cave

57

Coldeaton

Lees Barn

6

Gipsy Bank

Dove Top Farm

Iron Tors

Tissington Trail

Alsop Moor Cotts

CROSSLOW LA

Oxdales Farm

5

Gipsy La

Nettly Knowe

Oulds Barn

Coldeaton Bridge

56

Pine View

DE6

Oxdales House

Eatondale Wood

4

River Dove

Pinelow Plantation

Crosslow Bank Farm

Cross Low

Lode House

Greenlowfield

Manor Farm

3

Lode Plantation

LODE LA

Alsop en le Dale Hall

Alsop en le Dale

DAM LA

NEW COTT

Church Farm

55

Shining Tor

THE PINCH

OXCLOSE LA

Stonepit Plantation

Mill Dale

P

2

GREEN LA

New Inns Hotel

New Hanson Grange

1

GAG LA

A515

Baley Hill

Moat Low

54

14 A B 15 C D 16 E F

Derbyshire STREET ATLAS

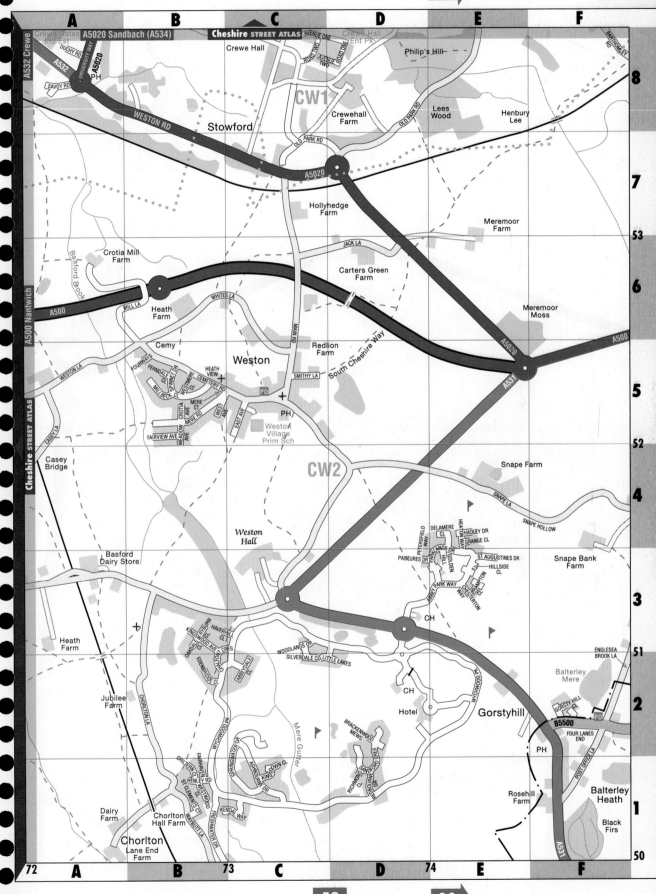

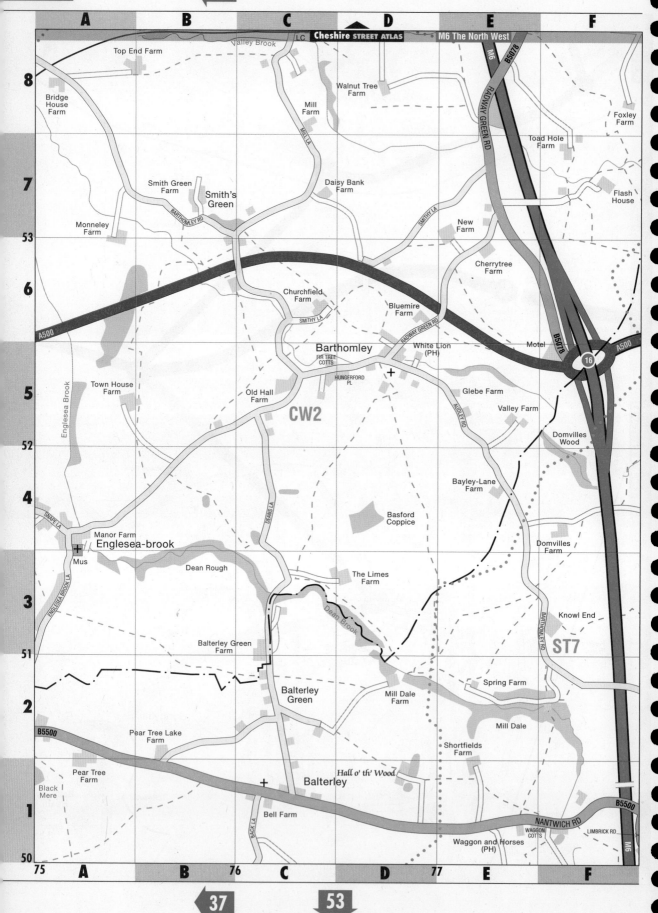

37

Cheshire STREET ATLAS

M6 The North West

A B C D E F

8

Top End Farm

Valley Brook

LC

Walnut Tree Farm

Bridge House Farm

Mill Farm

M6

B5078

Foxley Farm

7

Smith Green Farm

Smith's Green

Daisy Bank Farm

Toad Hole Farm

Flash House

BARTHOMLEY RD

MILL LA

SMITHY LA

RADWAY GREEN RD

53

Monneley Farm

New Farm

6

Churchfield Farm

Bluemire Farm

Cherrytree Farm

A500

SMITHY LA

RADWAY GREEN RD

B5078

Barthomley

White Lion (PH)

Motel

16

A500

FIR TREE COTTS

HUNGERFORD PL

5

Town House Farm

Old Hall Farm

CW2

Glebe Farm

Valley Farm

Englesea Brook

AUDLEY RD

Domvilles Wood

52

DEANS LA

Bayley-Lane Farm

4

SNAPE LA

Basford Coppice

Domvilles Farm

Manor Farm

Englesea-brook

Mus

ENGLESEA BROOK LA

Dean Rough

The Limes Farm

Knowl End

Dean Brook

BARTHOMLEY RD

ST7

3

Balterley Green Farm

51

Spring Farm

2

Balterley Green

Mill Dale Farm

Mill Dale

B5500

Pear Tree Lake Farm

Shortfields Farm

B5500

Pear Tree Farm

Hall o' th' Wood

Balterley

Black Mere

1

Bell Farm

NANTWICH RD

WAGGON COTTS

LIMBRICK RD

BACK LA

Waggon and Horses (PH)

M6

50

75 A 76 B C 76 D 77 E F

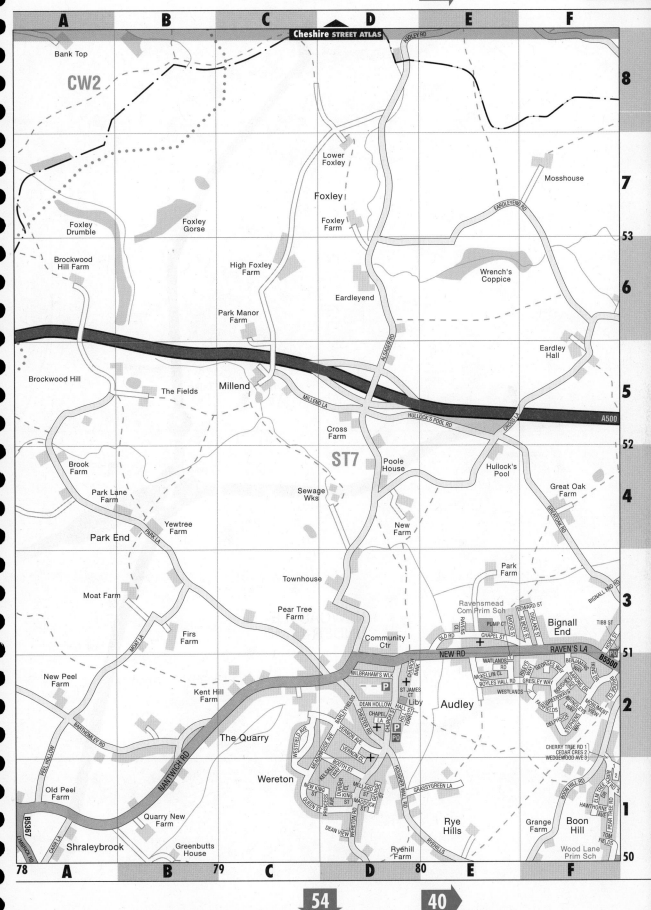

A   B   C   D   E   F

Cheshire STREET ATLAS

Bank Top

CW2

8

Lower
Foxley

Mosshouse

7

Foxley

EARDLEYEND RD

Foxley
Drumble

Foxley
Gorse

Foxley
Farm

53

Brockwood
Hill Farm

High Foxley
Farm

Eardleyend

Wrench's
Coppice

6

Park Manor
Farm

ALSAGER RD

Eardley
Hall

Brockwood Hill

The Fields

Millend

5

MILLEND LA

HULLOCK'S POOL RD

CROSS LA

A500

Cross
Farm

52

ST7

Poole
House

Hullock's
Pool

Brook
Farm

Sewage
Wks

Great Oak
Farm

4

Park Lane
Farm

New
Farm

GREAT OAK RD

Park End

PARK LA

Yewtree
Farm

Park
Farm

BIGNALL END RD

3

Moat Farm

Townhouse

Ravensmead
Com Prim Sch

EDWARD ST

Bignall
End

TIBB ST

MOAT LA

Firs
Farm

Pear Tree
Farm

RAVENS CL

PUMP CT

WOOD ST

DIGLAKE ST
ALBERT ST

51

Community
Ctr

CHAPEL ST

New Peel
Farm

NEW RD

RAVEN'S LA

B5500

PO

New Peel
Farm

WATLANDS
RD

RILEY'S WAY

GEORGES WAY

BENJAMINS
WAY

HOPE ST
IKINS DR

BARTHOMLEY RD

Kent Hill
Farm

WILBRAHAM'S WLK

P

ST JAMES
CT

Liby

McKELLIN CL
BOYLES HALL RD

GRESLEY WAY

WESTLANDS

ROUGHEY
GREENWAY'S
BRINDLE
BOUGHEY RD
AARONS DR

MONUMENT
VIEW

BRIDGE ST

2

WESTFIELD AVE

DEAN HOLLOW

CHESTER RD

CHAPEL LA

CHURCH
BANK

Audley

FAIRFIELDS
STEPHEN'S
WAY

DELPHSIDE

NANTWICH RD

The Quarry

MEADOWSIDE AVE

VERNON AVE

VERNON CL

HALL ST
CHURCH ST

PO

CHERRY TREE RD 1
CEDAR CRES 2
WEDGEWOOD AVE 3

PEEL HOLLOW

Wereton

KELSALL AVE

BOOTH ST

MELLARD ST
GEORGE ST

HOUGHER WALL RD

GRASSYGREEN LA

BOON HILL RD

HAWTHORNE
AVE

ELM TREE DR
PEAR TREE RD

1

Old Peel
Farm

NEW KING
ST
PRINCESS
AVE

QUEEN ST

DURBER
CL

KING ST
MADDOCK
ST

Rye
Hills

Grange
Farm

Boon
Hill

TOM
FIELDS

B5367

Quarry New
Farm

DEAN VIEW

WERETON RD

Ryehill
Farm

RYEHILLS

Wood Lane
Prim Sch

50

IMBROOK RD
CARR LA

Shraleybrook

Greenbutts
House

78   A   B   79   C   D   80   E   F

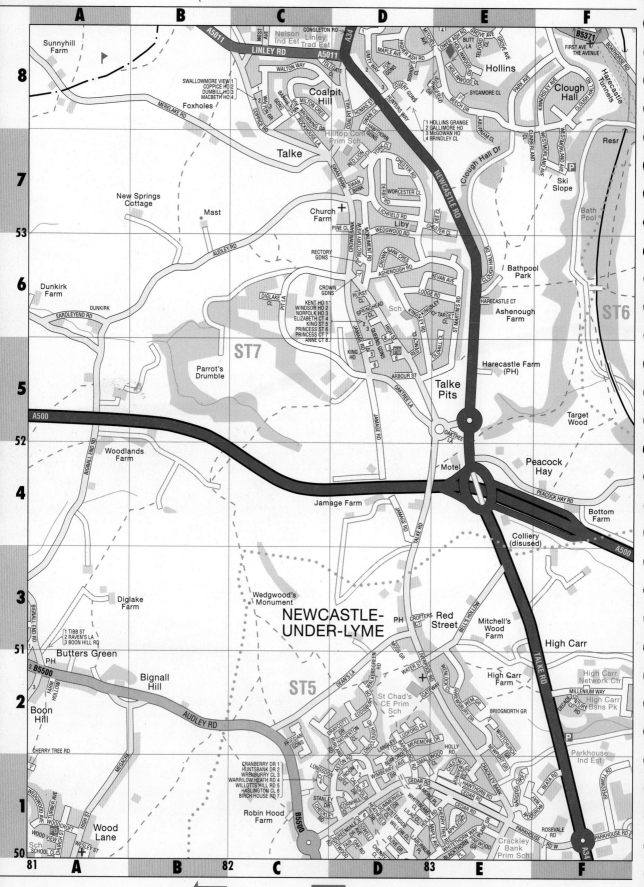

Sunnyhill Farm

Foxholes

SWALLOWMORE VIEW 1
COPPICE HO 2
DUMBILL HO 3
MACBETH HO 4

MERELAKE RD

Coalpit Hill

WALTON WAY

Talke

New Springs Cottage

Mast

Church Farm

Liby

Dunkirk Farm

Dunkirk

EARDLEYEND RD

AUDLEY RD

PINE CL

CROWN BANK CRES

RECTORY GDNS

DIGLAKE CL

CROWN GDNS

KENT HO 1
WINDSOR HO 2
NORFOLK HO 3
ELIZABETH CT 4
KING ST 5
PRINCESS ST 6
PRINCESS CT 7
ANNE CT 8.

HURST

SPRINGHEAD

KING HO

JAMAGE RD

QUEENS GDNS

ARBOUR ST

ST7

Parrot's Drumble

A500

Woodlands Farm

BIGNALL END RD

Jamage Farm

JAMAGE RD

TALKE RD

Motel

Talke Pits

OAKTREE LA

Peacock Hay

PEACOCK HAY RD

Colliery (disused)

Bottom Farm

A500

Target Wood

Harecastle Farm (PH)

Ashenough Farm

HARECASTLE CT

BEVAN AVE

LODGE RD

Sch

KINGSLEY RD

ST MARTIN'S RD

TARGET LA

REGENCY CT

Hollins

Clough Hall

1 HOLLINS GRANGE
2 GALLIMORE HO
3 McGOWAN HO
4 BRINDLEY CL

Clough Hall Dr

PARK AVE

CUMBERLAND

NEWCASTLE RD

CLOUGH HALL RD

Ski Slope

Bath Pool

Resr

Harecastle Tunnels

ST6

Bathpool Park

CONGLETON RD

LINLEY RD

A5011

Nelson Ind Est

Linley Trad Est

A34

A5011

UNITY WAY

FOX GDNS

COVERT GDNS

MAPLE AVE

HIGHER ASH RD

LOWER ASH RD

GROVE AVE

MITCHELL AVE

BUTT LA

TELFORD RD

GROVE AVE

FIRST AVE
THE AVENUE

B5371

BOATHORSE RD

HOLLINWOOD CL

SYCAMORE CL

BEECH DR

LABURNUM CL

WESTMORLAND AVE

B5500

Butters Green

PH

1 TIBB ST
2 RAVEN'S LA
3 BOON HILL RD

BIGNALL END RD

FARM HOLLOW

Boon Hill

CHERRY TREE RD

Diglake Farm

Bignall Hill

AUDLEY RD

MEGACRE

Wedgwood's Monument

NEWCASTLE-
UNDER-LYME

ST5

Red Street

CROFTERS CT

PH

BELLS HOLLOW

Mitchell's Wood Farm

High Carr Farm

High Carr

TALKE RD

High Carr Network Ctr

MILLENIUM WAY

High Carr Bsns Pk

Parkhouse Ind Est

P

CRANBERRY DR 1
HUNTSBANK DR 2
WRENBURRY CL 3
WARRILOW HEATH RD 4
WILLOTTS HILL RD 5
HASLINGTON CL 6
BIRCH HOUSE RD 7

Robin Hood Farm

B5500

St Chad's CE Prim Sch

DEAN'S LA

WATER ST

GATEWAY

LIVERPOOL RD

SHREWSBURY DR

BRIDGNORTH GR

HOLLY RD

CEDAR RD

Wood Lane

WEDGWOOD AVE

TURNER AVE

HIGH ST

WOODCROFT

WOOD VIEW

CHURCH

WESLEY ST

Sch

SCHOOL CL

PO

FRIESIAN GDNS

LONGSDON CL

WIMBERRY DR

STANLEY DR

CORNHILL

CREKLEY

MEREMORE DR

SMALLWOOD CL

NEWPORT GR

WHITCHURCH

CHESTNUT GR

CRACKLEY BANK

BEXTA RD

Crackley Bank Prim Sch

PARKHOUSE RD

ROSEVALE RD

SPEEDWELL RD

PARKHOUSE RD E

A34

Parkhouse

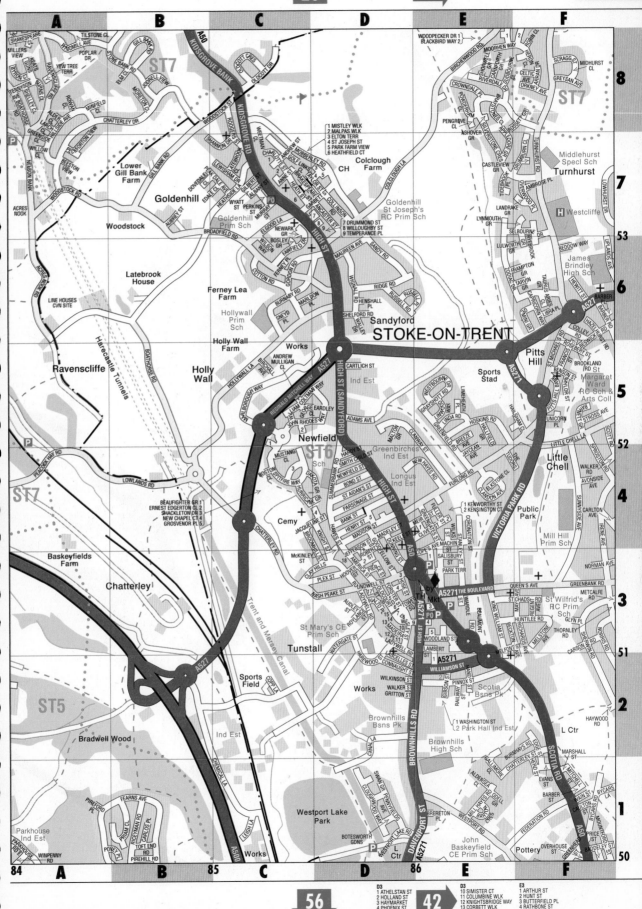

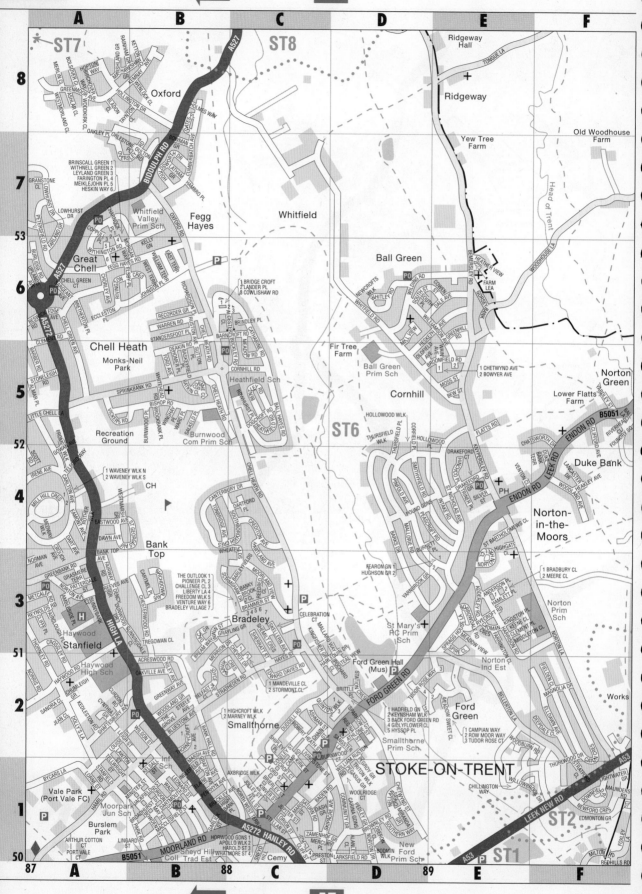

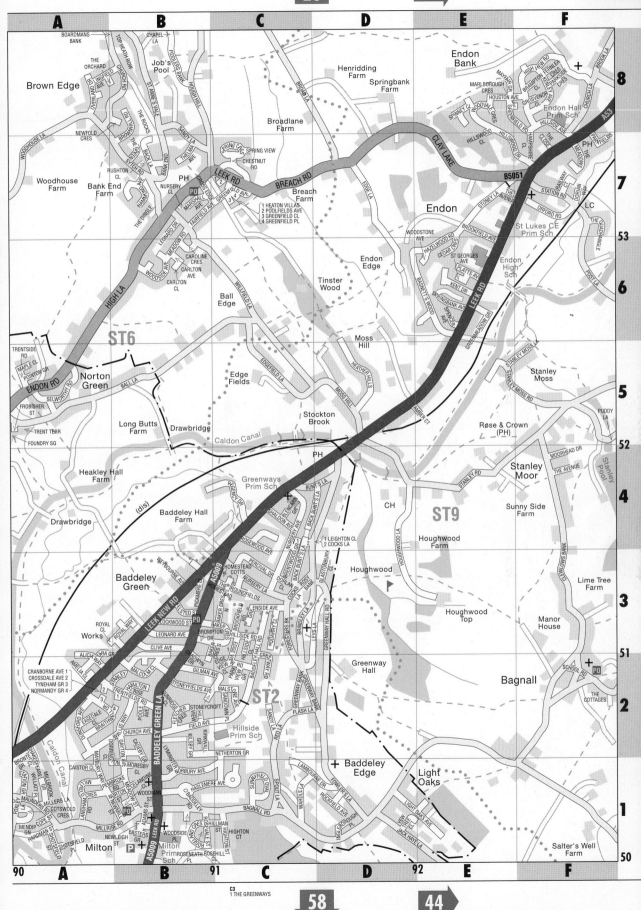

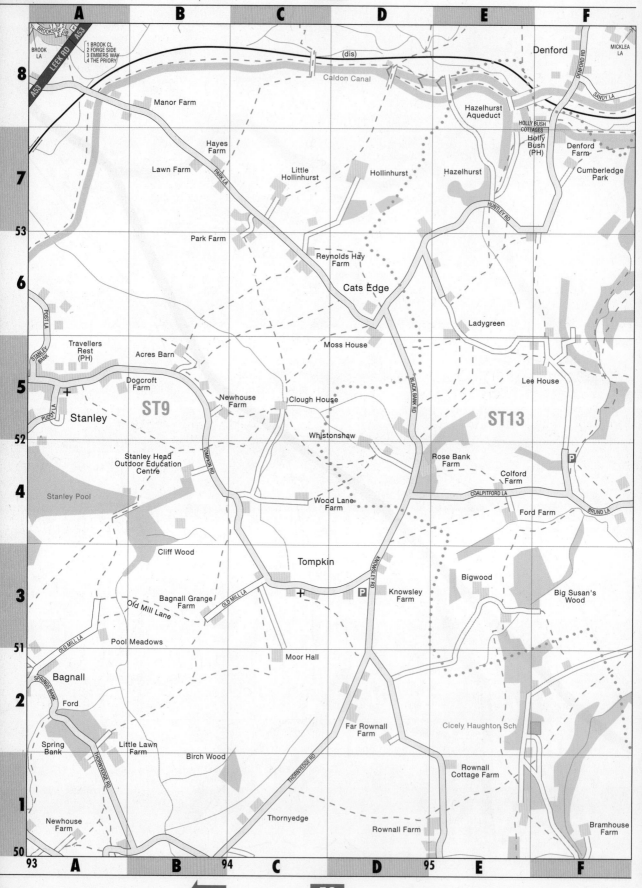

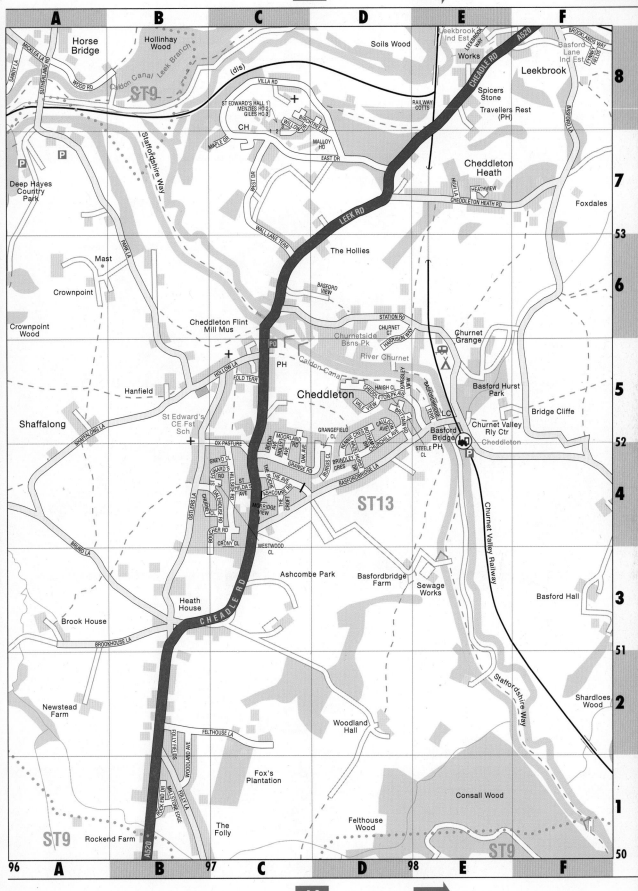

45
31

A | B | C | D | E | F

8

Brooklands Way

Roost Hill

Revedge

Fynneylane Farm

Yew Trees Farm

Ballfields

Sixoaks Farm

Apesford

7

Crowholt

P

Roughstone Hole

53

Combes Brook

Barnfield

Ringehay

6

Ferny Hill

Coombes Valley Nature Reserve

Sixoaks Wood

Oldfield

Cloughmeadow Cottage

Padwick

Padwick Wood

The Combes

Spiritholes Wood

Sharpcliffe Hall

Blackhill Wood

5

Lower House Farm

Upper Fernyhill Farm

Home Farm

52

Basford Grange

ST13

Sneyd Arms Farm

4

The Ridge

Low Wood

Whitehough Wood

Little Rocks Plantation

Basford Green

Mill Wood

Crab Tree Farm

ST10

Whitehough

3

Mosslee Mill Farm

Mosslee Barn

Brockholes

51

Collyhole

The Clough

2

Hills Farm

Mosslee Hall Farm

Stakebank Wood

Blackbank Wood

Coltstone

CHURCH LA

Middle Farm

Turner's Knipe

Intake Farm

Stocks Green

CHURCH MDW

1

Churnet Valley Railway

Rough Intake

Oddo Hall

CHURCHFIELD CT

River Churnet

ST9

50

99 | A | B | 00 | C | D | 01 | E | F

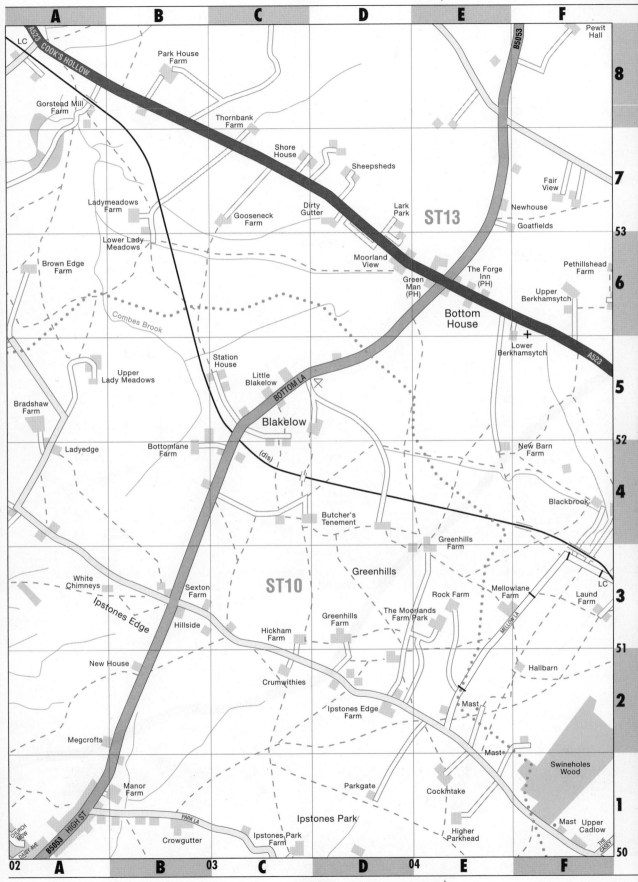

↑ 32

→ 48

↓ 62

→ 48

Grid references (top): A B C D E F

Grid references (right): 8 7 53 6 5 52 4 3 51 2 1 50

Grid references (bottom): A B C D E F — 02 03 04

LC
A523 COOK'S HOLLOW

Gorstead Mill Farm

Park House Farm

Thornbank Farm

Shore House

Sheepsheds

Brown Edge Farm

Ladymeadows Farm

Gooseneck Farm

Dirty Gutter

Lark Park

Lower Lady Meadows

Moorland View

ST13

Newhouse

Fair View

Goatfields

B5053

Pewit Hall

Combes Brook

Green Man (PH)

The Forge Inn (PH)

Pethillshead Farm

Upper Berkhamsytch

Bottom House

Lower Berkhamsytch

A523

Upper Lady Meadows

Station House

Little Blakelow

BOTTOM LA

Bradshaw Farm

Blakelow

Ladyedge

Bottomlane Farm

(dis)

New Barn Farm

Butcher's Tenement

Blackbrook

Greenhills Farm

White Chimneys

Sexton Farm

ST10

Greenhills

Ipstones Edge

Hillside

Hickham Farm

Greenhills Farm

The Moorlands Farm Park

Rock Farm

Mellowlane Farm

MELLOW LA

LC

Laund Farm

New House

Crumwithies

Hallbarn

Megcrofts

Ipstones Edge Farm

Mast

Mast

Swineholes Wood

Manor Farm

Parkgate

Cockintake

Higher Parkhead

Mast

Upper Cadlow

CHURCH MDW

DAISY AVE

B5053 HIGH ST

PARK LA

Crowgutter

Ipstones Park Farm

Ipstones Park

THE CASEY

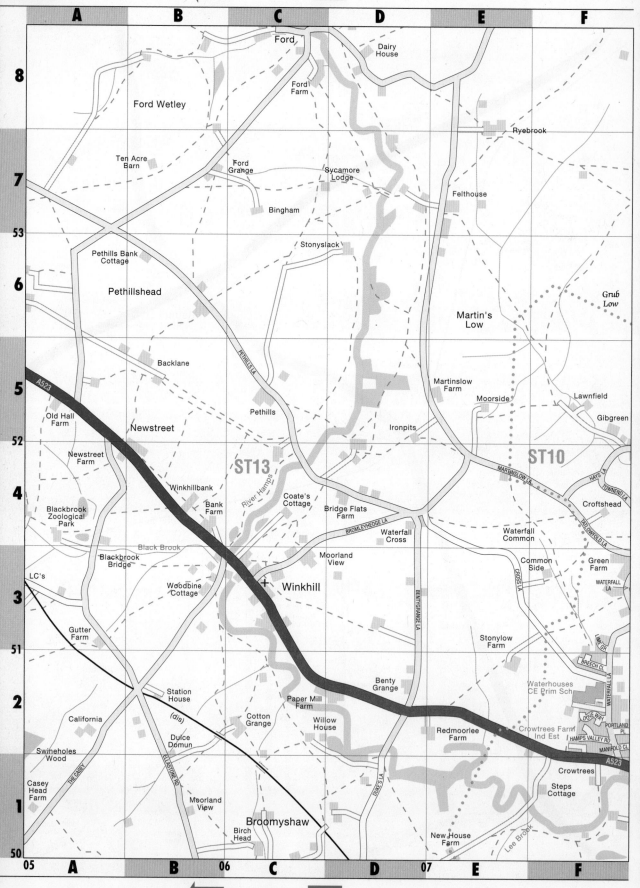

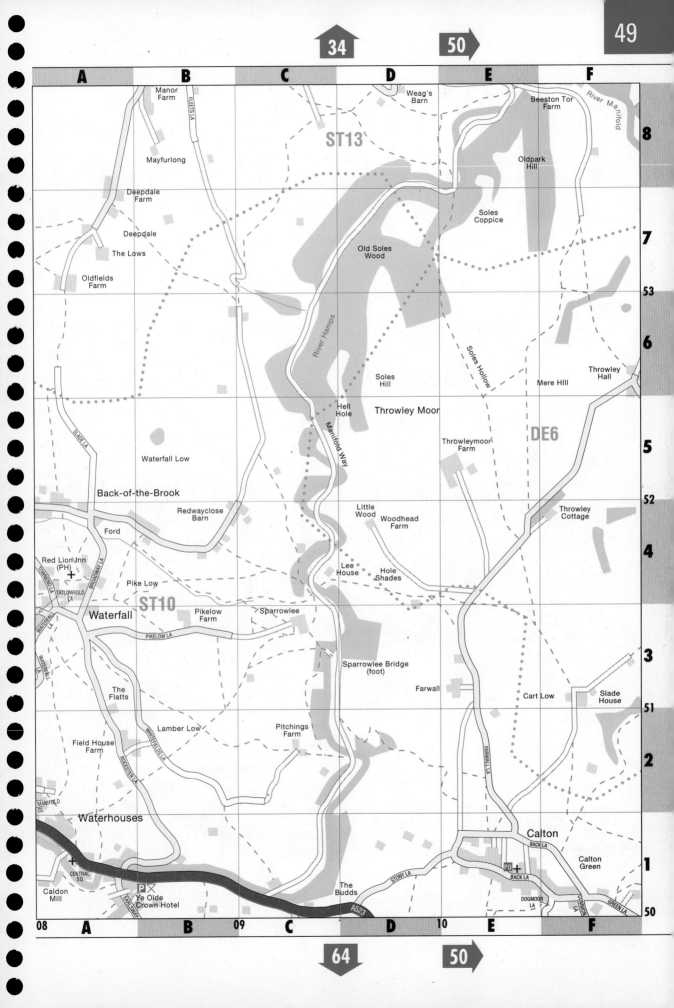

A B C D E F

8

ST13

Bincliff Mines (dis)

Long Low

Cheshire Wood

Damgate

Hall Dale

Hurt's Wood

7

53

Bingley Wood

Dove Dale

Hill Top Farm

Ilamtops Low

6

Castern

ILAM MOOR LA

Beechenhill

Ilam Tops

Ilamtops Farm

Castern Hall

Sandbroom Wood

5

52

DE6

River Lodge

Steeple House

Moor Plantation

4

River Manifold

Rushley Bridge

LODGE LA

Rushley Barn

Rushley

Bunster Hill

St Bertram's Well

Rushley Wood

Abbot's Banks

Musden Grange

Garden Farm

Ilam

Home Farm

3

Musden Wood

Ilam CE Prim Sch

Home Farm

51

Ilam Country Park

Cvn Pk

2

Upper Musden

Ilam Hall (Youth Hostel)

St Bertram's Bridge

Oxleisure Farm

ST10

Hinkley Wood

Doglane Farm

DERB LA

Fieldhead

Musden Low

1

Parson's Wood

50

11 A B 12 C D 13 E F

36

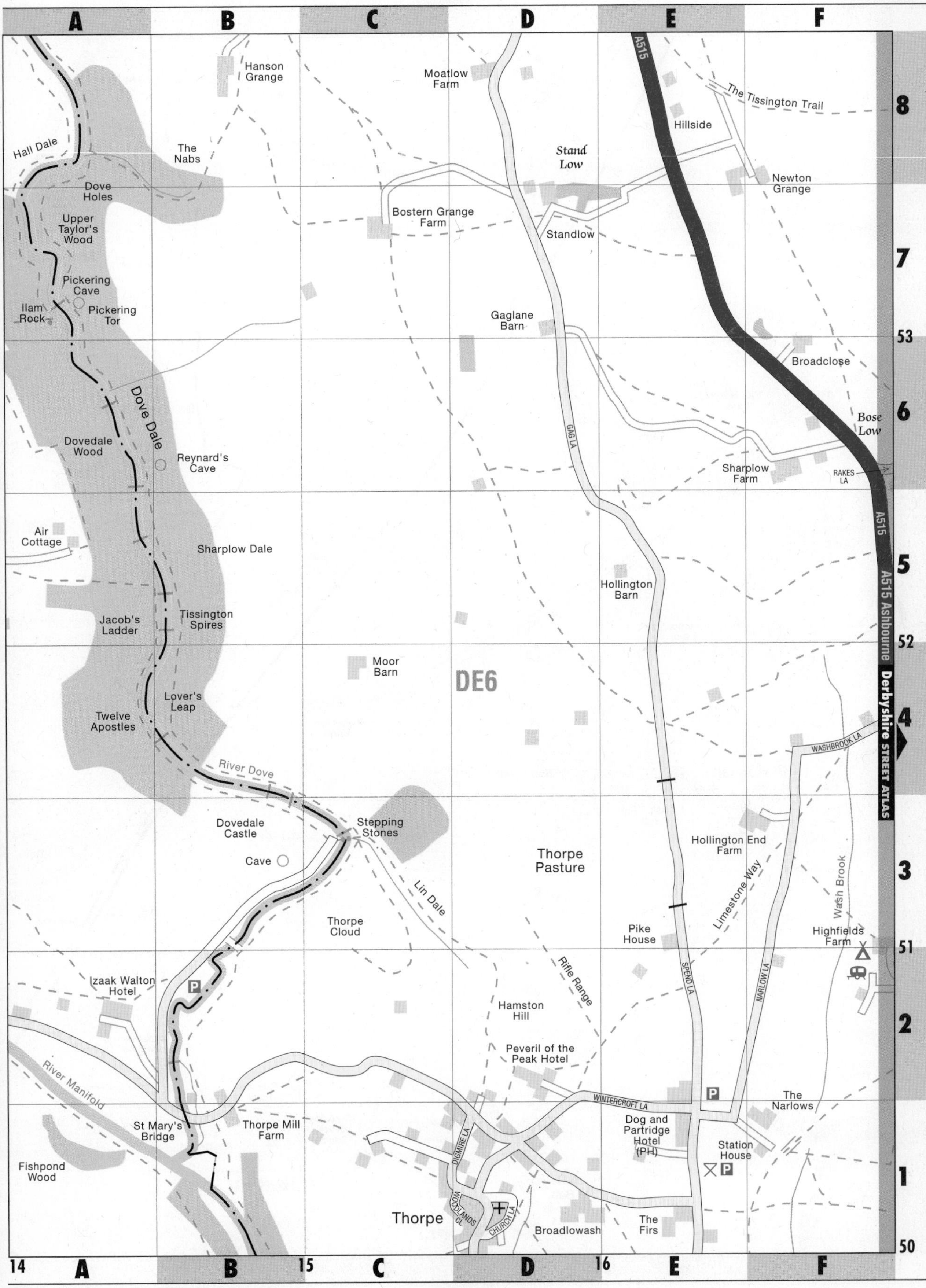
A
B
C
D
E
F
Hanson Grange
Moatlow Farm
A515
The Tissington Trail
8
Hillside
Hall Dale
The Nabs
Stand Low
Newton Grange
Dove Holes
Upper Taylor's Wood
Bostern Grange Farm
Standlow
7
Pickering Cave
Ilam Rock
Pickering Tor
Gaglane Barn
53
Broadclose
Dove Dale
Bose Low
6
Dovedale Wood
Reynard's Cave
GAG LA
Sharplow Farm
RAKES LA
Air Cottage
Sharplow Dale
5
Hollington Barn
Jacob's Ladder
Tissington Spires
A515 Ashbourne
52
Moor Barn
DE6
Lover's Leap
Twelve Apostles
4
WASHBROOK LA
River Dove
Dovedale Castle
Stepping Stones
Hollington End Farm
Thorpe Pasture
Cave
3
Lin Dale
Limestone Way
Wash Brook
Thorpe Cloud
Pike House
Highfields Farm
51
Izaak Walton Hotel
Rifle Range
SPEND LA
NARLOW LA
Hamston Hill
2
River Manifold
Peveril of the Peak Hotel
WINTERCROFT LA
The Narlows
St Mary's Bridge
Thorpe Mill Farm
Dog and Partridge Hotel (PH)
Station House
DIGMIRE LA
Fishpond Wood
1
WOODLANDS CL
CHURCH LA
Thorpe
Broadlowash
The Firs
50
14
15
16

66

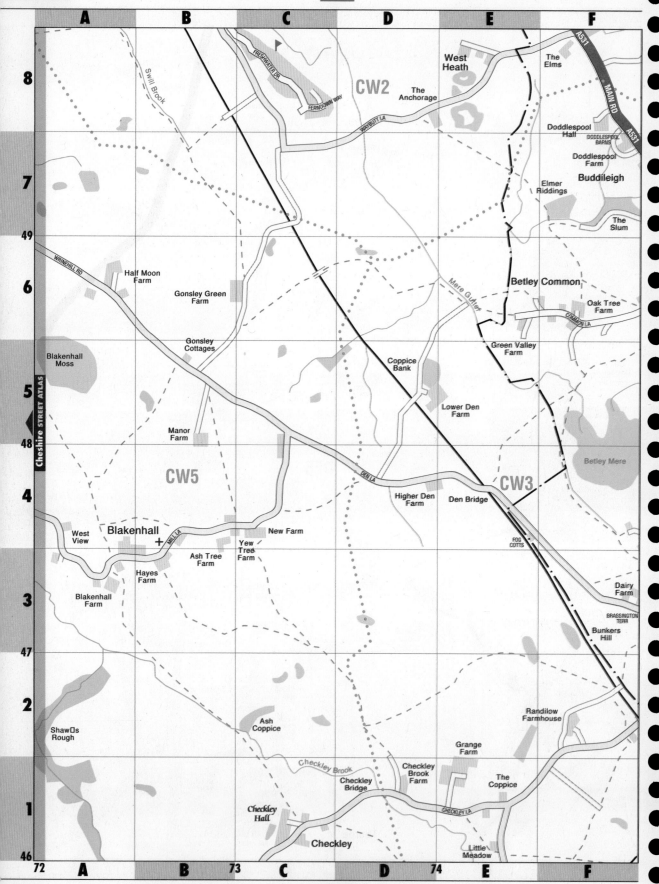

Cheshire STREET ATLAS

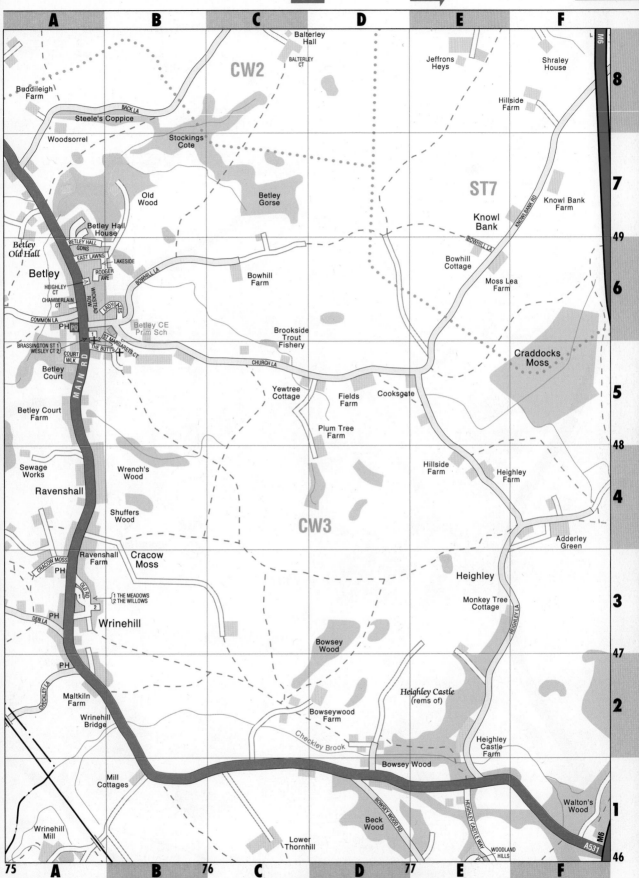

A   B   C   D   E   F

8
7
49
6
5
48
4
3
47
2
1
46

CW2

Balterley Hall
BALTERLEY CT

Jeffrons Heys

Shraley House

M6

Buddileigh Farm

BACK LA
Steele's Coppice
Woodsorrel

Stockings Cote

Hillside Farm

ST7

Old Wood

Betley Gorse

Knowl Bank

Knowl Bank Farm

KNOWL BANK RD

Betley Hall House

Betley Old Hall

BETLEY HALL GDNS
EAST LAWNS
LAKESIDE
RODGER AVE

Bowhill Farm

BOWHILL LA

Bowhill Cottage

Moss Lea Farm

Betley

HEIGHLEY CT
CHAMBERLAIN CT
COMMON LA
PH PO
BRASSINGTON ST 1
WESLEY CT 2
COURT WLK
THE BUTTS
ST MARGARETS CT
WICKSTEAD ROW
LADYGALES

Betley CE Prim Sch

Brookside Trout Fishery

CHURCH LA

Craddocks Moss

Betley Court

MAIN RD

Yewtree Cottage

Fields Farm

Cooksgate

Plum Tree Farm

Betley Court Farm

Sewage Works

Wrench's Wood

Hillside Farm

Heighley Farm

Ravenshall

Shuffers Wood

CW3

Adderley Green

Ravenshall Farm

Cracow Moss

CRACOW MOSS

OLD RD
1 THE MEADOWS
2 THE WILLOWS
1
2

PH

Heighley

Monkey Tree Cottage

PH
DEN LA
PH

Wrinehill

Bowsey Wood

HEIGHLEY LA

PH
CHECKLEY LA

Maltkiln Farm

Heighley Castle (rems of)

Wrinehill Bridge

Bowseywood Farm

Checkley Brook

Heighley Castle Farm

Mill Cottages

Bowsey Wood

BOWSEY WOOD RD

HEIGHLEY CASTLE WAY

Walton's Wood

Wrinehill Mill

Beck Wood

WOODLAND HILLS

M6

A531

Lower Thornhill

75   A   B   76   C   D   77   E   F   46

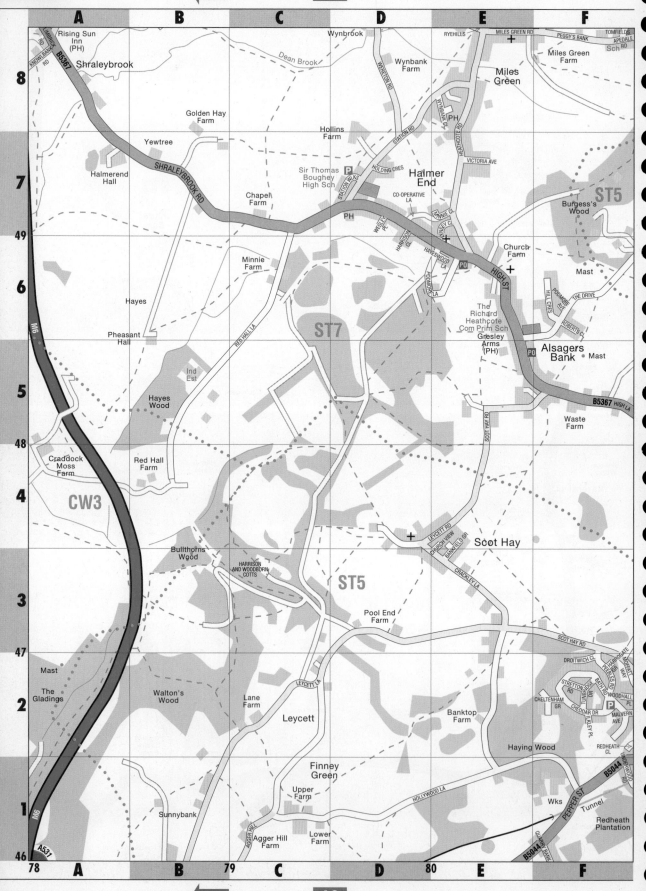

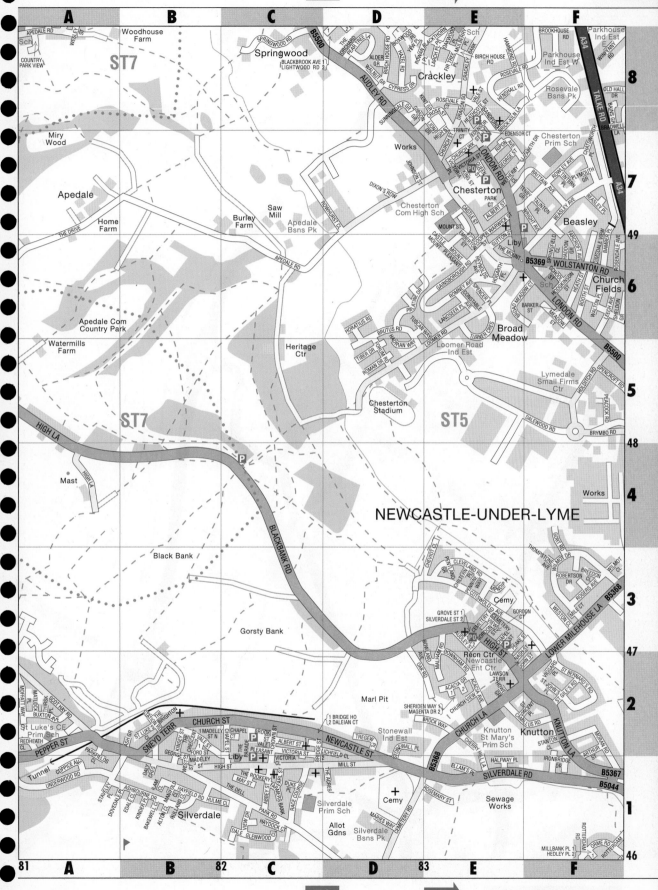

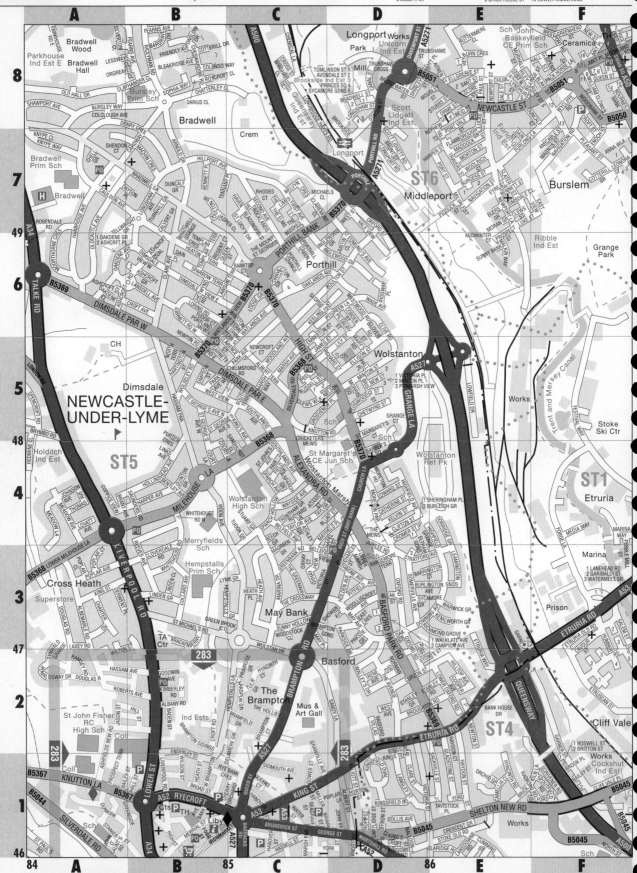

55
41

C5
1 WELLINGTON ST
2 PALMERSTON ST

E7
1 EMBLETON WLK
2 CLOVELLY WLK

E8
1 ENNERDALE CL
2 SANCTON GN
3 BULSTRODE ST
4 DALEHALL GDNS
5 TYLER GR
6 JOSEPH ST

F7
1 LESSWAYS WLK
2 BIGSBURY WLK
3 STROMA CL
4 BURMARSH WLK

F8
1 WEDGWOOD PL
2 JENKINS ST
3 NICHOLAS ST
4 WEDGWOOD ST
5 CLAYHANGER ST
6 BRICK HOUSE ST

7 KEATES ST
8 ST JOHNS SQ
9 FOUNTAIN PL
10 FOUNTAIN CT
11 FURLONG PAS
12 FURLONG PAR
13 LOWER HADDERIDGE

14 ROBIN CROFT
15 CLEVELAND ST
16 STEVENTON PL

For full street detail of the
highlighted area see page 283.

55
71

F2
1 LAKESIDE CL
2 WATER GLADES CL
3 WATERMEADOW GR
4 WATERSEDGE GR
5 MERE SIDE CL
6 BULLRUSHES CL

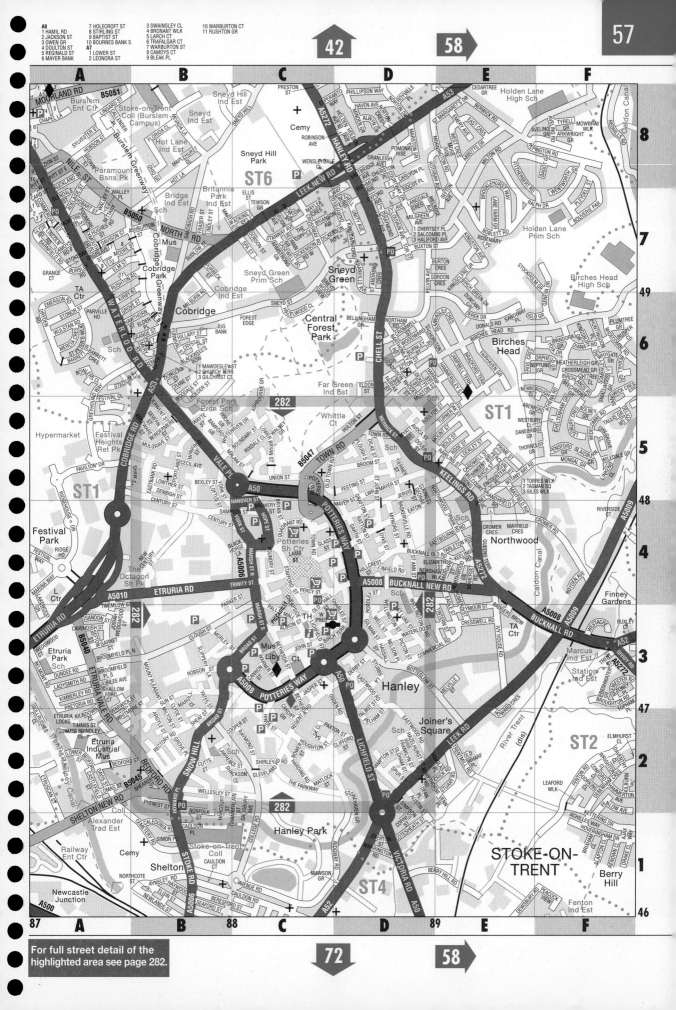

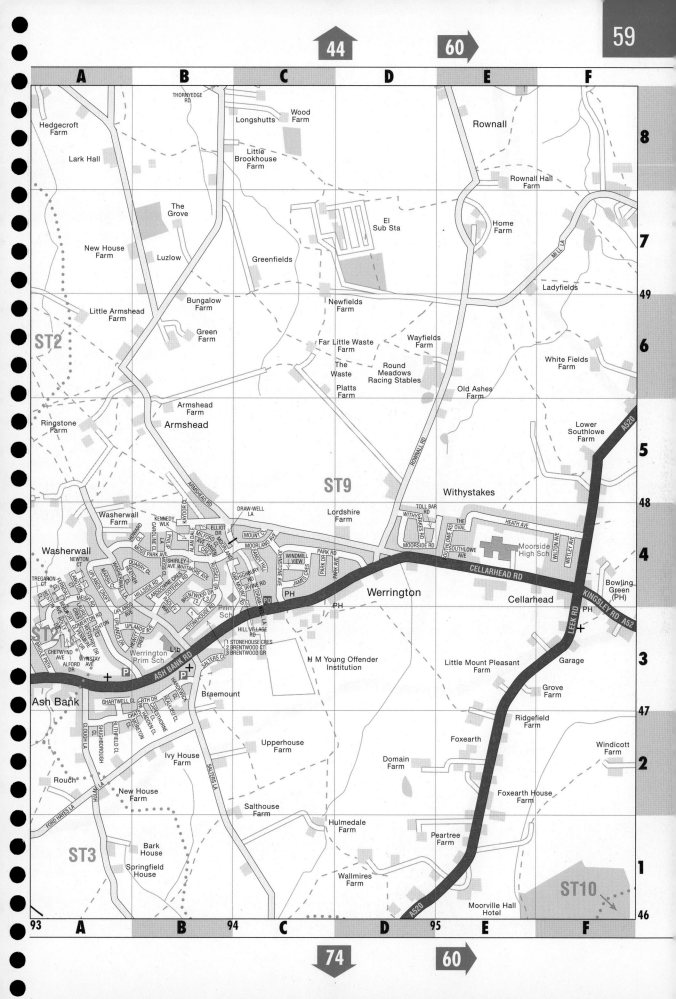

A B C D E F

8

7

49

6

ST2

5

ST9

48

4

3

47

2

ST3

1

46

Hedgecroft Farm
Lark Hall
THORNYEDGE RD
Longshutts
Wood Farm
Rownall
The Grove
New House Farm
Luzlow
Little Brookhouse Farm
Greenfields
El Sub Sta
Rownall Hall Farm
Home Farm
MILL LA
Ladyfields
Little Armshead Farm
Bungalow Farm
Newfields Farm
Green Farm
Far Little Waste Farm
Wayfields Farm
White Fields Farm
The Waste
Round Meadows Racing Stables
Platts Farm
Old Ashes Farm
Ringstone Farm
Armshead Farm
Armshead
Lower Southlowe Farm
A520
Withystakes
Washerwall Farm
DRAW-WELL LA
Lordshire Farm
TOLL BAR RD
THE OVAL
HEATH AVE
Moorside High Sch
ARMSHEAD RD
KENNEDY WLK
ELLIOT DR
MOUNT CL
WITHYSTAKES RD
MOORSIDE RD
SOUTHLOWE RD
SOUTHLOWE AVE
WILTON AVE
WETLEY AVE
Washerwall
HOWARD CL
CAROLINE CL
PHILIP LA
ALAN DALE
MILFORD AVE
MOORLAND AVE
MOORLAND RD
MOORLAND AVE
Lower Southlowe Farm
NEWTON CT
MOSS PARK AVE
SHIRLEY AVE
WHITMORE AVE
RUSSELL GR
PARK RD
PARK DR
PARK AVE
CELLARHEAD RD
Cellarhead
KINGSLEY RD A52
Bowling Green (PH)
TREGARON CT
FERNDALE
LANGTON CL
MARSH CL
QUARRY CL
WASHERWALL LA
HILLSIDE RD
LANSDOWNE CRES
COTEHILL RD
BRENTWOOD DR
OAK MOUNT RD
JAMES CRES
WINDMILL VIEW
Werrington
LEEK RD
PH
Garage
WESTON AVE
HOLLY AVE
MEIGH CT
LAUREL DR
UPLANDS AVE
UPLANDS AVE
RADLEY
STONEHOUSE RD
IRVINE RD
HIGHBURY DR
BELLE LA
PO
PH
PH
Little Mount Pleasant Farm
Grove Farm
ST2
ASHTON
SOMERTON RD
HEWITT CRES
UPLANDS DR
Prim Sch
HILL VILLAGE RD
1 STONEHOUSE CRES
2 BRENTWOOD CT
3 BRENTWOOD GR
H M Young Offender Institution
Ridgefield Farm
CHETWYND AVE
WYNSTAY AVE
ALFORD DR
Werrington Prim Sch
P
SALTERS CL
P
Windicott Farm
Ash Bank
BRIDLE PATH
ASH BANK RD
CHARTWELL CL
HARDWICK CL
BEAULIEU CL
Braemount
Foxearth
Domain Farm
CLOUGH LA
SHUGHBOROUGH CL
BLITHFIELD CL
CHATSWORTH DR
CRESTHORNE CL
WAM HAMDEN CL
Ivy House Farm
SALTERS LA
Upperhouse Farm
Foxearth House Farm
Rouch
HUTTON LA
FORD HAYES LA
New House Farm
Salthouse Farm
Hulmedale Farm
Peartree Farm
Bark House
Springfield House
ST3
Wallmires Farm
A520
ST10
Moorville Hall Hotel

93 A B 94 C D 95 E F 46

	A	B	C	D	E	F

8

Barns Farm

ST13

Park House

Consall Wood

Rock View Farm

Powys Arms (PH)

St John's CE Prim Sch

CHEADLE RD

Wetley Rocks

FOLLY LA

Spout House

Smithy Pool

7

MILL LA

MAIN RD

THE BUNTING

A522

Plough Inn (PH)

Long Meadows

Smithy Sprink

Old Hall Farm

49

OAKLANDS CL

PLOUGH BANK

MEADOW AVE

Knowle Bank Farm

CONSALL LA

Consall Hall

6

Platt Newhouse Farm

LEEK RD

Park House

RANDLES LA

ABBEY RD

Tunnel Farm

Consall

New Farm

Middle Farm

A520

Darleyshire

5

Wetley Abbey

Highfields Farm

Blackbank Plantation

ST9

Upper Farm

Keeper's Lodge Farm

CONSALL LA

Lodge Spinney

Wetley Abbey Farm

Ivy House Farm

48

Upper Ladypark Wood

Consall Wood

4

Gate House Cottage

Mast

Windyhouse Wood

Out Wood

Broadoak Wood

Rangemoor Farm

3

A52

New Park Farm

LEEK RD

A522

New Farm

Blakeley Farm

Little Broadoak Farm

Broadoak Farm

KINGSLEY RD

Overmoor

Richmoorhill Farm

Blakeley Lane

Youngsgreen Farm

Brough's Wood

47

MARCH LA

WINDYCOTE LA

ST10

2

Mount Pleasant

Little Abovepark

Abovepark Farm

Greenhead Farm

Greenhead

Moor Farm

DAIRYHOUSE LA

1

Bank Top Farm

Waggon and Horses Inn (PH)

A52

A522

Kingsley Moor

Little Bank Top Farm

TICKHILL LA

Dairy House Farm

Lower Above Park

46

DAIRYHOUSE LA

96	A	B	97	C	D	98	E	F

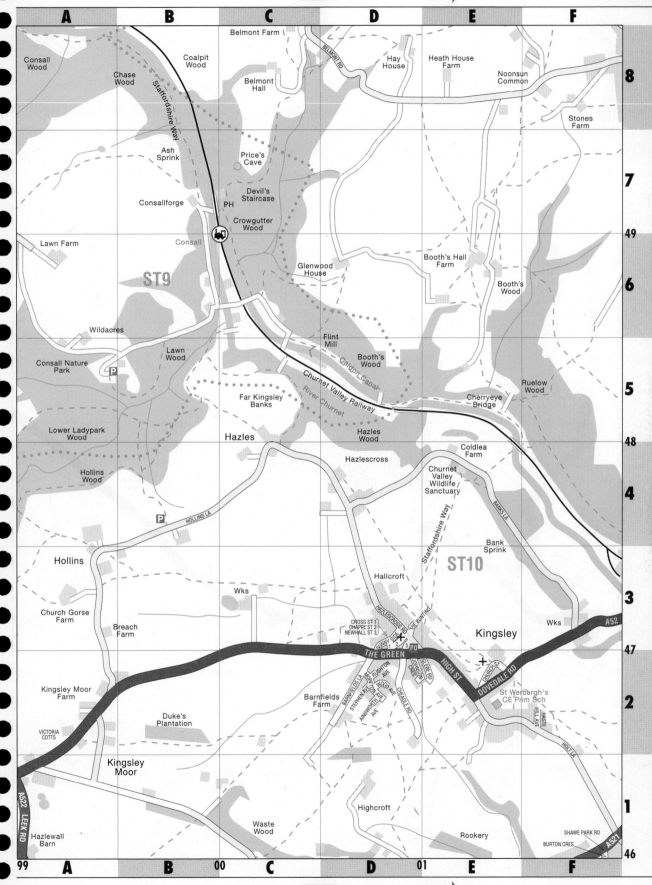

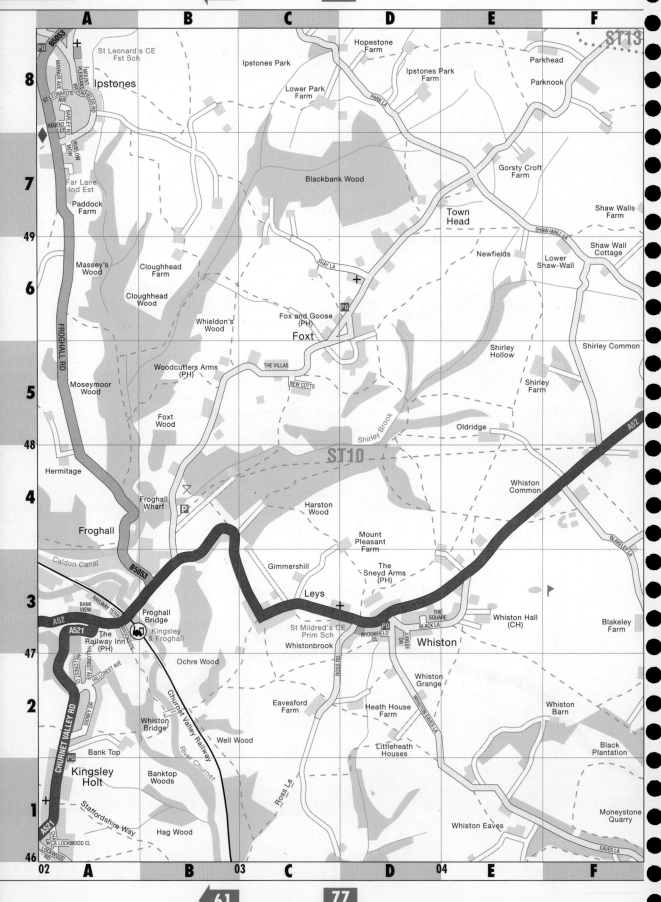

ST13

A B C D E F

8

ST Leonard's CE Fst Sch

St Leonard's CE Fst Sch

Ipstones

Ipstones Park

Hopestone Farm

Ipstones Park Farm

Parkhead

Parknook

PO B5053

MAYFAIR AVE
MOUNT PLEASANT RD
BROOKFIELDS RD
ST LEONARD'S AVE
BARLEY RD
BLUE LOW MDW
REGENT CT

Lower Park Farm

PARK LA

7

Far Lane Ind Est

Paddock Farm

Blackbank Wood

Town Head

Gorsty Croft Farm

Shaw Walls Farm

SHAW-WALL LA

49

FROGHALL RD

Massey's Wood

Cloughhead Farm

Newfields

Lower Shaw-Wall

Shaw Wall Cottage

6

Cloughhead Wood

Whieldon's Wood

SHAY LA

Fox and Goose (PH)

PO

Foxt

Shirley Hollow

Shirley Common

Moseymoor Wood

Woodcutters Arms (PH)

THE VILLAS

NEW COTTS

Shirley Farm

5

Foxt Wood

Shirley Brook

Oldridge

48

Hermitage

Froghall Wharf

P

ST10

Whiston Common

A52

4

Froghall

Harston Wood

BLAKELEY LA

Caldon Canal

B5053

Mount Pleasant Farm

The Sneyd Arms (PH)

3

RAILWAY TERR
BANK VIEW

Froghall Bridge

BROOKSIDE

Kingsley & Froghall

Gimmershill

Leys

THE SQUARE

BLACK LA

Whiston Hall (CH)

Blakeley Farm

A52

A521

The Railway Inn (PH)

St Mildred's CE Prim Sch

Whistonbrook

BROOKFIELD CL

PO

JUBILEE DR

Whiston

47

HILLCREST CT
HILLCREST AVE
RD JENNIS

Ochre Wood

Churnet Valley Railway

ROSS RD

WHISTON EAVES LA

Whiston Grange

Whiston Barn

2

CHURNET VALLEY RD

Whiston Bridge

Eavesford Farm

Heath House Farm

Black Plantation

PO

Bank Top

River Churnet

Well Wood

Littleheath Houses

1

A521

CHAPEL LA
LOCKWOOD CL

Kingsley Holt

Staffordshire Way

Banktop Woods

Hag Wood

ROSS LA

Whiston Eaves

Moneystone Quarry

EAVES LA

46

LOCKWOOD RD

02 A B 03 C D 04 E F

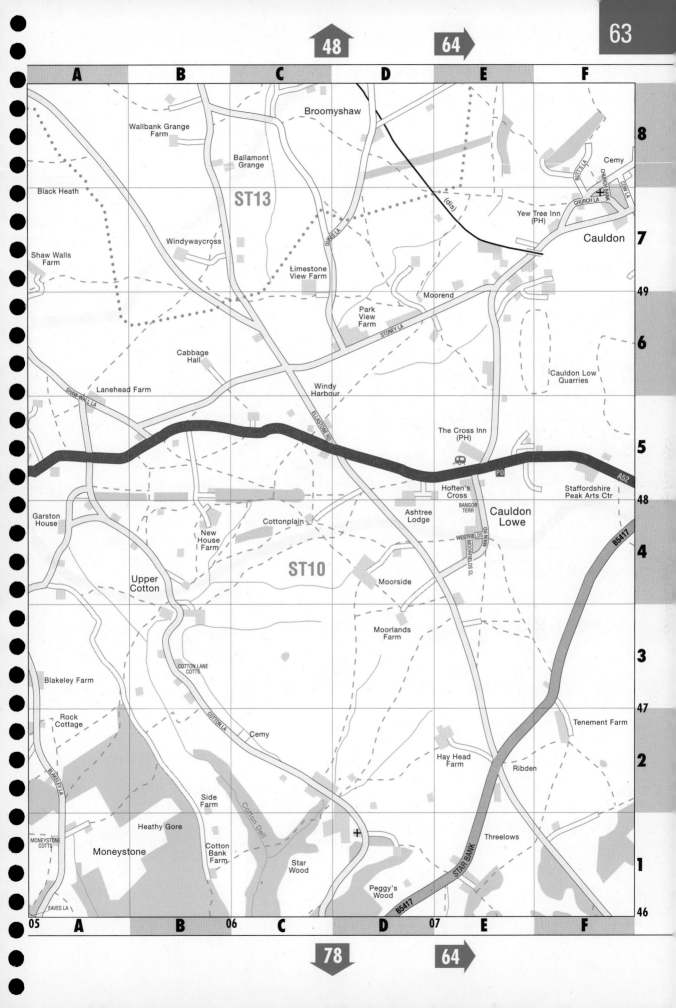

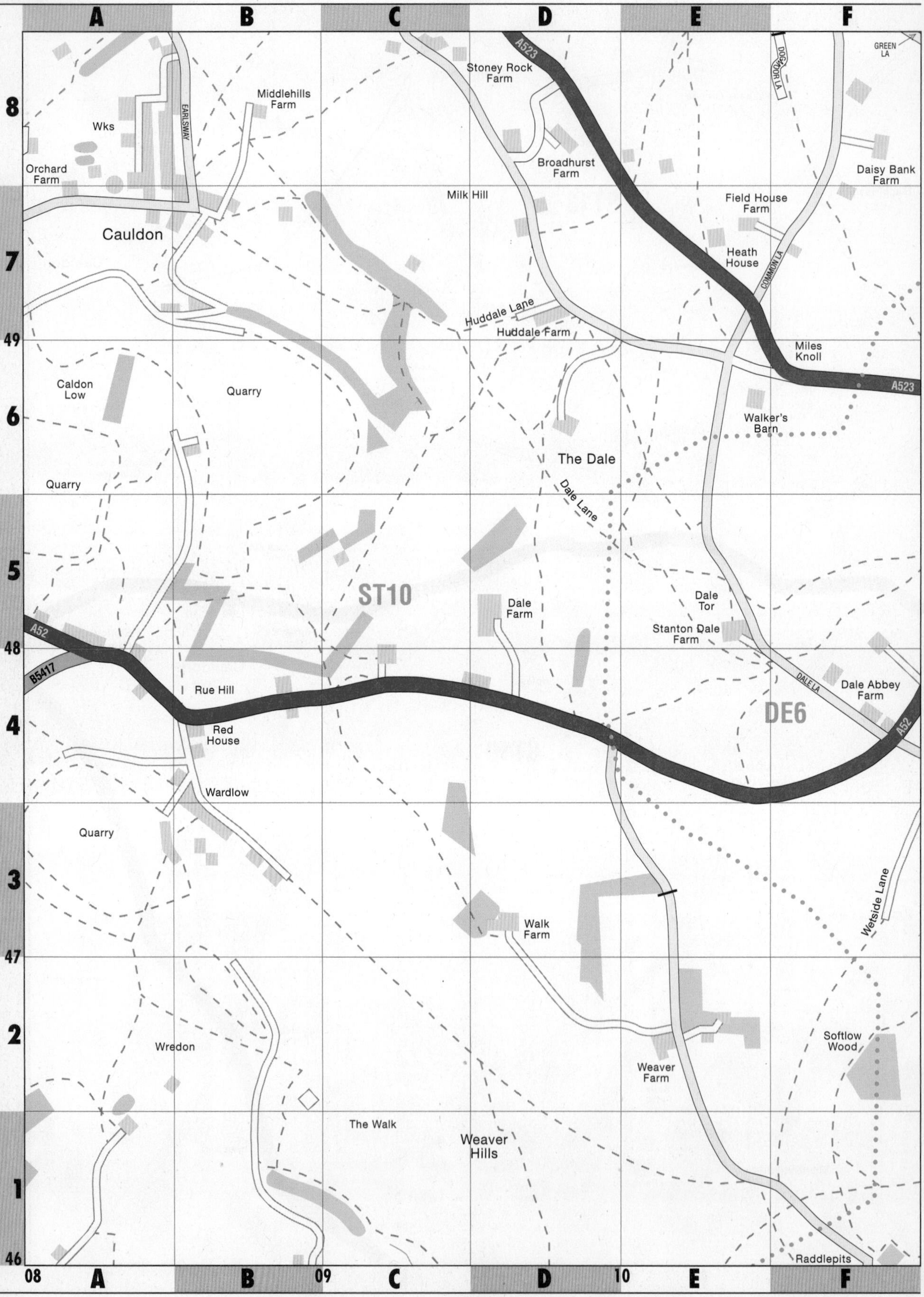

◀ 63
49 ⬆

A B C D E F

8

Wks

Middlehills Farm

EARLSWAY

Orchard Farm

A523

Stoney Rock Farm

GREEN LA

DOG POOL LA

Broadhurst Farm

Daisy Bank Farm

Milk Hill

Field House Farm

Cauldon

7

Heath House

COMMON LA

49

Huddale Lane

Huddale Farm

Miles Knoll

A523

Caldon Low

Quarry

Walker's Barn

6

The Dale

Quarry

Dale Lane

5

ST10

Dale Farm

Dale Tor

Stanton Dale Farm

A52

48

DALE LA

Dale Abbey Farm

B5417

Rue Hill

DE6

A52

4

Red House

Wardlow

Quarry

Walk Farm

Wetside Lane

3

47

2

Wredon

Weaver Farm

Softlow Wood

The Walk

Weaver Hills

1

46

Raddlepits

◀ 63
79 ⬇

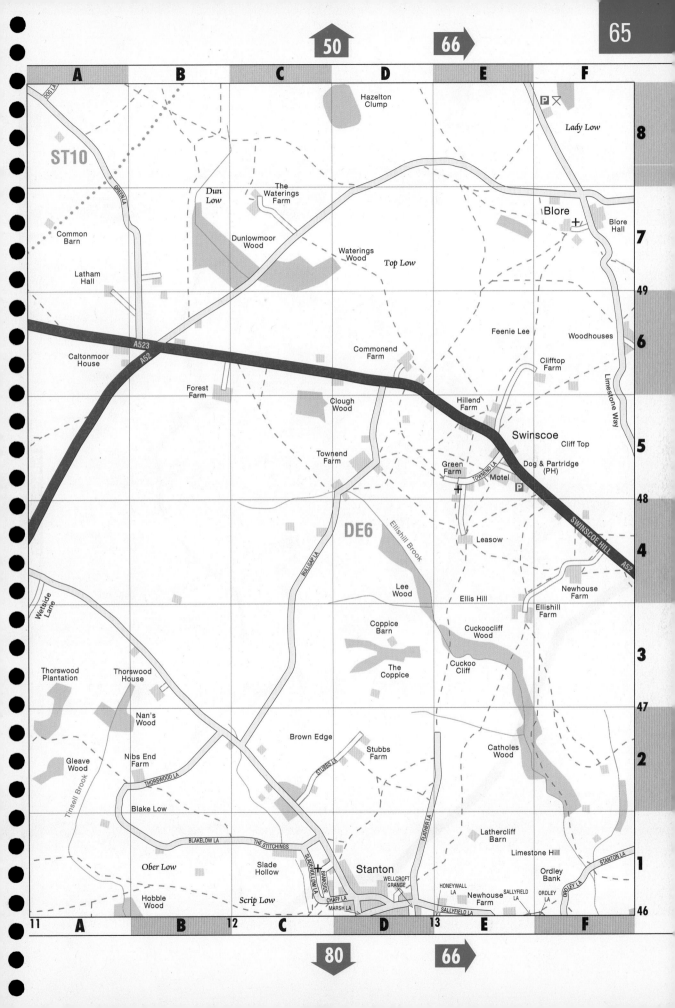

A   B   C   D   E   F

8

Coldwall
Bridge

Limestone Way

Coldwall
Farm

Little Peg's
Wood

Tissington Trail

Spendlane
Farm

SPEND LA

7

49

Littlepark

6

Lees House
Farm

Yerley
Farm

Kendar
Wood

Hinchley
Wood

YERLEY HILL

Hinchleywood

5

Cowclose
Wood

Okeover
Hall

Mill
Okeover
Bridge

Bank
Farm

DE6

Martin
Hill

48

Okeover
Arms
(PH)

Okeover
Park

Mapleton

4

Limestone Way

Marten
Hill

Lower
Grounds
Farm

Smythe's
Plantation

River Dove

Callowend
Farm

A52

Manor
House

3

The
Orchards

BIRDSGROVE LA

Callow
Hall

Cornpark

47

Snelsdale

Snelsdale
Wood

2

Throstle
Nest

Butler's
Holme

SWINSCOE HILL

Bentley Brook

Limestone Way

Lordspiece

The
Cliffs

Birdsgrove
Farm

STANTON LA

1

Harlow
Farm

Big
Quarry
Wood

Birdsgrove
House

Sewage
Wks

Upper
Mayfield

PICCADILLY LA

GALLOWSTREE LA

HOLLOW LA

A52

Buckholme

Cemy

SLACK LA

WATERY LA

46

14   A   B   15   C   D   16   E   F

Derbyshire STREET ATLAS

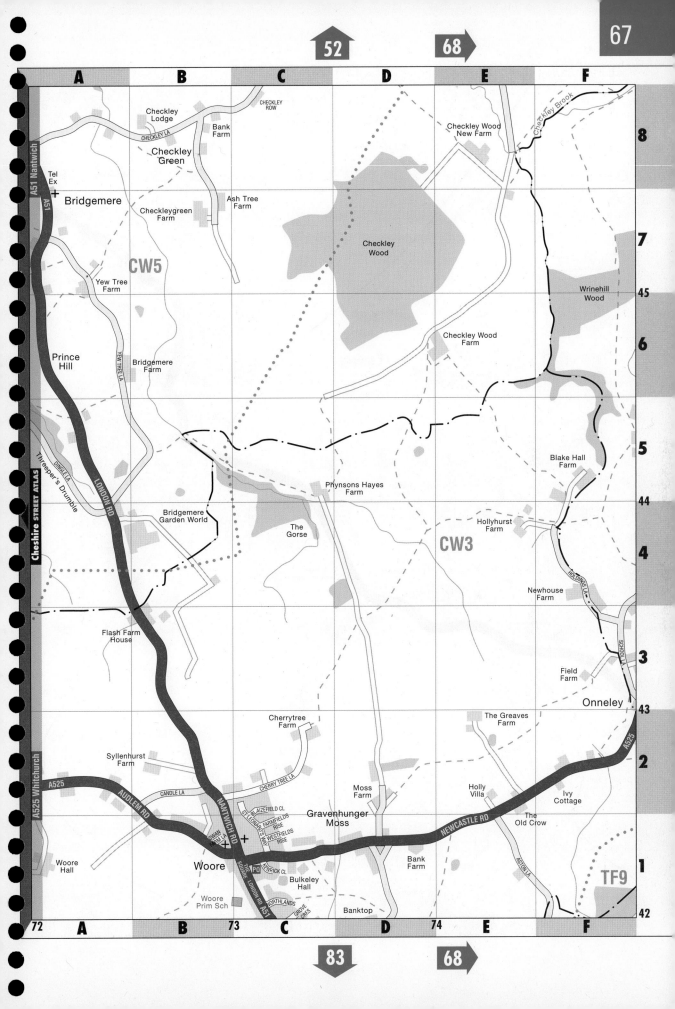

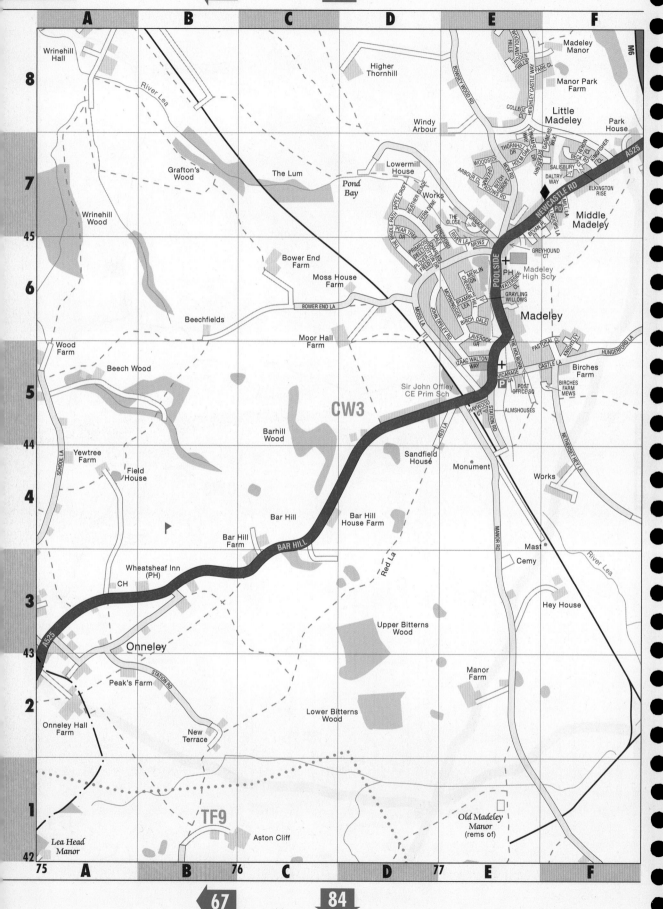

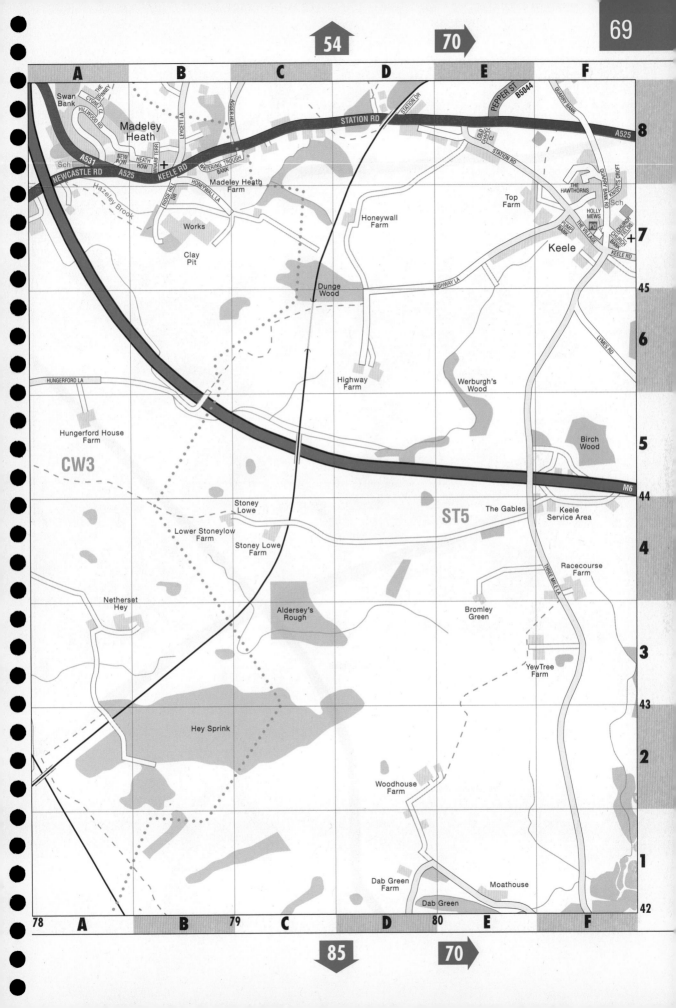

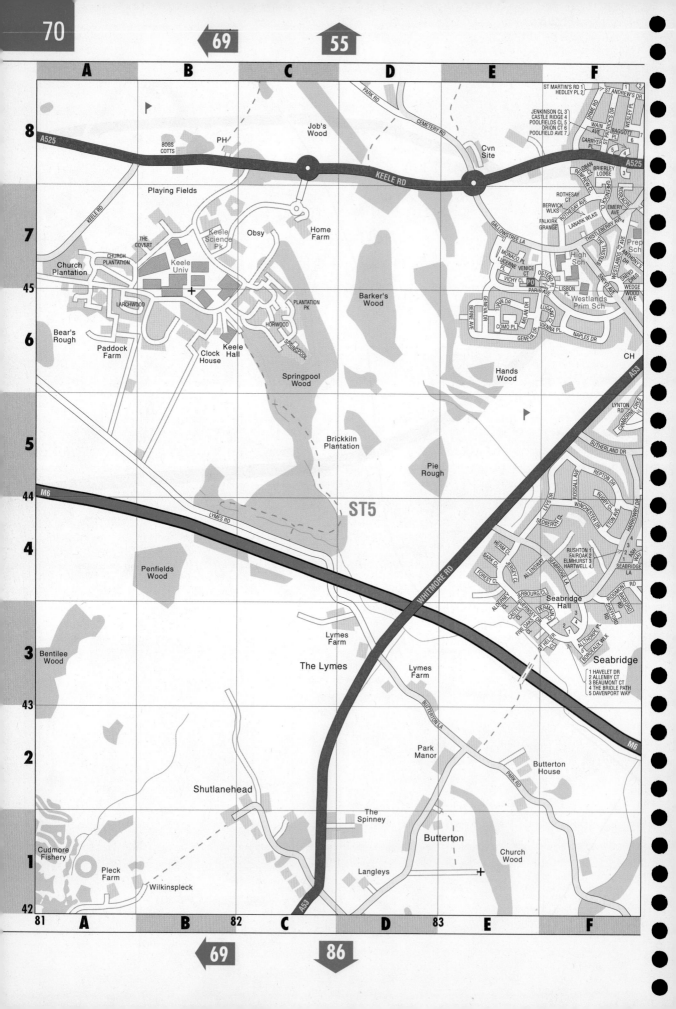

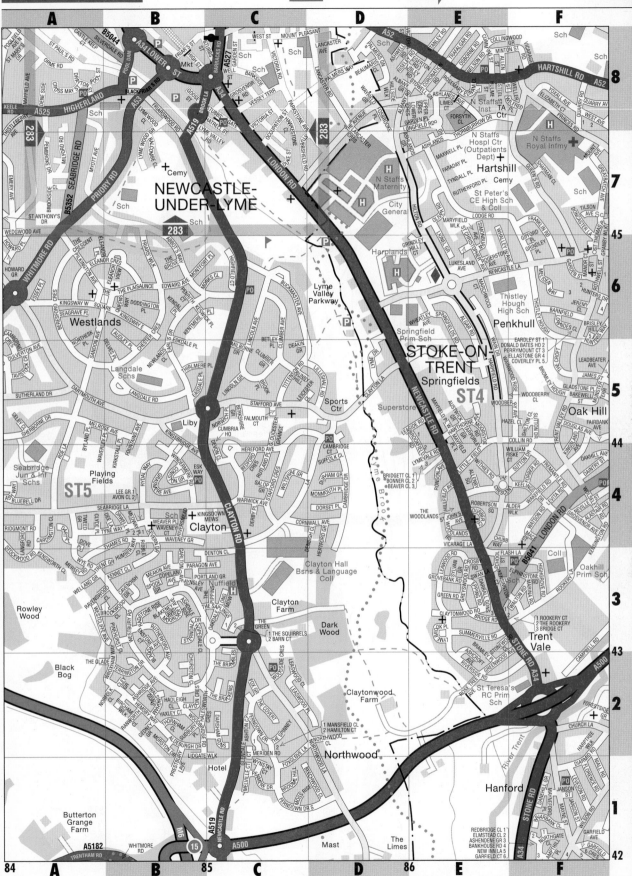

For full street detail of the highlighted area see page 283.

F8
1 CATHERINE HO
2 VICTORIA HO

71

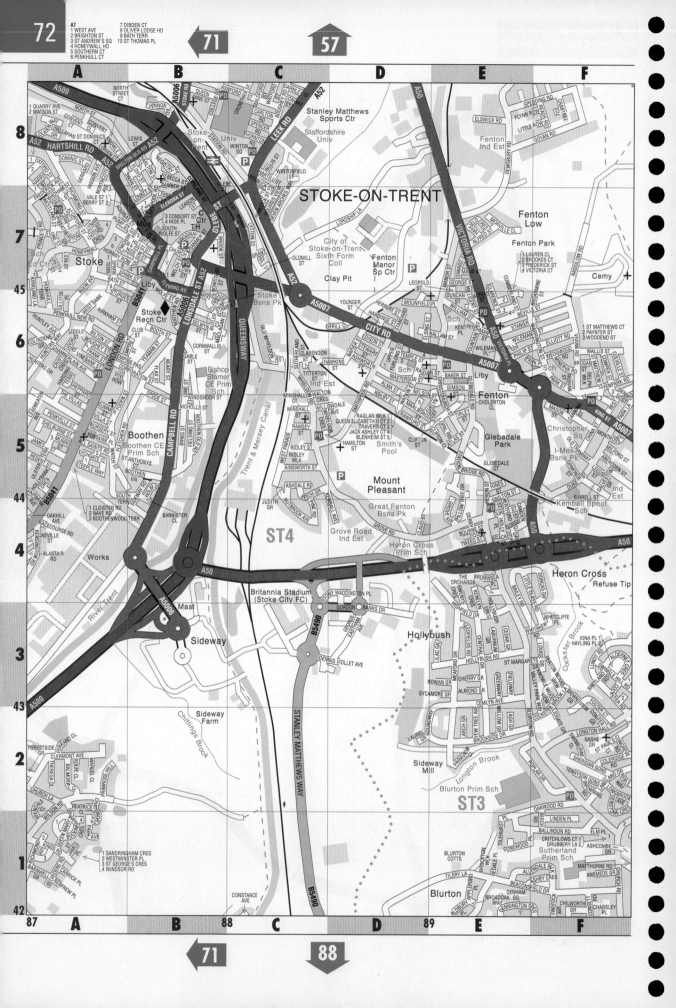

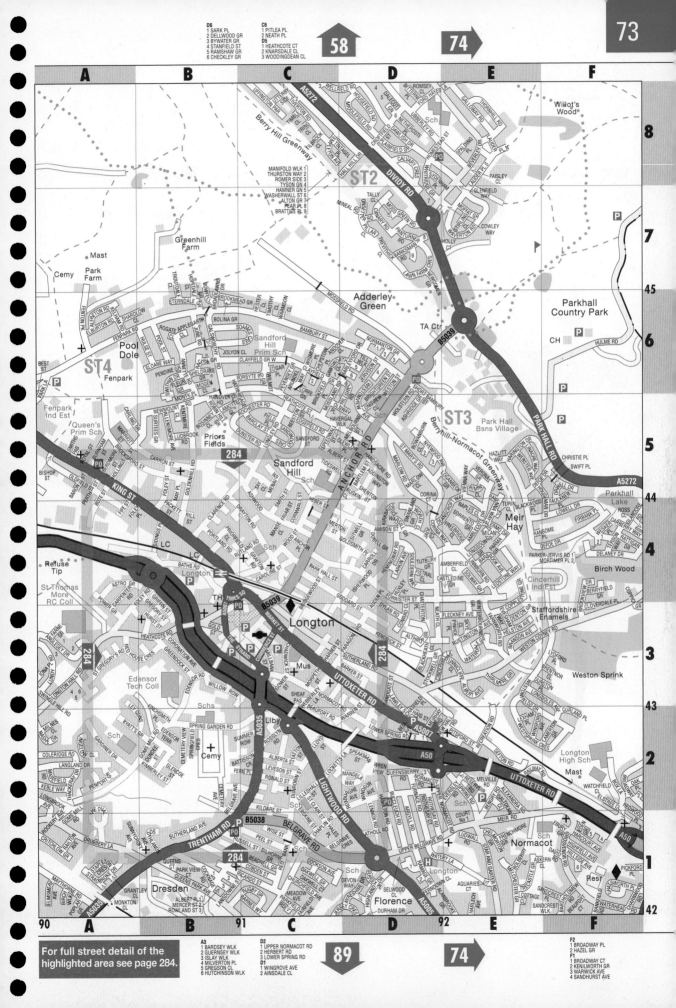

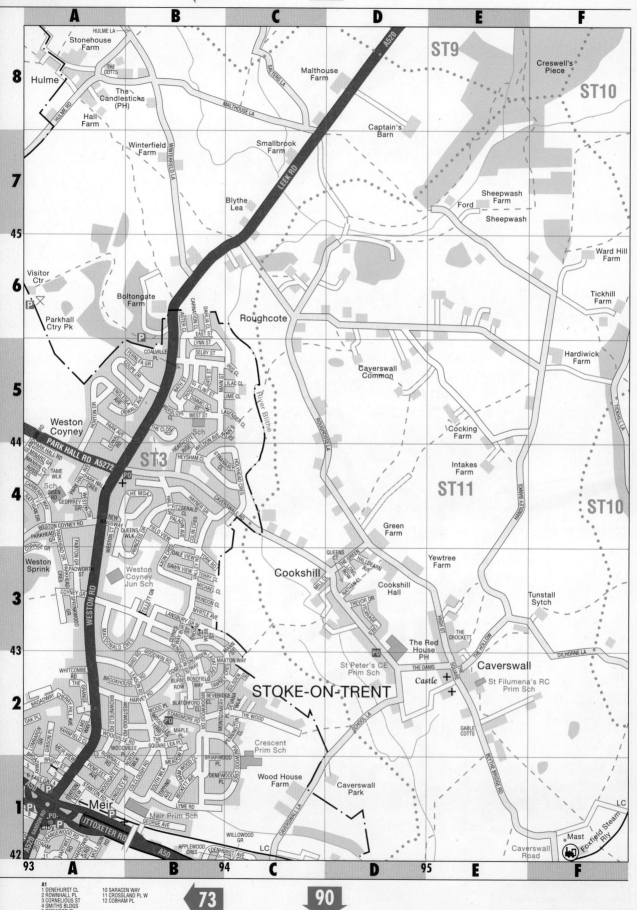

A1
1 DENEHURST CL
2 ROWNHALL PL
3 CORNELIOUS ST
4 SMITHS BLDGS
5 REDWOOD PL
6 BROADWAY CT
7 QUEENSWAY CT
8 PICKFORD PL
9 CHATSWORTH PL
10 SARACEN WAY
11 CROSSLAND PL W
12 COBHAM PL

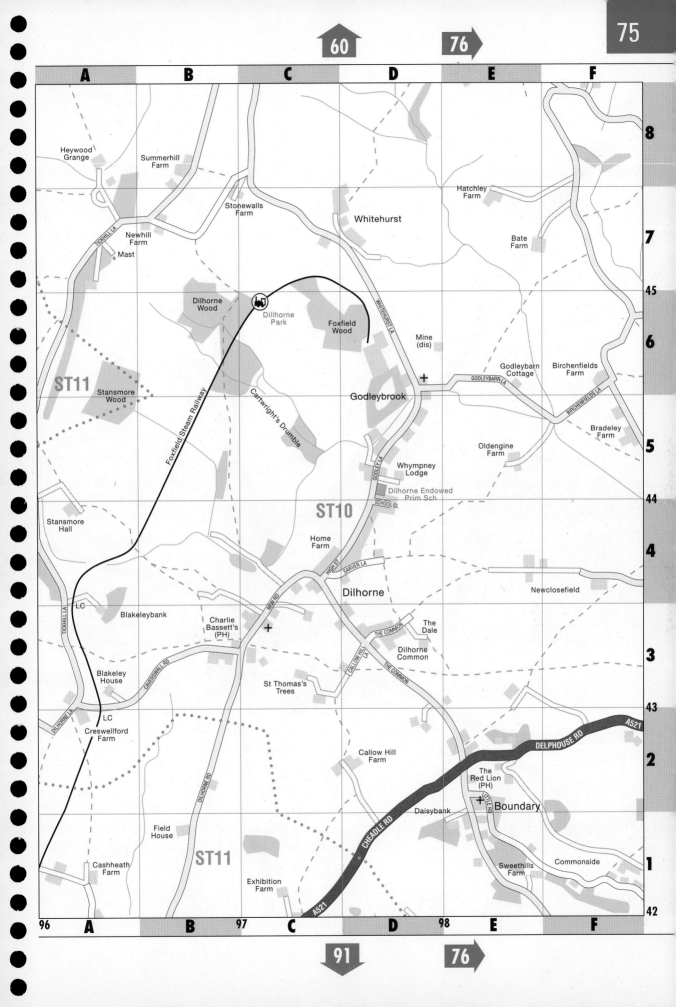

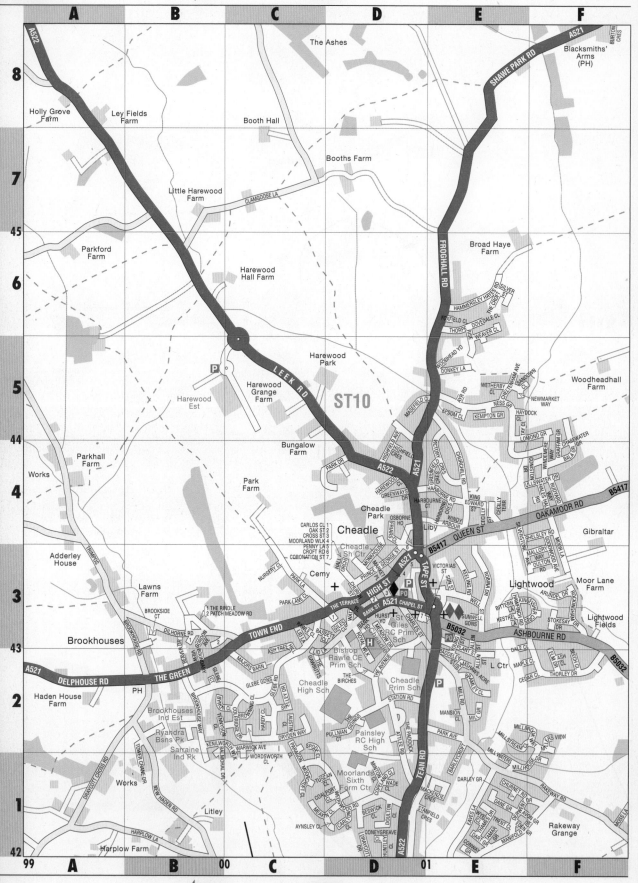

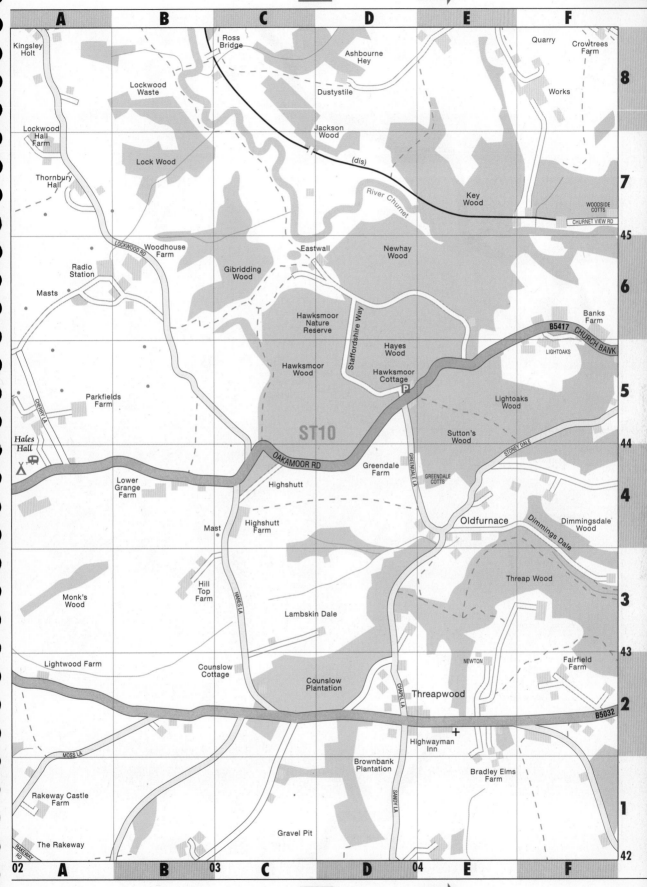

62
78

Kingsley Holt
Lockwood Waste
Ross Bridge
Ashbourne Hey
Quarry
Crowtrees Farm
Dustystile
Works
Lockwood Hall Farm
Lock Wood
Jackson Wood
(dis)
Thornbury Hall
River Churnet
Key Wood
WOODSIDE COTTS
CHURNET VIEW RD
LOCKWOOD RD
Woodhouse Farm
Eastwall
Newhay Wood
Radio Station
Gibridding Wood
Masts
Hawksmoor Nature Reserve
Staffordshire Way
Hayes Wood
Banks Farm
B5417 CHURCH BANK
LIGHTOAKS
Hawksmoor Wood
Hawksmoor Cottage
P
CHERRY LA
Parkfields Farm
Lightoaks Wood
Hales Hall
ST10
Sutton's Wood
STONEY DALE
OAKAMOOR RD
Greendale Farm
GREENDALE LA
GREENDALE COTTS
Lower Grange Farm
Highshutt
Oldfurnace
Dimmings Dale
Dimmingsdale Wood
Mast
Highshutt Farm
HARES LA
Threap Wood
Monk's Wood
Hill Top Farm
Lambskin Dale
NEWTON
Fairfield Farm
Lightwood Farm
Counslow Cottage
Counslow Plantation
CHAPEL LA
Threapwood
B5032
MOSS LA
Brownbank Plantation
Highwayman Inn
Bradley Elms Farm
Rakeway Castle Farm
SANDY LA
RAKEWAY RD
The Rakeway
Gravel Pit

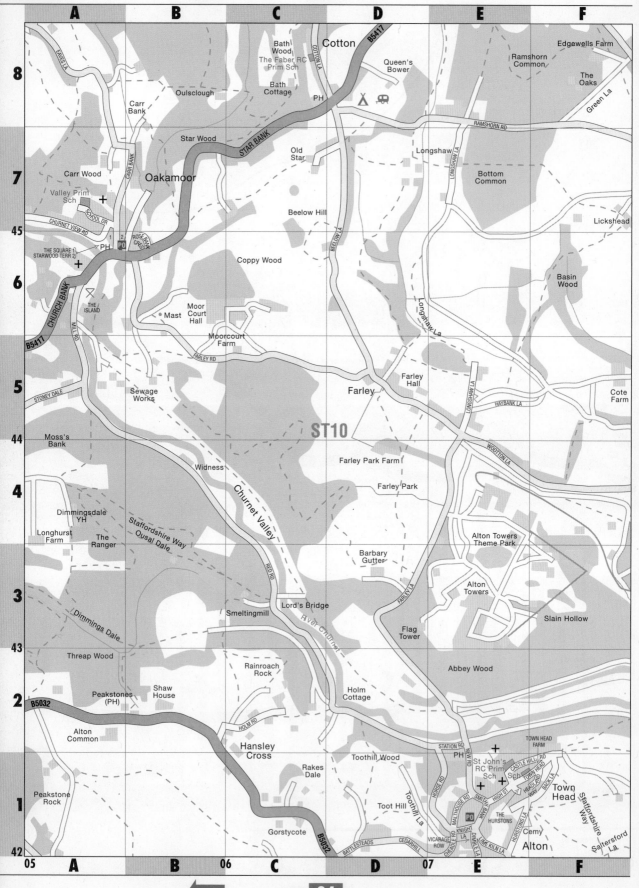

A B C D E F

8
7
45
6
5
44
4
3
43
2
1
42

Tinsell Wood

Wildhay Brook
Wildhay
Wildhay La
Hall La
Wildhay La

Bankerwall La
Field La
Willadding La

Marsh Brook

Honeywall La
Sallyfield La
Ordley La

Boldershaw
Eldergreave Cottage

Smithy Moor Farm

Griff Wood

Ray Wood

Rangemoor Wood

Rangemoor Brook
Rangemoor La

Motcarn Sprink

Stanton Wood

The Home Farm

Michael's Lane

Wooton Hall Farm

Ousley Wood

Gold's Wood

Dydon

Lee Wood

Far Wood

Ashfield Farm

Michael's La

Northwood La

Ousley La

The Hutts Farm

Limestone Way

DE6

Calwichbank Farm

B5032

Cliff Bridge

Northwood Farm

Stanton La

Upper Ellastone

Watery La

Churcha La

Back La

Sandford Brook

Duncombe Arms (PH)

Marlpit La

Ellastone

Tit Brook

The Boxes

Colwich Home Farm

Cockley

The Grove

Calwich Park

Calwich Abbey

Portobello Bridge

Hare Park

B5033

Mill La
PO

Lower Ellastone

Littlefield La

Dove St

River Dove

Knaveholm

Sides La

ST14

Norbury Hollow

Mill House

Mill La

Roughlow La

Norbury

Norbury Hall

Hope Wood

LLL Plantation

Lid La
Green La
B5033

B5032

11 A B 12 C D 13 E F

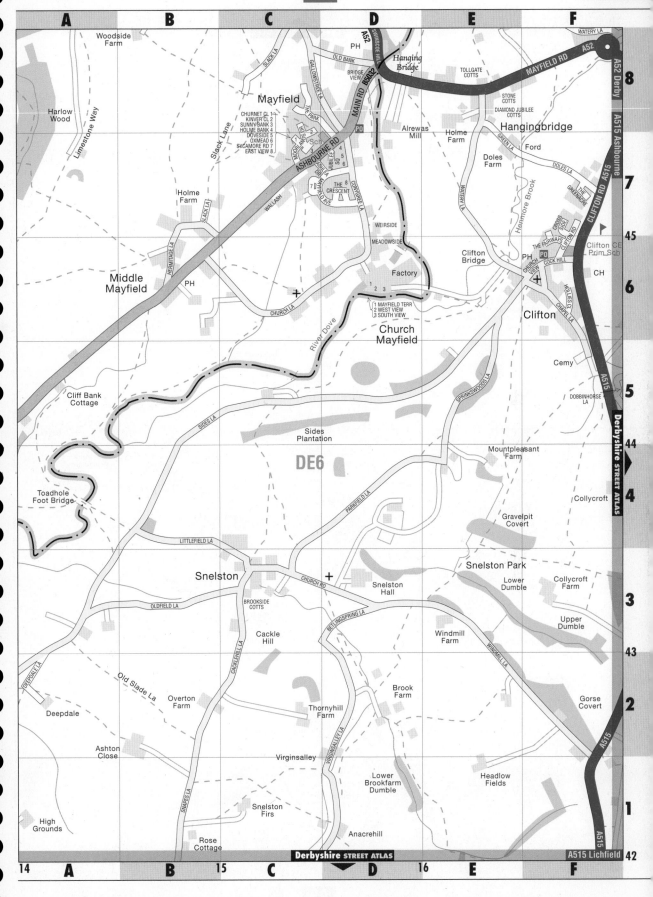

Derbyshire STREET ATLAS

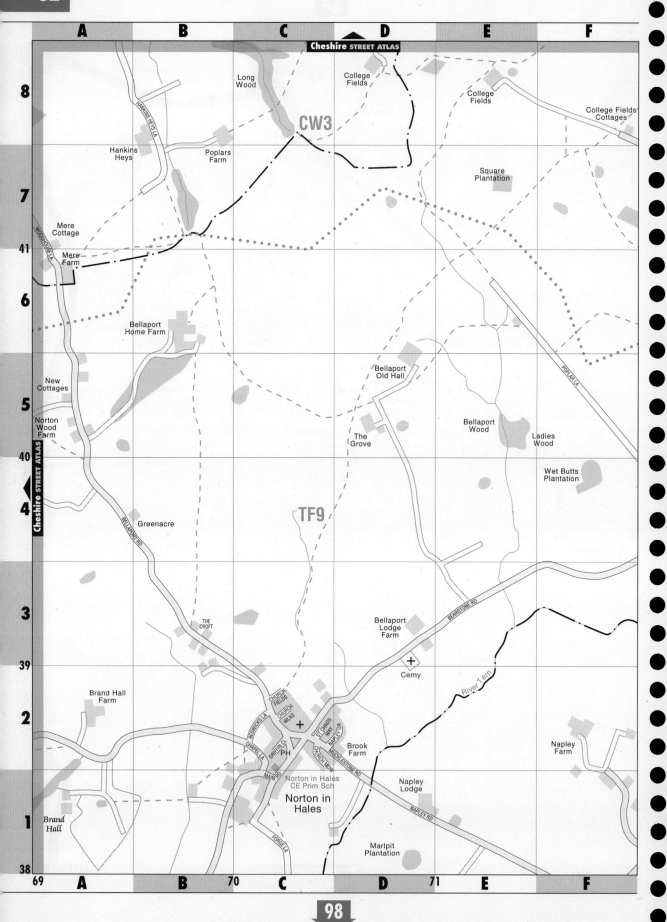

CW3

College Fields

College Fields

College Fields Cottages

Long Wood

HANKINS HEYS LA

Hankins Heys

Poplars Farm

Square Plantation

Mere Cottage

WOODHOUSE LA

Mere Farm

41

Cheshire STREET ATLAS

Bellaport Home Farm

POPLAR LA

Bellaport Old Hall

New Cottages

Bellaport Wood

Ladies Wood

Norton Wood Farm

The Grove

40

Wet Butts Plantation

TF9

Greenacre

BELLAPORT RD

THE CROFT

Bellaport Lodge Farm

BEARSTONE RD

Cemy

River Tern

Brand Hall Farm

CHURCH FIELDS

CHURCH WLKS

BESWICKS LA

ST CHADS WAY

NAPLEY DR

Napley Farm

Brook Farm

CHAPEL LA

GRIFFIN CL

PH

MUCKLESTONE RD

CHURCH MDW

Norton in Hales CE Prim Sch

Napley Lodge

Norton in Hales

MAIN RD

NAPLEY RD

Brand Hall

FORGE LA

Marlpit Plantation

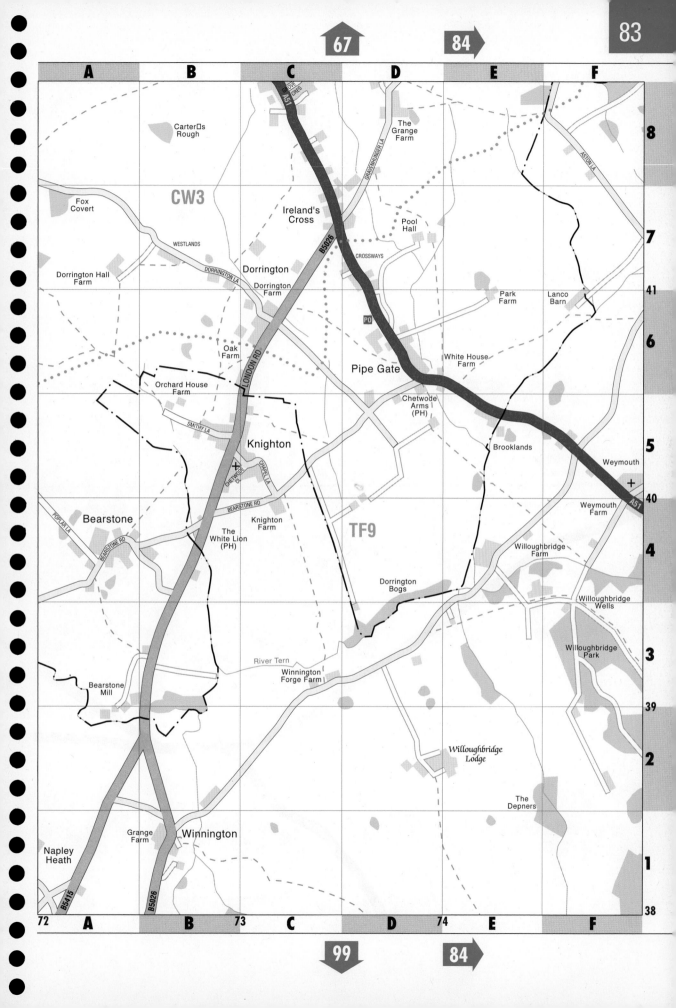

83
68

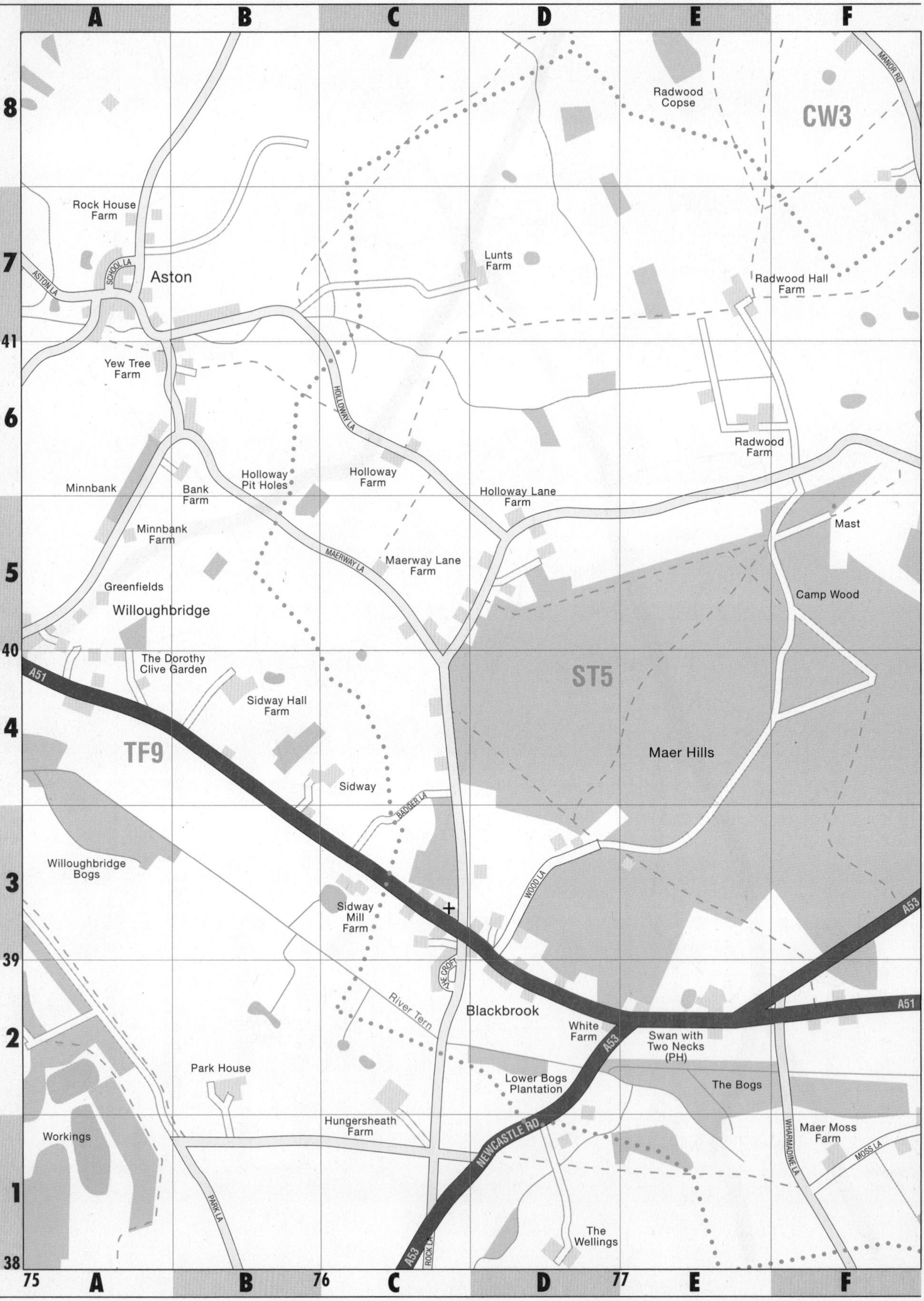

A B C D E F

8

Radwood Copse

CW3

Rock House Farm

7

Aston

Lunts Farm

Radwood Hall Farm

41

Yew Tree Farm

Radwood Farm

6

Holloway Pit Holes

Holloway Farm

Holloway Lane Farm

Minnbank

Bank Farm

Mast

Minnbank Farm

Maerway Lane Farm

Camp Wood

5

Greenfields

Willoughbridge

40

The Dorothy Clive Garden

ST5

A51

Sidway Hall Farm

4

TF9

Maer Hills

Sidway

Willoughbridge Bogs

3

Sidway Mill Farm

A53

39

River Tern

Blackbrook

Park House

White Farm

Swan with Two Necks (PH)

2

A51

Lower Bogs Plantation

The Bogs

Maer Moss Farm

Hungersheath Farm

Workings

NEWCASTLE RD.

The Wellings

1

A53

38

75 A B 76 C D 77 E F

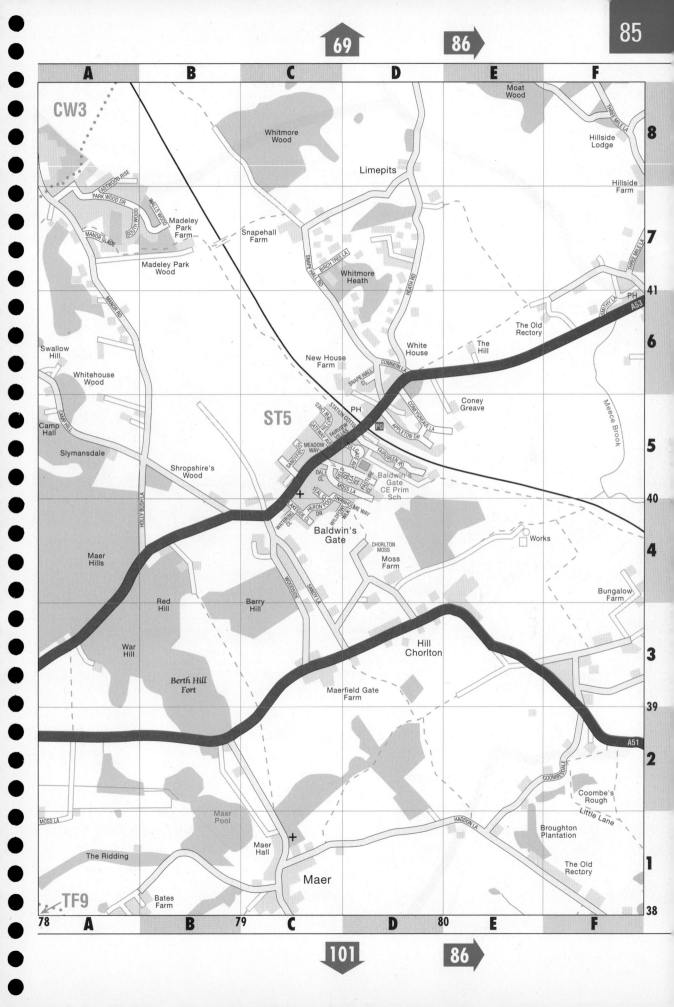

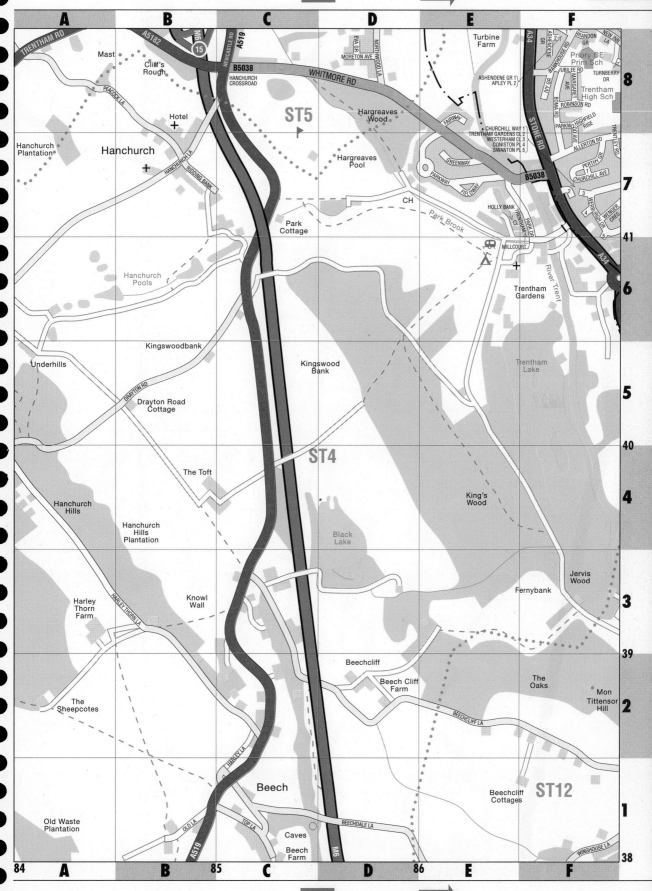

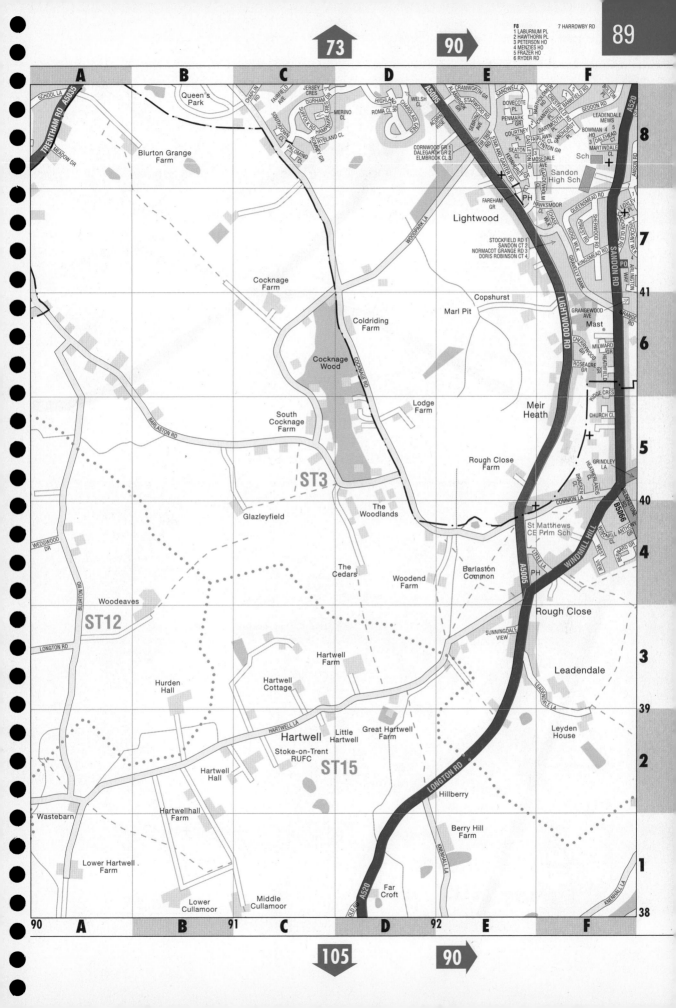

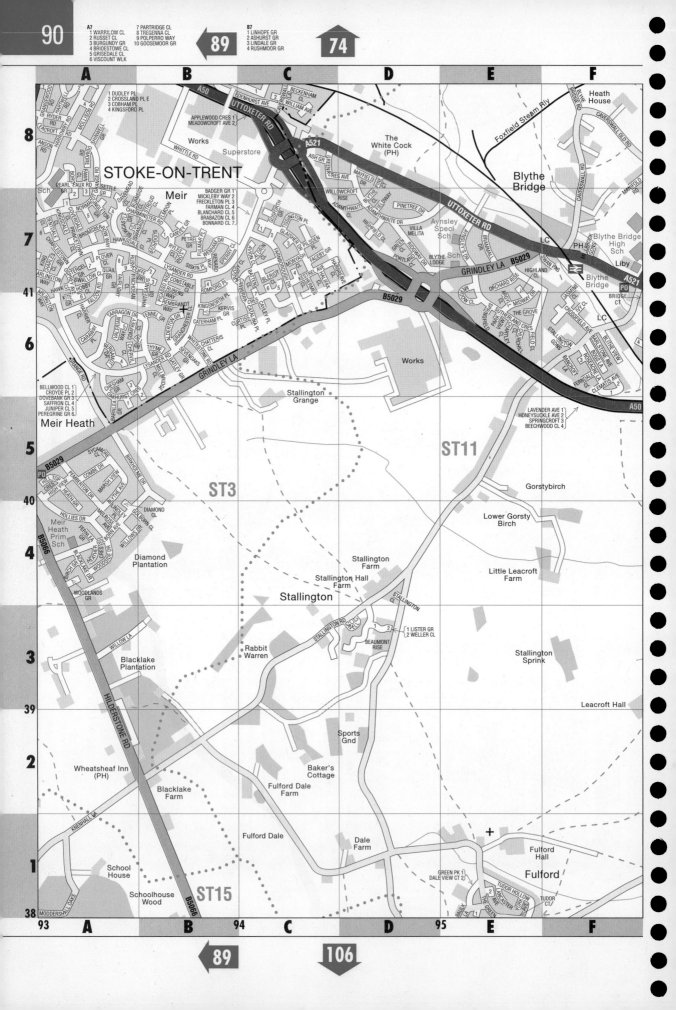

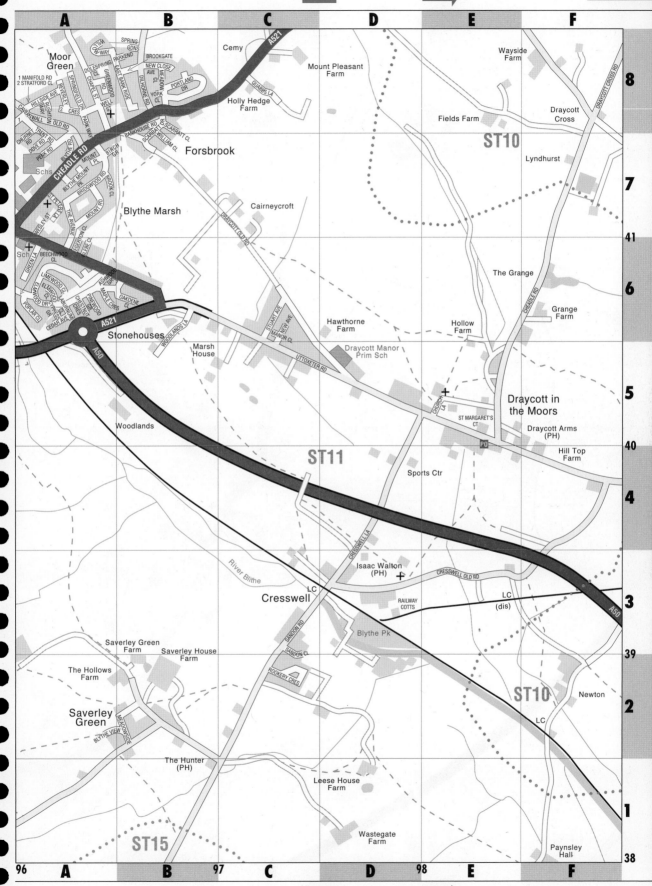

75
92
107
92

A   B   C   D   E   F

8

Moor Green

1 MANIFOLD RD
2 STRATFORD CL

Cemy

A521

Mount Pleasant Farm

Wayside Farm

Fields Farm

ST10

Draycott Cross

DRAYCOTT CROSS RD

SPRING GDNS
PARKEND
BROOKGATE
NEW CLOSE AVE
DOLESPRING CL
GREENWOOD
EAST BANK RIDE
CHAPEL ST
PORTLAND DR
DILHORNE RD
YORK CL

Holly Hedge Farm

QUABBS LA

Lyndhurst

7

BANKHOUSE RD
SCARRATT CL
WILLIAM CL
SCARRATT
BIRCH GR

Forsbrook

41

CHEADLE RD

Schs

Blythe Marsh

Cairneycroft

DRAYCOTT OLD RD

The Grange

CHEADLE RD

6

Sch

BEECHWOOD CL

LIMEWOOD CL
ELMWOOD DR
ASHWOOD GR
OAKDENE CL
MAPLE CRES
CHESTNUT
PINEWOOD GR

A521

Stonehouses

WOODLANDS LA

Marsh House

STUART AVE
MANOR CL
NEW AVE

Hawthorne Farm

UTTOXETER RD

Draycott Manor Prim Sch

Hollow Farm

Grange Farm

5

A50

Woodlands

Draycott in the Moors

CHURCH LA

ST MARGARET'S CT

Draycott Arms (PH)

PO

Hill Top Farm

40

ST11

Sports Ctr

4

River Blithe

CRESSWELL LA

Isaac Walton (PH)

CRESSWELL OLD RD

LC (dis)

A50

LC

Cresswell

RAILWAY COTTS

LC

3

Saverley Green Farm

SANDON RD

SANDON CL

Blythe Pk

Saverley House Farm

39

The Hollows Farm

ROOKERY CRES

ST10

Newton

2

Saverley Green

BLYTHE VIEW
MEADOWSIDE

LC

The Hunter (PH)

Leese House Farm

1

Paynsley Hall

ST15

Wastegate Farm

38

96   A   B   97   C   D   98   E   F

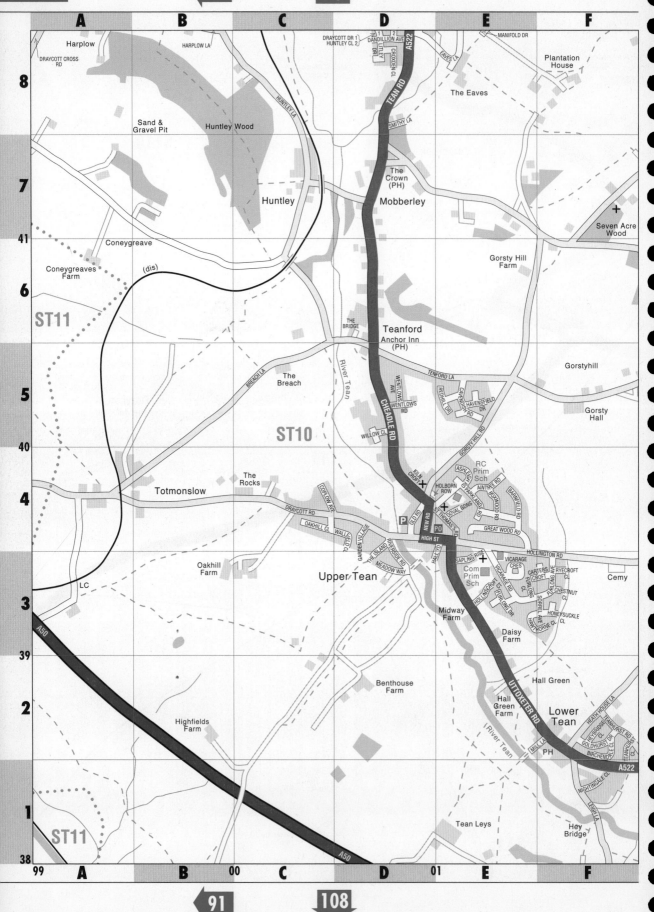

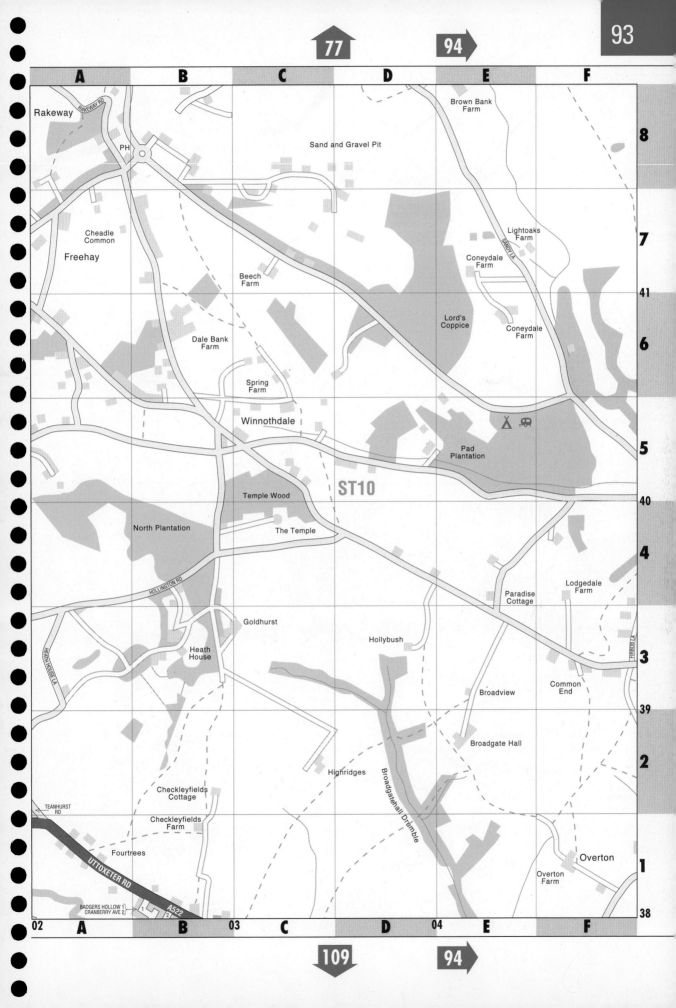

93
78

A   B   C   D   E   F

8

New Farm

B5032

Turnditch
Farm

GLENDA
DIMBLE LA
SHIRLEY DR
PEARTREE DR
BIRCH HILL
UTTOXETER RD
GLADSTONE
TERR
SALTERSFORD LA

Tithebarn

DENSTONE LA
B5032

7

Bradley in the
Moors

Spond
Farm

Gallows
Green

Newhouse
Farm

NABB LA

41

Bradley Hall
Farm

Jeffreymeadow

Eatonflats

Fields
House

6

Wood
Farm

Greatgate
Wood

5

Greatgate

SANDY LA

Ford

40

ST10

Croxden Brook

Abbey
Farm

Croxden

Highfields
Farm

4

Broadmoor
Wood

PH

QUARRY BANK

FERROR LA

Croxden
Abbey

QUARRY RD

ST14

3

Abbey View
Farm

Pointhorne

GROUNDHOLLOW

High Ridge
Farm

Vicarage

Butterley Bank
Farm

39

Upper
Whitley

PH

Hollington

MOUNT FIELDS

SCHOOL BANK

Wootons

2

Holly
Grove

Birchendale

RECTORY RD

The
Long Close

HOLLINGTON LA

Lower
Whitley

Chipperlee
Coppice

1

Hollingtonfields

Madeleypark

Gravelly
Bank

38

05   A   B   06   C   D   07   E   F

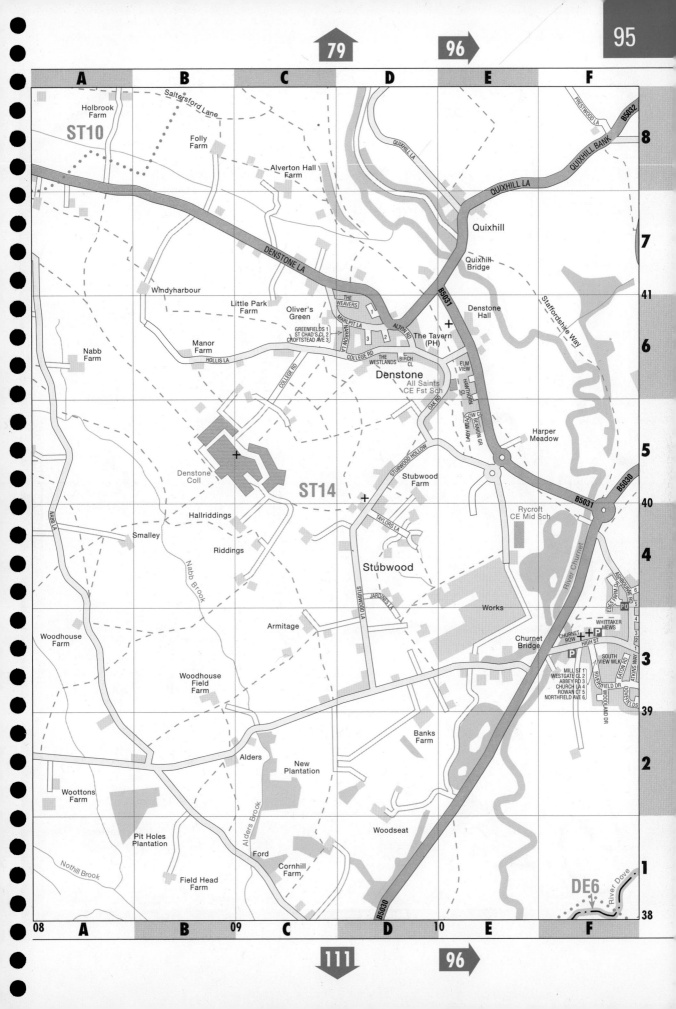

A B C D E F

8

7

41

6

5

40

4

39

2

1

38

Holbrook Farm

ST10

Saltersford Lane

Folly Farm

Alverton Hall Farm

QUIXHILL LA

PRESTWOOD LA

B5032

QUIXHILL BANK

QUIXHILL LA

Quixhill

Quixhill Bridge

DENSTONE LA

B5031

Denstone Hall

Windyharbour

Little Park Farm

Oliver's Green

THE WEAVERS

MARL PIT LA

NARROW LA

Staffordshire Way

GREENFIELDS 1
ST CHAD'S CL 2
CROFTSTEAD AVE 3

Manor Farm

HOLLIS LA

COLLEGE RD

ALTON RD

The Tavern (PH)

Nabb Farm

THE WESTLANDS

BIRCH CL

ELM VIEW

Denstone
All Saints
CE Fst Sch

HAWTHORN

COW CL

VERNON GR

OAK RD

Harper Meadow

Denstone Coll

ST14

STURWOOD HOLLOW

Stubwood Farm

Rycroft CE Mid Sch

B5031

B5030

Hallriddings

Smalley

NABB LA

Nabb Brook

Riddings

TAYLORS LA

Stubwood

River Churnet

ASHBOURNE RD

EAST FARM DR

PO

Woodhouse Farm

STUBWOOD LA

JARDINES LA

Armitage

Works

WHITTAKER MEWS

Churnet Bridge

CHURNET ROW

HIGH ST

SOUTH VIEW WLK

EATON RD

ATKINS WAY

RIVERSFIELD DR

WOODLAND DR

DOVEFIELDS

P

Woodhouse Field Farm

MILL ST 1
WESTGATE CL 2
ABBEY RD 3
CHURCH LA 4
ROWAN CT 5
NORTHFIELD AVE 6

Banks Farm

Alders

New Plantation

Alders Brook

Woottons Farm

Pit Holes Plantation

Nothill Brook

Ford

Field Head Farm

Cornhill Farm

Woodseat

DE6

River Dove

A | B | C | D | E | F

8

Ivy Cottages
Osier Plantation
Four Acre Plantation
Green Lane Farm
B5033 GREEN LA B5033
Woodend

Dovellys Manor Park
Alfross House
Norbury CE Prim Sch
Leigh's Plantation
Riverside Doveleys
New House Farm

7

Inge Cottages
Swinholm Farm
Roston Inn (PH)
Roston
BAG LA

41

Limestone Way
MILL LA
MEADOW LA
THE HOLLOW
Squashly Farm

6

Dalesgap
UNDERTOWN LA

Barrowhill
Dovecliff
Highfields House
DE6

5

B5030

ST14

40

Doveflats
River Dove
Shield House Farm
Hurd's Barn

4

WOODSEAT GR
The Shawleys
Long Chimneys

NORTHFIELD AVE
CORONATION CRES
Dove Fst Sch
DOVE LA
CHURCH LA
Rocester
Park Holme
Marston Park

3

SWINSCOE CL
ABBEY RD
CASTRUM CT
WEST VIEW
MILL ST
MILL BANK DR
Marston Lodge

VALLEY VIEW WLK
ABBEY CL
Rocester Bridge
White House

39

1 RIVERCROFT CL
2 DOVEFIELDS
3 RIVERSFIELD DR
Daisybank Farm

2

Staffordshire Way
Alder Carrs
Springfield House
CUBLEY LA

Abbotsholme Sch
Clowneholme Farm
Marstonbank Farm
Thurvaston
THURVASTON RD

1

Monk's Clownholme
Barway Cottages
WESTON BANK

Sedsall Rough
DE6
Marstonbrook Farm
Marston House Farm

38

Derbyshire STREET ATLAS

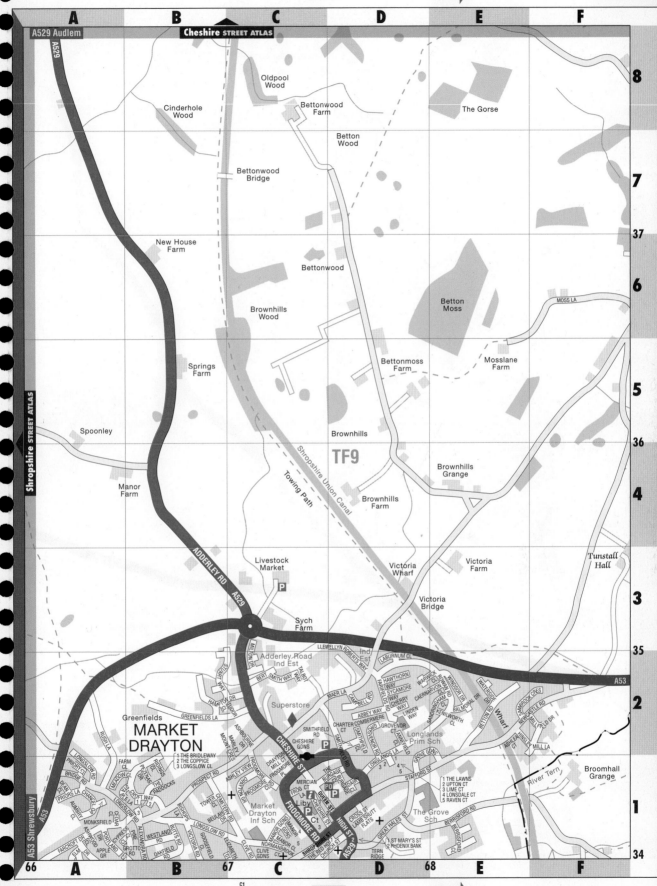

A529 Audlem

Cheshire STREET ATLAS

A529

Shropshire STREET ATLAS

8

7

37

6

36

5

4

3

35

2

1

34

Oldpool Wood

Cinderhole Wood

Bettonwood Farm

Bettonwood Bridge

Betton Wood

The Gorse

New House Farm

Bettonwood

Betton Moss

MOSS LA

Springs Farm

Brownhills Wood

Bettonmoss Farm

Mosslane Farm

Spoonley

Shropshire Union Canal

TF9

Brownhills

Brownhills Grange

Manor Farm

Towing Path

Brownhills Farm

Tunstall Hall

ADDERLEY RD

A529

Livestock Market

P

Victoria Wharf

Victoria Farm

Sych Farm

Victoria Bridge

LLEWELLYN ROBERTS WAY

Ind Est

LABURNUM CL

A53

Adderley Road Ind Est

MILTON DR

BERT SMITH WAY

ALBDT

MAER LA

CAMPBELL SO

HAWTHORN WAY

SYCAMORE WAY

WARWICK

ROWAN RD

WINDSOR DR

BALMORAL DR

BETTON RD

Wharf

WATERSIDE

SANDRINGHAM

KENILWORTH CL

CAMBROOK CRES

NEWCASTLE RD

Greenfields

GREENFIELDS LA

MARKET DRAYTON

HAMPTON DR

TUDOR

GREENFIELDS LA

Superstore

CHARTER COMBERMERE CT

LINDEN WAY

CAERNARVON CL

GROVENOR

Longlands Prim Sch

ASHLEA

TINSLEY CL

MILL LA

RUSH LA

LONGSLOW RD

PRIORS CT

FARM CL

RIDINGS

PECANS

THE PADDOCKS

ASHROUTHE

FROGMORE

ASHLEY VIEW

MAER LA

SMITHFIELD RD

SMITHFIELD

CHESHIRE GDNS

SMITHFORD RD

Longlands LA

GROVE GDNS

1 THE LAWNS
2 UPTON CT
3 LIME CT
4 LONSDALE CT
5 RAVEN CT

Broomhall Grange

BRIDGE CT

PRIORS LA

CHANCEL

MEADOW CL

CROFT WAY

LONGSLOW RD

PROSPECT RD

DRAYTON MILL CT

FROGMORE

MERCIAN CT

FROG

CHESHIRE ST

THE BURSAGE

Market Drayton Inf Sch

P

Liby

i

P

Ct

QUEEN ST

LAMB STUTT FLATS

HIGH ST

The Grove Sch

BERESFORD RD

BERESFORD RD

River Tern

TOWER LA

CEMETERY RD

BEULAH

FROGMORE RD

P

CROSS ST

MONKSFIELD

CEDAR

CYPRESS

WESTLAND CL

LONGSLOW RD

GOOSEFIELD

SHROP MILL ST

GREAT HALES ST

TERN RIDGE

1 ST MARY'S ST
2 PHOENIX BANK

FARCROFT DR

ELM

ASHFORD

PORTLAND

APPLE GR

GROTTO RD

OAKFIELD RD

NORMANBROOK RD

A529

CHURCH ST

THE RED HO

A53 Shrewsbury

A53

66

C1
1 WILKINSON WLK
2 THE BUTTERCROSS
3 RODENHURST HOUSE FLATS
4 CORBET CT
5 WARREN CT

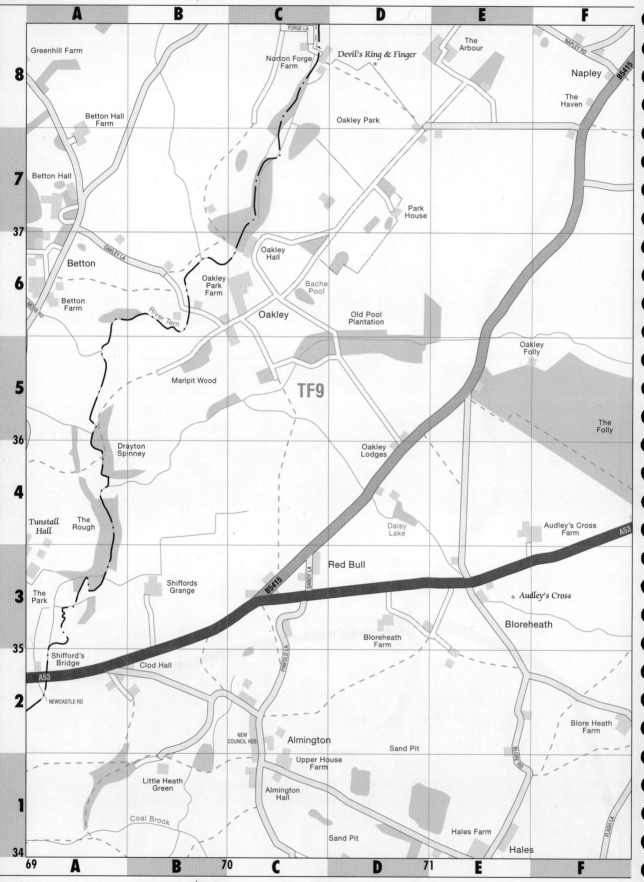

A B C D E F

8

7

37

6

5

36

4

3

35

2

34

69 A B 70 C D 71 E F

Greenhill Farm

Betton Hall Farm

Betton Hall

OAKLEY LA

Betton

MOSS RD

Betton Farm

River Tern

Oakley Park Farm

Marlpit Wood

Drayton Spinney

Tunstall Hall

The Rough

The Park

Shifford's Bridge

A53

NEWCASTLE RD

Clod Hall

Little Heath Green

Coal Brook

FORGE LA

Norton Forge Farm

Devil's Ring & Finger

Oakley Hall

Bache Pool

Oakley

TF9

Shiffords Grange

B5415

SANDY LA

Red Bull

NEW COUNCIL HOS

PINFOLD LA

Almington

Upper House Farm

Almington Hall

Sand Pit

Sand Pit

The Arbour

NAPLEY RD

Napley

B5415

The Haven

Oakley Park

Park House

Old Pool Plantation

Oakley Folly

The Folly

Oakley Lodges

Daisy Lake

Audley's Cross Farm

A53

Audley's Cross

Bloreheath

Bloreheath Farm

Blore Heath Farm

BLORE RD

Hales Farm

FLASH LA

Hales

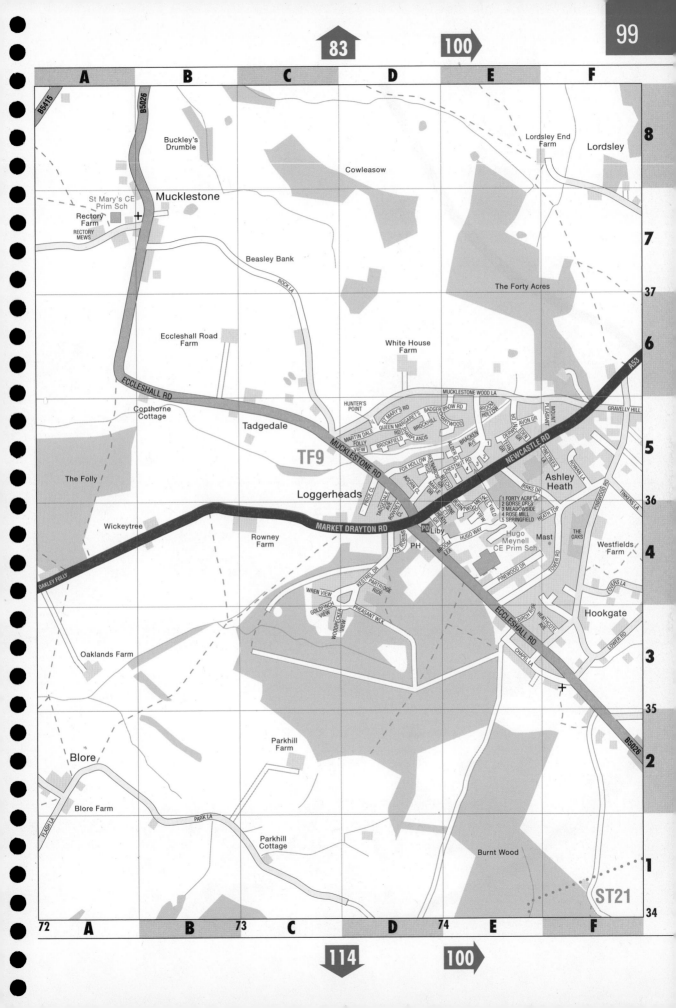

A B C D E F

8

7

37

6

5

36

4

35

3

2

1

34

75 A B 76 C D 77 E F

Manor House Farm

Birch House Rough

Manor Hill

Holly Croft Farm

LONGSLEY LA

A53

NEWCASTLE RD

PARK LA

SANDY LA

ELDERTREE LA

ROCK LA

A53

Castle Hill

WHARMADINE LA

Fields Farm

Oak Wood

Sniggle Pits

Akesworth Coppice

Rock House

The Oaks

WESLEYAN RD

SCHOOL LA

CHAPEL LA

ELDERTREE LA

CHURCH RD

GRAVELLY HILL

Peel Arms (PH)

Ashley

Ashley Dale

THE DALE

BACK LA

ST JOHNS WAY

ST JOHNS RD

DOCTOR'S BANK

ORCHARD PL

SOVEREIGN LA

NORRIS CL

ESSELIE AVE

CHARNES RD

GERARDS WAY

GREEN LA

WOODROW WAY

THE CRESCENT

BELL ORCH

CHURCH FARM

Middle Coppice

TF9

Greenlane Coppice

LARKHILL LA

LOWER RD

CHARNSFORD LA

JUG BANK

TIMBERS LA

The Robin Hood (PH)

Jugbank

RUDGE DALE RD

Podmore Pool

B5026

Broughton Birches

The Rudge

New Wood

Bromley Hall

Ashley Road Plantation

ST21

Broughton Folly

B5026

Broughton Wood

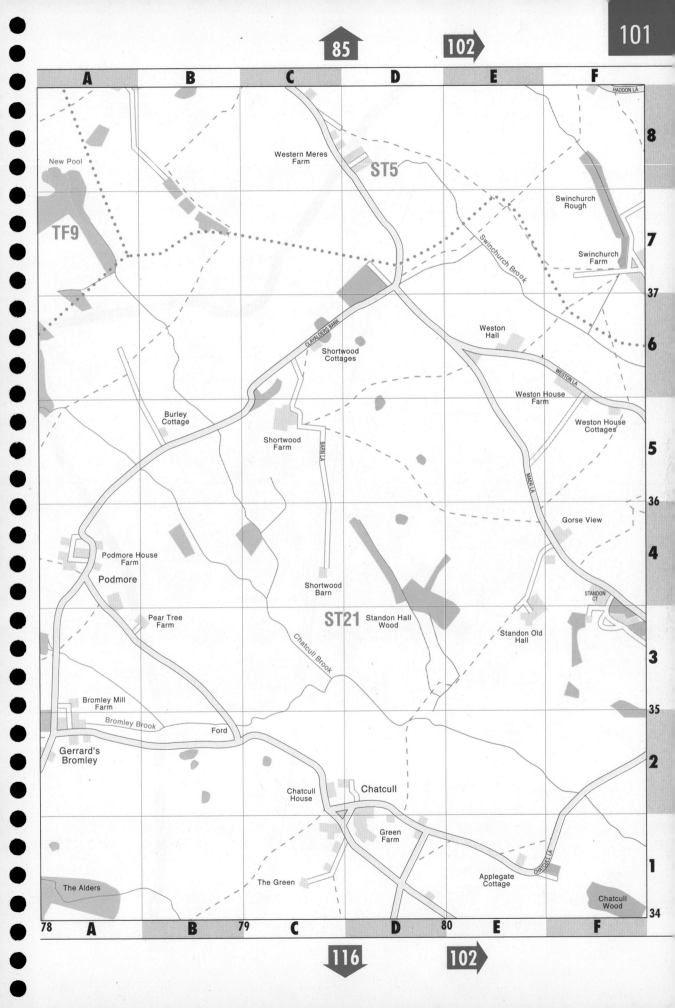

85
102

A B C D E F

8

7

37

6

5

36

4

3

35

2

1

34

New Pool

TF9

Western Meres
Farm

ST5

Swinchurch
Rough

Swinchurch Brook

Swinchurch
Farm

HADDON LA

Weston
Hall

WESTON LA

Weston House
Farm

Weston House
Cottages

MAER LA

CLAYALDERS BANK

Shortwood
Cottages

Burley
Cottage

Shortwood
Farm

BARN LA

Gorse View

Podmore House
Farm

Podmore

Shortwood
Barn

ST21

Standon Hall
Wood

Standon Old
Hall

STANDON
CT

Pear Tree
Farm

Chatcull Brook

Bromley Mill
Farm

Bromley Brook

Ford

Gerrard's
Bromley

Chatcull
House

Chatcull

Green
Farm

Applegate
Cottage

CHATCULL LA

The Alders

The Green

Chatcull
Wood

78 A B 79 C D 80 E F

116
102

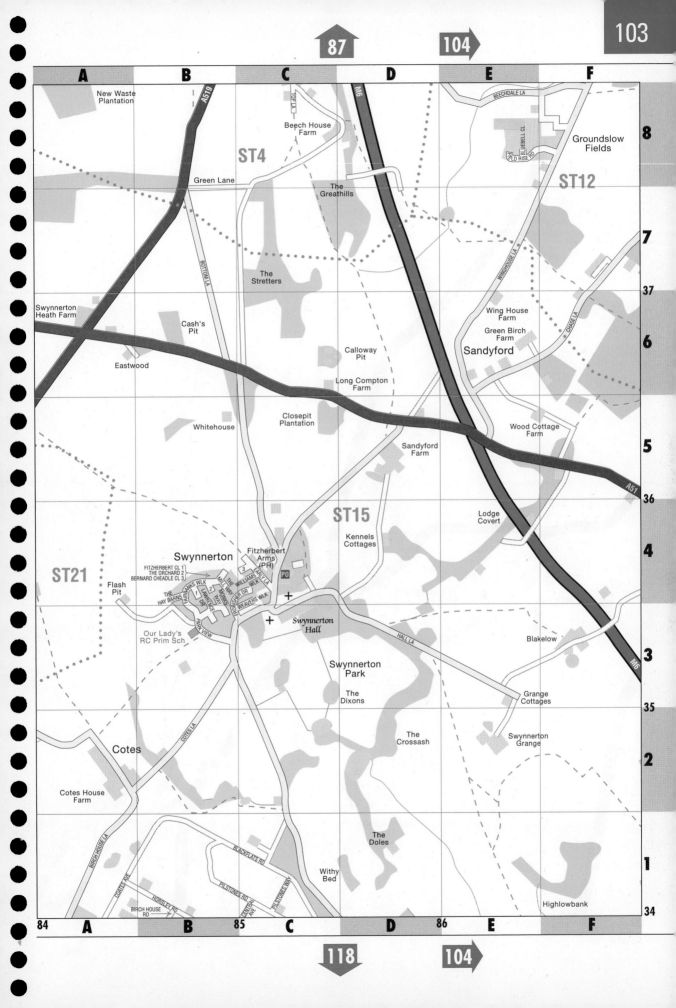

87
104

A B C D E F

8
7
37
6
5
36
4
35
2
1
34

New Waste Plantation

A519

ST4

Beech House Farm

Green Lane

The Greathills

M6

Beechdale La

BLUEBELL CL
OLD RISE RD

Groundslow Fields

ST12

WINGHOUSE LA

CHASE LA

BOTTOM LA

TOP LA

The Stretters

Swynnerton Heath Farm

Cash's Pit

Eastwood

Whitehouse

Closepit Plantation

Calloway Pit

Long Compton Farm

Wing House Farm

Green Birch Farm

Sandyford

Wood Cottage Farm

Sandyford Farm

A51

ST15

Kennels Cottages

Lodge Covert

ST21

Swynnerton

FITZHERBERT CL 1
THE ORCHARD 2
BERNARD CHEADLE CL 3

Fitzherbert Arms (PH)

EARLY LA

WILLIAMS WAY

PERSHER DR

MILL WAY

MONKS WAY

LAWRENCE DR

THE HAY BARNS

FAIRBANKS WLK

WEAVERS WLK

Flash Pit

PARK VIEW

Our Lady's RC Prim Sch

Swynnerton Hall

HALL LA

Blakelow

M6

Swynnerton Park

The Dixons

Grange Cottages

Swynnerton Grange

Cotes

COTES LA

The Crossash

Cotes House Farm

BIRCH HOUSE LA

COATES AVE

HORSLEY RD

BIRCH HOUSE RD

BLACKFLATS RD

PILSTONES RD

CEDERNAL LANE

PILSTONES WAY

Withy Bed

The Doles

Highlowbank

84 A B 85 C D 86 E F

Barton Land

ST12

Heyfields

Heyfields Farm

HEYFIELDS COTTS

TITTENSOR RD

RIDGE CL

DIAMOND RIDGE

DIAMOND CL

PARK DR

SILVER RIDGE

BOATYARD COTTS

Downs Banks

Inn

CH

Tittensor Chase

Spring Vale

Tittensor Chase

Warren House Farm

CHASE LA

Saxon's Lowe

Hilltop

Firs Cottage

Turnover Bridge

Ford

Meaford Farm

WASHDALE LA

MEAFORD RD

Bury Bank Farm

Bury Bank

BANKSIDE

Siddall's Bridge

Outlanes Mill Farm

ST15

River Trent

Marlpit House

Burybank

The Darlaston (PH)

Meaford

Meaford Hall

ST VINCENT MEWS

Meaford Old Hall Farm

Edge Hill

1 CRESSY CL
2 CALDON WAY
3 HARECASTLE BANK
4 SALTERSFORD RISE
5 RANGELEY VIEW
6 DARWIN CL
7 DIXON CL

Common Plot

Darlastonwood Farm

The Drumble

George and Dragon (PH)

Turnover Bridge

JERVIS LA

JOULES DR

BARNTON EDGE

ANDERTON

BENTLEY CL

RENDEL GR

FOAL

BRINDLEY CL

RUDYARD CL

NAVIGATION LOOP

Trent and Mersey Canal

Works

LC

Stonefield

Mount Ind Est

Darlaston Wood

Darlaston Park

Home Farm

MILLENNIUM WAY

WHITEBRIDGE

CENTRE RD

CANAL SIDE

WHITEBRIDGE WAY

WHITEBRIDGE CT

CHESTNUT CT

FIELD HOUSE CT

MOUNT RD

Whitebridge Ind Est

B5027

Stone

STATION APP

LC

KENT GR

MOUNT AVE

MEAFORD

BERKELEY CT

VICTOR ST

B5315

TUNLEY ST

STATION RD

ALMA ST

REGENT ST

B5315

NEWCASTLE RD

THE FILLYBROOKS

NEWCASTLE RD

TRENT RD

HARTLEY ST

YARNFIELD LA

A34

Darlaston Grange

St Dominic's Priory Sch

CAMEROON

WHARF

St Dominic's Priory Sch

A51

A34

STONE RD

A34

M6

A51

M6

F1
1 EDWARD ST
2 ALEXANDRA ST
3 KING'S AVE
4 NORTHESK ST
5 DOMINIC ST
6 MARGARET ST
7 RIVERSIDE GR
8 LIMEDALE CT

F2
1 CHESTNUT CT
2 STONEFIELD CT

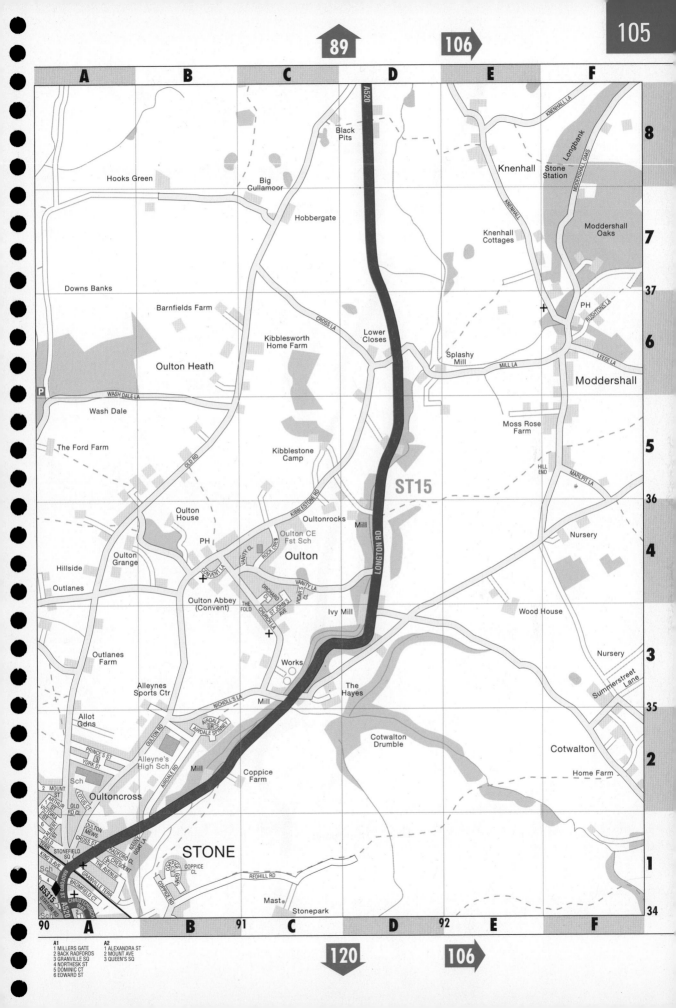

A B C D E F

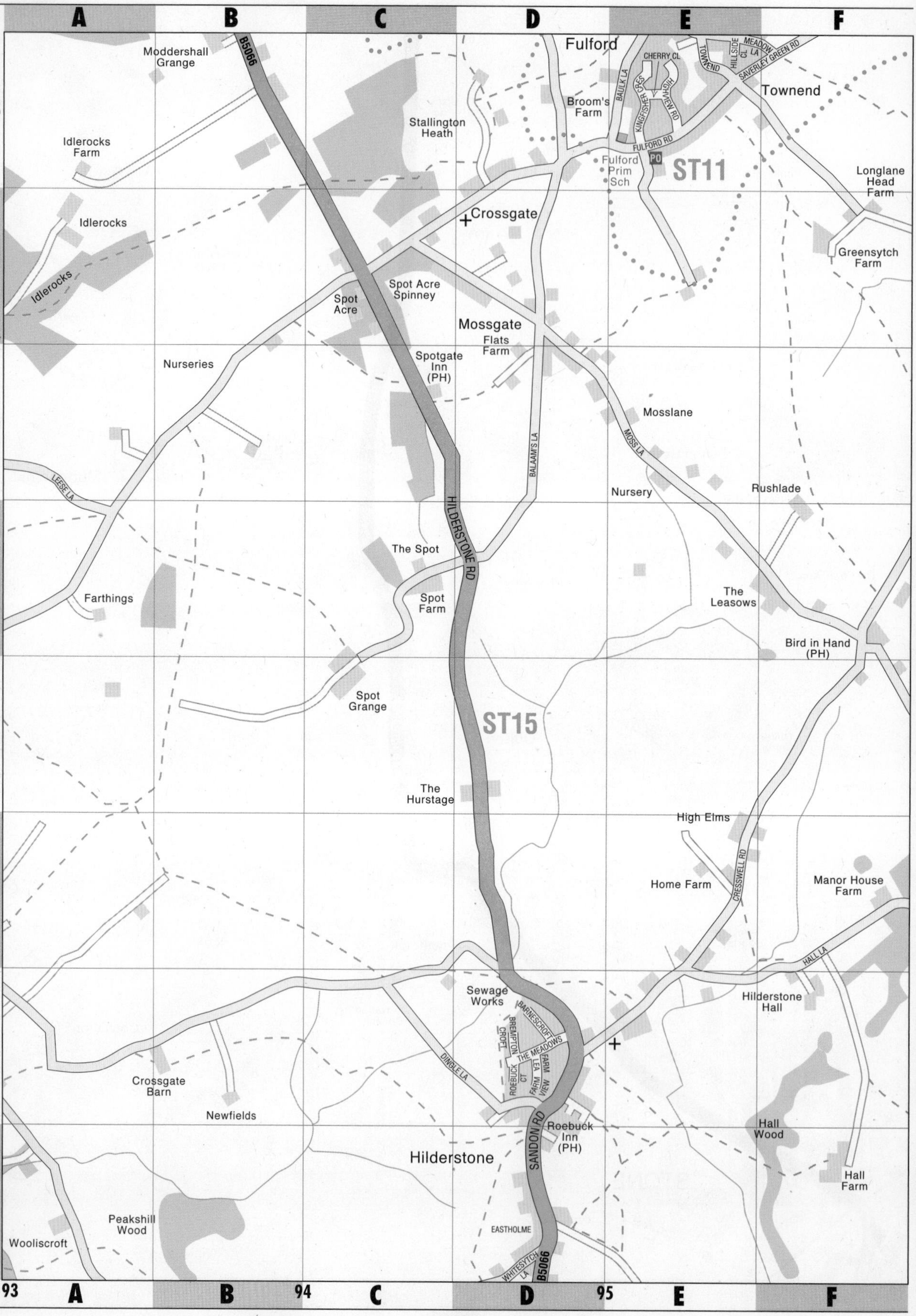

8

Moddershall
Grange

Fulford

Townend

Idlerocks
Farm

Stallington
Heath

Broom's
Farm

ST11

Longlane
Head
Farm

Fulford
Prim
Sch

PO

+ Crossgate

7

Idlerocks

Greensytch
Farm

Idlerocks

Spot Acre
Spinney

Spot
Acre

Mossgate

37

Nurseries

Spotgate
Inn
(PH)

Flats
Farm

Mosslane

6

Nursery

Rushlade

LESSE LA

The Spot

The
Leasows

5

Farthings

Spot
Farm

Bird in Hand
(PH)

36

Spot
Grange

ST15

4

The
Hurstage

High Elms

3

Home Farm

Manor House
Farm

35

Sewage
Works

Hilderstone
Hall

2

Crossgate
Barn

Hall
Wood

Newfields

Roebuck
Inn
(PH)

Hilderstone

1

Peakshill
Wood

Hall
Farm

Wooliscroft

EASTHOLME

B5066

34

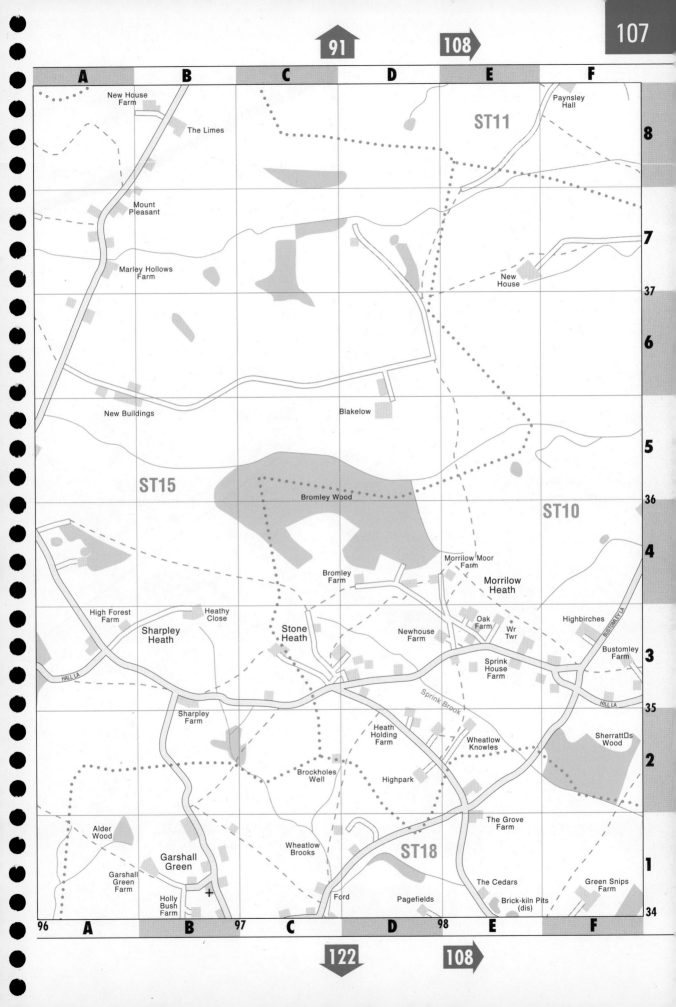

A B C D E F

8

New House Farm
The Limes
ST11
Paynsley Hall

7

Mount Pleasant
37
Marley Hollows Farm
New House

6

New Buildings
Blakelow

5

ST15
Bromley Wood
36
ST10

4

Morrilow Moor Farm
Bromley Farm
Morrilow Heath

High Forest Farm
Heathy Close
Sharpley Heath
Stone Heath
Newhouse Farm
Oak Farm
Wr Twr
Highbirches
BUSTOMLEY LA
Bustomley Farm

3

HALL LA
Sprink House Farm
HILL LA
35
Sharpley Farm
Sprink Brook
Heath Holding Farm
Wheatlow Knowles
Sherratt's Wood

2

Brockholes Well
Highpark
Alder Wood
The Grove Farm

1

Garshall Green
Wheatlow Brooks
ST18
Garshall Green Farm
The Cedars
Green Snips Farm
Holly Bush Farm
Ford
Pagefields
Brick-kiln Pits (dis)
34

96 A B 97 C D 98 E F

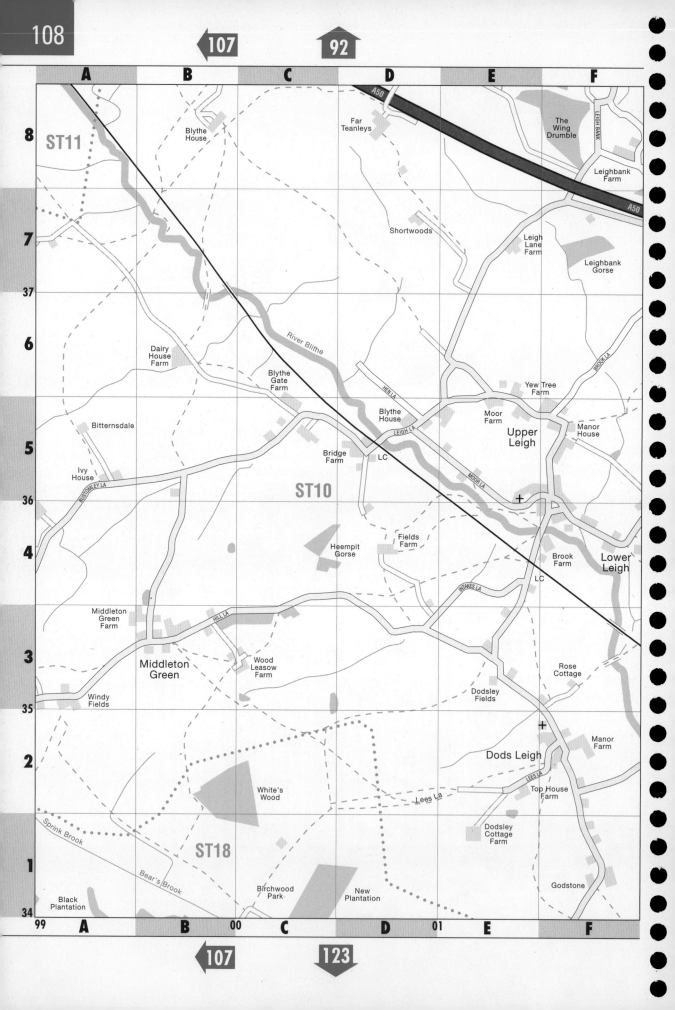

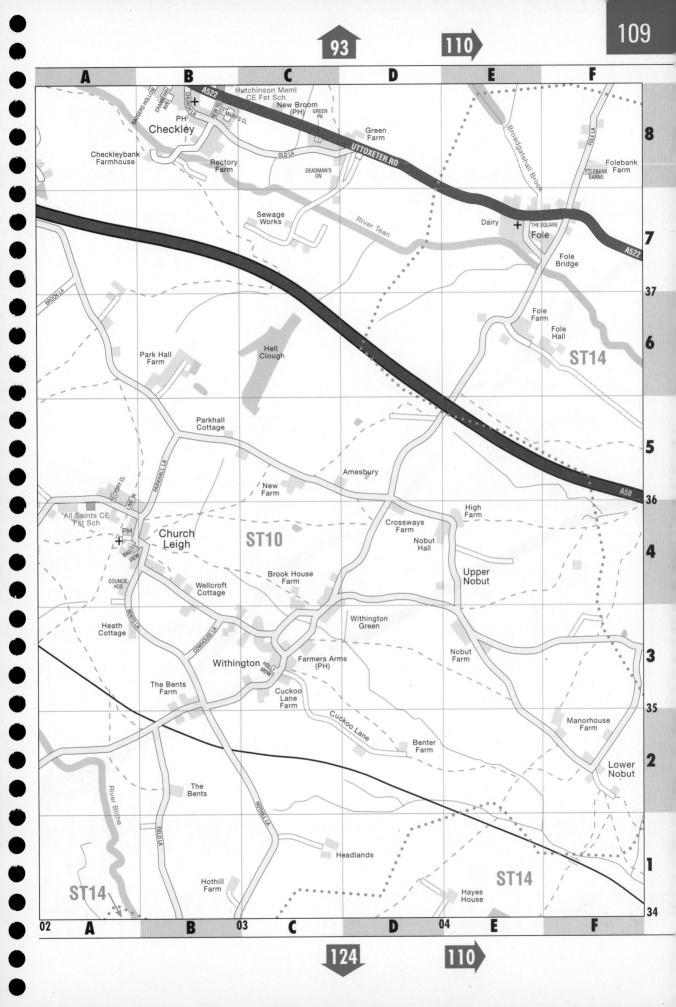

A   B   C   D   E   F

8   Oldwood   ST10   Hollywood Farm   Nothill Wood

Cotton's Wood   Nothill Farm

7   A522   Old Turnpike   Pale Flatts Farm

37   Madeley Farm   High Farm   Dove House   The Alders

6   Townend Farm   Lawn Farm   Creighton Park Farm

Beamhurst   Beamhursthall Farm   New House Farm

Oldwood

5   Overfole   Beamhurst Hall   Spar Flat Farm   Flashes Farm   Newhouse

PH   ST14   HOLLINGTON LA

36   A50   River Tean   Mill Farm   Springfields   Mount Pleasant   CEDAR DR 1 CHURCH FARM 2

4   Beamhurst Bridge   Beamhurst Lane   ST MICHAEL'S RD

Waterloo Farm   VICARAGE DR

3   Deggs Leasow   Park View

35   Broadoak Farm   Lightwoodfields   PIGEONRY LA   Parks' Farm

2   The Parks (PH)   A50

Dagdale Farm   Banktop   A522

FRADGLEY GR

1   Dagdale   BURTON MEWS 1
DERBY MEWS 2
NOTTINGHAM CT 3
LINCOLN CT 4
SHEFFIELD CT 5
LEICESTER CT 6
MANCHESTER CT 7   Moss Beds   Sch

34   Yew Tree Farm

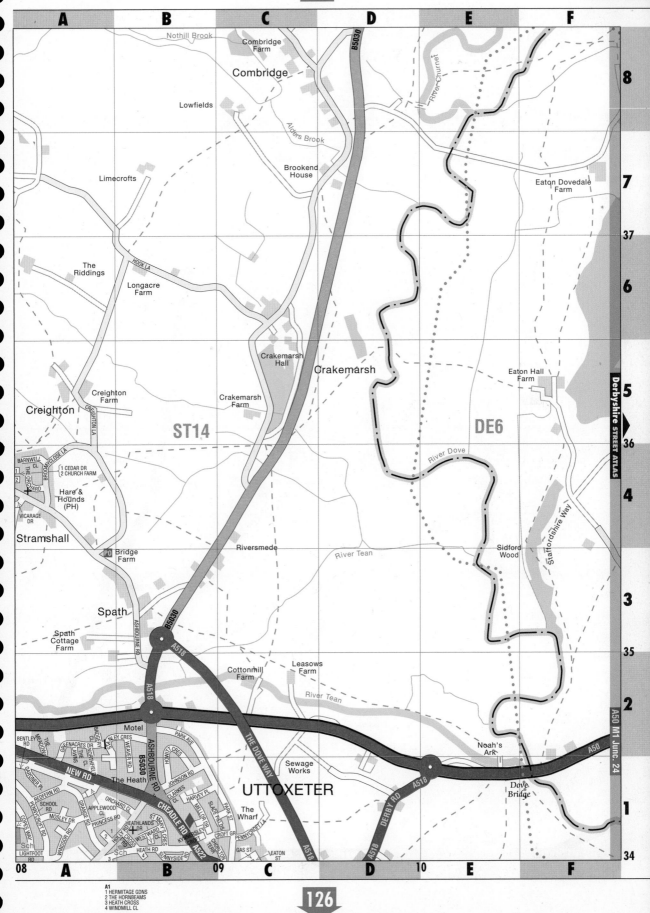

A1
1 HERMITAGE GDNS
2 THE HORNBEAMS
3 HEATH CROSS
4 WINDMILL CL

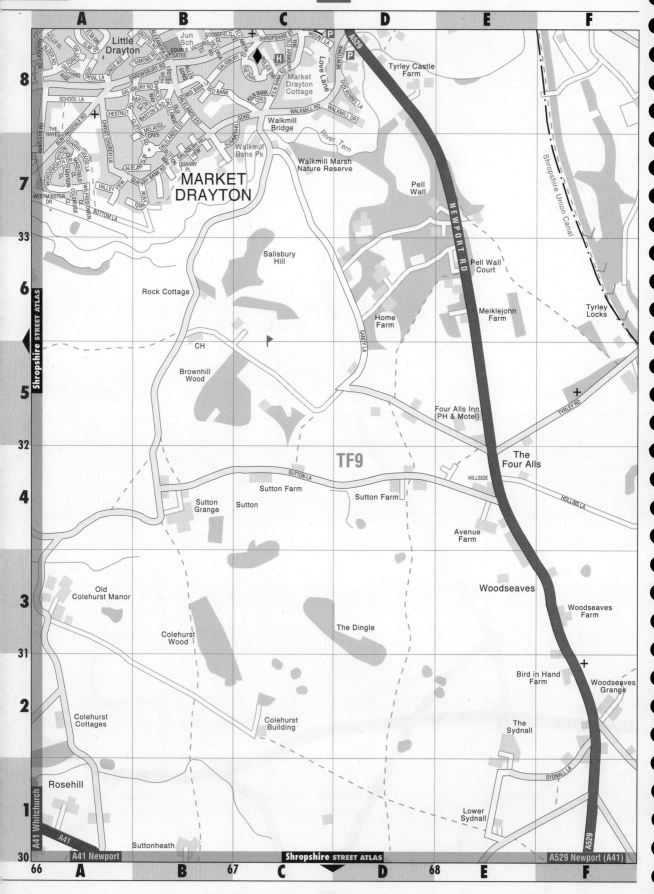

A8
1 PARKER BOWLES DR
2 GLENDON CL
3 ELLESMERE GR
4 SPRINGFIELD MOBILE HOME PK

Little Drayton

MARKET DRAYTON

Jun Sch
Goosefield Cl

Shropshire St
The Old Armoury
Market Drayton Cottage

Love Lane

Tyrley Castle Farm

Walkmill Bridge

River Tern

Walkmill Marsh Nature Reserve

Walkmill Bsns Pk

Pell Wall

Shropshire Union Canal

Salisbury Hill

Pell Wall Court

Rock Cottage

Meiklejohn Farm

Tyrley Locks

Home Farm

CH

Brownhill Wood

Four Alls Inn (PH & Motel)

Tyrley Rd

TF9

The Four Alls

Sutton La

HILLSIDE

Hollins La

Sutton Farm

Sutton Grange

Sutton

Sutton Farm

Avenue Farm

Woodseaves

Old Colehurst Manor

Woodseaves Farm

Colehurst Wood

The Dingle

Bird in Hand Farm

Woodseaves Grange

Colehurst Cottages

Colehurst Building

The Sydnall

Sydnall La

Rosehill

Lower Sydnall

Suttonheath

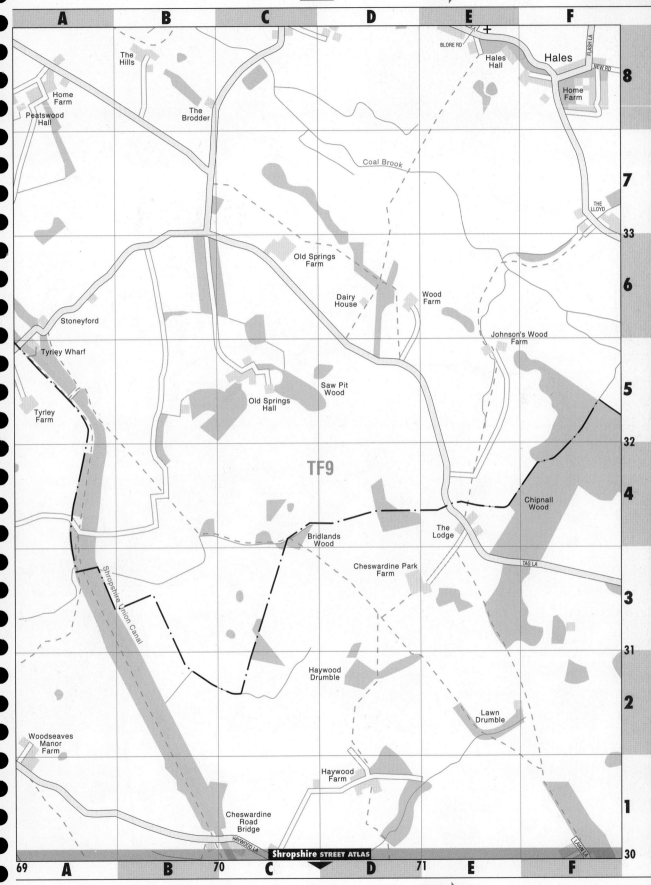

113
99

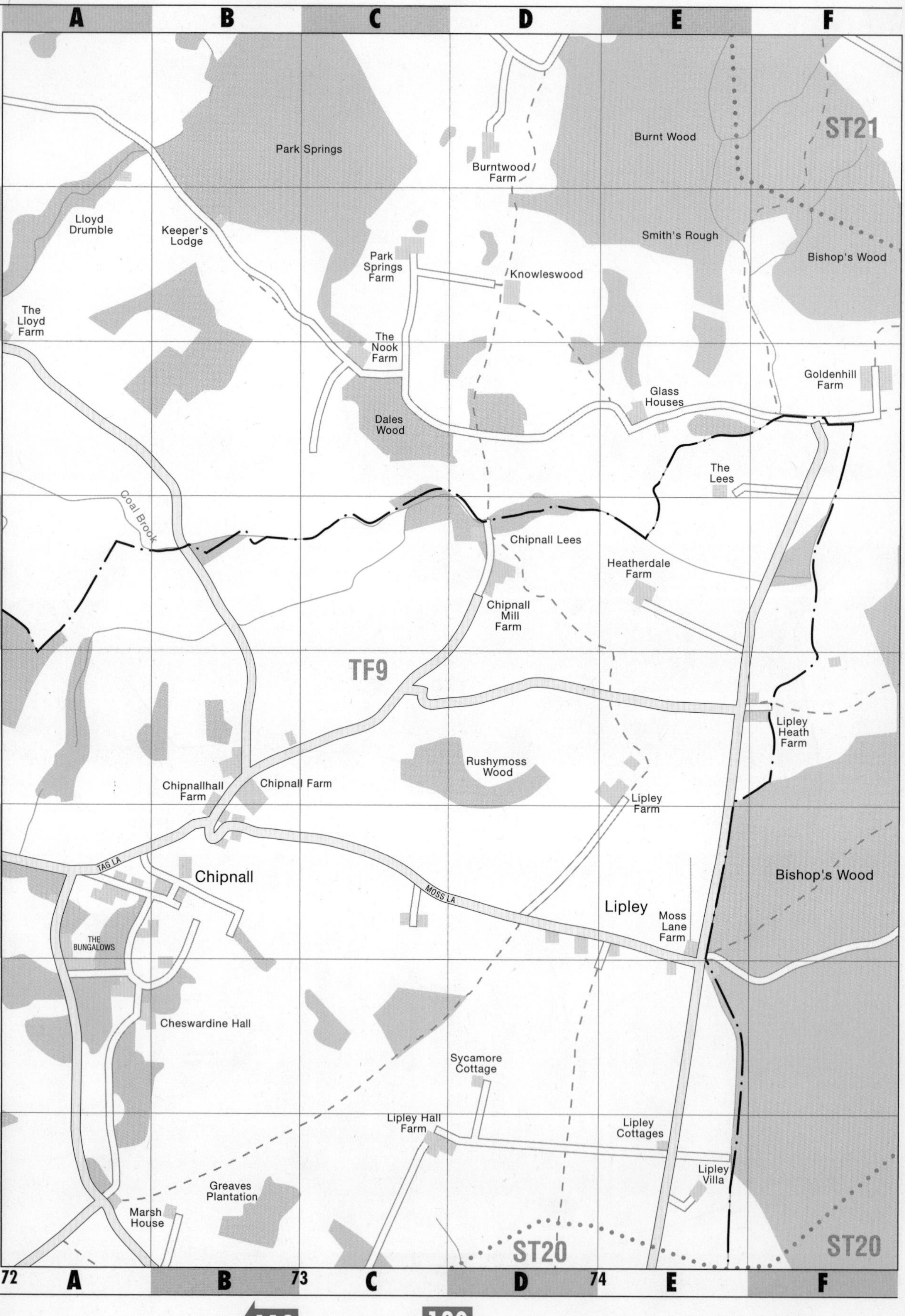

A
B
C
D
E
F
8
7
33
6
5
32
4
3
31
2
1
30
72
73
74
Park Springs
Burnt Wood
ST21
Burntwood Farm
Lloyd Drumble
Keeper's Lodge
Smith's Rough
Bishop's Wood
Park Springs Farm
Knowleswood
The Lloyd Farm
The Nook Farm
Goldenhill Farm
Glass Houses
Dales Wood
The Lees
Coal Brook
Chipnall Lees
Heatherdale Farm
Chipnall Mill Farm
TF9
Lipley Heath Farm
Rushymoss Wood
Chipnallhall Farm
Chipnall Farm
Lipley Farm
TAG LA
Chipnall
Bishop's Wood
MOSS LA
Lipley
Moss Lane Farm
THE BUNGALOWS
Cheswardine Hall
Sycamore Cottage
Lipley Hall Farm
Lipley Cottages
Lipley Villa
Greaves Plantation
Marsh House
ST20
ST20

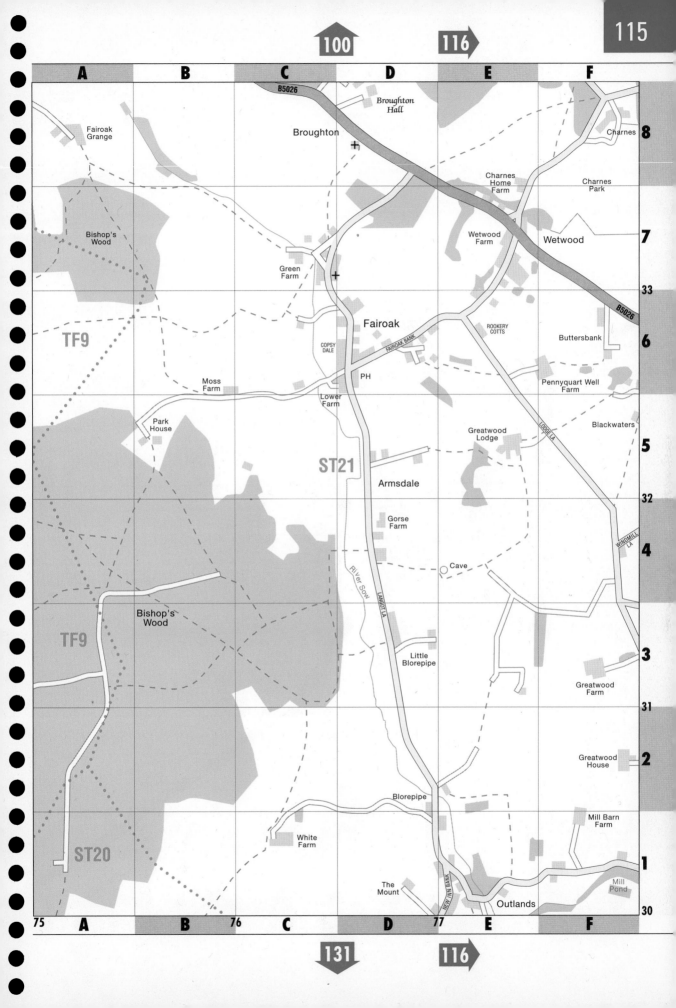

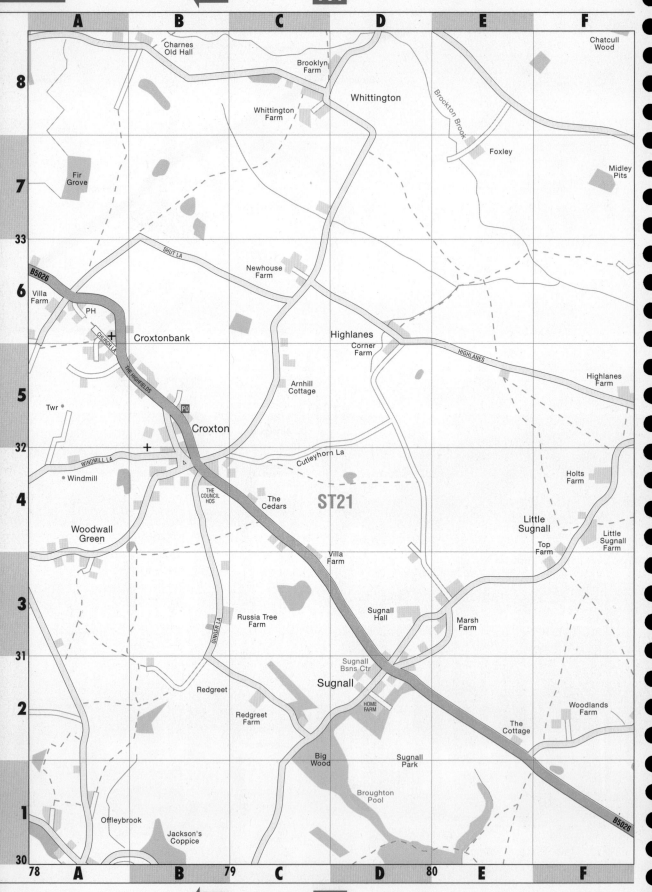

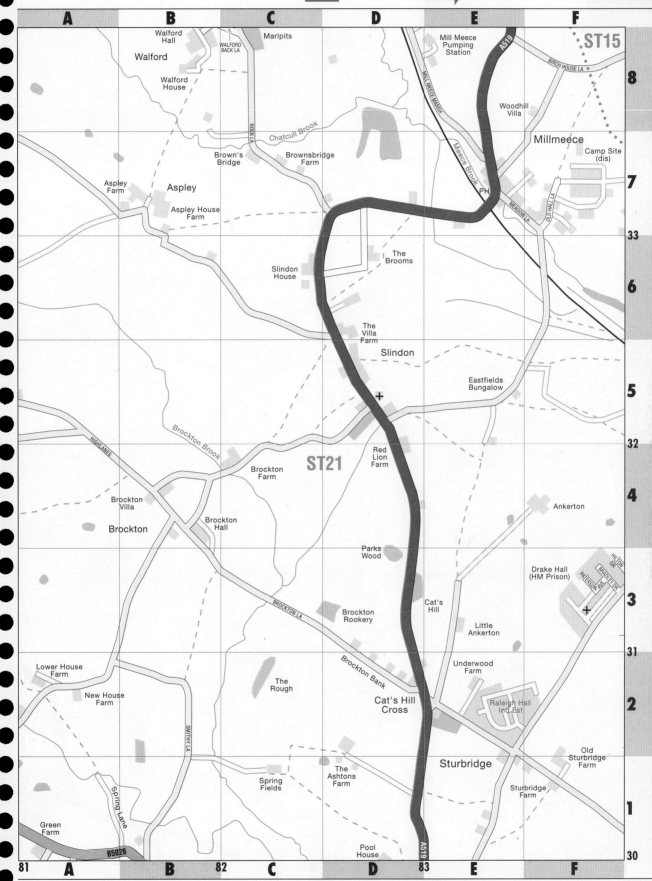

ST15

A B C D E F

8

Walford Hall
Marlpits
Walford
WALFORD BACK LA
Walford House
Mill Meece Pumping Station
A519
BIRCH HOUSE LA
Woodhill Villa
Millmeece
Camp Site (dis)

ROCK LA
Chatcull Brook
Brown's Bridge
Brownsbridge Farm
MILL MEECE MARSH
Meece Brook
PH
MEADOW LA
OLD HALL LA

7

Aspley Farm
Aspley
Aspley House Farm

33

The Brooms

6

Slindon House
The Villa Farm
Slindon
Eastfields Bungalow

5

Brockton Brook
+
ST21

32

HIGHLANES
Brockton Farm
Red Lion Farm
Ankerton

4

Brockton Villa
Brockton Hall
Brockton
Parks Wood
Drake Hall (HM Prison)
HILTON DR
BRADLEY DR
PATERSON RD
+

3

BROCKTON LA
Brockton Rookery
Cat's Hill
Little Ankerton

31

Lower House Farm
Brockton Bank
Underwood Farm
Raleigh Hall Ind Est
Old Sturbridge Farm

2

New House Farm
SMITHY LA
The Rough
Cat's Hill Cross
Sturbridge
Sturbridge Farm

1

Spring Lane
Spring Fields
The Ashtons Farm
Green Farm
B5026
Pool House
A519

30

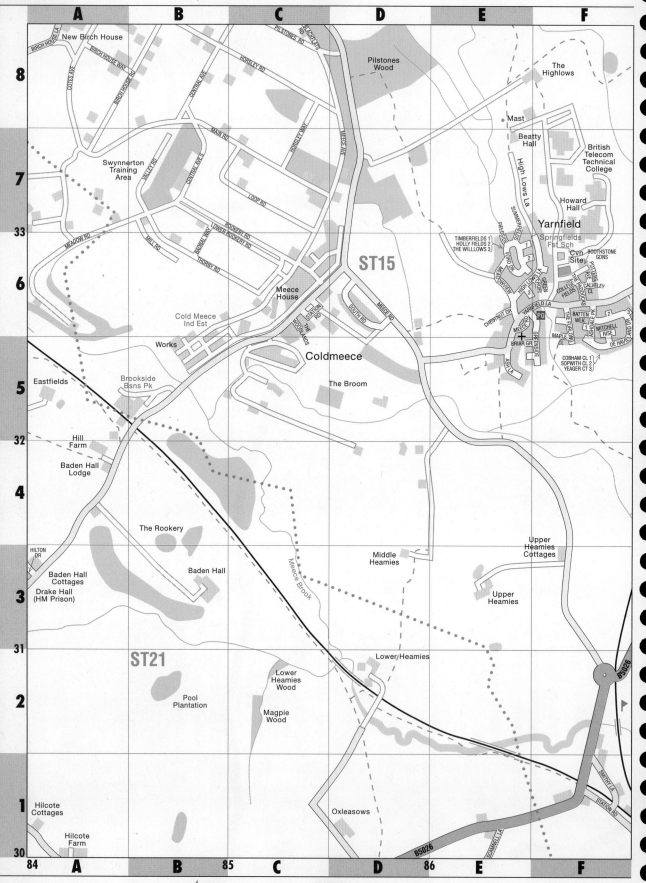

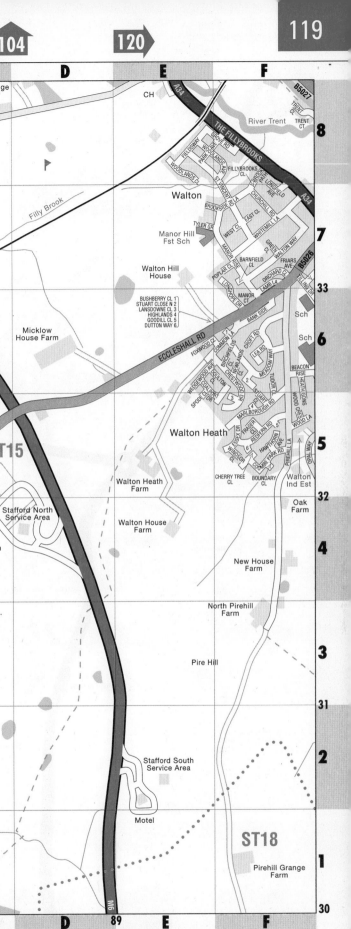

A B C D E F

8
7
33
6
5
32
4
3
31
2
1
30

A B C D E F

Darlaston Grange
CH
B5027
River Trent
TRENT CL
TRENT CT
THE FILLYBROOKS
A34
YARNFIELD LA
M6
Filly Brook
FIELDSWAY
GROVE RD
WOODLANDS AVE
ST VINCENT DR
WOODLANDS CL
FILLYBROOKS CL
BROOKSIDE PK
LONGFIELD AVE
A34
Walton
Whitemoor Farm
MOSS LA
Moss House
BROOKSIDE RD
CHURCHILL RD
EAST CL
TYLER GR
WEST CL
WHITMILL LA
Manor Hill Fst Sch
MANOR DR
GREEN CL
B5026
WALTON WAY
FRIARS AVE
FILING DR
Walton Hill House
BARNFIELD CL
POPLAR DR
ORCHARD CL
LAMB LA
Sch
LONGHOPE DR
MANOR CL
BUSHBERRY CL 1
STUART CLOSE N 2
LANSDOWNE CL 3
HIGHLANDS 4
GOODILL CL 5
DUTTON WAY 6
ECCLESHALL RD
FOXWOOD CL
COMMON LA
CROFT RD
BANK SIDE
Sch
Micklow House Farm
WETHEREWOOD AVE
DOULTON
COALPORT
CHALGORT
SPODE CL
CL DR
BIRCHFIELDS
COMMON LA
NEWLANDS
LEA RD
MCMEADOW
STUART
TUDOR RD
BEACON RISE
HEATH GDNS
WOOD CRES
WOOD LA
Cold Norton Farm
COLD NORTON COTTS
LAKESEDGE
ST15
MARLBOROUGH RD
FRASER CL
REDFERN RD
ESSEX CT
WINDSOR CL
HAWTHORN CL
CAMP PARK RD
PIREHILL LA
TRAIL WAY
Walton Heath
Motel
Works
Cold Norton
Walton Heath Farm
CHERRY TREE CL
BOUNDARY CL
Walton Ind Est
Cold Norton Gorse
Stafford North Service Area
Walton House Farm
Oak Farm
New House Farm
North Pirehill Farm
Pire Hill
White House Farm
CH
Norton Farm
STATION RD
Norton Bridge Junction
Norton Bridge
M6
Stafford South Service Area
Motel
ST18
Pirehill Grange Farm

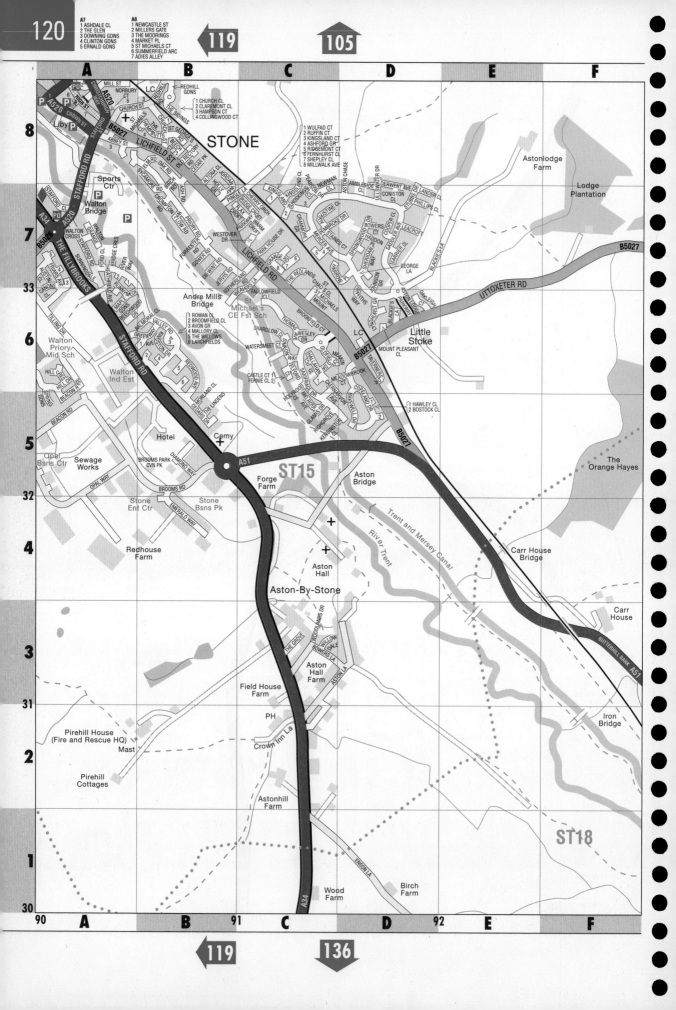

A7
1 ASHDALE CL
2 THE GLEN
3 DOWNING GDNS
4 CLINTON GDNS
5 ERNALD GDNS

A8
1 NEWCASTLE ST
2 MILLERS GATE
3 THE MOORINGS
4 MARKET PL
5 ST MICHAELS CT
6 SUMMERFIELD ARC
7 ADIES ALLEY

◄ 119
105

STONE

1 WULFAD CT
2 RUFFIN CT
3 KINGSLAND CT
4 ASHFORD GR
5 RIDGEMONT CT
6 FERNHURST CL
7 SHEPLEY CL
8 MILLWALK AVE

Astonlodge Farm

Lodge Plantation

B5027

Sports Ctr

Walton Bridge

LICHFIELD ST

UTTOXETER RD

B5027

Walton Cross

THE FILLYBROOKS

Andre Mills Bridge

St Michael's CE Fst Sch

1 ROWAN CL
2 BROOMFIELD CL
3 AVON GR
4 MALLORY CL
5 THE WILLOWS
6 LARCHFIELDS

Little Stoke

Walton Priory Mid Sch

STAFFORD RD

Walton Ind Est

1 CASTLE CT 1
2 FERNIE CL 2

MOUNT PLEASANT CL

1 HAWLEY CL
2 BOSTOCK CL

Opal Bsns Ctr

Sewage Works

Hotel

Cemy

A51

ST15

Forge Farm

Aston Bridge

The Orange Hayes

Stone Ent Ctr

Stone Bsns Pk

B5027

Redhouse Farm

Aston Hall

Trent and Mersey Canal

River Trent

Carr House Bridge

Aston-By-Stone

Carr House

Pirehill House (Fire and Rescue HQ)

Mast

THE GROVE

WOODLANDS DR

WILLOW DALE

BOWERS LA

Aston Hall Farm

ASTON LA

Field House Farm

BUTTERHILL BANK A51

PH

Iron Bridge

Pirehill Cottages

Crown Inn La

Astonhill Farm

ST18

A34

ENSON LA

Wood Farm

Birch Farm

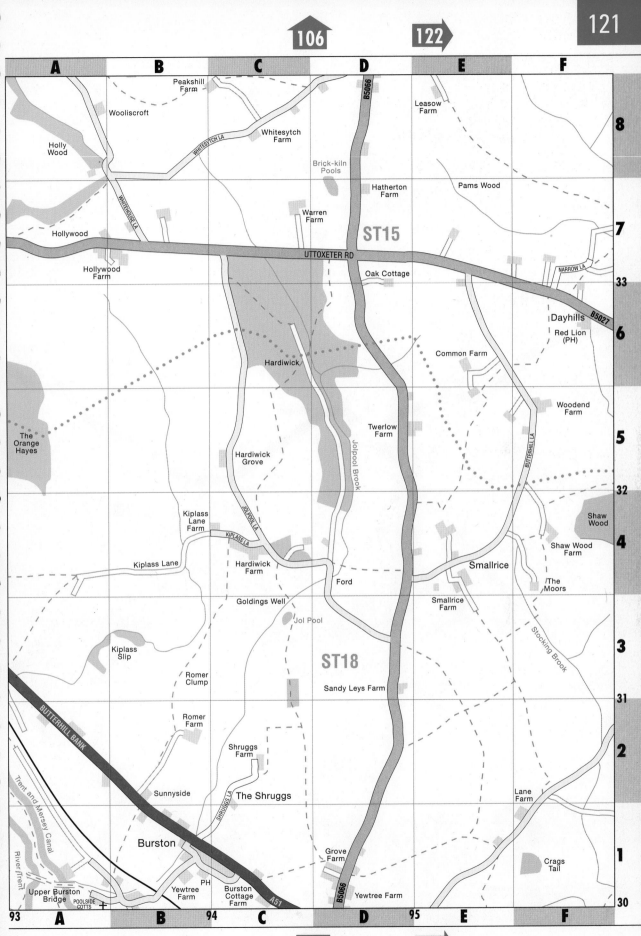

← 121
107

A B C D E F

8

Garshall
Green

Garshall
House

Castle
Farm

Summerhill

Withysitch Lane

Birch
Rough

Withysitch
Farm

7

Dayhills
Farm

Oulton
House

Wheatlow Brook

Potsmans La

Calloway
Farm

33

Grange
Farm

ST15

Coton
Hayes

Darley Lane

6

B5027

Grimblebrook
Farm

Burleypool
Bridge

Salt's
Bridge

THE ALWAYS

ALL WAYS

PO

B5027

Coton
Hill

Milwich

UTTOXETER RD

CROSSHILL BANK

5

Burley
Pool Farm

SANDON LA

The
Green Man
(PH)

Coton
Cottage

32

Milwich
Hall

+

Coton

Wheatsheaf
Inn
(PH)

Coton
Green
Farm

ST18

Park
Farm

4

Shaw
Wood

MILL LA

Green Lea
Fst Sch

3

Cromer Hill

Coton Mill
Farm

Mill Lane

WALBROOK RD

Fradswell Hall
Farm

31

Lander's Wood
Farm

Oxclose
Wood

Beacon Bank
Farm

Beacon
Bank

Model
Farm

HAWKINS LA

Lander's
Wood

2

Kendrick's Barn
Farm

Fox's Wood
Farm

Old Gayton
Gorse

The
Doglands

1

Sandon Wood
Farm

Gayton Brook

30

Kendrick's
Wood

DOGLANDS RD

96 A B 97 C D 98 E F

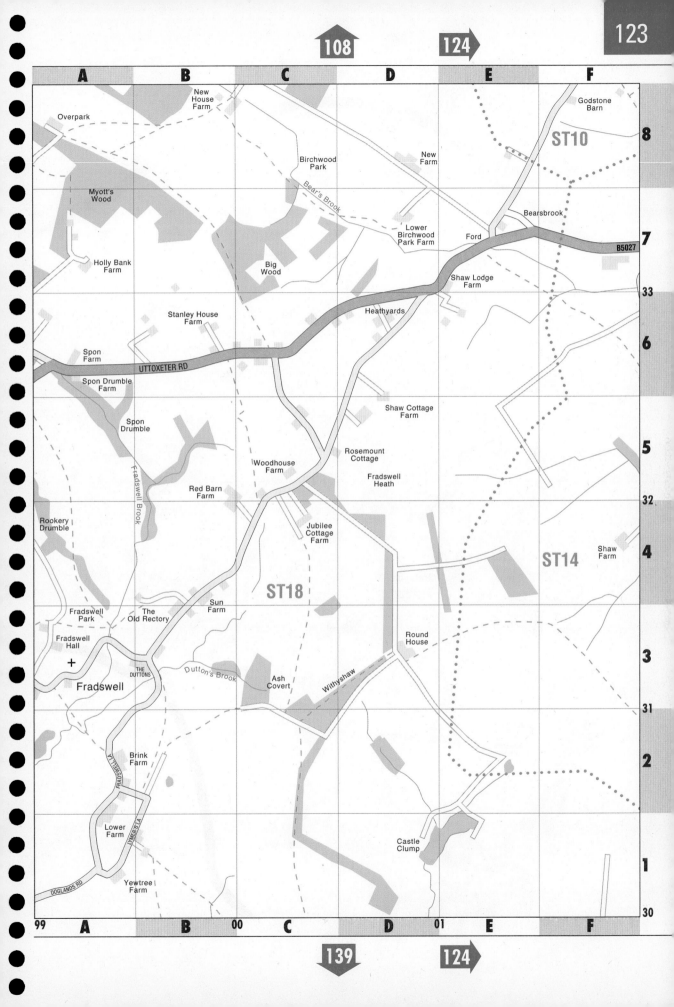

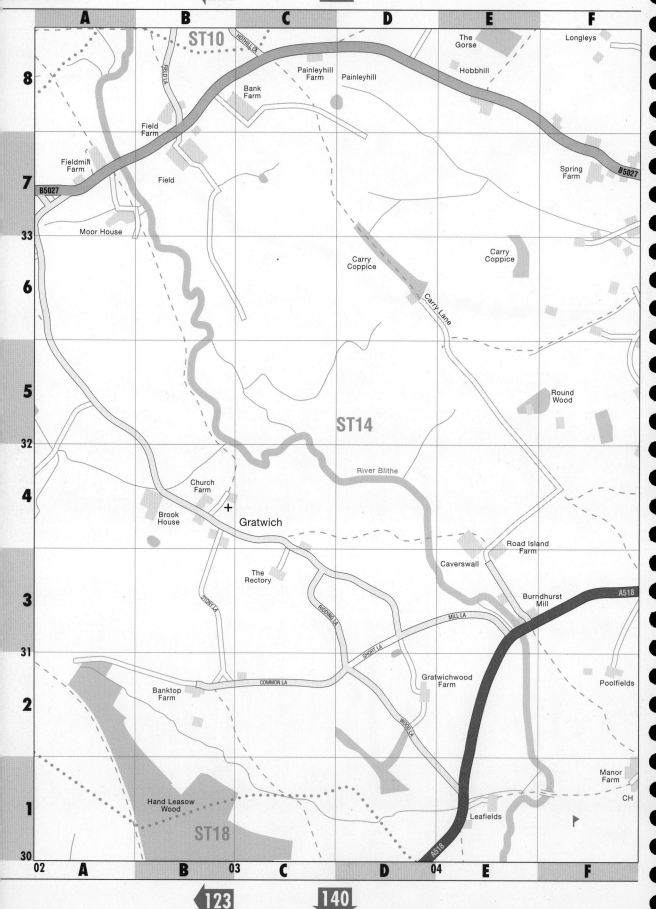

ST10

A B C D E F

Longleys

The
Gorse

Painleyhill
Farm   Painleyhill   Hobbhill

Bank
Farm

8

Field
Farm

Field   Spring
Farm   B5027

Fieldmill
Farm

7

B5027

Moor House

33

Carry
Coppice   Carry
Coppice

Carry
Coppice

6

Carry Lane

Round
Wood

5

ST14

32

River Blithe

Church
Farm

4

Brook
House   Gratwich

Road Island
Farm

The
Rectory   Caverswall

Burndhurst
Mill   A518

3

STONY LA

RIDDING LA

MILL LA

SHORT LA

31

Gratwichwood
Farm   Poolfields

Banktop
Farm   COMMON LA

2

WOOD LA

Manor
Farm

CH

Hand Leasow
Wood

1

ST18

Leafields

A518

30

02   A   B   03   C   D   04   E   F

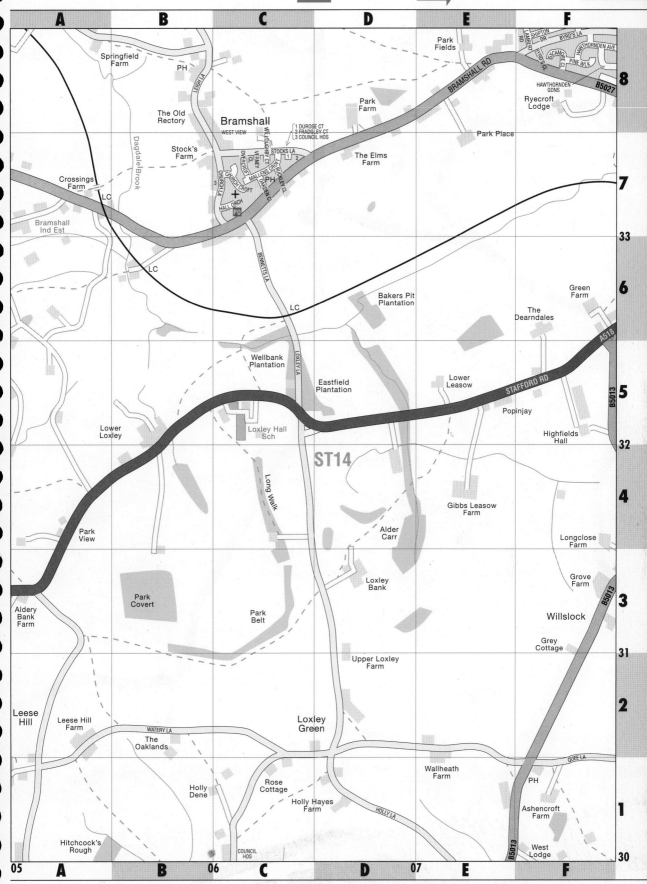

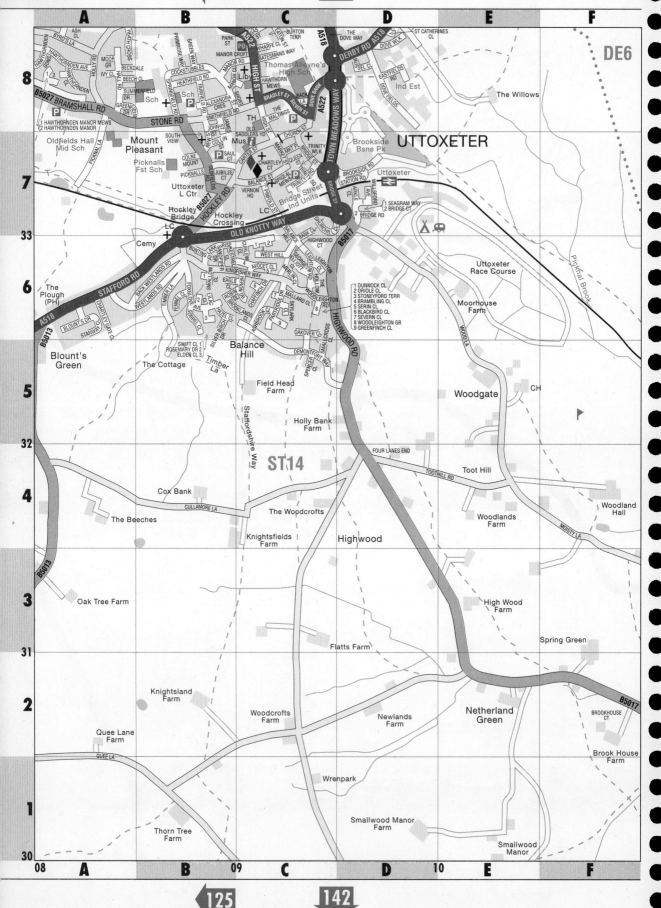

DE6

UTTOXETER

ST14

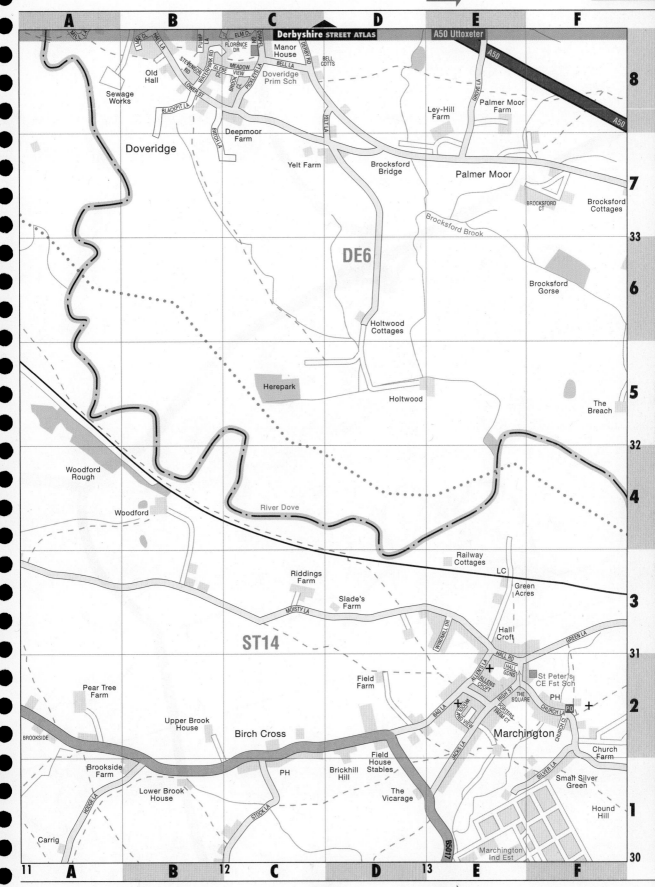

128
143
128

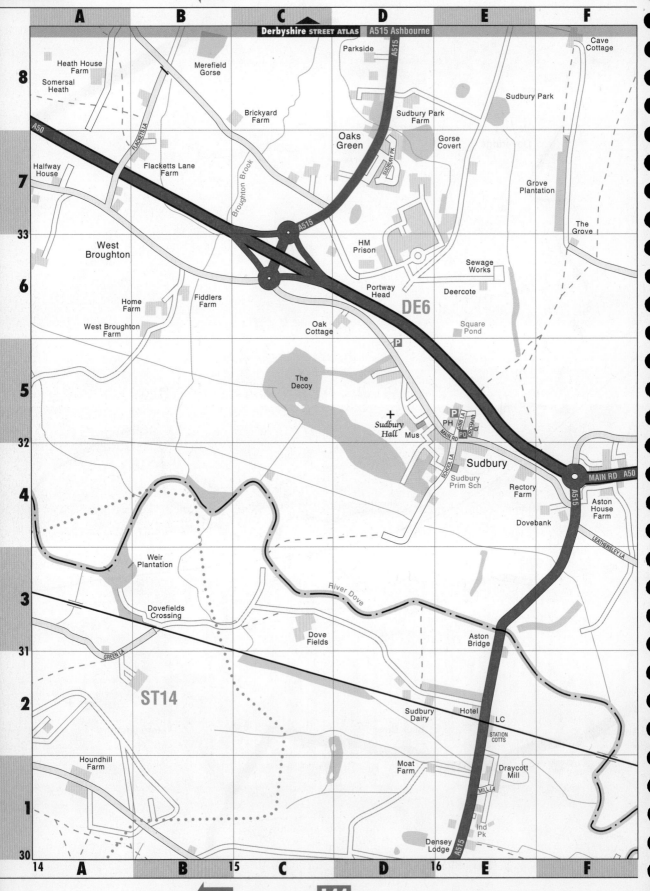

Derbyshire STREET ATLAS A515 Ashbourne

| A | B | C | D | E | F |

8
Heath House Farm
Somersal Heath
Merefield Gorse
Parkside
A515
Cave Cottage
Sudbury Park

Brickyard Farm
Sudbury Park Farm
Gorse Covert
Oaks Green

7
A50
FLACKETS LA
Halfway House
Flacketts Lane Farm
Broughton Brook
SUDBURY PK
Grove Plantation

33
West Broughton
A515
HM Prison
The Grove

6
Home Farm
Fiddlers Farm
Portway Head
Sewage Works
DE6
West Broughton Farm
Oak Cottage
Deercote

P
Square Pond

5
The Decoy
+ Sudbury Hall
P
PH
PO
Mus
CLUB LA
ORCHARD CL
MAIN RD

32
Sudbury
Sudbury Prim Sch
SCHOOL LA
Rectory Farm
MAIN RD A50
A515
Aston House Farm

4
Weir Plantation
Dovebank
LEATHERSLEY LA

3
Dovefields Crossing
Dove Fields
River Dove
Aston Bridge

31
GREEN LA

2
ST14
Sudbury Dairy
Hotel
LC
STATION COTTS
Moat Farm
Draycott Mill

1
Houndhill Farm
MILL LA
Densey Lodge
Ind Pk

30

| 14 | A | B | 15 | C | D | 16 | E | F |

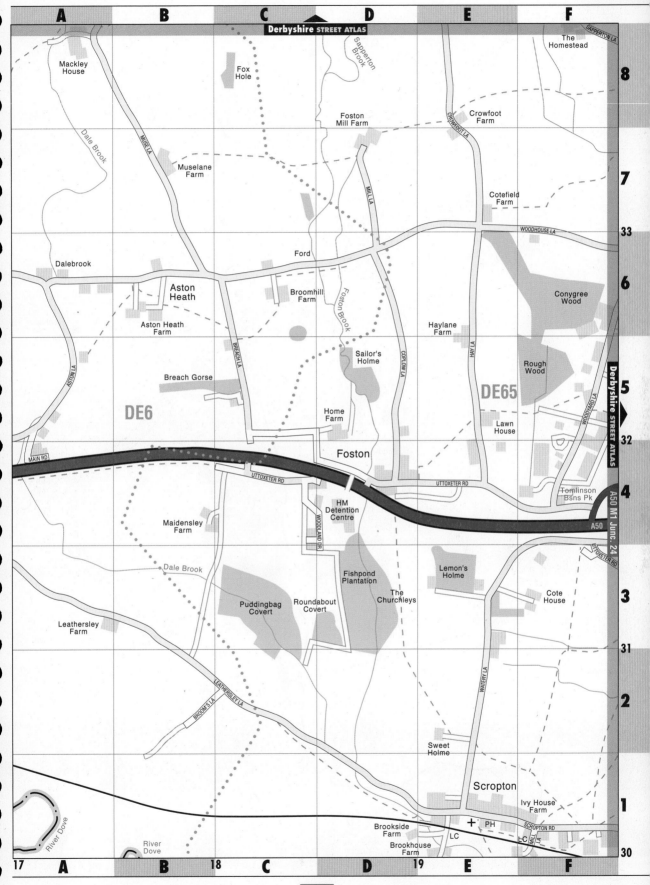

The Homestead

SAPPERTON LA

Mackley House

Fox Hole

Sapperton Brook

Foston Mill Farm

Crowfoot Farm

CROWFOOT LA

8

Muselane Farm

MUSE LA

Dale Brook

Cotefield Farm

7

MILL LA

WOODHOUSE LA

33

Dalebrook

Ford

Aston Heath

Broomhill Farm

Foston Brook

Conygree Wood

6

Aston Heath Farm

ASTON LA

BREACH LA

Haylane Farm

HAY LA

Rough Wood

Breach Gorse

Sailor's Holme

COPLOW LA

DE65

5

DE6

Home Farm

Lawn House

WOODYARD LA

32

Foston

Derbyshire STREET ATLAS

MAIN RD

UTTOXETER RD

UTTOXETER RD

A50

Tomlinson Bsns Pk

A50 M1 Junc. 24

4

Maidensley Farm

WOODLAND DRI

HM Detention Centre

UTTOXETER RD

Dale Brook

Fishpond Plantation

Lemon's Holme

Cote House

3

Leathersley Farm

Puddingbag Covert

Roundabout Covert

The Churchleys

31

LEATHERSLEY LA

BROOM'S LA

WATERY LA

2

Sweet Holme

Scropton

Ivy House Farm

1

River Dove

River Dove

Brookside Farm

+

PH

SCROPTON RD

Brookhouse Farm

LC

LC

MILL LA

30

17   A   B   18   C   D   19   E   F

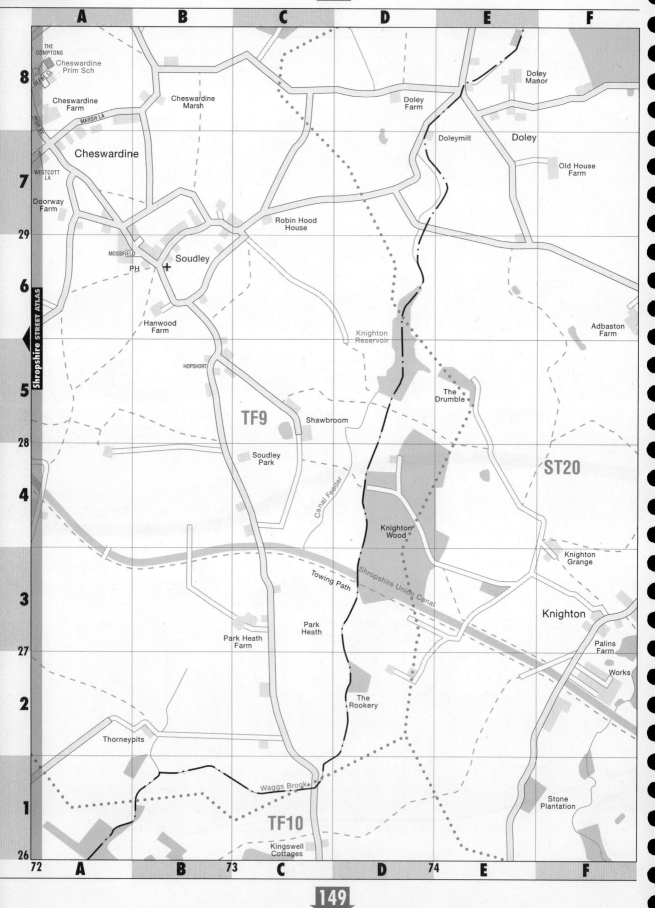

A B C D E F

8

7

29

6

5

28

4

3

27

2

1

26

Shropshire Street Atlas

THE COMPTONS
Cheswardine Prim Sch
GLEBE CL
HIGH ST
Cheswardine Farm
MARSH LA
Cheswardine Marsh
Cheswardine
WESTCOTT LA
Doorway Farm
Robin Hood House
MOSSFIELD
PH
Soudley
Hanwood Farm
HOPSHORT
TF9
Shawbroom
Soudley Park
Canal Feeder
Park Heath Farm
Park Heath
Thorneypits
Waggs Brook
TF10
Kingswell Cottages

Doley Manor
Doley Farm
Doleymill
Doley
Old House Farm
Adbaston Farm
Knighton Reservoir
The Drumble
ST20
Knighton Wood
Knighton Grange
Towing Path
Shropshire Union Canal
Knighton
Palins Farm
Works
The Rookery
Stone Plantation

72 73 74

A B C D E F

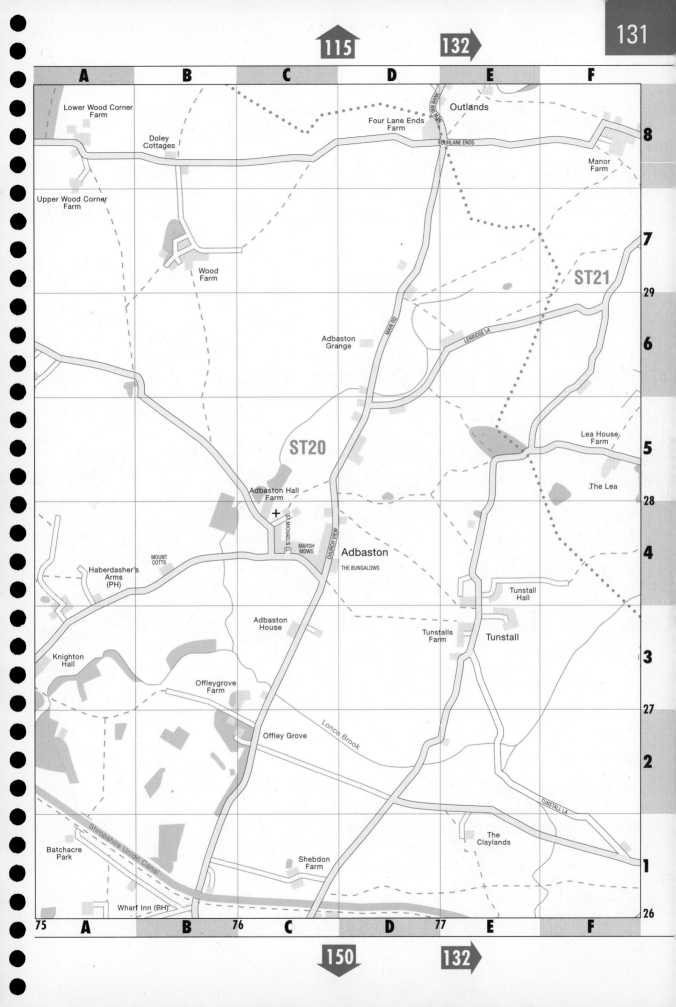

115
132

A B C D E F

Lower Wood Corner Farm

Doley Cottages

8

Outlands

Four Lane Ends Farm

FOURLANE ENDS

MAIN BANK

Manor Farm

Upper Wood Corner Farm

Wood Farm

7

ST21

29

Adbaston Grange

LERRIDGE LA

MAIN RD

6

ST20

Lea House Farm

5

The Lea

Adbaston Hall Farm

28

ST. MICHAEL'S CL.

MARSH MDWS

CHURCH VIEW

Adbaston

THE BUNGALOWS

4

Mount Cotts

Haberdasher's Arms (PH)

Tunstall Hall

Tunstalls Farm

Tunstall

Adbaston House

Knighton Hall

3

Offleygrove Farm

27

Offley Grove

Lonco Brook

2

TUNSTALL LA

Batchacre Park

Shropshire Union Canal

Shebdon Farm

The Claylands

1

Wharf Inn (PH)

26

150
132

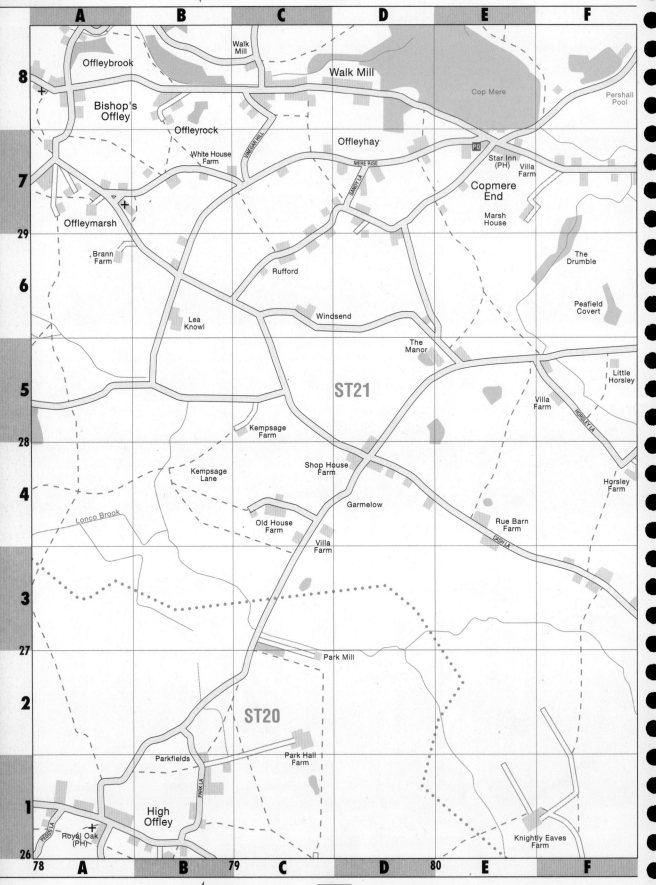

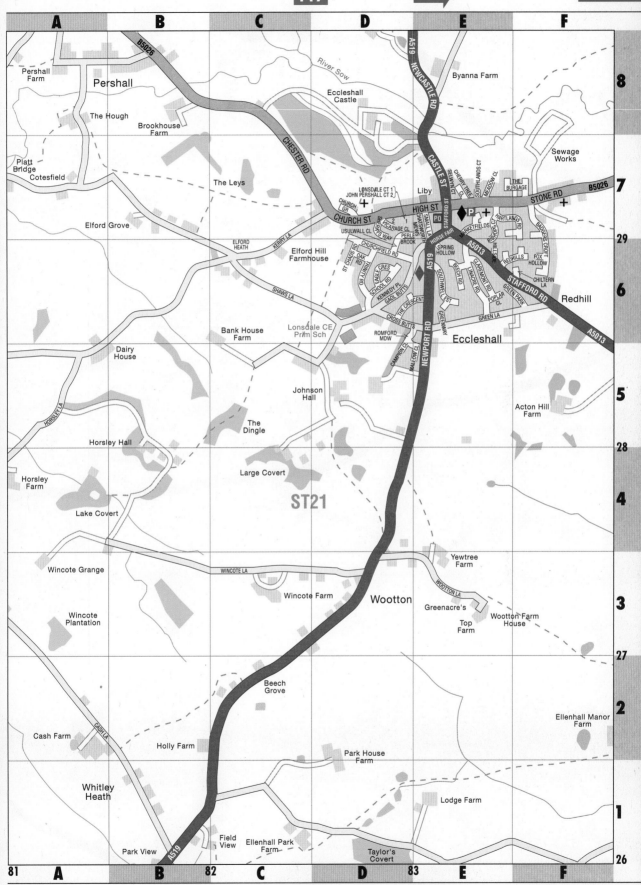

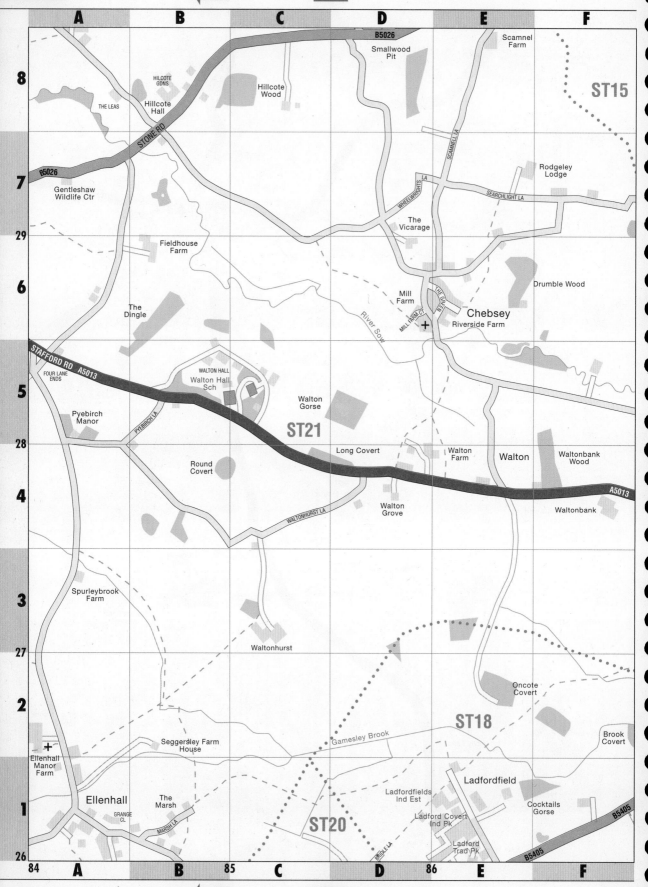

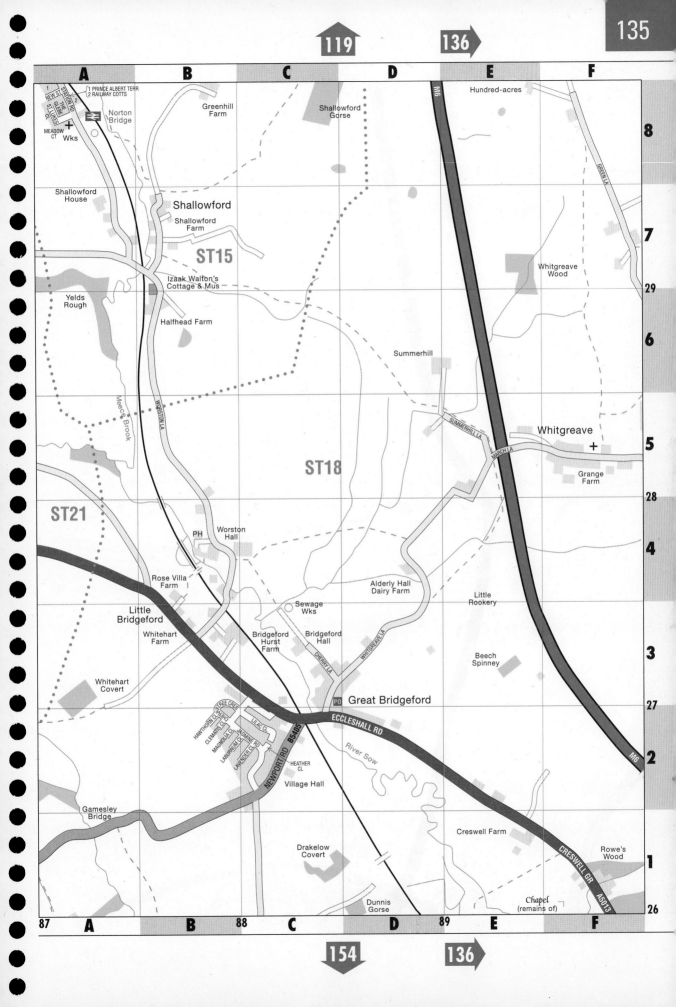

119
136
154
136

A B C D E F

8
7
29
6
5
28
4
3
27
2
1
26

1 PRINCE ALBERT TERR
2 RAILWAY COTTS

NEW ST
STATION RD
THE GLEBE
ST LUKES CL
MEADOW CT
Wks

Norton Bridge

Greenhill Farm

Shallowford Gorse

Hundred-acres

GREEN LA

Shallowford House

Shallowford

ST15

Shallowford Farm

Whitgreave Wood

Izaak Walton's Cottage & Mus

Yelds Rough

Halfhead Farm

Summerhill

Meece Brook

WORSTON LA

ST18

SUMMERHILL LA

Whitgreave

MARCH LA

Grange Farm

ST21

PH

Worston Hall

Alderly Hall Dairy Farm

Little Rookery

Rose Villa Farm

Little Bridgeford

Whitehart Farm

Sewage Wks

Bridgeford Hurst Farm

Bridgeford Hall

WHITGREAVE LA

CHERRY LA

Beech Spinney

Whitehart Covert

PO

Great Bridgeford

ECCLESHALL RD

M6

TREE CRES
HAWTHORN CL
CLEMATIS CL
MAGNOLIA CL
LABURNUM CL
JASMINE RD
LILAC CL
LAVENDER CL
NEWPORT RD
B5405
HEATHER CL

River Sow

Village Hall

Gamesley Bridge

Drakelow Covert

Creswell Farm

Rowe's Wood

CRESWELL GR
A5013

Dunnis Gorse

Chapel (remains of)

87 88 89

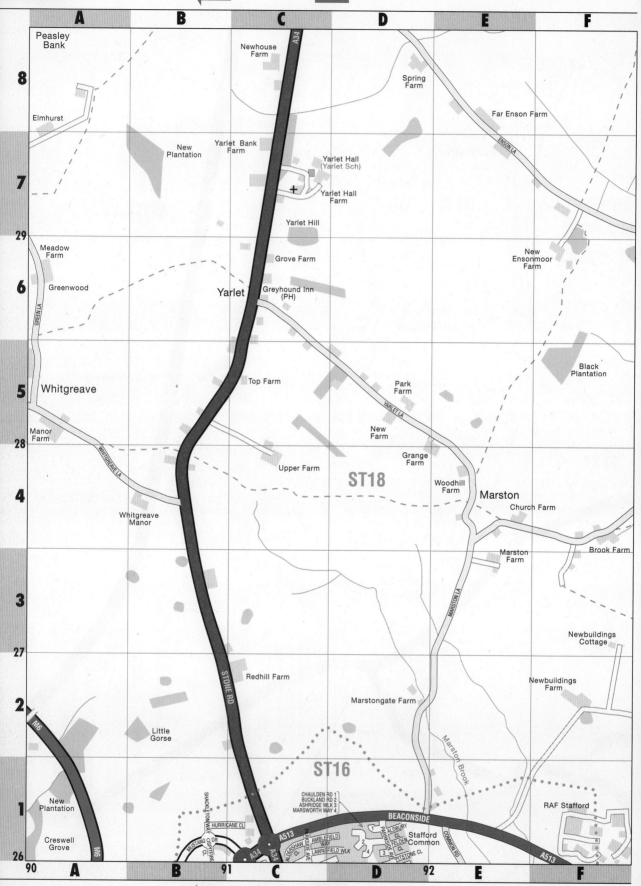

Peasley Bank

Newhouse Farm

Spring Farm

Far Enson Farm

Elmhurst

New Plantation

Yarlet Bank Farm

Yarlet Hall (Yarlet Sch)

Yarlet Hall Farm

ENSON LA

Meadow Farm

Greenwood

Yarlet Hill

Grove Farm

New Ensonmoor Farm

GREEN LA

Yarlet

Greyhound Inn (PH)

Black Plantation

Whitgreave

Top Farm

Park Farm

YARLET LA

Manor Farm

New Farm

Grange Farm

ST18

Woodhill Farm

Marston

Church Farm

WHITGREAVE LA

Upper Farm

Whitgreave Manor

Marston Farm

Brook Farm

MARSTON LA

STONE RD

Newbuildings Cottage

Redhill Farm

Marston Brook

Newbuildings Farm

M6

Little Gorse

Marstongate Farm

ST16

RAF Stafford

New Plantation

CHAULDEN RD 1
BUCKLAND RD 2
ASHRIDGE WLK 3
MARSWORTH WAY 4

Creswell Grove

M6

SHACKLETON WAY

HURRICANE CL

MUSTANG DR

SPITFIRE CL

A34

A513

BEACONSIDE

BRIGHTSIDE AVE

ALDERSHAW CL

AMBLEFIELD WAY

LAWNSFIELD WLK

ALDBURY CL

PARKSIDE AVE

FELDEN CL

PITSTONE CL

Stafford Common

COMMON RD

A513

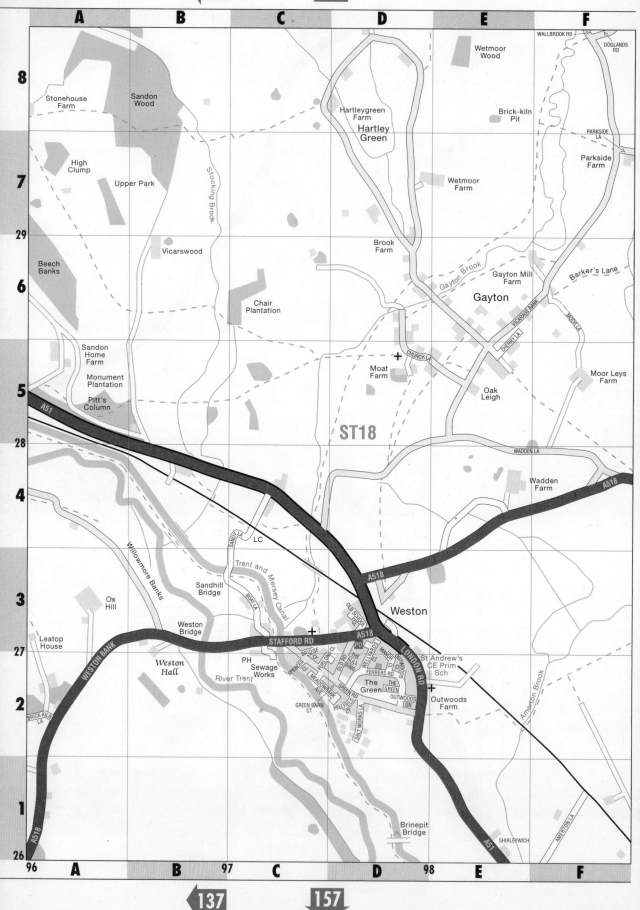

A · B · C · D · E · F

8
7
29
6
5
28
4
3
27
2
1
26

Stonehouse Farm
Sandon Wood
High Clump
Upper Park
Stocking Brook
Vicarswood
Beech Banks
Chair Plantation
Sandon Home Farm
Monument Plantation
Pitt's Column

Wetmoor Wood
Hartleygreen Farm
Hartley Green
Wetmoor Farm
Brook Farm
Gayton Brook
Gayton Mill Farm
Gayton
Moat Farm
CHURCH LA
CHERRY LA
VICARAGE BANK
Oak Leigh

Brick-kiln Pit
WALLBROOK RD
DOGLANDS RD
PARKSIDE LA
Parkside Farm
Barker's Lane
MOOR LA
Moor Leys Farm

ST18

WADDEN LA
Wadden Farm
A518

A51
Willowmore Banks
Ox Hill
Sandhill Bridge
Trent and Mersey Canal
SANDY LA
LC
BOAT LA
Weston Bridge
WESTON BANK
Leatop House
Weston Hall
Brick-kiln La
River Trent
PH
Sewage Works
STAFFORD RD
BRIDGE
SPENCER CT
MEADOWBANK AVE
GREEN BARN CT
GREEN RD
OLD RD
RUTLOW CT
OLD SCHOOL CT
A518
Weston
THE BULL RING
PO
WELLYARDS
FERRERS RD
THE GREEN
PELLFIELD CT
SALT WORKS LA
MANOR CL
OUTWOODS CL
LONDON RD
St Andrew's CE Prim Sch
THE GREEN
OUTWOODS GN
Outwoods Farm
A51
SHIRLEYWICH
Amerton Brook
AMERTON LA
Brinepit Bridge

96 · A · 97 · B · C · 98 · D · E · F

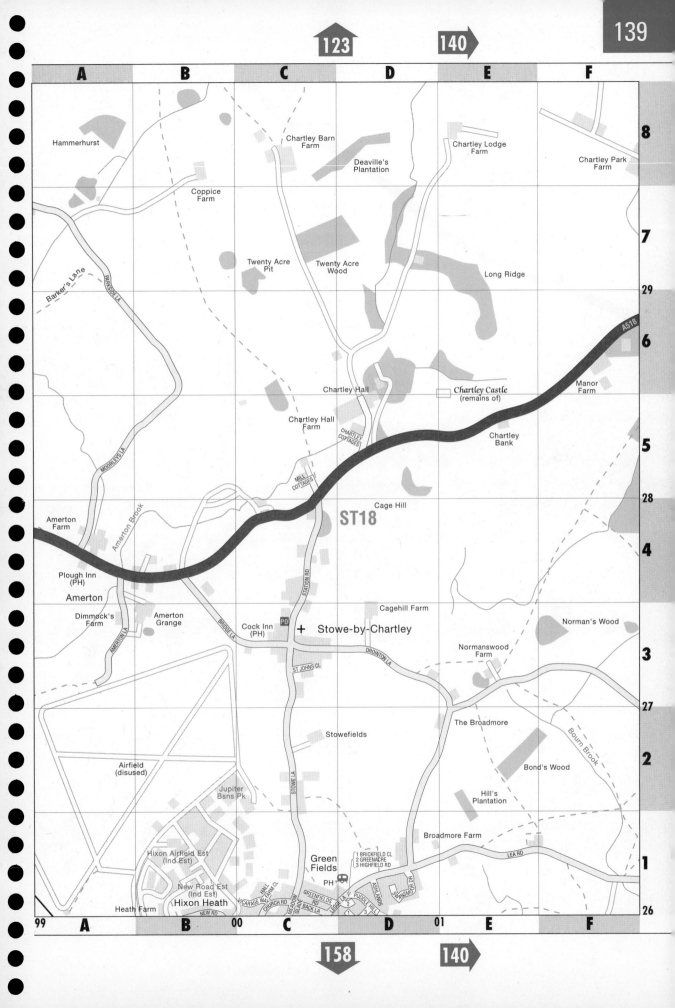

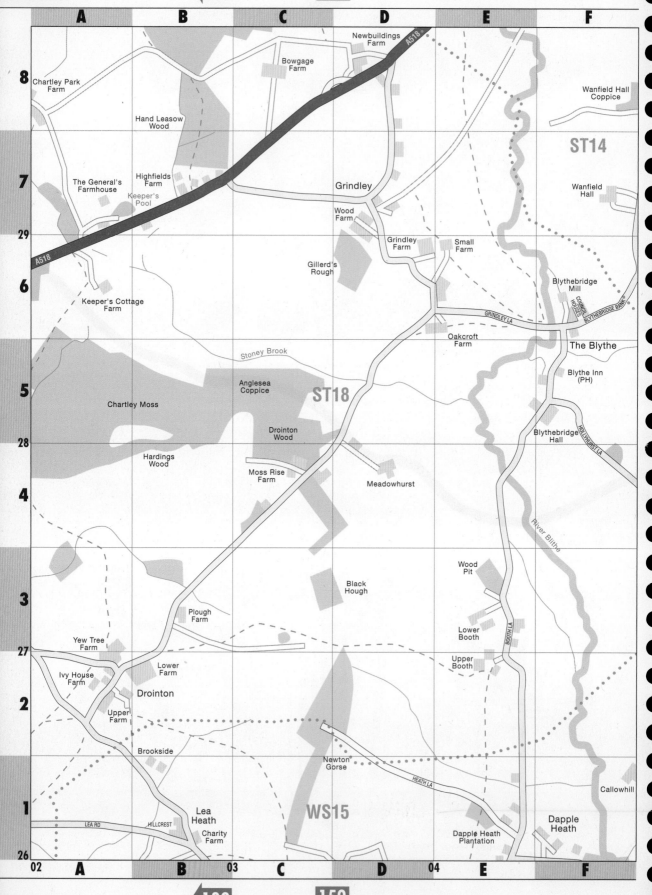

A B C D E F

8 | Chartley Park Farm | Hand Leasow Wood | Bowgage Farm | Newbuildings Farm | | Wanfield Hall Coppice

ST14

7 | The General's Farmhouse | Highfields Farm | | Grindley | | Wanfield Hall

Keeper's Pool | Wood Farm

29 | Grindley Farm | Small Farm

6 | Keeper's Cottage Farm | Gillerd's Rough | | Blythebridge Mill

GRINDLEY LA

COUNCIL HOUSES

BLYTHEBRIDGE BANK

Stoney Brook | Oakcroft Farm | The Blythe

Blythe Inn (PH)

5 | Chartley Moss | Anglesea Coppice | ST18

Drointon Wood | Blythebridge Hall

HOLLYHURST LA

28 | Hardings Wood | Moss Rise Farm | Meadowhurst

4 | River Blithe

Wood Pit

3 | Black Hough | Plough Farm | Lower Booth

BOOTH LA

27 | Yew Tree Farm | Lower Farm | Upper Booth

2 | Ivy House Farm | Drointon

Upper Farm

Brookside | Newton Gorse | Callowhill

HEATH LA

1 | Lea Heath | WS15 | Dapple Heath

LEA RD | HILLCREST | Charity Farm | Dapple Heath Plantation

26

02 A 03 B C 04 D E F

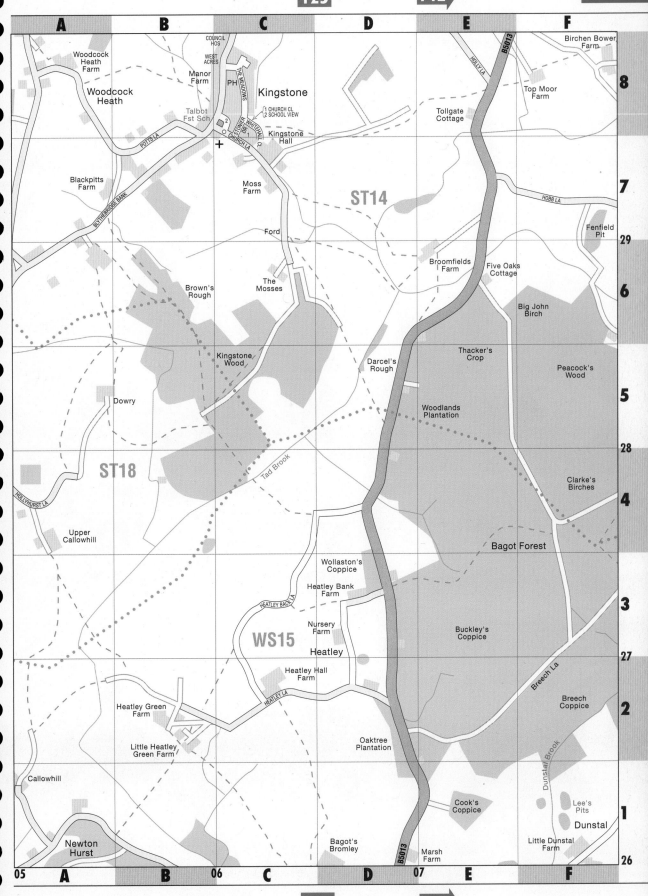

Birchen Bower Farm

Woodcock Heath Farm

Woodcock Heath

COUNCIL HOS
WEST ACRES
Manor Farm

THE MEADOWS

PH

Kingstone

1 CHURCH CL
2 SCHOOL VIEW

Talbot Fst Sch

POTTS LA

STONEY

WHITEHALL DR

CHURCH LA

Kingstone Hall

Top Moor Farm

Tollgate Cottage

HOLLY LA

B5013

Blackpitts Farm

Moss Farm

ST14

HOBB LA

Fenfield Pit

BLYTHEBRIDGE BANK

Ford

Broomfields Farm

Five Oaks Cottage

29

Brown's Rough

The Mosses

6

Big John Birch

Thacker's Crop

Peacock's Wood

Kingstone Wood

Darcel's Rough

Dowry

5

Woodlands Plantation

ST18

Tad Brook

28

Clarke's Birches

HOLLYHURST LA

4

Upper Callowhill

Bagot Forest

Wollaston's Coppice

Heatley Bank Farm

HEATLEY BACK LA

Nursery Farm

WS15

Buckley's Coppice

3

Heatley

27

Breech La

Heatley Hall Farm

Heatley Green Farm

HEATLEY LA

Breech Coppice

2

Little Heatley Green Farm

Oaktree Plantation

Callowhill

Dunstal Brook

Lee's Pits

Cook's Coppice

Dunstal

1

Newton Hurst

Bagot's Bromley

Marsh Farm

B5013

Little Dunstal Farm

26

05   06   07

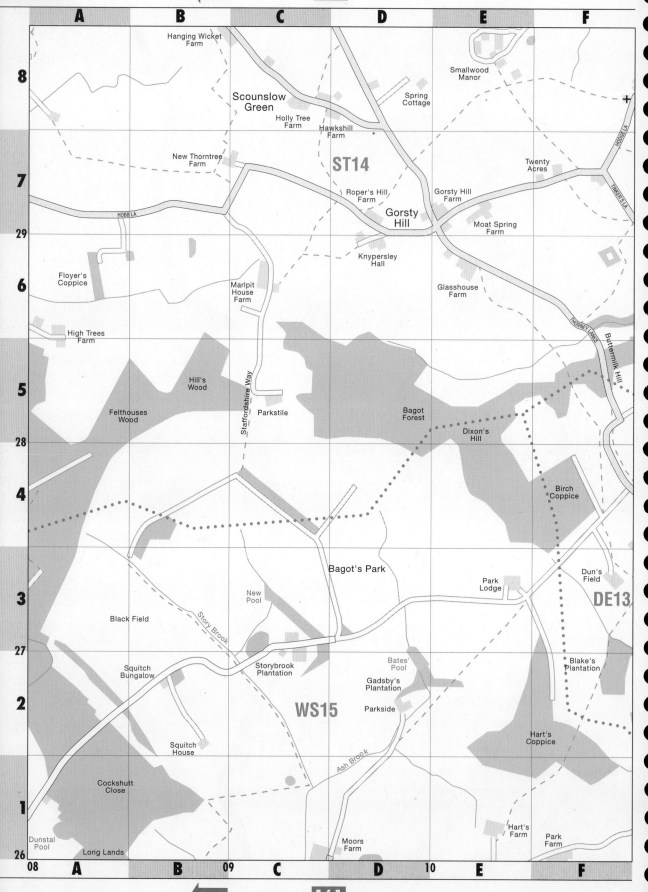

A   B   C   D   E   F

8

Hanging Wicket
Farm

Smallwood
Manor

Scounslow
Green

Spring
Cottage

Holly Tree
Farm

Hawkshill
Farm

New Thorntree
Farm

ST14

Twenty
Acres

HOBB LA

7

Roper's Hill
Farm

Gorsty Hill
Farm

TIMBER'S LA

29

HOBB LA

Gorsty
Hill

Moat Spring
Farm

Floyer's
Coppice

Knypersley
Hall

6

Marlpit
House
Farm

Glasshouse
Farm

THORNEY LANES

High Trees
Farm

Buttermilk Hill

Hill's
Wood

5

Staffordshire Way

Felthouses
Wood

Parkstile

Bagot
Forest

Dixon's
Hill

28

Birch
Coppice

4

Bagot's Park

Park
Lodge

Dun's
Field

3

New
Pool

DE13

Black Field

Story Brook

27

Blake's
Plantation

Squitch
Bungalow

Storybrook
Plantation

Bates'
Pool

Gadsby's
Plantation

2

WS15

Parkside

Hart's
Coppice

Squitch
House

Ash Brook

1

Cockshutt
Close

Dunstal
Pool

Long Lands

Moors
Farm

Hart's
Farm

Park
Farm

26

08   A   B   09   C   D   10   E   F

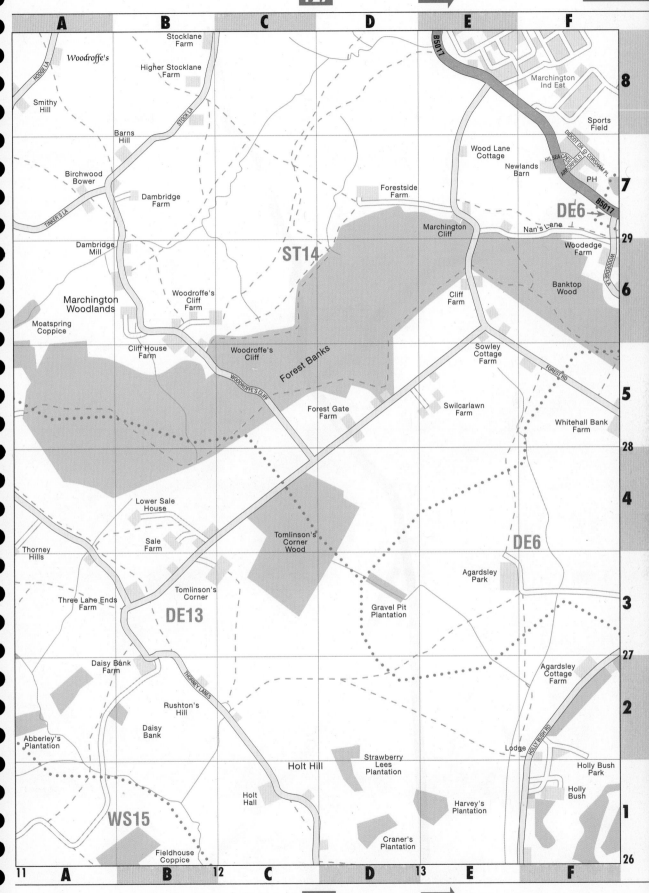

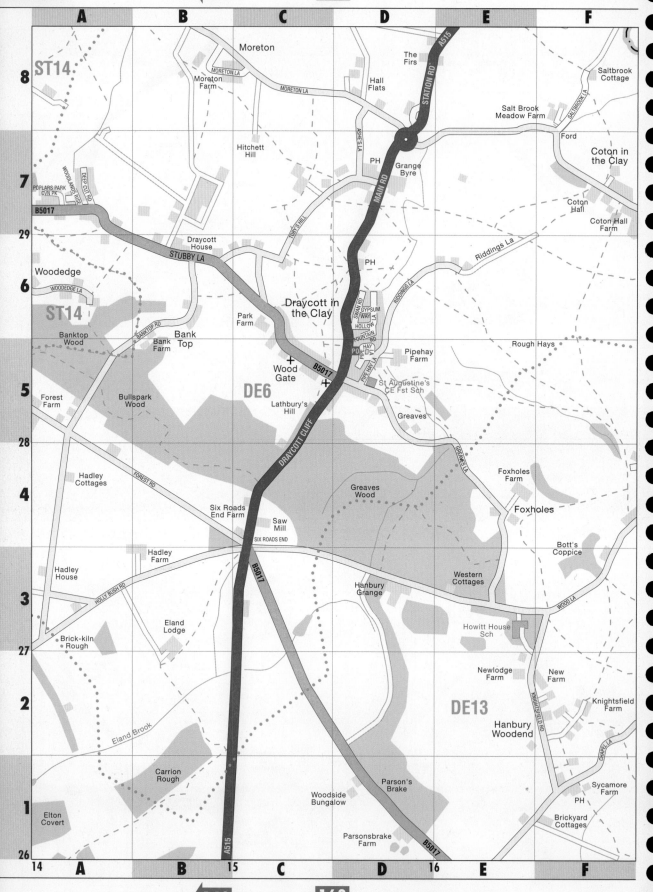

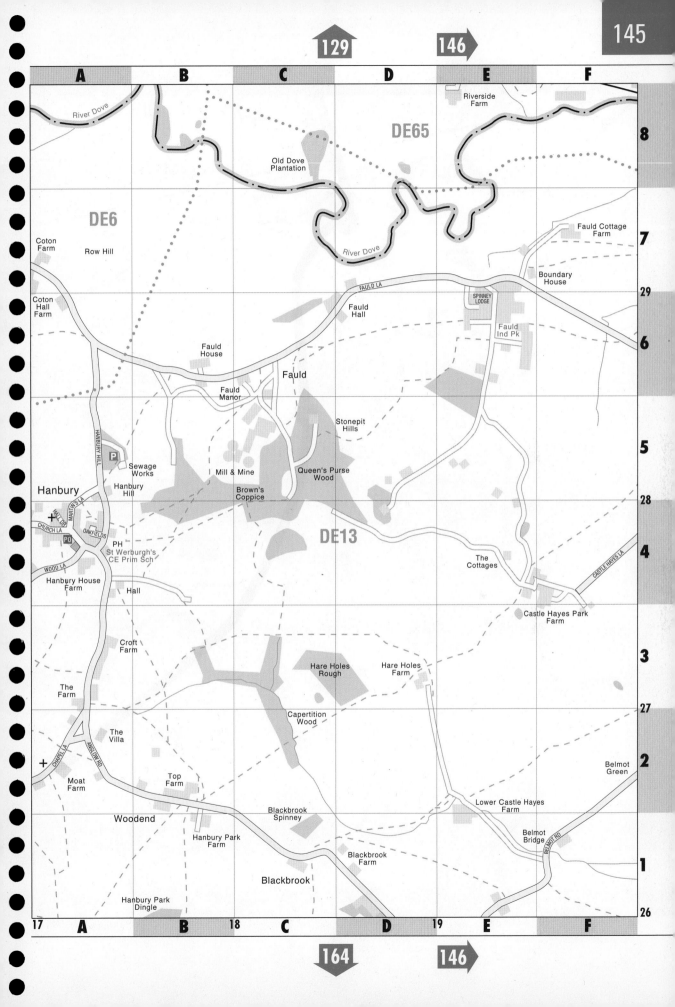

A B C D E F

River Dove

DE65

Riverside Farm

8

DE6

Coton Farm

Row Hill

Old Dove Plantation

River Dove

Fauld Cottage Farm

7

Coton Hall Farm

FAULD LA

Fauld Hall

Boundary House

SPINNEY LODGE

29

Fauld House

Fauld Ind Pk

6

Fauld Manor

Fauld

HANBURY HILL

Stonepit Hills

5

Sewage Works

Mill & Mine

Queen's Purse Wood

Hanbury Hill

Hanbury

Brown's Coppice

DE13

28

MARTIN'S LA

HALL CR

OAKFIELDS

CHURCH LA

PO

PH
St Werburgh's
CE Prim Sch

The Cottages

CASTLE HAYES LA

4

WOOD LA

Hanbury House Farm

Hall

Castle Hayes Park Farm

Croft Farm

Hare Holes Rough

Hare Holes Farm

3

The Farm

Capertition Wood

27

CHAPEL LA

ANSLOW RD

The Villa

Belmot Green

2

Moat Farm

Top Farm

Lower Castle Hayes Farm

Woodend

Blackbrook Spinney

Belmot Bridge

BELMOT RD

Hanbury Park Farm

Blackbrook Farm

1

Blackbrook

Hanbury Park Dingle

26

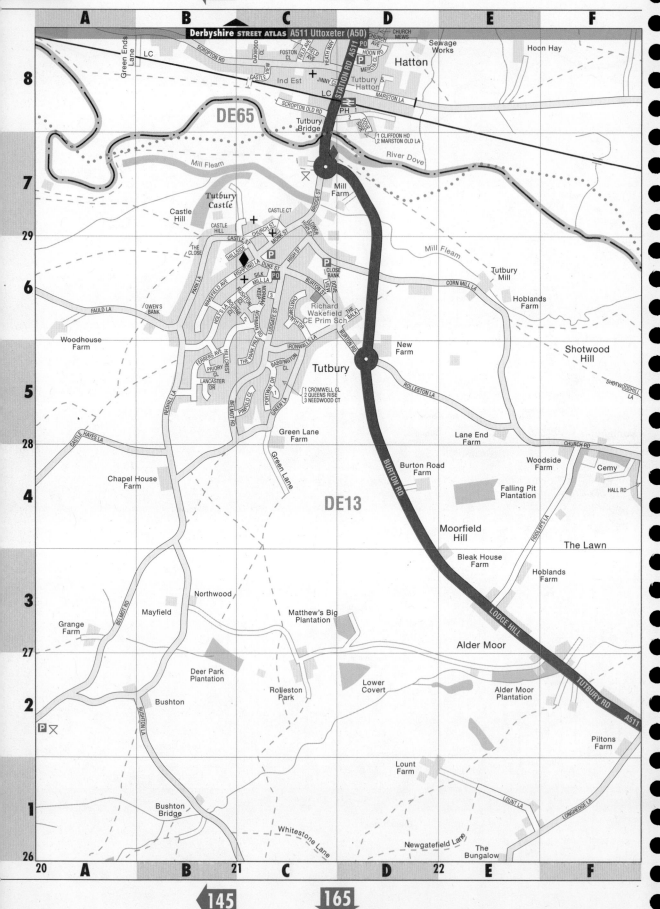

Derbyshire STREET ATLAS A511 Uttoxeter (A50)

Green Ends Lane
LC
SCROPTON RD
OAKWOOD CL
FOSTON CL
FIELD AVE
FIELD HAY
HEATH WAY
STATION RD A511
CHURCH MEWS
Sewage Works
Hoon Hay
Hatton
MERCIA CT
PO AVE
HOON RD
CASTLE VIEW
Ind Est
JINNY CL
Tutbury & Hatton
MARSTON LA
DE65
SCROPTON OLD RD
LC
PH 1
2
DOVE SIDE
1 CLIFFDON HO
2 MARSTON OLD LA
Tutbury Bridge
Mill Fleam
River Dove
Mill Farm
Tutbury Castle
Castle Hill
CASTLE CT
BRIDGE ST
CASTLE HILL
CASTLE ST
CHURCH ST
MONK ST
LOWER HIGH ST
THE CLOSE
HILLSIDE
FISHPOND LA
DUKE ST
HIGH ST
P
CLOSE BANK
CLOSE VIEW
Mill Fleam
CORN MILL LA
Tutbury Mill
PARK LA
P
SILK MILL LA
DOVE
BURTON ST
PO
3
Hoblands Farm
FAULD LA
OWEN'S BANK
WAKEFIELD AVE
HOLTS LA
BOURNE CT
RUSHTON
KEAY
MONK
2
1
LUDGATE ST
COMSTOW
SMYTH DR
Richard Wakefield CE Prim Sch
THE BALK
BURTON RD
Woodhouse Farm
REDHILL
FERRERS AVE
HILLCREST
THE PARK
PARK RD
MANWARD
BABBINGTON CL
IRONWALLS LA
Tutbury
New Farm
Shotwood Hill
PRIORY CL
LANCASTER DR
PORTWAY DR
GREEN LA
1 CROMWELL CL
2 QUEENS RISE
3 NEEDWOOD CT
SHOTWOODHILL LA
BELMOT RD
PINFOLD CL
Green Lane Farm
Lane End Farm
CHURCH RD
CASTLE HAYES LA
Green Lane
Woodside Farm
Cemy
HALL RD
Chapel House Farm
DE13
Burton Road Farm
Falling Pit Plantation
RIDDLERS LA
The Lawn
BURTON RD
Moorfield Hill
Northwood
Matthew's Big Plantation
Bleak House Farm
Hoblands Farm
BELMOT RD
Mayfield
Grange Farm
Alder Moor
LODGE HILL
Deer Park Plantation
BUSHTON LA
Rolleston Park
Lower Covert
Alder Moor Plantation
TUTBURY RD A511
Bushton
P
Piltons Farm
Lount Farm
Bushton Bridge
LOUNT LA
LONGHEDGE LA
Whitestone Lane
Newgatefield Lane
The Bungalow

ROLLESTON LA

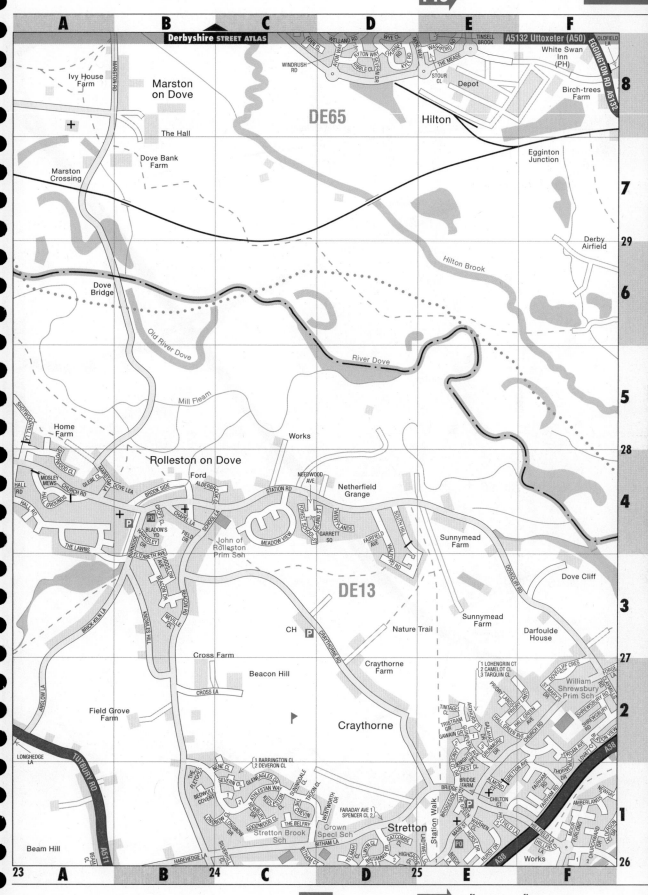

Derbyshire STREET ATLAS

A | B | C | D | E | F

8
7
29
6
5
28
4
3
27
2
1
26

Ivy House Farm

Marston on Dove

The Hall

Dove Bank Farm

Marston Crossing

MARSTON RD

WINDRUSH RD

DE65

Hilton

White Swan Inn (PH)

Depot

Birch-trees Farm

A5132 Uttoxeter (A50)

EGGINGTON RD

OLDFIELD LA

TINSELL BROOK

THE MEASE

STOUR CL

WASHFORD RD

RENE WAY

KYLE GR

AIRLEY RD

WYE CL

RYTON WAY

AVON WAY

SEVERN DR

RIBBLE CL

EDEN CL

WELLAND RD

A5132

Egginton Junction

Derby Airfield

Hilton Brook

Dove Bridge

Old River Dove

River Dove

Mill Fleam

Home Farm

Works

Rolleston on Dove

Ford

Needwood Grange

Netherfield Grange

Sunnymead Farm

Dove Cliff

Darfoulde House

SHOTWOOD HILL LA

HALL RD

HALL RD

MOSLEY MEWS

CHURCH RD

GLERE CL

MARSTON LA

DOVE LEA

BROOK SIDE

ALDERBROOK CL

STATION RD

FOREST SCHOOL RD

LADYS CROFT

TWENTY LANDS

GARRETT SQ

FAIRFIELD AVE

SOUTH HILL

WALFORD RD

DE13

DOVECLIFF RD

HALL GROUNDS

THE LAWNS

BURNSIDE

HAWKSLEY DR

BLADON'S YD

CROFT CL

CHAPEL LA

SCHOOL LA

FIELD DR

MEADOW VIEW

John of Rolleston Prim Sch

ELIZABETH AVE

BADSLOW DR

BEACON DR

BEACON RD

NEVILLE CL

BRICK KILN LA

KNOWLES HILL

Cross Farm

Beacon Hill

CROSS LA

Field Grove Farm

ANSLOW LA

Nature Trail

Craythorne Farm

Sunnymead Farm

Craythorne

CRAYTHORNE RD

CH

1 LOHENGRIN CT
2 CAMELOT CL
3 TARQUIN CL

William Shrewsbury Prim Sch

DOVE CLIFF CRES

FORGE LA

LAKENHEATH

ST MARY'S DR

SHREWSBURY RD

SHREWSBURY

TINTAGEL CL

TRISTRAM GR

GAWAIN GR

ARTHURS PL

JUBILEE PL

GALAHAD GR

GRISMORE

PRIORY LA

PRIORY LA

HALL GREEN AVE

HALL GREEN

CHURCH RD

JORDAN AVE

A38

DOVER VIEW

LONGHEDGE LA

TUTBURY RD

A511

BEAM HILL

Beam Hill

1 BARRINGTON CL
2 DEVERON CL

THE FLETCHES

NENE CL

SEVERN CL

GLENEAGLES DR

BEDWULF COVERT

ATHELSTAN WAY

KEDLESTON

SUNNINGDALE DR

WENTWORTH DR

TROON CL

THE CHEVIN

1 FARADAY AVE
2 SPENCER CL

Crown Specl Sch

Stretton Brook Sch

Stretton

CONGROW GR

LONGBOW GR

GOODWOOD CL

THE BELFRY

SILVERHILL

HAREHEDGE LA

BITHAM LA

BITHAM CT

ELWYN CL

BRITANNIA DR

HIGHGROVE

GATCOMBE CL

LADYWELL

Station Walk

BRIDGE FARM

CREST CL

ALMOND

GRETTON CL

CHILTON CT

MAIN ST

WARREN

HILLFIELD LA

HURST DR

BEECH

HILLFIELD

Works

AMBERLANDS

NEWBY

FAIRHAM RD

THORNE

CHURCHYARD

FURLONG

A38

23 | A | B | 24 | C | D | 25 | E | F | 26

E1
1 PRINCESS WAY
2 CARISBROOKE DR

F1
1 ALDERHOLME DR
2 MANTON CL

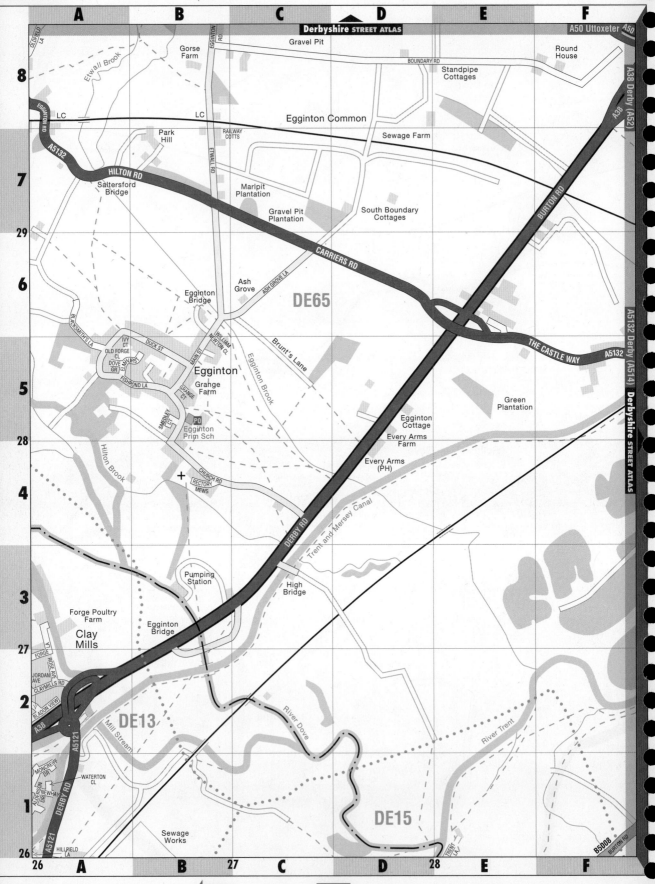

147

Derbyshire STREET ATLAS

A50 Uttoxeter A50

A38 Derby (A52)

A5132 Derby (A514)

Derbyshire STREET ATLAS

Gravel Pit

Round House

BOUNDARY RD

Standpipe Cottages

Gorse Farm

OLD FIELD LA

Etwall Brook

EGGINTON RD

Eggington Common

Sewage Farm

Park Hill

RAILWAY COTTS

LC

LC

A5132

EGGINTON RD

HILTON RD

Saltersford Bridge

ETWALL RD

Marlpit Plantation

Gravel Pit Plantation

South Boundary Cottages

BURTON RD

CARRIERS RD

Ash Grove

ASH GROVE LA

DE65

Eggington Bridge

WILLIAM NEWTON CL

Brunt's Lane

THE CASTLE WAY A5132

BLACKSMITH'S LA

IVY CT

DUCK ST

OLD FORGE CL

DOVE GR

ELM NURS

MAIN ST

Eggington

Eggington Brook

Green Plantation

FISHPOND LA

Grange Farm

SMEDLEY CT

GRANGE CT

PO

Eggington Prim Sch

Eggington Cottage

Every Arms Farm

Hilton Brook

CHURCH RD

RECTORY MEWS

Every Arms (PH)

Trent and Mersey Canal

DERBY RD

Pumping Station

High Bridge

Forge Poultry Farm

Eggington Bridge

Clay Mills

FORGE VW

ROSE AVE

JORDAN AVE

CLAYMILLS RD

BLADON VIEW

A38

DE13

Mill Stream

River Dove

River Trent

A5121

MONCREIFF DR

WATERTON CL

ALDERSON DR

NEWHAY

DERBY RD

DE15

BURTON RD

B5008

A5121

HILLFIELD LA

TRENT LA

Sewage Works

147

167

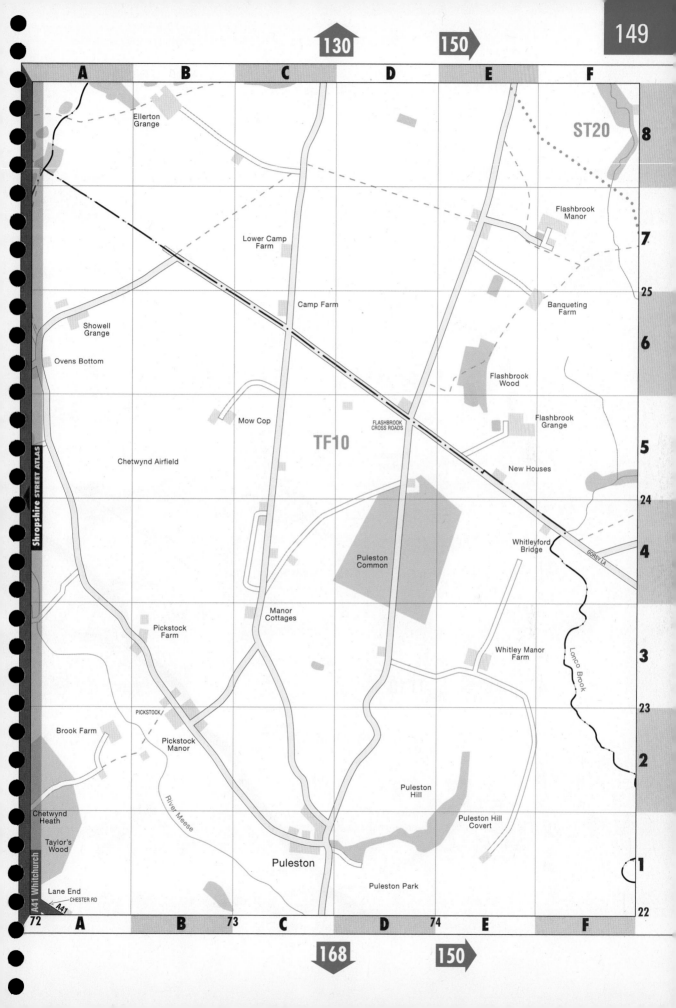

149
131

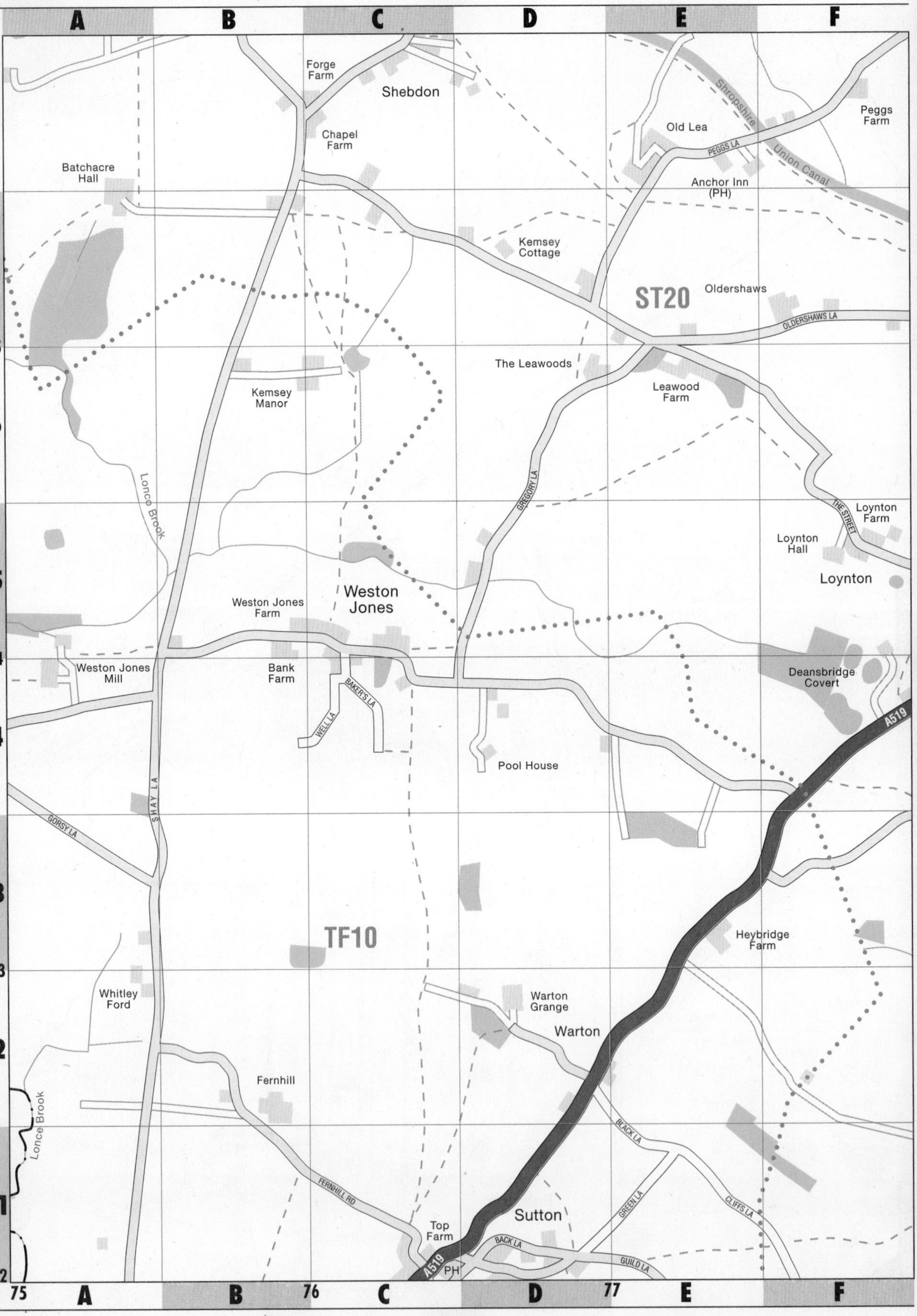

A B C D E F

8
7
25
6
5
24
4
23
3
2
22

75 A B 76 C D 77 E F

149
169

Forge Farm
Shebdon
Chapel Farm
Old Lea
Peggs Farm
PEGGS LA
Anchor Inn (PH)
Shropshire Union Canal
Batchacre Hall
Kemsey Cottage
ST20
Oldershaws
OLDERSHAWS LA
Kemsey Manor
The Leawoods
Leawood Farm
Lonco Brook
GREGORY LA
THE STREET
Loynton Farm
Loynton Hall
Loynton
Weston Jones Farm
Weston Jones
Weston Jones Mill
Bank Farm
BAKER'S LA
WELL LA
Deansbridge Covert
A519
SHAY LA
GORSY LA
Pool House
TF10
Heybridge Farm
Whitley Ford
Warton Grange
Warton
BLACK LA
Fernhill
Lonce Brook
FERNHILL RD
Top Farm
Sutton
A519
PH
BACK LA
GREEN LA
CLIFFS LA
GUILD LA

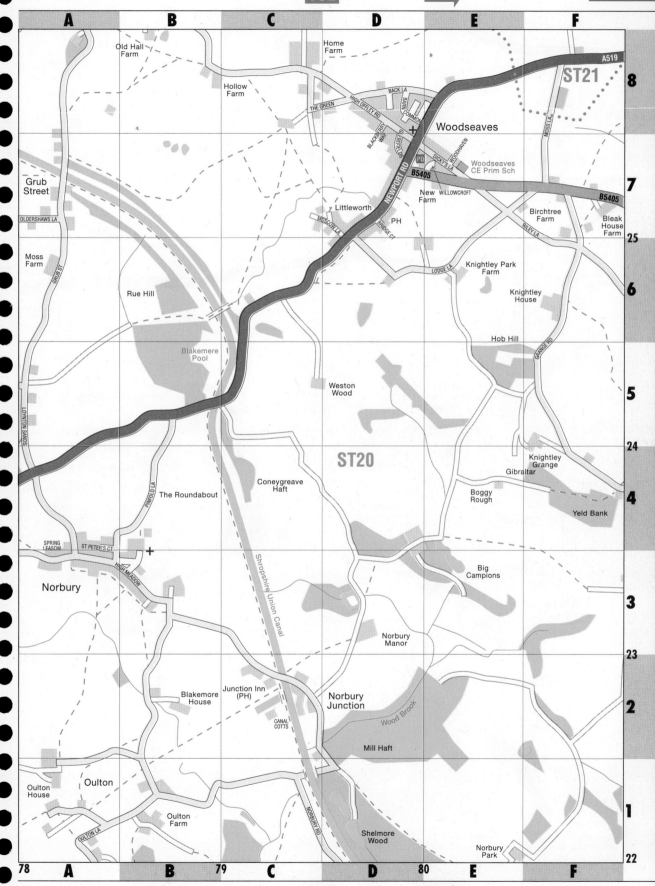

A B C D E F

A519

A519

8

ST21

Taylor's Covert

Knightley Gorse

7

Gorse Covert

Bond's Covert

Walton's Rough

B5405

25

Yewtree Farm

Hilltop Farm

Lawnhead

Woodhill Farm

Knightley

Depot

6

Addison's Covert

The Triangle

Common Belt

B5405

RILEY LA

Rose Tree Farm

Ashwoodhead Farm

Ash Wood

Wawell Lane

Ranton Abbey

5

Old Farm

LOWER RD

Green Farm

24

Humphrey's Wood

Yeld Bank Farm

ST20

4

GRANGE RD

Lower Knightley

Simpkin's Covert

Woise Lane

Knightley Green

Knightley Dale

New Covert

GNOSALL RD

Big Wood

Woodside

3

Knightley Hall

Yewtree Farm

Hollies Brook

Hollybank Farm

Prospect Hill

23

Bellingham's Covert

2

Ash's Covert

Brough Hall

Nut Wood

KNIGHTLEY RD

1

Moor End Farm

Hell Hole

Hollies Common

22

81 A 82 B 82 C 83 D 83 E F

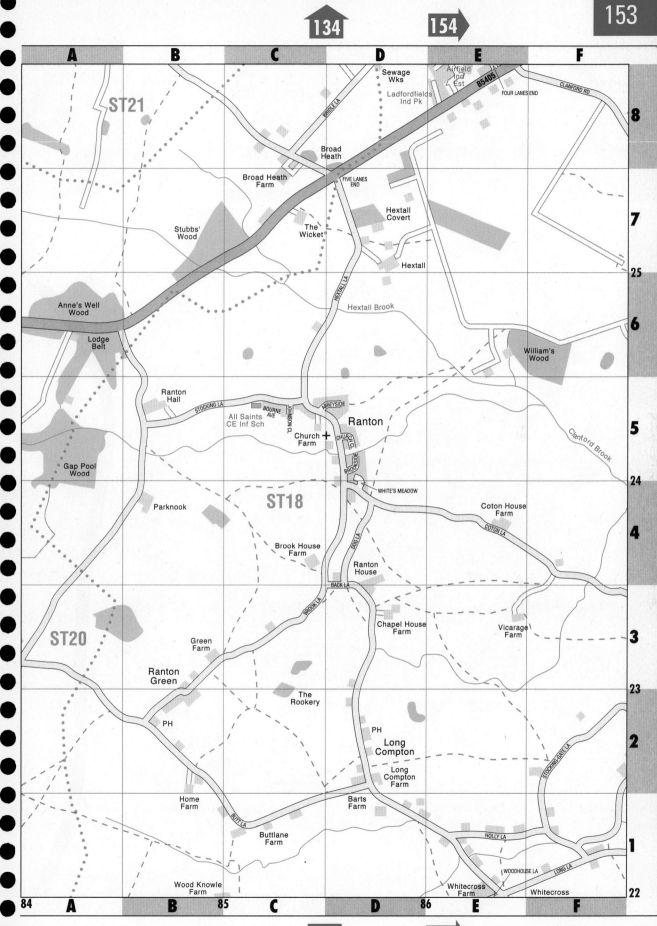

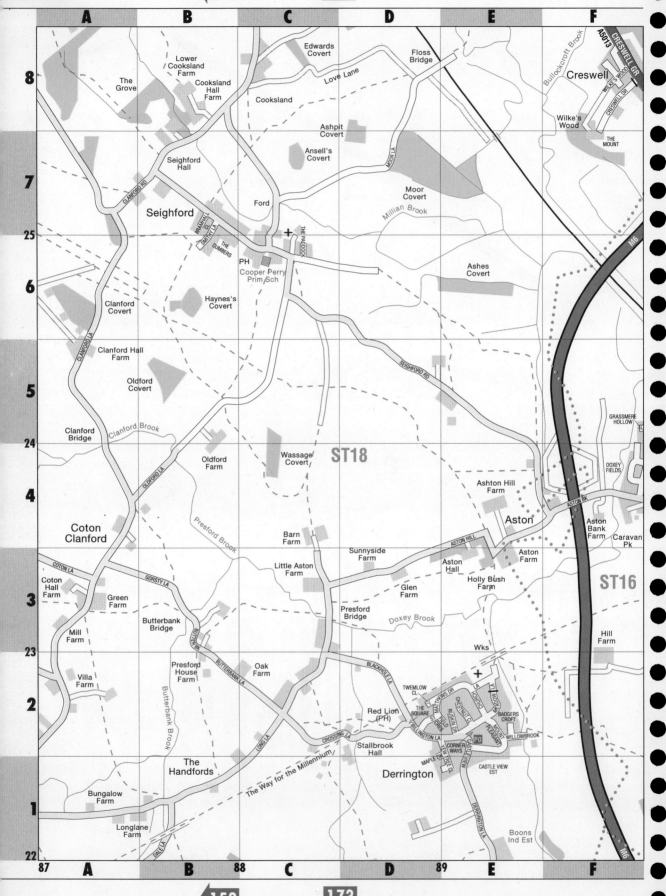

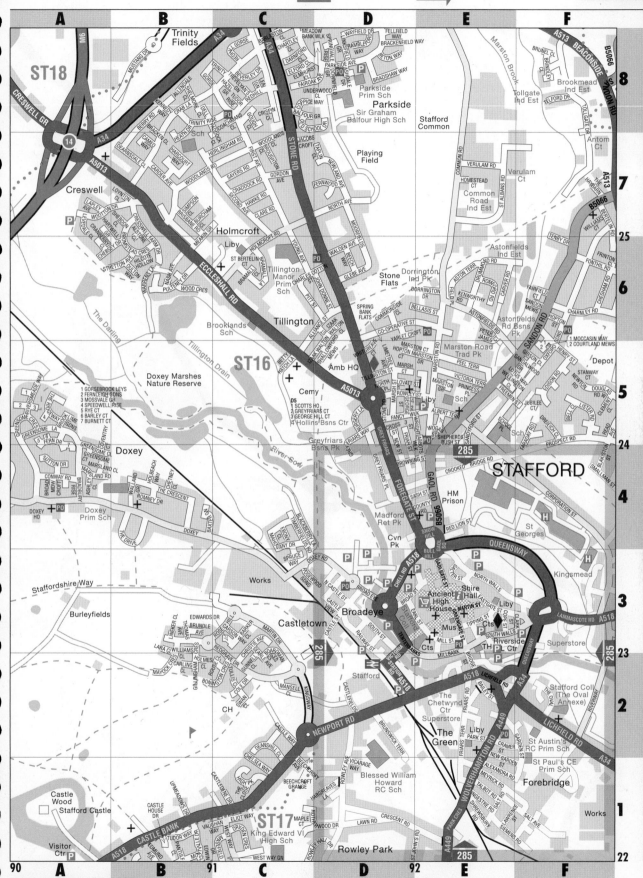

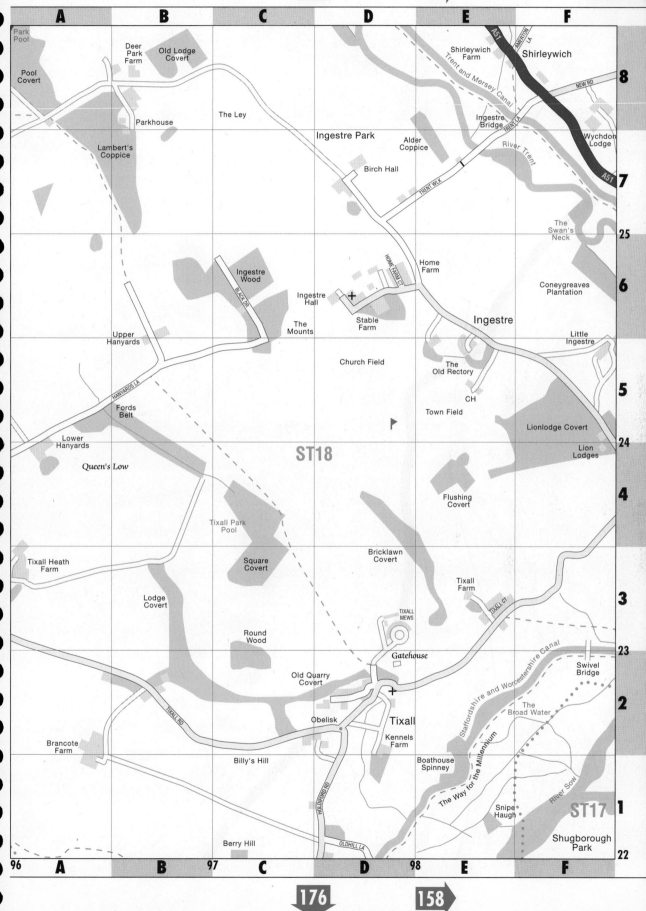

Park
Pool

Pool
Covert

Deer
Park
Farm

Old Lodge
Covert

Parkhouse

The Ley

Lambert's
Coppice

Ingestre Park

Shirleywich
Farm

Shirleywich

Trent and Mersey Canal

NEW RD

Ingestre
Bridge

Wychdon
Lodge

A51

River Trent

Birch Hall

Alder
Coppice

TRENT WLK

The
Swan's
Neck

Ingestre
Wood

BLACK DR

Ingestre
Hall

The
Mounts

Home Farm

Home
Farm

HOME FARM CT

Coneygreaves
Plantation

Ingestre

Stable
Farm

Little
Ingestre

Upper
Hanyards

HANYARDS LA

Fords
Belt

Church Field

The
Old Rectory

CH

Town Field

Lionlodge Covert

Lion
Lodges

Lower
Hanyards

Queen's Low

ST18

Flushing
Covert

Tixall Park
Pool

Square
Covert

Bricklawn
Covert

Tixall
Farm

TIXALL CT

Tixall Heath
Farm

Lodge
Covert

Round
Wood

TIXALL MEWS

Staffordshire and Worcestershire Canal

Swivel
Bridge

Gatehouse

Old Quarry
Covert

TIXALL RD

Obelisk

Tixall

Kennels
Farm

The
Broad Water

Brancote
Farm

Billy's Hill

Boathouse
Spinney

The Way for the Millennium

River Sow

HOLDIFORD RD

OLDHILL LA

Snipe
Haugh

ST17

Berry Hill

Shugborough
Park

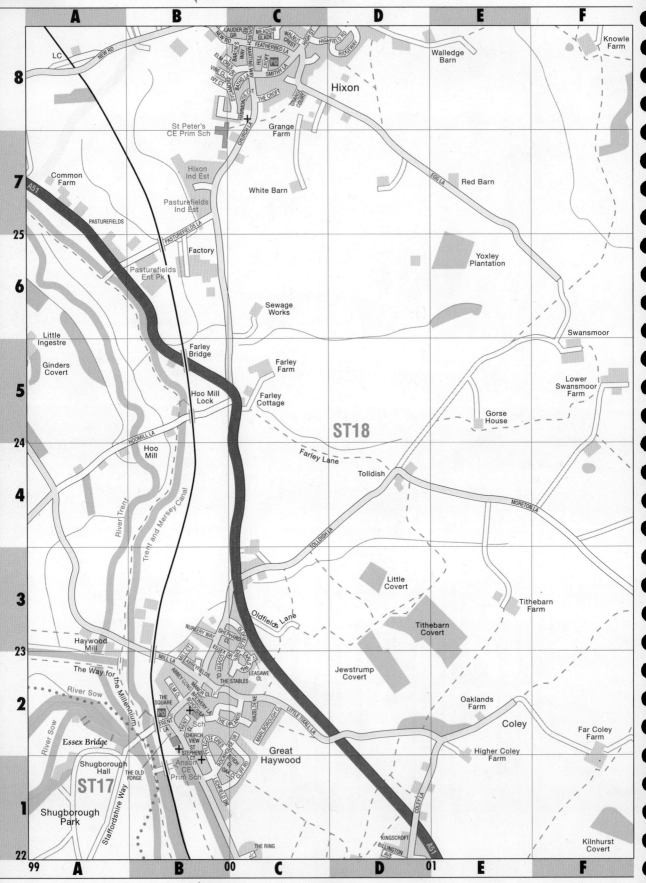

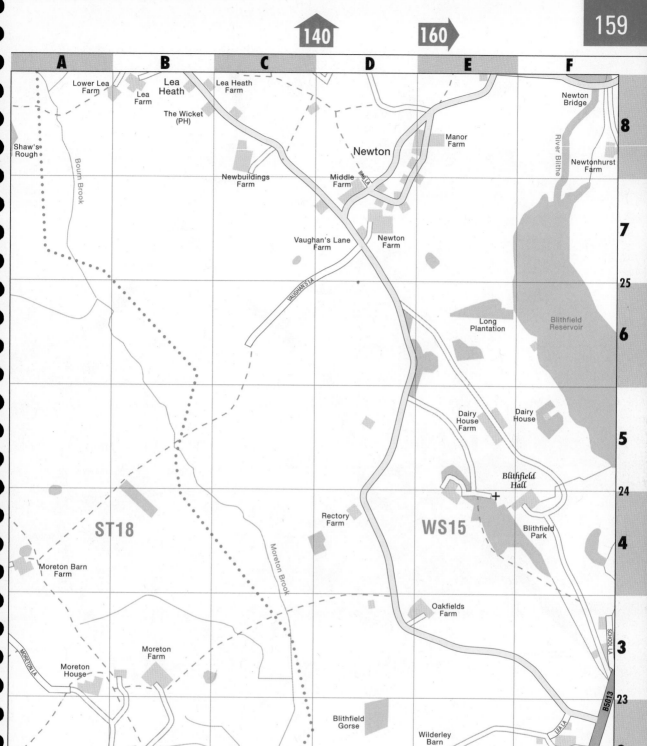

140 160

A B C D E F

8

Lower Lea Farm
Lea Heath
Lea Farm
Lea Heath Farm
The Wicket (PH)
Shaw's Rough
Bourn Brook
Newton
Manor Farm
River Blithe
Newton Bridge
Newtonhurst Farm

Newbuildings Farm
Middle Farm
BNG LA

7

Vaughan's Lane Farm
Newton Farm
VAUGHAN'S LA

25

Long Plantation
Blithfield Reservoir

6

Dairy House Farm
Dairy House

5

ST18
Moreton Brook
Rectory Farm
Blithfield Hall
+
WS15
Blithfield Park

24

Moreton Barn Farm

4

Oakfields Farm

Moreton Farm
SCHOOL LA
B5013

3

Moreton House
MORETON LA

Blithfield Gorse
LEA LA

23

Moreton Grange
Wilderley Barn
Lea Hall Farm

2

SHERRACOP LA

Spencer's Plantation

Upper Moreton
Flint's Barn
B5013

1

Jongham's Cottage

Moreton La

22

178 160

159
141

8

Newton Hurst

Dimsdale Plantation

Dimsdale

Mon

Bagots' Bromley

Dunstal Hall Farm

Dunstal Brook

Bagots' Bromley Cottages

7

Stansleywood Saw Mills

The Warren

Duckley Plantation

B5013

B5014

HARLEY LA

25

Stansley Wood

Leafields Farm

UTTOXETER RD

PAGET RISE

CECIL PAYTON CL

LOWLANDS PL

SALTERS GRANGE

6

Barn Farm

Yeatsall Cottages

ALFRED LYONS CL

B5014

BAGOT ST

COTTRELL CL

LINTAKE DR

ST NICHOLAS WAY

MIRES BROOK

FRIARY RD

FREEDINS PL

GOOSE LA

CHURCH LA

ABBOTS BROMLEY HOSPL

Narrow La

Yeatsall

5

Blithfield Reservoir

WS15

Wilversall House

YEATSALL RD

Highash

Mires Brook

Highelms

24

Causeway

P

Watery La

Black Wood

PORT LA

Hallhill La

Portfields

Yenbrook

4

P

Mickledale

SEEDCROFT LA

WATERS RD

3

Admaston Farm

B5013

Admaston

Seedcroft

23

St Stephen's Hill

STEENWOOD LA

Staffordshire Way

2

Round Plantation

Steenwood Cottages

Boat House

Tad Brook

River Blithe

Medleywood Barn

1

SHERRACOP LA

Newlands Cottage

22

Sherracop Plantation

Park Barn Farm

NEWLANDS LA

05   A   B   06   C   D   07   E   F

A   B   C   D   E   F

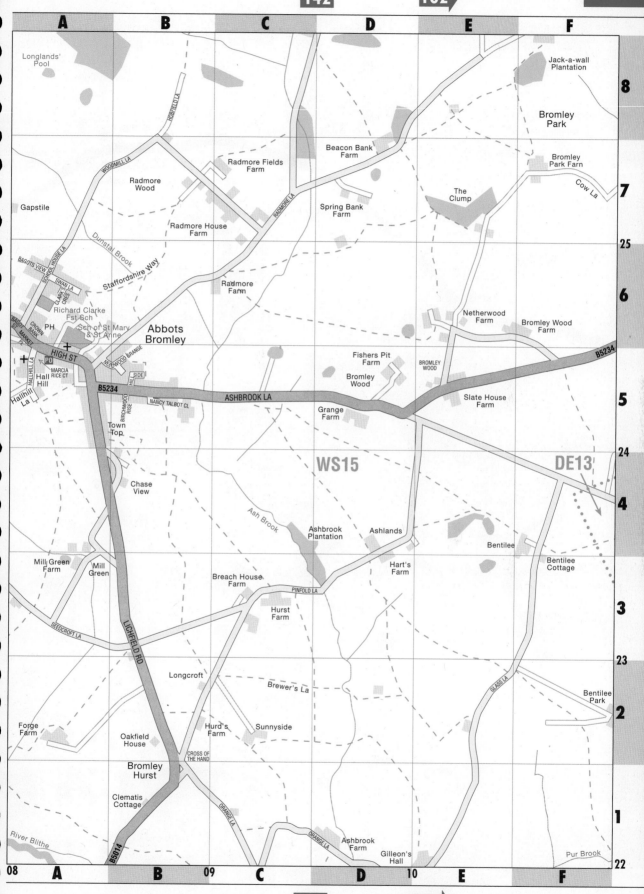

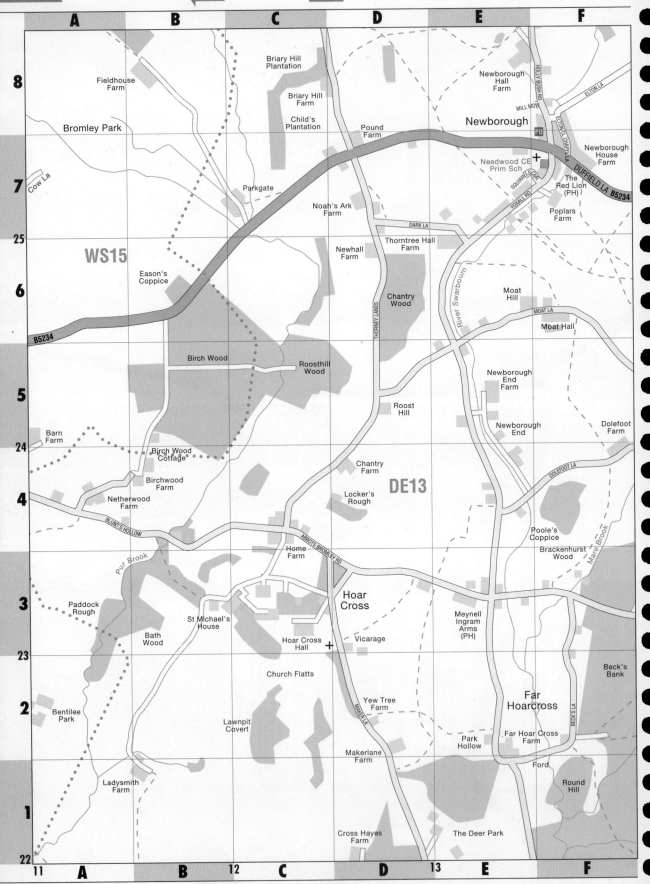

A B C D E F

8

Fieldhouse Farm

Briary Hill Plantation

Briary Hill Farm

Child's Plantation

Pound Farm

Newborough Hall Farm

HOLLY BUSH RD

ELTON LA

MILL MDW

Newborough

PO

ELTON CL CHAPEL LA

Bromley Park

Newborough House Farm

7

Cow La

Parkgate

Noah's Ark Farm

Needwood CE Prim Sch

The Red Lion (PH)

SQUIRREL SCRM

YOXALL RD

DUFFIELD LA B5234

Poplars Farm

DARK LA

25

WS15

Newhall Farm

Thorntree Hall Farm

River Swarbourn

Moat Hill

MOAT LA

6

Eason's Coppice

Chantry Wood

THORNEY LANES

Moat Hall

B5234

Birch Wood

Roosthill Wood

Newborough End Farm

5

Roost Hill

Newborough End

Dolefoot Farm

24

Barn Farm

Birch Wood Cottage

Chantry Farm

DOLEFOOT LA

Birchwood Farm

Locker's Rough

DE13

Poole's Coppice

Mare Brook

4

Netherwood Farm

BLUNT'S HOLLOW

Brackenhurst Wood

Pur Brook

Home Farm

ABBOTS BROMLEY RD

3

Paddock Rough

St Michael's House

Hoar Cross

Meynell Ingram Arms (PH)

Bath Wood

Hoar Cross Hall

Vicarage

23

Church Flatts

Beck's Bank

2

Bentilee Park

Lawnpit Covert

Yew Tree Farm

MAKER LA

Far Hoarcross

BECK LA

Far Hoar Cross Farm

Park Hollow

Makerlane Farm

Ford

1

Ladysmith Farm

Round Hill

Cross Hayes Farm

The Deer Park

22

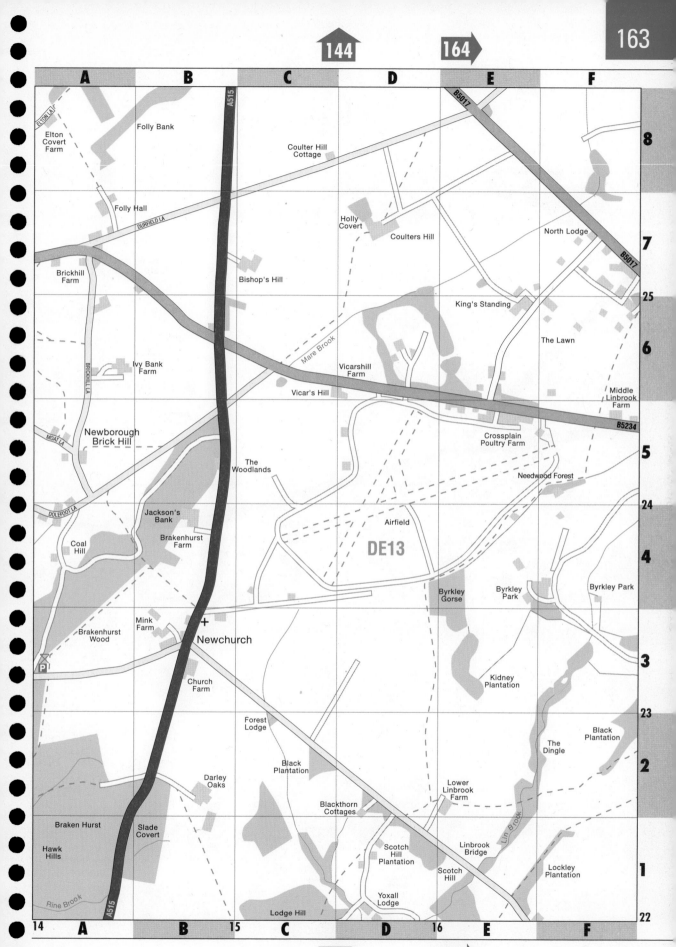

A B C D E F

8

ELTON LA

Elton
Covert
Farm

Folly Bank

Coulter Hill
Cottage

B5017

Folly Hall

DURFIELD LA

Holly
Covert

Coulters Hill

North Lodge

B5017

7

25

Brickhill
Farm

Bishop's Hill

King's Standing

The Lawn

6

BRICKHILL LA

Ivy Bank
Farm

Mare Brook

Vicarshill
Farm

Vicar's Hill

Middle
Linbrook
Farm

B5234

MOAT LA

Newborough
Brick Hill

The
Woodlands

Crossplain
Poultry Farm

5

DOLEFOOT LA

Jackson's
Bank

Needwood Forest

24

Coal
Hill

Brakenhurst
Farm

Airfield

DE13

Byrkley
Park

Byrkley Park

4

Brakenhurst
Wood

Mink
Farm

Newchurch

Byrkley
Gorse

23

Church
Farm

Kidney
Plantation

3

Forest
Lodge

Black
Plantation

The
Dingle

Black
Plantation

Darley
Oaks

Black
Plantation

Lower
Linbrook
Farm

2

Blackthorn
Cottages

Lin Brook

Braken Hurst

Slade
Covert

Scotch
Hill
Plantation

Linbrook
Bridge

Lockley
Plantation

Hawk
Hills

Scotch
Hill

1

Rine Brook

A515

Yoxall
Lodge

Lodge Hill

22

14 A B 15 C D 16 E F

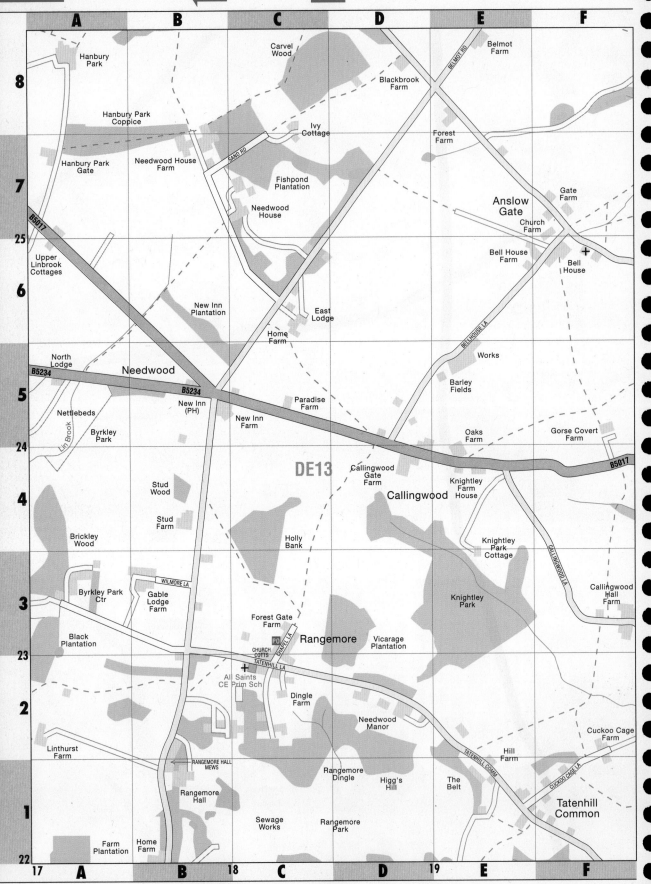

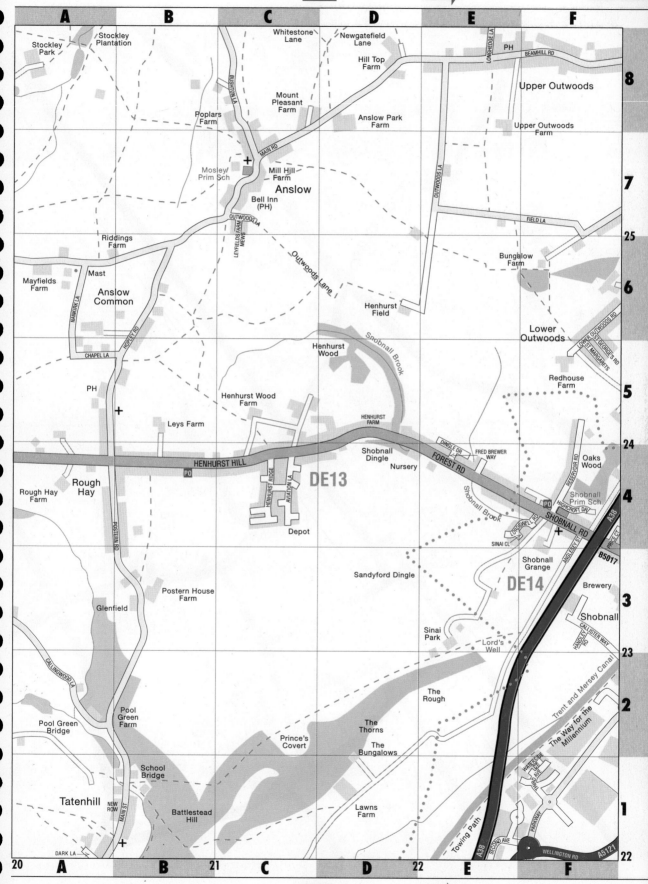

A **B** **C** **D** **E** **F**

Stockley Park
Stockley Plantation
Whitestone Lane
Newgatefield Lane
Hill Top Farm
Longhedge La
PH
BEAMHILL RD
Upper Outwoods

8

Poplars Farm
Mount Pleasant Farm
Anslow Park Farm
Upper Outwoods Farm
BUXTON LA
MAIN RD
OUTWOODS LA

Mosley Prim Sch
Mill Hill Farm
Anslow
Bell Inn (PH)
FIELD LA

7

Riddings Farm
LEYFIELDS FARM MEWS
OUTWOODS LA
Outwoods Lane
Bungalow Farm

25

Mayfields Farm
Mast
Anslow Common
NANKIRK LA
HOPLEY RD
Henhurst Field
Lower Outwoods
LOWER OUTWOODS RD
ST GEORGE'S RD
ST MARGARETS

6

CHAPEL LA
Snobnall Brook
Henhurst Wood
Redhouse Farm

5

PH
Henhurst Wood Farm
Leys Farm
HENHURST FARM
Shobnall Dingle
Nursery
DINGLE DR
FRED BREWER WAY
Oaks Wood
RESERVOIR RD

24

HENHURST HILL
PO
HENHURST RIDGE
AVIATION LA
DE13
FOREST RD
Shobnall Brook
Shobnall Prim Sch
HIGHCROFT DR
PO
SHOBNALL RD
ANGLESEY ST
A38
B5017

4

Rough Hay Farm
Rough Hay
POSTERN RD
Depot
Sandyford Dingle
SINAI CL
CROSSNEL RD
Shobnall Grange
DE14
Brewery
Shobnall
HANDLEY RD
CALLISTER WAY

3

Postern House Farm
Glenfield
Sinai Park
Lord's Well
PRIORY ST

23

CALLINGWOOD LA
Pool Green Farm
Prince's Covert
The Rough
The Thorns
Trent and Mersey Canal
The Way for the Millennium

2

Pool Green Bridge
School Bridge
The Bungalows
WATERSIDE CL
THIRD AVE
PARKWAY

Tatenhill
NEW ROW
MAIN ST
Battlestead Hill
Lawns Farm
Towing Path
A38
SECOND AVE
WELLINGTON RD
A5121

1

DARK LA

22

20 **A** **B** **21** **C** **D** **22** **E** **F**

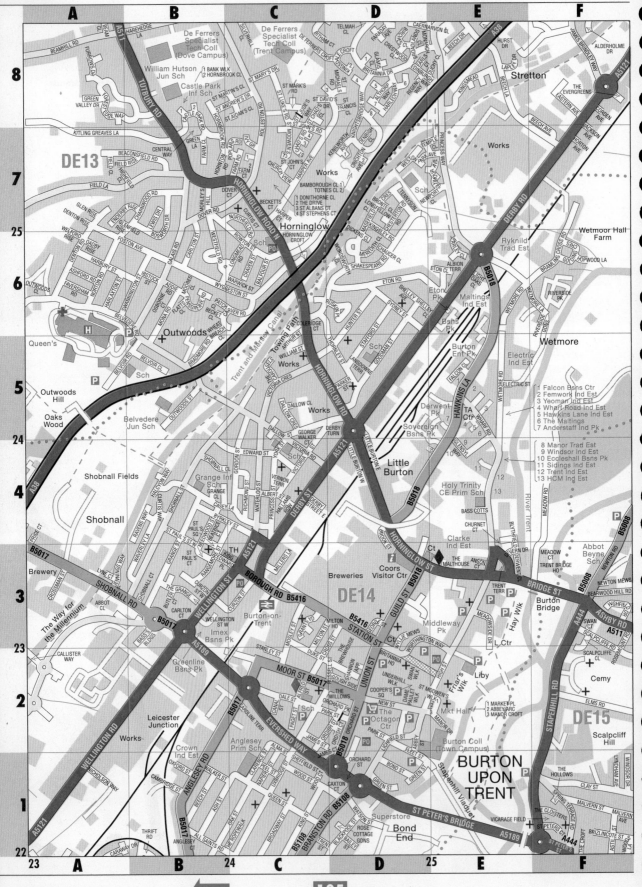

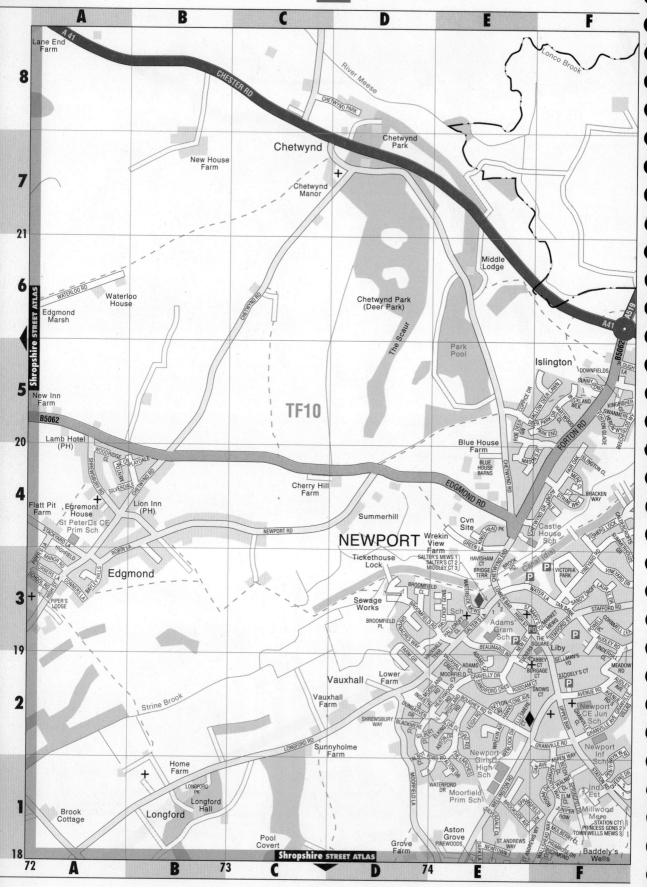

A B C D E F

Lane End Farm

CHESTER RD

A 41

River Meese

CHETWYND PARK

Lonco Brook

Chetwynd Park

8

Chetwynd

New House Farm

7

Chetwynd Manor

Chetwynd Park (Deer Park)

Middle Lodge

21

A41 A519

WATERLOO RD

Waterloo House

6

CHETWYND RD

The Scaur

Park Pool

B5062

Edgmond Marsh

Islington

DOWNFIELDS

SUNNY GDNS

FORTON RD

New Inn Farm

5

TF10

Blue House Farm

BLUE HOUSE BARNS

B5062

Lamb Hotel (PH)

20

WOODRIDGE CL

SHREWSBURY RD

MENTOR CR

PLAYDALE

CHETWYND RD

SILVERDALE

Cherry Hill Farm

EDGMOND RD

CHETWYND RD

Cvn Site

Castle House Sch

FISHER'S LOCK

Flatt Pit Farm

Egremont House

Lion Inn (PH)

4

St Peter's CE Prim Sch

Summerhill

KINGS HEAD PK

GREEN LA

Wrekin View Farm

NEWPORT RD

NEWPORT RD

STACKYARD LA

HIGHFIELD

ROBIN LA

NEWPORT

Tickethouse Lock

SALTER'S MEWS 1
SALTER'S CT 2
MIDGLEY CT 3

HAVISHAM CT

BRIDGE TERR

BROOK

Canal (dis)

Victoria Park

PIPER'S LA

LA MANOR RD

TURNERS LA

CONNERS LA

BATLEY HILLS

Edgmond

Sewage Works

BROOMFIELD CL

HALLCROFT GDNS

Sch

WATERSIDE MEWS

LOWER BAR

WATER LA

TAN BANK

SANDY CROFT

3

SCHOOL RD

PIPER'S LODGE

BROOMFIELD PL

FARM GR

VAUXHALL TERR

VAUXHALL CRES

ST MARY'S

HIGH ST

Adams Gram Sch

THE SQUARE

STAFFORD ST

POWELL RD

CORNMELL LEA

STAFFORD RD

19

BEAUMARIS RD

ADAMS CL

Liby

AUDLEY RD

UNDERHILL

MEADOW RD

Vauxhall

Lower Farm

MOORLAND CT

MOORFIELD CT

GRAVELLY DR

SANDFORD CRES

ABBEY CT

BURGAGE CT

RODDAM CT

SNOWS CT

BELLMAN'S YD

BADDELEY'S CT

AVENUE RD

AUDLEY AVE

2

Strine Brook

Vauxhall Farm

SHREWSBURY WAY

BLACKMERE CL

GILBERT

DUNGARVEN DR

INGESTRAE

HEATHROW

HIGHLAND

BOUCHEY RD

SANDFORD DR

SETTON

ONE AVE

HAWKS RD

UPPER BAR

Newport CE Jun Sch

GRANVILLE AVE

GRANVILLE RD

GRANT VILLAS

LONGFORD RD

Sunnyholme Farm

TALBOT

FORD RD

ELKINGTON

ELSTON

FORD CL

LEIGH RD

THE LARCHES

ELLESMERE

WREKIN

NEWLOCK DR

Newport Inf Sch

1

Home Farm

LONGFORD PK

Longford Hall

MOORFIELD LA

Waterford DR

Newport Girls High Sch

Moorfield Prim Sch

OAK AVE

ASPEN WAY

WALNUT

ELM CL

PSV

STATION RD

QUEENS DR

Ind Est

Millwood Mere

Brook Cottage

Longford

Pool Covert

Grove Farm

Aston Grove

PINEWOODS

ST ANDREWS WAY

NEWTOWN

DARK LA

PRIMROSE CL

RICHMOND

ST ANDREWS WAY

WALSHEAD WAY

MULBERRY CL

JUNIPER ROW

STATION CT 1
PRINCESS GDNS 2
TOWN WELLS MEWS 3

Baddeley's Wells

18

72 A B 73 C D 74 E F

Shropshire STREET ATLAS

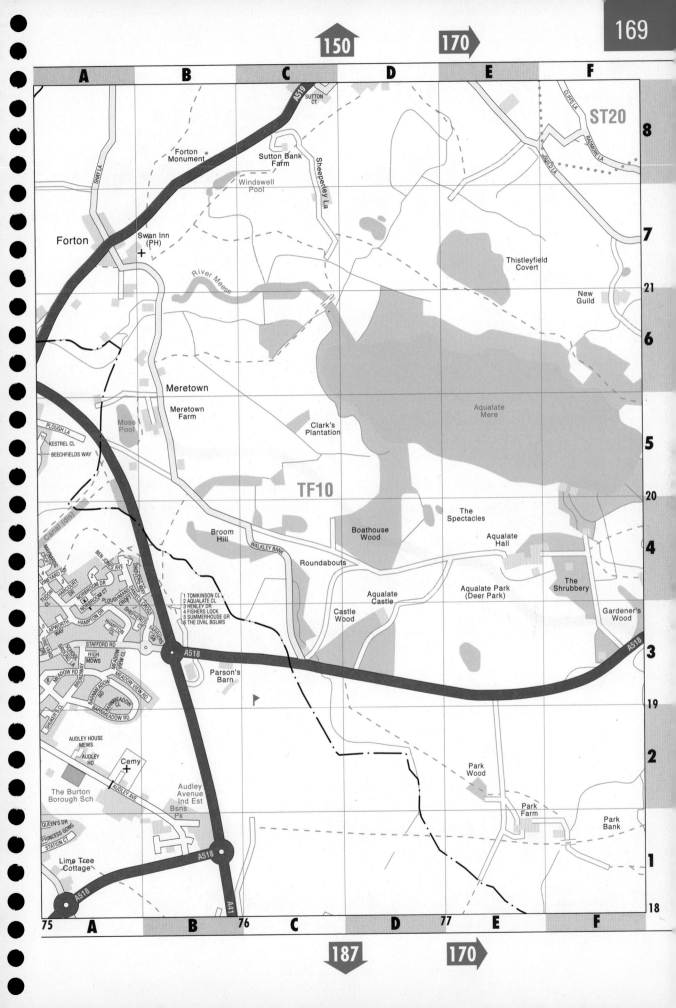

169
151

A B C D E F

8

Brook Covert

Shelmore Wood

Shropshire Union Canal

NORBURY RD

Ryland's Covert

Shelmore House

RADMORE LA

7

Wood Brook

Shelmore Valley Farm

Spring Coppice

Hatchwell's Covert

Radmore Lane Farm

Barn Bridge

21

6

GUILD LA

Guild of Monks

Hamesford Brook

Cotonwood

Pollymoor Farm

ST20

Weavers Hill

Swanpit Farm

A518

5

20

David's Pits Covert

TF10

Coley Brook

Broadhill

Windmill (dis)

4

A518

The Way for the Millennium

Lindore Wood

Broadhill

3

Coley Mill

Lindore Farm

Beffcote Farm

19

Back Brook

Polesworth

BEFFCOTE RD

Beffcote

2

Windmill Bank

Beffcote Manor

Wilbrighton Hall

GNOSALL RD

1

Tinwood Bank

Manor Farm

Bromstead Common

Back Brook

Euxley Farm

Outwoodsbank Farm

HEATH RD

18

Outwoods

Tavern Cottage

78 A B 79 C D 80 E F

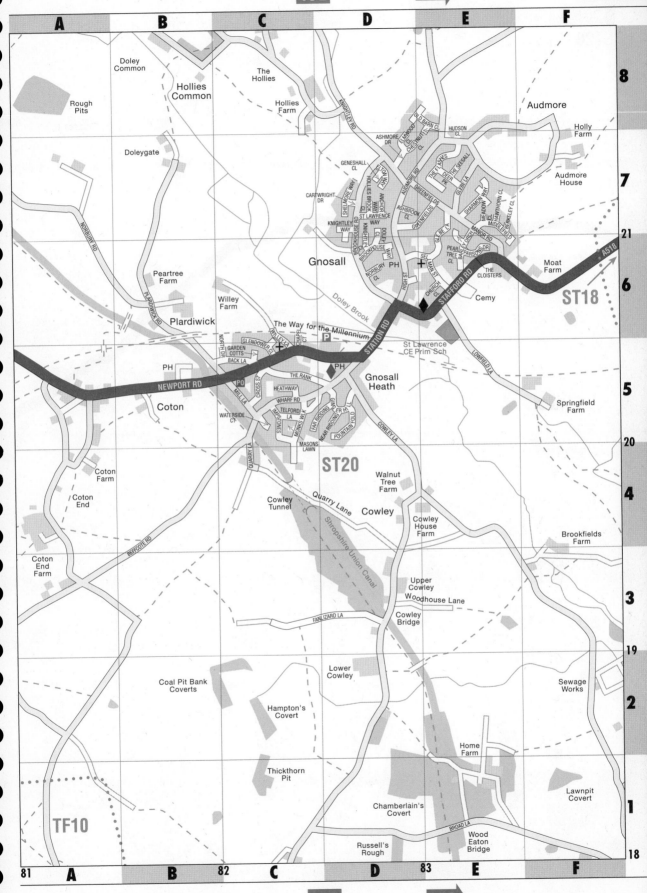

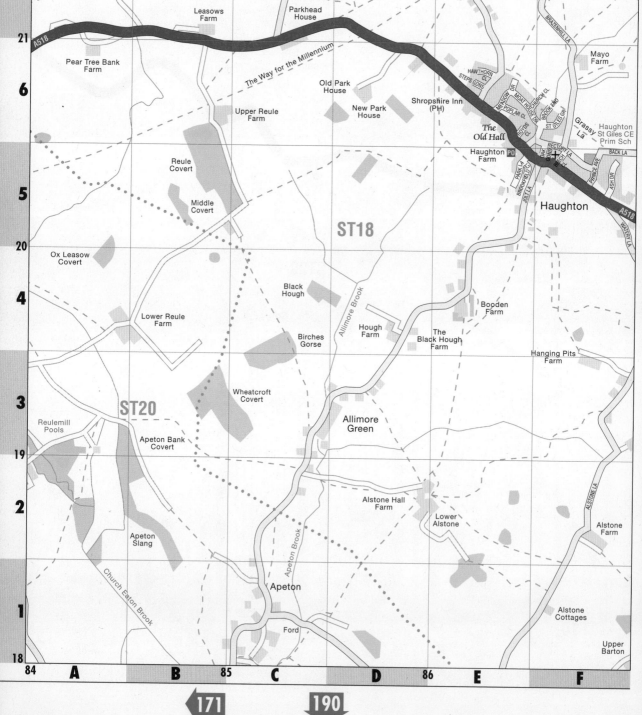

ST20

8

Bleak House
Farm

The Sheppy Farm

WOODHOUSE LA

Whitecross

Shut Heath
Farm

Shut
Heath

Brazenhill

7

Ivy House
Farm

Hurst
Farm

Woodhouse
Farm

P

STATION RD

Brazenhill
Farm

Leasows
Farm

Parkhead
House

BRAZENHILL LA

21

A518

Pear Tree Bank
Farm

The Way for the Millennium

Old Park
House

Mayo
Farm

6

Upper Reule
Farm

New Park
House

Shropshire Inn
(PH)

HAWTHORN
CL

STEPS GDNS

MEADOW

POPLAR CL

BROOK END

ST GILES GR

Grassy
La

Haughton
St Giles CE
Prim Sch

The
Old Hall

Haughton
Farm

PO

RECTORY LA

BACK LA

Reule
Covert

PARK LA

BROOKFIELD CL

JOAN LA

OAK
BUSH GR

PRINCE AVE

ASH DR

Haughton

A518

5

Middle
Covert

ST18

WATER LA

Ox Leasow
Covert

20

Black
Hough

Booden
Farm

4

Lower Reule
Farm

Birches
Gorse

Allimore Brook

Hough
Farm

The
Black Hough
Farm

Hanging Pits
Farm

Wheatcroft
Covert

3

Reulemill
Pools

ST20

Allimore
Green

ALSTONE LA

Apeton Bank
Covert

19

2

Apeton
Slang

Alstone Hall
Farm

Lower
Alstone

Alstone
Farm

Church Eaton Brook

Apeton Brook

Apeton

Alstone
Cottages

1

Ford

Upper
Barton

18

84   85   86

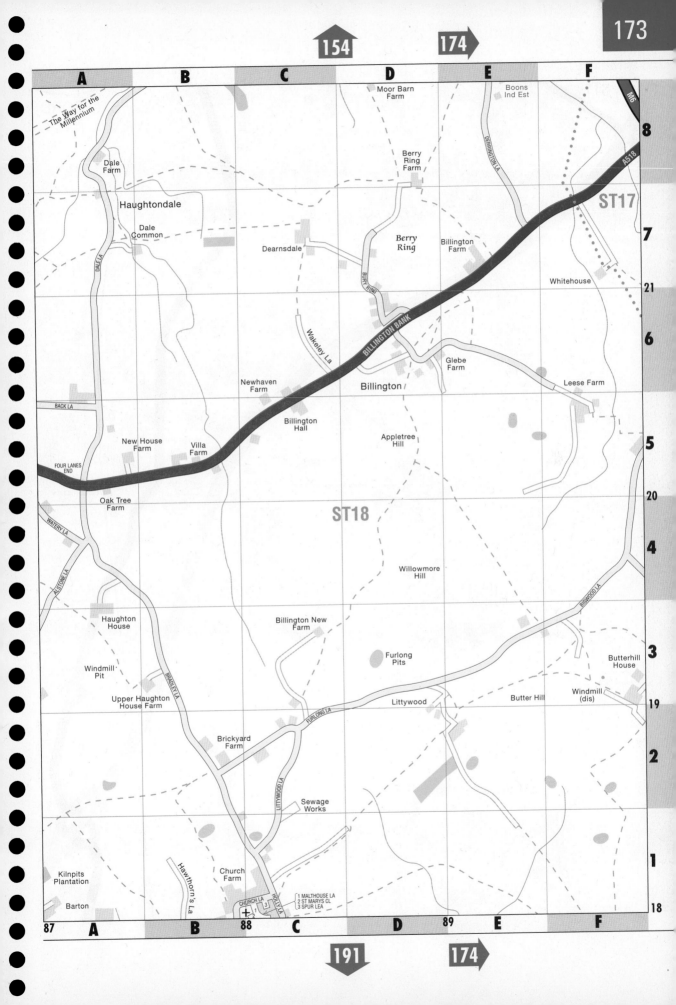

154
174

A B C D E F

Moor Barn
Farm

Boons
Ind Est

M6

The Way for the
Millennium

Dale
Farm

8

Berry
Ring
Farm

A518

DENNINGTON LA

ST17

Haughtondale

Berry
Ring

Billington
Farm

7

Dale
Common

Dearnsdale

Whitehouse

21

DALE LA

BURY RING

Wakeley La

Billington Bank

6

Glebe
Farm

Newhaven
Farm

Billington

Leese Farm

BACK LA

New House
Farm

Villa
Farm

Billington
Hall

Appletree
Hill

5

FOUR LANES
END

20

Oak Tree
Farm

ST18

WATERY LA

Willowmore
Hill

4

ALSTONE LA

BIGWOOD LA

Haughton
House

Billington New
Farm

Butterhill
House

3

Windmill
Pit

BRADLEY LA

Furlong
Pits

Butter Hill

Windmill
(dis)

19

Upper Haughton
House Farm

FURLONG LA

Littywood

Brickyard
Farm

2

LITTYWOOD LA

Sewage
Works

Kilnpits
Plantation

HOLLY DR

Church
Farm

1 MALTHOUSE LA
2 ST MARYS CL
3 SPUR LEA

1

Hawthorn's La

CHURCH LA

Barton

18

87 A B 88 C D 89 E F

191
174

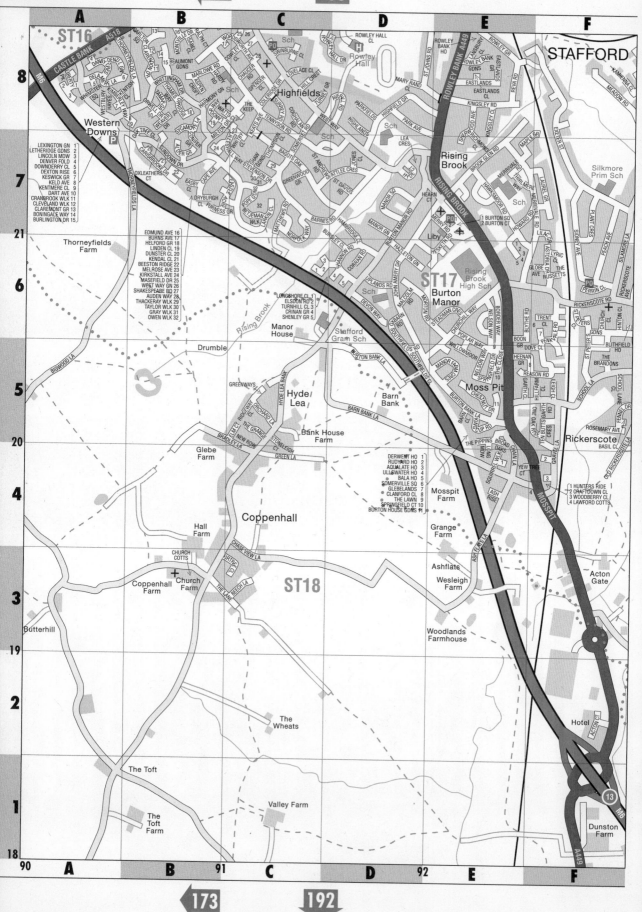

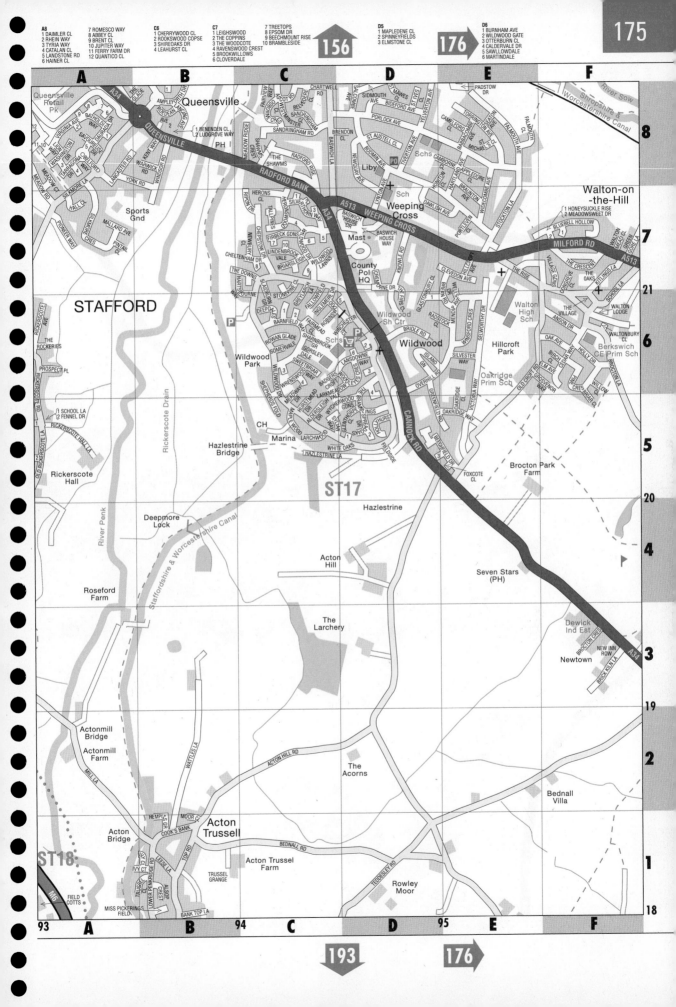

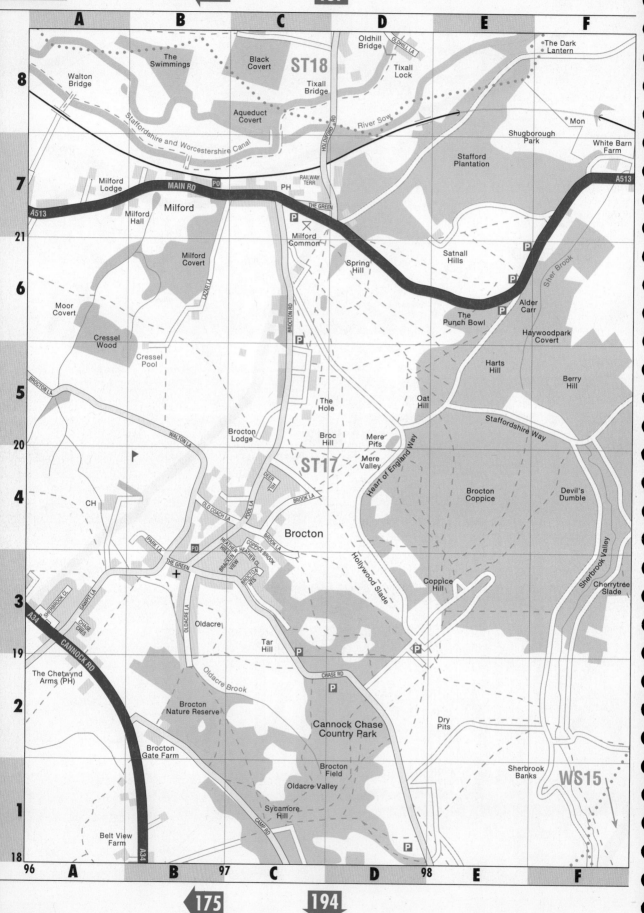

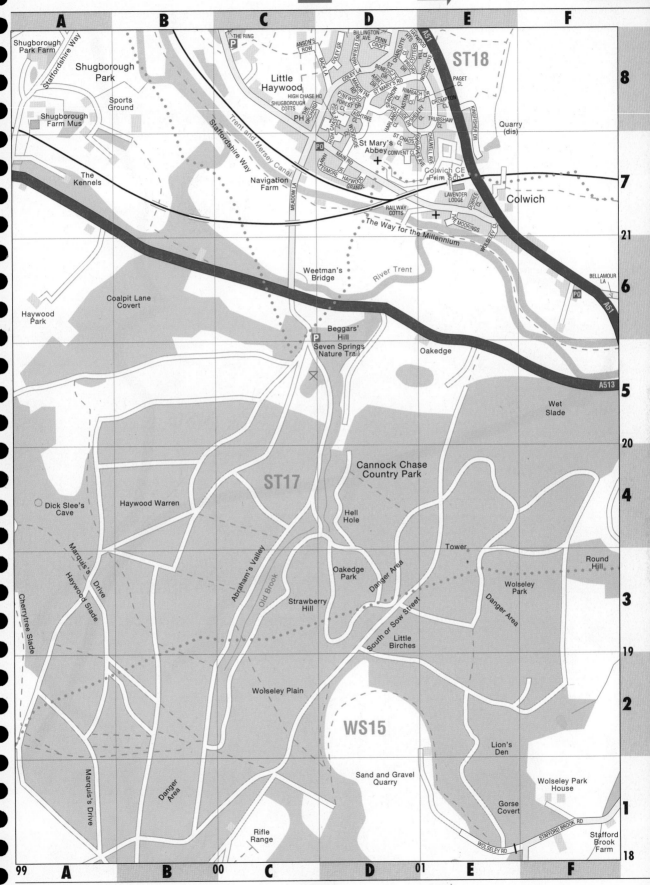

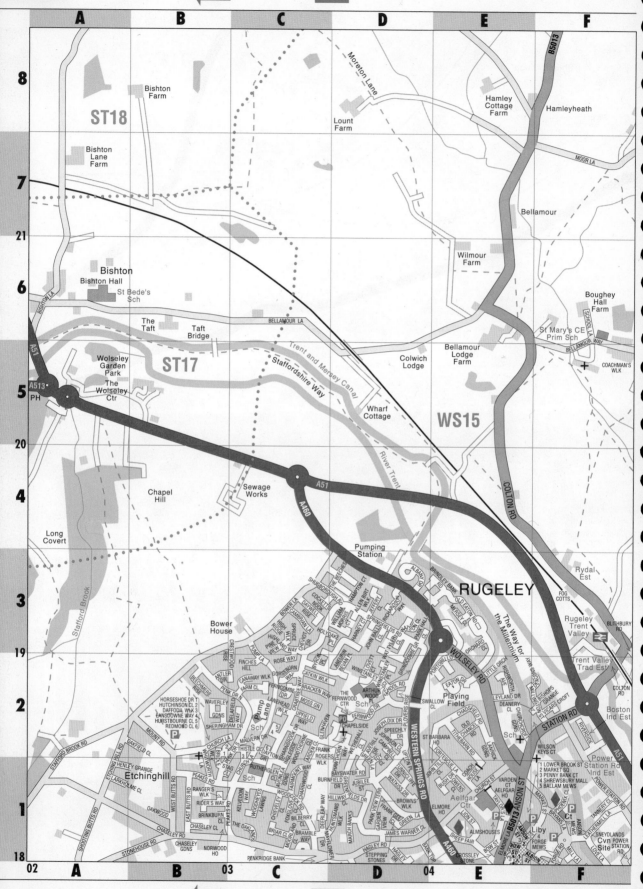

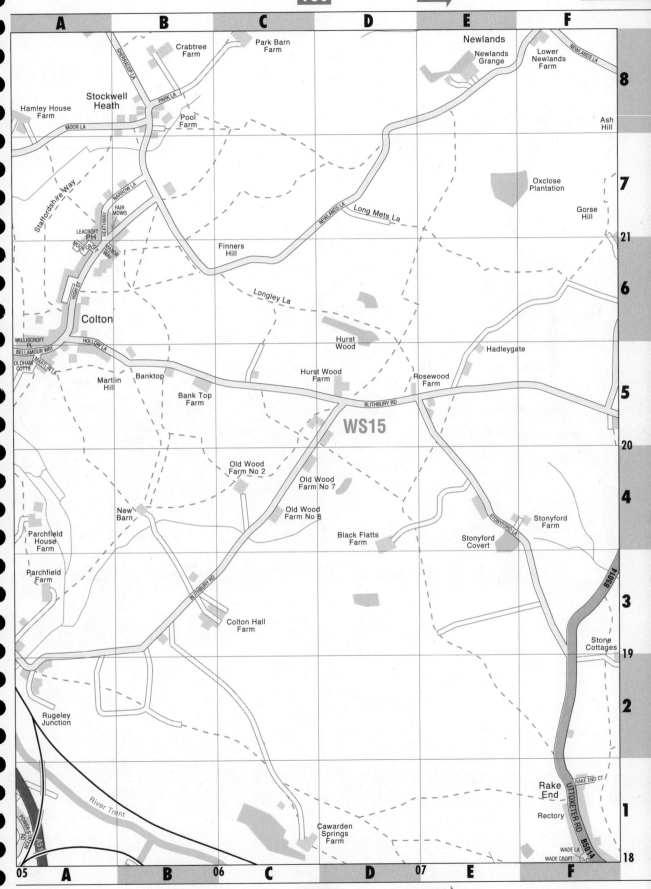

A B C D E F

DE13

8

Blithford Farm

Mount Pleasant

Poplar Farm

Rookery Farm

The Willows

ORANGE LA

Old Lane

Ash Hill

Little Blithe

The Hurst

7

Porter's Hill

NEWLANDS LA

B5014

21

NUNS LA

Priory Farm

Old Lane

6

Bank House Farm

PEARTREE LA

UTTOXETER RD

Blithbury Farm

River Blithe

Braddocks Barn

Pur Brook

5

Manor Farm

Blithbury

WS15

Hayend Wood

BLITHBURY RD

Longacres

20

PH

New House Farm

Hayend

4

B5014

Pipewood Cottage Farm

PIPE WOOD LA

Pipe Wood

Town End Farm

Hamstall Hall

Coatfield

BLITHBURY RD

3

Hamstall Ridware

19

Bentley Hall Farm

Goldhayfields

Hunger Hill

PH

BLYTHE VIEW

LICHFIELD RD

Cowley Hill

2

Woodhouse Farm

Cowley Hill Farm

Blythe House Farm

1

Quintin's Orchard

18

OAKLANDS CL CHADWICK CRES

08 A B 09 C D 10 E F

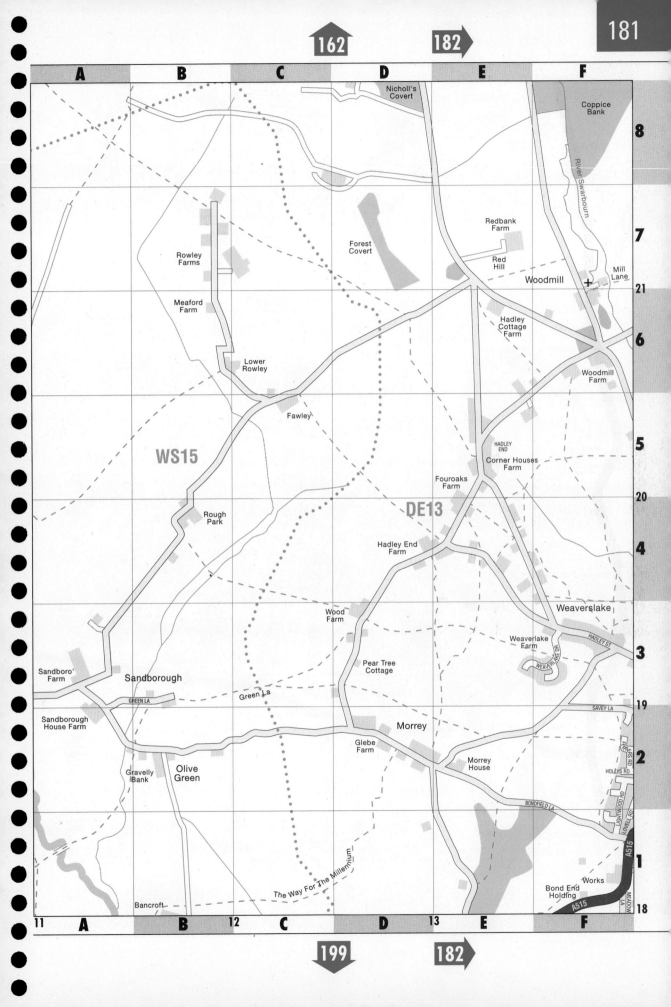

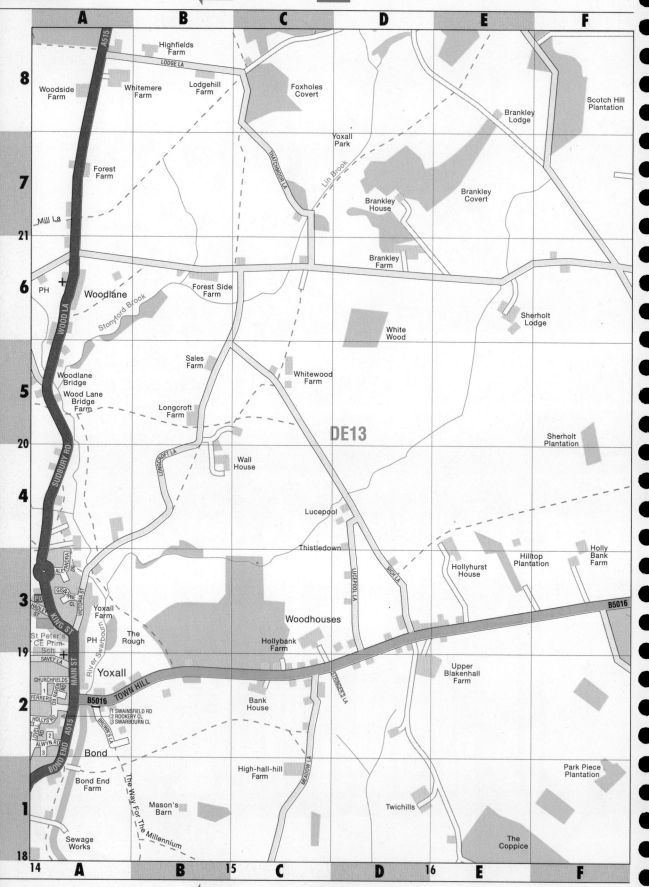

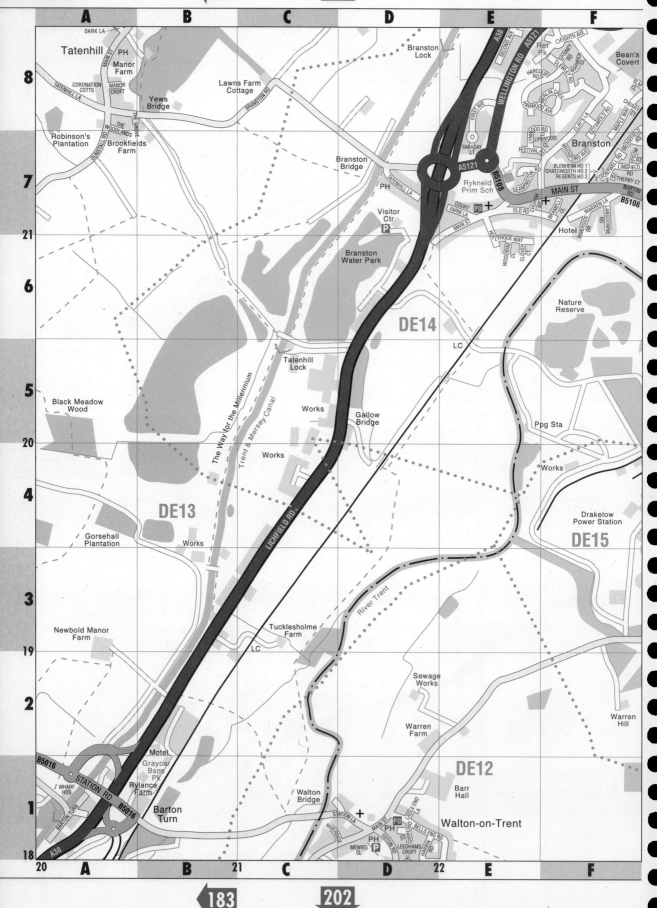

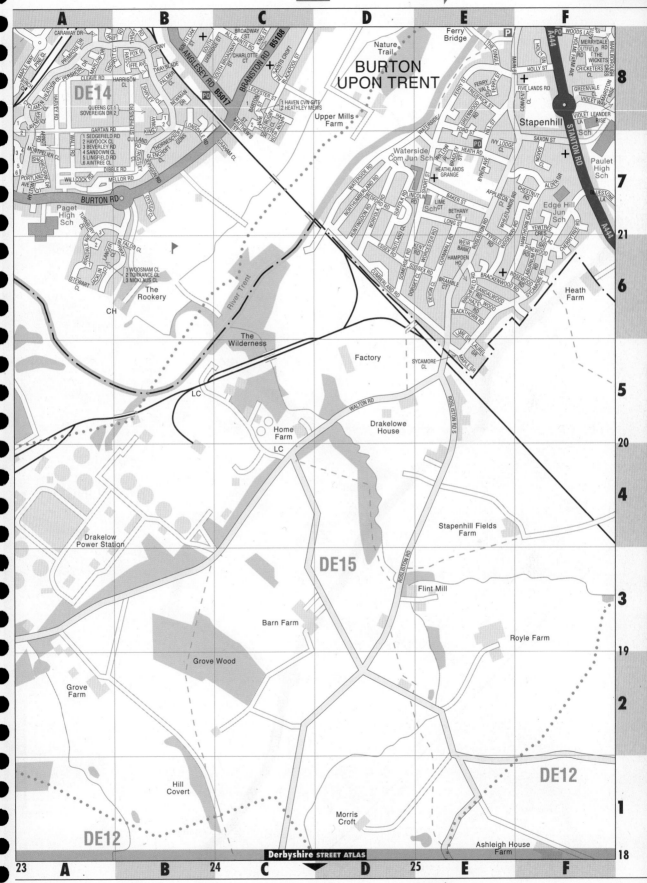

BURTON
UPON TRENT

DE14

Stapenhill

DE15

DE12

DE12

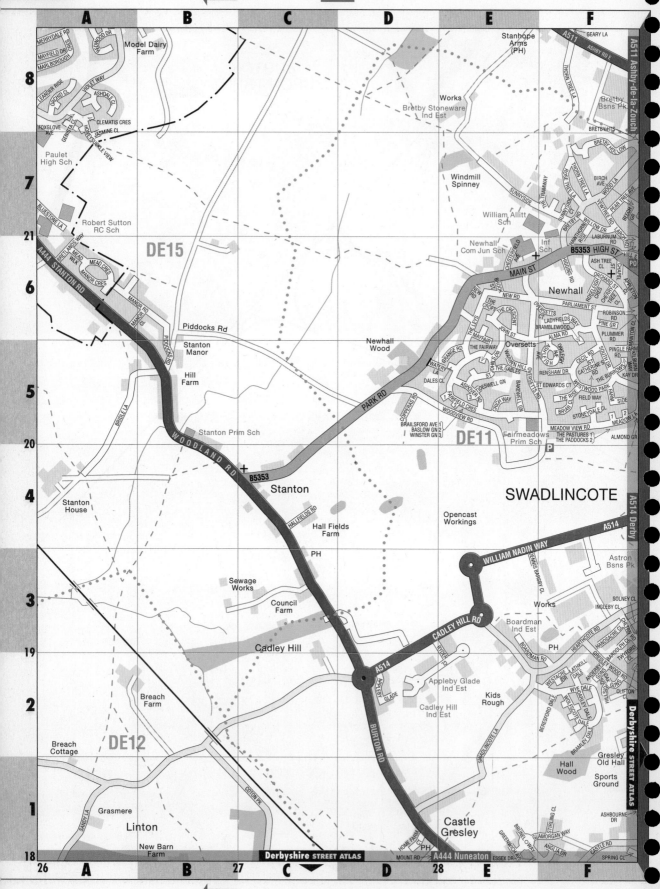

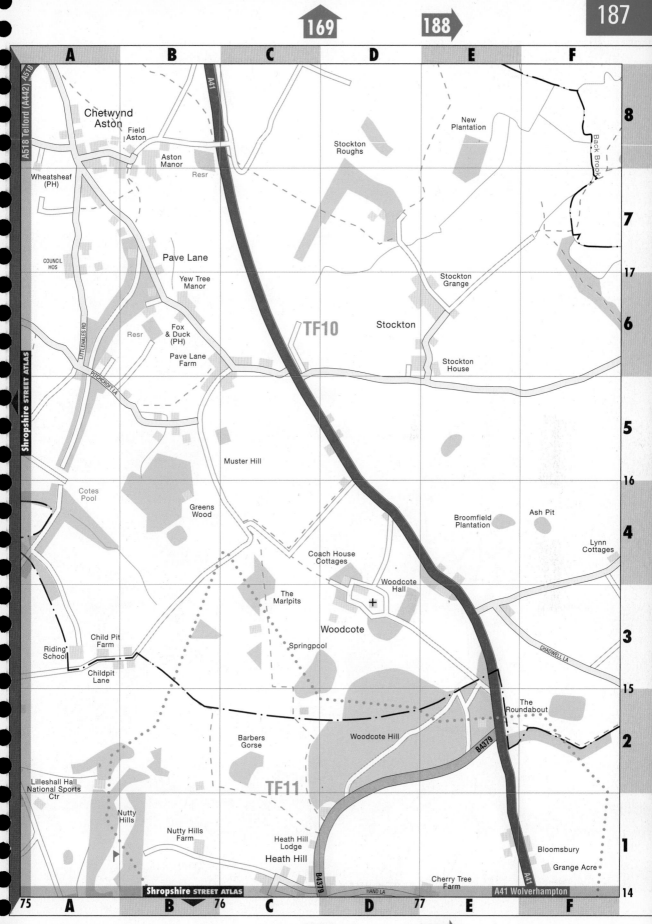

169

188

A   B   C   D   E   F

A518 Telford (A442)   A518

Chetwynd
Aston

Field
Aston

Aston
Manor

Resr

Wheatsheaf
(PH)

A41

Stockton
Roughs

New
Plantation

Back Brook

8

7

COUNCIL
HOS

Pave Lane

Yew Tree
Manor

LITTLEHALES RD

Resr

Fox
& Duck
(PH)

Pave Lane
Farm

PITCHCROFT LA

TF10

Stockton

Stockton
Grange

17

6

Stockton
House

Muster Hill

5

Cotes
Pool

Greens
Wood

Broomfield
Plantation

Ash Pit

Lynn
Cottages

16

4

Coach House
Cottages

Woodcote
Hall

The
Marlpits

Child Pit
Farm

Springpool

Woodcote

CHADWELL LA

3

Riding
School

Childpit
Lane

15

The
Roundabout

Barbers
Gorse

Woodcote Hill

B4379

2

Lilleshall Hall
National Sports
Ctr

Nutty
Hills

Nutty Hills
Farm

TF11

Heath Hill
Lodge

Heath Hill

B4379

Cherry Tree
Farm

Bloomsbury

Grange Acre

A41 Wolverhampton

1

14

Shropshire STREET ATLAS

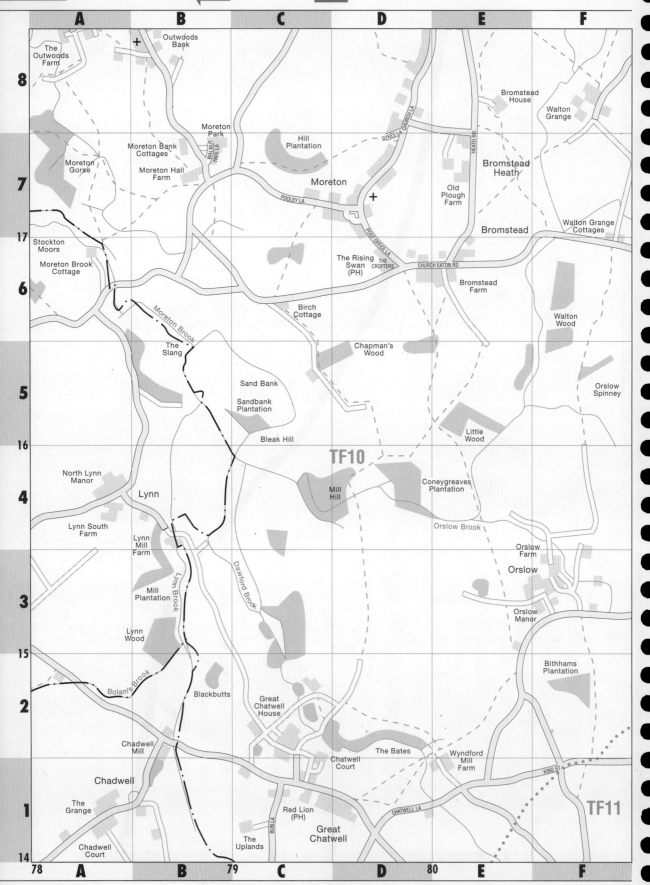

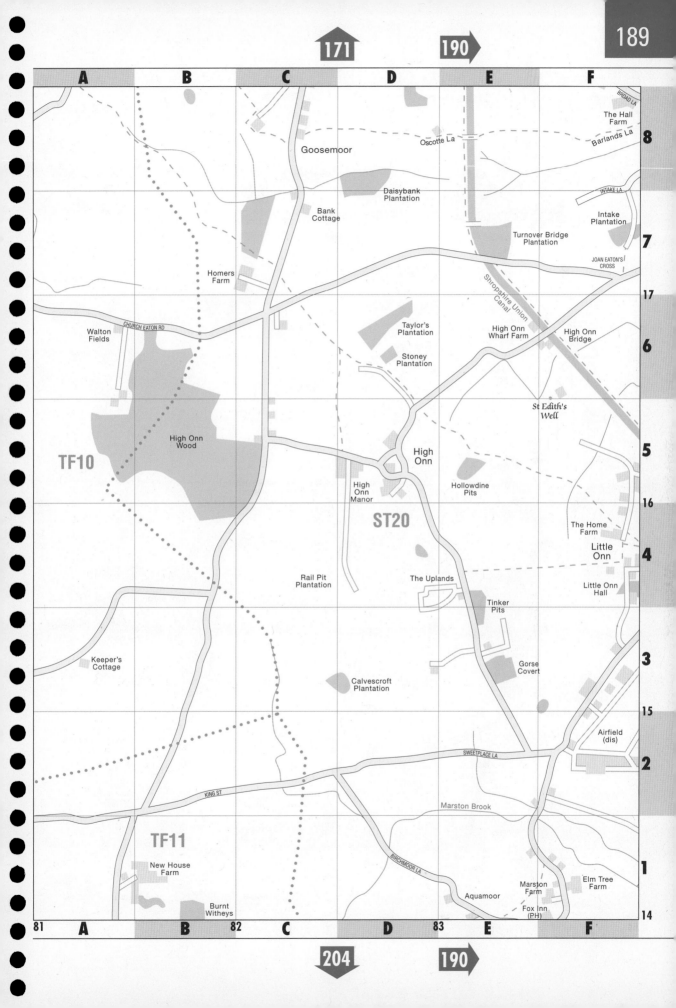

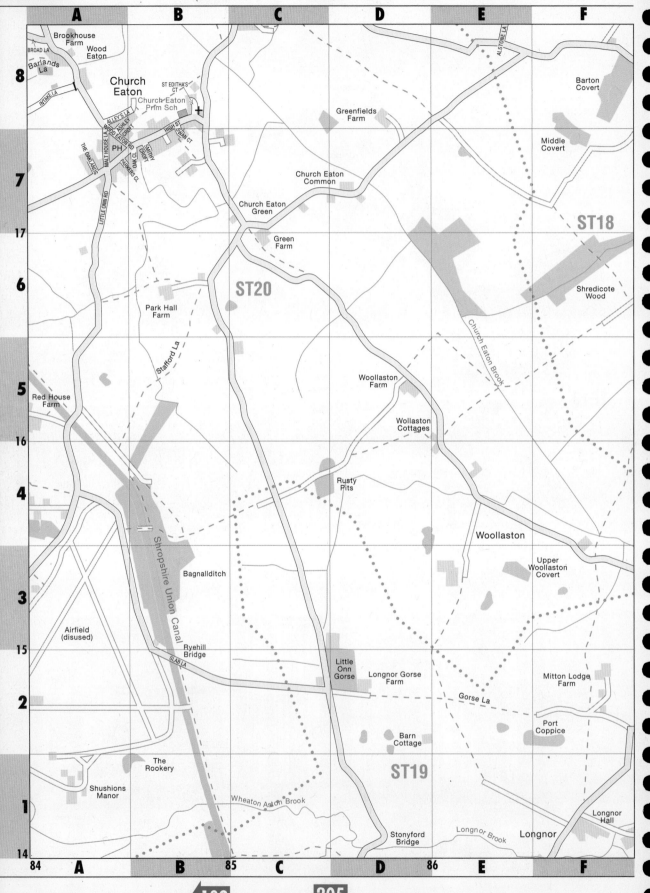

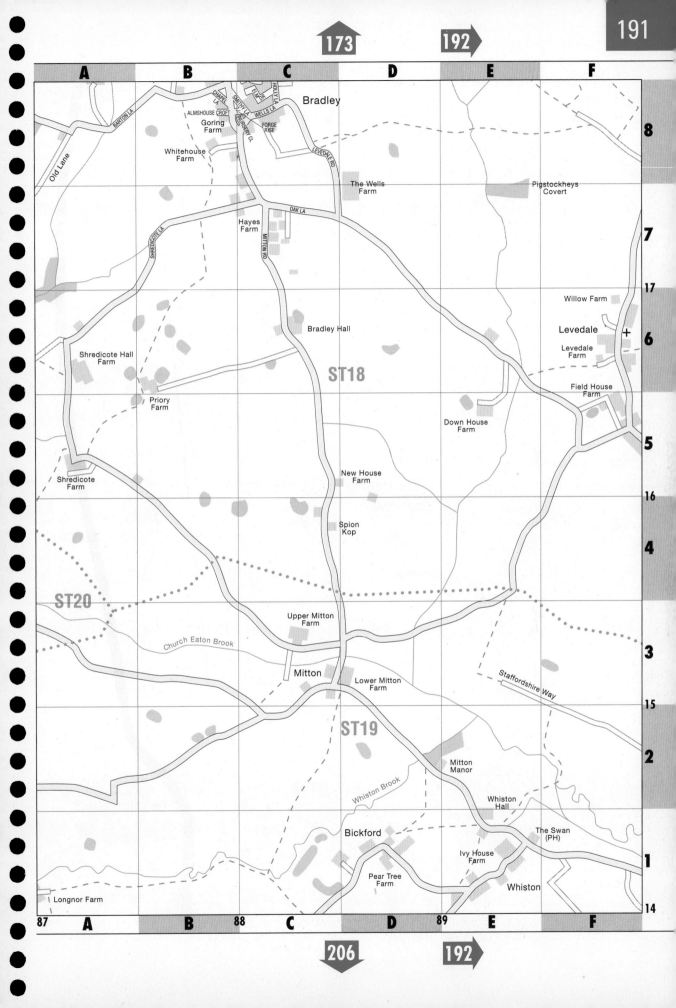

191
174

A B C D E F

8

Yew Tree Cottage

St Leonard's CE Fst Sch
Dunston House
Dunston
Dunston Hall

Little Heath

New Buildings Farm

Dunston Heath Farm
SCHOOL LA

Dunston Heath

7

Stanley Cottages

Home Farm
SWAN LA

17

Hay House

Drayton Manor

6

Hope Farm

ST18

5

Whittemore Farm

16

The Whittamoors

Honey Pots

4

Longridge

Longridge House

Lower Drayton Farm

LEVEDALE RD

3

Grassmere Farm

Chase View

15

Flax Ovens

2

Preston Vale

STAFFORD RD
River Penk
The Roller Mill

ST19

Penkridge

GOODS STATION LA
THE FLAX OVENS
NURSERY CL
COOME CL
GROCOTT CL
UPLANDS CL
Marshbrook Fst Sch

TEDDESLEY RD
HATHERTON RD
KEMPSON DR
FREDERICK PL
MILL CRES
ORCHARD CL
LITTLETON CL
MARSH LA
MARSH CL

Preston Hill

Staffordshire Way

Riverside Farm

CROWN BRIDGE 1
PALISADINGS 2
ALMSHOUSES 3
CUTTLESTONE HO 4
ST MICHAEL'S SQ 5
CHURCH COTTS 6
CHURCH FARM CL 7

Market Place

STONE CROSS
CHURCH RD
RIVERSIDE HO
STANFORD CL
MILL GDNS
GROSVENOR RD
MARKET PL
THE SAPLINGS
SAPLINGS CL
HALING CL
CHERRYBROOK DR

1

Whiston Mill

Whiston Brook

PRESTON VALE LA

CLAY ST A449
MILL ST
BELL BROOK
MARKET ST Y
NEW RD
CANNOCK RD
LITTLE MARSH
MARSH DR
BRAM DEAN DR

Liby

Hotel

PINFOLD LA
STATION RD

P Sch
P

14

90 A 91 B C 92 D E F

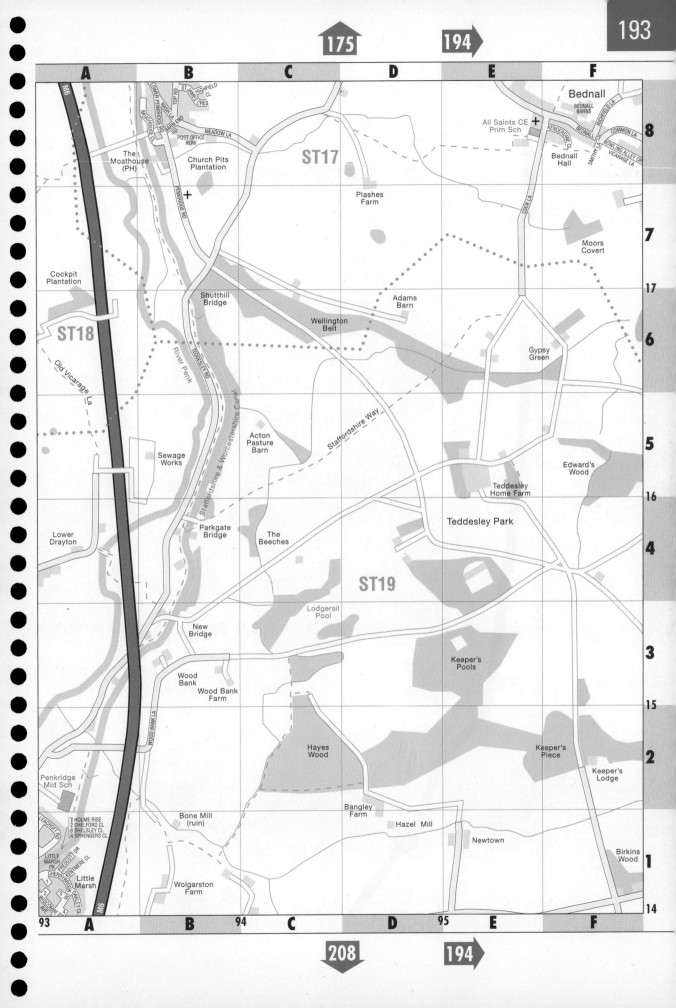

175
194

A B C D E F

M6

LOWER PENKRIDGE RD
MOATHOUSE CL
TOP RD
ST JAMES CRES
BARN END
HIGHFIELD CL
MEADOW LA
POST OFFICE ROW

The Moathouse (PH)

Church Pits Plantation

ST17

Bednall

BEDNALL BARNS

All Saints CE Prim Sch
KENDERDINE CL
BEDNALL CT
SMITHY LA
RICHFIELD LA
COMMON LA
BOWLING ALLEY OR
VICARAGE LA

8

Bednall Hall

Plashes Farm

Cockpit Plantation

PENKRIDGE RD

Shutthill Bridge

COCK LA

7

Moors Covert

17

ST18

Old Vicarage La

River Penk

TEDDESLEY RD

Wellington Belt

Adams Barn

6

Gypsy Green

Sewage Works

Staffordshire & Worcestershire Canal

Acton Pasture Barn

Staffordshire Way

Edward's Wood

5

Teddesley Home Farm

16

Lower Drayton

Parkgate Bridge

The Beeches

ST19

Teddesley Park

4

New Bridge

Lodgerail Pool

Keeper's Pools

3

Wood Bank
Wood Bank Farm

WOOD BANK LA

15

Hayes Wood

Keeper's Piece

2

Penkridge Mid Sch

Keeper's Lodge

LEACROFT RD
1 HOLME RISE
2 CHELFORD CL
3 SHELSLEY CL
4 SPRENGERS CL
LITTLE MARSH PK
PRESCOTT DR
KENTMERE CL
CHERRYBROOK DR
OAKLEY CL
WISCOMBE AVE

Bone Mill (ruin)

Bangley Farm

Hazel Mill

Newtown

Birkins Wood

1

Little Marsh

Wolgarston Farm

M6

14

93 A B 94 C D 95 E F

208
194

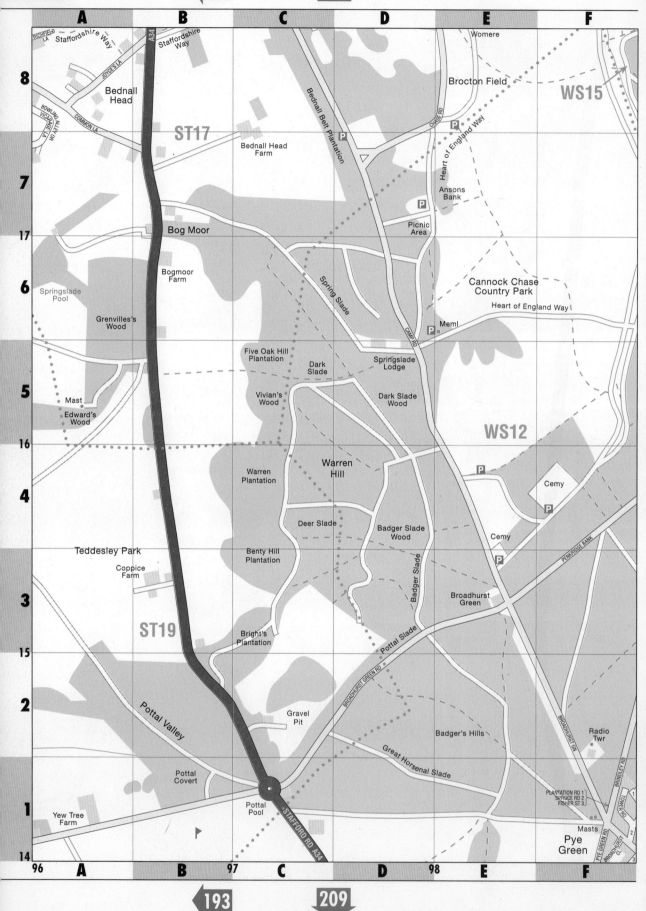

193
176

A B C D E F

RICHFIELD LA
Staffordshire Way
JOYCE'S LA
Staffordshire Way
A34

8

Womere

Brocton Field

WS15

Bednall Head

ST17

BOWLING ALLEY DR
VICAR'S LA

COMMON LA

Bednall Head
Farm

CHASE RD

7

Heart of England Way

Ansons
Bank

Bog Moor

17

Picnic
Area

Bogmoor
Farm

Spring Slade

Cannock Chase
Country Park

6

Springslade
Pool

Heart of England Way

Grenvilles's
Wood

Five Oak Hill
Plantation

Dark
Slade

Springslade
Lodge

CAMP RD

Meml

5

Mast

Edward's
Wood

Vivian's
Wood

Dark Slade
Wood

WS12

16

Warren
Plantation

Warren
Hill

Cemy

4

Deer Slade

Badger Slade
Wood

Cemy

Teddesley Park

Coppice
Farm

Benty Hill
Plantation

Badger Slade

Broadhurst
Green

PENKRIDGE BANK

3

ST19

Bright's
Plantation

Pottal Slade

15

BROADHURST GREEN RD

BROADHURST GN

2

Pottal Valley

Gravel
Pit

Badger's Hills

Great Horsenal Slade

Radio
Twr

BRINDLEY RD

Pottal
Covert

PLANTATION RD 1
SPRUCE RD 2
FISHER ST 3

1

Yew Tree
Farm

Pottal
Pool

STAFFORD RD A34

Masts

Pye
Green

PYE GREEN RD
BROADHURST CL
TOWER RD

14

96 A B 97 C D 98 E F

193
209

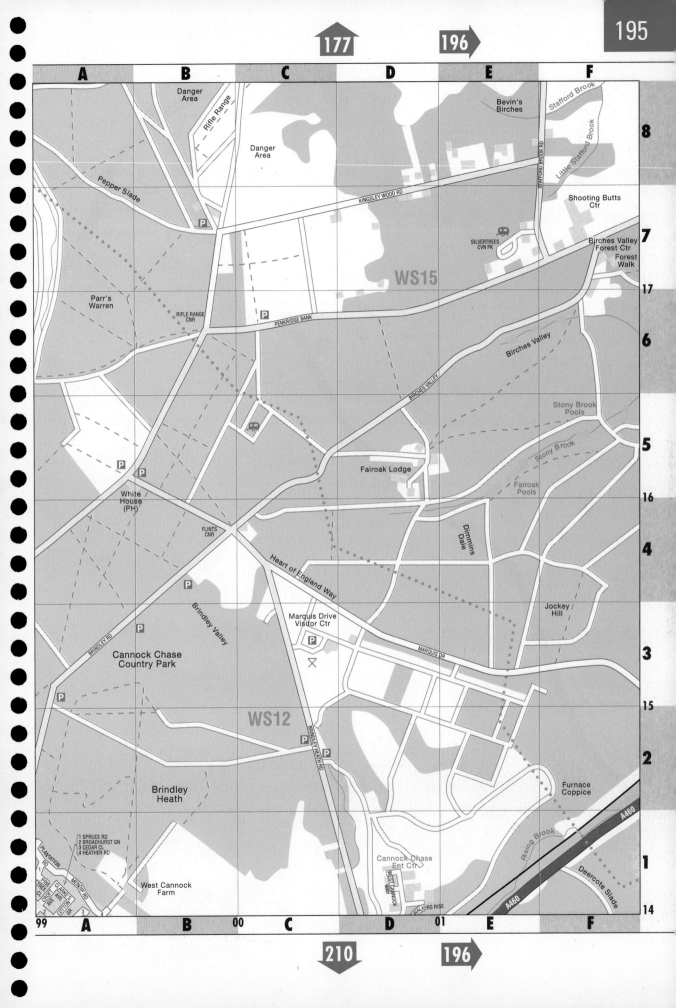

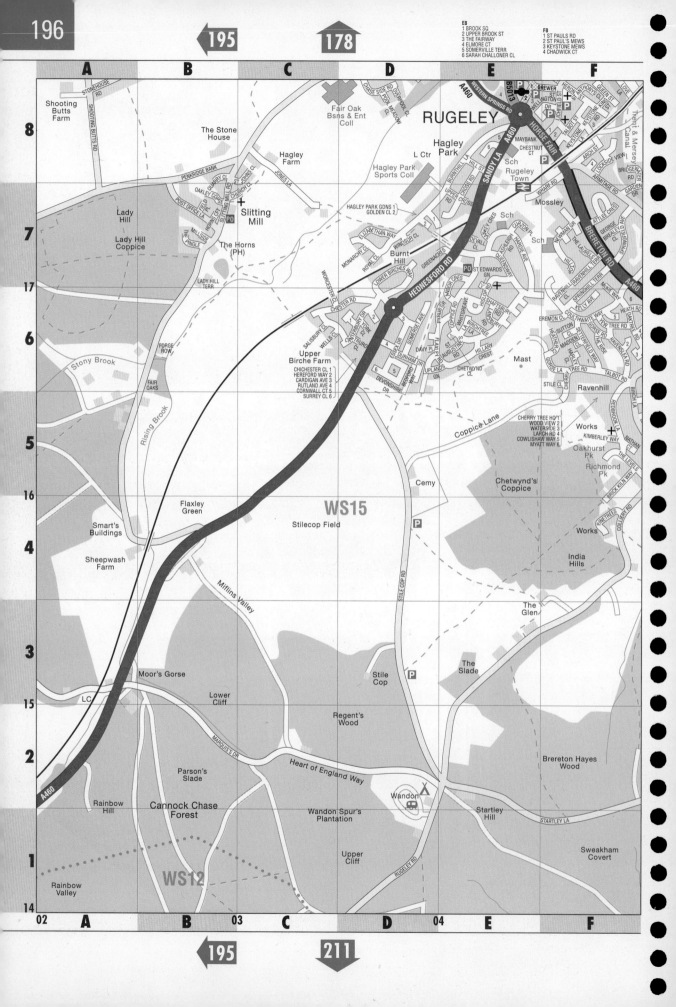

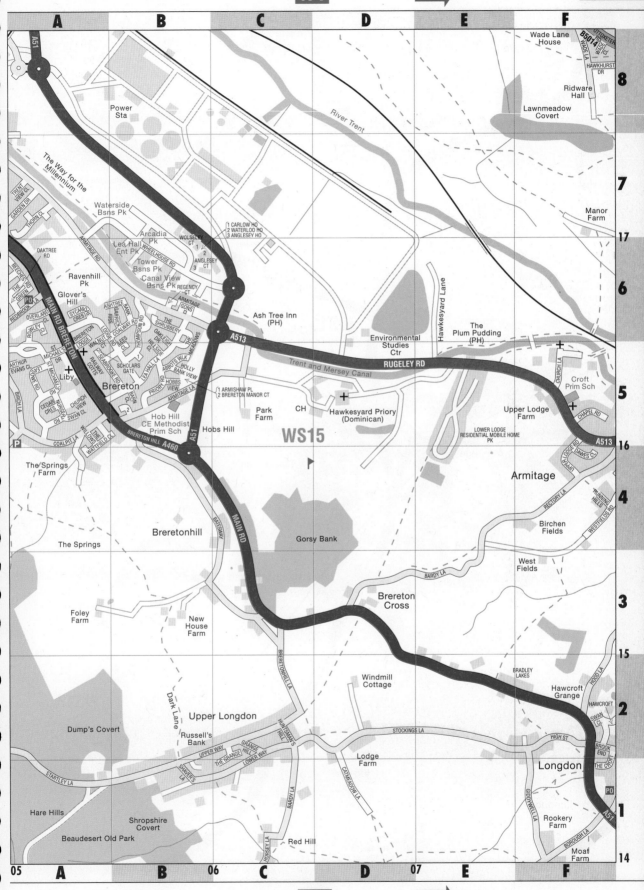

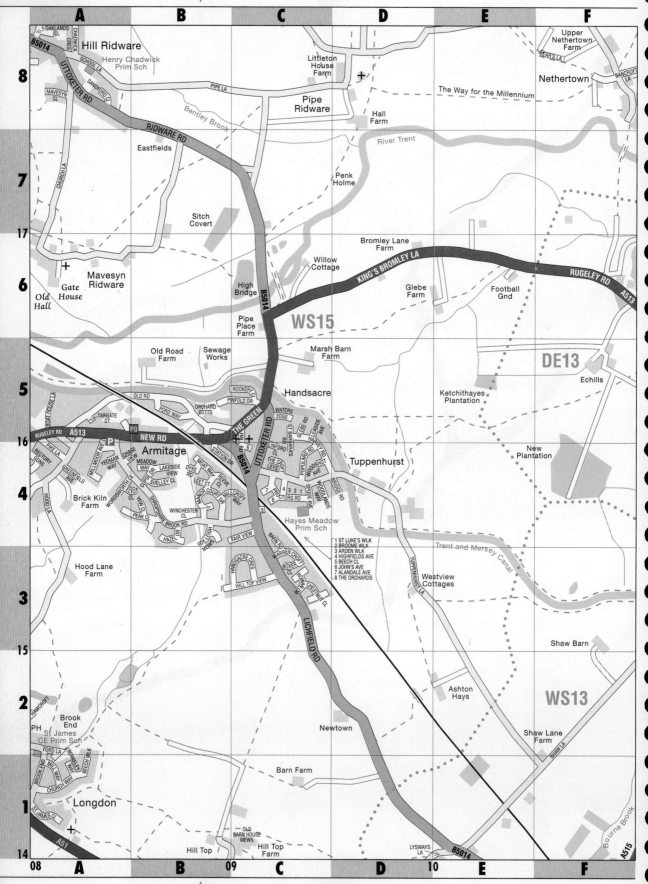

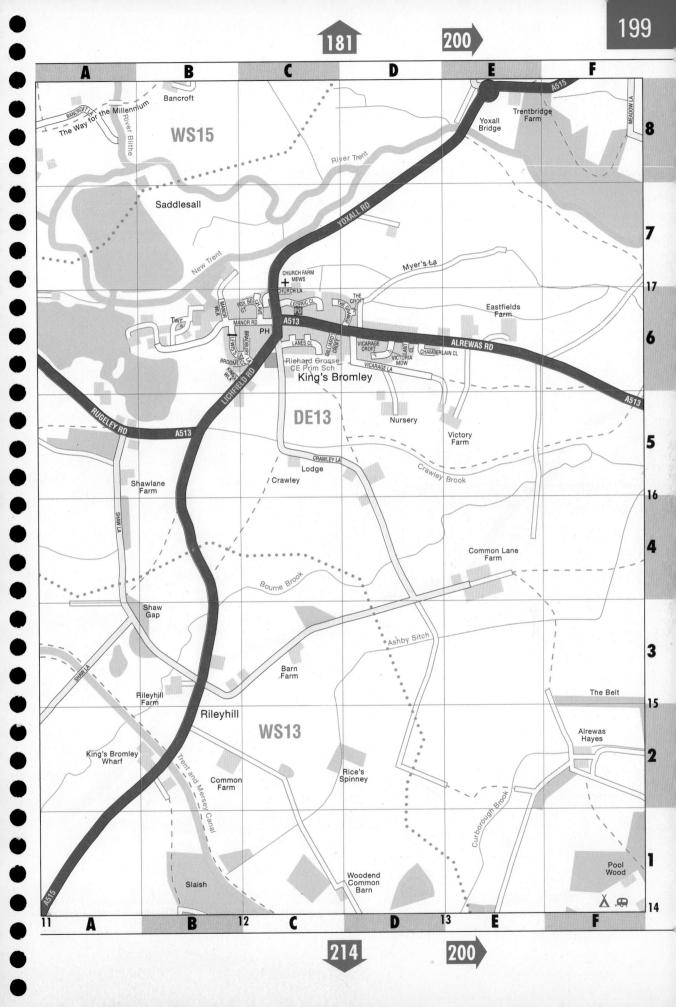

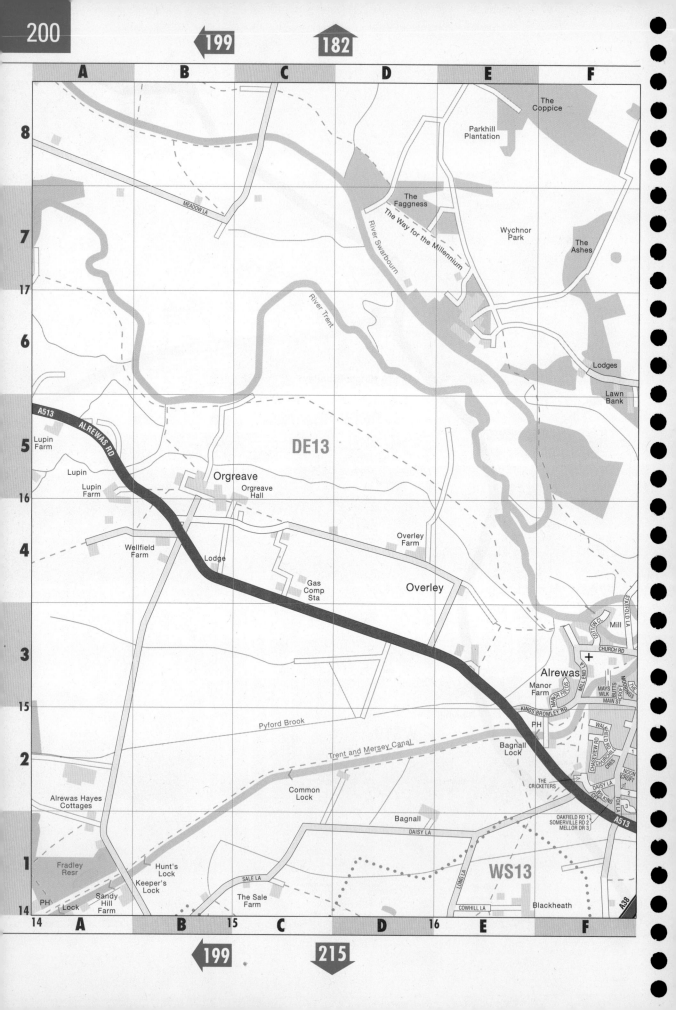

199
182

A B C D E F

8

7

17

6

5

DE13

16

4

3

15

2

1

14

A 15 B C 16 D E F

199
215

The Coppice
Parkhill Plantation
The Faggness
The Way for the Millennium
River Swarbourn
Wychnor Park
The Ashes
River Trent
Lodges
Lawn Bank

A513
ALREWAS RD

Lupin Farm
Lupin
Lupin Farm
Orgreave
Orgreave Hall
Overley Farm
Overley
Wellfield Farm
Lodge
Gas Comp Sta

Mill
STAFFOLD LA
COTTON CL
CHURCH RD
Alrewas
Manor Farm
MILL END
BUTTS
MAYS WLK
CROFT
MOOR RD
THE
MAIN ST
MANOR RISE
KINGS BROMLEY RD
PH
WALFIELD RD
CHASEVIEW RD
CHURCHILL CRES
DAISY LA
NOON CROFT
Bagnall Lock
THE CRICKETERS
WALKINS
FOX LA
Pyford Brook
Trent and Mersey Canal
Common Lock
Bagnall
DAISY LA
OAKFIELD RD 1
SOMERVILLE RD 2
MELLOR DR 3
A513
Alrewas Hayes Cottages
LONG LA
WS13
Fradley Resr
Hunt's Lock
Keeper's Lock
SALE LA
The Sale Farm
COWHILL LA
Blackheath
PH
Lock
Sandy Hill Farm
A38

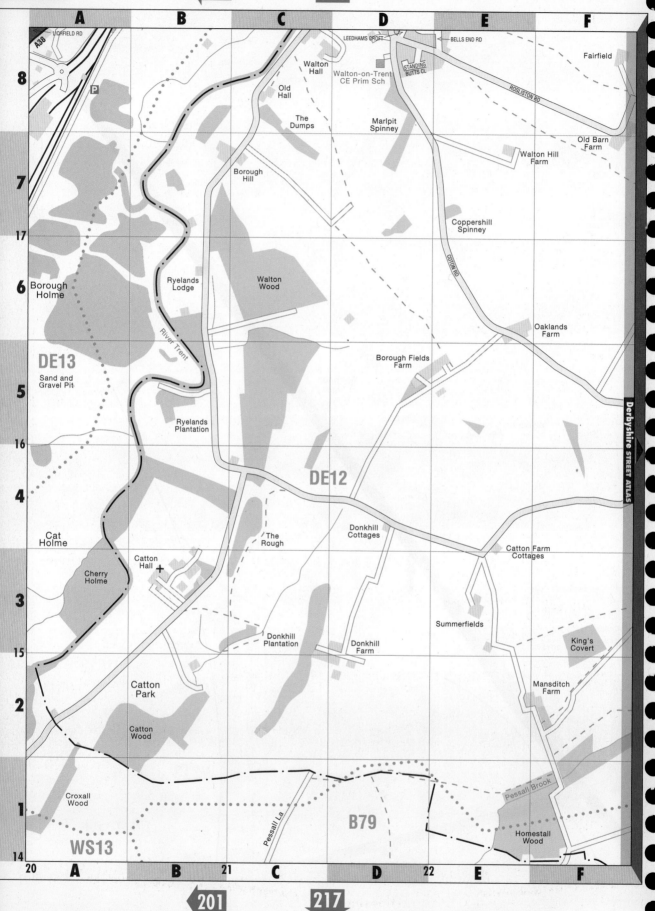

A   B   C   D   E   F

LICHFIELD RD
A38
P

8

Walton Hall
Old Hall
The Dumps
Walton-on-Trent CE Prim Sch
LEEDHAMS CROFT
STANDING BUTTS CL
BELLS END RD
Marlpit Spinney
Fairfield
ROSLISTON RD
Old Barn Farm
Walton Hill Farm

7

Borough Hill
Coppershill Spinney

17

6

Borough Holme
Ryelands Lodge
Walton Wood
River Trent
COTTON RD
Oaklands Farm

DE13
Sand and Gravel Pit

5

Ryelands Plantation
Borough Fields Farm

16

DE12

4

Cat Holme
Catton Hall
Cherry Holme
The Rough
Donkhill Cottages
Catton Farm Cottages

3

Summerfields
King's Covert

15

Donkhill Plantation
Donkhill Farm
Mansditch Farm

Catton Park

2

Catton Wood

Pessall Brook

1

Croxall Wood
Pessall La
B79
Homestall Wood

14

WS13

20   A   B   21   C   D   22   E   F

Derbyshire STREET ATLAS

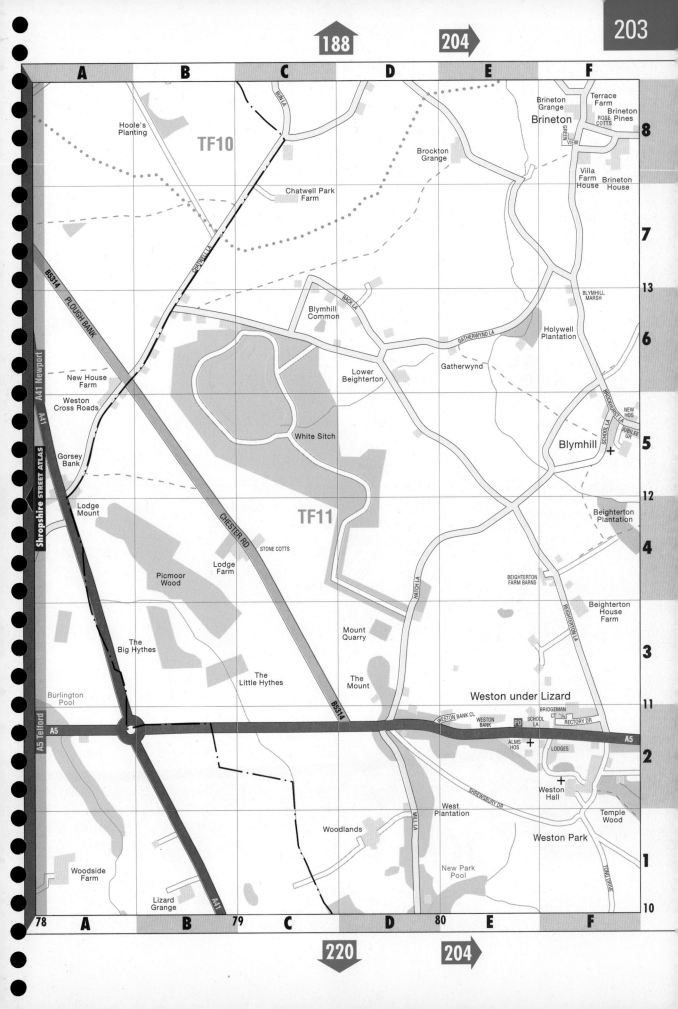

203
189

A B C D E F

8

7

13

6

Ryefield Lane

Wet Croft
Plantation

Wrestlers
Farm

Wrestlers
Wood

Marston

Manor
Farm

BIRCHMOOR LA

BRITCHILL LA

GAY LA

ST20

Mottymeadows Brook

Motty Meadows

Broadholes Lane

BROADHOLES LA

Beaudesert
Plantation

Brockhurst
Coppice

Lincoln Brook

5

Grove
Farm

Blymhill
Grange

12

High Hall

4

Lower
Brockhurst

BROCKHURST RD

Lucknow
Farm

Hartley's
Gorse

Brick Kiln
Lane

TF11

Brockhurst

ST19

New Buildings
Farm

Blymhill
Lawn

Blymhill Lawn
Farm

Brickyard
Plantation

Lawn
House

BROCKENHURST LA

BLYMHILL LAWN LA

3

11

Hurst
Plantation

Hurst
Farm

Ivetsey
Bank

IVETSEY RD

The Hurst

Wheaton Aston
New Hall

A5

Wall Plantations

WOLLEY LA

WATLING ST

Bradford
Arms
Hotel

A5

2

Temple
Pool

Cottage
Wood

East Park

Dogkennel
Wood

LICHFIELD DRIVE

Wheaton Aston
Old Hall

Ivetsey Bank
Farm

1

Weston
Park

Weston Park
Farm

SPRING LA

10

81 A B 82 C D 83 E F

203
221

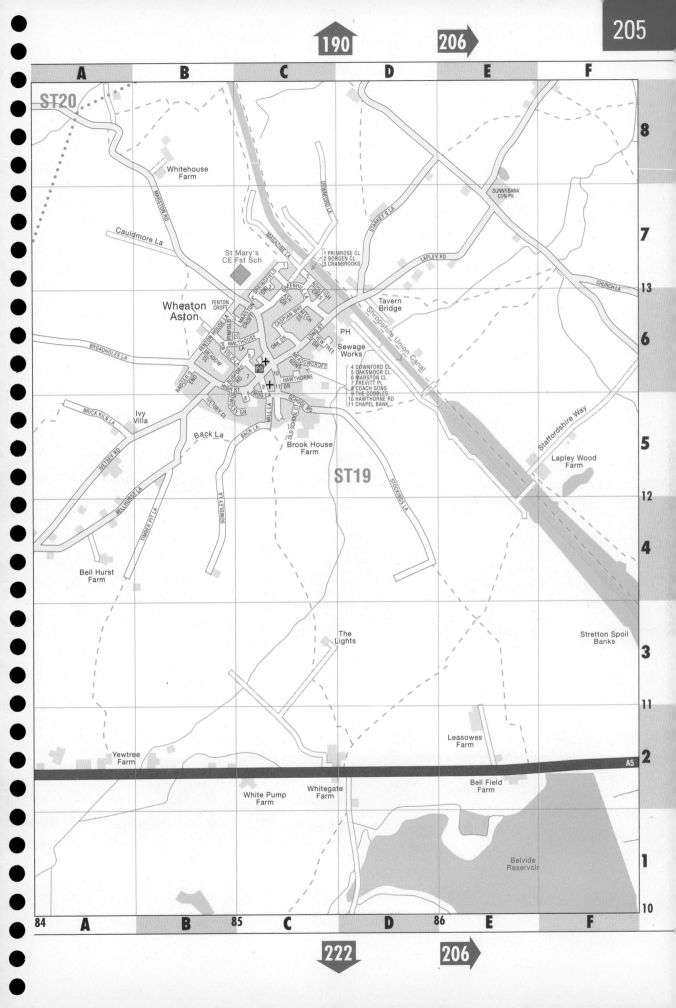

205
191

A　B　C　D　E　F

8

Pool
Plantation

Staffordshire Way

Bickford Grange
Farm

7

Bickford
Grange

Beacon
Hill

MERCIAN WAY
QUEENS
COTTAGES
PH
BICKFORD RD

13

CHURCH LA
BICKFORD CL
PRIORES PL
Lapley

+

PARK LA
LAPLEY HALL
MEWS

6

STRETTON RD
Lapley
Hall

Lapley
Gorse

Stretton
Wood

5

Keeper's
Cottage

ST19

Rabbit
Slack

12

The
Wilderness

Twenty Acre
Pit

LAPLEY LA

Home
Farm

ROWLEYHILL DR

4

The
Stubblers

WOOD LA

Wood
Farm

+

Stretton
Hall

Stretton Park

Rowleyhill
Plantation

SLING LA

GARDEN LA

3

Stretton
Spoil Banks

Stretton

STONEY LA

Upper
Pool

The
Pool

Lodge
Plantation

Vernon Lodge
Prep Sch

SCHOOL LA

PO

School
Farm

11

Aquaduct
House

Stretton
Wharf

Road
Farm

THE AVENUE

Crown
Farm

The Ivy
House

Stretton
Mill

2

A5

A5

The Bell Inn
(PH)

River Penk

Staffordshire Way

Shropshire Union Canal
Main Line

Horsebrook

Horsebrook
Hall

HORSEBROOK HALL LA

IVY HOUSE LA

Bell View
Farm

HORSEBROOK LA

Horse
Brook

Bungalow
Farm

1

Broom Hall
Farm

Horsebrook
Farm

Engleton
Hall

10

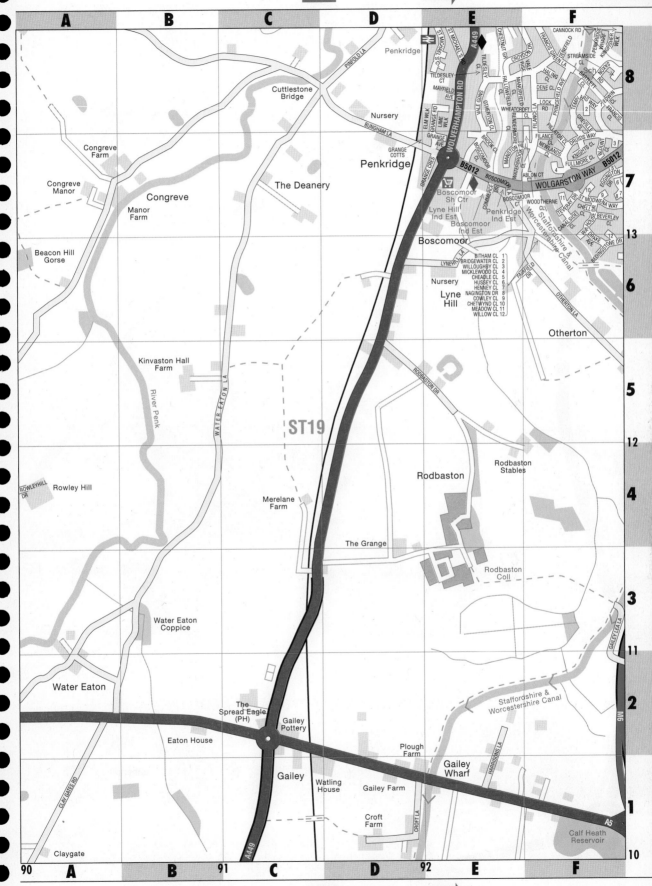

192
208

A B C D E F

8

7

13

6

5

12

4

3

11

2

1

10

Penkridge

Cuttlestone
Bridge

Nursery

Penkridge

Boscomoor
Sh Ctr

Lyne Hill
Ind Est

Boscomoor
Ind Est

Boscomoor

Lyne
Hill

Nursery

Congreve
Farm

Congreve
Manor

Congreve

Manor
Farm

The Deanery

Beacon Hill
Gorse

Kinvaston Hall
Farm

River Penk

ST19

Rowley Hill

Rowleyhill
Dr

Water Eaton
Coppice

Merelane
Farm

The Grange

Rodbaston

Rodbaston
Stables

Rodbaston
Coll

Otherton

Water Eaton

The Spread Eagle
(PH)

Eaton House

Gailey
Pottery

Gailey

Watling
House

Gailey Farm

Plough
Farm

Gailey
Wharf

Croft
Farm

Claygate

Clay Gates Rd

A449

Staffordshire &
Worcestershire Canal

M6

A5

Calf Heath
Reservoir

BITHAM CL   1
BRIDGEWATER CL 2
WILLOUGHBY CL   3
MICKLEWOOD CL   4
CHEADLE CL   5
HUSSEY CL   6
HENNEY CL   7
NAGINGTON DR   8
COWLEY CL   9
CHETWYND CL   10
MEADOW CL   11
WILLOW CL   12

WOLVERHAMPTON RD

B5012

B5012

WOLGARSTON WAY

Staffordshire &
Worcestershire Canal

Water Eaton La

Bungham La

Pinfold La

Grange Cres

Rodbaston Dr

Otherton La

Croft La

Gailey Lea La

Harrisons La

224
208

90   91   92

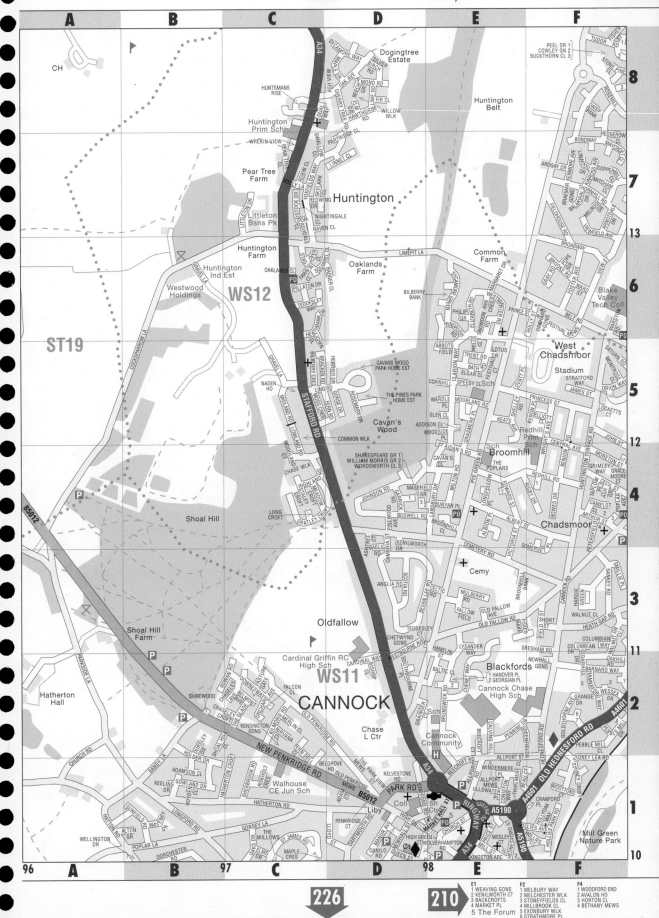

E1
1 WEAVING GDNS
2 KENILWORTH CT
3 BACKCROFTS
4 MARKET PL
5 The Forum

F2
1 MELBURY WAY
2 MELCHESTER WLK
3 STONEYFIELDS CL
4 MILLBROOK CL
5 EXONBURY WLK
6 STRATHMORE PL
7 HAWKESVILLE DR

F4
1 WOODFORD END
2 AVALON HO
3 HORTON CL
4 BETHANY MEWS

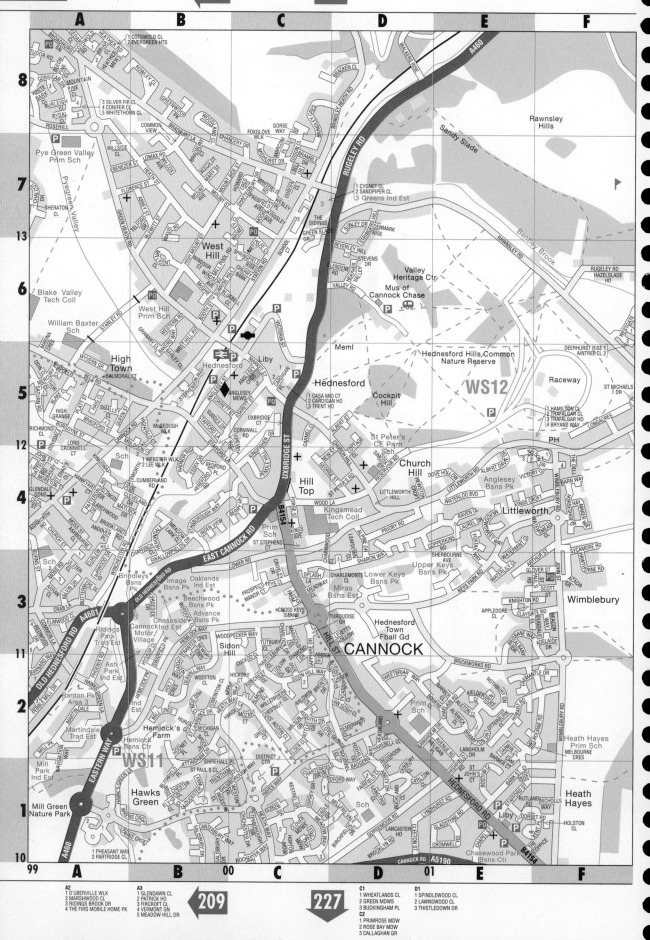

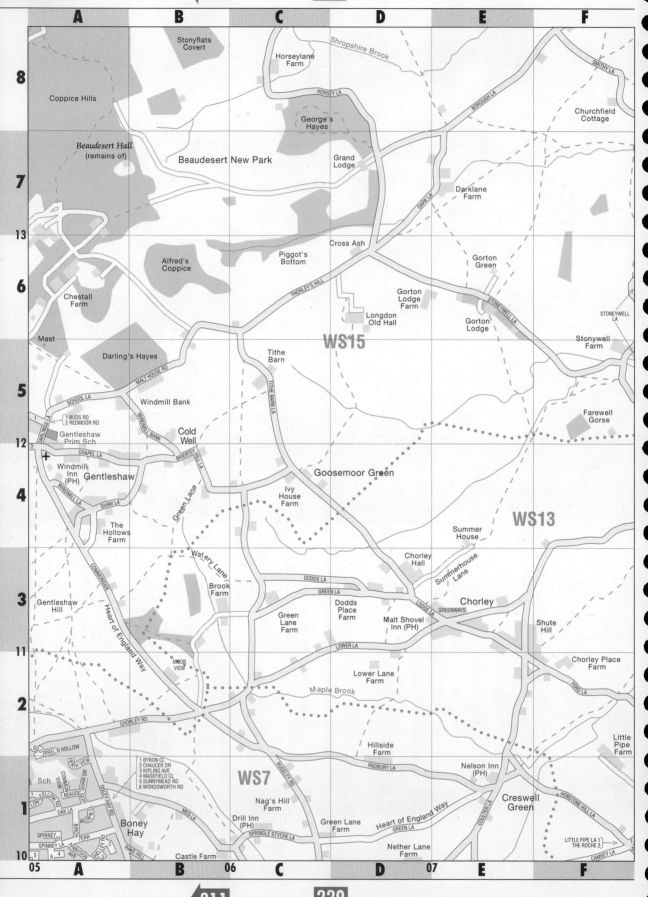

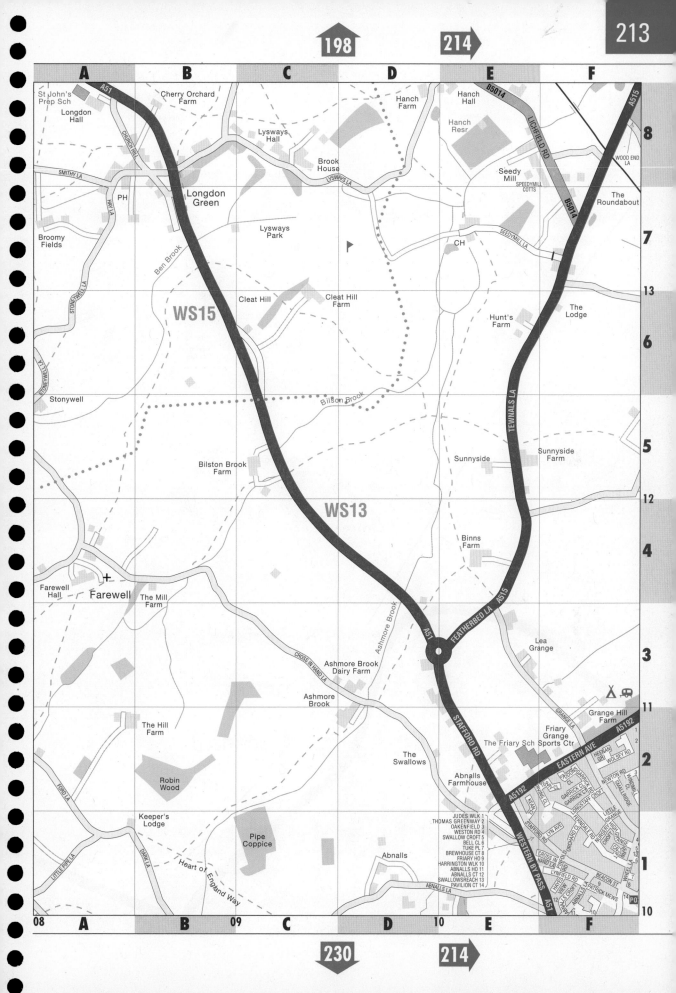

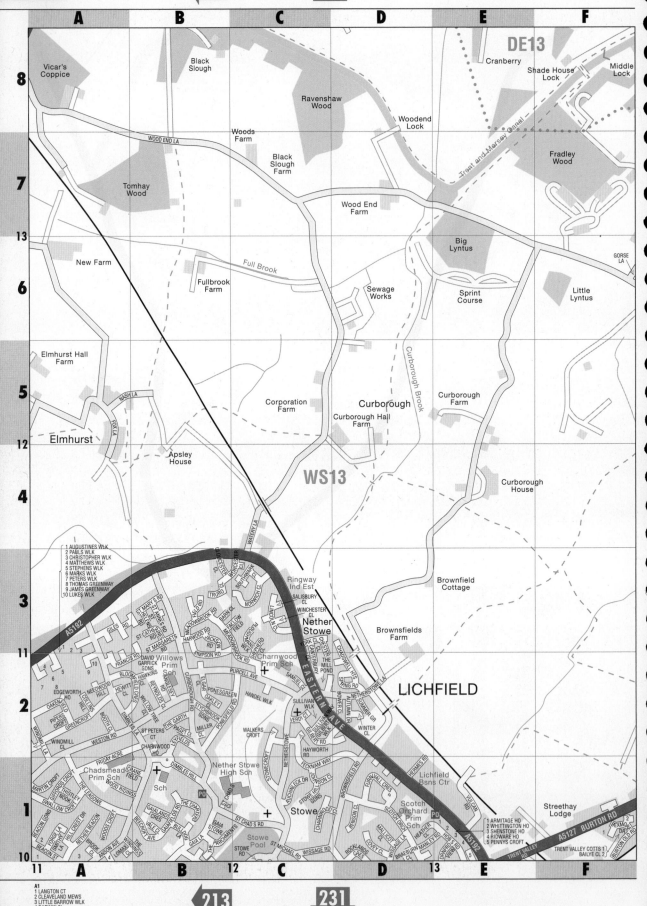

DE13

Cranberry

Shade House
Lock

Middle
Lock

Vicar's
Coppice

8

Black
Slough

Ravenshaw
Wood

Woodend
Lock

Fradley
Wood

WOOD END LA

Woods
Farm

Black
Slough
Farm

7

Tomhay
Wood

Trent and Marsey Canal

13

Wood End
Farm

Big
Lyntus

GORSE
LA

New Farm

Full Brook

6

Fullbrook
Farm

Sewage
Works

Sprint
Course

Little
Lyntus

Curborough Brook

Elmhurst Hall
Farm

5

Curborough
Farm

Curborough

MASH LA

Corporation
Farm

Curborough Hall
Farm

FOX LA

12

Elmhurst

Apsley
House

WS13

Curborough
House

4

Brownfield
Cottage

1 AUGUSTINES WLK
2 PAULS WLK
3 CHRISTOPHER WLK
4 MATTHEWS WLK
5 STEPHENS WLK
6 MARKS WLK
7 PETERS WLK
8 THOMAS GREENWAY
9 JAMES GREENWAY
10 LUKES WLK

WATERY LA

Ringway
Ind Est

Nether
Stowe

Brownsfields
Farm

3

SALISBURY
CL

WINCHESTER
CL

A5192

Charnwood Prim Sch

EASTERN AVE

LICHFIELD

David Willows
Prim Sch

11

THE
MILL
POND

Edgeworth
Ho

Handel Wlk

2

Hayworth
Rd

Nether Stowe
High Sch

Lichfield
Bsns Ctr

Chadsmead
Prim Sch

Sch

PO

1

Stowe

Scotch
Orchard
Prim Sch

1 ARMITAGE HO
2 WHITTINGTON HO
3 SHENSTONE HO
4 RIDWARE HO
5 PENNYS CROFT

Streethay
Lodge

A5127 BURTON RD

Stowe
Pool

PO

A5192

10

TRENT VALLEY
VIEW

TRENT VALLEY COTTS 1
BAILYE CL 2

A1
1 LANGTON CT
2 CLEAVELAND MEWS
3 LITTLE BARROW WLK
4 DARWIN CL

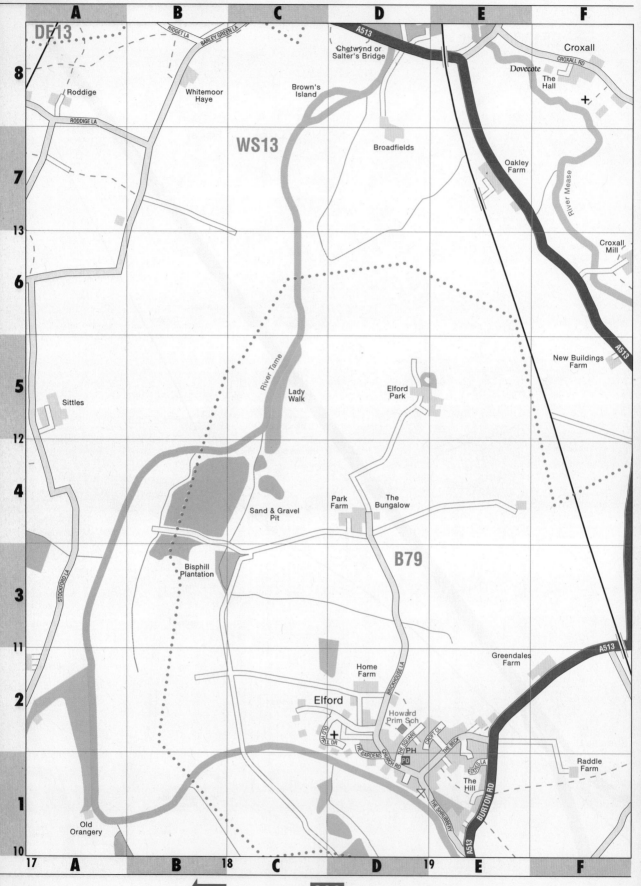

215
201

A B C D E F

DE13

8

Roddige

RIDGET LA

BARLEY GREEN LA

Whitemoor Haye

Chetwynd or
Salter's Bridge

A513

Croxall

CROXALL RD

Dovecote

The
Hall

Brown's
Island

WS13

7

RODDIGE LA

Broadfields

Oakley
Farm

River Mease

13

6

Croxall
Mill

River Tame

New Buildings
Farm

A513

5

Sittles

Lady
Walk

Elford
Park

12

STOCKFORD LA

4

Sand & Gravel
Pit

Park
Farm

The
Bungalow

B79

3

Bisphill
Plantation

11

Greendales
Farm

A513

2

Home
Farm

BRICKHOUSE LA

Elford

Howard
Prim Sch

THE BECK

CROFT CL

MILL DR

THE GARDENS

CHURCH RD

THE SQUARE

PH

PO

THE EDGES LA

Raddle
Farm

BURTON RD

The
Hill

1

Old
Orangery

THE SHRUBBERY

A513

10

17 A B 18 C D 19 E F

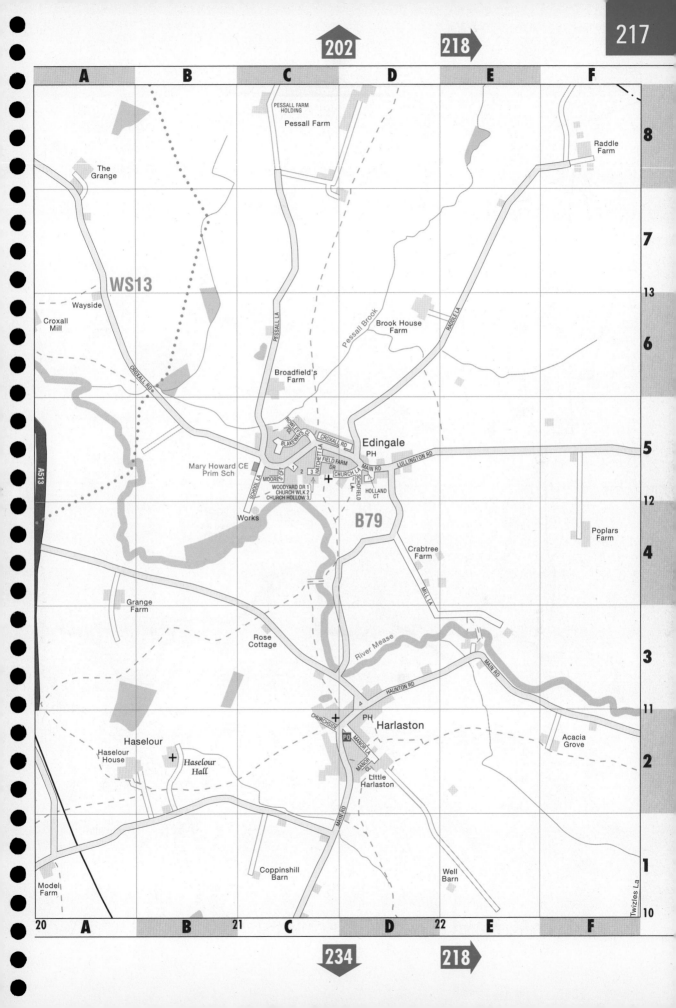

A B C D E F

8

7

13

6

5

12

4

3

11

2

1

10

The Grange

WS13

Wayside

Croxall Mill

PESSALL FARM HOLDING

Pessall Farm

CROXALL RD

PESSALL LA

Broadfield's Farm

Pessall Brook

Brook House Farm

RADDLE LA

Raddle Farm

A513

ROWLEYS CL
BLAKENALL

CROXALL RD

Edingale
PH

LULLINGTON RD

Mary Howard CE Prim Sch

SCHOOL LA

MOORE'S CFT

HATCHETT LA

FIELD FARM DR

CHURCH LA

MAIN RD

SCHOFIELD

HOLLAND CT

WOODYARD DR 1
CHURCH WLK 2
CHURCH HOLLOW 3

Works

B79

Crabtree Farm

MILL LA

Poplars Farm

Grange Farm

Rose Cottage

River Mease

HAUNTON RD

MAIN RD

Haselour

Haselour House

Haselour Hall

CHURCHSIDE

PH

Harlaston

PO

MANOR LA

MANOR CL

Acacia Grove

Little Harlaston

MAIN RD

Coppinshill Barn

Well Barn

Model Farm

Twizles La

217

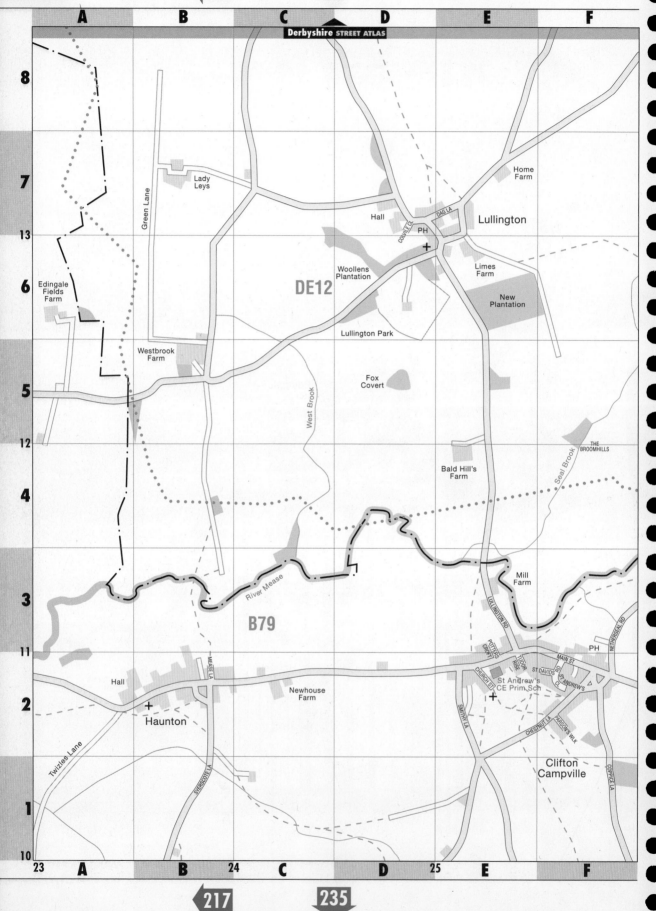

Derbyshire STREET ATLAS

Home Farm

Lady Leys

Green Lane

Hall

DAG LA

COLVILE CL

PH

Lullington

DE12

Woollens Plantation

Limes Farm

New Plantation

Edingale Fields Farm

Lullington Park

Westbrook Farm

Fox Covert

West Brook

THE BROOMHILLS

Seal Brook

Bald Hill's Farm

River Mease

Mill Farm

B79

LULLINGTON RD

NETHERSEAL RD

POTTERS CROFT

PH

TUDOR RISE

MAIN ST

ST DAVIDS

ST ANDREW'S

CHURCH ST

MEASE LA

Hall

Newhouse Farm

St Andrew's CE Prim Sch

Haunton

SMITH LA

CHESTNUT LA

PARSON'S WLK

COPPICE LA

Clifton Campville

Twizles Lane

STERSCOTE LA

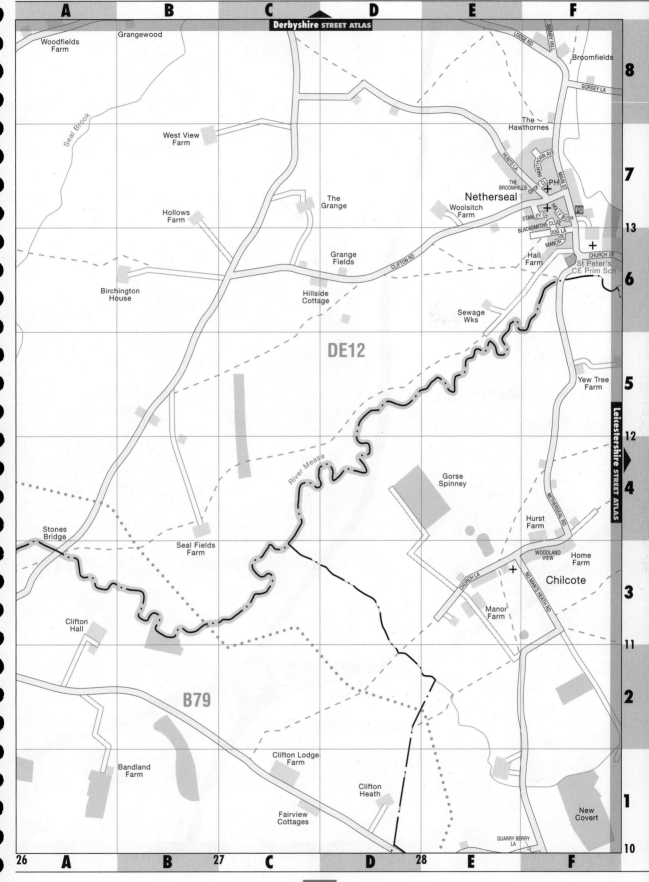

Derbyshire STREET ATLAS

Woodfields Farm

Grangewood

Broomfields

LODGE RD

GUNBY HILL

GORSEY LA

The Hawthornes

West View Farm

HUNTS LA

HAWTHORN AVE

THE BROOMHILLS

MAIN ST

CROFT CL

PH

Netherseal

Hollows Farm

The Grange

Woolsitch Farm

HOLLY BUSH

PO

STANLEY CL

13

BLACKSMITHS CL

DOG LA

MANOR

Grange Fields

CLIFTON RD

Hall Farm

CHURCH ST

St Peter's CE Prim Sch

6

Birchington House

Hillside Cottage

Sewage Wks

DE12

Yew Tree Farm

5

12

River Mease

Gorse Spinney

4

NETHERSEAL RD

Hurst Farm

Stones Bridge

Seal Fields Farm

WOODLAND VIEW

Home Farm

Clifton Hall

CHURCH LA

Chilcote

NO MAN'S HEATH RD

11

Manor Farm

B79

Bandland Farm

Clifton Lodge Farm

2

Clifton Heath

New Covert

1

Fairview Cottages

QUARRY BERRY LA

10

Seal Brook

Leicestershire STREET ATLAS

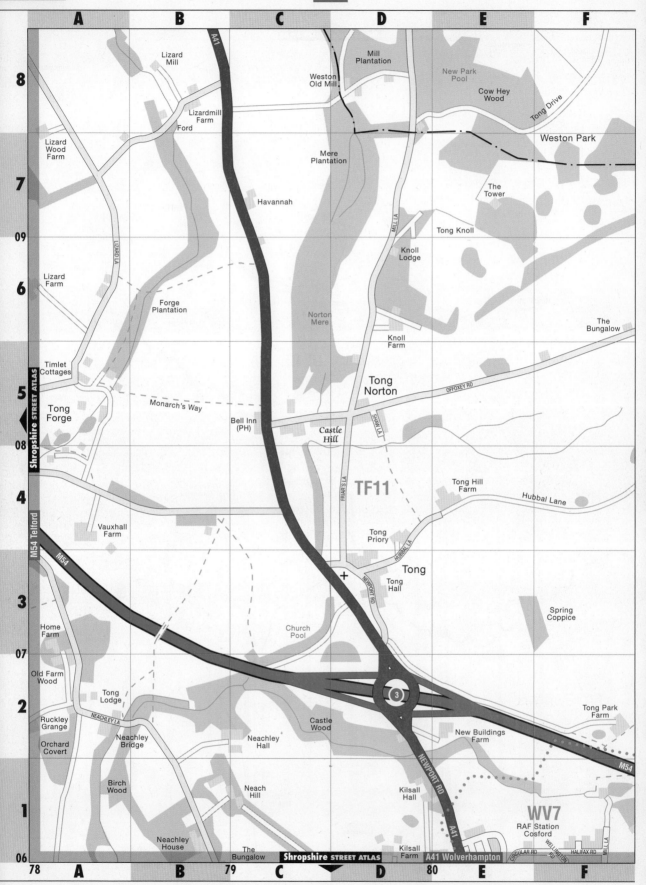

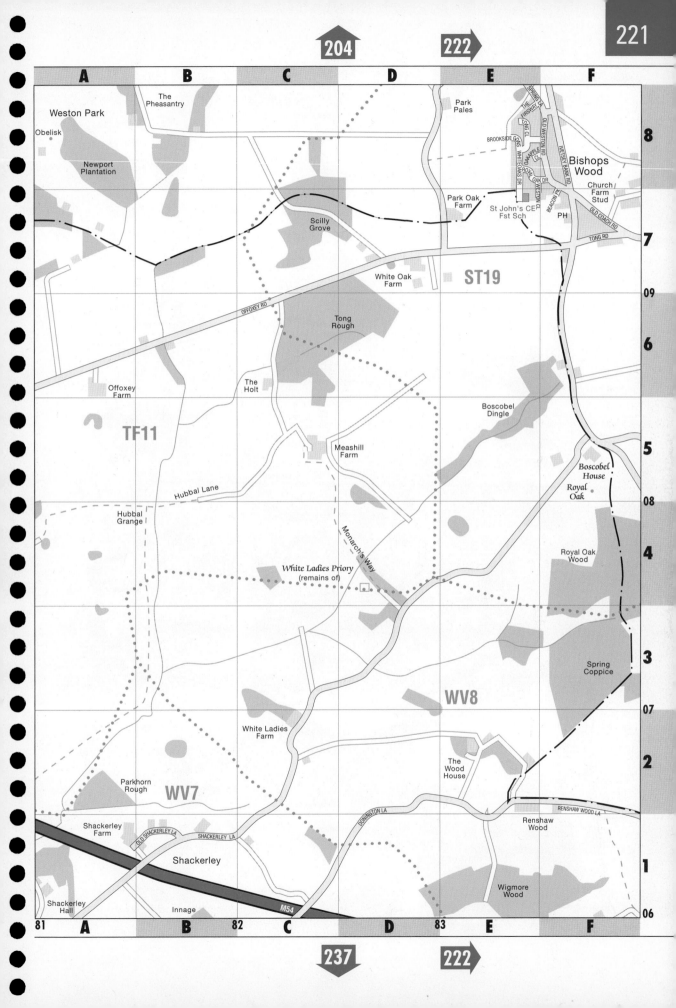

221
205

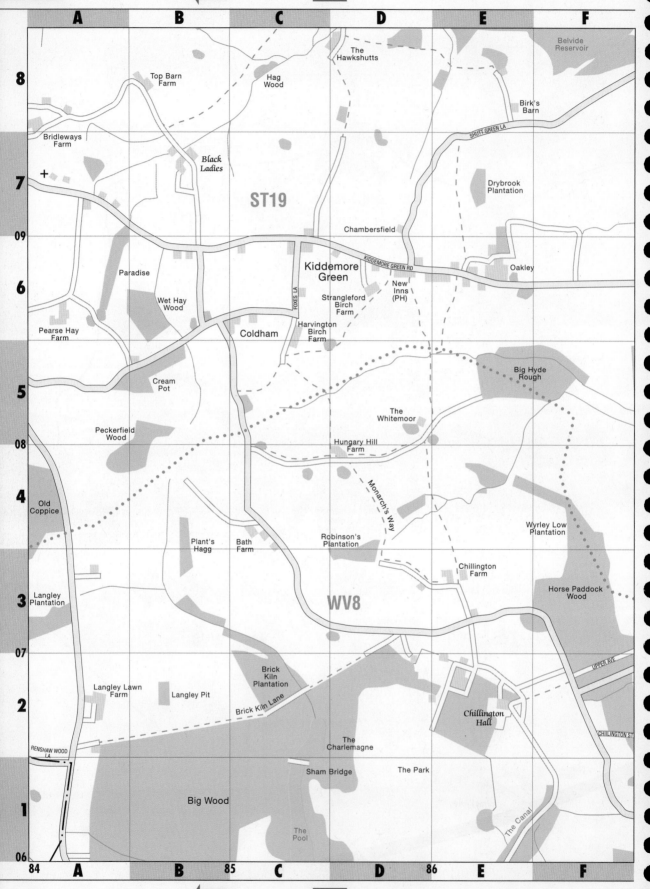

Belvide Reservoir

Top Barn Farm

Hag Wood

The Hawkshutts

Birk's Barn

SHUTT GREEN LA

Bridleways Farm

Black Ladies

ST19

Drybrook Plantation

Chambersfield

Paradise

Kiddemore Green

KIDDEMORE GREEN RD

Oakley

Wet Hay Wood

FOXES LA

Strangleford Birch Farm

New Inns (PH)

Pearse Hay Farm

Coldham

Harvington Birch Farm

Cream Pot

Big Hyde Rough

Peckerfield Wood

The Whitemoor

Hungary Hill Farm

Old Coppice

Monarch's Way

Plant's Hagg

Bath Farm

Robinson's Plantation

Wyrley Low Plantation

Chillington Farm

Horse Paddock Wood

Langley Plantation

WV8

Langley Lawn Farm

Langley Pit

Brick Kiln Plantation

Brick Kiln Lane

UPPER AVE

Chillington Hall

CHILLINGTON ST

RENSHAW WOOD LA

The Charlemagne

Sham Bridge

The Park

Big Wood

The Pool

The Canal

84   85   86

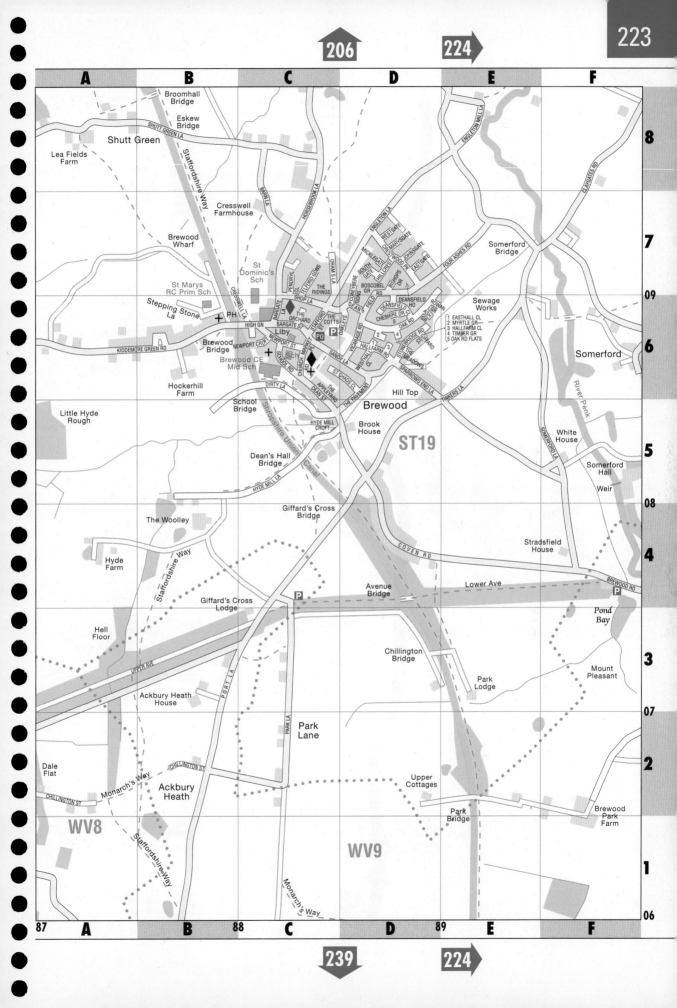

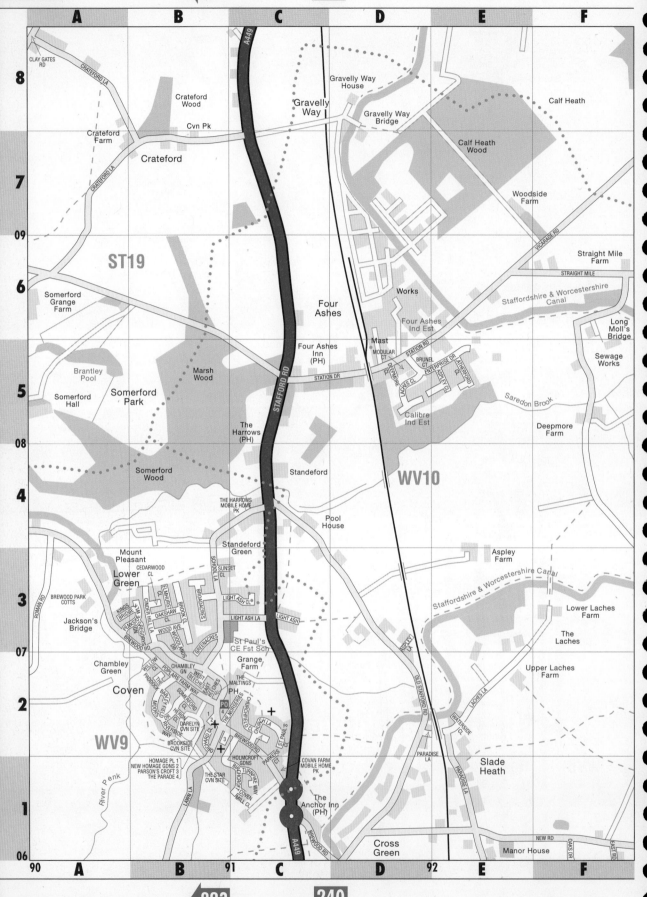

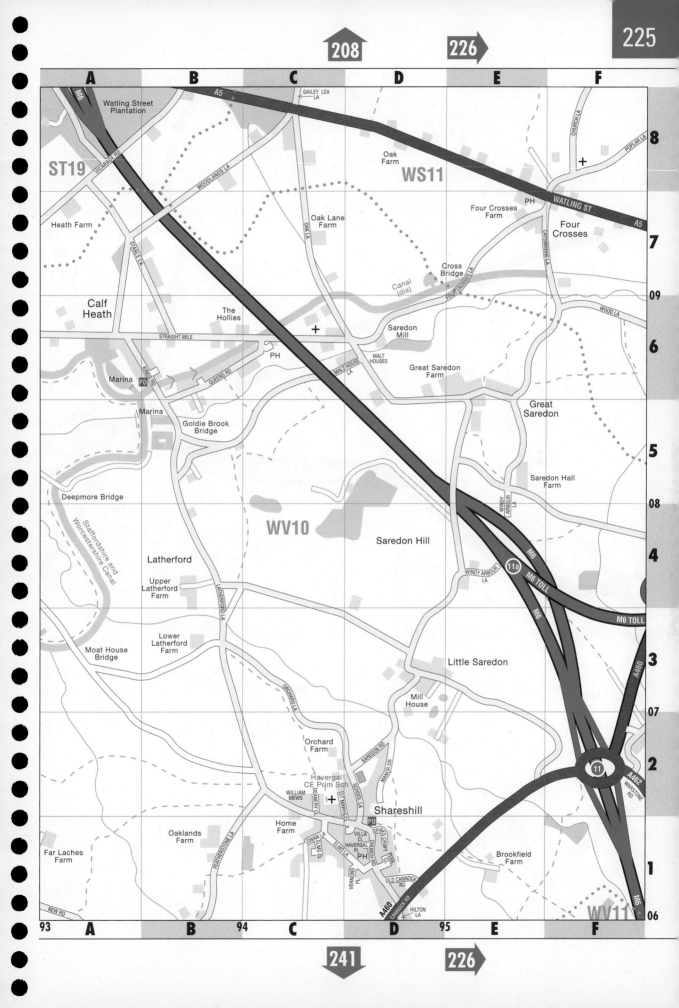

E8
1 BACKCROFTS
2 HALLCOURT CRES
3 HALLCOURT CL
4 CAXTON CT
5 FAIRMOUNT DR
6 NEW ST

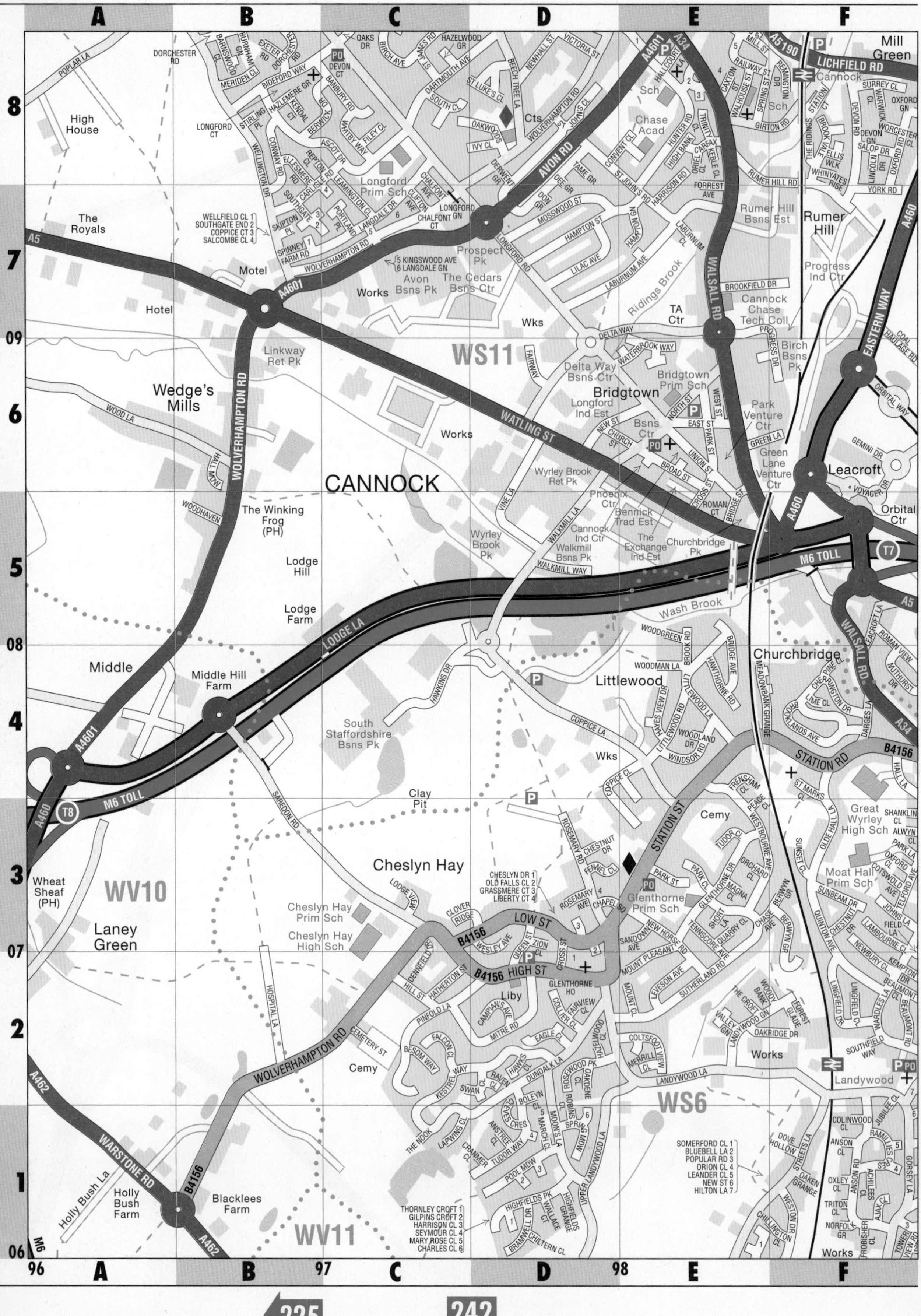

A B C D E F

CANNOCK

WS11

Bridgtown

WV10

Cheslyn Hay

Littlewood

Churchbridge

Leacroft

Rumer Hill

Mill Green

WS6

WV11

Wedge's Mills

Laney Green

Landywood

High House

The Royals

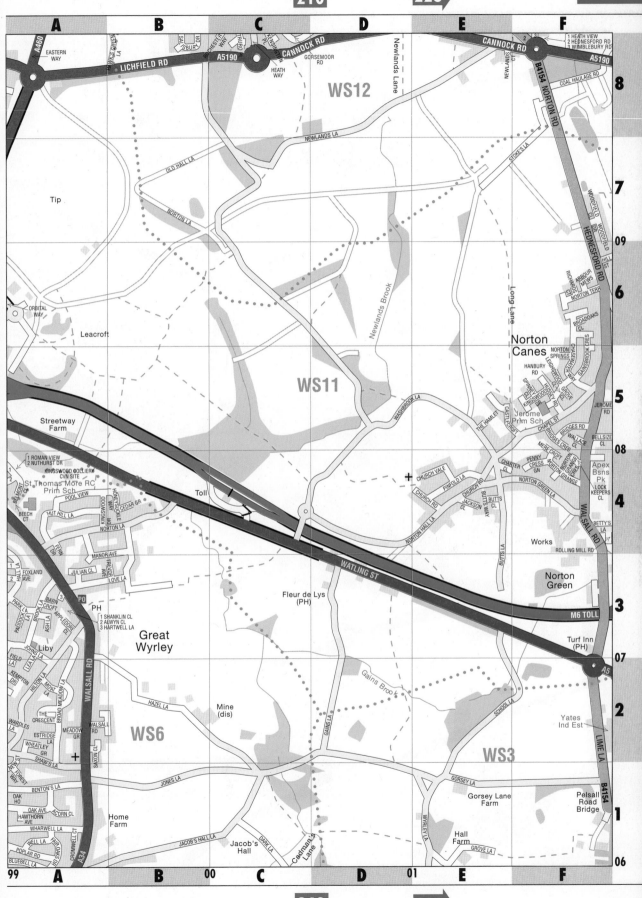

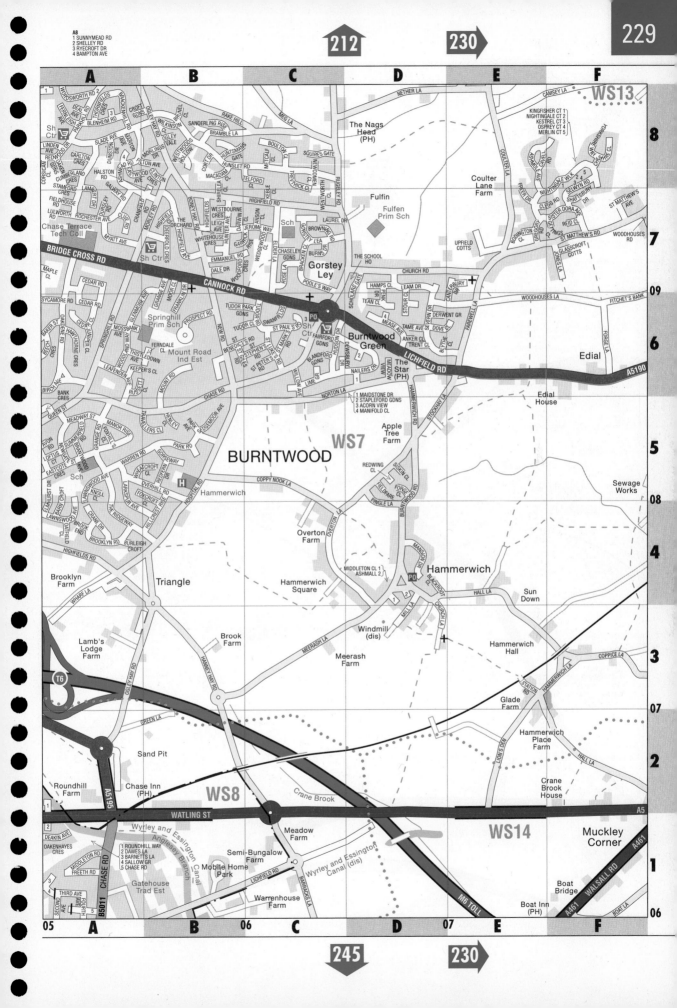

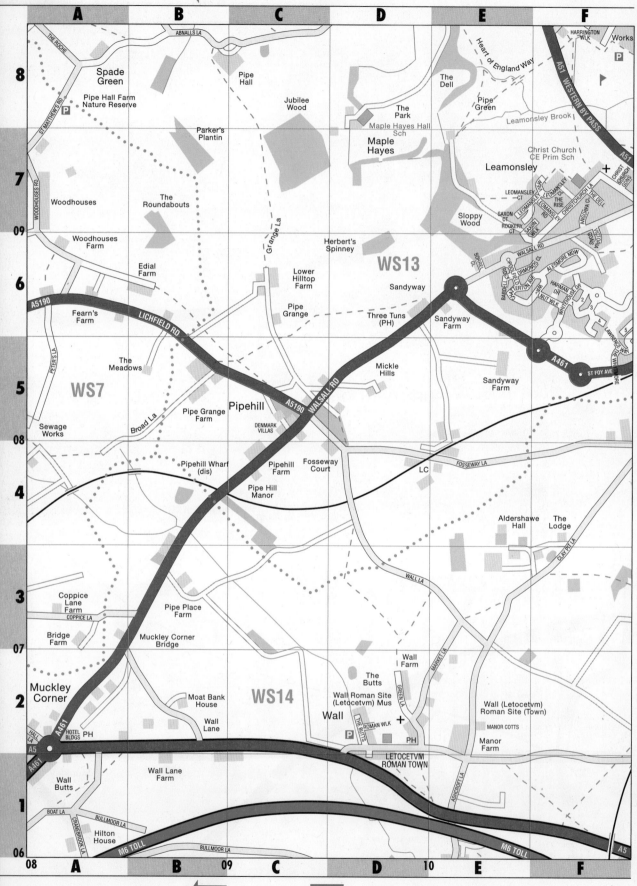

F6
1 BROADBENT CL
2 CATERBANCK WAY
3 COLLINS DR
4 MADDOCKE WLK
5 ALLINGTON AVE

HARRINGTON WLK
Works

THE ROCHE

ST MATTHEW'S RD

Spade Green

Pipe Hall Farm Nature Reserve

ABNALLS LA

Pipe Hall

Jubilee Wood

The Dell

Heart of England Way

Leamonsley Brook

A51 WESTERN BY PASS

A51

The Park

Maple Hayes Hall Sch

Pipe Green

Christ Church CE Prim Sch

CHRIST CHURCH GDNS

WOODHOUSES RD

Woodhouses

The Roundabouts

Parker's Plantin

Maple Hayes

Leamonsley

LEOMANSLEY CT
LEOMANSLEY RD
THE RISE
CHRISTCHURCH LA
THE DELL
ANGORFA CL
VICTORIA GDNS

Woodhouses Farm

Grange La

Herbert's Spinney

WS13

Sloppy Wood

SAXON CT
ROOKERY CT
SAXON WALK

WALSALL RD

Edial Farm

Lower Hilltop Farm

Sandyway

SORREL CL

ORMONDS CL
BARDELL CL
SHAW CL
LATERTON AVE

ALESMORE MDW

HARMAN DR

CHESTNUT WLK

A5190

Fearn's Farm

LICHFIELD RD

Pipe Grange

Three Tuns (PH)

Sandyway Farm

WHITEHORSE DR
LAWRENCE WAY
THE WHITMORE

A461

PETER'S LA

The Meadows

Pipehill

A5190

WALSALL RD

Mickle Hills

Sandyway Farm

ST FOY AVE

WS7

Broad La

Pipe Grange Farm

DENMARK VILLAS

Sewage Works

Pipehill Wharf (dis)

Pipehill Farm

Fosseway Court

LC

FOSSEWAY LA

Pipe Hill Manor

Aldershawe Hall

The Lodge

CLAY PIT LA

Coppice Lane Farm

Pipe Place Farm

Wall La

COPPICE LA

Bridge Farm

Muckley Corner Bridge

Wall Farm

MARKET LA

Muckley Corner

Moat Bank House

WS14

Wall Roman Site (Letocetvm) Mus

The Butts

Wall

Wall (Letocetvm) Roman Site (Town)

GREEN LA

MANOR COTTS

HALL LA

A461

A5

HOTEL BLDGS

PH

Wall Lane

ROMAN WLK
THE BUTTS

PH

Manor Farm

Wall Butts

Wall Lane Farm

LETOCETVM ROMAN TOWN

ASHCROFT LA

BOAT LA

BULLMOOR LA

Hilton House

M6 TOLL

BULLMOOR LA

M6 TOLL

A5

CRANEBROOK LA
A461

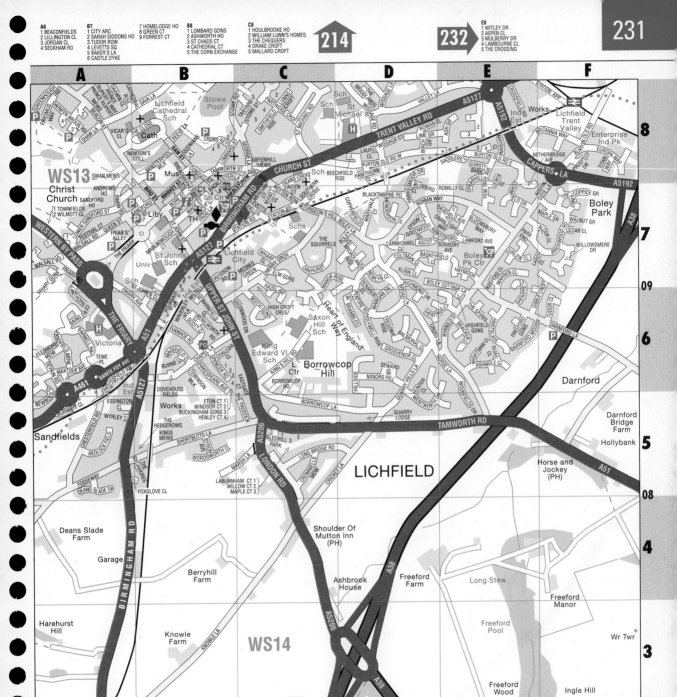

A8
1 BEACONFIELDS
2 LILLINGTON CL
3 JORDAN CL
4 SECKHAM RD

B7
1 CITY ARC
2 SARAH SIDDONS HO
3 TUDOR ROW
4 LEVETTS SQ
5 BAKER'S LA
6 CASTLE DYKE

B8
1 LOMBARD GDNS
2 ASHWORTH HO
3 ST CHADS CT
4 CATHEDRAL CT
5 THE CORN EXCHANGE

C8
1 HOULBROOKE HO
2 WILLIAM LUNN'S HOMES
3 THE CHEQUERS
4 DRAKE CROFT
5 MALLARD CROFT

7 HOMELODGE HO
8 GREEN CT
9 FORREST CT

E8
1 WITLEY DR
2 ASPEN CL
3 MULBERRY DR
4 LAMBOURNE CL
5 THE CROSSING

214

232

247

232

231
215

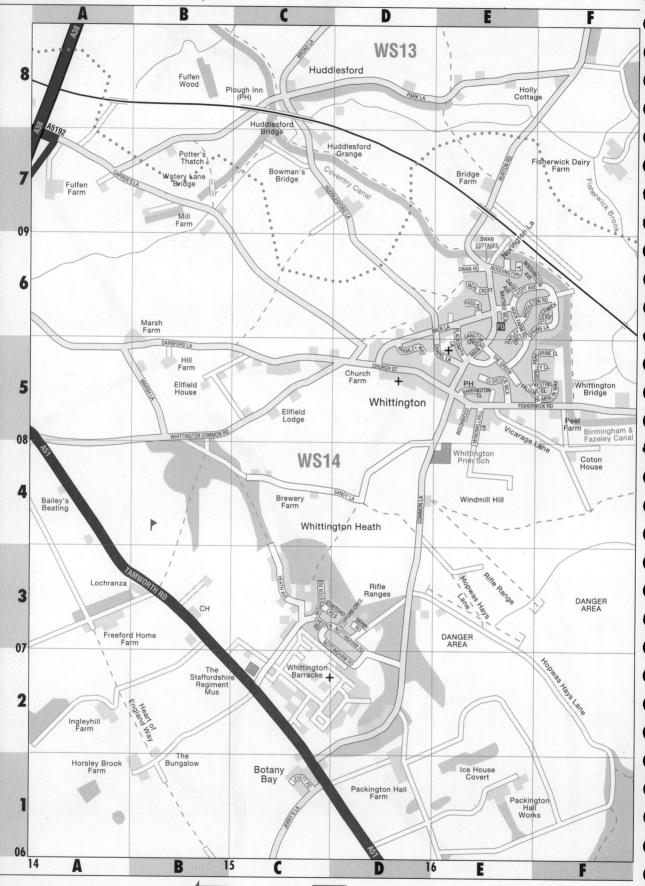

231
248

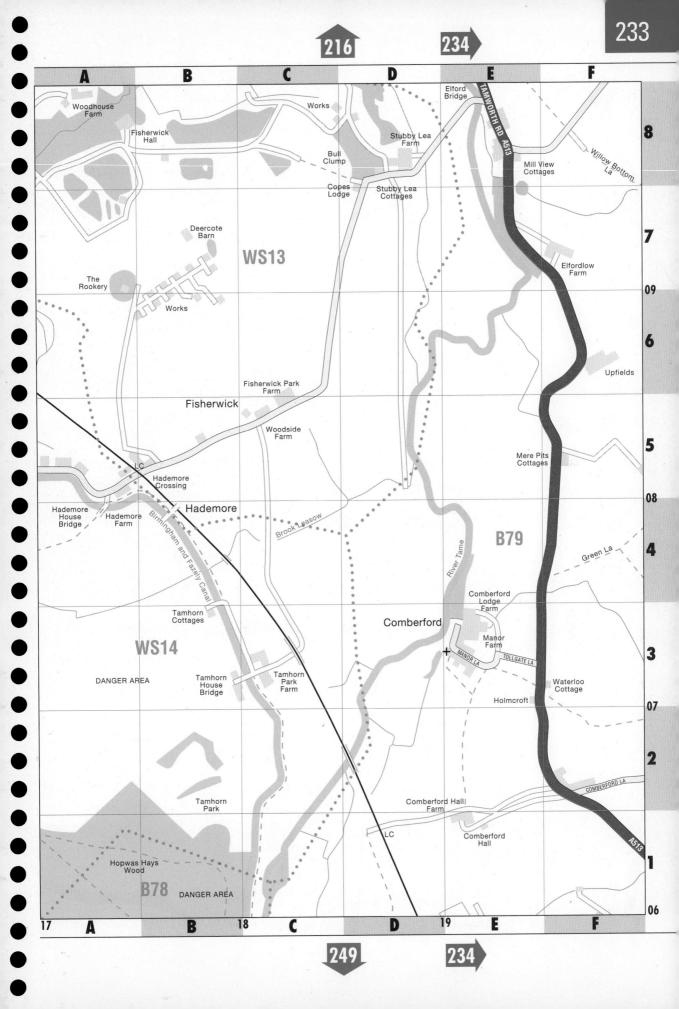

233 217

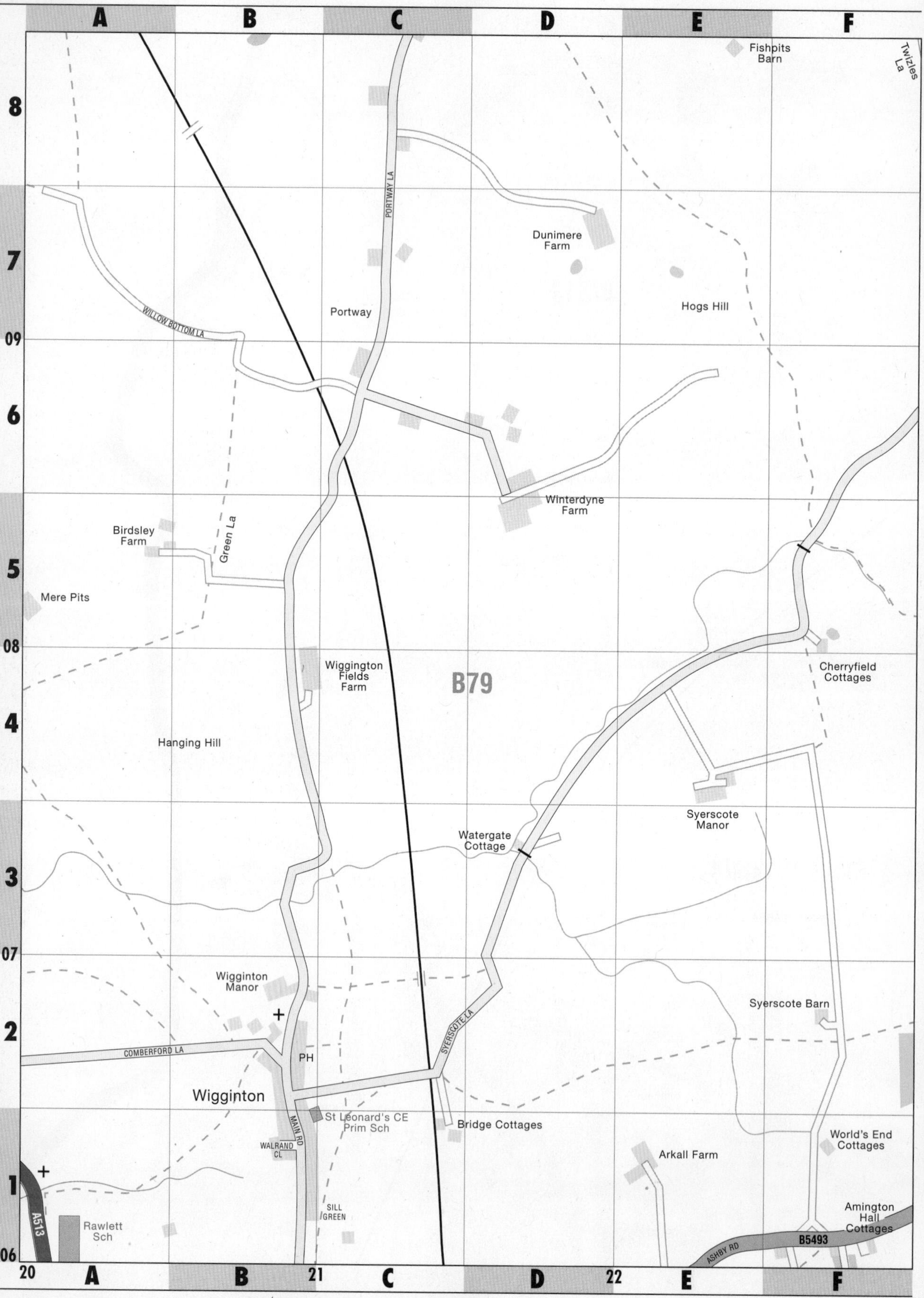

A B C D E F

8
7
09
6
5
08
4
3
07
2
1
06
20 A B 21 C D 22 E F

233 250

Twizles La
Fishpits Barn
Dunimere Farm
Hogs Hill
WILLOW BOTTOM LA
Portway
PORTWAY LA
Winterdyne Farm
Birdsley Farm
Green La
Mere Pits
Wiggington Fields Farm
B79
Cherryfield Cottages
Hanging Hill
Syerscote Manor
Watergate Cottage
Wigginton Manor
Syerscote Barn
SYERSCOTE LA
COMBERFORD LA
PH
Wigginton
MAIN RD
St Leonard's CE Prim Sch
Bridge Cottages
World's End Cottages
Arkall Farm
WALRAND CL
A513
Rawlett Sch
SILL GREEN
Amington Hall Cottages
ASHBY RD
B5493

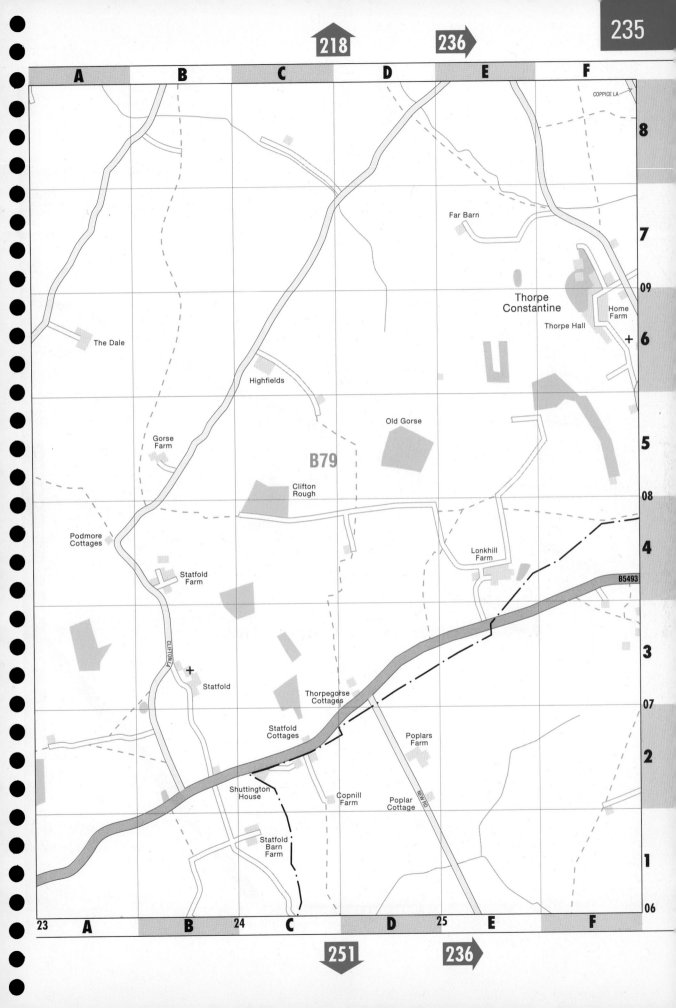

A B C D E F

8

COPPICE LA

Far Barn

7

Thorpe
Constantine

09

Home
Farm

Thorpe Hall

The Dale

+ 6

Highfields

Old Gorse

Gorse
Farm

B79

5

Clifton
Rough

08

Podmore
Cottages

Lonkhill
Farm

4

B5493

Statfold
Farm

CLIFTON

3

+

Statfold

Thorpegorse
Cottages

07

Statfold
Cottages

Poplars
Farm

2

NEW RD

Shuttington
House

Copnill
Farm

Poplar
Cottage

Statfold
Barn
Farm

1

06

23 A B 24 C D 25 E F

235
219

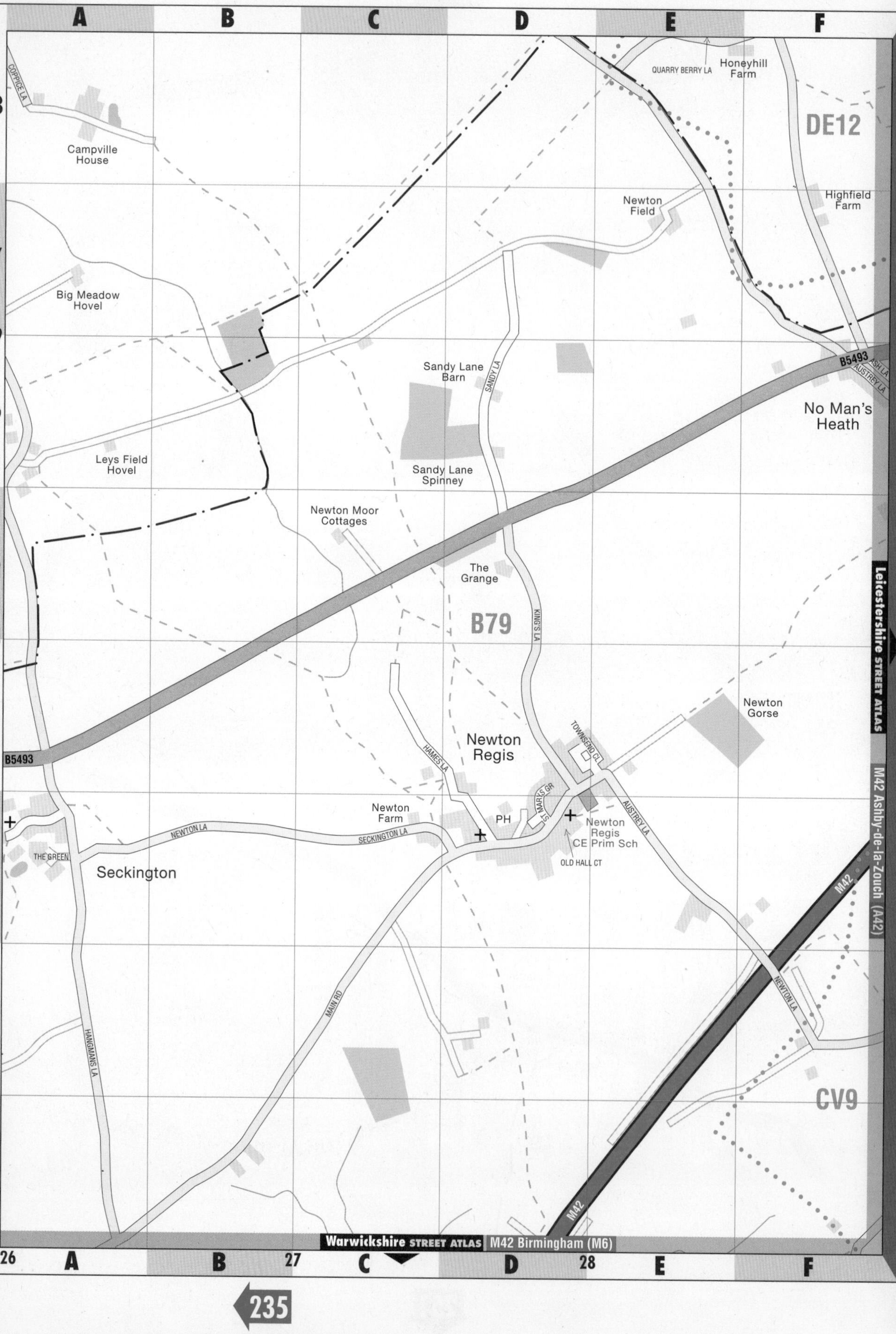

A **B** **C** **D** **E** **F**

DE12

8

Campville
House

Quarry Berry La

Honeyhill
Farm

Newton
Field

Highfield
Farm

7

Big Meadow
Hovel

09

B5493

No Man's
Heath

Sandy Lane
Barn

6

Leys Field
Hovel

Sandy Lane
Spinney

Newton Moor
Cottages

5

The
Grange

B79

08

4

Newton
Gorse

Newton
Regis

Newton
Farm

PH

Newton Regis
CE Prim Sch

OLD HALL CT

3

THE GREEN

Seckington

NEWTON LA

SECKINGTON LA

07

M42

2

HANGMANS LA

MAIN RD

NEWTON LA

CV9

1

06

26 **A** 27 **B** **C** 28 **D** **E** **F**

235

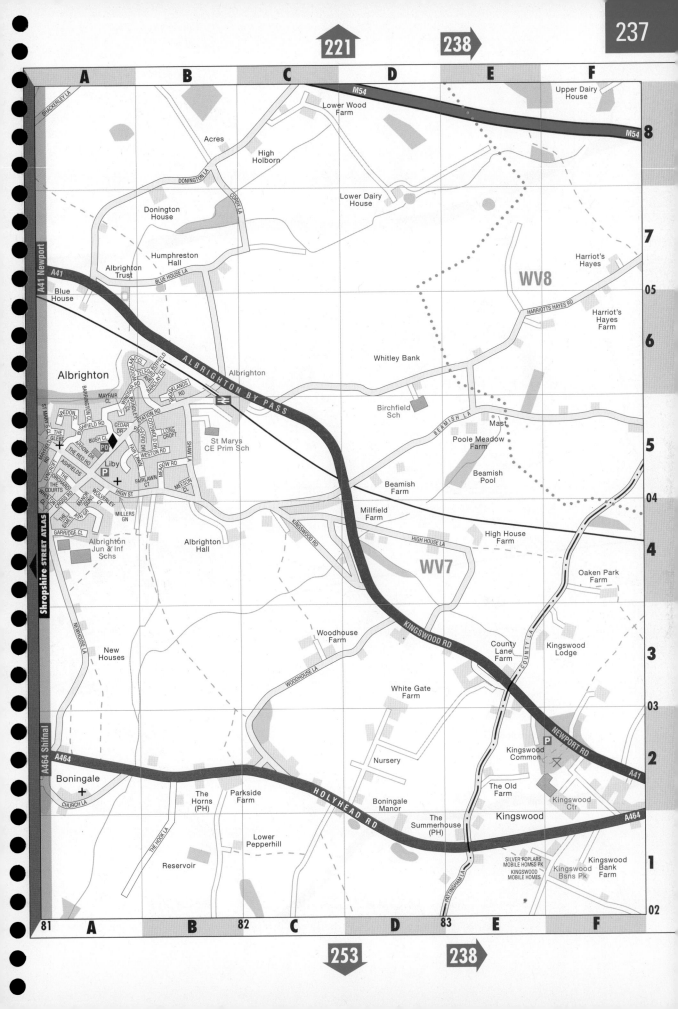

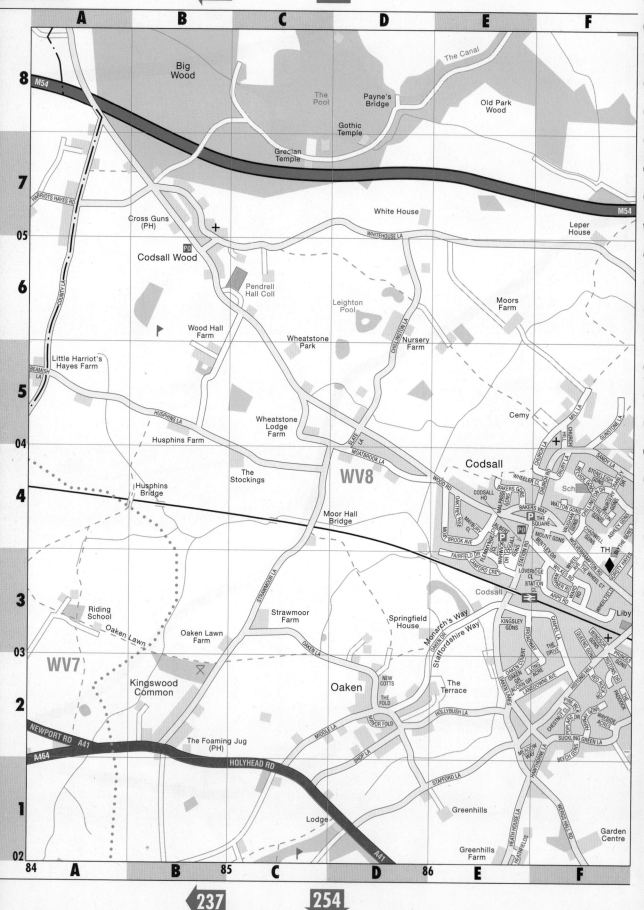

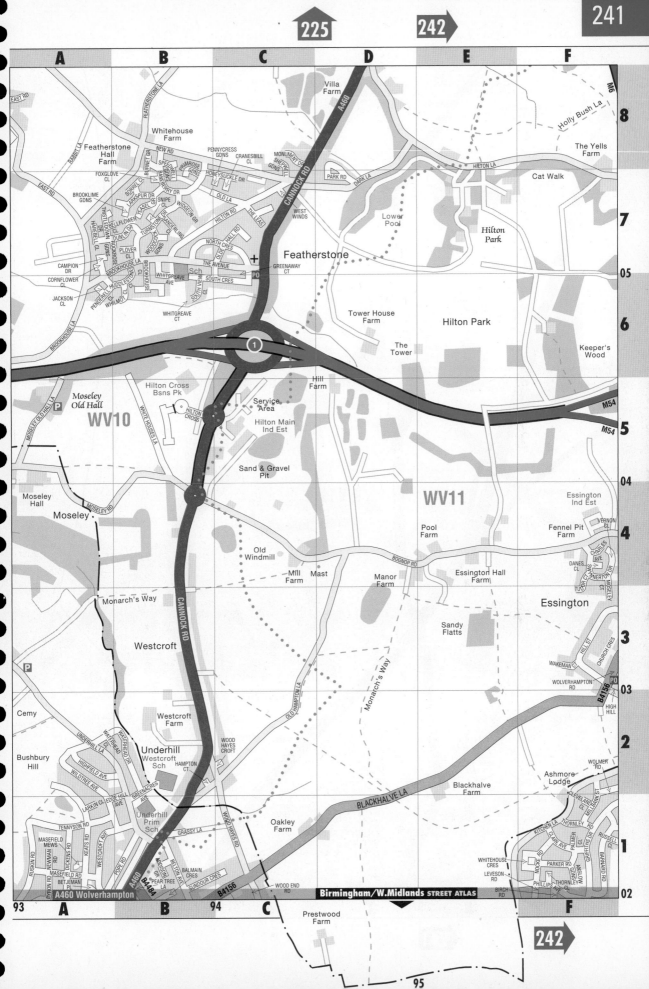

225

242

M6

8

Holly Bush La

The Yells Farm

EAST RD

Villa Farm

Whitehouse Farm

A460

Cat Walk

Featherstone Hall Farm

NEW RD

PENNYCRESS GDNS

CRANESBILL CL

MONUMENT DR

SHEPWELL GDNS

HILTON LA

PARK RD

DARK LA

FOXGLOVE CL

BURNET GR

PRIMROSE DR

SPEEDWELL

BANKSFRY DR

HONEYSUCKLE DR

OLD LA

WEST WINDS

Lower Pool

Hilton Park

7

SOHWEL CL

LARKSPUR DR

TEASEL

SNIPE

WIDGEON GR

THE LEASS

HILTON RD

BROOKLIME GDNS

HAREBELL CL

THISTLEDOWN

WOODCOCK

TURNSTONE

SANDERLING

WOODCOCK GDNS

NORTH CRES

OLDE HALL RD

Featherstone

05

CAMPION DR

PLOVER CL

BROOKHOUSE LA

BELLFLOWER CL

THE AVENUE

Sch

GREENAWAY CT

Tower House Farm

Hilton Park

6

CORNFLOWER CL

PENDEREL

HUDDLESTON

WHIMOT

SOUTH VIEW

WHITGREAVE AVE

SOUTH CRES

PO

The Tower

JACKSON CL

BROOKHOUSE LA

WHITGREAVE CT

Hill Farm

Keeper's Wood

Moseley Old Hall

P

Hilton Cross Bsns Pk

HILTON CROSS

Service Area

1

M54

M54

WV10

WHITE HOUSES LA

Hilton Main Ind Est

5

MOSELEY OLD HALL LA

Sand & Gravel Pit

04

Moseley Hall

MOSELEY RD

WV11

Essington Ind Est

Moseley

Pool Farm

Fennel Pit Farm

VERNON CL

4

Old Windmill

Mill Farm

Mast

Manor Farm

Essington Hall Farm

DANES CL

CHARLES AVE

TUCK OAKS

GLYNERTON DR

MOSELEY

Monarch's Way

BOGNOP RD

Essington

P

Sandy Flatts

HILL ST

CHURCH CRES

3

CANNOCK RD

Westcroft

Monarch's Way

WAKEMAN

WOLVERHAMPTON RD

B4156

PO

HIGH HILL

Cemy

OLD HAMPTON LA

03

Westcroft Farm

WOOD HAYES CROFT

HAMPTON CT

Ashmore Lodge

WOLMER RD

2

Bushbury Hill

UNDERHILL LA

WATERGLADE

WATERHEAD DR

HIGHFIELD AVE

WILDTREE AVE

Underhill

Westcroft Sch

BLACKHALVE LA

Blackhalve Farm

CLEVELAND

MILLBANKS ST

LARKIN CL

EDGE HILL AVE

GREENACRES AVE

GRASSY LA

Underhill Prim Sch

Oakley Farm

KITCHEN LA

CLARE AVE

THORNLEY

PALMER

THORNLEY DR

GRIFFITHS DR

RUSSELL CL

BARNARD RD

1

MASEFIELD MEWS

NEWMAN RD

DICKENS RD

KEATS RD

WESTCROFT AVE

POPE RD

PEAR TREE LA

BELTON AVE

BALMAIN CRES

SUNDOUR CRES

WOOD HAYES RD

WHITEHOUSE CRES

NOOKE

PARKER RD

ANGLOW

GONG

RUSKIN RD

BYRON RD

MASEFIELD RD

BETJEMAN PL

A460

B484

ADDISON GR

B4156

WOOD END RD

LEVESON RD

PHILLIPS AVE

BIRCH RD

02

Prestwood Farm

242

95

TENNYSON AVE

WILDTREE AVE

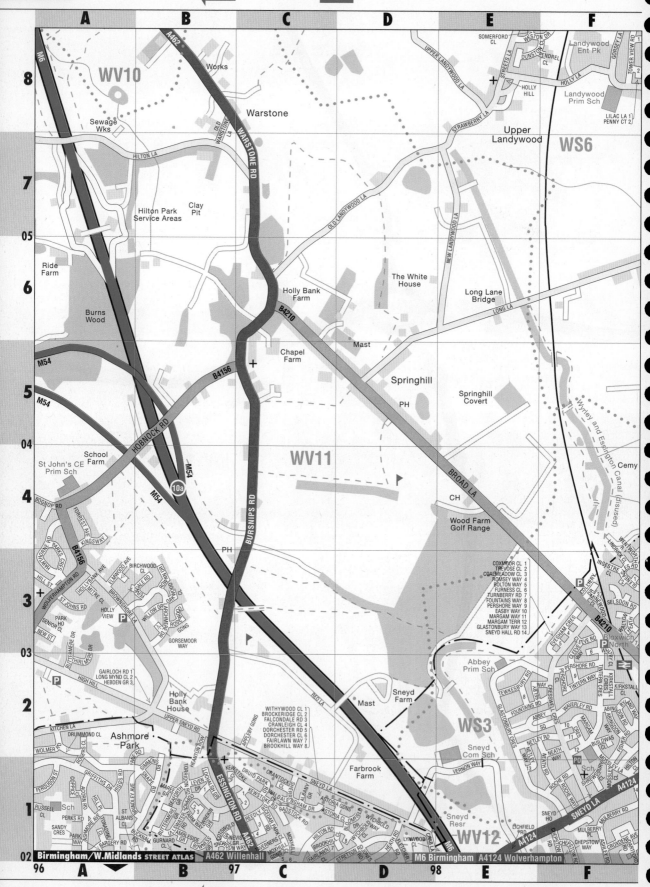

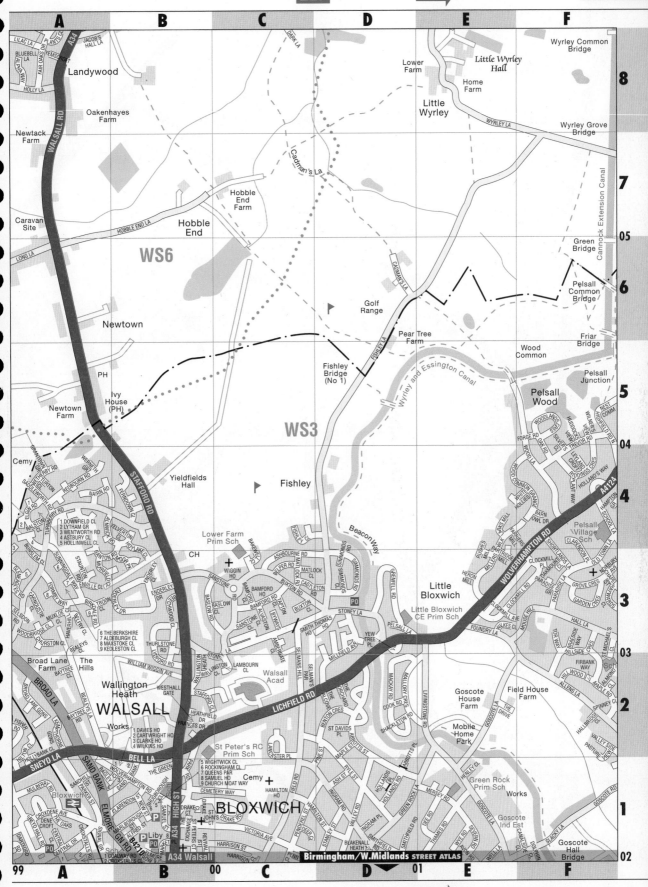

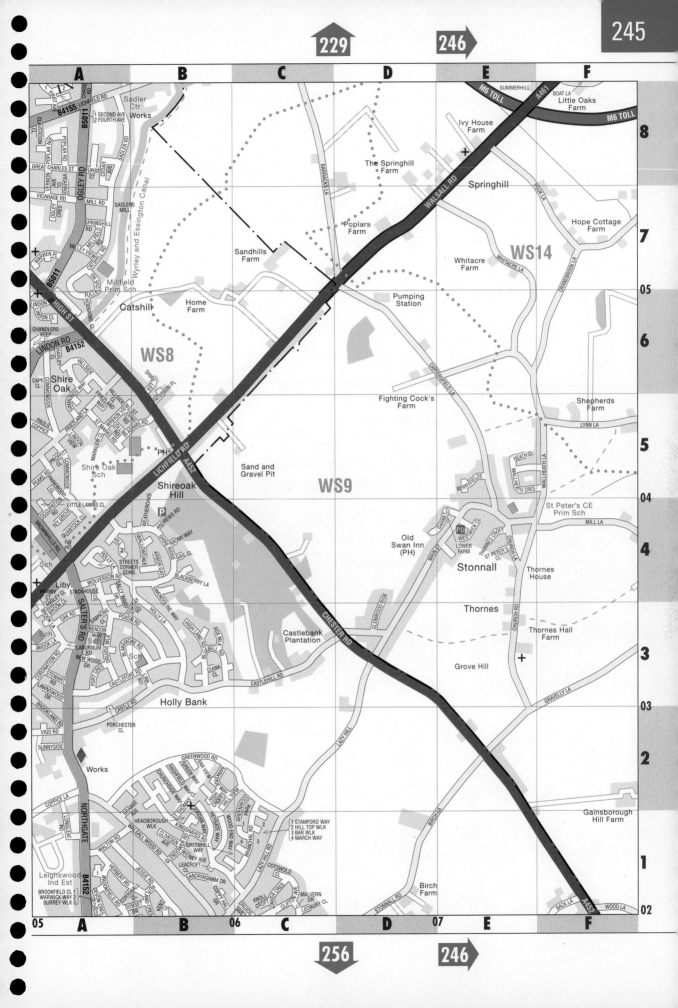

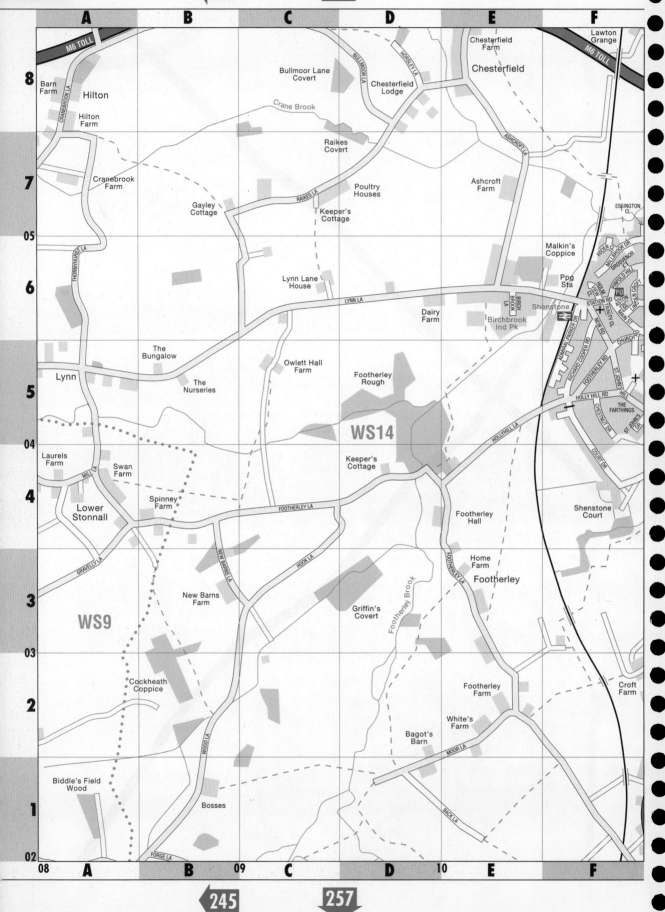

245
230
245
257

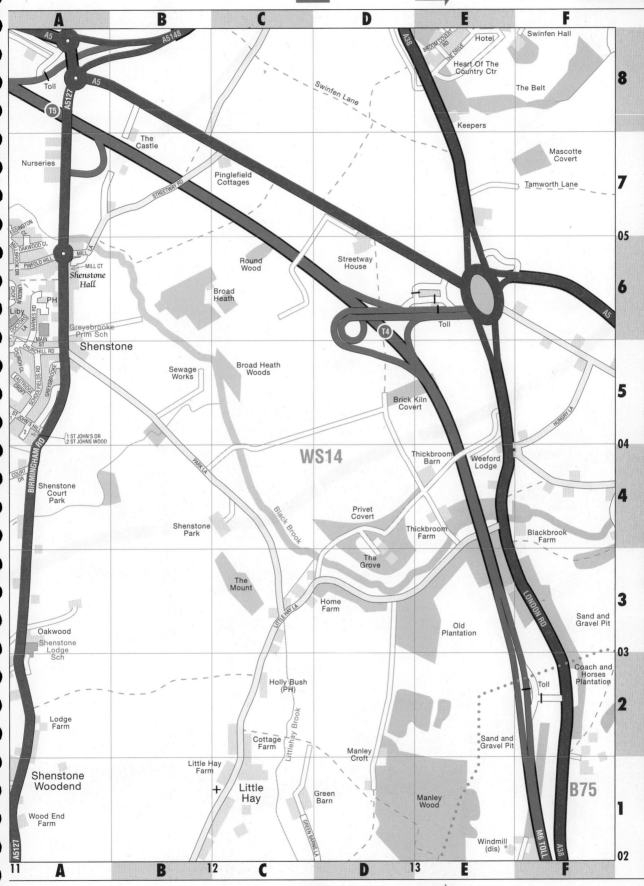

231
248

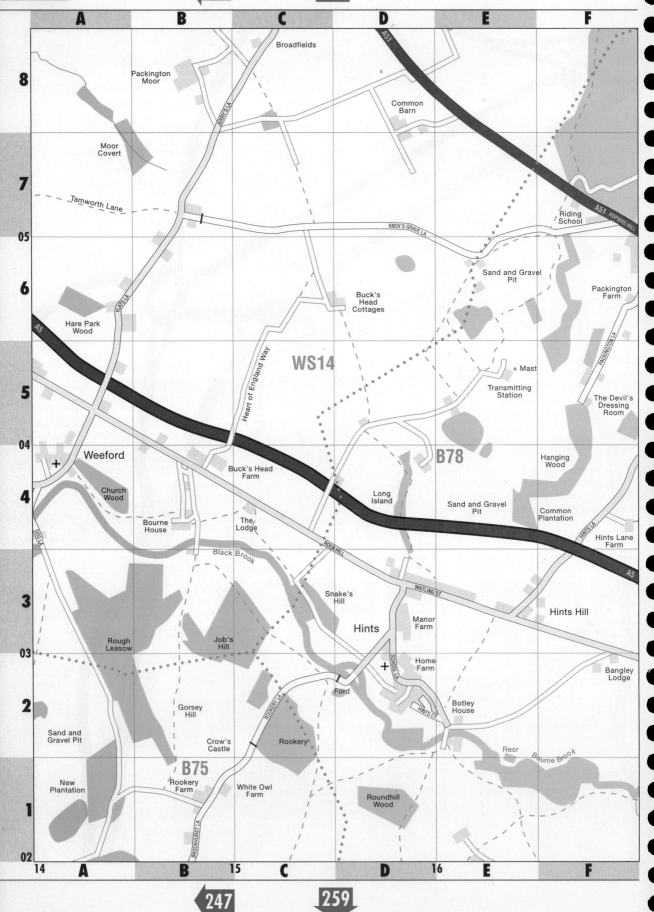

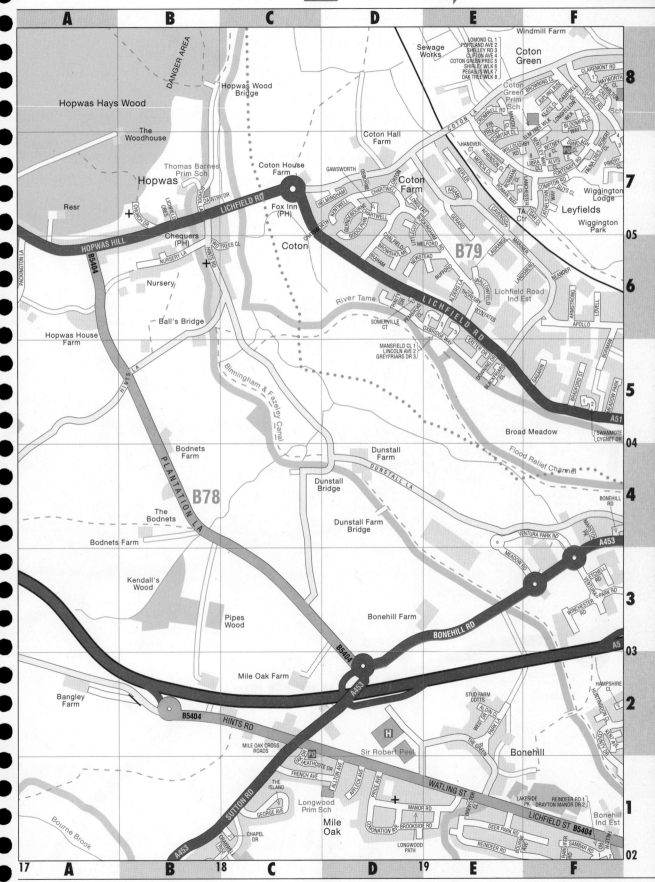

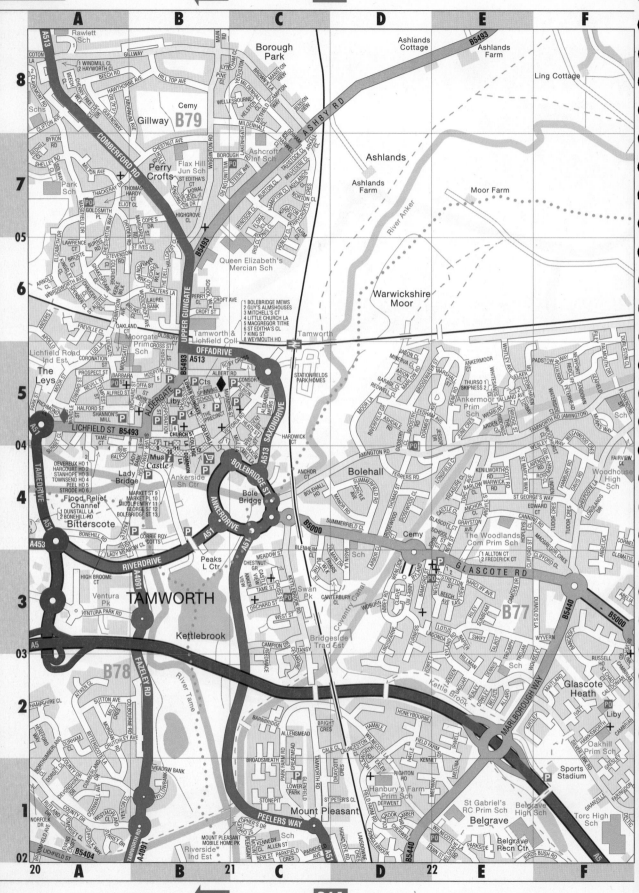

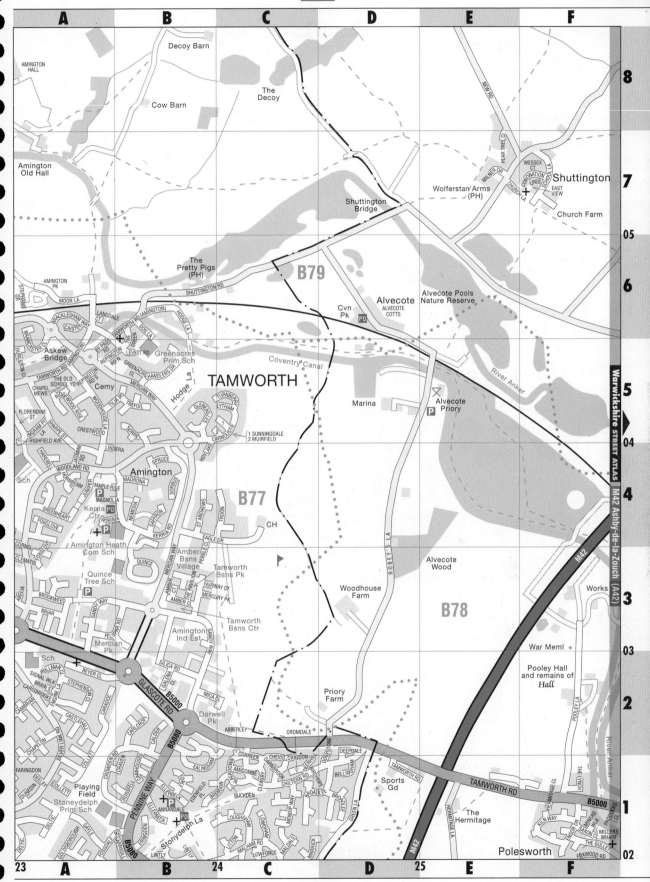

A B C D E F

8 7 05 6 5 04 4 3 03 2 1 02

23 A 24 B C 25 D E F

Decoy Barn
Amington Hall
Cow Barn
The Decoy
Amington Old Hall
NEW RD
PEAR TREE CL
MILNER DR
WESSEX CT
CORONATION CRES
CHURCH LA
SCHOOL LA
EAST VIEW
Shuttington
Wolferstan Arms (PH)
Church Farm
Shuttington Bridge
The Pretty Pigs (PH)
B79
SHUTTINGTON RD
Alvecote
ALVECOTE COTTS
Cvn Pk
Alvecote Pools Nature Reserve
River Anker
Coventry Canal
Marina
Alvecote Priory
TAMWORTH
Warwickshire STREET ATLAS
M42 Ashby-de-la-Zouch (A42)
STEPHANIE GR
AMINGTON PK
MOOR LA
LANGDALE
HODGE LA
BACKLESHAM WAY
CAISTER
BRANCASTER CL
DURLSTON CL
Askew Bridge
REPINGTON
TAMWORTH RD (AMINGTON)
THE GREEN
LEVETT RD
Greenacres Prim Sch
GREENACRE
HANDLERS DR
MERCIAN WAY
Hodge La
THE OLD SCHOOL YD
CHAPEL MEWS
Cemy
Cemy
WOODHOUSE LA
TILIA RD
TREFOIL
GLENEAGLES
TURNBERRY
LYTHAM
1 Sunningdale 2 Muirfield
CARNOUSTIE
HOYLAKE
FLORENDINE ST
INGRAM LA
SHARPE ST
HIGHFIELD AVE
CRESTWOOD
LINDERA
SPIRE
WOODLAND RD
HARNESS
JASMINE
WARNEAM
WOODBINE
Sch
MADRONA
Amington
SPRUCE
SORBUS
MAPLE RISE
MAGNOLIA
JUNIPER
NEMESIA
SAFFRON
KERRIA
ROBINIA
Kerria Ctr
GREENHEART
FOXGLOVE
CORNEL
CLEMATIS
Amington Heath Com Sch
QUINCE
B77
ST ANDREWS
TROON
EAGLE DR
PEBBLE CL
CH
MERCIAN WAY
Amber Bsns Village
Tamworth Bsns Pk
THE PAVILION
FAIRWAY CT
MERCURY PK
AMBER CT
AMBER CL
Quince Tree Sch
ABELIA
BROOKWEED
SANDY WAY
BRIAR
Mercian Pk
Amington Ind Est
Tamworth Bsns Ctr
Alvecote Wood
Woodhouse Farm
ROBEY'S LA
B78
Sch
BEYER CL
PULLMAN CL
SIGNAL WLK
BRAIN ST
CARISBROOKE
CAMBRIAN
CHAPELON
GLASCOTE RD
B5000
STEPHENSON CL
GALENA CL
SILICA RD
MICA GL
Darwell Pk
ABBERLEY
CROMDALE
War Meml
Pooley Hall and remains of Hall
POOLEY LA
M42
Works
B5080
CASTLEHAY
CARLCROFT
CALDER
PENNINE WAY
CROWDEN RD
CRAVEN
CAMPNESS
CROSSELL
CROSSDALE
ELLERBECK
ELLERBECK
Stonydelph La
ANNANDALE
FRIDGDEN
FRIDGDEN
LINTLY
FOSSDALE
CARRO HILL
CORREEN
CHEVIOT
CRIGDON
EALINGHAM
AMICOMBE
CLEASBY
BRENDON
BUCKDEN
EDENFIELD PL
CHILTERN RD
BROADLEE
BELLINGHAM
GREEN LA
DEEPDALE
DONSTONE
Priory Farm
Sports Gd
TAMWORTH RD
TAMWORTH RD
B5000
The Hermitage
HERMITAGE LA
M42
River Anker
KILN WAY
THE LYNCH
SAXON CT
MILLERS WHARF
THE GULLET
FOXWOOD RD
Polesworth
DEER PK
FARINGDON
DUNEDIN
Playing Field
Stoneydelph Prim Sch
GAYLE
GOODSBOROUGH
DELTIC
B5080
COLLETT
COLLETT
CADRIADOC
LOUGHSHAW
LITTON
MALHAM RD
LOWFORCE
MARRICK
MALDALE
MENDIP WAY
LOWDHAM

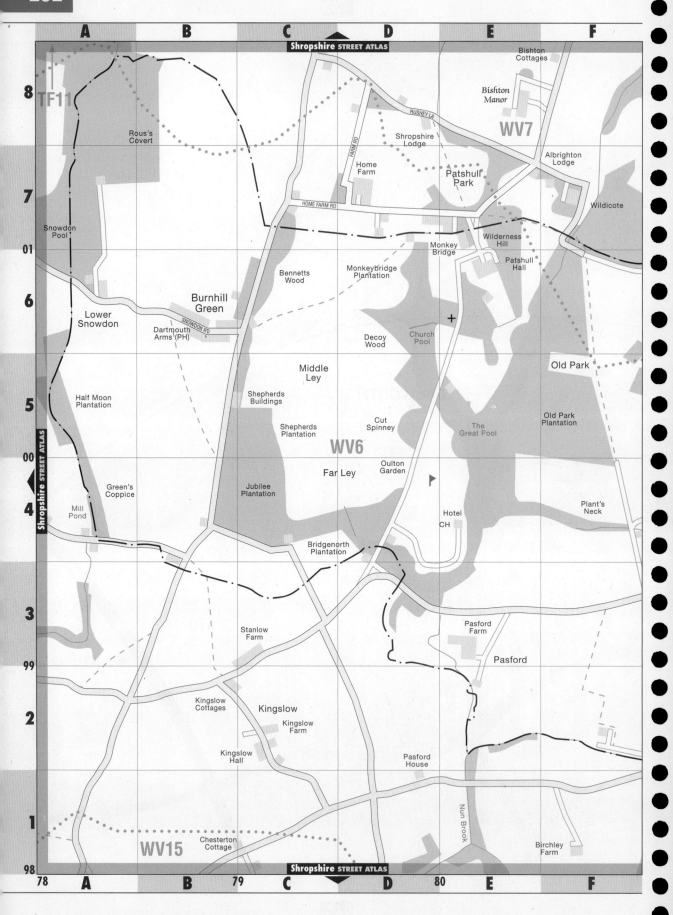

Shropshire STREET ATLAS

TF11

WV7

Bishton
Cottages

Bishton
Manor

RUSHEY LA

Shropshire
Lodge

Albrighton
Lodge

8

Rous's
Covert

FARM RD

Home
Farm

Patshull
Park

Wildicote

7

HOME FARM RD

Monkey
Bridge

Wilderness
Hill

Patshull
Hall

01

Snowdon
Pool

Bennetts
Wood

Monkeybridge
Plantation

6

Lower
Snowdon

Burnhill
Green

SNOWDON RD

Dartmouth
Arms (PH)

Decoy
Wood

Church
Pool

Old Park

Half Moon
Plantation

Middle
Ley

Old Park
Plantation

5

Shepherds
Buildings

Cut
Spinney

WV6

Shepherds
Plantation

The
Great Pool

00

Green's
Coppice

Far Ley

Oulton
Garden

4

Mill
Pond

Jubilee
Plantation

Plant's
Neck

Hotel
CH

Bridgenorth
Plantation

3

Stanlow
Farm

Pasford
Farm

Pasford

99

Kingslow
Cottages

Kingslow

2

Kingslow
Farm

Kingslow
Hall

Pasford
House

Nun Brook

1

WV15

Chesterton
Cottage

Birchley
Farm

98

Shropshire STREET ATLAS

78   A   B   79   C   D   80   E   F

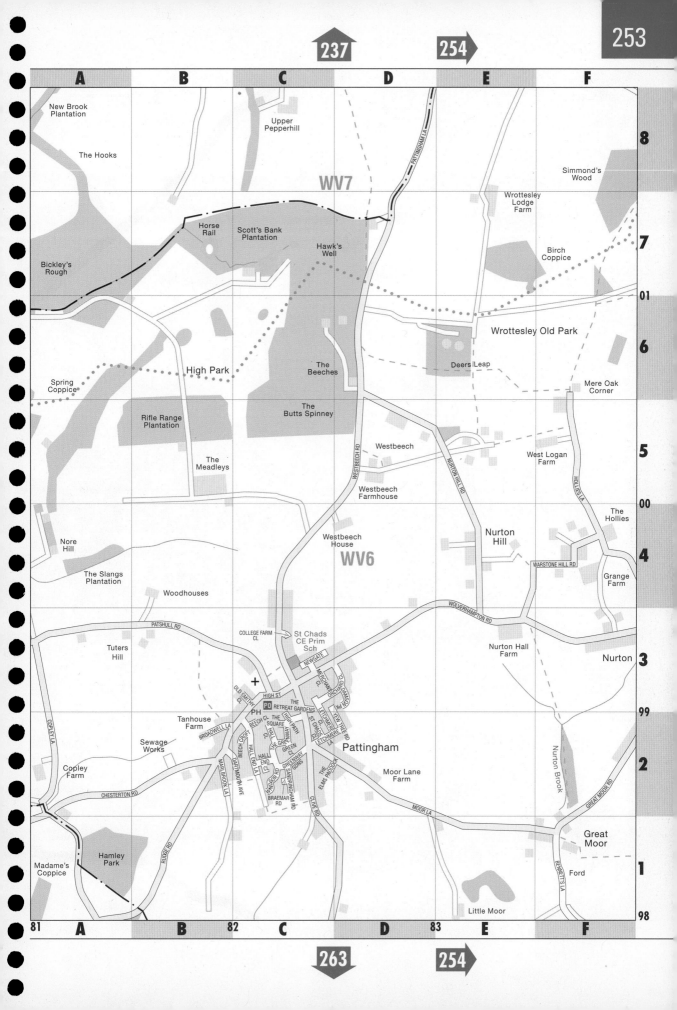

253 238

A B C D E F

8

WV7
Simmond's Wood
Wrottesley Hall
The Bradshaws

Bull Ride
WROTTESLEY CT
CH
Inland Pool
Heath House Farm
HEATHFIELDS
HEATH HOUSE LA
HOLYHEAD RD

7

Wrottesley Park
WV8
WERGS HALL
WERGS RD
River Penk
A41

01

Salt's Pool
Smith's Rough
The Grange
VEN TREE LA
WESTCROFT RD

6

Cranmoor
SCAMPTON CL 1
HUDSON GR 2
TANGMERE CL 3
LIVINGSTONE AVE 4
WROTTESLEY RD W
BOWEN-COOKE AVE
Dippons Lane

Cranmoor Lodge
HAWKSTONE CT
TURNBERRY GR
WENTWORTH GR
COLLET RD
BRUNEL RD
WEBB STEPHENSON DR
EDWARD RD
MERE OAK RD
EGERTON RD
IDONIA RD

HEPWORTH CL 1
LOWRY CL 2
MOORE CL 3
THIRLMERE GR 4
WASTWATER CT 5
BUTTERMERE CT 6
CHARTLEY CL 7
KENILWORTH RD 8

5

SUNNINGDALE AVE
TROON CT
FRANKWELL DR
BIGGIN
SHARBURY
COSFORD CT
ANSON GR
SHACKLET
GAYDON CL
KINGSBURY
MERLIN
HARWIN
ATHELSTAN
GUTHRUM
VINGTON
PENDA GR
REYNOLDS
GAINSBOROUGH RD

00

Perton
WROTTESLEY PARK RD
ANDREWS DR
MOOR PK
PORTRUSH RD
LYTHAM RD
GLENEAGLES RD
FORNEY
BERRY
CLOVERDALE
COOK CL
CABOT GR
STANLEY CT
DANVM
BROWNING
WORDSWORTH
MILTON CT
COLERIDGE DR
AUDEN
EPSOM CL
SEDGEFIELD
SANDOWN CT
LINGFIELD
HAYDERLAND
THE PARKWAY

4

Nurton
Staffordshire Way
Monarch's Way
THE PADDOCK 1
FALLOWFIELD 2
THE CARTWAY 3
THE WINDROW 4
THE SADDLESTONES 5
MEADOW CROFT 6
WORCESTER GR 7
WELLS CL
KELSO
LEASOWES
COUER GR
THE WEST LANDS
OATLANDS
MARBLE GR
CORMWL
TINTERN CT
ELGIN CT
HEDBURGH
CROWLAND GR
CANTERBURY RD
BADGER
CUNNINGHAM RD
CHESHIRE GR
GIBSON RD
MALLORY RD
SEVERN DR
TRENT CL
AVON
HAMBLE GR
CHUR
WYE
RYDAL CT
ENNERDALE CL
CHEPSTOW
SPENSER AVE
Sch
Liby
ANDERS SQ
RICHMOND DR
RIDGEACRE DR
RICHMOND RD
ARUNDEL

3

Perton Orchard
CH
WV6
WYKEHAM GR
WREN AVE
SWW
PAXTON
NASH AVE
ROWTON AVE
FOSTERTON
ROUGHEY
CHERITON GR
EDGE HILL DR
TURNHAM GR
THE GREENS
ROCKINGHAM DR
WINCEBY RD
CHOPTON CL
BERKELEY CL
WARWICK AVE
KINGSWEAR
DUNSTER GR
CRANBOROUGH GR
STOKESAY
CORFE
RAYMOND RD
ST MAWES
KINGSLEY
ELMLEY CL
WOLVERHAMPTON RD
BUTTERFIELD CL
VANBRUGH
Boundary Farm
THE HIGHFIELDS
THE WALLANDS
QUAIL GREEN
PERTON BROOK VALE
WIGHTWICK BK
OLD LA

99

Old Perton
Sling Wood
PATTINGHAM RD
WOLVERHAMPTON
Boundary Farm
BOUNDARY WAY
STOCKBRIDGE
PERTON RD

2

Perton House
Perton Court
Perton Green
RODWOOD
TINACRE HILL
Wightwick Hall Sch
Wightwick Manor
P
MAYSWOOD DR
RAVENSHOLME
HERONSWAY

1

Freehold Wood
Middle Wood
South Perton Farm
JENNY WALKERS LA
Wightwick
WIGHTWICK HALL RD
HEATH HILL RD
BRIDGNORTH RD
Cherringham
WV3
CASTLECROFT LA
HEADLAND
SABRINA RD
A454

98

84 A B 85 C D 86 E F

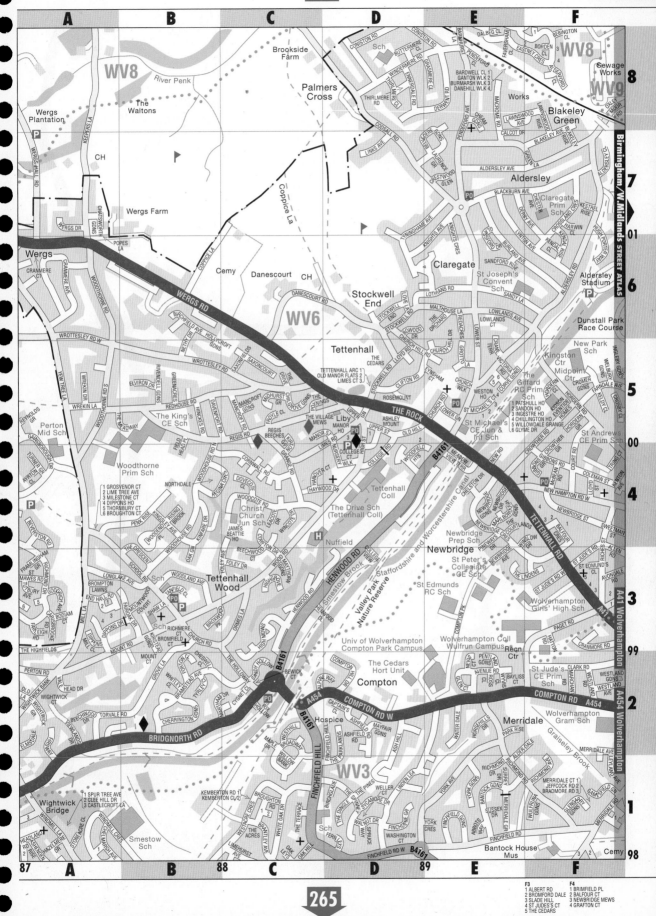

F3
1 ALBERT RD
2 BROMFORD DALE
3 SLADE HILL
4 ST JUDES'S CT
5 THE CEDARS

F4
1 BRIMFIELD PL
2 BALFOUR CT
3 NEWBRIDGE MEWS
4 GRAFTON CT

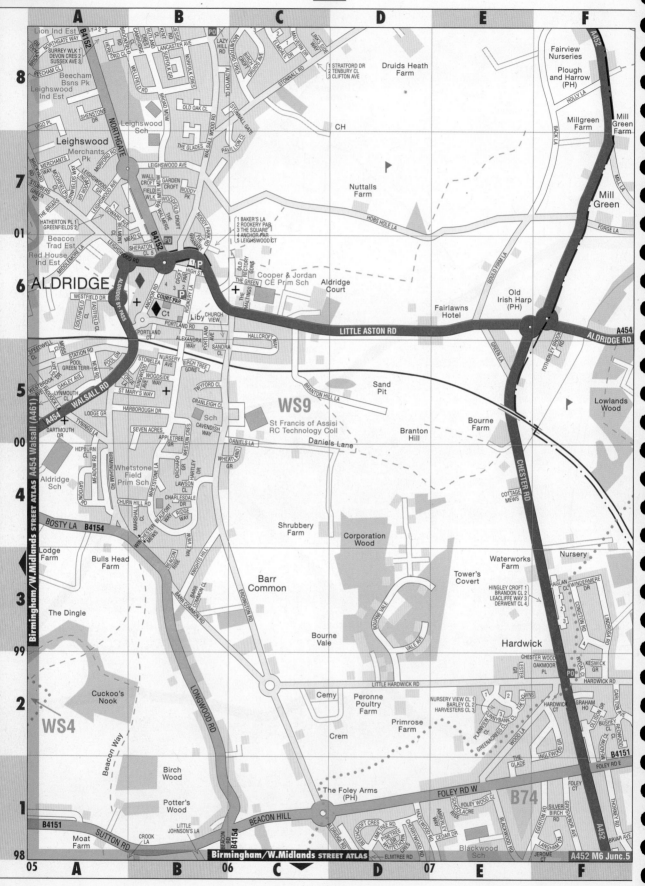

8

7

01

6

5

00

4

99

3

2

WS4

1

98

05   A   B   06   C   D   07   E   F

A   B   C   D   E   F

Lion Ind Est
NORTHGATE WAY
SURREY WLK 1
DEVON CRES 2
SUSSEX AVE 3
BEECHAM CL
Beecham
Bsns Pk
Leighswood
Ind Est
VIGO PL
SHENSTONE DR
Leighswood
Merchants
Pk
Merchants
Way
THE BRIARS
STUBBERS
GREEN
HATHERTON PL 1
GREENFIELDS 2
Beacon
Trad Est
Red House
Ind Est
ALDRIDGE
WESTFIELD DR
SOUTHFIELD
EASTFIELD CL
SPEEDWELL
CL
WESTBROOK
MOSS CL
STATION RD
Pool
Green Terr
POOL GR
WALSALL RD
A454
DARTMOUTH
DR
Aldridge
Sch
HEPBURN
CL
Whetstone
Field
Prim Sch
Aldridge
By-Pass
BOSTY LA   B4154
Lodge
Farm
Bulls Head
Farm
The Dingle
Birch
Wood
Potter's
Wood
Moat
Farm
SUTTON RD
CROOK LA
LITTLE
JOHNSON'S LA
B4151
BEACON RD
B4154
BEACON HILL
LONGWOOD RD
Cuckoo's
Nook
Beacon Way

B4152
NORTHGATE
Leighswood
Sch
OLD OAK CL
BROAD MDW
THE GLADES
LEIGHSWOOD AVE
WALL
CROFT
FIELD
GARDEN
CROFT
WOODY
PK
EDWARD AVE
BELMONT
LEIGHSWOOD RD
MEAD CL
THE WALTINGS
B4152
SHERATON
CL 5
ANCHOR RD
COURT PAR
Ct
PORTLAND RD
PORTLAND
CL
STONELEA
WOODSIDE
FORGE
ST MARY'S WAY
LODGE GR
HARBOROUGH DR
SEVEN ACRES
APPLETREE
GR
WESTON GR
ORCHARD
GR
HARTLEY
CL
LAWSON
CL
CHARLESDALE
DR
RIDGE
WAY
CHURCH HILL RD
WHETSTONE LA
MARSH
BEAUFORT
WINCHESTER
MEWS
VALE VIEW
KNIGHTS HILL
BARR COMMON CL
BARR COMMON RD
BMR
BMR

CAMBRIDGE RD
ROLAND
KENT
HEREF
CRD CL
AUBREYS
LANCASTER AVE
NORFOLK CRES
SUFFOLK GR
OLD OAK CL
LEIGHSWOOD AVE
PAVILION CL
RODDY PARK RD
ROOKERY LA
GRANARY
HIGH ST
LIBY
1P
P
Court Par
LAZY
HILL RD
CHURCH
VIEW
THE GREEN
THE MALTINGS
ALEXANDRA
WAY
HALLCROFT WAY
NURSERY AVE
BIRCH TREE
GDNS
TWYFORD CL
CRANLEIGH CL
SANDRA
CL
Sch
CAVENDISH
WAY
DANIELS LA
WHEATLEY
GR
1 BAKER'S LA
2 ROOKERY PAR
3 THE SQUARE
4 ANCHOR PAR
5 LEIGHSWOOD CT

STONNALL RD
DRUIDS AVE
STONNALL CL
WALSALL WOOD RD
STONNALL GATE
1 STRATFORD DR
2 TENBURY CL
3 CLIFTON AVE
OLD
RECTORY GDNS
Cooper & Jordan
CE Prim Sch
LITTLE ASTON RD
BRANTON HILL LA
WS9
St Francis of Assisi
RC Technology Coll
Daniels Lane
Shrubbery
Farm
Barr
Common
Bourne
Vale
VALE AVE
Cemy
Peronne
Poultry
Farm
Crem
Primrose
Farm
The Foley Arms
(PH)
FOLEY RD W
ALDRIDGE RD

LAZY
HILL RD
DRUNTFORD CRES
MALVERN DR
DRUIDS AVE
LINES SIDE
Druids Heath
Farm
CH
Nuttalls
Farm
HOBS HOLE LA
Aldridge
Court
Fairlawns
Hotel
Sand
Pit
Branton
Hill
Corporation
Wood
Bourne
Dale
Little Hardwick Rd
NURSERY VIEW CL 1
BARLEY CL 2
HARVESTERS CL 3

Fairview
Nurseries
A452
Plough
and Harrow
(PH)
HOLLY LA
BACK LA
Millgreen
Farm
Mill
Green
Farm
MILL LA
Mill
Green
FORGE LA
GOULD FIRM LA
Old Irish Harp
(PH)
GREEN LA
A454
ALDRIDGE RD
FOTHERLEY BROOK RD
Lowlands
Wood
Bourne
Farm
CHESTER RD
COTTAGE
MEWS
Waterworks
Farm
Tower's
Covert
Nursery
HINGLEY CROFT 1
BRANDON CL 2
LEACLIFFE WAY 3
DERWENT CL 4
RAGLAN CL
WINDERMERE
DR
CONISTON RD
LINDROSA RD
Hardwick
CHESTER WOOD
OAKMOOR
PL
LEISTER
KESWICK
GR
Hardwick Rd
RYDAL CL
PO
CHESTER WOOD
SUNNYBANK CL
PLANTREE
GREENACRES CL
WOOD LA
HARDWICK
CT
THE
GLADE
INGLEWOOD
GRAHAM
HO
OLLISON DR
BUSHEY
REDWOOD
CL
WINS
CARLTON
B4151
Foley Rd E
FOLEY
CT
B74
SILVER
BIRCH
RD
THORNEY RD
A452
A452 M6 Junc.5
EGERTON RD
GROSVENOR AVE
LANGHAM
JEROME
CT
BRIAR AVE
Blackwood
Sch

Birmingham/W.Midlands STREET ATLAS   A454 Walsall (A461)

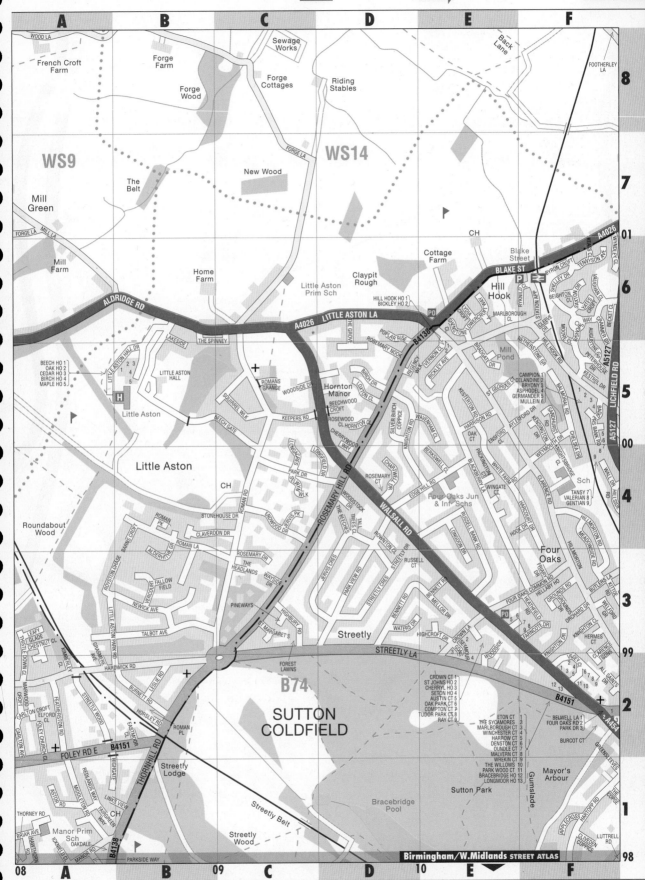

A   B   C   D   E   F

8

WS14

Joburns
Cottages

Alder
Farm

Brookfield

GREEN BARNS LA

Green
Wood

A38

M6 TOLL

LONDON RD

The Highwayman
(PH)

Blossom Hill
Farm

WOODLAND CT

SMARTS AVE

Camp
Farm

LITTLE HAY LA

Black Fir
Wood

7

BLAKE
ST

Biddles
Farm

WATFORD GAP RD

WATFORD GAP

A5127 LICHFIELD RD

BIRMINGHAM RD

A5127

Hovel
Covert

Weeford Park
Farm

01

WYNDLEY MANOR

CAMP RD

Pine Tree
Cottage

Springhill
Farm

6

B74

HILLWOOD COMMON RD

Hill
Common

Hill
Farm

Manorial
Wood

Springhill
Plantation

A38

TURF PITTS LA

5

Mast

Television
Station

Manorial
Farm

HILLWOOD RD

Spreading Tree
Hill

Hilltop
Farm

00

Hill

HAYCROFT
DR

BYRON
DR

KEATING
GDNS

WARDLE

STRINGER

DUNTON CL

DUNTON CL

Hill Wood

Hill Wood
Farm

Hillside Farm

B75

WORCESTER LA

1 PLOUGHMANS PL
2 TILLER GR
3 SOWERS CT
4 COMBINE CL

M6 TOLL

4

A5127

OAKLAND

HILLSIDE RD

HATHAWAY RD

GRESLEY CL

1 CHEVIOT CT
2 CHILTERN CT
3 BREDON CT
4 COTSWOLD CT

BEECH

WESTERN

MANOR

DAWNEY DR

HIGHOVER DR

GLANVILLE DR

SHENSTONE LA

CROSSFORD DR

Dale
Farm

MAYALL DR

ST
JOHNS
WOOD
DR

LOXLEY DR

AMINGTON

HARVEST
FIELDS
WAY

DUTTON'S LA

Piggery

WHEATSHEAF
CL

Woodside
Farm

CANWELL
GATE

RECROW

HARVEST FIELDS WAY

MANORIAL

FARM PL

ROUGHLEY
DR

B4151

BUTLERS LA

Butlers
Lane

HENLEY
DR

PEGASUS
CL

HILL VILLAGE RD

HOLLY

THE
DELL

KINGS
CT

DRAYTON
DR

BRENTHALL

WALCOT DR

GIBBONS RD

BOOTH RD

BUNCALFE

DUGDALE CR

GUDSEY
DR

TOWER RD

RANDLE DR

HOMESTEAD RD

EDWARDS RD

CARTWRIGHT

WILLMOTT
CL

WILLMOTT RD

MAIN
WAITING DR

CROFTERS LA

Little Sutton
Prim Sch

REDRIL

1

5

6

4

2

8

BRADWELL
CROFT

BOOTHE GR

BISHOPS
MDW

E3
1 MARLPIT RISE
2 WEEFORD DELL
3 WHEATCROFT CL
4 SHEARERS PL
5 WOODMAN GR
6 FARM HOUSE LA
7 BLACKSMITH DR
8 WEAVER CT

SLADE RD

3

BEACON RD

KITTOE RD

HOBART CT 1
BALFOUR CT 2

HARLAND

SARA CL

RED LA

BELWELL DR

HEATH RD

CLAYTON DR

CHARNLEY DR

Roughley

MARLPIT LA

PH

FOX HILL RD

The
Arthur Terry
Sch

99

PO

LICHFIELD RD

Mere
Green

CHURCH
TERR

ELISABETH
CT

Mere Green
Comb Sch

WILMCOTE DR

WHEATLEY
CL

ST JAMES CL

BORDESLEY
CT

BARN

MERE
GREEN
RD

MERE
GREEN
RD

Little Sutton Rd

HARVEY DR

ROUGHLEY DR

CLARENDON RD

GRANGE LA

GRANGE
AVE

PO

COBURN DR

PEROTT DR

MERE POOL RD

SHEPHERDS POOL RD

Moor Hall
Prim Sch

2

B4151

BELWELL LA

CARLTON
HO

Liby

P

ALL
SAINTS
DR

CLARENCE RD

3

1 DEVONSHIRE CT
2 HARBOROUGH CT
3 TUDOR CT

MERE DR

MUDEFORD

CREMORNE RD

CREMORNE
WLK

KINGSLEIGH
CROFT

JORDAN RD

ARLESCOTE

HOMER RD

ROWALLAN RD

ESSEX RD

FERRERS
CL

HOLTE DR

Hotel

CH

Fox Hill
Farm

SUTTON
COLDFIELD

1

A454

THE COPSE

B74

HARTOPP
RD

CRESSINGTON DR

ALSTON CL

4 MORE

ALSTON CL

MURSLEY

FOUR OAKS RD

BEECHCROFT
CT

HANSON
MAN

FOXTON
MAN

Ley
Hill

A5127

THE FURLONG

JORDAN

POWER RD

DEVEREUX RD

QUEENS
DOWNS

RIDGEWOOD
DR

LITTLE SUTTON LA

STREATHER RD

HANDFIELD
DR

GROSVENOR CR

HEATH CROFT RD

Moor
Hall

P

WYRLEY
RD

BROCKHURST
RD

MOOR HALL DR

Ashfurlong
Hall

A453 TAMWORTH RD

98

LUTTRELL RD

LADYWOOD

A454

FOUR
OAKS CT

PINE
LEIGH

WENT
WORTH
DR

TRINITY RD

LOCKHART DR

LEY HILL RD

Coppice
Sch

LAUREATES
WLK

HAZLEMERE DR

CEDARWOOD

11   A   B   12   C   D   13   E   F

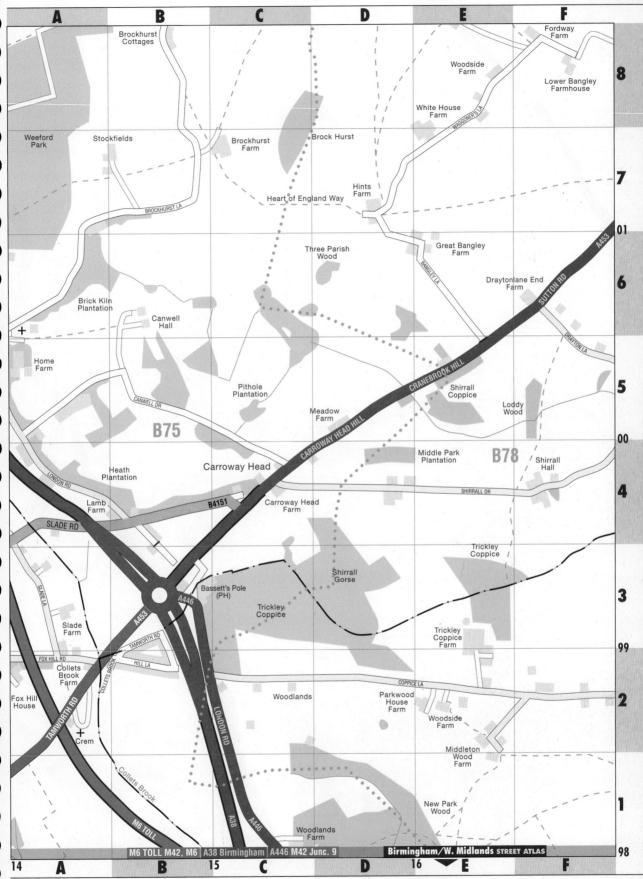

259
249

New House Farm
BANGLEY LA
SUTTON RD
Bourne Bridge
CAISTOR CL
GAINSBOROUGH DR
KIRKLAND WAY
CRANWELL RISE
A453
Alder Wood
A453
Hill Farm
Bourne Brook
Lodge Farm
Bourne Brook Cut
Seventeen Acre Wood
Duck Decoy
Longwood House
Fazeley
YORKSAND RD
REINDEER RD
DAMA RD
MAYAMA RD
DRAYTON MANOR DR
SWISS LODGE DR
Works
Drayton Manor Park
CH
DRAYTON MANOR DR
Longwood Stables
COLESHILL RD
A4091
Heathley Farm
HEATHLEY LA
Bullocks End Farm
Edden's Wood
Drayton Bassett
Oak Farm Craft Ctr
SHIRRAL DR
Stone House
DRAYTON LA
Heart of England Way
OLD MANOR CL
MOAT DR
CHURCH CL
EDDENS WOOD CL
PO
NEW ROW
PEEL CL
Manor Prim Sch
Sewage Works
Ashdene Farm
B78
RECTORY CL
SALTS LA
Drayton Brick Bridge
PORTLEYS LA
Brook End Farm
Brook Farm
Birmingham and Fazeley Canal
Heart of England Way
Upper House Farm
Gallows Brook
COPPICE LA
Quarry
Mill Plantation
Middleton
CHURCH ROW
SIMMONS CL
Highfields Farm
CHURCH LA
Walker's Spinney
Sewage Works
Park-gate Farm
Middleton Park
Newhouse Farm
Middleton Pool
The Green Man (PH)
VICARAGE HILL
PO
CRONKERRY LA
Langley Brook
A4091
Middleton Hall

259

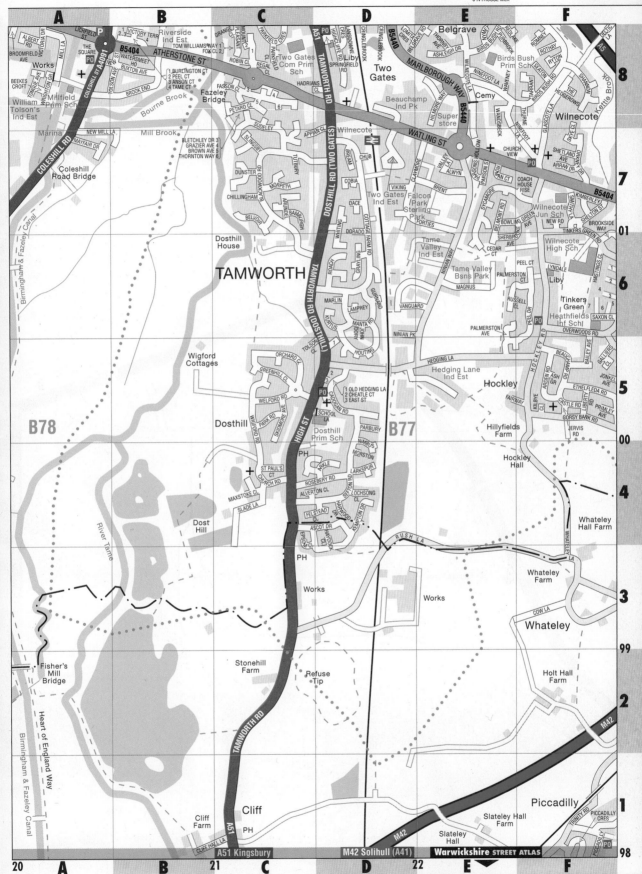

262

F6
1 BAKERS WLK
2 CALLIS WLK
3 LINTHOUSE WLK
4 COTTAGE WLK
5 STONEHILL WLK
6 IVYHOUSE WLK
7 LEISURE WLK

A B C D E F

8
7
01
6
5
00
4
3
99
2
1
98

TAMWORTH

B78

B77

Dosthill

Belgrave

Wilnecote

Hockley

Whateley

Piccadilly

Cliff

A51 Kingsbury   M42 Solihull (A41)   **Warwickshire** STREET ATLAS

20 A 21 B C 22 D E F

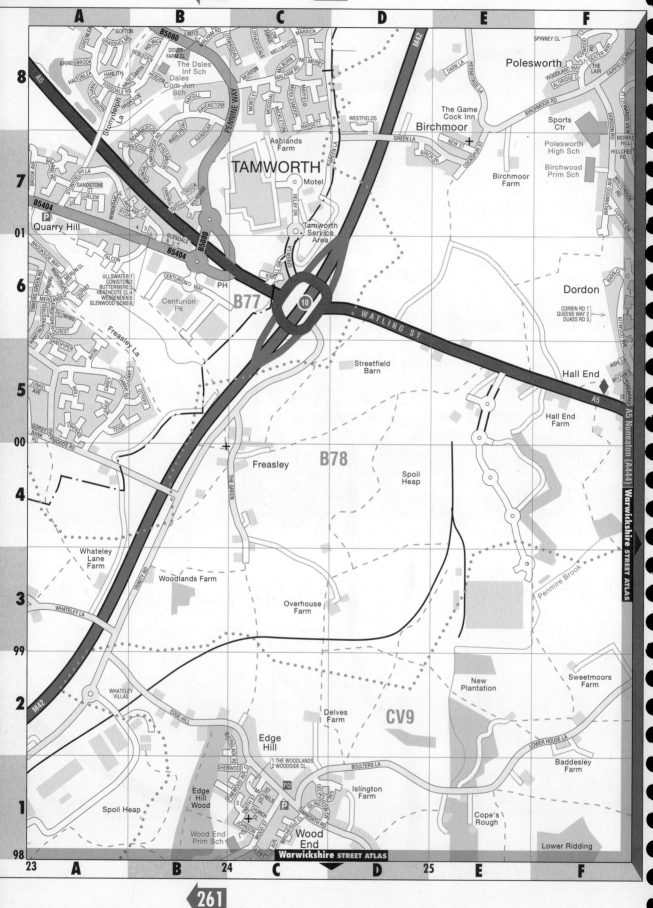

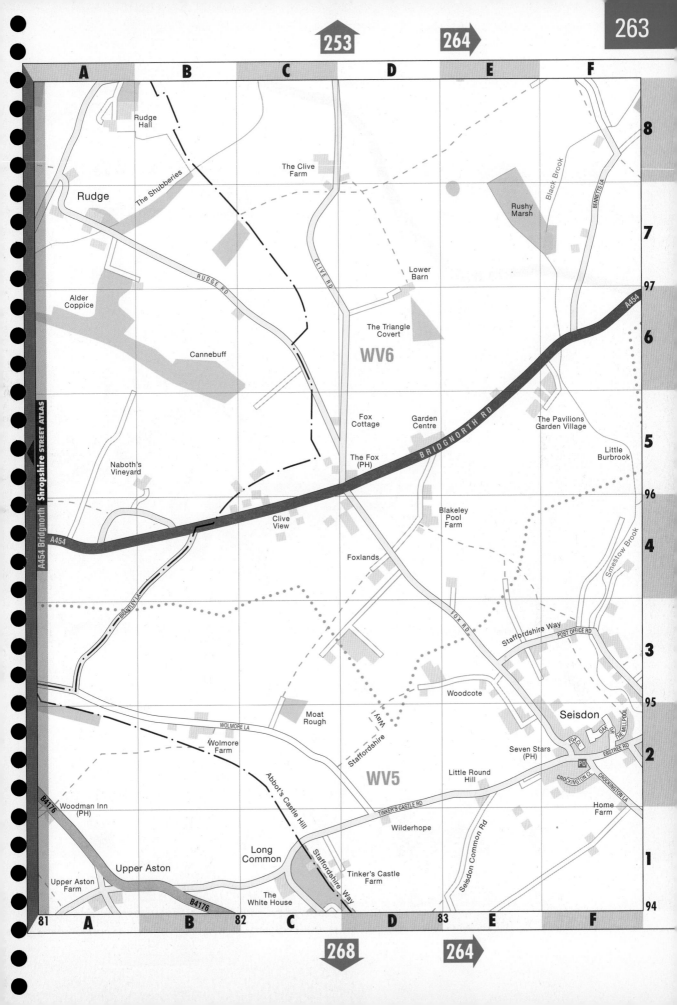

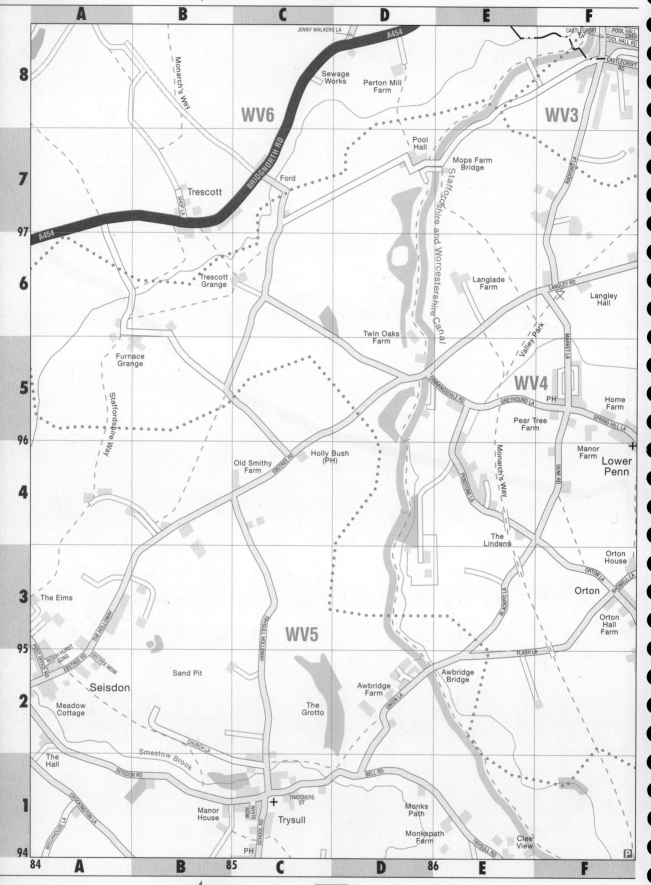

A B C D E F

8
7
97
6
5
96
4
3
95
2
1
94

WV3

WV4

WV5

WOLVERHAMPTON

Finchfield

Merry Hill

Oxbarn

Penn Fields

Penn

Castlecroft

Bradmore

BROAD LA

B4161

BIRCHES BARN RD

Bantock Park

Langley House

Nursery

Hill Croft Farm

Westcroft Farm

Lower Penn Farm

Springhill Farm

Spring Hill

Blazebank

Fox Hill

Orton Hill

Orchard Hill

Bearnett House

Bearnett Farm

Ladywell Wood

Bearnett La

Lloyd Farm

Lloyd House

St Anthony's Cheshire Home

The Penn Cottage (PH)

Lloyd Home Farm

Light Wood

Lloyd Wood

Grange Farm

St Bartholomew's CE Prim Sch

Nash's Coppice Farm

DY3

Bradney Wood

PENN RD

STOURBRIDGE RD

LLOYD HILL

A449

Highfields Science Specialist Sch

Springdale Jun & Inf Schs

Warstones Jun & Inf Sch

Woodfield Jun & Inf Schs

Penn Fields Sch

Penn Hall Sch

St Michael's RC Prim Sch

Castlecroft Prim Sch

Bhylls Acre Prim Sch

Uplands Jun Sch

265

C8
1 PAUL ST
2 BLOOMSBURY ST
3 St JOHNS RET PK
4 LITTLE POUNTNY ST
5 KING EDWARD'S ROW
6 STEVENS GATE

7 HOLLIES IND EST
8 RAINBOW ST

D8
1 DARTMOUTH ST
2 GORDON ST
3 GRANVILLE CL

265

271

F4
1 ELLIOT CT
2 HARDIE CT
3 MERIDEN CT
4 MORRIS CT
5 WESLEY CT
6 WARWICK CT
7 RYLCROFT
8 AVONCROFT
9 FIRCROFT
10 HOLMCROFT
11 GENTHORN CL
12 ASHCROFT
13 FLORENCE AVE
14 NORBURY CRES
15 CENTRAL AVE

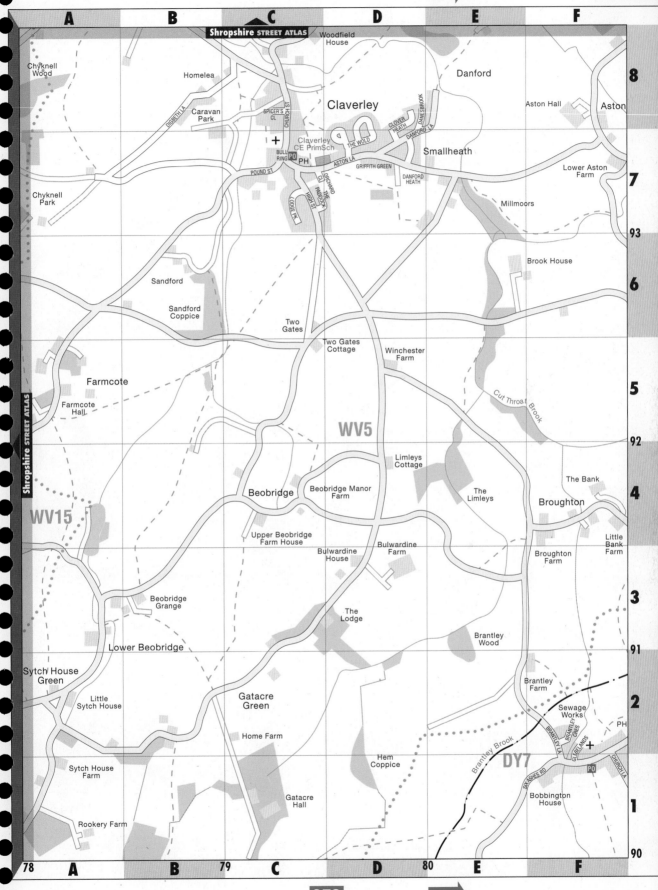

268

Shropshire STREET ATLAS

Woodfield House

Chyknell Wood

Homelea

Danford

Aston Hall

Aston

Caravan Park

DIGBETH LA

SPICER'S CL

CHURCH ST

Claverley

Clover Heath

Danford LA

DANESBROOK

Smallheath

Chyknell Park

Claverley CE PrimSch

BULL RING

PO

PH

THE WOLD

ASTON LA

GRIFFITH GREEN

Lower Aston Farm

POUND ST

ORCHARD CL

THE PADDOCK

DANFORD HEATH

Millmoors

LODGE PK

HIGH ST

Sandford

Brook House

Sandford Coppice

Two Gates

Two Gates Cottage

Winchester Farm

Cut Throat Brook

Farmcote

WV5

Farmcote Hall

Limleys Cottage

The Bank

Beobridge

Beobridge Manor Farm

The Limleys

Broughton

WV15

Upper Beobridge Farm House

Bulwardine House

Bulwardine Farm

Broughton Farm

Little Bank Farm

Beobridge Grange

The Lodge

Brantley Wood

Lower Beobridge

Sytch House Green

Gatacre Green

Brantley Farm

Little Sytch House

Sewage Works

PH

Home Farm

BRANTLEY CRES

Brantley Brook

GILRELANDS

DY7

PO

Sytch House Farm

Hem Coppice

BRANTLEY LA

SIX ASHES RD

CHURCH LA

Bobbington House

Rookery Farm

Gatacre Hall

272

268

Shropshire STREET ATLAS

267 263

A B C D E F

8

White House Farm

Long Common

Selsdon Common Rd

The Wellings

WV5

The Bungalow

Abbot's Castle Hill

7

The Wellings

Staffordshire Way

93

The Dwellings

Shellfields Farm

Gay Hills

Upper Whittimere Cottage

Gorse La

6

Admoor Cottage

Clan Park

Draycott

Heathton

Whittimere

Vineyard

Sand Pit

Upper Whittimere Farm

The Eaves

B4176

Old Gate Inn (PH)

5

Heathton House

Swan Cottage

Gayton

TOM LA

War Stone

Staffordshire Way

92

Cranmere

NEW RD

4

The Royal Oak (PH)

Halfpenny Green

Ferndale Farm

Blackhill Plantation

DY3

White Cross Farmhouse

Blakelands

+

Manor Farm

Gospel Ash

3

SIX ASHES RD

Blacklands Farm

DY7

Yew Tree Farm

Blacklands Plantation

91

White Cross

Wolverhampton Bsns Airport

Claire Hayes

GOSPEL ASH RD

Corbett Prim Sch

Saltershall Farm

FOREST LA

Forest Cottage

2

Bobbington

Twin Oaks

PEAR TREE LA

CRAB LA

WATER LA

Leaton Cottage

Crab Mill Farm

Forest Covert

Dogkennel Covert

Gorse Covert

Staffordshire Way

1

CHURCH LA

Leaton Lodge

Highgate Farm

DY3

LUTLEY LA

Highgate Country Park

P

90

Leaton Hall

WHITE HOUSE LA

81 A 82 B C 82 D 83 E F

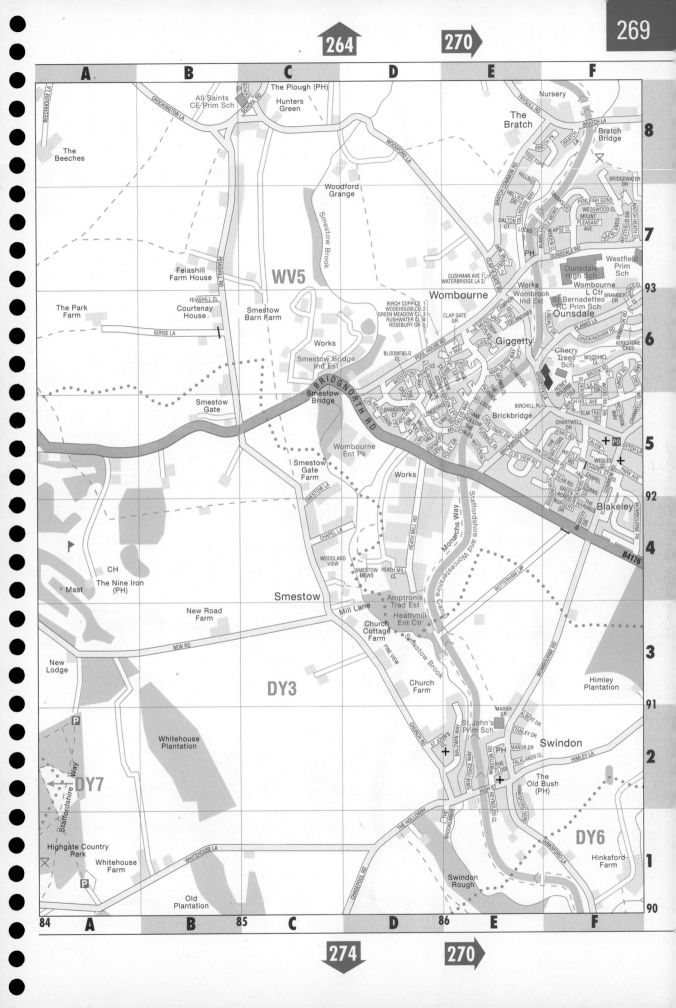

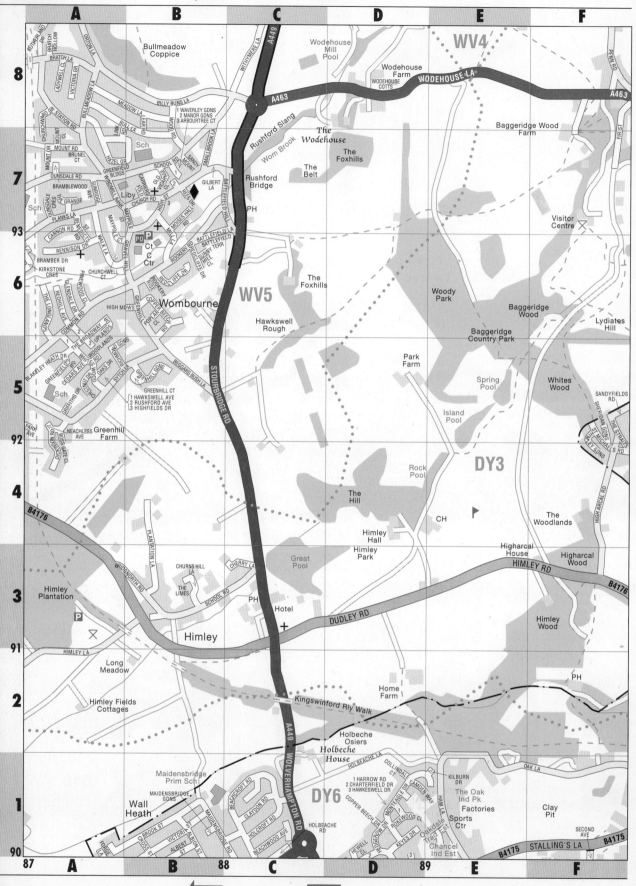

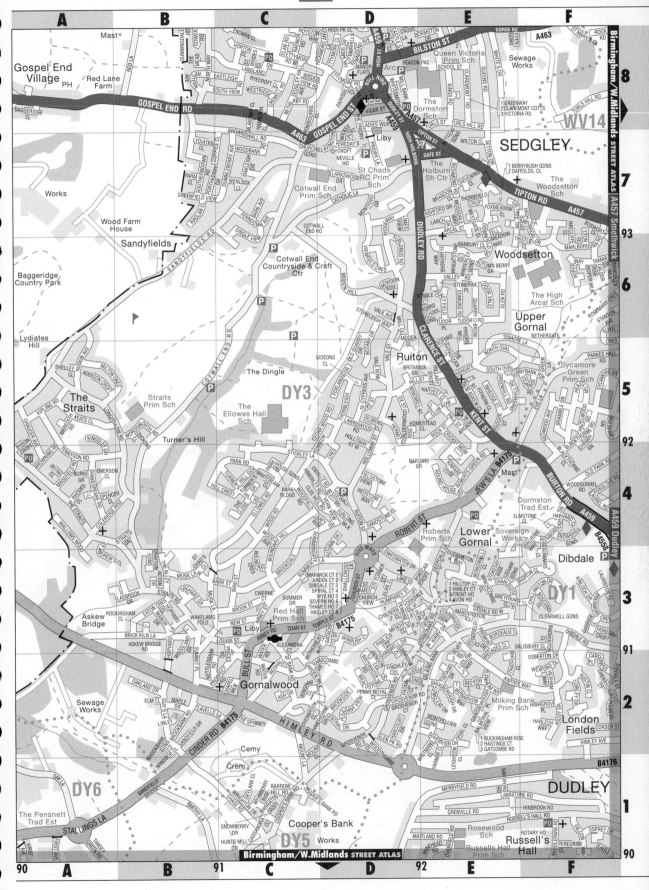

Birmingham/W.Midlands STREET ATLAS

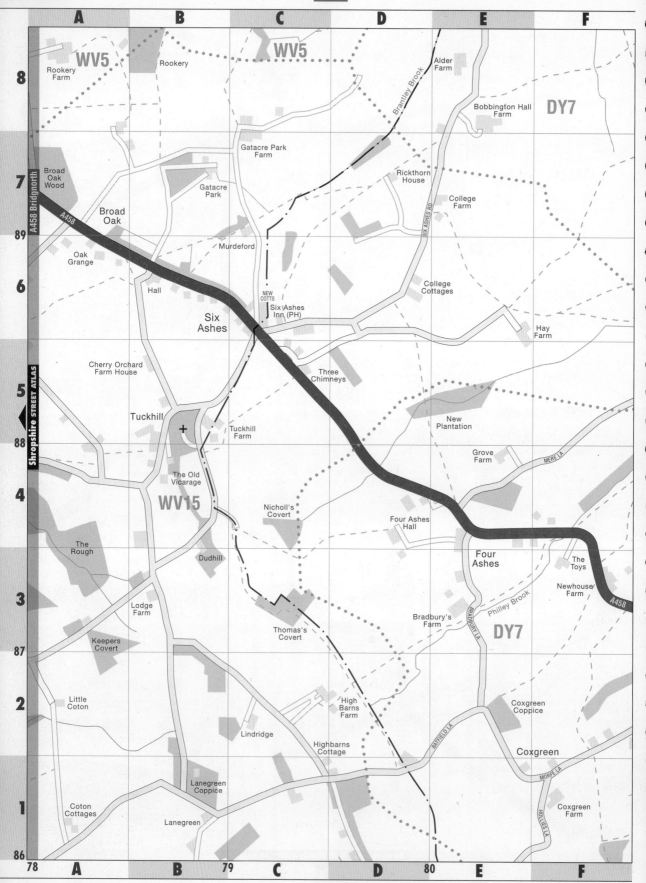

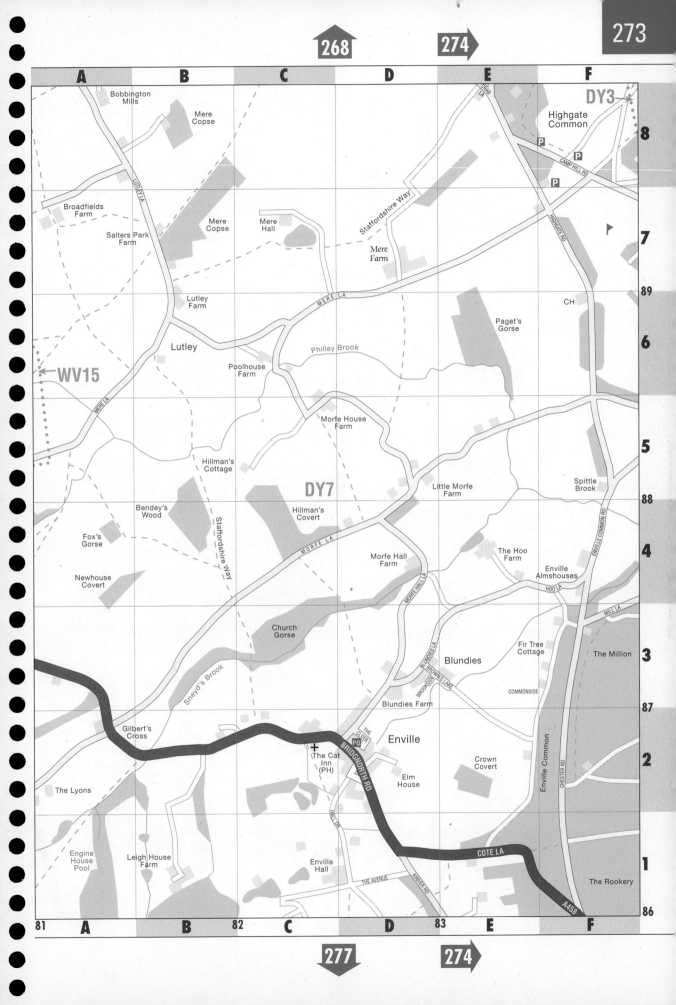

268
274

A B C D E F

DY3

Highgate Common

Bobbington Mills

Mere Copse

Broadfields Farm

Mere Copse

Mere Hall

Staffordshire Way

Mere Farm

Salters Park Farm

CAMP HILL RD

HIGHGATE RD

Lutley Farm

Mere La

CH

Lutley

Philley Brook

Paget's Gorse

Poolhouse Farm

WV15

MERE LA

Morfe House Farm

Hillman's Cottage

DY7

Little Morfe Farm

Spittle Brook

Bendey's Wood

Hillman's Covert

ENVILLE COMMON RD

Fox's Gorse

Staffordshire Way

MORFE LA

Morfe Hall Farm

The Hoo Farm

Enville Almshouses

HOO LA

Newhouse Covert

MORFE HALL LA

MILL LA

Church Gorse

Fir Tree Cottage

The Million

Sneyd's Brook

BLUNDIES LA

BROWN'S LAKE

Blundies

COMMONSIDE

Gilbert's Cross

BROOKSIDE

Blundies Farm

Enville Common

CHESTER RD

BRIDGNORTH RD

Enville

PO

The Close

The Cat Inn (PH)

Crown Covert

Elm House

The Lyons

HALL DR

Engine House Pool

Leigh House Farm

Enville Hall

THE AVENUE

KINVER RD

COTE LA

The Rookery

A458

81 A 82 B C 83 D E F 86

8 7 89 6 5 88 4 3 87 2 1

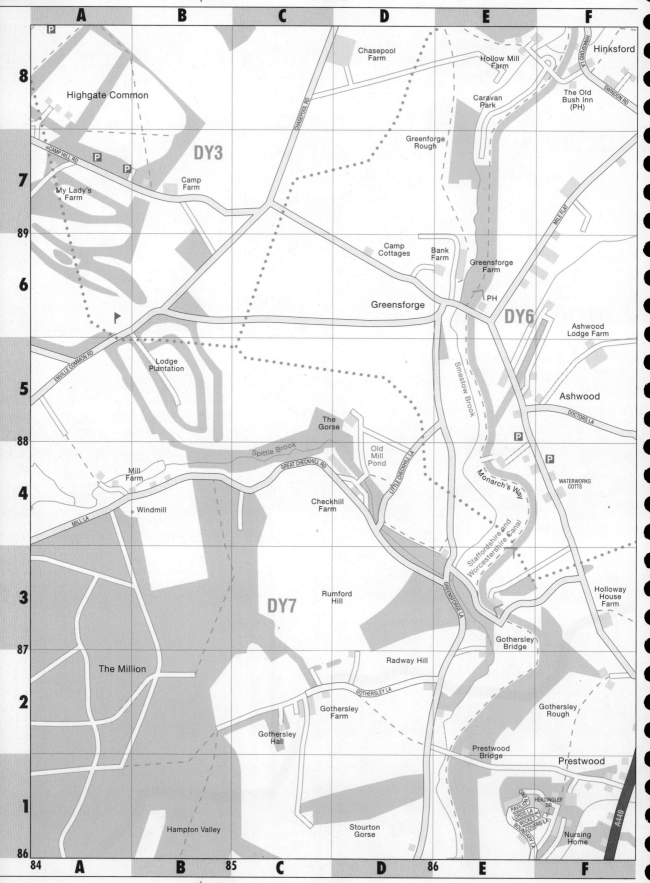

273
269

A B C D E F

8

Highgate Common

Chasepool Farm

Hollow Mill Farm

Hinksford

The Old Bush Inn (PH)

DY3

Greenforge Rough

7

My Lady's Farm

Camp Farm

Caravan Park

CAMP HILL RD

89

Camp Cottages

Bank Farm

Greensforge Farm

6

Greensforge

DY6

Ashwood Lodge Farm

ENVILLE COMMON RD

Lodge Plantation

PH

5

Smestow Brook

Ashwood

DOCTORS LA

88

The Gorse

Old Mill Pond

Spittle Brook

GREAT CHECKHILL RD

WATERWORKS COTTS

4

Mill Farm

Checkhill Farm

LITTLE CHECKHILL LA

Monarch's Way

Windmill

MILL LA

Staffordshire and Worcestershire Canal

3

DY7

Rumford Hill

GREENSFORGE LA

Holloway House Farm

87

The Million

Radway Hill

Gothersley Bridge

2

Gothersley Farm

GOTHERSLEY LA

Gothersley Rough

Gothersley Hall

Prestwood Bridge

Prestwood

1

PAVILION
LORDS LA
WICKET
COVERS LA
HEADINGLEY DR
BOUNDARY LA

Hampton Valley

Stourton Gorse

Nursing Home

A449

86

84 A 85 B C 86 D E F

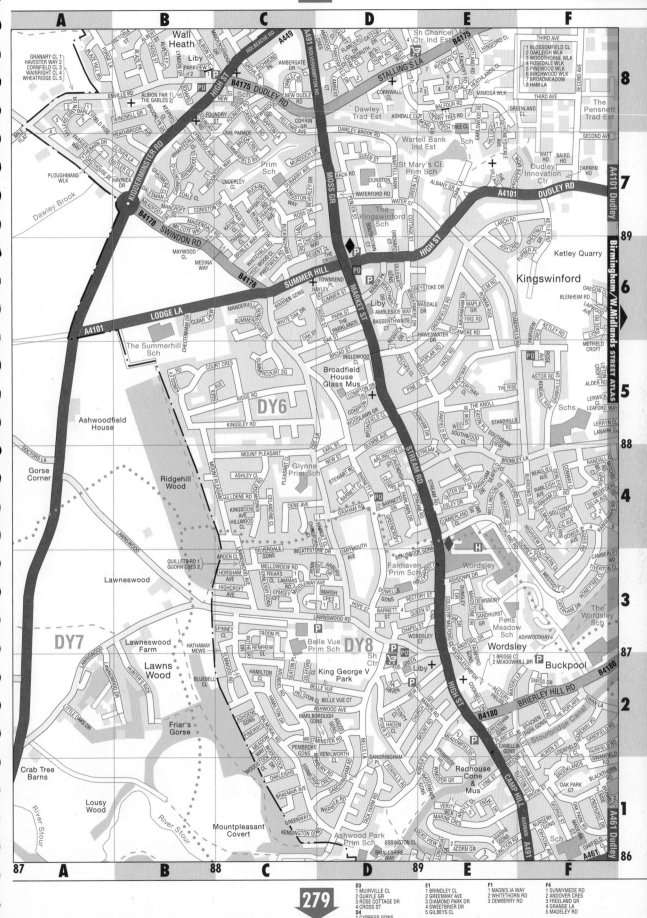

279

D3
1 MUIRVILLE CL
2 QUAYLE GR
3 ROSE COTTAGE DR
4 CROSS ST
D4
1 CYPRESS GDNS
2 THE SHOPS

E1
1 BRINDLEY CL
2 GREENWAY AVE
3 DIAMOND PARK DR
4 SWEETBRIER DR
5 GILBEYS CL

F1
1 MAGNOLIA WAY
2 WHITETHORN RD
3 DEWBERRY RD

F4
1 SUNNYMEDE RD
2 ANDOVER CRES
3 FREELAND GR
4 GRANGE LA
5 MADELEY RD

272

A442 Bridgnorth
A442 Kidderminster

Shropshire STREET ATLAS

Worcestershire STREET ATLAS

DY7
WV15
DY12
DY11

Chidleys Farm
Astley
Filletts
Barrets
The Hollies
Cains Coppice
Perry House
Leybrook Coppice
Perryhouse Dingle
Cains Gorse
No Man's Green
Birch Wood
HOLLIES LA
SHEEPWALKS LA
NO MAN'S GREEN LA
Herons Gate Farm
Howlet Hall
HERONS GATE RD
Herons Gate
Square Coppice
Bowhills Dingle
Roughpark Wood
New Barns
Lenmores
Hartsgreen
Compton Park Farm
Stoneacre
Heath House Farm
Cross Farm
BEACON LA
Hightrees Farm
Lower House Farm
Tucksash
Start's Green
Romsley
Tudor House
Brittle's Farm
DY12
Poolhouse Farm
Arley Wood
ROMSLEY LA
Brittle's Cottages
Castlehill Wood
Hammer Hill Farm
A442
Coldridge Wood
DY11

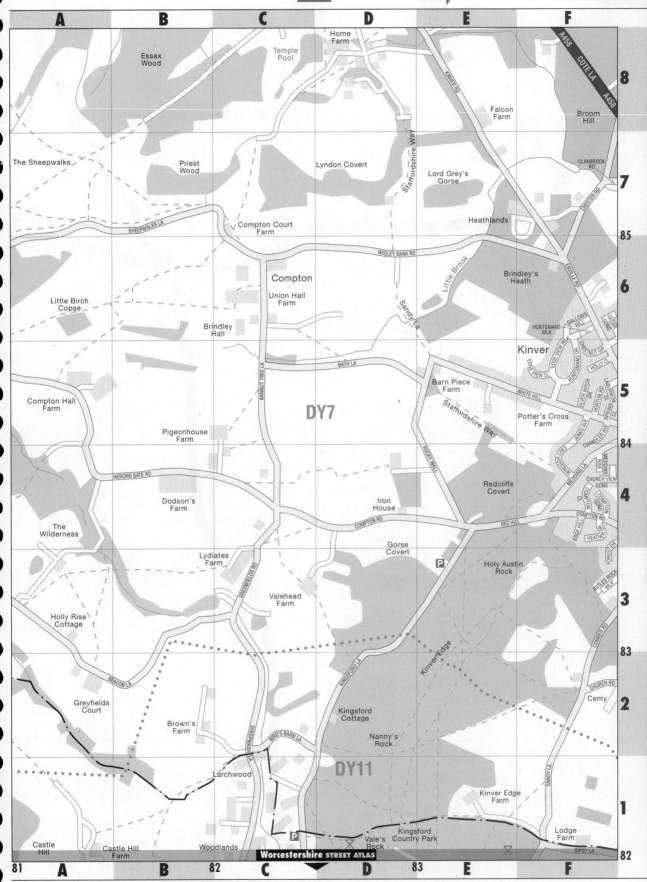

A   B   C   D   E   F

8

7

85

6

5

84

4

83

3

2

1

82

Essex Wood

Temple Pool

Home Farm

Falcon Farm

Broom Hill

A458

COTE LA

A458

The Sheepwalks

Priest Wood

Lyndon Covert

Staffordshire Way

Lord Grey's Gorse

CLANBROOK RD.

CHESTER RD

KINVER RD

SHEEPWALKS LA

Compton Court Farm

WIGLEY BANK RD

Heathlands

ENVILLE RD

Little Birch Copse

Compton

Union Hall Farm

Little Brook

Brindley's Heath

HUNTSMANS WLK

GALLOWS HILL

CEDAR GDNS

Brindley Hall

Sandy La

Kinver

EDGE VIEW WLK

HUNTSMANS

EDGE VIEW CL

CHESTNUT GR

HORTOM RD

HOLLY CL

Compton Hall Farm

BANNUT TREE LA

BATH LA

Barn Piece Farm

WHITE HILL

SILVER BIRCH DR

LABURNUM GRO

SPRING CL

DY7

Pigeonhouse Farm

Staffordshire Way

Potter's Cross Farm

JEAN'S AVE

CHANDLER AVE

MEADINS RISE

WINDSOR CRES

HERONS GATE RD

Dodson's Farm

ROCKY WALL

Redcliffe Covert

MEADINS LA

CHURCH VIEW GDNS

COMPTON RD

COMPTON GDNS

The Wilderness

Iron House

COMPTON RD

RED HILL

EDGE HILL CL

HEATH CL

FORDHO DR

Lydiates Farm

GREENFIELDS RD

Gorse Covert

P

Holy Austin Rock

ASTLES ROCK WLK

Holly Rise Cottage

Valehead Farm

Kinver Edge

CLUMBER RD

BEACON LA

KINGSFORD LA

CHURCH RD

Greyfields Court

Brown's Farm

SHEEPWASH LA

BIRD'S BARN LA

Kingsford Cottage

Cemy

SANDY LA

Nanny's Rock

DY11

Kinver Edge Farm

Larchwood

P

Vale's Rock

Kingsford Country Park

Lodge Farm

Castle Hill

Castle Hill Farm

Woodlands

GIPSY LA

81   82   83

A   B   C   D   E   F

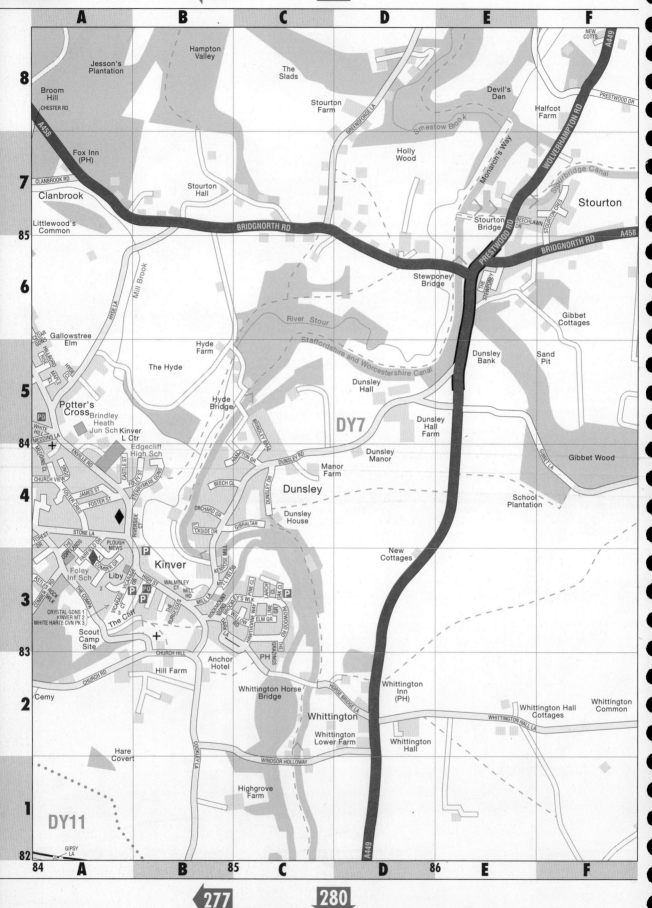

281

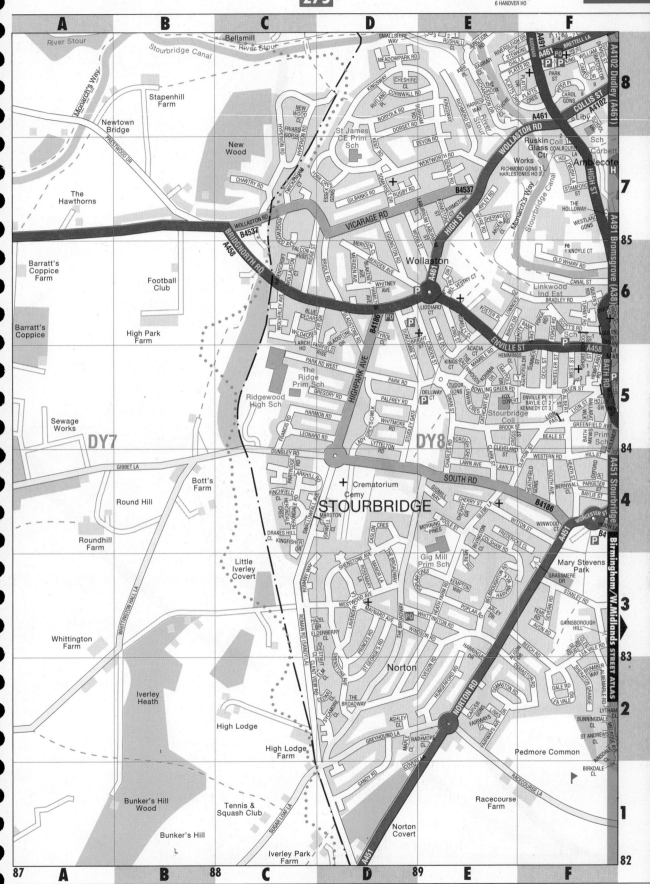

E8
1 THE JUNCTION
2 ALDRIDGE CL
3 LONGBOAT LA
4 STEWKINS CT

F8
1 CRYSTAL AVE
2 SURREY HO
3 WILTSHIRE HO
4 DEVON HO
5 LANCASTER HO
6 HANOVER HO

7 ALLAN CL
8 CORBETT HO
9 DENNIS HALL

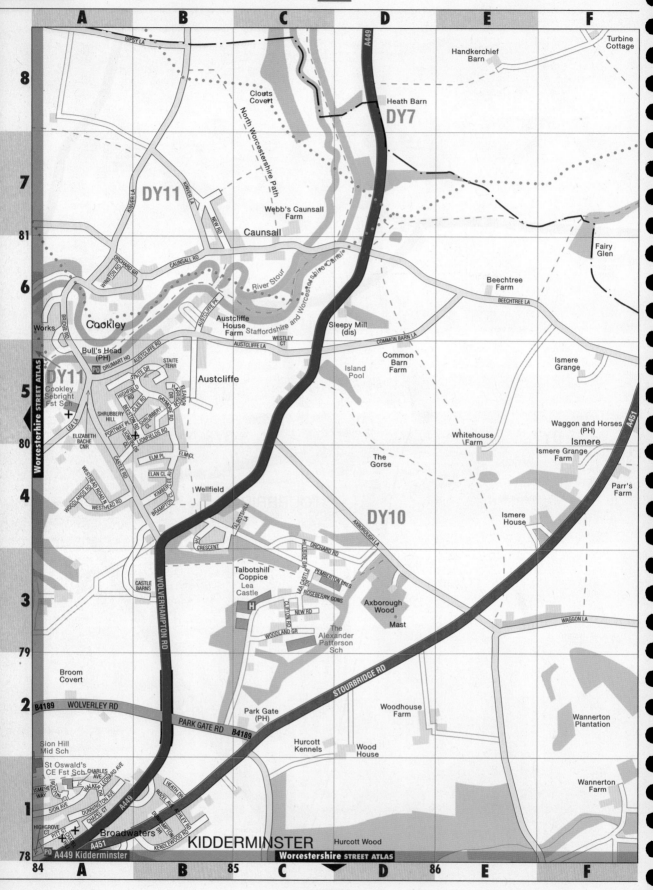

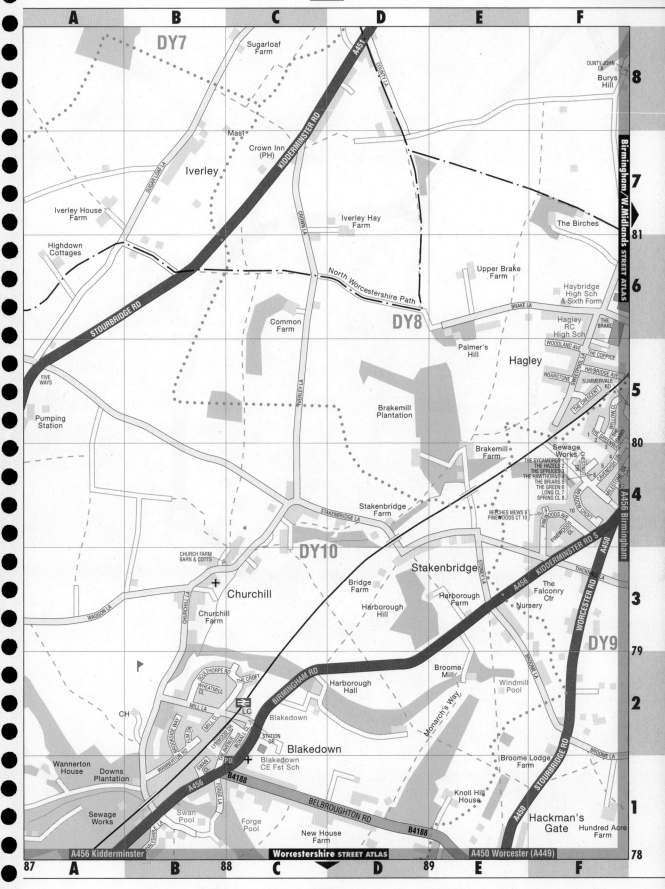

DY7

Sugarloaf Farm

Mast

Crown Inn (PH)

Iverley

Iverley House Farm

Highdown Cottages

STOURBRIDGE RD

FIVE WAYS

Pumping Station

KIDDERMINSTER RD

CROWN LA

Iverley Hay Farm

North Worcestershire Path

DY8

Common Farm

IVERLEY LA

Brakemill Plantation

Brakemill Farm

STAKENBRIDGE LA

Stakenbridge Farm

DY10

CHURCH FARM BARN & COTTS

Churchill

Churchill Farm

WAGGON LA

CHURCHILL LA

Bridge Farm

Harborough Hill

Stakenbridge

Harborough Farm

COUNTY LA

The Birches

81

Upper Brake Farm

BRAKE LA

Haybridge High Sch & Sixth Form

Hagley RC High Sch

THE BRAKE

THE COPPICE

WOODLAND AVE

Palmer's Hill

Hagley

HOARSTONE

SWEETPOOL LA

HAYBRIDGE AVE

SUMMERVALE RD

THE CRESCENT

WILTON CL

THE GREENWAY

THE GREENS

5

80

Sewage Works

CHESTNUT DR

CAVENDISH DR

MILLSTONE DR

MEADOW CROFT

THE SYCAMORES 1
THE HAZELS 2
THE SPRUCES 3
THE HAWTHORNS 4
THE BRIARS 5
THE GREEN 6
LONG CL 7
SPRING CL 8

BEECHES MEWS 9
PINEWOODS CT 10

PINEWOODS AVE

PINEWOODS CL

A456

KIDDERMINSTER RD S

THICKNALL

The Falconry Ctr

Nursery

STONEY LA

WORCESTER RD

A450

A456 Birmingham

DY9

3

79

Broome Mill

Windmill Pool

BROOME LA

Harborough Hall

BIRMINGHAM RD

Harborough Hall

SCULTHORPE RD

WHEATMILL CL

THE CROFT

MILL LA

MILL CL

BROOKSIDE WAY

ELM DR

WANNERTON RD

THE AVENUE

LYNWOOD DR

ROXALL CL

LC

Blakedown

STATION DR

Blakedown

PO

Blakedown CE Fst Sch

CH

Wannerton House

Downs Plantation

SWAN CL

FORGE LA

HALESHIRE LA

B4188

A456

Swan Pool

Forge Pool

Sewage Works

Monarch's Way

New House Farm

BELBROUGHTON RD

B4188

Knoll Hill House

Broome Lodge Farm

STOURBRIDGE RD

A450

Hackman's Gate

Hundred Acre Farm

2

1

78

Birmingham /W. Midlands STREET ATLAS

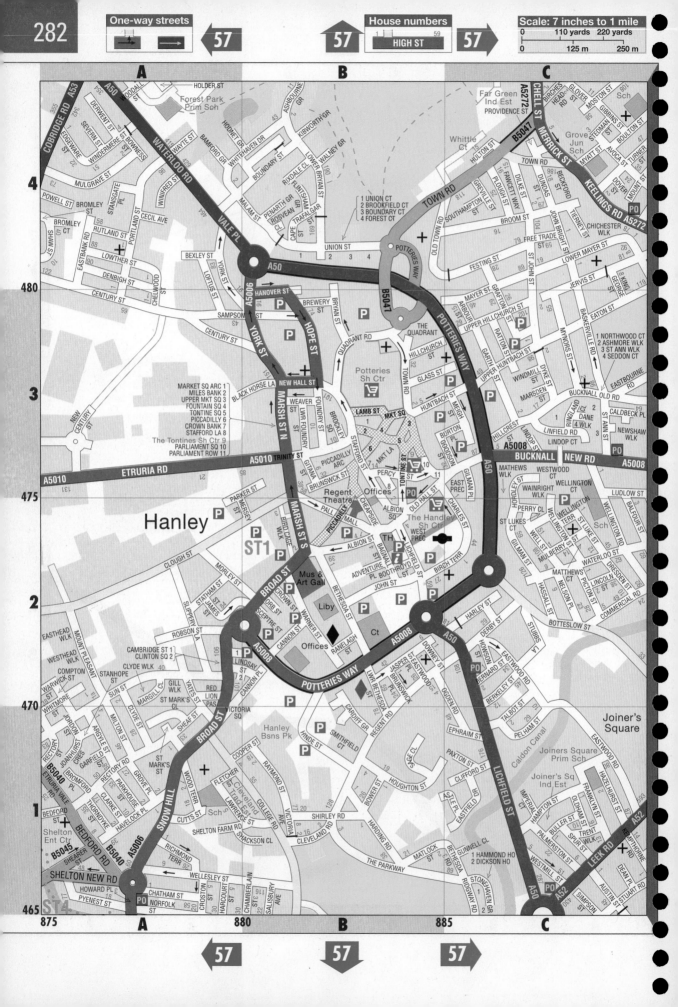

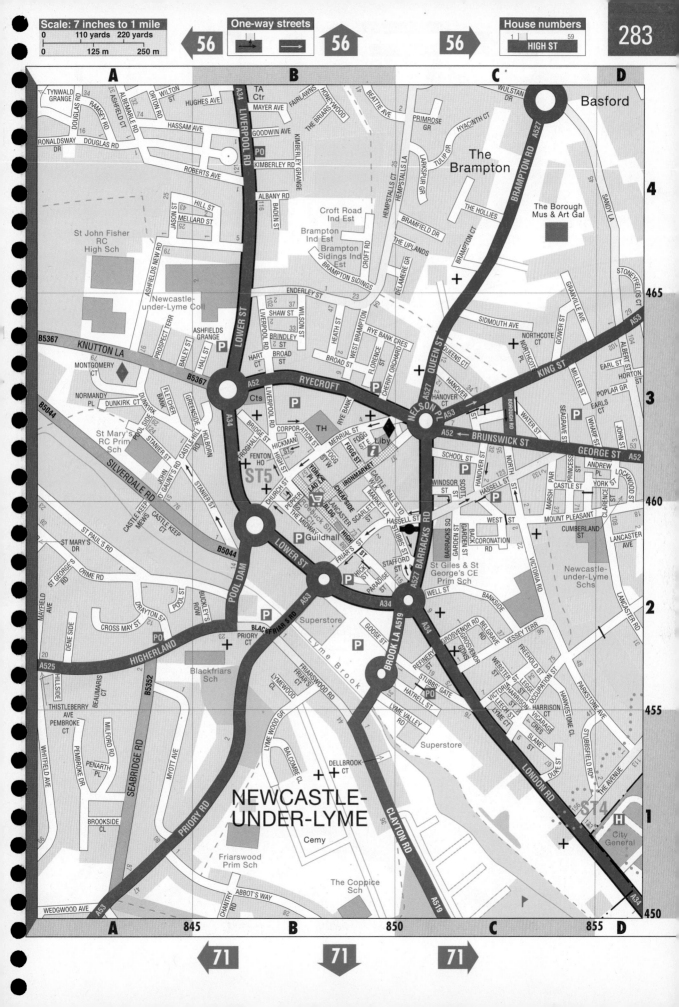

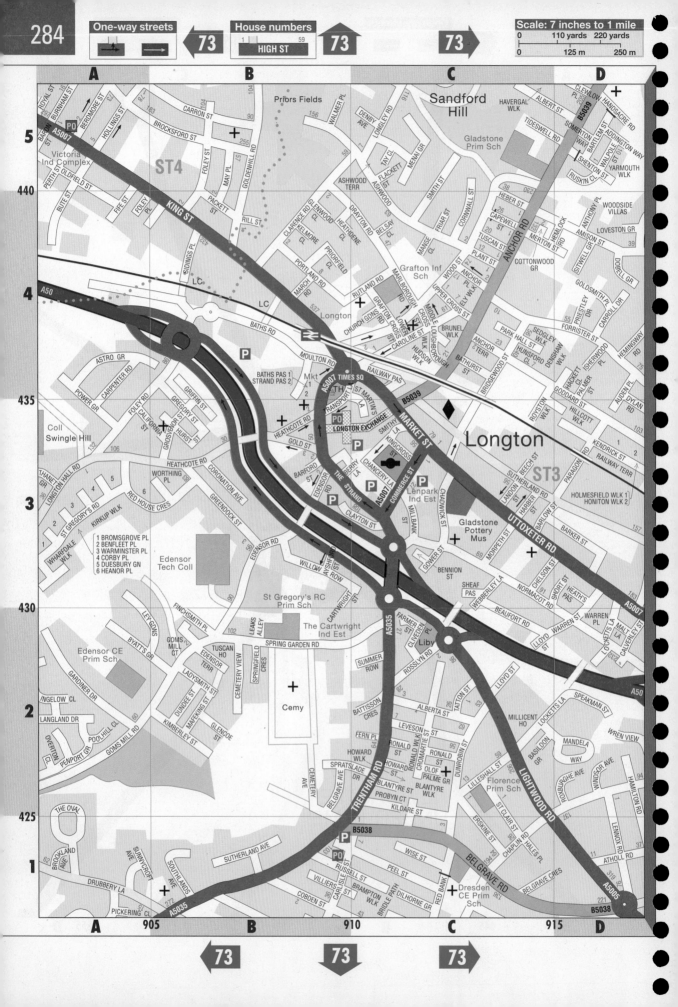

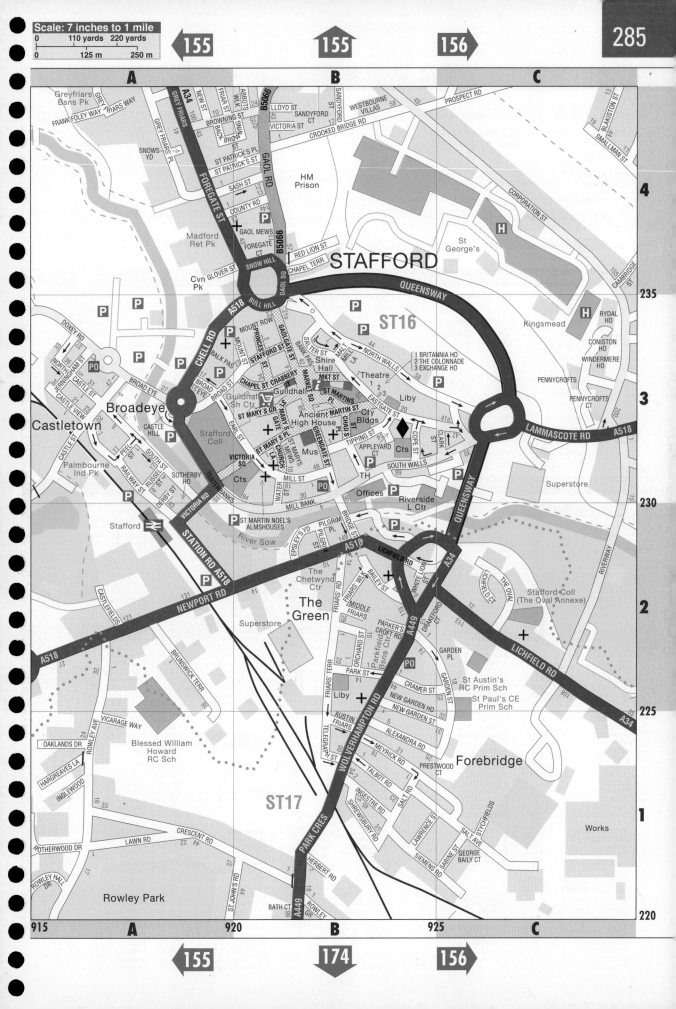

Index

Place name May be abbreviated on the map → **Church Rd**

Location number Present when a number indicates the place's position in a crowded area of mapping → **6**

Locality, town or village Shown when more than one place has the same name → Beckenham

Postcode district District for the indexed place → BR2

Page and grid square Page number and grid reference for the standard mapping → **53** C6

Church Rd **6** Beckenham BR2..........**53** C6

Public and commercial buildings are highlighted in **magenta** **Places of interest** are highlighted in **blue** with a star★

Abbreviations used in the index

Acad	**Academy**	Comm	**Common**	Gd	**Ground**	L	**Leisure**	Prom	**Promenade**
App	**Approach**	Cott	**Cottage**	Gdn	**Garden**	La	**Lane**	Rd	**Road**
Arc	**Arcade**	Cres	**Crescent**	Gn	**Green**	Liby	**Library**	Recn	**Recreation**
Ave	**Avenue**	Cswy	**Causeway**	Gr	**Grove**	Mdw	**Meadow**	Ret	**Retail**
Bglw	**Bungalow**	Ct	**Court**	H	**Hall**	Meml	**Memorial**	Sh	**Shopping**
Bldg	**Building**	Ctr	**Centre**	Ho	**House**	Mkt	**Market**	Sq	**Square**
Bsns, Bus	**Business**	Ctry	**Country**	Hospl	**Hospital**	Mus	**Museum**	St	**Street**
Bvd	**Boulevard**	Cty	**County**	HQ	**Headquarters**	Orch	**Orchard**	Sta	**Station**
Cath	**Cathedral**	Dr	**Drive**	Hts	**Heights**	Pal	**Palace**	Terr	**Terrace**
Cir	**Circus**	Dro	**Drove**	Ind	**Industrial**	Par	**Parade**	TH	**Town Hall**
Cl	**Close**	Ed	**Education**	Inst	**Institute**	Pas	**Passage**	Univ	**University**
Cnr	**Corner**	Emb	**Embankment**	Int	**International**	Pk	**Park**	Wk, Wlk	**Walk**
Coll	**College**	Est	**Estate**	Intc	**Interchange**	Pl	**Place**	Wr	**Water**
Com	**Community**	Ex	**Exhibition**	Junc	**Junction**	Prec	**Precinct**	Yd	**Yard**

Index of localities, towns and villages

A

Abbey Hulton **58** B7
Abbots Bromley **161** B6
Acton **86** C8
Acton Trussell **175** B1
Adbaston **131** D4
Admaston **160** A3
Albrighton **237** A6
Aldersley **255** F7
Aldridge **256** A6
Allgreave **1** C3
Allimore Green **172** D3
Almington **98** C2
Alrewas **200** F3
Alsagers Bank **54** F5
Alsop en le Dale **36** E3
Alstonefield **35** D4
Alton **78** F1
Alvecote **251** D6
Amblecote **279** F7
Amerton **139** A4
Amington **251** B4
Anslow **165** C7
Anslow Gate **164** E7
Apeton **172** C1
Armitage **198** B4
Armsdale **115** D5
Armshead **59** B5
Ash Bank **59** A3
Ashley **100** B5
Ashley Dale **100** B5
Ashmore park **242** A2
Ashwood **274** F5
Aspley **117** B7
Astbury **15** B7
Aston
Claverley **267** F8
Newcastle-under-Lyme **84** A7
Stafford **154** E4
Aston-By-Stone **120** C4
Aston Heath **129** B6
Audley **39** E2
Audmore **171** F8
Austcliffe **280** B5

B

Back of Ecton **34** F8
Baddeley Edge **43** D1
Baddeley Green **43** B3
Bagnall **43** F2
Balance Hill **126** C5
Baldwins Gate **85** C4
Ball Green **42** D6
Balterley **38** C1
Balterley Green **38** C2
Bank Top
Draycott in the Clay **144** B6
Stoke-on-Trent **42** B4
Barlaston **88** F2
Barlaston Park **88** F4
Barr Common **256** C3
Barthomley **38** C5
Barton Gate **183** B3
Barton Turn **184** B1
Barton-under-Needwood **183** C2
Basford **283** D4
Baswich **156** D1
Bath Vale **6** B3
Beaconside **156** B5
Beamhurst **110** B6
Beamhurst Lane **110** C4
Bearstone **83** A4
Beasley **55** F7
Bednall **193** F8
Bednall Head **194** A8
Beech **87** C1
Beffcote **170** F2
Belgrave **250** E1
Bemersley Green **27** D1
Bentilee **58** D2
Beobridge **267** C4
Berry Hill **57** F1
Betley **53** A6
Betley Common **52** F6
Betton **98** A6
Bickford **191** D1
Biddulph **27** B7
Biddulph Moor **17** B1
Bignall End **39** F3
Bignall Hill **40** B2
Bilbrook **239** C4
Billington **173** D6
Birch Cross **127** C2
Birches Head **57** E6
Birchmoor **262** D8
Bishop's Offley **132** A8
Bishops Wood **221** F8
Bishton **178** A6
Bitterscote **250** A4
Blackbrook
Baldwin's Gate **84** D2
Tutbury **145** C1
Blackfords **209** E2
Blackshaw Moor **20** E4
Blackwood Hill **28** F4
Blakedown **281** C2
Blakeley **269** F4
Blakeley Green **255** F8
Blakeley Lane **60** C3
Blakenhall
Chorlton **52** A4
Wolverhampton **266** B7
Blithbury **180** A5
Blore
Loggerheads **99** A2
Swinscoe **65** F7
Bloreheath **98** E3
Blount's Green **126** A5
Blundies **273** E3
Blurton **72** E1
Blymhill **203** F5
Blymhill Lawn **204** B3
Blythe Bridge **90** E8
Blythe Marsh **91** B7
Bobbington **268** A2
Bog Moor **194** B7
Bolehall **250** D4
Boley Park **231** F7
Bond End **166** D1
Bonehill **249** E2
Boney Hay **212** A1
Boningale **237** A2
Boon Hill **39** F1
Boothen **72** B5
Borough Park **250** C8
Borrowcop Hill **231** C6
Boscomoor **207** E6
Bosley **7** D8
Boundary **75** E2
Bowers **102** B4
Braddocks Hay **27** C8
Bradeley **42** C3
Bradley **191** C8
Bradley in the Moors **94** C7
Bradmore **265** E8
Bradnop **31** E3
Bradshaw **29** D4
Bradwell **56** B8
Bramshall **125** C8
Branston **184** F7
Brazenhill **172** F8
Brereton **197** B5
Brereton Cross **197** D3
Breretonhill **197** B4
Brewood **223** D5
Bridgemere **67** A7
Bridgtown **226** E6
Brindley Ford **27** B1
Brineton **203** F8
Brinsford **240** D7
Broadeye **285** A3
Broadhill **170** E3
Broad Meadow **55** E6
Broad Oak **272** A7
Broadwaters **280** A1
Brockton **117** B4
Brocton **176** C4
Bromley Hurst **161** B1
Bromstead **188** E7
Bromstead Heath **188** E7
Brookhouses **76** A3
Broomhill **209** E4
Broomyshaw **63** C8
Broughton
Claverley **267** F4
Loggerheads **115** C8
Brown Edge **43** A8
Brownhills **244** D8
Brown Lees **27** A5
Brund **23** E7
Bucknall **58** A4
Buckpool **275** F2
Buddileigh **52** F7
Buglawton **6** A4
Burnhill Green **252** B6
Burntwood **229** C5
Burntwood Green **229** D6
Burslem **56** F7
Burston **121** B1
Burton Manor **174** E6
Burton upon Trent **166** E1
Burybank **104** C4
Bushbury **240** E2
Butters Green **40** A2
Butterton
Leek **33** F5
Newcastle-under-Lyme **70** D1
Butterton Moor **33** B5
Butt Lane **25** D1
Buxton **4** D8

C

Calf Heath **225** A6
Callingwood **164** D4
Calton **49** E1
Cannock **209** D2
Cannock Wood **211** F5
Carmountside **58** B8
Carroway Head **259** C4
Castlecroft **265** B8
Castle Gresley **186** E1
Castletown **285** A3
Cats Edge **44** D6
Catshill **245** A6
Cat's Hill Cross **117** D2
Cauldon **63** F7
Cauldon Lowe **63** E4
Caunsall **280** C7
Caverswall **74** E2
Cellarhead **59** E4
Chadsmoor **209** F4
Chadwell **188** A1
Chapel Chorlton **102** B8
Chase Terrace **228** E8
Chasetown **228** F6
Chatcull **101** D2
Chatterley **41** B3
Cheadle **76** D4
Chebsey **134** E6
Checkley Madeley **52** C1
Upper Tean **109** B8
Checkley Green **67** B8
Cheddleton **45** D5
Cheddleton Heath **45** E7
Chell Heath **42** A5
Chelmorton **5** D8
Cheslyn Hay **226** C3
Chesterfield **246** E8
Chesterton **55** E7
Cheswardine **130** A7
Chetwynd **168** C7
Chetwynd Aston **187** A8
Chilcote **219** F3
Chipnall **114** B3
Chorley **212** E3
Chorlton **37** B1
Christ Church **231** A8
Churchbridge **226** F4
Church Eaton **190** A8
Churchill **281** C3
Church Lawton **25** C3
Church Leigh **109** B4
Church Mayfield **81** D6
Cinder Hill **266** F1
Clanbrook **278** A7
Claregate **255** E6
Claverley **267** D8
Clayhanger **244** D6
Clay Mills **148** A3
Clayton **71** B4
Cliff **261** C1
Cliff Vale **56** F2
Clifton **81** F6
Clifton Campville **218** F1
Cloud Side **7** B3
Clough Hall **40** F8
Coalpit Hill **40** C8
Cobridge **57** B6
Codsall **238** E4
Codsall Wood **238** B6
Coldeaton **36** B6
Coldmeece **118** C5
Cold Well **212** B5
Colshaw **3** E4
Colton **179** A6
Colton Hills **266** B3
Colwich **177** E7
Combridge **111** C8
Compton Kinver **277** C6
Wolverhampton **255** D2
Congleton **6** A4
Congreve **207** B7
Consall **60** D6
Cookley **280** A6
Cookshill **74** C3
Cooper's Bank **271** C1
Copmere End **132** E7
Coppenhall **174** C4

Cornhill 42 D5
Cotes 103 A2
Cotes Heath 102 D4
Coton
  Gnosall 171 B5
  Milwich 122 D5
  Tamworth 249 C6
Coton Clanford 154 A4
Coton Green 249 F8
Coton Hayes 122 F6
Coton Hill 122 F5
Coton in the Clay 144 F7
Cotonwood 170 E6
Cotton 78 D8
Cotwalton 105 F2
Coven 224 A2
Coven Heath 240 C6
Coven Lawn 240 A8
Cowall Moor 28 B4
Cowley 171 D4
Coxgreen 272 E2
Crackley 55 E8
Cracow Moss 53 B3
Craddocks Moss 53 F5
Crakemarsh 111 D5
Cranberry 102 D5
Crateford 224 B7
Craythorne 147 D2
Creighton 111 A5
Cresswell 91 C3
Creswell 155 A7
Creswell Green 212 E1
Crossgate 106 D7
Cross Green 224 D1
Cross Heath 56 A3
Crowborough 28 B7
Crowdecote 13 E7
Croxall 216 F8
Croxden 94 D4
Croxton 116 B5
Croxtonbank 116 B6
Curborough 214 D5

D

Dagdale 110 A1
Dales Green 26 C5
Danebridge 9 B7
Dane in Shaw 16 C8
Danford 267 E8
Dapple Heath 140 F1
Darnford 231 F6
Dayhills 121 F6
Denford 44 F8
Denstone 95 D6
Derrington 154 D1
Dibdale 271 F3
Dilhorne 75 D4
Dimsdale 56 B5
Dods Leigh 108 E2
Doley 130 E8
Dordon 262 F6
Dorrington 83 C7
Dosthill 261 C5
Dove Bank 26 A2
Dove Head 3 D6
Doveridge 127 B7
Doxey 155 B4
Draycott 268 A6
Draycott in the Clay 144 C6
Draycott in the Moors . . . 91 E5
Drayton Bassett 260 D5
Drointon 140 B2
Dudley 271 F1
Duke Bank 42 F4
Dunsley 278 C4
Dunstal 141 F1
Dunstall 183 D6
Dunston 192 F8
Dunston Heath 192 C7
Dunwood 29 D3

E

Earl Sterndale 5 C3
Eaton 6 A8
Eccleshall 133 E6
Ecton 23 D2
Edge Hill 262 C2
Edgmond 168 A3
Edial 229 F6
Edingale 217 D5
Efflinch 201 E7
Egginton 148 B5
Elford 216 C2
Ellastone 80 B3
Ellenhall 134 A1
Elmhurst 214 A5
Endon 43 E7
Endon Bank 43 E8
Englesea-brook 38 A4
Enson 137 C6
Enville 273 D2
Essington 241 F3
Etchinghill 178 B1
Etruria 56 F4
Ettingshall Park 266 D3

F

Fairoak 115 D6
Farewell 213 A4
Far Hoarcross 162 E2
Farley Park 78 D5
Farmcote 267 A5

Fauld 145 C6
Fawfieldhead 12 F3
Fazeley 260 F8
Featherstone 241 C7
Fegg Hayes 42 B7
Fenton 72 E5
Fenton Low 72 E7
Festival Park 57 A4
Finchfield 265 D8
Finney Green 54 C1
Fishley 243 C4
Flash 3 A3
Fole 109 E7
Footherley 246 E3
Ford Green 42 E2
Fordbridge 285 C1
Fordhouses 240 D2
Forebridge 285 C1
Forsbrook 91 B7
Forton 169 A7
Foston 129 D4
Four Ashes
  Coven 224 C6
  Enville 272 E3
Four Crosses 225 F7
Four Oaks 257 F5
Foxholes 144 E4
Foxley 39 D7
Foxt 62 C6
Fradley 215 E7
Fradswell 123 A3
Freasley 262 C4
Freehay 93 A7
Froghall 62 A4
Fulford 106 D8

G

Gailey 207 C1
Gailey Wharf 207 E1
Garshall Green 122 C8
Gateham 35 B6
Gayton 138 E6
Gentleshaw 212 A4
Gerrard's Bromley 101 A2
Giggetty 269 E6
Gillow Heath 16 C2
Gillway 250 B8
Glascote Heath 250 F2
Gnosall 171 D6
Gnosall Heath 171 D5
Goldenhill 41 B7
Goldthorn Hill 266 A5
Goldthorn Park 266 C5
Goodleybrook 75 D5
Goosemoor Green 212 C4
Gornalwood 271 C2
Gorstey Ley 229 C7
Gorstyhill 37 E2
Gorsty Hill 142 D7
Gospel Ash 268 D3
Gospel End Village 271 A4
Gradbach 10 A8
Gratton 29 A5
Gratwich 124 C4
Great Bridgeford 135 D3
Great Chatwell 188 C1
Great Chell 42 A6
Great Haywood 158 C2
Great Moor 253 F1
Great Saredon 225 E5
Great Wyrley 227 B3
Green Fields 139 C1
Greenhead 60 F2
Greenleighs 266 C3
Greensforge 274 D6
Grindley 140 D7
Grindon 34 B2
Groundslow Fields 103 D3
Grub Street 151 A7
Gunstone 239 A6

H

Hackman's Gate 281 F1
Hagley 281 E5
Hagley Park 196 D8
Hales 113 F8
Halfpenny Green 268 D4
Hall End 262 F5
Hall Green 25 E5
Halmer End 54 D7
Hammerwich 229 D4
Hamstall Ridware 180 E3
Hanbury 145 A5
Hanbury Woodend 144 E2
Hanchurch 87 B7
Handsacre 198 C8
Hanford 71 E1
Hangingbridge 81 E8
Hanley 282 A2
Hansley Cross 78 C2
Hardings Booth 12 D5
Harding's Wood 25 E2
Hardwick 256 E3
Harlaston 217 D2
Harper's Gate 29 E8
Harriseahead 26 E4
Hartington 24 D5
Hartley Green 138 D8
Hartsgreen 276 C4
Hartshill 71 E7
Hartwell 89 C2
Haselour 217 B2
Hatherton 208 E1
Hatton 146 D8
Haughton 172 F5

Haughtondale 173 B7
Haunton 218 B2
Hawks Green 210 B1
Hazelslade 211 B6
Hazles 61 C5
Heath End 244 A1
Heath Hayes 210 F1
Heath Hill 187 C1
Heathton 268 A5
Heatley 141 D3
Heaton 8 E2
Hednesford 210 D5
Heighley 53 E3
Hem Heath 88 D7
Heron Cross 72 F4
Highbridge 244 B6
High Carr 40 F3
Highfields
  Burntwood 228 F4
  Stafford 174 C8
High Heath 244 D2
Highlanes 116 D6
High Offley 132 B1
High Town 210 A5
Highwood 126 D4
Hilderstone 106 D1
Hill 258 A4
Hill Chorlton 85 D3
Hill Hook 257 C6
Hill Ridware 198 A8
Hill Top 210 C4
Hill Wood 258 C5
Hilton
  Egginton 147 E8
  Shenstone 246 A8
Himley 270 B3
Hinksford 274 F8
Hints 248 D3
Hints Hill 248 F3
Hixon 158 D8
Hixon Heath 139 B1
Hobble End 243 B7
Hockley 261 E5
Hodgefield 28 B2
Hollies Common 171 B8
Hollington 94 B2
Hollins
  Biddulph Moor 28 F8
  Kidsgrove 40 E8
  Kingsley 61 A3
Hollinsclough 4 C1
Holly Bank 245 B3
Hollybush 72 B3
Holly Wall 41 B5
Holmcroft 155 C7
Hookgate 99 F3
Hope 35 D3
Hopedale 35 C2
Hopton 137 D1
Hopton Heath 137 B1
Hopwas 249 B7
Horninglow 166 C7
Horse Bridge 45 A8
Horsebrook 206 D2
Horton 29 C7
Huddlesford 232 C8
Hulme 74 A4
Hulme End 23 F3
Huntington 209 D7
Huntley 92 C7
Hyde Lea 174 C5

I

Ilam 50 E3
Ingestre 157 E6
Ipstones 62 A8
Ireland's Cross 83 C7
Islington 168 F5
Ismere 280 F5
Iverley 281 B7
Ivetsey Bank 204 E3

J

Jack Hayes 58 E8
Joiner's Square 282 C1
Jugbank 100 A4

K

Keele 69 F7
Kerry Hill 58 F7
Kettlebrook 250 B3
Key Green 6 E4
Kiddemore Green 222 D6
Kidderminster 280 B1
Kidsgrove 26 B1
King's Bromley 199 C6
Kingsley 61 E3
Kingsley Holt 62 A1
Kingsley Moor 60 F1
Kingslow 252 C2
Kingstone 141 C8
Kingswinford 275 F6
Kingswood 237 C5
Kingswood Common 238 B2
Kinver 278 B3
Knightley 152 A6
Knightley Dale 152 B3
Knighton
  Adbaston 130 F3
  Loggerheads 83 C5
Knotbury 2 F5
Knowl Bank 53 E7

Knutton 55 F2
Knypersley 27 C5

L

Ladfordfield 134 E1
Landywood 243 A8
Lane Ends 27 A3
Lane Green 239 C3
Lanesfield 266 E4
Laney Green 226 A3
Lapley 206 B6
Lask Edge 28 C7
Latherford 225 B4
Lawnhead 152 E6
Lawns Wood 275 B2
Lawton-gate 25 A4
Leadendale 89 F3
Lea Heath 159 B8
Leamonsley 230 E1
Leek 30 E6
Leekbrook 45 F8
Leighswood 256 A7
Levedale 191 F6
Leycett 54 C2
Leyfields 249 F7
Ley Hill 258 B1
Leys 62 C3
Lichfield 231 D5
Light Oaks 43 E1
Lightwood
  Cheadle 76 F3
  Longton 89 E7
Limepits 85 D8
Linton 186 A1
Lipley 114 E3
Little Aston 257 B4
Little Bloxwich 243 E6
Little Bridgeford 135 B3
Little Burton 166 D4
Little Chell 41 F4
Little Drayton 112 A8
Little Hay 247 C1
Little Haywood 177 C8
Little Madeley 68 F7
Little Saredon 225 E3
Little Sugnall 116 F4
Littlewood 226 E4
Littleworth
  Cannock 210 E4
  Stafford 156 A4
Little Wyrley 243 E6
Loggerheads 99 C5
London Fields 271 F2
Long Common 268 C8
Long Compton 153 D2
Longdon 197 F1
Longdon Green 213 B7
Longford 168 B1
Longnor 13 A6
Longport 56 D8
Longridge 192 C4
Longsdon 29 F2
Longton 284 C3
Lower Beobridge 267 A3
Lower Elkstone 22 D1
Lower Ellastone 80 C2
Lower Gornal 271 E4
Lower Green 224 A3
Lower Hatton 102 B6
Lower Knightley 152 C4
Lower Leigh 108 F4
Lower Nobut 109 F2
Lower Penn 264 F4
Lower Stonnall 246 A4
Lower Tean 92 F2
Loxley Green 125 C2
Loynton 150 F5
Lullington 218 E7
Lynn 188 B4

M

Madeley 68 E6
Madeley Heath 69 B8
Maer 85 C1
Mapleton 66 F4
Marchington 127 E2
Marchington
  Woodlands 143 A6
Market Drayton 97 B2
Marsh Green 16 D3
Marston
  Stafford 136 E4
  Wheaton Aston 204 E8
Marston on Dove 147 B8
Mavesyn Ridware 198 A6
May Bank 56 C3
Mayfield 81 C8
Meaford 104 D4
Meerbrook 19 F7
Meir 74 A1
Meir Heath 90 A5
Mere Green 258 B3
Meretown 169 B6
Merridale 255 E2
Merry Hill 265 D7
Middle 226 A4
Middle Madeley 68 F7
Middle Mayfield 81 B6
Middleport 56 D7
Middleton 260 A1
Middleton Green 108 B3
Mile Oak 249 D1
Miles Green 54 E8
Milford 176 B7

Milldale 35 F2
Millend 39 C5
Mill Green
  Aldridge 256 F7
  Cannock 226 F8
Millmeece 117 F7
Milton 43 A8
Milwich 122 D5
Mitton 191 C3
Mobberley 92 D7
Moddershall 105 F6
Moneystone 63 A1
Moor Green 91 A8
Moor Hall 258 D1
Moreton
  Drayton in the Clay 144 C8
  Newport 188 D7
Morrey 181 D2
Morrilow Heath 107 E4
Mossgate 106 D7
Mossley
  Congleton 16 A8
  Rugeley 196 F7
Moss Pit 174 E5
Mount Pleasant
  Mow Cop 26 B5
  Stoke-on-Trent 72 D5
  Tamworth 250 C1
  Uttoxeter 126 B7
  Werrington 60 B2
Mow Cop 26 C7
Mucklestone 99 B7
Muckley Corner 230 A2

N

Napley 98 F8
Napley Heath 83 A1
Needwood 164 B5
Netherland Green 126 E2
Netherseal 219 E7
Nether Stowe 214 C3
Nethertown 198 B8
Newborough 162 E8
Newborough Brick Hill . . 163 A5
Newbridge 255 E3
Newcastle-under-Lyme . . 283 B1
Newchapel 26 E2
Newchurch 163 B3
Newfield 41 F4
Newhall 186 F6
Newpool 27 B6
Newport 168 D4
Newstead 88 E6
Newton 159 D8
Newton Hurst 141 A1
Newton Regis 236 D4
Newton Solney 167 E8
Newtown
  Biddulph 17 B5
  Great Wyrley 243 B6
  Longnor 12 C3
New Town 228 F2
No Man's Heath 236 F6
Norbury
  Gnosall 151 A3
  Roston 80 D1
Norbury Junction 151 D2
Northwood
  Hanley 57 E4
  Newcastle-under-Lyme . 71 D2
Norton 279 D2
Norton Bridge 119 A1
Norton Canes 227 F5
Norton East 228 A6
Norton Green 43 A5
Norton in Hales 82 C1
Norton-in-the-Moors 42 F4
Nurton 253 F3
Nurton Hill 253 E4

O

Oakamoor 78 B7
Oaken 238 D2
Oak Hill 71 F5
Oakley 98 C6
Oaks Green 128 D7
Offleybrook 132 A8
Offleyhay 132 D7
Offleymarsh 132 A7
Offleyrock 132 B7
Oldfallow 209 D4
Oldfurnace 77 E4
Old Perton 254 B2
Olive Green 181 B2
Onecote 32 F3
Onneley 68 A3
Orgreave 200 B5
Orslow 188 E3
Orton 264 F3
Otherton 207 F6
Oulton
  Newport 151 A1
  Stone 105 C4
Oulton Heath 105 B6
Ounsdale 269 C6
Outlands 115 E1
Outwoods
  Broadhill 170 A1
  Burton upon Trent 166 B6
Overley 200 D4
Overmoor 60 A3
Overton 93 F1
Oxbarn 265 E7
Oxford 42 B8

P

Packmoor ... 26 F1
Palmer Moor ... 127 E7
Palmers Cross ... 255 D8
Park End ... 39 A4
Parkfield ... 266 E5
Parkgate ... 79 F5
Parkside ... 155 D8
Pasford ... 252 D2
Pattingham ... 253 D2
Pave Lane ... 187 B7
Peacock Hay ... 40 F4
Pelsall ... 244 B3
Pelsall Wood ... 243 F5
Pendeford ... 239 F2
Penkhull ... 71 E6
Penkridge ... 192 E2
Penn ... 265 E5
Penn Fields ... 265 F6
Perry Crofts ... 250 B7
Pershall ... 133 B8
Perton ... 254 D4
Piccadilly ... 261 F1
Pillaton ... 208 C7
Pipe Gate ... 83 D6
Pipehill ... 230 C5
Pipe Ridware ... 198 C8
Pitts Hill ... 41 F5
Plardiwick ... 171 B6
Podmore ... 101 A4
Polesworth ... 262 F8
Poolend ... 19 B1
Poolfold ... 16 F4
Porthill ... 56 C6
Potter's Cross ... 278 A5
Prestwood Denstone ... 79 E1
  Kinver ... 274 F1
Prospect Village ... 211 C4
Puleston ... 149 C1
Pye Green ... 194 F1

Q

Quarry Hill ... 262 A7
Queensville ... 175 B8
Quixhill ... 95 E7

R

Rake End ... 179 F1
Rakeway ... 93 A8
Ramshorn ... 79 B7
Rangemore ... 164 C3
Ranton ... 153 D5
Ranton Green ... 153 B3
Ravenhill ... 196 F6
Ravenscliffe ... 41 A5
Ravenshall ... 53 A4
Rawnsley ... 211 B5
Red Bull ... 98 D3
Redhill ... 133 F6
Red Street ... 40 E3
Rickerscote ... 174 F5
Ridgeway ... 42 E8
Rileyhill ... 199 B2
Rising Brook ... 174 E7
Robin Hill ... 28 A8
Rocester ... 96 A3
Rock End ... 27 F6
Rodbaston ... 207 E4
Rolleston on Dove ... 147 B4
Romsley ... 276 A2
Rosehill ... 112 A1
Roston ... 96 E7
Rough Close ... 89 F3
Roughcote ... 74 C6
Rough Hills ... 266 F6
Roughley ... 258 D3
Rowley Park ... 285 A1
Rownall ... 59 E8

Rudge ... 263 A7
Rudyard ... 29 E8
Rugeley ... 196 E8
Ruiton ... 271 D5
Rumer Hill ... 226 F7
Rushton Spencer ... 8 B2
Russell's Hall ... 271 F1
Ryecroft Gate ... 18 C8
Rye Hills ... 39 E1

S

Salt ... 137 F4
Salt Heath ... 137 E3
Sandborough ... 181 B3
Sandfields ... 231 A5
Sandon ... 137 D7
Sandonbank ... 137 C5
Sandyfields ... 271 B6
Sandyford
  Stoke-on-Trent ... 41 D6
  Swynnerton ... 103 E6
Saverley Green ... 91 A2
Scholar Green ... 25 E8
Scot Hay ... 54 E4
Scounslow Green ... 142 C8
Scropton ... 129 E1
Seabridge ... 70 F3
Seckington ... 236 A3
Sedgley ... 271 F7
Seighford ... 154 B7
Seisdon ... 263 F2
Shackerley ... 221 B1
Shaffalong ... 45 A5
Shallowford ... 135 B7
Shareshill ... 225 D2
Sharpley Heath ... 107 B3
Shawfield ... 22 C8
Shebdon ... 150 C8
Sheen ... 24 A7
Sheepwash ... 74 E7
Shelfield ... 244 C1
Shelton ... 57 B1
Shelton under Harley ... 86 B3
Shenstone ... 247 A5
Shenstone Woodend ... 247 A1
Shire Oak ... 245 A6
Shirleywich ... 157 F8
Shobnall ... 166 A4
Shraleybrook ... 39 A1
Shut Heath ... 172 E8
Shutlanehead ... 70 B2
Shutt Green ... 223 A8
Shuttington ... 251 F7
Sideway ... 72 B3
Silverdale ... 55 B1
Six Ashes ... 272 B6
Slade Heath ... 224 E1
Slindon ... 117 D5
Slitting Mill ... 196 C7
Smallrice ... 121 E4
Smallthorne ... 42 C2
Smestow ... 269 C4
Smith's Green ... 38 B7
Snelston ... 81 C3
Sneyd Green ... 57 D7
Somerford ... 223 F6
Soudley ... 130 B6
Spade Green ... 230 A8
Sparklow ... 14 C8
Spath ... 111 B3
Springfields ... 71 E5
Springhill ... 245 E8
Spring Hill ... 265 C4
Springwood ... 55 C8
Stableford ... 86 B2
Stafford ... 285 B4
Stakenbridge ... 281 E3
Stallington ... 90 C4
Standon ... 102 A2
Stanfield ... 42 A3
Stanhope Bretby ... 167 F1
Stanley ... 44 A5

Stanley Moor ... 43 F4
Stanshope ... 35 D1
Stanton
  Mayfield ... 65 D1
  Swadlincote ... 186 C4
Stapenhill ... 185 F8
Stockton ... 187 D6
Stockton Brook ... 43 d5
Stockwell End ... 255 D6
Stockwell Heath ... 179 A8
Stoke ... 72 A7
Stoke-on-Trent ... 72 D7
Stone ... 120 B8
Stonefield ... 104 F2
Stone Heath ... 107 C3
Stonehouses ... 91 B6
Stonnall ... 245 E4
Stourbridge ... 279 D4
Stourton ... 278 F7
Stowe ... 214 C1
Stowe-by-Chartley ... 139 C3
Stowford ... 37 C8
Stramshall ... 111 A4
Streethay ... 215 A2
Streetley ... 257 C3
Streetly ... 257 D3
Stretton
  Brewood ... 206 C3
  Burton upon Trent ... 166 E8
Stubwood ... 95 D4
Sturbridge ... 117 E1
Sudbury ... 128 E4
Sugnall ... 116 D2
Sutton ... 150 D1
Sutton Coldfield ... 258 E1
Swadlincote ... 186 F4
Swindon ... 269 F2
Swinscoe ... 65 E5
Swynnerton ... 103 B4
Sytch House Green ... 267 A2

T

Tadgedale ... 99 C5
Talke ... 40 C7
Talke Pits ... 40 E5
Tamworth ... 250 B3
Tatenhill ... 165 A1
Tatenhill Common ... 164 F1
Teanford ... 92 D6
Tettenhall ... 255 D5
Tettenhall Wood ... 255 C8
The Bank ... 26 B7
The Blythe ... 140 F5
The Brampton ... 283 C4
The Bratch ... 269 E8
The Deanery ... 207 F2
The Four Alls ... 112 E4
The Green ... 285 B2
The Handfords ... 154 B1
The Leys ... 250 A4
The Lymes ... 70 C3
The Quarry ... 39 C2
The Rookery ... 26 C3
The Shruggs ... 121 C2
The Straits ... 271 E5
Thorncliffe ... 20 E2
Thornes ... 245 A4
Thorpe ... 51 C1
Thorpe Constantine ... 235 F6
Threapwood ... 77 E2
Thurvaston ... 96 F1
Tillington ... 155 C6
Timbersbrook ... 6 E2
Tittensor ... 88 B1
Tixall ... 157 D2
Tompkin ... 44 C3
Tong ... 220 D3
Tong Forge ... 220 A5
Tong Norton ... 220 D5
Totmonslow ... 92 B4
Townend ... 106 F8
Townhead ... 62 E7

Town Head ... 78 F1
Townsend ... 58 C3
Trentham ... 88 A6
Trent Vale ... 71 F3
Trescott ... 264 B7
Triangle ... 229 B4
Trinity Fields ... 155 B8
Trysull ... 264 C1
Tuckhill ... 272 B5
Tunstall
  Stoke-on-Trent ... 41 C3
  Woodseaves ... 131 E3
Tuppenhurst ... 198 D4
Turnhurst ... 41 F7
Tutbury ... 146 C5
Two Gates ... 261 D8

U

Ubberley ... 58 D1
Underhill ... 241 B2
Upper Aston ... 263 A1
Upper Cotton ... 63 B4
Upper Elkstone ... 22 A3
Upper Ellastone ... 80 B4
Upper Gornal ... 271 F6
Upper Hatton ... 102 D7
Upper Hulme ... 20 E7
Upper Landywood ... 242 E8
Upper Leigh ... 108 E5
Upper Longhorn ... 197 C2
Upper Mayfield ... 66 B1
Upper Nobut ... 109 E4
Upper Tean ... 92 D3
Uttoxeter ... 126 D7

V

Vauxhall ... 168 D2
Vigo ... 244 F2

W

Wain Lee ... 26 F4
Walford ... 117 B8
Walk Mill ... 132 D8
Wall ... 230 D2
Wallbridge Park ... 30 C4
Wall Heath ... 275 B8
Wallington Heath ... 243 B2
Walsall ... 243 B2
Walsall Wood ... 244 F4
Walton
  Eccleshall ... 134 E4
  Stone ... 119 E7
Walton Heath ... 119 E5
Walton-on-the-Hill ... 175 F7
Walton-on-Trent ... 184 E1
Warslow ... 23 B1
Warstone ... 242 C8
Warton ... 150 D2
Washerwall ... 59 A4
Water Eaton ... 207 A2
Waterhouses ... 49 A1
Waverslake ... 181 F3
Wedges Mills ... 226 B6
Weeford ... 248 A4
Weeping Cross ... 175 D7
Wereton ... 39 C1
Wergs ... 255 A6
Werrington ... 59 D4
West Broughton ... 128 A6
West Chadsmoor ... 209 F5
Westcroft ... 241 B3
Western Downs ... 174 A8
West Heath ... 52 E8
West Hill ... 210 B6
Westlands ... 71 A6
Weston
  Crewe ... 37 C5
  Stafford ... 138 D3

Weston Coyney ... 74 A5
Weston Jones ... 150 C5
Weston-under-Lizard ... 203 E3
Westwood ... 30 B6
Wetley Moor ... 58 F5
Wetley Rocks ... 60 B7
Wetmore ... 166 F5
Wetton ... 34 F4
Wetwood ... 115 F7
Whateley ... 261 F3
Wheaton Aston ... 205 B6
Whiston
  Cheadle ... 62 D3
  Penkridge ... 191 E1
Whitecross ... 172 F8
White Hill ... 26 B2
Whitehurst ... 75 D7
Whitemoor ... 16 D6
Whitfield ... 42 C7
Whitgreave ... 135 F5
Whitley Heath ... 133 A1
Whitmore ... 86 A6
Whittington
  Croxton ... 116 D8
  Kinver ... 278 C2
  Lichfield ... 232 D5
Whittington Heath ... 232 C4
Wigginton ... 234 B2
Wightwick ... 254 E1
Wildboarclough ... 1 E6
Wildwood ... 175 D6
Willoughbridge ... 84 A5
Willslock ... 125 F3
Wilnecote ... 261 F8
Wimblebury ... 210 F3
Wincle ... 9 A7
Winnington ... 83 B1
Winnothdale ... 93 C5
Winshill ... 167 B3
Withington ... 109 B3
Withystakes ... 59 E5
Wollaston
  Church Eaton ... 190 E4
  Stourbridge ... 279 D6
Wolstanton ... 56 D5
Wolverhampton ... 266 B7
Wombourne ... 269 E6
Woodcock Heath ... 141 A8
Woodcote ... 187 D3
Woodcroft ... 30 D5
Woodedge ... 144 A6
Woodend ... 145 B1
Wood End ... 262 C1
Woodgate ... 126 E5
Wood Gate ... 144 C5
Woodhouse Green ... 7 D2
Woodhouses ... 182 C3
Woodlane ... 182 D6
Wood Lane ... 40 A1
Woodmill ... 181 F7
Woodseaves
  Eccleshall ... 151 E8
  Market Drayton ... 112 E3
Woodsetton ... 271 E6
Woodshutts ... 25 F1
Woodwall Green ... 116 A4
Woore ... 67 B1
Wootton
  Eccleshall ... 133 D3
  Ellastone ... 79 E7
Wordsley ... 275 E3
Wrinehill ... 53 B3
Wychnor ... 201 B5

Y

Yarlet ... 136 C6
Yarnfield ... 118 F7
Yoxall ... 182 A2

Index of streets, hospitals, industrial estates, railway stations, schools, shopping centres, universities and places of interest

A

Aarons Dr ST7 . . . . **39** F2
Abberley Rd DY3 . . . . . **271** D4
Abberley B77 . . . . **251** C2
Abbey Arc DE14 . . . . . . **166** E2
Abbey Cl **8** Stafford ST17 **175** A8
Penkridge ST19 . . . . . **208** A8
Rocester ST14 . . . . **96** A3
Abbey Ct Bucknall ST2 . . . **58** B5
Newport TF10 . . . . **168** F2
Abbeydale Cl CW2 . . . . . **37** C2
Abbey Dr Colwich ST18 . . **177** D8
Walsall WS3 . . . . **244** A5
Abbeyfield Rd WV10 . . . **240** F4
Abbeyfields ST18 . . . . . **158** B2
Abbey Gdns ST18 . . . . . **158** B2
Abbey Green Rd ST13 . . . **30** D7
Abbey Hill Sch & Performing
Arts Coll ST2 . . . . **58** C5
Abbey Hulton Prim Sch
ST2 . . . . **58** A5
Abbey La ST2 . . . . **58** A5
Abbey Park Way CW2 . . . **37** E3
Abbey Prim Sch WS3 . . . **242** E2
Abbey Rd Bucknall ST2 . . . **58** B5
Dudley,Gornalwood DY3 . **271** C3
Rocester ST14 . . . . **95** F3
Tamworth B77 . . . . **250** D3
Wetley Rocks ST9 . . . . . **60** B6
Abbeyside ST18 . . . . . . **153** D5
Abbey Sq WS3 . . . . **242** E2
Abbey St Bucknall ST2 . . . **58** A6
Burton u T DE14 . . . . . **166** D2
Cannock WS12 . . . . **210** B7
Dudley DY3 . . . . **271** C3
Newcastle-u-L ST5 . . . . . **55** C1
Stone ST15 . . . . **120** A8
Abbey Way TF9 . . . . **97** D2
Abbey Wood Cl **1** ST13 . . **30** D6
Abbot Beyne Sch (Evershed
Bldg) DE15 . . . . **167** B4
Abbot Beyne Sch (Linnell
Bldg) DE15 . . . . **167** A3
Abbot Cl DE14 . . . . **166** A3
Abbots Bromley Hospl
WS15 . . . . **160** F6
Abbots Bromley Rd
DE13 . . . . **162** C4
Abbots Ct ST2 . . . . **58** B7
Abbots Field WS11 . . . . . **209** E5
Abbotsford Rd WS14 . . . **231** E4
Abbotsholme Sch ST14 . . . **96** A3
Abbots Pl ST2 . . . . **58** B6
Abbots Rd ST2 . . . . **58** B6
Abbot's Way ST5 . . . . . . **71** B6
Abbots Way WV3 . . . . . **255** E1
Abbots Wlk
Rugeley WS15 . . . . . . **197** B5
Stafford ST16 . . . . **155** C5
Abbott's Cl CW12 . . . . . . **16** B8
Abbotts Dr ST1 . . . . **57** E8
Abbotts Pl WS3 . . . . . . **243** D1
Abbott's Rd ST13 . . . . . . **31** A7
Abbotts St WS3 . . . . . . **243** D2
Abelia B77 . . . . **250** F3
Abercorn St ST4 . . . . **72** F5
Aberford Gr ST1 . . . . **57** F5
Abingdon Way
Stoke-on-T ST4 . . . . . . **88** B7
Walsall WS3 . . . . **242** F2
Ablon Ct ST19 . . . . **207** F7
Ablow St WV2 . . . . **266** C8
Abnalls Croft WS13 . . . . **213** C1
Abnalls Ct WS13 . . . . . . **213** F1
Abnalls La Lichfield WS13 **213** D1
Lichfield WS13 . . . . . . **213** C1
Abney Dr WV14 . . . . . . **266** F1
Acacia Ave ST5 . . . . **55** E2
Acacia Cres WV8 . . . . . **239** B4
Acacia Ct DY8 . . . . **279** E6
Acacia Gdns ST7 . . . . . . **26** C3
Acacia Gr WS12 . . . . . . **210** F3
Newcastle-u-L ST5 . . . . . **55** E2
Achilees Cl WS6 . . . . . . **226** F1
Achilles Way ST2 . . . . . . **57** F1
Ackleton Gdns WV3 . . . **265** F7
Acorn Cl Burntwood WS7 **212** A1
Cannock WS11 . . . . . . **210** C2
Great Wyrley WS6 . . . . **227** A4
Loggerheads TF9 . . . . . **99** D5
Acorn Gr Codsall WV8 . . **238** E2
Stourbridge DY8 . . . . . **275** C1
Acorn La CW12 . . . . **6** E3
Acorn Rd WV11 . . . . . . **242** A4
Acorn Rise ST3 . . . . **89** E8
Acorn Starter Units
WS7 . . . . **228** D7
Acorn View WS7 . . . . . . **229** C6
Acres Nook ST6 . . . . **41** A7
Acres Nook Rd ST6 . . . . . **41** A6
Acres The
Newcastle-u-L ST5 . . . . . **55** D1
Wolverhampton WV3 . . **255** C1
Acreswood Rd ST6 . . . . . **42** B2
Acton Ct ST18 . . . . **174** F2
Acton Dr DY3 . . . . **271** B3
Acton Hill Rd ST17 . . . . **175** C2
Acton St ST1 . . . . **57** D6
Adam Ct WS11 . . . . **209** D1

Adams Ave ST6 . . . . **41** D5
Adams Cl TF10 . . . . **168** E2
Adams Cres TF10 . . . . . **168** E2
Adams' Gram Sch TF10 . . **168** E3
Adams Gr ST13 . . . . **30** C4
Adamson Cl WS11 . . . . . **209** B1
Adams Rd Brownhills WS8 **245** B5
Wolverhampton WV3 . . **265** C8
Adams St
Newcastle-u-L ST5 . . . . . **56** C4
Stoke-on-T ST2 . . . . . . **43** B1
Adamthwaite Cl ST11 . . . **90** D7
Adamthwaite Dr ST11 . . . **90** D7
Adderley Pl ST12 . . . . . . **88** F3
Adderley Rd
Market Drayton TF9 . . . **97** B3
Stoke-on-T ST6 . . . . . . **42** E3
Adderley Road Ind Est
TF9 . . . . **97** C2
Addie Rd DE13 . . . . **166** B6
Addington Way ST3 . . . . **284** D5
Addison Pl WS11 . . . . . **209** E5
Addison Croft DY3 . . . . **271** A5
Addison Gr WV11 . . . . . **241** B8
Addison Rd WV3 . . . . . **265** F8
Addison St ST1 . . . . **57** D6
Adelaide Cres DE15 . . . **167** C2
Adelaide Dr WS12 . . . . **210** F3
Adelaide St ST6 . . . . **57** A7
Adelaide Wlk WV2 . . . . **266** E8
Adies Alley **7** ST15 . . . . **120** A8
Adkins St ST6 . . . . **57** C8
Admiral Parker Dr WS14 **246** F5
Adonis Cl B79 . . . . **250** C7
Adrian St ST4 . . . . **72** E6
Advance Bsns Pk WS11 . . **210** B3
Adventure Pl ST1 . . . . . **282** B2
Adwalton Rd WV6 . . . . **254** F3
Aegean Ct ST4 . . . . **88** C8
Aelfgar Ctr WS15 . . . . . **178** E1
Aelfgar Ho WS15 . . . . . **178** E1
Affleck Ave B79 . . . . . . **249** D1
Agenoria Dr DY8 . . . . . **279** F5
Agger Hill ST5 . . . . **54** C1
Aiden Ct WS13 . . . . **231** C1
Ainsdale Cl **2** Longton ST3 **73** D1
Stourbridge DY8 . . . . . **279** F2
Ainsley Cl ST2 . . . . **58** B6
Ainsworth Ave ST10 . . . . **61** D2
Ainsworth Rd WV10 . . . **240** D4
Ainsworth St ST4 . . . . . . **72** C5
Aintree Cl
Burton u T DE14 . . . . . **185** A7
Cannock WS12 . . . . . . **210** F6
Stoke-on-T ST4 . . . . . . **88** B7
Aintree Rd
Upper Tean ST10 . . . . . **92** E4
Wolverhampton WV10 . **240** D4
Aintree Way DY1 . . . . . **271** F2
Airdale Gr ST15 . . . . . . **105** B2
Airdale Rd ST15 . . . . . . **105** B2
Airdale Spinney ST15 . . . **105** B2
Airfield Ind Est ST18 . . . **153** E8
Aitken Cl B78 . . . . **250** A2
Aitken St ST6 . . . . **56** E8
Ajax Cl WS6 . . . . **226** F1
Ajax Way ST2 . . . . **57** F1
Akesmoor La Biddulph ST8 **27** A8
Mow Cop ST7 . . . . **26** F7
Alanbrook Gr ST3 . . . . . **89** E8
Alandale Ave WS15 . . . . **198** C4
Alan Dale ST7 . . . . **59** B4
Alanley Cl ST6 . . . . **42** D1
Alan Rd ST2 . . . . **58** C3
Alastair Rd ST4 . . . . **71** F4
Albany Dr Cannock WS12 **210** E3
Rugeley WS15 . . . . . . **178** D3
Albany Gr
Kingswinford DY6 . . . . **275** E7
Stoke-on-T ST4 . . . . . . **71** D8
Willenhall WV11 . . . . . **242** C1
Albany Rd
Newcastle-u-L ST5 . . . . **283** B4
Stoke-on-T ST4 . . . . . . **71** D8
Albany St ST6 . . . . **41** C7
Albemarle Rd
Newcastle-u-L ST5 . . . . . **56** A3
Stourbridge DY8 . . . . . **279** F2
Alberta St ST3 . . . . **284** C2
Albert Ave ST3 . . . . **73** E3
Albert Cl WV8 . . . . **238** E4
Albert Davie Dr WS12 . . **210** E4
Albert Dr DY3 . . . . **269** E2
Albert Pl ST3 . . . . **73** B1
Albert Rd Fazeley B78 . . **261** A8
Stoke-on-T ST4 . . . . . . **88** B6
Tamworth B79 . . . . . . **250** B5
Albert St **2** Leek ST13 . . . **30** E6
Audley ST7 . . . . **39** F3
Biddulph ST8 . . . . **27** D8
Broomhill WS11 . . . . . **209** E4
Burton u T DE14 . . . . . **166** C4
Cannock WS12 . . . . . . **210** D5
Kingswinford DY6 . . . . **275** B8
Longton ST3 . . . . **284** C4
Newcastle-u-L,Chesterton
ST5 . . . . **55** E7
Newcastle-u-L,Silverdale
ST5 . . . . **55** C2
Newcastle-u-L ST5 . . . . **283** C3
Stone ST15 . . . . **105** A1
Stourbridge DY8 . . . . . **279** F5

Albert Terr
Newcastle-u-L ST5 . . . . . **56** C5
Stafford ST16 . . . . **155** E5
Albion Par DY6 . . . . . . **275** B8
Albion Pl WS11 . . . . . . **209** E4
Albion Rd WS8 . . . . **244** E8
Albion Sq ST1 . . . . **282** B2
Albion St Hanley ST1 . . . **282** B2
Kingswinford DY6 . . . . **275** B8
Leek ST13 . . . . **30** E4
Rugeley WS15 . . . . . . **178** F1
Tamworth B79 . . . . . . **250** C5
Albion Terr DE14 . . . . . **166** E6
Albion Way DE14 . . . . . **166** E6
Albrighton By Pass WV7 **237** B6
Albrighton Jun & Inf Schs
WV7 . . . . **237** A4
Albrighton Sta WV7 . . . **237** B5
Albrighton Trust (for the
disabled)★ WV7 . . . . . **237** A7
Albutts Rd WS11 . . . . . **228** B3
Alcester Cl ST6 . . . . **42** B6
Alcove The WS3 . . . . . . **243** D2
Aldbury Cl ST16 . . . . . . **136** C3
Aldbury Pl ST3 . . . . **72** E1
Aldeburgh Cl WS3 . . . . **243** A3
Aldeburgh Dr ST5 . . . . . **71** B2
Alden Hurst WV7 . . . . . **228** F8
Alderbrook Cl
Rolleston on D DE13 . . **147** C4
Sedgley DY3 . . . . **266** B1
Alder Cl Kidsgrove ST7 . . **41** A8
Lichfield WS14 . . . . . . **231** F1
Loggerheads TF9 . . . . . **99** E5
Alder Coppice Prim Sch
DY3 . . . . **266** C1
Alder Coppice DY3 . . . . **266** C2
Alderdale Ave DY3 . . . . **266** C2
Alder Dale WV3 . . . . . . **255** E2
Alderflat Dr ST4 . . . . . . **88** D6
Alderford Cl WV8 . . . . . **255** F8
Aldergate B79 . . . . **250** B5
Alder Gr Burton u T DE15 **185** F7
Newcastle-u-L ST5 . . . . . **55** D8
Stafford ST17 . . . . **174** B7
Alderhay La ST7 . . . . . . **26** C4
Alderhithe Gr B74 . . . . **257** B3
Alderholme Dr **1** DE13 . . **147** F1
Alderney Cl ST5 . . . . . . **70** E4
Alderney Cres ST3 . . . . **72** F3
Alder Rd
Kingswinford DY6 . . . . **275** F5
Market Drayton TF9 . . . **112** A8
Aldersea Cl ST6 . . . . **41** E1
Aldershaw Cl ST16 . . . . **136** C1
Alders La B79 . . . . **249** E6
Aldersleigh Dr ST17 . . . **175** C5
Aldersley Ave WV6 . . . . **255** E7
Aldersley Dr WV6 . . . . . **255** F7
Aldersley High Sch WV8 **239** E1
Aldersley Rd WV6 . . . . . **255** F6
Aldersley Stadium WV6 . **255** F6
Alderson Dr DE13 . . . . **147** F1
Alderton Dr WV3 . . . . . **265** B6
Alderton Gr ST3 . . . . . . **90** B6
Alder Way WS12 . . . . . **211** A6
Alder Wlk ST4 . . . . **71** E4
Alderwood Prec DY3 . . . **266** C1
Alderwood Rise DY3 . . . **271** D5
Aldin Cl ST4 . . . . **249** E2
Aldridge By-Pass WS9 . . **256** A6
Aldridge Cl
2 Stourbridge DY8 . . . **279** E8
Polesworth B78 . . . . . **262** F8
Aldridge Rd Aldridge B74 **256** D1
Little Aston B74,WS9 . . **257** B6
Aldridge Sch WS9 . . . . **256** A4
Aldrin Cl Meir ST3 . . . . . **90** C7
Stafford ST16 . . . . **156** B5
Aldwych WS9 . . . . **256** B8
Aldwyck Dr WV3 . . . . . **265** A8
Alesmore Mdw WS13 . . **230** E4
Alexander Cl WS13 . . . . **215** D6
Alexander Patterson Sch The
DY10 . . . . **280** C3
Alexander Rd WV8 . . . . **239** C3
Alexander Trad Est ST4 . . **57** C7
Alexandra Cres ST14 . . . **126** B8
Alexandra Ct
Burton u T DE15 . . . . . **167** A3
Dudley DY3 . . . . **271** C3
Alexandra Dr DE13 . . . **182** A3
Alexandra Inf Sch ST3 . . **73** E2
Alexandra Jun Sch ST3 . . **73** F1
Alexandra Mews B79 . . . **250** C5
Alexandra Rd
Burton u T DE15 . . . . . **167** A3
Longton ST3 . . . . **73** E2
Market Drayton TF9 . . . **97** B1
Newcastle-u-L ST5 . . . . . **56** C4
Stafford ST17 . . . . **285** B1
Wolverhampton WV4 . . **266** A6
Alexandra St **2** ST15 . . . **104** F1
Alexandra Way WS9 . . . **256** B5
Alford Dr ST2 . . . . **59** A3
Alfred Lyons Cl WS15 . . **160** F6
Alfred St Burton u T DE14 **166** C2
Stoke-on-T ST4 . . . . . . **72** C2
Tamworth B79 . . . . . . **250** A5
Walsall WS3 . . . . **243** B1

Alfreton Rd ST4 . . . . **73** A6
Algar Rd ST4 . . . . **71** E6
Alicia Way ST2 . . . . **43** A2
Alison Dr DY8 . . . . **279** E3
Allan Cl **7** DY8 . . . . . . **279** F8
Allard B77 . . . . **250** E2
Allen Birt Wlk WS15 . . . **178** D3
Allenby Cl ST5 . . . . **70** F3
Allenby Sq ST4 . . . . **71** E4
Allendale ST16 . . . . **155** B8
Allendale Wlk ST3 . . . . . **72** F1
Allen Gdns TF9 . . . . . . **112** B8
Allens Croft ST14 . . . . . **127** E2
Allen's La ST14 . . . . **127** E2
Allens La WS3 . . . . **243** F2
Allensmead B77 . . . . . . **250** C2
Allensmore Ave ST4 . . . . **73** B5
Allen St Cheadle ST10 . . . **76** E2
Stoke-on-T ST4 . . . . . . **71** E8
Cheadle ST10 . . . . **76** E3
Stoke-on-T ST4 . . . . . . **71** E8
Tamworth B77 . . . . . . **250** C1
Allensway ST5 . . . . **70** C1
Allerdale Rd WS8 . . . . . **244** E6
Allerton Rd ST4 . . . . **87** F7
Alleston Rd WV10 . . . . **240** D1
Alleston Wlk WV10 . . . . **240** D2
Alleyne's High Sch ST15 **105** A1
Alley's La ST20 . . . . **190** A8
Alley The DY3 . . . . **271** B3
Alliance St ST16 . . . . . . **155** D6
Allington Ave **5** WS13 . . **230** F4
Alliss Cl ST16 . . . . **156** C4
Allport Mews WS11 . . . **209** E4
Allport Rd WS11 . . . . . **209** E4
Allport St WS11 . . . . . . **209** E2
All Saints CE Fst Sch
Church Leigh ST10 . . . **109** A4
Denstone ST14 . . . . . . **95** E6
Leek ST13 . . . . **30** F4
Standon ST21 . . . . **102** C3
All Saints CE Inf Sch
ST18 . . . . **153** C5
All Saints CE Prim Sch
Alrewas DE13 . . . . . . **201** A2
Bednall ST17 . . . . **193** E8
Rangemore DE13 . . . . . **164** C2
Trysull WV5 . . . . **269** C8
All Saints Croft DE14 . . . **185** C8
All Saints Dr B74 . . . . . **258** A2
All Saints Rd
Burton u T DE14 . . . . . **185** C8
Stoke-on-T ST4 . . . . . . **72** A5
Wolverhampton WV2 . . **266** D8
Allthorpe Pl ST5 . . . . . . **70** F3
Allton Ave B78 . . . . **249** D1
Allton Ct B77 . . . . **250** D1
Allways Cl ST18 . . . . . . **122** C5
All Ways ST18 . . . . **122** C5
Allways The ST18 . . . . . **122** C5
Alma Cl ST7 . . . . **25** E7
Alma Rd DE11 . . . . **186** F6
Almar Pl ST6 . . . . **42** A5
Alma St Burton u T DE14 **166** C2
Leek ST13 . . . . **30** D6
Stoke-on-T ST4 . . . . . . **72** D6
Stone ST15 . . . . **104** F1
Almond Cl Cannock WS11 **210** C2
Walsall WS3 . . . . **243** C3
Almond Ct DE13 . . . . . **147** E1
Almond Gr Stoke-on-T ST3 **72** B3
Swadlincote DE11 . . . . **186** F5
Almond Rd
Huntington WS12 . . . . **209** D8
Kingswinford DY6 . . . . **275** E8
Alms Hos TF11 . . . . . . **203** E2
Almshouse Croft ST18 . . **191** B8
Almshouses Biddulph ST8 **16** E3
Madeley CW3 . . . . **68** E5
Newton Solney DE15 . . **167** E8
Penkridge ST19 . . . . . **192** E1
Rugeley WS15 . . . . . . **178** E1
Wolverhampton WV4 . . **265** F3
Alnwick Cl WS12 . . . . . **210** E2
Alnwick Rd WS3 . . . . . **243** A4
Alpha Way WS6 . . . . . . **243** A8
Alpine Dr WS12 . . . . . . **210** D4
Alpine Way WV3 . . . . . **255** C2
Alrewas Rd DE13 . . . . . **199** E6
Alsager Rd ST7 . . . . **39** D5
Alsop Crest ST17 . . . . . **175** B1
Alsop Moor Cotts DE6 . . **36** D5
Alsop St ST13 . . . . **30** E5
Alston Cl Cannock WS12 **210** E2
Sutton Coldfield B74 . . **258** A2
Alstone Cl ST16 . . . . . . **155** B7
Alstonefield Youth Hostel★
DE6 . . . . **35** F4
Alstone La ST18 . . . . . . **172** F2
Alstonfield Ave ST2 . . . . **58** C7
Althorp Way DE13 . . . . **166** D8
Althrop Gr ST3 . . . . **73** D3
Altona St ST15 . . . . **120** B8
Alton Cl Newcastle-u-L ST5 **55** B1
Wolverhampton WV10 . **240** D1
Alton Gr Bucknall ST2 . . . **73** D7
Cannock WS11 . . . . . . **209** B1
Newport TF10 . . . . . . **168** E1
Alton Rd ST14 . . . . **95** D6
Alton Towers Theme Pk★
ST10 . . . . **78** E4
Alvaston Cl WS3 . . . . . **243** C3

Alvecote Cotts B79 . . . . **251** D6
Alvecote Pools Nature
Reserve★ B79 . . . . . . **251** E6
Alverley Cl DY6 . . . . . . **275** B8
Alverstoke Cl WV9 . . . . **240** A2
Alverton Cl B77 . . . . . . **261** C4
Alvis Cl B79 . . . . **249** F7
Alwen St DY8 . . . . **275** F2
Alwyn Cl WS6 . . . . **227** A3
Alwyn Cres ST6 . . . . **57** D8
Alwyn Rd DE13 . . . . . . **182** A2
Alwyn B77 . . . . **261** E7
Amanda Ave WV4 . . . . **265** F4
Amber Bsns Village B77 **251** B3
Amber Cl B77 . . . . **251** B3
Amber Ct Stoke-on-T ST9 **43** E5
Tamworth B77 . . . . . . **251** B3
Amberfield Cl ST3 . . . . . **73** E4
Ambergate Cl WS3 . . . . **243** C3
Ambergate Dr DY6 . . . . **275** C8
Amber Gn WS11 . . . . . **210** C2
Amber Gr WS11 . . . . . . **210** C2
Amberlands DE13 . . . . **147** F1
Amberley Way B74 . . . . **256** C6
Amblecote Dr ST3 . . . . . **73** E4
Amblecote Prim Sch
DY8 . . . . **279** F8
Amblefield Way ST16 . . **136** C1
Ambleside Cl ST15 . . . . **120** D7
Ambleside Gr WV11 . . . **242** B1
Ambleside Pl ST6 . . . . . **42** A3
Ambleside Way DY6 . . . **275** D6
Ambrose Cres DY6 . . . . **275** D8
Ambrose Pl ST6 . . . . . . **41** F7
Amelia Cl ST7 . . . . **43** A2
America St ST6 . . . . **41** D3
Amerton Farm★ ST18 . . **139** A4
Amerton La
Amerton ST18 . . . . . . **139** A3
Weston ST18 . . . . **138** F1
Amicable St ST6 . . . . . . **56** F7
Amicombe B77 . . . . **251** C1
Amington Cl B75 . . . . . **258** D3
Amington Hall B79 . . . . **251** A8
Amington Heath Com Sch
B77 . . . . **251** A4
Amington Ind Est B77 . . **251** B3
Amington Pk B77 . . . . . **251** A6
Amington Rd B77 . . . . . **250** D4
Amison St ST3 . . . . **73** D4
Ampleforth Dr ST17 . . . **156** B1
Ampthill Pl ST4 . . . . **71** F1
Amptronik Trad Est
WV5 . . . . **269** D4
Ancaster St ST6 . . . . . . **41** D7
Anchor Cl B77 . . . . **250** E4
Anchor Ct B77 . . . . **250** C4
Anchor Par WS9 . . . . . **256** B6
Anchor Pl ST3 . . . . **284** C4
Anchor Rd Aldridge WS9 **256** B6
Longton ST3 . . . . **284** C4
Anchor Terr ST3 . . . . . . **284** C4
Anchor Way ST20 . . . . . **171** D7
Ancient High House★
ST16 . . . . **285** B3
Anderby Gdns DE11 . . . **186** F2
Anderson Pl ST6 . . . . . . **42** E3
Anders Sq WV6 . . . . . . **254** E3
Anderstaff Ind Pk DE14 **166** C4
Anders B77 . . . . **250** A6
Anderton View ST15 . . . **104** E3
Andover Cl ST3 . . . . **73** C6
Andover Cres **2** DY6 . . **275** F4
Andover Pl WS11 . . . . . **210** A4
Andrew Mulligan Cl ST6 **41** C5
Andrew Pl ST5 . . . . **283** D3
Andrews Ho WS13 . . . . **231** A7
Andrews Rd WS9 . . . . . **245** A4
Andrew St ST6 . . . . **41** C7
Aneurin Bevan Pl WS15 **178** D2
Angel Croft WS7 . . . . . **211** E1
Angelica B77 . . . . **250** F4
Anglesey Bsns Pk WS12 **210** D4
Anglesey Cl WS7 . . . . . **228** F4
Anglesey Cres
Brownhills WS8 . . . . . **228** F2
Cannock WS12 . . . . . . **210** C5
Anglesey Ct
Burton u T DE14 . . . . . **166** B1
Rugeley WS15 . . . . . . **197** B6
Anglesey Dr ST3 . . . . . . **73** A3
Anglesey Ho WS15 . . . . **197** B6
Anglesey Mews WS15 . . **197** B6
Anglesey Prim Sch DE14 **166** C1
Anglesey Rd
Brownhills WS8 . . . . . **228** F2
Burton u T DE14 . . . . . **166** B1
Lichfield WS13 . . . . . . **214** B2
Anglesey St
Burton u T DE14 . . . . . **165** F4
Cannock WS12 . . . . . . **210** B5
Angle St **6** ST13 . . . . . **30** D6
Anglia Dr DE11 . . . . . . **186** F1
Anglia Rd WS11 . . . . . . **209** D3
Angorfa Cl WS13 . . . . . **230** F7
Angus Cl ST2 . . . . **58** C4
Anker Cl WV7 . . . . **229** D6
Ankerdrive B79 . . . . . . **250** B4
Ankermoor Ct B77 . . . . **250** E5

Ankermoor Prim Sch
 B77 . . . . 250 E5
Ankerside Sh Ctr B79 . . . 250 B4
Anker View B77 . . . . 250 C3
Annan Cl **3** CW12 . . . . 6 A1
Annandale B77 . . . . 251 B1
Anna Wlk ST6 . . . . 56 F7
Ann Cres WS11 . . . . 209 E6
Anne Ct ST7 . . . . 40 D6
Annefield Cl TF9 . . . . 97 D2
Anne Rd WV4 . . . . 266 B6
Anne St ST6 . . . . 41 C7
Annette Rd ST4 . . . . 73 B6
Anslow Gdns WV11 . . . . . 241 F1
Anslow La DE13 . . . . 147 A2
Anslow Rd DE13 . . . . 145 A2
Ansmede Gr ST3 . . . . 72 F1
Anson Ave WS13 . . . . 214 A1
Anson CE Prim Sch ST18 158 B2
Anson Cl Burntwood WS7 . 229 C7
 Great Wyrley WS6 . . . . . . 226 F1
 Perton WV6 . . . . 254 E5
Anson Ct Burton u T DE14 . 166 E3
 Fazeley B78 . . . . 261 B8
 Stafford ST18 . . . . 156 D5
Anson Dr ST17 . . . . 175 F6
Anson Mews WS15 . . . . . 178 E1
Anson Rd Alrewas DE13 . . 201 A2
 Great Wyrley WS6 . . . . . . 226 F1
 Meir ST3 . . . . 90 A8
Anson's Row ST18 . . . . . . 177 C8
Anson St WS15 . . . . 178 E1
Anstree Cl WS6 . . . . 226 D1
Ansty Dr WS12 . . . . 210 D1
Anthony Gr ST3 . . . . 89 F4
Anthony Pl ST3 . . . . 284 D4
Antler Dr WS15 . . . . 178 B2
Antom Ct ST16 . . . . 155 F7
Apedale Bsns Pk ST5 ★ . . 55 C7
Apedale Com Cntry Pk ★
 ST5 . . . . 55 A6
Apedale Rd
 Audley,Wood Lane ST7 . . . 55 A8
 Newcastle-u-L ST5 . . . . . 55 C6
Apex Bsns Pk WS11 . . . . 227 F4
Apex Rd WS8 . . . . 244 C7
Apley Pl ST4 . . . . 87 F8
Apley Rd DY8 . . . . 279 E7
Apollo Cl WS11 . . . . 210 A5
Apollo B79 . . . . 249 F6
Apollo Wlk ST6 . . . . 42 C1
Appian Cl B77 . . . . 261 D7
Appleby Gdns WV11 . . . . 242 C2
Appleby Glade Ind Est
 DE11 . . . . 186 E2
Appleby Glade DE11 . . . . 186 D2
Applecroft ST5 . . . . 40 E1
Applecross B74 . . . . 257 F1
Appledore Cl
 Cannock WS12 . . . . 210 E3
 Stafford ST17 . . . . 175 E8
Appledore Gr ST6 . . . . . . 41 E7
Appleford Pl ST3 . . . . 72 E1
Applegarth Cl ST4 . . . . . . 73 B6
Apple Gr TF9 . . . . 97 A1
Appleton Cl Biddulph ST8 . . 27 E6
 Burton u T DE15 . . . . . . 185 E7
 Congleton CW12 . . . . . . 15 E8
 Swadlincote DE11 . . . . . 186 F6
Appleton Cres WV4 . . . . . 266 A5
Appleton Dr ST5 . . . . 85 D5
Appletree Gr WS9 . . . . . . 256 B5
Applewood Cl ST14 . . . . . 111 A1
Applewood Cres ST3 . . . . 90 C8
Appleyard Ct ST16 . . . . . 285 B3
Appleyard The ST19 . . . . 223 C6
Apse Cl WV5 . . . . 269 F7
Apsley Gr ST12 . . . . 88 A1
Aqualate Cl TF10 . . . . . . 169 A4
Aqualate Ho ST17 . . . . . . 174 E6
Aquaries Ct ST3 . . . . 73 E1
Aquinas St ST4 . . . . 72 B7
Arbor B77 . . . . 250 D3
Arborfield Rd ST14 . . . . . 143 F7
Arbor Gate WS9 . . . . 245 B4
Arbour Cl CW3 . . . . 68 E7
Arbourfield Dr ST2 . . . . . . 58 A2
Arbour Mews WS11 . . . . . 227 F6
Arbour St Hanley ST1 . . . . 282 C3
 Talke Pits ST7 . . . . 40 D5
Arbourtree Ct WV5 . . . . . 270 B7
Arbury Dr DY8 . . . . 275 D3
Arcade The DY3 . . . . 271 E5
Arcadia Pk WS15 . . . . . . 197 B7
Arcal St DY3 . . . . 271 E7
Arch St WS15 . . . . 196 F8
Arclid Way ST2 . . . . 58 B2
Arctic Pl ST4 . . . . 88 B8
Arden Cl Leek ST13 . . . . . 31 B5
 Rugeley WS15 . . . . 178 C6
 Stourbridge DY8 . . . . . . 279 E7
 Stourbridge,Wordsley DY8 275 C3
 Tamworth B77 . . . . 250 E5
Arden Ct Congleton CW12 . 16 B7
 Dudley DY3 . . . . 271 D3
Arden Rd Barton-u-N DE13 201 E8
 Tamworth B77 . . . . 261 F5
Arden Wlk WS15 . . . . 198 C4
Ardgay Dr WV12 . . . . 209 F7
Argles Rd ST13 . . . . 31 A7
Argosy Cl ST3 . . . . 90 B7

Argyle Ave B77 . . . . 250 D4
Argyle Cl DY8 . . . . 275 E1
Argyle Rd WV2 . . . . 266 B6
Argyle St Hanley ST1 . . . . 282 A1
 Tamworth B77 . . . . 250 E4
Argyll Cl ST11 . . . . 90 E6
Argyll Rd ST3 . . . . 73 D1
Ariane B79 . . . . 249 E7
Aries Cl ST6 . . . . 41 F6
Arion Cl B77 . . . . 250 D5
Arkall Cl B79 . . . . 250 C7
Arkle Cl ST14 . . . . 126 D7
Arkle B77 . . . . 261 D6
Arkwright Gr ST1 . . . . 57 F8
Arlescote Cl B75 . . . . 258 C2
Arley Dr DY8 . . . . 279 E3
Arley Gr WV4 . . . . 265 D5
Arlington Ct DY6 . . . . 275 D4
Arlington Way Meir ST3 . . . 90 A7
 Stoke-on-T ST3 . . . . 89 F7
Armishaw Pl WS15 . . . . . 197 B5
Armitage Gdns WS15 . . . . 197 B6
Armitage Hill DE13 . . . . . 183 E4
Armitage Ho WS13 . . . . . 214 E1
Armitage La WS15 . . . . . . 197 B5
Armitage Rd WS15 . . . . . . 197 A6
Armshead Rd ST9 . . . . . . 59 B5
Armside Cl WS3 . . . . 244 B4
Armstead Rd WV4 . . . . . . 240 A3
Armstrong Ave ST16 . . . . 156 A4
Armstrong Gn ST6 . . . . . . 57 C7
Armstrong B79 . . . . 249 F6
Arnold Cl B79 . . . . 250 A6
Arnold Gr ST5 . . . . 56 B7
Arnotdale Dr WS12 . . . . . 209 F7
Arnot Dr DE14 . . . . 185 A7
Arps Rd WV8 . . . . 238 F3
Arran Cl ST1 . . . . 210 A3
Arran Dr Stoke-on-T ST7 . . 41 F8
 Tamworth B77 . . . . 261 F7
Arrow Dr WV7 . . . . 237 A5
Arthur Cotton Ct ST6 . . . . 42 A1
Arthur Evans Cl WS15 . . . 197 A5
Arthurs Ct DE13 . . . . 147 E2
Arthur St
 1 Stoke-on-T ST6 . . . . . 41 E3
 Burton u T DE14 . . . . . . 166 C5
 Cannock,Chadsmoor WS11 209 F4
 Cannock WS12 . . . . 210 F3
 Newcastle-u-L ST5 . . . . . 55 F2
 Stone ST15 . . . . 105 A2
 Wolverhampton WV2 . . . . 266 D7
Arthur Terry Sch The
 B74 . . . . 258 A3
Arthur Wood Pl WS15 . . . 178 E2
Arundel Dr ST10 . . . . 76 F3
Arundel Gr WV6 . . . . 254 F3
Arundel Rd
 Stourbridge DY8 . . . . . . 275 C2
 Wolverhampton WV10 . . . 240 B2
Arundel Cl B77 . . . . 261 C2
Arundel Way ST3 . . . . 73 C6
Ascot Cl Burton u T DE15 . 167 A3
 Lichfield WS13 . . . . 231 D7
Ascot Dr Cannock WS11 . . 226 C8
 Dudley DY1 . . . . 271 F2
 Tamworth B77 . . . . 261 D4
 Wolverhampton WV4 . . . . 266 A4
Ascot Gdns DY8 . . . . 275 D2
Ascot Rd ST17 . . . . 156 C1
Ash Bank Rd ST2,ST9 . . . 59 B3
Ashbourne Cl WS11 . . . . . 210 A4
Ashbourne Dr
 Chorlton CW2 . . . . 37 C1
 Market Drayton TF9 . . . . . 97 C2
 Newcastle-u-L ST5 . . . . . 55 B1
 Swadlincote DE11 . . . . . 186 F1
Ashbourne Gr ST1 . . . . . . 282 B4
Ashbourne La DE6 . . . . . . 35 A3
Ashbourne Rd
 Cheadle ST10 . . . . 76 F3
 Leek ST13 . . . . 31 B4
 Mayfield DE6 . . . . 81 C7
 Rocester ST14 . . . . 95 F4
 Uttoxeter,Spath ST14 . . . 111 B3
 Uttoxeter ST14 . . . . 111 B1
 Walsall WS3 . . . . 243 C3
 Wetton DE6 . . . . 35 B3
 Wolverhampton,Ettingshall Park
  WV4 . . . . 266 E3
Ashbrook DE15 . . . . 167 A1
Ashbrook Cl Gnosall ST20 . 171 D7
 Uttoxeter ST14 . . . . 126 C6
Ashbrook La WS15 . . . . . 161 C5
Ashburton St ST6 . . . . . . 57 B7
Ashby Cres ST3 . . . . 72 F1
Ashby Rd DE15 . . . . 167 B2
Ashby Rd E DE15 . . . . . . 167 E1
Ashby Rd B79 . . . . 250 C8
Ash Cl Cheadle ST10 . . . . 76 F2
 Codsall WV8 . . . . 239 A3
 Uttoxeter ST14 . . . . 126 A4
Ashcombe Gn ST3 . . . . . . 72 F1
Ashcombe Rd ST13 . . . . . 45 C4
Ashcombe Way ST13 . . . . 30 F4
Ashcott Wlk ST2 . . . . 58 C1
Ash Cres DY6 . . . . 275 E6
Ashcott **2** WV4 . . . . 266 F4
Ashcroft Cl ST5 . . . . 56 A4
Ashcroft Gr ST5 . . . . 56 B6
Ashcroft Inf Sch B79 . . . . 250 C7
Ashcroft La
 Lichfield WS14 . . . . 230 E1
 Shenstone WS14 . . . . . . 246 E7
Ashcroft Oval ST5 . . . . . . 56 B6
Ashcroft Pl ST5 . . . . 56 B6
Ashcroft Rd ST5 . . . . 56 A6

Ashdale Cl **1** Stone ST15 . 120 A7
 Burton u T DE15 . . . . . . 186 A8
 Huntington WS12 . . . . . . 209 C7
 Kingswinford DY6 . . . . . . 275 D8
Ashdale Dr ST16 . . . . 155 D8
Ashdale Pk ST15 . . . . 118 F6
Ashdale Rd Leek ST13 . . . 31 B6
 Stoke-on-T ST4 . . . . 72 C5
 Tamworth B77 . . . . 250 D5
Ashdale Rise ST5 . . . . . . 71 B3
Ashdene Gdns DY8 . . . . . 275 C2
Ashdown Dr DY8 . . . . 275 E3
Ash Dr ST18 . . . . 172 F5
Ashen Cl DY3 . . . . 266 C3
Ashendene Gr
 Stoke-on-T ST4 . . . . 71 F1
 Trentham ST4 . . . . 87 F8
Ashenden Rise WV3 . . . . . 265 A8
Ashenhurst Way ST13 . . . 30 F4
Ashenough Rd ST7 . . . . . . 40 D6
Ashe's La DE6 . . . . 144 D7
Ashfield Gr WV10 . . . . . . 240 C3
Ashfield Rd
 Wolverhampton,Compton
  WV3 . . . . 255 D2
 Wolverhampton,Fordhouses
  WV10 . . . . 240 C3
Ashfields WV7 . . . . 237 A5
Ashfields Grange ST5 . . . . 283 B3
Ashfields New Rd ST5 . . . . 283 A4
Ashfield Sq ST2 . . . . 58 A2
Ash Flats La ST17,ST18 . . 174 E4
Ashford Dr DY3 . . . . 271 E7
Ashford Gr ST15 . . . . 120 C7
Ashford Rd DE13 . . . . . . 166 A6
Ashford St ST4 . . . . 72 C8
Ash Gr Albrighton WV7 . . . 237 A4
 Barlaston ST12 . . . . 88 D1
 Blythe Bridge ST11 . . . . . 90 C8
 Brewood ST19 . . . . 223 D6
 Cannock WS11 . . . . 209 F4
 Dudley DY3 . . . . 271 C2
Ash Green Cl ST4 . . . . . . 88 A7
Ash Green Cl Prim ST4 . . . 88 B7
Ash Gr Lichfield WS14 . . . 231 E8
 Newcastle-u-L ST5 . . . . . 55 B2
Ashgrove WS7 . . . . 228 F5
Ash Grove La DE65 . . . . . 148 C6
Ash Gr Stoke-on-T ST3 . . . 72 E2
 Tamworth B77 . . . . 261 F5
 Werrington ST2 . . . . 58 F3
 Wheaton Aston ST19 . . . . 205 C6
Ash Hill WV3 . . . . 255 D2
Ash La WS6 . . . . 227 A3
Ashlands Ave ST4 . . . . . . 71 E8
Ashlands Cl B79 . . . . 250 C7
Ashlands Gr ST4 . . . . 71 E7
Ashlands ST18 . . . . 139 D1
Ashlands Rd ST4 . . . . 71 E7
Ashlands St WV3 . . . . . . 266 B8
Ash La B79 . . . . 236 F6
Ashlar Cl ST6 . . . . 42 A8
Ash La ST15 . . . . 118 E5
Ashlea Ct TF9 . . . . 97 E2
Ashlea B78 . . . . 262 F5
Ashlea Dr DE6 . . . . 81 D7
Ashleigh Ave DE11 . . . . . 186 F5
Ashleigh Cres ST19 . . . . . 205 C7
Ashleigh Dr
 Tamworth B77 . . . . 261 E8
 Uttoxeter ST14 . . . . 110 F1
Ashleigh Rd
 Rugeley WS15 . . . . 196 E7
 Upper Tean ST10 . . . . . . 92 E4
Ashley Cl Burton u T DE15 . 167 A3
 Kingswinford DY6 . . . . . . 275 C4
 Stafford ST16 . . . . 155 A4
 Stourbridge DY8 . . . . . . 279 D2
Ashley Croft ST20 . . . . . . 190 A8
Ashley Ct DE15 . . . . 167 A3
Ashley Gdns WV8 . . . . . . 238 F4
Ashley Gr ST5 . . . . 56 C4
Ashley Mount WV6 . . . . . 255 D5
Ashley Rd Burntwood WS7 211 E5
 Kidderminster DY10 . . . . 280 B1
 Walsall WS3 . . . . 242 F1
 Wolverhampton WV4 . . . . 265 E5
Ashley View TF9 . . . . 97 C1
Ashmall ST7 . . . . 229 D4
Ashman St ST6 . . . . 42 C2
Ashmead Rd WS7 . . . . . . 229 A8
Ashmole Ave WS7 . . . . . . 229 E8
Ashmole Cl WS14 . . . . . . 231 E6
Ashmore Ave WV11 . . . . . 242 A1
Ashmore Dr ST20 . . . . . . 171 D7
Ashmore Wlk ST1 . . . . . . 282 C3
Ashover Gr ST6 . . . . 41 E8
Ashover Rd DE11 . . . . . . 186 E5
Ash Park Ind Est WS11 . . . 210 B3
Ash Rd ST15 . . . . 120 B7
Ashridge Ave ST5 . . . . . . 71 B2
Ashridge Gr ST3 . . . . 73 D5
Ashridge Wlk ST16 . . . . . 136 D5
Ash Rise ST17 . . . . 174 E4
Ash St Burton u T DE14 . . . 166 B1
 Walsall WS3 . . . . 243 D1
Ashton Cl CW12 . . . . 6 B1
Ashton Ct
 Newcastle-u-L ST5 . . . . . 71 C2
 Werrington ST9 . . . . 59 A3
Ashton Dr WS4 . . . . 244 C2
Ashtree Bank WS15 . . . . . 197 B6
Ashtree Cl ST18 . . . . 177 D8
Ashtree Cl WS11 . . . . . . 209 D4
Ash Tree Hill ST10 . . . . . . 76 C2
Ash Tree La WS13 . . . . . . 215 A1

Ash Tree Rd DE13 . . . . . . 183 D1
Ashtree Rd WS3 . . . . 244 A3
Ashurst Gr **2** ST3 . . . . . 90 B7
Ash View
 Huntington WS12 . . . . . . 209 D8
 Kidsgrove ST7 . . . . 26 B2
Ash Way Newcastle-u-L ST5 71 A4
 Werrington ST2 . . . . 58 F3
Ashwell Rd ST4 . . . . 71 D8
Ashwells Gr WV9 . . . . 240 A2
Ashwood Ave DY8 . . . . . . 275 D2
Ashwood Cl TF9 . . . . 97 A1
Ashwood Gr
 Blythe Bridge ST11 . . . . . 91 A6
 Wolverhampton WV4 . . . . 266 A5
Ashwoodhay DY8 . . . . . . 275 F3
Ashwood St ST4 . . . . 284 C4
Ashwood Park Prim Sch
 DY8 . . . . 275 D1
Ashwood Terr ST3 . . . . . . 284 C5
Ashworth Ave DE15 . . . . . 167 C2
Ashworth Ho
 2 Lichfield WS13 . . . . . 231 B8
 Cannock WS11 . . . . 210 A4
Ashworth St ST4 . . . . 72 D6
Ashworth Way TF10 . . . . . 168 F1
Askerbank La SK11 . . . . . 8 A1
Askern Cl ST3 . . . . 73 E1
Askew Bridge Rd DY3 . . . . 271 B3
Askew Cl DY3 . . . . 271 E5
Aspen Cl
 2 Lichfield WS13 . . . . . 231 E8
 Harriseahead ST7 . . . . . . 26 E3
Aspen Croft ST17 . . . . . . 174 E8
Aspen Ct WS12 . . . . 211 A6
Aspen Gr WV7 . . . . 237 A4
Aspen Rd DE13 . . . . 201 D8
Aspen Way TF10 . . . . 168 F2
Asphodel B74 . . . . 257 F5
Aspley Cl WV10 . . . . 224 E5
Aspley La WV10 . . . . 224 D3
Asquith Cl ST8 . . . . 27 E8
Asquith Dr WS11 . . . . 210 C2
Astbury Cl Kidsgrove ST7 . . 26 C3
 Walsall WS3 . . . . 243 D1
Astbury Lane Ends CW12 . 15 F8
Astbury St Mary's CE Prim
 Sch CW12 . . . . 15 B8
Aster Cl ST3 . . . . 74 B6
Aster Wlk WV9 . . . . 240 A3
Astil St DE15 . . . . 166 F1
Astle Pl ST1 . . . . 282 C1
Astles Rock Wlk DY7 . . . . 278 A3
Aston Bk ST16,ST18 . . . . . 154 F4
Aston Chase ST15 . . . . . . 120 D7
Aston Cl Colwich ST18 . . . 177 D8
 Penkridge ST19 . . . . 208 A7
 Shenstone WS14 . . . . . . 246 F5
Aston Dr TF10 . . . . 168 F1
Aston La ST15 . . . . 120 D3
Aston St WV3 . . . . 266 A8
Aston Terr ST16 . . . . 155 E6
Astoria Cl WV12 . . . . 242 D1
Astoria Dr ST17 . . . . 174 F6
Astoria Gdns WV12 . . . . . 242 D1
Astor Rd Aldridge B74 . . . 257 A1
 Kingswinford DY6 . . . . . . 275 F5
Astro Gr ST3 . . . . 284 C4
Astron Bsns Pk DE11 . . . . 186 F3
Athelney St WS3 . . . . 244 A3
Athelstan Cl ST19 . . . . . . 208 A8
Athelstan Gr WV6 . . . . . . 254 F5
Athelstan **1** ST6 . . . . . . 41 D3
Athelstan Way B79 . . . . . 249 F6
Athelstan Way DE13 . . . . 147 C1
Athena Rd ST1 . . . . 57 F5
Atherstone Rd ST4 . . . . . 88 A7
Atherstone St B77,B78 . . . 261 B8
Athlestan Way DE13 . . . . 147 C1
Athlone Ct ST6 . . . . 42 D7
Atholl Rd ST3 . . . . 284 D1
Atkins Way ST14 . . . . 95 F3
Atlam Cl ST2 . . . . 58 A3
Atlantic Gr ST4 . . . . 88 B8
Atlas St ST4 . . . . 72 C5
Attingham Dr WS11 . . . . . 210 B2
Attlee Cres Rugeley WS15 . 196 F7
 Stafford ST17 . . . . 174 D7
Attlee Gr WS11 . . . . 210 C2
Attlee Rd ST10 . . . . 76 D2
Attwell Pk WV3 . . . . 265 D7
Attwood Gdns WV4 . . . . . 266 E5
Attwood Rd WS7 . . . . 228 C2
Attwood St ST7 . . . . 26 A2
Aubrey St ST6 . . . . 41 B7
Auchinleck Dr WS13 . . . . 214 C1
Auckland Rd DY6 . . . . 275 D5
Auckland St ST6 . . . . 57 A8
Auden Ct WV6 . . . . 254 F4
Auden Pl ST3 . . . . 284 D4
Auden Way ST17 . . . . 174 C9
Audlem Rd CW3 . . . . 67 B2
Audley Ave TF10 . . . . 169 A2
Audley Avenue Bsns Pk
 TF10 . . . . 169 B2
Audley Avenue Ind Est
 TF10 . . . . 169 B2
Audley Cl DE13 . . . . 201 A3

Audley Ho TF10 . . . . 169 A2
Audley House Mews
 TF10 . . . . 169 A2
Audley Pl ST5 . . . . 71 B5
Audley Rd Audley ST7 . . . . 39 D8
 Barthomley CW2 . . . . . . 38 E5
 Newcastle-u-L ST7,ST5 . . 40 B2
 Newport TF10 . . . . 168 F3
 Talke ST7 . . . . 40 B6
Audley St
 Newcastle-u-L ST5 . . . . . 55 E3
 Stoke-on-T ST6 . . . . 41 D3
Audmore Rd ST20 . . . . . . 171 D7
Audnam DY8 . . . . 275 F1
Augustine Cl ST15 . . . . . . 120 C7
Augustine Gr B74 . . . . . . 257 F5
Augustines Wlk WS13 . . . . 214 A3
Aulton Rd B75 . . . . 258 E2
Aumbry Cl TF9 . . . . 97 A1
Austcliffe La DY10 . . . . . . 280 C5
Austcliffe Pk DY10 . . . . . . 280 B6
Austcliffe Rd DY10 . . . . . . 280 B5
Austin Cl Cheadle ST10 . . . 76 C2
 Dudley DY1 . . . . 271 F2
 Stone ST15 . . . . 120 A7
Austin Cote La WS14 . . . . 231 F7
Austin Ct B74 . . . . 257 F5
Austin Friars ST17 . . . . . . 285 B1
Austin St ST1 . . . . 282 C1
Austrey La
 Newton Regis B79 . . . . . 236 E3
 No Man's Heath B79 . . . . 236 F6
Austwick Gr ST4 . . . . 71 E5
Autumn Berry Gr DY3 . . . . 271 E6
Autumn Cl WS4 . . . . 244 C1
Autumn Dr Dudley DY3 . . . 271 D4
 Lichfield WS13 . . . . 214 D2
 Walsall WS4 . . . . 244 C2
Avalon Ho **2** WS11 . . . . 209 F4
Aveling Gn ST1 . . . . 57 F8
Aveling Rd ST1 . . . . 57 F8
Avenue One CW1 . . . . . . 37 C8
Avenue Rd Cannock WS12 210 E2
 Newport TF10 . . . . 168 F2
Avenue Rd S TF10 . . . . . . 168 F2
Avenue Rd Stoke-on-T ST4 57 C1
 Wolverhampton WV3 . . . . 255 E2
Avenue The Bagnall ST9 . . 43 F4
 Blakedown DY10 . . . . . . 281 B2
 Blythe Bridge ST11 . . . . . 91 A7
 Cheadle ST10 . . . . 76 D2
 Cheddleton ST13 . . . . . . 45 C4
 Endon ST9 . . . . 43 E7
 Enville DY7 . . . . 273 D1
 Featherstone WV10 . . . . . 241 D7
 Kidsgrove ST7 . . . . 25 F1
 Newcastle-u-L,Basford ST5 . 56 D2
 Newcastle-u-L ST7 . . . . . 71 D8
 Stone ST15 . . . . 105 A1
 Stretton ST19 . . . . 206 D3
 Wolverhampton,Castlecroft
  WV3 . . . . 265 B8
 Wolverhampton,Penn WV4 265 E4
 Wootton DE6 . . . . 79 E5
Avenue Two CW1 . . . . . . 37 C8
Averill Dr WS15 . . . . 178 D2
Averill Rd ST17 . . . . 174 D8
Aviation La DE13 . . . . . . 165 C4
Avill B77 . . . . 262 A5
Avington Cl DY3 . . . . 271 D7
Avion Cl ST3 . . . . 90 C7
Avion Cl ST3 . . . . 90 C7
Avocet Cl ST14 . . . . 126 C6
Avoca St ST1 . . . . 282 C4
Avon Bsns Pk WS11 . . . . 226 C2
Avon Cl Kidsgrove ST7 . . . 26 B2
 Newcastle-u-L ST5 . . . . . 71 B4
 Perton WV6 . . . . 254 F4
 Stafford ST16 . . . . 156 B3
Avon Cres WS3 . . . . 244 A1
Avoncroft **8** WV4 . . . . . 266 F4
Avondale Cl DY6 . . . . 275 E8
Avon Dale TF10 . . . . 168 F4
Avondale Rd WV6 . . . . . . 255 F3
Avondale St ST6 . . . . 56 D8
Avon Gr Cheadle ST10 . . . 76 E1
 Loggerheads TF9 . . . . . . 99 E5
 Stone ST15 . . . . 120 B6
Avon Hill ST16 . . . . 156 C3
Avon Ho DY3 . . . . 271 E3
Avonlea Gdns WS15 . . . . 178 C1
Avon Rd Burntwood WS7 . . 228 F5
 Cannock WS11 . . . . 226 D8
 Stourbridge DY8 . . . . . . 279 F3
 Walsall WS3 . . . . 243 E1
Avon Rise ST16 . . . . 156 B3
Avonside Ave ST6 . . . . . . 41 F4
Avon B77 . . . . 262 A5
Avon Way
 Burton u T DE15 . . . . . . 167 A1
 Hilton DE65 . . . . 147 D8
Avonwick Gr ST1 . . . . 58 A6
Axborough La DY10 . . . . . 280 D4
Axbridge Wlk ST6 . . . . . . 42 C1
Axon Cres ST4 . . . . 74 B3
Aylesbury Rd ST2 . . . . . . 58 C2
Aylesford Cl DY3 . . . . 266 C2
Aylesford Dr B74 . . . . 257 F5
Aynsley Ave ST5 . . . . 71 B3
Aynsley Cl ST10 . . . . 76 D1
Aynsley Rd ST4 . . . . 57 B1
Aynsley Specl Sch ST11 . . 90 E7
Aynsley's Dr ST11 . . . . . . 90 E7
Ayreshire Gr ST3 . . . . 73 D1
Ayr Rd ST10 . . . . 76 E5
Ayrshire Way CW12 . . . . . 6 A1
Ayrton Cl WV6 . . . . 255 A4
Ayshford St ST3 . . . . 284 B3
Azalea Cl WV8 . . . . 239 B3

B

Babbacombe Ave ST17 . . 175 E8
Babbington Cl
Tutbury DE13 . . . . 146 C5
Whittington WS14 . . . . 232 E5
Babworth Cl WV9 . . . . 240 A2
Back Browning St ST16 . 285 A4
Back Bunt's La ST9 . . . . . . 43 D4
Backcester La WS13 . . . . 231 B8
Backcrofts 3 WS11 . . . . 209 E1
Back Cross La CW12 . . . . . 16 A8
Back Ford Green Rd ST6 . 42 D2
Back Garden St ST5 . . . . . . 283 C2
Back Heathcote St ST7 . . . 26 A2
Back La Aldridge WS9 . . . . 256 F8
Alstonefield DE6 . . . . 35 E3
Alton ST10 . . . . 78 F1
Ashley TF9 . . . . 100 A5
Betley CW3 . . . . 53 B8
Brown Edge,Hodgefield ST6 28 B1
Brown Edge ST6 . . . . 43 B7
Colwich ST18 . . . . 177 D8
Cotes Heath ST21 . . . . 102 D5
Ellastone DE6 . . . . 80 A3
Gnosall ST20 . . . . 171 C5
Haughton ST18 . . . . 173 A5
Hixon ST18 . . . . 139 C1
Leek ST13 . . . . 30 D6
Ranton ST18 . . . . 153 D4
Shenstone WS14 . . . . 246 E1
Sutton TF10 . . . . 150 D1
Uttoxeter ST14 . . . . 126 C8
Warslow SK17 . . . . 23 A2
Waterhouses ST10 . . . . 49 E1
Weston-Under-Lizard
TF11 . . . . 203 D6
Wheaton Aston ST19 . . . . . 205 C5
Whittington WS14 . . . . 232 E6
Woodseaves ST20 . . . . 151 D8
Wootton DE6 . . . . 79 F7
Back Radfords 2 ST15 . . 105 A1
Back Rd DY6 . . . . 275 D7
Back Westlands Rd ST14 126 B6
Baddeley Green La ST2 . . . 43 B1
Baddeley Hall Rd ST2 . . . . 43 C2
Baddeley Rd ST2 . . . . 43 B1
Baddeley St Burslem ST6 . . 41 F1
Cheadle ST10 . . . . 76 E2
Baddely's Ct TF10 . . . . 168 F2
Baden Powell Cl WS15 . . 211 F6
Baden Rd ST6 . . . . 42 C1
Baden St ST5 . . . . 283 B4
Bader Rd WV6 . . . . 254 E3
Badger Brow Rd TF9 . . . . . . 99 D5
Badger Cl WS12 . . . . 209 D6
Badger Gr ST3 . . . . 90 C7
Badger La TF9,ST5 . . . . 84 C3
Badgers Bank Rd B74 . . . 257 F5
Badgers Brow ST1 . . . . 57 E3
Badgers Cl WS3 . . . . 244 A5
Badgers Croft
Derrington ST18 . . . . 154 E2
Eccleshall ST21 . . . . 133 F7
Newcastle-u-L ST5 . . . . 40 E1
Stafford ST17 . . . . 175 C6
Badger's End ST19 . . . . . . 205 B6
Badgers Hollow ST10 . . . . 93 B1
Badgers Rise ST13 . . . . 30 E6
Badgers Sett ST13 . . . . 30 E6
Badger St DY3 . . . . 271 E5
Badgers Way WS12 . . . . . 210 D1
Badgery Cl ST14 . . . . 111 A2
Badminton Cl DY1 . . . . . . 271 F3
Badnall Cl ST13 . . . . 30 E6
Badnall St ST13 . . . . 30 D6
Baggeridge Cl DY3 . . . . . . 271 A8
Baggeridge Ctry Pk★
DY3 . . . . 270 E6
Baggott Pl ST5 . . . . 70 F8
Baggott St WV2 . . . . 266 C7
Bag La Marchington ST14 . . 127 E2
Newton WS15 . . . . 159 D7
Roston DE6 . . . . 96 E7
Bagnall Rd ST2 . . . . 43 C1
Bagnall St ST1 . . . . 282 B2
Bagot Gr ST1 . . . . 57 F8
Bagots Oak ST17 . . . . 174 C7
Bagot St WS15 . . . . 160 F6
Bagots View
Abbots Bromley WS15 . . . . 161 A6
Church Leigh ST10 . . . . . . 109 A4
Bagridge Cl WV3 . . . . 265 B8
Bagridge Rd WV3 . . . . 265 B8
Bailey Ave B77 . . . . 261 F5
Bailey Cl Burntwood WS7 . 228 D8
Cannock WS11 . . . . 210 A4
Bailey Cres CW12 . . . . 6 A4
Bailey Rd ST3 . . . . 72 E4
Bailey's Bank ST8 . . . . 16 D3
Bailey St Burton u T DE14 . 166 D1
Newcastle-u-L ST5 . . . . 283 A3
Stafford ST17 . . . . 285 B2
Stoke-on-T ST4 . . . . 56 F1
Bailye Cl WS13 . . . . 214 F1
Bainbridge Rd ST4 . . . . 88 A7
Bains Dr WS13 . . . . 231 A6
Bains Gr ST5 . . . . 55 F8
Baird Ho DY6 . . . . 275 F7
Baker Ave WV14 . . . . 266 F2
Baker Cl WS7 . . . . 228 F6
Baker Cres N ST2 . . . . 43 C3
Baker Cres S ST2 . . . . 43 B3
Baker Cres ST2 . . . . 43 C3
Baker Dr WS13 . . . . 215 C7
Bakers Gdns WV8 . . . . 238 E4
Baker's La
5 Lichfield WS13 . . . . 231 B7
Aldridge WS9 . . . . 256 B6
Weston Jones TF10 . . . . . . 150 C4
Baker St Burntwood WS7 . 228 F6
Burton u T DE15 . . . . 185 E7
Stoke-on-T ST4 . . . . 72 E6
Bakers Way
Cannock WS12 . . . . 210 B5
Codsall WV8 . . . . 238 F4
Bakers Wlk 1 B77 . . . . . . 261 F6
Bakewell Cl
Newcastle-u-L ST5 . . . . 55 B1
Walsall WS3 . . . . 243 C3
Bakewell Dr ST15 . . . . 120 D5
Bakewell Gn DE11 . . . . . . 186 E5
Bakewell St ST4 . . . . 71 F5
Balaam's La ST15 . . . . 106 D6
Bala Gr ST10 . . . . 76 F4
Bala Ho ST17 . . . . 174 E6
Balance Hill ST14 . . . . 126 C7
Balance St ST14 . . . . 126 C7
Balcombe Cl ST5 . . . . 283 B1
Baldwin Gr WS11 . . . . 210 C2
Baldwin's Gate CE Prim Sch
ST5 . . . . 85 D5
Baldwin Way DY3 . . . . 269 E2
Balfour Cres WV6 . . . . 255 F4
Balfour Ct
2 Wolverhampton WV6 . . 255 F4
Sutton Coldfield B74 . . . . . 258 A3
Balfour Gr Biddulph ST8 . . . 27 E8
Stafford ST16 . . . . 155 C8
Balfour Rd DY6 . . . . 275 E8
Balfour St
Burton u T DE13 . . . . 166 C6
Hanley ST1 . . . . 282 C2
Balfour B79 . . . . 250 A4
Balk Pas ST16 . . . . 285 A3
Balk The DE13 . . . . 146 D6
Ballam Mews WS15 . . . . . 178 E1
Ballarat Wlk DY8 . . . . 279 F5
Ball Green Prim Sch ST6 . 42 D5
Ball Haye Gn ST13 . . . . 31 A7
Ball Haye Rd ST13 . . . . 30 F6
Ball Hayes Rd ST6 . . . . 42 C5
Ball Haye St ST13 . . . . 30 F6
Ball Haye Terr ST13 . . . . . . 30 F6
Ballington Gdns ST13 . . . . 30 F5
Ballington View ST13 . . . . 30 F4
Ballinson Rd ST3 . . . . 72 F1
Balliol Bsns Pk WV9 . . . . 239 E3
Balliol St ST4 . . . . 72 A7
Ball La Coven Heath WV10 . 240 C6
Leek ST13 . . . . 30 E6
Stoke-on-T ST6 . . . . 43 B5
Balloon St ST4 . . . . 56 D1
Ball's Yd ST5 . . . . 283 B3
Balmain Cres WV11 . . . . . 241 B1
Balmoral Cl
Lichfield WS14 . . . . 231 D6
Stoke-on-T ST4 . . . . 72 A2
Stone ST15 . . . . 120 B6
Tamworth B79 . . . . 250 B7
Balmoral Ct WS11 . . . . . . 210 A5
Balmoral Dr
Cannock WS12 . . . . 209 F7
Cheadle ST10 . . . . 76 B2
Market Drayton TF9 . . . . 97 E2
Wombourne WV5 . . . . 265 A1
Balmoral Rd
Burton u T DE15 . . . . 167 A3
Stafford ST17 . . . . 156 C1
Stourbridge DY8 . . . . 275 C2
Sutton Coldfield B74 . . . . . 257 F5
Wolverhampton WV4 . . . . . 266 A5
Balmoral View DY1 . . . . . 271 E2
Balmoral Way WS7 . . . . . . 211 E1
Balterley Ct CW2 . . . . 53 C8
Baltic Cl Cannock WS11 . . . 209 E2
Stoke-on-T ST4 . . . . 88 B7
Balvenie Way DY1 . . . . 271 F4
Bamber Cl WV3 . . . . 265 E8
Bamber Pl ST5 . . . . 55 F6
Bamber St ST4 . . . . 72 B8
Bamborough Cl DE13 . . . 166 D7
Bamburgh B77 . . . . 261 C7
Bambury St ST3 . . . . 73 C6
Bamford Cl WS3 . . . . 243 C3
Bamford Gr Hanley ST1 . . 282 A4
Uttoxeter ST14 . . . . 110 F2
Bamford Ho WS3 . . . . 243 C3
Bamford Rd Walsall WS3 . 243 C3
Wolverhampton WV3 . . . . . 266 A8
Bamford St B77 . . . . 250 D3
Bampton Ave 4 WS7 . . . . 229 A8
Bampton Cl ST9 . . . . 43 F8
Banbery Dr WV5 . . . . 269 F4
Banbury Cl DY3 . . . . 271 E6
Banbury Gr ST8 . . . . 27 C7
Banbury Rd WS11 . . . . 226 C8
Banbury St ST7 . . . . 25 D1
Bancroft La
Blythe Bridge ST11 . . . . 90 F6
Nethertown WS15 . . . . 199 A8
Bancroft B77 . . . . 250 F3
Bandridge La SK11 . . . . 18 A8
Baneberry Dr WV10 . . . . . 241 B7
Bangley La
Drayton Bassett B78 . . . . . 259 E6
Mile Oak B78 . . . . 260 A8
Bangor Terr ST10 . . . . 63 E4
Bank Cl ST14 . . . . 126 C7
Bank Cres WS7 . . . . 228 F5
Bank Ct 5 ST7 . . . . 26 A2
Bank End ST6 . . . . 43 B7
Bankerwall La DE6 . . . . 80 C7
Bankfield Gr ST5 . . . . 54 E4
Bankfield Rd ST3 . . . . 89 F8
Bank Hall Rd ST6 . . . . 42 B2
Bank Ho ST10 . . . . 76 D3
Bankhouse Dr CW12 . . . . . . 6 A5
Bank House Dr ST5 . . . . . . 56 E2
Bankhouse Rd
Forsbrook ST11 . . . . 91 B8
Stoke-on-T ST4 . . . . 71 F1
Trentham ST4 . . . . 87 F8
Bank Pas ST16 . . . . 285 B3
Bank Rd DY3 . . . . 271 C2
Bank Side SK17 . . . . 24 D6
Bankside Meaford ST15 . . . 104 D4
Newcastle-u-L ST5 . . . . 283 C2
Stanton DE6 . . . . 65 C1
Bank Side ST15 . . . . 119 F6
Bankside Way WS9 . . . . . 245 B2
Bankside WV5 . . . . 269 F7
Banks La ST10 . . . . 61 E4
Banksman Rd ST2 . . . . 73 D7
Bank St Cannock WS12 . . . 210 E1
Cheadle ST10 . . . . 76 D3
Kidsgrove ST7 . . . . 26 C4
Stoke-on-T ST6 . . . . 41 D4
Bank The ST7 . . . . 26 B7
Bank Top Ave ST6 . . . . 42 A3
Banktop Ct ST5 . . . . 56 C6
Bank Top La ST17 . . . . 175 B1
Banktop Rd DE6 . . . . 144 B6
Bank Top WS15 . . . . 178 D1
Bank View ST10 . . . . 62 A3
Bank Wlk DE13 . . . . 166 B8
Banky Brook Cl ST6 . . . . . . 42 C3
Bannister Cl ST4 . . . . 72 B4
Bannut Tree La DY7 . . . . . 277 C5
Banstead Cl WV2 . . . . 266 E7
Bantock Ave WV3 . . . . 265 F8
Bantock Ct WV3 . . . . 265 E8
Bantock Gdns WV3 . . . . . . 255 E1
Bantock House Mus★
WV3 . . . . 255 F1
Bantock Prim Sch WV3 . . 266 A8
Baonal Way WS15 . . . . 118 B6
Baptist St 9 ST6 . . . . 57 A8
Barbara St B79 . . . . 250 A5
Barber Cl WS12 . . . . 210 E2
Barber Dr ST7 . . . . 25 E7
Barber Pl ST6 . . . . 41 F6
Barber Rd ST6 . . . . 41 F6
Barber's Sq ST5 . . . . 56 D4
Barber St ST6 . . . . 41 F1
Barbridge Rd ST5 . . . . 40 D1
Barbrook Ave ST3 . . . . 73 E4
Barclay Cl WV7 . . . . 237 B6
Barclay St ST3 . . . . 73 C5
Barcliff Ave B77 . . . . 250 E3
Bardell Cl WS13 . . . . 230 E6
Bardolph Cl DE11 . . . . 186 F3
Bardsey Wlk 1 ST3 . . . . . . 73 A3
Bardwell Cl WV8 . . . . 255 F8
Bardy La Armitage WS15 . . 197 E3
Longdon WS15 . . . . 197 C1
Barford Rd ST5 . . . . 70 F3
Barford St ST3 . . . . 284 B3
Bargate La ST19 . . . . 223 C6
Bargate St ST19 . . . . 223 C6
Bargery Rd WV11 . . . . 242 A1
Bargrave Dr ST5 . . . . 56 B8
Bargrave St ST2 . . . . 58 D1
Bar Hill CW3 . . . . 68 D4
Barker Cl ST16 . . . . 155 C3
Barker Ho ST3 . . . . 88 F8
Barker St Longton ST3 . . . . 284 D3
Newcastle-u-L ST5 . . . . 55 F6
Barks Dr ST6 . . . . 42 D4
Bar La DE13 . . . . 183 A2
Barlaston CE Fst Sch
ST12 . . . . 88 E1
Barlaston Cl ST16 . . . . 155 C8
Barlaston Hall★ ST12 . . . . 88 E3
Barlaston Old Rd ST4 . . . . . 88 D5
Barlaston Rd Barlaston ST3 89 B5
Stoke-on-T ST3 . . . . 88 F7
Barlaston Sta ST12 . . . . 88 D1
Barley Cl Aldridge WS9 . . . 256 E2
Burton u T DE14 . . . . 166 E6
Cannock WS12 . . . . 210 B5
Dudley DY3 . . . . 271 F7
Wolverhampton WV8 . . . . . 239 E1
Barleycorn Cl DE15 . . . . . 167 A1
Barleycroft ST10 . . . . 76 E1
Barley Croft WV6 . . . . 254 D3
Barleycroft Terr ST7 . . . . . 25 F7
Barley Croft WS14 . . . . . . 232 E6
Barley Ct ST16 . . . . 155 A5
Barley Field WV9 . . . . 224 B2
Barleyfield Rise DY6 . . . . 275 A8
Barleyfields Audley ST7 . . . 39 D2
Stoke-on-T ST6 . . . . 42 C3
Barleyford Dr ST3 . . . . 73 D6
Barley Green La DE13 . . . 201 C1
Barley Orch ST20 . . . . 171 E6
Barley Rd ST10 . . . . 62 A8
Barlow Cl B77 . . . . 250 E4
Barlow St ST3 . . . . 284 C3
Barlstone Ave ST11 . . . . . . 90 F6
Barmouth Cl ST8 . . . . 27 E6
Barmouth Gr ST8 . . . . 27 B2
Barnaby Sq WV10 . . . . 240 F4
Barnard Pl WV2 . . . . 266 E6
Barnard Rd WV11 . . . . 241 F1
Barnard Way WS11 . . . . . . 209 F2
Barn Ave DY3 . . . . 271 C7
Barn Bank La ST17,ST18 . 174 D5
Barnbridge Cl ST7 . . . . 25 E7
Barnbridge B77 . . . . 250 C2
Barn Cl Dordon B78 . . . . . . 262 F6
Lichfield WS13 . . . . 214 B3
Barn Cl *continued*
Rugeley WS15 . . . . 197 B5
Stafford ST17 . . . . 174 E5
Barn Comm ST20 . . . . 151 D8
Barn Croft
Burntwood WS7 . . . . 229 A4
Great Wyrley WS6 . . . . 227 A3
Barncroft Rd ST6 . . . . 42 C6
Barn Ct ST5 . . . . 71 C3
Barn End Rd ST17 . . . . 193 B8
Barnescroft ST15 . . . . 106 D2
Barnes Rd
Shenstone WS14 . . . . 247 A6
Stafford ST17 . . . . 174 C7
Barnes Way ST3 . . . . 73 C1
Barnett Cl DY6 . . . . 275 D4
Barnett Gn DY6 . . . . 275 D4
Barnett Gr ST6 . . . . 41 F5
Barnett La DY6,DY8 . . . . . . 275 D4
Barnetts La WS8 . . . . 228 F1
Barnett St DY8 . . . . 275 D3
Barnfield Cl
Lichfield WS14 . . . . 231 B6
Stone ST15 . . . . 119 F7
Barnfield Pl ST13 . . . . 30 E4
Barnfield Rd Burslem ST6 . 57 A7
Leek ST13 . . . . 30 D4
Upper Tean ST10 . . . . 92 E4
Barnfields Cl ST13 . . . . 30 D4
Barnfields Ind Est ST13 . . 30 D3
Barnfields La ST10 . . . . 61 D2
Barnfields Prim Sch
ST17 . . . . 175 C6
Barnfield ST4 . . . . 71 F6
Barnfield Way
Cannock WS12 . . . . 211 A6
Stafford ST17 . . . . 175 C6
Barngate St ST13 . . . . 30 D5
Barn Gn WV3 . . . . 265 F7
Barnhurst La WV8 . . . . 239 E2
Barn La Brewood ST19 . . . . 223 C7
Standon ST21 . . . . 101 C5
Barnlea Gr ST3 . . . . 90 A5
Barnmeadow Cl TF10 . . . 169 A3
Barnmeadow Rd TF10 . . . 169 A2
Barn Owl Dr WS3 . . . . 243 F4
Barn Rd WS15 . . . . 198 C4
Barns Cl WS9 . . . . 244 F4
Barns Croft B74 . . . . 257 B4
Barnsdale Cl ST4 . . . . 88 C5
Barnswood Cl WS11 . . . . . 226 B8
Barnton Edge ST15 . . . . . 104 E3
Barn Way WS12 . . . . 210 F4
Barnwell Cl ST14 . . . . 111 A4
Barnwell Gr ST4 . . . . 72 A1
Barnwood Rd WV8 . . . . . . 239 E1
Baron Cl WS7 . . . . 211 E1
Baron St ST4 . . . . 284 A5
Baron's Way ST18 . . . . 158 C8
Barracks La WS9,WS14 . . 245 C8
Barracks Rd ST5 . . . . 283 C2
Barracks Sq ST5 . . . . 283 C2
Barracks Way 2 ST13 . . . . 30 D6
Barrage Rd ST8 . . . . 28 B7
Barrar Cl DY8 . . . . 279 E8
Barratt Gdns ST2 . . . . 58 B8
Barratts Croft DY5 . . . . . . 271 C1
Barr Common Cl WS9 . . . . 256 B3
Barr Common Rd WS9 . . 256 B3
Barrett Cres ST6 . . . . 57 A6
Barrett Dr ST6 . . . . 57 A6
Barrie Gdns ST7 . . . . 40 C8
Barrington Cl
Albrighton WV7 . . . . 237 A5
Stretton DE13 . . . . 147 C1
Wolverhampton WV10 . . . . 240 C1
Barrington Ct ST5 . . . . 56 E3
Barrow Cl WS9 . . . . 244 F4
Barrow Hill Rd DY5 . . . . . 271 C1
Barr St DY3 . . . . 271 C3
Barry Ave ST2 . . . . 58 A4
Bartholomew Rd ST3 . . . . . 73 F1
Barthomley Rd Audley ST7 39 A2
Balterley ST7 . . . . 38 F3
Barthomley CW2 . . . . 38 B7
Hanley ST1 . . . . 57 D6
Bartic Ave DY6 . . . . 275 F4
Bartlem St ST3 . . . . 284 D5
Bartlett Cl ST19 . . . . 207 F8
Barton Cottage Hospl
DE13 . . . . 183 D1
Barton Cres ST6 . . . . 41 E1
Barton Gate DE13 . . . . 183 B2
Barton La Bradley ST18 . . . 191 A8
Kingswinford DY6 . . . . 275 C8
Barton Lodge DE13 . . . . . 183 D1
Barton Rd WV4 . . . . 266 F4
Barton's La TF9 . . . . 112 B8
Barton's Rd TF9 . . . . 112 B8
Barton St DE14 . . . . 185 C8
Barton Turn DE13 . . . . 184 A1
Bar Wlk WS9 . . . . 245 C1
Barwood Ave ST7 . . . . 25 A5
Basfordbridge La ST13 . . . 45 D4
Basfordbridge Terr ST13 . 45 E5
Basford La ST13 . . . . 45 F8
Basford Lane Ind Est
ST13 . . . . 45 F8
Basford Park Rd ST5 . . . . . 56 D3
Basford View ST13 . . . . 45 D6
Basford Villas ST5 . . . . 56 D2
Basil Cl ST17 . . . . 174 F5
Basildon Gr ST3 . . . . 284 C2
Basin La B77 . . . . 250 D3
Baskerville Rd ST1 . . . . . . 282 C3
Baskeyfield Cl WS14 . . . . 231 D7
Baskeyfield Pl ST6 . . . . 42 B5
Baslow Cl WS3 . . . . 243 C3
Baslow Gn DE11 . . . . 186 E5
Baslow Rd WS3 . . . . 243 B3
Basnett's Wood ST9 . . . . . . 43 E6
Bass Cotts DE14 . . . . 166 E4
Bassenthwaite Ct DY6 . . . 275 D6
Bassett Cl Cheadle ST10 . . . 76 D3
Wolverhampton WV4 . . . . . 265 C6
Bassilow Rd ST4 . . . . 72 F7
Bass's Bldgs DE14 . . . . . . 166 B3
Baswich Bsns Pk ST17 . . . 156 D2
Baswich Crest ST17 . . . . . 156 D1
Baswich House Dr ST17 . 175 D7
Baswich House Way
ST17 . . . . 175 D7
Baswich La ST17,ST18 . . . 156 D2
Batchelor Cl DY8 . . . . 279 F8
Batch La DE6 . . . . 127 B7
Bateman Ave ST8 . . . . 27 B5
Batesmans Way ST14 . . . 126 C8
Batesway WS15 . . . . 197 C4
Batfield La DY7 . . . . 272 E2
Bath Ct ST17 . . . . 285 B1
Bath La DY7 . . . . 277 D5
Bath Mews DY8 . . . . 279 F5
Batholdi Way ST17 . . . . . . 175 A8
Bath Rd Cannock WS11 . . . 209 E5
Newcastle-u-L ST5 . . . . 54 F2
Stourbridge DY8 . . . . 279 F5
Baths La ST18 . . . . 158 C8
Baths Pas ST3 . . . . 284 B4
Baths Rd ST3 . . . . 284 B4
Bath St Leek ST13 . . . . 30 F6
Meir ST3 . . . . 74 B5
Sedgley DY3 . . . . 266 E1
Stoke-on-T ST4 . . . . 72 A7
Bath Terr 9 ST4 . . . . 72 A7
Bathurst St ST3 . . . . 284 C4
Bath Vale Cotts CW12 . . . . . 6 A3
Batkin Cl ST6 . . . . 42 B5
Batten Cl ST3 . . . . 90 C7
Batten Wlk ST15 . . . . 118 F6
Battisson Cres ST3 . . . . . . 284 C2
Battlefield Hill WV5 . . . . . 270 B7
Battlefield La WV5 . . . . . . 270 B6
Battlefield Terr WV5 . . . . 270 B6
Battle Ridge ST18 . . . . 156 D8
Battlesteads ST10 . . . . 78 D1
Baulk La ST11 . . . . 106 E8
Baxter Gn ST16 . . . . 155 B4
Bayham Wlk ST2 . . . . 58 A4
Bayley Hills TF10 . . . . 168 A3
Baylie Ct DY8 . . . . 279 F5
Baylie St DY8 . . . . 279 F4
Bayliss Ct WV3 . . . . 255 E2
Bayston Ave WV3 . . . . 265 E8
Bayswater Rd
Dudley DY3 . . . . 271 D2
Rugeley WS15 . . . . 178 D1
Baytree Cl
Birches Head ST1 . . . . 57 F6
Walsall WS3 . . . . 243 A2
Baytree Rd WS3 . . . . 243 A2
Baytree Wlk WS14 . . . . . . 232 E6
Baywood Cl ST17 . . . . 156 C1
Beach Ave WV14 . . . . 266 F3
Beachcroft Rd DY6 . . . . . . 270 C1
Beachwood Ave DY6 . . . . 270 C1
Beacon Ctr for the Blind
WV4 . . . . 266 D4
Beacon Dr DE13 . . . . 147 B3
Beaconfields 1 WS13 . . . 231 A8
Beacon Gdns WS13 . . . . . 214 A1
Beacon Hill WS9 . . . . 256 C1
Beacon La Kinver DY7 . . . . 277 B2
Romsley DY11,DY12,WV15 276 E3
Sedgley DY3 . . . . 266 E1
Beacon Pas DY3 . . . . 266 D1
Beacon Pk ST19 . . . . 221 F7
Beacon Rd Aldridge WS9 . . 256 B1
Rolleston on D DE13 . . . . . 147 B3
Stone ST15 . . . . 120 A5
Beacon Rise
Aldridge WS9 . . . . 256 B3
Sedgley DY3 . . . . 266 E1
Stone ST15 . . . . 120 A5
Beaconsfield Ave WV4 . . 266 D5
Beaconsfield Dr
Stoke-on-T ST3 . . . . 72 E1
Stoke-on-T ST3 . . . . 88 E8
Wolverhampton WV4 . . . . . 266 D6
Beaconsfield ST5 . . . . 56 C7
Beaconsfield Rd DE13 . . . 166 B7
Beaconside Cl ST16 . . . . . 156 A5
Beaconside Sports Ctr
ST18 . . . . 156 D4
Beaconside
Stafford,Beaconside
ST16 . . . . 156 B5
Stafford ST16 . . . . 136 D1
Beacon St Lichfield WS13 . 231 A8
Wolverhampton WV14 . . . . 266 F1
Beacon Trad Est WS9 . . . . 256 A6
Beacon Way
Brownhills WS9 . . . . 245 A3
Cannock WS12 . . . . 210 F3
Beadnell Gr ST3 . . . . 73 C1
Beale St DY8 . . . . 279 F5
Bealeys Cl WS3 . . . . 243 A3
Bealeys La WS3 . . . . 243 A2
Beamhill Rd DE13 . . . . 165 F8
Beamish La WV7,WV8 . . . . 237 E5
Beard Gr ST2 . . . . 58 B7
Bearnett Dr WV4 . . . . 265 C2
Bearnett La WV4 . . . . 265 B2

Bearstone Rd
Bearstone TF9 . . . . 83 A4
Knighton TF9 . . . . 83 C4
Norton in H TF9 . . . . 82 E3
Bearwood Hill Rd DE15 . 167 A3
Beasley Ave ST5 . . . . 55 F7
Beasley Pl ST5 . . . . 55 F7
Beata Rd ST5 . . . . 40 F1
Beat La Ryecroft Gate SK11 . 18 A8
  Woodhouse Green ST8 . . . 17 E8
Beaton Rd B74 . . . . 258 A3
Beatrice Ct ST17 . . . . 72 A2
Beatrice St ST8 . . . . 27 B2
Beatrice Wlk ST8 . . . . . . 283 B4
Beattie Ave ST5 . . . . 283 B4
Beatty Dr CW12 . . . . 6 A4
Beatty Rd ST13 . . . . 31 A6
Beaubrook Gdns DY6 . . . 275 E3
Beauchamp Ind Pk B77 . 261 D8
Beauchamp Rd B77 . . . . 261 F5
Beau Ct WS11 . . . . 209 F1
Beaudesert WS7 . . . . 212 A1
Beaudesert View WS12 . . 211 A5
Beaufighter Gr ST6 . . . . . 41 C5
Beaufort Ct ST3 . . . . 73 F1
Beaufort Rd
  Burton u T DE15 . . . . . . 167 B1
  Longton ST3 . . . . 284 C2
Beaufort Way WS9 . . . . . 256 A4
Beaulieu Ave DY6 . . . . . . 275 F4
Beaulieu Cl ST9 . . . . 59 B3
Beaumaris Cl Dudley DY1 . 271 F4
  Stoke-on-T ST4 . . . . 71 D8
Beaumaris Ct ST4 . . . . . 283 A2
Beaumaris Rd TF10 . . . . 168 E3
Beaumont Cl Biddulph ST8 . 16 D3
  Great Wyrley WS6 . . . . . 226 F2
Beaumont Ct ST5 . . . . . . 70 F3
Beaumont Gdns ST17 . . 174 B8
Beaumont Rd
  Great Wyrley WS6 . . . . . 226 F2
  Stoke-on-T ST6 . . . . 41 E3
Beaumont Rise 90 D3
Beaumont Way WS11 . . . 228 A4
Beauty Bank Cres DY8 . . 279 F6
Beauty Bank Prim Sch
  DY8 . . . . 279 F6
Beaver Cl ST4 . . . . 71 E4
Beaver Dr ST10 . . . . 76 B2
Bebington Cl WV4 . . . . . 255 F8
Beckbury Ave WV4 . . . . . 265 C5
Beckdale ST14 . . . . 126 A8
Beckenham Cl ST3 . . . . . . 90 C8
Becket Cl Burton u T DE13 166 B6
  Sutton Coldfield B74 . . . 257 F6
Beckett Ave ST3 . . . . 74 B1
Becketts St DE13 . . . . . . 166 C7
Beckfields Cl ST8 . . . . 17 B1
Beckminster Rd WV3 . . . 265 F7
Beck's La DE13 . . . . 162 F2
Beck Rd CW3 . . . . 68 F7
Beck The B79 . . . . 216 E2
Beckton Ave ST6 . . . . 41 E3
Bedale Pl ST3 . . . . 72 E1
Beddow Way ST6 . . . . 41 F6
Bedford Ave ST16 . . . . . 156 A3
Bedford Cres ST5 . . . . . . 71 C4
Bedford Pl WS12 . . . . . . 210 B4
Bedford Rd
  Burton u T DE15 . . . . . . 185 D7
  Hanley ST1 . . . . 282 A1
  Kidsgrove ST7 . . . . 26 A3
Bedford St ST1 . . . . 57 A2
Bedford Way WS15 . . . . 196 D6
Bedingstone Dr ST19 . . . 208 A7
Bednall Barns ST17 . . . . 193 F8
Bednall Ct ST17 . . . . 193 F8
Bednall Rd ST17 . . . . 175 C1
Beecham Bsns Pk WS9 . . 256 A8
Beecham Cl WS9 . . . . . . 256 A8
Beech Ave
  Burton u T DE13 . . . . . . 166 F7
  Cheddleton ST13 . . . . 45 C4
  King's Bromley DE13 . . . 199 C6
  Tamworth B77 . . . . 250 E3
Beech Cl Armitage WS15 . 198 C4
  Biddulph ST8 . . . . 17 B1
  Cheadle ST10 . . . . 76 F2
  Dunsley DY7 . . . . 278 B4
  Haughton ST18 . . . . 172 F5
Beechcliff La ST4,ST12 . . 87 E2
Beech Cl Leek ST13 . . . . . 30 C2
  Newport TF10 . . . . 168 F1
  Pattingham WV6 . . . . . . 253 C2
  Sedgley DY3 . . . . 266 E1
  Sutton Coldfield B75 . . . 258 A4
  Tamworth B79 . . . . 250 A8
  Uttoxeter ST14 . . . . 126 A8
  Wheaton Aston ST19 . . . 205 C6
Beech Cres WS7 . . . . . . 228 F6
Beechcroft Ave ST16 . . . 155 C1
Beechcroft Ct ST12 . . . . . 88 F2
Beechcroft Cres B74 . . . 256 D1
Beechcroft Ct B74 . . . . . 256 A1
Beechcroft Grange ST16 155 C1
  Pattingham WV6 . . . . . . 253 C2
Beech Ct Cannock WS12 . 210 B7
  Great Wyrley WS6 . . . . . 227 A4
  Stone ST15 . . . . 120 B8
Beechdale La
  Beech ST4,ST12 . . . . 87 D1

Beechdale La continued
  Tittensor ST12 . . . . 103 E8
Beech Dr Burton u T DE13 . 166 E8
  Talke ST7 . . . . 40 E1
Beechen Gr WS7 . . . . . . 228 F8
Beeches Cl DY6 . . . . 275 D5
Beeches Croft WS13 . . . 215 D7
Beeches Mews DY9 . . . . 281 F4
Beeches Rd WS15 . . . . . 197 A6
Beeches The
  Newcastle-u-L ST5 . . . . . . 56 C7
  Rugeley WS15 . . . . 178 D3
  Sutton Coldfield,Little Aston
    B74 . . . . 257 D4
Beechfield Dr ST17 . . . . 175 D5
Beechfield Rd ST4 . . . . . 88 B6
Beechfield Rise WS14 . . 231 D8
Beechfields ST12 . . . . . . 88 F2
Beechfields Way TF10 . . 168 F5
Beech Gate B74 . . . . 257 C5
Beech Gdns Codsall WV8 238 F2
  Lichfield WS14 . . . . 231 C6
Beech Gr
  Huntington WS12 . . . . . 209 D8
  Leek ST13 . . . . 30 C6
  Loggerheads TF9 . . . . . . 99 E5
  Newcastle-u-L ST5 . . . . . 56 C4
  Stoke-on-T ST4 . . . . 72 C5
  Swadlincote DE11 . . . . . 186 F7
Beech Ho B74 . . . . 257 B5
Beechhouse La WV5 . . . 264 A1
Beech Hurst Gdns WV5 . 264 A1
Beech La Burton u T DE13 166 E8
  Coppenhall ST18 . . . . . . 174 C3
  Stretton DE13 . . . . 147 E1
Beechlawn Dr DY7 . . . . . 278 E7
Beechmere Rise WS15 . . 178 B2
Beechmont Gr ST1 . . . . . 57 F6
Beechmount Rise 9
  ST17 . . . . 175 C7
Beech Pine Cl WS12 . . . 210 A8
Beech Rd
  Barton-u-N DE13 . . . . . 183 D1
  Eccleshall ST21 . . . . . . 133 C4
  Kingswinford DY6 . . . . . 275 D5
  Stoke-on-T ST3 . . . . 72 F1
  Stourbridge DY8 . . . . . . 279 F3
  Tamworth B79 . . . . 250 A8
  Wolverhampton WV10 . . 240 B1
Beech St Burton u T DE14 . 166 B1
  Longton ST3 . . . . 284 C3
Beech Tree Cl DY6 . . . . . 275 E8
Beech Tree La WS11 . . . 226 D8
Beechtree La DY10 . . . . . 280 E6
Beech Tree Rd WS9 . . . . 244 F3
Beechway ST16 . . . . 155 D6
Beech Wlk WS15 . . . . . . 198 A1
Beechwood Bsns Pk
  WS11 . . . . 210 B3
Beechwood Cl
  Blythe Bridge ST11 . . . . . 91 A6
  Newcastle-u-L ST5 . . . . . . 71 D1
  Walsall WS3 . . . . 243 B3
Beechwood Cres ST5 . . . 250 F5
Beechwood Croft B74 . . 257 D5
Beechwood Ct WV6 . . . . 255 C3
Beechwood Dr
  Stone ST10 . . . . 120 A6
  Wolverhampton WV6 . . . 255 C3
Beechwood WS14 . . . . . 232 E5
Beecroft Ave WS13 . . . . 214 B1
Beecroft Ct WS11 . . . . . 209 E2
Beecroft Hill Sch WS11 . 209 E2
Beecroft Rd WS11 . . . . . 209 E1
Beekes Croft B78 . . . . . . 261 A8
Bee La WV10 . . . . 240 D3
Beelow La ST10 . . . . 78 D6
Bees La WS11 . . . . 178 E1
Beeston Rd DY10 . . . . . . 280 B5
Beeston Ridge ST17 . . . . 174 B7
Beeston St ST3 . . . . 73 C5
Beeston View ST7 . . . . . . 41 A7
Beffcote La ST20 . . . . . . 171 B4
Beggars Bush La WV5 . . 270 B5
Beggars La ST13 . . . . 30 C5
Beighterton Farm Barns
  TF11 . . . . 203 F4
Beighterton La TF11 . . . 203 F3
Beighton Cl B74 . . . . . . 257 F6
Belbroughton Rd
  Blakedown DY10 . . . . . . 281 D1
  Stourbridge DY8 . . . . . . 279 E3
Belfast Cl ST6 . . . . 42 B2
Belfield Ave ST5 . . . . 56 C4
Belford Pl ST4 . . . . 56 F1
Belfort Way ST17 . . . . . . 175 A8
Belfry Cl WS3 . . . . 243 A3
Belfry Dr DY8 . . . . 279 E3
Belfry The Perton WV6 . . 254 D4
  Stretton DE13 . . . . 147 C1
Belgrade Rd WV10 . . . . . 240 B1
Belgrave Ave ST3 . . . . . . 284 B2
Belgrave CE Prim Sch
  ST3 . . . . 73 D1
Belgrave Cres ST3 . . . . . 284 C1
Belgrave Ct DY6 . . . . 275 F4
Belgrave High Sch B77 . 250 C1
Belgrave Rd Longton ST3 284 C1
  Newcastle-u-L ST5 . . . . . 283 C2
  Tamworth B77 . . . . 261 E8
Belgrove Ho WS11 . . . . . 209 D1
Bellamour La WS15,ST17 . 178 C6
Bellamour Way WS15 . . 178 F5
Bellaport Rd TF9 . . . . 82 A4
Bellasis St ST16 . . . . 155 E6
Bell Ave ST3 . . . . 73 D2
Bellbrook ST19 . . . . 192 F1
Bell Cl Lichfield WS13 . . . 213 F1

Bell Cl continued
  Stafford ST16 . . . . 155 F5
Bell Cotts DE6 . . . . 127 D8
Bell Dr WS12 . . . . 210 C2
Bellefield View ST5 . . . . . 56 C3
Bellencroft Gdns WV3 . 265 C7
Bellerton La ST6 . . . . 42 E2
Belle Vue Ct DY6 . . . . . . 275 D2
Belle Vue ST13 . . . . 30 D6
Belle Vue Prim Sch DY8 . 275 C3
Belle Vue Rd ST13 . . . . . 30 D6
Belle Vue DY8 . . . . 275 D2
Bellevue St WV14 . . . . . 266 F2
Bellflower Cl WV10 . . . . 241 A7
Bell Heather Rd WS8 . . . 244 D6
Bell Ho ST3 . . . . 88 F8
Bellhouse La DE13 . . . . . 164 E6
Bellhurst La ST19 . . . . . 205 A5
Bellingham Gr ST1 . . . . . 57 D6
Bellingham B77 . . . . 251 D1
Bell La Barlaston ST12 . . . 88 E4
  Barton-u-N DE13 . . . . . 183 D2
  Doveridge DE6 . . . . 127 C8
  Walsall,Wallington Heath
    WS3 . . . . 243 B1
Bellman's Yd TF10 . . . . . 168 F2
Bell Orch TF9 . . . . 100 C5
Bell Pl WV2 . . . . 266 C8
Bell Rd WS5 . . . . 264 D1
Bellringer Cl ST8 . . . . 27 C7
Bellringer Rd ST8 . . . . . . 88 D7
Bells End Rd DE12 . . . . . 184 D1
Bell's Hollow ST5 . . . . . . 40 E3
Bellsize Cl WS11 . . . . . . 227 F5
Bells La Burntwood WS7 . 211 F1
  Stourbridge DY8 . . . . . . 275 D2
Bell St DY8 . . . . 279 F5
Bellwood Cl ST3 . . . . 90 A5
Belmont Ave WS11 . . . . 209 C2
Belmont Cl Aldridge WS9 . 256 A4
  Great Wyrley WS6 . . . . . 227 A4
Belmont Rd Hanley ST1 . 57 A3
  Ipstones ST10 . . . . 61 D8
  Tamworth B77 . . . . 261 E7
  Wolverhampton WV4 . . 266 A5
Belmot Rd DE13 . . . . 145 F1
Belper Rd WS3 . . . . 243 C3
Belsay Cl ST3 . . . . 284 C4
Belsize B77 . . . . 250 E2
Belton Ave WV11 . . . . . . 241 B1
Belt Rd WS12,WS11 . . . . 210 A5
Belvedere Ave WV4 . . . . 266 B5
Belvedere Cl
  Burntwood WS7 . . . . . . 228 F5
  Kingswinford DY6 . . . . . 275 F4
  Stafford ST17 . . . . 175 C8
  Tamworth B79 . . . . 250 C7
Belvedere Gdns WV6 . . . 255 E7
Belvedere Jun Sch DE14 166 B5
Belvedere Rd
  Burton u T DE13 . . . . . . 166 A6
  Stoke-on-T ST4 . . . . 72 A1
Belvide Gdns WV8 . . . . . 238 F4
Belvoir Ave ST4 . . . . 88 C5
Belvoir Cl Burton u T DE13 166 B5
  Dudley DY1 . . . . 271 E2
Belvoir Rd DE14 . . . . . . 166 A5
Belvoir B77 . . . . 261 C7
Belwell Dr B74 . . . . 258 A4
Belwell La B74 . . . . 258 A2
Bemersley Rd
  Chell Heath ST6 . . . . 27 C1
  Stoke-on-T ST6 . . . . 42 E6
Benches Cl WS7 . . . . 228 D6
Bencroft WS8 . . . . 239 B4
Bend Oak Dr DE15 . . . . . 167 C4
Bend Oak Jun Sch DE15 167 C3
Benedict Pl ST2 . . . . 58 A5
Benenden Ct ST17 . . . . . 156 B1
Benfleet Pl ST3 . . . . 284 A3
Bengal Gr ST4 . . . . 88 C8
Bengry Rd ST3 . . . . 73 E2
Benion Rd WS11 . . . . . . 209 F5
Benjamins Way ST7 . . . . 39 F2
Ben Jones Ave TF10 . . . . 169 A4
Bennett Pl ST5 . . . . 56 B7
Bennett Rd B74 . . . . 257 D3
Bennetts La Bosley SK11 . . 7 C1
  Bramshall ST14 . . . . . . 125 C6
Bennett's La WV6 . . . . . 253 F1
Bennetts La WV6 . . . . . . 263 F7
Benson Ave ST5 . . . . 56 E7
Benson Cl Lichfield WS13 214 D1
  Perton WV6 . . . . 254 E5
Benson St ST6 . . . . 41 F5
Benson View B79 . . . . . . 250 C8
Benson Cres WS3 . . . . . . 243 D2
Benton's La WS6 . . . . . . 227 A1
Bents La ST10 . . . . 109 A3
Bentygrange La ST13 . . . 48 D3
Beowulf Covert DE13 . . . 147 B1
Berdmore St ST4 . . . . . . 284 A5

Beresford Cres ST5 . . . . . 71 A6
Beresford Dale
  Madeley CW3 . . . . 68 D6
  Swadlincote DE11 . . . . . 186 F2
Beresford Meml CE Fst Sch
  ST13 . . . . 31 B7
Beresford St ST4 . . . . 57 B1
Bergamot Dr ST3 . . . . . . 90 A6
Berkeley Cl Gnosall ST20 . 171 E7
  Perton WV6 . . . . 254 F3
Berkeley Dr DY6 . . . . 275 C7
Berkeley St Hanley ST1 . . 282 C1
  Stone ST15 . . . . 104 F2
Berkeley Way WS11 . . . . 198 A1
Berkshire Gr ST5 . . . . 71 C5
Berkshire The WS3 . . . . . 243 A3
Berkswell Cl Dudley DY1 . 271 E6
  Sutton Coldfield B74 . . . 257 E4
Berkswich CE Prim Sch
  ST17 . . . . 175 F6
Bernard Cheadle Cl
  ST15 . . . . 103 C4
Bernard Gr ST3 . . . . 89 F4
Bernard St ST1 . . . . 282 C1
Berne Ave ST5 . . . . 70 E6
Bernwall Cl DY8 . . . . 279 F4
Berrisford Cl TF9 . . . . 97 E1
Berrisford Rd TF9 . . . . . . 97 E1
Berrybush Gdns DY3 . . . 271 E7
Berryfield Gr ST3 . . . . . . 73 F4
Berryfields WS9 . . . . 245 E5
Berry Gdns DE15 . . . . . . 167 C4
Berry Hedge La DE15 . . . 167 C4
Berry Hill WS12 . . . . 210 C4
Berry Hill High Sch ST2 . 58 A1
Berry Hill Rd ST2 . . . . . . 57 F1
Berry Hill Village ST2 . . . 58 A1
Berry La ST3 . . . . 284 B3
Berry Rd ST16 . . . . 155 D8
Berry St ST4 . . . . 72 B7
Bertelin Rd ST16 . . . . . . 155 F7
Bert Smith Way TF9 . . . . 97 C2
Berwick Dr WS11 . . . . . . 226 B8
Berwick Rd ST1 . . . . 57 E8
Berwick Wlks ST5 . . . . . . 70 F7
Berwyn Gr WS6 . . . . 226 F3
Besom Way WS6 . . . . . . 226 C2
Best Ave DE15 . . . . 167 B1
Best St ST4 . . . . 72 F5
Beswick Cl ST10 . . . . 76 D1
Beswick Rd ST6 . . . . 41 F6
Beswicks La TF9 . . . . 82 C2
Bethany Ct DE15 . . . . . . 185 E7
Bethany Mews 4 WS11 . 209 F4
Bethell Rd ST1 . . . . 57 D7
Bethesda Cl ST1 . . . . . . 282 C1
Bethesda St ST1 . . . . . . 282 B1
Betjeman Pl WV10 . . . . . 241 A1
Betjeman Wlk ST17 . . . . 174 C7
Betley CE Prim Sch CW3 . 53 B6
Betley Hall Gdns CW3 . . . 53 A6
Betley Pl ST5 . . . . 71 C6
Betlingspring La DE6 . . . 81 D3
Beton Way ST16 . . . . . . 155 D8
Betony Rd DE15 . . . . 167 C2
Bettany Glade WV10 . . . 240 E4
Bettany Rd ST5 . . . . 57 A7
Betton Rd TF9 . . . . 97 E2
Betty Hatch La ST16 . . . 155 C5
Betty's La WS11 . . . . 228 A4
Beulah Dr TF9 . . . . 97 B1
Bevan Ave Talke Pits ST7 . . 40 E6
  Wolverhampton WV4 . . 266 C4
Bevan Cl WS4 . . . . 244 C1
Bevandean Cl ST4 . . . . . 88 C5
Bevan Lee Rd WS11 . . . . 209 D3
Bevan Pl WV3 . . . . 68 E7
Beveridge Cl ST3 . . . . . . 74 E2
Beverley Cl ST19 . . . . . . 207 F7
Beverley Cres
  Forsbrook ST11 . . . . 91 A8
  Wolverhampton WV4 . . 266 F4
Beverley Dr Bucknall ST2 . 58 D2
  Kingswinford DY6 . . . . . 275 C7
  Stafford ST15 . . . . 155 C8
Beverley Hill WS12 . . . . 210 D6
Beverley Rd DE14 . . . . . 185 A7
Beverston Rd WV4 . . . . . 255 A4
Beville St ST4 . . . . 72 C6
Bevin La ST2 . . . . 58 A3
Bewcastle Gr ST3 . . . . . . 90 A7
Bewick Ct WV6 . . . . 255 C2
Bew St ST5 . . . . 42 E5
Bexhill Gr ST1 . . . . 57 F6
Bexley St ST1 . . . . 282 A4
Bexmore Dr WS13 . . . . . 214 F1
Beyer Cl B77 . . . . 251 A2
Bhylls Acre Prim Sch
  WV3 . . . . 265 B7
Bhylls Cres WV3 . . . . . . 265 C7
Bhylls La WV3 . . . . 265 C7
Bibbey's Gn WV10 . . . . . 240 F4
Bickford Cl ST19 . . . . . . 206 A6
Bickford Rd ST19 . . . . . . 206 B7
Bickley Ave B74 . . . . 257 E5
Bickley Ho B74 . . . . 257 E5
Bida La CW12 . . . . 16 B8
Biddles La ST21 . . . . 102 D4
Biddulph Common Rd
  ST8 . . . . 17 A7
Biddulph Grange Ctry Pk*
  ST8 . . . . 16 F3
Biddulph Grange Gdn*
  ST8 . . . . 16 F3
Biddulph High Sch ST8 . . 27 D5
Biddulph Park Rd ST8 . . . 17 A5

Biddulph Rd
  Congleton CW12 . . . . . . 16 B8
  Mow Cop ST7 . . . . 26 F6
  Stoke-on-T ST8 . . . . 42 B7
Biddulph St CW12 . . . . . 16 C7
Bideford Ave ST17 . . . . . 175 D8
Bideford Way WS11 . . . . 226 B8
Biggin St TF10 . . . . 254 E5
Bignall End Rd ST7 . . . . . 40 A4
Bigsbury Wlk 2 ST6 . . . . 56 F7
Bigwood La ST18 . . . . . . 173 F4
Bilberry Bank WS11 . . . . 209 E6
Bilberry Cl WS5 . . . . 178 C1
Bilberry Cres WS12 . . . . 209 C5
Bilbrook CE Mid Sch
  WV8 . . . . 239 B3
Bilbrook Cl WV8 . . . . . . 239 B3
Bilbrook Gr WV8 . . . . . . 239 B3
Bilbrook Rd WV8 . . . . . . 239 B4
Bilbrook Sta WV8 . . . . . 239 A2
Billinge St ST6 . . . . 56 E8
Billington Ave ST18 . . . . 158 C1
Billington Bank ST18 . . . 173 D6
Billington La ST18 . . . . . 154 D2
Billy Buns La WV5 . . . . . 270 B8
Billy Wright Cl WV4 . . . . 265 D6
Bilston Rd WV2 . . . . 266 F8
Bilston St DY3 . . . . 271 E8
Bilton St ST4 . . . . 72 A6
Bingley Ent Ctr WV3 . . . 266 A8
Bingley St WV3 . . . . 266 A8
Birchall Ave ST6 . . . . 41 C5
Birchall Cl ST13 . . . . 30 F2
Birchall La ST13 . . . . 30 F2
Birchall Park Ave ST13 . . 30 F1
Bircham Wlk ST5 . . . . . . 71 B2
Birch Ave Biddulph ST8 . . 27 A6
  Brownhills WS8 . . . . . . 244 E8
  Burntwood WS7 . . . . . . 228 F6
  Cannock WS11 . . . . 226 C8
  Swadlincote DE11 . . . . . 186 C8
Birchbrook Ind Pk WS14 246 E6
Birch Brook La WS14 . . . 246 E6
Birch Bsns Pk WS11 . . . . 226 F6
Birch Cl Burton u T DE14 . 185 A8
  Denstone ST14 . . . . 95 D6
  Great Haywood ST18 . . . 158 C2
  Walton-on-t-H ST17 . . . 175 F6
Birch Coppice WV5 . . . . 269 E6
Birch Croft WS9 . . . . 256 C8
Birchcroft WV9 . . . . 224 C1
Birch Dale ST3 . . . . 68 E6
Birchdown Ave ST6 . . . . 42 B3
Birch Dr Little Aston B74 . 257 D5
  Stourbridge DY8 . . . . . . 279 E6
Birchdale Cl ST10 . . . . . . 92 F2
Birchenfields La ST10 . . . 75 F5
Birchenwood Way ST7 . . 26 C1
Birchenwood Rd ST6 . . . 26 E1
Birches Ave WV8 . . . . . . 239 C1
Birches Barn Ave WV3 . . 265 F7
Birches Barn Rd WV3 . . . 265 F7
Birches Cl DE13 . . . . 166 D8
Birches Farm Mews CW3 . 68 F5
Birches Fst Sch WV8 . . . 239 B1
Birches Head High Sch
  ST1 . . . . 57 F7
Birches Head Rd
  Bucknall ST2 . . . . 58 A7
  Hanley ST1 . . . . 57 E6
Birches Park Rd WV8 . . . 239 A2
Birches Rd WV8 . . . . 239 B2
Birches The ST10 . . . . . . 76 D2
Birches Valley Forest Ctr &
  Wlk* WS15 . . . . 195 F7
Birches Valley WS15 . . . 195 D6
Birches Way 7 ST7 . . . . 26 B2
Birchfield Ave WV6 . . . . 255 B6
Birchfield Cl CV9 . . . . . . 262 C1
Birchfield Rd Bucknall ST2 . 58 C6
  Burton u T DE15 . . . . . . 185 D7
Birchfield St WV7 . . . . . . 237 D5
Birchfields Cl WS15 . . . . 119 F6
Birchfields Dr WS12 . . . . 210 D1
Birchgate ST2 . . . . 58 C4
Birchgate Gr ST2 . . . . . . 58 C4
Birchglade WV3 . . . . 255 D1
Birch Gr B78 . . . . 262 D7
Birch Green Gr ST1 . . . . . 57 E7
Birch Gr Forsbrook ST11 . . 91 A7
  Lichfield WS14 . . . . 231 D8
  Meir Heath ST3 . . . . 90 A4
Birch Hill Ave WV5 . . . . . 269 E6
Birch Ho B74 . . . . 257 B5
Birch House La
  Cotes ST15 . . . . 103 A1
  Millmeece ST21 . . . . . . 117 F8
Birch House Rd
  Coldmeece ST15 . . . . . . 118 A8
  Newcastle-u-L ST5 . . . . . 55 D8
Birch House Way ST15 . . 118 A8
Birchill Pl WV5 . . . . 269 F5
Birch La WS9 . . . . 245 D1
Birchlands Rd ST1 . . . . . 57 F6
Birch La Rugeley WS15 . . . 197 A5
  Walsall WS4 . . . . 244 C1
Birchmoor La ST20 . . . . 189 D1
Birchmoor Rd B78 . . . . . 262 F8
Birchover Way ST6 . . . . . 42 A8
Birch Rd Audley ST7 . . . . 39 F1
  Sedgley DY3 . . . . 266 F1
  Stone ST15 . . . . 120 B8
  Wolverhampton WV11 . . 241 F1
Birch Rise TF9 . . . . 99 E3
Birch St ST1 . . . . 57 E5
Birch Terr
  Burntwood WS7 . . . . . . 212 A1
  Hanley ST1 . . . . 282 B2

Birchtree Dr ST13. . . . . . . 45 C8
Birch Tree Gdns WS9 . . . 256 B5
Birchtree La WS15 . . . 196 E6
Birch Tree La
  The Bank ST7. . . . . 26 B8
  Whitmore ST5. . . . . 85 C7
Birch Valley Rd ST7 . . . . 26 C1
Birch Wlk ST5 . . . . 73 A1
Birchwood Ave B78 . . . . 262 F7
Birchwood Cl WV11 . . . 242 A3
Birchwood Prim Sch
  B78. . . . . 262 F7
Birchwood Rd
  Lichfield WS14 . . . . 231 F7
  Wolverhampton WV4. . . 266 A5
Birchwood Rise WS15 . . 161 B5
Birchwood Wlk DY6 . . . 275 E8
Bird Cage Wlk ST1. . . . . 282 B2
Birdhope B77. . . . . 251 C1
Bird Rd ST3 . . . . 74 B2
Bird's Barn La DY11. . . . 277 C2
Birds Bush Prim Sch
  B77. . . . . 261 E8
Birds Bush Rd B77 . . . . . 261 F8
Birdsgrove La DE6. . . . . . 66 D3
Bird St Dudley DY3. . . . . 271 C3
  Lichfield WS13. . . . . 231 B7
Birkdale Ave DE14 . . . . . 185 A6
Birkdale Cl DY8 . . . . 279 F2
Birkdale Dr Kidsgrove ST7 . . 26 C3
  Stafford ST16 . . . . 156 C3
Birkdale Rd WS3. . . . . . . 243 A3
Birkholme Dr ST3. . . . . . . 90 A5
Birks Dr TF9 . . . . 99 E5
Birks St ST4 . . . . 72 B5
Birmingham New Rd
  WV4. . . . . 266 E4
Birmingham Rd
  Aldridge WS9. . . . . 256 A4
  Blakedown DY10. . . . . . . 281 C2
  Lichfield WS14 . . . . 231 A4
  Shenstone WS14 . . . . 247 A4
  Wolverhampton WV2. . . 266 D7
Birrell St ST4. . . . . 72 F5
Biscay Gr ST4. . . . . 88 C8
Bishop Cl WS11. . . . . 209 D2
Bishop Cl ST2 . . . . 58 E5
Bishop Rawle CE Prim Sch
  ST10. . . . . 76 D3
Bishop Rd ST6 . . . . 42 B5
Bishop's Cl ST7 . . . . 40 D8
Bishops Ct ST21. . . . . . . 133 E7
Bishops Dr ST19 . . . . 223 D7
Bishops Grange WS15 . . 178 F2
Bishops La TF9 . . . . 97 B1
Bishops Mdw B75. . . . . . 258 E3
Bishop Stamer CE Prim Sch
  ST4. . . . . 72 B6
Bishop St ST3 . . . . 73 A5
Bishops Way B74 . . . . . . 257 F6
Bishton La ST17,ST18. . . 178 A6
Bitham Cl ST19 . . . . 207 F3
Bitham Ct DE13 . . . . 147 C1
Bitham La DE13. . . . . . . 147 D1
Bittell Cl WV10 . . . . 240 E7
Bitterne Pl ST2 . . . . 73 D8
Bittern La ST10 . . . . 76 E3
Bitterscote La B78. . . . . . 250 A2
Black Bank Rd ST13. . . . . 44 D5
Blackbank Rd ST5. . . . . . . 55 C4
Blackberry La
  Brownhills WS9. . . . . 245 B4
  Stafford ST16 . . . . 155 C4
  Sutton Coldfield B74. . . . 257 E4
Blackberry Way ST20. . . 151 D8
Blackbird Cl ST14. . . . . . 126 C6
Blackbird Way
  1 Packmoor ST7 . . . . . . 26 F1
  Biddulph ST8. . . . . 27 E8
  Stoke-on-T ST7 . . . . 41 F8
Blackbrook Ave ST5. . . . . 55 D8
Blackbrook Way WV10 . . 240 E4
Blackbrook Zoological Pk★
  ST13. . . . . 48 A4
Blackburn Ave WV6 . . . . 255 F7
Blackdown B77. . . . . 251 C1
Black Dr ST18 . . . . 157 C6
Blackflats Rd ST15. . . . . 103 C1
Blackfriars Cl ST3 . . . . . . 249 E5
Blackfriars F Ed Unit ST2. 58 F5
Blackfriar's Rd ST5 . . . . . 283 B2
Blackfriars Sch ST5. . . . . 283 B2
Blackhalve La WV11. . . . 241 D2
Blackheath Cl ST3 . . . . . . 73 D3
Blackheath La ST18 . . . . 156 E4
Blackhole La ST18 . . . . . 154 D2
Black Horse La ST1. . . . . 282 B3
Blackie's La Stone ST15. . 120 D6
  Stone ST15 . . . . 120 D7
Blacklake Dr ST3 . . . . 90 A4
Black La Sutton TF10. . . . 150 E1
  Whiston ST10. . . . . 62 D3
Blackmere Cl TF10. . . . . 168 D2
Blackpit La
  Doveridge DE6. . . . . 127 B8
  Orton WV4. . . . . 264 E3
Blackpool St DE14 . . . . . 185 C8
Blackroot Cl WS7 . . . . . . 229 D4
Blackshaw Cl CW12. . . . . .6 B1
Blackshaw Grange Cvn Pk
  ST13. . . . . 20 D3
Blackshaw Moor CE Prim
  Sch ST13. . . . . 20 E5
Blacksmith Dr **7** B75 . . . 258 E3
Blacksmith La WS14. . . . 232 E5
Blacksmiths Cl DE12 . . . 219 F7
Blacksmith's La
  Egginton DE65. . . . . 148 A6

Blacksmith's La continued
Newton Solney DE15 . . . 167 E8
Blackthorn Ave WS7 . . . 228 F4
Blackthorn Cres WS12 . . 211 A6
Blackthorn Cl DY1 . . . . . 271 F4
Blackthorne Rd
  Dudley DY1. . . . . 271 F5
  Lichfield WS14 . . . . 231 D7
Blackthorn Pl ST5 . . . . . . 55 E8
Blackthorn Rd
  Burton u T DE15. . . . . . . 185 E6
  Stourbridge DY8 . . . . . . 275 F1
Blackwell's Row ST6. . . . . 57 B6
Blackwood Pl ST3 . . . . . . 73 E4
Blackwood Rd
  Aldridge B74. . . . . 256 E1
  Tamworth B77. . . . . 261 C7
Blackwood Sch B74. . . . . 256 E1
Bladon Ave ST5. . . . . 71 B3
Bladon Cl ST6. . . . . 42 A8
Bladon House Sch DE15. 167 B6
Bladon St DE13 . . . . 167 C4
Bladon's Yd DE13 . . . . . 147 B4
Bladon View
  Burton u T DE13. . . . . . . 148 A2
  Stretton DE13 . . . . 147 F2
Blaizefield Cl CW3 . . . . . . 67 C2
Blakedown CE Fst Sch
  DY10. . . . . 281 C1
Blakedown Sta DY10 . . . 281 C2
Blakeley Ave WV6. . . . . . 255 F7
Blakeley Heath Dr WV5 . 270 A5
Blakeley Heath Prim Sch
  WV5. . . . . 270 A5
Blakeley La ST10. . . . . . . 63 A2
Blakeley Rise WV6. . . . . . 255 F7
Blakelow La DE6. . . . . . . 65 B1
Blakelow Rd ST2. . . . . 58 B6
Blakemore Rd WS9 . . . . 245 A3
Blakenall Heath WS3. . . 243 D1
Blakeney Ave
  Newcastle-u-L ST5. . . . . . 71 B3
  Stourbridge DY8 . . . . . . 279 D6
Blakeney Cl DY3 . . . . 271 C8
Blakenhall Gdns WV2 . . 266 D7
Blakenhall Ind Est WV2. 266 D7
Blake St ST6 . . . . 56 F8
Blake Street Sta B74 . . . 257 F6
Blake St B74. . . . . 257 E6
Blake Valley Tech Coll
  WS7. . . . . 209 F6
Blakeways Cl B79. . . . . . 217 C5
Blakiston St ST1. . . . . . . 285 C4
Blanchard Cl ST3 . . . . . . 90 C7
Blandford Dr DY8 . . . . . . 275 E3
Blandford Gdns WS7 . . . 229 C6
Blanefield WV8 . . . . 239 E2
Blanford Mere Prim Sch
  DY6 . . . . 275 E8
Blantyre St ST3. . . . . 284 C2
Blantyre Wlk ST3 . . . . . . 284 C2
Blatchford Cl ST3. . . . . . . 74 B2
Blaydon Ave B75. . . . . . . 258 E2
Blaydon Rd WV9,WV10. . 240 A1
Blaze Hill Rd DY6 . . . . . . 275 A8
Blaze Pk DY6 . . . . 275 B8
Bleak House Dr WS7 . . . 228 D8
Bleak Pl **9** ST6. . . . . 57 A7
Bleakridge Ave ST5 . . . . . 56 D3
Bleak St ST5. . . . . 56 D3
Bleeding Wolf La ST7 . . . 25 E5
Blencarn Gr ST9 . . . . 43 C4
Blenheim Cl
  Burton u T DE15. . . . . . . 167 C3
  Stafford ST18 . . . . 156 D3
  Tamworth B77. . . . . 250 C4
Blenheim Ho DE14 . . . . . 184 F7
Blenheim Rd
  Burntwood WS7. . . . . . . 229 A8
  Kingswinford DY6 . . . . . . 275 F6
  Norton Canes WS11 . . . 228 B4
Blenheim St ST4. . . . . 72 D5
Blenheim Way
  Dudley DY1 . . . . 271 E2
  Fradley WS13 . . . . 215 C5
Bleriot Cl ST3. . . . . 90 C7
Blessed Mother Teresa's RC
  Prim Sch ST14. . . . . 174 C8
Blessed William Howard RC
  Sch ST17 . . . . 285 A1
Bletchley Dr B77. . . . . . . 261 C8
Blewitt St WS12. . . . . 210 B7
Blithbury Rd Colton WS15 179 B3
  Hamstall Ridware WS15 . 180 E3
Blithe View ST11. . . . . 90 F6
Blithfield Cl ST9 . . . . 59 A2
Blithfield Ho ST17 . . . . . 174 F6
Blithfield Pl WS11 . . . . . 210 B1
Blithfield Rd WS8. . . . . . 228 C2
Bloomfield Cl WV5. . . . . 269 D6
Bloomfield Cres WS13 . . 214 B2
Bloomfield Dr WV12 . . . 242 D1
Bloomfield Way B79 . . . 249 E8
Bloomsbury St **2** WV2 . . 266 D7
Bloomsbury Way WS14 . 231 E7
Blore Rd TF9 . . . . 98 E1
Blossomfield Cl DY6 . . . . 275 E8
Blount Cl ST19 . . . . 207 F7
Blount's Dr ST14 . . . . . . 126 A6
Bloxwich CE Prim Sch
  WS3 . . . . 243 B1
Bloxwich North Sta WS3 242 F7
Bloxwich Sta WS3. . . . . . 243 A1
Bluebell Cl Biddulph ST8. . 27 E7
  Cannock WS12. . . . . 210 B6
  Stourbridge DY8 . . . . . . 275 C2
  Tittensor ST12. . . . . 103 E8

Bluebell Dr ST5. . . . . 71 A4
Bluebell Hollow ST17 . . 175 F7
Bluebell La WS6. . . . . . . 227 A1
Bluebell Rd WS9 . . . . . . 245 B3
Bluebird Cl WS14 . . . . . . 231 D8
Blue Cedars Dr DE15. . . 167 D2
Blue Cedars DY8. . . . . . . 279 C6
Blue House Barns TF10. . 168 C4
Blue House La WV7. . . . . 237 B7
Bluestone Ave ST6. . . . . . 42 B2
Bluestone La DE15. . . . . 186 A7
Bluestones ST13 . . . . 20 C4
Blundies La DY7. . . . . . . 273 D3
Blunt's Hollow WS15,
  DE13. . . . . 162 A4
Blunt St ST5 . . . . 56 D4
Blurton Cotts ST3. . . . . . . 72 E1
Blurton High Sch ST3 . . . 88 F8
Blurton Prim Sch ST3 . . . 72 E2
Blurton Priory ST3 . . . . . . 88 F8
Blurton Rd Barlaston ST12. 89 A4
  Newcastle-u-L ST5. . . . . . 72 E2
  Stoke-on-T ST3 . . . . 72 E2
Blymhill Lawn La TF11. . 204 C3
Blymhill Marsh TF11 . . . 203 F6
Blythe Ave ST3 . . . . 90 A5
Blythebridge Bank ST14,
  ST18. . . . . 141 A7
Blythe Bridge High Sch
  ST11. . . . . 90 F7
Blythe Bridge Rd
  Blythe Bridge ST11 . . . . . 90 D7
  Caverswall ST11 . . . . 74 E1
Blythe Bridge Sta ST11. . 90 F7
Blythe Cl
  Blythe Bridge ST11 . . . . . 90 D7
  Burntwood WS7. . . . . . . 229 D6
Blythe Gdns WV8. . . . . . 238 F4
Blythe Lodge ST11. . . . . . 90 D7
Blythe Mount Pk ST11 . . 91 A7
Blythe Pk ST11. . . . . 91 D3
Blythe Rd
  Blythe Bridge ST11 . . . . . 91 A7
  Stafford ST17 . . . . 174 E6
Blythe St B77 . . . . 250 C4
Blythe View
  Hamstall Ridware WS15 . 180 F2
  Saverley Green ST11. . . . . 91 A2
Blythfield DE14. . . . . 166 E3
Boardman Cres ST16. . . 155 C3
Boardman Ind Est DE11 . 186 E3
Boardman Rd DE11. . . . . 186 E2
Boardmans Bank ST6 . . . 41 D1
Board School Gdns DY3. 271 E6
Boathorse Rd
  Kidsgrove ST7. . . . . 41 A8
  Stoke-on-T ST6 . . . . 41 B5
Boat La
  Muckley Corner WS14. . . 229 F1
  Weston ST18. . . . . 138 C3
Boatman's La WS9. . . . . 244 E2
Boatyard Cotts ST12. . . . 104 D8
Bode Bsns Pk ST13. . . . . 31 A7
Bodiam Ct WV6. . . . . 255 A3
Bodicote Gr B75. . . . . . . 258 E3
Bodington Cl WV7 . . . . . 229 E7
Bodington Rd B75. . . . . . 258 E3
Bodmin Ave ST17 . . . . . 175 D8
Bodmin Wlk ST6. . . . . . . 42 D1
Bognop Rd WV11. . . . . . 241 D4
Bogs Cotts ST5. . . . . 70 B8
Bogs La ST11. . . . . 90 F6
Bolberry Cl ST3. . . . . 73 E1
Bold St ST1. . . . . 57 E5
Bolebridge Mews B79. . . 250 B5
Bolebridge St B79 . . . . . 250 B5
Bolehall Rd B77. . . . . 250 C4
Boley Cl WS14 . . . . 231 D7
Boley Cottage La WS14. 231 E7
Boley La WS14 . . . . 231 D7
Boleyn Cl WS6. . . . . 226 D2
Boley Park Ctr WS14. . . . 231 E7
Bolina Gr ST3. . . . . 73 B6
Bollin Gr ST1. . . . . 16 E1
Bolney Gr ST1 . . . . 57 F5
Bolsover Cl ST6. . . . . 42 A8
Bolton Pl ST3 . . . . 89 F8
Bolton Way WS3 . . . . . . 242 F3
Boma Rd ST4. . . . . 87 F8
Bond End DE13 . . . . 182 A2
Bondfield La DE13 . . . . . 181 F2
Bondfield Way ST3. . . . . . 74 B2
Bond St Burton u T DE14 . 166 D1
  Stoke-on-T ST6 . . . . 41 D4
Bondway WS12. . . . . 209 F7
Bonehill Ind Est B78 . . . 249 F1
Bonehill Rd B78. . . . . . . 249 E3
Boney Hay Prim Sch
  WS7. . . . . 211 F1
Boney Hay Rd WS7. . . . . 229 B7
Boningale Way ST17 . . . 174 B8
Bonington Cres ST16. . . 155 C2
Bonnard Cl ST3. . . . . 90 C6
Bonner Cl ST4. . . . . 71 E4
Bonville Gdns WV10. . . . 240 E4
Boon Ave ST4. . . . . 72 A7
Boon Gr ST17 . . . . 174 E6
Boon Hill Rd ST7. . . . . . . 39 F1
Boons Ind Est ST18 . . . . 154 E1
Booth Cl WS13. . . . . 214 A2
Boothen CE Prim Sch
  ST4. . . . . 72 A5
Boothen Gn ST4. . . . . 72 B5
Boothen Old Rd ST4. . . . . 72 B5
Boothen Rd ST4. . . . . 72 B5
Boothenwood Terr ST4. . 72 A5
Booth La ST18 . . . . 140 E3
Boothroyd St ST1. . . . . . 282 B2

Booth St Audley ST7 . . . . 39 D1
  Cannock WS12. . . . . 210 B6
  Newcastle-u-L ST5. . . . . . 283 C4
Boothstone Gdns ST15 . 118 F6
Booth St ST6 . . . . 72 B6
Booton Ct DY10 . . . . 280 A1
Bordeaux Cl DY1. . . . . . . 271 E3
Bordeaux Rd ST3. . . . . . . 90 A5
Bordeaux Wlk ST5 . . . . . 70 F3
Borden Cl
  Wheaton Aston ST19 . . . 205 C7
  Wolverhampton WV8. . . 255 F8
Border Way ST17 . . . . . . 174 F6
Borman B79. . . . . 249 F5
Borough Cres DY8 . . . . . 279 C6
Borough Mus & Art Gal The★
  ST5. . . . . 283 C4
Borough Rd
  Burton u T DE14. . . . . . . 166 C3
  Newcastle-u-L ST5. . . . . . 283 C3
  Tamworth B79. . . . . 250 C7
Borrowcop Ho WS14. . . 231 C6
Borrowcop La WS14 . . . 231 C5
Borrowdale Rd ST6 . . . . . 42 E3
  Penkridge ST19 . . . . 208 A7
Boscobel Cl DY1 . . . . 271 F3
Boscobel Gr ST19 . . . . . 223 C7
Boscobel Ho★ ST19 . . . 221 E5
Boscombe Gr ST4. . . . . . 88 C5
Boscomoor Cl ST19 . . . . 207 E2
Boscomoor Ct ST19 . . . . 207 E2
Boscomoor La ST19 . . . . 207 E2
Boscomoor Sh Ctr ST19. 207 E2
Bosinney Cl ST3. . . . . 73 B5
Bosley Brook CW12. . . . . 16 D5
Bosley Gr ST4. . . . . 41 C6
Bosley View CW12. . . . . . .6 B1
Boss Gate Cl WV5. . . . . . 270 A5
Bostock Cl ST15 . . . . 120 C5
Boston Cl Cannock WS12. 210 E1
  Stoke-on-T ST6 . . . . 41 C4
Boston Ind Est WS15 . . . 178 F2
Bosty La WS9. . . . . 256 A4
Boswell Rd WS11 . . . . . . 209 D4
Boswell St ST6 . . . . 56 F1
Bosworth Cl DY3. . . . . . . 271 C7
Bosworth Dr DE13 . . . . . 166 B7
Botany Bay Rd ST1. . . . . 57 E5
Botany Dr DY3 . . . . 271 D6
Botesworth Gdns ST6 . . . 41 D1
Botfield Cl WV7. . . . . 237 B6
Botham Dr ST3 . . . . 45 D5
Botterham La DY3,WV5. . 269 C4
Botteslow St ST1. . . . . . . 282 C2
Bottom La Ipstones ST10. . 47 C5
  Market Drayton TF9. . . . . 112 A7
  Swynnerton ST15. . . . . . 103 B7
Boucher Rd ST13. . . . . . . 45 C4
Boughey Rd Audley ST7 . . 39 F2
  Newport TF10. . . . . 168 E2
  Stoke-on-T ST4 . . . . 72 C8
Boughey St ST4. . . . . 72 A6
Boulevard The ST6. . . . . . 41 E3
Boulters La CV9. . . . . . . 262 D1
Boulton Cl WS7. . . . . 229 C8
Boulton St Hanley ST1 . . 282 C4
  Newcastle-u-L ST5. . . . . . 56 F5
Boundary Cl Leek ST13. . . 30 F3
  Stone ST15 . . . . 119 F5
Boundary Cres DY3. . . . . 271 C3
Boundary Ct ST1. . . . . . . 282 B4
Boundary Farm WV6. . . . 254 F2
Boundary Hill DY3 . . . . . 271 C4
Boundary Ind Est WV10 . 240 C5
Boundary La
  Congleton CW12. . . . . . . 16 B8
  Kinver DY7. . . . . 274 E1
Boundary Rd
  Brownhills WS9. . . . . 244 F3
  Egginton DE65. . . . . 148 D8
Boundary St Hanley ST1. . 282 B4
  Newcastle-u-L ST5. . . . . . 56 D1
Boundary View ST10. . . . 76 B2
Boundary Way
  Wolverhampton,Penn
  WV4. . . . . 265 C5
  Wolverhampton WV6. . . 254 F2
Bourne Ave Fazeley B78. . 249 E1
  Ranton ST18 . . . . 153 C5
Bourne Cl Cannock WS12. 210 E2
  Tutbury DE13 . . . . 146 B6
Bourne Pl ST13 . . . . 30 C6
Bourne Rd ST7 . . . . 25 F2
Bournes Bank ST6 . . . . . . 56 F8
Bournes Bank S **10** ST6. . 57 A8
Bourne St Mow Cop ST7. . 26 D7
  Stoke-on-T ST4 . . . . 72 E4
Bourne Vale WS9 . . . . . . 256 D3
Bouverie Par ST7. . . . . . . 57 F7
Bowden St ST6 . . . . 42 B1
Bowdler Rd WV2. . . . . . . 266 E8
Bowen-cooke Ave WV6. 254 E6
Bowen St WV4. . . . . 266 E5
Bower Cl WS13 . . . . 214 D2
Bower End La CW3. . . . . . 68 C6
Bower La WS15. . . . . 178 C3
Bowers Bent ST21. . . . . . 102 C4
Bowers Ct ST15. . . . . 120 D7
Bowers La Bowers ST21. . 102 B4
  Stone ST15 . . . . 120 D7
Bower St ST1. . . . . 282 B1
Bowes Dr WS11. . . . . 209 F4
Bowfell Gr ST3 . . . . 73 B6
Bowhill La Betley CW3. . . 53 B6
  Knowl Bank ST7. . . . . 53 E6
Bowland Ave ST5. . . . . . . 55 E2

Bowlers Cl ST6 . . . . 57 A6
Bowlingalley La DE6 . . . . 96 D8
Bowling Alley or Vicarage La
  ST17. . . . . 193 F8
Bowling Green Ave B77 . 261 F7
Bowling Green Rd DY8 . 279 E5
Bowman Gr ST6 . . . . 42 B7
Bowman Ho ST3 . . . . 89 F8
Bowmead Cl ST4. . . . . . . 88 C6
Bowmere Cl ST8 . . . . 16 C1
Bowness Gr WV11 . . . . . 242 B1
Bowness Rd ST4. . . . . . . 282 A4
Bowood Dr WV6 . . . . . . 255 D6
Bowsey Wood Rd CW3. . 68 E8
Bowstead St ST4. . . . . . . 72 B7
Bow St WS15 . . . . 178 E1
Bowyer Ave ST6 . . . . 42 E5
Boxer Cl WS15. . . . . 198 C3
Box La ST3 . . . . 73 F2
Boxwood Pl ST5 . . . . 55 D8
Boxwood Rd ST10. . . . . . 92 C4
Boyden Cl Cannock WS11. 209 B1
  Penkridge ST19 . . . . 208 A7
Boyles Hall Rd ST7. . . . . 39 E2
Brabazon Cl ST3 . . . . 90 C7
Bracebridge Ho B74 . . . 257 F6
Bracken Ave TF9 . . . . 99 E5
Brackenberry ST5. . . . . . 56 B3
Bracken Cl
  Burntwood WS7. . . . . . . 229 C7
  Cannock WS12. . . . . 210 D8
  Lichfield WS14 . . . . 231 E6
  Stafford ST16 . . . . 155 B7
  Stoke-on-T ST3 . . . . 89 F5
  Tittensor ST12. . . . . 88 A1
  Wolverhampton WV8. . . 239 E1
Bracken Dale ST13 . . . . . 30 B4
Brackenfield Ave ST2 . . . 58 C1
Brackenfield Way ST16. . 155 B6
Brackenhill Rd WS7. . . . 229 A8
Bracken Park Gdns DY8 . 275 F2
Bracken Rd WS12. . . . . . 209 C5
Brackens The ST5. . . . . . 71 C2
Bracken St ST4 . . . . 72 E4
Bracken View ST17 . . . . 176 C3
Bracken Way
  Newport TF10. . . . . 168 F4
  Rugeley WS15 . . . . 178 C2
Brackenwood Mews CW2 37 D2
Brackenwood Rd DE15 . 185 E6
Bracklesham Way B77 . . 251 A6
Brackley Ave ST6 . . . . . . 42 B1
Bradbury Cl
  Brownhills WS8 . . . . 244 F5
  Stoke-on-T ST6 . . . . 42 E3
Bradbury Ct WS12 . . . . . 210 B7
Bradbury Gdns CW12. . . 15 F8
Bradbury La
  Cannock WS12. . . . . 210 B8
  Enville DY7. . . . . 272 E3
  King's Bromley DE13 . . . 199 C6
Bradbury Rise ST16 . . . . 155 A4
Bradeley Village ST6. . . . 42 C3
Braden Rd WV4. . . . . 265 D4
Bradford Rd WS8. . . . . . 244 E8
Bradford St
  Cannock WS11. . . . . 210 A5
  Tamworth B79. . . . . 249 F5
Bradford Terr ST1. . . . . . 57 E6
Bradgate Dr B74. . . . . . . 257 E5
Bradley Ave ST18 . . . . . . 173 B3
Bradley La ST18 . . . . 174 C5
Bradley Lakes WS15 . . . 197 F2
Bradley La ST18 . . . . 174 C5
Bradley Rd
  Stourbridge DY8 . . . . . . 279 F6
  Wolverhampton WV2. . . 266 E7
Bradley St
  Burton u T DE15. . . . . . . 185 E7
  Uttoxeter ST14 . . . . 126 C8
Bradmore Rd
  Burton u T DE13. . . . . . . 166 B5
  Wolverhampton WV3. . . 265 F8
Bradshaw Way ST11 . . . 155 D8
Bradwell Croft B75 . . . . 258 E3
Bradwell Grange ST5 . . . 56 B7
Bradwell Hospl ST5 . . . . 56 A7
Bradwell La
  Cannock Wood WS15. . . 211 F5
  Newcastle-u-L ST5. . . . . . 56 B7
Bradwell Prim Sch ST5. . 56 B8
Bradwell St ST6 . . . . 56 D8
Braeburn Cl WS13 . . . . . 214 D1
Braemar Ave DY8 . . . . . . 275 C1
Braemar Cl Bucknall ST2 . 58 D3
  Sedgley DY3. . . . . 266 C3
Braemar Gdns WS12 . . . 209 F7
Braemar Rd
  Norton Canes WS11 . . . 228 B4
  Pattingham WV6 . . . . . . 253 C2
Braemore Rd ST2. . . . . . 58 B6
Braeside Way WS3 . . . . . 243 F3
Braham B79 . . . . 249 D6
Brailsford Ave DE11. . . . 186 E5
Brain St B77. . . . . 251 A2
Braithwaite Dr DY6 . . . . 275 D6
Braithwell Dr ST2. . . . . . 43 A2
Brake La DY8 . . . . 281 E6
Brakespeare St ST6. . . . . 41 C7
Brake The Hagley DY8. . . 281 F6
  The Bank ST7. . . . . 26 B7
Brake Village ST7. . . . . . 26 B7
Bramall Cl ST16. . . . . . . 155 C6
Bramall La ST16. . . . . . . 155 C6
Bramber Dr WV5. . . . . . . 269 F6

Bramber B77 . . . 250 D1
Bramber Way DY8 . . . 279 F2
Bramble Cl WS8 . . . 244 E5
Bramble Ct DE15 . . . 185 E6
Bramble Dr ST4 . . . 210 C7
Bramble Gn DY1 . . . 271 F5
Bramble La WS7 . . . 229 B8
Bramble Lea CW3 . . . 68 E6
Brambles Ct ST8 . . . 27 D7
Brambleside
  10 Stafford ST17 . . . 175 C7
  Stourbridge DY8 . . . 275 F1
Brambles The
  Lichfield WS14 . . . 231 D6
  Newcastle-u-L ST5 . . . 71 C2
  Norton Canes WS11 . . . 228 A5
Bramble Way WS15 . . . 178 C1
Bramblewood Dr WV3 . . . 265 E8
Bramblewood
  Swadlincote DE11 . . . 186 F6
  Wombourne WV5 . . . 270 A7
Brambling Cl ST14 . . . 126 C6
Bramblings The ST17 . . . 175 D5
Brambling B77 . . . 262 A5
Bramdean Dr ST19 . . . 192 F1
Bramdean Wlk WV4 . . . 265 C6
Bramell Cl DE14 . . . 184 F7
Bramfield Dr ST5 . . . 283 C4
Bramhall Cl ST18 . . . 154 E7
Bramley Cl ST10 . . . 76 E2
Bramley Dale DE11 . . . 186 F2
Bramley Pl ST4 . . . 71 E2
Bramley Way WS14 . . . 232 D5
Bramling Cross Rd DE14 . 166 F6
Brammall Dr ST11 . . . 90 E7
Brammer St ST6 . . . 42 C3
Brampton Cl
  Cookley DY10 . . . 280 B4
  Gorstyhill CW2 . . . 37 E3
  Stoke-on-T ST9 . . . 43 F8
Brampton Ct ST5 . . . 283 C4
Brampton Dr WS12 . . . 210 E2
Brampton Gdns ST5 . . . 56 C3
Brampton Ind Est ST5 . . . 283 B4
Brampton Rd ST5 . . . 283 C4
Brampton Sidings Ind Est
  ST5 . . . 283 B4
Brampton Sidings ST5 . . . 283 B4
Brampton Wlk ST3 . . . 284 C1
Bramshall Ind Est ST14 . 125 A7
Bramshall Rd ST14 . . . 125 E8
Bramshaws Acre ST10 . . . 76 E2
Bramstead Ave WS6 . . . 255 B2
Bramwell Dr WS6 . . . 226 D1
Brancaster Cl B77 . . . 251 A5
Branchal Rd WS9 . . . 245 C1
Brandon Cl Aldridge WS9 . 256 F3
  Sedgley DY3 . . . 271 E7
Brandon Gr ST4 . . . 87 F8
Brandon Pk WV3 . . . 265 E7
Brandons The ST17 . . . 174 F5
Bransdale Rd WS8 . . . 244 E6
Branson Ave ST3 . . . 73 E3
Branston Rd
  Burton u T DE14 . . . 185 C8
  Tatenhill DE13,DE14 . . . 184 C8
Branston Water Pk★
  DE14 . . . 184 D6
Bransty Gr ST4 . . . 88 C5
Brant Ave ST5 . . . 56 A4
Brantley Ave WV3 . . . 255 C1
Brantley Cres DY7 . . . 267 F2
Brantley La
  Bobbington DY7 . . . 267 F2
  Seisdon WV5,WV6 . . . 263 A3
Branton Hill La WS9 . . . 256 C5
Brantwood Ave WS7 . . . 229 A5
Brassington St CW3 . . . 53 A6
Brassington Terr ST4 . . . 52 F3
Brassington Way ST2 . . . 58 C1
Bratch Common Rd
  WV5 . . . 269 E7
Bratch Hollow WV5 . . . 270 A8
Bratch La WV5 . . . 269 F8
Bratch Pk WV5 . . . 269 F8
Brattice Cl ST2 . . . 73 D7
Brattswood Dr ST7 . . . 25 A3
Braunton Ave ST17 . . . 175 E7
Braystones Cl ST6 . . . 41 E8
Brazenhill La ST18 . . . 172 F7
Breach La Foston DE6 . . . 129 C5
  Upper Tean ST10 . . . 92 C5
Breach Rd ST6 . . . 43 C7
Breadmarket St WS13 . . . 231 B8
Breamore Cres DY1 . . . 271 F3
Bream B77 . . . 261 D7
Bream Way ST6 . . . 42 B3
Brean Rd ST17 . . . 175 E6
Brecon Way ST2 . . . 58 C2
Bredon Cl WV7 . . . 237 A5
Bredon Ct B75 . . . 258 A4
Breech Cl ST10 . . . 48 F2
Breedon Cl ST5 . . . 55 F3
Breedon Way WS4 . . . 244 C1
Breeze Ave
  Norton Canes WS11 . . . 228 B5
  Stoke-on-T ST6 . . . 41 E5
Brelades Cl DY1 . . . 271 C3
Brempton Croft ST15 . . . 106 D2
Brendale ST4 . . . 72 A1
Brendon Cl ST17 . . . 175 D8
Brendon B77 . . . 251 B1
Brent Cl **9** ST17 . . . 175 A8
Brentmill Cl WV10 . . . 240 F4
Brentnall Dr B75 . . . 258 B3

Brentnor Cl ST3 . . . 73 F3
Brenton Rd WV4 . . . 265 F3
Brent B77 . . . 261 E7
Brentwood Ct ST9 . . . 59 B4
Brentwood Dr ST9 . . . 59 B4
Brentwood Gr
  Stoke-on-T ST9 . . . 43 C3
  Werrington ST9 . . . 59 B4
Brenwood Cl DY6 . . . 275 B7
Breretonhill La WS15 . . . 197 C2
Brereton Lodge WS15 . . . 197 A6
Brereton Manor Ct
  WS15 . . . 197 B5
Brereton Pl WS15 . . . 41 E1
Brereton Rd WS15 . . . 196 F3
Bretby Bsns Pk DE15 . . . 186 F8
Bretby Fairways DE15 . . . 167 F2
Bretby Hollow DE11 . . . 186 F7
Bretby Hts DE11 . . . 186 F7
Bretby La DE15 . . . 167 E3
Bretby Rd DE11 . . . 186 F7
Bretby Stoneware Ind Est
  DE11 . . . 186 E8
Bretherton Pl ST6 . . . 42 A6
Bretlands Way DE15 . . . 186 A6
Brettell La DY8 . . . 279 E8
Brevitt Rd WV2 . . . 266 D6
Brewers Dr WS3 . . . 244 A1
Brewers Terr WS3 . . . 244 A2
Brewery La ST18 . . . 158 B2
Brewery St Hanley ST1 . . . 282 B3
  Rugeley WS15 . . . 196 F8
Brewester Rd ST2 . . . 57 F3
Brewhouse Ct WS13 . . . 213 F1
Brewhouse The DE14 . . . 166 D2
Brewood CE Mid Sch
  ST19 . . . 223 C6
Brewood Park Cotts
  WV9 . . . 224 A3
Brewood Rd
  Coven,Cross Green WV9 . 224 C1
  Coven WV9 . . . 224 C1
Brewster Cl B78 . . . 249 E1
Brianson Ave ST6 . . . 57 C7
Briar Ave B74 . . . 257 A1
Briarbank Cl ST4 . . . 71 F1
Briar Cl Cannock WS12 . . . 210 A8
  Rugeley WS15 . . . 178 C1
  Swadlincote DE11 . . . 186 F5
  Walton-on-t-H ST17 . . . 175 F6
Briar Gr ST15 . . . 118 E5
Briarsleigh ST17 . . . 175 C7
Briars The Aldridge WS9 . 256 A7
  Hagley DY9 . . . 281 D4
  Newcastle-u-L ST5 . . . 283 B4
Briars Way ST21 . . . 102 E2
Briarswood Biddulph ST8 . 16 C1
  Kidsgrove ST7 . . . 26 B1
Briar B77 . . . 251 A3
Briar Way ST21 . . . 102 E2
Briarwood Pl ST3 . . . 74 B2
Brickbridge La WV5 . . . 269 E5
Brickfield Cl ST18 . . . 139 D1
Brickfield Pl ST3 . . . 73 C6
Brickhill La DE13 . . . 163 A6
Brickhouse La B79 . . . 216 D2
Brick House St **6** ST6 . . . 56 F8
Bricknell St WS8 . . . 244 F7
Brick Kiln La
  Brocton ST17 . . . 175 F3
  Codsall Wood ST19 . . . 222 C2
  Dudley DY3 . . . 271 B3
  Hopton ST18 . . . 137 D1
Brick-Kiln La
  Newcastle-u-L ST5 . . . 55 E8
  Rolleston on D DE13 . . . 147 A3
Brick Kiln La
  Stoke-on-T ST4 . . . 56 E1
  Weston ST18 . . . 137 F2
  Wheaton Aston ST19 . . . 205 A3
Brick Kiln Way WS15 . . . 196 F3
Brick St DY3 . . . 271 D5
Brickworks Rd WS12 . . . 210 E2
Brickyard Rd
  Aldridge,Leighswood
  WS9 . . . 256 A7
  Aldridge,Leighswood WS9 256 A6
  Aldridge,Vigo WS9 . . . 244 F1
Bridestowe Cl **4** ST3 . . . 90 A7
Bridge Ave WS6 . . . 226 E4
Bridge Cl Audley ST7 . . . 39 F2
  Brownhills WS8 . . . 244 A6
  Weston ST18 . . . 138 C3
Bridge Cres ST15 . . . 120 A7
Bridge Croft ST6 . . . 42 B6
Bridge Cross Rd WS7 . . . 229 A7
Bridge Ct
  Blythe Bridge ST11 . . . 90 F8
  Stoke-on-T ST4 . . . 71 E3
  Stourbridge DY8 . . . 275 E2
  Uttoxeter ST14 . . . 126 D7
  Woodseaves ST20 . . . 151 D7
Bridge End ST13 . . . 30 C7
Bridge Farm DE13 . . . 147 E1
Bridgefoot Wlk WV8 . . . 239 D1
Bridge Ho ST5 . . . 55 C2
Bridge Ind Est ST6 . . . 57 B7
Bridge La ST18 . . . 139 B3
Bridgeman Ct TF11 . . . 203 F2
Bridgemary Cl WV10 . . . 240 E4
Bridgemere Garden World★
  CW5 . . . 67 B4
Bridge Rd Armitage WS15 . 198 C4
  Cookley DY10 . . . 280 A6
  Market Drayton TF9 . . . 97 A1
  Stoke-on-T ST4 . . . 71 E3
  Uttoxeter ST14 . . . 126 D7

Bridge Rd continued
  Walsall WS4 . . . 244 B1
Bridges Cres WS11 . . . 227 F5
Bridgeside DE13 . . . 147 E1
Bridgeside Trad Est B77 . 250 C3
Bridges Rd WS11 . . . 227 F5
Bridge St Brindley Ford ST8 . 27 B2
  Brownhills WS8 . . . 244 A6
  Burton u T DE14 . . . 166 F3
  Cannock WS11 . . . 226 E5
  Newcastle-u-L,Silverdale
  ST5 . . . 55 C2
  Newcastle-u-L ST5 . . . 283 B3
Bridge Street Ind Units
  ST14 . . . 126 C7
Bridge St Stafford ST16 . . . 285 B2
  Stourbridge DY8 . . . 275 E1
  Stretton DE13 . . . 147 E1
  Tamworth B77 . . . 250 E5
  Tutbury DE13 . . . 146 C7
  Uttoxeter ST14 . . . 126 C7
Bridge Terr Newport TF10 168 E3
  Upper Hulme ST13 . . . 20 E6
Bridge The ST10 . . . 92 D6
Bridget Cl ST4 . . . 71 E5
Bridge View DE6 . . . 81 D8
Bridgewater Cl
  Congleton CW12 . . . 6 B1
  Penkridge ST19 . . . 207 F8
Bridgewater Dr WV5 . . . 269 F7
Bridgewater Rd WS15 . . . 196 F3
Bridgewater St
  Burslem ST6 . . . 56 D8
  Tamworth B77 . . . 250 D5
Bridge Way WS8 . . . 244 E6
Bridgewood St ST3 . . . 284 C4
Bridgford Ave DE14 . . . 184 F4
Bridgnorth Ave WV5 . . . 269 F5
Bridgnorth Gr ST5 . . . 40 E2
Bridgnorth Rd
  Enville DY7 . . . 273 D2
  Himley DY3 . . . 270 B3
  Kinver DY7 . . . 278 C7
  Seisdon WV6 . . . 263 E5
  Stourbridge DY7,DY8 . . . 279 C6
  Trescott WV6 . . . 264 C3
  Wolverhampton WV6 . . . 255 B2
  Wombourne WV5 . . . 269 D5
Bridgtown Bsns Ctr
  WS11 . . . 226 E6
Bridgtown Prim Sch
  WS11 . . . 226 E6
Bridgwater Cl WS9 . . . 244 F3
Bridgwood Rd ST11 . . . 91 A7
Bridle La Ellenhall ST20 . 153 D8
  Stanton DE15 . . . 186 A5
Bridle Path ST3 . . . 284 C1
Bridleway The
  Madeley CW3 . . . 68 D7
  Newcastle-u-L ST5 . . . 70 F3
Bridle Path ST2 . . . 59 A3
Bridle Rd Stafford ST17 . 175 D6
  Stourbridge DY8 . . . 279 D6
Bridleway The TF9 . . . 97 B1
Bridle Wlk WS15 . . . 178 B1
Brierley Hill Rd DY8 . . . 275 F2
Brierley Rd CW12 . . . 6 B1
Brierley St ST6 . . . 42 C1
Brierlow Bar SK17 . . . 5 B8
Brier Sch The DY6 . . . 275 F5
Briertey Hill La WS15 . . . 212 B4
Brieryhurst Cl ST2 . . . 58 C5
Brieryhurst Rd ST7 . . . 26 B3
Bright Cres B77 . . . 250 C2
Brightgreen St ST3 . . . 73 D6
Brighton St **2** ST4 . . . 72 A7
Brighton The ST5 . . . 55 B2
Brights Ave **6** ST7 . . . 26 B2
Bright St **2** ST4 . . . 74 A1
Brightstone Cl WV10 . . . 240 F4
Bright St DY9 . . . 279 D6
Brimfield Pl **1** WV6 . . . 255 F4
Brindiwell Gr ST4 . . . 88 C6
Brindley Ave WV11 . . . 242 A1
Brindley Bank Rd WS15 . 178 E3
Brindley Brae DY7 . . . 278 C8
Brindley Cl
  1 Stourbridge DY8 . . . 275 E1
  Albrighton WV7 . . . 237 A6
  Kidsgrove ST7 . . . 25 E1
  Penkridge ST19 . . . 208 A7
  Stafford ST16 . . . 155 F8
  Stone ST15 . . . 104 E2
  Talke ST7 . . . 40 E8
  Wombourne WV5 . . . 269 D6
Brindley Cres
  Cannock WS12 . . . 210 C8
  Cheddleton ST13 . . . 45 D4
Brindley Heath Jun Sch
  DY7 . . . 278 A5
Brindley Heath Rd WS12 . 195 C2
Brindley La ST7 . . . 43 C3
Brindley Mill Mus The★
  ST13 . . . 30 D7
Brindley Pl ST6 . . . 42 C6
Brindley Rd WS12 . . . 195 A3
Brindleys Bsns Pk WS11 . 210 B3
Brindley St ST5 . . . 283 B3
Brindleys Way ST7 . . . 39 F2
Brindley Way CW12 . . . 6 B1
Brinkburn Cl WS15 . . . 178 B1
Brinkburn Ct ST13 . . . 74 B3
Brinkburn Cres ST17 . . . 175 F3
Brinley Way DY6 . . . 275 C6
Brinscall Gr ST6 . . . 42 A7
Brinsford La WV10 . . . 240 D7
Brinsford Rd WV10 . . . 240 C3
Brinsley Ave ST4 . . . 88 A6

Brisbane Rd ST16 . . . 155 B7
Brisbane Way WS12 . . . 210 E3
Brisley Hill ST4 . . . 71 F6
Bristol Cl WS11 . . . 210 B1
Bristol St
  Newcastle-u-L ST5 . . . 56 D5
  Wolverhampton WV3 . . . 266 B8
Britannia Dr
  Burton u T DE13 . . . 166 D8
  Stretton DE13 . . . 147 D1
Britannia Gn DY3 . . . 271 E5
Britannia Ho
  Burton u T DE14 . . . 166 D2
  Stafford ST16 . . . 285 B3
Britannia Park Ind Est
  ST6 . . . 57 B7
Britannia St **6** ST13 . . . 30 E6
Britannia Stadium (Stoke City
  FC) ST4 . . . 72 C3
Britannia Way ST13 . . . 231 F8
Britch La ST20 . . . 204 E8
Brittain Ave ST5 . . . 55 F7
Brittain Rd ST13 . . . 45 D5
Brittle Pl ST4 . . . 42 D2
Britton St ST4 . . . 56 F1
Brixham Ct ST4 . . . 57 F1
Brizlincote La DE15 . . . 167 D1
Brizlincote St DE15 . . . 166 F1
Broadacres WV3 . . . 224 B3
Broadbent Cl **1** WS13 . . . 230 F6
Broad Eye WS16 . . . 285 A3
Broadfield Cl DY6 . . . 275 D5
Broadfield House Glass
  Mus★ DY6 . . . 275 D5
Broadfield Rd ST6 . . . 41 C7
Broadholes La ST5 . . . 205 A6
Broadhurst Cl WS12 . . . 194 F1
Broadhurst Gn WS12 . . . 194 F2
Broadhurst Green Rd ST19,
  WS12 . . . 194 D2
Broadhurst St ST6 . . . 42 B1
Broad La Burntwood WS7 . 230 B5
  Church Eaton ST20 . . . 171 C1
  Lichfield WS14 . . . 231 D6
Broadlands DE13 . . . 166 D8
Broadlands Rise WS14 . . . 231 D7
Broadlands WV10 . . . 240 D5
Broad Lane Gdns WS3 . . . 243 A2
Broad La
  Stoke-on-T ST6,ST9 . . . 43 C8
  Walsall,Essington WS3 . 242 E4
  Walsall WS4 . . . 244 C2
  Whittington WS13 . . . 215 E1
Broadlawns Dr ST3 . . . 73 B6
Broad La WV3 . . . 265 E8
Broadlee B77 . . . 251 C1
Broad Mdw ST6 . . . 256 B8
Broad Meadow Croft
  ST16 . . . 155 A4
Broad Meadow Ct ST5 . . . 55 E6
Broadmeadow DY6 . . . 275 E8
Broad Meadow La ST6 . . . 227 A2
Broadmine St ST4 . . . 72 F6
Broadoaks Cl WS11 . . . 227 F6
Broad Oaks ST17 . . . 174 E5
Broadoak Way ST3 . . . 72 E1
Broadsmeath B77 . . . 250 C1
Broad St Cannock WS11 . 226 E6
  Hanley ST1 . . . 282 A1
  Kingswinford DY6 . . . 275 D5
  Leek ST13 . . . 30 E5
  Newcastle-u-L ST5 . . . 283 B3
Broadstone Cl WV4 . . . 266 D5
Broad St ST16 . . . 285 A3
Broadway Cannock WS12 . 209 F6
  Codsall WV8 . . . 238 C3
Broadway Ct **1** ST3 . . . 73 F1
Broadway Gdns WV10 . . . 240 E2
Broadway La ST10 . . . 49 A4
Broadway Longton ST3 . . . 73 F2
  Newport TF10 . . . 169 A3
Broadway Pl **1** ST3 . . . 73 F2
Broadway St DE14 . . . 166 C1
Broadway The
  Stourbridge DY8 . . . 279 D3
  Wombourne WV5 . . . 270 A5
Broad Way WS4 . . . 244 C2
Broadway
  Wolverhampton,Bushbury
  WV10 . . . 240 E2
  Wolverhampton,Compton
  WV3 . . . 255 C2
Broadwell La WV6 . . . 253 B2
Broc Cl ST19 . . . 208 A8
Brockbank Pl ST6 . . . 42 B5
Brockeridge Cl WV12 . . . 242 C1
Brockhill TF9 . . . 99 D5
Brockhurst La
  Blymhill Lawn TF11 . . . 204 B4
  Blymhill TF11 . . . 203 F5
  Weeford B75 . . . 259 B7
Brockhurst Rd
  Blymhill TF11 . . . 204 C6
  Sutton Coldfield B75 . . . 258 D1
Brocklehurst Way ST1 . . . 57 E8
Brockley Sq ST1 . . . 282 B3
Brockley's Wlk DY7 . . . 278 C8
Brocksford Ct DE6 . . . 127 F7
Brocksford St ST4 . . . 284 B5
Brockton La ST21 . . . 117 C3
Brockton Wlk ST3 . . . 72 E1
Brock Way ST5 . . . 55 E2
Brocton Cres ST17 . . . 175 F3
Brocton La ST17 . . . 175 F6
Brocton Rd ST17 . . . 176 C3
Brogan St ST4 . . . 72 F6
Bromfield Ct Stone ST15 . 105 A1

Bromfield Ct continued
  Wolverhampton WV6 . . . 255 B3
Bromford Dale **2** WV6 . . . 255 F3
Bromford Pl ST1 . . . 282 A1
Bromford Rise WV3 . . . 266 B8
Bromley Cl WS12 . . . 210 C2
Bromley Ct ST1 . . . 282 A4
Bromley Gdns WV8 . . . 239 A4
Bromleyhedge La ST13 . . . 48 D4
Bromley Hills Prim Sch
  DY6 . . . 275 F5
Bromley Hough ST4 . . . 71 F5
Bromley Ho WV4 . . . 266 A5
Bromley La DY6 . . . 275 E4
Bromley Lodge WV4 . . . 266 A5
Bromley Pl WV4 . . . 266 A5
Bromley St Hanley ST1 . . . 282 A4
  Wolverhampton WV2 . . . 266 C7
Bromley Wood WS15 . . . 161 E5
Brompton Dr ST2 . . . 43 B3
Brompton Lawns WV6 . . . 255 A3
Bromsberrow Way ST3 . . . 90 A7
Bromsgrove Pl ST3 . . . 284 A3
Bromstead Cres ST16 . . . 155 B6
Bromwich Dr WS13 . . . 215 D8
Bromwynd Cl WV2 . . . 266 B6
Bronant Wlk **4** ST6 . . . 57 A7
Bronte Cl DE14 . . . 166 D7
Bronte Ct B79 . . . 250 A6
Bronte Dr WS11 . . . 210 C2
Bronte Gr ST2 . . . 43 A2
Bronte Rd WV2 . . . 266 F6
Brook Ave B77 . . . 262 A7
Brook Cl
  Blythe Bridge ST11 . . . 91 A7
  Brownhills WS9 . . . 245 A3
  Coven WV9 . . . 224 D1
  Doveridge DE6 . . . 127 C8
  Endon ST9 . . . 44 A8
  Lichfield WS13 . . . 214 A1
  Penkridge ST19 . . . 207 E7
Brook Cres DY6 . . . 275 C7
Brookdale Dr WV4 . . . 265 E6
Brookdale DY3 . . . 271 C3
Brook End
  Burntwood WS7 . . . 229 A4
  Fazeley B78 . . . 261 B8
  Haughton ST18 . . . 172 F6
  Longdon WS15 . . . 198 A1
Brooke Rd WS12 . . . 209 F6
Brookes Ct ST4 . . . 72 E5
Brookfield Ave ST9 . . . 43 E7
Brookfield Cl
  Aldridge WS9 . . . 245 A1
  Whiston ST10 . . . 62 D3
Brookfield Ct Hanley ST1 . 282 B4
  Haughton ST18 . . . 172 E5
  Stone ST15 . . . 120 C6
Brookfield Dr WS11 . . . 226 E7
Brookfield TF9 . . . 99 D5
Brookfield Rd
  Aldridge WS9 . . . 245 A1
  Codsall WV8 . . . 239 B3
  Stoke-on-T,Baddeley Green
  ST2 . . . 43 C3
  Stoke-on-T,Springfields ST4 . 71 E5
Brookfields Rd ST10 . . . 62 B4
Brookgate ST11 . . . 91 B8
Brook Gdns ST8 . . . 16 E1
Brook Glen Rd ST17 . . . 174 E7
Brook Gr WV8 . . . 239 B2
Brookhay La WS13 . . . 215 E3
Brookhill Cl WV12 . . . 242 D1
Brookhill Way WV12 . . . 242 D1
Brook Ho TF10 . . . 168 E3
Brookhouse Cl WV10 . . . 241 B6
Brookhouse Ct ST14 . . . 126 F1
Brookhouse Dr ST12 . . . 88 D2
Brookhouse La
  Bucknall ST2 . . . 58 E4
  Cheddleton ST13 . . . 45 A3
  Congleton CW12 . . . 6 C2
  Featherstone WV10 . . . 241 B7
  Wolverhampton WV10 . . . 240 F6
Brookhouse Rd
  Cheadle ST10 . . . 76 B3
  Gnosall ST20 . . . 171 D7
  Meir ST3 . . . 74 B2
  Newcastle-u-L ST5 . . . 55 F8
Brookhouses Ind Est ST10 76 B2
Brookhouse Way
  Cheadle ST10 . . . 76 B2
  Gnosall ST20 . . . 171 D6
Brook La Brocton ST17 . . . 176 C4
  Brownhills WS9 . . . 244 F3
  Church Leigh ST10 . . . 108 F6
  Great Wyrley WS6 . . . 227 A3
Brookland Ave ST3 . . . 284 A1
Brookland Gr WS9 . . . 244 F3
Brookland Rd
  Brownhills WS9 . . . 244 F3
  Stoke-on-T ST6 . . . 41 F5
Brooklands Ave WS6 . . . 226 F4
Brooklands Cl ST14 . . . 126 B6
Brooklands Rd
  Albrighton WV7 . . . 237 B6
  Cannock WS11 . . . 210 A3
Brooklands Sch ST16 . . . 155 C6
Brooklands DY8 . . . 275 F1
Brooklands The DY3 . . . 269 E1
Brooklands Way
  Cheddleton ST13 . . . 46 A8
  Leek ST13 . . . 45 F8
Brook La
  Newcastle-u-L ST5 . . . 283 B2
  Ranton ST18 . . . 153 C3

Brook La *continued*
Stoke-on-T ST9 .... 43 F8
Brooklime Gdns
Featherstone WV10 ...... 241 B7
Stafford ST16 .... 155 A5
Brooklyn Gr DY6 .... 275 B8
Brooklyn Rd
Burntwood WS7 .... 229 A4
Cannock WS12 .... 210 D1
Brook Mdws WV8 .... 239 B4
Brookmead Gr ST3 .... 73 B6
Brookmead Ind Est ST16 155 F8
Brook Path ST15 .... 119 F8
Brook Pl Newcastle-u-L ST5 71 C5
Stoke-on-T ST4 .... 56 F1
Brook Prim Sch DY8 .... 275 F1
Brook Rd
Cheslyn Hay WS6 .... 226 E4
Stoke-on-T ST4 .... 88 A7
Wombourne WV5 .... 269 F6
Brookside Ave TF10 .... 168 E1
Brookside Bsns Ctr ST15 118 B5
Brookside Bsns Pk ST14 126 D7
Brookside Burslem ST6 .... 56 D7
Burton u T DE15 .... 167 B5
Brookside Cl
Newcastle-u-L ST5 .... 283 A1
Wombourne WV5 .... 269 E6
Brookside Cotts DE6 ..... 81 C3
Brookside Ct ST10 .... 76 B3
Brookside Cvn Site WV9. 224 B2
Brookside Dr Endon ST9... 44 A8
Stoke-on-T ST3 .... 72 E2
Brookside Dudley DY3 ... 271 D2
Enville DY7 .... 273 D3
Brookside Gdns ST19 ... 221 E8
Brookside Ind Est ST6 .... 56 D8
Brookside ST10 .... 62 A3
Brookside La ST15 ...... 119 F7
Brookside
Marchington ST14 .... 127 A2
Ranton ST18 .... 153 D5
Brookside Rd
Barton-u-N DE13 .... 183 C1
Tamworth B78 .... 249 D1
Uttoxeter ST14 .... 126 D7
Brook Side DE13 .... 147 B4
Brookside Way
Blakedown DY10 .... 281 B2
Kingswinford DY6 .... 275 C7
Tamworth B77 .... 262 A6
Brook Sq 1 WS15 .... 196 E8
Brook St Biddulph ST8 .... 27 A5
Burton u T DE14 .... 166 D4
Dudley,Gornalwood DY3 .. 271 C3
Kingswinford DY6 .... 270 B1
Leek ST13 .... 30 E5
Newcastle-u-L ST5 .... 55 C2
Stoke-on-T ST4 .... 72 B7
Stourbridge,Amblecote
DY8 .... 275 F1
Stourbridge DY8 .... 279 E5
Swadlincote DE11 .... 186 E6
Brook Vale WS11 .... 226 F8
Brookview Dr ST3 .... 73 F4
Brookweed B77 .... 251 A3
Brookwillows 5 ST17 ... 175 C7
Brookwood Cl ST5 .... 71 B3
Brookwood Dr ST3 .... 74 B2
Broom Covert Rd WS14 . 247 E8
Broome Cl DE13 .... 199 C6
Broome Hill ST5 .... 71 C1
Broome La DY9 .... 281 F2
Broome Wlk WS15 ...... 198 C4
Broomfield Ave B78 .... 261 A8
Broomfield Cl
Newport TF10 .... 168 D3
Stone ST15 .... 120 B6
Broomfield La ST14 ...... 79 F2
Broomfield Pl TF10 ..... 168 D3
Broomfield Pl N ST1 ..... 57 A3
Broomfield Pl S ST1 ..... 57 A3
Broomfield Rd
Newport TF10 .... 168 D3
Stoke-on-T ST6 .... 42 E5
Broomfields ST8 .... 17 B1
Broomhill Bank WS11 ... 209 E3
Broomhill Cl WS11 ...... 209 E4
Broomhills The DE12 .... 219 E7
Broomhill St ST6 .... 41 D4
Broom Hollow TF9 .... 99 E5
Broom Lea TF9 .... 99 D4
Broom's La DE6 .... 129 B2
Brooms Park Cvn Pk
ST15 .... 120 B5
Brooms Rd ST15 .... 120 B5
Broom St ST1 .... 282 C4
Broomyclose La ST14 ... 111 A4
Brough Cl Leek ST13 ...... 30 E6
Wolverhampton WV4,
WV14 .... 266 F3
Brough La ST4 .... 88 B7
Brough Rd DE15 .... 167 C3
Broughton Cl ST16 ...... 155 C7
Broughton Cres ST12 .... 88 E1
Broughton Ct WV6 ...... 255 A3
Broughton Rd Bucknall ST2 57 F3
Newcastle-u-L ST5 .... 56 D2
Wolverhampton WV3 ..... 255 C1
Brow Hill ST13 .... 30 E6
Brown Ave
Lawton-gate ST7 .... 25 A5
Tamworth B77 .... 261 C8
Brownfield Rd ST3 .... 74 A2
Brownhill Rd ST6 .... 43 B8
Brownhills Bsns Pk ST6 .. 41 D2
Brownhills Com Tech Coll
WS8 .... 228 F1
Brownhills High Sch ST6 . 41 E1
Brownhills Rd
Brownhills WS8 .... 245 A4
Norton Canes WS11 ..... 228 B4
Stoke-on-T ST6 .... 41 D2
Brownhills West Prim Sch
WS8 .... 228 C2
Brownhills West Sta★
WS7 .... 228 C3
Browning Cl Cheadle ST10. 76 C2
Tamworth B79 .... 249 F8
Browning Cres WV10 .... 240 C2
Browning Gr Perton WV6. 254 E4
Talke ST7 .... 40 C8
Browning Rd
Burntwood WS7 .... 229 C7
Dudley DY3 .... 271 A4
Stoke-on-T ST3 .... 72 F2
Browning St ST16 .... 285 A4
Brown La SK17 .... 3 B3
Brown Lees Ind Est ST8 .. 27 B4
Brown Lees Rd
Biddulph ST8 .... 27 A5
Biddulph ST8 .... 27 B4
Harriseahead ST7 .... 26 F4
Brownley Rd ST6 .... 42 D1
Brownsea Pl ST3 .... 72 E4
Brownsfield Rd WS13 ... 214 D1
Brownshill Bsns Pk WS8 244 F5
Brownshore La WV11 ... 242 A3
Brown's La B78 .... 262 F5
Brown's Lake DY7 ...... 273 D3
Brown's La Tamworth B79 250 C8
Yoxall DE13 .... 182 A2
Brown St Burslem ST6 .... 57 A8
Wolverhampton WV2 ..... 266 D7
Brownswall Rd DY3 ..... 271 C7
Browns Wlk WS15 ...... 178 D1
Browsholme B79 .... 249 D6
Broxwood Pk WV6 ...... 255 B3
Bruford Rd WV3 .... 266 A8
Brundall Oval ST2 .... 58 D2
Brund La ST13 .... 45 A3
Brundle Ave ST16 .... 155 B3
Brunel Cl Burntwood WS7. 229 B8
Stafford ST16 .... 155 F8
Tamworth B79 .... 250 B6
Brunel Ct
Four Ashes WV10 .... 224 D5
Wombourne WV5 .... 270 A7
Brunel Gr WV6 .... 254 E5
Brunel Way DE11 .... 186 E1
Brunel Wlk ST3 .... 284 C4
Brunslow Cl WV10 ...... 240 C1
Brunswick Mill 5 ST13 ... 30 E6
Brunswick Pl ST1 .... 282 B2
Brunswick Rd WS11 ..... 209 E2
Brunswick St 3 Leek ST13 30 F6
Hanley ST1 .... 282 B3
Newcastle-u-L ST5 ...... 283 C3
Brunswick Terr ST16 .... 285 A2
Brunt St ST6 .... 56 D7
Brutus Rd ST5 .... 55 D6
Bryan Ave WV4 .... 265 D4
Bryans La WS15 .... 178 F1
Bryan St ST1 .... 282 B3
Bryans Way WS12 ...... 210 F4
Bryant Rd ST2 .... 58 B5
Brymbo Rd ST5 .... 55 F5
Brynmawr Rd WV14 .... 266 F3
Bryony Burton u T DE14 .. 185 B8
Sutton Coldfield B74 .... 257 F5
Buccleuch Rd ST3 .... 73 D2
Buckden B77 .... 251 C1
Buckingham Cl
6 Burton u T DE13 ...... 166 D8
Stafford ST17 .... 156 C1
Buckingham Cres ST4 .... 72 A1
Buckingham Ct DE15 .... 167 C3
Buckingham Gdns WS14 231 B6
Buckingham Gr DY6 ..... 275 C7
Buckingham Pl 3 WS12. 210 C1
Buckingham Rd
Tamworth B79 .... 249 E7
Wolverhampton WV4 .... 266 A5
Buckingham Rise DY1 ... 271 E2
Buckland Cl WS12 ...... 210 D1
Buckland Gr ST4 .... 88 C5
Buckland Rd ST16 ...... 136 D1
Buckland Wlk TF10 ..... 168 F5
Buckley Cl ST14 .... 125 C7
Buckley Rd Stoke-on-T ST6. 42 C5
Wolverhampton WV4 ..... 265 D5
Buckley's Row ST5 ...... 283 B2
Buckmaster Ave ST5 ..... 71 C6
Bucknall Hospl ST2 ...... 58 C4
Bucknall New Rd ST1 ... 282 C3
Bucknall Old Rd ST1 .... 282 C3
Bucknall Rd Hanley ST1 ... 57 F3
Wolverhampton WV11 ... 242 B1
Buckthorn Cl WS12 ..... 209 F8
Buckton Cl B75 .... 258 E2
Bude Dr ST17 .... 156 E1
Buds Rd
Cannock Wood WS15 .... 211 F5
Gentleshaw WS15 ...... 212 A5
Buglawton Hall Specl Sch
CW12 .... 6 D5
Buglawton Prim Sch CW12 6 A4
Buildwas Cl WS3 .... 242 F2
Bulldog La WS13 .... 214 B1
Buller St Hanley ST1 .... 282 C1
Wolverhampton WV4 ..... 266 E6
Bullgap La DE6 .... 65 C4
Bull Hill ST16 .... 285 B3
Bull La Packmoor ST8 .... 27 A2
Wombourne WV5 .... 270 B7
Bullmeadow La WV5 .... 270 A8
Bullmoor La
Muckley Corner WS14 .... 230 A1
Muckley Corner WS14 .... 230 B1
Bullocks House Rd ST7 ... 26 E3
Bullows Rd WS8 .... 244 C6
Bull Ring Claverley WV5 .. 267 C7
Sedgley DY3 .... 271 D8
Bull Ring The ST18 ..... 138 D2
Bullrushes Cl
6 Hanley ST1 .... 56 F2
Stoke-on-T ST1 .... 57 A2
Bull St DY3 .... 271 C2
Bulrush Cl WS8 .... 244 E7
Bulstrode St 3 ST6 .... 56 E8
Bumblehole Mdws WV5 . 269 F7
Bungalows The
Adbaston ST20 .... 131 D4
Chipnall TF9 .... 114 A3
Leek ST13 .... 31 A5
Bungham La ST19 ...... 207 D8
Bun La Blymhill TF10 .... 188 C1
Great Chatwell TF10 ..... 203 C8
Bunny Hill ST5 .... 71 C5
Bunting Cl ST14 .... 126 B6
Buntingsdale Rd TF9 .... 112 A7
Bunting The Kingsley ST10. 61 D3
Wetley Rocks ST9 .... 60 A7
Bunt's La ST9 .... 43 D4
Bunyan Pl WS11 .... 209 E4
Burcham Cl ST16 .... 155 B7
Burcot Ct B74 .... 257 F2
Burdock Cl WS11 .... 210 B3
Burford Ave ST5 .... 40 D1
Burford Rd Stafford ST17 156 D1
Wheaton Aston ST19 .... 205 B6
Burford Way ST2 .... 58 A1
Burgage Cl TF9 .... 97 D1
Burgage Ct TF10 .... 168 F2
Burgage The
Eccleshall ST21 .... 133 F7
Market Drayton TF9 ...... 97 D1
Burgesses The DY7 ..... 278 B3
Burgess St ST6 .... 56 E7
Burgis Cl ST13 .... 45 D4
Burgoyne St WS11 ...... 210 A5
Burgundy Gr 3 ST3 ...... 90 A7
Burland Ave WV6 .... 255 E6
Burland Rd ST5 .... 40 D2
Burleigh Cl WS12 .... 210 A8
Burleigh Croft WS7 ..... 229 A4
Burleigh Gr ST5 .... 56 D3
Burleigh Rd WV3 .... 266 A8
Burlidge Rd ST6 .... 42 A6
Burlington Ave ST5 ...... 56 D3
Burlington Ct B78 ...... 261 B8
Burlington Dr ST17 ..... 174 B8
Burmarsh Wlk
4 Burslem ST6 .... 56 F7
Wolverhampton WV8 ..... 255 F8
Burnaby Rd ST6 .... 41 C6
Burnell Gdns WV3 ...... 265 E8
Burnet Gr WV10 .... 241 B8
Burnett Ct ST16 .... 155 A5
Burnett Pl ST6 .... 42 D4
Burnett Rd B74 .... 257 B2
Burnfield Dr WS15 ...... 178 D1
Burnfields Way WS9 .... 256 A7
Burnham Ave 1 ST17 ... 175 D6
Burnham Cl DY6 .... 275 F4
Burnham Gn WS11 ...... 226 B8
Burnham St ST4 .... 284 A5
Burnhays Rd ST6 .... 41 F2
Burnley St ST1 .... 57 D6
Burnsall Cl WV9 .... 240 A3
Burns Ave Stafford ST17 . 174 B8
Wolverhampton WV10 .... 240 D2
Burns Cl Kidsgrove ST7 .... 41 A8
Lichfield WS14 .... 231 B6
Burns Dr WS7 .... 229 C7
Burns Gr DY3 .... 271 A4
Burnside Cl ST3 .... 90 A7
Burnside DE13 .... 147 B4
Burns Rd Congleton CW12 .. 6 A2
Tamworth B79 .... 250 A6
Burns Row ST3 .... 74 B2
Burns St WS11 .... 210 A3
Burnthill La WS15 ...... 196 E8
Burntwood Bsns Pk
WS7 .... 228 D7
Burntwood Rd
Hammerwich WS7 .... 229 D4
Norton Canes WS11 ..... 228 A7
Burntwood Town Sh Ctr
WS7 .... 228 F7
Burntwood View TF9 ..... 99 E4
Burnwood Com Prim Sch
ST6 .... 42 B5
Burnwood Ct ST6 .... 42 D2
Burnwood Gr ST7 .... 26 B2
Burnwood Pl ST6 .... 42 B5
Burrington Dr ST4 .... 88 C6
Burrows Rd DY6 .... 275 F4
Burrows The DE11 ...... 186 F5
Burslem Cl WS3 .... 243 A3
Burslem Ent Ctr ST6 ..... 57 A8
Bursley Cl ST17 .... 174 D6
Bursley Prim Sch ST5 .... 56 B8
Bursley Rd ST6 .... 57 A7
Bursley Way ST5 .... 56 A8
Bursnips Rd WV11 ...... 242 C4
Burton Bank La
Stafford,Moss Pit ST17 ... 174 E5
Stafford ST17,ST18 ...... 174 D5
Burton Borough Sch The
TF10 .... 169 A2
Burton Cl B79 .... 250 C7
Burton Coll (Town Campus)
DE14 .... 166 E2
Burton Cres
Kingsley Holt ST10 .... 76 F8
Stoke-on-T ST1 .... 57 E7
Burton Ct ST17 .... 174 E7
Burton Ent Pk DE14 ..... 166 E5
Burton House Gdns
ST17 .... 174 E5
Burton Manor Prim Sch
ST17 .... 174 D6
Burton Manor Rd ST17 .. 174 D6
Burton Mews ST14 ...... 110 F1
Burton Old Rd E WS14 .. 231 E8
Burton Old Rd
Lichfield,Boley Park
WS14 .... 231 F8
Lichfield,Streethay WS13 .. 214 F1
Burton Old Rd W WS14 .. 231 D8
Burton-on-Trent Sta
DE14 .... 166 C3
Burton Pl ST1 .... 282 C3
Burton Rd Alrewas DE13 .. 201 B3
Burton u T DE14 .... 185 B7
Dudley DY1 .... 271 F4
Egginton DE65 .... 148 F7
Elford B79 .... 216 E1
Lichfield WS13 .... 214 F1
Newton Solney DE15,DE65 148 F1
Swadlincote DE11 .... 186 D2
Tutbury DE13 .... 146 D4
Whittington WS14 ...... 232 E7
Burton Sq ST17 .... 174 E7
Burton St Leek ST13 ..... 30 D5
Tutbury DE13 .... 146 C6
Burton Terr ST14 .... 126 C8
Burt St ST3 .... 74 B3
Burwaye Cl WS13 .... 231 A6
Burway Mdw DE13 ..... 201 A2
Bury Ring ST18 .... 173 D6
Bushberry Cl ST15 ...... 119 F6
Bushbury Hill Prim Sch
WV10 .... 240 F1
Bushbury La WV10 ...... 240 E2
Bush Cl WV7 .... 237 A5
Bush Dr WS15 .... 178 E1
Bushey Cl B74 .... 256 F2
Bushfield Rd WV7 ...... 237 A5
Bush Gr WS3 .... 244 A2
Bushton La DE13 .... 146 B2
Bustomley La ST10 ..... 108 A5
Bute St ST4 .... 284 A4
Butler Ct DE14 .... 166 B3
Butlers Lane Sta B74 .... 258 A3
Butlers La B74 .... 258 A3
Butler St ST4 .... 72 B6
Butterbank La ST18 ..... 154 B2
Butter Bk ST18 .... 154 B3
Buttercross The 2 TF9 ... 97 C1
Butterfield Cl WV6 ..... 254 D3
Butterfield Pl 3 ST6 ..... 41 E3
Butterhill Bank ST15 .... 121 A2
Butterhill La ST15 ...... 121 F5
Buttermere Cl
Burslem ST6 .... 56 E8
Cannock WS11 .... 210 A3
Wolverhampton WV6 .... 255 D8
Buttermere Ct WV6 ..... 254 F4
Buttermere Dr WV11 ... 242 A2
Buttermere Gr WV11 ... 242 B1
Buttermere B77 .... 262 B7
Butterton La ST5 .... 70 D2
Butthouse La ST21 ..... 102 C5
Butt La Ranton ST18 ..... 153 C1
Talke ST7 .... 40 E8
Buttons Farm Rd WV4 .. 265 D3
Butts Cl WS11 .... 227 E4
Butts Croft DE13 .... 200 F3
Butts Gn ST2 .... 58 C6
Butt's La ST10 .... 63 F8
Butts La
Norton Canes WS11 ..... 227 E4
Warslow SK17 .... 23 C2
Butts Rd
Market Drayton TF9 ...... 97 B1
Wolverhampton WV4 .... 265 F4
Butts The Betley CW3 ..... 53 A5
Lichfield WS14 .... 230 D2
Butts Way WS11 .... 227 E4
Buxton Ave Fazeley B78 .. 261 B8
Newcastle-u-L ST5 .... 55 A2
Buxton Cl WS3 .... 243 C3
Buxton Old Rd CW12 ...... 6 A4
Buxton Rd Congleton CW12 . 6 C6
Leek ST13 .... 31 B7
Longnor SK17 .... 13 B7
Walsall WS3 .... 243 C3
Wetton DE6 .... 35 B5
Buxton St ST1 .... 57 D7
Byatt's Gr ST3 .... 284 A2
Bycars Farm Croft WS13 215 E8
Bycars La ST6 .... 42 A1
Bycars Rd ST6 .... 41 F1
Byland Pl ST5 .... 71 A5
Byland B77 .... 250 D3
Byland Way WS3 .... 242 F2
By Pass Rd B77 .... 251 A5
Byrd's Cl ST14 .... 125 F8
Byrd's La ST14 .... 126 A8
Byrkley Park Ctr★ DE13 . 164 A3
Byrkley St DE14 .... 166 B4
Byrne Rd WV2 .... 266 D7
Byrom St 9 ST13 .... 30 D6
Byron Ave
Burton u T DE15 .... 185 E7
Lichfield WS14 .... 231 B5
Byron Cl Burntwood WS7 . 211 F1
Cheadle ST10 .... 76 B2
Market Drayton TF9 ..... 112 A7
Stafford ST16 .... 156 A5
Byron Croft Dudley DY3 .. 271 A5
Sutton Coldfield B74 .... 257 F6
Byron Ct Kidsgrove ST7 .... 41 A8
Sutton Coldfield B74 .... 258 A5
Byron Pl Cannock WS11 .. 209 F5
Rugeley WS15 .... 178 C2
Byron Rd Tamworth B79 .. 250 A7
Wolverhampton WV10 .... 241 A1
Byron St ST4 .... 56 D1
Bywater Gr 3 ST3 .... 73 D6
Byways WS3 .... 243 C3

C

Cable St WV2 .... 266 F8
Cabot Gr WV6 .... 254 E4
Cacklehill La DE6 .... 81 C2
Cadeby Gr ST2 .... 43 B2
Cadley Hill Ind Est DE11 186 D2
Cadley Hill Rd DE11 ..... 186 E3
Cadman Cres ST6 .... 42 E3
Cadman's La WS6,WS3 .. 243 D6
Cadogan Rd B77 .... 261 D5
Caernarvon Ave ST15 ... 120 C6
Caernarvon Cl
Burton u T DE13 .... 166 A8
Market Drayton TF9 ...... 97 E2
Caernarvon Way DY1 .... 271 E2
Cairn Cl ST2 .... 58 D3
Cairns Cl DE15 .... 167 C3
Cairns Dr ST16 .... 156 B5
Caister B77 .... 251 A6
Caistor Cl Mile Oak B78 .. 260 B8
Stoke-on-T ST2 .... 43 A1
Calais Rd DE13 .... 166 B6
Calcot Dr WV6 .... 255 E7
Caldbeck Pl ST1 .... 282 C3
Caldercrofts TF10 .... 168 F4
Calder Rise DY3 .... 271 F6
Calder B77 .... 251 B2
Caldervale Dr 4 ST17 ... 175 D6
Caldew Gr ST4 .... 88 C5
Caldon Way ST15 .... 104 E3
Cale Cl B77 .... 250 C2
Caledonian B77 .... 250 F2
Caledonia Rd Hanley ST4 .. 57 B1
Wolverhampton WV2 ..... 266 E8
Calgary Cres DE15 ...... 167 D3
Calibre Ind Est WV10 .... 224 D5
Californian Gr WS7 ..... 228 F8
California St ST3 .... 284 A3
Callaghan Gr 3 WS11 ... 210 C2
Callender Pl ST6 .... 57 A8
Callingwood La DE13 .... 164 F3
Callister Way DE14 ..... 165 F3
Callis Wlk 2 B77 .... 261 F6
Callow Hill La ST10 ...... 75 D3
Calrofold Dr ST5 .... 40 D1
Calvary Cres ST2 .... 73 D8
Calveley Cl ST15 .... 118 F6
Calverley St ST3 .... 284 D2
Calver St 5 ST6 .... 41 D3
Calvert Gr ST5 .... 56 B7
Calvin Cl
Wolverhampton WV10 .... 240 D3
Wombourne WV5 .... 269 F5
Calving Hill WS11 ...... 209 E2
Camberley Cres WV4 .... 266 E2
Camberley Dr WV4 ..... 266 A4
Camberley Rd DY8 ...... 275 F3
Camberwell Gr ST4 ...... 88 C6
Camborne Cl
Congleton CW12 .... 15 E8
Stafford ST17 .... 175 E8
Camborne Cres ST5 ...... 70 F5
Cambrian La WS15 ..... 178 C3
Cambrian B77 .... 251 A2
Cambrian Way ST2 ...... 58 C4
Cambria St WS11 ...... 209 D4
Cambridge Cl
Aldridge WS9 .... 256 B8
Biddulph ST8 .... 16 C1
Cambridge Ct ST5 .... 71 D4
Cambridge Dr ST5 .... 71 D4
Cambridge St
Burton u T DE14 .... 166 B1
Hanley ST1 .... 282 A2
Stafford ST16 .... 156 A4
Camden Dr B77 .... 250 E3
Camden St
Brownhills WS9 .... 244 F4
Stoke-on-T ST4 .... 72 E4
Camden Way DY6 ...... 270 D1
Camelford Cl ST17 ..... 175 E8
Camellia Cl ST4 .... 56 E1
Camellia Gdns
Stourbridge DY8 .... 275 E2
Wolverhampton WV9 .... 239 F3
Camelot Cl Cannock WS11 209 F4
Stoke-on-T ST4 .... 88 C4
Stretton DE13 .... 147 E2
Cameo Dr DY8 .... 279 F8
Cameo Way ST16 ...... 155 B7
Cameron Cl DE15 ...... 167 B1
Cameron Wharf ST15 ... 104 F1
Camhouses B77 .... 251 B1
Camillus Rd ST5 .... 55 F2
Camoys Ct 8 ST6 .... 57 A7
Camoys Rd ST6 .... 57 A7
Campbell Ave ST13 ...... 30 D4
Campbell Cl
Congleton CW12 .... 6 A4
Rugeley WS15 .... 178 D2
Tamworth B79 .... 249 F8

Campbell Pl ST4 . . . . 72 B7
Campbell Rd
 Market Drayton TF9 . . . . . 97 D2
 Stoke-on-T ST4 . . . . 72 B5
Campbell Terr ST1 . . . . . . 57 E6
Camp Hill Rd DY7 . . . . . 273 F8
Camp Hill
 Stourbridge DY8 . . . . . . 275 E1
 Whitmore ST5 . . . . 85 A5
Campian's Ave WS6 . . . . 226 D2
Campian Way ST6 . . . . . . 42 E2
Campion Cl ST5 . . . . 56 D3
Campion Cl
 Eccleshall ST21 . . . . 133 D6
 Wombourne WV5 . . . . . . 269 E6
Campion Dr
 Featherstone WV10 . . . . 241 A7
 Tamworth B77 . . . . 250 C3
Campion Rd
 Cannock ST17,WS12 . . . 194 D6
 Shenstone B75 . . . . 258 D6
 Stoke-on-T ST6 . . . . 42 C1
Camp Rd
 Cannock ST17,WS12 . . . 194 D6
 Shenstone B75 . . . . 258 D6
 Stoke-on-T ST6 . . . . 42 C1
Camrose Gdns WV9 . . . . 240 A3
Camsey La
 Burntwood WS7 . . . . 229 E8
 Creswell Green WS13 . . 212 F1
Canal Cotts ST20 . . . . . . 151 C2
Canal La ST6 . . . . 41 D2
Canal Mews The ST4 . . . 88 C6
Canal Rd CW12 . . . . 15 F8
Canal Side ST12 . . . . 88 D1
Canalside Cl
 Penkridge ST19 . . . . 207 F7
 Walsall WS3 . . . . 243 F1
Canalside Rd ST15 . . . . . 104 E2
Canal St Burslem ST6 . . . 56 D8
 Burton u T DE14 . . . . . . 166 C2
 Stourbridge DY8 . . . . . . 279 F6
Canal View Bsns Pk
 WS15 . . . . 197 B6
Canary Rd ST2 . . . . 73 D7
Canaway Wlk WS15 . . . . 178 C2
Canberra Cres ST3 . . . . . 90 C6
Canberra Dr ST16 . . . . . . 156 B4
Candle La CW3 . . . . 67 B2
Canford Cres WV8 . . . . . 238 E3
Cannel Rd WS7 . . . . 228 D6
Canning Rd B77 . . . . 250 F4
Canning St ST4 . . . . 72 F5
Cannock Chase Ctry Pk
 Brocton ST17 . . . . 176 D2
 Cannock WS12 . . . . 195 A3
Cannock Chase Ent Ctr
 WS12 . . . . 195 D1
Cannock Chase High Sch
 WS11 . . . . 209 E2
Cannock Chase Tech Coll
 Cannock,Blackfords
 WS11 . . . . 209 D1
 Cannock,Bridgtown WS11 . 226 E7
Cannock Com Hospl
 WS11 . . . . 209 E2
Cannock Ind Ctr WS11 . . 226 D5
Cannock Motor Village
 WS11 . . . . 210 B3
Cannock Rd Brocton ST17 176 A3
 Burntwood,Chase Terrace
 WS7 . . . . 228 D7
 Burntwood,Gorstey Ley
 WS7 . . . . 229 B7
 Cannock,Heath Hayes
 WS12 . . . . 227 C8
 Cannock WS12,WS11 . . 210 A5
 Featherstone WV10 . . . . 241 C7
 Huntington ST19 . . . . . . 208 B8
 Penkridge ST19 . . . . . . 192 F1
 Stafford ST17 . . . . 175 D5
Cannock Sh Ctr WS11 . . 209 E1
Cannock Sta WS11 . . . . . 226 F8
Cannock Wood Ind Est
 WS12 . . . . 211 C6
Cannock Wood Rd WS11 211 B5
Cannock Wood St WS12 . 211 A6
Cannon Cl ST1 . . . . 282 B2
Cannon Rd WV5 . . . . 270 A6
Cannon St ST1 . . . . 282 B2
Canons Cl ST15 . . . . 120 A6
Canterbury Cl
 Lichfield WS14 . . . . 214 C3
 Tamworth B77 . . . . 250 D3
 Walsall WS3 . . . . 244 A4
Canterbury Dr
 Burntwood WS7 . . . . 229 E7
 Perton WV6 . . . . 254 E4
 Rugeley WS15 . . . . 196 D6
 Stoke-on-T ST6 . . . . 42 C4
Canterbury Rd
 Burton u T DE15 . . . . . . 167 C2
 Wolverhampton WV4 . . . 265 E5
Canterbury Way WS12 . . 210 B1
Canvey Gr ST3 . . . . 90 B7
Canwell Dr B75 . . . . 259 B5
Canwell Gate B75 . . . . . . 258 E4
Cape Ave ST17 . . . . 174 E7
Cape Cl WS8 . . . . 245 A6
Cape St ST1 . . . . 282 B4
Capesthorne Cl ST9 . . . . 59 B3
Capewell St ST3 . . . . 284 C4
Capper Cl ST7 . . . . 26 A2
Cappers ST4,WS13,WS14 . 231 F8
Capper's La WS14 . . . . . 232 A7
Capper St 5 ST6 . . . . . . 41 E3
Capricorn Way ST6 . . . . . 41 F6
Captain's Cl WV3 . . . . . . 255 D2

Captain's La DE13 . . . . . 201 D8
Caradoc B77 . . . . 251 A2
Caraway Dr DE14 . . . . . . 185 A8
Caraway Pl ST3 . . . . 90 A6
Carberry Way ST3 . . . . . . 74 A4
Carder Ave ST16 . . . . . . 155 B7
Carder Gn SK17 . . . . 13 B6
Cardiff Gr ST1 . . . . 282 B1
Cardiff St WV3 . . . . 266 B8
Cardigan Ave WS15 . . . . 196 D6
Cardigan Gr ST4 . . . . 88 C6
Cardigan Ho WS12 . . . . . 210 C5
Cardigan Pl WS12 . . . . . 210 C5
Cardinal Griffin RC High Sch
 WS11 . . . . 209 D2
Cardinal Way WS11 . . . . 209 D2
Cardington St ST5 . . . . . . 71 A4
Cardoness Pl DY1 . . . . . 271 F2
Card St ST6 . . . . 57 A7
Cardway ST5 . . . . 56 B7
Cardwell St ST1 . . . . 57 E5
Carey B77 . . . . 262 A5
Carfax WS11 . . . . 226 E8
Carina Gdns ST6 . . . . 42 D1
Carisbrooke Dr
 2 Stretton DE13 . . . . . 147 E1
 Stafford ST17 . . . . 174 B7
Carisbrooke Gdns WV10 . 240 E3
Carisbrooke Rd
 Perton WV6 . . . . 255 A3
 Wolverhampton WV10 . . 240 E3
Carisbrooke B77 . . . . 251 A2
Carisbrooke Way ST4 . . . 88 C5
Carlcroft B77 . . . . 251 B2
Carling Cl ST16 . . . . 155 B2
Carling Gr ST4 . . . . 73 A5
Carlisle Rd WS11 . . . . . . 226 B7
Carlisle St ST3 . . . . 284 B1
Carlos Cl ST10 . . . . 76 D3
Carlos Pl ST5 . . . . 41 B1
Carlow Ho WS15 . . . . . . 197 B6
Carlton Ave Aldridge B74 . 257 A2
 Brown Edge ST6 . . . . . . 43 B6
 Newcastle-u-L ST5 . . . . . 71 B3
 Stoke-on-T ST6 . . . . 42 A4
Carlton Cl Brown Edge ST6 . 43 B6
 Cannock WS12 . . . . 210 D1
 Cheadle ST10 . . . . 76 D1
Carlton Cres
 Burntwood WS7 . . . . 229 A8
 Tamworth B79 . . . . 249 F8
Carlton Croft B74 . . . . . . 257 A2
Carlton Ho B75 . . . . 258 B2
Carlton Rd Stoke-on-T ST4 . 72 C8
 Wolverhampton WV3 . . . 266 A7
Carlton Sq ST17 . . . . 174 B8
Carlton St DE13 . . . . 166 B6
Carlton Terr ST13 . . . . 31 A6
Carlyon Pl ST1 . . . . 57 D8
Carmel Cl WS12 . . . . 210 C5
Carmichael Cl WS14 . . . 231 D7
Carmount Rd ST2 . . . . . . 58 B7
Carmountside Prim Sch
 ST2 . . . . 58 B7
Carnation Cl ST3 . . . . 74 B6
Carnforth Cl DY6 . . . . . . 275 D4
Carnforth Gr ST6 . . . . 41 E8
Carnoustie Cl WS3 . . . . . 243 A3
Carnoustie B77 . . . . 251 C5
Carol Gdns DY8 . . . . 279 B4
Caroline Cl ST9 . . . . 59 B4
Caroline Cres ST6 . . . . . . 43 B6
Caroline St ST3 . . . . 284 C4
Caroline St DE14 . . . . . . 166 C2
Carousels The DE14 . . . . 166 C5
Carpenter Cl DE15 . . . . . 167 C1
Carpenter Rd ST3 . . . . . . 284 A4
Carr Bank ST6 . . . . 78 B7
Carriage Dr ST8 . . . . 16 E1
Carrick Cl WS3 . . . . 244 A5
Carrick Pl ST4 . . . . 72 A1
Carriers Fold WV5 . . . . . 270 B7
Carriers Rd DE65 . . . . . . 148 D6
Carr La Audley ST7 . . . . . 39 A1
 Wetton ST13,DE6 . . . . . 34 F2
Carroll Dr ST3 . . . . 284 D4
Carron St ST4 . . . . 284 B5
Carroway Head Hill B78 . 259 D4
Carr St ST7 . . . . 26 F1
Carryer Pl ST5 . . . . 70 F8
Carshalton Gr WV2 . . . . 266 E4
Carson Rd ST4 . . . . 41 F3
Carson Way ST16 . . . . . . 155 C5
Carter Ave WV8 . . . . 239 B3
Carters Croft ST10 . . . . . . 92 F3
Cartersfield La WS9 . . . . 245 E6
Carter St ST14 . . . . 126 C7
Cartlich St ST6 . . . . 41 D5
Cartlidge St ST6 . . . . 56 D1
Cartmel Pl ST6 . . . . 42 B3
Cartway The WV6 . . . . . 254 D4
Cartwright Dr ST20 . . . . . 171 D7
Cartwright Ho WS3 . . . . 243 B1
Cartwright Ind Est The
 ST3 . . . . 284 B2
Cartwright Rd B75 . . . . . 258 C3
Cartwright St
 Longton ST3 . . . . 284 B3
 Wolverhampton WV2 . . . 266 D8
Carver Gdns DY8 . . . . . . 279 E2
Carver Rd
 Burton u T DE13 . . . . . . 166 C6
 Stafford ST16 . . . . 155 C6
Casa Mia Ct WS12 . . . . . 210 C5
Casewell Rd
 Kingswinford DY6 . . . . . 275 C8
 Stoke-on-T ST6 . . . . 57 C7

Casey La Burton u T DE14 . 166 B4
 Weston CW2 . . . . 37 A5
Casey The ST13 . . . . 48 A1
Cash La ST21 . . . . 132 C4
Caslon Cres DY8 . . . . . . 279 D4
Caspian Gr ST4 . . . . 88 B7
Caspian Way ST19 . . . . . 205 C6
Cassandra Cl DY5 . . . . . 271 C1
Castel Cl ST5 . . . . 70 E3
Castle Acre ST17 . . . . . . 174 B7
Castle Bank ST16,ST17 . . 174 A8
Castle Barns DY10 . . . . . 280 B3
Castlechurch Prim Sch
 ST17 . . . . 174 B8
 Tamworth B77 . . . . 250 E4
Castlecroft Gdns WV3 . . 265 C8
Castlecroft Ho WV3 . . . . 265 A8
Castlecroft La WV6 . . . . . 254 F1
Castlecroft WS11 . . . . . . 227 E5
Castlecroft Prim Sch
 WV3 . . . . 265 B8
Castlecroft Rd WV3 . . . . 265 B8
Castle Ct Stone ST15 . . . 120 C6
 Tutbury DE13 . . . . 146 C7
Castledene Dr ST16 . . . . 155 C1
Castledine Gr ST3 . . . . . . 73 E4
Castle Dyke 6 ST13 . . . . 231 B7
Castlefields ST16 . . . . . . 285 A2
Castlefield ST4 . . . . 57 A2
Castlefort Jun Mix Inf Sch
 WS9 . . . . 245 B3
Castlefort Rd WS9 . . . . . 245 A3
Castle Gr ST2 . . . . 58 B5
Castlehall B77 . . . . 251 A2
Castle Hayes La DE13 . . 146 A5
Castle Hill Rd ST10 . . . . . 78 E1
Castle Hill Rd ST5 . . . . . 283 A3
Castle Hill Stafford ST16 . 285 A3
 Tutbury DE13 . . . . 146 B7
Castle Ho ST7 . . . . 26 C3
Castle House Dr ST17 . . . 155 B1
Castle House St TF10 . . . 168 F4
Castle Inn Rd CW12 . . . . . 16 C7
Castle Keep Ct ST5 . . . . 283 A2
Castle Keep Mews ST5 . . 283 A2
Castle La CW3 . . . . 68 F5
Castle Mount ST5 . . . . . . 55 E6
Castle Park Inf Sch DE13 166 B8
Castle Park Rd DE13 . . . 166 B8
Castle Prim Sch ST7 . . . . 26 D6
Castle Rd Brownhills WS9 . 245 A3
 Cookley DY10 . . . . 280 A4
 Mow Cop ST7 . . . . 26 D7
 Swadlincote DE11 . . . . . 186 F1
 Tamworth B77 . . . . 261 F5
Castle Ridge ST5 . . . . 70 F8
Castle Ring Fort ★ WS15 211 E6
Castle St Brownhills WS8 . 228 F2
 Eccleshall ST21 . . . . . . 133 D4
 Kinver DY7 . . . . 278 A4
 Newcastle-u-L,Chesterton
 ST5 . . . . 55 E7
 Newcastle-u-L ST5 . . . . . 283 C3
 Sedgley DY3 . . . . 271 D8
 Stafford ST16 . . . . 285 A3
 Tutbury DE13 . . . . 146 C6
Castleton Rd
 Stoke-on-T ST4 . . . . 89 E8
 Walsall WS3 . . . . 243 C3
Castle View Biddulph ST8 . 27 C6
 Derrington ST18 . . . . . . 154 E2
Castle View Est ST18 . . . 154 E1
Castleview Gr ST6 . . . . . . 41 F7
Castle View DE65 . . . . . . 146 C8
Castleview Rd ST7 . . . . . . 26 B3
Castle View Stafford ST16 285 A3
 Tamworth B77 . . . . 250 C3
Castle Way ST16 . . . . . . 155 C2
Castle Way The DE65 . . . 148 F5
Castle Wlk ST5 . . . . 283 B3
Castrum Ct ST14 . . . . 96 A3
Caswell Rd DY3 . . . . 271 C8
Catalina Pl ST3 . . . . 90 C6
Cat And Kittens La
 WV10 . . . . 240 E6
Caterbanck Way 2
 WS3 . . . . 230 F6
Caterham Dr DY6 . . . . . . 275 F3
Caterham Pl ST3 . . . . 90 B6
Catesby Dr DY6 . . . . 275 D8
Catharine Rd ST6 . . . . . . 42 C6
Cathcart Rd DY8 . . . . 279 E5
Cathedral Ct 4 WS13 . . . 231 B8
Cathedral Rise WS13 . . . 231 A8
Catherine Ho 1 ST4 . . . . 71 F8
Catherine St ST5 . . . . 56 D4
Catholic La DY3 . . . . 271 D7
Catholme La DE13 . . . . . 201 F5
Catisfield Cres WV8 . . . . 239 F1
Catkin Wlk WS15 . . . . . . 178 C2
Catmeadow La WS15 . . . 197 D1
Caton Cres ST6 . . . . 42 F1
Catsbridge La WS11 . . . . 225 E2
Catshill Rd WS8 . . . . 245 A7
Cauldon Ave
 Cheddleton ST13 . . . . . . 45 D5
 Newcastle-u-L ST5 . . . . . 56 A7
Cauldon Cl ST13 . . . . 30 F4
Cauldon Ct ST4 . . . . 57 B1
Cauldon Pl ST4 . . . . 57 B1
Cauldon Rd ST4 . . . . 57 C1
Caulton St ST6 . . . . 41 F1
Caunsall Rd DY11 . . . . . . 280 B6
Causeley Gdns ST2 . . . . . 58 B3

Causeley Rd ST2 . . . . 58 B3
Causeway Pl ST13 . . . . . . 33 F6
Cavalier Circus WV10 . . . 240 E4
Cavan's Cl WS11 . . . . . . 209 E4
Cavans Wood Park Home Est
 WS12 . . . . 209 D5
Cavell Ct ST11 . . . . 90 D3
Cavell Rd WS7 . . . . 229 E8
Cavendish Cl DY6 . . . . . . 275 D4
Cavendish Dr DY9 . . . . . 281 F4
Cavendish Gr ST5 . . . . . . 71 B3
Cavendish Rd ST10 . . . . . 92 E5
Cavendish St ST1 . . . . . . 57 A3
Cavendish B79 . . . . 249 E7
Cavendish Way WS9 . . . 256 B5
Caverswall La ST3 . . . . . . 90 C8
Caverswall Old Rd ST11 . . 90 F8
Caverswall Rd
 Blythe Bridge ST11 . . . . 90 F8
 Dilhorne ST11 . . . . 75 B3
 Meir ST3 . . . . 74 C4
Caverswall Road Sta ★
 ST11 . . . . 74 F1
Cavour St ST1 . . . . 56 F3
Cawdry Bldgs 2 ST13 . . . 30 F6
Caxton Ct
 4 Cannock WS11 . . . . . 226 E8
 Burton u T DE14 . . . . . . 166 D1
Caxton St WS11 . . . . 226 E8
Cayley Pl ST3 . . . . 90 C6
Cecil Ave ST1 . . . . 282 A4
Cecilly St ST10 . . . . 76 E4
Cecilly Terr ST10 . . . . 76 E4
Cecil Payton Cl WS15 . . . 160 F6
Cecil Rd Biddulph ST8 . . . 16 C2
 Swadlincote DE11 . . . . . 186 F5
Cecil St Cannock WS11 . . 209 E4
 Stourbridge DY8 . . . . . . 279 F5
Cedar Ave
 Blythe Bridge ST11 . . . . 91 A6
 Brownhills WS8 . . . . 245 A8
 Kidsgrove ST7 . . . . 25 D1
Cedar Cl Burntwood WS7 . 229 A6
 Cannock WS12 . . . . 195 A1
 Cheadle ST10 . . . . 76 F2
 Lichfield WS14 . . . . 231 F7
 Market Drayton TF9 . . . . 97 A1
 Stourbridge DY8 . . . . . . 279 D2
 Uttoxeter ST14 . . . . 110 F1
Cedar Cres Audley ST7 . . . 39 F1
 Endon ST9 . . . . 43 E6
 Rugeley WS15 . . . . 197 A5
Cedar Ct Congleton CW12 . 15 F8
 Tamworth B77 . . . . 261 E6
Cedar Dr Albrighton WV7 . 237 A5
 Aldridge B74 . . . . 256 E1
 Stramshall ST14 . . . . . . 110 F4
 Tamworth B79 . . . . 250 A8
Cedar Gdns DY7 . . . . 277 F6
Cedar Gr Biddulph ST8 . . . 17 B1
 Codsall WV8 . . . . 239 B3
 Great Wyrley WS6 . . . . . 227 B4
 Stoke-on-T ST3 . . . . 72 E3
 Wolverhampton WV3 . . . 265 F7
Cedarhill ST10 . . . . 78 D1
Cedarhill Dr WS11 . . . . . 209 F3
Cedar Ho B74 . . . . 257 F5
Cedar Park Rd WV12 . . . 242 C1
Cedar Pk ST15 . . . . 120 B8
Cedar Rd
 Barton-u-N DE13 . . . . . 183 D1
 Burntwood WS7 . . . . 229 A7
 Newcastle-u-L ST5 . . . . . 40 D1
Cedars Ave
 Kingswinford DY6 . . . . . 275 D4
 Wombourne WV5 . . . . . 270 A5
Cedars Bsns Ctr The
 WS11 . . . . 226 C7
Cedars Dr ST15 . . . . 120 B5
Cedars Hort Unit The
 WV3 . . . . 255 D2
Cedars The
 5 Wolverhampton,Newbridge
 WV6 . . . . 255 F3
 Wolverhampton,Tettenhall
 WV6 . . . . 255 D5
Cedartree Gr ST1 . . . . . . 57 E8
Cedar Way ST17 . . . . . . 175 F6
Cedarwood Cl WV9 . . . . 224 B3
Cedar Wood Rd DY3 . . . . 271 D5
Celandine Cl
 Burton u T DE15 . . . . . . 167 C2
 Kingswinford DY6 . . . . . 275 C4
 Stoke-on-T ST3 . . . . 43 B1
Celandines The WV5 . . . 269 E6
Celandine
 Sutton Coldfield B74 . . . 257 F5
 Tamworth B77 . . . . 250 C3
Celebration Ct ST6 . . . . . 42 C3
Cellarhead Rd ST9 . . . . . . 59 E4
Celtic Ave ST4 . . . . 41 F8
Celtic Rd WS11 . . . . 209 C3
Cemetery Ave ST3 . . . . . 284 B2
Cemetery Rd
 Cannock WS11 . . . . 209 E4
 Hanley ST4 . . . . 57 B1
 Market Drayton TF9 . . . . 97 B3
 Newcastle-u-L,Knutton ST5 55 E3
 Newcastle-u-L,Silverdale
 ST5 . . . . 55 D1
 Weston CW2 . . . . 37 B5
Cemetery St WS6 . . . . . . 226 C2
Cemetery View
 Longton ST3 . . . . 284 B2
 Newcastle-u-L ST5 . . . . . 55 E3
Cemetery Way WS3 . . . . 243 B1
Cemlyn Ave ST3 . . . . 72 E3

Central Ave
 15 Wolverhampton WV4 . 266 F4
 Bucknall ST2 . . . . 58 B4
 Cannock WS11 . . . . 209 F5
 Coldmeece ST15 . . . . . . 118 B8
Central Ave S ST15 . . . . . 118 B7
Central Cl WS3 . . . . 243 A1
Central Dr
 Dudley,Gornalwood DY3 . 271 D2
 Stoke-on-T ST3 . . . . 72 E3
 Walsall WS3 . . . . 243 A1
Central Sq ST10 . . . . 49 A1
Central St ST7 . . . . 26 B6
Central Trad Est WV2 . . . 266 F8
Central Way DE13 . . . . . . 166 B7
Centre Rd ST15 . . . . 104 E2
Centrum East Ret Pk
 DE14 . . . . 184 F8
Centurion Pk B77 . . . . . . 262 B6
Centurion Way B77 . . . . . 262 B6
Century Rd ST5 . . . . 40 F2
Century St ST1 . . . . 282 A3
Ceramica ★ ST6 . . . . 56 F8
Chadsfield Rd WS15 . . . . 178 E2
Chadsmead Prim Sch
 WS13 . . . . 214 A1
Chadsmoor CE Jun Sch
 WS11 . . . . 210 A3
Chadsmoor Inf Sch
 WS11 . . . . 210 A4
Chadsfield Hts WS13 . . . 214 D2
Chadwell Gdns WV8 . . . . 238 F4
Chadwell Way ST2 . . . . . . 58 D1
Chadwick Cl WV4 . . . . . . 265 D6
Chadwick Cres WS15 . . . 198 A8
Chadwick Cl 4 WS15 . . . 196 F8
Chadwick St ST3 . . . . . . 284 C3
Chadwyn Dr ST2 . . . . 43 B2
Chaffinch Cl
 Cannock WS12 . . . . 210 B4
 Sedgley DY3 . . . . 266 C3
Chaffinch Dr Biddulph ST8 . 27 E8
 Uttoxeter ST14 . . . . 126 C6
Chaff La DE6 . . . . 65 D1
Chain La ST17 . . . . 174 E4
Chain St ST6 . . . . 42 C2
Chalcot Dr WS12 . . . . . . 210 A7
Chaldon Cl WV9 . . . . 240 A1
Chalfield B79 . . . . 249 D6
Chalfont Ave WS11 . . . . . 226 C7
Chalfont Cres CW2 . . . . . 37 B2
Chalfont Ct WS11 . . . . . . 226 C7
Chalfont Gn ST2 . . . . 58 B2
Challenge Cl ST6 . . . . 42 C3
Challinor Ave ST4 . . . . . . 72 A6
Chamberlain Cl DE13 . . . 199 D6
Chamberlain Ct CW3 . . . . 53 A6
Chamberlain's La WS4 . . 265 C3
Chamberlain St ST1 . . . . 282 B2
Chamberlain Way ST8 . . . 27 E8
Chambley Gn WV9 . . . . . 224 B2
Chance Hall La ST7 . . . . . 25 B8
Chancel Dr TF9 . . . . 97 A1
Chancel Ind Est DY6 . . . . 270 E1
Chancel Inf Sch WS15 . . . 178 E2
Chancery Dr WS12 . . . . . 210 C7
Chancery La ST3 . . . . . . 284 C3
Chandler Ave DY7 . . . . . . 277 F5
Chandler Dr WV4 . . . . . . 265 D3
Chandlers Cl WV9 . . . . . . 240 A1
Chandlers Dr B77 . . . . . . 251 B5
Chandlers Keep WS8 . . . 245 A6
Chanterelle Ct WV4 . . . . 266 B4
Chanterelle Gdns WV4 . . 266 B4
Chantry Rd
 Newcastle-u-L ST5 . . . . . 283 B1
 Stourbridge DY7 . . . . . . 279 C7
Chapel Ave WS8 . . . . 228 E2
Chapel Bank
 Kidsgrove ST7 . . . . 26 D6
 Wheaton Aston ST19 . . . 205 C6
Chapel Cl
 Mount Pleasant ST7 . . . . 26 B6
 Wombourne WV5 . . . . . 269 F5
Chapel Ct Barlaston ST12 . 88 C1
 Gnosall ST20 . . . . 171 C6
 Kidderminster DY10 . . . . 280 A1
 Newcastle-u-L ST5 . . . . . 55 C2
Chapel Dr Brownhills WS8 228 E2
 Mile Oak B78 . . . . 249 C1
Chapel Gn DE6 . . . . 127 C8
Chapel Hill DY10 . . . . . . 280 A1
Chapel La Anslow DE13 . . 165 A5
 Ashley TF9 . . . . 100 B6
 Audley ST7 . . . . 39 D2
 Biddulph ST8 . . . . 17 A1
 Bradley ST18 . . . . 191 B8
 Brown Edge ST6 . . . . . . 28 B1
 Burslem ST6 . . . . 57 A8
 Cannock Wood WS15 . . . 211 E5
 Cheadle ST10 . . . . 77 D2
 Clifton DE6 . . . . 81 F6
 Codsall WV8 . . . . 238 F3
 Gentleshaw WS15 . . . . . 212 A4
 Gratton ST9 . . . . 29 A5
 Hanbury DE13 . . . . 144 F2
 Harriseahead ST7 . . . . . 26 E4
 Kingsley Holt ST10 . . . . 62 A1
 Knighton TF9 . . . . 83 C5
 Lichfield WS14 . . . . 231 B6
 Loggerheads TF9 . . . . . . 99 E3
 Newborough DE13 . . . . 162 F7
 Norton in H TF9 . . . . 82 C2
 Rangemore DE13 . . . . . 164 C3
 Rolleston on D DE13 . . . 147 B4
 Smestow DY3 . . . . 269 C4
 Whittington WS14 . . . . . 232 E5

Chapel Mews B77 . . . . . . 251 A5
Chapel Mus Mow Cop★
ST7 . . . . 26 D7
Chapelon B77 . . . . 251 A4
Chapel Rd WS15 . . . . 197 F5
Chapelside WS15 . . . . . . 178 D2
Chapel Sq WS6 . . . . 226 D3
Chapel St Audley ST7 . . . . 39 E4
Brownhills WS8 . . . . 228 E2
Bucknall ST2 . . . . 58 B4
Burntwood WS7 . . . . . . 228 E6
Cannock WS12 . . . . 210 C1
Cheadle ST10 . . . . 76 D3
Forsbrook ST11 . . . . 91 A8
Kidsgrove ST7 . . . . 25 D2
Kingsley ST10 . . . . 61 D3
Kingswinford DY6 . . . . . 275 B6
Longnor SK17 . . . . 13 B6
Mount Pleasant ST7 . . . . 26 B6
Newcastle-u-L,Knutton ST5. 55 E4
Newcastle-u-L,May Bank
ST5. . . . . 56 D4
Newcastle-u-L,Silverdale
ST5. . . . . 55 C2
Norton Canes WS11 . . . . 227 D5
Stafford ST16 . . . . 285 B3
Stourbridge,Wordsley DY8 275 D3
Swadlincote DE11 . . . . . 186 F6
Walsall WS3 . . . . 244 A4
Wolverhampton WV2 . . . 266 D7
Wombourne WV5. . . . . . 269 F5
Chapel Terr ST16 . . . . . . 285 B4
Chapel Wlk DY3 . . . . 271 C2
Chaplain Rd WS12 . . . . . 210 E2
Chaplin Rd ST3. . . . . 284 C1
Chapter Wlk ST2. . . . . . . 58 A5
Charlecote Dr DY1 . . . . . 271 E4
Charlemonte CI WS12 . . . 210 D3
Charles Ave
Essington WV11 . . . . . . 241 F4
Kidderminster DY10 . . . . 280 A1
Wolverhampton WV4 . . . 266 B5
Charles CI WS6 . . . . 226 D1
Charles Cotton Dr CW3. . . 68 D6
Charles Cotton St ST16. . . 155 C6
Charles Cres WS3. . . . . . 244 A5
Charlesdale Dr WS9. . . . . 256 B4
Charles Hayward Bglws
WV4 . . . . 266 D3
Charles Rd DY8 . . . . 279 E4
Charles St Biddulph ST8 . . 27 D6
Cheadle ST10. . . . . 76 D3
Hanley ST1. . . . . 282 C2
Newcastle-u-L ST5. . . . . . 56 D3
Charlestown Gr ST3. . . . . 90 A7
Charlesway TF9. . . . . 112 B8
Charles Wesley Ct WV3 . . 266 A4
Charlock Gr WS11 . . . . . . 210 C3
Charlotte CI ST18 . . . . . . 177 D8
Charlotte Ct DE14 . . . . . . 185 C8
Charlotte St ST6 . . . . 41 C7
Charlton St ST4. . . . . 72 E4
Charminster Rd ST3. . . . . 90 B7
Charmouth CI ST1 . . . . . . 58 A6
Charnes Rd TF9 . . . . 100 C5
Charnley Dr B75 . . . . 258 E2
Charnley Rd ST16 . . . . . . 155 F6
Charnock PI ST3. . . . . 42 A7
Charnsford La TF9 . . . . . . 100 B4
Charnwood ⑪ ST7 . . . . . . 26 B1
Charnwood Ave DY3 . . . . 266 D2
Charnwood CI
Cannock WS12 . . . . 210 C3
Leek ST13 . . . . 30 C4
Lichfield WS13 . . . . 214 C1
Rugeley WS15 . . . . 178 C1
Charnwood Ho WS13 . . . . 214 B2
Charnwood Prim Sch
WS13 . . . . 214 C2
Charnwood Rd
Burton u T DE13. . . . . . 166 B7
Longton ST3. . . . . 73 F1
Charolais Cres ST3. . . . . . 89 D8
Charsley PI ST3. . . . . 72 F1
Charter CI WS11 . . . . 227 E4
Charter Ct TF9 . . . . 97 C3
Charterfield Dr
Cannock WS12 . . . . 210 C1
Kingswinford DY6 . . . . . 275 D8
Charterfields Sh Ctr
DY6 . . . . 275 D8
Charterhouse Dr ST17. . . 156 E1
Charter Rd ST5 . . . . 56 A3
Charters Ave B29. . . . . . . 239 B1
Charters The WS13 . . . . . 214 B1
Chartley CI
Blythe Bridge ST11 . . . . 90 E6
Perton WV6 . . . . 254 F4
Stafford ST16 . . . . 155 C8
Chartley Cotts ST18 . . . . 139 D5
Chartley Ct ST7 . . . . 126 C7
Chartley Gate CI ST14 . . . 126 A6
Chartway The WS3 . . . . . 244 B4
Chartwell CI ST9. . . . . . . 59 A3
Chartwell Dr
Sutton Coldfield B74 . . . 257 D4
Wolverhampton WV10. . . 240 E1
Wombourne WV5. . . . . . 269 F5
Chartwell Rd ST17 . . . . . 175 C8
Chartwell St DY7 . . . . . . 249 D2
Chartwood TF9 . . . . 99 E5
Chase Acad WS11 . . . . . . 226 E8
Chase Ave WS6. . . . . 226 E3
Chase Cres ST17. . . . . . . 176 A3
Chaselands ST7 . . . . 228 D7
Chase La ST15 . . . . 103 F6
Chase L Ctr WS11 . . . . . . 209 D2
Chaseley Ave WS11 . . . . . 209 C2

Chaseley CI WS15 . . . . . . 178 B1
Chaseley Croft WS11. . . . 209 C2
Chaseley Gdns
Burntwood WS7 . . . . . . 229 C7
Rugeley WS15 . . . . 178 B1
Chaseley Rd WS15 . . . . . 178 B1
Chase Park Ind Est WS7 . . 228 D7
Chasepool Rd DY3 . . . . . . 274 C8
Chase Rd Brocton ST17. . . 176 D2
Brownhills WS8 . . . . 229 A1
Burntwood WS7 . . . . . . 229 B6
Dudley DY3,DY5. . . . . . . 271 C1
Chaseside Dr WS11 . . . . . 210 B3
Chaseside Ind Est WS11. . 210 B3
Chase Side Rd WS15 . . . . 196 D8
Chase Terrace Prim Sch
WS7 . . . . 228 F7
Chase Terrace Tech Coll
WS7 . . . . 229 A7
Chasetown Com Sch
WS7 . . . . 228 E5
Chasetown Ind Est WS7. . 228 E4
Chasetown Specialist Sports
Coll WS7 . . . . 228 E4
Chasetown Sta★ WS7. . . 228 D5
Chase Vale WS7 . . . . 228 E6
Chase View WS7 . . . . 198 A4
Chase View Com Prim Sch
WS7. . . . . 196 E7
Chase View La ST18 . . . . 174 C3
Chaseview Rd DE13 . . . . . 200 F2
Chase View WV4. . . . . . . 266 E2
Chasewood Gr ST10 . . . . . 76 F4
Chasewater Country Pk★
WS7 . . . . 228 C5
Chasewater Heaths Sta★
WS7 . . . . 227 F5
Chasewater Rly★ WS11. . 228 B5
Chasewater Way WS11 . . 210 E1
Chase Wlk Cannock WS12. 209 C4
Stoke-on-T ST3 . . . . 89 F7
Chasewood Park Bsns Ctr
WS12 . . . . 210 E1
Chatcull La ST21. . . . . . . 101 F1
Chatfield CI DE15 . . . . . . 167 C1
Chatfield PI ST3 . . . . 73 D2
Chatham St ST1 . . . . 282 A1
Chatsworth Dr
Cannock WS11 . . . . 210 A4
Ford Green ST6 . . . . 42 F5
Tutbury DE13 . . . . 146 C6
Werrington ST9 . . . . 59 B3
Chatsworth Gdns WV6 . . 255 A7
Chatsworth Ho DE14 . . . . 184 F7
Chatsworth Mews ST21 . . 133 E7
Chatsworth Park Ave ST4 72 A1
Chatsworth PI Longton ST3 73 F1
Newcastle-u-L ST5. . . . . . 55 F7
Chatsworth B79 . . . . 249 C7
Chatteris CI ST3 . . . . 90 B6
Chatterley Ave WS13 . . . 230 F6
Chatterley Dr ST7. . . . . . 41 B8
Chatterley Rd ST6 . . . . . . 41 C4
Chatterley St ST1. . . . . . 41 F2
Chatterton Ave WS13 . . . 230 F6
Chatterton PI ST3. . . . . . 73 D3
Chatwell La Blymhill TF10 188 D1
Great Chatwell TF10,TF11. 203 B7
Chaucer Ave DY3 . . . . . . 271 A5
Chaucer CI
Burton u T DE14. . . . . . 166 D6
Lichfield WS14 . . . . 231 B6
Tamworth B79 . . . . 250 A6
Chaucer Dr WS7 . . . . 212 A1
Chaucer Rd ST17 . . . . . . 174 C8
Chaulden Rd ST16 . . . . . . 136 D1
Chawner CI WS7. . . . . . . 211 E1
Cheadle CI ST19 . . . . 207 F7
Cheadle High Sch ST10 . . 76 D2
Cheadle Hospl ST10. . . . . 76 D3
Cheadle Prim Sch ST10 . . 76 D2
Cheadle Rd Alton ST10 . . . 78 E1
Blythe Bridge ST11 . . . . 91 A7
Cheddleton ST13 . . . . . . 45 C3
Draycott i t M ST11. . . . . 91 F6
Kingsley ST10 . . . . 61 D2
Leek ST13 . . . . 45 E8
Upper Tean ST10 . . . . . . 92 D5
Uttoxeter ST14 . . . . 111 B1
Warslow SK17 . . . . 23 B2
Wetley Rocks ST9 . . . . . . 60 B7
Cheadle Sh Ctr ST10 . . . . 76 D3
Cheam Gdns WV6 . . . . . . 255 E8
Cheapside Hanley ST1 . . . 282 B2
Newcastle-u-L ST5. . . . . . 283 B3
Cheatle Ct B77 . . . . 261 D5
Chebsey CI ST2 . . . . 58 C4
Chebsey Dr ST16 . . . . . . 155 A6
Checkley Dr ST8 . . . . 16 D1
Checkley Gr ⑥ ST3 . . . . . 73 D4
Checkley La CW5 . . . . 52 E1
Checkley Rd ST5 . . . . 40 C1
Checkley Row CW5 . . . . . 67 C8
Cheddar Dr ST5. . . . . 54 F2
Cheddleton Flint Mill Mus★
ST13 . . . . 45 C6
Cheddleton Heath Rd
ST13. . . . . 45 E7
Cheddleton Park Ave
ST13. . . . . 45 D5
Cheddleton Rd ST13 . . . . 30 F4
Cheddleton Sta ST13. . . . 45 E5
Cheedale CI DE15 . . . . . . 167 B5
Cheddleton CI ST19 . . . . . 193 A1
Chell CI ST19 . . . . 207 F7
Chell Green Ave ST6. . . . . 42 A6
Chell Green Ct ST6. . . . . . 42 A6

Chell Gr ST5. . . . . 56 A7
Chell Heath Rd
Stoke-on-T ST6 . . . . 42 B5
Stoke-on-T ST6 . . . . 42 C4
Chell Rd ST16. . . . . 285 A3
Chell St ST1. . . . . 57 D6
Chelmarsh Ave WV3 . . . . 265 B8
Chelmorton Dr ST3 . . . . . 73 E1
Chelmsford Dr ST2. . . . . . 58 D1
Chelmsford Rd ST5. . . . . . 56 C5
Chelsea CI ST8 . . . . 16 C1
Chelsea Dr B74 . . . . 257 F4
Chelsea Way
Kingswinford DY6 . . . . . 275 C6
Stafford ST17 . . . . 155 C1
Chelson St ST3 . . . . 284 C3
Chelston Dr WV6 . . . . . . 255 E4
Cheltenham Ave ST10 . . . 76 E5
Cheltenham Dr
Kingswinford DY6 . . . . . 275 B6
Stafford ST17 . . . . 175 C7
Cheltenham Gr
Birches Head ST1 . . . . . 57 F5
Newcastle-u-L ST5. . . . . . 54 F2
Chelwood CI ST1 . . . . 282 A4
Chemical La ST6 . . . . 41 C1
Chenet Way WS11 . . . . . . 209 E2
Chepstow CI Biddulph ST8 . 16 C1
Perton WV6. . . . . 254 F4
Chepstow Dr ST17 . . . . . . 175 C7
Chepstow PI ST3. . . . . . . 73 C6
Chepstow Rd
Walsall WS3 . . . . 242 F1
Wolverhampton WV10. . . 240 D5
Chepstow Way WS3 . . . . 242 F1
Chequerfield Dr WV4 . . . 266 A6
Chequers Ave WV5. . . . . 265 A1
Chequers CI WS11 . . . . . . 228 A5
Chequers The ③ WS13 . . 231 C8
Chequer St WV3 . . . . 266 A6
Cheriton Gn ST2 . . . . 58 D1
Cheriton Gr WV6. . . . . . . 254 E3
Cherrington Dr WS6 . . . . 226 F4
Cherrington Gdns WV6 . . 255 B2
Cherry Bank ST6 . . . . 210 C6
Cherrybrook Dr ST19 . . . . 193 A1
Cherry CI Burntwood WS7. 228 F6
Fulford ST11 . . . . 106 E8
Newcastle-u-L ST5. . . . . . 40 D1
Cherry Ct DE14 . . . . 184 F8
Cherrydale Ct DY1. . . . . . 271 F2
Cherry Gn DY1. . . . . 271 F2
Cherry Gr Stoke-on-T ST3 . 72 E3
Stourbridge DY8 . . . . . . 279 E4
Cherry Hill Ave ST3 . . . . 74 A2
Cherry Hill La ST5 . . . . . . 55 E2
Cherry Hill CW3 . . . . 68 E6
Cherry La Cheadle ST10 . . 77 A5
Congleton CW12 . . . . . . 16 E8
Great Bridgeford ST18 . . 135 C3
Gayton ST18 . . . . 138 E5
Himley DY3 . . . . 270 C3
Cherry Leys DE15 . . . . . . 167 C4
Cherryl Ho B74 . . . . 257 E3
Cherry Orch
Lichfield WS14 . . . . 231 C7
Newcastle-u-L ST5. . . . . . 283 B3
Stone ST15 . . . . 120 C7
Cherry St Stourbridge DY8 279 E4
Tamworth B79 . . . . 250 B5
Cherry Tree Ave ST7 . . . . 25 A5
Cherry Tree CI
Eccleshall ST21 . . . . 133 E7
Stoke-on-T ST4 . . . . 88 A7
Stone ST15 . . . . 119 F5
Swadlincote DE11 . . . . . 186 F6
Cherrytree Cres ST18 . . . 135 B3
Cherry Tree Gdns WV8 . . 239 B3
Cherry Tree Ho WS15 . . . 196 E6
Cherry Tree La
Biddulph ST8 . . . . 17 B1
Codsall WV8 . . . . 239 B3
Woore CW3 . . . . 67 C2
Cherry Tree Rd ST7 . . . . . 39 F1
Cherrytree Rd DE15 . . . . . 185 F6
Cherry Tree Rd
Huntington WS12. . . . . . 209 D8
Kingswinford DY6 . . . . . 275 E8
Newcastle-u-L ST5. . . . . . 40 E1
Norton Canes WS11 . . . . 228 B5
Rugeley WS15 . . . . 196 F6
Cherry Trees Sch WV5 . . . 269 F6
Cherry Tree Wlk B79 . . . . 250 A8
Cherry Way TF9 . . . . 97 C2
Cherrywood CI ① ST17. . . 175 C6
Cherrywood Gr ST3 . . . . . 89 F6
Cherrywood Rd B74 . . . . . 256 D1
Cherrywood Way B74 . . . 257 D4
Chertsey PI ST7 . . . . 57 D4
Chervil CI ST3 . . . . 90 A6
Cherwell Dr WS8 . . . . . . 228 C2
Cherwell B77 . . . . 250 D1
Chesham Gr ST3 . . . . 90 A6
Chesham Rd ST16 . . . . . . 155 F6
Cheshire CI
Burntwood WS7. . . . . . . 229 F8
Stourbridge DY8 . . . . . . 279 D8
Cheshire Dr ST19 . . . . . . 223 D6
Cheshire Gdns TF9 . . . . . 97 C2
Cheshire Gr WV6 . . . . . . 254 E4
Cheshire St TF9. . . . . 97 C2
Cheslyn Dr WS6 . . . . 226 D2
Cheslyn Hay High Sch
WS6. . . . . 226 C3
Cheslyn Hay Prim Sch
WS6. . . . . 226 C3
Chessington Cres ST4. . . . 88 C7
Chestall Rd WS15 . . . . . . 211 F5

Chester Ave WV6 . . . . . . 255 F7
Chester CI Cannock WS11. 210 B1
Lichfield WS13 . . . . 214 C3
Talke ST7 . . . . 40 E7
Chester Cres ST5 . . . . . . 71 B5
Chester Ct WS9 . . . . 244 F4
Chesterfield Ave DE11. . . 186 E6
Chesterfield Ct WS9 . . . . 244 F4
Chesterfield Rd WS14 . . . 231 A5
Chester Rd Aldridge B74. . 256 E4
Audley ST7. . . . . 39 D2
Eccleshall ST21 . . . . 133 C7
Enville DY7 . . . . 273 F2
Kinver DY7 . . . . 277 F7
Rugeley WS15 . . . . 196 D6
Stonnall WS9 . . . . 245 D3
Talke ST7 . . . . 40 D7
Weston-Under-Lizard TF11 203 B4
Whittington WS14 . . . . . 232 C3
Chester Road N WS8 . . . . 228 D1
Chesterton Com High Sch
ST5. . . . . 55 F7
Chesterton Prim Sch ST5 . 55 F7
Chesterton Rd
Burton u T DE14. . . . . . 166 D7
Pattingham WV6 . . . . . . 253 A2
Chesterton Stadium ST5 . 55 D5
Chesterton Way
Gorstyhill CW2. . . . . . . 37 E3
Tamworth B79 . . . . 250 A7
Chester Wood WV6 . . . . . 256 F2
Chesterwood Rd ST6. . . . 42 B3
Chestnut Ave B79 . . . . . . 250 B7
Chestnut CI Aldridge B74 . 257 A3
Armitage WS15 . . . . 198 C3
Cannock WS11 . . . . 210 C2
Codsall WV8 . . . . 238 F2
Derrington ST18 . . . . . . 154 E2
Gnosall ST20 . . . . 171 D7
Stourbridge DY8 . . . . . . 279 D3
Upper Tean ST10 . . . . . . 92 F3
Chestnut Cres ST11 . . . . . 91 A6
Chestnut Ct
① Stone ST15 . . . . 104 F2
Burntwood WS7. . . . . . . 228 F4
Cotes Heath ST21 . . . . . 102 D2
Rugeley WS15 . . . . 196 E8
Chestnut Dr
Cheslyn Hay WS6. . . . . . 226 D3
Great Wyrley WS6 . . . . . 226 F3
Hagley DY9 . . . . 281 F4
Shenstone WS14 . . . . . . 246 F5
Stafford ST17 . . . . 174 E5
Wombourne WV5. . . . . . 270 A5
Yarnfield ST15 . . . . 118 E6
Chestnut Gr
Kingswinford DY6 . . . . . 275 F6
Kinver DY7 . . . . 277 F5
Newcastle-u-L ST5. . . . . . 40 E1
Penkridge ST19 . . . . 207 E8
Stone ST15 . . . . 104 F2
Tamworth B77 . . . . 250 C3
Chestnut La B79 . . . . 218 F2
Chestnut Rd
Brown Edge ST6 . . . . . . 43 C7
Burton u T DE15. . . . . . 185 F7
Loggerheads TF9 . . . . . . 99 E5
Market Drayton TF9 . . . . 112 A8
Chestnut Way WV3 . . . . . 265 B8
Cheswardine Prim Sch
TF9 . . . . 130 A8
Cheswardine Rd ST5. . . . 56 B8
Cheswell CI ST16 . . . . . . 155 B2
Chetney CI ST16 . . . . 155 B2
Chetton Gn WV10 . . . . . . 240 B3
Chetwode CI TF9 . . . . . . 83 C5
Chetwynd Ave
Stoke-on-T ST4 . . . . 42 E5
Werrington ST2 . . . . 59 A3
Chetwynd CI
Penkridge ST19 . . . . 207 F7
Rugeley WS15 . . . . 196 E6
Chetwynd Ctr The ST16. . 285 E2
Chetwynd End TF10 . . . . 168 E3
Chetwynd Gdns WS11 . . . 209 D3
Chetwynd Gr TF10 . . . . . 168 F4
Chetwynd Pk
Cannock WS12. . . . . 211 B5
Chetwynd TF10 . . . . 168 D8
Chetwynd Rd
Chetwynd TF10 . . . . 168 C6
Newcastle-u-L ST5. . . . . . 56 B6
Newport TF10 . . . . 168 E4
Wolverhampton WV2 . . . 266 B6
Chetwynd St
Newcastle-u-L ST5. . . . . . 56 D5
Stoke-on-T ST6 . . . . 42 D1
Chevening CI DY3 . . . . . . 271 E2
Chevin The DE13 . . . . . . 147 C1
Cheviot CI ST5 . . . . 55 E3
Cheviot Dr Rugeley WS15. 178 C3
Stoke-on-T ST6 . . . . 42 C2
Cheviot Rd WV2 . . . . 266 C5
Cheviot Rise WS12 . . . . . 210 C5
Cheviot B77 . . . . 251 C1
Chichester CI WS15 . . . . . 196 D6
Chichester Dr WS12 . . . . 210 C1
Chichester Wlk ST1. . . . . 282 C4
Chieveley CI ST5 . . . . . . 178 C1
Childerplay Rd ST8 . . . . . 27 C3
Chilgrove CI ST1. . . . . . . 57 F5
Chilgrove Gdns WV6 . . . . 255 C5
Chillingham B77 . . . . 261 C7
Chillington CI WS6. . . . . . 226 F1
Chillington Dr
Codsall WV8 . . . . 238 D7
Dudley DY1 . . . . 271 F3

Chillington Hall★ WV8 . . 222 E2
Chillington Ho WV6 . . . . . 255 C5
Chillington La WV8 . . . . . 238 D6
Chillington St
Codsall Wood WV8. . . . . 222 F2
Coven WV9 . . . . 223 A2
Chillington Way ST6 . . . . 42 E1
Chiltern CI
Cheslyn Hay WS6. . . . . . 226 D1
Chorlton CW2 . . . . 37 B1
Dudley DY3 . . . . 271 C3
Chiltern Ct B75 . . . . 258 A4
Chiltern La ST21 . . . . 133 F6
Chiltern PI ST5 . . . . 55 E3
Chiltern Rd
Swadlincote DE11 . . . . . 186 F3
Tamworth B77 . . . . 251 C1
Chilton Ct DE13 . . . . 147 E1
Chilton St ST4 . . . . 72 E5
Chilwell Ave ST18 . . . . . 177 E7
Chilworth Gr ST3 . . . . . . 72 F1
China St ST4. . . . . 72 E5
Chingford CI DY8 . . . . . . 275 C4
Chivelstone Gr ST4 . . . . . 88 C6
Cholerton CI ST4 . . . . . . 72 E5
Chorley Ave ST6 . . . . 42 A6
Chorley Rd WS7 . . . . 212 A2
Chorley St ST13. . . . . 30 E5
Chorlton La CW2. . . . . . . 37 B2
Chorlton Moss ST5. . . . . . 85 D4
Chorlton Rd ST1. . . . . . . 57 D6
Chorlton Terr ST1. . . . . . 111 C1
Christ Church CE Fst Sch
ST15. . . . . 105 A1
Christ Church CE Inf Sch
WV6 . . . . 255 B3
Christ Church CE Jun Sch
WV6 . . . . 255 C4
Christ Church CE Mid Sch
ST15. . . . . 105 A2
Christ Church CE Prim Sch
Lichfield WS13 . . . . 230 F7
Stoke-on-T ST4 . . . . 72 E6
Christ Church Gdns
WS13 . . . . 230 F7
Christ Church Inf Sch
DE14. . . . . 166 C2
Christchurch La WS13 . . . 230 F7
Christ Church La TF9 . . . . 112 A7
Christchurch St ST4. . . . . 72 E5
Christchurch Way ST15 . . 105 A1
Christie Ave ST16 . . . . . . 155 C3
Christie PI ST3. . . . . 73 F5
Christine St ST2 . . . . 58 A3
Christopher Rd WV2 . . . . 266 E8
Christopher Sq ST4. . . . . 72 F5
Christopher Terr ST17. . . 156 A2
Christopher Wlk WS13 . . 214 A3
Chubb Way ST4. . . . . 71 E4
Chubb St DY1 . . . . 261 D7
Chumleigh Gr ST6 . . . . . . 42 A2
Church Ave Grindon ST13. 34 B1
Hatton DE65 . . . . 146 D8
Stoke-on-T ST2 . . . . 43 B2
Church Bank Audley ST7 . 39 D2
Cauldon ST10. . . . . 63 F7
Keele ST5 . . . . 69 F7
Oakamoor ST10. . . . . . . 78 A6
Churchbridge Pk WS11. . . 226 E6
Church CI Biddulph ST8. . . 27 D6
Burton u T DE15. . . . . . 167 B3
Drayton Bassett B78 . . . 260 E5
Dunston ST18 . . . . 192 F8
Gnosall ST20 . . . . 171 E6
Haughton ST18 . . . . 172 E6
Kingstone ST14 . . . . 141 C8
Marchington ST14. . . . . 127 C2
Ranton ST18 . . . . 153 D5
Shenstone WS14 . . . . . . 247 A5
Stafford ST17 . . . . 174 F6
Stone ST15 . . . . 120 B8
Wood End CV9. . . . . 262 C1
Church Cotts
Biddulph Moor ST8 . . . . 17 B1
Coppenhall ST18 . . . . . . 174 B3
Penkridge ST19 . . . . 192 E1
Rangemore DE13. . . . . . 164 C2
Church Cres WV11 . . . . . . 241 F3
Church Croft ST14 . . . . . . 125 C7
Churchcroft Gdns WS15 . . 178 E2
Church Dr B78 . . . . 249 B7
Church Eaton Prim Sch
ST20 . . . . 190 A8
Church Eaton Rd TF10 . . . 188 E6
Church Farm TF9 . . . . . . 100 C4
Church Farm Barn & Cotts
DY10 . . . . 281 B3
Church Farm Mews
DE13 . . . . 199 C2
Church Farm ST14 . . . . . . 110 F4
Church Farm St ST3 . . . . 73 C1
Churchfield CI
Coven WV9 . . . . 224 C2
Stafford ST17 . . . . 156 C1
Churchfield Ct ST10. . . . . 46 F1
Churchfield St ST21 . . . . . 133 D6
Churchfields CE Jun Sch
WS15 . . . . 196 E8
Church Fields Keele ST5 . . 69 F7
Norton in H TF9 . . . . . . 82 C2
Churchfields Prim Sch
ST5 . . . . 55 F6

Churchfields DE13 . . . . .**182** A2
Church Gdns ST3 . . . .**284** C4
Church Gr ST21 . . . .**133** D7
Church Hill
 Cannock WS12 . . . .**210** D4
 Codsall WV8 . . . .**238** F5
Church Hill Dr WV6 . . . . .**255** E5
Church Hill Kinver DY7 . .**278** B2
 Longdon WS15 . . . .**213** A8
Church Hill Rd WV6 . . . . .**255** D5
Church Hill St DE15 . . . . .**167** B3
Church Hill WV4 . . . .**265** E4
Church Hollow B79 . . . . . .**217** C5
Churchill Ave
 Cheddleton ST13 . . . .**45** D5
 Trentham ST4 . . . .**87** F7
Churchill Cl
 Blythe Bridge ST11 . . . .**90** E6
 Uttoxeter ST14 . . . .**126** C7
Churchill Cres DE13 . . . . .**200** F2
Churchill Gdns DY3 . . . . .**271** C7
Churchill La DY10 . . . . . .**281** B3
Churchill Rd Cheadle ST10 . .**76** E4
 Shenstone WS14 . . . .**247** A5
 Stone ST15 . . . .**119** F7
Churchill Way
 Stafford ST17 . . . .**174** E6
 Trentham ST4 . . . .**87** F7
Church La
 Albrighton WV7 . . . .**237** A2
 Armitage WS15 . . . .**197** F5
 Barton-u-N DE13 . . . .**183** D1
 Betley CW3 . . . .**53** C5
 Biddulph ST8 . . . .**17** B1
 Bobbington DY7 . . . .**268** A1
 Bradley ST18 . . . .**173** C1
 Bramshall ST14 . . . .**125** C7
 Cannock WS11 . . . .**208** F1
 Cauldon ST10 . . . .**63** F7
 Checkley ST10 . . . .**109** B8
 Cheslyn Hay WS11 . . . .**225** F8
 Chilcote DE12 . . . .**219** E3
 Codsall WV8 . . . .**238** F4
 Coven WV9 . . . .**224** C2
 Croxton ST21 . . . .**116** A6
 Derrington ST18 . . . .**154** E2
 Draycott in t M ST11 . . . .**91** E5
 Edingale B79 . . . .**217** D5
 Ellastone DE6 . . . .**80** B4
 Endon ST9 . . . .**43** F8
 Fradley WS13 . . . .**215** E8
 Gayton ST18 . . . .**138** D5
 Gnosall TF10 . . . .**188** D8
 Hammerwich WS7 . . . .**229** D3
 Hanbury DE13 . . . .**145** A4
 Hill Ridware WS15 . . . .**198** A7
 Hixon ST18 . . . .**158** C8
 Ipstones ST10 . . . .**46** E1
 King's Bromley DE13 . . . . .**199** C6
 Kingstone ST14 . . . .**141** C7
 Lapley ST19 . . . .**206** A6
 Lawton-gate ST7 . . . .**25** C4
 Leek ST13 . . . .**30** E6
 Marchington ST14 . . . .**127** F2
 Mayfield ST6 . . . .**81** C6
 Middleton B78 . . . .**260** C1
 Mow Cop ST7 . . . .**26** E7
 Newcastle-u-L,Knutton ST5 . .**55** E2
 Newcastle-u-L,Wolstanton
  ST5 . . . .**56** D4
 Newton Solney DE15 . . . . .**167** D8
 Oulton ST15 . . . .**105** C3
 Rocester ST14 . . . .**96** A3
 Rugeley WS15 . . . .**178** B2
 Scholar Green ST7 . . . .**25** C7
 Seisdon WV5 . . . .**264** B2
 Shuttington B79 . . . .**251** E7
 Stafford ST16 . . . .**285** B3
 Standon ST21 . . . .**102** B3
 Stoke-on-T ST4 . . . .**71** F2
 Stonnall WS9 . . . .**245** E4
 Tamworth B79 . . . .**250** B5
 Thorpe DE6 . . . .**51** D1
Church Lawton Prim Sch
 ST7 . . . .**25** A5
Church Mdw Ipstones ST10 **46** F1
 Norton in H TF9 . . . .**82** C2
Church Mews DE65 . . . . .**146** D8
Church Moat Way WS3 . . .**243** B1
Church of the Ascension CE
 Prim Sch DY6 . . . .**275** C8
Church Plantation ST5 . . . .**70** A7
Church Rd Alrewas DE13 . .**200** F3
 Ashley TF9 . . . .**100** C6
 Biddulph ST8 . . . .**27** D6
 Brewood ST19 . . . .**223** C6
 Brown Edge ST6 . . . .**43** B8
 Brownhills WS8 . . . .**244** F7
 Burntwood WS7 . . . .**229** D7
 Burton u T DE14 . . . .**184** C7
 Codsall WV8 . . . .**238** A4
 Egginton DE65 . . . .**148** B4
 Elford B79 . . . .**216** D1
 Hixon ST18 . . . .**139** C1
 Huntington WS11 . . . .**209** A2
 Kinver DY7 . . . .**278** A2
 Norton Canes WS11 . . . . . .**227** C4
 Penkridge ST19 . . . .**192** E1
 Perton WV6 . . . .**254** E4
 Rolleston on D DE13 . . . . .**147** A4
 Shareshill WV10 . . . .**225** D2
 Shenstone WS14 . . . .**246** F5
 Snelston DE6 . . . .**81** C3
 Stoke-on-T ST3 . . . .**88** F8
 Stonnall WS9 . . . .**245** E3

Church Rd continued
 Stourbridge DY8 . . . .**275** E2
 Stretton DE13 . . . .**147** F2
 Swindon DY3 . . . .**269** D2
 Tamworth B77 . . . .**261** C4
 Walsall WS3 . . . .**244** A3
 Wolverhampton,Bradmore
  WV3 . . . .**265** F7
 Wolverhampton,Oxley
  WV10 . . . .**240** C1
 Wolverhampton,Tettenhall Wood
  WV6 . . . .**255** B3
 Wolverhampton,Tettenhall
  WV6 . . . .**255** B7
 Wombourne WV5 . . . .**270** B7
Church Row B78 . . . .**260** B1
Churchside B79 . . . .**217** C2
Churchside Way WS9 . . . .**245** B2
Church Sq ST6 . . . .**56** E8
Church St Alstonefield DE6 . .**35** E3
 Audley,Wereton ST7 . . . .**39** D2
 Audley,Wood Lane ST7 . . . . .**40** A1
 Brownhills WS8 . . . .**244** E6
 Burntwood WS7 . . . .**228** E5
 Cannock,Bridgtown WS11 . .**226** D6
 Cannock,Chadsmoor
  WS11 . . . .**210** A4
 Cannock WS11 . . . .**209** E1
 Cheadle ST10 . . . .**76** B3
 Claverley WV5 . . . .**267** C7
 Clifton Campville B79 . . . . .**218** E2
 Dudley,Gornalwood DY3 . . .**271** D3
 Eccleshall ST21 . . . .**133** D7
 Hartington SK17 . . . .**24** D5
 Kidsgrove,Butt Lane ST7 . . . .**25** D1
 Kidsgrove ST7 . . . .**26** C4
 Kingsley ST10 . . . .**61** E2
 Leek ST13 . . . .**30** E6
 Lichfield WS13,WS14 . . . . .**231** C8
 Longnor SK17 . . . .**13** B6
 Market Drayton TF9 . . . .**97** D1
 Mow Cop ST7 . . . .**26** C6
 Netherseal DE12 . . . .**219** F6
 Newcastle-u-L,Chesterton
  ST5 . . . .**55** E7
 Newcastle-u-L,Silverdale
  ST5 . . . .**55** B2
 Newcastle-u-L ST5 . . . .**283** B3
 Rugeley WS15 . . . .**178** E1
 Stoke-on-T ST4 . . . .**72** B7
 Stone ST15 . . . .**120** B8
 Tamworth B79 . . . .**250** B5
 Tutbury DE13 . . . .**146** C7
 Uttoxeter ST14 . . . .**126** C8
 Whittington WS14 . . . .**232** D5
Church Terr Burslem ST6 . . .**57** B6
 Sutton Coldfield B75 . . . . . .**258** C3
 Warslow SK17 . . . .**23** B2
Church Vale WS11 . . . . . .**227** E4
Church View
 Adbaston ST20 . . . .**131** C4
 Aldridge WS9 . . . .**256** B6
 Brownhills WS9 . . . .**244** F3
 Burton u T DE13 . . . .**166** C1
 Clifton DE6 . . . .**81** F6
 Cotes Heath ST21 . . . .**102** E2
 Dudley DY3 . . . .**271** D3
Church View Gdns DY7 . . .**278** A4
Church View
 Great Haywood ST18 . . . . .**158** B2
 Newcastle-u-L ST5 . . . .**55** E2
 Rugeley WS15 . . . .**197** A5
 Scot Hay ST5 . . . .**54** E4
 Tamworth B77 . . . .**261** F7
Churchward Dr DE13 . . . . .**147** F1
Churchward Gr WV5 . . . . .**270** A4
Church Way
 Longdon WS15 . . . .**198** A1
 Walsall WS4 . . . .**244** C2
Churchwell Ct WV5 . . . . . .**270** A6
Church Wlk Edingale B79 . .**217** C5
 Newcastle-u-L ST5 . . . .**55** E7
Church Wlks TF9 . . . .**82** C2
Church Wlk
 Wolverhampton,Penn
  WV3 . . . .**265** F7
 Wolverhampton,Tettenhall
  WV6 . . . .**255** E5
Churnet Cl
 Cheddleton ST13 . . . .**45** B4
 Mayfield DE6 . . . .**81** C7
Churnet Ct
 Burton u T DE14 . . . .**166** E3
 Cheddleton ST13 . . . .**45** D6
Churnet Gr WV6 . . . .**254** F4
Churnet Rd
 Blythe Bridge ST11 . . . .**91** A7
 Cheadle ST10 . . . .**76** E1
 Hilton DE65 . . . .**147** D8
Churnet Row ST14 . . . .**95** F3
Churnetside Bsns Pk
 ST13 . . . .**45** D6
Churnet Valley Railway ★
 ST13 . . . .**45** E4
Churnet Valley Rd ST10 . . .**62** A2
Churnet Valley Rly Ctr ★
 ST13 . . . .**45** E5
Churnet Valley Wildlife
 Sanctuary ★ ST10 . . . .**61** E4
Churnet View ST13 . . . .**31** A8
Churnet View Mid Sch
 ST13 . . . .**31** A8
Churnet View Rd ST10 . . . .**78** A7
Churn Hill Rd WS9 . . . . . .**256** B6
Churns Hill La DY3 . . . . . .**270** B3
Churston Cl
 Newcastle-u-L ST5 . . . .**71** B2
 Walsall WS3 . . . .**243** A3

Churston Pl ST1 . . . .**57** D8
Cicely Haughton Sch
 ST13 . . . .**44** F2
Cinderhill Ind Est ST3 . . . . .**73** E4
Cinder Hill La WV9 . . . . . .**224** B3
Cinderhill La ST3 . . . .**73** D3
Cinder-Hill La ST7 . . . .**25** C7
Cinder Rd
 Burntwood WS7 . . . .**228** E7
 Dudley DY3 . . . .**271** B2
Cinder Rock Way ST7 . . . . .**26** C1
Circular Rd WV7 . . . .**220** E1
City Arc 1 WS13 . . . .**231** B7
City Bank ST8 . . . .**16** C2
City La ST9 . . . .**30** A3
City of Stoke-on-Trent Sixth
 Form Coll ST4 . . . .**72** D7
City Rd ST4 . . . .**72** D6
Clamgoose La ST10 . . . .**76** C7
Clanbrook Rd DY7 . . . .**278** A7
Clandon Ave ST6 . . . .**41** E4
Clanford Cl ST17 . . . .**174** F5
Clanford La ST18 . . . .**154** A5
Clanford Rd ST18 . . . .**154** A7
Clanway St ST6 . . . .**41** E5
Clap Gate Gr WV5 . . . .**269** E6
Clap Gate Rd WV5 . . . .**269** C7
Clare Ave
 Newcastle-u-L ST5 . . . .**56** B6
 Wolverhampton WV11 . . . . .**241** F1
Clare Cres ST17 . . . .**174** B8
Claregate Prim Sch WV6 . .**255** F7
Claremont Cl
 Newcastle-u-L ST5 . . . .**56** C7
 Stone ST15 . . . .**120** B8
Claremont Cotts DY3 . . . . .**271** E8
Claremont Gr ST17 . . . . . .**174** B8
Claremont Mews WV3 . . . .**266** A7
Claremont Rd
 Eccleshall ST21 . . . .**133** E6
 Sedgley DY3 . . . .**271** E8
 Tamworth B79 . . . .**250** A8
 Wolverhampton WV3 . . . . .**266** B7
Clarence Gdns B74 . . . . . .**257** F3
Clarence Rd Longton ST3 . .**284** B4
 Sutton Coldfield B74 . . . . . .**257** F4
Clarence St
 Burton u T DE14 . . . .**166** C1
 Dudley DY3 . . . .**271** E5
 Newcastle-u-L,Porthill ST5 . .**56** B5
 Stoke-on-T ST4 . . . .**72** E6
Clarendon Dr ST17 . . . . . .**174** B8
Clarendon Pl WV3 . . . .**243** F3
Clarendon Rd
 Sutton Coldfield B75 . . . . . .**258** C3
 Walsall WS4 . . . .**244** C2
Clarendon St
 Stoke-on-T ST4 . . . .**72** C6
 Walsall WS3 . . . .**243** B1
Clare Rd ST16 . . . .**155** C7
Clare St Harriseahead ST7 . .**26** C6
 Mow Cop ST7 . . . .**26** C6
 Stoke-on-T ST4 . . . .**56** D1
Claridge Rd ST4 . . . .**56** E1
Clarion Way WS11 . . . . . .**209** E5
Clarke Ho WS3 . . . .**243** B1
Clarke's Ave WS12 . . . . . .**195** A1
Clarkes Cl ST14 . . . .**111** B1
Clarke St ST1 . . . .**282** A1
Clark Rd WV3 . . . .**255** F2
Clark's Cres WS15 . . . .**161** A6
Clark St Stafford ST16 . . . . .**285** C3
 Stourbridge DY8 . . . .**279** E4
Claud St ST4 . . . .**72** D4
Claverdon Cl WS8 . . . .**245** A8
Claverdon Dr B74 . . . .**257** B4
Claverhouse Rd DE15 . . . .**167** A2
Claverley CE Prim Sch
 WV5 . . . .**267** C7
Claverley Dr WV4 . . . .**265** D5
Clayalders Bank ST21 . . . .**101** C6
Claydon Cres ST5 . . . .**71** B2
Claydon Rd DY6 . . . .**270** C1
Clayfield Gr ST3 . . . .**73** C6
Clayfield Gr W ST3 . . . .**73** C6
Claygate Rd WS12 . . . .**210** E3
Claygates Rd ST19 . . . .**207** A1
Claygates Rd ST19 . . . .**223** F8
Clayhanger Cl ST5 . . . .**56** B8
Clayhanger La WS8 . . . . . .**244** D6
Clayhanger Rd WS8 . . . . . .**244** F6
Clayhanger St 5 ST6 . . . . . .**56** F8
Clay Hills ST9 . . . .**41** D3
Clay Lake ST9 . . . .**43** E7
Claymills Rd
 Burton u T DE13 . . . .**148** A2
 Stretton DE13 . . . .**147** F2
Claymore B77 . . . .**261** E2
Clay Pit La WS14 . . . .**230** F3
Clay St E DE15 . . . .**167** A1
Clay's La DE14 . . . .**184** F8
Clay St Burton u T DE15 . . .**166** F1
 Penkridge ST19 . . . .**192** E1
Clayton Ave CW12 . . . .**6** A5
Clayton Cl WV2 . . . .**266** C2
Clayton Hall Bsns &
 Language Coll ST5 . . . . . .**71** C3
Clayton La
 Newcastle-u-L ST5 . . . .**71** C4
 Stoke-on-T SY4,ST5 . . . .**71** D5
Clayton Rd ST5 . . . .**71** C4
Clayton St ST5 . . . .**284** C3
Claytonwood Rd ST4 . . . . . .**71** E3
Cleadon Pl ST2 . . . .**58** B6
Clear View DY6 . . . .**275** B6
Clearwater Ind Est WV2 . .**266** F7
Clearwell Gdns DY1 . . . . .**271** F3

Cleasby B77 . . . .**251** C1
Cleaveland Mews 2
 WS13 . . . .**214** A1
Cleave Rd DE14 . . . .**185** A8
Clee Hill Dr WV3 . . . .**255** A1
Clee Hill Rd DY3 . . . .**271** D4
Clee Rd DY10 . . . .**280** B5
Cleeton St WS12 . . . .**210** D1
Cleeve Dr B74 . . . .**257** F6
Cleeve Rd WS3 . . . .**242** F3
Cleeve B77 . . . .**250** D3
Cleeve Way WS3 . . . .**242** F3
Clee View Mdw DY3 . . . . . .**266** D2
Clee View Rd WV5 . . . .**269** E5
Clegg Rd WS7 . . . .**229** E7
Clematis Ave ST11 . . . .**90** F6
Clematis Cl ST1 . . . .**135** B2
Clematis Cres DE15 . . . . . .**186** A8
Clematis Dr WV9 . . . .**239** F3
Clematis B77 . . . .**250** F3
Clement Cl ST16 . . . .**155** F5
Clement Pl ST6 . . . .**42** E3
Clement Rd ST6 . . . .**42** A6
Clent View Rd DY8 . . . .**279** C2
Clerk Bank ST13 . . . .**30** E6
Clermont Ave ST4 . . . .**72** A2
Clevedon Ave ST17 . . . . . .**175** E7
Cleveland Cl WV11 . . . . . .**241** F1
Cleveland Ct DE15 . . . .**167** B3
Cleveland Dr WS11 . . . . . .**210** B4
Cleveland Rd Hanley ST1 . .**282** B1
 Newcastle-u-L ST5 . . . .**55** E3
Cleveland St
 15 Burslem ST6 . . . .**56** F8
 Stourbridge DY8 . . . .**279** E4
Cleveland Trad Est ST1 . . .**282** A1
Cleveland Wlk ST17 . . . . . .**174** B8
Cleves Cres WS6 . . . .**226** D1
Clewley Dr WV9 . . . .**240** B3
Clewley Rd DE14 . . . .**184** F8
Clewlow Pl ST3 . . . .**284** D5
Clewlows Bank ST9 . . . .**43** F3
Clews St ST6 . . . .**56** E7
Clews Wlk ST5 . . . .**56** C5
Cley Gr ST5 . . . .**71** B2
Cliffdon Ho DE65 . . . .**146** D8
Cliffe Pl ST3 . . . .**42** A3
Cliff Hall La B78 . . . .**261** C1
Clifford Ave ST6 . . . .**42** F5
Clifford Cl B77 . . . .**250** F3
Clifford Rd TF9 . . . .**112** B8
Clifford St Hanley ST1 . . . .**282** C1
 Tamworth B77 . . . .**250** E3
Cliff Rd ST18 . . . .**158** C1
Cliffs La TF10 . . . .**150** E1
Cliff St ST6 . . . .**42** C1
Cliff Vale Pl ST4 . . . .**56** F1
Clifton Ave Aldridge WS9 . .**245** C1
 Brownhills WS8 . . . .**244** D7
 Cannock WS11 . . . .**226** C2
 Tamworth B79 . . . .**250** B5
Clifton CE Prim Sch DE6 . . .**81** F6
Clifton Cl Stafford ST16 . . .**156** B3
 Stoke-on-T ST4 . . . .**72** E5
 Swadlincote DE11 . . . .**186** F2
Clifton Dr ST6 . . . .**156** B3
Clifton Gdns WV8 . . . .**239** C3
Clifton La B79 . . . .**235** B3
Clifton Rd Clifton DE6 . . . . .**81** F6
 Kidderminster DY10 . . . . . .**280** C3
 Netherseal DE12 . . . .**219** D6
 Wolverhampton WV6 . . . . .**255** D5
Clifton St
 Newcastle-u-L ST5 . . . .**56** D4
 Sedgley WV14 . . . .**266** F1
 Stoke-on-T ST4 . . . .**72** E5
 Stourbridge DY8 . . . .**279** F4
Clifton Way DE15 . . . .**167** B2
Clinton Cres WS7 . . . .**229** B8
Clinton Gdns 4 ST15 . . . .**120** A7
Clinton Sq ST1 . . . .**282** A4
Clive Ave ST2 . . . .**43** B3
Clive Cl B75 . . . .**258** D2
Cliveden Ave WS9 . . . .**245** B1
Cliveden Coppice B74 . . . .**257** F1
Cliveden Pl ST3 . . . .**284** C2
Cliveden Rd ST2 . . . .**58** B5
Clive Gdns TF9 . . . .**97** C2
Clive Ho DE15 . . . .**167** C3
Clive Rd Burntwood WS7 . . .**229** A7
 Market Drayton TF9 . . . .**97** C1
 Newcastle-u-L ST5 . . . .**56** D6
 Pattingham WV6 . . . .**263** C7
Clive St ST6 . . . .**41** E4
Clockmill Ave WS3 . . . .**243** B3
Clockmill Pl WS3 . . . .**243** B3
Clockmill Rd WS3 . . . .**243** B3
Cloister Rd ST4 . . . .**72** A5
Cloisters The
 Burton u T DE15 . . . .**166** F1
 Gnosall ST20 . . . .**171** E6
Cloister Wlk Bucknall ST2 . .**58** A5
 Whittington WS14 . . . .**232** E5
Close Bank DE13 . . . .**146** C6
Close La ST7 . . . .**26** D7
Close The Dudley DY3 . . . .**271** C4
 Enville DY7 . . . .**273** D2
 Lichfield WS13 . . . .**231** B8
 Madeley CW3 . . . .**68** E7
 Meir ST3 . . . .**74** B5
 Newton Solney DE15 . . . . .**167** B6
 Stafford,Moss Pit ST17 . . . .**174** E5
 Stafford,Rowley Park ST16 **155** C1
 Stoke-on-T ST9 . . . .**43** F7
 Swindon DY3 . . . .**269** C2
 Tutbury DE13 . . . .**146** B6
Cloud The ★ CW12 . . . .**7** A4
Cloud View CW12 . . . .**6** A2

Clough Hall Dr ST7 . . . .**40** E6
Clough Hall Rd ST7 . . . .**40** F8
Clough Hall Tech Sch ST7 . .**25** F1
Clough La ST9 . . . .**59** A2
Clough St ST1 . . . .**282** A2
Cloughwood Way ST6 . . . . .**41** D1
Clovelly Wlk 2 ST6 . . . .**56** E7
Clover Ct DE14 . . . .**184** E6
Cloverdale
 6 Stafford ST17 . . . .**175** C7
 Perton WV6 . . . .**254** D4
Cloverdale Pl ST3 . . . .**73** F3
Cloverdale Rd ST5 . . . .**56** B3
Clover Heath WV5 . . . .**267** D7
Clover La DY6 . . . .**275** B7
Clover Mdws WS12 . . . . . .**210** C1
Clover Rd ST5 . . . .**56** B6
Clover Ridge WS6 . . . .**226** C3
Clowes Rd ST2 . . . .**58** A3
Club Cotts WV10 . . . .**240** C6
Club La WV10 . . . .**240** C6
Club Row DY3 . . . .**271** E5
Club St ST4 . . . .**72** A6
Clumber Ave ST5 . . . .**71** C6
Clumber Gr ST5 . . . .**71** C5
Cluny Pl ST2 . . . .**58** A5
Clyde Ave ST8 . . . .**16** E1
Clyde Pl ST5 . . . .**71** A4
Clyde Rd ST6 . . . .**57** A7
Clydesdale Rd WS8 . . . . . .**244** E6
Clyde St ST1 . . . .**282** A1
Clyde Wlk ST1 . . . .**282** A1
Clynes Way ST3 . . . .**74** B3
Coach Gdns ST19 . . . .**205** C6
Coach Ho The ST7 . . . .**25** C4
Coach House La WS15 . . . .**178** E1
Coach House Rise B77 . . . .**261** F1
Coachmans Cl ST16 . . . . . .**155** C8
Coachman's Wlk WS15 . . . .**178** F5
Coalbourn La DY8 . . . .**279** F7
Coal Haulage Rd WS12 . . .**227** F8
Coalmeadow Cl WS3 . . . . .**242** F3
Coalpitford La ST13 . . . .**44** E4
Coalpit Hill ST7 . . . .**40** D8
Coalpit La WS15 . . . .**197** A5
Coalport Cl ST10 . . . .**76** D1
Coalport Dr ST15 . . . .**119** F5
Coalville Pl ST3 . . . .**74** B5
Coalway Ave WS3 . . . .**266** A6
Coalway Gdns WV3 . . . . . .**265** D6
Coalway Rd
 Rugeley WS15 . . . .**197** B6
 Walsall WS3 . . . .**243** B1
 Wolverhampton WV3 . . . . .**265** E6
Coates Pl ST6 . . . .**42** E8
Coatsgate Wlk WV8 . . . . . .**239** F1
Cobbett Rd WS7 . . . .**228** D7
Cobbles The ST19 . . . .**205** C6
Cobden Cl WS12 . . . .**210** C7
Cobden St Longton ST3 . . .**284** B1
 Newcastle-u-L ST5 . . . .**56** D6
 Stourbridge DY8 . . . .**279** C5
Cobham Cl ST15 . . . .**118** F6
Cobham Pl ST3 . . . .**90** A8
Cobia B77 . . . .**261** D7
Cob Moor Rd ST7 . . . .**26** A4
Cobridge Ind Est ST6 . . . . .**57** B7
Cobridge Rd ST1 . . . .**57** A5
Coburn Dr B75 . . . .**258** D2
Cocketts Nook WS15 . . . . .**178** C3
Cock Hill DE6 . . . .**81** F6
Cock La ST17 . . . .**193** E7
Cocknage Rd Longton ST3 . .**73** B1
 Meir Heath ST3 . . . .**89** C7
Cockshut Ind Est ST4 . . . . . .**56** F1
Cockshutts La WV2 . . . . . .**266** D3
Cocks La Stoke-on-T ST9 . . .**43** C3
 Stoke-on-T ST9 . . . .**43** C4
Cocksparrow La WS12,
 WS11 . . . .**209** B5
Cockspur St B78 . . . .**262** E7
Cockster Brook La ST3 . . . .**72** F3
Cockster Rd ST3 . . . .**72** F3
Cockstubbles ST14 . . . . . .**126** B8
Cocton Cl WV6 . . . .**254** E5
Codsall Com High Sch
 WV8 . . . .**239** A4
Codsall Gdns WV8 . . . .**238** E4
Codsall Ho WV8 . . . .**238** E4
Codsall Mid Sch WV8 . . . .**239** A3
Codsall Rd Codsall WV8 . . .**239** C1
 Wolverhampton WV6 . . . . .**255** D7
Codsall Sta WV8 . . . .**238** E3
Coghlan Ct ST17 . . . .**174** C6
Colbourne Rd B78 . . . .**250** A2
Colbrook B77 . . . .**250** D1
Colclough Ave ST5 . . . .**56** A8
Colclough La ST6 . . . .**41** D7
Colclough Rd ST3 . . . .**74** B1
Cold Meece Ind Est
 ST5 . . . .**118** B6
Cold Norton Cotts WS15 . .**119** C5
Coldridge Cl WV8 . . . .**239** F1
Coldstream Dr DY8 . . . . . .**275** E3
Cole Dr ST16 . . . .**155** C2
Coleford Cl DY8 . . . .**275** C2
Colehill B79 . . . .**250** B5
Coleman St WS6 . . . .**255** F4
Colenso Way ST5 . . . .**56** B8
Coleridge Cl
 Market Drayton TF9 . . . . . .**112** A7
 Tamworth B79 . . . .**250** A6
 Walsall WS3 . . . .**244** A5
Coleridge Ct DE14 . . . .**166** C6
Coleridge Dr Cheadle ST10 . .**76** C2
 Perton WV6 . . . .**254** E4
 Stafford ST17 . . . .**174** C8
Coleridge Rd ST3 . . . .**73** A2

Coleridge Rise DY3 . . . . . 271 A4
Colesden Wlk WV4 . . . . . 265 C6
Coleshill Rd B78 . . . . . 261 A4
Coleshill St B78 . . . . . 261 A8
Cole St ST8 . . . . . 27 C7
Coley Gr ST18 . . . . . 177 D8
Coley La ST18 . . . . . 158 D1
Colin Cres ST4 . . . . . 74 B4
Colindene Gr ST4 . . . . . 72 A6
Colinwood WS6 . . . . . 226 F1
Collard Ave ST5 . . . . . 56 B3
College Cl CW3 . . . . . 68 E8
College Ct WV6 . . . . . 255 D4
College Farm Cl WV6 . . . . . 253 C3
College Fields ST15 . . . . . 118 F6
College La B79 . . . . . 250 B5
College Rd Denstone ST14 . 95 D6
  Hanley ST1,ST4 . . . . . 57 C1
  Wolverhampton WV6 . . . . . 255 D4
College View ST15 . . . . . 255 D3
Collet Rd WV6 . . . . . 254 E5
Collets Brook B75 . . . . . 259 A2
Collett B77 . . . . . 251 A1
Colley Rd ST6 . . . . . 41 F6
Collier Cl
  Cheslyn Hay WS6 . . . . . 226 D2
  Walsall WS8 . . . . . 244 C7
Colliers Way ST8 . . . . . 27 C7
Colliery Dr WS3 . . . . . 242 F3
Colliery Rd WS15 . . . . . 196 F4
Collinbourne Cl ST4 . . . . . 88 B6
Collindale Cl DY6 . . . . . 270 D1
Collingwood Ct ST14 . . . . . 120 B8
Collingwood Dr ST4 . . . . . 71 E8
Collingwood Rd WV10 . . . . . 240 E2
Collin Rd ST4 . . . . . 71 F5
Collins Dr 3 WS13 . . . . . 230 F6
Collins Hill WS13 . . . . . 214 A2
Collinson Rd
  Barton-u-N DE13 . . . . . 183 D1
  Stoke-on-T ST6 . . . . . 41 D7
Collins Rd WS8 . . . . . 245 A5
Collin St ST14 . . . . . 126 B7
Collis Ave ST4 . . . . . 56 D1
Collis St DY8 . . . . . 279 F8
Colne Mount ST14 . . . . . 126 B7
Colonnade St ST16 . . . . . 285 B3
Colshaw Rd DY8 . . . . . 279 E4
Coltman Cl WS14 . . . . . 231 D7
Colton Hills Com Sch
  WV4 . . . . . 266 B4
Colton Rd ST4 . . . . . 178 E4
Coltsfoot View WS6 . . . . . 226 E2
Columbian Cres WS7 . . . . . 228 F8
Columbian Dr WS11 . . . . . 209 F3
Columbian Way WS11 . . . . . 209 F3
Columbine Wlk 11 ST6 . . 41 D3
Colvile Cl DE12 . . . . . 218 D7
Colville St ST4 . . . . . 72 F6
Colwall Rd DY3 . . . . . 271 D4
Colwich CE Prim Sch
  ST17 . . . . . 177 E7
Colwich Cres ST16 . . . . . 156 C3
Colwyn Dr ST8 . . . . . 27 D5
Combe Dr ST3 . . . . . 90 A5
Comberford Ave ST14 . . . . . 234 A2
Comberford Rd B79 . . . . . 250 A7
Comber Gr DY7 . . . . . 278 A3
Combermere TF9 . . . . . 97 D2
Comber Rd DY7 . . . . . 278 A3
Combine Cl B75 . . . . . 258 D4
Comfrey Cl ST3 . . . . . 90 A6
Commerce Dr ST19 . . . . . 207 E7
Commerce St ST3 . . . . . 284 C3
Commercial Rd ST1 . . . . . 282 C2
Commercial St ST6 . . . . . 57 A7
Common Barn La Bednall ST17. 194 A8
  Betley CW3 . . . . . 52 F6
  Cannock WS11 . . . . . 210 A3
  Fradley WS13 . . . . . 215 D7
  Gratwich ST14 . . . . . 124 C2
  Stoke-on-T ST3 . . . . . 89 F4
  Stone ST15 . . . . . 119 E6
  Tamworth B79 . . . . . 250 B4
  Upper Hatton ST21 . . . . . 102 E7
  Waterhouses ST10 . . . . . 64 F7
  Whitmore ST5 . . . . . 85 D6
  Whittington WS14 . . . . . 232 D4
Common Rd
  Stafford ST16 . . . . . 155 E7
  Wombourne WV5 . . . . . 270 A6
Common Road Ind Est
  ST16 . . . . . 155 E7
Commonside
  Brownhills WS8 . . . . . 245 A6
  Burntwood WS15 . . . . . 212 A4
Commonside Cl ST16 . . . . . 155 D6
Commonside Enville DY7. 273 E3
  Walsall WS3 . . . . . 244 A2
Common The ST10 . . . . . 75 D3
Common View
  Burntwood WS7 . . . . . 212 A4
  Cannock WS12 . . . . . 210 B7
Common Wlk WS12 . . . . . 209 C5
Community Dr ST6 . . . . . 42 D1
Como Pl ST5 . . . . . 70 E6
Compa The DY3 . . . . . 278 A3
Compton Cl Kinver DY7 . 277 C2
  Stafford ST17 . . . . . 156 A1
Compton Ct B74 . . . . . 257 F3
Compton Dr DY6 . . . . . 275 D5
Compton Gdns DY7 . . . . . 277 C4
Compton Gr DY6 . . . . . 275 D5
Compton Hill Dr WV3 . . 255 D2
Compton Ho 6 ST13 . . 30 E5
Compton ST13 . . . . . 30 E5

Compton Mews ST13 . . . 30 F5
Compton Pk WV6 . . . . . 255 E3
Compton Rd Kinver DY7 . 277 D4
  Stafford ST17 . . . . . 156 D1
  Tamworth B79 . . . . . 249 F7
  Wolverhampton WV3 . . . . . 255 F2
Compton Rd W WV3 . . . . . 255 D2
Compton St ST1 . . . . . 282 A2
Comptons The TF9 . . . . . 130 A8
Condlyffe Rd ST13 . . . . . 30 E4
Condor Gr WS12 . . . . . 210 C1
Conduit Rd WS11 . . . . . 228 A4
Conduit St ST13 . . . . . 231 B8
Conewood Pl ST3 . . . . . 72 E1
Coneybere Gdns ST19 . . 223 D7
Coneygreave Cl ST10. . . . . 76 D1
Coneygreave La ST5 . . . . . 85 D5
Coney Gr ST3 . . . . . 74 A3
Conford St ST2 . . . . . 57 F2
Congleton Edge Rd CW12 16 B6
Congleton Rd
  Biddulph,Braddocks Hay
    ST8 . . . . . 27 D8
  Biddulph,Marsh Green ST8 . 16 D2
  Kidsgrove ST7 . . . . . 25 D1
  Mow Cop ST7 . . . . . 26 E8
Congleton Rd N ST7 . . . . . 25 E6
Congleton Rd S ST7 . . . . . 25 D2
Congleton Rd ST7 . . . . . 40 D8
Congleton Sta CW12 . . . . . 6 A1
Congreve Cl ST17 . . . . . 175 F7
Congreve Rd ST3 . . . . . 72 F2
Conifer Cl WS12 . . . . . 210 A8
Conifer Gr Stafford ST17 . 174 M7
  Stoke-on-T ST3 . . . . . 72 F2
Coniston Cl ST3 . . . . . 120 D7
Coniston Dr Cheadle ST10 . 76 F4
  Kingswinford DY6 . . . . . 275 B7
Coniston Gr ST5 . . . . . 71 B4
Coniston Ho ST16 . . . . . 285 C3
Coniston Pl ST4 . . . . . 87 F7
Coniston Rd Aldridge B74 . 256 F3
  Wolverhampton WV6 . . . . . 255 D8
Coniston B77 . . . . . 262 B7
Coniston Way WS11 . . . . . 209 E1
Connaught Dr WV5 . . . . . 265 A1
Connaught St ST6 . . . . . 41 D2
Conners La TF10 . . . . . 168 A3
Conrad Cl ST3 . . . . . 73 D3
Consall Gr ST4 . . . . . 88 C6
Consall La ST9 . . . . . 60 D6
Consall Nature Pk★ ST9. 61 A5
Consall Station ST9 . . . . . 61 B6
Consett Rd ST3 . . . . . 88 F8
Consort Pl B79 . . . . . 250 C5
Consort St ST4 . . . . . 72 B7
Constable Ave ST5 . . . . . 55 E6
Constable Cl ST3 . . . . . 90 A7
Constance Ave ST4 . . . . . 88 B8
Convent Cl
  Burton u T DE15 . . . . . 185 F8
  Cannock WS11 . . . . . 226 D8
  Colwich ST18 . . . . . 177 D7
  Stoke-on-T ST4 . . . . . 72 A8
Convent Ct ST4 . . . . . 72 A8
Convent La ST15 . . . . . 105 B4
Conway Cl
  5 Burton u T DE13 . . . . . 166 D8
  Kingswinford DY6 . . . . . 275 F4
Conway Gr ST10 . . . . . 76 L1
Conway Rd Biddulph ST8 . 27 C6
  Cannock WS11 . . . . . 226 B8
  Perton WV6 . . . . . 254 F3
  Stafford ST16 . . . . . 155 A4
Conway St ST4 . . . . . 72 C8
Conygree La DE6 . . . . . 81 D7
Cook Cl WV6 . . . . . 254 E4
Cooke Cl ST19 . . . . . 192 E4
Cooke St WV2 . . . . . 266 C8
Cookley La DY7 . . . . . 278 B1
Cookley Sebright Fst Sch
  DY10 . . . . . 280 A5
Cooknell Dr DY8 . . . . . 275 D5
Cook Rd WS3 . . . . . 243 D2
Cook's Bank ST17 . . . . . 175 B1
Cook's Hollow ST13 . . . . . 47 A8
Cook's La ST13 . . . . . 32 A1
Cookson Ave ST3 . . . . . 73 C1
Coolidge St 18 ST6 . . 41 D3
Coombe Croft WV9 . . . . . 240 A3
Coombe Park Rd ST13 . . 119 F5
Coombesdale ST5 . . . . . 85 F2
Coombes Valley Nature
  Reserve★ ST13 . . . . . 46 D6
Co-Operative La ST7 . . . . . 54 D7
Co-operative St ST16 . . 155 D6
Cooper Ave ST5 . . . . . 56 B2
Cooper Cl ST15 . . . . . 120 D7
Cooper & Jordan CE Prim
  Sch WS9 . . . . . 256 C6
Cooper Perry Prim Sch
  ST18 . . . . . 154 C6
Cooper's Bank Rd DY5 . . 271 A2
Coopers Cl ST13 . . . . . 30 C5
Cooper's Sq DE14 . . . . . 166 D2
Cooper St Hanley ST1 . . 282 A1
  Newcastle-u-L ST5 . . . . . 55 E6
  Wolverhampton WV2 . . . . . 266 F8
Coopers Way ST8 . . . . . 27 B8
Coors Visitor Ctr★ DE14 166 D3
Copeland Ave
  Newcastle-u-L ST5 . . . . . 71 B3
  Tittenson ST12 . . . . . 88 A1
Copeland Cl ST10 . . . . . 76 D1
Copeland Cl ST15 . . . . . 120 D5
Copelands The DY7 . . . . . 278 A3
Copeland St ST4 . . . . . 72 B7
Cope's Ave ST6 . . . . . 41 E3

Cope's Dr B79 . . . . . 250 B7
Cope St Stafford ST16 . . . 285 B3
  Stoke-on-T ST2 . . . . . 43 A1
Copes Way ST14 . . . . . 111 A1
Copley La WV6 . . . . . 253 A2
Coplow Ave ST10 . . . . . 92 C4
Copperas Rd DE11 . . . . . 186 D5
Copper Beech Dr
  Kingswinford DY6 . . . . . 270 D1
  Wombourne WV5 . . . . . 270 D6
Copperfields WS14 . . . . . 231 D7
Copper Glade ST16 . . . . . 156 B3
Copperhill Rd CW12 . . . . . 16 B7
Copperkins Rd WS12 . . 210 E4
Coppermill Cl WS12 . . . . . 209 F7
Coppice Ave ST5 . . . . . 55 A1
Coppice Brook ST17 . . . . . 176 C4
Coppice Cl Biddulph ST8. . 27 D7
  Burntwood WS7 . . . . . 228 B8
  Cheslyn Hay WS6 . . . . . 226 D4
  Sedgley ST15 . . . . . 271 C7
  Stone ST15 . . . . . 105 A1
  Wolverhampton WV11 . . 242 A1
Coppice Cres WS8 . . . . . 244 D7
Coppice Ct WS11 . . . . . 226 B7
Coppice Dr Newport TF10 168 E5
  Polesworth B79 . . . . . 262 F7
Coppice Farm Way
  WV11 . . . . . 242 B1
Coppice Gdns ST15 . . . . . 105 B1
Coppice Gr
  Lichfield WS14 . . . . . 231 F7
  Meir ST3 . . . . . 74 A3
Coppice Ho ST7 . . . . . 40 C8
Coppice La Aldridge WS9 . 244 F1
  Brownhills WS8 . . . . . 244 F4
  Cheslyn Hay WS6 . . . . . 226 D4
  Clifton Campville B79 . . 218 F1
  Middleton B78 . . . . . 259 D2
  Muckley Corner WS7,
    WS14 . . . . . 230 A3
  Wolverhampton WV6 . . . . . 255 B6
Coppice Prim Sch B75 . . 258 B1
Coppice Rd
  Brownhills WS8,WS9 . . 244 F4
  Rugeley WS15 . . . . . 196 F6
  Stone ST15 . . . . . 105 A1
  Talke ST7 . . . . . 40 C8
  Wolverhampton WV3 . . 265 D8
Coppice Sch The ST5 . . 283 B1
Coppice Side WS8 . . . . . 244 D7
Coppice Side Ind Est
  WS8 . . . . . 244 C8
Coppice The
  Cannock WS12 . . . . . 210 L1
  Hagley DY8 . . . . . 281 F6
  Market Drayton TF9 . . . . . 97 B1
  Stoke-on-T ST4 . . . . . 57 C7
Coppice View ST5 . . . . . 56 A4
Coppice Way ST16 . . . . . 155 C8
Coppins The
  2 Stafford ST17 . . . . . 175 C7
  Leek ST13 . . . . . 30 C5
Copp La ST6 . . . . . 41 C2
Copplestone Gr ST3 . . . . . 73 E3
Coppull Pl ST6 . . . . . 42 A7
Coppy Hall Gr WS9 . . . . . 245 A1
Coppy Nook La WS7 . . . . . 229 C5
Copse Cres WS3 . . . . . 244 A4
Copse Dr WS15 . . . . . 198 B4
Copse The B74 . . . . . 257 F1
Copsy Dale ST21 . . . . . 115 C6
Copthorne Ave WS7 . . . . . 228 F4
Copthorne Rd WV3 . . . . . 266 A7
Coracle Gr ST8 . . . . . 27 C6
Coral Gr ST4 . . . . . 88 B7
Corbet Ct 4 TF9 . . . . . 97 C1
Corbett Ho 8 DY8 . . . . . 279 F8
Corbett Hospl DY7 . . . . . 279 F7
Corbett Prim Sch DY7 . . 268 A2
Corbett Wlk 13 ST6 . . . . . 41 D3
Corbin Rd B78 . . . . . 262 F6
Corby Pl ST3 . . . . . 284 A3
Corden Ave DE13 . . . . . 166 F8
Cordy La WV7 . . . . . 237 C7
Corfe Cl WV6 . . . . . 254 F3
Corfe Gn ST3 . . . . . 73 C6
Corfield Pl ST6 . . . . . 42 D5
Corfton Dr WV6 . . . . . 255 C3
Corina Way ST3 . . . . . 73 D4
Corinth Way 15 ST6 . . . . . 41 D3
Cormie Cl ST6 . . . . . 42 B5
Corncrake Rd DY1,DY3 . . 271 E3
Cornelious St 3 ST3 . . . . . 74 A1
Cornel Ho ST3 . . . . . 73 E1
Corner Ways ST18 . . . . . 154 E2
Cornes St 57 D1
Corneville Rd ST2 . . . . . 58 C3
Corn Exchange The 5
  WS13 . . . . . 231 B8
Cornfield Cl DY6 . . . . . 275 A8
Cornfield Dr WS14 . . . . . 231 E7
Cornfield Rd ST8 . . . . . 27 E7
Cornfield WV8 . . . . . 239 F2
Cornflower Cl WV10 . . . . . 241 A7
Cornflower Rd WS8 . . . . . 244 D6
Cornhill WS11 . . . . . 209 E5
Cornhill Cl ST5 . . . . . 40 D1
Cornhill Gdns ST13 . . . . . 30 E4
Cornhill Rd ST6 . . . . . 42 C5
Cornhill St 10 ST13 . . . . . 30 E5
Cornmell Lea TF10 . . . . . 168 F3
Cornmill Gr WV6 . . . . . 254 D3
Corn Mill La DE13 . . . . . 146 E6
Cornovian Cl WV6 . . . . . 254 C4
Corns Gr WV5 . . . . . 269 F5

Cornwall Ave
  Newcastle-u-L ST5 . . . . . 71 D4
  Tamworth B78 . . . . . 250 A1
Cornwall Cl
  4 Congleton CW12 . . . . . 6 A1
  Aldridge WS9 . . . . . 245 A1
  Kingswinford DY6 . . . . . 275 D8
Cornwall Ct WS15 . . . . . 196 D6
Cornwall Dr ST17 . . . . . 156 D1
Cornwallis St ST4 . . . . . 72 B6
Cornwall Rd
  Burton u T DE15 . . . . . 185 E6
  Cannock WS12 . . . . . 210 B5
  Stourbridge DY8 . . . . . 279 D8
  Wolverhampton WV6 . . . . . 255 C4
Cornwall St ST3 . . . . . 284 C4
Cornwood Gr ST3 . . . . . 89 E8
Coronation Ave
  Biddulph ST8 . . . . . 27 B5
  Longton ST3 . . . . . 284 B3
  Mile Oak B78 . . . . . 250 B1
Coronation Cotts DE13 . . 184 A8
Coronation Cres
  Kidsgrove ST7 . . . . . 25 E1
  Rocester ST14 . . . . . 96 A4
  Shuttington B79 . . . . . 251 F7
Coronation Rd
  Brownhills WS9 . . . . . 245 A3
  Newcastle-u-L ST5 . . . . . 283 C2
  Stafford ST16 . . . . . 156 A6
  Stoke-on-T,Hartshill ST4 . 71 E8
  Walsall WS4 . . . . . 244 B2
Coronation St
  Cheadle ST10 . . . . . 76 D3
  Stoke-on-T ST6 . . . . . 41 E4
  Tamworth B79 . . . . . 250 A5
Corporation St
  Newcastle-u-L ST5 . . . . . 283 B3
  Stafford ST16 . . . . . 285 C4
  Stoke-on-T ST4 . . . . . 72 B6
  Tamworth B79 . . . . . 250 B6
Corran Rd ST17 . . . . . 174 D6
Correen B77 . . . . . 251 C1
Corrie Roy Cotts B78 . . . . . 250 A4
Corrin Gr DY6 . . . . . 275 C8
Corser St DY1 . . . . . 271 F2
Corsham Pl ST14 . . . . . 143 F7
Corsican Cl WS7 . . . . . 229 A8
Corsican Dr WS12 . . . . . 210 A8
Cort Dr WS7 . . . . . 229 B8
Corve Gdns WV6 . . . . . 255 E5
Corve View DY3 . . . . . 266 C1
Corvedale Cl ST3 . . . . . 90 A7
Coseley St ST6 . . . . . 42 C2
Cosford Ct WS11 . . . . . 254 E5
Cosgrove Wlk WV8 . . . . . 239 F1
Cotehill Rd ST9 . . . . . 59 B4
Cote La DY7 . . . . . 273 C1
Coteheath St ST1 . . . . . 57 D1
Cotes La
  Cotes Heath ST21 . . . . . 102 F2
  Swynnerton ST15 . . . . . 103 B2
Cot La DY6,DY8 . . . . . 275 C5
Coton Ave ST16 . . . . . 156 B3
Coton Green Prec B79 . . 249 F7
Coton Green Prim Sch
  B79 . . . . . 249 F8
Coton La
  Coton Clanford ST18 . . . . . 154 A3
  Ranton ST18 . . . . . 153 E4
  Tamworth B79 . . . . . 249 E8
Coton Pk DE12 . . . . . 186 C1
Coton Rd
  Walton-On-Trent DE12 . . 202 E6
  Wolverhampton WV4 . . 266 B5
Coton Rise ST12 . . . . . 88 E1
Cotsdale Rd WV4 . . . . . 265 E3
Cotswold Ave
  Great Wyrley WS6 . . . . . 226 F3
  Newcastle-u-L ST5 . . . . . 55 E3
Cotswold Cl
  Aldridge WS9 . . . . . 245 C1
  Cannock WS12 . . . . . 210 A8
Cotswold Cres ST2 . . . . . 43 A1
Cotswold Ct
  Sutton Coldfield B75 . . 258 A4
  Wolverhampton WV3 . . 266 B6
Cotswold Dr WV7 . . . . . 237 B5
Cotswold Gr WV12 . . . . . 242 B1
Cotswold Rd
  Burton u T DE14 . . . . . 184 F8
  Cannock WS12 . . . . . 210 A8
  Wolverhampton WV2 . . 266 F7
Cottage Cl
  Burntwood WS7 . . . . . 228 F5
  Cannock WS12 . . . . . 210 D5
  Longton ST3 . . . . . 73 E1
Cottage Ct WS7 . . . . . 228 F5
Cottage Farm Rd B77 . . 261 D7
Cottage La
  Biddulph Moor ST8 . . . . . 28 A8
  Burntwood WS7 . . . . . 228 F5
  Wolverhampton WV10 . . 240 D3
Cottage Mews WS9 . . . . . 256 E4
Cottages The Bagnall ST9 . 43 F2
  Brewood ST19 . . . . . 223 C6
Cottage St DY6 . . . . . 275 D7
Cottage View WV8 . . . . . 239 B4
Cottage Wlk 4 B77 . . . . . 261 F6
Cotterill Dr ST5 . . . . . 56 B8
Cotterill Gr ST5 . . . . . 56 B8
Cotters Hill Cl ST18 . . . . . 177 D8
Cottesmore Ct DE15 . . . . . 167 A1
Cotton Cl DE13 . . . . . 200 F3
Cotton Gr WS12 . . . . . 195 A1
Cotton La ST10 . . . . . 63 B2
Cotton Lane Cotts ST10 . 63 B3
Cotton Rd ST6 . . . . . 41 C6
Cotton Way WS7 . . . . . 211 F1

Cottonwood Gr
  Harriseahead ST7 . . . . . 26 E4
  Longton ST3 . . . . . 284 C4
Cottrell Cl WS15 . . . . . 160 F6
Cotts The ST3 . . . . . 74 A8
Cotwall End Countryside &
  Craft Ctr★ DY3 . . . . . 271 C6
Cotwall End Ho DY3 . . . . . 271 C7
Cotwall End Prim Sch
  DY3 . . . . . 271 D7
Cotwall End Rd DY3 . . . . . 271 C5
Coulson Cl WS7 . . . . . 211 D1
Coulter Gr WV6 . . . . . 254 D4
Coulter La ST7 . . . . . 229 E8
Coulthwaite Way WS15 . . 196 F6
Council Hos
  Bramshall ST14 . . . . . 125 C7
  Chetwynd Aston TF10 . . 187 A7
  Church Leigh ST10 . . . . . 109 A4
  Kingstone ST14 . . . . . 125 C1
  Kingstone,The Blythe ST18 140 F6
Council Hos The ST21 . . 116 B4
Country Park View ST5 . . 55 A8
County Dr B78 . . . . . 250 A2
County La
  Codsall WV7,WV8 . . . . . 237 E3
  Iverley DY8 . . . . . 281 D8
County Rd ST16 . . . . . 285 B4
Coupe Dr ST3 . . . . . 74 A5
Court Cres DY6 . . . . . 275 C5
Court Dr WS14 . . . . . 246 F4
Court Farm La DE14 . . . . . 184 E7
Courtland Mews ST16 . . 155 F5
Courtland Rd DY6 . . . . . 275 C8
Courtlands The WV6 . . . . . 255 E4
Court La ST5 . . . . . 56 B4
Courtney Pl ST3 . . . . . 89 E8
Court No 1 ST3 . . . . . 73 E1
Court Par WS9 . . . . . 256 B6
Court Rd WV6 . . . . . 255 F4
Courts The WV7 . . . . . 237 A4
Courtway Dr ST1 . . . . . 57 D8
Court Wlk CW3 . . . . . 53 A5
Cousins St WV2 . . . . . 266 D7
Covan Farm Mobile Home Pk
  WV9 . . . . . 224 C1
Coven Cl WS3 . . . . . 244 A5
Coven Mill Cl WV9 . . . . . 224 C1
Coven Rd WV9 . . . . . 223 D4
Coventry Ct ST16 . . . . . 155 A5
Coverdale Cl ST3 . . . . . 90 A7
Coverley Pl ST4 . . . . . 71 F6
Covers La DY7 . . . . . 274 E1
Covert Cl ST18 . . . . . 158 B2
Covert Gdns ST7 . . . . . 40 D8
Covert La DY8 . . . . . 279 D2
Covert The Keele ST5 . . . . . 70 B7
  Newcastle-u-L ST5 . . . . . 71 C2
  Wolverhampton WV8 . . 239 E1
Covey Cl WS13 . . . . . 214 D1
Cowallmoor La ST13 . . . . . 28 B5
Cowan Dr ST16 . . . . . 156 A4
Cowen St ST6 . . . . . 42 E6
Cowhill La WS13 . . . . . 200 E1
Cowhouse La ST10 . . . . . 109 B3
Cow La Cauldon ST10 . . . . . 63 F7
  Whateley B78 . . . . . 261 F3
Cowley Cl Penkridge ST19 . 207 F7
  Stafford ST17 . . . . . 174 C8
Cowley Dr DY1 . . . . . 271 F2
Cowley Gn WS12 . . . . . 209 E8
Cowley La ST20 . . . . . 171 D5
Cowley B77 . . . . . 250 D2
Cowley Way ST2 . . . . . 73 E7
Cowlishaw Cl ST8 . . . . . 27 B5
Cowlishaw Rd ST5 . . . . . 42 C6
Cowlishaw Way WS15 . . 196 F6
Cowlow La SK17 . . . . . 23 D3
Cowper St ST4 . . . . . 72 F6
Coxmoor Cl WS3 . . . . . 242 F3
Coyney Gr ST3 . . . . . 74 A3
Crabbery St ST16 . . . . . 285 B3
Crab La Bobbington DY7 . 268 C2
  Cannock WS11 . . . . . 210 A3
  Stafford ST16 . . . . . 155 B8
  Willenhall WV12 . . . . . 242 D1
Crabtree Ave ST8 . . . . . 27 C7
Crabtree Cl ST4 . . . . . 72 F8
Crabtree Way WS15 . . . . . 178 C2
Cracklehill La DE6 . . . . . 81 C3
Crackley Bank ST5 . . . . . 40 E1
Crackley Bank Prim Sch
  ST5 . . . . . 40 E1
Crackley La ST5 . . . . . 54 E3
Cracow Moss CW3 . . . . . 53 A3
Craddock Rd ST5 . . . . . 155 C7
Craftdown Cl ST17 . . . . . 174 F4
Craigside 5 ST8 . . . . . 27 C8
Cramer St ST17 . . . . . 285 B2
Cranberry Ave ST10 . . . . . 93 B1
Cranberry Cl ST16 . . . . . 155 A6
Cranberry Dr ST2 . . . . . 43 B2
Cranberry Marsh ST21 . . 102 D3
Cranbone Ave ST2 . . . . . 43 B2
Cranbourne Ave WV4 . . 266 E3
Cranbrook Cl ST4 . . . . . 88 A7
Cranbrook Gr WV6 . . . . . 254 F3
Cranbrooks ST19 . . . . . 205 C7
Cranbrook Wlk ST7 . . . . . 174 B8
Cranbrook Hill B78 . . . . . 259 E5
Cranebrook La
  Stonnall WS14 . . . . . 245 F7
  Wall WS14 . . . . . 246 A8
Crane Dr WS7 . . . . . 229 A4
Crane Field WS13 . . . . . 214 B1

Crane Hollow WV5......269 E5
Cranesbill Cl WV10.....241 C7
Crane St ST1..........57 B6
Crane Terr WS4........255 E5
Cranfield Pl ST2........58 B2
Cranfield Rd WS7......229 A7
Cranford Pl WS11......209 F1
Cranford Rd WV3......265 D8
Cranford Way ST2......58 D3
Cranham Dr DY6......275 E5
Cranleigh Ave ST1.....57 D8
Cranleigh Cl
  Aldridge WS9.........256 B5
  Willenhall WV12......242 C1
Cranleigh Way WS14...231 E7
Cranley Dr WS8........238 F4
Cranmer Ave WV6......255 A6
Cranmere Ave WV6.....255 A6
Cranmere Ct ST4.......255 A6
Cranmer Gr B74.......257 F6
Cranmer St ST4........72 B7
Cranmore Gr ST15.....120 C7
Cranmore Rd WV3......255 F3
Cranswick Gr ST2......58 D1
Crantock Cl WV11......242 C1
Cranwell Gn WV5......269 F5
Cranwell Pl ST3........89 F8
Cranwell Rise B78......249 C1
Cranwood Rd ST12.....88 A1
Cranworth Gr ST3......89 E8
Crateford La ST19......224 B7
Crathorne Ave WV10...240 C1
Crauford Rd CW12......6 A8
Craven Cl ST4..........88 A4
Craven St Burton u T DE13 166 C6
  Wolverhampton WV2...266 F6
Craven ST5............251 B1
Crawford Ave WV4.....266 F3
Crawfurd St ST4.......72 C5
Crawley La DE13.......199 C5
Crayford Ave CW12.....6 A5
Craythorne Rd DE13....147 D3
Crediton Ave ST6.......42 C4
Creighton La ST14......111 A5
Cremorne Dr ST17......175 D7
Cremorne Rd B75.......258 B2
Cremorne Wlk B75......258 B2
Crescent Gr ST4........56 E1
Crescent Prim Sch ST3..74 C1
Crescent Rd ST17......285 A1
Crescent The Ashley TF9 100 C5
  Burntwood WS7.......211 F1
  Cookley DY10........280 B4
  Eccleshall ST21......133 D6
  Great Wyrley WS6....227 A2
  Hagley DY8..........281 F5
  Leek ST13...........31 A7
  Mayfield DE6.........81 D7
  Newcastle-u-L,Silverdale
    ST5...............55 B2
  Newcastle-u-L ST5....71 A6
  Rudyard ST13........18 D1
  Stafford,Doxey ST16...155 B4
  Stoke-on-T ST4.......71 E4
  Stone ST15..........105 A1
  Swadlincote DE11.....186 E6
  Walton-on-t-H ST17...175 F7
  Wolverhampton WV6...255 B3
Cressington Dr ST4.....258 A1
Cresswell Ave ST5.......40 D1
Cresswell Cres WS3.....242 F2
Cresswell Ct WV10.....240 A3
Cresswell La
  Brewood ST19.........223 C6
  Cresswell ST11.......91 D4
Cresswell Old Rd ST11..91 E3
Cresswell Rd Hanley ST1.57 E3
  Hilderstone ST15......106 E3
Cressy ST15...........104 E3
Crestbrook Rd ST2......58 C6
Crest Cl DE13.........147 E1
Crestfield Rd ST3.......89 F8
Crestway Rd ST2........43 C2
Crestwood Cl DE13.....166 D8
Crestwood Dr ST15.....119 F6
Crestwood Glen WV6...255 E7
Crestwood Pk ST19.....223 D7
Crestwood Rise WS14...178 C3
Crestwood Sch The DY6.275 F5
Crestwood B77.........251 A5
Creswell Dr ST18......154 F8
Creswell Farm Dr ST16..155 B7
Creswell Gr
  Creswell ST18........154 F8
  Stafford ST18........155 A8
Crewe Gates Ind Est CW1 37 A8
Crewe Hall Ent Pk CW1..37 D8
Crichton Ave DE13.....166 D7
Crich Way DE11........186 E5
Cricket Cl DE15.......167 E8
Cricketers Cl DE15.....185 F8
Cricketers Mews ST5....56 C5
Cricketers The DE13....200 F2
Cricket La WS14.......231 C5
Cricket Mdw Dudley DY3.271 E5
  Wolverhampton WV10..240 D4
Crick Rd ST1..........57 E2
Crigdon B77...........251 C1
Crinan St ST4.........174 D6
Cringlebrook B77.......250 D4
Crispin Cl ST15........155 C8
Critchlow Gr ST3.......73 A1
Critchlows Ct ST3......72 F1
Crockett The ST11......74 E3
Crockford Dr B75......258 B3

Crockington Cl WV5....263 F2
Crockington La WV5....264 A1
Crocus Cres WV9......240 A3
Croft Ave Cannock WS12.195 A1
  Newcastle-u-L ST5....56 B6
  Tamworth B79........250 B6
Croft Cl Elford B79.....216 E2
  Netherseal DE12......219 F7
  Rolleston on D DE13...147 B4
Croft Cres
  Brownhills WS8.......244 D7
  Stoke-on-T ST4.......72 A6
Croft Ct ST6...........42 C1
Crofter Cl ST8.........27 B8
Crofters Ct ST5.........40 D3
Crofters La B75........258 E3
Crofters The TF10......188 D6
Crofters Wlk WS14.....239 E1
Croftfield St ST2........73 D8
Croft Gdns WS7........229 A8
Croft Gr ST14.........111 C1
Croft La ST19.........207 D1
Croft Leys The WS15...198 C4
Croft Par WS9.........256 B6
Croft Prim Sch WS15...197 F5
Croft Rd Cheadle ST10..76 D3
  Newcastle-u-L ST5....283 B4
  Stone ST15..........119 F6
Croft Road Ind Est ST5.283 B4
Croft St ST6...........56 E7
Croftstead Ave ST14....95 D6
Croft B79.............250 B6
Croft The
  Blakedown DY10......281 C2
  Burton u T DE15......166 F1
  Cheadle ST10........76 E6
  Cheddleton ST13......45 C4
  Cheslyn Hay WS6.....226 C2
  Hixon ST18..........158 C8
  King's Bromley DE13...199 D6
  Longdon WS15.......197 F1
  Maer ST5............84 C2
  Norton in H TF9......82 B3
  Sedgley DY3.........266 E1
  Stoke-on-T ST4.......71 F5
  Swadlincote DE11.....186 A6
  Wombourne WV5......269 D5
Croft Way TF9..........97 B1
Cromartie St ST3......284 C2
Cromdale B77..........251 C1
Cromer Cres ST1.......57 E4
Cromer Gdns WV6.....255 F5
Cromer Rd ST1.........57 F4
Cromer St ST5.........56 D4
Crompton Cl
  Colwich ST18........177 E8
  Congleton CW12......6 A6
Crompton Ct WV8......239 B4
Crompton Gr ST4.......88 C5
Crompton Rd ST15.....120 B7
Cromwell Cl Hopton ST18 137 D1
  Tutbury DE13........146 C5
Cromwell Ct WS6......227 A1
Cromwell Rd
  Cannock WS12.......210 A1
  Tamworth B79........249 E8
  Wolverhampton WV10.240 E4
Cromwells Mdw WS14..231 C5
Cromwell St Biddulph ST8.27 C8
  Hanley ST1..........57 D6
Cromwell Terr ST13.....30 F5
Crony Cl ST13.........145 C4
Crooked Bridge Rd ST16 285 B4
Crook La WS9.........256 B5
Crosby Cl WV6.........255 F5
Crosby Rd ST4.........71 E3
Cross Butts ST1........133 D6
Crossdale Ave ST2.....43 A2
Cross Edge ST6........43 B7
Crossfield B77.........251 B1
Crossfield Ave
  Biddulph ST8.........27 C6
  Blythe Bridge ST11....90 F6
Crossfield Rd Ind Est
  WS13..............231 E8
Crossfield Rd WS13....231 E8
Crosshill Bank ST18....122 F5
Cross Hill ST6.........56 E7
Cross Ho WV2.........266 C7
Crossing La ST18......154 C2
Crossings The ST5......231 E8
Cross In Hand La
  Lichfield,Farewell WS13.213 C3
  Lichfield WS13......213 F1
Cross Keys Island WS12 210 C3
Cross Keys WS13......231 B8
Cross La Audley ST7....39 E5
  Congleton CW12......6 A6
  Lichfield WS14......231 D6
Crossland Cres WV6....255 F7
Crossland Pl E ST3.....90 A8
Crossland Pl W ST3....74 A1
Crosslands CW12......6 A1
Cross La Oulton ST15...105 C6
  Rolleston on D DE13...147 B2
  Sedgley DY3.........266 E1
  Waterhouses ST10.....48 E3
Crossley Rd ST6........42 A5
Crossley Stone WS15...178 E1
Crosslow La DE6........36 E5
Crossman St DE14.....166 A3
Cross May St ST5......283 A2
Crossmead Gr ST1......57 F6
Cross of the Hand WS15.161 B2
Cross Pl DY3..........266 E1
Cross Rd Albrighton WV7 237 A5
  Rugeley WS15........196 F2
  Uttoxeter ST14......111 B1

Cross St S WV2........266 C7
Cross Side DE6.........81 F7
Cross St
  [4] Stourbridge,Wordsley
    DY6...............275 D3
  [7] Leek ST13........30 F5
  Biddulph ST8........27 C8
  Burntwood WS7......228 E8
  Burton u T DE14......166 C3
  Cannock,Bridgtown WS11 226 E5
  Cannock WS12.......210 C1
  Cheadle ST10........76 D3
  Cheslyn Hay WS6.....226 D2
  Gnosall ST20........171 C5
  Kingsley ST10.......61 D3
  Kingswinford DY6....275 D6
  Kingswinford,Wall Heath
    DY6...............275 B8
  Market Drayton TF9...97 D1
  Meir ST3............74 B5
  Newcastle-u-L ST5....55 E8
  Stafford ST16.......155 D5
  Stone ST15..........105 A1
  Stourbridge DY8......279 E5
  Tamworth B79........250 B5
  Tamworth,Kettlebrook
    B77...............250 C3
  Tunstall ST6.........56 C8
  Walsall WS3.........244 A1
Cross The DY6.........275 D6
Crossway Rd ST6.......57 C7
Crossways Biddulph ST8..16 A1
  Pipe Gate TF9........83 D7
Crossways Rd ST7......25 A4
Crossway ST16........156 A3
Crossway The ST5......56 C3
Croston St ST1........282 A1
Crotia Ave CW2........37 B5
Crouch Ave ST6........42 A4
Crouch La ST12........6 D4
Crowberry Cl WS8......244 D6
Crowberry La B83......183 D2
Crowborough Rd ST8,
  ST13..............28 B6
Crowcrofts Rd ST4......88 E7
Crowden Rd B77........251 A1
Crowfoot La DE65......129 E8
Crowland Ave WV6.....254 E4
Crown Bank WS15......161 A6
Crown Bank Cres ST7...40 D6
Crown Bank Hanley ST1.282 B3
  Talke Pits ST7........40 D6
Crown Bridge ST19.....192 E1
Crown Cl DY3.........266 D1
Crown Ct B74..........257 E3
Crowndale Pl ST6.......41 E8
Crown Gdns ST7........40 D6
Crown Ind Est DE14....166 B1
Crown La Iverley ST7....281 C7
  Stourbridge DY8......279 E5
  Sutton Coldfield B74...257 E3
Crown Specl Sch DE13..147 D1
Crown St Hanley ST1...282 B2
  Newcastle-u-L ST5....55 C2
  Stone ST15..........120 A8
Crowther Gr WV6......255 F4
Crowther Rd WV6......255 F5
Crowther St ST4.......72 C8
Crowtrees Farm Ind Est
  ST10..............48 F2
Croxall Rd Alrewas DE13 201 B2
  Edingale B79........217 C5
  Edingale B79,WS13...217 B6
Croxden Cl ST10.......92 D8
Croxdene Ave WS3......243 A1
Croxden Rd ST2........58 B6
Croxley Dr WS12......210 C3
Croxstalls Cl WS3......243 A1
Croyde Pl ST4.........90 B6
Croydon Dr ST19......207 F8
Cruso St ST13.........30 E5
Crutchley Ave B78.....250 A2
Crystal Ave DY8.......275 F1
Crystal Gdns DY7......278 A3
Crystal St ST3.........57 B6
Cubley La DE6.........96 C2
Cuckoo Cage La DE13..164 F1
Cuckoo Cl WS11.......210 C2
Cullamore La ST14.....126 B4
Culland Rd DE14......185 B7
Cull Ave ST16.........156 A3
Cumberbatch Ave ST6..42 B7
Cumberland Cl
  Kingswinford DY6....275 E4
  Talke ST7...........40 D6
Cumberland Cres WS7..229 A8
Cumberland Dr B78.....250 A1
Cumberland Rd
  Burton u T DE15......185 D6
  Cannock WS11.......210 A4
Cumberland St
  Newcastle-u-L ST5....283 C3
  Stoke-on-T ST4.......72 E6
Cumberledge Hill WS15.211 C5
Cumbers The ST18.....154 B6
Cumbria Ho ST5.......71 C5
Cumming St ST4.......71 E8
Cunningham Rd WV6...254 E4
Curborough Rd WS13..214 B2
Curland Pl ST3........73 F2
Curlew Cl Lichfield WS14 231 E7
  Uttoxeter ST14......126 C6
Curlew Dr WS8........244 E7
Curlew Hill WS11......210 A3
Curlew Rd ST7.........26 E1
Curlew B77...........262 A7
Curtis Ct DE13........166 C7

Curtiss Pl ST3.........90 C6
Curtis Way DE14......166 B4
Curzon Rd ST6.........42 A2
Curzon Rise ST13......30 B5
Curzon St W DE14......166 B3
Curzon St
  Burton u T DE14......166 C3
  Newcastle-u-L ST5....56 D2
  Wolverhampton WV2...266 D7
Cushman Ave WV5.....269 E7
Cuttlestone Ho ST19...192 E1
Cutts St ST1..........282 A1
Cwerne Ct DY3........271 C3
Cyclamen Cl DE14.....185 A8
Cygnet Cl Cannock WS12 210 C7
  Madeley Heath CW3...69 A8
  Wolverhampton WV6...255 C2
Cygnet Dr Brownhills WS8 244 E7
  Tamworth B79........249 F5
Cynthia St ST4........42 A2
Cypress Ave DY3......271 D5
Cypress Cl
  Market Drayton TF9...97 A1
  Stafford ST17.......156 C1
Cypress Gdns [1] DY6..275 D4
Cypress Gr
  Blythe Bridge ST11....91 A6
  Newcastle-u-L ST5....55 D8
Cypress Rise WS12.....211 A6
Cyprus St WV2........266 C6

D

Dace Gr ST6...........42 B3
Dace B77.............261 D7
Daffodil Cl DY3........271 E7
Daffodil Wlk WS15.....178 C2
Dag La DE12...........218 E7
Dahlia Cl ST3..........74 B6
Daimler Cl [1] ST17....175 A8
Dain Pl ST5...........56 B6
Dain St ST6...........56 E7
Daintry Cl ST13........30 E5
Daintry Dr B78.........249 E8
Daintry St Leek ST13....30 E5
  Stoke-on-T ST4.......71 F4
Dairy Cl Leek ST13.....31 A6
  Market Drayton TF9...97 D1
Dairyfields Way ST1....57 D7
Dairyhouse La
  Dilhorne ST10........60 B2
  Overmoor ST10.......60 E1
Dairylands Rd ST7......25 A4
Daisy Bank WS12......209 F8
Daisy Bank Cl WS3.....244 A1
Daisy Bank ST13.......30 E6
Daisy La Alrewas DE13..200 D1
  Alrewas DE13........200 F2
Daisy Pl ST4..........72 E4
Daisy Wlk WV9........240 A3
Dakota Gr ST6.........41 D4
Dalbeg Cl WV8........255 F5
Dalbrook Rd DE15.....167 B5
Dale Ave ST6..........42 E6
Dalebrook Cl WS3......244 A1
Dale Cl Cheadle ST10....76 E2
  Whitmore ST5........85 C5
Dalecot Gn ST2........73 D8
Dale Cres CW12........6 A2
Dale Dr WS7..........229 B7
Dalegarth Gr ST3.......89 E8
Dale Gr CW12.........6 A2
Dalehall Gdns [4] ST6..56 E8
Dalehead Ct ST3.......89 F8
Dalehouse Rd ST13.....45 C4
Daleian Ct ST5........55 C1
Dale La ST18..........173 A7
Dalelands Est TF9......112 B8
Dalelands W TF9......112 B7
Dale La DE6..........64 F4
Dale Rd DY8..........279 F2
Dales Cl Biddulph Moor ST8 28 B8
  Swadlincote DE11.....186 E5
Dales Com Jun Sch B77 262 B8
Dales Green Rd ST7.....26 C5
Daleside DE15........167 B1
Dales Inf Sch The B77..262 B8
Dalesman Cl DY6......275 B7
Dale St Burslem ST6....56 E8
  Burton u T DE14......166 C2
Dale The Ashley TF9....100 B5
  Warslow DE6,SK17....23 C2
Dale View Ct ST11......90 E1
Daleview Dr ST5.......55 C1
Dale View
  Earl Sterndale SK17....5 B3
  Meir ST3............74 B3
  Mow Cop ST7.........26 C5
Dalewood Rd ST5.......55 F5
Dallow Cl DE15........166 C5
Dallow Cres DE14......166 C5
Dallow St DE14........166 C5
Dalton Ave DE15......167 B1
Dalton Ct WV5.........269 E7
Dalton Gr ST2.........58 D1
Dalton St WV3........266 B8
Daltry Way CW3.......68 F7
Daly Cres ST5.........55 B1
Dama Rd B78..........260 F8
Dame Paulet Wlk DE14.166 C1
Dam La Alsop en le D DE6 36 E3
  Biddulph ST8........17 B2
Dampier St ST13.......30 E5
Damson Pk WV6.......253 D3
Dams The ST11........74 D2
Dam St WS13..........231 B8
Danbury Gdns WV10..240 C2

Danby Crest ST17......174 A8
Danby Dr WS12........211 D4
Dandillion Ave ST10....92 D8
Danebower Rd ST4.....88 C6
Danebridge Gr ST1......57 F5
Dane Dr ST8...........16 E1
Dane Gdns ST7.........26 C2
Dane Gr ST10..........76 E1
Danehill Gr ST4........71 F1
Danehill Wlk WV8......255 F8
Danelagh Cl B79......249 F7
Danemead Cl ST3......90 A7
Danesbrook WV5......267 D8
Danes Cl WV11........241 F4
Danescourt Rd WV6....255 C6
Danes Croft ST4.......88 B7
Danesmore Park Jun & Inf
  Sch WV11..........242 A1
Daneswood Dr WS9....244 F3
Dane Wlk ST1..........282 C3
Danford Heath WV5....267 D7
Danford La WV5.......267 D7
Daniels Cross TF10.....169 B4
Daniels La WS9........256 C5
Danilo Rd WS11.......209 D1
Danta Way ST17.......156 C1
Darby Ave WS14......232 E6
Darelyn Cvn Site WV9..224 B2
Darges La WS6........226 F4
Darius Cl ST5..........56 B8
Dark La Alrewas DE13...201 A3
  Birchmoor B78........262 E8
  Brinsford WV10......240 D8
  Featherstone WV10...241 D7
  Great Wyrley WS6....227 C1
  Kinver DY7..........278 B3
  Lichfield WS13......213 B1
  Longdon WS15.......212 D7
  Newborough DE13.....162 D7
  Newport TF10.......168 E1
Darley Cl DE15........167 C1
Darley Dale DE11......186 F2
Darley Gr ST10........76 E1
Darlings La WS15......212 A5
Darnbrook B77........251 C1
Darnel Hurst Rd B75...258 D3
Darnford Cl ST16......155 C8
Darnford La
  Lichfield WS14......231 F6
  Whittington WS14....232 B5
Darnford Moors WS14.231 E6
Darnford View WS13...214 E1
Darnley St ST4........72 C8
Darrall Gdns ST4......71 E3
Darsham Gdns ST5.....71 C2
Dart Ave Stafford ST17.174 B8
  Stoke-on-T ST6......42 A4
Dart Cl ST8...........16 D1
Dartford Pl ST6........42 C4
Dartford Rd WS3......242 F1
Dart Gr ST10..........76 E1
Dartmouth Ave
  Cannock WS11.......226 C8
  Newcastle-u-L ST5....71 A5
  Pattingham WV6.....253 C2
  Stourbridge DY8......275 D3
Dartmouth Dr WS9.....256 A5
Dartmouth Pl ST3.......89 F8
Dartmouth Rd WS11...209 D1
Dartmouth St
  [1] Wolverhampton WV2 266 D8
  Stafford ST16.......156 A3
  Stoke-on-T ST6......42 B1
  Wolverhampton WV2...266 E8
Dart Pl ST5...........71 A4
Dart B77.............262 A5
Darwell Pk B77........251 B2
Darwin Cl Burntwood WS7 229 B7
  Burton u T DE15......167 C1
  Cannock WS12.......210 E2
  Lichfield WS13......231 A8
  Stafford ST16.......156 C4
  Stone ST15..........104 E2
Darwin Dr WV6........254 E4
Darwin Ho DY6........275 F7
Dash Gr ST6...........42 C1
Datteln Rd WS11......210 A4
Daurada Dr ST17......175 A8
Davenport Cl ST13.....30 B4
Davenport Rd WV6....255 B5
Davenport St ST6......41 E1
Davenport Way ST5....70 F3
Daventry Cl ST2........57 F2
Davey Cl WS7.........228 F4
David Garrick Gdns
  WS13..............214 B2
David Rd ST3..........73 F1
Davidson Ave CW12....6 A5
Davidson Rd WS14.....231 B7
Davies Dr ST14........110 F1
Davies Ho WS3........243 B1
Davis Cl ST16.........156 A4
Davison St ST6........57 A7
Davis Rd B77..........250 D4
Davis St ST4..........57 A2
Davy Cl ST2...........58 A3
Davy Pl WS15.........196 D6
Dawes Cl WS15.......197 F4
Dawes La WS8.........229 A1
Dawley Brook Prim Sch
  DY6...............275 C7
Dawley Brook Rd DY6..275 D7
Dawley Rd DY6........275 D8
Dawley Trad Est DY6..275 D8
Dawlish Dr ST17......175 D7
Dawlish Dr Bucknall ST2..58 C1
  Bucknall ST2........73 D8
Dawn Ave ST6.........42 A4

Dawney Dr B75 .... 258 A4
Dawn View ST3 .... 74 B3
Dawson Ave WV14 .... 266 F2
Dayson Pl ST5 .... 56 A7
Dayton Dr WS15 .... 178 C2
Daywell Rise WS15 .... 178 C3
Deacons Way WS15 .... 178 F2
Deadman's Gn ST10 .... 109 C8
Deakin Ave WS8 .... 228 F1
Deakin Gr ST5 .... 71 C5
Deakin Rd ST6 .... 42 B5
Deal Ave WS7 .... 229 A8
Dean Cl TF9 .... 97 A1
Dean Ct WV6 .... 254 E6
Deanery Cl Rugeley WS15 178 F2
Shareshill WV10 .... 225 C2
Dean Hollow ST7 .... 39 D2
Dean Pl ST1 .... 282 C1
Dean Rd WV5 .... 269 F5
Deansberry Cl ST4 .... 88 A8
Deans Croft WS14 .... 231 C8
Deanscroft Way ST3 .... 73 E4
Deansfield Cl ST19 .... 223 D6
Deansfield Ho ST19 .... 223 C7
Deansfield Rd ST19 .... 223 D6
Deansgate 1 ST13 .... 30 F6
Deanshill Cl ST16 .... 155 C2
Deans La CW2 .... 38 C4
Dean's La ST5 .... 40 D2
Deans Slade Dr WS14 ... 231 A5
Dean St Brewood ST19 ... 223 C6
Bucknall ST2 .... 58 C4
Sedgley DY3 .... 271 D8
Deansway ST4 .... 88 B6
Dean View ST7 .... 39 D1
Dearnsdale Cl ST16 .... 155 B7
Deavall Way WS11 .... 210 B2
Deaville Rd ST2 .... 58 C3
Debenham Cres ST2 .... 58 A2
Deborah Cl WV4 .... 266 C4
Decade Cl ST5 .... 40 F2
Deebank Ave ST13 .... 31 B6
Dee Cl Biddulph ST8 .... 16 E1
Talke ST7 .... 40 E7
Dee Gr WS11 .... 226 D8
Dee La ST5 .... 71 B4
Deeley B77 .... 251 A1
Deep Cut Rd DE6 .... 144 A7
Deepdale Cl
Burton u T DE15 .... 167 B5
Stoke-on-T ST6 .... 42 F2
Deepdale La Dudley DY3 . 271 E3
Snelston DE6 .... 81 A2
Deepdales Stafford ST17 . 175 C6
Wombourne WV5 .... 269 E6
Deepdale B77 .... 251 D2
Deep Hayes Ctry Pk★
ST13 .... 45 A7
Deepmore Cl
Alrewas DE13 .... 201 A2
Four Ashes WV10 .... 224 D5
Deer Cl Huntington WS12 . 209 C6
Norton Canes WS11 .... 228 B7
Walsall WS3 .... 243 C1
Dee Rd WS3 .... 243 E1
Deerfold Cres WS7 .... 229 B7
Deer Hill ST17 .... 176 C4
Deerhill B77 .... 251 C1
Deerhurst Rise WS12 .... 210 F6
Deerleap Way WS15 .... 178 C1
Deer Park Dr TF10 .... 168 F5
Deer Park Rd B78 .... 249 E1
Deer Pk ST20 .... 171 E7
Deer Wlk WV8 .... 239 F2
De Ferrers Croft DE13 ... 166 D8
De Ferrers Specialist Tech Coll (Dove Campus)
DE13 .... 166 B8
De Ferrers Specialist Tech Coll (Trent Campus)
DE13 .... 166 C8
Defford Ave WS4 .... 244 C1
Defoe Dr ST3 .... 73 E4
De Havilland Dr ST15 .... 118 F6
Delafield Way WS15 .... 178 C2
Delamere Cl CW2 .... 37 E4
Delamere Gr
Newcastle-u-L ST5 .... 283 C4
Stoke-on-T ST4 .... 88 A7
Delamere La ST17 .... 174 A8
Delaney Dr ST3 .... 73 F4
Delhi Cl DE15 .... 167 C3
Delhurst Ave WV4 .... 266 E3
Delius Gr ST1 .... 57 F5
Dellbrook Ct ST5 .... 283 B1
Dell Cl ST16 .... 155 B8
Dell The Cannock WS12 ... 210 F4
Lichfield WS13 .... 230 F7
Newcastle-u-L ST5 .... 55 C1
Stourbridge DY8 .... 279 E6
Tamworth B79 .... 250 B6
Dellway Ct DY8 .... 279 E5
Dellwood Gr 2 ST3 .... 73 D6
Delphouse Rd
Boundary ST10 .... 75 F2
Cheadle ST10 .... 76 A2
Delphside ST7 .... 39 F2
Delph Wlk ST4 .... 72 F6
Delta Way Bsns Ctr
WS11 .... 226 D6
Delta Way WS11 .... 226 D7
Deltic B77 .... 251 A1
Delves Cres CV9 .... 262 C1
Delves Pl ST5 .... 71 B5
Demontfort Way ST14 ... 126 C5
Denbigh Cl Biddulph ST8 .. 27 C6
Burton u T DE13 .... 166 D7
Dudley DY1 .... 271 F2
Denbigh Cl *continued*
Newcastle-u-L ST5 .... 71 D4
Denbigh St ST1 .... 282 A4
Denbury Cl WS12 .... 210 D1
Denby Ave ST3 .... 284 C5
Dency Gr ST6 .... 42 A3
Dene Ave DY6 .... 275 C4
Dene Cl ST19 .... 207 F8
Dene Croft WS3 .... 243 A1
Denefield ST19 .... 207 F8
Denehurst Cl 1 ST3 .... 74 A2
Dene Rd Lower Penn WV4 . 264 F4
Stourbridge DY8 .... 279 F3
Dene Side ST5 .... 283 A2
Denewood Pl ST3 .... 74 B1
Denford Rd ST9 .... 44 F8
Denham Gdns WV3 .... 265 B8
Denham Sq ST3 .... 72 E1
Den La CW3 .... 52 D4
Denleigh Rd DY6 .... 275 F4
Denmark Rise WS12 .... 210 D7
Denmark Villas WS13 .... 230 C5
Dennfield Dr WS6 .... 226 C2
Dennington Cres ST3 .... 72 E1
Dennis Barsby Cl DE11 .. 186 E3
Dennis Hall 9 DY8 .... 279 F8
Dennis St Stoke-on-T ST4 .. 72 F5
Stourbridge DY8 .... 279 F8
Dennis B77 .... 250 E2
Dennis Viollet Ave ST4 ... 72 C3
Denry Cres ST5 .... 56 B8
Denshaw Wlk ST3 .... 284 C4
Denston Ct B74 .... 257 F2
Denstone Ave ST17 .... 156 B1
Denstone Coll ST14 .... 95 B5
Denstone Cres ST3 .... 72 F2
Denstone Gdns WV10 .... 240 F3
Denstone La ST14 .... 95 C7
Dentdale Cl ST3 .... 90 A7
Denton Cl ST5 .... 71 C3
Denton Gr ST3 .... 73 E3
Denton Rd DE13 .... 166 A6
Denton Rise DE13 .... 166 A7
Dent St B79 .... 250 C5
Denver Fold ST17 .... 174 A8
Denyer Ct WS13 .... 215 C6
Denzil Gn ST17 .... 174 A8
Derby Ave WV6 .... 255 F7
Derby Mews ST14 .... 110 F1
Derby Pl ST5 .... 71 C4
Derby Rd
Burton u T DE13,DE14 .... 166 E7
Doveridge DE6 .... 127 C8
Egginton DE65 .... 148 C4
Stretton DE13 .... 148 A1
Talke ST7 .... 40 D7
Uttoxeter ST14 .... 111 D1
Whittington WS14 .... 232 D3
Derby St E DE14 .... 166 C4
Derby St Burton u T DE14 . 166 C4
Hanley ST1 .... 282 C2
Leek ST13 .... 30 F5
Stafford ST16 .... 285 A3
Derby Turn DE14 .... 166 D5
Dereham Way ST2 .... 58 D1
Derek Dr ST1 .... 57 E6
Deroen Hill WS15 .... 197 B5
Derrington La
Bradley ST18 .... 173 E8
Derrington ST18 .... 154 E1
Derry St Stoke-on-T ST4 ... 72 E4
Wolverhampton WV2 .... 266 D8
Derwent Ave ST15 .... 120 D7
Derwent Cl Aldridge WS9 . 256 F3
Burton u T DE14 .... 166 E3
Derwent Cres ST7 .... 26 C2
Derwent Dr
2 Congleton CW12 .... 6 A1
Biddulph ST8 .... 16 E1
Cheadle ST10 .... 76 E1
Loggerheads TF9 .... 99 E5
Derwent Gr
Burntwood WS7 .... 229 D6
Cannock WS11 .... 226 D8
Derwent Ho ST17 .... 174 E6
Derwent Pk DE14 .... 166 E5
Derwent Pl ST5 .... 56 A3
Derwent Rd
Burton u T DE15 .... 167 A1
Wolverhampton WV6 .... 255 E8
Derwent St ST1 .... 282 A4
Derwent B77 .... 250 D1
Devall Cl WS15 .... 196 E7
Devana Wlk ST3 .... 74 C2
Devereux Ho B79 .... 250 A4
Devereux Rd B75 .... 258 C1
Deveron Cl DE13 .... 147 C1
Devil's La ST9,ST13 .... 29 E5
Devon Cl Burton u T DE15 . 185 E6
Newcastle-u-L ST5 .... 71 C4
Devon Cres WS9 .... 245 A1
Devon Ct WS11 .... 226 C8
Devon Gn WS11 .... 226 F8
Devon Gr ST8 .... 16 C1
Devon Ho 4 DY8 .... 279 F8
Devonport Ct 7 ST13 .... 30 E6
Devon Rd Cannock WS11 . 226 F8
Stourbridge DY8 .... 279 E7
Devonshire Ct B74 .... 258 A2
Devonshire Dr
Rugeley WS15 .... 196 D6
Tamworth B78 .... 250 A1
Devonshire Sq ST2 .... 58 C1
Devon Way ST17 .... 174 D6
Dewberry Rd 3 DY8 .... 275 F1
Dewick Ind Est ST17 .... 175 F3
De-Wint Rd ST15 .... 120 B7
Dewsbury Cl DY8 .... 275 E3
Dewsbury Dr
Burntwood WS7 .... 229 C6
Wolverhampton WV4 .... 266 A4
Dewsbury Rd ST4 .... 72 E8
Dexter Way B78 .... 262 F8
Dexton Rise ST17 .... 174 A8
Deykin Rd WS13 .... 231 A6
Dial La Biddulph CW12,SK11 .. 7 B1
Stourbridge DY8 .... 279 E8
Diamond Ave 8 ST7 .... 26 B2
Diamond Cl
Barlaston ST12 .... 104 C8
Biddulph ST8 .... 27 C8
Meir Heath ST3 .... 90 A4
Diamond Gr WS11 .... 210 C3
Diamond Jubilee Cotts
DE6 .... 81 E8
Diamond Park Dr 3
DY8 .... 275 E1
Diamond Ridge ST12 .... 104 C8
Diamond Way ST15 .... 120 B5
Diana Cl WS9 .... 245 B3
Diana Rd ST1 .... 57 F6
Diarmid Rd ST4 .... 71 F1
Dibble Rd DE14 .... 185 A7
Dibdale Ct DY3 .... 271 D3
Dibdale Rd DY1 .... 271 F3
Dibdale Rd W DY1 .... 271 E3
Dibdale St DY1 .... 271 F2
Dibden Ct 7 ST4 .... 72 A7
Dickens Cl
Burton u T DE14 .... 166 D6
Dudley DY3 .... 271 B5
Dickenson Rd E ST6 .... 57 C7
Dickenson Rd W ST6 .... 57 C7
Dickens Rd WV10 .... 241 A1
Dickens St ST2 .... 58 C4
Dickinson Rd WV5 .... 270 A4
Dickson Ho ST1 .... 282 C1
Dickson Rd ST16 .... 156 A5
Dicky's La ST20 .... 151 E7
Didcot Dr ST14 .... 143 F7
Digbeth La WV5 .... 267 B8
Digby Rd DY6 .... 275 D8
Diglake Cl ST7 .... 40 C6
Diglake St ST7 .... 39 F3
Digmire La DE6 .... 51 D1
Dig St SK17 .... 24 D6
Dilhorne Endowed Prim Sch
ST10 .... 75 D5
Dilhorne Gr ST3 .... 284 C1
Dilhorne La
Caverswall ST10 .... 74 F3
Dilhorne ST10 .... 75 A2
Dilhorne Rd Cheadle ST10 . 76 B3
Forsbrook ST11 .... 75 B2
Dilke St ST1 .... 282 C4
Dill Gr ST3 .... 90 B6
Dilhorne Park★ ST10 .... 75 C6
Dimble La ST10 .... 94 E8
Dimbles Hill WS13 .... 214 B1
Dimbles La WS13 .... 214 A2
Dimmelow St ST3 .... 74 B5
Dimmingsdale Rd WV4 ... 264 E5
Dimmingsdale YH★ ST10 . 78 A4
Dimmock St WV4 .... 266 E5
Dimsdale Par E ST5 .... 56 C5
Dimsdale Par W ST5 .... 56 A6
Dimsdale St ST6 .... 56 E7
Dimsdale View E ST5 .... 56 B6
Dimsdale View ST5 .... 55 F6
Dimsdale View W ST5 .... 56 B6
Dingle Dr DE13 .... 165 E4
Dingle La Bridgemere CW5 . 67 A5
Hilderstone ST15 .... 106 D2
Woodhouse Green ST8 .... 17 E7
Dingle Rd Brownhills WS8 244 E6
Wombourne WV5 .... 269 F6
Dingle The Brown Edge ST6 43 B7
Burton u T DE15 .... 185 E8
Wolverhampton WV3 .... 255 D1
Dingle View DY3 .... 271 C7
Dinham Gdns DY1 .... 271 E3
Dippons Dr WV6 .... 255 A3
Dippons Ho WV6 .... 255 A3
Dippons Mill Cl WV6 .... 255 A3
Dirtyfoot La WV4 .... 265 A5
Dirty La ST19 .... 223 C6
District Ctr WS12 .... 210 C2
Ditch Cotts SK17 .... 5 F8
Ditch The SK17 .... 5 F8
Dividy Rd ST2 .... 58 B2
Dixon Cl ST15 .... 104 E2
Dixon Rd CW12 .... 6 A5
Dixon's Row ST5 .... 55 D7
Dixon St WV2 .... 266 E7
Dobbinhorse La DE6 .... 81 F5
Dobbs St WV2 .... 266 C8
Dobell Gr ST3 .... 284 D4
Dobree Cl ST17 .... 177 E7
Dobson St ST6 .... 57 C7
Dock Rd DY8 .... 275 F2
Doctor's Bank TF9 .... 100 C5
Doctors Cl ST8 .... 27 C8
Doctors La
Kingswinford DY6 .... 275 A4
Kinver DY6 .... 274 F5
Shenstone WS14 .... 247 A6
Doddington Pl ST5 .... 71 B6
Doddlespool Barns CW3 .. 52 F7
Dodds La Astbury CW12 ... 15 C6
Chorley WS13 .... 212 C3
Dodslow Ave DE13 .... 147 B3
Dogcroft Rd ST6 .... 42 C5
Dog Kennel La TF9 .... 112 D8
Dog La Butterton ST13 .... 33 E7
Calton ST10 .... 50 A1
Leek ST13 .... 30 E5
Doglands Rd ST18 .... 123 A1
Dog La Netherseal DE12 .. 219 F6
Ranton ST18 .... 153 D4
Stableford ST4,ST5 .... 86 C3
Tamworth B77 .... 251 B6
Weeford WS14 .... 248 A4
Dogmoor La ST10 .... 64 F8
Dogshead La DE13 .... 201 C7
Dolefoot La DE13 .... 162 F4
Doles La DE6 .... 81 F7
Dolespring Cl ST11 .... 91 A8
Doley Cl ST20 .... 171 D6
Dolly's La ST6 .... 42 A2
Dolphin Cl Stafford ST17 . 156 C1
Walsall WS3 .... 243 F1
Dominic St 5 Stone ST15 104 F1
Stoke-on-T ST4 .... 72 A8
Donald Bates Ho ST4 .... 71 F6
Donald Rd ST1 .... 57 E6
Doncaster La ST4 .... 71 F7
Don Gr WS11 .... 226 D7
Donington La WV7 .... 237 B8
Donithorne Cl DE13 .... 166 C7
Donkey La ST10 .... 76 E5
Dorado B77 .... 261 D7
Dorcas Dr ST3 .... 72 F4
Dorchester Cl ST7 .... 26 A3
Dorchester Rd
Cannock WS11 .... 209 B1
Willenhall WV12 .... 242 C1
Dorchester Wlk ST2 .... 58 C2
Dordon Rd B78 .... 262 F8
Doreen Ave CW12 .... 16 B8
Dorian Way ST9 .... 43 F7
Doris Robinson Ct ST3 ... 89 F7
Dorking Cl ST2 .... 57 F2
Dorlan Cl ST9 .... 43 C3
Dormer Ave B77 .... 250 D5
Dormston Dr DY3 .... 271 E8
Dormston Sch The DY3 .. 271 E8
Dormston Trad Est DY1 .. 271 F4
Dorothy Clive Garden The★
TF9 .... 84 A4
Dorridge Gr ST5 .... 56 E4
Dorrington Cl ST2 .... 43 A1
Dorrington Dr ST16 .... 155 E6
Dorrington Gr ST5 .... 56 C6
Dorrington Ind Pk ST16 . 155 E6
Dorrington La CW3 .... 83 B7
Dorset Cl Bucknall ST2 .... 58 C3
Burton u T DE15 .... 185 E6
Tamworth B78 .... 250 A1
Dorset Dr Aldridge WS9 .. 245 B1
Biddulph ST8 .... 27 B8
Dorset Pl Kidsgrove ST7 ... 26 A2
Newcastle-u-L ST5 .... 71 D4
Dorset Rd Cannock WS12 . 210 E1
Stourbridge DY8 .... 279 D8
Dosthill Prim Sch B77 ... 261 D5
Dosthill Rd (Two Gates)
B77 .... 261 D7
Double Gates TF9 .... 112 B8
Douglas Ave Biddulph ST8 . 27 D7
Stoke-on-T ST4 .... 71 F5
Douglas Pl ST1 .... 57 E2
Douglas Rd
Newcastle-u-L ST5 .... 56 A3
Stafford ST16 .... 156 A5
Douglas Rd W ST16 .... 156 A5
Douglas St ST1 .... 57 B6
Doulton Cl Cheadle ST10 .. 76 D1
Stone ST15 .... 119 E6
Doulton Dr ST5 .... 56 B7
Doulton Rd ST18 .... 156 B8
Doulton St 4 ST6 .... 57 A8
Douse La ST13 .... 32 D4
Doval Gdns ST10 .... 92 E4
Dovebank Gr ST3 .... 90 A6
Dove Bank Prim Sch ST7 . 26 A2
Dove Bank ST14 .... 126 C8
Dove Cl Burntwood WS7 .. 229 D6
Fradley WS13 .... 215 B5
Dovecliff Cres DE13 .... 147 F2
Dovecliff Rd DE13 .... 147 E3
Dove Cl ST17 .... 174 F5
Dovecote Cl WV6 .... 255 C4
Dovecote Pl ST3 .... 89 E8
Dovecotes Prim Sch
WV8 .... 239 F1
Dovecotes The B75 .... 258 B3
Dovedale Ave WS3 .... 244 B5
Dovedale WS11 .... 210 A5
Dovedale Cl
Burton u T DE15 .... 167 B5
Cheadle ST10 .... 76 E6
Congleton CW12 .... 6 A4
Stoke-on-T ST6 .... 41 B7
Dovedale Ct WV4 .... 266 F2
Dovedale Pl ST5 .... 55 A1
Dovedale Rd Kingsley ST10 61 E2
Kingswinford DY6 .... 275 E8
Wolverhampton WV4 .... 266 E3
Dovefields ST14 .... 95 F3
Dove Fields ST14 .... 126 D8
Dove Fst Sch ST14 .... 96 A3
Dove Gr Biddulph ST8 .... 16 D1
Egginton DE65 .... 148 A5
Dove Ho ST7 .... 26 C3
Dove Hollow
Cannock WS12 .... 210 E4
Great Wyrley WS6 .... 226 F1
Dovehouse Fields WS14 . 231 B6
Dove La ST14 .... 96 A4
Dove Lea DE13 .... 147 B4
Dove Pl ST5 .... 71 A4
Dover Ct DE13 .... 166 C7
Dove Rd ST11 .... 91 A7
Dover Farm Cl B77 .... 262 B8
Dove Ridge SK17 .... 13 C6
Doveridge Prim Sch
DE6 .... 127 C8
Doveridge Rd DE15 .... 167 B1
Dover Rd DE13 .... 166 B7
Dover St ST1 .... 282 C4
Dove Side DE65 .... 146 D8
Doveside DE6 .... 81 D7
Dove St DE6 .... 80 B2
Dovestone B77 .... 251 D1
Dove View DE13 .... 146 C6
Dove Way The ST14 .... 111 C2
Dove Way ST10 .... 48 F2
Dove Wlk ST14 .... 126 D8
Dowells Gdns DY8 .... 275 D3
Dower Rd B75 .... 258 B1
Downderry Cl ST17 .... 174 A8
Downend Cl WV10 .... 240 F4
Downesway WS11 .... 209 C2
Downey St ST1 .... 282 B2
Downfield Cl WS3 .... 243 A4
Downfield Dr DY3 .... 271 E6
Downfield Gr ST16 .... 155 D8
Downfield Pl ST2 .... 42 F1
Downfields TF10 .... 168 F5
Downford Cl ST19 .... 205 C6
Downford La ST19 .... 205 C6
Downham Pl WV3 .... 265 F8
Downham Rd ST5 .... 55 E2
Downie Rd WV8 .... 239 C3
Downing Ave ST5 .... 56 E3
Downing Dr B79 .... 249 E5
Downing Gdns 3 ST15 .. 120 A7
Downs The Aldridge WS9 . 256 E2
Stafford ST17 .... 175 C7
Downsview Gr ST3 .... 72 F3
Dowty Way WV9 .... 240 A3
Doxey Fields ST16 .... 154 F4
Doxey Ho ST16 .... 155 A4
Doxey Prim Sch ST16 ... 155 B4
Doxey ST16 .... 155 B4
Dragon Sq ST5 .... 55 E8
Drake Ave ST19 .... 207 F6
Drake Cl Berry Hill ST2 .... 57 F1
Walsall WS3 .... 243 B1
Drake Croft 4 WS13 .... 231 C8
Drake Ct WS3 .... 243 B1
Drakeford Ct
Stafford ST17 .... 285 B2
Stoke-on-T ST6 .... 42 E4
Drakeford Gr ST6 .... 42 E4
Drake Rd WS3 .... 243 C1
Drakes Hill Cl DY8 .... 279 C4
Draw-Well La ST9 .... 59 C4
Draycott Cliff DE6 .... 144 C5
Draycott Cl WV4 .... 265 C5
Draycott Cres B77 .... 250 D1
Draycott Cross Rd
Cheadle ST10 .... 76 A1
Draycott in t M ST10 .... 91 F8
Draycott Dr Cheadle ST10 . 76 D1
Newcastle-u-L ST5 .... 40 D2
Draycott Manor Prim Sch
ST11 .... 91 D5
Draycott Old Rd ST11 .... 91 C7
Draycott Rd ST10 .... 92 C4
Drayton Cl B75 .... 258 B3
Drayton Gn ST2 .... 58 A2
Drayton Gr TF9 .... 97 C1
Drayton La B78 .... 260 C5
Drayton Manor Dr
Drayton Bassett B78 .... 260 F7
Fazeley B78 .... 260 F8
Drayton Manor Pk B78 .. 260 E7
Drayton Mill Ct TF9 .... 97 C1
Drayton Rd Hanchurch ST4 . 87 B5
Longton ST3 .... 284 C4
Drayton St
Newcastle-u-L ST5 .... 283 A2
Wolverhampton WV2 .... 266 C8
Dreieich Cl ST15 .... 155 F5
Drenfell Rd ST7 .... 25 F7
Dresden CE Prim Sch
ST3 .... 284 C1
Dresden St ST1 .... 282 C2
Dreys The ST4 .... 88 B7
Driffield Cl ST2 .... 58 E1
Drive Fields WV4 .... 265 B6
Drive Sch (Tettenhall Coll)
The WV6 .... 255 D4
Drive The
Alsagers Bank ST7 .... 54 F6
Burton u T DE13 .... 166 C7
Codsall WV8 .... 238 F3
Rudyard ST13 .... 29 E8
Shenstone WS14 .... 247 E8
Stafford ST16 .... 155 B4
Walsall,Pelsall WS3 .... 243 E2
Walsall WS4 .... 244 C1
Wolverhampton WV6 .... 255 C5
Drointon La ST18 .... 139 D3
Droitwich Cl ST5 .... 54 F2
Drovers Way TF10 .... 169 A4
Droveway The WV9 .... 239 F2
Droxford Wlk WV8 .... 239 E1
Drubbery La ST3 .... 284 A1
Druid Park Rd WV12 .... 242 C1
Druids Ave WS9 .... 256 C8
Druids Way ST19 .... 207 F7
Druids Wlk WS9 .... 245 A3
Drumart Ho DY10 .... 280 A5
Drumber La ST7 .... 26 B8
Drumburn Cl ST6 .... 41 F7
Drummond Cl WV11 .... 242 A2
Drummond Rd ST16 .... 155 E6

Drummond St ST6 41 D7
Drury La WV8 238 F4
Dryburgh Cl ST17 174 B7
Dryburg Wlk ST2 58 A4
Dryden Cres ST17 155 C1
Dryden Rd Burslem ST6 57 A6
Tamworth B79 250 A6
Wolverhampton WV10 240 F1
Dryden Way ST10 76 C2
Dual Way WS12 209 D8
Dubarry Ave DY6 275 C7
Duchy Cl DE13 166 E8
Duchy Rd CW1 37 A8
Duck La WV8 239 B3
Duck St DE65 148 B5
Duddell Rd ST6 42 C2
Dudding Rd WV4 266 D5
Dudley Innovation Ctr DY6 275 F7
Dudley Pl ST3 90 A8
Dudley Rd Dudley DY3 271 E6
Himley DY3 270 D3
Kingswinford DY6 275 F7
Kingswinford,Wall Heath DY6 275 C8
Wolverhampton WV2 266 D7
Dudley St DY3 271 D8
Dudley Wlk WV4 266 C5
Dudmaston Way DY1 271 E3
Duesbury Gn ST3 284 A3
Duffield Cl WV8 239 F1
Duffield La DE13 162 F7
Dugdale Cl WS12 210 F3
Dugdale Cres B75 258 C3
Duke Bank Terr ST6 42 F4
Duke Pl ST5 55 C1
Duke Rd WS7 211 E1
Dukes La ST13,ST10 63 D7
Dukes Rd B78 262 F6
Duke St Biddulph ST8 27 D7
Burton u T DE14 166 C2
Dudley DY3 271 D5
Leek ST13 30 F5
Newcastle-u-L ST5 283 C1
Stoke-on-T ST4 72 E4
Stoke-on-T ST4 72 F5
Tutbury DE13 146 C6
Wolverhampton,Penn Fields WV3 266 A7
Dulverton Ave ST5 71 A5
Dumbill Ho ST7 40 C8
Dumbleberry Ave DY3 271 C7
Dumolo's La B77 250 F3
Dumore Hay La WS13 215 F8
Duncalfe Dr B75 258 B3
Duncalf Gr ST5 56 B7
Duncalf St ST6 56 F8
Duncan St Stoke-on-T ST4 72 E6
Wolverhampton WV2 266 C7
Duncombe St DY8 279 D5
Dundalk La WS6 226 D2
Dundas St ST1 282 C4
Dundee Rd ST1 57 A3
Dundee St ST3 284 B2
Dunedin Cres DE15 167 C2
Dunedin B77 251 A1
Dungarven Dr TF10 168 D2
Dunhampton Dr DY10 280 B1
Dunkirk ST7 40 A6
Dunkirk Ct ST5 283 A3
Dunkirk ST5 283 A3
Dunlin Dr WV10 241 B7
Dunnerdale Rd WS8 244 D6
Dunning St ST6 41 D3
Dunnington Ave DY10 280 A1
Dunnock Cl ST14 126 C6
Dunnock Way ST8 27 E8
Dunrobin St ST3 284 C2
Dunsany Gr ST1 57 E6
Dunsford Ave ST2 43 A2
Dunsley Dr Dunsley DY7 278 C4
Stourbridge DY8 275 E3
Dunsley Gr WV4 266 A4
Dunsley Rd Dunsley DY7 278 C4
Stourbridge DY8 279 C4
Dunstall Brook DE15 167 A1
Dunstall Cross DE13 183 A6
Dunstall Hill DE13 183 B6
Dunstall La B78 249 D4
Dunstall Rd
Barton-u-N DE13 183 E3
Tatenhill DE13 184 A7
Dunster Cl ST17 174 B7
Dunster Gr WV6 254 F3
Dunster Rd ST3 73 C5
Dunster B77 261 C7
Dunston Cl
Great Wyrley WS6 242 E8
Kingswinford DY6 275 D7
Dunston Dr WS7 229 A8
Dunton Cl B75 258 A4
Dunwood Dr ST6 42 A3
Dunwood La ST9,ST13 29 D4
Durban Cl DE15 167 C3
Durber Cl Audley ST7 39 D1
Stoke-on-T ST4 71 E4
D'Urberville Cl WV2 266 F6
D'Urberville Rd WV2 266 F6
D'Urberville Wlk 1 WS11 210 A2
Durfield La DE13 163 B7
Durham Cl B78 250 A2
Durham Dr Rugeley WS15 196 D6
Stoke-on-T ST3 89 C8
Durham Gr ST5 71 D4
Durham Rd DY8 279 D8
Durlston Cl B77 250 F5
Durose Ct ST14 125 C7
Dursley Dr WS11 209 B2
Dursley Rd WS7 229 A7
Durston Pl ST3 73 E3
Dutton's La B75 258 E4
Duttons The ST18 123 B3
Dutton Way ST15 119 F5
Dyke Rd WS15 198 B4
Dykes La TF10 188 D8
Dyke St ST1 282 C3
Dylan Rd Biddulph ST8 27 E6
Longton ST3 73 D3
Dyott Ave WS14 232 E6
Dyott Cl WS13 215 A1
Dyson Ct ST18 156 C5
Dyson Way ST18 156 C5

E

Eagle Cl Cheslyn Hay WS6 226 D2
Dudley DY1 271 F1
Uttoxeter ST14 126 B6
Eagle Cres ST21 133 D6
Eagle Ct
Wolverhampton,Pendeford WV10 240 B3
Wolverhampton,Penn Fields WV3 266 A7
Eagle Dr B77 251 C4
Eagle Gr WS12 210 C1
Eagle Hts DE15 167 D3
Eagle Mill 1 ST13 30 F5
Eagle St Hanley ST1 57 E3
Wolverhampton,Monmore Green WV2 266 E8
Wolverhampton,Penn Fields WV3 266 A7
Ealand St DE13 147 D4
Ealingham B77 251 B1
Eamont Ave ST6 42 A4
Eardleyend Rd ST7 39 F7
Eardley St ST4 71 F6
Earl Dr WS7 211 E1
Earlsbrook Dr ST4 88 C7
Earls Ct Burton u T DE13 166 D8
Newcastle-u-L ST5 283 D3
Earl's Dr ST5 71 B5
Earls Rd ST4 88 E7
Earl Sterndale CE Prim Sch SK17 5 C3
Earl St Kingswinford DY6 275 D4
Leek ST13 30 F6
Newcastle-u-L,Silverdale ST5 55 C1
Newcastle-u-L ST5 283 B3
Stafford ST16 285 B3
Earls Way ST18 158 C2
Earlsway ST10 64 B8
Earlswood Cres WV9 240 A3
Earlswood Rd Bucknall ST1 58 A6
Kingswinford DY6 275 E8
Early La ST15 103 C4
Easby Cl ST17 174 B7
Easby Way WS3 242 F2
Easdale Pl ST5 71 B5
Easedale Cl ST2 43 A2
Easing La ST13 31 E8
East Ave CW2 37 C5
Eastbank Rd ST1 282 A4
East Bank Ride ST11 91 B8
East Beeches WV9 224 B2
Eastbourne Cl ST13 30 D6
Eastbourne Rd ST1 57 E4
Eastbridge Ave ST1 57 D8
East Butts Rd WS15 178 B1
East Cannock Rd WS12 210 C4
East Cl ST15 119 F7
Eastcote Cres WS7 229 A5
East Cres
Newcastle-u-L ST5 56 D3
Stoke-on-T ST1 57 E8
East Croft Rd WV4 265 C5
Eastdean Ave ST2 58 A2
East Dr Biddulph ST8 27 D8
Cheddleton ST13 45 D7
Eastern Ave
Burton u T DE13 166 F8
Lichfield WS13 214 C2
Eastern Way WS11 210 A2
Easters Gr ST2 43 B1
Eastfield Cl Aldridge WS9 256 A6
Stoke-on-T ST3 88 E8
Eastfield Dr ST1 282 C1
Eastfields Rd ST14 126 D8
Eastgate Brewood ST19 223 D7
Cannock WS12 211 A5
Eastgate Ct WS14 231 C6
Eastgate St
Burntwood WS7 228 E8
Stafford ST16 285 B3
East Gn WV4 265 D6
East Gr ST3 74 A1
Easthall Cl ST19 223 D6
Easthead Wlk ST1 282 A2
Eastholme ST15 106 D1
Eastlands Cl ST17 174 E8
Eastlands Gr ST17 174 E8
Eastlands ST17 174 E8
East Lawns CW3 53 A6
Eastleigh DY3 271 C8
Eastmoor Cl B74 257 B2
Eastney Cres WV8 255 F8
East Prec ST1 282 C3
East Rd
Featherstone WV10 241 A7
East Rd *continued*
Wolverhampton WV4 266 F4
Eastridge Croft WS14 247 A5
East St Burton u T DE15 167 C3
Cannock WS11 226 E6
Dudley,Gornalwood DY3 271 D3
Leek ST13 31 A6
Meir ST3 74 B6
Tamworth B77 261 D5
East Terr ST6 42 B6
East View Burslem ST6 56 F7
Mayfield DE6 81 D7
Shuttington B79 251 F7
Tamworth B77 250 E3
Eastward Glen WV8 239 C1
Eastwick Cres ST4 88 A8
Eastwood Ave
Burntwood WS7 229 A8
Stoke-on-T ST6 42 A4
Eastwood Pl ST1 282 B2
Eastwood Rd ST1 282 C1
Eastwood Rise ST5 85 A7
Eaton Cres DY3 271 B3
Eaton Dr WS15 178 E2
Eaton Park Prim Sch ST2 58 A2
Eaton Pl DY6 275 E5
Eaton Rd ST14 95 F3
Eaton St ST1 282 C3
Eaves Court Dr DY3 266 C1
Eaves La Bucknall ST2 58 D5
Cheadle ST10 76 E1
Oakamoor ST10 78 A8
Whiston ST10 62 F1
Eaveswood Rd ST2 58 C6
Ebenezer St WS12 210 A7
Ebony Cl ST16 155 C4
Ebstree Mdw WV5 264 A2
Ebstree Rd Seisdon WV5 264 A2
Seisdon WV5 264 C4
Ebury Gr ST3 73 F1
Eccleshall Bsns Pk DE14 166 E4
Eccleshall Rd
Great Bridgeford ST18 135 D2
Loggerheads,Hookgate TF9 99 E3
Loggerheads,Tadgedale TF9 99 B6
Stafford ST16 155 C6
Stone ST15 119 E6
Eccleston Pl ST6 42 A6
Edale Cl Kingswinford DY6 275 B7
Newcastle-u-L ST5 55 B1
Stoke-on-T ST6 41 B7
Wolverhampton WV4 266 E3
Edale B77 251 B1
Eddens Wood Cl B78 260 E5
Eddies La B79 216 E1
Eddisbury Dr ST5 40 D2
Edenbridge Cl CW2 37 B2
Edenbridge View DY1 271 E3
Eden Cl Biddulph ST8 16 E1
Cannock WS12 210 E2
Hilton DE65 147 C8
Kidsgrove ST7 26 B2
Eden Ct WV10 240 F8
Edenfield Pl B77 251 B1
Eden Gdns DY3 271 E8
Eden Gr Cheadle ST10 76 E1
Loggerheads TF9 99 E5
Longton ST3 73 F1
Edenhurst Ave ST3 90 C8
Edenhurst Prep Sch ST5 70 F7
Edensor CE Prim Sch ST3 284 A2
Edensor Ct ST5 55 E7
Edensor Rd ST3 284 B3
Edensor St ST5 55 E7
Edensor Tech Coll ST3 284 B3
Edensor Terr ST3 284 B2
Edes Farm Dr ST14 95 F4
Edgar Cl B79 249 F7
Edgar Pl ST3 73 C6
Edgbaston Dr ST4 88 D7
Edge Ave ST6 42 A6
Edgecliff High Sch DY7 278 A4
Edgefield La ST6,ST9 43 C5
Edgefield Rd ST3 73 C5
Edge Hill Ave WV10 241 B1
Edge Hill Dr Perton WV6 254 E3
Sedgley DY3 266 C2
Edge Hill Jun Sch DE15 185 F7
Edge Hill DY7 277 F4
Edgehill Rd ST13 30 C5
Edge Hill Rd B74 257 E4
Edge Hill CV9 262 B2
Edge La ST9 43 D7
Edgeley Rd ST8 27 D7
Edgemoor Mdw WS12 210 C1
Edge St ST6 41 F2
Edge View Cl Kinver DY7 277 F5
Stoke-on-T ST2 43 C2
Edge View Ct ST8 27 C7
Edgeview Rd CW12 16 B7
Edge View Rd ST2 43 C2
Edge View Wlk DY7 277 F5
Edgeware St ST1 282 A4
Edgeworth Ho WS13 214 A2
Edgmond Rd TF10 168 E4
Edinburgh Cres DY8 275 C1
Edinburgh Rd CW12 6 A2
Edinburgh Way DE13 166 D8
Edison Cl WS12 210 C7
Edison Rd ST16 155 F5
Edison St ST4 72 D6
Edmonton Cl WS11 210 B2
Edmonton Gr ST2 42 F1
Edmonton Pl DE15 167 D2
Edmund Ave ST17 174 B8
Edmund Rd DY3 271 E6
Ednam Gr WV5 265 A1
Ednam Pl ST3 74 A1
Ednam Rd WV4 266 C5
Edwal Rd ST3 74 A4
Edward Ave Aldridge WS9 256 A7
Newcastle-u-L ST5 71 B6
Stoke-on-T ST4 88 B7
Edward Ct B77 250 F4
Edward Davies Rd ST6 42 C2
Edward Rd WV6 254 E5
Edwards Dr ST16 155 C3
Edwards Farm Rd WS13 215 E8
Edwards Rd
Burntwood WS7 228 F5
Sutton Coldfield B75 258 D3
Edward St 6 Stone ST15 105 A1
Audley ST7 39 F3
Burton u T DE14 166 C4
Cannock WS11 209 E4
Newcastle-u-L ST5 56 D4
Stoke-on-T ST4 72 E7
Tamworth B79 250 A5
Wolverhampton WV4 266 F5
Edwin Cl Penkridge ST19 207 F8
Stafford ST17 155 B1
Efflinch La DE13 201 E7
Egelwin Cl WV6 254 E5
Egerton Cl ST11 91 A6
Egerton Rd Aldridge B74 256 F1
Stoke-on-T ST4 71 E8
Wolverhampton WV10 240 E3
Egerton St ST1 57 D1
Eggington Dr ST19 207 F7
Eggington Rd Hilton DE65 147 F8
Stourbridge DY8 279 D6
Egginton Prim Sch DE65 148 B5
Egginton Rd DE65 148 B8
Egg La ST18 158 E7
Eighth Ave DE14 184 F8
Eights Croft WS7 228 D8
Elaine Ave ST6 42 B1
Elan Cl Cookley DY10 280 B4
Dudley DY3 271 D3
Elan Rd DY3 271 C8
Elburton Rd ST4 73 A6
Elderberry Cl DY8 279 C3
Elder Cl Cannock WS11 210 C2
Uttoxeter ST14 126 B6
Elder Gr WV5 269 F6
Elder La WS7 229 C7
Elder Pl ST6 57 B6
Elder Rd ST6 57 B6
Elderside Cl WS8 244 F8
Eldertree La TF9 100 C6
Eldon St Burton u T DE15 167 B3
Hanley ST1 57 D6
Eldridge Cl WV9 239 F2
Eleanor Cres ST5 71 A6
Eleanor Harrison Dr DY10 280 B5
Eleanor Pl ST5 71 A6
Eleanor View ST5 71 B6
Electric Ind Est DE14 166 E5
Electric St DE14 166 E5
Elenora St ST4 72 B7
Elers Gr ST6 56 E7
Elford Cl Aldridge B74 257 A2
Stafford ST16 155 C8
Elford Heath ST21 133 C6
Elgar Cl Cannock WS11 209 E5
Lichfield WS13 214 B2
Elgar Cres ST1 58 A5
Elgin Cl DY3 266 E1
Elgin Ct WV6 254 E4
Elgin Rd WS3 243 A4
Elgin St ST4 57 B1
Elgood La ST6 41 C7
Elias Cl WS14 231 E6
Eliases La ST8 17 B2
Eliot Cl Armitage WS15 198 B4
Tamworth B79 250 A7
Eliot Way ST17 155 C1
Elisabeth Ct B74 258 B3
Elizabethan Way WS15 196 D7
Elizabeth Ave
Rolleston on D DE13 147 B3
Wolverhampton WV4 266 B5
Elizabeth Bache Cnr DY10 280 A5
Elizabeth Ct
Burton u T DE15 167 C3
Market Drayton TF9 112 C8
Stoke-on-T ST4 71 F8
Talke Pits ST7 40 D5
Elizabeth Dr
Newcastle-u-L ST5 55 E7
Tamworth B79 250 A6
Elizabeth Rd WS11 209 E6
Elizabeth St ST1 57 E4
Elkes Gr ST14 110 F2
Elkington Cl TF10 168 E2
Elkington Rise CW3 68 F7
Elkstone Cl ST6 41 E4
Ellam's Pl ST5 55 E1
Ellastone Gr ST4 71 F6
Ellastone Rd ST10 63 C5
Elldawn Ave ST6 42 F2
Ellerbeck B77 251 B1
Ellerby Rd ST3 88 E8
Ellesmere Ct TF10 168 E2
Ellesmere Gr 3 TF9 112 A8
Ellesmere Rd WS11 226 B8
Ellgreave St ST6 56 E8
Ellington Ave ST16 156 B5
Ellington Cl ST2 58 A2
Elliot Ct 1 WV4 266 F4
Elliot Dr ST9 59 B4
Elliott Cl WS11 209 F5
Elliott Rd ST4 72 F6
Elliotts La WV8 239 A3
Elliott St ST5 56 D1
Ellison Prim Sch ST5 56 D5
Ellison St ST5 56 D5
Ellis St ST6 57 C7
Ellis Wlk WS11 226 F8
Ellowes Hall Sch The DY3 271 C5
Ellowes Rd DY3 271 C4
Ellsmore Mdw WS13 231 A6
Elm Ave ST17 175 F6
Elmbridge Way DY3 271 E6
Elmbrook Cl ST3 89 E8
Elm Cl Burton u T DE14 184 F8
Cookley DY10 280 B4
Doveridge DE6 127 C8
Dudley DY3 271 B2
Great Haywood ST18 158 B2
Kidsgrove ST7 41 B8
Leek ST13 30 C5
Newport TF10 168 F1
Stourbridge DY8 279 D2
Elm Cres ST18 158 C8
Elmcroft Gdns WV10 240 E3
Elmcroft Rd ST2 58 B6
Elm Ct ST18 174 C5
Elmdale Dr WS9 256 C8
Elm Dale Rd WV4 266 A5
Elmdon Cl
Penkridge ST19 208 A8
Wolverhampton WV10 240 A1
Elmdon Pl ST3 90 B7
Elmdon Rd WV10 240 A1
Elm Dr Blakedown DY10 281 B2
Bradley ST18 191 C8
Cheadle ST10 76 F2
Market Drayton TF9 112 A8
Elm Farm Rd WV2 266 D7
Elm Gdns WS14 231 C7
Elm Gr Codsall WV8 239 A3
Huntington WS12 209 D8
Kinver DY7 278 C3
Elmhurst Cl Berry Hill ST2 57 F2
Coven WV9 224 B3
Stafford ST16 155 C8
Elmhurst Dr
Burntwood WS7 229 A4
Kingswinford DY6 275 F4
Elmhurst Egginton DE65 148 A5
Newcastle-u-L ST5 70 F4
Elmley Gr WV6 254 F3
Elmore Ct 4 WS15 196 E8
Elmore Green Prim Sch WS3 243 B1
Elmore Green Rd WS3 243 B1
Elmore Ho WS15 178 E1
Elmore La WS15 178 E1
Elmore Row WS3 243 B1
Elm Pl Cookley DY10 280 B4
Stoke-on-T ST3 72 F1
Elm Rd Kingswinford DY6 275 E6
Norton Canes WS11 228 B5
Stone ST15 120 B8
Elms Cl WV10 225 C1
Elmsdale WV6 255 A2
Elms Dr WS11 209 C1
Elms La WV10 225 C1
Elmsmere Ave ST3 73 A1
Elmsmere Rd ST2 58 B6
Elms Paddock The WV6 253 C2
Elms Rd DE15 166 F2
Elm St ST6 57 A7
Elmstead Cl ST4 71 F1
Elms The ST5 56 C7
Elm St ST5 56 D3
Elmstone Cl
3 Stafford ST17 175 D5
Dudley DY3 271 F4
Elms Way ST3 74 A2
Elm Tree Cl WV5 269 F5
Elm Tree Dr ST7 39 F1
Elmtree Rd B74 256 D1
Elm Tree Wlk B79 249 F8
Elm View ST14 95 E6
Elm Wlk ST19 207 E8
Elmwood Ave WV11 242 A3
Elmwood Cl
Blythe Bridge ST11 91 A6
Cannock WS11 210 A3
Gnosall ST20 171 D7
Lawton-gate ST7 25 A4
Elmwood Dr ST11 91 A6
Elmwood Gr ST14 110 F1
Elmwood Rd DY8 275 C2
Elmwood Rise DY3 266 B1
Elphinstone Rd ST4 71 F3
Elsby Pl ST6 42 A6
Elsdon Rd ST18 174 C6
Elsing St ST4 72 D6
Elston Hall La WV10 240 D1
Elston Hall Prim Sch WV10 240 D2
Elstree Cl ST3 73 F2
Elstree Gr ST1 58 A6
Elswick Rd ST4 72 E8
Eltham Gdns ST5 56 D3
Elton Cl Newborough DE13 162 F8
Wolverhampton WV10 240 E4
Elton La DE13 162 F8
Elton Terr ST6 41 D7
Elton Way ST20 171 D7
Elunda Gr WS7 228 E5
Elviron Dr WV6 255 B5
Elwell Cres DY1 271 F6
Elworthy Cl ST16 156 A5
Elwyn Cl DE13 147 D1
Ely Cl WS11 210 B1
Ely Wlk ST3 284 C4

Emanuals La SK17 . . . . 23 B2
Embers Way ST9 . . . . 44 A8
Emberton St
 Newcastle-u-L,Chesterton
  ST5 . . . . 55 E6
 Newcastle-u-L,Wolstanton
  ST5 . . . . 56 C5
Emberton Way B77 . . . . . . 250 F5
Embleton Wlk **1** ST6 . . . . 56 E7
Embry Ave ST16 . . . . 156 A5
Emerald Way ST15 . . . . . . 120 B4
Emerson Cl DY3 . . . . 271 A4
Emerson Rd Burslem ST6 . . 57 A6
 Wolverhampton WV10 . . . . 240 F1
Emery Ave
 Newcastle-u-L ST5 . . . . . . 71 A7
 Stoke-on-T ST1 . . . . 57 E8
Emery St ST6 . . . . 57 B6
Emmanuel Rd WS7 . . . . . . 229 B7
Empire Ind Est WS9 . . . . . 244 F1
Empire Pas ST4 . . . . 72 A6
Empire Rd DE15 . . . . 167 D3
Empire St ST4 . . . . 72 A6
Emsworth Cres WV9 . . . . . 240 A2
Emsworth Rd ST3 . . . . 88 E8
Encounter Pl ST1 . . . . 57 E5
Enderby Dr WV4 . . . . 266 A5
Enderby Rise DE13 . . . . . . 166 B7
Enderley Cl WS3 . . . . 243 B3
Enderley Dr WS3 . . . . 243 B3
Enderley St ST5 . . . . 283 B4
End Hall Rd WV6 . . . . 255 A3
Endon Dr ST8 . . . . 27 D7
Endon Hall Prim Sch ST9 . 43 F8
Endon High Sch ST9 . . . . . 43 E6
Endon St ST6 . . . . 42 F5
End The DE15 . . . . 167 E8
Endwood Dr B74 . . . . 257 C4
Engine La Tamworth B77 . . 251 B2
 Walsall WS8 . . . . 244 C8
Englesea Ave ST3 . . . . 74 A5
Englesea Brook La CW2 . . . 38 A3
Englesea Brook Mus of
 Primitive Methodism★
  CW2 . . . . 38 A3
Engleton La ST19 . . . . 223 D7
Engleton Mill La ST19 . . . . 223 E8
English Martyrs RC Prim Sch
 ST8 . . . . 27 D7
Ennerdale Cl
 1 Burslem ST6 . . . . 56 E8
 Brownhills WS8 . . . . 244 E7
Ennerdale Dr WV6 . . . . . . 254 F4
Ennerdale Rd WV6 . . . . . . 255 D8
Enoch St ST6 . . . . 56 F7
Ensall Dr DY8 . . . . 275 E1
Ensford Cl B74 . . . . 257 E5
Enson La Marston ST18 . . . 137 B7
 Stone ST15 . . . . 120 D1
Ensor Dr B78 . . . . 251 F1
Enstone Cl ST3 . . . . 88 E8
Enstone Ct ST5 . . . . 71 B3
Enterprise Dr WV10 . . . . . 224 E5
Enterprise Gr WS3 . . . . . . 244 B5
Enterprise Ind Pk WS13 . . 231 F8
Enville Cl WS3 . . . . 243 A3
Enville Common Rd
 Enville DY7 . . . . 273 F5
 Kinver DY7 . . . . 274 A5
Enville Pl DY8 . . . . 279 E5
Enville Rd Dudley DY3 . . . . 271 D4
 Kingswinford DY6 . . . . . . 275 B6
 Kinver DY7 . . . . 278 A5
 Wolverhampton WV4 . . . . 265 C4
Enville St DY8 . . . . 279 F5
Ephraim St ST1 . . . . 282 C1
Epping Rd ST4 . . . . 71 E3
Epsley's Yd ST5 . . . . 285 B2
Epsom Cl Burton u T DE14 . 184 F7
 Cheadle ST10 . . . . 76 E5
 Lichfield WS14 . . . . 231 D7
 Perton WV6 . . . . 254 F4
 Tamworth B77 . . . . 261 C4
Epsom Dr **8** ST17 . . . . . 175 C7
Epworth Ho DE15 . . . . 167 D3
Epworth St ST4 . . . . 72 A7
Erasmus Way WS13 . . . . . 231 A8
Erdington Rd WS9 . . . . . . 256 C5
Eremon Cl WS15 . . . . 196 F6
Eringden B77 . . . . 251 B1
Ermington Rd WV4 . . . . . . 266 D4
Ernald Gdns **5** ST3 . . . . 120 A7
Ernest Edgerton Cl ST6 . . . 41 C5
Eros Cres ST1 . . . . 57 E6
Errill Cl ST4 . . . . 72 D6
Erskine St ST3 . . . . 284 C1
Eskdale Pl
 Newcastle-u-L ST5 . . . . . . 71 B5
 Stoke-on-T ST4 . . . . 88 A7
Eskrett St WS12 . . . . 210 C5
Esk Way ST1 . . . . 71 B4
Esperanto Way ST6 . . . . . . 57 C8
Esselie Ave TF9 . . . . 100 C5
Essex Ave DY6 . . . . 275 B5
Essex Dr Biddulph ST8 . . . . 16 D2
 Cannock WS12 . . . . 210 B4
 Castle Gresley DE11 . . . . . 186 E1
 Great Haywood ST18 . . . . 158 B3
 Kidsgrove ST7 . . . . 25 E2
 Rugeley WS15 . . . . 196 D6
 Stone ST15 . . . . 119 F5
Essex Gdns DY8 . . . . 279 D7
Essex Pl ST1 . . . . 71 A6
Essex Rd Burton u T DE15 . 185 D6
 Sutton Coldfield B75 . . . . 258 D2
Essington Cl
 Alrewas DE13 . . . . 201 A3
 Lichfield WS14 . . . . 231 A5

Essington Cl continued
 Shenstone WS14 . . . . 247 A7
 Stourbridge DY8 . . . . 275 D3
Essington Ind Est WV11 . . 241 F4
Essington Rd WV12 . . . . . 242 B1
Estridge La WS6 . . . . 227 A2
Etchell Rd B78 . . . . 249 F3
Etching Hill CE Prim Sch
 WS15 . . . . 178 C2
Ethelfleda Rd WS15 . . . . . 178 A2
Ethelfleda Rd B77 . . . . 261 F5
Ethelred Cl B74 . . . . 258 A3
Ethelred Cl ST17 . . . . 175 C6
Eton Ave ST5 . . . . 70 F4
Eton Cl Burton u T DE14 . . 166 E6
 Dudley DY3 . . . . 271 F6
 Stafford ST17 . . . . 156 B1
Eton Ct Lichfield WS14 . . . 231 B6
 Sutton Coldfield B74 . . . . 257 F2
Eton Park Jun Sch DE14 . . 166 D7
Eton Pk DE14 . . . . 166 E6
Eton Rd DE14 . . . . 166 D6
Etruria Industrial Mus★
 ST4 . . . . 57 A2
Etruria Locks ST1 . . . . 57 A2
Etruria Old Rd ST1 . . . . . . 56 F3
Etruria Rd
 Hanley,Etruria ST5 . . . . . . 56 F3
 Hanley ST1 . . . . 282 A3
Etruria Vale Rd ST1 . . . . . 57 A3
Etruria Way ST5 . . . . 56 E2
Etruscan Prim Sch ST1 . . . 57 A3
Etruscan St ST1 . . . . 56 F2
Etruscan Wlk ST12 . . . . . . 88 F4
Ettingshall Park Farm La
 WV4 . . . . 266 E4
Ettymore Cl DY3 . . . . 271 D8
Ettymore Rd DY3 . . . . 271 D8
Ettymore Rd W DY3 . . . . . 271 C8
Etwall Rd DE65 . . . . 148 B7
Europa Way WS13 . . . . . . 231 F8
Eva Gr ST5 . . . . 87 D8
Evans Croft B78 . . . . 250 A1
Evans St Burslem ST6 . . . . 41 F1
 Wolverhampton,Cinder Hill WV4,
  WV10 . . . . 266 F1
Eve La DY1 . . . . 271 F5
Evelyn St ST4 . . . . 72 E5
Everest Rd ST7 . . . . 26 C3
Everglade Rd CV9 . . . . 262 C1
Evergreen Hts WS12 . . . . 210 A8
Evergreens The DE13 . . . . 166 F8
Evershed Way DE14 . . . . . 166 C2
Eversley Ave ST13 . . . . 30 E4
Eversley Gr DY3 . . . . 266 C2
Eversley Rd ST3 . . . . 73 E3
Evesham Cres WS3 . . . . . . 242 F3
Evesham St ST3 . . . . 73 E3
Eveson Rd DY8 . . . . 279 C2
Ewe Dale La DE6 . . . . 35 A3
Exbury Cl WV9 . . . . 239 F2
Excelsior Gr WS3 . . . . 244 B5
Exchange Ho ST16 . . . . . . 285 B3
Exchange Ind Est The
 WS11 . . . . 226 E5
Exchange Rd DE13 . . . . . . 201 A3
Exchange The WS3 . . . . . . 243 B1
Exeter Dr B79 . . . . 249 E5
Exeter Gn ST2 . . . . 58 C2
Exeter Rd WS11 . . . . 226 B8
Exeter St ST17 . . . . 174 F4
Exley B77 . . . . 250 D1
Exmouth Gr ST6 . . . . 57 A7
Exonbury Wlk **5** WS11 . . 209 F2
Eyam Cl DE15 . . . . 167 B2
Eynsham Ct WV6 . . . . 255 E5
Eyre St ST6 . . . . 56 E7
Eyrie The DE15 . . . . 167 C3

F

Faber RC Prim Sch The
 ST10 . . . . 78 C8
Faceby Gr ST3 . . . . 90 C7
Fairbank Ave ST4 . . . . 71 F5
Fairbanks Wlk ST15 . . . . . 103 B4
Fairburn Cres WS3 . . . . . . 244 B5
Fairclough Pl ST6 . . . . 42 A3
Fairfax Rd WV10 . . . . 240 E3
Fairfax St ST1 . . . . 57 D6
Fairfield Ave
 Brown Edge ST6 . . . . 43 B7
 Newcastle-u-L ST5 . . . . . . 56 C4
 Rolleston on D DE13 . . . . . 147 D4
 Stoke-on-T ST3 . . . . 89 C8
Fairfield Cl WS12 . . . . 210 D1
Fairfield Cres DE11 . . . . . . 186 E5
Fairfield Ct ST16 . . . . 155 F6
Fairfield Dr Codsall WV8 . . 238 E4
 Kinver DY7 . . . . 278 A3
 Penkridge ST19 . . . . 207 F6
 Walsall WS3 . . . . 244 B4
Fairfield Rd
 Stourbridge DY8 . . . . 275 F2
 Uttoxeter ST14 . . . . 126 B8
Fairfield Rise DY8 . . . . 279 D5
Fairfields ST7 . . . . 39 F2
Fairfields Hill B78 . . . . 262 F8
Fairfields Rd ST8 . . . . 17 B1
Fairford Gdns
 Burntwood WS7 . . . . 229 C6
 Stourbridge DY8 . . . . 275 E3
Fairgreen Rd ST5 . . . . 85 D5
Fairgreen Way B74 . . . . . . 257 A1
Fairham Rd DE13 . . . . 147 F1
Fairhaven CW2 . . . . 37 B1
Fairhaven Gr ST1 . . . . 57 E6
Fairhaven Prim Sch DY8 . . 275 D3

Fairhills DY3 . . . . 271 D8
Fair Lady Dr WS7 . . . . 228 D8
Fair Lawn WV7 . . . . 237 A5
Fairlawn Cl Stoke-on-T ST3 . 89 E8
 Willenhall WV12 . . . . 242 C1
Fairlawn Ct WV7 . . . . 237 B5
Fairlawn Dr DY6 . . . . 275 D4
Fairlawns ST3 . . . . 283 B4
Fairlawns Way WV12 . . . . 242 C1
Fairlight Gr ST3 . . . . 90 A7
Fair Mdws WS15 . . . . 179 A7
Fairmead Cl ST17 . . . . 175 C6
Fairmeadows Prim Sch
 DE11 . . . . 186 E5
Fairmount Rd **5** WS11 . . 226 E8
Fairmount Way WS15 . . . . 178 C1
Fairoak Ave ST16 . . . . 155 C8
Fairoak Bank ST21 . . . . . . 115 D6
Fairoak Dr WV6 . . . . 255 B3
Fairoak St ST5 . . . . 70 F4
Fair Oak TF10 . . . . 168 F4
Fair Oaks Bsn & Ent Coll
 WS15 . . . . 196 D8
Fair Oaks Dr WS6 . . . . 243 A8
Fair Oaks WS15 . . . . 196 B6
Fair View WS15 . . . . 198 C4
Fairview Ave
 Cheslyn Hay WS6 . . . . 226 D2
 Tamworth B79 . . . . 250 F5
Fairview Cres DY6 . . . . 275 F6
Fair View Rd ST13 . . . . 31 A4
Fairview Rd WV4 . . . . 265 C4
Fairview Villas ST5 . . . . . . 85 C5
Fairview Way ST17 . . . . . . 156 C1
Fairway Burton u T DE14 . . 185 B6
 Cannock WS11 . . . . 226 D6
Fairway Ct B77 . . . . 251 B3
Fairway Rd ST6 . . . . 42 A3
Fairways Ave DY8 . . . . 279 E2
Fairways Cl DY8 . . . . 279 E2
Fairway ST16,ST17 . . . . . . 156 A2
Fairways The DE6 . . . . 81 F6
Fairway B77 . . . . 261 F5
Fairway The
 3 Rugeley WS15 . . . . . . 196 E8
 Swadlincote DE11 . . . . . . 186 E5
Fairway Trentham ST4 . . . . 87 E8
 Walsall WS4 . . . . 244 D1
Falcon Bsns Ctr DE14 . . . . 166 E5
Falcon Cl Burton u T DE14. 166 E5
 Cannock WS11 . . . . 209 C2
 Cheslyn Hay WS6 . . . . 226 C2
Falcon Cres WV14 . . . . . . 266 F2
Falcondale Rd WV12 . . . . 242 C1
Falcon Dr WS14 . . . . 232 E5
Falcon Pk B77 . . . . 261 E7
Falcon Rd ST3 . . . . 90 A6
Falcon Rise DY8 . . . . 279 C6
Falconry Ctr The★ DY9 . . . 281 F3
Falcon B77 . . . . 262 A6
Falcon Way DY1 . . . . 271 F1
Faldo Cl DE14 . . . . 185 B6
Falkirk Grange ST5 . . . . . . 70 F7
Falklands Cl DY3 . . . . 269 E2
Fallow Deer Lawn TF10 . . 168 F5
Fallow Field WS11 . . . . . . 209 E4
Fallowfield Cl
 Penkridge ST19 . . . . 207 E8
 Stone ST15 . . . . 120 C6
Fallowfield Dr DE13 . . . . . 183 C2
Fallow Field
 Lichfield WS13 . . . . 214 C3
 Little Aston B74 . . . . 257 B3
Fallowfield Perton WV6 . . 254 D4
 Stafford ST17 . . . . 175 C6
 Stoke-on-T ST3 . . . . 88 F8
 Wolverhampton WV8 . . . . 239 E2
Fallow Rd B78 . . . . 249 F1
Falmouth Ave ST17 . . . . . 175 E8
Falmouth Cl ST17 . . . . 175 E8
Falmouth Ct ST5 . . . . 71 C5
Falmouth Dr B77 . . . . 250 F5
Falmouth Rd CW12 . . . . . . 15 E8
Falna Cres B79 . . . . 249 F7
Fancourt Ave WV4 . . . . . . 265 D4
Fancy Wlk ST16 . . . . 155 D5
Fane Rd WV11 . . . . 242 B2
Fanlizard La ST20 . . . . 171 D3
Faraday Ave DE13 . . . . . . 166 D8
Faraday Ct DE14 . . . . 184 E7
Faraday Pl ST4 . . . . 71 E7
Faraday Rd ST16 . . . . 155 F5
Farcroft Ave ST5 . . . . 55 F6
Farcroft Dr TF9 . . . . 97 A1
Fareham Cres WV4 . . . . . . 265 C6
Farewell La WS7 . . . . 229 E6
Far Green Ind Est ST1 . . . . 57 D6
Farifields Rd TF9 . . . . 97 D2
Faringdon B77 . . . . 250 F1
Farington Dr ST6 . . . . 42 A6
Farland Gr ST6 . . . . 42 A6
Far Lane Ind Est ST10 . . . . 62 A7
Farleigh Dr WV3 . . . . 265 A8
Farleigh Gr ST2 . . . . 58 C1
Farleigh Rd WV6 . . . . 255 A3
Farley La ST10 . . . . 78 D3
Farley Rd ST10 . . . . 78 B5
Farmadine St ST4 . . . . 88 B7
Farman Cl ST4 . . . . 90 C7
Farmbrook Ave WV10 . . . . 240 D3
Farm Cl Burton u T DE13 . . 166 B7
 Cannock WS11 . . . . 210 C3
 Codsall WV8 . . . . 239 B2
 Market Drayton TF9 . . . . . 97 A1
 Rugeley WS15 . . . . 178 C2

Farm Cl continued
 Sedgley DY3 . . . . 271 B7
 Tamworth B79 . . . . 250 C7
Farm Ct DE13 . . . . 166 C7
Farmdown Rd ST17 . . . . . 156 C1
Farmers Bank ST5 . . . . . . 55 C1
Farmer St ST3 . . . . 284 C2
Farmfields Rise CW3 . . . . . 67 C1
Farm Gr TF10 . . . . 168 D3
Farm Hollow ST7 . . . . 40 A2
Farm House La **6** B75 . . 258 E3
Farm La DE15 . . . . 167 E7
Farm Lea
 Hilderstone ST15 . . . . 106 D2
 Stoke-on-T ST6 . . . . 42 E6
Farmoor Way WV10 . . . . . 240 E4
Farm Rd
 Burnhill Green WV6 . . . . . 252 D7
 Burton u T DE13 . . . . 166 C7
 Wolverhampton WV3 . . . . 265 C8
Farmside GN WV9 . . . . 239 F2
Farmside La ST8 . . . . 17 B1
Farm Side DE11 . . . . 186 F5
Farm View ST15 . . . . 106 D2
Farm Wood Cl ST3 . . . . . . 74 B1
Farnborough Ct B75 . . . . . 258 C2
Farnborough Dr ST3 . . . . . 90 C7
Farncote Dr B74 . . . . 257 F3
Farndale Ave WV6 . . . . . . 255 F6
Farndale St **9** ST6 . . . . . 41 D3
Farne Gr ST3 . . . . 73 A3
Farnham Dr ST8 . . . . 27 B5
Farnworth Cl ST8 . . . . 27 B6
Farnworth Rd ST3 . . . . 73 E3
Far Ridding ST20 . . . . 171 C5
Farrier Cl ST15 . . . . 120 D7
Farriers Gn TF10 . . . . 169 B3
Farriers Mill WS3 . . . . 243 E4
Farrier Way DY6 . . . . 275 A7
Farrington Cl ST15 . . . . . . 42 E3
Farrington Rd WV4 . . . . . . 266 E3
Farthings The WS14 . . . . . 246 F5
Far View WS9 . . . . 245 B2
Farway Gdns WV8 . . . . . . 238 F2
Fasson Cl B77 . . . . 261 C8
Fauld Ind Pk DE13 . . . . . . 145 E6
Fauld La Tutbury DE13 . . . 146 A6
 Tutbury,Fauld DE13 . . . . . 145 D7
Faulkner Cl DY8 . . . . 279 F4
Faulkner Pl ST3 . . . . 73 C7
Faversham Wlk **3** 255 E8
Faversham Rd DE13 . . . . . 166 A6
Fawcett Way ST1 . . . . 282 C4
Fawfield Dr ST6 . . . . 41 C6
Fawn Dr Huntington WS12 . 209 C6
 Meir ST3 . . . . 90 A8
Fazeley Rd Tamworth B78 . 250 A4
 Tamworth,Fazeley B78 . . . 250 B2
Fearns Ave ST5 . . . . 41 B1
Fearon Gn ST6 . . . . 42 E3
Featherbed La
 Hixon ST18 . . . . 158 C3
 Lichfield WS13 . . . . 213 E3
Featherston Gr ST4 . . . . . . 72 A7
Featherstone La
 Featherstone WV10 . . . . . 241 B8
 Shareshill WV10 . . . . 225 B1
Featherston Rd B74 . . . . . 257 A2
Fecknam Way WS13 . . . . . 214 C1
Federation Rd ST6 . . . . . . 41 F1
Fegg Hayes Rd ST6 . . . . . 42 A6
Feiashill Cl WV5 . . . . 269 B7
Feiashill Rd WV5 . . . . 269 B7
Felcourt Gdns ST1 . . . . . . 57 E5
Felden St ST16 . . . . 136 D1
Fellbrook Ct ST2 . . . . 58 A4
Fellbrook La ST2 . . . . 58 A4
Fellfield Way ST16 . . . . . . 155 D8
Fellmeadow Way DY3 . . . . 271 C7
Fellows Ave DY6 . . . . 275 C8
Fellows St WV2 . . . . 266 C8
Fell St ST6 . . . . 42 C1
Felspar Rd B77 . . . . 251 B3
Felstead Cl B77 . . . . 261 C4
Felsted St ST2 . . . . 43 B3
Felthouse La ST13 . . . . . . 45 B2
Femcroft Ind Est DE14 . . . 166 E5
Fence La CW12 . . . . 15 D4
Fenlow Ave ST2 . . . . 57 F2
Fenmere Cl WV4 . . . . 266 D5
Fennel Cl
 Cheslyn Hay WS6 . . . . 226 D3
 Uttoxeter ST14 . . . . 126 B6
Fennel Dr ST17 . . . . 174 F5
Fennel Gr ST3 . . . . 90 B6
Fenners Gr ST4 . . . . 88 B7
Fenn Rise DY8 . . . . 275 D3
Fenn St B77 . . . . 250 D5
Fenpark Ind Est ST4 . . . . . 73 A5
Fenpark Rd ST4 . . . . 73 A6
Fenton Cl CW12 . . . . 6 A1
Fenton Ct ST19 . . . . 205 C6
Fenton Ho ST5 . . . . 283 B3
Fenton House La ST5 . . . . 205 B6
Fenton Ind Est ST4 . . . . . . 72 E8
Fenton Pk ST4 . . . . 73 A6
Fenton Berry Hill ST2 . . . . 57 F2
 Bucknall ST2 . . . . 58 A3
Fereday Rd WS9 . . . . 245 B3
Fereday's Croft DY3 . . . . . 271 B7
Ferguson St WV11 . . . . . . 242 A1
Fermain Cl ST5 . . . . 70 F2
Fern Cl Mow Cop ST7 . . . . 26 C6
 Walsall WS4 . . . . 244 D1
Fern Cres CW12 . . . . 6 A3
Ferncroft Cl ST4 . . . . 88 B7

Ema – Fie **303**

Fern Croft WS13 . . . . 213 F1
Ferndale Cl
 Blythe Bridge ST11 . . . . . . 90 F6
 Burntwood WS7 . . . . 229 B6
 Werrington ST9 . . . . 59 A4
 Weston CW2 . . . . 37 B5
Ferndale Gdns ST7 . . . . . . 26 E3
Ferndale Rd
 Essington WV11 . . . . 242 B3
 Lichfield WS13 . . . . 213 F1
Fern Dell Cl WS11 . . . . . . 209 C2
Fern Dene CW3 . . . . 68 D7
Ferndown Ave DY3 . . . . . . 271 C7
Ferndown Cl Longton ST3 . 73 D1
 Walsall WS3 . . . . 243 B4
Ferndown Dr ST5 . . . . 71 C2
Ferndown Dr S ST5 . . . . . . 71 C1
Ferndown Way CW2 . . . . . 52 C8
Fern Dr Great Wyrley WS6 . 227 A4
 Stafford ST16 . . . . 155 A5
Ferney Pl ST6 . . . . 41 C6
Fernhill Rd TF10 . . . . 150 C1
Fernhurst Cl ST15 . . . . . . 120 C7
Fernie Cl ST15 . . . . 120 C6
Fernlea Cres ST9 . . . . 43 F8
Fernlea Gr Meir Heath ST3 . 90 A4
 Meir ST3 . . . . 74 B5
Fernleigh Ave WS7 . . . . . . 229 A8
Fernleigh Gdns
 Stafford ST16 . . . . 155 A5
 Stourbridge DY8 . . . . 275 C3
Fern Leys WV3 . . . . 255 D1
Fern Pl ST3 . . . . 284 C2
Fern Rd Huntington WS12 . 209 D5
 Wolverhampton WV3 . . . . 266 B8
Fernwood Croft ST13 . . . . 30 C4
Fernwood Ctr The WS15 . . 178 C4
Fernwood Dr Leek ST13 . . . 30 C4
 Rugeley WS15 . . . . 178 C4
Fernwood Gn ST4 . . . . 88 C7
Fernwood Rd ST16 . . . . . . 155 D7
Ferrand Cl ST4 . . . . 72 A2
Ferrers Ave DE13 . . . . 146 B5
Ferrers Cl B75 . . . . 258 D2
Ferrers Rd Tamworth B77 . 250 D4
 Weston DE13 . . . . 138 C2
 Yoxall DE13 . . . . 182 A2
Ferrie Gr WS8 . . . . 244 E8
Ferry St DE15 . . . . 185 E8
Ferry Vale Cl DE15 . . . . . . 185 E8
Festival Cl ST6 . . . . 57 A5
Festival Ct Cannock WS11 . 209 E5
 Lichfield WS13 . . . . 231 A7
Festival Heights Ret Pk
 ST1 . . . . 57 A5
Festival Mews WS12 . . . . 209 F6
Festival Rd DE14 . . . . 184 E7
Festival Way ST1 . . . . 56 F5
Fiddlers Bank ST6 . . . . 43 B8
Fiddler's La DE13 . . . . 146 F4
Field Ave Hatton DE65 . . . . 146 C8
 Stoke-on-T ST2 . . . . 43 B7
Field Cl Blythe Bridge ST11 . 90 E6
 Burton u T DE13 . . . . 166 A7
 Walsall WS4 . . . . 244 B2
 Whitmore ST5 . . . . 85 C5
Field Cotts ST18 . . . . 175 A1
Field Cres ST18 . . . . 154 D2
Field Ct WS4 . . . . 244 B2
Field Dr DE13 . . . . 147 B4
Fielden Cl ST6 . . . . 42 F2
Field End Cl ST4 . . . . 88 B7
Fieldfare WS7 . . . . 229 D5
Field Farm Dr B79 . . . . . . 217 C5
Field Farm Rd B77 . . . . . . 250 D1
Field Head Pl WV6 . . . . . . 255 B4
Field House Ct ST15 . . . . . 104 F2
Fieldhouse Rd
 Burntwood WS7 . . . . 229 A7
 Cannock WS12 . . . . 209 F7
 Wolverhampton WV4 . . . . 266 E4
Fielding St ST4 . . . . 72 B5
Field La Burton u T DE13 . . 166 A7
 Church Leigh ST10 . . . . . . 109 B1
 Great Wyrley WS6 . . . . . . 226 F3
 Stanton DE6 . . . . 80 C8
 Walsall WS4 . . . . 244 B2
Field Pl Longton ST3 . . . . . 73 C5
 Rugeley WS15 . . . . 196 B7
 Stafford ST16 . . . . 155 E6
Field Rd Lichfield WS13 . . . 214 B3
 Walsall WS3 . . . . 243 C1
Field Rise DE13 . . . . 166 B7
Field Rise Rd ST12 . . . . . . 103 E8
Fieldside Stafford ST17 . . . 175 D5
 Yarnfield ST15 . . . . 118 E6
Fields Rd CW12 . . . . 15 F8
Field St WS11 . . . . 209 F3
Fields The WV8 . . . . 239 B4
Field St ST13 . . . . 30 E5
Fieldstone View DY3 . . . . . 271 C4
Fieldsway ST15 . . . . 119 E8
Field Terr ST15 . . . . 105 A1
Field View Biddulph ST8 . . 16 F7
 Meir ST3 . . . . 74 B4
Fieldway
 Blythe Bridge ST11 . . . . . . 90 D7
 Stoke-on-T ST3 . . . . 72 E3
Field Way DE11 . . . . 186 F5
Fieldway Trentham ST4 . . . 87 E7
 Werrington ST2 . . . . 58 F3
Field Wlk WS9 . . . . 256 B7

Fife St ST4 . . . . 284 A4
Fifth Ave ST7 . . . . 25 E1
Filance Cl ST19 . . . . 207 F7
Filance La ST19 . . . . 207 F8
Filey Cl Bucknall ST2 . . . . 58 D2
Cannock WS11 . . . . 226 C8
Filey Rd WV10 . . . . 240 B2
Filey B77 . . . . 250 F6
Fillybrooks Cl ST15 . . . . 119 F8
Fillybrooks The ST15 . . . 119 F8
Filton Ave WS7 . . . . 229 A8
Fincham Cl WV3 . . . . 240 A3
Finchdean CI WV3 . . . . . . 255 D1
Finchdene Gr WV3 . . . . . . 255 C1
Finches Hill WS15 . . . . . . 178 C2
Finchfield Cl DY8 . . . . . . 279 C4
Finchfield Gdns WV3 . . . . 255 E1
Finchfield Hill WV3 . . . . . 255 C1
Finchfield La WV3 . . . . . . 265 C8
Finchfield Rd WV3 . . . . . . 255 D1
Finchfield Rd W WV3 . . . . 255 D1
Finchley Cl DY3 . . . . 271 D2
Finch Pl ST8 . . . . 27 B2
Finchsmith Pl ST3 . . . . . 284 B2
Finch St ST8 . . . . 27 B1
Finch Way WS13 . . . . 215 E8
Fine La WS13 . . . . 215 E6
Finger Post Dr WS3 . . . . 244 A5
Finney Gn ST2 . . . . 58 A3
Finstock Ave ST3 . . . . 88 E8
Firbank Pl ST3 . . . . 73 F4
Firbank Way WS3 . . . . . . 243 F2
Firbeck Gdns ST17 . . . . . 175 C7
Firbob La ST10 . . . . 93 F3
Fir Cl WV12 . . . . 209 D8
Fircroft 9 WV4 . . . . 266 F4
Fircroft 3 WS11 . . . . 210 A3
Firecrest Cl WS11 . . . . . . 210 C2
Fir Gr DY8 . . . . 279 D6
Firmstone Dr DY8 . . . . . . 279 E7
Firmstone St DY8 . . . . . . 279 E7
Firs Cl The ST17 . . . . 175 D7
Firs Mobile Home Pk The 4
WS11 . . . . 210 A2
Firs Rd DY6 . . . . 275 E6
First Ave Brownhills WS8 . 245 A8
Bucknall ST2 . . . . 58 D3
Burton u T DE14 . . . . . . 184 E8
Kidsgrove ST7 . . . . 25 F1
Kingswinford DY6 . . . . . 271 A1
Newcastle-u-L ST5 . . . . . 56 C7
Stafford ST16 . . . . 155 C7
Firs The WS15 . . . . 211 F5
Fir St DY3 . . . . 270 F7
Firsway The ST19 . . . . . . 221 E8
Firsway WV6 . . . . 255 A2
Firtree Cl ST18 . . . . 174 C3
Fir Tree Cl B79 . . . . 249 E2
Fir Tree Cotts CW2 . . . . . 38 C5
Fir Tree Dr DY3 . . . . 271 E7
Fir Tree Pl ST5 . . . . 55 E8
Fir Tree Rd Stoke-on-T ST3 . 89 E8
Wolverhampton WV3 . . . 265 D8
Firwood Rd ST8 . . . . 16 F1
Fisher Rd WS3 . . . . 242 F2
Fishers Lock TF10 . . . . . 168 F4
Fisher St Brindley Ford ST8 . 27 B2
Cannock WS12 . . . . 209 F8
Wolverhampton WV3 . . . 266 B8
Fisherwick Cl WS14 . . . . 232 F6
Fisherwick Rd WS14 . . . . 232 F5
Fishley Cl WS3 . . . . 243 C4
Fishley La WS3 . . . . 243 D5
Fishpond La
Egginton DE65 . . . . 148 A3
Tutbury DE13 . . . . 146 C6
Fishpond Way ST2 . . . . . . 58 A7
Fistral Cl ST3 . . . . 73 D4
Fistral Gdns WV3 . . . . . . 265 F7
Fitchet's Bank WS7 . . . . . 229 F6
Fithern Cl DY3 . . . . 271 E5
Fitzgerald Cl ST3 . . . . 74 B4
Fitzherbert Cl ST15 . . . . 103 B4
Fitzherbert Rd ST11 . . . . . 57 E8
Five Lands Rd DE15 . . . . 185 F8
Five Lanes End ST20 . . . . 153 D7
Five Oaks Cl ST5 . . . . 70 E3
Fives Gr WS7 . . . . 228 C8
Five Ways Dudley DY3 . . . 271 D3
Iverley DY10 . . . . 281 A5
Five Ways Prim Sch
WS12 . . . . 210 D2
Five Ways WV3 . . . . 265 C2
Flackets La DE6 . . . . 128 B7
Flackett St ST3 . . . . 284 C5
Flamborough Gr ST6 . . . . . 56 E7
Flanders Dr DY6 . . . . 275 D8
Flashbrook Cross Roads
TF10 . . . . 149 D5
Flash CE Prim Sch SK17 . . . 3 B3
Flashes The ST20 . . . . . . 171 E7
Flash La Blore TF9 . . . . . . 98 F1
Orton WV4 . . . . 264 C2
Stoke-on-T,Baddeley Edge
ST2 . . . . 43 C2
Stoke-on-T,Trent Vale ST4 . 71 E3
Flash Ley Prim Sch ST17 174 F2
Flash The CW12 . . . . 15 E6
Flather La DE6 . . . . 65 D1
Flats La WS14 . . . . 248 A6
Flatts Cl DE13 . . . . 166 B6
Flatts Rd ST6 . . . . 42 E5
Flavells La DY3 . . . . 271 B2
Flaxcroft Ct ST12 . . . . 88 C2
Flax Croft ST15 . . . . 120 B7

Flax Hill Jun Sch B79 . . . 250 B7
Flaxley Rd WS15 . . . . . . 196 D6
Flaxman Cl ST12 . . . . 88 F4
Flax Ovens The ST19 . . . 192 E2
Flax St ST4 . . . . 72 B6
Fleckney Rd ST3 . . . . 73 E3
Fleets La ST13 . . . . 49 B8
Fleet St DE14 . . . . 166 D1
Fleming Rd ST4 . . . . 72 B7
Flemmynge Cl WV8 . . . . . 238 E4
Fletcher Bank ST5 . . . . . 283 A3
Fletcher Cres ST2 . . . . . . 43 B2
Fletcher Dr WS13 . . . . . . 215 C6
Walsall WV12 . . . . 242 D1
Fletcher St ST1 . . . . 282 A1
Fletches The DE13 . . . . . 147 B1
Fleur Gr ST4 . . . . 73 B6
Flinn Cl WS14 . . . . 231 D7
Flints Cnr WS12 . . . . 195 B4
Flintsham Gr ST1 . . . . . . 282 B4
Flint St ST5 . . . . 74 B5
Flora Cl B79 . . . . 250 C7
Florence Ave 13 WV4 . . . 266 F4
Florence Dr DE6 . . . . 127 C8
Florence Prim Sch ST3 . . 284 C2
Florence Rd Codsall WV8 . 239 C3
Trentham ST4 . . . . 71 C1
Florence St
Cannock WS12 . . . . 210 B7
Newcastle-u-L ST5 . . . . . 283 B3
Florence Terr ST9 . . . . . . 29 A1
Florendine Com Prim Sch
B77 . . . . 250 F5
Florendine St B77 . . . . . . 250 F5
Florida Cl ST6 . . . . 57 B8
Floyd St ST4 . . . . 72 B8
Flynn Row ST4 . . . . 72 F8
Foden Ave ST7 . . . . 25 A3
Foden Cl WS14 . . . . 246 F6
Foden St ST4 . . . . 72 A5
Fog Cotts Rugeley WS15 . 178 E1
Wrinehill CW3 . . . . 52 E4
Fogg St E ST5 . . . . 283 B3
Fogg St W ST5 . . . . 283 B3
Fogg St ST5 . . . . 283 B3
Fold La ST8 . . . . 16 E4
Fold Terr ST13 . . . . 45 C5
Fold The Oaken WV8 . . . . 238 D2
Oulton ST15 . . . . 105 C3
Wolverhampton WV4 . . . 265 D2
Folebank Barns ST14 . . . 109 F8
Fole La ST14 . . . . 109 F8
Foley Ave WV6 . . . . 255 C3
Foley Church Cl B74 . . . . 257 A4
Foley Ct B74 . . . . 256 F1
Foley Dr WV6 . . . . 255 C3
Foley Gr WV5 . . . . 269 E5
Foley Inf Sch DY7 . . . . . . 278 A3
Foley Pl ST4 . . . . 284 A4
Foley Rd E B74 . . . . 257 A2
Foley Rd ST3 . . . . 284 A3
Foley Rd W B74 . . . . 256 E1
Foley St Dunsley DY7 . . . 278 B4
Longton ST3 . . . . 284 B5
Foley Wood Cl B74 . . . . . 256 E1
Folly Fields ST13 . . . . 45 B2
Folly La ST9 . . . . 60 C7
Folly View TF9 . . . . 99 D5
Fontaine Pl ST4 . . . . 72 A5
Fontenaye Rd B79 . . . . . 249 F7
Fonthill Wlk ST2 . . . . 58 A4
Fonthill Rd ST16 . . . . . . 155 F6
Fontwell Rd
Burton u T DE14 . . . . . . 184 F7
Wolverhampton WV10 . . 240 D4
Footherley La WS14 . . . . 246 C4
Footherley Rd WS14 . . . . 246 F5
Forber Rd ST4 . . . . 71 F4
Ford Ave ST6 . . . . 42 B5
Ford Brook La WS3 . . . . . 244 B2
Ford Cl ST15 . . . . 120 A7
Ford Dr ST15 . . . . 118 E6
Ford Green Hall (Mus)★
ST6 . . . . 42 D2
Ford Green Rd ST6 . . . . . . 42 D2
Fordham Gr WV9 . . . . . . 240 A3
Ford Hayes La
Bucknall ST2 . . . . 73 D8
Bucknall ST3 . . . . 58 F1
Werrington ST3 . . . . 59 A1
Fordhouse Rd Ind Est
WV10 . . . . 240 D1
Fordhouse Rd WV10 . . . . 240 D1
Ford La
Creswell Green WS13 . . 212 F2
Longdon WS15 . . . . 198 A3
Ford Rd TF10 . . . . 168 E1
Fordrough The B74 . . . . . 258 A1
Fords La ST7 . . . . 26 C6
Ford St Burton u T DE15 . 185 E7
Leek ST13 . . . . 30 F6
Newcastle-u-L ST5 . . . . . 55 B2
Stoke-on-T ST4 . . . . 56 E1
Ford Way WS15 . . . . 198 B5
Foregate Ct ST16 . . . . . . 285 B4
Foregate St ST16 . . . . . . 285 A4
Forest Cl Colwich ST18 . . 177 D8
Newcastle-u-L ST5 . . . . . 70 E4
Forest Ct ST1 . . . . 282 B4
Forest Dr DY7 . . . . 277 F4
Forest Edge ST6 . . . . 57 C6
Forest Edge Way DE13 . . 166 A8
Forest Glade WS6 . . . . . . 226 F2
Forest La DY7 . . . . 268 E2
Forest Lawns B74 . . . . . . 257 C3
Forest Park Prim Sch
ST1 . . . . 282 A4

Forest Rd Burton u T DE13 165 E4
Draycott in t C DE6 . . . . 144 B4
Dunstall ST19 . . . . 183 B5
Market Drayton TF9 . . . 112 A8
Stoke-on-T ST3 . . . . 89 F7
Forest School St DE13 . . 147 C4
Forestside Gr ST4 . . . . . . 72 A2
Forest Way WS6 . . . . 227 A1
Forge Cl
Hammerwich WS7 . . . . . 229 D5
Wolverhampton WV8 . . . 239 F1
Forge La
Aldridge,Leighswood
WS9 . . . . 256 A5
Aldridge,Mill Green WS9 . 256 F7
Blakedown DY10 . . . . . . 281 B1
Burntwood WS7 . . . . . . 229 F6
Burton u T DE13 . . . . . 148 A2
Hanley ST1 . . . . 56 F4
Kingswinford DY6 . . . . . 275 A8
Lichfield WS13 . . . . 214 A1
Norton in H TF9 . . . . 82 C1
Shenstone B74,WS14 . . 257 C7
Stretton DE13 . . . . 147 F2
Forge Leys WV5 . . . . 269 E6
Forge Mews WS15 . . . . . 178 F1
Forge Rd Rugeley WS15 . 178 F1
Stourbridge DY8 . . . . . . 279 F6
Walsall WS3 . . . . 243 F5
Forge Rise ST18 . . . . 191 C8
Forge Row WS15 . . . . . . 196 B6
Forge Side ST9 . . . . 44 A8
Forge St WS12 . . . . 210 C4
Forge Valley Way WV5 . . 269 C6
Forge Way ST8 . . . . 27 B4
Formby Ave WV6 . . . . . . 254 D4
Formby Way WS3 . . . . . . 243 A3
Forrest Ave
Cannock WS11 . . . . 226 E8
Essington WV11 . . . . . . 242 A4
Forrest Ct 9 WS13 . . . . . 231 B7
Forrester Cl
3 Biddulph ST8 . . . . . . 27 C8
Fradley WS13 . . . . 215 D6
Forrester Rd ST15 . . . . . 120 B7
Forresters Bank ST2,ST9 . 43 C3
Forrister St ST3 . . . . 73 D4
Forsbrook CE Prim Sch
ST11 . . . . 91 A7
Forster St ST6 . . . . 41 D3
Forsyth Cl ST4 . . . . 71 E8
Forsythia Gr WV8 . . . . . . 239 A3
Fort Cres WS9 . . . . 245 A3
Fortescue La WS15 . . . . . 178 E2
Forties B77 . . . . 261 E7
Forton Cl WV6 . . . . 255 B2
Forton Glade TF10 . . . . . 168 F5
Forton Rd TF10 . . . . 168 F5
Forty Acre Cl TF9 . . . . 99 E5
Forum Rd ST5 . . . . 55 D5
Forum The 5 WS11 . . . . 209 E1
Fosbrooke Pl ST4 . . . . . . 71 D8
Fossdale Rd B77 . . . . 262 A8
Fosseway La WS13,WS14 . 230 E4
Fosseway WS14 . . . . 231 A5
Foster Ave WS12 . . . . . . 209 F6
Foster Cres DY7 . . . . 278 A4
Foster Ct ST3 . . . . 72 F3
Foster Gn WV6 . . . . 254 E3
Foster Pl DY8 . . . . 279 E6
Foster Rd CW12 . . . . 6 A5
Foster St DY7 . . . . 278 A4
Foston Ave DE13 . . . . . . 166 B6
Foston Cl DE65 . . . . 146 C8
Fotherley Brook Rd WS9 . 256 F5
Foundry La Bucknall ST2 . . 58 A3
Scholar Green ST7 . . . . . 25 F7
Walsall WS3 . . . . 243 F7
Foundry Rd DY6 . . . . 275 C8
Foundry Sq ST6 . . . . 43 A5
Foundry St Hanley ST1 . . 282 B3
Kingswinford DY6 . . . . . 275 C8
Fountain Ct
10 Burslem ST6 . . . . 56 F8
Biddulph ST8 . . . . 16 D1
Fountain Fold ST20 . . . . 171 D5
Fountain Pl 9 ST6 . . . . . . 56 F8
Fountain Rd DE6 . . . . . . 144 D6
Fountains Ave ST5 . . . . . . 71 B5
Fountains Rd WS3 . . . . . 242 E2
Fountain Sq ST1 . . . . . . 282 B3
Fountain St Leek ST13 . . . 30 F6
Stoke-on-T ST6 . . . . 72 E6
Fountains Way WS3 . . . . 242 E2
Four Ashes Ind Est
WV10 . . . . 224 D6
Four Ashes Rd ST19 . . . . 223 E7
Four Crosses La WS11 . . 225 E7
Four Crosses Rd WS4 . . . 244 C1
Fourlane Ends ST20,ST21 131 E8
Four Lane Ends
Eccleshall ST21 . . . . . . 134 A5
Milwich ST18 . . . . 122 B8
Four Lanes End
Gorstyhill CW2 . . . . 37 F2
Haughton ST18 . . . . . . 173 A5
Seighford ST18 . . . . . . 153 E8
Uttoxeter ST14 . . . . . . 126 D4
Four Oaks Common Rd
B74 . . . . 257 F3
Four Oaks Ct B74 . . . . . . 258 B1
Four Oaks Inf Sch B74 . . 257 E4
Four Oaks Jun Sch B74 . 257 E4
Four Oaks Rd B74 . . . . . 258 A1
Fourth Ave
Brownhills WS8 . . . . 229 A1
Bucknall ST2 . . . . 58 E4

Fourth Ave continued
Kidsgrove ST7 . . . . 25 F1
Fourways CW2 . . . . 37 B5
Fowlchurch Rd ST13 . . . . 30 F7
Fowler Cl WV6 . . . . 254 E6
Fowler's La ST1 . . . . 43 D1
Fowler St WV2 . . . . 266 C6
Fox Cl Burton u T DE14. . 185 B8
Seisdon WV5 . . . . 263 F2
Tamworth B77 . . . . 261 C8
Foxcote Cl ST17 . . . . 175 E5
Foxcroft WS7 . . . . 229 B5
Fox Ct DE13 . . . . 199 C6
Foxes La ST19 . . . . 222 C6
Foxes Rake WS11 . . . . . . 209 E3
Foxfield Cl ST10 . . . . 76 E6
Foxfield Steam Railway★
ST10,ST11 . . . . 75 B5
Foxfield Steam Rly★
ST11 . . . . 90 B5
Foxfields Way WS12 . . . . 209 C7
Foxfield Way ST3 . . . . . . 88 B8
Fox Gdns ST7 . . . . 40 D8
Foxglove Ave
Burton u T DE15. . . . . . 186 A8
Uttoxeter ST14 . . . . . . 126 B6
Foxglove Cl
Featherstone WV10 . . . . 241 B7
Lichfield WS14 . . . . 231 A5
Meir ST3 . . . . 74 B5
Rugeley WS15 . . . . 178 C1
Walsall WS3 . . . . 244 A5
Foxglove La ST5 . . . . 71 C2
Foxglove Rd DY1 . . . . . . 271 F4
Foxgloves Ave ST18 . . . . 177 E7
Foxglove B77 . . . . 251 A4
Foxglove Wlk WS12 . . . . 210 C7
Fox Gr ST5 . . . . 71 C2
Foxhill Cl WS12 . . . . 210 D2
Fox Hill Rd B75 . . . . 258 F2
Foxhill's Cl WS7 . . . . 229 A5
Foxhills Rd
Stourbridge DY8 . . . . . . 275 D1
Wolverhampton WV4 . . . 265 C4
Fox Hollow
Eccleshall ST21 . . . . . . 133 F6
Loggerheads TF9 . . . . . . 99 D5
Wolverhampton WV6 . . . 255 C2
Fox La Alrewas DE13 . . . 200 F2
Lichfield WS13 . . . . 214 A5
Foxland Ave WS6 . . . . . . 227 A3
Foxlands Ave WV4 . . . . . 265 D3
Foxlands Cl ST2 . . . . 58 D3
Foxlands Cres WV4 . . . . . 265 C3
Foxlands Dr Dudley DY3 . 271 C6
Wombourne WV4 . . . . . 265 D3
Fox Leigh Mdws WS15 . . 198 B4
Foxley La ST2 . . . . 43 A1
Foxmeadow Cl DY3 . . . . 271 C6
Fox Rd WV5,WV6 . . . . . . 263 E3
Foxtail Way WS12 . . . . . 210 E4
Foxton Cl DE13 . . . . 201 A2
Foxton Man B74 . . . . . . 258 A1
Fox Wlk WS9 . . . . 245 B3
Foxwood Cl ST15 . . . . . . 119 E6
Foxwood Rd B78 . . . . . . 262 F8
Fradgley Cl ST14 . . . . . . 125 C7
Fradgley Gr ST14 . . . . . . 110 F2
Fradley La WS13 . . . . . . 215 C7
Fradswell La ST18 . . . . . 123 A2
Framlingham Gr WV6 . . . 255 A3
Frampton Gr ST6 . . . . 41 E6
Frances Dr WS3 . . . . 243 B2
Francis Cl
1 Kingswinford DY6. . . 275 D8
Penkridge ST19 . . . . . . 208 A8
Francis Green La ST19 . . 207 F8
Francis Rd Lichfield WS13 214 A2
Stourbridge DY8 . . . . . . 279 C5
Francis St ST6 . . . . 41 F5
Frank Foley Way ST16 . . 285 A4
Frank Gee St ST15. . . . . 178 D1
Franklin Cl DE15 . . . . . . 167 B1
Franklin Dr WS7 . . . . . . 229 B7
Franklin Rd ST4 . . . . 71 F7
Franklyn Cl WV6 . . . . . . 254 E5
Franklyn St ST1 . . . . 282 C1
Frank Rogers Wlk WS15 . 178 D2
Frank St ST4 . . . . 72 A6
Fraser Cl ST15 . . . . 119 F5
Fraser St ST6 . . . . 57 B7
Frayne Ave DY6 . . . . 275 C7
Frazer Ho 6 ST3 . . . . 89 F8
Freckleton Pl ST3 . . . . . . 90 C7
Fred Brewer Way DE13 . . 165 E4
Frederick Ave ST4 . . . . . . 72 A7
Frederick Ct B77 . . . . . . 250 E3
Frederick Rd ST19 . . . . . 192 F1
Fredericks Cl DY8 . . . . . . 279 E4
Frederick St
Burton u T DE15 . . . . . 185 E4
Stoke-on-T ST4 . . . . 72 E6
Wolverhampton WV2 . . . 266 C8
Freebridge Cl ST3 . . . . . . 73 C4
Freedom Dr ST7 . . . . 26 E3
Freedom Wlk ST6 . . . . . . 42 C3
Freeford Gdns WS14 . . . 231 E6
Freehold St ST5 . . . . 283 C1
Freeland Gr 3 DY6 . . . . . 275 F4
Freemen St ST16 . . . . . . 155 E5
Freer Dr WS7 . . . . 229 B7
Freeth Rd WS8 . . . . 229 A1
Free Trade St ST1 . . . . . . 282 C4
Fremantle Dr WS12 . . . . 210 F2
Fremantle Rd ST4 . . . . . . 71 F4
Fremont Dr DY1 . . . . 271 E3
French Ave B78 . . . . 249 C1

Frenchmore Gr ST3 . . . . . 73 E1
Frensham Cl WS6 . . . . . . 226 E4
Freshwater Dr
Chorlton CW2 . . . . 37 B1
Weston CW2 . . . . 52 C8
Freshwater Gr ST2 . . . . . 57 F3
Freville Cl B79 . . . . 250 A5
Frew Cl ST16 . . . . 156 A4
Friar's Alley WS13 . . . . . 231 B7
Friars Ave ST15 . . . . 120 A7
Friars Cl 7 Cheadle ST10 . 76 D4
Stourbridge DY8 . . . . . . 275 C3
Friar's Ct ST5 . . . . 283 B2
Friars Gorse DY7 . . . . . . 279 C8
Friar's La TF11 . . . . 220 D4
Friars Pl ST2 . . . . 58 B7
Friars Rd ST2 . . . . 58 B7
Friars Rd ST17 . . . . 285 B3
Friar's St ST5 . . . . 283 B2
Friars' Terr ST17 . . . . . . 285 B2
Friar St Longton ST3 . . . . 284 C4
Stafford ST16 . . . . 155 D5
Friars' Wlk
Newcastle-u-L ST5 . . . . . 71 B6
Stafford ST17 . . . . 285 B2
Friars Wlk B77 . . . . 250 C3
Friarswood Prim Sch
ST5 . . . . 283 B1
Friarswood Rd ST5. . . . . 283 B2
Friary Ave
Abbots Bromley WS15 . . 160 F5
Lichfield WS13 . . . . 231 A6
Friary Dr B74 . . . . 257 F3
Friary Gdns WS13 . . . . . 231 A7
Friary Grange Sports Ctr
WS13 . . . . 213 F2
Friary Ho WS13 . . . . 213 F1
Friary Rd WS13 . . . . 231 A7
Friary Sch The WS13 . . . 213 E2
Friary The WS13 . . . . . . 231 A7
Friday Acre WS13 . . . . . . 214 A2
Friendly Ave ST5 . . . . 56 B8
Friesian Gdns ST5 . . . . . . 40 C2
Friezland La WS8 . . . . . . 245 A5
Friezland Way WS8 . . . . 245 A5
Frinton Cl ST16 . . . . 155 F6
Frith St ST13 . . . . 30 D6
Frobisher Cl WS6 . . . . . . 226 F1
Frobisher Dr ST15 . . . . . 103 B4
Frobisher St ST6 . . . . 43 A5
Frodingham Rd ST2 . . . . . 58 E1
Froghall ST5 . . . . 283 B3
Froghall Rd Cheadle ST10 . 76 E6
Ipstones ST10 . . . . 62 A6
Froghall Wharf★ ST10 . . 62 B4
Frog La Lichfield WS13 . . 231 B7
Market Drayton TF9 . . . . 97 C1
Wheaton Aston ST19 . . . 205 C6
Frogmore Cl TF9 . . . . 97 C1
Frogmore Pl TF9 . . . . 97 C1
Frogmore Rd TF9 . . . . . . 97 C1
Frome Cl DY3 . . . . 271 D2
Frome Wlk ST6 . . . . 42 A4
Froyle Cl WV6 . . . . 255 C5
Fuchsia Dr WV9 . . . . 239 F3
Fulfen Prim Sch WS7 . . . 229 D7
Fulford Prim Sch ST11 . . 106 E8
Fulford Rd ST11 . . . . 106 E8
Fullbrook Ave DE13 . . . . 201 E8
Fullelove Rd WS8 . . . . . . 245 A7
Fuller St ST6 . . . . 41 E4
Fullerton Cl WV8 . . . . . . 239 E1
Fullmore Cl ST19 . . . . . . 207 F7
Fullwood Wlk ST2 . . . . . . 58 C1
Fulmar Pl ST3 . . . . 90 B7
Furber Cl DY6 . . . . 275 F6
Furlong Ave ST10 . . . . . . 92 C3
Furlong Cl Alrewas DE13 . 201 A2
Upper Tean ST10 . . . . . . 92 E3
Weston ST18 . . . . 138 C2
Furlong Dr ST10 . . . . 92 E3
Furlong Ind Est ST6 . . . . 56 E7
Furlong La Alrewas DE13 . 201 A2
Bradley ST18 . . . . 173 C2
Burslem ST6 . . . . 56 E7
Hope DE6 . . . . 35 C4
Furlong Par 12 ST6 . . . . . 56 F8
Furlong Pas 11 ST6 . . . . . 56 F8
Furlong Rd ST6 . . . . 41 E4
Furlongs Rd DY3 . . . . . . 271 D6
Furlong The ST15 . . . . . . 118 F6
Furlong Wlk DY3 . . . . . . 271 C4
Furmston Pl ST13 . . . . . . 31 A7
Furnace Cl WV5 . . . . 269 E5
Furnace La CW3 . . . . 68 C7
Furnace Rd ST3 . . . . 73 D2
Furness Cl WS3 . . . . 242 F3
Furness Gr ST17 . . . . . . 174 B7
Furness B77 . . . . 250 D3
Furnivall Cres WS13 . . . . 214 A1
Furnival St ST6 . . . . 57 B6
Furrows Dr DE13 . . . . . . 166 A4
Furst St WS8 . . . . 245 A8
Fyfield Rd DE15 . . . . 185 E6
Fynney Fields ST13 . . . . . 45 F3
Fynney St ST13 . . . . 30 F5

G

Gable Cotts ST11 . . . . . . 74 E2
Gable Croft WS14 . . . . . . 231 F6
Gables The
Kingswinford DY6 . . . . . 275 B8
Swadlincote DE11 . . . . . 186 E5
Gable St ST4 . . . . 72 B6
Gaelic Rd WS11 . . . . 209 D4
Gagarin B79 . . . . 249 F5

Gag La DE6 . . . . 51 D6
Gaiafields Rd WS13 . . . . 214 B1
Gaia La WS13 . . . . 231 B8
Gaia Stowe WS13 . . . . . . 214 B1
Gail Cl WS9 . . . . 245 B4
Gailey Lea La ST19 . . . . . 208 B2
Gailey Pottery★ ST19 . . . 207 C2
Gail Pk WV3 . . . . 265 D7
Gainford Cl WV8 . . . . . . 239 F1
Gainsborough Dr
  Mile Oak B78 . . . . 260 B8
  Perton WV6 . . . . 255 A4
Gainsborough Hill DY8 . . 279 F3
Gainsborough Pl DY1 . . . 271 E2
Gainsborough Rd
  Newcastle-u-L ST5. . . . . 55 E6
  Stoke-on-T ST3 . . . . 88 E8
Gainsborough Way DE15 167 B3
Gainsbrook Cres ST27 . . . 227 F5
Gains La WS3,WS11 . . . . 227 D2
Gairloch Rd WV11 . . . . . 242 B1
Galahad Dr DE13 . . . . . . 147 E2
Galena B77 . . . . 251 B2
Galleys Bank ST7 . . . . . . 26 B3
Galliers Cl B77 . . . . 261 F5
Gallimore Cl ST6 . . . . 41 E1
Gallimore Ho ST7 . . . . . . 40 D8
Galloway Rd ST2 . . . . 73 E8
Gallows Hill DY7 . . . . . . 277 F6
Gallowstree La
  Mayfield DE6 . . . . 81 C8
  Newcastle-u-L ST5. . . . . 70 E7
Galsworthy Rd ST3. . . . . . 73 B6
Galveston Gr ST4 . . . . 72 F5
Galway Rd WS7 . . . . 229 A7
Gamesfield Gn WV3 . . . . 255 F1
Ganton Rd WS3 . . . . 243 A3
Ganton Wlk WV8 . . . . . . 255 F8
Gaol Butts ST21 . . . . 133 D6
Gaolgate St ST16 . . . . . . 285 B3
Gaol Mews ST16 . . . . . . 285 B4
Gaol Rd ST16 . . . . 285 B4
Gaol Sq ST16 . . . . 285 B4
Garage Cl B77 . . . . 250 D5
Garbett St ST6. . . . . 41 D7
Garden Cotts ST27 . . . . . 171 C5
Garden Cres WS3 . . . . . . 243 F1
Garden Croft WS9 . . . . . 256 B7
Garden Dr WV5 . . . . 197 A4
Gardeners Cl ST8 . . . . 27 B5
Gardeners Way WV5 . . . . 269 F5
Gardenholm Cl ST3 . . . . . 89 F8
Garden La ST19 . . . . 206 D4
Garden Pl Stafford ST17 . . 285 C2
  Stoke-on-T ST4 . . . . 71 E8
Gardens The Elford B79 . . 216 D2
  Lawton-gate ST7 . . . . . . 25 C4
Garden St Leek ST13 . . . . . 30 D6
  Newcastle-u-L ST5. . . . . 283 C1
  Stafford ST17 . . . . 285 C2
  Stoke-on-T ST4 . . . . 71 F6
Garden View WS15 . . . . 178 D1
Garden Village ST10 . . . . . 92 D4
Garden Wlk DY3 . . . . . . 271 C2
Gardiner Dr ST8 . . . . 284 A2
Gardner Pl ST14 . . . . 111 A1
Garfield Ave ST4 . . . . 71 F1
Garfield Cres ST4 . . . . 71 F1
Garfield Ct ST4 . . . . 71 F1
Garfield St ST1 . . . . 282 A1
Garibaldi St ST1 . . . . 56 F3
Garlick St ST6 . . . . 42 B1
Garner St ST4 . . . . 56 E3
Garners Wlk CW3 . . . . . . 68 E7
Garnet Cl WS9 . . . . 245 A4
Garnet St ST1 . . . . 57 A3
Garnett Rd E ST5 . . . . 56 B5
Garnett Rd W ST5. . . . . . . 56 B6
Garret Cl DY6 . . . . 275 D8
Garrett Sq DE13 . . . . . . 147 C4
Garrick Cl Dudley DY1. . . 271 F3
  Lichfield WS13 . . . . . . 213 F2
Garrick Ct WS13 . . . . . . 213 F2
Garrick Rd Cannock WS11 209 D4
  Lichfield WS13 . . . . . . 213 F2
Garrick Rise
  Burntwood WS7 . . . . . . 229 B7
  Rugeley WS15 . . . . . . 197 B6
Garridge Cl WV7 . . . . . . 237 A4
Garrigill B77 . . . . 251 B1
Garrod Sq ST16 . . . . 156 B5
Garsdale Cres ST3 . . . . . . 88 F8
Gartan Rd DE14 . . . . . . 185 A8
Garth Cl ST17 . . . . 174 F5
Garth Rd ST17 . . . . 174 F5
Garth St ST1. . . . . 282 C3
Garth The WS13 . . . . . . 214 B2
Gaskell Rd ST2 . . . . 58 D3
Gas St ST13. . . . . 111 C1
Gas Works Ind Est ST7 . . . 25 E2
Gatacre St DY3 . . . . 271 C2
Gatcombe Cl
  Stretton DE13 . . . . 147 D1
  Wolverhampton WV10. . 240 F4
Gatcombe Rd DY1 . . . . . 271 E2
Gatehouse Trad Est WS8. 229 B1
Gate St Meir ST3 . . . . 74 B5
  Sedgley DY3. . . . . 271 E7
Gateway Ave ST5 . . . . . . 85 C5
Gateway ST5 . . . . 40 D2
Gatherwynd La TF11 . . . 203 E6
Gatley Gr ST3. . . . . 90 B6
Gauledge La SK17. . . . . . 13 B6
Gaunt St 8 ST13. . . . . . . 30 D6
Gawbutts The ST10 . . . . . 76 C2
Gawsworth Cl ST3 . . . . . . 73 C6

Gawsworth B79. . . . . . . 249 D7
Gaydon Cl WV6 . . . . 254 E5
Gaydon Rd WS9. . . . . . . 256 A4
Gay La ST20 . . . . 204 F8
Gayle B77 . . . . 251 A1
Gaymore Rd DY10. . . . . 280 B5
Gayton Ave ST2 . . . . 43 B2
Geary La DE15 . . . . 167 F2
Gedney Gr ST5. . . . . 71 B2
Geen St ST4 . . . . 72 B7
Gemini Dr WS11 . . . . . . 226 F6
Gemini Gr ST6. . . . . 41 F6
Geneshall Cl ST20. . . . . . 171 D7
Geneva Dr
  Birches Head ST1 . . . . . 57 F6
  Newcastle-u-L ST5. . . . . 70 E6
Genge Ave WV4 . . . . . . 266 E4
Genista Cl DE15 . . . . . . 186 A8
Genthorn Cl 11 WV4 . . . 266 F4
Gentian B74 . . . . 257 F4
Gentleshaw Prim Sch
  WS15 . . . . 212 A5
Gentleshaw Wildlife Ctr★
  ST21 . . . . 134 V2
Geoffrey Ave ST3 . . . . . . 30 D5
Geoffrey Gr ST3 . . . . 74 A4
George Ave Meir ST3 . . . . 74 B1
  Mile Oak B78 . . . . 249 C1
George Baily Ct ST17. . . . 285 C1
George Brealey Cl WS15 196 F7
George Eardley Cl ST6 . . . 41 C5
George Eastham Ave ST4 . 72 F6
George Elliott Cl ST14. . . 126 C6
George Hill Ct 3 ST16 . . . 155 F5
  Stone ST15 . . . . 120 D7
George La Lichfield WS13. 231 C8
George St Audley ST7 . . . . 39 D1
  Burton u T DE14. . . . . 166 D3
  Cannock WS12. . . . . . 210 C4
  Newcastle-u-L,Chesterton
    ST5. . . . . 55 E7
  Newcastle-u-L,Porthill ST5 56 D6
  Newcastle-u-L,Silverdale
    ST5. . . . . 55 B1
  Newcastle-u-L ST5. . . . 283 D3
  Stafford ST16 . . . . . . 155 D3
  Stoke-on-T ST4 . . . . 72 C7
  Stourbridge DY8 . . . . . 275 F1
  Tamworth B79 . . . . . . 250 B4
Georges Way ST7 . . . . . . 39 F2
George Walker Ct DE14 . 166 C5
Georgian Pl WS11. . . . . . 209 E2
Gerald Rd DY8. . . . . 279 F7
Gerards Way TF9 . . . . . . 100 C5
Gerard B79 . . . . 249 E7
Gerrard St ST4 . . . . 72 A8
Gettings Cl WS7 . . . . . . 229 A7
Gibbet La Kinver DY7. . . 278 F4
  Stourbridge DY7 . . . . . 279 B4
Gibbins St ST1. . . . . 282 C4
Gibb La DE6 . . . . 128 C5
Gibbons Gr WV6 . . . . . . 255 F4
Gibbons Hill Rd DY3 . . . 266 D2
Gibbons Rd
  Sutton Coldfield B75 . . . 258 B3
  Wolverhampton WV6. . . 255 F4
Gibraltar DY7 . . . . 278 C4
Gibson Cl ST16 . . . . 155 F5
Gibson Pl ST3 . . . . 74 A2
Gibson Rd WV6 . . . . 254 E3
Gibson St ST6 . . . . 41 E2
Giddywell La WS15 . . . . 197 F1
Gideons Cl DY3 . . . . 271 D5
Giffard Cl ST19 . . . . 223 D6
Giffard RC Prim Sch The
  WV6 . . . . 255 F5
Giffard Rd WV10 . . . . . . 240 F3
Gifford Pl ST4 . . . . 71 F6
Giffords Croft WS13 . . . . 214 A1
Giggetty La WV5 . . . . . . 269 F8
Gig Mill Prim Sch DY8 . . 279 E4
Gigmill Way DY8 . . . . . . 279 E4
Gilbanks Rd DY8 . . . . . . 279 D7
Gilbern Dr ST8. . . . . 27 B5
Gilbert Cl 2 Kidsgrove ST7 26 A2
  Newport TF10 . . . . 168 D3
Gilbert La WV5 . . . . 270 B7
Gilbert Rd WS13 . . . . . . 214 C2
Gilbert St ST6 . . . . 41 C7
Gilbert Wlk WS13 . . . . . 214 C2
Gilbeys Cl 5 DY8 . . . . . 275 E1
Gilchrist Ct ST6 . . . . 57 B6
Giles Ho WS13. . . . . 45 C8
Giles Rd WS13 . . . . 214 A3
Giles Wlk ST1. . . . . 57 E5
Gill Bank Rd Kidsgrove ST7 41 B8
  Stoke-on-T ST6 . . . . 41 B7
Gillespie Cl WS13 . . . . . 215 D6
Gillette Cl ST18 . . . . 156 C5
Gilliard's Croft DE13 . . . 199 C6
Gilliat Wlk ST2. . . . . 58 C1
Gillingham Cres ST16 . . . 155 B2
Gillway B79 . . . . 250 B8
Gill Wlk ST1 . . . . 282 A2
Gillyflower Cl ST6. . . . . . 42 D2
Gilman Ave ST2. . . . . . . 43 B2
Gilman Pl ST1 . . . . 282 C3
Gilman St ST1 . . . . 282 C2
Gilmour La DE13 . . . . . . 183 E1
Gilpin Cres WS3 . . . . . . 244 A4
Gilpins Croft WS6. . . . . . 226 D1
Gilwell Rd WS15 . . . . . . 211 F5
Gimson St ST4 . . . . 72 E6
Ginger Hill ST20 . . . . . . 171 D5
Ginger La ST21 . . . . 116 B3

Gipsy La Alstonefield DE6 . . 35 F4
  Cookley DY7,DY11. . . . 280 A8
Girsby Ct ST4 . . . . 88 C5
Girton Rd WS11 . . . . . . 226 F3
Gisborne Cl DE13 . . . . . 182 A3
Gitana St ST1. . . . . 282 B3
Glades The WS9 . . . . . . 256 B7
Glade The Aldridge B74. . 256 E1
  Cannock WS11. . . . . . 209 C2
  Newcastle-u-L ST5. . . . . 71 B2
  Stafford ST17 . . . . . . 175 B8
  Wolverhampton WV8. . . 239 E1
Gladman Bsns Quarter
  WV9 . . . . 239 F3
Gladstone Dr DY8. . . . . . 279 D8
Gladstone Gr
  3 Kingswinford DY6. . . 275 D8
  Biddulph ST8 . . . . 27 D8
Gladstone Pl ST1 . . . . . . 71 F5
Gladstone Pottery Mus★
  ST3 . . . . 284 C3
Gladstone Prim Sch
  Longton ST3. . . . . 284 C5
  Longton ST3 . . . . 73 D5
Gladstone Rd
  Cannock WS12. . . . . . 210 C1
  Stourbridge DY8 . . . . . 279 D8
Gladstone St Leek ST13 . . 30 E5
  Stoke-on-T ST4 . . . . 56 E1
Gladstone Terr ST10 . . . . . 94 E8
Gladstone Way ST18 . . . . 156 C5
Gladwyn St ST2. . . . . . . 58 C4
Glaisher Dr ST3. . . . . . . 90 C7
Glamis Cl DE13 . . . . 166 D8
Glamis Dr ST15 . . . . 120 C5
Glamorgan Way DE11 . . 186 F1
Glandore Rd ST3. . . . . . . 73 F4
Glanville Dr B75 . . . . . . 258 A4
Glascote Ct B77 . . . . 250 E4
Glascote Heath Prim Sch
  B77. . . . . 251 A2
Glascote La B77 . . . . . . 261 F8
Glascote Rd
  Tamworth B77 . . . . . . 251 B2
  Tamworth,Glascote Heath
    B77. . . . . 250 E3
Glasscroft Cotts WS7 . . . 229 F7
Glassford Dr WV6. . . . . . 255 F8
Glasshouse Coll DY8 . . . 279 F7
Glass La WS15 . . . . 161 E2
Glass St ST1. . . . . 282 B3
Glastonbury Cl
  Stafford ST17 . . . . 175 D6
  Stoke-on-T ST9 . . . . . . 43 D3
Glastonbury Cres WS3 . . 242 E2
Glastonbury Way WS3. . . 242 E1
Glebe Ave ST16 . . . . 155 D6
Glebe Cl Blythe Bridge ST11 91 A6
  Cheswardine TF9 . . . . . 130 A8
  Doveridge DE6. . . . . . . 127 B8
  Rolleston on D DE13 . . . 147 A4
Glebe Ct Cheadle ST10 . . . 76 B2
  Stoke-on-T ST4 . . . . 72 C7
Glebedale Ct ST4 . . . . . . 72 E5
Glebedale Rd ST4. . . . . . 72 E5
Glebefields ST20. . . . . . . 151 D7
Glebe Gdns ST10. . . . . . 76 C2
Glebe La ST20 . . . . 171 E7
Glebelands
  Bobbington DY7 . . . . ., 267 F2
  Stafford ST17 . . . . 174 F4
Glebe La DY8. . . . . 279 E4
Glebe Prim Sch ST4. . . . . 72 F6
Glebe Rd Armitage WS15 198 C5
  Cheadle ST10. . . . . . . 76 C2
  Kingsley ST10 . . . . 61 C2
Glebe St Kidsgrove ST7 . . 25 D2
  Stoke-on-T ST4 . . . . 72 B7
Glebe The
  Albrighton WV7 . . . . . . 237 A5
  Norton Bridge ST15. . . . 135 A8
Glebeville ST13 . . . . 30 E4
Gledhill Pk WS14 . . . . . 231 C5
Glencastle Way ST4. . . . . 88 C5
Glen Cl WS11 . . . . 209 E5
Glencoe Dr WS11 . . . . . 210 A4
Glencoe St ST3 . . . . 284 B2
Glencroft Cl DE14. . . . . . 185 B7
Glen Ct Codsall WV8 . . . 239 A4
  Wolverhampton WV6. . . 255 C2
Glendale Cl WV3 . . . . . . 265 C8
Glendale Ct
  Newcastle-u-L ST5. . . . . 71 C2
  Tamworth B79 . . . . . . 262 B6
Glendale Dr WV5 . . . . . . 270 A6
Glendale Gdns WS11 . . . 210 A4
Glendale St ST6 . . . . 57 A7
Glendawn Cl 1 WS11 . . . 210 A3
Glendene Rd ST4. . . . . . . 210 D6
Glendon Cl 2 TF9 . . . . . 112 A8
Glendower Cl ST20. . . . . 171 C6
Glendower Rd WS9 . . . . 245 B1
Glen Dr ST10 . . . . 94 E8
Glendue Gr ST4. . . . . . . 88 C6
Gleneagles Cres ST1. . . . 57 E6
Gleneagles Dr
  Stafford ST16 . . . . 156 C3
  Stretton DE13 . . . . 147 C1
Gleneagles Rd
  Perton WV6 . . . . 254 D5
  Walsall WS3 . . . . 242 F3
Gleneagles B77 . . . . 251 B5
Glenfield Rise DE13 . . . . 166 B7
Glenfield B77 . . . . 250 C1
Glenfield Way ST2 . . . . . 73 E7
Glenfield WV8 . . . . 239 E2
Glengarry Gdns WV3 . . . 255 F1
Glenhaven WS15 . . . . . . 178 C2

Glenmore Ave WS7 . . . . 229 A6
Glenmore Cl WV3 . . . . . 265 E7
Glen Park Rd DY3 . . . . . 271 D2
Glen Rd Dudley DY3. . . . 271 E6
  Stourbridge DY8 . . . . . 279 F3
Glen Rise DE13 . . . . 166 A7
Glenroyd Ave ST2. . . . . . 58 A1
Glenroyd Wlk ST2. . . . . . 58 C1
Glensyl Way DE14. . . . . . 166 E4
Glen The 2 ST15 . . . . . . 120 A7
Glenthorne Cl ST17 . . . . 175 D5
Glenthorne Dr WS6 . . . . 226 E3
Glenthorne Ho WS6 . . . . 226 D2
Glenthorne Prim Sch
  WS6 . . . . 226 E3
Glenville Ave CV9 . . . . . 262 C1
Glenwood Cl Longton ST3 284 B4
  Newcastle-u-L ST5. . . . . 55 C1
Glenwood Gdns ST7 . . . . 262 B6
Glenwood Rise WS9. . . . 245 D3
Globe Ave ST17 . . . . 174 F6
Globe St ST6 . . . . 56 E8
Gloucester Cl WS13 . . . . 214 B3
Gloucester Grange ST5. . . 71 C5
Gloucester Rd ST7 . . . . . 26 A3
Gloucester Way
  Burton u T DE15. . . . . 167 B1
  Cannock WS11. . . . . . 210 B1
Glovers Cl WS12 . . . . . . 211 A5
Glover St Cannock WS12. 210 F3
  Hanley ST1 . . . . 282 C4
  Stafford ST16 . . . . . . 285 A4
Glyme Dr WV6 . . . . 255 C5
Glyndebourne B79 . . . . . 249 D7
Glynne Ave DY6 . . . . . . 275 D5
Glynne Prim Sch DY6 . . . 275 D5
Glyn Pl ST6. . . . . 41 F3
Gnosall Rd
  Gnosall,Knightley Dale
    ST20. . . . . 152 B3
  Gnosall TF10 . . . . 170 D2
Goddard St ST3. . . . . . . 284 D4
Godfrey Rd ST2. . . . . . . 58 B3
Godleybarn La ST10. . . . . 75 E6
Godley La ST10 . . . . 75 D5
Godolphin B79. . . . . 249 D7
Gofton ST7 . . . . 262 A8
Golborn Ave ST3. . . . . . . 90 A4
Golborn Cl ST3 . . . . 90 B4
Goldcrest B77 . . . . 262 A6
Goldcrest Way ST8. . . . . . 27 E8
Golden Cl WS15 . . . . . . 196 D7
Golden Hill CW2 . . . . . . 37 E3
Goldenhill Prim Sch ST6 . 41 C7
Goldenhill Rd ST4. . . . . . 284 B5
Goldenhill St Joseph's RC
  Prim Sch ST6. . . . . 41 D7
Goldfinch Rd 5 ST7 . . . . 26 F1
Goldfinch View TF1 . . . . 99 C3
Goldhurst Dr ST10 . . . . . 92 F4
Golding Cres DE14. . . . . 166 F6
Goldsborough B77. . . . . . 251 A1
Goldsmith Pl
  Longton ST3. . . . . 284 D4
  Tamworth B79 . . . . . . 250 A7
Gold St ST3 . . . . 284 B3
Goldthorn Ave WV4 . . . . 266 B6
Goldthorn Cres WV4 . . . 266 A6
Goldthorn Ave WS11 . . . 209 C4
Goldthorn Hill WV2,WV4 . 266 C6
Goldthorn Park Prim Sch
  WV4 . . . . 266 D5
Goldthorn Rd WV2,WV3. . 266 B6
Golf Links Cl ST6 . . . . . . 41 C7
Goms Mill Cl ST3 . . . . . . 284 B2
Goms Mill Rd ST3 . . . . . 284 A2
Goodfellow St ST6 . . . . . 41 D4
Goodill Cl ST15 . . . . 119 F5
Goodman St DE14. . . . . 166 D5
Goodrich Ave WV6 . . . . . 255 A3
Goodson Dr ST1. . . . . . . 282 C3
Goods Station St ST19 . . 192 E2
Goodwick Cl ST4. . . . . . . 88 C5
Goodwin Ave ST5 . . . . . 283 B4
Goodwin Rd ST3 . . . . . . 74 B2
Goodwood Ave ST10 . . . . 76 F3
Goodwood Cl
  Cannock WS12. . . . . . 211 A5
  Lichfield WS14. . . . . . 231 D7
  Stretton DE13 . . . . 147 C1
Goodwood Pl ST4. . . . . . 88 B7
Goosefield Cl TF9 . . . . . . 97 B1
Goose La WS15 . . . . 160 F5
Goosemoor Cl 10 ST3. . . 90 A7
Goose St ST5 . . . . 283 C4
Goostry Cl ST7 . . . . 250 D5
Goostry Rd B77. . . . . . . 250 D5
Gordale Cl CW12. . . . . . . 6 A5
Gordon Ave Cheadle ST10 . 76 B3
  Stafford ST16 . . . . . . 155 C7
  Stoke-on-T ST6 . . . . 57 C7
  Wolverhampton WV4. . . 266 F3
Gordon Banks Dr ST4 . . . 72 F2
Gordon Cl ST13 . . . . 30 C4
Gordon Cres ST7 . . . . . . 57 E7
Gordon Cres ST5. . . . . . . 55 E3
Gordon Rd ST6 . . . . 41 C6
Gordon St
  2 Wolverhampton WV2. 266 D8
  Burton u T DE14. . . . . 166 C4
  Newcastle-u-L ST5. . . . . 55 E3
  Stoke-on-T ST6 . . . . 42 B1
Gorge Rd Sedgley DY3. . . 271 E8
  Wolverhampton WV14,DY3 266 F1
Gorsebrook Leys ST15 . . 185 A5
Gorseburn Way WS15. . . 178 C2
Gorse Cres TF9 . . . . 99 E5
Gorse Dr WS12 . . . . 209 D5

Gorse La Astbury CW12. . . 15 D5
  Church Eaton ST19 . . . . 190 E2
  Fradley WS13 . . . . 215 A7
  Gnosall ST20,ST21 . . . 152 A7
  Lichfield WS14. . . . . . 231 E6
  Rugeley WS15 . . . . . . 196 F6
  Wombourne WV5. . . . . 269 B6
Gorsemoor Prim Sch
  WS12 . . . . 210 D1
Gorsemoor Rd WS12 . . . 210 D1
Gorsemoor Way WV11 . . 242 B3
Gorse Rd WS15 . . . . 196 F6
Gorse St ST4 . . . . 72 E4
Gorseway WS7 . . . . 229 B5
Gorse Way WS12. . . . . . 210 C8
Gorsey Bank ST6 . . . . . . 42 E6
Gorsey La Cannock WS11 209 C1
  Great Wyrley WS6 . . . . 226 F1
  Nethersael DE12 . . . . . 219 F8
  Norton Canes WS3 . . . . 227 E1
Gorsley Dale ST17 . . . . . 175 C6
Gorstey Lea WS7. . . . . . 229 C7
Gorsty Bank WS14 . . . . . 231 E8
Gorsty Hayes WV8 . . . . . 238 F3
Gorsty Hill Cl CW2 . . . . . 37 F2
Gorsty Hill Rd ST10 . . . . 92 E5
Gorsty La ST18. . . . . 154 B3
Gorsy Bank Rd B77 . . . . 261 F5
Gorsy La
  Cotes Heath ST21 . . . . 102 E5
  Weston Jones TF10 . . . 150 A3
Gort Rd ST5 . . . . 55 F4
Gosberryhole La CW12 . . 7 A2
Goscote Ind Est WS3 . . . 243 E1
Goscote La WS3 . . . . . . 243 E1
Goscote Rd WS3. . . . . . . 244 A1
Gosforth Gr ST3 . . . . 90 C7
Gospel Ash Rd DY7. . . . . 268 D2
Gospel End Rd DY3 . . . . 271 B8
Gospel End St DY3. . . . . 271 D8
Gothersley La DY7 . . . . . 274 D2
Gough Cl ST16 . . . . 155 C8
Gough Side DE14. . . . . . 166 D2
Gould Firm La WS9 . . . . 256 E6
Govan Rd ST4 . . . . 72 E4
Gowan Ave ST6 . . . . 42 A4
Gower Ave DY6 . . . . 275 F4
Gower Rd Sedgley DY3 . . 271 B8
  Stone ST15 . . . . 120 B7
Gower St Longton ST3. . . 284 C3
  Newcastle-u-L ST5. . . . . 283 C3
  Wolverhampton WV2. . . 266 E8
Gowland Dr WS11. . . . . . 209 B1
Goya Cl WS11. . . . . 210 D2
Grace Moore Ct WS11 . . 209 C6
Grace St ST13 . . . . 30 C6
Gradbach Mill★ SK17 . . . 2 A1
Graffam Gr ST10 . . . . . . 76 F4
Grafton Ave ST6 . . . . . . 42 B1
Grafton Ct 4 WV6 . . . . . 255 F4
Grafton Gdns DY3. . . . . . 271 B3
Grafton Ho WV4 . . . . . . 266 E5
Grafton Inf Sch ST4 . . . . 284 C4
Grafton Rd
  Burton u T DE15. . . . . 167 B1
  Longton ST3. . . . . 284 C4
Grafton St ST1 . . . . 282 C3
Graham Cl DE14 . . . . . . 185 C7
Graham Ho B74. . . . . . . 256 F2
Graham Rd DY6,DY8. . . . 275 D4
Graham St ST2 . . . . 58 A3
Grainger Ct WS11. . . . . . 209 D2
Graiseley Hill WV2. . . . . 266 C8
Graiseley Prim Sch WV2 266 C8
Graiseley Row WV2 . . . . 266 C8
Granary Cl Cannock WS12 210 B5
  Kingswinford DY6 . . . . 275 A8
Granary Rd WV8 . . . . . . 239 E1
Granary The WS9 . . . . . 256 B6
Granby Wlk ST4 . . . . 71 F6
Granchester Cl ST3 . . . . 90 B6
Grange Ave Aldridge WS9. 245 A1
  Burntwood WS7 . . . . . . 229 B7
  Penkridge ST19 . . . . . 207 F2
  Sutton Coldfield B75 . . . 258 C3
Grange Cl
  Burton u T DE14. . . . . 166 B4
  Ellenhall ST21 . . . . . . 134 A1
  Gorstyhill CW2. . . . . . 37 E4
  Tamworth B77 . . . . . . 261 C8
Grange Cotts ST19 . . . . . 207 D7
Grange Court ST18. . . . . 158 C8
Grange Cres ST19 . . . . . 207 E7
Grange Ct Biddulph ST8 . . 16 D2
  Burslem ST6 . . . . 57 A7
  Egginton DE65 . . . . . . 148 B5
  Newcastle-u-L ST5. . . . . 56 D5
Grange Dr WV11 . . . . . . 209 F2
Grangefield Cl
  Cheddleton ST13 . . . . . 45 C4
  Wolverhampton WV8. . . 239 F1
Grangefields ST8 . . . . . . 16 E3
Grange Gdns ST13 . . . . . 30 D4
Grange Hill WS15 . . . . . 197 C8
Grange Inf Sch DE14 . . . 166 B4
Grange La
  4 Kingswinford DY6. . . 275 F4
  Lichfield WS13 . . . . . . 213 C2
  Newcastle-u-L ST5. . . . . 56 D4
  Sutton Coldfield B75 . . . 258 C3
Grange Park Dr ST8. . . . . 16 E3
Grange Prim Sch ST4 . . . 90 A7
Grange Rd Biddulph ST8 . . 16 E4
  Burntwood WS7 . . . . . . 229 A5
  Cheddleton ST13 . . . . . 45 C4

Grange Rd *continued*
Meir ST3 . . . . **90** A6
Norton Canes WS11 . . **228** B6
Penkridge ST19 . . . . . **207** E8
Stone ST15 . . . . **120** C7
Swadlincote DE11 . . . . **186** E5
Uttoxeter ST14 . . . . . . **111** A1
Wolverhampton,Blakenhall
WV2 . . . . **266** B6
Wolverhampton,Tettenhall
WV6 . . . . **255** C4
Woodseaves ST20 . . . . **151** F5
Grange St Burslem ST6 . . **57** B6
Burton u T DE14 . . . . **166** B3
Grange The
Burton u T DE14 . . . . **166** B3
King's Bromley DE13 . . **199** D6
Longdon WS15 . . . . . . **197** C2
Meir ST3 . . . . **74** A2
Stafford ST18 . . . . . . **174** C5
Wombourne WV5 . . . . . **270** A7
Grangewood Ave ST3 . . **89** F6
Grangewood Rd ST3 . . . **74** A1
Granstone Cl ST6 . . . . . . **42** A7
Grant Cl DY6 . . . . **275** D8
Grantham Pl ST2 . . . . . . **58** A6
Grantley Cl ST3 . . . . **73** A1
Grantley Cres DY6 . . . . **275** C7
Grantown Gr WS3 . . . . . **243** A4
Grant St ST4 . . . . **72** C7
Grants Yd DE14 . . . . . . **166** C3
Granville Ave
Newcastle-u-L ST5 . . . **283** C3
Newport TF10 . . . . **168** F2
Stoke-on-T ST1 . . . . **57** D7
Granville Cl
3 Wolverhampton WV2 . . **266** D8
Newport TF10 . . . . **168** F2
Granville Dr DY6 . . . . . **275** F5
Granville Rd Bucknall ST2 . . **58** B5
Newport TF10 . . . . **168** F2
Granville Sq 3 WS15 . . **105** A1
Granville St WV2 . . . . . **266** D8
Granville Terr WS15 . . . **105** A1
Granville Villas TF10 . . **168** F2
Grasmere Ave
Aldridge B74 . . . . **257** A2
Newcastle-u-L ST5 . . . . **71** B4
Perton WV6 . . . . **254** F4
Grasmere Cl
Burton u T DE15 . . . . **167** B1
Kingswinford DY6 . . . . **275** B7
Wolverhampton,Tettenhall
WV6 . . . . **255** E8
Grasmere Pl WS11 . . . . **209** E5
Grasmere Terr ST6 . . . . . **42** A3
Grassholme B77 . . . . . . **262** A8
Grassmere Ct WS6 . . . . **226** D3
Grassmere Dr DY8 . . . . **279** F3
Grassmere Hollow ST16 . . **154** F5
Grassygreen La ST7 . . . . **39** E1
Grassy La WV10,WV11 . . **241** B1
Gratley Croft WS12 . . . **209** C4
Gratton La ST9 . . . . **29** A3
Gratton Rd ST2 . . . . **58** D3
Gravel Hill WV5 . . . . . . **270** B6
Gravel La
Huntington WS12 . . . . **209** C5
Stafford ST17 . . . . **174** F4
Gravelly Bank ST3 . . . . . **89** F7
Gravelly Dr TF10 . . . . . . **168** E2
Gravelly Hill TF9 . . . . . **100** A5
Gravelly La WS9 . . . . . . **245** F3
Gravenhunger La CW3 . . . **83** D8
Graycar Bsns Pk DE13 . . **184** B1
Grayling Gr ST6 . . . . **42** B3
Grayling B77 . . . . **261** D6
Grayling Willows CW3 . . . **68** E6
Gray Rd WS12 . . . . **209** F6
Gray's Cl ST7 . . . . **26** B7
Grayshott Rd ST6 . . . . . . **41** E5
Grayston Ave B77 . . . . . **250** E4
Gray Wlk ST17 . . . . **174** C7
Grazier Ave B77 . . . . . . **261** C8
Grazings The DY7 . . . . . **278** C3
Greasley Rd ST2 . . . . **58** B6
Greatbatch Ave ST4 . . . . **71** F7
Great Charles St WS8 . . **244** F8
Great Checkhill Rd DY7 . . **274** C4
Great Fenton Bsns Pk
ST4 . . . . **72** D4
Great Furlong ST1 . . . . . **201** A2
Great Hales St TF9 . . . . . **97** D1
Greatmead B77 . . . . **250** C1
Great Moor Rd
Nurton WV6 . . . . **254** A3
Pattingham WV6 . . . . **253** F2
Greatoak Rd ST7 . . . . **39** F4
Great Wood Com Prim Sch
ST10 . . . . **92** E4
Great Wood Rd ST10 . . . . **92** E4
Great Wyrley High Sch
WS6 . . . . **226** F3
Greaves La DE6,DE13 . . **144** E4
Greenacre Cl B77 . . . . . **251** B5
Greenacre Dr WV8 . . . . **239** B2
Greenacre ST18 . . . . . . **139** D1
Greenacres Ave
Blythe Bridge ST11 . . . . **90** C8
Wolverhampton WV10 . . **241** B2
Greenacres Cl WS9 . . . . **256** E2
Greenacres WV9 . . . . . . **224** B3
Greenacres Dr ST14 . . . **111** A2

Greenacres Prim Sch
B77 . . . . **251** B5
Greenacres
Rugeley WS15 . . . . . . **196** E7
Sedgley DY3 . . . . **266** B1
Greenacres Way TF10 . . **168** D3
Greenacres WV6 . . . . . . **255** B5
Green Acres WV5 . . . . . **269** F5
Greenacre The DE6 . . . . . **81** F7
Greenaway Cl WV10 . . . **241** C7
Greenbank Gdns DY8 . . **275** E2
Greenbank Rd
Newcastle-u-L ST5 . . . . **56** C3
Stoke-on-T ST6 . . . . . . **42** A3
Green Barn Ct ST18 . . . **138** D2
Green Barns La WS14 . . **258** C8
Greenbirches Ind Est ST6 . . **41** D4
Green Brook Ct ST5 . . . . . **56** B3
Green Cl Barlaston ST12 . . **88** D1
Blythe Bridge ST11 . . . . **90** D7
Pattingham WV6 . . . . **253** C2
Stone ST15 . . . . **119** F7
Greencroft
Kingswinford DY6 . . . . **275** D4
Lichfield WS13 . . . . . . **214** A2
Green Croft ST15 . . . . . **118** F6
Green 8 WS13 . . . . **231** B7
Greendale Cotts ST10 . . . **77** E4
Greendale Dr ST5 . . . . . . **40** D1
Greendale La ST10 . . . . . **77** D4
Greendock St ST3 . . . . . **284** B3
Greenfield Ave
Armitage WS15 . . . . . **198** A4
Brown Edge ST6 . . . . . . **43** C7
Stourbridge DY8 . . . . . **279** F5
Greenfield St **27** D6
Greenfield Bldgs WV5 . . **270** A7
Greenfield Cl ST6 . . . . . . **43** C7
Greenfield Cres ST10 . . . **76** E4
Greenfield Dr ST14 . . . . **126** A8
Greenfield La WV10 . . . **240** E5
Greenfield Pl ST6 . . . . . . **43** C7
Greenfield Prim Sch
DY8 . . . . **279** F5
Greenfield Rd Endon ST9 . . **43** C8
Stafford ST17 . . . . . . **175** D5
Stoke-on-T ST6 . . . . . . **41** E5
Greenfields Aldridge WS9 . . **256** B7
Cannock WS11 . . . . . . **209** E2
Denstone ST14 . . . . **95** D6
Greenfields Dr WS15 . . . **178** D1
Greenfields ST20 . . . . . **171** E7
Greenfields La TF9 . . . . . **97** B2
Greenfields Rd
Hixon ST18 . . . . **139** C1
Kingswinford DY6 . . . . **275** E6
Kinver DY7 . . . . **277** C3
Walsall WS4 . . . . **244** D2
Wombourne WV5 . . . . **270** A5
Greenfield View DY3 . . . **271** B7
Greenfinch Cl ST14 . . . . **126** C6
Greengates St ST6 . . . . . **41** E4
Green Gore La ST14 . . . . **175** F7
Greenhall Com Specl Sch
ST16 . . . . **155** B7
Greenhead St ST6 . . . . . . **56** F8
Greenheart B77 . . . . . . **251** A4
Green Heath Rd WS12 . . **210** A7
Greenhill Cl B77 . . . . . . **261** C5
Greenhill Ct WV5 . . . . . **270** B5
Greenhill Gdns WV5 . . . **270** B5
Greenhill La ST19 . . . . . **205** C7
Greenhill WS13 . . . . . . **231** C8
Greenhill Mews WS13 . . **231** C8
Greenhill Rd Dudley DY3 . . **271** E5
Stoke-on-T ST6 . . . . . . **42** E6
Greenhill Way WS9 . . . **245** B1
Greenhill WS15 . . . . . . **270** B5
Greenhough Rd WS13 . . **231** A8
Green La Aldridge WS9 . . **256** E5
Alsop en le D DE6 . . . . . **36** C2
Ashley TF9 . . . . **100** D5
Birchmoor B77,B78 . . . **262** D7
Blythe Bridge ST11 . . . . **91** A6
Brownhills WS8 . . . . . **229** B2
Burntwood WS7 . . . . . **212** D1
Burton u T DE13 . . . . **166** B7
Cannock WS11 . . . . . . **226** E6
Chorley WS13 . . . . . . **212** C3
Clifton Campville DE12 . . **218** B7
Clifton DE6 . . . . **81** E7
Dudley DY3 . . . . **271** F5
Eccleshall ST21 . . . . . **133** E6
Hamstall Ridware WS15 . . **181** B3
Kingswinford DY6 . . . . **275** D7
Lichfield WS14 . . . . . . **230** D2
Marchington ST14 . . . . **128** A2
Greenland Cl DY6 . . . . . **275** D8
Greenlands WV5 . . . . . . **269** F7
Green Lane Venture Ctr
WS11 . . . . **226** E6
Green La Newport TF10 . . **168** E4
Roston DE6 . . . . **96** F8
Rudyard ST13 . . . . **18** F2
Rugeley WS15 . . . . . . **178** D1
Stafford ST18 . . . . . . **174** C4
Sutton TF10 . . . . **150** E1
Tamworth B77 . . . . . . **262** C6
Tutbury DE13 . . . . **146** C5
Walsall,High Heath WS4,
WS9 . . . . **244** D3
Walsall,Pelsall WS3 . . . **244** A4
Waterhouses DE6 . . . . . **65** A7
Whitgreave ST18 . . . . **135** F7
Wolverhampton WV6 . . **255** F7
Greenlea Cl ST4 . . . . **88** C5
Green Lea Fst Sch ST18 . . **122** D4

Greenlea B77 . . . . **262** A8
Greenleighs DY3 . . . . . . **266** D3
Greenline Bsns Pk DE14 . . **166** B3
Greenly Rd WV4 . . . . . . **266** D5
Green Mdws 2 WS12 . . . **210** C1
Green Meadow Cl WV5 . . **269** C6
Greenmeadow Gr ST9 . . . **43** E6
Greenmeadows Rd CW3 . . **68** E7
Greenmoor Ave ST6 . . . . **42** A8
Green Oak Rd WV8 . . . . **239** B2
Green Pk Checkley ST10 . . **109** C8
Eccleshall ST21 . . . . . **133** F6
Fulford ST11 . . . . **90** E1
Green Rd Stoke-on-T ST4 . . **71** E3
Weston ST18 . . . . **138** D2
Green Rock La WS3 . . . . **243** D1
Green Rock Prim Sch
WS3 . . . . **243** E1
Greensforge La
Kinver DY7 . . . . **274** E3
Stourton DY7 . . . . **278** D8
Greenside Ave ST9 . . . . . **43** C3
Greenside Cl ST7 . . . . . . **41** A7
Greenside
Newcastle-u-L ST5 . . . **283** A3
Yarnfield ST15 . . . . . . **118** F6
Greenslade Rd DY3 . . . . **266** B2
Green's La ST2 . . . . **58** E3
Greensleeves B74 . . . . . **257** F1
Greensmith Cl DE15 . . . **167** C3
Greensome Cl ST16 . . . . **155** A5
Greensome Ct ST16 . . . . **155** A4
Greensome La ST16 . . . . **155** A5
Green St ST4 . . . . **166** D1
Greens The WV6 . . . . . . **254** E3
Green St DY9 . . . . **279** F5
Green The Aldridge WS9 . . **256** C5
Armitage WS15 . . . . . **198** C5
Barton-u-N DE13 . . . . **183** C1
Brocton,Milford ST17 . . **176** C7
Brocton ST17 . . . . **176** B3
Brown Edge ST6 . . . . . . **43** B7
Caverswall ST11 . . . . . . **74** D3
Cheadle ST10 . . . . **76** B2
Chebsey ST21 . . . . **134** E6
Fazeley B78 . . . . **249** E2
Fulford ST11 . . . . **90** E1
Kingsley ST10 . . . . **61** D2
Lawton-gate ST7 . . . . . . **25** A4
Newcastle-u-L ST5 . . . . **71** C3
Rugeley WS15 . . . . . . **197** A6
Seckington B79 . . . . . . **236** A3
Stourbridge DY8 . . . . . **275** D2
Stretton DE13 . . . . . . **147** E1
Tamworth B77 . . . . . . **251** B5
Walsall WS3 . . . . **243** B1
Weston ST18 . . . . **138** D2
Whittington WS14 . . . . **232** E5
Wood End B78 . . . . . . **262** C4
Woodseaves ST20 . . . . **151** C8
Greenvale DE15 . . . . . . **185** F8
Green Valley Dr DE13 . . **166** A8
Green View TF11 . . . . . . **203** F8
Green Way WS9 . . . . . . **245** B2
Greenway Ave
2 Stourbridge DY8 . . . **275** E1
Stoke-on-T ST6 . . . . . . **42** B2
Stone ST15 . . . . **120** B6
Greenway Bank ST8 . . . . **27** D3
Greenway Bank Ctry Pk★
ST8 . . . . **27** D3
Greenway Bank ST2 . . . . **43** C2
Greenway
Burton u T DE15 . . . . **167** A4
Eccleshall ST21 . . . . . **133** E6
Greenway Gdns
Pattingham WV6 . . . . **253** C2
Sedgley DY3 . . . . **266** C1
Greenway Hall Rd ST2,
ST9 . . . . **43** D3
Greenway Pl ST2 . . . . . . **58** B7
Greenway Rd ST3 . . . . . . **16** E2
Greenways Audley ST7 . . . **39** F2
Chorley WS13 . . . . . . **212** E3
Greenways Dr ST10 . . . . **76** D4
Greenway DY3 . . . . **266** B1
Greenways ST19 . . . . . . **208** A8
Greenways Prim Sch ST9 . . **43** C4
Greenways Stafford ST18 . . **174** C5
Stourbridge DY8 . . . . . **275** C1
Greenway ST16 . . . . **156** A3
Greenways The 1 ST2 . . **43** C3
Greenway ST3 . . . . **72** E3
Greenway The
Hagley DY9 . . . . **281** F5
Newcastle-u-L ST5 . . . . **56** C3
Pattingham WV6 . . . . **253** C2
Greenway ST4 . . . . **87** E2
Green Way ST14 . . . . . . **126** B8
Greenwich Ave DE11 . . . **186** E1
Greenwood Ave ST4 . . . . **71** E2
Greenwood Dr WS14 . . . **231** B6
Greenwood Gr ST17 . . . **174** C7
Greenwood Pk
Aldridge WS9 . . . . **245** C2
Cannock WS12 . . . . . . **210** B8
Greenwood Rd
Aldridge WS9 . . . . **245** B2
Burton u T DE15 . . . . **185** E8
Forsbrook ST11 . . . . . . **91** A4
Greenwoods The DY8 . . **279** E5
Gregory La ST20 . . . . . . **150** D6

Gregory Rd
Burntwood WS7 . . . . . **229** E7
Wolverhampton WV9 . . **279** D5
Gregorys Gn WV9 . . . . . **224** B3
Gregory St ST3 . . . . **284** B3
Gregson Cl 5 ST3 . . . . . **73** A3
Greig Ct WS11 . . . . **210** C2
Grenadier Ct ST14 . . . . . **88** C4
Grendon Gdns WV3 . . . **265** D6
Grendon Gn ST2 . . . . **58** C2
Grenfell Rd WS3 . . . . . . **243** D3
Grenville Cl ST14 . . . . . . **110** F1
Grenville Rd DY1 . . . . . . **271** E1
Gresham Rd WS11 . . . . . **209** F3
Gresley Cl B74 . . . . **258** A4
Gresley Row WS13 . . . . **231** C8
Gresley B77 . . . . **250** F1
Gresley Way ST7 . . . . . . **39** F2
Gresley Wood Rd DE11 . . **186** F2
Gresty St ST4 . . . . **72** A7
Gretton Ave DE13 . . . . . **147** E1
Greville Cl ST19 . . . . . . **207** F8
Greville St ST1 . . . . **282** C4
Greyfriars Bsns Pk ST16 . . **285** A4
Greyfriars Cl DY1 . . . . . **271** E3
Greyfriars Cl 2 ST16 . . . **155** D5
Greyfriars Dr B79 . . . . . **249** E6
Greyfriars Rd ST2 . . . . . . **58** A5
Grey Friars' Pl ST16 . . . **285** A4
Greyfriars Rd ST2 . . . . . . **58** A5
Grey Friars ST16 . . . . . . **155** D5
Grey Friars Way ST16 . . **155** D5
Greyhound Ct CW3 . . . . . **68** E6
Greyhound La
Lower Penn WV4 . . . . **264** E5
Stourbridge DY8 . . . . . **279** D2
Greyhound Way ST1,ST6 . . **57** A5
Greylarch La ST17 . . . . . **175** C7
Greysan Ave ST4 . . . . . . **41** F8
Greysbrooke Prim Sch
WS14 . . . . **247** A6
Greysbrooke WS14 . . . . **247** A5
Greystoke Dr DY6 . . . . . **275** D6
Greyswood Rd ST4 . . . . . **71** E3
Grice Rd ST4 . . . . **71** E8
Griffin Cl Burntwood WS7 . . **228** E8
Norton in H TF9 . . . . . . **82** C7
Griffin St ST3 . . . . **284** B3
Griffithgreen WV5 . . . . . **267** D7
Griffiths Dr
Wolverhampton WV11 . . **242** A1
Wombourne WV5 . . . . **270** A5
Griffiths Way WS15 . . . . **120** D6
Grimley Way WS11 . . . . **209** F4
Grindcobbe Gr WV5 . . . **178** D3
Grindley Hill Ct ST4 . . . . **71** E6
Grindley La
Kingstone ST18 . . . . . . **140** E6
Meir ST3,ST11 . . . . **90** B6
Grindley Pl ST4 . . . . **71** F6
Grindsbrook B77 . . . . . . **262** A8
Grisedale Cl 3 ST3 . . . . . **90** A7
Grissom Cl 6 ST16 . . . . **156** A5
Gritton St ST6 . . . . **41** D2
Grizedale Cl DE15 . . . . . **167** B1
Grocott Cl ST19 . . . . . . **192** E2
Grosvenor Ave
Aldridge B74 . . . . **256** F1
Stoke-on-T ST4 . . . . . . **71** F4
Grosvenor Cl
Lichfield WS14 . . . . . . **231** D6
Penkridge ST19 . . . . . **192** F1
Stoke-on-T ST6 . . . . . . **43** F8
Sutton Coldfield B75 . . **258** C1
Wolverhampton WV10 . . **240** D2
Grosvenor Cres WV10 . . **240** D2
Grosvenor Ct Dudley DY3 . . **271** D2
Shenstone WS14 . . . . . **246** F6
Wolverhampton,Tettenhall
WV6 . . . . **255** A3
Grosvenor Gdns ST5 . . . **283** C2
Grosvenor Pk WV4 . . . . **265** F9
Grosvenor Pl
Newcastle-u-L ST5 . . . . **56** C5
Stoke-on-T ST5 . . . . . . **41** F4
Grosvenor Rd
Dudley DY3 . . . . **271** D2
Longton ST3 . . . . **73** F1
Market Drayton TF9 . . . **97** D2
Newcastle-u-L ST5 . . . **283** C2
Wolverhampton,Bushbury
WV10 . . . . **240** D2
Wolverhampton,Ettingshall Park
WV4 . . . . **266** E3
Grosvenor Road S DY3 . . **271** D2
Grosvenor St Leek ST13 . . **30** F5
Longton ST3 . . . . **284** B3
Grosvenor Way WS17 . . **175** F6
Grotto La WV6 . . . . **255** E5
Grotto Rd TF9 . . . . **112** B8
Groundhollow ST10 . . . . **94** A3
Grounds Dr B74 . . . . . . **257** F3
Grounds Rd B74 . . . . . . **257** F3
Grove Ave Kidsgrove ST7 . . **25** E1
Lawton-gate ST7 . . . . . . **25** A4
Stoke-on-T ST4 . . . . . . **72** E4
Talke ST7 . . . . **40** E8
Grovebank Rd ST4 . . . . . **71** E3
Grove Cl WS11 . . . . **227** F5
Grove Cres Walsall WS3 . . **243** C4
Woore CW3 . . . . **83** C8
Grove Gdns TF9 . . . . **97** D1
Grove Jun Sch ST1 . . . . **282** C4
Grove La DE6 . . . . **127** C8
Grovelands Cres WV10 . . **240** D3
Grove La
Norton Canes WS3 . . . **227** E1
Wolverhampton WV6 . . **255** B2

Grovenor Ct TF9 . . . . **97** D2
Grove Park Ave ST7 . . . . **25** A4
Grove Pk DY6 . . . . **275** C8
Grove Pl ST1 . . . . **282** A1
Grove Prim Sch The
ST17 . . . . **174** D8
Grove Prim Sch WV2 . . . **266** E8
Grove Rd Stoke-on-T ST4 . . **72** D4
Stone ST15 . . . . **119** F8
Grove Road Ind Est ST4 . . **72** D4
Grove Sch The TF9 . . . . . **97** D1
Groveside Way WS3 . . . **244** A5
Grove St Burslem ST6 . . . **57** A6
Leek ST13 . . . . **30** D6
Newcastle-u-L ST5 . . . . **55** E3
Wolverhampton WV2 . . **266** D8
Grove Terr 11 ST13 . . . . **30** D6
Grove The
Blythe Bridge ST11 . . . . **90** E6
Burntwood WS7 . . . . . **228** D8
Lawton-gate ST7 . . . . . . **25** A4
Little Aston B74 . . . . . **257** D6
Newcastle-u-L ST5 . . . . **71** B6
Stoke-on-T ST6 . . . . . . **42** B2
Stone ST15 . . . . **120** C3
Tatenhill DE13 . . . . . . **184** A8
Wolverhampton,Lanesfield
WV4 . . . . **266** E5
Grub St ST20 . . . . **151** A6
Grunmore Dr DE13 . . . . **147** E2
Guernsey Cl CW12 . . . . . . **6** A1
Guernsey Dr ST5 . . . . . . **70** E3
Guernsey Wlk 2 ST3 . . . **73** A3
Guildford La TF10 . . . . . **169** F8
Guildhall Sh Ctr ST16 . . **285** B3
Guild La TF10 . . . . **169** F8
Guild St DE14 . . . . **166** D3
Guinevere Ave DE13 . . . **147** E2
Gullet The B78. . . . . **251** F1
Gullick Way WS7 . . . . . **228** D8
Gun Battery La ST8 . . . . . **28** A8
Gunby Hill DE12 . . . . . . **219** F8
Gunnell Cl Hanley ST1. . . **282** C1
Stafford ST16 . . . . **155** C2
Gunn St ST6 . . . . **27** C8
Gunstone La WV8 . . . . . **238** F5
Gurnard Cl WV12 . . . . . **242** B1
Gurnard B77 . . . . **261** D6
Guthrum Cl WV6 . . . . . . **254** F5
Guy's Almshouses B79 . . **250** B5
Guys Cl B79 . . . . **249** F7
Guy's La DY3 . . . . **271** B2
Guy St ST2 . . . . **58** B4
Gwendoline Way WS9 . . **245** B4
Gwenys Cres ST3 . . . . . . **72** E4
Gwyn Ave ST8 . . . . **27** D5
Gypsum Way DE6 . . . . . **144** D6

H

Hackett Cl Longton ST3. . **284** D4
Wolverhampton WV14 . . **266** F1
Hackford Rd WV4 . . . . . **266** F4
Hackwood Cl ST12 . . . . . **88** F4
Hadden Cl ST9 . . . . **59** B2
Haddon Gr ST5 . . . . **55** F6
Haddon La ST5 . . . . **85** E1
Haddon Pl Bucknall ST2 . . **58** C5
Stone ST15 . . . . **120** D7
Haden Cl DY8 . . . . **275** D2
Hadfield Gn ST6 . . . . **42** D2
Hadleigh Cl ST5 . . . . **71** B2
Hadleigh Rd ST2 . . . . . . **58** B6
Hadley Dr CW2 . . . . **37** E4
Hadley End DE13 . . . . . **181** E5
Hadley Park Sports Coll
WS15 . . . . **196** D8
Hadley St DE13 . . . . . . **181** F3
Hadrians Dr B77 . . . . . . **261** D8
Hadrian Way ST5 . . . . . . **55** D5
Haggar St WV2 . . . . **266** C6
Hagley Ct DY3 . . . . **271** D3
Hagley Dr WS15 . . . . . . **178** D3
Hagley Park Gdns WS15 . . **196** D7
Hagley RC High Sch DY8 . . **281** F6
Hagley Rd WS15 . . . . . . **178** D1
Haig Cl WS11 . . . . **210** A5
Haigh Cl ST13 . . . . **45** D5
Haig Rd ST13 . . . . **31** A7
Haig St ST3. . . . . **73** D2
Hailes Park Cl WV2 . . . . **266** E6
Hailsham Cl ST6 . . . . **41** F5
Hainer Cl 6 ST17 . . . . . **175** A8
Hainult Cl ST5 . . . . **275** D4
Halcyon Way DE14 . . . . **166** B4
Hales Hall Rd ST10 . . . . . **76** F4
Hales Pl ST3 . . . . **284** C1
Halesworth Cres ST5 . . . . **71** B2
Halesworth Rd WV9 . . . **239** F2
Halford St B79 . . . . **250** A5
Halfpenny Green Vineyard★
DY7 . . . . **268** D6
Halfshire La DY10 . . . . . **281** B1
Halfway Pl ST5 . . . . **55** E1
Halifax Cl ST13 . . . . **90** C7
Halifax Rd WV7 . . . . **220** F1
Haliford Ave ST1 . . . . **57** D7
Haling Cl ST19 . . . . **207** F8
Haling Rd ST19 . . . . **192** F1
Hallahan Cl ST15 . . . . . **120** C6
Hallahan Gr ST4 . . . . **72** A8
Hallam Rd ST4 . . . . **110** F1
Hallams Row DE14 . . . . **166** C4
Hallam St ST4 . . . . **72** E6
Hall Ave ST13 . . . . **31** A7
Hall Bank SK17 . . . . **24** E5
Hallbridge Cl WS3 . . . . . **243** F2

Hall Cl Pattingham WV6 . . . . 253 C2
Stafford ST17 . . . . 175 A7
Hallcourt Cl 3 WS11 . . . 226 E8
Hallcourt Cres 2 WS11 . . 226 E8
Hallcourt La WS11 . . . . . 226 E8
Hallcroft Cl TF10 . . . . 168 E3
Hallcroft Gdns TF10 . . . . 168 E3
Hallcroft Way WS9 . . . . . 256 C5
Halldearn Ave ST11 . . . . . 74 D3
Hall Dr Enville DY7 . . . . . 273 C1
Hanbury DE13 . . . . 145 A4
Meir ST3 . . . . 74 B4
Hall End Cl WV6 . . . . . . 253 C2
Hall End La WV6 . . . . . . 253 C2
Hallfarm ST17 . . . . 223 D6
Hall Farm Cl ST18 . . . . . 139 C1
Hall Farm Cres DE13 . . . 137 F4
Hallfarm Rd ST19 . . . . . . 223 D6
Hallfield Gr ST6 . . . . 41 E5
Hallfields Rd DE15 . . . . . 186 C4
Hall Gdns ST14 . . . . 127 E2
Hall Green Ave DE13 . . . 147 F2
Hall Grounds DE13 . . . . 147 A4
Hall Hill Dr ST2 . . . . 73 D8
Hallhill La WS15 . . . . 161 A5
Hall La Brownhills WS9 . . 244 E3
Cotes Heath ST21 . . . . 102 D3
Doveridge DE6 . . . . 127 B8
Great Wyrley WS6 . . . . 227 A3
Hammerwich WS7 . . . . 229 E4
Hilderstone ST15 . . . . . 106 F3
Muckley Corner WS7,
WS14 . . . . 229 F2
Stanton DE6 . . . . 80 A7
Swynnerton ST15 . . . . 103 D3
Walsall WS3 . . . . 243 F2
Wolverhampton WV14 . . 266 F1
Wootton DE6 . . . . 79 F7
Hall Mdw WS11 . . . . 226 B6
Hall Orch Bramshall ST14 . 125 C7
Cheadle ST10 . . . . 76 D3
Hall Pl ST5 . . . . 56 D5
Hall Rd Armitage WS15 . . 198 C5
Marchington ST14 . . . . 127 C2
Rolleston on D ST13 . . . 146 F4
Rolleston on D DE13 . . . 147 A4
Uttoxeter ST14 . . . . . . 126 A8
Halls Rd Biddulph ST8 . . . 16 C1
Mow Cop ST7 . . . . 26 C7
Hall St Audley ST7 . . . . . . 39 D2
Burslem ST6 . . . . 56 F8
Newcastle-u-L ST5 . . . . 283 B3
Sedgley DY3 . . . . 271 D8
Hall Yd ST10 . . . . 92 E4
Halston Rd WS7 . . . . 229 B8
Halton Gn ST3 . . . . 88 E8
Haltonlea B77 . . . . 262 A8
Hambledon Cl WV9 . . . . 240 A2
Hamble Gr ST4 . . . . 254 E4
Hamble Rd WV4 . . . . 265 C6
Hamble B77 . . . . 250 D2
Hambleton Pl ST8 . . . . 27 B5
Hamble Way ST2 . . . . 58 D1
Hambridge Cl ST17 . . . . . 174 D7
Hambro Pl ST6 . . . . 42 B7
Hamelin St WS11 . . . . . . 209 E3
Hames La B79 . . . . 236 D3
Hamil Dr ST13 . . . . 30 D6
Hamil Rd ST6 . . . . 42 A1
Hamilton Ave DY8 . . . . . 279 D6
Hamilton Cl
Cannock WS12 . . . . . . 210 F4
Sedgley DY3 . . . . 271 C8
Stourbridge DY8 . . . . . 275 C2
Hamilton Ct ST5 . . . . 71 C2
Hamilton Dr DY8 . . . . . . 275 C2
Hamilton Fields DE15 . . . 167 A2
Hamilton Gdns WV10 . . . 240 F3
Hamilton Ho WS3 . . . . . . 243 C1
Hamilton Inf Sch ST1 . . . . 57 D6
Hamilton Lea WS11 . . . . 228 A6
Hamilton Rd
Burton u T DE15 . . . . . 167 A2
Longton ST3 . . . . 284 D2
Hamilton Rise ST2 . . . . . . 43 B2
Hamilton St
Stoke-on-T ST4 . . . . 72 C5
Walsall WS3 . . . . 243 C1
Ham La DY6 . . . . 270 E1
Hamlet The WS11 . . . . . . 227 B6
Hamlett Pl ST6 . . . . 42 E3
Hammersley Hayes Rd
ST10 . . . . 76 E6
Hammersley St ST1 . . . . . 57 E6
Hammerton Ave ST2 . . . . . 57 F2
Hammerwich Hospl
WS7 . . . . 229 B5
Hammerwich La WS7 . . . 229 F3
Hammerwich Rd WS7 . . . 229 D5
Hammond Ave ST6 . . . . . . 43 B7
Hammond Ho ST1 . . . . . . 282 C1
Hammond Rd ST5 . . . . . . 55 E8
Hammonds Croft ST18 . . 158 C8
Hammoon Gr ST2 . . . . . . 58 B2
Hamner Gn ST2 . . . . 73 D8
Hampden Ho DE15 . . . . . 185 E6
Hamps Cl WS7 . . . . 229 D7
Hampshire Ave
Stoke-on-T ST9 . . . . 43 F7
Tamworth B78 . . . . 249 F2
Hampshire Cres ST3 . . . . . 89 C3
Hampson Ct ST15 . . . . . . 120 B8
Hampstead Gr ST4 . . . . . . 88 C7
Hamps Valley Rd ST10 . . . 48 F2
Hampton Cl
Newport TF10 . . . . 169 A3
Tamworth B79 . . . . 250 C7
Hampton Ct Leek ST13 . . . 30 D5

Hampton Ct continued
Rugeley WS15 . . . . 178 D3
Wolverhampton WV10 . . 241 B2
Hampton Dr
Market Drayton TF9 . . . . . 97 B2
Newport TF10 . . . . 169 A3
Hampton Gdns ST18 . . . . 156 D3
Hampton Gn WS11 . . . . . 226 E7
Hampton Gr Dunsley DY7 . 278 C4
Walsall WS3 . . . . 244 A4
Hampton Rd WV10 . . . . . 240 B1
Hampton St
Cannock WS11 . . . . . . 226 D7
Hanley ST1 . . . . 282 C1
Hams Cl ST8 . . . . 27 C7
Hanbridge Ave ST5 . . . . . . 56 C7
Hanbury Cres WS11 . . . . 265 E6
Hanbury Hill DE13 . . . . . 145 A5
Hanbury Rd
Brownhills WS8 . . . . . . 228 F2
Norton Canes WS11 . . . 227 F5
Tamworth B77 . . . . 250 F4
Hanbury's Farm Com Prim
Sch B77 . . . . 250 D1
Hanchurch Cl DE15 . . . . . 167 A4
Hanchurch Crossroad
ST5 . . . . 87 C8
Hanchurch Hills Circular
Wlks★ ST4 . . . . 86 F4
Hanchurch La ST4 . . . . . . 87 B7
Hancock St ST4 . . . . 72 C7
Handel Ct WS11 . . . . 210 C2
Handel Gr ST1 . . . . 58 A6
Handel Wlk WS13 . . . . . . 214 C2
Hand La TF11 . . . . 187 D1
Handley Banks ST11 . . . . . 74 E4
Handley Dr ST8 . . . . 27 C2
Handley Rd DE14 . . . . . . 165 F3
Handley Sh Ctr The ST1 . . 282 B2
Handley St ST7 . . . . 27 A2
Handsacre Cl DE11 . . . . . 186 F3
Handsacre Cres WS15 . . . 198 C3
Handsacre Rd ST3 . . . . . . 284 D5
Hand St ST6 . . . . 41 D2
Hangmans La B79 . . . . . . 236 A2
Hankins Heys La CW3 . . . . 82 B8
Hanley Bsns Pk ST1 . . . . . 282 B1
Hanley Rd ST6,ST1 . . . . . . 57 D8
Hanlith B77 . . . . 262 A8
Hannaford Way WS11 . . . 209 E3
Hanney Hay Rd WS7,WS8 . 229 B3
Hanover Ct
Newcastle-u-L ST5 . . . . 283 C3
Tamworth B79 . . . . 249 E7
Wolverhampton WV6 . . . 255 C4
Hanover Ho
6 Stourbridge DY8 . . . 279 F8
Longton ST4 . . . . 73 B5
Hanover Pl WS11 . . . . . . 209 E2
Hanover St Hanley ST1 . . . 282 B3
Newcastle-u-L ST5 . . . . 283 C3
Hanson Man B74 . . . . . . 258 A1
Hanyards La ST18 . . . . . . 156 F4
Harald Cl WV6 . . . . 254 E5
Harber St ST3 . . . . 284 C3
Harbin Rd DE12 . . . . 184 D1
Harborne Cres ST10 . . . . . 76 E4
Harborne Rd ST10 . . . . . . 76 E4
Harborough Ct B74 . . . . . 258 A2
Harborough Dr WS9 . . . . 256 B5
Harbourne Ct ST10 . . . . . . 76 E4
Harbury St DE13 . . . . 166 A6
Harcourt Ave ST3 . . . . 73 F1
Harcourt Dr Dudley DY3 . . 271 C2
Newport TF10 . . . . 169 A4
Sutton Coldfield B74 . . . 257 F4
Harcourt Ho B79 . . . . 250 A4
Harcourt Rd DE14 . . . . . . 184 F8
Harcourt St ST1 . . . . 282 A1
Harcourt Way ST16 . . . . . 155 B7
Hardewick Cl ST9 . . . . 59 B3
Hardie Ave WS16 . . . . . . 196 E7
Hardie Ct 2 WV4 . . . . . . 266 F4
Hardie Gn WS11 . . . . 209 F3
Hardinge St ST4 . . . . 72 D6
Harding Rd ST1 . . . . 282 B1
Hardings Mdw ST7 . . . . . . 25 E1
Hardingswood Rd ST7 . . . . 25 E2
Harding Terr ST4 . . . . 72 A6
Hardman St ST2 . . . . 43 A1
Hardon Rd WV4 . . . . 266 F5
Hardwick Cl ST4 . . . . 88 C4
Hardwick Ct Aldridge B74 . 256 F2
Tamworth B79 . . . . 250 C5
Hardwick Rd B74 . . . . . . 257 A4
Hardy Cl Barton-u-N DE13 . 201 E7
Cheadle ST10 . . . . 76 C2
Hardy Rd ST17 . . . . 174 B8
Hardy Sq WV2 . . . . 266 F6
Hardy St ST6 . . . . 41 D4
Harebell Cl
Cannock WS12 . . . . . . 210 D2
Featherstone WV10 . . . . 241 A7
Harebell Gr ST7 . . . . 26 F1
Harebell Rd B77 . . . . 251 A4
Harecastle Ave ST7 . . . . . . 25 E1
Harecastle Bank ST15 . . . 104 E3
Harecastle Ct ST7 . . . . 40 E6
Haregate Rd ST13 . . . . . . 31 A8
Haregate Terr ST13 . . . . . . 31 A7
Harehedge La
Burton u T DE13 . . . . . 166 B8
Stretton DE13 . . . . 147 B1
Hareshaw Gr ST6 . . . . 42 A8
Harewell Dr B75 . . . . 258 C1
Harewood Cl ST10 . . . . . . 76 D4
Harewood Est ST10 . . . . . 76 B5

Harewood St ST6 . . . . 41 D2
Hargate Rd DE15 . . . . . . 167 C1
Hargreave Cl ST13 . . . . . . 30 E5
Hargreaves Ct 5 ST13 . . . 30 E5
Hargreaves La ST17 . . . . 285 A1
Harington Dr ST3 . . . . 73 E5
Harland Cl ST18 . . . . 177 D8
Harland Rd B74 . . . . 258 A3
Harlech Ave ST3 . . . . 73 E1
Harlech Dr ST8 . . . . 27 C6
Harlech Way
Burton u T DY8 . . . . . . 166 D8
Dudley DY1 . . . . 271 F2
Harlequin Dr ST6 . . . . 42 C2
Harlestones Ho DY8 . . . . 279 F7
Harley Cl Brownhills WS8 . 245 A6
Rugeley WS15 . . . . 196 F6
Harley La
Abbots Bromley WS15 . . 160 F7
Beech ST4 . . . . 87 C1
Harley St ST1 . . . . 282 C2
Harley Thorn La ST4 . . . . . 87 B3
Harman Dr WS13 . . . . . . 230 F6
Harmon Rd DY8 . . . . 279 C5
Harmony Gn ST17 . . . . . . 174 B8
Harney Ct WS15 . . . . 178 D3
Harold St ST6 . . . . 42 C1
Harper Ave
Burton u T DE13 . . . . . 166 C7
Newcastle-u-L ST5 . . . . . 56 B4
Harper Ct DE13 . . . . 166 C7
Harper St ST6 . . . . 56 E7
Harpfield Prim Sch ST4 . . . 71 D8
Harpfield Rd ST4 . . . . 71 E5
Harplands Hospl ST4 . . . . 71 D6
Harplow La ST10 . . . . 76 B1
Harptree Wlk ST4 . . . . 71 F2
Harpur-Crewe Cotts DE6 . . 35 D3
Harrier Cl ST3 . . . . 90 A6
Harringay Dr DY8 . . . . . . 279 F5
Harrington Cl ST13 . . . . . . 30 E3
Harrington Wlk WS13 . . . 213 F1
Harriotts Hayes Rd WV7 . . 237 F6
Harriseahead La ST7 . . . . . 26 D4
Harrison Cl
Burton u T DE14 . . . . . 185 B8
Cheslyn Hay WS6 . . . . . 226 D1
Halmer End ST7 . . . . 54 D7
Walsall WS3 . . . . 243 C1
Harrison Ct ST5 . . . . 283 C1
Harrison Rd
Cannock WS11 . . . . . . 226 E7
Stoke-on-T ST6 . . . . 42 C3
Sutton Coldfield B74 . . . 257 E5
Walsall WS4 . . . . 244 C2
Harrisons La ST19 . . . . . . 207 E1
Harrison St
Newcastle-u-L ST5 . . . . 283 C3
Walsall WS3 . . . . 243 C1
Harrison Way ST11 . . . . . . 45 D5
Harrison & Woodburn Cotts
ST5 . . . . 54 C3
Harris Rd ST16 . . . . 156 B4
Harris St ST4 . . . . 72 A8
Harrogate Dr ST5 . . . . 54 F2
Harrop St ST1 . . . . 57 D6
Harrop Way DY8 . . . . 279 E8
Harrots La SK17 . . . . 24 D6
Harrowby Cr WV10 . . . . . 240 B3
Harrowby Dr ST5 . . . . 70 F4
Harrowby Rd Meir ST3 . . . 90 A8
Wolverhampton WV10 . . 240 C2
Harrowby St ST16 . . . . . . 156 A3
Harrow Ct B74 . . . . 257 F2
Harrow Dr DE14 . . . . 185 C8
Harrow Pl ST13 . . . . 120 D7
Harrow Rd DY6 . . . . 270 D1
Harrows Mobile Home Pk
The WV9 . . . . 224 C4
Hart Ct ST5 . . . . 283 B3
Hartill Rd WV4 . . . . 265 D3
Hartill St ST4 . . . . 72 C8
Hartington CE Prim Sch
SK17 . . . . 24 D5
Hartington Hall Youth
Hostel★ SK17 . . . . 24 E5
Hartington Dr Leek ST13 . . 30 E5
Newcastle-u-L ST5 . . . . . 56 B5
Hartland Ave
Stafford ST16 . . . . 175 A8
Stoke-on-T ST6 . . . . 42 C3
Hartlands Rd ST21 . . . . . 133 E7
Hartlebury Pl WS11 . . . . . 210 C2
Hartleyburn B77 . . . . 262 A8
Hartley Dr Aldridge WS9 . . 256 B4
Stone ST15 . . . . 104 F1
Hartley Gdns CW12 . . . . . 16 B8
Hartsbourne Way ST17 . . 175 C7
Hartshill Rd ST4 . . . . 71 F8
Hartslade WS14 . . . . 231 E6
Hartwell Gr ST16 . . . . . . 155 F4
Hartwell Cl
Great Wyrley WS6 . . . . 227 A3
Hartwell ST15 . . . . 89 C2
Hartwell ST5 . . . . 70 F4
Hartwell Rd ST3 . . . . 90 A8
Hartwood Cl TF10 . . . . . . 168 F5
Hartwood Cres WV3 . . . . 265 F5
Harvard Cl DY1 . . . . 271 F4
Harvest Cl DY3 . . . . 271 C5
Harvesters Cl WS9 . . . . . . 256 E2
Harvesters Wlk WV8 . . . . 239 E1
Harvester Way DY6 . . . . . 275 D4
Harvest Fields Way
Sutton Coldfield B75 . . . 258 D4
Sutton Coldfield B75 . . . 258 E3
Harvey Dr B75 . . . . 258 C2

Harvey Pl ST14 . . . . 111 B1
Harvey Rd Armitage WS15 . 198 C4
Burton u T DE14 . . . . . 185 A8
Congleton CW12 . . . . 6 A5
Meir ST3 . . . . 74 B2
Harvine Wlk DY8 . . . . . . 279 E3
Harwell Cl B79 . . . . 250 C7
Harwin Cl WV6 . . . . 255 F7
Harwood Ave DE14 . . . . . 184 F8
Harwood Rd B77 . . . . . . 261 D4
Harwood Rd WS13 . . . . . 214 B3
Haslemere Ave ST2 . . . . . . 43 B1
Haslington Cl ST5 . . . . . . 40 D1
Hassall St ST1 . . . . 282 C2
Hassall Ave ST5 . . . . 283 A4
Hassam Par ST5 . . . . 56 B5
Hassell St ST5 . . . . 283 C3
Haste Hill Ave ST10 . . . . . 61 F2
Hastings Cl ST5 . . . . 261 F6
Hastings Ct DY1 . . . . 271 C2
Hatchett Cl B79 . . . . 217 C5
Hatch Heath Cl WV5 . . . . 269 F7
Hatch La TF11 . . . . 203 D4
Hateley Dr WV4 . . . . 266 E4
Hatfield Cres ST3 . . . . 88 E8
Hathaway Mews DY8 . . . . 275 C3
Hathaway Rd B74 . . . . . . 258 A4
Hathersage Cl ST3 . . . . . . 73 C5
Hatherton Cl ST5 . . . . 40 D2
Hatherton Croft WS11 . . . 209 C1
Hatherton Gdns WV10 . . 240 E2
Hatherton Pl WS9 . . . . . . 256 A7
Hatherton Rd
Cannock WS11 . . . . . . 209 C1
Penkridge ST19 . . . . . . 192 F1
Hatherton St
Cheslyn Hay WS6 . . . . . 226 C2
Stafford ST16 . . . . 156 A3
Hatrell St ST5 . . . . 283 C1
Hatton Rd Cannock WS11 . 209 A1
Wolverhampton WV6 . . . 255 F7
Hattons Gr WV8 . . . . 239 B2
Hatton Waterworks Cotts
ST21 . . . . 102 D7
Haughton St Giles CE Prim
Sch ST18 . . . . 172 F5
Haunton Rd B79 . . . . 217 D3
Havannah La CW12 . . . . . . 6 A5
Havannah Prim Sch CW12 . 6 A5
Havefield Ave WS14 . . . . 231 E7
Havelet Dr ST5 . . . . 70 F3
Havelock Cl WV3 . . . . . . 265 F8
Havelock Gr ST8 . . . . 27 C7
Havelock Pl ST1 . . . . 282 A1
Haven Ave ST5 . . . . 57 D8
Haven Cres ST9 . . . . 59 B4
Haven Cvn Site DE14 . . . . 185 C8
Haven Gr ST5 . . . . 56 C7
Havensfield Dr ST10 . . . . . 92 E5
Haven The
Stourbridge DY8 . . . . . 275 D2
Wolverhampton WV2 . . . 266 C8
Havergal CE Prim Sch
WV10 . . . . 225 D1
Havergal Pl WV10 . . . . . . 225 D1
Havergal Wlk ST3 . . . . 73 C5
Haverhill Cl Chorlton CW2 . 37 B3
Walsall WS3 . . . . 243 A3
Havisham Ct TF10 . . . . . . 168 E3
Hawcroft WS15 . . . . 197 F2
Hawes St ST6 . . . . 41 D4
Haweswater Dr DY6 . . . . 275 D6
Hawfield La
Burton u T DE15 . . . . . 167 C3
Burton u T DE15 . . . . . 167 D4
Hawfinch Rd ST10 . . . . . . 76 E3
Hawk Cl B77 . . . . 262 A6
Hawk Cl ST3 . . . . 90 A7
Hawke Rd ST16 . . . . 155 C7
Hawkesford Cl B74 . . . . . 258 B1
Hawkesmoor Dr WS14 . . . 231 D8
Hawkesmore Dr ST18 . . . 177 D7
Hawkestone Cl ST5 . . . . . 283 C2
Hawkesville Dr 7 DY6 . . 275 D8
Hawkeswell Dr 4 DY6 . . . 275 D8
Hawkhurst Dr WS15 . . . . 197 F8
Hawkins Cl WS13 . . . . . . 214 B2
Hawkins Dr WS11 . . . . . . 226 C4
Hawkins La
Burton u T DE14 . . . . . 166 E5
Fradswell ST18 . . . . . . 122 F2
Hawkins Lane Ind Est
DE14 . . . . 166 E5
Hawks Cl WS6 . . . . 226 D2
Hawksdale Cl ST3 . . . . . . 90 A7
Hawk's Dr DE15 . . . . 167 D3
Hawks Green La WS11 . . . 210 A1
Hawkside B77 . . . . 262 B8
Hawksley Dr DE13 . . . . . 147 B4
Hawksmoor Cl ST3 . . . . . . 89 E7
Hawksmoor Dr WV6 . . . . 254 D3
Hawksmoor Rd ST17 . . . . 174 E2
Hawkstone Ave TF10 . . . . 168 E2
Hawkstone Cl WV6 . . . . . 254 D5
Hawkswell Ave WV5 . . . . 270 A5
Hawksworth Ave ST13 . . . 30 D4
Hawksworth Cl ST13 . . . . . 30 D4
Hawksworth B77 . . . . . . 250 F2
Hawkyard Cl WS11 . . . . . 210 A4
Hawley St ST15 . . . . 120 D5
Haworth Ave CW12 . . . . . . 6 A5
Hawthorn Ave
Great Wyrley WS6 . . . . 227 A1
Netherseal DE12 . . . . . 219 F7
Stone ST15 . . . . 119 F5
Hawthorn Cl
Denstone ST14 . . . . 95 E6

Hawthorn Cl continued
Gnosall ST20 . . . . 171 E7
Great Bridgeford ST18 . . 135 B2
Haughton ST18 . . . . . . 172 E6
Lichfield WS14 . . . . 231 D8
Hawthorn Cres DE15 . . . 185 F7
Hawthornden Ave ST14 . . 126 A8
Hawthornden Cl ST14 . . . 126 A8
Hawthornden Gdns ST14 . 125 F8
Hawthornden Manor Mews
ST14 . . . . 126 A8
Hawthornden Manor
ST14 . . . . 126 A8
Hawthorne Ave Audley ST7 . 71 E5
Stoke-on-T ST4 . . . . 71 E5
Hawthorne Cl ST10 . . . . . 92 F3
Hawthorne Cres WS7 . . . 229 A6
Hawthorne Dr ST19 . . . . 205 C6
Hawthorne Gr DY3 . . . . . 271 D2
Hawthorne La WV8 . . . . . 238 F2
Hawthorne Rd
Cannock WS12 . . . . . . 210 F3
Cheslyn Hay WS6 . . . . . 226 E4
Essington WV11 . . . . . . 242 A3
Huntington ST17 . . . . . 209 D8
Wheaton Aston ST19 . . . 205 C6
Wolverhampton WV2 . . . 266 D6
Hawthorne Terr ST13 . . . . 30 F6
Hawthorne Way DY7 . . . . 278 C3
Hawthorn Gdns ST7 . . . . . 40 D8
Hawthorn Gr ST8 . . . . 27 E7
Hawthorn Mews ST14 . . . 126 C8
Hawthorn Pl 2 ST3 . . . . . 89 F8
Hawthorn Rd
Aldridge B74 . . . . 257 A1
Newcastle-u-L ST5 . . . . . 40 E1
Walsall WS4 . . . . 244 B1
Hawthorn Rise DE11 . . . . 186 F7
Hawthorn St ST6 . . . . 57 B6
Hawthorns The
Hagley DY9 . . . . 281 F4
Keele ST5 . . . . 69 F7
Hawthorn Way
Market Drayton TF9 . . . . . 97 D2
Rugeley WS15 . . . . 178 D2
Stafford ST17 . . . . 156 A1
Haybank La ST10 . . . . 78 E5
Hay Barns The ST15 . . . . 103 B4
Haybarn The ST16 . . . . . . 155 F7
Haybridge Ave DY8 . . . . . 281 B5
Haybridge High Sch & Sixth
Form DY8 . . . . 281 F6
Haycroft Dr B74 . . . . 258 A4
Haydock Cl
Burton u T DE14 . . . . . 185 A7
Cheadle ST10 . . . . 76 E5
Tamworth B77 . . . . 261 D4
Haydock Ct ST5 . . . . 55 C1
Haydon Ct ST4 . . . . 56 E2
Haydon St ST4 . . . . 56 E1
Hay End La WS13 . . . . . . 215 C8
Hayes Cl ST13 . . . . 30 F7
Hayes Meadow Prim Sch
WS15 . . . . 198 C4
Hayes St ST6 . . . . 42 C2
Hayes The TF9 . . . . 112 A7
Hayes View Dr WS6 . . . . 226 E4
Hayes View WS13 . . . . . . 213 F1
Hayes Way WS12 . . . . . . 210 C1
Hayeswood La ST7 . . . . . . 54 E6
Hayfield Cres ST4 . . . . 72 E7
Hayfield Hill WS15 . . . . . 211 B4
Hayfield Rd ST5 . . . . 55 B1
Hay Gr WS8 . . . . 244 A4
Hayhead Cl ST7 . . . . 26 B2
Hay La Ellastone DE6 . . . . 79 E4
Foston DE65 . . . . 129 E5
Longdon WS15 . . . . . . 213 A7
Hayle Cl ST17 . . . . 156 E1
Hayle B77 . . . . 250 D2
Hayley Ct DY6 . . . . 275 D6
Hayling Ct WS4 . . . . 244 D1
Hayling Gr WV2 . . . . 266 B6
Hayling Pl ST3 . . . . 72 F3
Haymaker Way WS12 . . . . 210 F4
Haymarket 3 ST6 . . . . . . 41 D3
Haymarket The WV8 . . . . 239 E1
Haymoor WS14 . . . . 231 E2
Hayner Gr ST3 . . . . 74 B4
Hayrick Dr DY6 . . . . 275 B7
Hays La ST10 . . . . 48 F4
Haywain Cl WV9 . . . . 239 F2
Haywards Cl WS3 . . . . . . 243 F3
Haywood Cl CW3 . . . . 68 C5
Haywood Dr WV6 . . . . . . 255 D4
Haywood Grange ST18 . . . 177 D7
Haywood High Sch ST6 . . . 42 A2
Haywood Hospl ST6 . . . . . 42 A3
Haywood Hts ST18 . . . . . 177 D8
Haywood La TF9 . . . . 113 C1
Haywood Rd ST6 . . . . 42 A2
Haywood St Leek ST13 . . . 30 F5
Stoke-on-T ST6 . . . . 57 B1
Hayworth Cl B79 . . . . 249 E6
Hayworth Rd WS13 . . . . . 214 C2
Hazel Cl Kidsgrove ST7 . . . 26 B3
Stoke-on-T ST4 . . . . 71 F5
Uttoxeter ST14 . . . . . . 126 B6
Hazeldene ST18 . . . . 158 C4
Hazeldene St4 . . . . 88 C7
Hazel Dr Armitage WS15 . . 198 B4
Cannock WS12 . . . . . . 211 A6
Hazelgarth B77 . . . . 262 B8
Hazel Gdns WV8 . . . . 239 A4

Hazel Gr 2 Longton ST3 . . . . . 73 F2
Biddulph ST8 . . . . 17 B1
Lawton-gate ST7 . . . . 25 A2
Leek ST13 . . . . 30 C5
Lichfield WS14 . . . . 231 C7
Stafford ST16 . . . . 155 C8
Stourbridge DY8 . . . . 279 C3
Wombourne WV5 . . . . . . 270 A7
Hazelhurst Dr ST13 . . . . 45 D4
Hazelhurst Rd ST6 . . . . 41 F6
Hazelhurst ST1 . . . . 282 C1
Hazel La WS6 . . . . 227 B2
Hazelmere Dr
Burntwood WS7 . . . . 228 F4
Wolverhampton WV3 . . . 255 A1
Hazel Rd
Kingswinford DY6 . . . . . . 275 E5
Newcastle-u-L ST5 . . . . . . 55 D8
Wolverhampton WV3 . . . 265 C7
Hazel Slade Com Prim Sch
WS12 . . . . 211 A6
Hazelslade Ho WS12 . . . . . 210 F6
Hazelslade Nature Reserve★
WS12 . . . . 211 B6
Hazels The DY9 . . . . 281 F5
Hazelwood Cl
Cheslyn Hay WS6 . . . . . . 226 D2
Hanley ST6 . . . . 57 C6
Hazelwood Gr WS11 . . . . 226 C8
Hazelwood Rd
Aldridge B74 . . . . 256 D1
Burton u T DE15 . . . . 185 E6
Dudley DY1 . . . . 271 F6
Endon ST9 . . . . 43 E6
Hazlemere Dr B74 . . . . 258 B1
Hazlemere Gr WS11 . . . . . 226 B8
Hazlescross Rd ST10 . . . . . . 61 D3
Hazleton Gn ST17 . . . . 174 D6
Hazlitt Way ST3 . . . . 73 D5
HCM Ind Est DE14 . . . . . . 166 E4
Headborough Wlk WS9 . . 245 B1
Headingley Dr DY7 . . . . . . 274 F1
Headingley Gr ST4 . . . . 88 D7
Headland Rd WV3 . . . . . . 255 A1
Headlands The ST3 . . . . . . 257 C3
Headland Way ST10 . . . . . . 78 F1
Heakley Ave ST6 . . . . 42 F4
Healey Ave ST8 . . . . 27 B5
Healey B77 . . . . 250 E2
Heanor Pl ST3 . . . . 284 A3
Heantun Row WV11 . . . . . 242 B2
Hearn Ct ST17 . . . . 174 D7
Hearthcote Rd DE11 . . . . 186 F3
Heart Of The Country Ctr★
WS14 . . . . 247 E8
Heath Ave
Newcastle-u-L ST5 . . . . . . 56 C3
Werrington ST9 . . . . 59 E4
Whittington WS14 . . . . . 232 C3
Heathbank Dr WS12 . . . . . 209 C6
Heathbrook Ave DY6 . . . . 275 B7
Heath Cl WS14 . . . . 245 E5
Heathcote Ave TF9 . . . . 99 F3
Heathcote Cl ST3 . . . . . . 73 D5
Heathcote Ct 1 ST3 . . . . 73 D5
Heathcote Dr B78 . . . . . . 249 C1
Heathcote Rd
Halmer End ST7 . . . . 54 E7
Longton ST3 . . . . 284 B3
Heathcote Rise ST3 . . . . . . 74 B5
Heathcote St
Kidsgrove ST7 . . . . 26 A2
Longton ST3 . . . . 73 C5
Newcastle-u-L ST5 . . . . . . 55 E8
Heath Croft Rd B75 . . . . . 258 D1
Heath Cross ST14 . . . . . . 126 A8
Heath Cvn Pk WV10 . . . . 240 C6
Heathdene Cl ST3 . . . . . . 284 B4
Heath Dr
Kidderminster DY10 . . . . 280 B1
Stafford ST16 . . . . 155 B7
Heather Cl Brocton ST17 . 176 C4
Burton u T DE14 . . . . 185 A8
Great Bridgeford ST18 . . 135 C2
Lichfield WS13 . . . . 214 D1
Rugeley WS15 . . . . 196 F6
Werrington ST9 . . . . 59 A4
Heather Cres ST3 . . . . 90 A4
Heather Dr
Huntington WS12 . . . . . . 209 D5
Kinver DY7 . . . . 277 F4
Heather Glade CW3 . . . . . . 68 D7
Heather Hill ST17 . . . . . . 176 C4
Heather Hills ST9 . . . . 43 D5
Heatherlands Cl ST3 . . . . . 89 F5
Heatherleigh Gr ST1 . . . . . 57 F6
Heather Mews WS12 . . . . 210 A8
Heather Rd WS12 . . . . . . 210 A8
Heatherside ST7 . . . . 26 C6
Heather Valley WS12 . . . . 210 D6
Heather View ST6 . . . . 42 E6
Heath Farm Rd
Codsall WV8 . . . . 239 B2
Stourbridge DY8 . . . . . . 279 E3
Heathfield Ave ST5 . . . . . 120 A7
Heathfield Ct ST6 . . . . 41 C7
Heathfield Dr
Newcastle-u-L ST5 . . . . . . 40 D1
Walsall WS3 . . . . 243 B1
Heathfield Gdns DY8 . . . 279 E3
Heathfield Gr ST3 . . . . 89 F6
Heathfield Rd
Stoke-on-T ST6 . . . . 42 C5

Heathfield Rd continued
Sutton Coldfield B74 . . . 257 F3
Uttoxeter ST14 . . . . 126 B8
Heathfields WV8 . . . . 238 E1
Heathfields Inf Sch B77 . 261 F6
Heathfield Specl Sch ST6 42 C5
Heath Gap WS13 . . . . . . 215 D7
Heath Gap Rd WS11 . . . 209 F3
Heath Gdns ST15 . . . . . . 119 F6
Heath Gn DY1 . . . . 271 F5
Heath Gr Codsall WV8 . . 239 B3
Loggerheads TF9 . . . . 99 D4
Meir Heath ST3 . . . . 90 A5
Heath Hayes Prim Sch
WS12 . . . . 210 F2
Heath Hill Rd WV6 . . . . . 254 E1
Heath House Dr WV5 . . . 269 D5
Heath House La
Bucknall ST2 . . . . 58 A4
Codsall WV8 . . . . 238 E1
Lower Tean ST10 . . . . 93 A3
Rudyard ST13 . . . . 18 C1
Heathland Cl WS12 . . . . . 210 D2
Heathlands Cl DY6 . . . . . 275 E8
Heathlands Dr ST14 . . . . 111 B1
Heathlands Grange
DE15 . . . . 185 E7
Heathlands The WV5 . . 269 D5
Heath La Newton WS15 . . 140 D1
Stourbridge DY8 . . . . . . 279 F4
Heathley La B78 . . . . 260 E5
Heathley Mews DE14 . . . 185 C8
Heath Mill Cl WV5 . . . . . 269 D4
Heath Mill Rd WV5 . . . . . 269 D4
Heath Pl ST5 . . . . 56 C3
Heath Rd Burton u T DE15 . 185 E7
Gnosall TF10 . . . . 188 E7
Rugeley WS15 . . . . 196 F6
Uttoxeter ST14 . . . . 111 B1
Whitmore ST5 . . . . 85 D7
Willenhall WV12 . . . . . . 242 D1
Heath Row CW3 . . . . 69 B8
Heathside Dr WS3 . . . . . . 244 A4
Heathside La ST6 . . . . 41 C7
Heath's Pas ST3 . . . . . . 284 D3
Heath St Biddulph ST8 . . . . 27 C7
Cannock WS12 . . . . 210 B7
Newcastle-u-L,Broad Meadow
ST5 . . . . 55 F6
Newcastle-u-L ST5 . . . . . 283 B8
Stoke-on-T ST6 . . . . 41 C7
Tamworth B79 . . . . 250 C5
Heath Top TF9 . . . . 99 F4
Heath View
Burntwood WS7 . . . . 212 A1
Cannock WS12 . . . . 227 E8
Heathview ST13 . . . . 45 E7
Heath View CW2 . . . . 37 B5
Heath Way WS11 . . . . . . 210 B2
Heathway Colton WS15 . . 179 A7
Gnosall ST20 . . . . 171 C5
Heath Way DE65 . . . . 146 C8
Heathwood Rd TF10 . . . . 168 E2
Heatley Back La WS15 . . . 141 C3
Heatley La WS15 . . . . . . 141 C2
Heaton Cl WV10 . . . . 240 E5
Heaton Terr
Endon Bank ST9 . . . . 29 A1
Newcastle-u-L ST5 . . . . . . 56 B6
Heaton Villas ST6 . . . . 43 C7
Heaton Way CW2 . . . . 37 E4
Hebden Gr WV11 . . . . . . 242 B1
Hebden B77 . . . . 262 B8
Heber St ST3 . . . . 284 C4
Hedgerow Cl WS12 . . . . 209 F7
Hedgerow Dr DY6 . . . . . . 270 D7
Hedgerows The
Lichfield WS14 . . . . 231 B5
Tamworth B77 . . . . 261 F8
Hedgerow Wlk WV8 . . . . 239 E1
Hedges The WV5 . . . . . . 269 E6
Hedging Lane Ind Est
B77 . . . . 261 E5
Hedging La B77 . . . . 261 E5
Hedley Pl ST5 . . . . 70 F8
**Hednesford Hills Common
Nature Reserve**★
WS12 . . . . 210 E5
Hednesford Rd
Brownhills WS8 . . . . 228 C2
Cannock,Blackfords WS11 209 F2
Cannock WS12 . . . . 210 E1
Norton Canes WS11 . . . . 227 F6
Rugeley WS15 . . . . 196 D7
Hednesford Sta WS12 . . . 210 B5
Hednesford St WS11 . . . . 209 E1
Heenan Gr Lichfield WS13 213 F2
Stafford ST17 . . . . 174 E5
Heighley Castle Way CW3 68 E8
Heighley Ct CW3 . . . . 53 A6
Heighley La CW3 . . . . 53 F3
Heights The ST13 . . . . 30 B2
Helen Sharman Dr ST16 . 156 B5
Helford Gr ST17 . . . . 174 B8
Heligan Pl WS12 . . . . 210 E2
Hellaby Ho B74 . . . . 257 F3
Hellier Dr WV5 . . . . 269 E7
Hellier Rd WV10 . . . . 240 E2
Helmingham B79 . . . . . . 249 D7
Helston Ave ST3 . . . . 73 E3
Helston Cl Stafford ST17 . 156 E1
Stourbridge DY8 . . . . . . 275 C2
Tamworth B79 . . . . 250 C8
Heming Rd ST3 . . . . 73 D4
Hemingway Rd ST3 . . . . . 73 D4
Hemlock Bsns Ctr WS11 210 B2
Hemlock Pk WS11 . . . . . . 210 B2

Hemlock Rd ST3 . . . . 284 D4
Hemlock Way WS11 . . . . 210 B3
Hemmings Cl DY8 . . . . . . 279 F5
Hempbutts The ST15 . . . . 120 B8
Hempits Gr ST17 . . . . 175 B1
Hemplands Rd DY8 . . . . . 279 F5
Hempstalls Ct ST5 . . . . . . 283 B4
Hempstalls Gr ST5 . . . . . . 56 B3
Hempstalls La ST5 . . . . . . 283 C4
Hempstalls Prim Sch ST5 56 B3
Hemsby Way ST5 . . . . 71 B2
Hencroft ST13 . . . . 30 E6
Henderson Cl WS14 . . . . 231 D7
Henderson Gr ST3 . . . . . . 74 B2
Hendon Cl DY3 . . . . 271 D2
Henhurst Farm DE13 . . . 165 D5
Henhurst Hill DE13 . . . . . 165 C4
Henhurst Ridge DE13 . . . 165 C4
Hen La ST10 . . . . 108 D6
Henley Ave ST8 . . . . 27 A4
Henley Cl Barlaston ST12 . 88 E4
Burntwood WS7 . . . . 229 B5
Tamworth B79 . . . . 250 C6
Walsall WS3 . . . . 243 E1
Henley Ct WS14 . . . . 231 B6
Henley Dr Newport TF10 . 169 A4
Sutton Coldfield B74 . . . 258 A3
Henley Grange WS15 . . . 178 A1
Henley Gr ST Chorlton CW2 . 37 B1
Wolverhampton WV10 . . 240 B1
Henney Cl ST19 . . . . 207 F7
Henry Chadwick Prim Sch
WS15 . . . . 198 A8
Henry Prince CE Fst Sch The
DE6 . . . . 81 D7
Henry St Stafford ST16 . . 155 F5
Stoke-on-T ST6 . . . . 41 D4
Hensel Dr WV3 . . . . 265 C8
Henshall Hall Dr CW12 . . . . 6 B1
Henshall Pl ST6 . . . . 41 C4
Henshall Rd ST5 . . . . 55 E8
Henshaw Way ST15 . . . . . 119 A6
Henwood Cl WV6 . . . . . . 255 C3
Henwood Rd WV6 . . . . . . 255 D3
Hepburn Cl WV9 . . . . 256 A4
Hepworth Cl WV6 . . . . . . 254 F4
Herbert Rd 2 Longton ST3 73 D2
Aldridge WS9 . . . . 245 A1
Stafford ST17 . . . . 285 B1
Herbert St
Burton u T DE15 . . . . 167 B3
Stoke-on-T ST4 . . . . 72 D6
Herbhill Cl WV4 . . . . 266 D4
Herd St ST5 . . . . 41 F1
Hereford Ave ST5 . . . . 71 C4
Hereford Cl WS9 . . . . 256 A8
Hereford Gr ST2 . . . . 58 D2
Hereford Rd WS12 . . . . . 210 B4
Hereford Way
Rugeley WS15 . . . . 196 D6
Tamworth B79 . . . . 250 A2
Heritage Ct WS14 . . . . . . 231 D6
Heritage Way DE15 . . . . . 167 A1
Herm Cl ST5 . . . . 70 E4
Hermes Cl ST3 . . . . 90 C7
Hermes Rd WS13 . . . . . . 214 D1
Hermitage Cl B74 . . . . . . 257 F3
Hermitage Gdns ST14 . . 111 A1
Hermitage La Mayfield DE6 81 B6
Polesworth B78 . . . . 251 E1
Hermit St DY3 . . . . 271 D5
Heron Cl Brownhills WS8 . 244 E7
Coven WV9 . . . . 224 B2
Madeley CW3 . . . . 68 F7
Stoke-on-T ST7 . . . . 41 F8
Heron Cross Prim Sch
ST4 . . . . 72 D4
Heron Ct DE13 . . . . 201 A2
Herondale WS12 . . . . . . 210 B4
Herondale Cres DY8 . . . . 279 C4
Herondale Rd DY8 . . . . . 279 C4
Heron Dr Penkridge ST19 . 208 A6
Uttoxeter ST14 . . . . 126 C6
Heron Mill WS3 . . . . 243 E3
Heron Pool Dr ST5 . . . . . . 85 C4
Heronry The WV6 . . . . . . 254 F2
Herons Cl ST17 . . . . 175 C7
Herons Gate Rd DY7 . . . . 277 B4
Heron St Rugeley WS15 . . 196 F8
Stoke-on-T ST4 . . . . 72 E5
Heronswood ST17 . . . . . 175 C7
Heron Way TF10 . . . . 168 F5
Hertford Gr ST5 . . . . 71 D4
Hertford St ST4 . . . . 72 E4
Hesketh Ave ST6 . . . . 42 D6
Hesketh Rd ST17 . . . . . . 174 E6
Heskin Way ST6 . . . . 42 A6
Hesleden B77 . . . . 262 B8
Hester Cl ST3 . . . . 73 C6
Hethersett Wlk ST2 . . . . . 58 D2
Hever Cl DY1 . . . . 271 E3
Hewell Cl DY6 . . . . 270 D1
Hewitt Cl WS13 . . . . 214 A2
Hewitt Cres ST9 . . . . 59 B3
Hewitt St ST6 . . . . 41 F6
Hewston Croft WS12 . . . 210 D4
Hexham Way DY1 . . . . . . 271 F2
Hextall La ST18 . . . . 153 D6
Heybridge Cl ST10 . . . . . . 92 F2
Heyburn Cres ST6 . . . . . . 56 E8
Heyfields Cotts ST12 . . . 104 B8
Heygate Way WS9 . . . . . 245 B1
Heysham Cl ST3 . . . . 74 B4
Hickmerelands La DY3 . . 266 C1
Hickory Ct WS11 . . . . . . 210 C2
Hick St ST5 . . . . 283 B2

Hidden Hills CW3 . . . . 68 E8
Hide La Hartington SK17 . . 24 E7
Sparklow SK17 . . . . 14 F1
Hide Pl ST4 . . . . 72 B7
Hide St ST4 . . . . 72 B7
Higginson Cl CW12 . . . . . 16 C8
Higgins Rd DE11 . . . . 186 F6
Higgott Cl DE14 . . . . 185 B8
Higgs Rd WV11 . . . . 242 A1
High Arcal Dr DY3 . . . . . . 271 F7
High Arcal Rd DY3 . . . . . . 270 F4
High Arcal Sch The DY3 . 271 F6
High Bank WS11 . . . . 226 E8
High Bank Pl ST6 . . . . 42 B1
High Bank Rd DE15 . . . . . 167 B3
Highbrook Cl WV9 . . . . . 240 A2
High Broome Ct B78 . . . . 250 A3
Highbury Rd
Sutton Coldfield B74 . . . 257 C3
Werrington ST9 . . . . 59 C4
High Carr Bsns Pk ST5 . . 40 F2
High Carr Network Ctr
ST5 . . . . 40 F2
High Chase Ho ST18 . . . . 177 D8
High Chase Rise ST18 . . . 177 D8
Highcliffe Rd B77 . . . . . . 261 D8
High Croft WS9 . . . . 245 B2
Highcroft Ave DY8 . . . . . 275 C3
High Croft Cres WS14 . . . 231 C7
Highcroft Dr
Burton u T DE14 . . . . 165 F4
Sutton Coldfield B74 . . . 257 E3
Highcroft WS3 . . . . 244 B6
Highcroft Wlk ST6 . . . . . . 42 B2
High Cross SK17 . . . . 24 F5
Higher Ash Rd ST7 . . . . . . 40 D8
Higherland ST5 . . . . 283 A2
Higherland Ct 6 ST7 . . . . 26 A2
Higher Woodcroft ST13 . . 30 D4
Higher Works Cotts SK11 . . 7 C6
Highfield Ave
Burntwood WS7 . . . . 229 B7
Cheadle ST10 . . . . 76 D4
Kidsgrove ST7 . . . . 26 B2
Longton ST3 . . . . 73 F1
Newcastle-u-L ST5 . . . . . . 56 D4
Tamworth B77 . . . . 251 A5
Wolverhampton WV10 . . 241 A2
Highfield Cl
Acton Trussell ST17 . . . . 193 B8
Blythe Bridge ST11 . . . . . 90 D7
Burntwood WS7 . . . . 229 B7
Burton u T DE13 . . . . 166 B7
Highfield Cres ST10 . . . . . 76 D4
Highfield Dr
Burton u T DE13 . . . . 166 F3
Colwich ST18 . . . . 177 D8
Stoke-on-T ST3 . . . . 72 E3
Highfield TF10 . . . . 168 A3
Highfield Gdns WS14 . . . 231 E6
Highfield Grange ST5 . . . . 56 E4
Highfield Gr ST17 . . . . . . 174 C8
Highfield La SK17 . . . . 24 F5
Highfield Rd
Burntwood WS7 . . . . 229 C4
Cannock WS12 . . . . 210 E1
Cookley DY10 . . . . 280 A5
Highfield Rd E ST8 . . . . . . 27 D8
Highfield Rd ST18 . . . . . . 158 D8
Highfield Rd N WS3 . . . . 243 F5
Highfield Rd Sedgley DY3 266 D1
Walsall WS3 . . . . 244 A4
Highfield Rd W ST8 . . . . . 27 D8
Highfield Rise ST4 . . . . . . 87 F8
Highfields Ave WS15 . . . 198 C4
Highfields The
Croxton ST21 . . . . 116 B5
Wolverhampton WV6 . . . 255 A3
Highfield Way WS9 . . . . . 245 A4
Highgate ST4 . . . . 257 A1
Highgate Ave WV4 . . . . . 265 D6
Highgate Cl ST6 . . . . 42 E4
Highgate Country Pk★
DY3 . . . . 269 A1
Highgate DY3 . . . . 271 E5
Highgate Rd DY7 . . . . . . 273 F7
High Gn Brewood ST19 . . 223 C6
Cannock WS11 . . . . 209 D1
High Grange
Cannock WS11 . . . . 210 A5
Lichfield WS13 . . . . 213 F1
High Green St WS11 . . . . 209 D1
Highgrove Cl
Stretton DE13 . . . . 147 D1
Tamworth B79 . . . . 250 B7
Highgrove Ct DY10 . . . . . 280 A1
Highgrove Pl DY1 . . . . . . 271 F2
Highgrove Rd ST4 . . . . . . 71 F3
Highgrove Stone ST15 . . 120 C5
Wolverhampton WV6 . . . 255 C3
High Hill WV1 . . . . 242 A2
High Holborn DY3 . . . . . . 271 D7
High House La WV7 . . . . . 237 D4
High La Alsagers Bank ST7 . 55 A5

High La continued
Brown Edge ST6 . . . . 43 B6
Leek ST13 . . . . 45 E7
Highland Cl
Biddulph Moor ST8 . . . . . 28 B8
Blythe Bridge ST11 . . . . . 90 E7
Highland Dr Longton ST3 . 73 D1
Stoke-on-T ST3 . . . . 89 D8
High Land Rd WS9 . . . . . 245 B3
Highland Rd
Cannock WS12 . . . . 209 C4
Newport TF10 . . . . 168 E2
Highlands Dr DE15 . . . . . 167 A4
Highlands Rd WV3 . . . . . 265 D8
Highlands Stafford ST17 . 174 D8
Stone ST15 . . . . 119 F5
Highland Way WS15 . . . . 178 C3
Highlanes ST21 . . . . 116 E5
High La ST6 . . . . 42 A3
High Lowe Ave CW12 . . . . 6 A4
High Lows La WS15 . . . . . 118 F6
High Mdw
Cannock Wood WS15 . . . 211 F5
Norbury ST20 . . . . 151 B3
High Mdws Newport TF10 169 A3
Wolverhampton WV6 . . . 255 C3
Wombourne WV5 . . . . . . 270 A6
High Mount St WS12 . . . 210 B6
High Offley Rd ST20 . . . . 151 D8
Highover Dr B75 . . . . 258 A4
Highpark Ave DY8 . . . . . 279 D5
High Park Cl DY3 . . . . . . 271 D8
High Park Cres DY3 . . . . 266 D1
High Path WV6 . . . . 253 C2
High Pk SK17 . . . . 155 C1
High Ridge WS15 . . . . . . 178 C3
High St (May Bank) ST5 . . 56 D4
High St (Sandyford) ST6 . 41 D5
High St
Abbots Bromley WS15 . . 161 A5
Albrighton WV7 . . . . 237 A5
Aldridge WS9 . . . . 256 B6
Alsagers Bank ST7 . . . . . 54 E6
Alton ST10 . . . . 78 E1
Audley ST7 . . . . 40 A1
Biddulph ST8 . . . . 27 C8
Brownhills,Clayhanger
WS8 . . . . 244 E6
Brownhills,Vigo WS9 . . . 244 F3
Brownhills WS8 . . . . 244 F8
Burntwood,Chasetown
WS7 . . . . 228 B4
Burntwood WS7 . . . . 211 E1
Burton u T DE14 . . . . 166 E2
Caverswall ST11 . . . . 74 E3
Cheadle ST10 . . . . 76 D3
Cheslyn Hay WS6 . . . . . . 226 D2
Cheswardine TF9 . . . . . . 130 A8
Church Eaton ST20 . . . . . 190 B8
Claverley WV5 . . . . 267 C7
Colton WS15 . . . . 179 A6
Dilhorne ST10 . . . . 75 C4
Eccleshall ST21 . . . . 133 E7
Edgmond TF10 . . . . 168 A3
Gnosall ST20 . . . . 171 D6
Harriseahead ST7 . . . . . . 26 E5
Hixon ST18 . . . . 158 C8
Ipstones ST10 . . . . 47 A1
Kidsgrove,The Rookery ST7 26 C4
Kingsley ST10 . . . . 61 E2
Kingswinford DY6 . . . . . 275 C6
Kingswinford,Wall Heath
DY6 . . . . 275 C8
Kinver DY7 . . . . 278 B3
Leek ST13 . . . . 30 E6
Longdon WS15 . . . . 197 F2
Longnor SK17 . . . . 13 C6
Market Drayton TF9 . . . . . 97 D1
Mow Cop ST7 . . . . 26 D7
Newcastle-u-L,Chesterton
ST5 . . . . 55 E7
Newcastle-u-L,Knutton ST5 55 E3
Newcastle-u-L,Silverdale
ST5 . . . . 55 B1
Newcastle-u-L ST5 . . . . . 283 B2
Newcastle-u-L,Wolstanton
ST5 . . . . 56 C5
Newchapel ST7 . . . . 26 E2
Newport TF10 . . . . 168 E3
Norton Canes WS11 . . . . 228 B5
Pattingham WV6 . . . . . . 253 C3
Rocester ST14 . . . . 95 F3
Sedgley DY3 . . . . 271 D8
Stoke-on-T,Golden Hill ST6 . 41 D7
Stoke-on-T,Newfield ST6 . 41 D4
Stoke-on-T,Tunstall ST6 . . 41 E3
Stone ST15 . . . . 120 A8
Stourbridge,Amblecote
DY8 . . . . 279 F7
Stourbridge,Wollaston
DY8 . . . . 279 E7
Stourbridge,Wordsley DY8 275 E2
Swadlincote DE11 . . . . . 186 F6
Swindon DY3 . . . . 269 E2
Talke Pits ST7 . . . . 40 D6
Tamworth B77 . . . . 261 C5
Tutbury DE13 . . . . 146 C6
Upper Tean ST10 . . . . 92 D4
Uttoxeter ST14 . . . . 126 C8
Walsall,Wallington Heath
WS3 . . . . 243 B1
Walsall WS3 . . . . 244 A4
Wheaton Aston ST19 . . . 205 B6
Wolverhampton WV6 . . . 255 D4
Wombourne WV5 . . . . . . 270 B7
Highton Ct ST2 . . . . 43 C1
Highton St ST2 . . . . 43 C1

Highup Rd ST13. . . . . 19 C1
Highview Dr DY6. . . . . . . 275 F4
High View Meir Heath ST3 . 90 A1
  Mount Pleasant ST7 . . . . . 26 B5
Highview Rd ST11. . . . . . 106 E8
High View Rd Leek ST13 . . 31 B5
  Stoke-on-T ST9 . . . . 43 F8
High View WV14 . . . . . . 266 F1
Highway La ST5. . . . . 69 E7
High Wood ST4. . . . . 72 A8
High Wood Cl DY6 . . . . . 275 C6
Highwood Ct ST14. . . . . . 126 C6
Highwood Rd ST14. . . . . . 126 D5
Higson Ave ST4. . . . . 72 A8
Hilary Dr Aldridge WS9 . . 256 A5
  Wolverhampton WV3. . . . 265 D7
Hilcote Gdns ST21 . . . . . 134 B8
Hilcote Hollow ST16 . . . . 155 B6
Hilderstone Rd
  Hilderstone ST15. . . . . . 106 D5
  Meir Heath ST3,ST15. . . . 90 A2
Hillary Ave CW12 . . . . 6 A2
Hillary Crest Dudley DY3 . 271 E5
  Rugeley WS15. . . . . 196 E6
Hillary Rd ST7 . . . . 26 B3
Hillary St ST6. . . . . 57 B6
Hill Avenue Prim Sch
  WV4 . . . . 266 F3
Hill Ave WV4 . . . . 266 F3
Hillberry Cl ST2. . . . . 58 A2
Hillboro Rise DY7 . . . . . . 278 A5
Hillchurch St ST1 . . . . . . 282 B3
Hill Cl Sedgley DY3. . . . . 266 E1
  Uttoxeter ST14 . . . . 110 F1
Hillcott Wlk ST3. . . . . . . 284 D3
Hill Cres Alsagers Bank ST7 54 F6
  Stone ST15 . . . . 120 A6
Hillcrest Ave
  Burton u T DE15. . . . . . 167 A4
  Kingsley Holt ST10 . . . . . 62 A2
  Wolverhampton WV10. . . 240 E1
Hillcrest ST19 . . . . 223 D7
Hillcrest Cl
  Kingsley Holt ST10 . . . . . 62 A2
  Tamworth B79 . . . . 250 B6
Hill Crest Dr WS13 . . . . . 214 A1
Hill Crest DY3 . . . . 271 C4
Hillcrest Hixon WS15. . . . 140 B1
  Leek ST13 . . . . 30 D6
Hillcrest Rd B78 . . . . 262 F7
Hillcrest Rise WS7 . . . . . 229 B4
Hill Crest ST17 . . . . 174 C8
Hillcrest ST1 . . . . 282 C3
Hillcrest DE13 . . . . 146 B5
Hillcroft Ave ST17. . . . . . 175 E7
Hillcroft Rd DY6 . . . . 275 C7
Hilldene Rd DY6 . . . . 275 C4
Hill Dr ST15 . . . . 120 A6
Hill End ST15 . . . . 105 E5
Hillfarm Cl ST17 . . . . . . 174 C8
Hillfield Ave ST4. . . . . 71 E4
Hillfield La DE13 . . . . . . 147 F1
Hillgreen Rd ST3. . . . . . . 73 D5
Hill Hook Ho B74 . . . . . . 257 E5
Hill Hook Rd B74 . . . . . . 257 F5
Hill La Burntwood WS7 . . 211 E1
  Church Leigh ST10 . . . . . 108 B3
  Middleton B75 . . . . 259 B2
Hillman Dr ST2. . . . . 43 B1
Hillman St B77 . . . . 250 E2
Hillmorton Rd B74 . . . . . 257 F4
Hillmorton B74 . . . . 257 F3
Hill Pk WS9. . . . . 245 A4
Hillport Ave ST5 . . . . 56 B7
Hill Pl WV11 . . . . 242 A1
Hillrise ST10. . . . . 94 E8
Hill Rise ST18 . . . . 137 F4
Hillsdale La ST13 . . . . 33 F3
Hillsdale Rd DE15 . . . . . 167 A4
Hillside ST16. . . . . 161 B5
Hillside Ave
  Forsbrook ST11 . . . . 91 A8
  Kidsgrove ST7 . . . . 41 A8
  Longton ST3. . . . . 73 F1
  Stoke-on-T ST9 . . . . 43 F8
Hillside WS8. . . . . 245 A6
Hillside Cl Biddulph ST8 . . 17 B1
  Brownhills WS8 . . . . 245 A6
  Burntwood WS7. . . . . . . 228 E5
  Cannock WS12. . . . . . . 210 A7
  Fulford ST11 . . . . 106 E8
  Gorstyhill CW2. . . . . 37 E3
  Kidsgrove ST7 . . . . 26 D7
  Rugeley WS15. . . . . 197 B5
  Stoke-on-T ST2 . . . . 43 C3
Hillside Cres ST3 . . . . . . 243 F3
Hillside Dr Colwich ST18. . 177 D8
  Leek ST13 . . . . 30 C4
Hillside ST21 . . . . 133 E6
Hillside Gdns DE11. . . . . 186 F2
Hillside Gr DY10 . . . . . . 280 C3
Hillside Lichfield WS14 . . 231 D6
  Market Drayton TF9. . . . 112 E4
  Newcastle-u-L ST5. . . . . 283 A4
Hillside Prim Sch ST2. . . . 43 C2
Hillside Rd
  Cheddleton ST13 . . . . . . 45 C4
  Stoke-on-T ST2 . . . . 43 C3
  Sutton Coldfield B74 . . . 258 A4
  Werrington ST9. . . . . 59 B4
Hillside DE13 . . . . 146 C6
Hillside Wlk ST4 . . . . 71 D8
Hillside WV5. . . . . 269 C8
Hill St Burntwood WS7. . . 228 E5
  Burton u T DE15. . . . . . 185 E8
  Cannock WS12. . . . . . . 210 C3
  Cheslyn Hay WS6. . . . . . 226 C2

Hill St continued
  Dudley,Upper Gornal DY3 . 271 D5
  Essington WV11 . . . . . . 241 F3
  Newcastle-u-L ST5. . . . . 283 B4
  Norton Canes WS11 . . . . 227 F6
  Rugeley WS15 . . . . 196 E8
  Stoke-on-T ST4 . . . . 72 B7
  Stourbridge,Amblecote
    DY8. . . . . 279 F8
  Stourbridge DY8 . . . . . . 279 F4
  Swadlincote DE11. . . . . . 186 F6
Hillswood Ave ST13 . . . . . 30 D6
Hillswood Cl ST9 . . . . 43 F7
Hillswood Dr ST9 . . . . 43 F7
Hill Terr ST7. . . . . 39 D2
Hilltop Ave ST5 . . . . 56 E2
Hill Top Ave B79 . . . . . . 250 B8
Hill Top ST6 . . . . 28 B2
Hill Top ST8 . . . . 28 B1
Hilltop Com Prim Sch
  ST7 . . . . 40 D7
Hill Top Cres ST3 . . . . 90 A5
Hilltop Ct DY3 . . . . 271 E3
Hilltop WS15 . . . . 196 F7
Hill Top View WS15 . . . . 198 C3
Hill Top Wlk WS9 . . . . . . 245 C1
Hill View WS9 . . . . 245 B2
Hillview Cres ST5 . . . . 85 C5
Hill View Leek ST13 . . . . . 31 A5
  Stoke-on-T ST2 . . . . 43 B2
Hill Village Rd
  Sutton Coldfield B75 . . . 258 A4
  Werrington ST9 . . . . 59 C4
Hillway Cl WS15 . . . . . . 178 D1
Hill West Prim Sch B74 . . 257 F4
Hillwood Cl DY6 . . . . 275 C4
Hillwood Common Rd
  B75 . . . . 258 B6
Hillwood Rd
  Madeley Heath CW3 . . . . 69 A8
  Sutton Coldfield B75 . . . 258 C5
Hill Wood WS3 . . . . 243 F2
Hilmore Way B77 . . . . . . 261 E8
Hilsea Cl WV8 . . . . 239 F1
Hilsea Cres ST14. . . . . . 143 F7
Hilston Ave WV4 . . . . . . 265 C4
Hilton Cl WS3 . . . . 243 A2
Hilton La
  Featherstone WV10,
    WV11 . . . . 241 E8
  Great Wyrley,Warstone
    WV11 . . . . 242 B7
  Great Wyrley WS6 . . . . . 227 A2
Hilton Main Ind Est
  WV11 . . . . 241 C5
Hilton Park Service Area
  WV11 . . . . 242 B7
Hilton Rd Burntwood WS7. 228 C8
  Egginton DE65. . . . . 148 B7
  Featherstone WV10. . . . . 241 F7
  Stoke-on-T ST4 . . . . 71 E7
  Willenhall WV12 . . . . . . 242 C1
  Wolverhampton WV4. . . . 266 F4
Hilton Trad Est WV4. . . . 266 F4
Himley Ave DY1. . . . . . . 271 F2
Himley Cres WV4 . . . . . . 266 B5
Himley Ct DY3 . . . . 271 E3
Himley Gdns DY3 . . . . . . 270 F4
Himley Hall* DY3. . . . . . 270 D4
Himley La DY3 . . . . 269 F2
Himley Rd DY1,DY3. . . . . 271 C2
Hinbrook Rd DY1 . . . . . . 271 E1
Hinchco Pl TF9. . . . . 42 E4
Hinckes Rd WV6. . . . . . . 255 F5
Hinckley Gr ST4 . . . . 88 B5
Hinde St ST1 . . . . 282 B1
Hines St ST4. . . . . 72 E5
Hingley Croft WS9 . . . . . 256 F3
Hinksford Gdns DY3. . . . 269 E1
Hinksford La DY3,DY6 . . . 269 F1
Hinsford Cl DY6. . . . . . . 275 E8
Hinsley Mill La TF9. . . . . . 97 E2
Hinstock Cl WV4 . . . . . . 266 A4
Hinton Cl Stafford ST17. . 174 F6
  Stoke-on-T ST3 . . . . 88 F8
Hints Ct B78 . . . . 248 F2
Hints La Hopwas B78. . . . 249 B5
  Weeford B78 . . . . 248 F4
Hints Rd Hopwas B78 . . . 249 B6
  Mile Oak B78. . . . . 249 C2
Hislop Rd WS15. . . . . . . 196 B6
Histons Dr WV8. . . . . . . 238 F2
Histons Hill WV8. . . . . . 238 F2
Hitchman St ST4. . . . . . . 72 E6
Hixon Airfield Est (Ind Est)
  ST18. . . . . 139 B1
Hixon Ind Est ST18. . . . . 158 B7
HM Young Offender Inst
  (Swinfen Hall) WS14 . . . 231 C1
Hoarstone DY8 . . . . 281 F5
Hobart Cl DE15 . . . . 167 C2
Hobart Ct B74. . . . . 258 A3
Hobart Rd WS12 . . . . . . 210 E2
Hobart St ST6 . . . . 57 A7
Hobb La ST14. . . . . 142 A7
Hobble End La WS6. . . . . 243 B7
Hobbs View WS15. . . . . . 197 B5
Hobby Cl ST3 . . . . 90 A7
Hobfield La WS15. . . . . . 161 B8
Hob Hill CE Methodist Prim
  Sch WS15 . . . . 197 B5
Hobnock Rd WV11. . . . . 242 B5
Hobs Hole La WS9 . . . . . 256 D7
Hobson St ST6. . . . . 57 A8

Hob's Rd WS13 . . . . 214 E1
Hobstone Hill La WS13 . . 212 F1
Hockley Rd
  Tamworth B77. . . . . . . 261 F5
  Uttoxeter ST14 . . . . 126 B7
Hodge La
  Marchington ST14. . . . . 127 A1
  Tamworth B77 . . . . 251 B6
Hodgkins Cl WS8 . . . . . . 245 A6
Hodgkinson St ST5. . . . . . 55 F6
Hodnet Gr ST1. . . . . 282 A4
Hodnet Pl WS11 . . . . . . 210 B2
Hodson Way ST16. . . . . . 156 C4
Hogan Way ST16. . . . . . 156 C4
Hogarth Pl ST5 . . . . 55 E6
Holbeach Ave ST2 . . . . . . 58 A2
Holbeache La DY6 . . . . . 270 D1
Holbeache Rd DY6 . . . . . 275 C6
Holbeach Way ST16. . . . 155 B4
Holborn ST5. . . . . 283 B3
Holborn Row ST10 . . . . . 92 E4
Holborn Sh Ctr The DY3 . 271 D7
Holborn The CW3 . . . . . . 68 E5
Holbrook Wlk ST2 . . . . . . 58 C1
Holbury Cl WV9. . . . . . . 240 C2
Holcroft Rd DY6 . . . . . . 270 C1
Holdcroft Rd ST2 . . . . . . 58 C5
Holden Ave ST5. . . . . 56 D3
Holden Ave N ST6. . . . . . 57 D8
Holden Ave S ST6. . . . . . 57 D8
Holden Lane High Sch
  ST1. . . . . 57 F8
Holden Lane Prim Sch
  ST1. . . . . 57 F7
Holden Rd WV4 . . . . 265 D3
Holder Dr WS11 . . . . . . 209 B2
Holder St ST1 . . . . 57 B6
Holdiford Rd
  Brocton ST18. . . . . 176 C3
  Tixall ST18 . . . . 157 D1
Holding Cres ST7 . . . . 54 D7
Holdings La CW3 . . . . 67 F4
Holditch Ind Est ST5 . . . . 56 A4
Holditch Rd ST5. . . . . 55 F5
Holecroft St [7] ST6 . . . . . 57 A8
Holehouse La
  Endon ST6,ST9. . . . . 28 C2
  Scholar Green ST7. . . . . . 25 D8
Holehouse Rd ST2 . . . . . . 58 C6
Holendene Way WV5. . . . 269 E7
Holland Cl WS13 . . . . . . 215 A1
Holland Pk DE13 . . . . . . 183 E2
Hollands Pl WS3 . . . . . . 243 D1
Hollands Rd WS3 . . . . . . 243 D1
Holland St [2] ST6. . . . . . 41 D3
Hollands The ST8 . . . . . . 17 C3
Holland's Way WS3 . . . . 243 F4
Hollies Ave WS11 . . . . . . 209 F1
Hollies Brook Cl ST20. . . 171 C2
  Newton Solney DE15. . . . 167 E8
Hollies Cl WS11. . . . . . . 209 F1
Hollies Dr ST3 . . . . 90 A4
Hollies Ind Est [7] WV2 . . 266 C8
Hollies La Enville DY7 . . . 276 F8
  Nurton WV6. . . . . 254 A4
  Pattingham WV6. . . . . . 253 F5
Hollies Park Rd WS11 . . . 209 F1
Hollies The
  Newcastle-u-L ST5. . . . . 283 C4
  Wolverhampton WV2. . . . 266 C8
Hollings St ST4 . . . . 284 A5
Hollington Dr ST6. . . . . . . 42 B8
Hollington La ST14 . . . . . 110 F5
Hollington Rd ST10 . . . . . 93 B4
Hollins Bsns Ctr [4] ST16 155 D5
Hollinsclough CE Prim Sch
  SK17. . . . . 4 D2
Hollinsclough Rake SK17. . 4 B2
Hollins Cres ST7. . . . . 25 E1
Hollinscroft Ct ST10. . . . . 92 E3
Hollins Grange ST7 . . . . . 40 D8
Hollinshead Ave ST5. . . . . 56 B4
Hollinshead Cl ST7. . . . . . 25 C7
Hollins La ST10 . . . . 61 B4
Hollinwell Cl WS3. . . . . . 243 A4
Hollinwood Cl ST7 . . . . . . 40 E8
Hollinwood Rd ST7 . . . . . 40 E8
Hollis La ST14 . . . . 95 B6
Holloway Dr WV5 . . . . . . 269 C5
Holloway La ST5. . . . . 84 C6
Holloway St W DY3 . . . . 271 D4
Holloway St DY3. . . . . . . 271 D4
Holloway B79. . . . . 250 B4
Holloway The
  Seisdon WV5. . . . . 264 A3
  Stourbridge DY8 . . . . . . 279 F7
  Swindon DY3. . . . . 269 D1
  Wolverhampton WV6. . . . 255 C2
Hollow Cres DE15. . . . . . 167 C4
Hollow La
  Burton u T DE15. . . . . . 167 C4
  Cheddleton ST13 . . . . . . 45 C5
  Colton WS15 . . . . 179 A5
  Draycott in t C DE6 . . . . 144 A4
  Mayfield DE6. . . . . 66 C1
Hollowood Pl ST6. . . . . . . 42 E5
Hollowood Wlk ST6. . . . . 42 D5
Hollows The DE15. . . . . . 166 F1
Hollow The
  Caverswall ST11 . . . . . . 74 E3
  Mount Pleasant ST7 . . . . 26 B5
  Roston DE6 . . . . 96 C7
  Uttoxeter ST14 . . . . 126 C6
Holly Ave WS13. . . . . 45 C4
Hollybank Ave WV11 . . . 242 A3
Hollybank Cl WS3. . . . . . 243 A2

Hollybank Cres ST4 . . . . . 72 A5
Holly Bank ST4 . . . . 87 E7
Holly Bank View WS15 . . 197 B5
Holly Bush Cl DE12. . . . . 219 F7
Holly Bush Cotts ST13. . . . 44 F8
Hollybush Cres ST3 . . . . . 72 E3
Hollybush La WV8 . . . . . 238 E2
Holly Bush Rd ST3. . . . . . 85 B4
Hollybush La
  Stourbridge DY8 . . . . . . 279 F7
  Wolverhampton WV4. . . . 265 D4
Holly Bush Rd DE13 . . . . 143 F2
Hollybush Rd ST3. . . . . . . 72 E3
Holly Cl Kinver DY7 . . . . 277 F5
  Market Drayton TF9. . . . 112 A8
  Tamworth B79 . . . . 250 B7
Hollycroft Gdns WV6. . . . 255 B6
Holly Ct ST2 . . . . 73 E7
Holly Dr Fradley WS13. . . 215 D8
  Walton-on-t-H ST17. . . . 175 F6
  Werrington ST9 . . . . 59 A3
Holly Fields ST15 . . . . . . 118 E6
Holly Gn DE15 . . . . 185 F8
Holly Grove La WS7 . . . . 211 E1
Holly Grove Prim Sch
  WS7 . . . . 211 E1
Holly Gr Stone ST15 . . . . 120 B7
  Stourbridge DY8 . . . . . . 279 F5
  Wolverhampton WV3. . . . 265 F7
Holly Hill WS6 . . . . 242 E8
Hollyhill La WS14 . . . . . 246 E5
Holly Hill Rd
  Cannock Wood WS15. . . . 211 E6
  Shenstone WS14 . . . . . . 246 F5
Hollyhock Way ST14 . . . . 184 E6
Hollyhurst Dr DY6. . . . . . 275 E3
Hollyhurst La ST18 . . . . . 140 F5
Hollyhurst ST17 . . . . 175 D5
Holly La Aldridge WS9 . . . 256 F8
  Bradley WS8 . . . . 173 C1
  Brownhills WS9 . . . . . . 245 A4
  Great Wyrley WS6 . . . . . 242 F8
  Harriseahead ST7 . . . . . . 26 F5
  Huntington WS12. . . . . . 209 C7
  Ranton ST18 . . . . 153 E1
  Sutton Coldfield B74 . . . 258 A3
  Uttoxeter ST14 . . . . 125 D1
Holly Mdw ST10 . . . . . . 109 C3
Holly Mews ST5. . . . . 69 F7
Hollyoak Way WS11 . . . . 209 F1
Holly Pl ST4 . . . . 72 E4
  Newcastle-u-L ST5. . . . . . 40 C1
  Uttoxeter ST14 . . . . 111 B1
Hollys Rd DE13 . . . . 182 A2
Holly St Burton u T DE15 . 185 F8
  Cannock WS12. . . . . . . 209 F6
Holly Tree Dr ST8. . . . . . . 16 C2
Holly View WV11. . . . . . 242 A3
Hollywall La ST6 . . . . 41 C5
Hollywall Prim Sch ST6 . . 41 C6
Hollywood La ST5. . . . . . . 54 D1
Holmbridge Gr WS4. . . . 244 D2
Holm Cl ST4 . . . . 72 B5
Holmcroft [10] WV4 . . . . 266 F4
Holmcroft Rd ST16. . . . . 155 C6
Holme Bank DE6. . . . . . . 81 D7
Holme Farm Ave DE15. . . 185 F8
Holme Mill WV10 . . . . . . 240 D4
Holme Rise ST19. . . . . . . 193 A1
Holmes Cl ST16. . . . . . . 155 B2
Holmesfield Wlk ST3. . . . 284 D3
Holmes The WV10 . . . . . 240 D3
Holmes Way ST6. . . . . . . 42 B8
Holm Oak Dr CW3. . . . . . 68 E7
Holm Rd ST10 . . . . 78 C2
Holmroft Gdns WV9. . . . 224 C2
Holm View Cl WS14 . . . . 246 F6
Holst Dr ST1. . . . . 58 A6
Holston Cl ST12. . . . . . . 210 F1
Holsworth Cl B77. . . . . . 250 D1
Holt Cres WS11 . . . . 210 B2
Holte Dr B75 . . . . 258 D2
Holt La ST10 . . . . 61 F2
Holt's La DE13 . . . . 146 B6
Holwick B77. . . . . 262 B8
Holy Austin Rock* DY7 . . 277 E3
Holyhead Cres ST3. . . . . . 74 C4
Holyhead Rd
  Albrighton WV7 . . . . . . 237 C2
  Codsall WV8. . . . . 238 C1
Holyoake Pl WS15 . . . . . 178 D3
Holyrood Cl
  Stafford ST18 . . . . 156 C3
  Stone ST15 . . . . 120 C6
Holy Rosary RC Prim Sch
  DE15. . . . . 167 A3
Holy Trinity CE Prim Sch
  Brownhills WS8 . . . . . . 244 E6
  Burton u T DE14. . . . . . 166 E4
Holywell Cl ST18 . . . . 27 E6
Holywell Rise WS14 . . . . 231 D6
Home Farm Cotts SK17. . . 5 C2
Home Farm Ct
  Castle Gresley DE11 . . . 186 D1
  Ingestre ST18 . . . . 157 D6
Home Farm Rd WV6 . . . . 252 C7
Home Farm ST21 . . . . . . 116 D2
Homefield Rd WV8. . . . . 239 C3
Homelands Park The
  WV10. . . . . 240 C6
Homelodge Ho [7] WS13. 231 B7
Homer Pl ST6. . . . . 42 B5
Homer Rd B75 . . . . 258 D2
Homer St ST1. . . . . 57 E4
Homestead Cl DY3 . . . . . 271 E5
Homestead Cotts ST2. . . . 43 C3
Homestead Ct ST16. . . . . 155 E7

Homestead Dr B75 . . . . . 258 C3
Homestead St ST2 . . . . . . 73 D8
Homestead The ST9. . . . . 43 C3
Honesty Cl WS8. . . . . . . 244 D6
Honeybourne Cres WV5 . 269 F5
Honeybourne B77. . . . . . 250 D2
Honeysuckle Ave
  Blythe Bridge ST11 . . . . . 90 F6
  Kingswinford DY6 . . . . . 275 E7
Honeysuckle Cl ST10. . . . . 92 F3
Honeysuckle Dr WV10. . . 241 C7
Honeysuckle La ST5. . . . . 29 C2
Honeysuckle Rise ST17. . 175 F7
Honeysuckle View ST6 . . 186 A8
Honeysuckle Way WS6 . . 227 B4
Honeytree Cl DY6 . . . . . . 275 F3
Honeywall Ho [4] ST4. . . . 72 A7
Honeywall La
  Madeley Heath CW3 . . . . 69 B7
  Stanton DE6. . . . . 80 E8
Honeywall ST4. . . . . 72 A7
Honeywood ST5 . . . . 283 B4
Honiton Cl ST17 . . . . 175 D8
Honiton Wlk ST3. . . . . . . 284 D3
Honor Ave WV4 . . . . 266 C5
Hood La Armitage WS15 . 198 A4
  Longdon WS15. . . . . . . 197 F2
Hook Dr B74. . . . . 257 F4
Hook La Shenstone WS14 . 246 C3
  Stramshall ST14 . . . . . . 111 B6
Hook La The WV7. . . . . . 237 B1
Hoo La DY7. . . . . 273 F4
Hoomill La ST18 . . . . . . 158 B5
Hoon Ave ST5 . . . . 56 B4
Hoon Rd DE65 . . . . 146 D8
Hoover St ST6 . . . . 41 D3
Hopedale Cl Longton ST4 . 73 B6
  Newcastle-u-L ST5. . . . . . 71 B3
Hope St Audley ST7 . . . . . 39 F3
  Hanley ST1 . . . . 282 B4
  Stourbridge DY8 . . . . . . 275 D3
Hopley Rd DE13. . . . . . . 165 B5
Hopleys Cl B77 . . . . 250 E4
Hopmeadow Way DE15. . 167 A1
Hopshaw TF9 . . . . 130 B5
Hopstone Gdns WV4 . . . 265 F4
Hopton Bank ST18 . . . . . 137 C1
Hopton Cl WV6 . . . . 254 F3
Hopton Ct ST16. . . . . . . 155 D5
Hoptonhall La ST18 . . . . 137 D1
Hopton La ST18 . . . . 137 C1
Hopton Mdw WS12. . . . . 210 C1
Hopton St ST16 . . . . 155 F6
Hopton Way ST6 . . . . 42 A8
Hopwas Hill B78 . . . . . . 249 A6
Hopwood La DE14 . . . . . 166 F6
Hopwood Pl ST2 . . . . 58 B3
Hopyard Cl DY3 . . . . 271 B3
Hopyard La DY3 . . . . 271 B3
Horatius Rd ST5 . . . . 55 D6
Hordern Cl WV6 . . . . 255 F5
Hordern Gr WV6 . . . . . . 255 F5
Hordern Rd WV6. . . . . . . 255 F5
Hordley St ST1 . . . . 282 C3
Hornbeam Cres WS12. . . 211 A6
Hornbeams [2] ST14. . . . 111 A1
Hornbeam B77 . . . . 251 A4
Hornbrook Cl DE13 . . . . 166 B8
Hornbrook Rd DE13 . . . . 166 B7
Hornby Rd WV4. . . . . . . 266 C5
Hornby Row ST4. . . . . . . 72 A7
Horner Ave WS13 . . . . . 215 C6
Horninglow Croft DE13. . 166 C6
Horninglow Inf Sch
  DE13. . . . . 166 C6
Horninglow Rd DE14. . . . 166 C5
Horninglow Road N
  DE13. . . . . 166 C7
Horninglow St DE14. . . . 166 D3
Horns Croft WS15. . . . . . 196 B7
Hornton Cl B74 . . . . 257 D5
Hornton Rd DE13 . . . . . . 166 B7
Horse Bridge La DY7 . . . 278 D2
Horsebrook Hall La
  ST19. . . . . 206 D1
Horsebrook La ST19 . . . . 223 C8
Horsecroft Cres ST13 . . . . 31 A7
Horsecroft St ST13 . . . . . 31 B7
Horse Fair
  Eccleshall ST21 . . . . . . 133 E7
  Rugeley WS15. . . . . 196 E8
Horsehills Dr WV3 . . . . . 255 E2
Horse Rd ST10 . . . . 78 E1
Horseshoe Dr
  Cannock WS12. . . . . . . 210 F4
  Rugeley WS15. . . . . 178 B2
Horsey La WS15 . . . . . . 212 C8
Horsham Ave DY8. . . . . . 275 C3
Horsley Gr ST3 . . . . 88 E8
Horsley La
  Eccleshall ST21 . . . . . . 132 F5
  Shenstone WS14 . . . . . . 246 D8
Horsley Rd
  Coldmeece ST15 . . . . . . 118 C3
  Little Aston B74. . . . . . . 257 B2
Horsley Way ST15 . . . . . 118 C7
Horton Ave DE13. . . . . . 166 F7
Horton Cl
  [3] Cannock WS11 . . . . 209 F4
  Sedgley DY3. . . . . 271 C8
Horton Dr ST3 . . . . 74 A5
Horton Lodge Com Specl Sch
  ST13 . . . . 18 D2
Horton Rd DY7. . . . . 277 F5
Horton St Leek ST13 . . . . 30 F6

Horton St continued
Newcastle-u-L ST4. . . . . .56 D1
Horwood Gdns ST6 . . . . .42 C1
Horwood ST5. . . . . .70 C6
Hose St ST6 . . . . .41 D3
Hoskings Cl ST15 . . . . .120 C7
Hoskins Rd ST6. . . . . .41 E5
Hospital La
Cheslyn Hay WS6. . . . . .226 B2
Market Drayton TF9. . . . . . .112 A8
Hospital Rd WS7. . . . . .229 B5
Hospital St B79 . . . . .250 B5
Hotel Bldgs WS14. . . . . . . .230 A2
Hothill La ST10 . . . . .109 C1
Hot La Biddulph ST8 . . . . . . .17 C2
Burslem ST6. . . . . .57 B8
Hot Lane Ind Est ST6. . . . . .57 B8
Hougher Wall Rd ST7 . . . . . .39 D1
Hough Hill ST6 . . . . .43 B8
Houghton St ST1. . . . . .282 B1
Houghwood La ST9 . . . . .43 E4
Houlbrooke Ho 1 WS14. . . .231 C8
Houldsworth Dr ST6 . . . . . . .42 B7
Housefield Rd ST2. . . . . . . .73 D8
Houseman Dr ST3 . . . . .73 F4
Houston Ave ST9 . . . . .43 E8
Houting B77 . . . . .261 D5
Houx The DY8 . . . . .279 E8
Hoveringham Dr
Berry Hill ST2 . . . . .57 F1
Bucknall ST2 . . . . .58 A1
Howard Cl Leek ST13 . . . . . . .30 C4
Werrington ST9 . . . . .59 B4
Howard Cres
Cannock WS12. . . . . .210 C7
Hanley ST1 . . . . .57 E2
Howard Gr ST5. . . . . .71 A6
Howard Pl Hanley ST1. . . . . .282 A1
Newcastle-u-L ST5. . . . . .71 A6
Howard Prim Sch B79. . . . . .216 D2
Howard Rd ST17 . . . . .174 E7
Howard St Longton ST3. . . . .284 C2
Wolverhampton WV2. . . . . . .266 D8
Howard Wlk ST3 . . . . .284 C2
Howdle's La WS8 . . . . .228 F3
Howe Gr ST5 . . . . .55 E2
Howell Rd WV2 . . . . .266 E7
Howitt Cres ST14 . . . . .111 B2
Howitt House Sch DE13 . . .144 E3
Howland Cl WV9 . . . . .239 F2
Howson St ST1 . . . . .282 C2
Hoylake Cl WS3. . . . . .243 B4
Hoylake Rd WV6 . . . . .254 D5
Hoylake B77 . . . . .251 B4
Hubbal La TF11 . . . . .220 D3
Huddlesford La WS14 . . . . .232 D7
Huddlestone Cl WV10 . . . . .241 B6
Huddocks View WS3 . . . . . .243 F5
Hudson Cl Cannock WS11. . .210 B2
Gnosall ST20 . . . . .171 E8
Hudson Dr WS7. . . . . .229 C6
Hudson Gr WV6. . . . . .254 E5
Hudson Wlk ST3 . . . . .284 C4
Hugh Bourne Pl ST8 . . . . . . .27 B2
Hughes Ave
Newcastle-u-L ST5. . . . . . . .283 B4
Wolverhampton WV3. . . . . . .265 F8
Hughes St ST6. . . . . .57 A7
Hugh Porter Way WV6 . . . . .255 F6
Hughson Gr ST5. . . . . .42 E3
Hugo Meynell CE Prim Sch
TF9 .99 E4
Hugo St ST13 . . . . .30 E1
Hugo Way TF9 . . . . .99 E4
Hulland Cl ST5. . . . . .55 B1
Hullock's Pool Rd ST7. . . . . .39 E5
Hulme Cl ST5. . . . . .55 B1
Hulme La ST3,ST9 . . . . .59 A2
Hulme Rd ST3 . . . . .73 F6
Hulme St ST4. . . . . .71 E8
Hulse St ST4. . . . . .73 B6
Hulton Cl CW12. . . . . .6 B1
Hulton Rd ST2 . . . . .58 B6
Hulton St ST1. . . . . .282 C4
Humber Dr ST8 . . . . .27 E8
Humbert Rd ST1. . . . . .56 F3
Humber Way ST5 . . . . .71 B3
Humphrey St DY3 . . . . .271 D3
Humphries Ho WS8 . . . . . . .244 F7
Hungerford La CW3 . . . . . . .68 F5
Hungerford Pl CW2 . . . . .38 D5
Hungerford Rd DY8 . . . . . . .279 E2
Hungry La WS14 . . . . .247 F5
Hunsford Cl ST3 . . . . .284 C4
Hunslet Rd WS7 . . . . .229 B8
Huntbach St ST1. . . . . .282 B3
Hunter Ave WS7 . . . . .229 B7
Hunter Cl WS14. . . . . .231 D6
Hunter Rd WS11 . . . . .226 E8
Hunters Cl ST18 . . . . .137 F4
Hunters Ct ST18 . . . . .137 F4
Hunters Dr ST4 . . . . .71 F6
Hunter's Point TF9. . . . . . . .99 D5
Hunters Ride ST17 . . . . . . .174 E4
Hunter's Ride DY7 . . . . .275 B2
Hunter St DE14. . . . . .166 D6
Hunters Way
Stoke-on-T ST4 . . . . .72 A6
Talke ST7. . . . . .40 D8
Huntilee Rd ST6. . . . . .41 F3
Huntingdon B78. . . . . .249 F2
Huntingdon Pl ST1. . . . . . . .57 F6
Huntingdon Rd DE15. . . . . .185 D7
Huntington Ind Est
WS12 . . . . .209 B6

Huntington Prim Sch
WS12 . . . . .209 C8
Huntington Terrace Rd
WS11 . . . . .209 F4
Huntley Ave ST4 . . . . .72 A6
Huntley Cl ST10. . . . . .76 D1
Huntley La ST10 . . . . .92 C8
Huntley Rd ST13 . . . . .44 E7
Hunts La DE12 . . . . .219 E7
Huntsbank Dr ST5 . . . . .40 D1
Huntsmans Gate WS7 . . . . .229 B8
Huntsman's Hill WS15. . . . .197 C2
Huntsmans Rise WS12 . . . .209 C8
Huntsmans Wlk
Kinver DY7 . . . . .277 F6
Rugeley WS15 . . . . .178 D1
Hunts Mill Dr DY5. . . . . . . .271 C1
Hunt St 2 ST6 . . . . .41 E3
Hurlingham Rd ST16 . . . . . .155 C7
Huron Cl WS11 . . . . .210 B2
Huron Gr ST4. . . . . .88 A8
Hurricane Cl ST16 . . . . .136 B1
Hurricane Gr ST6. . . . . .41 C4
Hurstbourne Cl WS15 . . . . .178 C2
Hurst Cl ST7 . . . . .40 D6
Hurst Dr DE13 . . . . .147 E1
Hurstmead Dr ST17 . . . . . . .175 C5
Hurstons La ST10 . . . . .78 E1
Hurstons The ST10 . . . . .78 E1
Hurst Rd Biddulph ST8. . . . . .17 A3
Sedgley WV14 . . . . .266 F1
Hurst St ST3 . . . . .284 B3
Hurst Yd ST10 . . . . .76 D3
Husphins La WV8. . . . . .238 B5
Hussey Cl ST19 . . . . .207 F7
Hussey Rd
Brownhills WS8 . . . . .244 E8
Norton Canes WS11 . . . . . . .227 F5
Hutchinson Cl WS15 . . . . . .178 D2
Hutchinson Meml CE Fst Sch
ST10 . . . . .109 B8
Hutchinson Wlk 6 ST3. . . . .73 A3
Hut Hill La WS6 . . . . .227 A4
Hutton Dr CW12 . . . . .6 A2
Hutton Way ST2 . . . . .58 D2
Huxley Cl WV9. . . . . .240 A3
Huxley Pl ST3. . . . . .73 D4
Hyacinth Cl ST5 . . . . .283 C4
Hyacinth Rd ST4 . . . . .56 E1
Hyde Cl DY7 . . . . .278 A5
Hyde Cl ST17. . . . . .174 D7
Hyde La DY7 . . . . .278 A6
Hyde Lea Bank ST10 . . . . . .174 C5
Hyde Mill Croft ST19 . . . . . .223 C5
Hyde Mill La ST19. . . . . . . .223 C5
Hylton Cl DE14. . . . . .185 A7
Hyndley Cl ST2 . . . . .58 A3
Hyperion Dr WV4 . . . . .266 A3
Hyperion Rd DY7 . . . . .279 C7
Hyssop Cl WS11 . . . . .210 B3
Hyssop Pl ST6. . . . . .42 D2

I

Ian Rd ST7 . . . . .26 D3
Ibsen Rd ST3 . . . . .74 A4
Ibstock Dr DE13 . . . . .166 B6
Icknield Cl B74 . . . . .257 A1
Idonia Rd WV6. . . . . .254 F5
Ikins Dr ST7 . . . . .39 F2
Ilam Ctry Pk Inf Sch DE6. . . .50 E2
Ilam Cl ST5. . . . . .55 B1
Ilam Ctry Pk* DE6 . . . . .50 E2
Ilam-Moor La DE6. . . . . .50 E4
Ilford Side ST3 . . . . .88 E8
Ilkley Pl ST5 . . . . .54 F2
Illshaw WV9. . . . . .240 A3
Image Bsns Pk WS11. . . . . .210 B3
Imandra Cl ST4. . . . . .88 A8
Imex Bsns Pk DE14. . . . . . .166 B3
I-Mex Bsns Pk ST4. . . . . . . .72 F5
Imex Bsns Pk WV2. . . . . . . .266 C7
Imex Ho WV2 . . . . .266 B7
Imex Tech Pk ST4. . . . . .88 D7
Imogen Cl ST4. . . . . .73 B6
Imperial Ct ST1. . . . . .282 C1
Impstones ST20 . . . . .171 C5
Ingatestone Dr DY8 . . . . . . .275 C3
Inge Dr DE13 . . . . .201 A2
Ingelow Cl ST3 . . . . .73 A2
Ingestre Ho WV6. . . . . .255 E5
Ingestre Rd Stafford ST17 . .285 B1
Wolverhampton WV10. . . . . .240 C1
Ingestre Sq ST3. . . . . .88 F8
Ingleborough Pl ST2. . . . . . .43 D1
Ingleby Cl DE11. . . . . .186 F3
Ingleby Rd ST3 . . . . .88 E8
Inglefield Ave ST6 . . . . .42 B1
Inglemere Dr ST17 . . . . . . .175 C6
Ingleside ST10 . . . . .178 C1
Ingleton Gr ST3 . . . . .90 A7
Inglewood Ave WV3. . . . . . .265 F4
Inglewood Cl DY6. . . . . .275 D5
Inglewood Dr ST5. . . . . .56 D6
Inglewood Gr
Aldridge B74 . . . . .256 C6
Newcastle-u-L ST5. . . . . .56 C6
Inglewood ST17 . . . . .285 A1
Inglis St ST4 . . . . .72 C8
Ingram Pit La B77. . . . . . . .251 A5
Ingram Pl WS3 . . . . .243 D1
Ingram Rd WS3 . . . . .243 D1
Inhedge St DY3 . . . . .271 E5

Intake La ST20 . . . . .190 A8
Intake Rd ST6 . . . . .42 E4
Intake La ST10 . . . . .108 E4
Inworth WV9. . . . . .240 A3
Iona Pl ST3 . . . . .72 F3
Irene Ave
Newcastle-u-L ST5. . . . . .56 D2
Stoke-on-T ST6 . . . . .41 F4
Ireton Rd WV10 . . . . .240 E3
Iris Cl Meir ST11. . . . . .74 C5
Tamworth B79 . . . . .250 C4
Irnham Rd B74. . . . . .258 B1
Ironbridge Dr ST5. . . . . .55 F1
Ironmarket ST5. . . . . .283 B3
Ironstone La WS13 . . . . . . .215 E5
Ironstone Rd
Burntwood WS7. . . . . .228 E8
Prospect Village WS12 . . . . .211 B3
Ironwalls La DE13. . . . . . . .146 C5
Irvine Rd ST9 . . . . .59 C4
Irving Cl Dudley DY3 . . . . . .271 A4
Lichfield WS13. . . . . .213 E2
Irwell B77. . . . . .250 E2
Isabel Cl ST7. . . . . .174 B8
Isherwood Pl ST3 . . . . .284 D4
Island Gn ST17. . . . . .175 D6
Island The Mile Oak B78 . . .249 C1
Oakamoor ST10. . . . . .78 A6
Upper Tean ST10 . . . . .92 D4
Islay Wlk 3 ST3 . . . . .73 A3
Islington Cl TF10. . . . . .168 F4
Islington Cres CV9 . . . . . . .262 C1
Ismere Way DY10 . . . . .280 A1
Itchen Gr WV6. . . . . .254 A1
Ivanhoe Rd WS14 . . . . .231 B6
Ivatt B77 . . . . .250 F2
Iverley La DY10,DY8. . . . . . .281 C5
Ivetsey Bank Rd ST19 . . . . .221 F8
Ivetsey Cl ST19 . . . . .205 B5
Ivetsey Rd
Ivetsey Bank ST19. . . . . . . .204 F3
Wheaton Aston ST19. . . . . . .205 A5
Ivy Cottage Mobile Home Pk
ST18. . . . . .137 D2
Ivy Cotts ST13 . . . . .20 A6
Ivycourt ST17 . . . . .175 B1
Ivy Croft WV9. . . . . .239 F3
Ivy Ct Acton Trussell ST17. . .175 B1
Eggington DE65. . . . . .148 A3
Hixon ST18 . . . . .158 B8
Ivy Gdns WS11. . . . . .228 A5
Ivy Gr Brownhills WS8 . . . . .245 A4
Burton u T DE13. . . . . .166 C7
Trentham ST4 . . . . .87 F8
Ivy Ho WS9 . . . . .245 A4
Ivy House La ST19 . . . . .206 E1
Ivy House Rd Biddulph ST8. . .16 C2
Hanley ST1 . . . . .57 B3
Ivyhouse Wlk 6 B77 . . . . . .261 F6
Ivy La WS15 . . . . .211 F5
Ivy Lodge Cl DE15. . . . . . . .185 E7
Izaac Walton Way CW3. . . . .68 E5
Izaak Walton Cl ST6 . . . . . .155 D6
Izaak Walton's Cottage &
Mus* ST15. . . . . .135 B7
Izaak Walton St ST16. . . . . .155 D5

J

Jack Ashley Ct ST4. . . . . . . .72 D6
Jackdaw Cl ST6 . . . . .266 C2
Jackfield Inf Sch ST6. . . . . . .42 B1
Jackfield St ST6 . . . . .42 B1
Jack Haye La Bagnall ST2 . . .58 E8
Stoke-on-T ST2 . . . . .43 D1
Jack La CW2. . . . . .37 D6
Jacklin Cl DE14 . . . . .185 A6
Jackman Cl WS13. . . . . .215 D6
Jackman Rd WS13. . . . . . . .215 D6
Jacks La ST14 . . . . .127 E2
Jackson Ave DE13 . . . . .166 F7
Jackson Cl
Featherstone WV10 . . . . . . .241 A6
Norton Canes WS11 . . . . . . .227 A4
Jackson Rd WS13 . . . . .214 B3
Jackson St 2 ST6 . . . . .57 A8
Jacobean Ct DE15 . . . . .167 C4
Jacobs Croft ST16 . . . . .155 C7
Jacob's Hall La WS6 . . . . . .227 B1
Jacqueline St ST6 . . . . .41 D4
Jade Ct ST3 . . . . .73 D4
Jade Gr WS11 . . . . .210 C2
Jaguar B77 . . . . .250 E2
Jamage Rd
Newcastle-u-L ST7. . . . . .40 D4
Talke Pits ST7. . . . . .40 D5
James Beattie Ho WV6. . . . .255 C4
James Brindley Cl ST1. . . . . .57 A2
James Brindley High Sch
ST6. . . . . .41 F6
James Brindley Way
DE13 . . . . .166 F3
James Cres ST9 . . . . .59 C4
James Ct DE14. . . . . .166 C1
James Greenway WS13. . . . .214 A2
James Hutchens Ct ST6. . . .228 F5
James St Burton u T DE14. . .166 C2
Cannock WS11. . . . . .209 F5
Kinver DY7 . . . . .278 A4
Leek ST13 . . . . .30 D5
Newcastle-u-L ST5. . . . . .56 D6
Stoke-on-T ST4 . . . . .72 A5

James St continued
Uttoxeter ST14 . . . . .126 B8
James Warner Cl WS15 . . . .178 D1
James Way ST8. . . . . .27 A6
Janet Pl ST1. . . . . .57 E4
Janson St ST4 . . . . .71 F1
Jardines La ST14 . . . . .95 D4
Jasmine Cl
Blythe Bridge ST11. . . . . . . .90 F6
Burton u T DE15. . . . . .186 A7
Wolverhampton WV9. . . . . . .240 A3
Jasmine Cres ST7. . . . . .26 D2
Jasmine Gr WV8 . . . . .239 B3
Jasmine Rd
Great Bridgeford ST18 . . . . .135 C2
Tamworth B77 . . . . .251 A4
Jasmin Way ST7 . . . . .27 A2
Jason Cl B77 . . . . .250 D5
Jason St ST5 . . . . .283 A4
Jasper Cl Barlaston ST12 . . . .88 F4
Newcastle-u-L ST5. . . . . .56 B7
Jasper St ST1. . . . . .282 B2
Java Cres ST4 . . . . .88 B7
Jaycean Ave ST6. . . . . .41 E4
Jay Rd DY6 . . . . .275 D8
Jean Cl ST6 . . . . .42 A2
Jedburgh Ave WV6 . . . . . . .254 E4
Jeddo St WV2 . . . . .266 C8
Jeffcock Rd WV3 . . . . .266 A7
Jefferson St ST6. . . . . .41 D4
Jeffery Cl WS15. . . . . .178 D3
Jeffrey Ave WV4 . . . . .266 F5
Jeffs Ave WV2 . . . . .266 D8
Jenkinson Cl ST5 . . . . .70 F8
Jenkins St 2 ST6. . . . . .56 F8
Jenkinstown Rd WS12. . . . .211 A6
Jenks Ave DY7. . . . . .277 F5
Jenks Rd WV5 . . . . .269 F5
Jennings St DE14 . . . . .166 A3
Jenny Walkers La WV6. . . . .254 D1
Jensen B77. . . . . .250 E2
Jephson Rd DE14 . . . . .185 B7
Jerbourg Ct ST5 . . . . .70 E4
Jeremy Cl ST4. . . . . .71 F6
Jeremy Rd WV4. . . . . .266 C5
Jerningham St ST16 . . . . . .285 A3
Jerome Cl B74. . . . . .256 F1
Jerome Dr WS11. . . . . .228 A5
Jerome Prim Sch WS11 . . . .227 F5
Jerome Rd WS11 . . . . .228 A5
Jerome Way WS7 . . . . .229 C7
Jerry's La WS14 . . . . .248 B5
Jersey Cl Congleton CW12. . . .6 A2
Newcastle-u-L ST5. . . . . .70 E4
Jersey Cres ST3 . . . . .73 D1
Jervis Cres B74 . . . . .257 D3
Jervis Ct ST15 . . . . .104 C3
Jervison St ST3 . . . . .73 D6
Jervis Pk B74. . . . . .257 C4
Jervis Rd Stone ST15. . . . . .120 B7
Tamworth B77 . . . . .261 F5
Jervis St ST1. . . . . .282 C4
Jesmond Cl WS12. . . . . . . .211 A6
Jesmond Gr ST3 . . . . .88 E8
Jessie Rd WS9. . . . . .245 B1
Jessop Dr B77. . . . . .250 E5
Jew's La DY3 . . . . .271 E4
Jinny Cl DE65. . . . . .146 C8
Joan Eaton's Cross ST20 . . .189 E7
Joanhurst Cres ST1 . . . . . . .282 A1
Joan St WV2 . . . . .266 E6
Jockey Field DY3 . . . . .271 E6
Jodrell View WV7 . . . . .41 B8
Joe Jones Ct DY3 . . . . .266 D1
Joeys La WV8. . . . . .239 C3
John Amery Dr ST17 . . . . . .174 D6
John Ball Cl WS15 . . . . .178 D3
John Bamford Prim Sch
WS15 . . . . .178 C1
John Baskeyfield CE Prim
Sch
Burslem ST6 . . . . .41 E1
Burslem ST6 . . . . .56 F8
John Bright St ST1. . . . . . . .282 C4
John Donne St ST16 . . . . . .155 D6
Johndory B77 . . . . .261 D6
John Offley Rd CW3. . . . . . . .68 E6
John of Rolleston Prim Sch
DE13 . . . . .147 C3
John O' Gaunt's Rd ST5. . . .283 A3
John Pershall Ct ST21. . . . .133 D7
John Rhodes Way ST6. . . . . .41 D5
Johns Ave WS15 . . . . .198 C4
Johnsgate ST19. . . . . .223 D7
Johns La WS6 . . . . .227 A3
Johnson Ave ST5 . . . . .56 A4
Johnson Cl Congleton CW12. . .6 B1
Lichfield WS13. . . . . .214 C1
Ranton ST18 . . . . .153 C5
Rugeley WS15 . . . . .178 D2
Johnson Cres ST10 . . . . .61 D2
Johnson Gr ST15. . . . . .120 D7
Johnson Pl ST6. . . . . .42 B6
Johnson Rd
Burntwood WS7. . . . . .228 F8
Cannock WS11. . . . . .209 D4
Uttoxeter ST14 . . . . .111 B1
Johnson St
Newcastle-u-L ST5. . . . . .55 D7
Wolverhampton,Cinder Hill
WV14 . . . . .266 F1
Wolverhampton WV2. . . . . . .266 D7
Wood End CV9 . . . . .262 C1
John St Biddulph ST8 . . . . . . .27 C8
Cannock,Chadsmoor
WS11 . . . . .210 A4
Cannock,Wimblebury
WS12 . . . . .210 F3

John St continued
Hanley ST1 . . . . .282 B2
Leek ST13 . . . . .30 E5
Newcastle-u-L,Knutton St5. . .55 E2
Newcastle-u-L ST5. . . . . . . .283 D1
Johnstone Ave ST9 . . . . .59 C4
John St Stafford ST16 . . . . . .156 A4
Stourbridge DY8 . . . . .275 F1
Swadlincote DE11 . . . . .186 E6
Tamworth B77 . . . . .250 E4
Uttoxeter ST14 . . . . .126 B8
John Taylor High Sch
DE13. . . . . .183 E2
John Till Cl WS15 . . . . .178 E1
John Wheeldon Prim Sch
ST16. . . . . .155 E5
Joiner's Square Ind Est
ST1. . . . . .282 C1
Joiner's Square Prim Sch
ST1. . . . . .282 C1
Jolley St ST6 . . . . .42 C1
Jolliffe St 11 ST13 . . . . .30 E5
Jolpool La ST18. . . . . .121 C4
Jolt La ST18 . . . . .172 E5
Jolyon Cl ST4 . . . . .73 B6
Jonathan Rd ST4 . . . . .88 C5
Jones Cl Fradley WS13 . . . . .215 E8
Stafford ST17 . . . . .174 D7
Jones La Burntwood WS7 . . .229 F7
Great Wyrley WS6 . . . . .227 B1
Rugeley WS15 . . . . .196 C8
Jones Rd WV12 . . . . .242 D1
Jonkel Ave B77 . . . . .262 A5
Jordan Ave DE13. . . . . .147 F2
Jordan Cl
3 Lichfield WS13. . . . . .231 A8
Fradley WS13 . . . . .215 D6
Sutton Coldfield B75 . . . . . .258 B1
Jordan Croft WS13. . . . . . . .215 D7
Jordan Rd B75. . . . . .258 C2
Jordan Way Aldridge WS9 . .245 B1
Stone ST15 . . . . .120 B7
Jordon St ST1 . . . . .282 A1
Joseph Dewsbury Cl
WS7. . . . . .228 F8
Joseph Dix Dr WS15. . . . . .178 D2
Joseph St 6 ST6 . . . . .56 E8
Josiah Wedgwood St ST1 . . .57 A3
Joules Dr ST15 . . . . .104 E3
Jowett B77 . . . . .250 E2
Joyce Ave ST6 . . . . .42 B2
Joyce's La ST4 . . . . .194 A8
Jubilee Ave ST1 . . . . .57 A3
Jubilee Cl Biddulph ST8 . . . . .27 D8
Great Wyrley WS6 . . . . .226 F2
Jubilee Ct Stafford ST16. . . .155 F5
Uttoxeter ST14 . . . . .126 B7
Jubilee Dr ST10. . . . . .62 D3
Jubilee Gr TF11 . . . . .203 F5
Jubilee Rd
Newcastle-u-L ST5. . . . . .56 D3
Trentham ST4 . . . . .87 F8
Jubilee Rise DE15. . . . . . . .167 C3
Jubilee Sq DE6 . . . . .81 D7
Jubilee St WS15 . . . . .178 D1
Jubilee Terr 12 ST13 . . . . . .30 D6
Judes Wlk WS13 . . . . .213 F2
Judgefield La ST6 . . . . .28 A2
Judith Gr ST4. . . . . .72 C5
Jug Bank Ashley TF9 . . . . . .100 B4
Burslem ST6 . . . . .57 B6
Julian Cl WS6 . . . . .227 A3
Junction St Leek ST13 . . . . . .30 E4
Stourbridge,Amblecote
DY8. . . . . .275 C1
Junction The 1 DY8 . . . . . . .279 E8
June Cres B77 . . . . .250 E5
June Rd ST4 . . . . .73 B6
Juniper Cl
Burntwood WS7. . . . . .229 A6
Cannock WS12. . . . . .211 A6
Meir ST3 . . . . .90 A6
Newcastle-u-L ST5. . . . . .40 E1
Juniper Row TF10. . . . . . . .168 F1
Juniper B77 . . . . .251 A4
Jupiter St ST6 . . . . .42 C1
Jupiter Way 10 ST17 . . . . .175 A8
Justin Cl ST5 . . . . .56 C5

K

Kamienna Cl ST17 . . . . .174 F8
Kara Pl ST4. . . . . .88 B8
Kaydor Cl ST9 . . . . .59 B4
Kay Dr DE11 . . . . .186 F5
Kayne Cl DY6. . . . . .275 C7
Kean Cl WS13. . . . . .213 E2
Kearsley Way ST3. . . . . .88 E8
Keary St ST4. . . . . .72 B6
Keates St 7 ST6. . . . . .56 F8
Keating Gdns B75. . . . . . . .258 A4
Keats Ave Cannock WS11. . .209 E5
Stafford ST17 . . . . .174 C8
Keats Cl Dudley DY3 . . . . . .271 A5
Sutton Coldfield B74 . . . . . .257 F6
Tamworth B79 . . . . .249 F8
Keats Gdns ST7 . . . . .41 A8
Keats Rd WV10 . . . . .241 A1
Keble Cl Burntwood WS7. . . .229 C7
Burton u T DE15. . . . . .167 C2
Cannock WS11. . . . . .226 E8
Keble Way ST3 . . . . .73 D2
Keble Wlk B79 . . . . .250 A6
Kedleston Cl
Stretton DE13 . . . . .147 C1
Walsall WS3 . . . . .243 A3

Ked – Lad 311

Kedleston Rd ST6 42 A2
Keele Rd Keele ST5 70 A7
Madeley Heath CW3 69 B8
Newcastle-u-L ST5 70 D8
Keele Science Pk ST5 70 B7
Keele Service Area ST5 69 F4
Keele St ST6 41 D4
Keele Univ ST5 70 B7
Keeling Dr WS11 209 B1
Keeling Rd ST10 76 E3
Keelings Dr ST4 71 F4
Keelings Rd ST1 57 E5
Keeling St ST5 56 C6
Keene Cl ST6 42 E3
Keepers Cl WS9 244 F3
Keeper's Cl WS7 229 A6
Keepers Cl
Kingswinford DY6 275 B8
Lichfield WS14 231 E7
Keepers La Codsall WV8 239 A1
Wolverhampton WV6,WV8 255 A7
Keepers Rd B74 257 C5
Keep The ST17 174 C8
Keir Pl DY8 279 E8
Keld Ave ST17 174 A8
Keldy Cl WV6 255 F5
Kelham Rd ST4 73 A6
Kelly Ave WS15 196 F6
Kelly Gn ST6 42 B6
Kelmore Cl ST3 284 B4
Kelsall St ST6 42 B1
Kelsall Way ST7 39 D1
Kelso Gdns WV6 254 D4
Kelvedon Way WS15 178 C1
Kelvestone Ho WS11 209 D1
Kelvin Ave ST1 57 D7
Kelvin Dr WS11 210 A3
Kelvin St ST5 56 D4
Kemball Ave ST4 72 D4
Kemball Specl Sch ST4 72 F5
Kemberton Cl WV3 255 C1
Kemberton Rd WV3 255 C1
Kemnay Ave ST6 42 B8
Kempson Rd ST19 192 F1
Kempthorne Ave WV10 240 E1
Kempthorne Gdns WS3 243 A2
Kempthorne Rd ST1 282 C1
Kempton Cl WS12 211 A6
Kempton Dr
Great Wyrley WS6 226 F2
Tamworth B77 261 D4
Kempton Gr ST10 76 E5
Kempton Rd DE15 167 A3
Kempton Way DY8 279 E3
Kendal Cl Stafford ST17 174 B7
Wolverhampton WV6 255 F6
Kendal Ct Brownhills WS9 244 F4
Cannock WS11 226 B8
Kendal Gr ST2 58 D2
Kendall Rise DY6 275 F5
Kendal Pl ST5 71 B6
Kendal Rise WV6 255 F6
Kendal Way CW2 37 C1
Kenderdine Cl ST17 193 F8
Kendlewood Rd DY10 280 B1
Kendrick St ST3 73 D3
Kenelyn Cres ST3 72 E4
Kenilworth Ave DE13 166 D7
Kenilworth Cl
Market Drayton TF9 97 E2
Penkridge ST19 208 A8
Stourbridge DY8 275 D2
Kenilworth Cres WV4 266 E4
Kenilworth Ct 2 WS11 209 E1
Kenilworth Dr WS11 209 D4
Kenilworth Gr
2 Longton ST3 73 F1
Newcastle-u-L ST5 56 E3
Kenilworth Rd
Lichfield WS14 231 B6
Perton WV6 254 F4
Tamworth B77 250 E4
Kenilworth Wlk ST10 76 B2
Kenley Ave ST9 43 F8
Kenmore Ave WS12 209 F7
Kennedy Cl B77 250 C1
Kennedy Cres DY3 271 D4
Kennedy Ct DY8 279 F5
Kennedy Pl ST21 133 D6
Kennedy Rd ST4 88 B6
Kennedy Way ST16 155 B8
Kennedy Wlk ST9 59 B4
Kennermont Rd ST2 58 C6
Kennet Cl Brownhills WS8 228 C2
Newcastle-u-L ST5 71 B3
Kennet B77 250 D1
Kennington Oval ST4 88 D8
Kenrick Cl CW3 67 C1
Kenrose Mill DY7 278 B3
Kensington Cl ST15 120 C5
Kensington Ct
Stoke-on-T,Trent Vale ST4 71 E3
Stoke-on-T,Tunstall ST6 41 E4
Kensington Dr
Stafford ST18 156 C3
Sutton Coldfield B74 257 F5
Tamworth B79 250 B7
Kensington Gdns
Cannock WS11 209 C2
Stourbridge DY8 275 C1
Kensington Pl WS12 227 C8
Kensington Rd
Burton u T DE15 167 A3
Stoke-on-T ST4 72 A4
Kensworth Cl ST5 71 A3
Kent Ave B78 249 F2
Kent Cl WS9 245 B1
Kent Dr ST9 43 E6
Kent Gr Newcastle-u-L ST5 55 E8
Stone ST15 104 F2
Kent Ho ST7 40 D6
Kentish Cl ST17 174 A8
Kentmere Cl Longton ST4 73 B5
Penkridge ST19 193 A1
Stafford ST17 174 A8
Kentmere Pl ST5 71 B6
Kenton Ave WV6 255 F4
Kent Pl Cannock WS12 210 F1
Stoke-on-T ST4 72 E6
Kent Rd Burton u T DE15 185 E6
Stourbridge DY8 279 D7
Wolverhampton WV2 266 E7
Kents Row ST12 88 E2
Kent St DY3 271 E5
Kent Way ST17 175 B8
Kentwell B79 249 D7
Kenworthy Rd ST16 155 E6
Kenworthy St ST6 41 E4
Kepler B79 249 E7
Kerria Ctr B77 251 A4
Kerria Rd B77 251 B4
Kerridge Cl WV9 240 A2
Kerry La ST21 133 C6
Kersbrook Cl ST4 88 C6
Kervis Gr ST3 90 B6
Kesterton Rd B74 257 E5
Kesteven Wlk ST2 58 B3
Kestrel Ave ST3 90 C7
Kestrel Cl Biddulph ST8 27 B6
Newport TF10 169 A5
Stafford ST17 156 C1
Uttoxeter ST14 126 B6
Whittington WS14 232 F5
Kestrel Ct WS7 229 F8
Kestrel Dr
Loggerheads TF9 99 D4
Sutton Coldfield B74 257 F5
Kestrel Gr WS12 210 C1
Kestrel La ST10 76 E3
Kestrel Rise WV6 255 F7
Kestrel B77 262 A6
Kestrel Way
Burton u T DE15 167 D3
Cheslyn Hay WS6 226 C2
Keswick Dr DY6 275 D6
Keswick Gr Aldridge B74 256 F2
Stafford ST17 174 A8
Keswick Pl ST5 71 B6
Ketley Rd
Kingswinford DY6 275 F6
Kingswinford DY6 275 F7
Kettering Dr Berry Hill ST2 57 F1
Bucknall ST2 58 A1
Kettlebrook Rd B77 250 C3
Kettlesbank Rd DY3 271 B2
Ketton Cl ST6 42 B8
Kewstoke Cl WV12 242 B1
Kewstoke Rd WV12 242 C1
Keyes Dr DY6 270 D1
Keynsham Wlk ST6 42 D2
Keys Cl WS12 210 C3
Keys Park Rd WS12 210 E3
Keystone La WS15 196 F8
Keystone Mews 3 WS15 196 F8
Keystone Rd WS15 196 F8
Keyworth Wlk ST2 58 A2
Kibblestone Rd ST15 105 C5
Kibworth Gr ST1 282 B4
Kidbrooke Pl ST3 88 E8
Kiddemore Green Rd
Brewood ST19 223 A6
Kiddemore Green ST19 222 D6
Kidderminster Rd
Iverley DY8 281 C7
Kingswinford DY6 275 B7
Kidderminster Rd S DY9 281 F3
Kidsgrove Bank ST7 41 B8
Kidsgrove Rd ST6 41 C8
Kidsgrove Sta ST7 25 F1
Kidson Eventide Homes
WV6 255 F5
Kielder Cl WS12 210 E2
Kilburn Dr DY6 270 E1
Kilburn Pl ST2 57 F2
Kilburn Way DE11 186 F5
Kilbye Cl B77 261 F5
Kildare St ST3 284 C2
Kilmorie Rd WS11 209 C2
Kiln Bank Cres TF9 112 C8
Kiln Bank Rd TF9 112 C8
Kiln Croft ST10 92 D4
Kilndown Cl ST1 57 A2
Kiln La ST13 30 C6
Kiln Way B78 251 F1
Kilsby Gr ST2 43 B2
Kimberlee Ave DY10 280 B4
Kimberley Cl B74 257 A2
Kimberley Dr
Burton u T DE15 167 C3
Uttoxeter ST14 110 F1
Kimberley Grange ST5 283 B4
Kimberley Rd Hanley ST1 57 A3
Newcastle-u-L ST5 283 B4
Kimberley St Longton ST3 284 B2
Wolverhampton WV3 266 A8
Kimberley B77 261 F7
Kimberley Way
Rugeley WS15 196 F5
Stafford ST17 174 A8
Kinder Pl ST5 55 B1
Kineton Rise DY3 266 C2
Kinfare Dr WV6 255 B4
Kinfare Rise DY3 271 E4
King Charles Cl ST3 90 A7
Kingcross St ST3 284 C3
Kingcup Rd ST17 174 E5
King Edward Pl DE14 166 B3
King Edward's Row 5
WV2 266 C8
King Edward St ST10 76 E4
King Edward VI High Sch
ST17 155 C1
King Edward VI Sch
WS14 231 C6
Kingfisher Cl
Brownhills WS8 244 E7
Madeley CW3 68 F7
Newport TF10 168 F5
Sedgley DY3 266 C2
Kingfisher Cres
Cheadle ST10 76 F3
Fulford ST11 106 E8
Kingfisher Ct WS7 229 F8
Kingfisher Dr
Cannock WS12 210 C5
Colwich ST18 177 E8
Stourbridge DY8 279 C4
Kingfisher Gr ST6 42 C3
Kingfisher B77 262 A6
Kingfisher Way ST14 126 C6
Kingfisher Wlk ST19 207 F8
King George St ST1 282 C4
Kingham Cl DY3 271 C2
King Ho ST7 40 D5
Kings Ave Cannock WS12 210 C4
Market Drayton TF9 112 A8
King's Ave
Newcastle-u-L ST5 56 C5
Stone ST15 105 A1
Kingsbridge Ave ST5 71 B5
Kings Bridge WV9 224 A3
King's Bromley La WS15 198 D6
Kings Bromley Rd DE13 200 F2
Kingsbury Cl DE15 167 A4
Kingsbury Gr ST1 57 F6
King's CE Sch The WV6 255 B5
Kingsclere Gr ST1 57 E7
Kingsclere Wlk WV4 265 C6
Kings Croft WS12 210 E4
Kingscroft ST18 158 D1
King's Croft ST4 56 D1
Kings Ct Stourbridge DY8 279 E5
Sutton Coldfield B75 258 B3
Kingsdale Cl ST3 90 A7
Kingsdale Croft DE13 166 D8
Kingsdene Ave DY6 275 C4
Kingsdown Cl CW2 37 C1
Kingsdown Mews ST5 71 C4
Kingsdown Rd WS7 211 E1
Kings Dr ST18 156 D8
Kingsfield Cres ST8 27 D8
Kingsfield Fst Sch ST8 27 C8
Kingsfield Oval ST4 56 D1
Kingsfield Rd Biddulph ST8 27 D8
Stoke-on-T ST4 56 D1
Kingsford Country Park★
DY11 277 D1
Kingsford La DY7,DY11 277 D2
Kingsford Pl ST3 90 A8
Kingshayes Rd WS9 245 B1
Kings Head Pk TF10 168 E4
King's Hill Rd WS14 231 C6
Kingside Gr ST4 88 C5
Kingsland Ave ST4 71 F4
Kingsland CE Prim Sch
ST2 58 C4
Kingsland Cl ST15 120 C7
Kingsland Ct ST15 120 C7
Kingsland Rd ST15 120 C7
King's La B79 236 C5
Kingsleigh Croft B75 258 B2
Kingsley Ave
Cannock WS12 210 C7
Wolverhampton WV6 255 B4
Kingsley Cl Stafford ST17 174 E8
Talke Pits ST7 40 D6
Tamworth B79 250 A6
Kingsley & Froghall Sta★
ST10 62 B3
Kingsley Gdns WV8 238 E3
Kingsley Gr DY3 271 A5
Kingsley Rd
Burton u T DE14 166 D6
Congleton CW12 6 A3
Kingswinford DY6 275 C5
Overmoor ST9 60 B3
Stafford ST17 174 E8
Talke Pits ST7 40 D6
Werrington ST9 59 F3
Kingsley St ST3 74 A1
Kingsley View ST13 45 D5
Kingsley Wood Rd WS15 195 D7
Kingslow Ave WV4 265 D6
Kingsmead DE13 166 E8
Kingsmead Hospl ST16 285 C3
Kingsmead Rd ST3 89 F7
Kingsmead Tech Coll
WS12 210 C4
Kings Mews WS14 231 B5
Kingsnorth Pl ST3 90 B6
Kings Pl ST4 56 D2
Kings Rd Sedgley DY3 271 E8
Shareshill WV10 225 A6
Stoke-on-T ST4 72 A1
King St Audley ST7 39 D1
Biddulph ST8 27 C8
Blymhill TF10,TF11 189 A1
Brownhills WS9 244 F2
Burntwood WS7 228 F5
Burton u T DE14 166 C1
Kings Terr ST4 56 D1
King St Kidsgrove ST7 26 A2
Leek ST13 30 E5
Longton ST3,ST4 284 B4
King St *continued*
Newcastle-u-L,Chesterton
ST5 55 E7
Newcastle-u-L,Cross Heath
ST5 56 A3
Newcastle-u-L ST5 283 C3
Kingston Arc WS11 209 E1
Kingston Ave
Stafford ST16 156 B4
Stoke-on-T ST1 57 E7
Kingston Cl B79 250 C7
Kingston Ctr WV6 255 F5
Kingston Dr ST15 120 B6
Kingston Hill Ct ST16 156 C3
Kingston Pl Biddulph ST8 16 E2
Stoke-on-T ST6 42 E3
Kingston Rd DE15 167 C2
Kingston Row ST16 156 A3
Kingston Way DY6 275 C7
King St Rugeley WS15 196 F8
Stourbridge DY8 279 E6
Talke Pits ST7 40 D5
Tamworth B79 250 B5
Yoxall DE13 182 A3
Kingsway Burton u T DE14 185 B8
Cannock WS11 210 A4
Kingsway E ST5 71 B6
Kingsway Essington WV11 242 A4
Stafford ST16 155 C2
Stoke-on-T ST4 72 B7
Stourbridge DY8 279 E8
Kingsway W ST5 71 A6
Kingswear Ave WV6 254 F3
Kingswell Rd ST4 56 D1
Kingswinford Pl ST4 57 D7
Kingswinford Sch The
DY6 275 D7
Kings Wlk DE13 199 B6
Kingswood Ave
Cannock WS11 226 C7
Chorlton CW2 37 B3
Kingswood Bsns Pk WV7 237 F1
Kingswood Colliery Cvn Site
WS6 227 A4
Kingswood Ctr WV7 237 F2
Kingswood Dr
Great Wyrley WS6 227 A4
Norton Canes WS11 227 F5
Kingswood Gdns WV4 265 F6
Kingswood ST7 26 B1
Kingswood Mobile Homes
WV7 237 E1
Kingswood Rd
Albrighton WV7 237 C4
Albrighton WV7 237 D3
Kingswinford DY6 275 C4
King William St
Stoke-on-T ST6 41 E3
Stourbridge DY8 279 F8
Kinlet Cl WV3 265 A8
Kinloch Dr DY1 271 F3
Kinnersley Ave ST7 40 F8
Kinnersley St 1 ST7 26 A2
Kinross Ave WS12 209 F7
Kinsall Gn B77 262 C6
Kinsey St ST5 55 B2
Kinver Cl DE6 81 C8
Kinver Cres WS9 245 C1
Kinver Dr WV4 265 C5
Kinver Edge★ DY7 277 E2
Kinver La DY11 280 B7
Kinver Mt DY7 278 A3
Kinver Rd
Burton u T DE15 167 A4
Kinver DY7 277 E8
Kinver St Stoke-on-T ST6 42 C1
Stourbridge DY8 275 E1
Kiplass La ST18 121 C4
Kipling Ave WS7 212 A1
Kipling Rd Dudley DY3 271 A5
Wolverhampton WV10 240 D2
Kipling Rise B79 249 F8
Kipling Way ST2 58 D1
Kirby Dr DY1 271 E3
Kirby St ST6 57 A6
Kirkbride Cl ST3 73 D4
Kirkham St ST4 72 A6
Kirkland La ST4 72 A6
Kirkland Way B78 260 B8
Kirkside Gr WS8 244 F7
Kirkstall Ave ST17 174 B7
Kirkstall Cl WS3 242 F2
Kirkstall Cres WS3 242 F2
Kirkstall Pl ST5 71 B5
Kirkstone Cres WV5 269 F6
Kirk St ST6 42 C1
Kirkup Wlk ST3 284 A3
Kirkwall Gr ST2 43 B2
Kirstead Gdns WV6 255 B3
Kirtley B77 250 E2
Kirton Gr WV6 255 C4
Kitchen La WV11 241 F1
Kite Gr Kidsgrove ST7 26 D3
Meir ST3 90 B6
Kitling Greaves La DE13 166 A7
Kitlings La ST17 175 F7
Kittoe Rd B74 258 A3
Kitwood Ave B78 262 F6
Knarsdale Cl 2 ST3 73 D5
Knaves Castle Ave WS8 228 F2
Knebworth Ct CW12 16 B8
Knenhall La
Moddershall ST3,ST15 89 F1
Stone ST15 89 F1
Knenhall ST15 105 E7
Knight Ave ST16 156 A4
Knight La ST10 78 E1
Knightley Cl ST20 171 D6
Knightley CW3 68 F5
Knightley Rd ST20 171 D8
Knightley Way ST20 171 D7
Knighton Cl B74 257 F3
Knighton Dr B74 257 F3
Knighton Rd
Cannock WS12 210 E3
Sutton Coldfield B74 257 D5
Knight Rd WS7 211 E1
Knights Ave WV6 255 E6
Knightsbridge Cl B74 257 F4
Knightsbridge Way
12 Stoke-on-T ST6 41 D3
Burton u T DE13 166 D7
Knights Cl ST19 207 F7
Knights Cres WV6 255 E7
Knights Croft ST5 69 F7
Knights Ct
Norton Canes WS11 228 A4
Stretton DE13 147 E2
Knightsfield Rd DE13 144 E2
Knights Hill WS9 256 B3
Knight St ST6 41 D4
Kniveden La ST13 31 B5
Knoll Cl WS7 229 A5
Knoll Croft WS9 245 C1
Knoll The DY6 275 E5
Knotty La CW12 17 A8
Knowlbank Rd ST7 53 F7
Knowle La WS14 231 B3
Knowle Rd Biddulph ST8 27 C7
Stafford ST17 175 D7
Knowles Hill DE13 147 B3
Knowle St ST4 72 A8
Knowle Wood View ST3 72 F3
Knowsley La Kidsgrove ST7 26 A4
Lawton-gate ST7 25 F4
Knowsley Rd ST9 44 D3
Knox Rd WV2 266 D6
Knox's Grave La WS14,
B78 248 D7
Knoyle Ct 1 DY8 279 F6
Knutsford Rd ST7 25 A6
Knutton La ST5 55 F2
Knutton Rd ST5 56 C5
Knutton St Mary's Prim Sch
ST5 55 E2
Knype Cl ST5 56 A7
Knypersley Fst Sch ST8 27 B6
Knypersley Rd ST6 42 E4
Knype Way Biddulph ST8 27 B6
Newcastle-u-L ST5 56 A7
Kohima Dr DY8 279 E5
Kurtus B77 261 D6
Kyffin Rd ST2 58 B6
Kyle Cl WV10 240 B1
Kyle Rd DE65 147 D8
Kynaston Cres WV8 239 B2
Kynnersley Croft ST14 111 B1

L

Laburnam Cl ST7 40 E7
Laburnham Ct WS14 231 C5
Laburnham Rd DY6 275 E6
Laburnum Ave
Cannock WS11 226 E7
Tamworth B79 250 B8
Laburnum Cl
Blythe Bridge ST11 91 A6
Cannock WS11 226 E7
Great Bridgeford ST18 135 B2
Kinver DY7 277 F5
Market Drayton TF9 97 D2
Stourbridge DY8 279 E7
Walsall WS3 244 A2
Laburnum Gr
Burntwood WS7 228 F6
Stoke-on-T ST3 72 E3
Laburnum Ho WS4 244 D1
Laburnum Pl
1 Stoke-on-T ST3 89 F8
Newcastle-u-L ST5 40 D1
Laburnum Rd
Brownhills WS9 245 A3
Burton u T DE15 185 F6
Swadlincote DE11 186 F6
Wolverhampton WV4 266 F3
Laburnum St DY8 279 E7
Laches Cl WV10 224 D5
Laches La WV10 224 E2
Ladbrook Gr DY3 271 B3
Ladderedge Ctry Pk★
ST13 30 B4
Ladderedge ST13 30 C2
Ladford Covert Ind Pk
ST18 134 E1
Ladfordfields Ind Est
ST18 134 D1
Ladfordfields Ind Pk
ST18 153 D8
Ladford Trad Pk ST18 134 E1
Ladies Wlk DY3 271 D8
Lad La ST5 283 B3
Ladle End La DE12 184 D1
Ladybank Gr ST3 88 E8
Lady Bank B79 250 B4
Ladydale Cl ST13 30 F4
Ladyfields Way DE11 186 F6
Ladygates CW3 53 B6
Lady Grey's Wlk DY8 279 D5
Lady Hill Terr WS15 196 B7
Lady Meadow Cl
Denstone ST14 95 E5

Lady Meadow Cl continued
Tamworth B78 . . . .**250** A3
Ladymoor La ST6 . . . . **28** B3
Ladysmith Rd ST1 . . . . **57** A3
Ladysmith St ST3 . . . . **57** A3
Ladywell Cl Stretton DE13 .**147** E1
Wombourne WV5 . . . .**270** A8
Ladywell Rd ST6 . . . . **41** D3
Lagonda Cl ST8 . . . . **27** B6
Lagonda B77 . . . .**250** E3
Lagrange B79 . . . .**249** E6
Lair The B78 . . . .**262** F8
Lakeland Dr B77 . . . .**262** B7
Lakenheath B79 . . . .**250** C7
Lake Rd ST13 . . . . **18** E1
Lakesedge ST15 . . . .**119** B5
Lakeside Betley CW3 . . . . . . **53** A6
Bosley SK11 . . . . **7** D8
Lakeside Cl 1 Hanley ST1. . **56** F2
Whitmore ST5 . . . . **85** C4
Lakeside Dr WS11 . . . .**228** B6
Lakeside B74 . . . .**257** B5
Lakeside Pk B78 . . . .**249** F1
Lakeside Prim Sch B77. .**250** E2
Lakeside View WS15 . . . .**198** B4
Lake St ST13 . . . .**271** D3
Lakewood Dr ST12 . . . . . . **88** E4
Lakewood Gr ST1 . . . . **57** A3
Lally Pl ST8. . . . . **27** B2
Lamb Cres WV5 . . . .**269** F6
Lambert Cl DY6 . . . .**275** D8
Lambert Dr WS7 . . . .**229** A8
Lambert Rd ST14 . . . .**110** F1
Lambert St ST6 . . . . **41** E3
Lamb La ST15. . . . .**119** F7
Lambourn Cl WS3. . . . . . .**243** C2
Lambourne Cl
4 Lichfield WS14 . . . . . .**231** E8
Great Wyrley WS6 . . . . . .**226** F1
Lambourne Dr ST2 . . . . . . **43** C1
Lambourne Way WS11 . . .**228** A5
Lambourn Pl ST3 . . . . **88** E8
Lamb Shutt Flats TF9 . . . . **97** D1
Lamb St Hanley ST1. . . . . .**282** B3
Kidsgrove ST7 . . . . **26** A2
Lamerton Gr ST3 . . . . **73** F2
Lammas Rd DY8 . . . .**275** C3
Lamorna Cl WV3 . . . .**265** B8
Lamotte Cl ST4 . . . . **73** B5
Lamprey B77 . . . .**261** D6
Lanark Cl DY6 . . . .**275** F5
Lanark Wlks ST5. . . . . **70** F7
Lancaster Ave
Aldridge WS9 . . . .**256** B8
Fulford ST11 . . . . **90** E1
Leek ST13 . . . . **30** F7
Newcastle-u-L ST5. . . . . .**283** D2
Lancaster Bldg ST5 . . . . .**283** B2
Lancaster Cres ST4 . . . . . **71** D8
Lancaster Dr
Stoke-on-T ST6 . . . . **42** F4
Tutbury DE13 . . . .**146** B3
Lancaster Gdns WV4 . . . .**265** E5
Lancaster Ho
5 Stourbridge DY8. . . . . .**279** F8
Cannock WS12 . . . .**210** D1
Lancaster Pl WS3 . . . .**243** C2
Lancaster Rd
Fradley WS13 . . . .**215** C3
Newcastle-u-L ST5. . . . . .**283** D2
Stafford ST17 . . . .**175** A8
Lance Dr WS7 . . . .**211** F1
Lancelot Dr DE13 . . . .**147** E2
Lanchester Cl Biddulph ST8 **27** B6
Tamworth B79 . . . .**249** E7
Lancia Cl ST8. . . . . **27** B5
Lancing Ave ST17 . . . .**175** B8
Lander Cl ST15 . . . .**120** D7
Lander Pl ST6 . . . . **42** B6
Landon St ST3 . . . .**284** C3
Landor Cres WS15 . . . . . .**196** E7
Landor Way ST17 . . . .**174** B8
Landport Rd WV2 . . . .**266** F8
Landrake Gr ST6. . . . . **41** F7
Landsberg B79 . . . .**249** F6
Landseer Pl ST5 . . . . **55** E6
Landstone Rd 5 ST17. . . .**175** A8
Landywood Ent Pk WS6 . .**242** F8
Landywood Gn WS6 . . . . .**226** E2
Landywood La WS6 . . . . . .**226** E2
Landywood Prim Sch
WS6 . . . .**242** F8
Landywood Sta WS6 . . . . .**226** F2
Lane End SK17 . . . . **23** D7
Lane Farm Gr ST1. . . . . . . **57** E7
Lane Green Ave WV8 . . . .**239** C1
Lane Green Ct WV8 . . . . . .**239** B3
Lane Green Fst Sch WV8 .**239** B4
Lane Green Rd WV8 . . . . .**239** C2
Lane Green Rd Masionettes
WV8. . . . .**239** B3
Lane Green Sh Par WV8. .**239** B3
Lane Head SK17 . . . . **13** B7
Lanehead Rd ST1. . . . . **56** F7
Lanehead Wlk WS15 . . . .**178** C2
Lanes Cl
King's Bromley DE13 . . . .**199** C6
Wombourne WV5. . . . . . .**269** E5
Lane The ST18. . . . .**174** C3
Langdale Cl ST8. . . . .**244** E6
Langdale Cres ST1. . . . . . . **57** D7
Langdale Ct B77 . . . .**251** A6
Langdale Dr WS11 . . . . . .**226** C7

Langdale Gn WS11 . . . . . .**226** C7
Langdale Jun & Inf Schs
ST5 . . . . **71** B5
Langdale Rd ST5. . . . . **71** B5
Langer Cl DE14 . . . .**185** B6
Langford Rd Bucknall ST2 . **58** C3
Newcastle-u-L ST5. . . . . . **71** A4
Langford St ST13 . . . . **30** D5
Langham Gn B74 . . . .**256** F1
Langham Rd ST2. . . . . **43** A1
Langholm Dr WS12 . . . . . .**210** E2
Langland Dr Longton ST3 . . **73** A2
Sedgley DY3. . . . .**271** C8
Langley Cl
Brownhills WS9 . . . .**245** A3
Newcastle-u-L ST5. . . . . . **40** D2
Langley Gdns WS9 . . . . . .**265** D7
Langley Rd WV3,WV4 . . . .**265** B7
Langley St ST4. . . . . **56** D1
Langot La ST21 . . . .**115** D4
Langton Cres WS14 . . . . .**232** E6
Langton Ct
1 Lichfield WS13 . . . . . .**214** A1
Werrington ST9 . . . . **59** A4
Lanrick Gdns WS15 . . . . .**178** E2
Lansbury Cl ST17 . . . .**174** E8
Lansbury Dr ST11 . . . .**209** E4
Lansbury Gr ST3 . . . . **74** B3
Lansbury Rd WS15 . . . . . .**196** E6
Lansdell Ave ST5 . . . . **56** B6
Lansdowne Ave WV8 . . . .**238** F2
Lansdowne Cl Leek ST13 . . **30** C5
Stone ST15 . . . .**119** F5
Lansdowne Cres
Tamworth B77 . . . .**261** D8
Werrington ST9 . . . . **59** B4
Lansdowne Inf Sch
DE14 . . . .**166** D5
Lansdowne Rd
Burton u T DE14 . . . .**184** F7
Stoke-on-T ST4 . . . . **56** E1
Lansdowne St ST3 . . . . . . **73** B1
Lansdowne Terr DE14 . . .**166** D5
Lansdowne Way
Rugeley WS15 . . . .**178** C2
Stafford ST17 . . . .**175** D6
Lant Cl DE13 . . . .**199** D6
Lanthorn Cl WS13 . . . .**231** A7
Lapley Ave ST16 . . . .**155** A7
Lapley Dr DE13 . . . .**166** E8
Lapley Hall Mews ST19 . .**206** A6
Lapley La ST19 . . . .**206** C4
Lapley Rd ST19 . . . .**205** D7
Lapper Ave WV4 . . . .**266** F2
Lapwing Cl
2 Packmoor ST7 . . . . **26** F1
Brownhills WS8 . . . .**244** E7
Cheslyn Hay WS6. . . . . . .**226** C1
Lapwing Rd ST7 . . . . **26** D3
Lapwing B77 . . . .**262** A6
Lapwood Ave DY6 . . . .**275** F6
Lapworth Way TF10 . . . . .**169** A3
Lara Cl ST16 . . . .**155** B3
Larch Cl Kidsgrove ST7 . . . **41** A8
Kinver DY7 . . . .**278** C3
Lichfield WS14 . . . .**231** E7
Larch Ct 5 ST6. . . . . **57** A7
Larches The TF10 . . . .**168** E2
Larchfields ST15 . . . .**120** B6
Larch Gr Sedgley DY3 . . . .**271** E7
Stoke-on-T ST3 . . . . **72** C2
Larch Ho DY8. . . . .**279** C6
Larchmere Dr WV11 . . . . .**242** B3
Larchmount ST4 . . . . **88** B7
Larch Pl ST5. . . . . **55** E8
Larch Rd
Kingswinford DY6 . . . . . .**275** E7
Rugeley WS15 . . . .**196** F6
Swadlincote DE11 . . . . . .**186** F6
Larchwood Dr WS11 . . . . .**210** A4
Larchwood Keele ST5 . . . . **70** A6
Stafford ST17 . . . .**175** C5
Larcombe Dr WV4 . . . .**266** D5
Lark Ave ST7 . . . . **26** D3
Larkfield ST7 . . . . **26** B1
Lark Hall Com Inf Sch
B79 . . . .**250** A8
Larkhill La TF9 . . . .**100** A4
Larkhill Rd DY8 . . . .**279** C4
Larkholme Cl WS15 . . . . .**178** A1
Larkin Ave ST3 . . . . **73** D4
Larkin Cl Stafford ST17 . . .**174** C7
Wolverhampton WV10 . . .**241** A1
Lark Rise ST14 . . . .**126** B6
Larksfield Rd ST6. . . . . . . **42** D1
Larksmeadow Vale ST17 .**175** D6
Larks Mill WS3 . . . .**243** B6
Larkspur Ave WS7 . . . . . .**229** A5
Larkspur Dr WV10 . . . . . .**241** B7
Larkspur Gr ST5 . . . .**283** C4
Larkspur B77 . . . .**261** D4
Larkspur Way WS8 . . . . . .**244** D6
Larkstone La ST13,DE6. . . **34** E1
Larkswood Dr
Sedgley DY3. . . . .**271** D7
Wolverhampton WV4 . . . .**265** C3
Lascelles St ST6 . . . . **41** D2
Lask Edge Rd ST9,ST13 . . **28** D7
Laski Cres ST3. . . . . **74** B2
Latebrook Cl ST8 . . . . **26** A8
Latham Cl DE11 . . . .**167** C2
Latham Gr ST6. . . . . **42** B7
Latherford Cl WV10 . . . . .**224** E5
Latherford La WV10 . . . . .**225** B4
Lathkill Dale DE11 . . . . . .**186** F2
Latimer Way ST2. . . . . **58** C2

Lauder Cl DY3 . . . .**266** C1
Lauderdale Cl WS8. . . . . .**244** E6
Lauderdale Gdns WV10 . .**240** E3
Lauder Gr ST18 . . . .**158** C8
Lauder Pl N ST2 . . . . **73** E8
Lauder Pl S ST2. . . . . **73** E8
Launceston Cl B77 . . . . . .**250** D2
Laureates Wlk B74. . . . . .**258** A1
Laurel Bank B79 . . . .**250** B6
Laurel Cl WS14 . . . .**231** D8
Laurel Cres ST9. . . . . **59** A3
Laurel Dr Burntwood WS7.**229** C7
Cannock WS12 . . . .**210** E4
Harriseahead ST7 . . . . . . **26** E3
Newport TF10 . . . .**168** F3
Laurel Gr Burton u T DE15.**185** E5
Stafford ST17 . . . .**174** F7
Stoke-on-T ST3 . . . . **72** D2
Wolverhampton WV4 . . . .**265** E6
Laurel Rd DY1 . . . .**271** F4
Laurels The WS15 . . . . . .**196** F1
Laurence Gr WV6 . . . .**255** E7
Lauren Cl ST4 . . . . **72** E6
Lauriston Cl DY1. . . . .**271** F3
Lavender Ave ST11 . . . . . . **90** F5
Lavender Cl
Burton u T DE14 . . . .**185** A8
Great Bridgeford ST18 . . .**135** C2
Meir ST3 . . . . **74** C5
Wolverhampton WV9. . . .**239** F3
Lavender La ST3 . . . .**279** D3
Lavender Lodge ST17 . . . .**177** E7
Lavender Rd ST7 . . . .**250** F4
Laverock Gr CW3 . . . . **68** E6
Lawford Ave WS14 . . . . . .**231** E7
Lawford Cotts ST17 . . . . .**174** F4
Lawley Cl WS4 . . . .**244** B1
Lawley St ST3 . . . . **73** D3
Lawn Ave DY8 . . . .**279** E4
Lawn Farm Cres ST17 . . . **73** D7
Lawn La Cheswardine TF9 .**113** A1
Coven Heath WV9 . . . . . .**240** A7
Lawnoaks Cl WS8. . . . . . .**228** D2
Lawn Rd Stafford ST17 . . .**285** A1
Wolverhampton WV2 . . . .**266** F6
Lawnsfield Wlk ST16 . . . .**136** C1
Lawns The
Market Drayton TF9. . . . . **97** D1
Rolleston on D DE13 . . . .**147** A4
Uttoxeter ST14 . . . .**111** A2
Lawn St DY8 . . . .**279** E4
Lawnswood Ave
Burntwood WS7 . . . .**228** F5
Stourbridge DY8 . . . .**275** C3
Wolverhampton,Parkfield
WV4 . . . .**266** A4
Wolverhampton,Tettenhall
WV6 . . . .**255** E8
Lawnswood Cl 2 WS12 .**210** D1
Lawnswood Dr
Brownhills WS9 . . . .**245** A3
Stourbridge DY7 . . . .**275** A2
Lawnswood Rd
Dudley DY3 . . . .**271** D5
Stourbridge DY8 . . . .**275** D3
Lawnswood Rise WV6 . . .**255** F8
Lawnswood DY7 . . . .**275** A2
Lawn The ST17 . . . .**174** E5
Lawrence Ct B79 . . . .**250** A6
Lawrence St ST15 . . . .**103** B4
Lawrence St Hanley ST1. .**282** A1
Stafford ST17 . . . .**285** B1
Lawrence Way WS13 . . . .**230** F5
Lawson Cl WS9 . . . .**256** B4
Lawson Terr
Newcastle-u-L,Knutton
ST5. . . . . **55** E2
Newcastle-u-L,Porthill ST5 . **56** C6
Lawton Ave ST7 . . . . **25** D3
Lawton Coppice ST7 . . . . **25** E4
Lawton Cres ST8. . . . . **27** D8
Lawtongate Est ST7 . . . . . **25** A5
Lawton Hall ST7 . . . . **25** C4
Lawton St Biddulph ST8 . . **27** D8
Kidsgrove ST7 . . . . **26** C4
Stoke-on-T ST6 . . . . **42** A2
Laxey Rd ST5 . . . . **56** A3
Laxton Gr ST4 . . . . **88** C4
Lazar La ST17 . . . .**176** B6
Lazy Hill Rd WS9 . . . .**245** C1
Lazy Hill WS9. . . . .**245** D2
Lea Castle Dr DY10. . . . . .**280** C3
Lea Castle Hospl DY10 . . .**280** C3
Leacliffe Way WS9 . . . . . .**256** F3
Lea Cl ST5. . . . . **85** D5
Leacote Dr WV6 . . . .**255** C4
Lea Cres ST17 . . . .**174** D7
Leacroft Ave WV10. . . . . .**240** F1
Leacroft Cl WS9 . . . .**245** B1
Leacroft WS15 . . . .**179** A7
Leacroft Rd
Kingswinford DY6 . . . . . .**275** E8
Meir ST3 . . . . **90** A8
Penkridge ST19 . . . .**193** A1
Leacroft ST15 . . . .**120** D7
Leadbeater Ave ST4. . . . . **71** F5
Leadendale La ST3 . . . . . . **89** F8
Leadendale Mews ST3 . . . **89** F8
Leafdown Cl WS12 . . . . . .**210** D3
Leafenden Ave WS7. . . . .**229** A6
Leaford Way DY6 . . . .**275** F5
Leaford Wlk WV6 . . . . **57** F2
Leafy Glade B74 . . . .**257** A3
Leafy Rise DY3. . . . .**271** D4
Lea Gdns WV3 . . . .**266** B8
Lea Gn ST16 . . . .**155** C8
Lea Hall Dr WS7 . . . .**211** D1

Lea Hall Ent Pk WS15 . . .**197** B6
Lea Hall La WS15 . . . .**197** B5
Leahurst Cl 4 ST17 . . . . .**175** C6
Leaks Alley ST3 . . . .**284** C2
Lea La Admaston WS15 . . .**159** F2
Cookley DY10 . . . .**280** A5
Great Wyrley WS6 . . . . . .**227** A3
Lea Manor Dr WV4. . . . . .**265** E4
Leam Dr WS7 . . . .**229** D7
Leamington Cl WS11 . . . .**226** C7
Leamington Gdns ST5. . . **56** C3
Leamington Rd DE14 . . . .**184** E7
Leander Cl
Burntwood WS7 . . . .**211** B1
Great Wyrley WS6 . . . . . .**226** F1
Leander Rise DE15 . . . . . .**186** A8
Lea Pl ST3. . . . . **74** B2
Lea Rd Hixon ST18 . . . . . .**139** C1
Stone ST15 . . . .**119** F6
Wolverhampton WV3 . . . .**266** B8
Lear Rd WV5 . . . .**270** B8
Leasawe Cl ST18 . . . .**158** C2
Leaside Ave WS15 . . . . . .**198** C5
Leaside Rd ST4 . . . . **71** E5
Leason Rd ST3 . . . . **74** B2
Leason St ST4 . . . . **72** B7
Leasowe Rd WS15 . . . . . .**197** A5
Leasowes Dr Perton WV6 .**254** D4
Wolverhampton WV4 . . . .**265** D6
Leasowes Jun & Inf Schs
ST17 . . . .**175** D8
Leasowe The WS13 . . . . .**214** A1
Leas The Eccleshall ST21.**134** A8
Featherstone WV10 . . . . .**241** C7
Leaswood Cl ST5 . . . . **71** C2
Leaswood Pl ST5 . . . . **71** C2
Leathermill La WS15 . . . .**178** F1
Leathersley La DE6,DE65 .**129** C2
Lea The ST4 . . . . **88** B7
Leaton Hall DY7 . . . .**268** B1
Lea Vale Rd DY8 . . . .**279** F3
Leawood Rd ST4 . . . . **71** E3
Lebanon Gr WS7 . . . .**228** F8
Ledbury Cl WS9 . . . .**245** C1
Ledbury Cres ST1 . . . . **57** F5
Ledstone Way ST3 . . . . . . **73** E4
Leech Ave ST5. . . . . **55** F6
Leech St ST5 . . . .**283** C1
Lee Ct WS9 . . . .**244** F3
Leedham Ave B77. . . . . . .**250** D5
Leedhams Croft DE12 . . .**202** D8
Leek Coll of F Ed & Sch of
Art ST13 . . . . **30** F7
Leek Fst Sch ST13 . . . . . . **31** A5
Leek High Sch ST13 . . . . . **31** A6
Leek La ST8 . . . . **28** B8
Leek Morlands Hospl
ST13 . . . . **31** A5
Leek New Rd ST1,ST2,ST6 . **42** F1
Leek Old Rd ST9 . . . . **29** E1
Leek Rd Brown Edge ST6. . **43** C7
Bucknall ST2 . . . . **58** A6
Cheadle ST10. . . . . **76** C5
Cheddleton ST9,ST10. . . . **60** C3
Cheddleton ST9,ST10,ST6 . **45** D7
Congleton CW12 . . . . **16** A8
Endon ST9 . . . . **43** E6
Hanley ST1 . . . . **57** E2
Longnor SK17 . . . . **13** B6
Longsdon ST2 . . . . **43** B1
Stoke-on-T ST6 . . . . **42** F4
Warslow SK17 . . . . **23** A2
Werrington ST9 . . . . **59** F3
Wetley Rocks ST9 . . . . . . **60** A6
Wetton DE6 . . . . **34** D3
Leek Road Ind Est SK17 . **23** A2
Lees Cl WS15 . . . .**197** B5
Leese La
Acton Trussell ST17 . . . .**175** B1
Moddershall ST15 . . . . . .**105** F6
Leese St ST4 . . . . **72** B7
Lees La ST10 . . . .**108** E2
Leet Ct WS15 . . . .**198** B4
Lee Wlk WS11 . . . .**210** B4
Legge La ST18 . . . .**139** D1
Legge St
Newcastle-u-L ST5. . . . . .**283** C5
Wolverhampton WV2 . . . .**266** E6
Legion Cl WS11 . . . .**228** A6
Legs La WV10 . . . .**240** F3
Leicester Cl ST5 . . . . **71** C5
Leicester Cl ST14 . . . .**110** F1
Leicester Pl ST12 . . . . **58** C2
Leicester St DE14 . . . .**185** C8
Leigh Ave WS7 . . . .**229** B7
Leigh Bank ST10 . . . .**108** F8
Leigh Cl ST17 . . . .**174** E5
Leigh La Bramshall ST14 . .**125** B8
Church Leigh ST10. . . . . .**108** C3
Lower Tean ST10 . . . . **92** F1
Stoke-on-T ST6 . . . . **41** D7
Leigh Rd Congleton CW12 . . **6** B5
Newport TF10 . . . .**168** E2
Leighs Cl WS4 . . . .**244** C1
Leighs Rd WS4 . . . .**244** C1
Leigh St ST6. . . . . **42** B2
Leighswood 1 ST17 . . . .**175** C7
Leighswood Ave WS9 . . . .**256** B7
Leighswood Cl WS11 . . . .**227** F5
Leighswood Ct WS9 . . . . .**256** B6
Leighswood Gr WS9 . . . . .**256** A7
Leighswood Ind Est
WS9 . . . .**256** A8

Leighswood Rd WS9 . . . . .**256** A6
Leighswood Sch WS9 . . . .**256** B8
Leighton Cl Dudley DY1 . . .**271** E2
Stoke-on-T ST4 . . . . **43** C4
Uttoxeter ST14 . . . .**126** C6
Leighton Rd
Uttoxeter ST14 . . . .**126** C6
Wolverhampton WV4 . . . .**265** D6
Leisure La SK17 . . . . **24** E5
Leisure Wlk 7 B77 . . . . . .**261** F6
Lema Way ST6. . . . .**156** C3
Le More B74. . . . .**258** A2
Lennox Gdns WV3 . . . . . .**266** A8
Lennox Rd ST3. . . . .**284** D1
Lenpark Ind Est ST3 . . . . .**284** C3
Lenthall Ave CW12 . . . . . . **15** F8
Leofric Cl DE13 . . . .**199** C6
Leomansley Cl WS13 . . . .**230** F7
Leomansley Ct WS13 . . . .**230** E7
Leomansley Rd WS13 . . . .**230** F7
Leomansley View WS13 . .**230** E7
Leonard Ave
Kidderminster DY10 . . . .**280** A1
Stoke-on-T ST3 . . . . **43** B3
Leonard Dr ST6. . . . . **43** B7
Leonard Rd DY8 . . . .**279** C5
Leonard St Leek ST13 . . . . **30** F5
Stoke-on-T ST6 . . . . **42** B1
Leonora St ST6 . . . . **56** F7
Leopold St ST4 . . . . **72** E7
Lerridge La ST20. . . . .**131** E6
Lerryn Cl DY6. . . . .**275** F5
Lerwick Cl DY6 . . . .**275** F5
Lesley Dr DY6 . . . .**275** E4
Leslie Rd B74. . . . .**257** B2
Lesscroft Cl WV9 . . . .**240** A3
Lessways Cl ST5 . . . . **56** A8
Lessways Wlk 1 ST6. . . . **56** F7
Lester Gr WS9 . . . .**256** E2
Letchmere Cl WV6 . . . . . .**253** C2
Letchmere La WV6 . . . . . .**253** C2
Letheridge Gdns ST17. . .**174** A8
Levedale Cl ST16. . . . .**155** A7
Levedale Rd Bradley ST18 .**191** C8
Penkridge ST18,ST19 . . . .**192** C3
Levels The WS15. . . . .**196** F5
Leven Dr WV11 . . . .**242** B1
Lever St WV2 . . . .**266** D8
Leveson Ave WS6 . . . .**226** E2
Leveson Rd Trentham ST4 . **71** F1
Wolverhampton WV11. . . .**241** F1
Leveson St ST3 . . . .**284** C2
Levett Rd Tamworth B77. .**251** B5
Whittington WS14 . . . . . .**232** C1
Levetts Fields WS14. . . . .**231** C7
Levetts Hollow WS12. . . .**210** D3
Levetts Sq 4 WS13 . . . . .**231** B7
Levington Cl WV6 . . . .**254** F5
Levita Rd ST4. . . . . **71** F4
Lewis Cl WS14 . . . .**231** E7
Lewis Dr DE13 . . . .**166** B7
Lewisham Dr ST6 . . . . **41** C7
Lewisham Rd WV10 . . . . .**240** B2
Lewis's La DE13. . . . .**199** B6
Lewis St ST4. . . . . **72** B8
Lewthorn Rise WV4 . . . . .**266** D4
Lexham Pl ST3 . . . . **73** E2
Lexington Gn ST17 . . . . . .**174** A8
Leybourne Cres WV9 . . . .**239** F2
Leycett La ST5 . . . . **54** C2
Leycett Rd ST5 . . . . **54** E4
Leyfield Rd ST4 . . . . **88** B6
Leyfields Farm Mews
DE13 . . . .**165** C7
Leyfields WS13 . . . .**214** B2
Ley Gdns ST3 . . . .**284** A2
Ley Hill Rd B75 . . . .**258** C1
Leyland Ave WV3 . . . .**255** B6
Leyland Croft WS3. . . . . .**243** F4
Leyland Dr ST5 . . . .**178** E2
Leyland Gn ST6. . . . . **42** A6
Leyland Rd B77 . . . .**250** E3
Ley Rise DY3 . . . .**266** C3
Leys Dr ST5 . . . . **70** F4
Leys La ST2. . . . . **43** C3
Leys The DE11 . . . .**186** E6
Liberty Cl WS6. . . . .**226** D3
Liberty La ST6 . . . . **42** C3
Liberty Pk ST17 . . . .**174** A8
Liberty Rd B77. . . . .**261** F5
Libra Cl B79 . . . .**249** F7
Libra Pl ST6 . . . . **41** F6
Lichen Cl WS12 . . . .**209** C6
Lichfield Bsns Ctr WS13 .**214** D1
Lichfield Cathedral Sch
WS13 . . . .**231** B8
Lichfield Cath ★ WS13 . . .**231** B8
Lichfield City Sta WS14. .**231** B7
Lichfield Cl ST5. . . . . **55** D2
Lichfield Cres B78 . . . . . .**249** B8
Lichfield Ct ST17. . . . .**285** C2
Lichfield Dr
Blymhill Lawn TF11 . . . . .**204** B1
Great Haywood ST18. . . .**158** B1
Lichfield Rd
Abbots Bromley WS15. . . .**161** B3
Armitage WS15 . . . .**198** C3
Brownhills,Shireoak Hill WS9,
WS9. . . . .**245** B5
Brownhills WS8,WS14. . . .**245** A8
Burntwood WS7. . . . .**229** D6
Burton u T DE13,DE14. . .**184** C4
Cannock WS11. . . . .**227** B8
Hamstall Ridware WS15 . .**180** F2
King's Bromley DE13. . . .**199** C6
Lichfield SW7,SW13 . . . .**230** B6
Sandon ST18 . . . .**137** D8
Stafford ST17 . . . .**285** B2

Lichfield Rd *continued*
Stafford ST17 285 C2
Stone ST15 120 C7
Sutton Coldfield B74 258 A3
Talke ST7 40 D7
Tamworth B78,B79 249 E6
Walsall,Highbridge WS3 244 B5
Walsall,New Invention WS3,WS4, WS8,WS9 242 E1
Walsall,Shelfield WS4 244 C1
Walsall,Wallington Heath WS3 243 C2
Lichfield Road Ind Est B79 249 E6
Lichfield St
Burton u T DE14 166 D2
Fazeley B78 249 F1
Hanley ST1 282 C1
Rugeley WS15 196 F8
Stone ST15 120 A8
Tamworth B79 250 A5
Lichfield Trent Valley Sta WS13 231 F8
Liddiard Ct DY8 279 E6
Liddle St ST4 72 A6
Lidgate Gr ST3 72 F2
Lidgate Wlk ST5 71 B2
Lid La Cheadle ST10 76 C3
Roston DE6 96 E7
Liffs Rd DE6,SK17 36 C7
Lifton Croft DY6 275 F5
Light Ash Cl WV9 224 C3
Light Ash WV9 224 C3
Light Ash La WV9 224 C3
Lightfoot Rd ST14 110 F1
Light Oaks Ave ST2 43 D1
Light Oaks Cl DE14 166 E6
Lightoaks ST10 77 F5
Lightwater Gr ST2 42 F1
Lightwood Rd
Longton ST3 284 C2
Newcastle-u-L ST5 40 D1
Stoke-on-T ST3 89 F6
Yoxall DE13 181 F2
Lilac Ave WS11 226 D7
Lilac Cl
Great Bridgeford ST18 135 C2
Meir ST3 74 C5
Newcastle-u-L ST5 40 D1
Uttoxeter ST14 126 B6
Lilac Dr WV5 269 F6
Lilac Gr Burntwood WS7 228 F7
Burton u T DE15 185 F6
Stafford ST17 174 F7
Stoke-on-T ST3 72 E3
Lilac Ho WS4 244 D1
Lilac La WS6 243 A8
Lilac Rd B79 250 A8
Lilleshall Cres WV2 266 D7
Lilleshall Hall National Sports Ctr TF10 187 A2
Lilleshall Rd ST5 71 D5
Lilleshall St ST3 284 C2
Lilleshall Way ST17 174 B7
Lillington Cl 2 WS13 231 A8
Lillydale Rd ST2 58 B3
Lily St ST5 56 D5
Limbrick Rd ST7 39 A1
Lime Cl Church Leigh ST10 109 A4
Doveridge DE6 127 B8
Great Wyrley WS6 226 F4
Meir ST3 74 C5
Lime Ct Burton u T DE15 185 E7
Market Drayton TF9 97 D1
Limedale Ct 8 ST15 104 F1
Lime Gr Barlaston ST12 88 F4
Burntwood WS7 229 C6
Burton u T DE15 185 E5
Kinver DY7 278 C3
Lichfield WS14 231 D8
Waterhouses ST10 48 F3
Limeheath Pl ST6 41 E5
Limehurst Ave WV3 255 C1
Lime Kiln La Alton ST10 78 E1
Kidsgrove ST7 25 E2
Lime La
Norton Canes WS3 228 A1
Walsall WS3 244 A7
Limepit La WS11,WS12 209 D6
Lime Rd Huntington WS12 209 D8
Sedgley DY3 266 F1
Limes Ave ST9 30 A1
Limes Ct Stoke-on-T ST4 71 E8
Wolverhampton WV6 255 D5
Limes Rd WV6 255 D4
Limes The
Albrighton WV7 237 A4
Himley DY3 270 B3
Newcastle-u-L ST5 56 C7
Lime St Stoke-on-T ST4 72 B6
Wolverhampton WV3 266 B8
Limes View DY3 271 D7
Limetree Ave ST16 155 D5
Lime Tree Ave WV6 255 A3
Lime Tree Gdns WV8 239 B3
Limetree Rd B74 256 D1
Lime Tree Rd WV8 239 B4
Lime Wlk ST19 207 E8
Limewood Cl ST11 91 A6
Linacre Rd ST21 133 E6
Linacre Way ST3 73 E5
Lincoln Ave
Newcastle-u-L ST5 71 C5
Tamworth B79 249 E6
Lincoln Cl WS13 214 C3
Lincoln Croft WS14 246 F6
Lincoln Ct ST14 110 F1
Lincoln Dr WS11 226 F8
Lincoln Gn WV10 240 D2
Lincoln Gr ST5 71 C5
Lincoln Mdw ST17 174 A8
Lincoln Rd Burslem ST6 57 A7
Burton u T DE15 185 D7
Kidsgrove ST7 25 F2
Lincoln St ST1 282 C2
Lindale Cl CW12 6 A5
Lindale Dr WV5 269 F6
Lindale Gr 3 ST3 90 B7
Linda Rd ST6 41 E5
Linden Ave WS7 229 A8
Lindenbrook Vale ST17 175 C7
Linden Cl Congleton CW12 16 A8
Newcastle-u-L ST5 56 B3
Stafford ST17 174 B8
Tamworth B77 250 F4
Linden Dr ST8 16 C1
Linden Gr Biddulph ST8 16 C1
Newcastle-u-L ST5 56 B3
Linden Lea WV3 255 D1
Linden Pl ST3 72 F1
Linden Rd DE13 183 D1
Lindens The Stone ST15 120 B5
Wolverhampton WV6 255 E3
Linden View WS12 210 B4
Linden Way TF9 97 D2
Lindera B77 251 A4
Lindisfarne B77 250 D3
Lindley Pl ST3 90 A4
Lindley St ST6 57 B7
Lindon Cl WS8 245 A6
Lindon Dr WS8 244 F7
Lindon Rd WS8 244 F5
Lindon View WS8 245 A5
Lindop Ct ST1 282 C3
Lindops La CW3 68 F7
Lindop St ST1 282 C3
Lindrick Cl WS3 242 F3
Lindrosa Rd B74 256 F3
Lindsay St ST1 282 A2
Lindum Ave ST4 88 C7
Line Houses Cvn Site ST6 41 A6
Lineker Cl ST16 155 B3
Linet Gr ST7 26 E1
Linfield Gdns DY3 266 C1
Linfield Rd ST1 282 C3
Linford Cl WS15 198 C4
Lingard St ST6 57 A8
Lingfield Ave
Stoke-on-T ST6 43 A8
Wolverhampton WV10 240 D5
Lingfield Cl WS6 226 F2
Lingfield Dr WS6 226 F2
Lingfield Gr WV6 254 F4
Lingfield Rd
Burton u T DE14 184 F7
Norton Canes WS11 228 A5
Lingmoor Gr WS9 256 A7
Ling Rd WS12 209 C5
Linhope Gr 1 ST3 90 B7
Linkend Cl ST1 57 F5
Link Rd Brownhills WS9 245 B3
Wombourne WV5 270 A7
Links Ave
Newcastle-u-L ST5 56 B4
Wolverhampton WV6 255 D7
Links Dr DY8 279 E2
Linksfield Gr ST16 155 D8
Links Rd WV4 266 A3
Links Side Way WS9 256 C8
Links View B74 257 B1
Linksway Cl CW12 15 F8
Linksway CW12 15 E8
Linkway Ret Pk WS11 226 B6
Linkwood Ind Est DY8 279 F6
Linley Dr WV10 240 E1
Linley Gr Dudley DY3 271 B2
Lawton-gate ST7 25 A3
Linley La ST7 25 A2
Linley Rd Lawton-gate ST7 25 A2
Stoke-on-T ST4 71 E8
Talke ST7 40 C8
Linley Trad Est
Kidsgrove ST7 25 C1
Talke ST7 40 C8
Linnburn Rd ST3 73 E4
Linnet Cl WS12 209 D7
Linnet Way ST8 27 E8
Linslade Cl WV4 266 D4
Lintake Dr WS15 160 F6
Linthouse Wlk 3 B77 261 F6
Lintly B77 251 B1
Linton Rd WV4 265 E5
Linwood Dr WS12 209 F7
Linwood Way ST6 41 E5
Lionel Gr ST4 71 E6
Lionfields Cl DY10 280 A5
Lionfields Rd DY10 280 B5
Lion Gr ST5 55 E8
Lion Ind Est WS9 256 A8
Lion Pas DY8 279 F5
Lion's Den WS7,WS14 229 E2
Lion St Rugeley WS15 178 E1
Stoke-on-T ST4 72 A7
Stourbridge DY8 279 F5
Lion Way ST17 175 A8
Lisbon Pl ST5 70 F7
Liskeard Cl ST2 58 A1
Lister Gr ST11 90 D3
Lister Rd ST16 155 F5
Litley Dr ST10 92 D8
Little Aston Hall Dr B74 257 B5
Little Aston Hall B74 257 B5
Little Aston Hospl B74 257 B5
Little Aston La B74 257 D6
Little Aston Park Rd B74 257 A3
Little Aston Prim Sch B74 257 C6
Little Aston Rd WS9 256 D6
Little Barrow Wlk 3 WS13 214 A1
Little Birches WV3 265 F8
Little Bloxwich CE Prim Sch WS3 243 D3
Little Burton E DE14 166 D4
Little Burton W DE14 166 D4
Little Checkhill La DY7 274 D4
Little Chell La ST6 41 F5
Little Church La B79 250 B5
Little Cliffe Rd ST3 72 E4
Little Comm WS3 244 A4
Littlecote B79 249 D7
Little Eaves La ST2 58 C6
Littlefield La Ellastone DE6 80 A2
Snelston DE6 81 B4
Little-Field ST4 71 E4
Little Grange WS13 213 F1
Littlehales Rd TF10 187 A6
Little Hardwick Rd WS9 256 D2
Little Hay La WS14 247 C3
Little Johnson's La WS9 256 B1
Little Lakes CW2 37 D2
Little La ST3 89 F4
Little Lawns Cl WS9 245 A4
Little Marsh Gr ST19 192 F1
Little Marsh Pk ST19 193 A1
Little Moss Cl ST7 25 E5
Little Moss La ST7 25 E5
Little Oaks Dr DY7 275 A2
Little Onn Rd ST20 190 A7
Little Orch WS15 178 E2
Little Pipe La
Creswell Green WS13 212 F1
Lichfield WS13 213 A1
Little Pountney St 4 WV2 266 C8
Little Rd ST10 75 E2
Little Row
5 Kidsgrove ST7 26 B2
Stoke-on-T ST4 72 F8
Little Sutton La B75 258 C1
Little Sutton Prim Sch B75 258 D3
Little Sutton Rd B75 258 D2
Little Tixall La ST18 158 C2
Littleton Bsns Pk WS12 209 C7
Littleton Cl ST16 156 A3
Littleton Cres ST19 192 F1
Littleton Dr WS12 209 C7
Littleton Way WS7 211 D1
Littlewood La WS6 226 E4
Littlewood Rd WS6 226 E4
Littleworth Hill WS12 210 D4
Littleworth Rd WS12 210 E4
Littondale Cl CW12 6 A5
Litton B77 251 C1
Littywood La ST18 173 C2
Liverpool Rd E ST7 25 E2
Liverpool Rd
Kidsgrove ST7 26 A1
Newcastle-u-L,Cross Heath ST5 56 A3
Newcastle-u-L,Red Street ST5 40 D2
Newcastle-u-L ST5 283 B3
Stoke-on-T ST4 72 B7
Liverpool Rd W ST7 25 B4
Livingstone Ave WV6 254 E5
Livingstone Rd WS3 243 E2
Livingstone St Leek ST13 30 F5
Stoke-on-T ST6 42 C2
Lizard La TF11 220 A6
Llewellyn Roberts Way TF9 97 D2
Lloyd Dr WV4 265 C2
Lloyd George Gr WS11 210 C2
Lloyd Hill WV4 265 C3
Lloyd Rd WV6 255 D5
Lloyd Roberts Bldgs WV4 265 F1
Lloyd St Cannock WS11 209 D1
Longton ST3 284 C2
Stafford ST16 285 B4
Wolverhampton WV6 255 F4
Lloyd The TF9 113 F7
Lochalsh Gr WV11 242 B1
Lochsong Cl B77 261 D4
Lockerbie Cl ST13 31 B5
Locketts Ct WS11 209 F5
Locketts La ST3 284 D2
Lockett St ST1 57 D6
Locke Way ST16 156 B3
Lockfield Cl DY8 275 F2
Lockhart Dr B75 258 C1
Lockington Ave ST2 58 D1
Lock Keepers Cl WS11 227 F4
Lockley St ST1 57 E5
Lock Rd ST19 207 F8
Lockside Dr DY7 278 B4
Lockside View WS15 196 F8
Lockside WV5 269 E7
Locks View DY8 275 E1
Lockwood Cl ST10 62 A1
Lockwood Rd ST10 77 B6
Lockwood St
Newcastle-u-L ST5 283 D3
Stoke-on-T ST2 43 B3
Lode La DE6 35 F4
Lodge Barn Rd ST8 27 F6
Lodgefield Mobile Home Pk ST17 156 D2
Lodge Gr Aldridge WS9 256 A5
Newcastle-u-L ST5 56 C6
Lodge Hill DE13 146 E3
Lodge La
Cheslyn Hay WS11 226 C5
Chorley WS15 212 D3
Fairoak ST21 115 F5
Hope DE6 35 B3
Ilam DE6 50 D3
Kingswinford DY6 275 B6
Woodseaves ST20 151 E6
Yoxall DE13 182 B8
Lodge Pk WV5 267 C7
Lodge Rd Burntwood WS7 211 F1
Netherseal DE12 219 E8
Rugeley WS15 197 A6
Stoke-on-T ST4 71 E7
Talke Pits ST7 40 D6
Walsall WS4 244 B1
Lodges TF11 203 F2
Lodge View WS6 226 C3
Loftus Ct WS7 229 A5
Loftus St ST1 282 A4
Loganbeck Gr ST3 73 E5
Lohengrin Ct DE13 147 E2
Lomas St ST4 57 A2
Lomax Cl WS13 214 A1
Lomax Rd WS12 210 B7
Lombard Gdns 1 WS13 231 B8
Lombard St WS13 231 B8
Lombardy Gr
Burntwood WS7 228 F8
Meir ST3 74 A2
Lomita Cres B77 261 D8
Lomond Cl B79 249 F8
Lomond Gr ST10 76 F5
Lomond Rd DY3 266 C1
Lomond Wlk ST3 88 F7
London Rd
Bridgemere CW5 67 A5
Knighton CW3,TF9 83 C6
Lichfield WS14 231 C5
Newcastle-u-L,Chesterton ST5 55 E7
Newcastle-u-L,City General Hospl ST5 283 C1
Shenstone B75,WS14 258 F7
Stoke-on-T ST4 72 A6
Sutton Coldfield B75 259 A4
Weeford WS14 247 F3
Weston ST18 138 D2
London St ST13 30 F5
Long Acre WV8 238 F2
Longacres Cannock WS12 210 F5
Little Aston B74 257 C4
Longboat La DY8 275 E1
Longbow Cl DE13 147 C1
Longbow Gr DE13 147 C1
Longbridge Hayes Rd ST5 56 C8
Long Bridge Rd WS14 231 C5
Longbrook Ave ST3 72 F2
Longclough Rd ST5 40 D2
Long Croft
Albrighton WV7 237 B5
Cannock WS12 209 C4
Longcroft La DE13 182 B4
Longdoles Ave ST3 73 F3
Longdon Ave WV4 266 D5
Longdon Dr B74 257 E4
Longfellow Cl DE14 166 D7
Longfellow Pl WS11 209 E4
Longfellow Rd
Burntwood WS7 212 A1
Dudley DY3 271 B5
Longfellow Wlk B79 249 F8
Longfield Ave ST15 119 F7
Longfield Cl B77 250 E4
Longfield Dr B74 257 D4
Longfield Rd ST4 71 E8
Longford Cl
Burton u T DE15 167 B2
Wombourne WV5 269 D5
Longford Ct WS11 226 B8
Longford Gn WS11 226 C7
Longford Ind Est WS11 226 D6
Longford Pk TF10 168 B1
Longford Prim Sch WS11 226 C8
Longford Rd
Cannock WS11 226 D7
Newport TF10 168 C2
Longford Wlk ST2 58 A2
Long Furrow WV8 239 E1
Longhedge La DE13 146 F1
Longhope Dr ST15 119 F6
Longhurst Dr ST16 156 C4
Long La Alrewas WS13 200 E1
Derrington ST18 154 C2
Great Wyrley WS6 242 E6
Harriseahead ST7 26 E4
Longlake Ave WV6 255 B3
Longlands Dr B77 250 F4
Longlands La TF9 97 D1
Longlands Pl WS15 160 F6
Longlands Prim Sch TF9 97 D2
Longlands The WV5 270 A6
Long La DE6 35 B5
Longleat Dr DY1 271 E2
Longleat Rd WS9 245 A1
Longleat B79 249 D7
Longley Rd ST3 73 C5
Long Mdw
Newcastle-u-L ST5 71 C3
Stafford ST17 174 E5
Long Meadow Dr DY3 266 B2
Longmead Rd DE13 166 C6
Longmoor Ho B74 257 F2
Long Mynd Cl WV11 242 B1
Longnor Craft Ctr★ SK17 13 B6
Longnor Pl ST2 58 A2
Longport Rd ST6 56 D7
Longport Sta ST6 56 D7
Long Row Caverswall ST11 74 D3
Kidsgrove ST7 26 A1
Longsdon Cl ST5 40 C1
Longsdon Gr ST3 73 E4
Longshaw Ave ST5 56 B7
Longshaw La Alton ST10 78 E5
Oakamoor ST10 78 E7
Longshaw St ST6 56 D8
Longshore Cl ST18 174 C6
Longslow Cl TF9 97 B1
Longslow Rd TF9 97 A1
Longstaff Ave WS12 211 C4
Longstaff Croft WS13 213 F2
Long St Burton u T DE15 185 E7
Wheaton Aston ST19 205 C6
Longton Exchange ST3 284 C3
Longton Hall Rd ST3 72 F2
Longton High Sch ST3 73 F2
Longton Hospl ST3 73 D1
Longton Rd Barlaston ST12 88 F2
Oulton ST15 105 D4
Stoke-on-T ST4 88 B6
Longton Sta ST3 284 B4
Longus Ind Est ST6 41 D4
Long Valley Rd ST8 16 C2
Longview Cl ST3 73 D5
Longwood Path B78 249 D1
Longwood Prim Sch B78 249 D1
Longwood Rd WS9 256 B2
Lonsdale CE Prim Sch ST21 133 D6
Lonsdale Ct
Eccleshall ST21 133 D7
Market Drayton TF9 97 D1
Lonsdale Rd
Burton u T DE14 185 B8
Wolverhampton WV3 266 B7
Lonsdale St ST4 72 B6
Loomer Rd ST5 55 E6
Loomer Road Ind Est ST5 55 E5
Loop Rd ST15 118 C7
Lord Cromwell Ct WS11 210 A5
Lords Cl ST4 88 D7
Lordship La ST4 72 D7
Lordshire Pl ST7 26 F2
Lords La DY7 274 E1
Lordsley La TF9 100 A7
Lord St Biddulph ST8 27 D7
Stoke-on-T ST6 42 C1
Lordswell Rd DE14 165 F4
Lordswood Rd ST4 88 D7
Lorien Cl ST13 30 C4
Lorien Ct ST4 72 A8
Loring Rd ST5 56 B6
Loring Terr S ST5 56 C6
Lorne St Burntwood WS7 228 E8
Stoke-on-T ST6 42 A1
Lorraine St ST7 26 F1
Lorton B79 249 D7
Lothersdale B77 262 C8
Lothians Rd Walsall WS3 244 A5
Wolverhampton WV6 255 E6
Lotus Ave ST8 27 B6
Lotus Ct ST15 105 A2
Lotus Dr WS11 209 E5
Lotus B77 250 E3
Lotus Way ST16 155 F5
Loughborough Wlk ST3 284 C4
Loughshaw B77 251 C1
Louise Dr ST3 72 F3
Louise St Dudley DY3 271 C3
Stoke-on-T ST6 42 A2
Lount La DE13 146 E1
Louvain Ave ST1 57 D7
Lovage Gr ST2 58 A3
Lovatt Ave ST5 56 A4
Lovatt Cl DE13 147 F2
Lovatt Pl WS11 209 E5
Lovatt St Stafford ST16 155 D5
Stoke-on-T ST4 72 B7
Lovelace Cl ST17 174 C8
Love La Great Wyrley WS6 227 B3
Rugeley WS15 178 F1
Wolverhampton WV6 255 D6
Lovell Dr ST16 156 B5
Lovell Rd DE13 182 A2
Lovell B79 249 F6
Loveridge Cl WV8 238 F3
Lovers La TF9 99 F4
Loveston Gr ST3 284 D4
Lovett Ct WS15 178 D2
Lowdham B77 251 C1
Lowe Dr DY6 275 E4
Lowell Dr ST3 73 F4
Lower Ash Rd ST7 25 E1
Lower Bar TF10 168 E3
Lower Bedford St ST4 57 A2
Lower Bethesda St ST1 282 B2
Lower Birches Way WS15 196 D7
Lower Brook St WS15 178 E1
Lower Bryan St ST1 282 B4
Lower Cres ST4 71 E8
Lowercroft Way B74 257 E6
Lower Cross St ST3 284 C4
Lower Farm Prim Sch WS3 243 C3
Lower Farm WS9 245 E4
Lower Foundry St ST1 282 B3
Lower Gn WV6 255 E5
Lower Gungate B79 250 B5
Lower Hadderidge 13 ST6 56 F8

Lower High St
Mow Cop ST7. . . . . 26 D7
Stourbridge DY8 . . . . 279 F6
Tutbury DE13. . . . . 146 C7
Lower House La CV9 . . . . . 262 F2
Lower Keys Bsns Pk
WS12 . . . . 210 D3
Lower La Chorley WS13. . . 212 D3
Hopton ST18. . . . . 156 D8
Lower Lodge Residential
Mobile Home Pk WS15 197 E5
Lower Mayer St ST1. . . . . 282 C4
Lower Milehouse La ST5. 55 F3
Lower Outwoods Rd
DE13. . . . . 165 F4
Lower Oxford Rd ST5. . . . . 56 E2
Lowerpark B77. . . . . 250 C1
Lower Penkridge Rd
ST17. . . . . 175 B1
Lower Rd Ashley TF9. . . . . 100 B4
Cannock WS12. . . . . 210 C3
Gnosall ST20. . . . . 152 B5
Lower Rookery Rd ST15. 118 C6
Lower Sandford St
WS13. . . . . 231 A7
Lower Spring Rd ST3. . 73 D2
Lower St 1 Burslem ST6. . 57 A7
Doveridge DE6. . . . . 127 B8
Newcastle-u-L ST5. . . . . . 283 B3
Wolverhampton WV4. . . . 255 E5
Lower Villiers St WV2. . 266 C7
Lower Way WS15. . . . . 197 C1
Lowe St ST4. . . . . 72 B7
Loweswater Dr DY3. . . . . 271 D3
Lowfield St ST5. . . . . 56 E5
Lowfield La ST20. . . . . 171 E5
Lowforce B77. . . . . 251 C1
Lowhurst Dr ST6. . . . . 42 A7
Lowland Rd WS12. . . . . . . 209 C5
Lowlands Ave WV6. . . . . . 255 E6
Lowlands Ct WV6. . . . . . . 255 E6
Lowlands Rd ST6. . . . . 41 B4
Lowndes Cl ST4. . . . . 71 F6
Lowndes Rd DY8. . . . . 279 E6
Lowry Cl WV6. . . . . 254 F4
Low St WS6. . . . . 226 D3
Lowther Pl ST13. . . . . 31 A5
Lowther St ST1. . . . . 282 A4
Lowthorpe Way ST4. . . . . . 58 E1
Loxley Hall Sch ST14. . . . 125 C5
Loxley La ST14. . . . . 125 C5
Loxley Pl ST3. . . . . 89 F7
Loxley Rd B75. . . . . 258 D3
Loxton Cl B74. . . . . 257 D5
Loynton Cl ST16. . . . . 155 B7
Loynton Sands ST20. . . . . 151 A5
Lucas St ST6. . . . . 56 E8
Lucepool La DE13. . . . . . . 182 D3
Lucerne Pl ST5. . . . . 70 E7
Ludbrook Rd ST4. . . . . 73 B5
Ludford Cl ST5. . . . . 40 D2
Ludgate St DE13. . . . . 146 C6
Ludgate B79. . . . . 250 A5
Ludgrove Way ST17. . . . . 175 B8
Lud La B79. . . . . 250 A5
Ludlow Cl WS11. . . . . 210 C2
Ludlow St ST1. . . . . 282 C3
Ludlow Way DY1. . . . . 271 E2
Ludstone Ave WV4. . . . . . 265 D5
Ludwall Rd ST3. . . . . 73 E1
Lugano Cl ST5. . . . . 70 F6
Lukesland Ave ST4. . . . . . . 71 E6
Luke St ST6. . . . . 56 E7
Lukes Wlk WS13. . . . . 214 A2
Lullington Rd
Clifton Campville B79 . . . . 218 E3
Edingale B79. . . . . 217 D5
Lulworth Gr ST6. . . . . 41 E6
Lulworth Rd WS7. . . . . . . 229 A7
Lulworth Wlk WV4. . . . . . 265 C6
Lundy Cl ST3. . . . . 72 F3
Lune Cl 1 CW12. . . . . 6 A1
Lunns Croft WS13. . . . . . . 231 C8
Lunts Moss ST7. . . . . 25 C7
Lutley Cl WV3. . . . . 265 E7
Lutley La DY7. . . . . 273 B8
Luttrell Rd B74. . . . . 258 A1
Lychgate Cl ST4. . . . . 72 A5
Lydford Pl ST3. . . . . 73 F3
Lydford Rd WS3. . . . . 243 B3
Lydgate Rd DY6. . . . . 275 F6
Lydia Croft B74. . . . . 257 E6
Lydia Dr ST1. . . . . 57 F6
Lydiates Cl DY3. . . . . 271 B7
Lyme Brook Pl ST4. . . . . . . 71 E3
Lyme Ct ST5. . . . . 283 C1
Lymedale Small Firms Ctr
ST5. 55 F5
Lyme Dr ST4. . . . . 71 D5
Lyme Gr ST5. . . . . 56 C3
Lyme Gr ST3. . . . . 74 B1
Lymer Rd WV10. . . . . 240 C1
Lymer's La ST18. . . . . 123 A1
Lymes Rd ST5. . . . . 70 B4
Lymevale Rd ST4. . . . . 71 E4
Lyme Valley Rd ST5. . . . . 283 C1
Lymewood Cl ST5. . . . . . . 283 B2
Lyme Wood Gr ST5. . . . . 283 B1
Lymington Rd
Burntwood WS7. . . . . 211 F1
Stafford ST16. . . . . 156 C4
Lyminster Gr ST2. . . . . 43 B1
Lymsey Croft DY8. . . . . . . 275 C3
Lynam St ST4. . . . . 72 A7
Lynam Way CW3. . . . . 68 E7

Lyn Ave WS13. . . . . 213 F1
Lynch The B78. . . . . 251 F1
Lyncroft WV7. . . . . 237 A5
Lyndale Rd DY3. . . . . 266 B2
Lyndale B77. . . . . 261 F6
Lyndham Ave DE15. . . . . 166 F1
Lyndhurst Dr Biddulph ST8. 27 A6
Stourbridge DY8. . . . . 275 F1
Lyndhurst Gr ST15. . . . . . 120 D6
Lyndhurst Rd
Cannock WS12. . . . . 210 E1
Wolverhampton WV3. . . . 266 A7
Lyndhurst St ST6. . . . . 56 E8
Lyndon Cl DY3. . . . . 266 E1
Lyndon Gr DY6. . . . . 275 B8
Lyne Ct DE14. . . . . 166 A3
Lyneham Cl B79. . . . . 250 C8
Lynehill La ST17. . . . . 207 E6
Lyneside Rd ST8. . . . . 27 B5
Lynfield Rd WS13. . . . . . . 213 F1
Lynmouth Cl
Aldridge WS9. . . . . 256 A5
Biddulph ST8 . . . . 27 C6
Lynmouth Gr ST6. . . . . 41 F7
Lynn Ave ST7. . . . . 40 C8
Lynn La WS14. . . . . 246 D6
Lynn St ST3. . . . . 74 B5
Lynsey Cl ST7. . . . . 54 E7
Lynton Ave Stafford ST17 175 D8
Wolverhampton WV6. . . . 255 F6
Lynton Gr ST3. . . . . 89 E8
Lynton Rd ST5. . . . . 70 F5
Lynwood Ave DY6. . . . . . 275 B7
Lynwood Cl
Burton u T DE14. . . . . 184 F7
Walsall WV12. . . . . 242 E1
Lynwood Dr DY10. . . . . . 281 C2
Lynwood Rd DE14. . . . . . 184 E8
Lyric Cl ST17. . . . . 174 F6
Lysander Rd ST3. . . . . 90 B7
Lysander Way WS11. . . . . 209 E3
Lysways ST13,WS15 . . . . 213 C8
Lytham Cl DY8. . . . . 279 F2
Lytham Dr ST16. . . . . 156 C3
Lytham Gr WS3. . . . . 243 F4
Lytham Rd WV6. . . . . 254 D4
Lytham B77. . . . . 251 C5
Lyttelton Rd DY8. . . . . . . 279 D5
Lytton Ave WV4. . . . . 265 E4
Lytton St ST4. . . . . 72 C7

M

Macadam Cl WS7 . . . . . . 229 B8
McAdam Cl DE15 . . . . . . 167 B2
McBean Rd WV6 . . . . 255 F4
Macbeth Ho ST7 . . . . 40 C8
Macclesfield Rd
Congleton CW12 . . . . 6 A8
Leek ST13 . . . . 30 C1
Macclesfield St ST6 . . . . . . 42 B1
Macdonald Cres ST3 . . . . . 74 A3
Mace St ST4 . . . . 71 F4
McGeough Wlk WS11 . . . 210 B5
McGhie St WS11 . . . . 210 B6
McGough St 8 ST6 . . . . . . 41 D3
McGowan Ho ST7 . . . . 40 D8
Macgregor Cres B77 . . . . 250 F3
Macgregor Tithe B79 . . . 250 B5
Machin Cres ST5 . . . . 56 B7
Machin St ST6 . . . . 41 E4
Macintyre St ST6 . . . . 57 A7
Mackay Rd WS3 . . . . 243 D2
McKellin Cl ST7 . . . . 39 E2
Mackenzie Cres ST10 . . . . 76 E1
McKie Way WS15 . . . . . . 196 F6
McKinley St ST6 . . . . 41 D3
Maclagan St ST4 . . . . 72 B6
McLean Rd WV10 . . . . . . 240 C1
Macrome Rd WV6 . . . . . . 255 E8
Madden Cl WS15 . . . . 196 F6
Maddocke Wlk 4 WS13 . 230 F6
Maddock St Audley ST7 . . 39 D1
Burslem ST6 . . . . 56 E7
Madeira Ave WV8 . . . . . . 239 A2
Madeira Ct DY8 . . . . 275 F1
Madeira Pl ST5 . . . . 41 D3
Madeley High Sch CW3 . . 68 E6
Madeley Rd 5 DY6 . . . . . 275 F4
Madeley St N ST5 . . . . 55 B2
Madeley St
Newcastle-u-L ST5. . . . . . 55 B1
Stoke-on-T ST6 . . . . 41 D4
Madford Ret Pk ST16 . . . 285 A4
Madison St ST6 . . . . 41 D4
Madox Rd ST8 . . . . 249 E8
Madras Rd DE15 . . . . 167 C3
Madrona B77 . . . . 251 B4
Maer La TF9 . . . . 97 D2
Maer Lane Ind Est TF9 . . . 97 D2
Maer La ST21. . . . . 101 E5
Maerway La ST5 . . . . 84 C5
Mafeking St ST3 . . . . 284 B2
Magazine La ST19. . . . . . 205 C7
Magdalen Rd ST3 . . . . 88 E8
Magdalen Wlk ST3 . . . . . . 88 E7
Magenta Dr ST5 . . . . 55 C2
Magna Cl WS6 . . . . 226 C3
Magnolia Cl ST18 . . . . . . 135 B2
Magnolia Dr ST6 . . . . 42 F2
Magnolia Gr WV8 . . . . . . 239 B3
Magnolia B77 . . . . 251 A4
Magnolia Way 1 DY8 . . . 275 F1
Magnus St ST6 . . . . 56 F7
Magnus B77 . . . . 261 E6
Magpie Cres 9 ST7. . . . . . 26 B2

Mahogany Dr ST16. . . . . 155 C4
Maidendale Rd DY6 . . . . 275 B7
Maidensbridge Dr DY6 . . 275 C8
Maidensbridge Gdns
DY6 . . . . 270 B1
Maidensbridge Prim Sch
DY6. . . . . 270 B1
Maidensbridge Rd DY6. . 270 B1
Maidstone Dr
Burntwood WS7. . . . . 229 D6
Stourbridge DY8. . . . . 275 E3
Maidstone Gr ST2. . . . . 58 C2
Main Rd Adbaston ST21. . 131 D6
Anslow DE13. . . . . 165 C7
Armitage WS15 . . . . 197 C4
Betley CW3. . . . . 53 A5
Main Rd Brereton WS15. 197 A6
Main Rd Cauldon Lowe ST10 63 E4
Coldmeece ST15 . . . . 118 B7
Colwich ST18. . . . . 177 D7
Draycott in t C DE6 . . . . . 144 D7
Edingale B79. . . . . 217 D5
Harlaston B79. . . . . 217 D3
Harlaston B79. . . . . 217 E3
Mayfield DE6 . . . . 81 D8
Newton Regis B79. . . . . . 236 C2
Norton in H TF9 . . . . 82 C1
Stafford ST17. . . . . 176 B7
Sudbury,Aston Heath DE6 . 129 A4
Sudbury DE6. . . . . 128 E5
Tamworth B79. . . . . 250 B8
Weston CW2. . . . . 37 C6
Wetley Rocks ST9 . . . . . . 60 B7
Wigginton B79. . . . . 234 B2
Main Road Brereton
WS15. . . . . 197 A6
Main St Alrewas DE13 . . . 201 A3
Barton-in-N DE13 . . . . . . 183 C2
Burton u T DE14. . . . . 184 F7
Burton u T,Stapenhill DE15 185 E8
Clifton Campville B79 . . . 218 F3
Egginton DE65 . . . . 148 B5
Meir ST3. . . . . 74 B5
Netherseal DE12 . . . . 219 F7
Newton Solney DE15. . . . 167 E8
Shenstone WS14 . . . . 246 F6
Stonnall WS9 . . . . 245 D4
Stretton DE13 . . . . 147 E1
Swadlincote DE12 . . . . . . 186 E6
Tatenhill DE13. . . . . 183 B1
Walton-on-T DE12 . . . . . 184 D1
Whittington WS14 . . . . . . 232 E5
Yoxall DE13 . . . . 182 A2
Mainwaring Dr B75 . . . . . 258 E2
Maitland Gr ST4 . . . . 88 B6
Maitland Rd DY1. . . . . . . 271 E1
Maitland B77. . . . . 250 F2
Majors Barn ST10 . . . . 76 C2
Major St WV2. . . . . 266 F7
Maker La DE13. . . . . 162 D2
Malam St ST1. . . . . 282 B4
Malcolm Cl ST2. . . . . 43 B2
Malcolm Ct ST5. . . . . 58 C5
Malcolm Dr ST2. . . . . 58 C5
Malcolm Rd ST17. . . . . . . 174 D6
Maldale B77. . . . . 251 C1
Malhamdale Rd CW12 . . . . 6 A5
Malham Rd
Newcastle-u-L ST5. . . . . . 55 E2
Tamworth B79. . . . . 262 C8
Malins Rd WV4. . . . . 266 E5
Malkin Way ST6. . . . . 56 E6
Mallard Ave ST17. . . . . . . 175 A7
Mallard Cl Uttoxeter ST14. 126 C6
Walsall WS3 . . . . 244 A5
Mallard Croft 5 WS13 . . 231 C8
Mallard Way
Penkridge ST19. . . . . 208 A6
Stoke-on-T ST6 . . . . 42 D3
Mallens Croft ST14 . . . . . 125 C7
Mallicot Cl WS13 . . . . . . 214 D1
Mallorie Rd ST6. . . . . 42 D4
Mallory Cl ST15. . . . . 120 B6
Mallory Cres WS3 . . . . . . 243 D2
Mallory Rd WV6. . . . . 254 E3
Mallory Way ST10. . . . . . . 76 F3
Mallow Cl ST21. . . . . 133 E5
Mallow B74. . . . . 251 C1
Mallowdale Cl ST4. . . . . . . 88 C6
Malloy Ho ST13. . . . . 45 D7
Malpass Gdns WV8. . . . . 238 E4
Malpas Wlk ST6. . . . . 41 C7
Malstone Ave ST2. . . . . . . 43 C2
Malthouse La
Barlaston ST12 . . . . 88 F2
Bradley ST18. . . . . 173 C1
Caverswall ST11 . . . . 74 C8
Malt House La
Church Eaton ST20 . . . . . 190 A7
Shareshill WV10 . . . . 225 C6
Malthouse La
Wheaton Aston ST19. . . . 205 C6
Wolverhampton WV6. . . . 255 E6
Malthouse Rd Alton ST10. 78 E1
Bucknall ST2 . . . . 58 B3
Malt House Rd WS15. . . . 212 B5
Malt Houses WV10 . . . . . 225 D6
Malthouse The DE14 . . . . 166 E3
Maltings Ind Est DE14. . . 166 E6
Maltings The
Aldridge WS9. . . . . 256 C6
Burton u T,Stapenhill DE15 167 A1
Burton u T,Wetmore DE14. 166 E5
Coven WV9 . . . . 224 B2
Uttoxeter ST14 . . . . 126 C8
Malton Gr ST6 . . . . 41 D5

Malvern Ave
Burton u T DE15. . . . . 167 A1
Newcastle-u-L ST5. . . . . . . 54 F2
Malvern Cl Stafford ST17 . 156 B1
Stoke-on-T ST4 . . . . 88 A7
Malvern Ct B74. . . . . 257 F2
Malvern Dr Aldridge WS9 . 256 C8
Rugeley WS15. . . . . 178 C2
Malvern St DE15 . . . . 166 F1
Malvern View Rd DY3 . . . 271 D4
Mamble Rd DY8. . . . . 279 E5
Manchester Ct ST14. . . . . 110 F1
Mancroft Cl DY6 . . . . 275 B7
Mancroft Gdns WV6. . . . 255 C5
Mancroft Rd WV6. . . . . . 255 C5
Mandela Way ST3. . . . . . 284 D2
Manderley Cl DY3. . . . . . 266 C2
Manderston Cl DY1. . . . . 271 E3
Mander St WV3. . . . . 266 B8
Manderville Gdns DY6. . . 275 C6
Mandeville Cl ST6 . . . . 42 C3
Manifold CE Prim Sch
SK17 . . . . 23 A2
Manifold Cl
Burntwood WS7. . . . . 229 D6
Newcastle-u-L ST5. . . . . . . 55 B1
Waterhouses ST10 . . . . . . 48 F2
Manifold Dr ST4. . . . . 76 E1
Manifold Rd ST11. . . . . 90 F8
Manifold Valley Visitor Ctr
SK17 . . . . 23 E3
Manifold Wlk ST2. . . . . 58 C1
Manley Rd WS13. . . . . . . 214 D1
Manlove St WV3. . . . . . . 266 A8
Mannin Cl ST3 . . . . 74 A4
Mann St ST3. . . . . 74 C3
Manor Ave
Cannock WS11. . . . . 209 D1
Great Wyrley WS6. . . . . . 227 A4
Manor Cl Codsall WV8. . . 239 B4
Congleton CW12 . . . . 6 A1
Draycott in t M ST11. . . . . 91 C6
Great Haywood ST18. . . . 158 B2
Harlaston B79. . . . . 217 D2
Market Drayton TF9. . . . . 97 C1
Stanton DE15. . . . . 186 A6
Uttoxeter ST14 . . . . 126 B8
Weston ST18. . . . . 138 D2
Wolverhampton WV4. . . . 265 F4
Manor Cotts WS14 . . . . . 230 E2
Manor Court Dr WS15. . . 198 B4
Manor Cres DE15 . . . . . . 186 A6
Manor Croft
Burton u T DE14. . . . . 166 D2
Tatenhill DE13. . . . . 184 A8
Uttoxeter ST14 . . . . 126 C8
Manor Ct
Barton-u-N DE13 . . . . . . 183 D2
Stone ST9. . . . . 119 F6
Manor Ct St ST4 . . . . 71 F6
Manor Dr Burton u T DE14 166 E2
Dudley DY3. . . . . 271 B3
Netherseal DE12 . . . . 219 F6
Shareshill WV10 . . . . 225 D2
Swindon DY3. . . . . 269 E2
Manor Farm Cres ST17 . . 174 E5
Manor Farm Rd ST18. . . . 177 D8
Manorfield Cl ST19 . . . . . 207 E8
Manor Fields DE13 . . . . . 200 F3
Manor Flats DY3. . . . . . . 271 D8
Manor Fold WV8. . . . . . . 238 D2
Manor Gdns
Albrighton WV7 . . . . 237 A5
Market Drayton TF9. . . . . 97 C1
Wombourne WV5. . . . . . . 270 B7
Manor Glade ST5 . . . . 85 A7
Manor Gn ST17 . . . . 174 D7
Manor Hill Fst Sch ST15. 119 F7
Manor House Pk WV8. . . 239 B4
Manor Ho WV6 . . . . 255 D5
Manorial Rd B75. . . . . . . 258 E3
Manor La Harlaston B79 . 217 D2
Stourbridge DY8. . . . . 279 D3
Wigginton B79. . . . . 233 E3
Manor Pk DY6 . . . . 275 D6
Manor Prim Sch
Aldridge WS9. . . . . 257 A1
Drayton Bassett B78. . . . 260 C5
Manor Rd Aldridge B74 . . 257 A1
Edgmond TF10 . . . . 168 A3
Gnosall ST20 . . . . 171 E7
King's Bromley DE13 . . . 199 C6
Madeley CW3 . . . . 68 E3
Mile Oak B78. . . . . 249 D1
Stanton DE15. . . . . 186 A6
Stourbridge DY8. . . . . 275 E2
Tamworth B79. . . . . 250 D4
Uttoxeter ST14 . . . . 126 C8
Whitmore ST5. . . . . 85 A7
Wolverhampton,Penn WV4 265 F4
Manor Rise
Burntwood WS7. . . . . 229 A5
Lichfield WS14 . . . . 231 C7
Stone ST9. . . . . 119 F7
Manor Sq ST17 . . . . 174 D7
Manor St Stoke-on-T ST4. . 72 E7
Wolverhampton WV6. . . . 255 D5
Manor Trad Est DE14. . . . 166 E4
Manor Way WS15 . . . . . . 179 A6
Manor Wlk DE13 . . . . 199 B6
Mansard Cl WV3 . . . . 265 F8
Manse Cl ST3. . . . . 284 C4
Mansell Cl ST16. . . . . 155 C7
Mansfield Cl
Newcastle-u-L ST5. . . . . . . 71 C4
Tamworth B79. . . . . 249 E6
Mansfield Dr ST8 . . . . 27 A5

Mansion Cl ST10 . . . . 76 E2
Mansion Ct WV5. . . . . . . 269 D5
Mansion Dr WV7. . . . . . . 229 D4
Manson Ct WV4. . . . . 265 D5
Manston Dr WV6. . . . . . . 254 E5
Manston Hill ST19 . . . . . . 207 F7
Manston View B79 . . . . . 250 C8
Manta Rd B77. . . . . 261 D6
Manton Cl
2 Stretton DE13. . . . . . . 147 F1
Swadlincote DE11 . . . . . . 186 F6
Maple Ave
Newcastle-u-L ST5. . . . . . . 40 E1
Talke ST7. . . . . 40 E8
Maple Cl Burntwood WS7 . 228 F7
Cheadle ST10. . . . . 76 F2
Kinver DY7. . . . . 278 A5
Stoke-on-T ST6 . . . . 43 A5
Stourbridge DY8. . . . . 279 D2
Yarnfield ST15. . . . . 118 F5
Maple Cres
Blythe Bridge ST11 . . . . . 91 A5
Cannock WS11. . . . . 209 C1
Maple Cl Lichfield WS14 . 231 C5
Stafford ST17. . . . . 155 C1
Mapledene Cl 1 ST17. . . 175 D5
Maple Dr Derrington ST18 154 D1
Dudley DY3. . . . . 271 B2
Huntington WS12. . . . . . . 209 D8
Loggerheads TF9 . . . . 99 D5
Maple Gdns ST15 . . . . . . 120 A6
Maple Gr Burton u T DE15. 185 E5
Cheddleton ST13 . . . . 45 C7
Kingswinford DY6 . . . . . . 275 E6
Lichfield WS14. . . . . 231 F7
Stafford ST17. . . . . 174 E7
Wolverhampton WV3. . . . 255 C2
Maple Hayes Hall Sch
WS13 . . . . 230 D8
Maple Ho Little Aston B74. 257 B5
Walsall WS4. . . . . 244 D1
Maplehurst Cl ST6 . . . . . . 57 B8
Maple Pl ST3 . . . . 74 B2
Maple Rd Walsall WS3 . . 243 F2
Wolverhampton WV3. . . . 265 E8
Maple Rise B77. . . . . 251 A4
Maple St WS3. . . . . 243 D2
Maple Way DE14 . . . . . . 184 E4
Maple Wood ST17 . . . . . . 175 C5
Marcel St ST4 . . . . 72 A2
Marchant Rd WV6 . . . . . 255 F2
March Banks WS15 . . . . . 178 D1
March Cl WS6 . . . . 226 D1
Marchington Ind Est
ST14. . . . . 143 F8
March La Overmoor ST9 . . 60 A3
Whitgreave ST18. . . . . . . 135 E5
March Rd ST3 . . . . 284 B4
March Way WS9 . . . . 245 C1
Marchwood Ct ST4. . . . . . 71 E6
Marcia Rice Ct WS15. . . . 161 A5
Marconi Gate ST18. . . . . 156 C5
Marconi Pl WS12 . . . . . . 210 C2
Marcus Ind Est ST1 . . . . . 57 F3
Mardale Cl CW12 . . . . 6 A5
Maree Gr WV11. . . . . 242 B1
Margam Cres WS3 . . . . . 242 F2
Margam Terr WS3 . . . . . . 242 F2
Margam Way WS3 . . . . . 242 F2
Margaret Ave ST4 . . . . 87 F8
Margaret Dr WS11 . . . . . 209 E6
Margaret St
6 Stone ST15. . . . . 104 F1
Hanley ST1. . . . . 57 E4
Margery Ave ST7 . . . . 25 E7
Margill Cl ST1. . . . . 282 A2
Marholm Cl WV9. . . . . . . 239 F2
Maries Way ST5 . . . . 55 D1
Marigold Cl WS11 . . . . . . 210 C3
Marina Cres WS12 . . . . . 210 A5
Marina Dr ST5 . . . . 56 C3
Marina Rd ST4. . . . . 71 F3
Marina Way ST1 . . . . 57 A4
Marine Cres DY6 . . . . 275 E1
Marine Gdns DY8 . . . . . . 275 E1
Mariner B79 . . . . 249 E6
Market Drayton Cottage
Hospl TF9. . . . . 112 C8
Market Drayton Inf Sch
TF9. . . . . 97 C1
Market Drayton Jun Sch
TF9. . . . . 112 B8
Market Drayton Rd TF9 . . 99 D4
Marketfields ST21 . . . . . . 133 E7
Market Hall St WS11 . . . 209 E1
Market La Hanley ST1. . . 282 B3
Lichfield WS14. . . . . 230 C2
Lower Penn WV4. . . . . . . 264 F5
Newcastle-u-L ST5. . . . . . 283 B4
Market Mews TF10. . . . . 168 F3
Market Pl 10 Leek ST13 . . 30 E6
4 Cannock WS11. . . . . . 209 E1
4 Stone ST15. . . . . 120 A8
Abbots Bromley WS15 . . 161 A6
Brewood ST19 . . . . 223 C6
Burslem ST6 . . . . 56 F8
Burton u T DE14. . . . . . . 166 E2
Cheadle ST10. . . . . 76 D3
Hartington SK17 . . . . 24 C5
Longnor SK17 . . . . 13 B6
Penkridge ST19 . . . . 192 E1
Tamworth B79. . . . . 250 B4
Uttoxeter ST14 . . . . 126 C7
Walsall WS3. . . . . 243 B1
Market Sq Arc ST7. . . . . . 282 B3
Market Sq Hanley ST1 . . 282 B3
Rugeley WS15. . . . . 178 E1
Stafford ST16. . . . . 285 B3

Market St Cannock WS12 . **210** C5
Kidsgrove ST7 . . . . **26** A1
Kingswinford DY6 . . . . . . **275** D6
Leek ST13 . . . . **30** F6
Lichfield WS13 . . . . **231** B8
Longton ST3 . . . . **284** C3
Penkridge ST19 . . . . **192** E1
Rugeley WS15 . . . . **178** F1
Stafford ST16 . . . . **285** B3
Tamworth B79 . . . . **250** B4
Uttoxeter ST14 . . . . **126** C7
Markham Croft WV9 . . . . **240** A2
Markham Dr DY6 . . . . . . **275** E4
Marklew Cl WS8 . . . . **245** A5
Marklin Ave WV10 . . . . . **240** D1
Marks Wlk WS13 . . . . **214** A2
Marlborough Ave ST16 . **156** C4
Marlborough Cl
　Great Haywood ST18 . . . **158** C2
　Sutton Coldfield B74 . . . . **257** E6
Marlborough Cres
　Burton u T DE15 . . . . **186** A8
　Endon ST9 . . . . **43** E8
Marlborough Ct
　Lichfield WS13 . . . . **231** B8
　Sutton Coldfield,Four Oaks
　B74 . . . . **257** F2
Marlborough Gdns
　Stourbridge DY8 . . . . **275** D2
　Wolverhampton WV6 . . . . **255** E4
Marlborough Ind Est
　WV2 . . . . **266** D7
Marlborough Rd
　Dudley DY3 . . . . **271** F6
　Longton ST3 . . . . **284** C4
　Stone ST15 . . . . **119** F5
Marlborough St
　Stoke-on-T ST4 . . . . **72** D5
　Walsall WS3 . . . . **243** B1
Marlborough Way
　Stoke-on-T ST6 . . . . **41** C5
　Tamworth B77 . . . . **250** F2
　Uttoxeter ST14 . . . . **110** F1
Marlbrook Dr WV4 . . . . . **266** B6
Marlbrook La WV6 . . . . . **253** B2
Marlburn Way WV5 . . . . **269** E6
Marldon PI ST6 . . . . **41** F5
Marley Mount Cres TF9 . **97** C2
Marlin B77 . . . . **261** D6
Marlow ST3 . . . . **73** D5
Marlow Dr DE14 . . . . **185** A8
Marlowe Rd ST17 . . . . . . **174** B8
Marlow Rd Longton ST3 . **73** D5
　Tamworth B77 . . . . **250** D5
Marlpit La Denstone ST14. **95** D6
　Ellastone DE6 . . . . **80** A3
　Moddershall ST15 . . . . . . **105** F5
　Sutton Coldfield B75 . . . . **258** D3
Marlpit Rise 🔢 B75 . . . . . **258** E3
Marlpool Dr WS3 . . . . . . **244** A1
Marmion Pk B79 . . . . . . **250** B6
Marmion St B79 . . . . **250** B5
Marnel Dr WV3 . . . . **265** E7
Marney Wlk ST6 . . . . **42** B2
Marquis Dr WS12,WS15 . **195** D3
Marquis Drive Visitor Ctr★
　WS15 . . . . **195** D3
Marquis's Dr WS15 . . . . . **196** B2
Marrick B77 . . . . **251** C1
Marriott St ST4 . . . . **73** A5
Marsden St ST1 . . . . **282** C3
Marsett B77 . . . . **262** C8
Marshall Ave ST6 . . . . . . **43** B7
Marshall Cl WS9 . . . . **256** B4
Marshall Gr CW12 . . . . . . **6** A3
Marshalls Ind Est WV2 . **266** C7
Marshall St Burslem ST6 . **41** F1
　Tamworth B79 . . . . **250** E5
Marsh Ave
　Newcastle-u-L ST5 . . . . . **56** C5
　Newchapel ST7 . . . . **26** E2
　Stoke-on-T ST6 . . . . **42** B2
Marshbrook Fst Sch
　ST19 . . . . **192** F1
Marsh Cl ST9 . . . . **59** A4
Marsh Cres DY8 . . . . **275** D3
Marsh Ct ST16 . . . . **155** D5
Marshfield La ST8 . . . . . . **16** C2
Marsh Gr ST8 . . . . **16** C3
Marsh Green Cl ST8 . . . . **16** D2
Marshgreen Rd ST8 . . . . **16** D3
Marsh Gr DY3 . . . . **269** E2
Marsh La
　Cheswardine TF9 . . . . . . **130** A8
　Ellenhall ST21 . . . . **134** B1
　Lichfield WS14 . . . . **231** C5
Marshland Gr ST6 . . . . . . **42** A8
Marshlands Sch ST17 . . **175** C6
Marsh Lane Par WV10 . . **240** C2
Marsh La Penkridge ST19 . **192** F1
　Stanton DE6 . . . . **80** D8
　Whittington WS14 . . . . . . **232** B5
　Wolverhampton WV10 . . . **240** B2
Marsh Mdws ST20 . . . . . **131** C4
Marsh Par ST5 . . . . **283** C3
Marsh Prim Sch ST11 . . . **91** A6
Marsh St N ST1 . . . . **282** B3
Marsh St S ST1 . . . . **282** B2
Marsh St ST16 . . . . **155** D5
Marsh View ST3 . . . . **90** A5
Marsh Way ST5 . . . . **56** C5
Marshwood Cl 🔢 WS11 . . **210** A3
Marsland Cl ST16 . . . . . . **155** A4
Marsland Rd ST16 . . . . . **155** A4
Mars St ST5 . . . . **42** C1
Marston Cl
　Stourbridge DY8 . . . . **279** D4
　Wheaton Aston ST19 . . . . **205** C6

Marston Croft ST19 . . . . . **205** C6
Marston Ct ST16 . . . . **155** D5
Marston Dr ST16 . . . . **155** E5
Marston Gr Stafford ST16. **155** E5
　Stoke-on-T ST1 . . . . **57** D8
Marston Ind Est WV2 . . **266** C7
Marston La Hatton DE65 . **146** D8
　Marston ST18 . . . . **147** A4
　Rolleston on D DE13 . . . . **147** A4
Marston Old La DE65 . . . **146** D8
Marston Pk B78 . . . . **249** F4
Marston Rd
　Cannock WS12 . . . . **209** F6
　Marston-On-Dove DE65 . . **147** B8
　Stafford ST16 . . . . **155** E5
　Wheaton Aston ST19 . . . . **205** B7
　Wolverhampton WV2 . . . . **266** C7
Marston Rise DE14 . . . . . **185** B8
Marsworth Way ST16. . . . **136** D1
Martham Dr WV6 . . . . . . **255** B2
Martin Croft WS13 . . . . . **214** A1
Martindale
　🔢 Stafford ST17 . . . . **175** D6
　Cannock WS11 . . . . **210** A2
Martindale Cl ST3 . . . . . . **89** F8
Martin Dale TF9 . . . . **99** D5
Martindale Trad Est
　WS11 . . . . **210** A2
Martin Dr ST16 . . . . **155** C3
Martin's La DE13 . . . . **145** A4
Martinslow La ST10,ST13. **48** E4
Martins Mill CW12 . . . . . . **16** C8
Martin St Burslem ST6 . . . **57** B7
　Stafford ST16 . . . . **285** B3
　Wolverhampton WV4 . . . . **266** F5
Martins Way ST18 . . . . . **158** C8
Martley Rd WS4 . . . . **244** C2
Martlin La WS15 . . . . **179** A5
Marton Ave WS7 . . . . **229** A8
Marwood Croft B74 . . . . **257** A2
Marychurch Rd ST4 . . . . . **58** B3
Maryfield Wlk ST4 . . . . . . **71** E7
Maryhill Cl ST7 . . . . **26** A3
Maryhill High Sch ST7 . . . **26** A3
Maryhill Prim Sch ST7 . . . **26** A3
Mary Howard CE Prim Sch
　B79 . . . . **217** C5
Mary Rand Cl ST1 . . . . . . **174** D8
Mary Rose Cl Bucknall ST2. **58** B3
　Cheslyn Hay WS6 . . . . . . **226** D1
Marysgate ST19 . . . . **223** D7
Mary St WS12 . . . . **210** B7
Maryvale Ct WS14 . . . . . **231** C5
Masefield Cl
　Burntwood WS7 . . . . **212** A1
　Cheadle ST10 . . . . **76** D5
　Lichfield WS14 . . . . **231** B6
　Market Drayton TF9 . . . . **112** A7
Masefield Cres DE14 . . . **166** D7
Masefield Dr
　Stafford ST17 . . . . **155** C1
　Tamworth B79 . . . . **250** A7
Masefield Gr WS11 . . . . **209** E4
Masefield Mews WV10 . . **241** A1
Masefield Rd Dudley DY3 . **271** A4
　Longton ST3 . . . . **73** A2
　Wolverhampton WV10 . . . **241** A1
Mason Cres WV4 . . . . . . **265** C5
Mason Dr ST8 . . . . **27** B8
Masons Lawn ST20 . . . . . **171** C5
Masons Pl TF10 . . . . **168** E4
Mason's Pl TF10 . . . . **168** E5
Mason St Stoke-on-T ST4 . **72** F5
　Wolverhampton WV2 . . . . **266** C7
Masterson St ST4 . . . . . . **72** D6
Mathews Wlk ST1 . . . . . . **282** C3
Matlock Cl WS3 . . . . **243** C3
Matlock Dr WS11 . . . . . . **210** A4
Matlock Pl ST5 . . . . **55** A2
Matlock Rd WS3 . . . . **243** C3
Matlock St ST1 . . . . **282** B1
Matthews Ct ST1. . . . . . . **282** C2
Matthews Pl CW12 . . . . . . **6** A2
Matthews Rd ST17 . . . . . **174** C7
Matthews Wlk WS13 . . . **214** A2
Maud St ST4 . . . . **72** E7
Maunders Rd ST2 . . . . . . **43** A1
Maureen Ave ST6 . . . . . . **41** D6
Maureen Gr ST5 . . . . **56** C3
Mavesyn Cl WS15 . . . . . **198** A8
Mavis Rd WS12 . . . . **210** B7
Mavor Ave WS7 . . . . **211** D1
Mawdesley St ST6 . . . . . . **57** B6
Mawgan Dr WS14 . . . . . **231** D6
Mawson Gr ST4 . . . . **57** D1
Maxstoke Cl
　Tamworth B77 . . . . **261** C4
　Walsall WS3 . . . . **243** A3
Maxtock Ave WS13 . . . . . **231** A6
Maxton Way ST3 . . . . **74** B2
Maxwell Cl WS14 . . . . . . **231** C7
Maxwell Pl ST4 . . . . **71** E7
Maxwell Rd
　Congleton CW12 . . . . . : . **16** A8
　Wolverhampton WV2 . . . . **266** D8
Mayall Dr B75 . . . . **258** D4
Mayama Rd B78 . . . . **260** F8
May Ave Newcastle-u-L ST5. **56** D3
　Stoke-on-T ST6 . . . . **41** F3
Maybank Cl WS14 . . . . . . **231** E8
May Bank Inf Sch ST5 . . . **56** D3
Maybank WS15 . . . . **196** E4
Maybrook Ind Est WS8 . **244** F5
Maybrook Rd WS8 . . . . . **244** F5
Maybury Cl WV8 . . . . **238** E4
Maybury Way ST2 . . . . . . **43** A1

Maybush Gdns WV10 . . . . **240** C1
May Cl WS7 . . . . **211** F1
Maycroft WS12 . . . . **209** F7
Mayer Ave ST5. . . . . **283** B4
Mayer Bank 🔢 ST6. . . . . . **57** A8
Mayers Ct 🔢 ST13 . . . . . . **30** E5
Mayer St ST1 . . . . **282** C3
Mayfair Ave ST10 . . . . **62** A8
Mayfair Cl WV7 . . . . **237** A5
Mayfair Gr ST9 . . . . **43** E8
Mayfair Gdns
　🔟 Stoke-on-T ST6. . . . . . . **41** D3
　Wolverhampton WV3 . . . . **255** D2
Mayfair Gr ST9 . . . . **43** E8
Mayfair DE11 . . . . **186** E6
Mayfield Hanley WS1 . . . . **57** C7
　Mayfield DE6 . . . . **81** C7
　Newcastle-u-L ST5. . . . . . **283** A2
　Penkridge ST19 . . . . **207** E8
Mayfield Cl ST13 . . . . **30** B5
Mayfield Cres ST1 . . . . . . **57** E4
Mayfield Dr
　Blythe Bridge ST11 . . . . . . **90** D8
　Burton u T DE15 . . . . **186** A8
Mayfield Pl E ST4 . . . . **71** E5
Mayfield Pl N ST4 . . . . . . **55** C4
Mayfield Pl W ST4 . . . . . . **71** E5
Mayfield Rd
　Albrighton WV7 . . . . **237** A5
　Biddulph ST8 . . . . **27** D6
　Burton u T DE15. . . . . **167** A3
　Hangingbridge DE6 . . . . . . **81** F8
　Stafford ST17 . . . . **156** C1
Mayfields Dr WS8 . . . . . . **228** B2
Mayfield B77 . . . . **262** C6
Mayfield Terr DE6 . . . . **81** D6
Mayflower Dr WS15 . . . . **178** C1
Maygrove Rd DY6 . . . . . . **275** C7
Maynard Ave DY8 . . . . . . **279** D3
Maynards Croft TF10 . . . **169** A4
Mayneford Pl ST4. . . . . . . **71** F1
Mayne St ST4. . . . . **71** F1
Mayock Cres ST16 . . . . . **155** B2
Maypole Ct WV5 . . . . **270** A6
Maypole Dr DY8 . . . . **279** C5
Maypole St WV5 . . . . **270** B7
May St Newcastle-u-L ST5 . **55** F6
　Stoke-on-T ST6 . . . . **42** B1
Mays Wlk DE13 . . . . **200** F3
Mayswood Dr WV6 . . . . . **254** F1
Maythorne Rd ST3 . . . . . . **73** A1
Maythorn Gdns
　Codsall WV8 . . . . **239** A4
　Wolverhampton WV6 . . . . **255** C3
Maywood Cl DY6 . . . . **275** B6
Mead Ave ST7 . . . . **25** E7
Mead Cl WS9 . . . . **256** B5
Mead Cres DE14 . . . . **186** A6
Meadfoot Dr DY6 . . . . . . **275** B7
Meadlands The WV5 . . . . **269** E6
Meadow Ave Longton ST3 . **73** A1
　Newcastle-u-L ST5. . . . . . **56** A4
　Weston CW2 . . . . **37** B5
　Wetley Rocks ST9 . . . . **60** B6
Meadowbank Ave ST18. . **138** C2
Meadowbank Grange
　WS6 . . . . **226** E4
Meadow Bank B78 . . . . . **250** B1
Meadow Bank Wlk ST16 . **155** C8
Meadowbrook Ct ST15 . . **120** D6
Meadowbrook Gdns
　WV8 . . . . **239** B4
Meadowbrook Rd WS13 . **214** B3
Meadow Cl Aldridge B74. . **256** F2
　Blythe Bridge ST11 . . . . . . **90** E6
　Eccleshall ST21 . . . . **133** C7
　Forsbrook ST11 . . . . **91** B8
　Gnosall ST20 . . . . **171** E7
　Leek ST13 . . . . **31** A5
　Market Drayton TF9 . . . . . **97** A1
　Penkridge ST19 . . . . **207** F7
　Wheaton Aston ST19 . . . . **205** B6
Meadowcroft Ave ST3 . . . **90** C8
Meadow Croft ST3 . . . . . **209** C6
Meadowcroft Gdns ST19 . **205** C6
Meadow Croft
　Hagley DY9 . . . . **281** F4
　Perton WV6 . . . . **254** A3
　Streetway WS13. . . . . **215** A1
Meadow Ct Barlaston ST12. **88** C2
　Burton u T DE14 . . . . **166** F3
　Newchapel ST7 . . . . **26** E2
　Norton Bridge ST15. . . . . **135** A8
　Stafford ST17 . . . . **175** A8
Meadow Dr Cheadle ST10 . **76** D3
　Haughton ST18 . . . . **172** E6
　Stoke-on-T ST3 . . . . **89** A8
Meadowfields DY8 . . . . . **275** E2
Meadow Glade ST18 . . . . **158** C8
Meadow Gr WS14 . . . . . . **227** A2
Meadow Hill Dr 🔢
　WS11 . . . . **210** A3
Meadowhill Dr DY8 . . . . **279** C7
Meadow La
　Acton Trussell ST17 . . . . . **193** B8
　Burton u T DE13. . . . . **167** A8
　Colwich ST18 . . . . **177** C7
　Coven Heath WV10 . . . . . . **240** C1
　Derrington ST18 . . . . **154** E2
　Fulford ST11 . . . . **106** E8
　Millmeece ST21. . . . . **117** E7
Meadowlands Dr WS4. . . **244** D1
Meadow La ST5. . . . . **56** A4

Meadow Lark Cl WS12 . . **210** B4
Meadow La Roston DE6 . . **96** C7
　Stoke-on-T ST4 . . . . **88** C7
　Swadlincote DE11 . . . . . . **186** F5
　Wombourne WV5. . . . . . . **270** B8
　Yoxall DE13 . . . . **200** B7
Meadowpark Rd DY8. . . . **279** D8
Meadow Pk B79 . . . . **249** F5
Meadow Pl ST3 . . . . **74** B1
Meadow Rd
　Albrighton WV7 . . . . **237** B5
　Aldridge WS9 . . . . **256** A4
　Barlaston ST12 . . . . **88** D1
　Brown Edge ST6 . . . . **43** B6
　Burton u T DE14. . . . . **166** F4
　Coldmeece ST15 . . . . **118** A6
　Newport TF10 . . . . **169** A3
　Stafford ST17 . . . . **174** F8
　Stoke-on-T ST6 . . . . **42** C5
　Tamworth B78 . . . . **249** E3
　Wolverhampton WV3 . . . . **265** D8
Meadow Ridge ST17 . . . . **175** C8
Meadow Rise DE13 . . . . . **183** E1
Meadows Gr WS8 . . . . . . **239** A4
Meadow Side ST8 . . . . **27** B6
Meadowside Ave ST7 . . . . **39** D2
Meadowside Dr DE14 . . . **166** E3
Meadowside La ST7 . . . . . **26** B7
Meadowside
　Loggerheads TF9 . . . . **99** E5
　Mayfield DE6 . . . . **81** D6
Meadowside Rd B74 . . . **257** F3
Meadowside
　Saverley Green ST11. . . . . **91** B2
　Stoke-on-T ST4 . . . . **88** B7
Meadows Prim Sch CW3. **69** A8
Meadows Rd ST7 . . . . **25** F1
Meadows The
　Brewood ST19 . . . . **223** D6
　Hilderstone ST15. . . . . . . **106** C2
　Kingstone ST14 . . . . **141** C8
　Rugeley WS15 . . . . **197** B6
　Salt ST18 . . . . **137** F4
　Stoke-on-T ST9 . . . . **43** F7
　Uttoxeter ST14 . . . . **111** A2
　Wrinehill CW3 . . . . **53** A3
Meadow Stile Home Park
　Cvn Site ST8 . . . . **27** A6
Meadow St
　Newcastle-u-L ST5 . . . . . **55** F6
　Stoke-on-T ST2 . . . . **43** B1
　Tamworth B77 . . . . **250** C3
Meadow Sweet Cl ST6 . **42** E2
Meadowsweet Dr ST17 . **175** F7
Meadowsweet Way
　WS12. . . . . **210** A4
Meadow Vale WV8 . . . . . **239** B2
Meadow View WS7 . . . . . **229** D6
Meadow View TF10. . . . . **169** A3
Meadow View Cvn Pk
　WV10. . . . . **240** C6
Meadow View DE6 . . . . . **127** C8
Meadow View Rd
　Newport TF10 . . . . **169** A3
　Swadlincote DE11 . . . . . . **186** F5
Meadow View
　Rolleston on D DE13 . . . . **147** C4
　Sedgley DY3. . . . . **266** C1
Meadowview ST6 . . . . **42** E3
Meadow View Terr WV6. **255** E5
Meadowview ST15 . . . . . **118** E6
Meadow Way
　Armitage WS15 . . . . **198** B4
　Cannock WS12 . . . . **210** C1
　Codsall WV8 . . . . **238** E2
　Lawton-gate ST7 . . . . **25** A5
　Stone ST15 . . . . **119** F6
　Stourbridge DY8 . . . . **275** C6
　Upper Tean ST10 . . . . **92** D3
　Whitmore ST5 . . . . **85** D5
Mead The Sedgley DY3 . . **271** B8
　Stoke-on-T ST4 . . . . **88** B7
Meadway Cl WS12 . . . . . **210** C3
Meadway Dr ST17. . . . . . **175** C6
Meadway WS7 . . . . **229** D6
Meadway The WV6. . . . . **255** A5
Mead Wlk DE15 . . . . **186** A6
Meaford Ave ST15 . . . . . **104** F2
Meaford Dr ST3 . . . . **72** E3
Meaford Rd ST12,ST15. . **104** D6
Meakin Ave ST5 . . . . **71** B3
Meakin Cl Cheadle ST10 . . **76** C1
　Congleton CW12 . . . . **6** B1
　Stone ST15 . . . . **120** C6
Meakin Gr ST16 . . . . **155** B6
Meakin Ho ST15 . . . . **104** F1
Mear Greaves La DE15 . . **167** B4
Mear's La WS15. . . . . **198** F8
Mease La B79 . . . . **218** B2
Mease The DE65 . . . . **147** E8
Media Way ST1 . . . . **56** F4
Medina Cl WV10 . . . . **240** F4
Medina ST3 . . . . **250** E1
Medina Way Kidsgrove ST7 . **26** B2
　Kingswinford DY6 . . . . . . **275** C6
Medway Dr ST8 . . . . **16** D1
Medway Pl ST5 . . . . **71** B4
Medway Rd WS8 . . . . **228** C2
Medway B77 . . . . **250** E1
Medway Wlk
　Brownhills WS8 . . . . **228** C1
　Stoke-on-T ST6 . . . . **42** A4
Meece Ave ST15 . . . . **118** D7
Meece Rd ST15 . . . . **118** D5

Meerash La WS7 . . . . **229** C3
Meerbrook Cl ST4 . . . . **88** B5
Meerbrook Rd ST13 . . . . . **19** D1
Meerbrook Youth Hostel★
　ST13 . . . . **19** F6
Meere Cl ST6 . . . . **42** E3
Meeson Ct WV7. . . . . **237** B5
Megacre ST7 . . . . **40** A1
Meg La WS7 . . . . **212** B1
Meigh Rd ST2,ST9 . . . . . . **59** A4
Meigh St ST1 . . . . **282** C3
Meiklejohn Pl ST6. . . . . . . **42** A6
Meirhay Rd ST3. . . . . **73** D2
Meir Heath Prim Sch ST3 . **90** A4
Meir Prim Sch ST3. . . . . . . **74** B1
Meir Rd ST3 . . . . **73** C1
Meir St ST6 . . . . **41** E4
Meir View ST3 . . . . **74** A1
Melbourne Ave DE15 . . . **167** C3
Melbourne Cl DY6 . . . . . . **275** E4
Melbourne Cres
　Cannock WS12 . . . . **210** F2
　Stafford ST16 . . . . **156** B5
Melbourne Rd WS12 . . . **210** F2
Melbourne St ST3. . . . . . . **73** D5
Melbury Way 🔟 WS11. . . **209** E8
Melchester Gr ST3 . . . . . . **73** C1
Melchester Wlk 🔢 WS11 **209** F2
Melfont St ST6. . . . . **41** E3
Melford Cl DY3 . . . . **266** C2
Melford Grange WS7. . . . **211** F1
Melford Rise WS7. . . . . . **211** F1
Melford B77 . . . . **249** E2
Meliden Way ST4 . . . . **71** F6
Mellard St Audley ST7. . . . **39** D1
　Newcastle-u-L ST5. . . . . . **283** A4
Mellor Dr Alrewas DE13 . . **200** F2
　Sutton Coldfield B74 . . . . **257** F3
　Uttoxeter ST14 . . . . **111** B1
Mellor Rd DE14 . . . . **185** B7
Mellors Bank ST7 . . . . . . **26** D6
Mellor St ST7 . . . . **26** F2
Mellowdew Rd DY8 . . . . **275** C3
Mellow La ST10,ST13 . . . . **47** E3
Mellor St ST7 . . . . **26** F2
Mellwaters B77 . . . . **262** C6
Melmerby B77 . . . . **262** C8
Melrose Ave
　Meir Heath ST3 . . . . **90** A4
　Newcastle-u-L ST5. . . . . . **71** A5
　Stafford ST17 . . . . **174** C8
　Stoke-on-T ST1 . . . . **57** D7
　Stone ST15 . . . . **120** C5
　Stourbridge DY8 . . . . **279** F2
Melrose Cres TF9 . . . . . . **112** B8
Melrose Dr
　Cannock WS12 . . . . **209** F7
　Perton WV6 . . . . **254** E4
Melrose Pl ST13 . . . . **30** B5
Melstone Ave ST6. . . . . . . **41** F3
Melville Ct ST5 . . . . **71** C1
Melville Rd ST3 . . . . **73** E2
Melville St ST3 . . . . **57** E3
Melvyn Cres ST6. . . . . **56** C7
Menai Dr ST8. . . . . **27** D6
Menai Gr ST3 . . . . **284** C5
Mendip Ave ST17 . . . . . . **175** C5
Mendip Cl Dudley DY3. . . **271** C3
　Wolverhampton WV2. . . . **266** D3
Mendip Gn ST2 . . . . **43** A1
Mendip Pl ST5 . . . . **55** C3
Mendip Rd WS12. . . . . . . **195** A1
Mendip Way B77. . . . . . . **251** C1
Mentone Cres TF10 . . . . . **168** B4
Menzies Ho
　🔢 Stoke-on-T ST3 . . . . **89** F8
　Cheddleton ST13. . . . . **45** C7
Meon Gr WV6. . . . . **254** F1
Mercer Ave ST15. . . . . . . **120** C7
Mercer St ST3 . . . . **73** B1
Merchant Cl WV6 . . . . . . **253** C3
Merchants Pk WS9. . . . . **256** A7
Merchants Way WS9 . . . . **256** A7
Mercia Cl Hatton DE65 . . **146** D8
　Tamworth B79 . . . . **249** E7
Mercia Cres ST6 . . . . **57** A6
Mercia Dr WV6 . . . . **254** E5
Mercian Ct
　Lichfield WS14 . . . . **231** C7
　Market Drayton TF9. . . . . . **97** C1
Mercian Pk B77. . . . . **251** A3
Mercian Way Lapley ST19 **206** A7
　Tamworth B77 . . . . **251** B3
Mercury Pk B77 . . . . **251** B3
Mercury Pl ST6 . . . . **42** C1
Mercury Rd WS11. . . . . . **210** A5
Mere Cl TF10 . . . . **168** F4
Mere Croft WS11 . . . . . . **227** F4
Mere Ct CW2 . . . . **37** B5
Meredith Cl DE14 . . . . . . **166** D6
Meredith Rd DY3 . . . . . . **271** A4
Mere Dr B75. . . . . **258** B2
Mere Green Cl B75. . . . . . **258** C2
Mere Green Comb Sch
　B75. . . . . **258** B2
Mere Green Rd B75. . . . . **258** C2
Mere La DY7 . . . . **273** C6
Merelake Rd ST7 . . . . **40** B8
Meremore Dr ST5. . . . . . . **40** D2
Mere Oak Rd WV6 . . . . . **254** E5
Mere Pool Rd B75 . . . . . **258** C4
Mere Rd Stourbridge DY8 . **279** E3
　Weston CW2 . . . . **37** B5
Mere Rise ST21 . . . . **132** D7
Mere Side Cl 🔢 ST1. . . . . . **56** F2
Merevale Ave ST2. . . . . . . **58** A2

Merganser B77 . . . . 262 A6
Meriden Ave DY8 . . . . 279 D6
Meriden Cl
Cannock WS11. . . . . 226 B8
Stourbridge DY8 . . . . 279 D6
Meriden Ct 3 WV4 . . . . . 266 F4
Meriden Rd
Newcastle-u-L ST5. . . . . 71 C2
Wolverhampton WV10. . . . 240 B1
Merino Cl ST3 . . . . 89 C8
Merlin Cl Cannock WS11. . 209 C2
Stoke-on-T ST6 . . . . 42 A8
Tamworth B77. . . . . 262 A6
Uttoxeter ST14 . . . . 126 C6
Merlin Cres DE14 . . . . 184 F8
Merlin Ct WS7. . . . . 229 F8
Merlin Gn CW3 . . . . 68 E6
Merlin Way Kidsgrove ST7 . 26 D3
Whittington WS14 . . . . 232 F5
Merrial St ST5. . . . . 283 B3
Merrick St ST1 . . . . 282 C4
Merridale Ave WV3 . . . . . 255 F2
Merridale Ct WV3. . . . . 255 F1
Merridale Gr WV3. . . . . . . 255 E1
Merridale St W WV3 . . . . 266 A8
Merrill Cl WS6. . . . . 226 E2
Merrion Dr ST6. . . . . 42 B3
Merrivale Rd ST17 . . . . . . 174 E7
Merrydale Rd DE15 . . . . . . 186 A8
Merryfield Rd DY1 . . . . . . 271 E1
Merryfields Sch ST5 . . . . . 56 B4
Merry Rd ST17. . . . . 174 E7
Mersey Cl WS15 . . . . 178 E3
Mersey Rd
Newcastle-u-L ST5. . . . . 71 A3
Walsall WS3 . . . . 243 E1
Mersey St ST1 . . . . 282 A2
Merthyr Gr ST8 . . . . 27 E6
Merton Ct WS7 . . . . 228 F5
Merton St ST3. . . . . 284 C4
Mervyn Rd DE15 . . . . 167 A3
Mesnes Gn WS14 . . . . 231 C7
Metcalf Cl WS7. . . . . 229 C8
Metcalfe Cl WS12. . . . . 210 C6
Metcalfe Rd ST6. . . . . 42 A3
Metfield Cl B79. . . . . 250 C8
Metfield Croft DY6. . . . . . . 275 F6
Mewies Cl DE12. . . . . 184 D1
Mews Cl ST2 . . . . 58 A2
Mews The Cannock WS11 209 D1
Newcastle-u-L ST5. . . . . 56 D4
Meynell Cl DE15 . . . . 167 B1
Meynell Field TF9. . . . . 99 E4
Meyrick Rd ST17 . . . . 285 B1
Mica Cl B77 . . . . 251 B2
Michael Cl ST3 . . . . 74 B3
Michaels Cl ST5 . . . . 56 C7
Michael's La DE6 . . . . 81 C5
Michigan Cl WS11 . . . . 210 B2
Michigan Gr ST4. . . . . 88 B8
Micklea La ST9 . . . . 29 F1
Mickleby Way ST3 . . . . 90 C7
Micklegate ST19. . . . . 223 D7
Micklehome Dr DE13. . . . . 201 B3
Mickleton B77. . . . . 262 C8
Micklewood Cl ST19 . . . . . 207 F7
Micklewood La ST19 . . . . . 208 B4
Middle Cross St ST3 . . . . . 284 C4
Middle Entry B79 . . . . 250 B4
Middlefield ST20. . . . . 171 E7
Middlefield Rd ST2 . . . . 73 D8
Middlefield WV8. . . . . 239 E2
Middle Friars ST17. . . . . . . 285 B2
Middlehurst Specl Sch
ST7 . . . . 41 F7
Middle La Codsall WV8 . . . 238 C2
Congleton CW12 . . . . 6 D4
Wolverhampton WV9. . . . . . 240 A5
Middlemore La WS9 . . . . . 256 A6
Middlepark Rd DY1 . . . . . 271 F1
Middlesmoor B77. . . . . 262 C8
Middleton Cl
Hammerwich WS7. . . . . 229 D4
Stoke-on-T ST6 . . . . 42 E3
Middleton Hall★ B78. . . . 260 E1
Middleton Rd
Aldridge B74 . . . . 257 A1
Brownhills WS8. . . . . 229 A1
Whittington WS14 . . . . 232 E6
Middleway Ave DY8. . . . . . 275 C3
Middleway WS12 . . . . 211 A6
Middleway Pk DE14. . . . . . 166 E3
Midfield Cl ST8 . . . . 16 C2
Midgley Ct TF10 . . . . 168 E3
Midgley Dr B74. . . . . 258 A2
Midhurst Cl ST7 . . . . 41 F8
Midhurst Dr WS12 . . . . 210 C7
Midhurst Gr WV6. . . . . 255 C5
Midland Rd WS12. . . . . 209 C5
Midpoint Ctr WV6. . . . . 255 F5
Midway Dr ST11 . . . . 90 E6
Midway The ST5 . . . . 283 B2
Midwinter Ct ST6. . . . . 56 E6
Milan Dr ST5 . . . . 70 E6
Milan Gr ST3 . . . . 73 E4
Milborne Dr ST5. . . . . 71 C5
Milburn Rd ST6. . . . . 57 B6
Milburn B77. . . . . 262 C8
Milcote Way DY6 . . . . 275 B7
Mildenhall B79 . . . . 250 C8
Mile Ct ST5. . . . . 55 F3
Mile Flat
Kingswinford DY6 . . . . 275 A7
Kinver DY6. . . . . 274 F7
Milehouse La ST5. . . . . 56 B4
Mile Oak Cross Rds B78 . 249 C2
Miles Bank ST1. . . . . 282 B3
Miles Green Rd ST7 . . . . . . 54 E8
Milestone Ct WV6. . . . . 255 A3
Milestone Dr DY9 . . . . 281 F4
Milford Ave ST9 . . . . 59 B4
Milford Cl DY8. . . . . 275 E3
Milford Rd
Newcastle-u-L ST5. . . . . . . 283 A1
Walton-on-t-H ST17. . . . . . 175 F7
Wolverhampton WV2. . . . . 266 C7
Milford St ST4 . . . . 72 F5
Milgreen Ave ST1. . . . . 57 D7
Milking Bank DY1. . . . . 271 E2
Milking Bank Prim Sch
DY1 . . . . 271 E2
Milk St ST13. . . . . 30 F7
Mill Bank Dr ST14. . . . . 96 A3
Millbank Pl ST5. . . . . 55 F1
Mill Bank Sedgley DY3. . . . 271 D8
Stafford ST16 . . . . 285 B3
Millbank St Longton ST3. . 284 C3
Wolverhampton WV11. . . . 241 F1
Millbeck Cl CW2 . . . . 37 B5
Millbridge Cl ST3 . . . . 90 B6
Millbrook Cl 4 WS11 . . . . 209 F2
Millbrook Dr WS14 . . . . . . 246 F6
Millbrook Gdns ST11. . . . . . 90 F7
Millbrook Gr ST2 . . . . 43 A1
Millbrook Way ST10. . . . . . . 76 F2
Mill Cl Blakedown DY10 . . . 281 B2
Caverswall ST3 . . . . 74 C3
Dudley DY3 . . . . 271 D6
Newton Solney DE15 . . . . . 167 E8
Mill Cotts Sandon ST18 . . . 137 D7
Stowe-by-Chartley ST18 . . 139 C5
Millcourt ST4. . . . . 87 F7
Mill Cres Barton-u-N DE13 201 E8
Cannock WS11. . . . . 210 B2
Millcroft Way WS15 . . . . . . 198 C4
Mill Ct
Great Haywood ST18. . . . . . 158 B2
Shenstone WS14 . . . . 247 A6
Milldale Cres WV10 . . . . . . 240 D3
Milldale Rd WV10. . . . . 240 D4
Mill End La DE13. . . . . 200 F3
Millend La ST7. . . . . 39 C5
Millenium Way ST5 . . . . 40 F2
Millennium Cl WS3 . . . . . . 244 A4
Millennium Way
Codsall WV8 . . . . 239 B4
Stone ST15 . . . . 104 E2
Miller Cl WS13. . . . . 214 B2
Millersdale Cl DE15 . . . . . . 167 B5
Millers Gate 2 ST15 . . . . . 120 A8
Millers Gn WV7. . . . . 237 A5
Millers Green Dr DY6 . . . . 275 A8
Millers La
Burton u T DE14. . . . . 166 C3
Stoke-on-T ST2 . . . . 43 A1
Miller St ST5 . . . . 283 C3
Millers Vale
Cannock WS12. . . . . 210 D1
Wombourne WV5. . . . . 269 D5
Millers View Cheadle ST10. 76 F2
Kidsgrove ST7 . . . . 26 A1
Millers Wharf B78 . . . . 251 F1
Millers Wlk WS3 . . . . 243 E3
Millett Rd ST2 . . . . 58 A3
Mill Farm Ct ST21. . . . . 134 D6
Millfield Ave
Walsall,Little Bloxwich
WS3 . . . . 243 D3
Walsall WS4 . . . . 244 B1
Millfield Cres ST2. . . . . 43 A1
Millfield Dr TF9. . . . . 97 F2
Millfield Prim Sch
Brownhills WS8. . . . . 245 A7
Fazeley B78 . . . . 261 A8
Millfield Rd WS8. . . . . 245 A7
Mill Fields DY7 . . . . 278 B3
Millfields Way WV5 . . . . . . 269 E5
Mill Gn WV10. . . . . 240 D4
Mill Gr Cheadle ST10 . . . . . . 76 E2
Codsall WV8 . . . . 239 C3
Mill Green Nature Pk★
WS11 . . . . 209 F1
Mill Gr ST7 . . . . 25 D1
Mill Hayes Rd
Biddulph ST8. . . . . 27 C4
Burslem ST6 . . . . 41 E1
Mill Hill Cres ST6. . . . . 42 A4
Mill Hill Dr DE15 . . . . 167 B4
Mill Hill La DE15 . . . . 167 B4
Mill Hill Prim Sch ST6 . . . . 41 F4
Mill Ho DY7 . . . . 278 B3
Millhouse Dr ST10 . . . . 76 E1
Millhouse Gdns ST19. . . . . 192 F1
Millicent Cl WS12. . . . . 210 B6
Millicent Ho ST3. . . . . 284 C2
Millicent St ST4. . . . . 72 E6
Millington St WS15 . . . . . . 178 F2
Mill La
Acton Trussell ST17 . . . . . . 175 A2
Albrighton WV7 . . . . 220 F1
Aldridge WS9. . . . . 256 F7
Barthomley CW2 . . . . 38 C7
Barton-u-N DE13 . . . . 201 E8
Blakedown DY10 . . . . 281 B2
Blakenhall CW5 . . . . 52 B4
Codsall WV8 . . . . 238 F5
Congleton CW12 . . . . 16 C8
Doveridge DE6. . . . . 127 A8
Edingale B79 . . . . 217 D4
Ellastone DE6 . . . . 80 B2
Fazeley B78. . . . . 261 A8
Foston DE65 . . . . 129 D7
Gnosall ST20 . . . . 171 C5
Mill La *continued*
Gratwich ST14. . . . . 124 E3
Great Haywood ST18. . . . . 158 B2
Hammerwich WS7. . . . . 229 D3
Hartington SK17 . . . . 24 D5
Kinver,Blundies DY7. . . . . . 274 A4
Kinver DY7. . . . . 278 B3
Little Aston WS9 . . . . 257 A7
Lower Tean ST10. . . . . 92 F2
Madeley CW3 . . . . 68 F7
Milwich ST18. . . . . 122 D4
Moddershall ST15 . . . . 105 E6
Roston DE6 . . . . 96 D7
Rugeley WS15 . . . . 178 F1
Scropton DE65. . . . . 129 F1
Shenstone WS14 . . . . 247 A6
Standon ST21 . . . . 102 C3
Stonnall WS9,WS14. . . . . . . 246 A4
Sudbury DE6 . . . . 128 E1
Tamworth B79. . . . . 250 C5
Tettenhall Wood WV6 . . . . 255 A3
The Bank ST7. . . . . 26 A7
Weston CW2. . . . . 37 B6
Weston-u-L TF11 . . . . 220 D7
Weston-Under-Lizard
TF11 . . . . 203 D1
Wetley Rocks ST9 . . . . 59 F7
Wheaton Aston ST19. . . . . . 205 C5
Wombourne WV5. . . . . 270 B6
Mill Mdw DE13. . . . . 162 F8
Mill Meece Marsh ST21 . 102 D1
Mill Meece Pumping
Station★ ST21. . . . . 117 E8
Millmoor Ave WS15 . . . . . . 198 A4
Mill Park Ind Est WS11. . . 210 A1
Mill Pk WS11 . . . . 210 A2
Mill Pond The WS13 . . . . . 214 C2
Mill Pool Cl WV5. . . . . 269 D5
Mill Pool Rd WS12 . . . . 210 B6
Millpool The WV5. . . . . 263 F2
Mill Rd Brownhills WS8 . . . 245 A7
Cheadle ST10. . . . . 76 E2
Coldmeece ST15 . . . . 118 B6
Oakamoor ST10. . . . . 78 A6
Walsall WS4 . . . . 244 C1
Mill Rise ST7 . . . . 26 A1
Millrise Rd ST2 . . . . 43 A1
Mills Cres WV2 . . . . 266 E8
Millside Rugeley WS15 . . . 196 B7
Wombourne WV5. . . . . 269 E5
Mills Rd WV2 . . . . 266 E8
Mill St Cannock WS11 . . . . 209 E1
Leek ST13 . . . . 30 D6
Newcastle-u-L ST5. . . . . 55 D1
Millstone Ave ST7. . . . . 25 E1
Millstone Edge ST13 . . . . . . 45 B1
Mill St ST19 . . . . 192 E1
Millstream Cl ST10. . . . . 76 E2
Mill Stream Cl WV8 . . . . . . 239 B4
Mill St Rocester ST14. . . . . . 96 A3
Stafford ST16 . . . . 285 B3
Stone ST15 . . . . 120 A8
Stourbridge DY8 . . . . 275 F2
Mill The ST7. . . . . 26 C5
Milltown Way ST13. . . . . 31 A4
Mill View ST6. . . . . 42 D6
Millwalk Ave ST15 . . . . 120 C7
Millwalk Dr WV9. . . . . 240 A3
Millward Rd ST2 . . . . 58 C3
Mill Waters ST10. . . . . 76 E1
Millway La DE6 . . . . 35 F3
Mill Way WS15. . . . . 198 A1
Mill Way The ST15 . . . . 103 B4
Milne Ave WS13. . . . . 215 D6
Milner Dr B79 . . . . 251 E7
Milner Terr ST13. . . . . 31 A7
Milnes Cl ST3. . . . . 73 A2
Milo Cres B78 . . . . 250 A2
Milton Ave B79 . . . . 250 A7
Milton Cres Dudley DY3 . . 271 A5
Talke ST7 . . . . 40 C8
Milton Ct WV6. . . . . 254 E4
Milton Dr TF9. . . . . 97 C2
Milton Gr ST17. . . . . 174 B8
Milton Ho DE14 . . . . 166 D3
Milton Prim Sch ST2. . . . . . 43 B1
Milton Rd Cannock WS11 . 209 E4
Stoke-on-T ST1 . . . . 42 F1
Stoke-on-T ST1 . . . . 57 E8
Milton St Burton u T DE14. 166 C3
Hanley ST1 . . . . 282 A1
Milvale St ST6. . . . . 56 E7
Milverton Dr ST14 . . . . 110 F1
Milverton Pl 4 ST3. . . . . . . 73 A3
Milward Gr ST3. . . . . 89 F6
Mimosa Wlk DY6. . . . . 275 E8
Minard Gr ST3. . . . . 74 A4
Minden Gr ST6 . . . . 57 D8
Mineal Rd ST2 . . . . 73 D7
Minehead Rd Dudley DY1. 271 E1
Wolverhampton WV10. . . . . 240 B2
Miners Way WS7. . . . . 228 C7
Miners Wlk B78. . . . . 251 F1
Minerva Cl Biddulph ST8. . . 27 B5
Tamworth B77 . . . . 250 D5
Minerva Rd ST4. . . . . 72 F6
Minewood Cl WS3 . . . . 242 F3
Minfield Cl ST7 . . . . 41 A8
Minn-End-La SK11. . . . . 8 B6
Minnie Cl ST7 . . . . 54 E7
Minors Hill WS14 . . . . 231 D6
Minshall Ct ST4. . . . . 72 C5
Minshall St ST4. . . . . 72 C5
Minsterley Cl WV3 . . . . 265 E8
Minsterpool Wlk WS13. . . 231 B8
Minster St ST6. . . . . 42 B1
Minster The WV3 . . . . 266 A7
Minstrel Ct ST8 . . . . 27 D7
Minton Cl Cheadle ST10 . . . 76 D1
Congleton CW12 . . . . 6 B1
Minton Pl ST5 . . . . 56 D5
Minton St
Newcastle-u-L ST5. . . . . 56 D5
Stoke-on-T ST4 . . . . 71 E8
Miranda Gr ST6. . . . . 42 D1
Miras Bsns Est WS12 . . . . 210 D3
Mires Brook La WS15 . . . . 160 F6
Mires The DE6. . . . . 35 A3
Mirfield Cl WV9. . . . . 240 A3
Miss Pickerings Field
ST17. . . . . 175 B1
Mistley Wlk ST6 . . . . 41 C7
Mitcham Cl WS12. . . . . 209 F7
Mitchell Ave ST7. . . . . 25 D1
Mitchell Cl WS13 . . . . 215 C6
Mitchell Dr ST7. . . . . 25 D1
Mitchell High Sch ST2 . . . 58 C3
Mitchell Rise ST15 . . . . 118 F6
Mitchell's Ct B79 . . . . 250 B5
Mitchell St ST6 . . . . 41 F1
Mitchel Rd DY6 . . . . 275 F4
Mitre Cl WV11 . . . . 242 A3
Mitre Rd WS6. . . . . 226 D2
Mitton Rd ST18 . . . . 191 C7
Moat Bank DE15 . . . . 167 D2
Moat Brook Ave WV8. . . . . 238 E4
Moatbrook La WV8 . . . . . . 238 D4
Moat Dr B78. . . . . 260 E5
Moat Farm Way WS3. . . . . 244 A5
Moat Hall Prim Sch WS6 226 F3
Moathouse Cl ST17 . . . . . . 193 B8
Moat House Dr ST18 . . . . . 172 E6
Moat La Audley ST7 . . . . 39 B3
Great Wyrley WS6 . . . . 227 A2
Newborough DE13. . . . . 162 F6
Moatside Cl WS3 . . . . 244 A5
Moat The ST3. . . . . 74 B4
Moat Way WS15 . . . . 198 B4
Mobberley Rd ST6 . . . . 41 C7
Mob La WS4. . . . . 244 C3
Moccasin Way ST16. . . . . . 155 F5
Moddershall Oaks ST3,
ST15. 90 A1
Moden Cl DY3 . . . . 271 D6
Moden Hill DY3 . . . . 271 D6
Modular Ct WV10 . . . . 224 D5
Moffat Gr ST2 . . . . 73 E7
Moffatt Way ST5. . . . . 55 A2
Moises Hall Rd WV5. . . . . 270 B7
Moisty La
Marchington ST14 . . . . 127 C3
Uttoxeter ST14 . . . . 126 F4
Mollatts Cl ST13 . . . . 30 B2
Mollatts Wood Rd ST13 . . 30 B1
Mollison Rd ST3 . . . . 90 A8
Monaco Pl ST5 . . . . 70 E7
Monarch Cl DE13. . . . . 166 D8
Monarchy Cl WS15. . . . . . . 196 D7
Mona Rd DE13. . . . . 166 B6
Moncreiff Dr DE13. . . . . . . 148 A1
Moneystone Cotts ST10 . . 63 A1
Monkhouse ST10 . . . . 76 D3
Monkleigh Cl ST4. . . . . 88 B5
Monks Cl
Newcastle-u-L ST5. . . . . 71 C6
Wombourne WV5. . . . . 269 E6
Monksfield TF9. . . . . 97 A1
Monk St DE13 . . . . 146 C7
Monks Way
Swynnerton ST15. . . . . 103 B4
Tamworth B77. . . . . 250 F5
Monks Wlk ST20 . . . . 171 C5
Monkton Cl ST3 . . . . 73 A1
Monmore Bsns Pk WV2 . 266 F7
Monmouth Pl ST5. . . . . 71 D4
Monsaldale Cl
Brownhills WS8 . . . . 244 D7
Burton u T DE15. . . . . 167 B4
Monsal Gr ST1. . . . . 57 F5
Monteagle Dr DY6 . . . . 270 D1
Montford Gr DY3 . . . . 271 D7
Montfort Pl ST5. . . . . 71 B5
Montgomery Ct ST5. . . . . . 283 A3
Montgomery Pl ST3. . . . . . . 74 B2
Montley B77. . . . . 262 C8
Montpelier Cl DE14 . . . . . . 185 A7
Montpellier Gdns DY1. . . 271 E2
Montrose Cl WS11 . . . . 209 F5
Montrose St ST4. . . . . 72 F5
Montville Dr ST17 . . . . 155 B1
Monty Pl ST4 . . . . 73 B6
Monument Cl ST12. . . . . 88 A2
Monument Dr WV10. . . . . . 241 C8
Monument La
Sedgley DY3. . . . . 266 E1
Tittensor ST12. . . . . 88 A2
Monument Rd ST7 . . . . 40 D6
Monument View ST7. . . . . . 39 F2
Monyash Cl ST3 . . . . 90 C7
Monyash Dr ST13 . . . . 31 A5
Moon's La WS6. . . . . 226 D1
Moor Cl
Acton Trussell ST17 . . . . . . 175 B1
Biddulph ST8 . . . . 16 E1
Burntwood WS7. . . . . 229 B7
Moorcroft Ave ST5. . . . . 71 B3
Moorcroft Cl ST10 . . . . 76 C1
Moor Croft WS15 . . . . 179 A6
Moorcroft Mus★ ST6. . . . . . 57 B7
Moore Cl Perton WV6 . . . . . 254 F4
Sutton Coldfield B74 . . . . . 257 F6
Moores Cl DE13. . . . . 166 B6
Moores Croft B79. . . . . 217 C5
Moore St Burslem ST6. . . . . . 57 A7
Cannock WS12. . . . . 210 C7
Moorfield Ave ST8 . . . . 27 C8
Moorfield Ct TF10. . . . . 168 E2
Moorfield La TF10 . . . . 168 D1
Moorfield Prim Sch
TF10 . . . . 168 E1
Moorfield Rd WV2 . . . . 266 C7
Moorfields Cl
Aldridge WS9. . . . . 256 A7
Cauldon Lowe ST10. . . . . 63 E4
Moorfields Ind Est ST21. 102 F3
Moorfields Leek ST13 . . . . . 30 F5
Stafford ST16 . . . . 155 D7
Moor Fst Sch ST8. . . . . 17 B1
Moor Furlong DE13 . . . . . . 147 F1
Moorgate Com Prim Sch
B79. 250 A5
Moorgate B79 . . . . 250 A5
Moor Gr ST14. . . . . 126 A8
Moor Hall Dr B75 . . . . 258 D1
Moor Hall La ST19 . . . . 208 A7
Moor Hall Prim Sch B75 258 D2
Moorhead Dr ST9. . . . . 43 F4
Moorhen Cl WS8. . . . . 244 E7
Moorhen Way ST6 . . . . 41 E8
Moorhill Prim Sch
Cannock WS11. . . . . 209 E4
Cannock WS11. . . . . 209 E5
Moorhouse Ct ST15 . . . . . . 119 A6
Moorhouse St ST13 . . . . 30 F5
Moorings The
3 Stone ST15. . . . . 120 A8
Alrewas DE13 . . . . 200 F3
Colwich ST17. . . . . 177 E7
Wolverhampton WV9. . . . . 239 F2
Moor La Cheadle ST10. . . . . . 76 F3
Church Leigh ST10. . . . . 108 E5
Colton WS15 . . . . 179 A8
Gayton ST18 . . . . 138 F6
Moorland Ave ST9 . . . . 59 C4
Moorland Cl
Rugeley WS15 . . . . 178 C1
Werrington ST9. . . . . 59 B4
Moorland Rd Biddulph ST8. 27 D8
Burslem ST6 . . . . 57 A8
Cannock WS11. . . . . 209 E5
Cheddleton ST13 . . . . 45 C5
Leek ST13 . . . . 31 B5
Mow Cop ST7. . . . . 26 D7
Newport TF10 . . . . 168 E2
Stoke-on-T ST6 . . . . 42 B1
Moorlands Dr DE6 . . . . 81 C7
Moorlands Farm Pk The★
ST10. 47 D3
Moorlands Sixth Form Ctr
ST10. 76 D1
Moorland View ST6. . . . . . . 42 C3
Moorland Wlk ST10. . . . . . . 76 D3
Moor La Pattingham WV6 . 253 D2
Seighford ST18 . . . . 154 D7
Shenstone WS14 . . . . 246 E2
Tamworth,Amington B79. . 251 A6
Tamworth,Bolehall B77 . . 250 D5
Moorleys La ST18 . . . . 139 A5
Moorpark Jun Sch ST6. . . 42 A1
Moor Pk Perton WV6. . . . . . 254 D5
Walsall WS3 . . . . 243 B3
Moor St S WV2 . . . . 266 C7
Moors Dr WV9. . . . . 224 B2
Moors Hill Cotts DE13. . . . 183 F8
Moorside High Sch ST9 . . 59 E4
Moorside Rd ST9 . . . . 59 D4
Moorson Ave ST7. . . . . 25 F8
Moor St Burton u T DE14 . . 166 C2
Tamworth B79. . . . . 250 A5
Moorsyde Rd ST4. . . . . 71 E5
Moor The WS13. . . . . 215 D8
Moorthorne Cres ST5 . . . . . 56 A6
Moor View WS7 . . . . 212 B2
Moorview Gdns ST7. . . . . . . 26 E6
Moran Gr ST6 . . . . 56 E7
Moran Rd ST5 . . . . 55 F2
Mordaunt Dr B75 . . . . 258 E2
Mordern Mobile Home Pk
WV10. . . . . 240 C6
Moresby Cl ST2. . . . . 43 B1
Moreton Ave
Hanchurch ST5 . . . . 87 D8
Kingsley ST10 . . . . 61 D2
Wolverhampton WV4. . . . . . 266 E4
Moreton Cl Kidsgrove ST7 . 41 B8
Werrington ST9. . . . . 59 B2
Moreton Com Sch WV10. 240 F1
Moreton Ho ST5 . . . . 56 D4
Moreton La
Draycott in t C DE6 . . . . . . 144 C8
Great Haywood ST18. . . . . 158 E4
Moreton Par ST5 . . . . 56 D4
Moreton Pl ST7. . . . . 25 E6
Moreton Rd WV10 . . . . 240 D1
Moreton St WS11 . . . . 209 F4
Morfe Hall La DY7 . . . . 273 D4
Morfe La DY7. . . . . 273 C4
Morford Rd WS9. . . . . 256 A7
Morgan Rd B78. . . . . 250 A2
Morgan Way ST6 . . . . 42 B6
Morland Cl ST15 . . . . 120 B5
Morley Cl DE15 . . . . 167 B2
Morley Dr CW12 . . . . 6 A1
Morley Rd WS7 . . . . 229 B7
Morley Road Sh Ctr WS7 229 B7
Morley's Hill DE13 . . . . 166 B7
Morley St Hanley ST1 . . . . . 282 A2
Leek ST13 . . . . 30 D5
Morlings Dr WS7 . . . . 229 B8
Morning Pines DY8 . . . . . . 279 E4
Morningside CW3. . . . . 68 E6
Mornington Rd ST1 . . . . 57 E8
Morpeth St ST3. . . . . 284 C3
Morpeth B77 . . . . 261 C7

Morridge Side ST13 ...... 32 A1
Morridge View ST13 ..... 45 C4
Morris Ct 4 WV4 .... 266 F4
Morris Dr ST16 .... 156 C3
Morris Hill B78 .... 262 F7
Morris Sq ST5 .... 56 D5
Morston Dr ST5 .... 71 B2
Morston B77 .... 261 D4
Mortimer Pl ST3 .... 73 F4
Morton Rd ST17 .... 174 D6
Morton St ST6 .... 56 E7
Morville Cl ST4 .... 72 E7
Moscow La ST20 .... 151 D7
Mosedale Ave ST3 .... 89 E8
Moseley Ct WV11 ...... 241 F3
Moseley Old Hall★
WV10 .... 241 A5
Moseley Old Hall La
WV10 .... 241 A5
Moseley Rd WV10 ...... 241 A4
Moseley Row ST18 ..... 137 C1
Mosley Dr ST14 .... 111 A1
Mosley Mews DE13 ..... 147 A4
Mosley Prim Sch DE13 .. 165 C7
Mosley St DE14 .... 166 C3
Mossbank Ave WS7 ..... 229 A6
Moss Cl Aldridge WS9 .... 256 A5
Werrington ST9 .... 59 B4
Moss Cres WS12 .... 209 C5
Mossdale B77 .... 262 C8
Mossdale Way DY3 ...... 271 E7
Mossfield TF9 .... 130 A6
Mossfield Cres 4 ST7 .... 26 B2
Mossfield Dr ST8 .... 27 E7
Mossfield Rd ST3 .... 73 C6
Moss Gn WS15 .... 178 C2
Moss Green Rd ST2 ...... 73 D7
Moss Gr Kingswinford DY6 275 D7
Newcastle-u-L ST5 .... 40 D3
Moss Hill ST9 .... 43 D5
Moss La Betton TF9 .... 97 F6
Cheadle ST10 .... 77 A2
Chipnall TF9 .... 114 C3
Hilderstone ST15 .... 106 E6
Lawton-gate ST7 .... 25 F4
Madeley CW3 .... 68 D6
Maer ST5 .... 84 F1
Mossland Rd ST3 .... 73 C5
Moss La Whitmore ST5 .... 85 C5
Woodseaves ST20,ST21 .. 151 F8
Yarnfield ST15 .... 119 A7
Mossley CE Prim Sch
CW12 .... 16 B8
Mossley Cl WS3 .... 242 F1
Mossley Ct CW12 .... 15 F8
Mossley Garth Cl 5 CW12 . 6 A1
Mossley La WS3 .... 242 F2
Mossley Prim Sch WS3 .. 242 F2
Moss Park Ave ST9 ...... 59 B4
Mosspit ST17 .... 174 F4
Moss Pl ST7 .... 26 B3
Moss Rd Cannock WS11 .. 210 A3
Congleton CW12 .... 15 E7
Moss Rise ST5 .... 71 C1
Moss Side ST1 .... 57 E8
Moss St Cannock WS11 ... 210 A4
Stoke-on-T ST6 .... 42 E5
Mossvale Gr ST16 ...... 155 A5
Mosswood St WS11 ..... 226 D7
Moston St ST1 .... 57 D6
Mostyn Cl ST8 .... 27 E6
Mott Pl ST6 .... 56 D8
Moulton Rd ST3 .... 284 B4
Mounfield Pl ST4 .... 72 D6
Mountain Ash Rd WS8 .. 244 E5
Mountain Pine Cl WS12 . 210 A8
Mount Ave Cannock WS12 210 B7
Stoke-on-T ST4 .... 71 F7
Stone ST15 .... 104 F2
Mountbatten Cl
1 Burton u T DE13 ...... 166 D8
Burntwood WS7 .... 211 F1
Mount Cl
Cheslyn Hay WS6 .... 226 E2
Dudley DY3 .... 271 C2
Stone ST15 .... 120 D6
Werrington ST9 .... 59 C4
Wombourne WV5 .... 270 A7
Mount Cotts ST20 .... 131 B4
Mount Cres ST15 .... 104 F2
Mount Ct WV6 .... 255 B2
Mount Dr WV5 .... 270 A7
Mount Edge ST18 .... 137 B1
Mount Fields ST10 .... 94 B2
Mountford Cres WS9 .... 256 C8
Mountford St ST6 .... 41 F1
Mount Gdns WV8 .... 238 F4
Mount Ind Est ST15 ..... 104 F2
Mount La Dudley DY3 .... 271 C2
Market Drayton TF9 ..... 112 C8
Mount Pleasant Ave
WV5 .... 269 F7
Mount Pleasant WS6 .... 226 E2
Mount Pleasant Cl ST15 120 D6
Mount Pleasant
Derrington ST18 .... 154 E2
Hanley ST1 .... 282 A2
Ipstones ST10 .... 62 A8
Kidsgrove ST7 .... 26 A1
Kingswinford DY6 ...... 275 C4
Leek ST13 .... 30 E6
Loggerheads TF9 .... 99 F5
Mount Pleasant Mobile
Home Pk B77 .... 250 C1
Mount Pleasant
Newcastle-u-L,Chesterton
ST5 .... 55 E6
Newcastle-u-L ST5 ...... 283 C2
Mount Pleasant Rd ST7 .. 26 B7
Mount Pleasant B77 .... 261 C8
Mount Pl ST11 .... 91 A7
Mount Rd
Blythe Bridge ST11 .... 91 A7
Burntwood WS7 .... 229 B6
Castle Gresley DE11 ..... 186 D1
Kidsgrove ST7 .... 26 B1
Leek ST13 .... 31 B5
Rugeley WS15 .... 178 B2
Stone ST15 .... 104 F2
Stourbridge,Wordsley DY8 275 E2
Walsall WS3 .... 244 A4
Wolverhampton,Goldthorn Hill
WV4 .... 266 A4
Wolverhampton,Lanesfield
WV4 .... 266 F2
Wolverhampton,Tettenhall Wood
WV6 .... 255 A3
Wombourne WV5 .... 270 A7
Mount Road Ind Est
WS7 .... 229 B6
Mount Row ST16 .... 285 B3
Mount St Georges The
ST5 .... 56 C6
Mountside Gdns ST13 .... 31 B6
Mount Side St WS12 .... 210 C7
Mountsorrel Cl ST4 ...... 88 C6
Mount St Burton u T DE15 . 167 A3
Cannock WS12 .... 210 B7
Hanley ST1 .... 57 E5
Newcastle-u-L ST5 .... 55 E6
Stafford ST16 .... 285 B3
Stone ST15 .... 105 A2
Mount The Creswell ST18 . 154 F7
Kidsgrove ST7 .... 26 A1
Newcastle-u-L ST5 .... 55 E6
Scholar Green ST7 .... 25 E7
Mountwood Covert WV6 255 B3
Mouse Hill WS3 .... 243 F3
Mousley St ST6 .... 56 E8
Mowbray Croft WS7 ..... 211 E1
Mowbray Wlk ST1 .... 57 F8
Mow Cop Rd ST7 .... 26 D6
Mow La Biddulph ST7,ST8 .. 16 B2
Mount Pleasant ST7 .... 26 B5
Mow Cop CW12 .... 15 F4
Moxhull Cl WV12 .... 242 C1
Moxhull Gdns WV12 ..... 242 C1
Moxley Ave ST1 .... 57 D7
Mozart Ct WS11 .... 210 C2
Muchall Rd WV4 .... 266 A5
Mucklestone Rd
Loggerheads TF9 .... 99 D5
Norton in H TF9 .... 82 D2
Mucklestone Wood La
TF9 .... 99 E6
Muirfield Cl WS3 .... 243 A3
Muirfield B77 .... 251 C5
Muirville Cl 1 DY8 ..... 275 D3
Mulberry Cl TF10 .... 168 F1
Mulberry Dr 3 WS13 .... 231 E8
Mulberry Gn DY1 .... 271 F5
Mulberry Pl
Newcastle-u-L ST5 .... 55 E8
Walsall WS3 .... 242 F1
Mulberry Rd
Cannock WS11 .... 209 E3
Walsall WS3 .... 243 A1
Mulberry St ST1 .... 282 C2
Mulberry Way ST13 ...... 31 A4
Muldoon Cl WS11 .... 210 B4
Mulgrave St ST1 .... 282 A4
Mullein B74 .... 257 F5
Mulliner Cl ST2 .... 58 D3
Munro St ST4 .... 72 A5
Munster Terr ST4 .... 71 F5
Murdoch Dr DY6 .... 275 C7
Murhall St ST6 .... 56 E8
Murray St ST6 .... 41 C7
Murton B77 .... 262 C8
Muse La DE6 .... 129 B7
Musk La DY3 .... 271 B3
Musk La W DY3 .... 271 B3
Mus of Cannock Chase★
WS12 .... 210 D6
Mustang Cl ST6 .... 41 C4
Mustang Dr ST16 .... 155 B8
Muxloe Cl WS3 .... 243 A3
Myatt Ave
Burntwood WS7 .... 229 A7
Wolverhampton WV2 .... 266 E6
Myatt Cl WV2 .... 266 E6
Myatt St ST1 .... 282 C4
Myatt Way WS15 .... 196 D6
Mynors St Hanley ST1 ... 282 C3
Stafford ST16 .... 156 A3
Myott Ave ST5 .... 283 A1
Myrtle Ave ST3 .... 74 B3
Myrtle Gr Brewood ST19 .. 223 D6
Wolverhampton WV3 .... 265 E6
Myrtle St WV2 .... 266 F6

N

Nabb La Alton ST10 .... 94 F7
Denstone ST14 .... 95 A4
Nabbs Cl ST7 .... 26 B2
Nabbswood Rd ST7 .... 26 B2
Nab Hill Ave ST13 .... 30 D6
Nab Hill Ct ST13 .... 30 C6
Naden Ho WS12 .... 209 C5
Naesby Rd WV6 .... 254 F3
Nagington Dr ST19 ..... 207 F7
Nailers Dr WS7 .... 229 D6
Nairn Rd WS3 .... 243 A4
Nancy Talbot Cl WS15 ... 161 B5
Nankirk La DE13 .... 165 A6
Nanny Goat La ST15 ..... 105 A1
Nantwich Rd Audley ST7 .. 39 B1
Balterley ST7 .... 38 F1
Woore CW3 .... 67 B1
Naomi Way WS9 .... 245 B4
Napier Gdns 3 ST7 .... 26 A2
Napier Rd WV2 .... 266 D7
Napier St Burton u T DE14 . 166 C1
Stoke-on-T ST4 .... 72 D6
Napier B77 .... 250 E3
Naples Cl ST3 .... 73 E4
Naples Dr ST5 .... 70 F6
Napley Dr TF9 .... 82 C2
Napley Rd TF9 .... 82 D1
Narlow La DE6 .... 51 F2
Narrow La
Brownhills WS8 .... 244 F8
Colton WS15 .... 179 B7
Denstone ST14 .... 95 D6
Milwich ST15 .... 121 F7
Narvik Cres ST6 .... 42 C2
Nash Ave Perton WV6 .... 254 E3
Stafford ST16 .... 155 B6
Nashe Dr ST3 .... 73 A2
Nash La
Acton Trussell ST17 ..... 193 B8
Lichfield WS13 .... 214 A5
Nash Peake St ST6 .... 41 D3
Nash St ST5 .... 55 E2
Natham Cl ST11 .... 74 D3
Nathan Ct WS15 .... 196 F5
Nathans Mdw CW12 ...... 16 C7
National Meml Arboretum
The★ DE13 .... 201 C2
Nave Rd ST4 .... 72 A5
Navigation Loop ST15 ... 104 E2
Navigation Rd ST6 .... 56 F7
Navigation St ST6 .... 56 E7
Navigation Way WS11 ... 210 A2
Naylors Gr DY3 .... 271 E4
Naylor St ST6 .... 41 F5
Naylor Yd 1 ST13 .... 30 E6
Neachless Ave WV5 ..... 270 A5
Neachley La TF11 .... 220 A2
Neal Croft WS14 .... 232 E6
Neale Ho WV2 .... 266 C7
Neale Pl ST2 .... 58 B5
Neander B79 .... 249 F6
Near Ridding ST20 ...... 171 D5
Neath Cl ST3 .... 73 D3
Neath Pl 2 ST3 .... 73 C6
Neath Rd WS3 .... 242 F2
Neath Way WS3 .... 242 F2
Needwood Ave DE13 .... 147 C4
Needwood CE Prim Sch
DE13 .... 162 F7
Needwood Cl WV2 ...... 266 B6
Needwood Ct DE13 ..... 146 C6
Needwood Dr WV4 ..... 266 F4
Needwood Grange
WS15 .... 161 A5
Needwood Hill WS13 ... 214 A2
Needwood Pk DE13 ..... 183 D1
Needwood St DE14 ..... 166 B4
Nellan Cres ST6 .... 42 D1
Nelson Bank ST6,ST7 ..... 41 A7
Nelson Bldgs ST7 .... 26 A1
Nelson Cres ST21 .... 102 E2
Nelson Dr WS12 .... 210 F4
Nelson Ind Est ST7 .... 25 C1
Nelson Pl Hanley ST1 .... 282 C2
Newcastle-u-L ST5 ...... 283 C3
Nelson Rd ST4 .... 71 E8
Nelson St Burton u T DE15 167 C4
Leek ST13 .... 30 F7
Newcastle-u-L ST5 .... 56 C5
Stoke-on-T ST4 .... 72 D6
Nelson Way ST17 .... 174 E6
Nemesia B77 .... 251 B4
Nene Cl DE13 .... 147 C1
Nene Way DE65 .... 147 D8
Nephew St ST6 .... 56 E8
Neptune Gr ST1 .... 57 F6
Ness Gr ST10 .... 76 E5
Nest Comm WS3 .... 243 F5
Nether Beacon WS13 .... 214 A1
Netherbridge Ave WS14 . 231 E7
Netherby Rd DY3 .... 271 C8
Nethercote Pl ST2 .... 73 D8
Nethergate DY3 .... 271 F5
Nether La WS7 .... 229 D8
Netherseal Rd
Chilcote DE12 .... 219 F4
Clifton Campville B79 ... 218 F2
Netherset Hey La CW3 ... 68 F4
Netherstone Gr B74 ..... 257 F5
Nether Stowe High Sch
WS13 .... 214 B1
Netherstowe La WS13 ... 214 D2
Netherstowe WS13 ...... 214 C2
Netherton Gr ST2 .... 43 C2
Nethy Dr WV6 .... 255 B5
Netley Pl ST3 .... 88 E7
Netley Rd WS3 .... 242 E2
Netley Way WS3 .... 242 E2
Nevada La ST6 .... 57 B8
Neve Ave WV10 .... 240 F1
Neville Ave WV4 .... 266 D5
Neville Cl DE13 .... 147 B3
Neville Ho DY3 .... 271 D7
Neville St Stoke-on-T ST4 .. 71 F4
Tamworth B77 .... 250 E3
Nevill St B79 .... 250 A5
Nevin Ave ST8 .... 27 D5
Nevis Ct WV6 .... 255 E2
Nevis Gr WV12 .... 242 B1
Newall Ave ST16 .... 156 B5
Newark Gr ST6 .... 41 C7
New Ave ST11 .... 91 C6
New Barns La WS14 .... 246 B3
New Bldgs Barlaston ST12 . 88 D1
Biddulph ST8 .... 27 C3
Newbold Cl WS13 ...... 231 A5
Newborough Cl ST1 ...... 57 F6
Newbridge Ave WV6 .... 255 E3
Newbridge Cres WV6 ... 255 E4
Newbridge Dr WV6 ..... 255 E4
Newbridge Gdns WV6 ... 255 E4
Newbridge Mews 3
WV6 .... 255 F4
Newbridge Prep Sch
WV6 .... 255 E4
Newbridge Rd DY6 ..... 275 C8
Newbridge St WV6 ..... 255 F4
Newburn Gr ST4 .... 88 B8
Newbury Cl
Great Wyrley WS6 ...... 226 F2
Stafford ST17 .... 175 C7
Newbury Dr DE13 ...... 147 C1
Newbury Gr ST3 .... 88 E7
Newbury Rd
Norton Canes WS11 .... 228 A5
Stourbridge DY8 .... 275 D1
Wolverhampton WV10 ... 240 C2
Newby Cl DE15 .... 167 B1
Newcastle Com High Sch
ST5 .... 70 F7
Newcastle Ent Ctr ST5 ... 55 E2
Newcastle La ST4 .... 71 E6
Newcastle Rd Ashley TF9 . 100 B7
Astbury CW12 .... 15 A7
Cotes Heath ST21 .... 102 F3
Eccleshall ST21 .... 133 E8
Leek ST13 .... 30 D4
Loggerheads TF9 .... 99 E5
Madeley CW3 .... 68 F7
Market Drayton TF9 ...... 97 F2
Newcastle-u-L ST5 .... 71 C1
Stoke-on-T ST4 .... 71 E5
Stone ST15 .... 104 E1
Talke ST7 .... 40 E7
Woore CW3 .... 67 E1
Newcastle St Burslem ST6 . 56 E8
Newcastle-u-L ST5 .... 55 D2
Stone ST15 .... 104 F1
Newcastle-under-Lyme Coll
ST5 .... 283 A3
Newcastle-under-Lyme Schs
ST5 .... 283 C2
New Century St ST1 ..... 282 A3
New Chapel Ct ST6 ...... 41 D4
Newchapel Observatory★
ST7 .... 26 E2
Newchapel Rd ST7 .... 26 C3
New Close Ave ST11 ..... 91 B8
Newcomen Cl WS7 ..... 229 C8
Newcomen Gr ST2 .... 73 D7
New Cott DE6 .... 36 E3
Newcott Cl WV9 .... 239 F2
New Cotts Foxt ST10 ..... 62 C5
Oaken WV8 .... 238 D2
Six Ashes WV15 .... 272 C6
Stourton DY7 .... 278 F8
New Council Hos TF9 .... 98 C2
Newcroft Ct ST5 .... 56 C5
Newcrofts Wlk ST6 ...... 42 D6
New Dudley Rd DY6 .... 275 C8
Newfield Dr DY6 .... 275 E4
Newfield Rd DE15 ...... 167 B4
Newfield St ST6 .... 41 D4
Newfold Cres ST6 .... 43 B8
Newford Cres ST2 .... 42 F1
New Ford Prim Sch ST6 .. 42 D1
New Garden Ho ST17 ... 285 B2
New Garden St ST17 .... 285 B1
Newgate WV6 .... 253 C3
Newgate St WS7 .... 229 A5
New Gdns WS7 .... 228 F5
New Haden Rd ST10 ...... 76 B1
Newhall Com Jun Sch
DE11 .... 186 E6
Newhall Cres WS11 .... 210 B3
Newhall Gdns WS11 .... 209 F2
Newhall Inf Sch DE11 ... 186 F7
New Hall Rd ST3 .... 73 E2
Newhall St WS11 .... 209 D1
New Hall St ST1 .... 282 B3
Newhall St ST10 .... 61 D3
New Hampton Rd W
WV6 .... 255 F4
Newhaven Gr ST4 .... 88 B5
New Hayes Rd
Prospect Village WS12 ... 211 C4
Stoke-on-T ST6 .... 41 E4
Newhay DE13 .... 147 F1
New Homage Gdns WV9 . 224 B2
New Horse Rd WS6 ..... 226 E3
New Hos TF11 .... 203 F5
Newhouse Ct ST2 .... 58 B5
Newhouse La WV7 ..... 237 A3
Newhouse Rd ST2 .... 58 B5
Newick Ave B74 .... 257 B3
Newington Gr ST4 .... 88 C5
New Inn Bank ST21 ..... 131 D8
New Inn La ST4 .... 88 A7
New Inn Row ST17 ..... 175 F3
New King St ST7 .... 39 C1
New Kingsway ST3 .... 74 A4
New La ST6 .... 28 B1
Newland Ave ST16 ..... 155 D7
Newland Cl WS4 .... 244 C2
Newlands Cl
Newcastle-u-L ST5 .... 71 B5
Penkridge ST19 .... 207 F7
Stone ST15 .... 119 F6
Newlands Ct WS12 ..... 227 E8
Newlands La
Colton WS15 .... 179 D7
Norton Canes WS12 ..... 227 D8
Newlands St ST4 .... 57 B1
New Landywood La WS6 242 E7
Newleigh St ST2 .... 43 B1
Newlyn Ave CW12 .... 15 F8
Newlyn Cl WS14 .... 231 D7
Newman Ave WV4 ...... 266 F4
Newman Cl ST15 .... 120 C7
Newman Dr DE14 ...... 185 B8
Newman Gr WS15 ...... 196 F7
Newman Rd WV10 ..... 241 A1
Newmarket Rd WS11 ... 228 B4
Newmarket Way ST10 .... 76 E5
New Mill La B78 .... 261 A7
Newmill St ST2 .... 43 B1
Newmount Rd ST4 .... 73 B5
New Park Gdns ST4 ...... 88 C5
New Park Sch WV6 ..... 255 F5
New Penkridge Rd
WS11 .... 209 C1
New Plant La WS7 ..... 228 C8
Newpool Cotts ST8 .... 27 B5
Newpool Rd ST8 .... 27 B6
Newpool Terr ST8 .... 27 B5
Newport CE Jun Sch
TF10 .... 168 F2
Newport Cl DE14 ...... 166 E7
Newport Croft ST19 .... 223 C6
Newport Girls' High Sch
TF10 .... 168 E1
Newport Gr ST5 .... 40 E2
Newport Inf Sch TF10 ... 168 F2
Newport La ST6 .... 56 E7
Newport Rd
Albrighton TF11,WV7 .... 220 D1
Codsall WV7 .... 237 F2
Eccleshall ST21 .... 133 E6
Edgmond TF10 .... 168 C4
Gnosall ST20 .... 171 B5
Great Bridgeford ST18 ... 135 C2
Market Drayton TF9 .... 112 E6
Stafford ST16 .... 285 A2
Tong TF11 .... 220 D3
Woodseaves ST20 ...... 151 D7
Newport St
Brewood ST19 .... 223 C6
Burslem ST6 .... 56 E8
Newport B77 .... 250 F5
Newquay Ave ST17 ..... 175 D8
Newquay Ct CW12 .... 15 E8
New Rd Aldridge WS9 ... 256 A5
Alton ST10 .... 78 E1
Armitage WS15 .... 198 B5
Astbury CW12 .... 15 B4
Audley ST7 .... 39 E3
Brownhills WS8 .... 244 F7
Burntwood WS7 .... 229 B6
Checkley ST10 .... 109 B8
Cookley DY11 .... 280 B7
Dilhorne ST10 .... 75 C4
New Rd Est (Ind Est)
ST18 .... 139 B1
New Rd Flash SK17 .... 3 A3
Hales TF9 .... 113 F8
Halfpenny Green DY3 ... 268 F4
Hixon ST18 .... 158 A8
Kidderminster DY10 .... 280 C3
Madeley CW3 .... 68 E7
Penkridge ST19 .... 192 E1
Shenstone WS14 .... 246 F6
Shuttington B79 .... 251 E8
Slade Heath WV10 ...... 224 F1
Smestow DY3 .... 269 B3
Swadlincote DE11 ...... 186 E6
Tamworth B77 .... 261 F7
Upper Tean ST10 .... 92 D4
Uttoxeter ST14 .... 111 A1
Werrington ST2 .... 58 F3
Wolverhampton,Newbridge
WV6 .... 255 E4
New Row
Drayton Bassett B78 .... 260 E5
Madeley Heath CW3 ...... 69 A8
Stafford ST18 .... 174 C5
Tatenhill DE13 .... 165 A1
Newshaw Wlk ST1 ...... 282 C3
New Sreet Cotts CW12 .... 6 A6
New St
6 Cannock,Mill Green
WS11 .... 226 E8
Biddulph Moor ST8 .... 28 A8
Biddulph ST8 .... 27 F7
Birchmoor B78 .... 262 E7
Burntwood,Chase Terrace
WS7 .... 228 E8
Burntwood,Chasetown
WS7 .... 228 E5
Burslem ST6 .... 56 F8
Burton u T DE14 .... 166 D2
Cannock,Bridgtown WS11 226 D6
Cannock WS12 .... 210 C4
Dudley,Gornalwood DY3 .. 271 C3
Newstead Prim Sch ST3 .. 88 F6
Newstead Rd ST2 .... 58 B5
Newstead B79 .... 249 D6
Newstead Trad Est ST4 ... 88 D7
New St Essington WV11 ... 242 A3
Fazeley B78 .... 261 B8
Great Wyrley WS6 ...... 227 A1
Kingswinford DY6 ...... 275 D4
Kingswinford,Wall Heath
DY6 .... 275 C8

New St continued
Leek ST13 . . . . 30 F6
Newcastle-u-L ST5. . . . . . 56 D5
Newport TF10 . . . . 168 E3
Norton Bridge ST15. . . . 135 A8
Stafford ST16 . . . . 155 D5
Stourbridge DY8 . . . . . . 279 F5
Stourbridge,Wordsley DY8 275 D2
Tamworth,Bolehall B77 . . 250 E4
Tamworth,Mount Pleasant
 B77 . . . . 250 C1
Uttoxeter ST14 . . . . 126 B7
Walsall,Wallington Heath
 WS3 . . . . 243 B1
Walsall WS4 . . . . 244 D1
Wolverhampton,Merry Hill
 WV3 . . . . 265 D7
Wolverhampton,Parkfield
 WV4 . . . . 266 E6
Newton Cl DE15 . . . . . . 167 E8
Newton Ct ST9. . . . . 59 A4
Newton La
 Newton Regis CV9 . . . . 236 F2
 Newton Solney DE15. . . 167 F7
 Seckington B79 . . . . . . 236 B3
Newton Leys DE15. . . . . 167 C4
Newton Mews DE15. . . . 166 F3
Newton ST10. . . . . 77 E2
Newton Rd Lichfield WS13 213 F2
 Newcastle-u-L ST5. . . . . 56 B5
 Newton Solney DE15. . . 167 B6
 Stafford ST16 . . . . 155 F5
Newton Regis CE Prim Sch
 B79 . . . . 236 C3
Newton's Coll WS13. . . . 231 B8
Newton Solney CE Inf Sch
 DE15. . . . . 167 E8
Newton St ST4. . . . . 56 E2
Newtown
 Market Drayton TF9. . . . 112 D8
 Newchapel ST7 . . . . 26 E2
 Newport TF10 . . . . 168 E1
New Wood Cl DY7 . . . . . 279 C8
New Wood Gr WS9. . . . . 245 A3
Niall Rd ST4. . . . . 71 F1
Nicholas Gr ST13 . . . . . . 30 B5
Nicholas St 3 ST6. . . . . . 56 F8
Nicholl's La ST15 . . . . . . 105 B3
Nicholls St ST4. . . . . 72 B5
Nicholls Way WS12 . . . . 210 F1
Nicholson Way
 Burton u T DE14. . . . . . 166 A1
 Leek ST13 . . . . 30 D6
Nicklaus Cl DE14. . . . . . 185 A7
Nidderdale Cl CW12. . . . . 6 A5
Nightingale Cl
 Huntington WS12. . . . . 209 C7
 Lower Tean ST10 . . . . . . 92 F1
Nightingale Ct WS7 . . . . 229 B8
Nightingale B77 . . . . 262 A6
Nightingale Wlk WS7 . . . 229 F8
Nile St ST6 . . . . 57 A8
Nimbus B77 . . . . 261 D4
Ninefoot La
 Tamworth,Belgrave B77 . . 261 E8
 Tamworth,Wilnecote B77 . 261 F7
Ninian Pk B77 . . . . 261 D6
Ninian Way B77 . . . . 261 E6
Nirvana Cl WS11 . . . . . . 209 C2
Noblett Rd ST1 . . . . 57 E7
Nocke Rd WV11 . . . . 241 F1
Noddington Ave WS14 . . 232 E6
Noddington La WS14. . . . 232 E6
Noddy Park Rd WS9. . . . 256 B7
Noddy Pk WS9. . . . . 256 B7
No Man's Green La DY7 . 276 E6
No Man's Heath Rd DE12 219 F3
No Name Rd WS7 . . . . . . 228 E7
Nook The WS6. . . . . 226 C1
Noon Croft DE13 . . . . . . 200 F2
Norbroom Ct TF10 . . . . . 169 A4
Norbroom Dr TF10 . . . . . 169 A4
Norbury Ave
 Stoke-on-T ST2 . . . . 43 A3
 Walsall WS3 . . . . 244 A3
Norbury CE Prim Sch DE6 96 E7
Norbury Cl ST20 . . . . 171 D6
Norbury Cres 14 WV4 . . 266 F4
Norbury Ct ST15 . . . . . . 120 A8
Norbury Hollow DE6 . . . . 80 D1
Norbury Rd ST20. . . . . . . 171 A7
Norfolk Cl ST5. . . . . 71 B2
Norfolk Cres WS6. . . . . . 256 B8
Norfolk Dr B78 . . . . 250 A1
Norfolk Gr Biddulph ST8 . . 16 C1
 Great Wyrley WS6 . . . . 226 F1
Norfolk Ho ST7 . . . . 40 D6
Norfolk Rd
 Burton u T DE15. . . . . . 185 D7
 Kidsgrove ST7 . . . . 25 F2
 Stourbridge DY8 . . . . . 279 D8
 Wolverhampton WV3 . . . 266 A8
Norfolk St ST1. . . . . 282 A1
Norfolk Way ST17. . . . . . 174 C7
Normacot Grange Rd ST3 90 A7
Normacot Rd ST3 . . . . . . 284 C3
Norman Ave ST6. . . . . 41 F3
Normanbrook Ct TF9. . . . . 97 C1
Norman Cl B79 . . . . 249 E7
Normandy Gr ST2 . . . . . . 43 A2
Normandy Pl ST5 . . . . . . 283 A3
Norman Gr ST5 . . . . 56 D2
Norman Keep DE13 . . . . 146 C6
Norman Rd
 Penkridge ST19 . . . . . . 208 A8

Norman Rd continued
 Tutbury DE13. . . . . 146 C6
Normanton Gr ST3. . . . . . 73 D6
Norris Cl TF9 . . . . 100 C5
Norris Rd ST6 . . . . 41 F3
Northam Rd ST1 . . . . 57 D6
North Ave Leek ST13 . . . . 30 D5
 Stafford ST16 . . . . 155 D7
North Castle St ST16 . . . 285 A3
Northcliffe 4 ST13 . . . . . 30 D6
Northcote Ave ST4 . . . . . . 72 A8
Northcote Ct ST18 . . . . . 177 E8
Northcote Ct ST5 . . . . . . 283 C3
Northcote Pl ST5 . . . . . . 283 C3
Northcote St ST4 . . . . 57 B1
North Cres WV10 . . . . . . 241 C7
Northdale WV6 . . . . 255 B4
North Dr ST20. . . . . 171 C5
Northesk Pl ST5 . . . . 71 A5
Northesk St 4 ST15. . . . 105 A1
Northfield Ave ST14. . . . . 96 A4
Northfield Cl ST14 . . . . . 111 A2
Northfield Dr ST8 . . . . 16 E2
Northfield Gr WV3 . . . . . 265 C7
Northfield Rd DE13 . . . . 166 C7
Northfields Way WS8 . . . 244 D7
Northfleet St ST2 . . . . 58 A3
Northgate WS9 . . . . 256 A7
Northgate St ST4 . . . . 71 F1
Northgate Way WS9 . . . . 256 A8
North Gn WV4 . . . . 265 D6
Northicote Recn Ctr
 WV10 . . . . 240 E3
Northicote Sch The
 WV10 . . . . 240 E3
Northlands CW3 . . . . 67 C1
North Oval DY3 . . . . 271 E5
Northover Cl WV9. . . . . . 240 A2
North Pl Bucknall ST2 . . . . 58 B6
 Stafford ST16 . . . . 155 D5
North Prim Sch ST6. . . . . 57 B7
North Rd Burslem ST6. . . . 57 B7
 Wolverhampton,Parkfield
 WV4 . . . . 266 F5
North Springfield DY3 . . 266 E1
North Staffordshire Hospl
 Ctr (Outpatients Dept)
 ST4 . . . . 71 E8
North Staffordshire Medical
 Inst ST4 . . . . 71 E8
North Staffordshire Nuffield
 Hospl The ST5 . . . . 71 C3
North Staffordshire Royal
 Infmy ST4 . . . . 71 F7
North St Burntwood WS7. . 211 F1
 Burton u T DE15. . . . . . 167 B3
 Cannock WS11. . . . . . . 226 E6
 Leek ST13 . . . . 30 D6
 Mount Pleasant ST7 . . . . 26 B6
 Newcastle-u-L ST5. . . . . 283 C3
North Street Ct ST4 . . . . . 72 A8
North St ST4. . . . . 72 A8
North Terr ST5 . . . . 56 B5
Northumberland Cl B78. . 250 A1
Northumberland Rd
 DE15 . . . . 185 D7
North Walls ST16 . . . . . . 285 B3
Northway DY3 . . . . 266 C2
North West Terr ST6 . . . . 42 C1
North Wlk ST3 . . . . 74 B1
Northwood Cl ST5 . . . . . . 71 D7
Northwood Ct ST1 . . . . . 282 C3
Northwood Gn ST1. . . . . . 57 E4
Northwood Inf Sch ST1 . . 57 E4
Northwood La
 Ellastone DE6 . . . . 80 C5
 Newcastle-u-L ST5. . . . . 71 D2
Northwood Park Cl
 WV10 . . . . 240 E3
Northwood Park Prim Sch
 WV10 . . . . 240 E3
Northwood Park Rd
 Hanley ST1 . . . . 57 E4
 Wolverhampton WV10 . . 240 E3
Northycote Farm & Ctry Pk★
 WV10 . . . . 240 F3
Northycote La WV10 . . . . 240 F4
Norton Ave ST6. . . . . 42 A3
Norton Bridge Sta ST15. 135 A8
Norton Canes High Sch
 WS11 . . . . 228 A7
Norton Canes Prim Sch
 WS11 . . . . 228 A6
Norton Cl Tamworth B79. . 250 C7
 Wolverhampton WV4. . . 265 C3
Norton Cres ST6 . . . . 57 D8
Norton Dr ST6 . . . . 57 D8
Norton East Rd WS11 . . . 228 B6
Norton Grange Cres
 WS11. . . . . 227 F4
Norton Grange WS11. . . . 227 F4
Norton Green La WS11 . . 227 F4
Norton Hall Cl ST6 . . . . . . 42 E3
Norton Hall La WS11 . . . 227 D4
Norton Ind Est ST6 . . . . . 42 E2
Norton in Hales CE Prim Sch
 TF9 . . . . 82 C2
Norton La
 Burntwood WS7 . . . . . . 229 C6
 Great Wyrley WS6 . . . . 227 A4
Norton Lakeside Sta★
 WS11 . . . . 228 C6
Norton La
 Norton Canes WS12 . . . 227 F3
 Stoke-on-T ST6 . . . . 42 F3
Norton Prim Sch ST6 . . . . 42 F3
Norton Rd
 Burton u T DE13. . . . . . 166 A6

Norton Rd continued
 Norton Canes WS11,WS12 227 F8
 Stourbridge DY8 . . . . . . 279 E2
 Walsall WS3 . . . . 244 A5
Norton Springs WS11 . . . 227 F5
Norton St ST2 . . . . 43 B1
Norton Terr WS11. . . . . . 227 F6
Norwich Cl WS13 . . . . . . 214 C3
Norwich Pl ST5 . . . . 71 C5
Norwich Rd ST2 . . . . 58 D2
Norwood Ho WS15 . . . . . 178 B1
Nottingham Ct ST14. . . . 110 F1
Nottingham Rd WS14 . . . 232 D3
Novi La ST15 . . . . 31 A7
Nuffield Hospl WV6 . . . . 255 C4
Nunn's Cl ST3 . . . . 74 C5
Nunn St ST13 . . . . 30 D6
Nuns La WS15 . . . . 180 B6
Nurseries The WV9 . . . . . 224 B2
Nursery Ave
 Aldridge WS9 . . . . 256 B5
 Stoke-on-T ST9 . . . . 43 C4
Nursery Cl Bradley ST18. . 191 C8
 Brown Edge ST6 . . . . . . 43 B7
 Cheadle ST10. . . . . 76 C3
 Kidsgrove ST7 . . . . 25 D1
Nursery Croft WS13 . . . . 213 F1
Nursery Dr Biddulph ST8. . 16 C2
 Penkridge ST19 . . . . . . 192 E2
 Wombourne WV5. . . . . . 269 F4
Nursery Gdns
 Codsall WV8 . . . . 238 F4
 Stourbridge DY8 . . . . . 275 F1
Nursery La Hopwas B78 . . 249 B6
 Stafford ST16 . . . . 155 D5
 Stoke-on-T ST9 . . . . 43 C3
 Sutton Coldfield B74 . . 257 A1
Nursery Rd Rugeley WS15 197 A5
 Scholar Green ST7. . . . . 25 E5
Nursery St ST4 . . . . 72 A5
Nursery View Cl WS9. . . . 256 E2
Nursery Way ST18 . . . . . 158 B3
Nursery Wlk WV6 . . . . . . 255 D4
Nurton Bank WV6. . . . . . 254 A3
Nurton Hill Rd WV6 . . . . 253 E6
Nutbrook Ave ST4 . . . . . . 72 C4
Nuthurst Dr WS11. . . . . . 226 F4
Nyewood Ave ST3. . . . . . . 73 D5
Nymet B77 . . . . 261 E8

O

Oadby Rise DE13 . . . . . . 166 A6
Oakamoor Rd ST10. . . . . . 77 C4
Oakapple Cl ST18 . . . . . . 221 E8
Oak Ave Cheddleton ST13 . 45 C4
 Great Wyrley WS6 . . . . 227 A1
 Huntington WS12. . . . . 209 D8
 Newport TF10 . . . . 168 F1
 Walton-on-T ST17. . . . . 175 F6
Oak Cl Church Eaton ST20 . 190 B7
 Great Haywood ST18. . . 158 C1
 Kinver DY7. . . . . 278 C3
 Uttoxeter ST14 . . . . . . 110 F1
Oak Ct B74 . . . . 257 E5
Oakdale B74. . . . . 257 A1
Oakdale Cl CW2 . . . . 37 B3
Oakdale ST5. . . . . 71 C3
Oakdale Trad Est DY6 . . . 270 E1
Oakden Cl ST14 . . . . 125 C7
Oakdene Ave ST5 . . . . . . 56 A6
Oakdene Cl
 Cheslyn Hay WS6. . . . . 226 D2
 Forsbrook ST11. . . . . . . 91 B6
 Newcastle-u-L ST5. . . . . 56 A6
Oakdene Gr ST5 . . . . 56 A6
Oakdene Rd WS7 . . . . . . 229 A6
Oakdene ST8 . . . . 27 D7
Oak Dr Mile Oak B78 . . . 249 C1
 Scholar Green ST7. . . . . 25 E6
 Seisdon WV5 . . . . 263 F2
 Wheaton Aston ST19. . . 205 C6
Oaken Covert WV8. . . . . . 238 E2
Oaken Dr WS8. . . . . 238 E3
Oakenfield WS13 . . . . . . 214 A2
Oaken Gdns WS7 . . . . . . 229 A8
Oaken Grange WS6 . . . . . 226 F1
Oaken Gr WV8 . . . . 238 E2
Oakenhayes Cres WS8 . . 228 F1
Oakenhayes Dr WS8 . . . . 228 F1
Oaken La WV8 . . . . 238 C3
Oaken Lanes WV8. . . . . . 238 E2
Oaken Pk WV8. . . . . 239 A2
Oak Farm Craft Ctr★
 B78. . . . . 260 B5
Oakfield Ave DY6 . . . . . . 275 E5
Oakfield Cl Rugeley WS15 178 A2
 Stourbridge DY8 . . . . . 275 F1
Oakfield Dr WS3 . . . . 244 B5
Oakfield Gr ST8. . . . . 27 E7
Oakfield Rd
 Alrewas DE13 . . . . 201 A4
 Codsall WV8 . . . . 239 C2
 Market Drayton TF9. . . . 97 B1
Oakfields DE13 . . . . 145 A4
Oak Gdns ST18 . . . . 172 F5
Oak Gn WV6 . . . . 255 B3
Oakham Way ST2 . . . . . . 58 C2
Oakhill Ave ST4. . . . . 71 F4
Oakhill Cl ST10 . . . . 92 C4
Oakhill Prim Sch
 Stoke-on-T ST4 . . . . 71 F3
 Tamworth B77 . . . . 250 F2
Oakhill Rd WS11 . . . . . . 209 F2
Oak Hill WV3 . . . . 255 C1
Oak Ho Great Wyrley WS6. 227 A1
 Little Aston B74. . . . . . 257 B5

Oakhurst Cres ST3 . . . . . . 90 A6
Oakhurst WS14 . . . . 231 C7
Oakhurst Pk WS15 . . . . . 196 F5
Oak Ind Pk The DY6 . . . . 270 E1
Oak La Astbury CW12. . . . 15 B4
 Bradley ST18. . . . . 191 C7
 Burntwood WS7. . . . . . 212 A1
 Cheslyn Hay WV10 . . . . 225 C7
 Kingswinford DY6 . . . . 271 A1
Oakland Ct B79 . . . . 250 A5
Oakland Dr DY3. . . . . . . 271 B2
Oakland Ho B74 . . . . 258 A4
Oaklands Ave ST5. . . . . . . 56 C6
Oaklands Cl
 Fradley WS13 . . . . 215 D6
 Hill Ridware WS15. . . . 198 A8
 Huntington WS12. . . . . 209 C6
 Wetley Rocks ST9 . . . . . 60 A6
Oaklands Dr ST17. . . . . . 175 A6
Oaklands Ind Est WS12. . 210 B3
Oaklands Rd WV3 . . . . . . 266 B8
Oaklands The
 Church Eaton ST20 . . . . 190 A7
 Rugeley WS15 . . . . 178 C1
Oaklands Way WS3 . . . . 244 B3
 Walsall WS3 . . . . 266 B8
Oakleigh Ave DE11 . . . . . 186 F5
Oakleigh Ct ST15 . . . . . . 120 D6
Oakleigh Dr Codsall WV8 . 239 A3
 Rugeley WS15 . . . . 197 B6
 Sedgley DY3. . . . . 271 C7
Oakleigh Wlk DY6. . . . . . 275 E8
Oakley Ave WS9 . . . . 256 A5
Oakley Cl Lichfield WS13. . 214 B2
 Penkridge ST19 . . . . . . 193 A1
Oakley Copse WS15 . . . . 196 B7
Oakley Folly TF9 . . . . 99 A4
Oakley Gr WV4 . . . . 265 D5
Oakley La TF9 . . . . 98 A6
Oakley Pl ST6. . . . . 42 A7
Oakley Rd WV4 . . . . 265 D5
Oakleys ST19 . . . . 223 D6
Oak Leys WV3 . . . . 255 C1
Oakmoor Pl WS9. . . . . . . 256 F2
Oakmount Cl WS11. . . . . 243 F3
Oak Mount Rd ST9 . . . . . . 59 C4
Oakover Cl ST14 . . . . 126 C6
Oak Park Ct
 Stourbridge DY8 . . . . . 275 F1
 Sutton Coldfield B74 . . 257 E3
Oak Park Rd DY8. . . . . . . 275 F1
Oak Pl ST3 . . . . 74 C5
Oak Rd Barton-u-N DE13 . 201 D8
 Brewood ST19 . . . . 223 D6
 Brownhills WS9 . . . . . . 245 A3
 Denstone ST14 . . . . 95 D5
 Eccleshall ST21 . . . . . . 133 D6
Oak Rd Flats ST19. . . . . . 223 D6
Oak Rd Newcastle-u-L ST5. 56 D2
 Stone ST15 . . . . 120 B8
 Walsall,Pelsall Wood WS3. 244 F1
 Walsall WS4 . . . . 244 C1
Oakridge Cl ST17 . . . . . . 175 E5
Oakridge Dr WS6 . . . . . . 226 E2
Oakridge Prim Sch ST17 175 E6
Oakridge Way ST17 . . . . 175 E5
Oaks Dr Cannock WS11 . . 209 C1
 Featherstone WV10. . . . 240 F8
 Wombourne WV5. . . . . . 270 A5
Oakshaw Cl WV9 . . . . . . 224 B3
Oakshaw Gr ST4 . . . . 88 B8
Oaksmoor Cl ST19 . . . . . 205 C6
Oak Sq ST6. . . . . 57 E5
Oak St Burton u T DE14. . 166 C1
 Cheadle ST10. . . . . 76 D3
 Hanley ST1 . . . . 57 E5
Oaks The Loggerheads TF9 . 99 F4
 Walsall WS3 . . . . 243 A1
 Walton-on-t-H ST17. . . . 175 F7
Oak St Kingswinford DY6 . 275 D6
 Newcastle-u-L ST5. . . . . 56 D3
Oak Tree Ct ST17 . . . . . . 174 B8
Oaktree La ST7 . . . . 40 D5
Oaktree Rd Rugeley WS15 196 F6
 Stoke-on-T ST4 . . . . 88 B6
Oaktree Rise WS8 . . . . . 238 E4
Oak Tree Wlk B79. . . . . . 249 F7
Oakville Ave ST6. . . . . . . 42 B2
Oakwell Cl ST3 . . . . 73 C1
Oakwell Gr ST3 . . . . 73 C1
Oakwood Cl
 Brownhills WS9 . . . . . . 244 E4
 Essington WV11. . . . . . 242 B3
 Hatton DE65 . . . . 146 C8
 Shenstone WS14 . . . . . 247 A6
Oakwood Pl ST5 . . . . 55 E8
Oakwood Rd Leek ST13 . . 30 C6
 Stoke-on-T ST3 . . . . 72 F2
Oakwood WS15 . . . . 178 B1
Oakwoods WS11. . . . . . . 226 D8
Oakwood Sch WS9. . . . . . 245 A3
Oasis The DY9 . . . . 281 F5
Oasthouse Cl DY6. . . . . . 275 A7
Oatfield Cl WS7. . . . . 229 A4
Oatlands Way WV6. . . . . 254 D3
Oban Cl ST5 . . . . 70 F8
Oberon Cl ST6 . . . . 42 D1
Occupation Rd WS8. . . . . 245 A4
Occupation St ST5 . . . . . 283 C2
Octagon Ctr The DE14. . . 166 D2
Octagon Sh Pk The ST1 . . 57 A4
Odell Gr ST5 . . . . 41 E1
Odger Cl ST3 . . . . 74 B2
Odiham Cl B79. . . . . 250 C7
Odin Cl WS11 . . . . 210 A5
Offadrive B79. . . . . 250 B5

Offa's Dr WV6 . . . . 254 E5
Offa St B79 . . . . 250 B5
Offoxey Rd TF11,ST19. . . 221 C6
Ogden Rd ST1 . . . . 282 C2
Ogley Cres WS8 . . . . 245 A7
Ogley Hay Rd
 Burntwood,Boney Hay
 WS7 . . . . 229 B8
 Burntwood,Triangle WS7,
 WS8 . . . . 229 A3
Ogley Rd WS8 . . . . 245 A7
Ogley Vale WS7. . . . . 229 B8
Ogmore Gr ST3 . . . . 90 A8
O'Hare Pl ST13 . . . . 31 B7
Ohio Gr ST6 . . . . 57 B8
Oldacre La ST17 . . . . 176 B3
Oldacres Rd ST4 . . . . 88 C5
Old Armoury The TF9 . . . 112 C8
Old Bank DE6. . . . . 81 D8
Old Barn Cl ST20. . . . . . . 171 E8
Old Barn House Mews
 WS15 . . . . 198 C1
Oldbury Ct B79 . . . . 250 B5
Old Butt La ST7 . . . . 25 D2
Old Cannock Rd WV10 . . 225 D1
Oldcastle Ave ST5 . . . . . . 56 A6
Old Castle Gr WS8 . . . . . 228 F2
Old Chancel Rd WS15 . . . 178 E2
Old Chapel Cl ST5. . . . . . . 69 E8
Old Coach La ST17 . . . . . 176 B4
Old Coach Rd ST19. . . . . 221 F7
Old Coalpit La SK17 . . . . . 5 E8
Old Colehurst Manor★
 TF9 . . . . 112 A3
Old Cottage Hospl The 4
 ST13. . . . . 30 F6
Oldcott Cres ST7. . . . . 41 C8
Oldcott Dr ST7. . . . . 41 C8
Oldcourt St ST6. . . . . 41 D3
Old Croft Rd ST17. . . . . . 175 E6
Old Daleands TF9 . . . . . 112 B8
Old Eaton Rd WS15 . . . . 178 E3
Olde Hall La WS6 . . . . . . 226 F3
Olde Hall Rd WV10 . . . . 241 C7
Oldershaws La ST20. . . . 150 F7
Old Fallings La WV10. . . 240 F5
Old Fallow Ave WS11. . . 209 E3
Old Fallow Rd WS11. . . . 209 E3
Old Falls Cl WS6 . . . . 226 D3
Old Farm Dr WV8 . . . . . . 239 A4
Old Farm Mdw WV3 . . . . 265 C8
Oldfield Ave ST6. . . . . 42 D5
Oldfield Dr ST15 . . . . . . 120 C6
Oldfield Ind Est ST4. . . . . 72 F5
Oldfield La Egginton DE65 148 A8
 Snelston DE6 . . . . 81 B3
Oldfields Cres ST18 . . . . 158 C3
Oldfields Hall Mid Sch
 ST14. . . . . 126 A7
Oldfields Rd ST14. . . . . . 126 B7
Oldfield St ST4 . . . . 73 A5
Oldford La ST18 . . . . 154 B4
Old Forge Cl DE65 . . . . . 148 A5
Old Forge The ST18 . . . . 158 B2
Old Hall Ct B79 . . . . 236 D3
Old Hall Dr Elford B79. . . 216 C2
 Newcastle-u-L ST5. . . . . 56 A8
Old Hall La Fradley WS13 215 D8
 Millmeece ST21. . . . . . 117 F7
 Norton Canes WS11,WS12 227 B7
Old Hall St ST1 . . . . 282 B3
Oldham Cotts WS15 . . . . 179 A5
Oldham St ST1. . . . . 282 C1
Old Hedging La B77. . . . . 261 D5
Old Hednesford Rd
 WS11. . . . . 210 A3
Oldhill Cl ST7. . . . . 40 E5
Oldhill La ST18 . . . . 157 C1
Old Hill WV6. . . . . 255 D5
Oldicote La DE15 . . . . . . 167 E3
Old Knotty Way ST14. . . . 126 C7
Old La Beech ST4 . . . . 87 B1
 Brown Edge ST6 . . . . . . 28 A1
 Checkley ST10. . . . . . . 109 D8
 Featherstone WV10. . . . 241 D7
Old Landywood La WS6 . 242 D7
Old La WV6. . . . . 254 F2
Old Lodge Hill Ctry Pk★
 WS15 . . . . 211 E3
Old London Rd WS14. . . 231 C1
Old Man of Mow★ ST7. . . 26 D8
Old Manor Cl B78 . . . . . 260 E5
Old Manor Flats WV6 . . . 255 D5
Old Mill Gdns WS4 . . . . 244 C2
Old Mill House Cl WS4 . . 244 B1
Old Mill La Bagnall ST9. . . 44 A3
 Bagnall,Tompkin ST9 . . . 44 C3
Oldmill St ST4 . . . . 72 C7
Old Mill The 9 ST13 . . . . 30 E6
Old Oak Cl WS9 . . . . 256 B8
Old Park Rd
 Cannock WS12. . . . . . . 211 A5
 Dudley DY1. . . . . 271 F4
 Stowford CW1. . . . . 37 C7
 Stowford CW1. . . . . 37 D8
Old Penkridge Mews
 WS11. . . . . 209 D1
Old Penkridge Rd WS11 . 209 C2
Old Quarry Dr DY3 . . . . . 271 D5
Old Rd Armitage WS15. . . 198 B5
 Audley ST7. . . . . 39 E3
 Burton u T DE14. . . . . . 184 E7
Old Rd Cl ST15. . . . . 105 A1
Old Rd Oulton ST15 . . . . 105 B5
 Stoke-on-T ST4,ST12. . . 88 C3
 Upper Tean ST10 . . . . . . 92 D4
 Weston ST18 . . . . 138 D2

Old Rd *continued*
Wrinehill CW3 . . . . 53 A3
Old Rectory Gdns WS9 . . 256 C6
Old Rectory Rd ST15 . . . 120 B8
Old Rickerscote La ST17. 175 A5
Old Saddler's Yd ST14. . 126 C7
Old School Cl
  Kidsgrove ST7 . . . . 26 A1
  Weston ST18 . . . . .138 D3
Old School Ct ST19 . . . . . 205 C5
Old School Dr ST16 . . . . . 155 C8
Old School Pl 🖪 ST13. . . . 30 E5
Old School Wlk B79 . . . . . 250 B6
Old School Yd The B77. . 251 A5
Old Shackerley La WV7. .221 B1
Old Smithy Cl WV6. . . . . .253 C3
Old Stafford Rd
  Brinsford WV10 . . . . 240 C8
  Slade Heath WV10 . . . . . . 224 D2
Old Town La WS3 . . . . 243 F3
Old Town Rd ST1 . . . . 282 B4
Old Tramway ST4 . . . . 72 F5
Old Vicarage Cl
  Walsall WS3 . . . . .244 A2
  Wombourne WV5 . . . . . . .270 B7
Old Warstone La WV11. .242 B8
Oldway Pl ST3 . . . . .73 C5
Old Weston Rd ST19 . . . 221 F8
Old Wharf Pl ST1 . . . . 57 E2
Old Wharf Rd DY8. . . . . . 279 F6
Old Whieldon Rd ST4 . . . 72 C6
Olive Ave WV4 . . . . 266 E5
Olive Gr ST5. . . . . 40 C1
Oliver Lodge Ho 🖪 ST4 . 72 A7
Oliver Rd ST4. . . . . 71 E7
Ollison Dr B74. . . . . 256 F2
Olof Palme Gr ST3 . . . . . 284 C2
Omega Way ST4 . . . . 88 A8
One Oak Rise ST17 . . . . . 174 F5
Onsetter Rd ST2 . . . . 73 D7
Onslow Dr ST5. . . . . 56 B8
Ontario Cl ST4 . . . . 88 A8
Opal Bsns Ctr ST15. . . . . 120 A5
Opal Rd ST4 . . . . 72 E5
Opal Way ST15. . . . . 120 A5
Oram's La ST19 . . . . 223 C7
Orange La WS15 . . . . 161 C1
Orbital Way WS11. . . . . . 226 F6
Orb St ST1 . . . . 282 B2
Orchard Ave WS11. . . . . . 209 C2
Orchard Cl Ashley TF9 . . 100 C5
  Cheslyn Hay WS6. . . . . . .226 E3
  Claverley WV5 . . . . .267 C7
  Coven WV9 . . . . .224 B2
  Lichfield WS13. . . . . .213 F1
  Oulton ST15. . . . . .105 C4
  Pattingham WV6 . . . . . . .253 D3
  Penkridge ST19 . . . . .192 F1
  Rugeley WS15 . . . . .178 E3
  Stone ST15 . . . . .119 F7
  Sudbury DE6 . . . . .128 E5
  Tamworth B77 . . . . .261 C5
  Uttoxeter ST14 . . . . .111 B1
  Walton-on-T DE12 . . . . . .184 D1
Orchard Cotts WS15 . . . 198 B5
Orchard Cres
  Kidsgrove ST7 . . . . 25 D1
  Penkridge ST19 . . . . .192 F1
  Wolverhampton WV3. . . . .265 B7
Orchard Ct
  Kingswinford DY6 . . . . . . .275 D6
  Leek ST13 . . . . 30 C6
  Wolverhampton WV3. . . . .265 B7
Orchard Gdns
  Cannock WS12. . . . . .209 F6
  Leek ST13 . . . . 30 C6
Orchard Gr Aldridge WS9 . 256 B4
  Cookley DY11. . . . . .280 A6
  Dudley DY3 . . . . .271 B3
  Dunsley DY7 . . . . .278 B4
  Sutton Coldfield B74. . . . .257 F3
  Wolverhampton WV4. . . . .266 C5
Orchard La Codsall WV8. .239 B3
  Shareshill WV10 . . . . . . .225 C3
  Stafford ST18 . . . . .174 C5
Orchard Mobile Home Pk
  ST18. . . . . .137 C2
Orchard Pk DE14. . . . . . . 166 D2
Orchard Pl ST12 . . . . 88 D1
Orchard Rd DY10 . . . . 280 C3
Orchard Rise
  Blythe Bridge ST11 . . . . . .90 E7
  Market Drayton TF9. . . . . .112 A8
Orchard St DE14 . . . . 166 D2
Orchards The
  Armitage WS15 . . . . .198 C4
  Stoke-on-T ST3 . . . . 72 A4
Orchard St
  Newcastle-u-L ST5. . . . . . . 56 D5
  Stafford ST17 . . . . .285 B2
  Swadlincote DE11 . . . . . .186 F6
  Tamworth,Kettlebrook
    B77. . . . . 261 C5
  Tamworth,The Leys B79 . 250 B5
Orchard The
  Albrighton WV7 . . . . .237 A5
  Brewood ST19 . . . . .223 C6
  Burntwood WS7. . . . . . . .229 B7
  Colwich ST18. . . . . .177 D8
  Newcastle-u-L ST5. . . . . . 55 D8
  Stoke-on-T ST6 . . . . 43 A8
  Stramshall ST14 . . . . . . .111 A4
  Swynnerton ST15. . . . . . .103 B3
  Walsall WS3 . . . . .243 D2
  Wolverhampton WV6. . . . .255 C6
Orchid Cl DE15 . . . . 186 A8
Orchid Gr ST4 . . . . 56 E1
Ordish Ct DE14. . . . . 166 D2

Ordish St DE14. . . . . 166 D2
Ordley La DE6 . . . . 65 F1
Oregon Cl DY6. . . . . 275 F6
Oregon Gdns WS7 . . . . . . 228 F8
Orford Rd ST9 . . . . 43 F7
Orford St ST5. . . . . 56 D7
Orford Way ST3. . . . . 88 E8
Orgreaves Cl ST5 . . . . 56 B8
Orgreave St ST6 . . . . 57 A7
Oriel Cl Cannock WS11 . . 226 E8
  Dudley DY1 . . . . .271 E2
Oriel Dr WV10 . . . . 240 D3
Oriel St ST4 . . . . 72 A7
Oriole Cl ST14 . . . . 126 C6
Orion Cl WS6 . . . . 226 F1
Orion Ct ST5. . . . . 70 F8
Orion St ST6. . . . . 42 C1
Orion Way WS11. . . . . 209 F5
Orkney Ave ST7. . . . . 41 F8
Orkney Dr B77. . . . . 261 F7
Orlestone Pl ST6. . . . . 42 B7
Orme Rd Biddulph ST8. . . 27 D5
  Newcastle-u-L ST5. . . . . .283 A2
  Newcastle-u-L ST5. . . . . . 55 F1
Ormes La WV6. . . . . 255 C3
Orme St ST6. . . . . 56 E8
Ormonde St ST4 . . . . 72 F5
Ormonds Cl WS13. . . . . . 230 E6
Orpheus Gr ST1. . . . . 57 F6
Orton Gr WV4 . . . . 265 D4
Orton La WV4,WV5. . . . . 265 A2
Orton Rd ST5. . . . . 283 A4
Orwell Cl ST8. . . . . 279 D4
Orwell Dr Longton ST3 . . 73 F5
  Stafford ST17 . . . . .174 B8
Orwell Pl ST5. . . . . 71 B4
Osberton Dr DY1. . . . . . . 271 E7
Osborne Cres ST17. . . . . . 175 C8
Osborne Ct DE13. . . . . . . 166 B6
Osborne Ho ST10 . . . . 76 F3
Osborne Rd Stoke-on-T ST4 71 E8
  Wolverhampton WV4. . . . .265 D4
Osborne St
  Burton u T DE15. . . . . . . .167 A3
  Leek ST13 . . . . 31 A6
Osborne St B79 . . . . 249 D7
Osbourne Gdns DE15. . . 167 A3
Oslo Gr ST1. . . . . 57 F6
Osmaston Rd DY8. . . . . . 279 F2
Osprey Ave ST3 . . . . 90 A7
Osprey Cl
  Burton u T DE15. . . . . . . .167 D4
  Whittington WS14 . . . . . .232 F5
Osprey Ct WS7. . . . . 229 F8
Osprey Dr DY1. . . . . 271 F1
Osprey Gr WV12 . . . . 210 C1
Osprey B77. . . . . 262 A6
Osprey View ST7. . . . . 26 D3
Ostend Pl ST5 . . . . 70 F7
Ostler Cl DY6 . . . . 275 B7
Ostlers La ST13 . . . . 45 B4
Oswald Ave ST3 . . . . 74 B5
Otherton Cl ST19 . . . . . . 207 E8
Otherton La ST19 . . . . . . 207 F6
Otterburn Cl
  🖪 Stafford ST17 . . . . . . .175 D6
  Cannock WS12 . . . . .210 E2
Otterstone Cl DY3. . . . . . 266 C2
Ottery B77. . . . . 262 B5
Oulton CE Fst Sch ST15. 105 C4
Oulton La ST10,ST10. . . 170 A8
Oulton Mews ST15 . . . . . 105 A1
Oulton Rd Cheadle ST10 . 76 F3
  Stoke-on-T ST6 . . . . 42 B7
  Stone ST15 . . . . .105 B2
Oulton Way ST16 . . . . . . 155 B6
Oundle Ct B74. . . . . 257 F2
Ounsdale Cres WV5 . . . . 270 A7
Ounsdale High Sch WV5. 269 F7
Ounsdale Rd WV5. . . . . . 269 F7
Our Lady & St Benedict RC
  Prim Sch ST2. . . . . 58 A5
Our Lady & St Werburgh's RC
  Prim Sch ST5. . . . . 71 B4
Our Lady's RC Prim Sch
  ST4. . . . . 72 D6
Our Lady's RC Prim Sch
  ST15 . . . . .103 B3
Ousley La DE6 . . . . 80 C5
Outclough Rd ST8 . . . . . . 27 B1
Outfield Rd DE15. . . . . . . 185 F8
Outlook The ST6 . . . . 42 C3
Outwoods Cl
  Burton u T DE13. . . . . . . .166 A6
  Weston ST18 . . . . .138 D2
Outwoods Gn ST18. . . . . 138 D2
Outwoods La
  Anslow DE13 . . . . .165 C7
  Burton u T DE13. . . . . . . .165 E7
Outwoods St DE14 . . . . . 166 B5
Oval Bglws The TF10 . . . 169 A3
Ovaldene Way ST4. . . . . . 88 C5
Oval The Longton ST3 . . 284 A2
  Market Drayton TF9. . . . . .112 C8
  Stafford ST17 . . . . .285 C2
  Werrington ST9 . . . . 59 E4
Overbrook Cl DY3. . . . . . 271 C2
Overcroft ST14 . . . . 125 C7
Overdale Pl ST13 . . . . 30 B5
Overfield Rd DY1 . . . . . . 271 E1
Overhill Rd
  Burntwood WS7. . . . . . . .229 B5
  Stafford ST17 . . . . .175 D6
Overhouse La ST6. . . . . . . 41 F1
Overland Cl WS15. . . . . . 197 A6
Overland Dr ST6 . . . . 43 A8
Overpool Cl WS15. . . . . . 196 D8
Oversetts Rd DE11. . . . . . 186 F5

Oversetts Rd DE11 . . . . . 186 E5
Oversley Rd ST6 . . . . 42 B7
Overstrand WV9 . . . . 239 F3
Over The Hill ST8 . . . . 17 A2
Overton Bank 🖪 ST13. . . 30 E6
Overton Cl ST3 . . . . 284 A2
Overton La WS7 . . . . 229 C4
Overton Rd ST6 . . . . 16 F6
Overton Wlk WV4 . . . . . . 265 C6
Overwood Pl ST6 . . . . 41 F7
Overwoods Rd B77. . . . . 262 A4
Owen Gr 🖪 ST6. . . . . 57 A8
Owen Rd WV3 . . . . 266 A8
Owen's Bank DE13 . . . . . 146 B6
Owen Wlk ST17 . . . . 174 C7
Owens Cl WS15 . . . . 178 E1
Oxbarn Ave WV3. . . . . . . 265 E7
Oxbarn Rd ST17. . . . . 174 D6
Oxbridge Way B79 . . . . . 249 E6
Oxclose La DE6 . . . . 36 C2
Oxford Ave ST1 . . . . 57 D7
Oxford Cl WS6. . . . . 226 F3
Oxford Cres ST4 . . . . 72 A7
Oxford Dr DY8 . . . . 279 F4
Oxford Gdns ST16. . . . . . 155 F5
Oxford Rd Cannock WS11 . 226 F8
  Newcastle-u-L ST5. . . . . . . 56 D3
  Stoke-on-T ST6 . . . . 42 B7
Oxford St Burton u T DE14. 166 B1
  Stoke-on-T ST4 . . . . 72 A7
  Stoke-on-T ST4 . . . . 72 A8
Oxhay Ct ST5 . . . . 56 C3
Oxhay View ST5 . . . . 56 C3
Ox-Hey Cres ST8 . . . . 16 D1
Ox-Hey Dr ST8. . . . . 16 D1
Oxhey Fst Sch ST8 . . . . . . 16 E1
Oxleathers Ct ST17. . . . . 174 B7
Oxley Cl WS6 . . . . 226 F1
Oxley Moor Rd
  Wolverhampton,Blakeley Green
    WV9 . . . . 255 F8
  Wolverhampton,Oxley WV9,
    WV10 . . . . 240 B1
Oxley Rd DE15 . . . . 167 A3
Oxmead DE6. . . . . 81 D7
Ox Pasture ST13 . . . . 45 C5
Ox St DY3 . . . . 271 D5
Oyster Cl DE14. . . . . 185 B7

P

Pacific Rd ST4 . . . . 88 B7
Packett St ST4. . . . . 284 B4
Pack Horse La ST6. . . . . . . 56 F8
Packington Ct B74. . . . . . 257 E4
Packington La B78. . . . . . 248 F5
Packmoor Prim Sch ST7 . 26 F1
Padarn Cl DY3. . . . . 266 C1
Padbury La WS7 . . . . 212 D1
Padbury WV9 . . . . 240 B3
Paddock Cl ST16. . . . . . . 155 C8
Paddock Cotts ST4. . . . . . 88 A6
Paddock La Aldridge WS9 256 A5
  Great Wyrley WS6. . . . . . .227 A3
Paddock Rise ST4. . . . . . . 88 A6
Paddocks Cl B78. . . . . . . 251 F1
Paddocks Gn CW12 . . . . . 15 F8
Paddocks The
  Market Drayton TF9. . . . . .97 B3
  Swadlincote DE11 . . . . . .186 F5
  Yarnfield ST15 . . . . .118 F6
Paddock The
  Burton u T DE15. . . . . . . .167 B4
  Cheadle ST10. . . . . 76 D2
  Claverley WV5 . . . . .267 C7
  Codsall WV8 . . . . .238 F2
  Coven WV9 . . . . .224 B2
  Dudley DY3 . . . . .271 E5
  Lichfield WS14. . . . . .231 C5
  Perton WV6 . . . . .254 D4
  Seighford ST18 . . . . .154 C6
  Wombourne WV5. . . . . . .269 E6
Padstow Dr ST17 . . . . . . 156 E1
Padstow B77 . . . . 250 F5
Padstow Way ST4. . . . . . . 88 C5
Padworth St ST3. . . . . 74 A3
Paget Cl Colwich ST18. . . 177 E8
  Lichfield WS13. . . . . .214 B2
  Penkridge ST19 . . . . .208 A7
Paget Dr WS7 . . . . 211 E1
Paget High Sch DE14 . . . 185 A7
Paget Rd WV3,WV6. . . . . 255 F6
Paget Rise WS15 . . . . . . 160 F6
Pagets Chase WS12. . . . . 211 C4
Paget St DE14 . . . . 166 C2
Pagham Cl WV9 . . . . 239 F2
Painsley RC High Sch
  ST10 . . . . 76 D2
Paisley Cl ST2 . . . . 73 E8
Paladin Ave ST3 . . . . 74 B4
Palatine Dr ST5. . . . . 55 D6
Palermo Dr ST3. . . . . 73 E4
Pale St DY3 . . . . 271 E5
Palfrey Rd DY8 . . . . 279 D5
Palisadings ST19. . . . . . . 192 E1
Pall Mall ST1 . . . . 282 B2
Palmbourne Ind Pk
  ST6. . . . . .285 A3
Palmer Cl
  Barton-u-N DE13 . . . . . . .183 D2
  Burton u T DE14. . . . . . . .185 B8
  Stafford ST17 . . . . .156 B4
  Wolverhampton WV11 . . .241 F1
Palmers Cl WV8 . . . . 239 C1
Palmers Cross Prim Sch
  WV6 . . . . .255 D8

Palmers Gn ST4 . . . . 71 D8
Palmer St ST3 . . . . 284 D4
Palmerston Ave B77 . . . . 261 E6
Palmerston Ct B77. . . . . . 261 F6
Palmerston St
  🖸 Newcastle-u-L ST5. . . . . 56 C5
  Hanley ST1 . . . . .282 C1
Palmerston Way ST8 . . . . 16 D1
Palmers Way
  Codsall WV8 . . . . .239 C1
  Newcastle-u-L ST5. . . . . . . 71 D8
Palomino Cl ST3. . . . . 89 C8
Pandora Gr ST1. . . . . 57 F6
Panton Cl ST16 . . . . 156 B4
Pantulf Cl ST17 . . . . 155 B1
Panturner Rd ST2. . . . . . . 73 D7
Parade The
  Brownhills WS8. . . . . . . .228 E1
  Coven WV9 . . . . .224 B2
  Kingswinford DY6 . . . . . . .275 B7
  Newcastle-u-L ST5. . . . . . . 55 C1
Parade View WS8 . . . . . . 244 E8
Paradise Gr WS3. . . . . . . 243 F3
Paradise La
  Slade Heath WV10 . . . . . .224 D2
  Walsall WS3 . . . . .243 F3
  Wolverhampton WV10. . . .240 E8
Paradise St
  🖸 Stoke-on-T ST6. . . . . . . 41 D3
  Newcastle-u-L ST5. . . . . .283 B2
Paragon Ave ST5 . . . . 71 B3
Paragon Cl ST10 . . . . 76 C1
Paragon Rd ST3 . . . . 284 D3
Paramount Bsns Pk ST6. . 57 A8
Parbury B77. . . . . 261 D5
Parchments The WS13 . . 214 B1
Pargeter St DY8 . . . . 279 F4
Paris Ave ST5 . . . . 70 E6
Park Ave Burntwood WS7. 229 B5
  Cheadle ST10. . . . . 76 E2
  Meir ST3 . . . . 74 A5
  Newcastle-u-L ST5. . . . . . . 56 C5
  Norton Canes WS11 . . . . .228 A5
  Stafford ST17 . . . . .174 D8
  Stone ST15 . . . . .119 E8
  Talke ST7 . . . . 40 E8
  Uttoxeter ST14 . . . . .111 B2
  Werrington ST9 . . . . 59 D4
Park Ave W ST5. . . . . 56 B5
Park Ave
  Wolverhampton,Goldthorn Park
    WV4 . . . . 266 C6
  Wombourne WV5. . . . . . .269 F5
Park Bldgs ST5 . . . . 271 C4
Park Cl Barton-u-N DE13 . 183 C1
  Brownhills WS8. . . . . . . .244 F8
  Cheslyn Hay WS6. . . . . . .226 E3
  Madeley CW3 . . . . 68 E8
Park Cres ST17 . . . . 285 B1
Park Croft WS7 . . . . 228 C8
Park Ct ST5 . . . . 55 E7
Parkdale DY3 . . . . 271 D8
Park Dr Barlaston ST12 . . 104 D8
  Cheadle ST10. . . . . 76 D4
  Little Aston B74. . . . . . . .257 C4
  Sutton Coldfield B74 . . . .257 F2
  Trentham ST4 . . . . 87 F7
  Werrington ST9 . . . . 59 C4
  Wolverhampton WV4. . . . .266 C5
Parkend ST11 . . . . 91 B8
Park End Lichfield WS14. 231 E7
  Newport TF10 . . . . .168 F5
Parker Bowles Dr 🖪
  TF9. . . . . .112 A8
Parker-Jervis Rd ST3 . . . 73 F4
Parker Paul Ind Est WV2 266 C7
Parker Rd WV11 . . . . 241 F1
Parkers Cl ST20. . . . . 190 A7
Parker's Croft Rd ST17. . 285 B1
Parkers Ct ST5 . . . . 224 C1
Parker St Burton u T DE14 166 D5
  Hanley ST1 . . . . .282 A3
  Leek ST13 . . . . 31 A5
  Walsall WS3 . . . . .243 A1
Parkes Ave WV8 . . . . 239 B2
Parkes Hall Rd DY1 . . . . 271 F5
Park Farm Rd B77 . . . . . 250 C1
Park Farm View ST6 . . . . 41 D7
Parkfield Ave B77. . . . . . 250 C1
Parkfield Bsns Ctr ST17 . 285 C8
Parkfield Chalet Pk
  WV2. . . . . .266 D6
Parkfield Cl B77 . . . . 261 C8
  Wolverhampton WV2. . . . .266 E6
Parkfield Colliery WV4. . 266 F5
Parkfield Cres
  Tamworth B77 . . . . .261 C8
  Wolverhampton WV2. . . . .266 E6
Parkfield Gr WV2. . . . . . . 266 E6
Parkfield High Sch WV4. 266 E5
Parkfield La DE6. . . . . 81 D4
Parkfield Prim Sch WV4. 266 E6
Parkfield Rd Longton ST3. 73 C1
  Wolverhampton WV2,WV4. 266 E6
Parkfields Cl
  Barlaston ST12 . . . . 88 C1
  Newcastle-u-L ST5. . . . . . . 55 A2
Parkfields Farm ST12 . . . 88 C1
Parkfields Stafford ST17. 174 D8
  Stoke-on-T ST9 . . . . 43 F7
Parkgate La DE6. . . . . 79 F5
Park Gate Rd
  Cannock Wood WS15 . . . .211 F5
  Kidderminster DY10 . . . . .280 B2
Park Hall Ave ST3. . . . . . . 74 A4
Park Hall Bsns Village
  ST3 . . . . 73 E5
Park Hall Cl WS15 . . . . . 178 D3
Park Hall Cres ST3. . . . . . 74 A4

Parkhall Ctry Pk★ ST3 . . 74 A6
Parkhall Cty Pk★ ST3 . . . 73 F6
Park Hall Ind Est ST6. . . . 41 E2
Parkhall La ST10. . . . . . . 109 B5
Park Hall Prim Sch ST3 . . 74 A4
Park Hall Rd Longton ST3. 73 E5
  Meir ST3 . . . . 74 A4
  Wolverhampton WV4. . . . .266 D5
Park Hall St ST3 . . . . 284 C4
Parkhead Cres ST3 . . . . . 74 A3
Parkhead Dr ST3. . . . . 74 A3
Parkhead Gr ST3. . . . . 74 A4
Parkhill Rd WS7 . . . . 229 A8
Park Ho WV11 . . . . 242 A3
Park House Dr ST15 . . . . 120 C7
Parkhouse Gdns DY3 . . . 271 C4
Parkhouse Ind Est E ST5. 56 A8
Parkhouse Ind Est W ST5 55 F8
Parkhouse Rd E ST5 . . . . 40 F1
Parkhouse Rd W ST5. . . . 40 E1
Parkhouse St ST2 . . . . . . 282 A1
Park La Ashley TF9 . . . . . 100 B8
  Audley ST7. . . . . 39 B4
  Biddulph ST8 . . . . 27 D6
  Blore TF9 . . . . 99 B1
  Brewood WV9 . . . . .223 C2
  Brocton ST17 . . . . .176 B4
  Cheadle ST10. . . . . 76 C3
  Cheddleton ST13 . . . . 45 B6
  Colton WS15 . . . . .179 B8
  Congleton CW12 . . . . 6 A1
  Endon ST9 . . . . 44 B7
  Fazeley B78 . . . . .249 E2
  Great Wyrley WS6 . . . . . .227 A3
  Haughton ST18 . . . . .172 E5
  High Offley ST20 . . . . . . .132 B1
  Ipstones ST10 . . . . 47 B1
  Kingswinford DY6 . . . . . . .275 E7
Parklands ST8 . . . . 17 B1
Parklands Dr CW2 . . . . . . 37 E3
Parklands Rd ST10 . . . . . 92 E4
Parklands The
  Congleton CW12 . . . . 6 A2
  Kingswinford DY6 . . . . . . .275 D6
  Wolverhampton WV3. . . . .255 D1
Park Lane Cl ST10 . . . . . . 76 C3
Park La Shenstone WS14. 247 B4
  Stoke-on-T ST4 . . . . 72 F5
  Stretton ST19 . . . . .206 A6
  Tutbury DE13 . . . . .146 B6
  Whittington WS13 . . . . . .232 D8
Park Mid Sch ST8. . . . . . . 27 C6
Park Pale The DE13 . . . . 146 C5
Park Pl Stoke-on-T ST4 . . 72 F6
  Uttoxeter ST14 . . . . .126 C8
Park Rd Alrewas DE13. . . 201 A3
  Barton-u-N DE13 . . . . . . .183 C2
  Burntwood,Chase Heath
    WS7 . . . . 228 F8
  Burntwood,Triangle WS7. 229 B5
  Cannock WS11. . . . . .209 D1
  Dudley,Lower Gornal DY3 .271 C4
  Featherstone WV10. . . . . .241 D8
  Leek ST13 . . . . 30 E7
  Newcastle-u-L,Butterton
    ST5. . . . . 70 E2
  Newcastle-u-L,Silverdale
    ST5. . . . . 70 D8
  Newcastle-u-L ST5. . . . . . . 55 C1
  Norton Canes WS11 . . . . .228 A5
  Stoke-on-T ST6 . . . . 42 B7
  Stourbridge DY8 . . . . . . .279 D5
  Swadlincote DE15,DE11 . .186 D5
  Tamworth B77 . . . . .261 C6
  Walsall,Wallington Heath
    WS3 . . . . 243 B1
  Werrington ST9 . . . . 59 C4
Park Rd W DY8 . . . . 279 D5
Park St S WV2 . . . . 266 C6
Park Sch B79. . . . . 250 A7
Parks Cres WV11 . . . . . . 242 A3
Parkside Ave ST16 . . . . . 155 D8
Parkside Cres ST9 . . . . . . 43 F8
Parkside Dr ST5 . . . . 56 C3
Parkside Gr ST5 . . . . 56 C3
Parkside Ind Est WV1 . . 266 F8
Parkside La Gayton ST18 139 A7
  Huntington WS11. . . . . . .209 A2
Parkside Prim Sch ST16 155 D8
  Tamworth B77 . . . . .250 E1
Parkside Way B74 . . . . . 257 A1
Park St Burton u T DE14. 166 C2
  Cannock WS11. . . . . .226 E6
  Cheslyn Hay WS6. . . . . . .226 E3
Parks The ST4 . . . . 88 D7
Park St DY6 . . . . 275 D6
Parkstone Ave ST5 . . . . . 283 C4
Parkstone Cl WS4. . . . . . 244 C1
Park St Stafford ST17. . . 285 B2
  Stoke-on-T ST4 . . . . 72 F6
  Stourbridge DY8 . . . . . . .279 F8
  Tamworth B79 . . . . .250 A5
  Uttoxeter ST14 . . . . .111 C1
Park Terr ST6 . . . . 41 E3
Park The DE6. . . . . 81 C8
Park Venture Ctr WS11 . 226 E6
Park View
  Blythe Bridge ST11 . . . . . .90 E6
  Burntwood WS7. . . . . . . .228 E8
Parkview ST3 . . . . 72 E2
Park View Ct ST11 . . . . . 209 D1

Parkview Ct DY6 . . . . 275 B8
Park View Ct ST3 . . . . 73 B1
Parkview Dr WS8 . . . . 228 F2
Park View Gr ST2 . . . . 43 C2
Park View Rd
  Kidsgrove ST7 . . . . 26 B3
  Sutton Coldfield B74 . . . . 257 D3
Park View ST15 . . . . 103 B3
Park View Terr WS15 . . . 178 D1
Parkway DE14 . . . . 165 F1
Park Way ST11 . . . . 91 A8
Parkway ST15 . . . . 120 C7
Parkway The Hanley ST1 . 282 B1
  Perton WV6 . . . . 254 F4
Park Way WV11 . . . . 242 A1
Parkwood Ave ST4 . . . . . . 87 F8
Parkwood Cl WS1 . . . . . . 245 A5
Park Wood Ct B74 . . . . . . 257 F2
Park Wood Dr ST5 . . . . . . 85 A7
Parkyn St WV2 . . . . 266 E8
Parliament Row ST1 . . . . 282 B3
Parliament Sq ST1 . . . . . 282 B3
Parliament St DE11 . . . . 186 F6
Parma Gr ST3 . . . . 73 E4
Parnell Ave WS13 . . . . . . 231 A6
Parnell Sq CW12 . . . . 6 A2
Parsonage St 41 D4
Parsons Cl SK17 . . . . 24 D5
Parson's Croft WV9 . . . . 224 B2
Parsons Dr ST20 . . . . 171 E6
Parsons Hollow B77 . . . . 261 E2
Parsons La ST13 . . . . 33 D3
Parson St B77 . . . . 261 E7
Parson's Wlk B79 . . . . . . 218 F2
Parton Gr ST3 . . . . 74 A3
Partridge Cl [7] Meir ST3 . 90 A7
  Cannock WS11 . . . . 210 A1
  Huntington WS12 . . . . . . 209 D7
Partridge Croft WS13 . . . 231 C8
Partridge Dr ST14 . . . . . . 126 C6
Partridge Mill WS3 . . . . . 243 E3
Partridge Rd DY8 . . . . . . 279 C4
Partridge Ride TF9 . . . . . . 99 D4
Parva Ct ST14 . . . . 110 F1
Parville Ho ST6 . . . . 57 A6
Paskin Cl WS13 . . . . 215 C1
Pass Ave WS14 . . . . 232 E6
Passfield Ave WS12 . . . . 210 C2
Pastoral Cl CW3 . . . . 68 F5
Pasture Cl ST5 . . . . 85 D5
Pasturefields Ent Pk
  ST18 . . . . 158 B6
Pasturefields ST18 . . . . . 158 A7
Pasturefields Ind Est
  ST18 . . . . 158 B7
Pasturefields La ST18 . . . 158 B7
Pasture Gate WS11 . . . . . 209 C2
Pasture La DE6 . . . . 35 E1
Pastures Dr CW2 . . . . 37 D3
Pastures The
  Perton WV6 . . . . 254 D4
  Swadlincote DE11 . . . . . . 186 F5
Pasture View WS3 . . . . . 243 F2
Patch Cl DE13 . . . . 166 B6
Patch Meadow Rd ST10 . . 76 B3
Paterson Ave ST21 . . . . . 117 F3
Paterson Pl WS8 . . . . 245 B5
Patricia Ave WV4 . . . . . . 266 C5
Patrick Ho [2] WS11 . . . . 210 A3
Patrick Mews WS13 . . . . 213 F1
Patrick Pl ST8 . . . . 27 B2
Patshull Ave WV10 . . . . . 240 B3
Patshull Cl WV10 . . . . . . 240 B3
Patshull Gr WV10 . . . . . . 240 B3
Patshull Ho WV6 . . . . . . 255 C6
Patshull Rd WV6 . . . . 253 B3
Patterdale Rd WS11 . . . . 210 A4
Patterdale St ST6 . . . . 42 A3
Pattingham La WV7 . . . . 253 D8
Pattingham Rd WV6 . . . . 254 C2
Paulet High Sch DE15 . . . 185 F7
Pauls Coppice WS8 . . . . . 245 A5
Paul St [1] WV2 . . . . 266 C8
Pauls Wlk WS13 . . . . 214 A1
Pavement The ST19 . . . . 223 D6
Pavilion Ct WS13 . . . . . . 213 F1
Pavilion Dr ST1 . . . . 57 A5
Pavilion End DY7 . . . . . . 274 E1
Pavilions Garden Village
  The ★ WV6 . . . . 263 F5
Pavilion The B77 . . . . 251 B3
Pavillion Cl WV9 . . . . 256 C7
Pavior's Rd WS7 . . . . 228 E4
Paxton Ave WV6 . . . . . . 254 E3
Paxton St ST1 . . . . 282 C1
Paynter St ST4 . . . . 72 F5
Peace Cl WS6 . . . . 226 E3
Peacehaven Gr ST4 . . . . . 88 C5
Peach Ave ST4 . . . . 174 F7
Peacock Hay Rd ST7 . . . . . 40 F4
Peacock La ST4,ST5 . . . . . 87 A8
Peacock Rd ST5 . . . . 55 F5
Peacock View ST4 . . . . . . 57 F1
Peak Cl WS15 . . . . 198 B4
Peak Dale Ave ST6 . . . . . . 41 C7
Peak Dr DY3 . . . . 271 E2
Peake Cres WS8 . . . . 244 F5
Peake Rd WS8 . . . . 245 A5
Peakes Rd WS15 . . . . 178 B1
Peake St ST5 . . . . 55 E3
Peaks L Ctr B79 . . . . 250 B3
Peak View ST13 . . . . 31 A5
Pearis Dr ST10 . . . . 94 E8
Pearl Gr ST3 . . . . 90 A8

Pear Pl ST2 . . . . 73 D7
Pearson Dr ST15 . . . . . . 120 C7
Pearson St WV2 . . . . 266 C8
Pear Tree Ave DE11 . . . . 186 F7
Peartree Cl ST12 . . . . 88 D1
Pear Tree Cl
  Gnosall ST20 . . . . 171 E6
  Huntington WS12 . . . . . . 209 D1
  Shuttington B79 . . . . 251 E7
Pear Tree Dr CW3 . . . . 68 D7
Peartree La WS15 . . . . . . 180 B6
Pear Tree La
  Bobbington WV5 . . . . . . 268 A4
  Brownhills WS8 . . . . 228 C2
  Newcastle-u-L ST5. . . . . . 55 D8
  Wolverhampton WV11 . . . 241 B1
Pear Tree St ST7 . . . . 39 F1
Peascroft Rd ST6 . . . . 42 D4
Pebble Dr ST3 . . . . 251 B3
Pebble Mill Cl WS11 . . . . 209 F2
Pebble Mill Dr WS11 . . . . 210 A2
Pebble Mill St ST1 . . . . . . 56 F4
Peckforton View ST7 . . . . 41 A7
Peck Mill La ST8 . . . . 27 C1
Pedley Cl ST3 . . . . 88 F8
Pedley Gr ST6 . . . . 42 D1
Pedley La CW12 . . . . 6 F4
Peebles Gn ST2 . . . . 58 C2
Peebles Rd ST5 . . . . 54 F2
Peel Cl B78 . . . . 260 E5
Peel Cl [4] Kidsgrove ST7 . 26 A2
  Fazeley B78 . . . . 261 B8
  Tamworth B77 . . . . 261 F6
Peel Dr Astbury CW12 . . . 15 B7
  Cannock WS12 . . . . 209 F8
  Tamworth B77 . . . . 261 F6
Peelers Way B77 . . . . 250 C1
Peel Hollow ST7 . . . . 39 A2
Peel Ho B79 . . . . 250 A4
Peel La CW12 . . . . 15 D7
Peel St Burton u T DE14 . . 166 C1
  Longton ST3 . . . . 284 C1
  Newcastle-u-L ST5 . . . . . . 56 C5
  Stafford ST16 . . . . 285 A3
  Tunstall ST6 . . . . 56 C8
Peel Terr ST16 . . . . 155 E5
Pegasus Ct B74 . . . . 258 A3
Pegasus Gr ST6 . . . . 42 D1
Pegasus Wlk B79 . . . . . . 249 F7
Peggs La ST20 . . . . 150 E8
Peggy's Bank ST7 . . . . . . 54 F8
Pegroy Gr ST6 . . . . 42 D2
Pelham St ST1 . . . . 282 C1
Pellfield Ct ST18 . . . . 138 D2
Pelsall La
  Walsall,Little Bloxwich
  WS3 . . . . 243 D3
  Walsall WS3,WS4 . . . . . . 244 A1
Pelsall Rd WS8 . . . . 244 D7
Pelsall Village Sch WS3 . 243 F6
Pemberton Cres DY10 . . 280 C3
Pemberton Dr ST3 . . . . . . 90 A5
Pembridge Rd ST3 . . . . . . 88 E7
Pembroke Cl B79 . . . . . . 249 D6
Pembroke Ct ST5 . . . . . . 283 A1
Pembroke Dr
  Newcastle-u-L ST5 . . . . . 283 A4
  Stone ST15 . . . . 120 C7
Pembroke Gdns DY8 . . . 275 C2
Pembroke Rd ST2 . . . . . . 43 B1
Penarth Gr ST1 . . . . 282 B4
Penarth Pl ST5 . . . . 283 A1
Pencombe Dr WV4 . . . . . 266 D5
Penda Gr WV6 . . . . 254 F5
Pendeford Ave WS5 . . . . 255 E8
Pendeford Bsns Pk WV9 . 239 F3
Pendeford Hall La WV9 . 239 D5
Pendeford High Sch
  WV10 . . . . 240 B2
Pendeford La WV9 . . . . . 240 A3
Pendeford Mill La WV9 . 239 C3
Pendeford Mill Nature
  Reserve ★ WV9 . . . . . . 239 E4
Pendene Dr WV4 . . . . . . 266 A5
Penderell Cl WV10 . . . . . 241 A6
Penderel St WS3 . . . . 243 C1
Pendinas Dr WV8 . . . . . . 239 B3
Pendine Gr ST4 . . . . 73 B6
Pendle Hill WS12 . . . . . . 210 C4
Pendrel Cl WS6 . . . . 242 F8
Pendrell Cl WV8 . . . . 239 A3
Pendrell Hall Coll WV8 . . 238 C6
Pendrill Rd WV10 . . . . . . 240 E3
Pendryl Cl ST19 . . . . 223 C7
Penfleet Ave ST3 . . . . 74 A1
Pengrove Cl ST6 . . . . 41 E8
Penhallow Dr WV4 . . . . . 266 E5
Penk Dr WS7 . . . . 229 D6
Penk Dr N WS15 . . . . 178 C2
Penk Dr S WS15 . . . . 178 C2
Penkhull Ct [6] ST4 . . . . . 72 A7
Penkhull Ed Ctr ST4 . . . . 72 A7
Penkhull New Rd ST4 . . . 72 A6
Penkhull Terr ST4 . . . . . . 72 A6
Penk Rd ST11 . . . . 91 A7
Penkridge Bank WS12,
  WS15 . . . . 196 B8
Penkridge Ct WS11 . . . . 209 D1
Penkridge Ind Est ST19 . 207 E7
Penkridge Mid Sch ST19 193 A2
Penkridge Rd ST17 . . . . 193 B7
Penkridge Sta ST19 . . . . 207 E8
Penkridge Wharf ST19 . . 207 F8
Penk Rise WV6 . . . . 255 B4
Penkside Wlk WV9 . . . . . 224 B3
Penkvale Rd ST17 . . . . . 174 F6
Penkville St ST4 . . . . 72 A5

Penleigh Gdns WV5 . . . . 269 F7
Penmark Gr ST3 . . . . 89 E8
Penmere Dr
  Newcastle-u-L ST5. . . . . . 71 C1
  Werrington ST9 . . . . 59 A3
Pennant Ct WV3 . . . . 266 B8
Penn Bridge SK11 . . . . 7 C1
Penn Cl WS3 . . . . 243 C1
Penn Common Rd WV4. . 265 F1
Penn Croft ST3 . . . . 177 D8
Penn Croft La WV4 . . . . . 266 A1
Penncroft WV4 . . . . 265 E4
Pennell St ST2 . . . . 58 B4
Penn Fields Sch WV3 . . . 265 F7
Penn Hall Sch WV4 . . . . 265 E3
Penn Hospl WV4 . . . . . . 265 E4
Pennhouse Ave WV4 . . . 265 F5
Pennine Dr
  Cannock WS11 . . . . 209 E2
  Dudley DY3 . . . . 271 D6
Pennine Way Biddulph ST8 . 16 E1
  Newcastle-u-L ST5 . . . . . . 55 E3
  Tamworth B77 . . . . 262 C8
Pennington St ST3 . . . . . . 74 C2
Penn Rd Sedgley DY3 . . . 270 F8
  Wolverhampton WV2,WV3,
  WV4 . . . . 266 A6
Penn St WV3 . . . . 266 B8
Penns Wood Cl DY3 . . . . 266 C2
Pennwood Ct WV4 . . . . . 265 D6
Pennwood La WV4 . . . . . 265 F3
Penny Bank Ct WS15 . . . 178 E1
Penny Bank La DY5 . . . . . 30 F5
Pennycress Gdns WV10 . 241 C2
Penny Cress Gn WS11 . . . 227 F4
Pennycroft La WV11 . . . . 111 C1
Pennycroft Rd ST14 . . . . 111 A1
Pennycrofts Ct ST16 . . . 285 C3
Pennycrofts ST16 . . . . . . 285 C3
Penny Ct WS6 . . . . 242 F8
Penny Farthing Arc DY3 . 271 D6
Pennyfields Ave ST6 . . . . 41 D1
Pennyfields Rd ST7 . . . . . 26 D2
Penny La ST10 . . . . 76 D3
Pennymoor Rd B77 . . . . 262 B7
Pennymore Cl ST4 . . . . . . 88 B8
Penny Royal Cl DY3 . . . . 271 D2
Pennys Croft WS13 . . . . 214 E1
Penport Gr ST3 . . . . 284 A2
Penrhyn Ave ST6 . . . . 42 B1
Penrith Cl ST4 . . . . 88 C6
Penrith Gr ST5 . . . . 71 B6
Pensett Trad Est The
  DY6 . . . . 271 A1
Pensford Gr ST1 . . . . 57 F5
Pensgreave Rd DE13 . . . 166 B6
Penshaw Cl WV9 . . . . . . 240 A2
Pens Meadow Sch DY8. . 275 E3
Pensnett Trad Est The
  DY6 . . . . 275 F8
Penstone La WV4 . . . . . . 264 E4
Pentire Rd WS14 . . . . . . 231 D6
Pentland Gdns WV6 . . . . 255 E2
Pentland Gr ST5 . . . . 55 E3
Penton Pl ST3 . . . . 88 E7
Penton Wlk ST3 . . . . 88 E7
Pen-Y-Bont Wlk ST8 . . . . 27 C6
Pen-Y-Bryn Way TF10 . . 168 F2
Penzance Way ST17 . . . . 156 C1
Penzer St DY6 . . . . 275 D7
Peolsford Rd WS3 . . . . . 244 A4
Peover La CW12 . . . . 6 F6
Pepper St
  Newcastle-u-L,Silverdale
  ST5 . . . . 54 F1
  Newcastle-u-L ST5. . . . . . 283 B2
Perceval St ST1 . . . . 57 E5
Percival Dr ST9 . . . . 43 C3
Percy St ST1 . . . . 282 B3
Peregrine Dr
  Burton u T DE15 . . . . . . 167 D3
  Dudley DY1 . . . . 271 F1
  Whittington WS14 . . . . . 232 F5
Peregrine Gr ST3 . . . . 90 A6
Perivale Cl ST1 . . . . 58 A6
Periwinkle Cl WS8 . . . . . 244 D6
Perkins St ST6 . . . . 41 C7
Perks Rd WV11 . . . . 242 A1
Perle Brook ST21 . . . . . . 133 D7
Perott Dr B75 . . . . 258 D2
Perrin Cl ST17 . . . . 174 F6
Perry Cl Hanley ST1 . . . . 282 C2
  Tamworth B79 . . . . 250 B6
Perrycrofts Cres B79 . . . 250 C7
Perrymount Ct ST4 . . . . . 71 F6
Pershore Cl WS3 . . . . 242 F2
Pershore Dr DE14 . . . . . . 185 A8
Pershore Rd WS3 . . . . . . 242 F2
Pershore Way WS3 . . . . . 242 F2
Persia Wlk [16] ST6 . . . . . 41 D3
Perth Cl DE15 . . . . 167 C2
Perth St ST4 . . . . 284 A1
Perthy Gr ST4 . . . . 87 F7
Perton Brook Vale WV6 . 254 F5
Perton Fst Sch WV6 . . . . 254 E5
Perton Gr WV6 . . . . 254 F2
Perton Mid Sch WV6 . . . 255 A5
Perton Rd WV6 . . . . 254 F2
Perton Sandown Fst Sch
  WV6 . . . . 254 F4
Perton Wood View ST3. . 72 F3
Pessall Farm Holding
  B79 . . . . 217 C8
Pessall La B79 . . . . 217 C6
Petard Cl B77 . . . . 261 C6
Peterborough Dr WS12. . 210 C1
Peterdale Dr WV4 . . . . . . 265 F3
Peterhead B77 . . . . 250 F5

Peter James Ct ST16 . . . 155 E6
Petersfield WS11 . . . . . . 209 F4
Petersfield Rd ST6 . . . . . . 42 A7
Petershouse Dr B74 . . . . 257 F5
Peterson Ho [3] ST3 . . . . 89 F8
Peters Wlk ST3 . . . . 214 A2
Peterway Gr ST3 . . . . 73 C6
Pezenas Dr TF9 . . . . 97 B1
Pheasant Way WS11 . . . . 210 A1
Pheasant Wlk TF9 . . . . . . 99 D3
Philip Gr WS11 . . . . 209 E6
Philip La ST9 . . . . 59 B4
Philip St ST4 . . . . 72 E6
Phillips Ave WV11 . . . . . . 241 F1
Phillips Cl ST15 . . . . 120 D7
Phillipson Way ST6 . . . . . 57 D8
Phoenix Bank TF9 . . . . . . 97 D1
Phoenix Cl Kidsgrove ST7 . 26 C2
  Rugeley WS15 . . . . 178 F1
Phoenix Ctr WS11 . . . . . 226 E6
Phoenix Rd WS11 . . . . . . 210 A2
Phoenix Rise WV2 . . . . . 266 C6
Phoenix St
  [4] Stoke-on-T ST6. . . . . . 41 D3
  Wolverhampton WV2. . . . 266 D6
Picasso Cl WS11 . . . . 210 D2
Picasso Rise ST3 . . . . 90 B7
Piccadilly Arc ST1 . . . . . . 282 B3
Piccadilly Cres B78 . . . . 261 F1
Piccadilly ST1 . . . . 282 B2
Piccadilly La DE6 . . . . 66 C1
Piccadilly B78 . . . . 261 F1
Piccadilly St [7] ST6 . . . . . 41 D3
Pickering Dr ST3 . . . . . . 284 A1
Pickford Pl [8] ST3 . . . . . . 74 A1
Pickleys La DE6 . . . . 127 C8
Pickmere Cl ST2 . . . . 43 B3
Picknal La ST5 . . . . 56 E7
Picknalls Fst Sch ST14 . . 126 B7
Picknalls St ST14 . . . . . . 126 B7
Pickstock TF10 . . . . 149 B2
Pickwick Pl ST7 . . . . 25 D2
Pickwood Ave ST13 . . . . . 31 A5
Pickwood Cl ST13 . . . . . . 31 A5
Picton St Hanley ST1 . . . 282 C2
  Leek ST13 . . . . 30 D5
Piddocks Rd DE15 . . . . . 186 B5
Pidduck St ST6 . . . . 56 E7
Pierce St ST6 . . . . 41 D3
Pier St WS8 . . . . 244 F7
Pigeonhay La ST14 . . . . . 110 C2
Piggott St ST2 . . . . 58 A3
Pike Cl ST16 . . . . 156 A5
Pike La WS15 . . . . 198 A4
Pikelow La ST10 . . . . 49 B3
Pilgrim Pl ST16 . . . . 285 B2
Pilgrim St ST16 . . . . 285 B2
Pilkington Ave ST5. . . . . . 71 A6
Pillar Ct ST2 . . . . 73 D7
Pillaton Cl ST19 . . . . 207 F7
Pillaton Dr WS12 . . . . . . 209 C6
Pillaton Hall Farm ST19 . 208 C3
Pilsbury St ST5 . . . . 56 D6
Pilsden Pl ST3 . . . . 90 C7
Pilstones Rd ST15 . . . . . 103 C1
Pilstones Way ST15 . . . . 103 C1
Pimlico Ct DY3 . . . . 271 D3
Pinch The DE6 . . . . 36 B2
Pine Cl Burton u T DE14 . . 185 A8
  Great Wyrley WS6 . . . . . 226 F4
  Kingswinford DY6 . . . . . . 275 D5
  Kinver DY7 . . . . 278 C3
  Market Drayton TF9 . . . . . 97 B1
  Talke ST7 . . . . 40 D7
  Tamworth B79 . . . . 250 B8
Pine Cres ST17 . . . . 175 F6
Pine Ct Blythe Bridge ST11 . 90 D8
  Loggerheads TF9 . . . . 99 E4
Pine Gr Burntwood WS7 . 228 F5
  Swadlincote DE11 . . . . . . 186 F6
Pinehurst Cl ST5 . . . . 71 B3
Pine Leigh B74 . . . . 258 B1
Pine Rd ST4 . . . . 72 C4
Pineside Ave WS15 . . . . 211 F5
Pines Park Home Est The
  WS12 . . . . 209 D5
Pines The Lichfield WS14 . 231 F7
  Wolverhampton WV3. . . . 255 D1
Pine St WS3 . . . . 243 D2
Pine Tree Cl WS12 . . . . . 195 A1
Pinetree Dr Aldridge B74 . 256 D1
  Blythe Bridge ST11 . . . . . 90 D7
Pinetrees La TF9 . . . . 99 F5
Pinetrees WS15 . . . . 196 F4
Pine View Rugeley WS15 . 178 C3
  Smestow DY3 . . . . 269 D3
Pineways Dr WV6 . . . . . . 255 E4
Pineways Stourbridge DY8 275 C2
  Sutton Coldfield B74 . . . . 257 C3
Pine Wlk Codsall WV8 . . . 238 F2
  Uttoxeter ST14 . . . . 125 F8
Pinewood Ave
  Cannock WS11 . . . . 209 D4
  Wood End CV9 . . . . 262 C1
Pinewood Cl
  Brownhills WS8 . . . . 228 E2
  Wolverhampton WV3. . . . 265 A8
  Wombourne WV5. . . . . . . 270 A6
Pinewood Cres ST3 . . . . . 74 C1
Pinewood Dr
  Colwich ST18 . . . . 177 D8

Pinewood Dr continued
  Loggerheads TF9 . . . . 99 E4
Pinewood Gr
  Blythe Bridge ST11 . . . . . 91 A6
  Newcastle-u-L ST5. . . . . . 40 E1
Pinewood Rd
  Burton u T DE15 . . . . . . 185 F6
  Loggerheads TF9 . . . . 99 F5
Pinewoods Ave DY9 . . . . 281 F4
Pinewoods Cl DY9 . . . . . 281 F4
Pinewoods Ct DY9 . . . . . 281 F4
Pinewoods TF10 . . . . 168 E1
Pinewood Wlk DY6 . . . . . 275 E8
Pinfold Ave ST6 . . . . 42 C4
Pinfold Cl Tutbury DE13 . 146 C5
  Wheaton Aston ST19 . . . 205 B6
Pinfold Cres WV4 . . . . . . 265 D6
Pinfold Gr WS15 . . . . . . 198 C5
Pinfold Gr WV4 . . . . 265 D6
Pinfold Hill WS14 . . . . . . 246 F6
Pinfold La
  Abbots Bromley WS15 . . . 161 C3
  Blore TF9 . . . . 98 C2
  Cheslyn Hay WS6 . . . . . . 226 C2
  Norbury ST20 . . . . 151 B4
  Norton Canes WS11 . . . . 227 E4
  Penkridge ST19 . . . . 192 D1
  Wheaton Aston ST19 . . . 205 B6
  Wolverhampton WV4. . . . 265 E5
Pinfold Rd WS13 . . . . . . 213 F1
Pinfold St ST14 . . . . 126 C7
Pingle Farm Rd DE11 . . . 186 F5
Pingle La
  Hammerwich WS7 . . . . . 229 D5
  Stone ST15 . . . . 120 B7
Pingle The WS15 . . . . . . 196 B7
Pinhoe Pl ST3 . . . . 73 E3
Pinnox St ST6 . . . . 41 E2
Pintail Cl ST17 . . . . 175 A7
Pioneer Pl ST6 . . . . 42 C3
Pioneer Way ST17 . . . . . 175 A7
Pipe Hall Farm Nature
  Reserve ★ WS13. . . . . . 230 A8
Pipe Hay La DE6 . . . . 144 D5
Pipe La WS15 . . . . 198 B8
Piper Cl WV6 . . . . 254 F4
Piper Pl DY8 . . . . 279 F8
Piper Rd WV3 . . . . 265 C8
Pipers Croft WS13 . . . . . 214 A2
Piper's La TF10 . . . . 168 A3
Piper's Lodge TF10 . . . . . 168 A3
Pipe Wood La WS15. . . . . 180 B4
Pippins The
  Newcastle-u-L ST5. . . . . . 71 C3
  Stafford ST17 . . . . 174 E5
Pireford Pl ST5 . . . . 41 A1
Pirehill La ST15 . . . . 119 F5
Pirehill Prim Sch ST15 . . 119 F6
Pirehill Rd ST5 . . . . 41 B1
Pirie Cl CW12 . . . . 6 A4
Pirie Rd CW12 . . . . 6 A4
Pitchcroft La TF10 . . . . . 187 A5
Pitcher La ST13 . . . . 31 B5
Pitfield Ave ST5 . . . . 56 D3
Pitgreen La ST5 . . . . 56 D6
Pit La ST7 . . . . 40 C6
Pitlea Pl [1] ST3 . . . . 73 C6
Pitmarsh View ST5. . . . . . 56 D5
Pitsford St ST3 . . . . 73 E2
Pitstone Cl ST16 . . . . . . 136 D1
Pitt St E ST6 . . . . 57 A8
Pitt St W ST6 . . . . 57 A8
Pitts Hill Bank ST6 . . . . . 41 F5
Pitt St Kidderminster DY10 280 A1
  Stafford ST16 . . . . 155 C6
Plainfield Gr ST2 . . . . 73 D8
Plainview Cl WS9 . . . . . . 256 E2
Plaisaunce The ST5 . . . . . 71 B6
Plane Gr ST5 . . . . 40 E1
Planks La WV5 . . . . 269 F6
Plantation La Himley DY3. 270 B3
  Hopwas B78 . . . . 249 B4
Plantation Pk ST5 . . . . . . 70 C6
Plantation Rd
  Cannock WS12 . . . . 195 A1
  Stoke-on-T ST4 . . . . 88 D7
Plant Cres ST17 . . . . 174 F7
Plant La WS7 . . . . 228 E7
Plants Cl WS6 . . . . 243 A8
Plant St Cheadle ST10 . . . 76 E2
  Longton ST3 . . . . 284 C4
  Stourbridge DY8 . . . . 275 E2
Plant Way WS3 . . . . 243 F4
Plardiwick Rd ST20 . . . . 171 B6
Platts Ave ST9 . . . . 43 E6
Platts Cres DY8 . . . . 279 E8
Platts Dr DY8 . . . . 279 F8
Platts Rd DY8 . . . . 279 E8
Platt St WS11 . . . . 210 A5
Playdale TF10 . . . . 168 B4
Pleasant Cl DY6 . . . . 275 C4
Pleasant St ST6 . . . . 56 F7
Pleasant View DY3 . . . . . 271 D2
Plex St ST6 . . . . 41 D3
Pleydell St ST7 . . . . 57 F7
Plough Bank
  Weston-Under-Lizard
  TF11. . . . . 203 A6
  Wetley Rocks ST9 . . . . . . 60 B7
Plough La TF10 . . . . 168 F5
Ploughmans Croft TF10 . 169 A4
Ploughmans Pl B75 . . . . 258 D4
Ploughmans Wlk
  Kingswinford DY6 . . . . . . 275 A2
  Lichfield WS13 . . . . 214 C3
  Wolverhampton WV8. . . . 239 F1
Plough Mews DY7 . . . . . 278 A3
Plough St ST1 . . . . 282 C4

Plover Cl
Featherstone WV10 241 B7
Meir ST3 90 A7
Plover Dr ST8 27 E8
Plover Field CW3 68 D6
Plovers Rise WS15 178 D2
Plummer Rd DE11 186 F6
Plumtree Gr ST1 57 F6
Plymouth Gr ST5 55 F7
Pochard Cl ST6 42 C2
Podmore Ave ST7 54 F6
Podmore La ST7 54 E6
Podmore St ST6 57 A7
Pointon Gr ST6 43 A5
Polesworth High Sch
B78 262 F7
Police Dr TF9 112 C8
Polperro Way 9 ST3 90 A7
Pomona Rise ST1 57 D8
Pond Cres WV2 266 E7
Pond Gr WV2 266 E7
Pond La WV2 266 D7
Ponesfield Rd WS13 214 B2
Ponesgreen WS13 214 B2
Pool Ave WS11 228 B5
Pool Cl WV10 225 D1
Pool Dam ST5 283 B2
Poole Ave ST2 43 B2
Poole Cres WS8 228 D2
Pooles Rd ST8 17 B1
Poole St DY8 279 E4
Poole's Way WS7 229 C7
Pooley La Gnosall TF10 188 C7
Polesworth B78 251 F2
Poolfield Ave ST5 70 F8
Poolfield Ave N ST5 71 A8
Poolfield Rd WS13 230 E6
Poolfields Ave ST6 43 C7
Poolfields Cl ST5 70 F8
Pool Gn WS9 256 A5
Pool Green Terr WS9 256 A5
Pool Hall Cres WV3 265 A8
Pool Hall Rd WV3 265 A8
Poolhill Cl ST3 284 A2
Pool House Rd WV5 269 D6
Pool La ST17 176 C4
Pool Mdw WS6 226 D1
Pool Meadow Cl WS15 196 D8
Pool Rd Brownhills WS7 228 E3
Burntwood WS7 228 E4
Poolside Cotts ST18 121 A1
Poolside CW3 68 E6
Pool Side
Newcastle-u-L ST5 283 A3
Scholar Green ST7 25 A8
Poolside ST3 88 F8
Pool St Longton ST4 73 B6
Newcastle-u-L ST5 283 A2
Wolverhampton WV2 266 C8
Pool View WS6 227 A4
Pope Gdns ST17 174 C7
Pope Gr WS12 209 F6
Pope Rd WV10 241 B1
Popes La WV6 255 A6
Poplar Ave
Brownhills WS8 245 A8
Burntwood WS7 228 F6
Cannock WS11 209 F4
Newcastle-u-L ST5 56 A3
Poplar Cl
Blythe Bridge ST11 91 A6
Eccleshall ST21 133 E6
Haughton ST18 172 E6
Newcastle-u-L ST5 56 A3
Stone ST15 119 F7
Uttoxeter ST14 110 F1
Wombourne WV5 270 B6
Poplar Cres DY8 279 D3
Poplar Ct ST5 56 A3
Poplar Dr Kidsgrove ST7 26 A1
Stoke-on-T ST3 72 F2
Poplar Gr Longton ST3 73 A1
Newcastle-u-L ST5 283 D3
Poplar La Bearstone TF9 82 F5
Cannock WS11 209 B1
Poplar Rd Brownhills WS8 245 A8
Great Wyrley WS6 227 A1
Kingswinford DY6 275 E5
Stourbridge DY8 279 E3
Wolverhampton WV3 266 A6
Poplar Rise B74 257 D6
Poplars Dr WV8 238 F2
Poplars Farm Way WV9 224 B2
Poplars Park Cvn Pk
DE6 144 A7
Poplars Rd
Armitage WS15 198 C4
Burton u T DE13 166 C7
Poplars The
Cannock WS11 209 E4
Stourbridge DY8 275 F2
Poplar St
Norton Canes WS11 228 A6
Wolverhampton WV2 266 D6
Poplar Way ST17 174 E6
Poppit's La ST14 110 F4
Poppy Gdns DE13 201 A2
Porchester Cl WS9 245 A2
Porlock Ave ST17 175 D8
Porlock Gr ST4 88 B6
Portal Rd ST16 156 B5
Porters Farm Ct ST14 127 E2
Porters La ST13 31 F3
Porthill Bank ST5 56 C6
Porthill ST6 56 D7
Porthill Gn ST5 56 C6
Porthill Grange ST5 56 C6
Porthill Rd ST6 56 D7
Porthkerry Gr DY3 271 B7
Port La
Abbots Bromley WS15 160 E5
Brewood WV9 223 B3
Portland Ave
Aldridge WS9 256 B5
Burton u T DE14 185 A7
Tamworth B79 249 F8
Portland Cl ST11 90 D7
Portland Ct WS9 256 B6
Portland Dr Biddulph ST8 16 D2
Forsbrook ST11 91 B8
Market Drayton TF9 97 A1
Scholar Green ST7 25 E6
Portland Gr ST5 71 B3
Portland Mews ST5 56 B6
Portland Pl Barlaston ST12 88 F4
Cannock WS11 226 C7
Waterhouses ST10 48 F2
Portland Rd Aldridge WS9 256 B6
Longton ST3 284 B4
Portland St N ST13 30 F6
Portland St S ST13 30 F6
Portland St Hanley ST1 282 A4
Leek ST13 30 F6
Portleven Cl ST17 175 E7
Portleys La B78 260 D4
Portobello WS15 178 E2
Portrush Rd WV6 254 D4
Port St ST6 56 E7
Portswood Cl WV9 239 F1
Port Vale Ct ST6 42 A1
Port Vale St ST6 56 E8
Portway Cl DY6 275 E5
Portway Dr DE13 146 C5
Portway La B79 234 C7
Portway Pl DY10 280 A5
Portway The DY6 275 E5
Postern Rd DE13 165 B3
Post La ST9 43 F6
Post Office La
Gnosall TF10 188 D6
Gorstyhill CW2 37 F1
Rugeley WS15 196 B7
Post Office Rd
Alrewas DE13 201 A3
Seisdon WV5 263 F3
Post Office Row ST17 193 B8
Post Office Sq CW3 68 E5
Pothooks La ST13 33 F4
Potsmans La ST18 122 D7
Potteries Mus & Art Gall
The★ ST1 282 B2
Potteries Sh Ctr ST1 282 B3
Potteries Way ST1 282 C3
Potters Ave ST15 118 F6
Potters Croft B79 218 E2
Potters End ST8 16 C1
Potts La ST14 141 B7
Pouk La WS14 245 F7
Poulson St ST4 72 B7
Pound Gdns ST6 42 D4
Poundsgate Gr ST4 88 B8
Pound St WV5 267 C7
Pountney St WV2 266 C8
Pourbaix Ho WS13 231 B6
Povey Pl ST5 41 B1
Powderham Cl ST6 41 E8
Powell Pl TF10 168 F3
Powell St ST1 282 A4
Power Gr ST3 284 A4
Power Station Rd WS15 178 F1
Power Station Road Ind Est
WS15 178 F1
Power Wash Ind Est ST8 27 B4
Pown St SK17 23 F6
Powy Dr ST7 26 B2
Poxon Rd WS9 245 A3
Poynings The WV6 255 C5
Precinct The B79 250 B5
Preedys Cl WS15 160 F5
Prescott Ave ST16 156 A4
Prescott Dr ST19 193 A1
Prestbury Ave ST5 71 B2
Preston St ST6 57 C8
Preston Vale La ST19 192 C1
Prestwick Rd DY6 275 C6
Prestwood Ct ST17 285 B1
Prestwood Dr
Stourbridge DY7 279 A7
Stourton DY7 278 F8
Prestwood La ST14 79 E1
Prestwood Rd DY7 278 E6
Pretoria Rd ST1 57 A3
Priam Cl ST5 41 B1
Priam Gr WS3 244 B5
Price Ave B78 249 D1
Price Cl TF9 99 D5
Price Ct Burton u T DE14 165 F4
Burton u T DE14 166 A4
Prices Rd DY3 271 C3
Price St Burslem ST6 56 F8
Cannock WS11 209 E1
Priestley Dr ST3 284 D4
Prime St ST1 57 E5
Primitive St ST7 26 C7
Primley Ave B77 261 F5
Primrose Ave WV10 240 D3
Primrose Cl Walsall WS3 244 A5
Wheaton Aston ST19 205 C7
Primrose Dell CW3 68 D6
Primrose Dr
Burton u T DE14 185 A8
Newport TF10 168 F1
Primrose Gdns
Codsall WV8 239 A3
Featherstone WV10 241 B7
Primrose Gr ST5 283 C4
Primrose Hill
Stoke-on-T ST4 72 A2
Stourbridge DY8 275 E1
Primrose Mdw 1 WS11 210 C2
Primrose Way ST14 126 B8
Prince Albert Terr ST15 135 A8
Prince Ave ST18 172 F5
Prince Charles Ave ST13 31 B7
Princefield Ave ST19 207 F8
Princefield Fst Sch ST19 207 F8
Prince George St ST10 76 D3
Prince Rupert Mews
WS13 231 A8
Prince Rupert's Way
WS13 231 A8
Princes Dr WV8 239 A2
Princes Gdns WV8 239 A2
Princes Rd Stoke-on-T ST4 71 F8
Stourbridge DY8 279 D3
Princess Ave Audley ST7 39 D1
Leek ST13 31 B8
Princess Cl WS7 228 E7
Princess Ct ST7 40 D5
Princess Dr ST3 74 B4
Princess Gdns TF10 168 F1
Princess Pl ST16 155 E5
Princes Sq ST6 56 D8
Princess Rd ST14 111 A1
Princess St Biddulph ST8 27 D7
Burntwood WS7 228 E8
Burton u T DE14 166 C4
Cannock WS11 209 F5
Newcastle-u-L ST5 283 C3
Talke Pits ST7 40 D5
Princes St ST16 285 B3
Prince's St ST15 105 A2
Princess Way DE13 166 E7
Prince St Brownhills WS9 244 F2
Cannock WS12 209 E6
Leek ST13 31 A6
Princeton Gdns WV9 239 F2
Princetown Cl ST3 90 A7
Priorfield Cl ST3 284 B4
Priors La TF9 97 A1
Priors Mill DY3 271 E5
Prior's Pl ST19 206 A6
Priory Ave ST13 31 A8
Priory CE Prim Sch ST4 87 F8
Priory Cl Congleton CW12 16 B7
Tamworth B79 249 F7
Tutbury DE13 146 B5
Priory Ct Brownhills WS9 245 A4
Market Drayton TF9 97 A1
Newcastle-u-L ST5 283 B2
Priory Dr ST18 177 D8
Priory Field Cl WV14 266 F1
Priory Green Prim Sch
WV9 240 A2
Priory Lands DE13 147 F2
Priory La DY3 271 D7
Priory Pl ST7 26 A3
Priory Rd Bucknall ST2 58 B6
Cannock WS12 210 D4
Newcastle-u-L ST5 283 B1
Rugeley WS15 197 B5
Stone ST15 120 B7
Priory The Endon ST9 44 A8
Sedgley DY3 271 D8
Pritchett Ave WV4 266 F3
Probert Rd WV10 240 B1
Probyn Ct ST3 284 C2
Proctors Rd WS15 198 C4
Proffitt Cl WS8 245 A5
Progress Dr WS11 226 F6
Progress Ind Ctr WS11 226 F7
Prospect Dr WS13 231 F8
Prospect Manor Ct
WS12 210 C3
Prospect Pk WS11 226 D7
Prospect Pl 9 Leek ST13 30 E5
Stafford ST17 175 A6
Prospect Rd
Burntwood WS7 229 B6
Dudley DY3 271 C2
Leek ST13 31 A5
Market Drayton TF9 97 B1
Stafford ST16 155 F5
Prospect St Burslem ST6 56 E7
Tamworth B79 250 A5
Prospect Terr ST5 283 A3
Prosper Mdw DY6 275 F7
Providence St ST1 282 C4
Provost Pl ST13 31 A7
Pruden Ave WV4 266 F3
Puddle Bank La CW12 15 F5
Puddle Hill ST18 139 D1
Puddy La ST9 44 A5
Pudsey Dr B75 258 C3
Pugh Rd WV4,WV14 266 F2
Pugin Cl WV6 254 D3
Pullman Cl B77 251 A2
Pullman Ct ST10 76 D2
Pulteney Dr ST16 155 B6
Pump Bank ST5 69 F7
Pump Ct ST7 39 E2
Pump La Doveridge DE6 127 B8
Rugeley WS15 178 C3
Pump St Leek ST13 31 A7
Stoke-on-T ST4 72 A7
Purbeck St ST6 57 B7
Purbrook Rd WV1 266 F8
Purbrook B77 261 E8
Purcell Ave WS13 214 C2
Purser Cres ST5 56 B5
Pyebirch La ST21 134 B5
Pye Green Rd WS11 209 E4
Pye Green Valley Prim Sch
WS12 210 A7
Pyenest St ST1 282 A1
Pyrus Gr WS15 196 D6

Q

Quabbs La ST11 91 C8
Quadrangle The ST9 43 F7
Quadrant Rd ST1 282 B3
Quadrant The Hanley ST1 282 B3
Sedgley DY3 266 D1
Quadrille Lawns WV9 239 F2
Quail Gn WV6 254 F2
Quail Gr ST3 90 A7
Quantico Cl 12 ST17 175 A8
Quantock Cl WS8 245 A4
Quarry Ave ST4 71 F8
Quarry Bank
Hollington ST10 94 A4
Keele ST5 69 F8
Quarry Bank Rd Keele ST5 69 F8
Market Drayton TF9 112 B7
Quarry Berry La DE12 236 E7
Quarry Brow DY3 271 E6
Quarry Cl
Cheslyn Hay WS6 226 E3
Rugeley WS15 196 B8
Stoke-on-T ST9 43 C3
Werrington ST9 59 B4
Quarry Hills La WS14 231 D6
Quarry House La TF9 112 A7
Quarry La ST20 171 C4
Quarry Lodge WS14 231 D5
Quarry Pl TF9 112 B7
Quarry Rd Hollington ST10 94 A3
Stoke-on-T ST4 71 F8
Quarry Terr ST7 26 A1
Quarter La SK17 23 B2
Quayle Gr 2 DY8 275 D3
Quee La ST14 126 B1
Queen Anne St ST4 72 B8
Queen Elizabeth II Ct ST4 72 D6
Queen Elizabeth's Mercian
Sch B79 250 C6
Queen Margaret's Rd TF9 99 D5
Queen Mary Rd ST4 72 A1
Queen Mary's Dr ST12 88 E3
Queen's Ave ST6 41 F3
Queensberry Rd ST3 73 D2
Queens Cotts ST19 206 B7
Queen's Croft Com Sch
WS13 231 B7
Queens Ct
Burton u T DE14 185 B8
Caverswall ST11 74 D3
Longton ST3 73 B1
Newcastle-u-L ST5 283 C3
Queen's Dr ST8 27 D6
Queens Dr
Burntwood WS7 228 F5
Leek ST13 31 B8
Newport TF10 168 F1
Queens Gdns
Codsall WV8 238 F3
Talke Pits ST7 40 D5
Queen's Hospl DE13 166 A6
Queensland Cres DE15 167 C2
Queensmead Rd ST3 89 F7
Queens Park Ave ST3 73 B1
Queens Par WS3 243 B1
Queen's Prim Sch ST4 73 A5
Queens Rd Sedgley DY3 271 E8
Shareshill WV10 225 B6
Queen's Rd Stoke-on-T ST4 71 F7
Stourbridge DY8 279 F6
Queens Rise DE13 146 C6
Queen's Row ST12 88 F2
Queen's Sq 3 ST15 105 A2
Queens Sq WS11 209 E1
Queen St Audley ST7 39 C1
Brownhills WS9 244 F2
Burntwood WS7 228 F5
Burslem ST6 56 F8
Burton u T DE14 166 C1
Cannock,Blackfords WS11 209 D1
Cannock WS11 210 A5
Cheadle ST10 76 E4
Cheslyn Hay WS6 226 D3
Queens Terr ST1 57 E4
Queen St Kidsgrove ST7 26 A2
Kingswinford DY6 275 D7
Leek ST13 30 F6
Lichfield WS13 231 A7
Longnor SK17 13 B6
Market Drayton TF9 97 C1
Newcastle-u-L,Chesterton
ST5 55 E7
Newcastle-u-L,Porthill ST5 56 B6
Newcastle-u-L ST5 283 C3
Rugeley WS15 196 F8
Stourbridge DY8 279 F6
Stourbridge,Wordsley DY8 275 E3
Uttoxeter ST14 126 C7
Queensville Ave ST17 156 A1
Queensville Bridge ST17 156 A1
Queensville Ret Pk ST17 175 A8
Queensville Stafford ST17 156 A1
Stafford ST17 175 B8
Queensway Ct 7 ST3 74 A1
Queens Way B78 262 F6
Queensway Ind Est ST6 56 C8
Queensway
Newcastle-u-L ST5 71 B6
Rugeley WS15 196 E7
Stafford ST16 285 B4
Stoke-on-T ST4 72 C6
Tamworth B79 250 A8
Queens Wlk ST3 74 B4
Queenswood Rd B75 258 B1
Queen Victoria Prim Sch
DY3 271 E8
Quendale WV5 269 E6
Quillets Rd DY8 275 C3
Quince B77 251 B3
Quince Tree Sch B77 251 A3
Quinton Ave WS6 226 F3
Quinton Gr ST5 56 B4
Quinton Pl WS11 228 A4
Quinton Wlk ST6 42 C2
Quixhill Bank ST14 95 F8
Quixhill La ST14 95 E8
Quonians La WS13 231 B8
Quorn Cl DE15 167 A1
Quorn Cres DY8 275 C3

R

Rabbit La WV10 241 A8
Raby St WV2 266 D8
Racecourse La DY8 279 F1
Race Course ST5 55 C1
Racecourse Rd ST4 72 A4
Rachel Gr ST4 73 B6
Raddle La B79 217 E5
Radford Bank ST17 175 C8
Radford Cl ST15 105 A1
Radford Dr WS4 244 C2
Radford La WV3,WV4 264 F7
Radford Rd ST4 56 F1
Radford Rise ST17 175 C8
Radford St ST15 105 A1
Radhurst Rise DE13 183 C2
Radley Way ST9 59 B3
Radmore Cl WS7 228 D8
Radmore La
Abbots Bromley WS15 161 C7
Gnosall TF10,ST20 170 D7
Radnor Ct WS9 244 F4
Radnor Rd DY3 271 C8
Radnor Rise WS12 210 B4
Radstock Cl ST17 175 E6
Radstock Rd WV12 242 C1
Radstone Rise ST5 71 B3
Radway Green Rd
Barthomley CW2 38 D6
Barthomley CW2 38 E8
Ragees Rd DY6 275 F4
Raglan Ave WV6 254 F3
Raglan Cl
8 Burton u T DE13 166 D8
Aldridge WS9 256 F3
Sedgley DY3 271 B7
Raglan St ST4 72 D6
Raglan Wlk ST4 72 D6
Ragley Cl WS3 243 A1
Raikes La WS14 246 C7
Railswood Dr WS3 244 B3
Railton Ave ST3 73 A1
Railway Cotts
Colwich ST17 177 D7
Congleton CW12 6 A1
Cotes Heath ST21 102 D3
Cresswell ST11 91 D3
Egginton DE65 148 B7
Leek ST13 30 E1
Leek ST13 45 E8
Norton Bridge ST15 135 A8
Rugeley WS15 197 A5
Railway Ct ST9 43 F7
Railway Ent Ctr ST4 57 A1
Railway La WS7 211 E1
Railway Pas ST3 284 C4
Railway Rd ST3 73 E2
Railway St Cannock WS11 226 E8
Norton Canes WS11 228 A5
Stafford ST16 285 A3
Stoke-on-T ST6 41 E2
Railway Terr
Brocton ST17 176 C7
Kingsley Holt ST10 62 A3
Longton ST3 284 D3
Rainbow St 8 WV2 266 C8
Rainford Cl ST7 26 F1
Rainham Gr ST6 42 A8
Rainscar B77 262 B7
Rake End Ct WS15 179 F1
Rakegate Prim Sch
WV10 240 B1
Rake Hill WS7 229 B8
Rakes La DE6 51 F6
Rakeway Rd ST10 76 F1
Raleigh Hall Ind Est
ST21 117 E2
Ralph Ct ST17 174 B8
Ralph Dr ST1 57 F7
Ralston Cl WS3 243 A4
Ramage Gr ST3 73 D1
Rambleford Way ST16 155 D8
Ramillies Cres WS6 226 F1
Ramsay Cl ST12 88 E4
Ramsey Rd ST5 283 A4
Ramsey St ST4 72 C5
Ramshaw Gr 5 ST3 73 D6
Ramshaw View ST13 31 B8
Ramshorn Rd ST10 78 E8
Randall Cl DY6 275 F4
Randle Dr B75 258 C3
Randles La ST9 60 B6
Randle's View CW12 16 C8
Ranelagh Ho WV2 266 D7
Ranelagh Rd WV2 266 D6
Ranelagh St ST1 282 B2

Rangeley View ST15 ... 104 E2
Rangemoor La DE6 ... 80 D6
Rangemore Hall Mews
DE13 ... 164 B1
Rangemore Hill DE13 ... 183 B7
Rangemore St DE14 ... 166 B3
Rangemore Terr ST5 ... 56 D3
Ranger's Wlk WS15 ... 178 B1
Rangeways Rd DY6 ... 275 F4
Rangifer Rd B78 ... 249 F1
Rank The ST20 ... 171 C5
Ranleigh Ave DY6 ... 275 F4
Ranscombe Dr DY3 ... 271 D2
Ransome Pl ST3 ... 73 E4
Ranton Park Area 3
WS11 ... 210 A2
Ranworth Cl ST5 ... 71 B2
Ranworth Rise WV4 ... 266 D4
Ratcliffe Ave DE14 ... 185 B8
Ratcliffe Cl DY3 ... 271 F6
Rathbone Ave ST5 ... 56 D3
Rathbone St 4 ST6 ... 41 E3
Rathlin Cl WV9 ... 240 A3
Rathmore Cl DY8 ... 279 E2
Rathwell Cl WV9 ... 240 A1
Rattigan Dr ST3 ... 73 F4
Ratton St ST1 ... 282 C3
Raven Cl Cannock WS12 ... 210 E4
Cheslyn Hay WS6 ... 226 D2
Huntington WS12 ... 209 C7
Raven Ct
Market Drayton TF9 ... 97 D1
Wolverhampton WV10 ... 240 B3
Ravenhill Cl WS15 ... 196 F6
Ravenhill Dr WV8 ... 239 A4
Ravenhill Terr WS15 ... 196 F7
Ravenna Way ST3 ... 73 E4
Raven Rd DE13 ... 182 A2
Ravensbank Mobile Home Pk
ST18 ... 137 D2
Ravens Cl ST7 ... 39 E3
Ravenscliffe Rd ST7 ... 41 A8
Ravenscroft DY8 ... 279 C6
Ravens Ct WS8 ... 244 F7
Ravensholme WV6 ... 254 F2
Raven's La ST7 ... 39 F3
Ravenslea Rd WS15 ... 196 F6
Ravensmead Com Prim Sch
ST7 ... 39 E3
Ravenstone B77 ... 262 B8
Ravens Way DE14 ... 166 B4
Ravenswood Cl ST5 ... 71 B3
Ravenswood Crest 4
ST17 ... 175 C7
Rawle Cl ST10 ... 76 C3
Rawlett Sch
Tamworth B79 ... 250 A8
Wigginton B79 ... 234 A1
Rawlins St ST1 ... 57 E5
Rawnsley Rd WS12 ... 210 E6
Ray Ct B74 ... 257 F3
Raygill B77 ... 262 B8
Rayleigh Rd WV3 ... 266 A8
Rayleigh Way ST2 ... 58 D1
Raymond Ave ST1 ... 57 D7
Raymond St ST1 ... 282 B1
Reacliffe Rd SK11,ST13 ... 18 B4
Read Ave ST16 ... 155 F5
Reade's La CW12 ... 16 D8
Reading Way ST2 ... 58 D2
Reads Rd ST4 ... 72 F8
Reapers Wlk WV8 ... 239 F1
Reason Rd ST17 ... 174 F5
Rebecca Gdns WV4 ... 265 F4
Rebecca St ST4 ... 72 B8
Recorder Gr ST6 ... 42 B6
Recreation Rd ST3 ... 73 E2
Rectory Cl
Church Leigh ST10 ... 109 A5
Drayton Bassett B78 ... 260 E5
Rectory Dr TF11 ... 203 F2
Rectory Fields DY8 ... 275 E2
Rectory Gdns
Armitage WS15 ... 198 A4
Talke Pits ST7 ... 40 D6
Rectory La
Armitage WS15 ... 197 F4
Haughton ST18 ... 172 F5
Rectory Mews
Egginton DE65 ... 148 B4
Mucklestone TF9 ... 99 A7
Rectory Rd Hanley ST1 ... 282 A1
Hollington ST10 ... 94 C2
Rectory St Hanley ST1 ... 282 A1
Stourbridge DY8 ... 275 E3
Rectory View ST7 ... 40 D6
Redacres WV6 ... 255 E6
Red Bank La TF9 ... 112 B8
Red Bank Longton ST3 ... 73 C1
Market Drayton TF9 ... 112 B8
Redbourne Dr CW2 ... 37 D1
Redbourn Rd WS3 ... 243 A4
Redbridge Cl ST4 ... 71 F1
Redbrook Cl WS12 ... 210 D2
Redbrook La WS15 ... 196 F5
Redcar Rd Stoke-on-T ST4 ... 88 B7
Wolverhampton WV10 ... 240 D4
Redcliffe Dr WV5 ... 270 B6
Redcliff B77 ... 250 F5
Redfern Dr WS7 ... 229 B5
Redfern Rd Stone ST15 ... 119 F5
Uttoxeter ST14 ... 111 A1
Redford Dr WV7 ... 237 B5
Redgrave Dr ST16 ... 155 C2
Red Hall La ST7 ... 54 C5
Red Hall Prim Sch DY3 ... 271 C3
Redhall Rd DY3 ... 271 C2
Redheath Cl ST5 ... 55 A2
Redhill Ave WV5 ... 270 A6
Redhill Cl B79 ... 250 A7
Redhill Dr ST10 ... 92 E5
Redhill Gdns ST15 ... 120 B8
Redhill Gorse ST16 ... 155 C8
Red Hill DY7 ... 277 E4
Redhill La DE13 ... 146 B5
Redhill Prim Sch WS11 ... 209 F4
Redhill Rd Cannock WS11 ... 209 F4
Stone ST15 ... 105 C1
Redhills ST21 ... 133 E6
Redhills Rd Bucknall ST2 ... 58 A7
Stoke-on-T ST2 ... 57 F8
Redhill ST16 ... 155 C8
Red Ho The
Albrighton WV7 ... 237 A5
Market Drayton TF9 ... 97 C1
Redhouse Cone & Mus★
DY8 ... 275 E1
Red House Cres ST3 ... 284 A3
Red House Ind Est WS9 ... 256 A6
Redhouse Rd WV6 ... 255 B5
Redhurst Dr WV10 ... 240 B3
Red La WV11 ... 242 C3
Redlake B77 ... 261 E8
Red La CW3 ... 68 E5
Redland Dr ST2 ... 58 D3
Redlands The ST15 ... 120 C7
Redlands Way B74 ... 257 A1
Red La Sedgley DY3 ... 271 B8
Stoke-on-T ST2 ... 43 C2
Red Lion Ave WS11 ... 228 A4
Red Lion Cl ST7 ... 40 D7
Red Lion Cres WS11 ... 228 A4
Red Lion La WS11 ... 228 B4
Red Lion Pas ST1 ... 282 A2
Red Lion St ST16 ... 285 B4
Redlock Field WS14 ... 231 A5
Redman Gr ST6 ... 57 C7
Redmine Cl ST5 ... 56 A4
Redmond Cl WS15 ... 178 C2
Redmoor Cl DE15 ... 167 B3
Redmoor Gdns WV4 ... 266 A5
Redmoor Rd WS15 ... 211 F4
Rednall Dr B75 ... 258 C3
Red Rd ST10 ... 78 C3
Redrock Cres ST7 ... 26 C1
Red Rock Dr WV8 ... 238 F2
Redruth Cl DY6 ... 275 D8
Redruth Dr ST17 ... 156 D1
Redstone Way DY3 ... 271 D4
Redwell Cl B77 ... 250 D5
Redwing Cl
3 Packmoor ST7 ... 26 F1
Hammerwich WS7 ... 229 D5
Redwing Dr Biddulph ST8 ... 27 E8
Huntington WS12 ... 209 C7
Redwing B77 ... 262 A6
Redwood Ave Dudley DY1 ... 271 F5
Stone ST15 ... 120 B5
Redwood Cl B74 ... 256 F2
Redwood Dr
Burntwood WS7 ... 228 F8
Burton u T DE15 ... 186 A8
Cannock WS11 ... 210 A3
Redwood Pl ST3 ... 73 F1
Redwood Rd DY7 ... 278 C3
Reedbed Gr ST6 ... 42 C3
Reedham Gdns WV4 ... 265 D5
Reedham Way ST2 ... 58 D2
Reedly Rd WV12 ... 242 C1
Reedmace B77 ... 250 C2
Rees Dr WV5 ... 270 B7
Reeve Cl WS15 ... 198 B4
Reeve La WS13 ... 231 B8
Reeves Ave
Newcastle-u-L ST5 ... 56 B3
Stoke-on-T ST6 ... 42 A3
Reeves Gdns WV8 ... 239 A4
Refinery St ST5 ... 283 C2
Regal Cl B77 ... 261 C8
Regency Cl ST7 ... 40 D5
Regency Ct WS15 ... 197 B6
Regency Dr ST9 ... 43 C4
Regency Way DE13 ... 166 D8
Regency Wlk B74 ... 257 D5
Regent Ave ST6 ... 41 F3
Regent Cl DY6 ... 275 C6
Regent Coll ST4 ... 57 A2
Regent Ct Ipstones ST10 ... 62 A8
Newcastle-u-L ST5 ... 56 B6
Regent Rd Hanley ST1 ... 282 B1
Wolverhampton WV4 ... 265 E5
Regents Ho DE14 ... 184 F7
Regent St Leek ST13 ... 30 F6
Stoke-on-T ST4 ... 72 A5
Stone ST15 ... 104 F1
Regent Theatre★ ST1 ... 282 B2
Regina Cres WV6 ... 255 B4
Reginald Mitchell Prim Sch
The ST7 ... 25 D1
Reginald Mitchell Way
ST6 ... 41 C5
Reginald St 5 ST6 ... 57 A8
Regina St ST6 ... 42 D2
Regis Beeches WV6 ... 255 C5
Regis Rd WV6 ... 255 C5
Registry St ST4 ... 72 B8
Reid Cl WS7 ... 229 F7
Reid St ST6 ... 56 E8
Reindeer Rd B78 ... 249 E1
Relay Dr B77 ... 262 C7
Rembrandt Cl WS11 ... 210 D2
Rembrandt Way ST3 ... 90 B6
Remer St ST6 ... 57 B6
Remington Dr WS11 ... 226 F8
Renard Way ST3 ... 90 B7
Rendel Gr ST15 ... 104 E2
Rendermore Cl ST19 ... 207 E7
Rene Rd B77 ... 250 E5
Renfrew Cl
Newcastle-u-L ST5 ... 70 F8
Stourbridge DY8 ... 275 C3
Renfrew Pl ST4 ... 72 A1
Rennie Cres ST13 ... 45 D5
Rennison Dr WV5 ... 270 A6
Renown Cl ST2 ... 57 F1
Renshaw Dr DE11 ... 186 F5
Renshaw Wood La WV8 ... 221 F2
Renton Gr WV10 ... 240 A1
Renton Rd WV10 ... 240 A1
Repington Rd N B77 ... 251 A5
Repington Rd S B77 ... 251 A5
Repington Rd ST1 ... 57 F8
Repton Ave WV6 ... 254 E3
Repton Cl Cannock WS11 ... 226 B8
Stafford ST17 ... 156 B1
Repton Dr ST5 ... 70 F5
Repton Rd DE15 ... 167 E8
Reservoir Rd
Burton u T DE14 ... 165 F4
Cannock WS12 ... 210 D4
Longton ST3 ... 73 E2
Retreat Gdns DY3 ... 271 E7
Retreat Gdns The WV6 ... 253 C3
Retreat St WV3 ... 266 B8
Reva Rd ST17 ... 174 E8
Revival St WS3 ... 243 B1
Reynards La SK17 ... 24 E4
Reynards Rise TF9 ... 99 D5
Reynolds Ave ST5 ... 55 E6
Reynolds Cl
Lichfield WS13 ... 214 B2
Swindon DY3 ... 269 E2
Reynolds Gr WV6 ... 254 F5
Reynolds Rd ST6 ... 42 A3
Rhein Way 2 ST17 ... 175 A8
Rhodes Cl DY3 ... 271 A4
Rhodes Ct ST5 ... 56 C7
Rhodes Ho DE15 ... 167 C3
Rhodes St ST1 ... 57 D6
Rhondda Ave ST6 ... 57 C7
Rialto Pl ST6 ... 41 D3
Ribble Cl Hilton DE65 ... 147 D8
Newcastle-u-L ST5 ... 71 B4
Ribble Dr ST8 ... 16 E1
Ribble Ind Est ST6 ... 56 F6
Ribblesdale Ave CW12 ... 6 A5
Ribblesdale B77 ... 262 B7
Ricardo St ST3 ... 73 C1
Riceyman Rd ST5 ... 56 B8
Richard Clarke Fst Sch
WS15 ... 161 A6
Richard Cooper Rd
WS14 ... 246 F5
Richard Crosse CE Prim Sch
DE13 ... 199 C6
Richard Heathcote Com Prim
Sch The ST7 ... 54 E6
Richards Ave
Stafford ST16 ... 156 A4
Stoke-on-T ST6 ... 41 F3
Richards Ct WS11 ... 227 F6
Richardson Ct WS7 ... 228 E8
Richardson Dr DY8 ... 279 E8
Richardson Pl ST6 ... 42 B6
Richardson Way WS15 ... 178 D3
Richard Wakefield CE Prim
Sch DE13 ... 146 C6
Richborough Dr DY1 ... 271 F4
Riches St WV6 ... 255 F3
Richfield La ST17 ... 193 F8
Richmere Ct WV6 ... 255 B3
Richmond Ave
Stoke-on-T ST1 ... 57 D8
Wolverhampton WV3 ... 255 F1
Richmond Cl
Cannock WS11 ... 210 A5
Chorlton CW2 ... 37 D1
Newport TF10 ... 168 F1
Stafford ST17 ... 174 E7
Tamworth B79 ... 250 A5
Richmond Dr
Lichfield WS14 ... 231 D7
Perton WV6 ... 254 F3
Wolverhampton WV3 ... 255 E1
Richmond Gdns
Stourbridge DY8 ... 279 F7
Wombourne WV5 ... 270 A5
Richmond Grove ST5 ... 56 D3
Richmond Gr DY8 ... 279 E8
Richmond Pk
Kingswinford DY6 ... 275 C8
Rugeley WS15 ... 196 F5
Richmond Rd
Sedgley DY3 ... 271 E7
Stoke-on-T ST4 ... 72 E1
Wolverhampton WV3 ... 255 E1
Richmond St
Burton u T DE14 ... 166 C4
Stoke-on-T ST4 ... 72 A7
Richmond Terr ST1 ... 282 A1
Rickerscote Ave ST17 ... 175 A6
Rickerscote Hall La
ST17 ... 175 A5
Rickerscote Rd ST17 ... 174 F6
Ridding Bank ST4 ... 87 B7
Ridding La Denstone ST14 ... 79 E2
Gratwich ST14 ... 124 C3
Riddings Cres WS3 ... 243 F4
Riddings La DE6 ... 144 D6
Riddings The B77 ... 250 E5
Rider's Way WS15 ... 178 B1
Ridge Cl ST12 ... 104 C8
Ridge Cres ST3 ... 89 F6
Ridge Croft ST15 ... 120 C7
Ridgefields ST8 ... 17 B1
Ridge Hill Dr CW3 ... 69 B7
Ridge Ho ST1 ... 57 A4
Ridgehouse Dr ST1 ... 57 A4
Ridgemont Ct ST15 ... 120 C7
Ridge Prim Sch The DY8 ... 279 C5
Ridge Rd
Kingswinford DY6 ... 275 C5
Stoke-on-T ST6 ... 41 D6
Ridge St DY8 ... 279 C6
Ridge The DE15 ... 167 B6
Ridget La WS13 ... 201 B1
Ridge Way WS9 ... 256 B4
Ridgeway Cl Hopton ST18 ... 156 B8
Stafford ST18 ... 174 C5
Ridgeway Dr WV4 ... 265 F3
Ridgeway ST18 ... 158 D8
Ridgeway Prim Sch WS7 ... 229 A5
Ridgeway Rd
Burton u T DE15 ... 185 E6
Stourbridge DY8 ... 275 F2
Ridgeway Ridgeway ST6 ... 42 E8
Sedgley DY3 ... 271 D7
Ridgeway The
Burntwood WS7 ... 229 A4
Stafford ST16 ... 155 A5
Ridge Wlk ST3 ... 89 F7
Ridgewood Ave DY8 ... 279 C7
Ridgewood Dr B75 ... 258 B1
Ridgewood High Sch
DY8 ... 279 C5
Ridgewood Rise B77 ... 251 A5
Ridgmont Rd ST5 ... 70 F4
Ridgway Dr ST11 ... 90 D7
Ridgway Pl ST5 ... 56 D6
Ridgway Rd ST1,ST4 ... 57 D1
Ridings Brook Dr 3
WS11 ... 210 A2
Ridings Cl TF9 ... 97 B1
Ridings Park Trad Est
WS11 ... 210 A3
Ridings The
Brewood ST19 ... 223 C7
Cannock WS11 ... 226 F8
Ridley St ST4 ... 72 C5
Ridley Wlk ST4 ... 72 C5
Ridware Ho WS13 ... 214 E1
Ridware Rd WS15 ... 198 B7
Rifle Range Cnr WS15 ... 195 B6
Rigby Dr WS11 ... 209 F4
Rigby Rd ST7 ... 26 B3
Righton Ho B77 ... 250 D1
Riley Ave ST6 ... 42 B2
Riley Cres WV4 ... 266 A6
Riley La ST20 ... 151 F7
Riley St N ST6 ... 56 E8
Riley St S ST6 ... 56 F8
Rileys Way ST7 ... 39 F2
Riley B77 ... 250 E3
Rill St ST4 ... 284 B4
Rimbach Dr ST18 ... 177 D8
Rimini Cl ST3 ... 73 E5
Rindleford Ave WV4 ... 265 C6
Rindle The ST10 ... 76 B3
Ringhills Rd WV8 ... 239 B2
Ringland Cl ST1 ... 282 C3
Ring Rd WS7 ... 228 E7
Ring The ST18 ... 158 C1
Ringway WS11 ... 209 E1
Ringway Ind Est WS13 ... 214 C3
Ringwood Ave WS9 ... 256 B5
Ringwood Rd WV10 ... 240 D1
Ripon Ave ST5 ... 55 E7
Ripon Dr ST17 ... 175 C7
Ripon Rd ST3 ... 88 F8
Riseley Rd ST4 ... 71 D8
Rise The
Kingswinford DY6 ... 275 E5
Lichfield WS13 ... 230 F7
Rugeley WS15 ... 196 F6
Stafford ST17 ... 175 E7
Swadlincote DE11 ... 186 F5
Rishworth Ave WS15 ... 178 E2
Rising Brook High Sch
ST17 ... 174 E6
Rising Brook
Stafford ST17 ... 174 E7
Wolverhampton WV6 ... 255 B4
Rivendell Gdns WV6 ... 255 B5
Rivendell La ST13 ... 30 F2
Rivercroft Cl ST14 ... 96 A3
Riverdale Cl DE15 ... 167 B5
Riverdale Dr ST6 ... 41 E8
Riverdrive B78,B79 ... 250 B3
Riverfield Gr B77 ... 250 D5
Riverhead Cl ST6 ... 42 F5
River Lea Mews CW3 ... 68 E6
Riversfield Dr ST14 ... 95 F3
Riverside Ct Bucknall ST1 ... 57 F4
Dunsley DY7 ... 278 B4
Riverside Dr DE14 ... 184 F7
Riverside Gdns
Burton u T DE14 ... 166 F6
Codsall WV8 ... 239 B5
Riverside Gr 7 ST15 ... 104 F1
Riverside Ho ST19 ... 192 E1
Riverside Ind Est B78 ... 250 B1
Riverside L Ctr ST16 ... 285 B3
Riverside Pk DE14 ... 166 F6
Riverside Rd
Stoke-on-T ST4 ... 71 E2
Upper Tean ST10 ... 92 D4
Riverside Rugeley WS15 ... 178 F2
Walton-on-T DE12 ... 184 C1
Riverside Way WV9 ... 224 B2
Riversleigh Dr DY8 ... 279 E8
Riversmeade Way ST16 ... 155 A5
Riversmead ST5 ... 71 B4
River View SK17 ... 13 B6
Riverway ST17 ... 285 C2
River Way ST15 ... 120 A7
Rivington Cl DY8 ... 279 E4
Rivington Cres ST6 ... 42 A6
Rixdale Cl ST1 ... 282 B4
Roaches Sch ST8 ... 27 C6
Roaches The★ ST13 ... 10 C2
Roach B77 ... 261 D6
Road One CW1 ... 37 D8
Road Two CW1 ... 37 C8
Robert Cl B79 ... 249 F7
Robert Heath St ST6 ... 42 C2
Roberts Ave ST5 ... 283 B4
Roberts Cl
Alsagers Bank ST7 ... 54 F6
Brownhills WS9 ... 244 F2
Roberts Green Rd DY3 ... 271 E4
Robertson Dr ST5 ... 55 F3
Robertson Sq ST4 ... 71 E4
Roberts Prim Sch DY3 ... 271 D4
Robert St Dudley DY3 ... 271 D4
Stoke-on-T ST6 ... 41 D4
Robert Sutton RC Sch
DE15 ... 186 A7
Robertville Rd ST2 ... 58 B3
Robey's La B78 ... 251 D3
Robina Dr ST10 ... 76 E3
Robin Cl Huntington WS12 ... 209 C7
Stoke-on-T ST7 ... 41 F8
Tamworth B77 ... 261 C8
Uttoxeter ST14 ... 126 B6
Robin Croft 14 ST6 ... 56 F8
Robin Hill ST8 ... 28 A7
Robin Hill Gr ST4 ... 73 B5
Robinia B77 ... 251 A4
Robin La TF10 ... 168 A4
Robins Cl WS6 ... 226 D1
Robins Croft WS11 ... 210 A1
Robinson Ave ST6 ... 57 D8
Robinson Cl B79 ... 249 E7
Robinson Ct ST3 ... 88 F8
Robinson Rd
Burntwood WS7 ... 228 F8
Swadlincote DE11 ... 186 F6
Trentham ST4 ... 87 F8
Robins Rd WS7 ... 228 E7
Robins The TF9 ... 99 D4
Robinswood ST17 ... 175 C6
Robson Cl WS8 ... 244 F5
Robson St ST1 ... 282 A2
Rocester La ST10 ... 49 A2
Roche Ave ST13 ... 31 A8
Roche Rd WS3 ... 242 F1
Rochester Ave WS7 ... 229 A7
Rochester Rd ST3 ... 73 C5
Rochester Way WS12 ... 210 C1
Roche The
Burntwood WS13 ... 230 A8
Cheddleton ST13 ... 45 C4
Creswell Green WS13 ... 212 F1
Roche Way WS3 ... 242 F1
Rochford Cl ST13 ... 30 C5
Rochford Gr WV4 ... 265 D5
Rochford Way ST2 ... 58 D1
Rock Cres ST15 ... 105 C4
Rock End Dr ST13 ... 45 B1
Rockeries The ST17 ... 175 A6
Rock Farm Rd WS14 ... 232 E6
Rockfield Ave ST2 ... 43 D1
Rock Hill B78,WS14 ... 248 C4
Rock House Dr ST12 ... 88 D1
Rockhouse Dr ST18 ... 158 B2
Rockhouse La ST7 ... 40 C7
Rockingham Cl
Dudley DY3 ... 271 B3
Walsall WS3 ... 243 B1
Rockingham Dr
Cheadle ST10 ... 76 F3
Perton WV6 ... 254 F3
Rock La Ashley TF9 ... 100 C8
Mucklestone TF9 ... 99 C7
Rocklands Cres WS13 ... 214 D1
Rocklands ST5 ... 56 C7
Rocklands Sch WS13 ... 231 D8
Rock La ST21 ... 102 B1
Rockmount Gdns DY7 ... 278 B3
Rock Rd WV14 ... 271 F8
Rockrose Gdns WV10 ... 241 A7
Rockside ST7 ... 26 C6
Rock St DY3 ... 271 E5
Rocks The Brown Edge ST6 ... 43 B8
Standon ST21 ... 102 C2
Rock The WV6 ... 255 D5
Rocky Wall DY7 ... 277 E4
Rodbaston Coll ST19 ... 207 E3
Rodbaston Dr ST19 ... 207 E5
Roddam Ct TF10 ... 168 E2
Roddige La WS13 ... 216 A8
Rode Hall★ ST7 ... 25 B7
Rodenhurst House Flats 3
TF9 ... 97 C1
Rodger Ave CW3 ... 53 A6
Rodgers St ST6 ... 41 C7
Rodway Cl WV4 ... 266 D3
Roebuck Ct ST15 ... 106 D2
Roebuck Sh Ctr ST5 ... 283 B2
Roebuck St ST4 ... 72 C7
Roedean Ave ST17 ... 175 B8
Roe Deer Gn TF10 ... 168 E5
Roe La ST5 ... 71 A4
Roe Pk ST7 ... 15 E1
Roford Ct DY3 ... 271 E5
Rogate Cl ST4 ... 73 B6
Rogers Ave ST5 ... 55 F3

Rogers Cl WV11 242 A2
Rogerson Rd WS13 215 D6
Rogerstone Ave ST4 71 E6
Rokewood Cl DY6 270 D1
Rokholt Cres WS11 209 C1
Rolfe Cl ST4 72 A2
Rolleston La DE13 146 D5
Rolleston Rd DE13 166 C8
Rolling Mill Rd WS11 227 F4
Rolt Cl ST15 104 E3
Roma Cl ST3 89 D8
Roman Cl WS8 228 E2
Roman Ct Cannock WS11 226 E5
Tamworth B77 261 E7
Roman Dr ST5 55 D5
Roman La B74 257 B4
Roman Pk B74 257 B4
Roman Pl B74 257 B2
Roman Rd Coven WV9 224 A3
Little Aston B74 257 C4
Roman Rd (Sandy La) DY8 279 C3
Romans Grange B74 257 C5
Roman View WS11 226 F5
Roman Way
Lichfield WS14 231 D7
Tamworth B79 249 E7
Roman Wlk WS14 230 D2
Romany Way DY8 279 C3
Romer Side ST2 73 C8
Romesco Way
7 Stafford ST17 175 A8
Stafford ST17 175 A8
Romford Mdw ST21 133 D6
Romford Pl ST3 90 B7
Romford Rd ST16 155 E6
Romilly Cl Lichfield WS14 231 E7
Stourbridge DY8 279 E6
Romney Ave ST5 55 E6
Romney Dr ST16 155 B4
Romney Gr ST3 89 C8
Romney B77 261 F8
Romsey Cl ST2 73 D8
Romsey Gr WV10 240 C3
Romsey Rd WV10 240 C3
Romsey Way WS3 242 F3
Romsley Cl WS4 244 C2
Romsley La WV15 276 A2
Ronald St ST3 284 C2
Ronaldsway Dr ST5 283 A4
Ronald Wlk ST3 284 C2
Ronson Ave ST4 71 E4
Rooker Ave WV2 266 F6
Rooker Cres WV2 266 F6
Rookery Ave ST3 73 A1
Rookery Cl
Armitage WS15 198 C5
Yoxall DE13 182 A2
Rookery Cotts ST21 115 E6
Rookery Cres ST11 91 C2
Rookery Ct
Lichfield WS13 230 E7
Stoke-on-T ST4 71 E3
Rookery La Aldridge WS9 256 B6
Stoke-on-T ST4 71 F3
Weeford B75,B78 248 C2
Wolverhampton WV2 266 B6
Rookery Par WS9 256 B6
Rookery Rd
Coldmeece ST15 118 C7
Kidsgrove ST7 26 C3
Wombourne WV5 270 B6
Rookery Rise WV5 270 B6
Rookery The
Newcastle-u-L ST5 55 C1
Stoke-on-T ST4 71 E3
Rookswood Copse 2 ST17 175 C6
Rookwood Dr WV6 254 F2
Roper Way DY3 271 F6
Roper Wlk DY3 271 F6
Rope St ST4 56 D1
Ropewalk The DE14 166 C1
Roseacre Gr ST3 89 F6
Roseacre La ST11 90 F6
Roseacre ST5 70 F7
Rose Ave Burton u T DE13 148 A2
Kingswinford DY6 275 F5
Rose Bank Cres ST10 78 B6
Rose Bank St ST13 30 F6
Rose Bank Terr ST13 30 F6
Rose Bay Mdw 2 WS11 210 C2
Roseberry Dr CW3 68 E7
Roseberry Gdns DY10 280 C3
Rosebery Cl ST8 27 E8
Rosebery Rd B77 261 D4
Rosebery St ST6 41 F5
Rosebury Gr WV5 269 E6
Rose Cottage Dr 3 DY8 275 D3
Rose Cottage Gdns DE14 166 D1
Rose Cotts ST11 203 F8
Rosedale Wlk DY6 275 E8
Rose Dr WS8 244 E5
Rosehill WS12 209 F8
Rosehill Cl ST2 43 B1
Rose Hill ST16 155 C3
Rose La WS7 229 C7
Roseland Cres ST2 43 B1
Roseleigh Cres DE11 186 F6
Rosemary Ave
Cheslyn Hay WS6 226 D3
Stafford ST17 174 F5
Wolverhampton WV4 266 C6
Rosemary Cl WS8 244 D6
Rosemary Cres
Dudley DY1 271 F6
Wolverhampton WV4 266 C5
Rosemary Cres W WV4 266 B5
Rosemary Ct B74 257 D4
Rosemary Dr
Huntington WS12 209 D5
Little Aston B74 257 C3
Uttoxeter ST14 126 B6
Rosemary Ednam Cl ST4 71 E8
Rosemary Hill Rd B74 257 D4
Rosemary La DY8 279 D3
Rosemary Nook B74 257 D5
Rosemary Pl ST1 57 E7
Rosemary Rd
Cheslyn Hay WS6 226 D3
Tamworth B77 250 F4
Rosemary St ST5 55 E1
Rose Mill TF9 99 E5
Rosemount Rd DE15 166 F3
Rosemount WV6 255 D5
Rosendale Ave ST5 55 F6
Rosendale Rd ST5 56 A5
Roseneath Pl ST2 43 B1
Rose St ST1 57 E5
Rose Tree Ave ST4 71 E2
Rose Tree La DE11 186 F7
Rosevale Bsns Pk ST5 55 F8
Rosevale Ct ST5 55 E8
Rosevale Rd ST5 55 E8
Rosevale St ST2 43 B1
Roseville Dr CW12 16 B8
Roseville Gdns WV8 239 A4
Rose Way WS15 178 C2
Rosewood Ave ST9 43 C4
Rosewood Cl
Little Aston B74 257 D5
Tamworth B77 250 D4
Rosewood Ct B77 250 D4
Rosewood Gdns
Essington WV11 242 B3
Stafford ST16 155 C3
Rosewood Pk WS6 226 D2
Rosewood Rd DE15 185 F6
Rosewood Sch DY1 271 E1
Rosliston Rd DE15 185 E7
Rosliston Rd S DE15 185 E5
Rosliston Rd
Swadlincote DE15 185 D3
Walton-On-Trent DE12 202 E8
Rossall Ave ST5 70 F5
Ross Cl Longton ST3 74 A4
Wolverhampton WV6 255 E2
Ross Dr DY6 275 C7
Rossett Gr ST6 41 F8
Rosslyn Rd ST3 284 C2
Ross Rd ST10 62 C2
Rosvean Cl ST1 282 B4
Rosy Bank ST9 43 C3
Rosy Cross B79 250 B5
Rotary Ho DY1 271 F1
Rothay B77 261 F8
Rothbury Gn WS12 210 E2
Rother Wlk ST6 42 A4
Rotherwood Dr ST17 285 A1
Rothesay Ave ST5 70 F7
Rothesay Ct Longton ST3 73 D2
Newcastle-u-L ST5 70 F7
Rothesay Dr DY8 275 C3
Rothesay Rd ST3 73 D2
Rothley Gn ST3 88 F7
Rothsay Ave ST1 57 D8
Rothwell St ST4 71 F6
Rotten Row WS14 231 C7
Rotterdam ST5 55 F1
Rotterdam Rd ST5 55 F1
Rough Bank CW12 16 E8
Roughcote La ST11 74 C5
Rough Hills Cl WV2 266 F6
Rough Hills Rd WV2 266 F6
Roughley Dr B75 258 C2
Roughley Farm Rd B75 258 E3
Roughlow La DE6 80 D1
Roundfields ST9 43 C3
Round Hill DY3 266 D2
Roundhill Way WS8 229 A2
Round House Rd DY3 271 E4
Roundway Down WV6 254 F3
Roundway ST3 72 D2
Roundwell St ST6 41 D3
Rouse Cl ST16 155 C2
Rowallan Rd B75 258 D2
Rowanburn Cl ST3 73 D5
Rowan Cl
Biddulph Moor ST8 28 B8
Kidsgrove ST7 41 A8
Lichfield WS14 231 D8
Stone ST15 120 B6
Rowan Cres WV3 265 E7
Rowan Ct ST14 95 F4
Rowan Dr Armitage WS15 198 C3
Essington WV11 242 B3
Newport TF10 168 F1
Rowan Glade ST17 175 C6
Rowan Gr Brewood ST19 223 D6
Burntwood WS7 228 F7
Stoke-on-T ST3 72 E3
Rowan La TF9 99 F5
Rowan Pl ST5 55 D8
Rowan Rd Cannock WS11 209 C2
Market Drayton TF9 97 E2
Sedgley DY3 266 F1
Rowan Rise DY6 275 E6
Rowbury Dr DE15 167 B2
Rowena Gdns DY3 266 C2
Rowhurst Cl ST5 55 D7
Rowhurst Pl ST6 42 C5
Rowland St ST3 73 B1
Rowley Ave
Newcastle-u-L ST5 55 F7
Stafford ST17 285 A1
Rowley Bank Gdns ST17 174 E8
Rowley Bank Ho ST17 174 E8
Rowley Bank ST17 174 E8
Rowley Cl Cannock WS12 210 B8
Edingale B79 217 C5
Rugeley WS15 197 A6
Rowley Gr ST17 174 E8
Rowley Hall Cl ST17 174 C8
Rowley Hall Dr ST17 174 C8
Rowley Hall Hospl ST17 174 D8
Rowleyhill Dr ST19 206 F4
Rowley St ST16 155 D5
Row Moor Way ST6 42 E2
Rownall Pl 2 ST3 74 A2
Rownall Rd Meir ST3 74 A1
Werrington ST9 59 D5
Rownall View ST13 30 C4
Rowney Cl TF9 99 D4
Rownton Cl B74 257 D4
Row The ST18 137 F4
Rowton Ave WV6 254 E3
Rowton St DE13 166 C6
Roxall Cl DY10 281 C2
Roxburghe Ave ST3 284 D2
Royal Cl Rugeley WS15 196 D7
Stoke-on-T ST2 43 A3
Royal Oak Dr ST19 221 E8
Royal St ST4 284 A5
Royal Way ST2 43 B3
Royal Wlk ST10 76 D3
Royal Wolverhampton Sch The WV3 266 B7
Royce Ave ST8 27 B5
Roycroft Cl ST5 56 B8
Royden Ave ST1 57 F4
Royds Cl ST18 172 E6
Roylance St ST6 41 D3
Royston Chase B74 257 A3
Royston Way DY3 271 C8
Royston Wlk ST3 284 C3
Royville Pl ST6 57 D8
Rozel Ave DY10 280 B1
Ruabon Cl ST8 27 E6
Rubens Cl DY3 271 D5
Rubens Way ST3 90 B7
Rubian St ST4 72 F6
Rudge Dale Rd TF9 100 A4
Rudge Rd WV6 263 B7
Rudyard Cl Stone ST15 104 E2
Wolverhampton WV10 240 E4
Rudyard Gr ST5 56 C4
Rudyard Ho ST17 174 E5
Rudyard Lake Steam Rly★ ST13 18 E2
Rudyard Lake Visitors Ctr★ ST13 18 E1
Rudyard Rd Biddulph ST8 17 C1
Poolend ST13 19 A1
Rudyard ST13 29 E8
Rudyard Vale Cvn Pk ST13 18 D2
Rudyard Way ST10 76 F4
Ruelow Mdw ST10 62 A7
Ruffin Ct ST15 120 C7
Rufford B79 249 E6
Rugby Cl Burton u T DE14 185 C8
Newcastle-u-L ST5 70 F4
Rugby Dr ST3 73 C1
Rugby Rd DY8 279 D7
Rugeley Rd
Armitage WS15 197 D5
Burntwood,Chase Terrace WS7 211 F2
Burntwood,Gorstey Ley WS7 229 C7
Cannock WS12 211 B7
King's Bromley DE13 199 A5
Rugeley WS15 196 D1
Rugeley Town Sta SW15 196 E8
Rugeley Trent Valley Sta WS15 178 F3
Ruiton St DY3 271 D4
Rumbold Ave WS13 215 D6
Rumer Hill Bsns Est WS11 226 E7
Rumer Hill Rd WS11 226 F8
Running Hills WS15 197 F4
Runnymede Cl ST2 58 B3
Runnymede ST15 120 A6
Rupert St 1 ST8 27 C8
Rushall Cl DY8 279 E8
Rushall JMI Sch WS4 244 B1
Rushall Rd WV10 240 E2
Rushbrook Cl WS8 244 D6
Rushcliffe Dr ST3 90 B7
Rushes Mill WS3 243 E3
Rushey La WV7 252 D8
Rushford Ave WV5 270 A6
Rush La
Market Drayton TF9 97 A2
Tamworth B77,B78 261 D4
Rushmoor Gr 4 ST3 90 B7
Rushton Ave ST10 61 D2
Rushton CE Prim Sch SK11 8 B2
Rushton Cl Brown Edge ST6 43 B7
Tutbury DE13 146 C6
Rushton Gr 11 ST6 57 A7
Rushton Mews WS12 211 C4
Rushton ST5 70 F4
Rushton Rd ST6 57 A7
Rushtons La ST15 105 F6
Rushton Way ST11 91 A8
Rushwater Cl WV5 269 E6
Ruskin Ave Dudley DY3 271 A5
Wolverhampton WV4 266 F2
Ruskin Cl ST3 284 D5
Ruskin Dr ST18 154 E2
Ruskin Glass Ctr★ DY8 279 F7
Ruskin Pl DE14 166 D6
Ruskin Rd WV10 241 A1
Rusper Cl ST1 57 F6
Russell Bank Rd B74 257 E4
Russell Cl Congleton CW12 16 A8
Tamworth B77 261 E6
Uttoxeter ST14 126 D8
Wolverhampton WV11 241 F1
Russell Ct B74 257 D3
Russell Gr ST9 59 B4
Russell Ho B77 250 F2
Russell Pl ST6 41 D6
Russell Rd ST6 41 D6
Russells Hall Prim Sch DY1 271 E1
Russell's Hall Rd DY1 271 F1
Russell St
Burton u T DE14 166 D2
Leek ST13 30 E5
Longton ST3 284 B1
Newcastle-u-L ST5 56 C5
Russel St ST16 285 A3
Russet Cl 2 ST3 90 A7
Russett Cl WS7 229 A6
Russetts The ST17 174 F6
Russet Wlk WV8 239 E1
Rustington Ave ST3 73 E3
Ruston Ave ST6 42 B6
Rutherford Ave ST5 71 B3
Rutherford Ct ST18 156 C5
Rutherford Pl ST4 71 E7
Rutherglen Cl WS15 178 C1
Ruthin Gr ST8 27 E6
Ruthin Rd ST2 58 D2
Rutland Ave
Rugeley WS15 196 D6
Wolverhampton WV4 265 D4
Rutland Cl DE15 185 D6
Rutland Cres WS9 245 B1
Rutland Dr B78 250 A1
Rutland Pl
Newcastle-u-L ST5 71 C4
Stourbridge DY8 279 D8
Rutland Rd
Cannock WS12 210 E1
Kidsgrove ST7 26 A2
Longton ST3 284 C4
Rutland St ST1 282 A4
Ruxley Ct ST2 57 F3
Ruxley Rd ST2 58 A3
Ryandra Bsns Pk ST10 76 B2
Ryburn Cl CW2 37 B3
Rycroft CE Mid Sch ST14 95 E4
Rydal Cl Aldridge B74 256 F2
Cannock WS12 210 A8
Rydal Dr WV6 254 F4
Rydal Est WS15 178 F3
Rydal Ho ST16 285 C3
Rydal B77 262 A7
Rydal Way ST5 71 B4
Ryder Cl DE11 186 E2
Ryder Rd ST3 90 A8
Ryders Hayes Com Sch WS3 244 A5
Ryders Hayes La WS3 244 B4
Ryder St DY8 275 D2
Rye Bank Cres ST5 283 B3
Rye Bank ST5 283 B3
Ryebrook Gr ST6 41 F6
Ryecroft Ave WV4 266 B5
Ryecroft Cl Sedgley DY3 271 C8
Upper Tean ST10 92 F3
Ryecroft Cotts WV4 266 B5
Ryecroft Dr 3 WS7 229 A8
Ryecroft ST5 283 B3
Ryecroft Rd ST6 42 E3
Ryecroft Sh Ctr WS7 229 A8
Rye Ct ST16 155 A5
Ryedale Way CW12 16 C8
Ryefield WV8 239 E1
Ryehills ST7 39 E1
Ryeland Cl ST3 89 C8
Ryhope Wlk WV9 240 A3
Rykneld Prim Sch DE14 184 E7
Rykneld St WS13 215 E7
Ryknild Cl B74 257 F6
Ryknild St Alrewas DE13 201 A2
Lichfield WS14 231 E6
Ryknild Trad Est DE14 166 E6
Rylands Dr WV4 266 A4
Rylcroft 7 WV4 266 F4
Rylestone Cl ST3 90 B7
Ryle St WS3 243 D1
Ryton B77 261 F8
Ryton Way DE65 147 D8

S

Sabine St ST17 285 C1
Sabrina Rd WV6 254 E1
Sackville St ST4 56 E1
Saddler Ave ST15 120 D7
Saddlers Cl WS14 231 E8
Saddlestones The WV6 254 D4
Saddleworth Rd WS3 243 A4
Sadler Ctr WS8 245 A8
Sadler Rd WS8 245 A8
Sadlers Mill WS8 245 A7
Saffron Cl
Barton-u-N DE13 183 C1
Meir ST3 90 A6
Saffron Gdns WV4 266 A4
Saffron B77 251 B4
Sage Cl ST1 282 B1
St Aidan's Cl DE13 166 C8
St Aidan's Ct WV4 266 A5
St Aidan's Rd WS11 209 E5
St Aidan's St ST6 41 D4
St Albans Cl WV11 242 A1
St Albans Ct DE13 166 C7
St Albans Rd ST16 155 E7
St Andrew Cl WS12 211 A5
St Andrews Ave WS3 244 B4
St Andrew's CE Prim Sch B79 218 E1
St Andrews CE Prim Sch
Weston ST18 138 D2
Wolverhampton WV6 255 F4
St Andrew's Cl
Clifton Campville B79 218 F2
Dudley DY3 271 A3
St Andrews Cl DY8 279 F2
St Andrews Cres ST1 57 D7
St Andrew's Dr DE13 166 C8
St Andrews Dr ST7 26 C3
St Andrew's Dr ST5 70 F8
St Andrews Dr WV6 254 D5
St Andrews Rd ST17 174 C7
St Andrew's Sq 3 ST4 72 A7
St Andrews B77 251 B4
St Andrews Way TF10 168 E1
St Anne's CE Prim Sch ST6 28 B1
St Anne's Cl WS7 228 E4
St Anne's RC Prim Sch ST17 175 D7
St Annes Rd WS13 214 B3
St Anne's Rd WV10 240 B1
St Anne's Vale ST6 43 B8
St Ann St ST1 282 C3
St Ann Wlk ST1 282 C3
St Anthonys Cl WS15 196 F8
St Anthonys Ct ST4 72 B5
St Anthony's Dr ST5 71 A7
St Anthonys Dr WS3 244 B5
St Anthony's RC Prim Sch WV10 240 D3
St Augustine's CE Fst Sch DE6 144 D5
St Augustines Dr CW2 37 E3
St Augustine's RC Prim Sch ST3 89 F8
St Augustine's Rd WS15 196 E6
St Austell Cl
Stafford ST17 175 D8
Tamworth B79 250 A6
St Austin's RC Prim Sch ST17 285 C2
St Barbara Ho WS15 178 E1
St Barbara's Rd WS15 198 C5
St Bartholomew's CE Prim Sch SK17 13 B7
St Bartholomew's CE Prim Sch WV4 265 E3
St Bartholomews Cl ST6 42 E4
St Bede's Sch WS15 178 A6
St Benedict Bishop CE Prim Sch WV5 270 B7
St Benedict's Dr ST18 177 D8
St Benedict's Rd WS7 229 B6
St Benedicts Rd WV5 270 A6
St Bernadette's RC Prim Sch WS8 244 F8
St Bernadettes RC Prim Sch WV5 269 F6
St Bernard Pl ST2 58 A5
St Bernards Cl WS12 211 D4
St Bernard's Rd ST5 55 F2
St Bertelin Ct ST16 155 C6
St Blaise Rd B75 258 D3
St Brides Cl Sedgley DY3 271 C8
Wombourne WV5 269 F6
St Catherines Cl ST14 126 D8
St Catherine's Cres WV4 265 F4
St Catherines Rd WS13 214 B3
St Catherine's Rd DE11 186 F5
St Chad Ct B77 250 F2
St Chad's CE Prim Sch
Lichfield WS13 231 C8
Newcastle-u-L ST5 40 D2
St Chads CE Prim Sch WV6 253 C3
St Chads Cl ST19 223 D6
St Chad's Cl
Burton u T DE13 166 C8
Cannock WS11 210 A4
St Chads Cl ST18 177 D7
St Chad's Cl
Denstone ST14 95 D6
Dudley DY3 271 B3
St Chads Cl
Lichfield WS13 214 B1
Pattingham WV6 253 C2
St Chad's Cl ST15 120 C7
St Chads Ct 3 WS13 231 B8
St Chad's Pl ST16 285 B3
St Chads RC Prim Sch DY3 271 D7
St Chad's Rd DE13 166 C7
St Chads Rd ST21 133 D6
St Chad's Rd WS13 214 C1
St Chads Rd ST6 41 E3
St Chads Way TF9 82 C2
St Christopher Ave ST4 71 E6
St Christopher Cl WS12 211 A5
St Christopher's Dr B77 250 C1
St Christophers RC Prim Sch WV8 239 A3
St Clair St ST3 284 C2
St Clements Ct CW2 37 B1
St David Cl WS12 211 A6
St Davids Cl WS3 244 B5

St David's Dr DE13 ...... 166 D8
St Davids Pl WS3 ...... 243 D2
St Davids Rd
  Clifton Campville B79 ... 218 F2
  Stafford ST17 ...... 174 D7
St Davids Way ST8 ...... 27 E6
St Dominics Ct ST4 ...... 72 A8
St Dominics Ind Jun Sch
  ST4 ...... 71 F8
St Dominic's Priory Sch
  ST15 ...... 104 F1
St Dominic's RC Prim Sch
  ST15 ...... 105 A1
St Dominic's Sch ST13 .. 223 C7
St Editha's Cl B79 ...... 250 B5
St Editha's Ct
  Church Eaton ST20 ...... 190 B8
  Tamworth B79 ...... 250 B7
St Edmund's Ave ST5 .. 56 B6
St Edmund's Cl WV6 ... 255 F3
St Edmunds RC Sch
  WV3 ...... 255 E3
St Edward's CE Fst Sch
  ST13 ...... 45 B5
St Edwards CE Mid Sch
  ST13 ...... 30 C5
St Edwards Ct DE11 .... 186 F4
St Edwards Gn WS15 ... 196 E2
St Edward's Hall ST13 .. 45 C7
St Edward's Rd ST13 ... 45 C4
St Edward St ST13 ...... 30 E5
Sainte Foy Ave WS13... 231 A6
St Elizabeth's RC Prim Sch
  B79 ...... 249 F8
St Filumena's RC Prim Sch
  ST11 ...... 74 E2
St Foy Ave WS13 ...... 230 F5
St Francis Cl
  Burton u T DE13 ...... 166 D8
  Cannock WS12 ...... 211 A5
  Walsall WS3 ...... 244 B5
St Francis of Assisi RC Sch
  WS9 ...... 256 C5
St Francis RC Prim Sch
  WS4 ...... 244 C1
St Gabriel's RC Prim Sch
  B77 ...... 250 E1
St George Dr WS12 ...... 211 A5
St George & St Martin's RC
  Prim Sch ST1 ...... 282 C4
St Georges Ave ST9 .... 43 E6
St George's Ave N ST5 .. 56 B5
St George's Ave S ST5... 56 B5
St Georges Ave ST5 .... 42 B4
St George's Ave W ST5... 56 B5
St George's Cres ST4 ... 72 A1
St Georges Ct B74 ...... 257 E5
St Georges Hospl ST16.. 285 C4
St George's Rd
  Burton u T DE13 ...... 165 F5
  Newcastle-u-L ST5 ...... 283 A2
  Stafford ST17 ...... 156 A2
  Stone ST15 ...... 120 B8
  Stourbridge DY8 ...... 279 D2
St George's St 4 ST13 .... 30 E6
St George's Way B77.... 250 F4
St Giles Gr ST18 ...... 172 F6
St Giles' RC Prim Sch
  ST10 ...... 76 D3
St Giles Rd WS7 ...... 229 B6
St Gile's Rd ST5 ...... 55 F2
St Giles & St George's CE
  Prim Sch ST5 ...... 283 C4
St Gregory's RC Prim Sch
  ST3 ...... 284 B2
St Gregory's Rd ST3.... 284 A3
St Helens Rd WS13..... 214 B3
St Helier Cl ST5 ...... 70 F3
St Hilda's Ave ST13 ... 45 C4
St Ives Cl Stafford ST17 .. 175 D8
  Tamworth B79 ...... 250 B6
St James CE Prim Sch
  Longdon WS15 ...... 198 A2
  Stourbridge DY8 ...... 279 D7
St James Cl
  Longdon WS15 ...... 198 A1
  Walsall WS3 ...... 244 B5
St James Cres ST17 .... 193 B8
St James Ct Audley ST7 .. 39 D2
  Barton-u-N DE13 ...... 183 D2
St James' Ct ST8 ...... 16 E3
St James Gdns WS8 .... 244 F7
St James Gn ST21 ...... 102 E3
St James Pl ST4 ...... 72 A1
St James Prim Sch WS8. 244 F8
St James' Rd DE13 ...... 183 D1
St James Rd
  Cannock WS11 ...... 209 C1
  Norton Canes WS11 ... 228 B5
  Sutton Coldfield B75 ... 258 C2
St James' St DY3 ...... 271 D3
St James Wlk WS8 ...... 244 F7
St John Cl B75 ...... 258 D4
St John Fisher RC High Sch
  ST5 ...... 283 A4
St John's Ave
  Newcastle-u-L ST5 ...... 56 C4
  Oulton ST15 ...... 105 C3
  Stoke-on-T ST4 ...... 71 E4
St John's CE Fst Sch
  ST19 ...... 221 D4
St Johns CE Prim Sch
  WS9 ...... 245 A3

  Cheddleton ST9 ...... 60 A7
  Essington WV11 ...... 242 A4
  Keele ST5 ...... 69 F7
  Stafford ST16 ...... 156 B4
St Johns Cl WS9 ...... 244 F3
St Johns Cl WS7 ...... 211 E1
St John's Cl
  Cannock WS11 ...... 226 D8
  Lichfield WS13 ...... 231 B6
St Johns Cl
  Rugeley WS15 ...... 196 C8
  Stowe-by-Chartley ST18 .. 139 C3
St John's Ct DY3 ...... 269 D2
St John's Ct
  Burton u T DE13 ...... 166 C7
  Cannock WS12 ...... 210 E1
  Walsall WS3 ...... 243 B1
St John's Dr
  Shenstone WS14 ...... 246 F5
  Swadlincote DE11 ...... 186 E5
St Johns Hill WS14 ...... 246 F5
St Johns Ho B74 ...... 257 E5
St Johns Pl ST8 ...... 27 D7
St John's Pl Biddulph ST8.. 27 D7
  Newcastle-u-L ST5 ...... 55 F2
St John's Prep Sch
  WS15 ...... 213 A8
St John's Prim Sch DY3. 269 E2
St John's RC Prim Sch
  ST10 ...... 78 E1
St John's RC Prim Sch
  ST18 ...... 158 B2
St Johns Rd TF9 ...... 100 C5
St Johns Rd ST8 ...... 27 C5
St Johns Rd WS8 ...... 245 A5
St John's Rd
  Burton u T DE13 ...... 166 C7
  Cannock WS11 ...... 226 E7
  Congleton CW12 ...... 6 A5
St Johns Rd
  Essington WV11 ...... 242 A3
  Stafford ST17 ...... 174 D8
St Johns Rd ST17 ...... 174 D8
St Johns Rd WS3 ...... 244 B5
St Johns Ret Pk 3 WV2 266 C8
St Johns Sch WS13 ...... 231 B7
St John's Sq
  8 Burslem ST6 ...... 56 F8
  Uttoxeter ST14 ...... 110 F1
St John's St B79 ...... 250 B5
St John St Hanley ST1... 282 C4
  Lichfield WS13 ...... 231 B7
St Johns Way TF9 ...... 100 C5
St John's Wlk ST16 ...... 156 A3
St Johns Wood WS14 ... 247 A5
St John The Evangelist RC
  Prim Sch (Annexe) ST7 . 25 F1
St Joseph & St Theresa RC
  Prim Sch WS7 ...... 228 C6
St Josephs Cl WS3 ...... 244 A4
St Joseph's Coll ST4 .... 71 F3
St Joseph's Convent Sch
  WV6 ...... 255 E6
St Josephs Ct WV4 ...... 265 D6
St Joseph's RC Prim Sch
  Cannock WS12 ...... 210 C4
  Lichfield WS14 ...... 231 C1
  Rugeley WS15 ...... 196 F7
  Uttoxeter ST14 ...... 126 B8
St Joseph St ST6 ...... 41 D7
St Jude's CE Prim Sch
  WV3 ...... 255 E5
St Jude's Ct 4 WV6 .... 255 F3
St Jude's Rd WV6 ...... 255 F3
St Jude's Rd W WV6 .... 255 F3
St Jude's Way DE13 .... 166 C8
St Lawrence CE Prim Sch
  ST20 ...... 171 E6
St Lawrence Dr WS11 ... 210 B2
St Lawrence View SK17 .. 23 B2
St Lawrence Way ST20 .. 171 D7
St Leonard's Ave
  Ipstones ST10 ...... 62 A8
  Stafford ST17 ...... 156 A1
St Leonard's CE Fst Sch
  Dunston ST18 ...... 192 F8
  Ipstones ST10 ...... 62 A8
St Leonard's CE Prim Sch
  B79 ...... 234 C1
St Leonard's Prim Sch
  ST17 ...... 156 A1
St Leonards View ST18 .. 262 F8
St Leonard's Way CW3 .. 67 C1
St Lucy's Dr ST5 ...... 56 C7
St Lukes CE Prim Sch
  ST9 ...... 43 E7
St Luke's CE Prim Sch
  Hanley ST1 ...... 282 C2
  Newcastle-u-L ST5 ...... 55 A2
St Luke's CE Prim Sch
  WV2 ...... 266 B7
St Lukes Cl
  Cannock WS11 ...... 226 D8
  Newcastle-u-L ST5 ...... 55 B2
St Lukes Cl ST15 ...... 135 A8
St Lukes Ct ST11 ...... 91 A7
St Lukes Prim Sch (Inf Site)
  WV2 ...... 266 C7
St Luke's Rd
  Barton-u-N DE13 ...... 183 D1
  Burntwood WS7 ...... 229 C6
  Burton u T DE13 ...... 166 C8
St Luke St ST1 ...... 282 C2
St Luke's Wlk WS15 .... 198 C4
St Margarets DE13 ...... 165 F5

St Margaret's CE Jun Sch
  ST5 ...... 56 D4
St Margarets Ct CW3 ... 53 B6
St Margaret's Ct
  Draycott in t M ST11 ... 91 E5
  Newcastle-u-L ST5 ...... 56 D5
St Margaret's Dr ST1.... 57 E8
St Margarets Gr ST3 .... 72 F3
St Margarets Rd WS13 .. 214 B3
St Margaret's Rd B79 ... 250 B7
St Margarets Rd WS3 ... 244 A4
St Margaret's B74 ...... 257 C3
St Margaret Ward RC Sch &
  Arts Coll ST6 ...... 41 F5
St Maria Goreti RC Prim Sch
  ST2 ...... 58 C2
St Mark's CE Prim Sch
  ST1 ...... 282 A1
St Marks Cl WS6 ...... 226 F4
St Mark's Cl ST1 ...... 282 A2
St Marks Rd WS8 ...... 245 A5
St Mark's Rd
  Burntwood WS7 ...... 229 C6
  Burton u T DE13 ...... 166 C8
St Marks Rd WS3 ...... 244 A4
St Mark's St ST1 ...... 282 A1
St Martin Noel's Almshouses
  ST16 ...... 285 B3
St Martin's Cl
  Burton u T DE13 ...... 166 C8
  Wolverhampton WV2 ... 266 E6
St Martin's La ST3 ...... 284 C4
St Martin's Pl ST16..... 285 B3
St Martin's Rd
  Newcastle-u-L ST5 ...... 70 F8
  Talke Pits ST7 ...... 40 E6
St Mary of the Angels RC
  Prim Sch WV10 ...... 256 B5
St Mary & St Chad CE Prim
  Sch ST19 ...... 223 C6
St Marys CE Fst Sch
  Uttoxeter ST14 ...... 111 B1
  Wheaton Aston ST19 ... 205 C7
St Marys CE Prim Sch
  WV7 ...... 237 B5
St Mary's CE Prim Sch
  Bosley SK11 ...... 7 D8
  Colton WS15 ...... 178 F6
  Kingswinford DY6 ...... 275 D7
  Mucklestone TF9 ...... 99 A7
  Stoke-on-T ST6 ...... 41 D3
St Mary's Cl WV7 ...... 237 A5
St Marys Cl ST18 ...... 173 C1
St Mary's Cl
  Checkley ST10 ...... 109 B8
  Newton Solney DE15 ... 167 E8
  Sedgley DY3 ...... 271 F8
St Marys Ct WV10 ...... 225 C2
St Mary's Cres ST14 .... 111 B1
St Mary's Ct 7 ST13 ... 30 E5
St Mary's Dr
  Burton u T DE13 ...... 166 C8
  Newcastle-u-L ST5 ...... 71 A8
  Stretton DE13 ...... 147 F2
St Mary's Gate ST16 .... 285 B3
St Marys Gr ST18 ...... 236 D3
St Marys Gr ST16 ...... 285 B3
St Marys Mews ST16 ... 285 B3
St Mary's Pl ST16 ...... 285 B3
St Marys RC Prim Sch
  ST19 ...... 223 B6
St Mary's RC Prim Sch
  WS11 ...... 226 E8
St Mary's RC Prim Sch
  Leek ST13 ...... 30 E5
  Newcastle-u-L ST5 ...... 283 A3
  Stoke-on-T ST6 ...... 42 D3
St Mary's Rd
  Colwich ST18 ...... 177 D8
  Lichfield WS13 ...... 214 B3
  Loggerheads TF9 ...... 99 D5
  Longton ST3 ...... 73 D5
  Newcastle-u-L ST5 ...... 56 D5
St Mary's & St John's RC Sch
  WV2 ...... 266 D8
St Mary's St
  Market Drayton TF9 .... 97 D1
  Newport TF10 ...... 168 F3
St Mary's Way
  Aldridge WS9 ...... 256 B5
  Tamworth B77 ...... 250 E4
St Matthew Cl WS12 .... 211 A5
St Matthews Ave WS7 .. 229 F7
St Matthews CE Prim Sch
  ST3 ...... 89 E4
St Matthews Cl WS3 .... 244 B5
St Matthews Cl ST4 .... 72 F6
St Matthews Dr ST18 ... 154 D2
St Matthew's Rd WS7 .. 229 F7
St Matthew's St DE14 .. 185 C8
St Matthew St ST4 ...... 72 F6
St Mawes Cl ST17 ...... 175 D8
St Mawes Rd WV6 ...... 255 A3
St Michael Rd WS13..... 231 C8
St Michaels CE Fst Sch
  ST19 ...... 192 E1
St Michael's CE Fst Sch
  Rudyard ST13 ...... 18 C2
  Stone ST15 ...... 120 C6
St Michael's CE Jun & Inf Sch
  WV6 ...... 255 E5
St Michaels CE Prim Sch
  Annexe WS3 ...... 244 A3
St Michael's CE Prim Sch
  Lichfield WS14 ...... 231 C7
  Lichfield WS14 ...... 231 C8
St Michaels CE Prim Sch
  WS3 ...... 243 F2

St Michael's Cl
  Adbaston ST20 ...... 131 C4
  Penkridge ST19 ...... 207 E8
  Stafford ST17 ...... 175 E8
St Michaels Cl ST15 .... 120 B8
St Michael's Cl WS3 .... 244 A2
St Michaels Cl CV9 ...... 262 C1
St Michaels Ct 5 ST15 .. 120 A8
St Michaels Ct WV6 .... 255 E5
St Michaels Dr WS12 ... 211 A5
St Michael's Dr WS15 ... 197 A5
St Michael's Hospl
  WS13 ...... 231 D8
St Michaels RC Prim Sch
  WV3 ...... 265 D7
St Michaels Rd
  Burton u T DE13 ...... 166 D8
  Dudley DY3 ...... 270 F5
St Michael's Rd
  Newcastle-u-L ST5 ...... 56 B3
  Penkridge ST19 ...... 207 E8
  Rugeley WS15 ...... 197 A5
  Stoke-on-T ST4 ...... 41 F5
  Stramshall ST14 ...... 110 F4
St Michael's Sq ST19 ... 192 E1
St Mildred's CE Prim Sch
  ST10 ...... 62 D3
St Modwena Way ST19 .. 207 F7
St Modwen's Cl DE13 ... 166 C7
St Modwen's RC Prim Sch
  DE13 ...... 166 B5
St Modwen's Wlk DE14.. 166 E2
St Nicholas Ave ST6..... 42 E4
St Nicholas CE Prim Sch
  WV8 ...... 238 F4
St Nicholas Cl WS3 ...... 244 A4
St Nicholas Way WS15 .. 160 F6
St Oswald's CE Fst Sch
  DY10 ...... 280 A1
St Patrick Cl WS12 ...... 211 A6
St Patrick's Dr ST5 ...... 70 F3
St Patrick's Pl ST16 ...... 285 B3
St Patrick's RC Prim Sch
  ST16 ...... 155 E5
St Patricks Rd 3 DE13 .. 166 D8
St Patricks's Pl ST16 .... 285 B4
St Patrick's St ST16 .... 285 B4
St Paul's CE Fst Sch
  WV9 ...... 224 B3
St Paul's CE Prim Sch
  ST17 ...... 285 C2
St Pauls CE Prim Sch
  WV9 ...... 240 A2
St Paul's Cl
  Cannock WS11 ...... 210 B1
  Coven WV9 ...... 224 C2
St Pauls Cres WS3 ...... 244 B5
St Paul's Ct
  Burton u T DE14 ...... 166 B3
  Stoke-on-T ST3 ...... 72 F2
  Tamworth B77 ...... 261 C4
St Paul's Mews 2 WS15. 196 F8
St Pauls Rd 1 WS15 .... 196 F8
St Paul's Rd
  Burntwood WS7 ...... 229 C6
  Cannock WS12 ...... 210 F3
  Newcastle-u-L ST5 ...... 283 A2
St Paul's St W DE14 .... 166 B4
St Paul's Sq DE14 ...... 166 B3
St Paul St ST6 ...... 72 F6
St Peter & St Paul RC Sch
  Lichfield WS13 ...... 214 B3
  Newport TF10 ...... 168 B3
St Peter's Bridge DE14 . 166 E1
St Peter's CE Fst Sch
  Alton ST10 ...... 78 E1
  Marchington ST14 ...... 127 F2
St Peter's CE High Sch &
  International Language Coll
  ST4 ...... 71 F7
St Peter's CE Prim Sch
  WS12 ...... 210 D4
St Peter's CE Prim Sch
  Caverswall ST11 ...... 74 D2
  Edgmond TF10 ...... 168 A4
  ST18 ...... 158 B7
St Peter's CE Prim Sch
  Netherseal DE12 ...... 219 F6
  Stonnall WS9 ...... 245 E4
  Yoxall DE13 ...... 182 A3
St Peters Cl ST17 ...... 174 F6
St Peter's Cl
  Stonnall WS9 ...... 245 E4
  Tamworth B77 ...... 250 D1
St Peter's Collegiate CE Sch
  WV3 ...... 255 E3
St Peters Ct
  Burton u T DE15 ...... 166 F1
  Lichfield WS13 ...... 214 B2
St Peter's Ct ST20 ...... 151 A4
St Peters Ct WS3 ...... 243 B1
St Peters Dr WS3 ...... 244 A4
St Peter's Gdns ST17 ... 174 F5
St Peters La ST11 ...... 91 A7
St Peter's RC Prim Sch
  Burslem ST6 ...... 57 A6
  Walsall WS3 ...... 243 B2
St Peter's Rd
  Burntwood WS7 ...... 229 C6
  Cannock WS12 ...... 210 D4
St Peter's St DE15 ...... 166 F1
St Peter's Wlk ST6 ...... 57 A6
St Phillip's Ave WV3 .... 265 F8
St Phillips Ave WV3 .... 265 F8
St Phillip's Gr WV3 ..... 265 F8

St Saviour's CE Prim Sch
  ST7 ...... 25 D1
St Saviour's Cl WV2 .... 266 F6
St Saviour's St ST7 ...... 25 D1
St Stephens Ct
  Burton u T DE13 ...... 166 C7
  Cannock WS12 ...... 210 C4
  Great Haywood ST18 ... 158 B2
St Stephen's Prim Sch
  WS13 ...... 215 D7
St Stephen's Rd WS7.... 229 C6
St Teresa's RC Prim Sch
  ST4 ...... 71 F2
St Teresa's RC Prim Sch
  WV4 ...... 266 E5
St Thomas Aquinas RC Prim
  Sch ST4 ...... 56 F1
St Thomas CE Prim Sch
  ST7 ...... 26 A1
St Thomas' Cl WS9 ...... 245 B1
St Thomas Dr WS12 .... 211 A5
St Thomas La ST18 ...... 156 D3
St Thomas More RC Coll
  ST3 ...... 73 A3
St Thomas More RC Prim
  Sch WS6 ...... 227 A4
St Thomas' Pl ST4 ...... 71 F7
St Thomas' RC Prim Sch
  ST10 ...... 92 E4
St Thomas's Rd ST10 ... 92 E4
St Thomas St Mow Cop ST7 26 E7
  Stafford ST16 ...... 156 A3
St Vincent Mews ST15 .. 104 D4
St Vincent St ST15 ...... 55 F2
St Vincent Rd ST15 ...... 119 C7
St Werburgh's CE Prim Sch
  Hanbury DE13 ...... 145 A4
  Kingsley ST10 ...... 61 D2
St Wilfrid's RC Prim Sch
  ST6 ...... 41 F3
St Wulstan's CE Prim Sch
  ST5 ...... 56 D4
Salcombe Ave ST17 .... 175 D8
Salcombe Cl WS11 ...... 226 C7
Salcombe Pl ST1 ...... 57 D7
Sale La DE13 ...... 200 C1
Salem St ST1 ...... 56 F3
Sales La DE15 ...... 167 C4
Salisbury Ave
  Burton u T DE15 ...... 167 D3
  Hanley ST1 ...... 282 A3
Salisbury Cl Dudley DY1. 271 F3
  Lichfield WS13 ...... 214 C3
  Madeley CW3 ...... 68 C7
  Rugeley WS15 ...... 196 C6
Salisbury Dr
  Cannock WS12 ...... 210 B1
  Stafford ST16 ...... 156 B4
Salisbury Hill View TF9. 112 B3
Salisbury Rd
  Market Drayton TF9 .... 112 B8
  Stafford ST16 ...... 156 B4
Salisbury St Leek ST13 .. 30 E6
  Stoke-on-T ST6 ...... 41 E3
Salkeld Pl ST6 ...... 42 B5
Sallow Gr WS8 ...... 229 A1
Sallyfield La DE6 ...... 65 E1
Sally Ward Dr WS9 ...... 245 A4
Salmond Ave ST16 ...... 156 B5
Salop Dr WS11 ...... 226 F8
Salop Gr ST5 ...... 71 C4
Salop Pl ST7 ...... 26 A3
Salt Ave ST17 ...... 285 C1
Salt Banks ST18 ...... 137 C3
Saltbrook La DE6 ...... 144 F8
Saltdean Cl ST3 ...... 73 E2
Salters Cl ST9 ...... 59 B3
Salter's Ct ST10 ...... 168 E3
Saltersford La ST10 .... 94 F8
Saltersford Rise ST15 ... 104 E3
Salters Grange WS15 ... 160 F6
Salters Green Way DE13. 201 B3
Salter's La TF10 ...... 168 E3
Salters La Tamworth B79 . 250 B6
  Werrington ST9 ...... 59 B2
Salter's Mews TF10 .... 168 E3
Salter's Rd WS9 ...... 245 A3
Salter St ST16 ...... 285 B3
Saltheath La ST18 ...... 137 E3
Saltings Mobile Home Pk
  The ST18 ...... 156 D2
Salt La ST18 ...... 137 D5
Salt Rd Salt ST18 ...... 137 E4
  Stafford ST17 ...... 285 B1
Salts La B78 ...... 260 E5
Salt Works La ST18 ...... 138 D2
Sam Barber Ct WS12 ... 210 E1
Sambar Rd B78 ...... 249 F1
Sambrook Cres TF9 ...... 97 E2
Sampson St ST1 ...... 282 A3
Samuel Cl WS13 ...... 214 C2
Samuel Ho WS3 ...... 243 B1
Samuel Johnson's Birthplace
  Mus ✶ WS13 ...... 231 B8
Samuel St Packmoor ST7 . 26 A1
  Walsall WS3 ...... 243 B1
Sancton Gn 2 ST6 ...... 56 E8
Sandalwood Dr ST16 ... 155 F5
Sandalwood Rd DE15 ... 185 E6
Sandbach Rd ST6 ...... 57 B7
Sand Bank WS3 ...... 243 B1
Sandcrest Pl ST3 ...... 73 F1
Sandcrest Wlk ST3 ...... 73 F1
Sanderling Cl WV10..... 241 B7
Sanderling Rise WS7.... 229 B8
Sandfield Bridge DY5 ... 271 B3
Sandfield Gr DY3 ...... 271 B2
Sandfield Mdw WS13.... 231 A6

Sandfield Rd DY8 . . . . 275 F2
Sandford Cl WS15. . . . . . . 198 A8
Sandford Cres CW2 . . . . 37 D1
Sandford Hill Prim Sch
ST3 . . . . 73 C6
Sandford Ho WS13 . . . . . . 231 A7
Sandford Rd DY1 . . . . 271 E1
Sandford Rise WV6 . . . . . 255 E6
Sandford St
Lichfield WS13. . . . . 231 B7
Longton ST3. . . . . 73 C5
Newcastle-u-L ST5. . . . . 55 E8
Sandgate St ST3 . . . . 73 D3
Sandhill St WS3 . . . . 243 A1
Sandhurst Ave 4 ST3 . . . . 73 F1
Sandhurst Cl ST5 . . . . 56 C4
Sandhurst Dr WV4 . . . . . . 266 A4
Sandhurst Gr DY8. . . . . . . 275 E3
Sandhurst Pl ST3 . . . . 89 F8
Sandhurst Rd B74. . . . . . . 257 F5
Sandiford Cres TF10 . . . . . 168 E2
Sandiway DE13 . . . . 201 E8
Sandiway Pl ST1. . . . . 57 E6
Sandmere Rise WV10 . . . 240 E1
Sandon Ave ST5 . . . . 71 A5
Sandon Cl ST11. . . . . 91 C2
Sandon Ct ST3. . . . . 89 F7
Sandon High Sch ST3 . . . . 89 F8
Sandon Ho WV6 . . . . 255 E5
Sandon La ST18. . . . . 122 C5
Sandon Mews ST16 . . . . . 155 F6
Sandon Old Rd ST3 . . . . . . 89 F7
Sandon Rd Cresswell ST11. 91 C3
Hilderstone ST15. . . . . 106 D1
Hopton ST18 . . . . 137 C2
Stafford ST16,ST18 . . . . 155 F6
Stoke-on-T ST3 . . . . 89 F7
Wolverhampton WV10. . . . 240 B2
Sandon St Hanley ST1. . . . . 57 A3
Leek ST13 . . . . 30 E3
Sandown Ave WS6 . . . . . . 226 E3
Sandown Cl
Burntwood WS7. . . . . 211 F1
Burton u T DE14. . . . . 185 A7
Cannock WS12. . . . . 211 A6
Cheadle ST10. . . . . 76 E5
Sandown Dr WV6 . . . . 254 F4
Sandown Pl ST2 . . . . 43 C2
Sandown B77. . . . . 250 F5
Sandpiper Cl WS12 . . . . . 210 C7
Sandpiper Ct ST7 . . . . 26 C2
Sandpiper Dr ST14. . . . . . . 126 B6
Sandpiper B77. . . . . 262 A5
Sandra Cl Aldridge WS9 . . 256 B5
Stoke-on-T ST6 . . . . 42 A2
Sand Rd DE13 . . . . 164 C7
Sandringham Ave DE15 . 167 A1
Sandringham Cl
Burntwood WS7. . . . . 211 E1
Market Drayton TF9. . . . . . . 97 E2
Stafford ST17 . . . . 175 C8
Sandringham Cres ST4. . . 72 A1
Sandringham Dr WS9 . . . 245 B1
Sandringham Pl DY8. . . . 275 D1
Sandringham Rd
Pattingham WV6 . . . . 253 C2
Stafford ST17 . . . . 175 C8
Stourbridge DY8 . . . . 275 D1
Wolverhampton WV4. . . . . 266 A4
Wombourne WV5. . . . . 269 F6
Sandsdown Cl ST8 . . . . 16 C1
Sands La ST6 . . . . 28 B2
Sands Rd ST7. . . . . 26 E6
Sandstone Cl DY3. . . . . . . 271 D4
Sandstone Ct B77. . . . . . . 262 A7
Sandwell Pl ST3 . . . . 89 E8
Sandwell Rd WV10. . . . . . 240 B1
Sandwick Cres ST1 . . . . . . 57 F6
Sandwood Cres ST3. . . . . . 73 C5
Sandy Bank ST21 . . . . 102 C4
Sandybrook Cl ST13. . . . . . 30 F3
Sandybrook La ST13 . . . . . 30 F2
Sandy Cres WV11 . . . . 242 A1
Sandy Croft TF10 . . . . 168 F3
Sandyfield Ct ST8. . . . . 16 C1
Sandyfield Rd ST1 . . . . 57 E5
Sandyfields Rd DY3 . . . . . 271 B6
Sandyfields ST5 . . . . 85 C5
Sandyford Ct ST16 . . . . . . 285 B4
Sandyford St ST16 . . . . . . 155 E5
Sandy Gr WS8 . . . . 228 F1
Sandy Hill ST9. . . . . 59 C4
Sandy Hollow WV6. . . . . . . 255 C2
Sandy La Ashley TF9 . . . . . 100 B7
Blore TF9. . . . . 98 C3
Brewood ST19. . . . . 223 C6
Brown Edge ST6 . . . . 43 B7
Cannock WS11. . . . . 209 B1
Chapel Chorlton ST5 . . . . . . 85 C4
Codsall WV8 . . . . 238 F4
Copmere End ST21 . . . . . . 132 D7
Cotes Heath ST21 . . . . 102 D4
Hollington ST10. . . . . 93 E7
Kinver DY7,DY11 . . . . 277 F1
Linton DE12. . . . . 186 A1
Longsdon ST9 . . . . 44 F8
Market Drayton TF9. . . . . . 112 D6
Newcastle-u-L ST5. . . . . . . 283 D4
Newton Regis B79. . . . . . . 236 D6
Rugeley WS15 . . . . 196 E8
Stoke-on-T ST2 . . . . 43 C2
Weston ST18 . . . . 138 C4
Whittington WS14 . . . . 232 D4
Wolverhampton,Bushbury
WV10. . . . . 240 E1
Wolverhampton,Tettenhall
WV6 . . . . 255 E6
Sandy Mount WV5 . . . . . . 270 B7
Sandy Rd Biddulph ST8 . . . . 16 C2
Stoke-on-T ST6 . . . . 41 D6
Stourbridge DY8 . . . . 279 D1
Sandy Way B77 . . . . 251 B3
Sangster La ST6 . . . . 42 D2
Sankey Cres WS15 . . . . . . 196 E7
Sankey Rd WS11. . . . . 209 F3
Sankey's Cnr WS7 . . . . . . 228 F7
Sanstone Cl WS3 . . . . 243 C3
Sanstone Rd WS3 . . . . 243 C3
Sant St ST6. . . . . 56 E8
Sapling Rise ST10. . . . . 92 E3
Saplings Cl ST19. . . . . 192 F1
Saplings The
Newcastle-u-L ST5. . . . . 71 C3
Penkridge ST19 . . . . 192 F1
Stafford ST17 . . . . 156 A1
Sapperton La DE65. . . . . . 129 F8
Sapphire Dr WS11 . . . . . . 210 C3
Saracen Way 10 ST3 . . . . . 74 A1
Sara Cl B74. . . . . 258 A3
Sarah Challinor Cl 6
WS15. . . . . 196 E8
Sarah Siddons Ho 2
WS13. . . . . 231 B7
Saredon Cl WS3 . . . . 244 A1
Saredon Rd
Shareshill WV10 . . . . 225 D2
Wedges Mills WS6,WS11,
WV10 . . . . 226 B3
Sargeant Ave ST6. . . . . 42 A6
Sark Cl ST5. . . . . 70 E4
Sark Pl 1 ST3 . . . . 73 D6
Sarraine Ind Pk ST10. . . . . 76 B2
Sarver La ST10. . . . . 75 D4
Sash St ST16 . . . . 285 B4
Saturn Rd Cannock WS11 . 210 A5
Stoke-on-T ST6 . . . . 42 C1
Saul Ct ST14. . . . . 126 B7
Saunders Cl WS12 . . . . . . 211 A6
Saunders Rd ST5 . . . . 56 B4
Saverley Green Rd ST11 . 106 E8
Savey La DE13 . . . . 181 F2
Savoureuse Dr ST17. . . . . 175 A8
Savoy Rd CW1 . . . . 37 A8
Sawpit La ST17 . . . . 176 A3
Sawyer Dr ST8. . . . . 16 C1
Saxifrage Dr ST15. . . . . . . 120 C6
Saxon Cl Burton u T DE15 . 185 F7
Great Wyrley WS6 . . . . 227 A2
Polesworth B78. . . . . 251 F1
Tamworth B79 . . . . 261 F6
Saxoncourt WV6. . . . . 255 C5
Saxon Ct WS13 . . . . 230 E7
Saxondrive B79 . . . . 250 C5
Saxonfields WV6. . . . . 255 C5
Saxon Hill Sch WS14 . . . . 231 C6
Saxon Mill La B79. . . . . . . 250 C4
Saxon Rd ST19. . . . . 207 F8
Saxon St DE15 . . . . 185 F7
Saxon Wlk WS13. . . . . 230 E7
Saxton Dr B74 . . . . 257 F6
Sayers Rd ST16 . . . . 155 C7
Scalpcliffe Cl DE15. . . . . . 166 F3
Scalpcliffe Rd DE15 . . . . . 166 F3
Scammerton B77 . . . . 262 B7
Scamnell La ST21 . . . . 134 E7
Scampton Cl WV6. . . . . . . 254 E5
Scampton Way B79 . . . . . 250 C8
Scarecrow La B75 . . . . . . 258 E4
Scarlett St ST5 . . . . 283 B2
Scarratt Cl ST11 . . . . 91 B8
Scarratt Dr ST11 . . . . 91 B8
Sceptre St ST1. . . . . 282 B2
Schofield La B79. . . . . 217 D5
Sch of St Mary & St Anne
WS15 . . . . 161 A6
Scholar Green Prim Sch
ST7 . . . . 25 E6
Scholars Gate
Burntwood WS7. . . . . 229 D7
Rugeley WS15 . . . . 197 A5
Schoolacre Rise B74 . . . . 256 E1
School Ave WS8 . . . . 244 F8
School Bank ST10. . . . . 94 B2
School Cl Audley ST7. . . . . . 40 A1
Burntwood WS7. . . . . 228 D8
Codsall WV8 . . . . 239 A4
Dilhorne ST10 . . . . 75 D4
Leek ST13 . . . . 30 C4
Norton Canes WS11 . . . . . 228 B6
Trysull WV5 . . . . 269 C8
Wolverhampton WV3. . . . . . 265 B7
School Cres WS11 . . . . . . 228 A6
School Ct WS12. . . . . 210 C6
School Dr Oakamoor ST10 . 78 A7
Stourbridge DY8 . . . . 279 F8
Schoolfields Rd WS14. . . 247 A5
Schoolgate Cl WS4 . . . . . 244 D1
School Ground La TF10. . 169 A3
School Ho The WS7. . . . . 229 D7
School House La WS15. . 161 A6
School La
Admaston WS15 . . . . 159 F3
Ashley TF9 . . . . 100 B6
Astbury CW12 . . . . 15 B8
Biddulph ST8 . . . . 17 B1
Bradnop ST13 . . . . 31 E3
Burntwood WS7. . . . . 228 D8
Caverswall ST3,ST11. . . . . . 74 D2
Colton WS15 . . . . 178 F6
Coven WV9 . . . . 224 B3
Dunston ST18 . . . . 192 D7
Edingale B79 . . . . 217 C5
Gentleshaw WS15. . . . . . . 212 A5
Great Haywood ST18. . . . . . 158 B2
Hill Ridware WS15. . . . . . . 198 A8
Hopwas B78 . . . . 249 B7
School La *continued*
Longsdon ST9 . . . . 30 A2
Maer TF9 . . . . 84 A7
Market Drayton TF9. . . . . . 112 A8
School Lane Cl ST17 . . . . 174 F5
School La
Norton Canes WS3 . . . . . . 227 E2
Onneley CW3. . . . . 68 A4
Rolleston on D DE13 . . . . . 147 B4
Sandon ST18 . . . . 137 E7
Shareshill WV10 . . . . 225 D2
Shuttington B79. . . . . 251 F7
Stafford,Rickerscote ST17. 174 F5
Stoke-on-T ST3 . . . . 89 A8
Stretton ST19 . . . . 206 C3
Sudbury DE6 . . . . 128 E4
Tamworth B77 . . . . 261 D5
Walsall WS3 . . . . 243 F4
Walton-on-t-H ST17. . . . . . 175 F6
Warslow SK17. . . . . 23 B1
Weeford B78 . . . . 248 D2
Weston-Under-Lizard TF11 203 E2
Wolverhampton WV10. . . . 240 E2
School Pl ST16 . . . . 155 E5
School Rd Bagnall ST9 . . . . 43 F2
Brewood ST19. . . . . 223 C6
Bucknall ST2 . . . . 58 A5
Eccleshall ST21 . . . . 133 D6
Edgmond TF10. . . . . 168 A3
Himley DY3 . . . . 270 B3
Norton Canes WS11 . . . . . 228 A6
Rugeley WS15 . . . . 178 D2
Trysull WV5 . . . . 269 C8
Uttoxeter ST14 . . . . 110 F1
Wheaton Aston ST19. . . . . 205 C5
Wolverhampton,Tettenhall
WV6 . . . . 255 B3
Wombourne WV5. . . . . 270 B7
School St 3 Leek ST13. . . . 30 E6
Newcastle-u-L,Broad Meadow
ST5 . . . . 55 F6
Newcastle-u-L ST5. . . . . . . 283 C3
Sedgley DY3. . . . . 271 E8
Stoke-on-T ST4 . . . . 71 E3
Stourbridge DY8 . . . . 279 F6
Tamworth B77 . . . . 250 E4
Walsall WS4 . . . . 244 D1
School View ST14. . . . . . . 141 C8
School Wlk
Burntwood WS7. . . . . 228 D8
Tamworth B79 . . . . 250 B6
Scimitar Cl B79. . . . . 249 E7
Scotch Orchard Prim Sch
WS13 . . . . 214 D1
Scotch Orch WS13 . . . . . . 214 D1
Scot Hay Rd
Alsagers Bank ST7 . . . . 54 E5
Newcastle-u-L ST5. . . . . 54 F3
Scotia Bsns Pk ST6 . . . . . . 41 E2
Scotia Rd Burslem ST6 . . . . 41 F1
Cannock WS11. . . . . 209 D3
Scott Ave WV4. . . . . 265 E4
Scott Cl WS14 . . . . 231 B6
Scott Lidgett Ind Est ST6. 56 D8
Scott Lidgett Rd ST6. . . . . . 56 D7
Scott Rd Stoke-on-T ST6 . . . 41 F5
Tamworth B77 . . . . 250 E4
Scotts Ho 1 ST16. . . . . . . 155 D5
Scott's Rd DY8. . . . . 279 F6
Scott St Cannock WS12. . . 210 F3
Newcastle-u-L ST5. . . . . . . 283 C3
Scott Way WS7 . . . . 211 F1
Scragg St ST7 . . . . 41 F8
Scrimshaw Dr ST6 . . . . 42 C3
Scrivener Rd ST4 . . . . 56 F1
Scropton Old Rd DE65. . . 146 C8
Scropton Rd Hatton DE65. 146 B8
Scropton DE65. . . . . 129 F1
Sculthorpe Rd DY10. . . . . 281 B2
Seabridge Jun & Inf Schs
ST5 . . . . 71 A4
Seabridge La ST5 . . . . 71 B4
Seabridge Rd ST5. . . . . . . 283 A1
Seabrooke Rd WS15 . . . . 197 A5
Seafield Cl DY6 . . . . 275 E4
Seafield B77 . . . . 250 F5
Seaford St ST4 . . . . 57 B1
Seaforth Gr WV11. . . . . . . 242 B1
Seagram Way ST14 . . . . . 126 D7
Seagrave Pl ST5 . . . . 71 A6
Seagrave St ST5 . . . . 283 C3
Searchlight La ST21. . . . . . 134 E7
Searle Ave ST16 . . . . 155 C2
Seaton Ave ST17. . . . . 175 E8
Seaton Cl ST3 . . . . 89 E8
Seaton Pl DY8 . . . . 275 C2
Seaton B77. . . . . 261 F8
Sebring Ave ST3. . . . . 89 E8
Seckham Rd 4 WS13 . . . . 231 A8
Seckington La B79. . . . . . 236 C3
Second Ave
Branston DE14. . . . . 165 E1
Brownhills WS8 . . . . 229 A1
Bucknall ST2 . . . . 58 D4
Kidsgrove ST7 . . . . 25 E1
Kingswinford,Wall Heath
DY6. . . . . 275 F8
Newcastle-u-L ST5. . . . . 56 C7
Stafford ST16 . . . . 155 C7
Sedbergh Cl ST5. . . . . 70 F4
Seddon Ct ST1. . . . . 282 C3
Seddon Rd ST3 . . . . 89 F8
Sedgefield Cl DY1 . . . . . . 271 E3
Sedgefield Gr WV6. . . . . . 254 F4
Sedgefield Rd DE14 . . . . . 184 F7
Sedgemoor Ave WS7. . . . 229 B5
Sedgfield Way WS11 . . . . 228 B4
Sedgley Hall Ave DY3 . . . 271 C8
Sedgley Rd WV4 . . . . 265 F2
Sedgley St WV2. . . . . 266 C7
Sedgley Wlk ST3. . . . . 284 C4
Seedcroft La WS15. . . . . . 160 F4
Seedfields Rd ST3 . . . . 72 E3
Seeds La WS8 . . . . 244 F8
Seedymill La WS13. . . . . . 213 E7
Seesall The ST20. . . . . 171 E7
Sefton Ave Congleton CW12 . 6 A1
Stoke-on-T ST1 . . . . 57 E7
Sefton Cl DE15. . . . . 167 B1
Sefton Rd Longton ST3 . . . . 73 E2
Tamworth B77 . . . . 261 D4
Sefton St ST1. . . . . 57 A3
Seighford Rd ST18 . . . . . . 154 D5
Seisdon Rd WV5 . . . . 264 A1
Selborne Rd ST13 . . . . 30 E4
Selbourne Dr ST6. . . . . 41 F7
Selby Cl ST5. . . . . 71 A5
Selby St ST3. . . . . 74 B5
Selby Way WS3 . . . . 242 E2
Selby Wlk ST3 . . . . 88 E7
Selker Dr B77 . . . . 250 F5
Sellman St ST20 . . . . 171 E6
Selmans Hill WS3. . . . . . . 243 C2
Selman's Par WS3 . . . . 243 C2
Selsdon Rd WS3 . . . . 242 F3
Selwood Cl ST3. . . . . 73 D1
Selworthy Dr ST17. . . . . . . 175 E6
Selworthy Rd ST6. . . . . 43 A5
Selwyn Cl Alrewas DE13 . . 201 A3
Wolverhampton WV2. . . . . . 266 C7
Selwyn Ct ST21 . . . . 133 E7
Selwyn Rd WS7. . . . . 229 F8
Selwyn St ST4 . . . . 72 B6
Selwyn Wlk B74 . . . . 257 C4
Semper Cl CW12. . . . . 6 A4
Senior Cl WV11 . . . . 242 A3
Serin Cl ST14 . . . . 126 C6
Seton Ho B74. . . . . 257 E2
Setterfield Way WS15 . . . 196 F6
Settle Gr ST3 . . . . 90 A7
Setton Dr DY3 . . . . 271 E7
Seven Acres WS9 . . . . 256 B5
Seven Arches Way ST4. . . 72 C7
Sevenoaks Gr ST3 . . . . 90 B6
Seven Springs Nature Trail★
ST17. . . . . 177 D5
Sevens Rd WS12. . . . . 211 D3
Severn Cl Biddulph ST8. . . . 16 E1
Congleton CW12 . . . . 6 A1
Stretton DE13 . . . . 147 C1
Uttoxeter ST14 . . . . 126 C6
Severn Dr
Burntwood WS7. . . . . 229 D6
Burton u T DE14. . . . . 166 E3
Hilton DE65 . . . . 147 D8
Newcastle-u-L ST5. . . . . 71 B4
Perton WV6 . . . . 254 E4
Severn Ho DY3 . . . . 271 D3
Severn Rd
Brownhills WS8 . . . . 228 C2
Stourbridge DY8 . . . . 279 F3
Walsall WS3 . . . . 243 E1
Severn St ST1 . . . . 282 A4
Seward Cl WS14 . . . . 231 D6
Seymour Ave DE14. . . . . . 166 E7
Seymour Cl WS6. . . . . 226 D1
Seymour Gdns B74. . . . . . 257 E3
Seymour St ST1. . . . . 57 E3
Shackerley La WV7 . . . . . 221 B1
Shackleton Dr
Perton WV6. . . . . 254 E5
Stoke-on-T ST6 . . . . 41 C4
Shackleton Rd WS3 . . . . . 243 D2
Shackleton Way ST16 . . . 136 B1
Shackson Cl ST1. . . . . 282 B1
Shadwell Dr DY3. . . . . 271 D3
Shaffalong La ST13 . . . . . . 45 A5
Shaftesbury Ave ST6 . . . . . 42 A2
Shaftesbury Dr WS12 . . . 210 C7
Shaftsbury Dr WS7. . . . . . 229 F7
Shaftsbury Rd WS15 . . . . 196 E6
Shakespeare Ave WS14 . 231 B6
Shakespeare Cl
Kidsgrove ST7 . . . . 41 A8
Stoke-on-T ST2 . . . . 43 A2
Tamworth B79 . . . . 250 A6
Shakespeare Ct ST8. . . . . . 27 C7
Shakespeare Gr WS11. . . 209 D4
Shakespeare Rd
Burntwood WS7. . . . . 228 F8
Burton u T DE14. . . . . 166 D6
Dudley DY3 . . . . 271 A4
Stafford ST17 . . . . 174 C8
Shaldon Ave ST9. . . . . 43 C4
Shales The WV5 . . . . 269 E5
Shallcross La DY3. . . . . . . 271 D3
Shallowford Ct ST1 . . . . . . 57 A3
Shallowford Mews ST16 155 D5
Shanklin Cl WS6 . . . . 227 A3
Shannon App DE14. . . . . . 166 D2
Shannon Dr
Brownhills WS8 . . . . 228 C2
Stoke-on-T ST6 . . . . 41 C7
Shannon Rd ST17 . . . . 174 D6
Shannon's Mill B79 . . . . . 250 A5
Shannon B77 . . . . 261 F8
Shannon Wlk WS8 . . . . . . 228 C2
Shanti Niketan WV2. . . . . 266 D7
Shardlow Cl Longton ST4 . . 73 A6
Stone ST15 . . . . 120 C6
Sharman Cl ST4 . . . . 71 F7
Sharmon Way ST20 . . . . . 171 E7
Sharnbrook Dr WS15. . . . 178 C2
Sharnbrook Gr ST17 . . . . 175 C6
Sharon Cl WV4 . . . . 266 E5
Sharon Way WS12 . . . . . . 210 D3
Sharpe St B77 . . . . 251 A5
Sharplands TF9. . . . . 99 D5
Sharrat Field B75 . . . . 258 D2
Sharron Dr ST13 . . . . 31 B5
Shaver's La WS15. . . . . . . 197 B1
Shawbury Gr WV6 . . . . . . 254 E5
Shaw Cl WS13 . . . . 215 D8
Shaw Ct WS11 . . . . 228 A5
Shaw Dr Burntwood WS7 . 212 A1
Fradley WS13 . . . . 215 C6
Shawe Park Rd ST10 . . . . . 76 E8
Shaw Gdns ST17 . . . . 174 C7
Shaw Hall La WV9 . . . . . . 240 C7
Shaw La Albrighton WV7. . 237 B5
Armitage WS13 . . . . 198 F2
Gentleshaw WS15 . . . . 212 A4
King's Bromley WS13 . . . . 199 A4
Lichfield WS13. . . . . 231 A8
Tong TF11 . . . . 220 D5
Wolverhampton WV6. . . . . . 255 B3
Shawmans La ST18 . . . . . 172 E8
Shawms Crest ST17 . . . . . 175 C8
Shawm s The ST17. . . . . . 175 C8
Shaw Pl ST13 . . . . 31 A6
Shawport Ave ST5 . . . . 56 A8
Shaw Rd WV4 . . . . 266 C6
Shaws La ST21 . . . . 133 C6
Shaw's La WS6 . . . . 227 A2
Shaw St Biddulph ST8 . . . . . 27 C7
Hanley ST1 . . . . 282 A4
Newcastle-u-L ST5. . . . . . . 283 B3
Shaw-Wall La ST10 . . . . . . 62 F7
Shay La Foxt ST10 . . . . 62 C6
Weston Jones TF10. . . . . . 150 A4
Shayler Gr WV2. . . . . 266 D7
Sheaf Pas ST3 . . . . 284 C3
Sheaf St ST1. . . . . 282 A1
Shearers Pl 4 B75. . . . . . 258 E3
Shearer St ST1 . . . . 282 A1
Shearwater Ct WV10 . . . . 240 B3
Shebdon Cl ST16. . . . . 155 B7
Sheepcote La B77 . . . . . . 250 F4
Sheep Fair WS15. . . . . 178 E1
Sheep Market ST13 . . . . . . 30 E6
Sheepwalks La DY7 . . . . . 277 B7
Sheepwash La DY11. . . . . 277 C2
Sheffield Ct ST14 . . . . 110 F1
Sheffield St DE14 . . . . 166 C1
Shefford Rd ST5 . . . . 70 F3
Shelburne St ST4 . . . . 72 A5
Sheldon Ave CW12. . . . . 6 A1
Sheldon Gr ST5. . . . . 55 F6
Sheldon Rd WV10. . . . . . . 240 A1
Sheldrake Gr ST4 . . . . 73 B6
Shelfield Sports & Com Coll
WS4 . . . . 244 C2
Shelford Rd ST6 . . . . 41 D6
Shelley Ave DE14 . . . . 166 D6
Shelley Cl Armitage WS15 198 B4
Burton u T DE14. . . . . 166 D6
Colwich ST18. . . . . 177 D8
Dudley DY3 . . . . 271 A5
Kidsgrove ST7 . . . . 41 A8
Stafford ST16 . . . . 156 A5
Shelley Dr Cheadle ST10. . . 76 C2
Sutton Coldfield B74 . . . . . 257 F6
Shelley Rd Bucknall ST2 . . . 58 B6
Burntwood WS7. . . . . 212 A1
Cannock WS11. . . . . 209 E5
Tamworth B79 . . . . 250 A7
Wolverhampton WV10. . . . 240 D2
Shelmore Cl ST16. . . . . . . 155 B8
Shelmore Way ST20. . . . . 171 D7
Shelsley Cl ST19 . . . . 193 A1
Shelsley Rd ST10 . . . . 76 F4
Shelton Ent Ctr ST1. . . . . 282 A1
Shelton Farm Rd ST1 . . . 282 A1
Shelton New Rd ST4 . . . . . 56 E1
Shelton Old Rd ST4 . . . . . . 72 B8
Shelton St B77. . . . . 261 F7
Shemilt Cres ST6 . . . . 42 C3
Shendon Ct ST5 . . . . 56 A7
Shenfield Gn ST2 . . . . 58 C2
Shenley Gr ST17 . . . . 174 D6
Shenstone Ave DY8 . . . . . 279 D3
Shenstone Cl B74. . . . . . . 257 E6
Shenstone Ct WV3. . . . . . . 266 A6
Shenstone Dr WS9. . . . . . 256 A8
Shenstone Ho WS13 . . . . . 214 E1
Shenstone Lodge Sch
WS14 . . . . 247 A3
Shenstone Sta WS14 . . . . 246 F6
Shenton St ST3 . . . . 284 D5
Shephard Cl ST18. . . . . . . 158 B3
Shepherd Cl WS13 . . . . . . 214 C3
Shepherds Bush St ST16 155 E5
Shepherds Ct TF10. . . . . . 169 A3
Shepherds Fold ST17. . . . 175 C6
Shepherds Pool Rd B75 . 258 E2
Shepherd St ST8. . . . . 27 C7
Shepherds Wlk WV8 . . . . 239 F2
Shepley Cl ST15 . . . . 120 C7
Shepley Gr ST3 . . . . 88 E7
Sheppard St ST4. . . . . 72 A6
Shepwell Gdns WV10. . . . 241 C7
Sheraton Cl Aldridge WS9 256 B6
Cannock WS12. . . . . 210 A7
Sheraton Grange DY8 . . . 279 F2
Sherborne Cl ST3. . . . . 88 E7
Sherborne Ct WV10 . . . . . 240 E1
Sherborne Dr ST5. . . . . 71 A5
Sherborne Gdns WV8 . . . 239 A3
Sherborne Rd WV10. . . . . 240 D1
Sherbourne Ave WS12 . . 210 E4
Sherbourne Dr DE14 . . . . 185 A7

Sherbrook Cl ST17 . . . . . 176 A3
Sherbrooke Ave B77 . . . . 261 E6
Sherbrook Rd WS11 . . . . 209 C1
Sheridan Gdns
　Dudley DY3 . . . . 270 F5
　Stoke-on-T ST3 . . . . 72 C7
Sheridan St ST4 . . . . 156 A4
Sheridan Way ST15 . . . . 120 D7
Sheriden Way ST5 . . . . . . 55 E2
Sheriffs Cl WS14 . . . . . . 231 E6
Sheriffs Way ST21 . . . . . 133 D7
Sherifoot La B75 . . . . . . 258 B4
Sheringham Covert
　ST16 . . . . 156 C4
Sheringham Dr WS15 . . . 178 B2
Sheringham Pl ST5 . . . . . 56 D4
Sherington Dr WV4 . . . . 266 D5
Sherracop La WS15 . . . . 160 A1
Sherrans Dell WV4 . . . . 266 D4
Sherratt St ST6 . . . . 42 C3
Sherringham Dr WV11 . . 242 C1
Shervale Cl WV4 . . . . . . 266 A6
Sherwin St ST6 . . . . 41 F3
Sherwood Ave ST17 . . . . 174 E8
Sherwood CV9 . . . . 262 C1
Sherwood Dr WS11 . . . . 210 A3
Sherwood Rd
　Stoke-on-T ST3 . . . . 89 F7
　Stourbridge DY8 . . . . . . 279 C7
Shetland Ave B77 . . . . . 261 F7
Shetland Rd ST3 . . . . 72 F3
Shillingford Dr ST4 . . . . . 88 B8
Shilton Cl ST4 . . . . 71 F5
Shinwell Gr ST3 . . . . 90 A8
Shipley Cl DE14 . . . . 185 B8
Shipley Pl ST6 . . . . 42 C2
Shippy La ST18 . . . . 172 C8
Shipston Rd ST17 . . . . . 156 D1
Shipton Dr ST14 . . . . . . 110 F1
Shirburn Rd ST13 . . . . . . 31 A6
Shirebrook Cl ST13 . . . . . 88 E7
Shirehall Pl WS11 . . . . . 210 B2
Shire Lea WS8 . . . . 245 B6
Shirelea Cl WS7 . . . . . . 229 B8
Shireoaks Dr ST17 . . . . . 175 C6
Shire Ridge WS9 . . . . . . 245 B4
Shires Ind Est WS14 . . . . 231 A6
Shireview Gdns WS3 . . . 244 B4
Shireview Rd WS3 . . . . . 244 B4
Shirewood WS11 . . . . . . 209 B2
Shirley Ave ST9 . . . . 59 B4
Shirley Dr ST10 . . . . 94 E8
Shirley Rd ST1 . . . . 282 B1
Shirley St Burslem ST6 . . . 56 D8
　Leek ST13 . . . . 30 C5
Shirleywich ST18 . . . . . . 138 E1
Shirley Wlk B79 . . . . 249 F7
Shirrall Dr B78 . . . . 259 E4
Shoal Hill Cl WS11 . . . . . 209 B2
Shobnall Cl DE14 . . . . . 166 A4
Shobnall Ct DE14 . . . . . 166 B3
Shobnall Prim Sch DE14 165 F4
Shobnall Rd DE14 . . . . . 166 A3
Shobnall St DE14 . . . . . 166 B4
Sholing Cl WV8 . . . . 239 F1
Shoobridge St ST13 . . . . . 30 F5
Shooting Butts Rd WS15 196 A8
Shop La Brewood ST19 . . 223 C6
　Oaken WV8 . . . . 238 D2
　Trescott WV6 . . . . 264 B7
Shops The 2 DY6 . . . . . 275 D4
Short Bambury St ST3 . . . 73 D6
Shortbutts La ST17 . . . . 281 B5
Short La Barton-u-N DE13 183 D1
　Cheslyn Hay WS6 . . . . . 226 E3
　Gratwich ST14 . . . . 124 D3
Shortlands La WS3 . . . . 243 F3
Short Rd WV10 . . . . 240 E1
Short St Brownhills WS8 . 244 F7
　Burton u T DE15 . . . . . 185 E7
　Cannock WS11 . . . . 209 F4
　Longton ST3 . . . . 284 D3
Short Street Com Inf Sch
　DE15 . . . . 185 E7
Short St Stourbridge DY8 . 279 F5
　Uttoxeter ST14 . . . . . . 126 B8
Shorwell St ST6 . . . . 41 E8
Shotsfield Pl ST2 . . . . 43 A1
Shotsfield St ST2 . . . . 43 A1
Shotwood Cl DE13 . . . . . 147 A4
Shotwoodhill La DE13 . . 147 A5
Showan Ave ST5 . . . . 56 D3
Showell La WV4 . . . . 265 B3
Shraleybrook Rd ST7 . . . . 54 B7
Shredicote La ST18 . . . . 191 B7
Shrewsbury Cl WS3 . . . . 242 F1
Shrewsbury Dr
　Newcastle-u-L ST5 . . . . . 40 E2
　Weston-Under-Lizard TF11 203 E2
Shrewsbury Mall WS15 . 178 F1
Shrewsbury Rd
　Edgmond TF10 . . . . . . 168 A4
　Market Drayton TF9 . . . 112 B8
　Stafford ST17 . . . . 285 B1
　Stretton DE13 . . . . 147 F2
Shrewsbury Way TF10 . . 168 E2
Shropshire Brook Rd
　WS15 . . . . 198 B4
Shropshire St TF9 . . . . . . 97 C1
Shrubbery Cl DY10 . . . . 280 A5
Shrubbery Hill DY10 . . . 280 A5
Shrubbery The
　Elford B79 . . . . 216 E1

Shrubbery The continued
　Rugeley WS15 . . . . 197 B6
Shruggs La ST18 . . . . . . 121 C1
Shugborough Cl WS3 . . . 243 B1
Shugborough Cotts
　ST18 . . . . 177 C8
Shugborough Dr DY1 . . . 271 E2
Shugborough Farm Mus★
　ST17 . . . . 177 A8
Shugborough Hall★
　ST17 . . . . 158 A1
Shugborough Rd WS15 . . 178 C3
Shugborough Way
　WS11 . . . . 210 C1
Shughborough Cl ST9 . . . 59 A2
Shuker's Cl TF10 . . . . . . 169 A2
Shut La ST21 . . . . 116 B6
Shutt Green La
　Brewood ST19 . . . . 223 B8
　Kiddemore Green ST19 . . 222 E8
Shuttington Rd B77,B79 . 251 B6
Sich La DE13 . . . . 182 D4
Sidcot Pl ST1 . . . . 57 D8
Siddalls St DE15 . . . . . . 167 B3
Siddons Cl WS13 . . . . . . 213 F2
Sides La DE6 . . . . 81 B5
Sidestrand WV9 . . . . 239 F1
Sideway Rd ST4 . . . . 72 B5
Sidings Ind Est DE14 . . . 166 E4
Sidings Pl ST3,ST4 . . . . . 284 B4
Sidings The
　Cannock WS12 . . . . 210 C7
　Cheadle ST10 . . . . 76 D2
　Stone ST15 . . . . 120 B8
Sidmouth Ave
　Newcastle-u-L ST5 . . . . 283 C3
　Stafford ST17 . . . . 156 D1
Sidney Ave ST17 . . . . . . 174 E7
Sidney Dr ST10 . . . . 62 A3
Sidney St WV2 . . . . 266 C8
Sidon Hill Way WS11 . . . 210 C2
Siemens Rd ST17 . . . . . . 285 B1
Signal Gr WS3 . . . . 243 A1
Signal Wlk B77 . . . . 251 A2
Silica Rd B77 . . . . 251 B2
Silk Mill La DE13 . . . . . . 146 C6
Silkmore Cres ST17 . . . . 175 A7
Silkmore La ST17 . . . . . . 175 A8
Silkmore Prim Sch ST17 174 F7
Silk St ST13 . . . . 30 E6
Sill Gn B79 . . . . 234 C1
Sillitoe Pl ST4 . . . . 72 A6
Silsden Gr ST3 . . . . 74 C2
Silva Ave DY6 . . . . 275 F4
Silver Birch Coppice
　B74 . . . . 257 D5
Silver Birch Dr
　Kinver DY7 . . . . 277 F5
　Uttoxeter ST14 . . . . . . 126 B6
Silver Birch Rd
　Aldridge B74 . . . . 256 F1
　Huntington WS12 . . . . . 209 D8
　Norton Canes WS11 . . . 228 B5
　Wolverhampton WV2 . . 266 F2
Silver Cl ST8 . . . . 27 C8
Silver Court Gdns WS8 . . 244 F7
Silver Ct WS8 . . . . 244 F7
Silverdale Cl Chorlton CW2 37 C3
　Newport TF10 . . . . 168 E1
Silverdale Dr WS7 . . . . . 228 D7
Silverdale TF10 . . . . 168 A4
Silverdale Gdns DY8 . . . . 279 C3
Silverdale Prim Sch ST5 . 55 C1
Silverdale Rd
　Newcastle-u-L,Knutton
　ST5 . . . . 55 E1
　Newcastle-u-L,Wolstanton
　ST5 . . . . 56 C5
Silverdale St ST5 . . . . 55 E3
Silver Fir Cl WS12 . . . . . 210 A8
Silvergate Ct CW12 . . . . . 15 E8
Silverhill Cl DE13 . . . . . 166 C8
Silverstone Ave ST10 . . . . 76 E3
Silverstone Cres ST6 . . . . 41 E8
Silver St Stoke-on-T ST6 . . 42 E4
　Tamworth B79 . . . . 250 B5
　Uttoxeter ST14 . . . . . . 126 E4
Silverthorn Way ST17 . . . 175 C7
Silverton Cl ST5 . . . . 56 A8
Silvertrees Cvn Pk WS15 195 E7
Silverwood ST7 . . . . 26 B1
Silvester Way ST17 . . . . 175 E6
Simcox St WS12 . . . . . . 210 D4
Simeon Way WS15 . . . . 120 C6
Simister Ct 10 ST6 . . . . . . 41 D3
Simmonds Cl WS3 . . . . . 243 D3
Simmonds Rd WS3 . . . . 243 D3
Simmonds Way WS8 . . . 245 A6
Simmons Cl B78 . . . . . . 260 B1
Simmons Rd WV11 . . . . 242 B1
Simonburn Ave ST4 . . . . . 71 E6
Simon Pl ST4 . . . . 57 B1
Simons Rd TF9 . . . . 112 B8
Simpkins Cl WS9 . . . . . . 245 A3
Simpson Cl ST16 . . . . . . 155 B7
Simpson Rd WS13 . . . . . 214 B2
Simpson St Hanley ST1 . . 282 C1
　Newcastle-u-L ST5 . . . . . 56 B5

Sinai Cl DE13 . . . . 165 E4
Sion Ave DY10 . . . . 280 A1
Sion Hill Mid Sch DY10 . 280 A1
Sir Graham Balfour High Sch
　ST16 . . . . 155 D8
Sir John Offley CE Prim Sch
　CW3 . . . . 68 E5
Sir Robert Peel Hospl
　B78 . . . . 249 D2
Sir Thomas Boughey High
　Sch ST7 . . . . 54 D7
Siskin Cl WS7 . . . . 229 D5
Siskin Pl ST3 . . . . 90 B7
Sister Dora Ave WS7 . . . 229 F7
Sitwell Gr ST3 . . . . 284 D4
Six Ashes Rd
　Bobbington DY7 . . . . . . 267 F1
　Halfpenny Green DY7 . . 268 A3
　Six Ashes WV15 . . . . . . 272 D7
Six Roads End DE6 . . . . 144 C4
Skeath La ST18 . . . . 137 C4
Skellern Ave ST6 . . . . 42 C3
Skellern St ST7 . . . . 25 D2
Skidmore Ave
　Tamworth B77 . . . . 261 C5
　Wolverhampton WV3 . . 265 F8
Skipacre Ave ST6 . . . . 42 D1
Skipness B77 . . . . 250 E5
Skipton Pl WV3 . . . . 226 B7
Skye Cl Longton ST3 . . . . 73 C3
　Wolverhampton WV3 . . 261 F7
Skylark Cl Dudley DY5 . . 271 C1
　Huntington WS12 . . . . . 209 C7
　Uttoxeter ST14 . . . . . . 126 C6
Slab La ST9,ST20 . . . . . . 190 B2
Slacken La ST7 . . . . 25 D2
Slack La Mayfield DE6 . . . 81 C8
　Mayfield,Middle Mayfield
　DE6 . . . . 81 B7
Slacky La WS3 . . . . 243 F1
Slade Ave WS7 . . . . 229 A8
Slade Fields ST14 . . . . . 111 B1
Slade Gdns WV8 . . . . . . 239 A4
Slade Hill 3 WV6 . . . . . 255 F3
Sladehollow La DE6 . . . . 65 C1
Slade La
　Sutton Coldfield B75 . . . 259 A3
　Tamworth B77 . . . . 261 C4
　Waterhouses ST10 . . . . . 49 A5
Slade Rd
　Sutton Coldfield B75 . . . 258 E3
　Wolverhampton WV10 . . 240 C3
Slade View Rise WS12 . . 211 A6
Slaidburn Gr
　Birches Head ST1 . . . . . . 57 F5
　Stafford ST17 . . . . 175 C7
Slaney St ST5 . . . . 283 C1
Slang La WS15 . . . . 211 F5
Slapton Cl ST2 . . . . 57 F1
Slate La WV8 . . . . 238 D5
Slater St Biddulph ST8 . . . 27 C7
　Burslem ST6 . . . . 56 E7
Sleeve The ST13 . . . . 30 C4
Sleigh Gr ST13 . . . . 30 E5
Slessor Rd ST16 . . . . . . 156 A5
Slindon Cl ST5 . . . . 40 D1
Sling La ST19 . . . . 206 B4
Slingsby B77 . . . . 261 C2
Slippery La ST1 . . . . 282 A2
Slitting Mill Rd WS15 . . . 196 B7
Sloane Way ST4 . . . . 73 B6
Smallbrook La WV5 . . . . 270 B2
Smallcross Cl ST14 . . . . 126 C5
Smalley Cl WS11 . . . . . . 210 A5
Small La ST21 . . . . 133 E7
Smallman St ST16 . . . . . 285 C4
Small Mdws DE13 . . . . . 183 E2
Smallridge WS13 . . . . . . 213 F2
Smallshire Way DY8 . . . . 279 E8
Smallthorne Prim Sch
　ST6 . . . . 42 D2
Smallwood Cl ST5 . . . . . . 40 D1
Smallwood Gr ST1 . . . . . . 57 F6
Smallwood Rd WV8 . . . . 239 E2
Smarts Ave WS14 . . . . . 258 A4
Smedley Ct DE65 . . . . . . 148 B5
Smestow Bridge Ind Est
　WV5 . . . . 269 C6
Smestow La DY3 . . . . . . 269 C5
Smestow Mews WV5 . . . 269 D4
Smestow Sch WV3 . . . . . 255 B1
Smillie Pl WS11 . . . . 209 F3
Smith Child St ST6 . . . . . . 41 D4
Smithfield Cl TF9 . . . . 97 D2
Smithfield Ct ST1 . . . . . . 282 B1
Smithfield Ctr The 4
　ST13 . . . . 30 F5
Smithfield Ho 2 ST13 . . . 30 F5
Smithfield Rd
　Market Drayton TF9 . . . . 97 D2
　Uttoxeter ST14 . . . . . . 126 B8
　Walsall WS3 . . . . 243 D1
Smithfield Rise WS13 . . . 231 C8
Smith Ho WS3 . . . . 243 C3
Smithpool Rd ST4 . . . . . . 72 D5
Smiths Bldgs 4 ST3 . . . . 74 A1
Smith's Cl WS7 . . . . 228 D6
Smiths Pas ST4 . . . . 73 A5
Smith St Longton ST3 . . . 284 C5
　Wood End CV9 . . . . 262 C1
Smithy Bank ST10 . . . . . . 78 E1
Smithy Croft ST20 . . . . . 190 B7
Smithy Dr WS3 . . . . 244 A4
Smithy La Barthomley CW2 38 C6
　Barthomley CW2 . . . . . . 38 D7
　Bednall ST17 . . . . 193 F8
　Biddulph ST8 . . . . 16 D2

Smithy La continued
　Bosley SK11 . . . . 7 E6
　Bradley ST17 . . . . 191 C8
　Cheadle ST10 . . . . 92 D8
　Clifton Campville B79 . . 218 E2
　Dudley DY5 . . . . 271 B1
　Eccleshall ST21 . . . . . . 117 B2
　Hixon ST18 . . . . 158 C8
　Knighton TF9 . . . . 83 B5
　Lichfield WS13 . . . . 214 A1
　Longdon WS15 . . . . . . 212 F8
　Longton ST3 . . . . 284 C3
　Norton Bridge ST15 . . . 118 F1
　Seighford ST18 . . . . . . 154 B7
　Tamworth B77 . . . . 261 F7
　Weston CW2 . . . . 37 C5
　Whitmore ST5 . . . . 85 F6
Smokies Way ST8 . . . . . . 16 C1
Smout Cres WV14 . . . . . 266 F2
Snape Hall Cl ST5 . . . . . . 85 D6
Snape Hall Rd ST5 . . . . . 85 C7
Snape Hollow CW2 . . . . . 37 F4
Snape La CW2 . . . . 37 F4
Snape Rd WV11 . . . . 242 B1
Snapes La DE6 . . . . 81 B1
Snead Cl ST16 . . . . 156 C4
Sneyd Ave Leek ST13 . . . . 30 E5
　Newcastle-u-L ST5 . . . . . 70 F7
Sneyd Cl ST13 . . . . 45 C4
Sneyd Com Sch WS3 . . . 242 E2
Sneyd Cres ST5 . . . . 70 F7
Sneyd Green Prim Sch
　ST6 . . . . 57 C7
Sneyd Hall Rd WS3 . . . . 243 A1
Sneyd Hill ST6 . . . . 57 C8
Sneyd Hill Ind Est ST6 . . . 57 B8
Sneyd Ind Est ST6 . . . . . . 57 B8
Sneyd Ho WS3 . . . . 242 F1
Sneydlands WS15 . . . . . 178 F1
Sneyd La Walsall WS3 . . 242 F1
　Willenhall WV11 . . . . . 242 C1
Sneyd Pl ST6 . . . . 41 C6
Sneyd St Hanley ST6,ST1 . . 57 C6
　Leek ST13 . . . . 30 E5
Sneyd Terr ST5 . . . . 55 B2
Sneyd Wood View ST6 . . . 57 C7
Snipe Cl WV10 . . . . 241 B7
Snowberry Dr DY5 . . . . . 271 C1
Snowden Way ST3 . . . . . . 74 B2
Snowdon Rd
　Burnhill Green WV6 . . . 252 B6
　Cannock WS11 . . . . 209 E6
Snowdon Rise DY3 . . . . 271 D6
Snowdon Way WV12 . . . 242 B1
Snowdrop Cl WS8 . . . . . 244 D6
Snow Hill Hanley ST1 . . . 282 A1
　Stafford ST16 . . . . 285 B4
Snows Ct TF10 . . . . 168 F2
Snowshill Gdns DY1 . . . 271 F4
Snows Yd ST16 . . . . 285 A4
Soames Cres ST3 . . . . . . 73 C6
Solent Cl WV9 . . . . 239 F2
Solney Cl DE11 . . . . 186 F3
Solway Cl B79 . . . . 250 A7
Solway Gr ST3 . . . . 73 E4
Somerfield Cl WS4 . . . . . 243 C1
　Great Wyrley WS6 . . . . 226 E1
Somerford Gdns WV10 . . 240 E2
Somerford La ST19 . . . . 223 F5
Somerley Rd ST1 . . . . 57 F6
Somerset Ave
　Kidsgrove ST7 . . . . 25 F2
　Rugeley WS15 . . . . 196 D6
Somerset Cl B78 . . . . . . 250 A1
Somerset Dr DY8 . . . . . . 279 D7
Somerset Pl WS11 . . . . . 209 F3
Somerset Rd
　Burton u T DE15 . . . . . 185 D6
　Hanley ST1 . . . . 57 E4
　Stafford ST17 . . . . 174 C7
Somerton Rd ST9 . . . . . . 59 A3
Somerton Way ST3 . . . . 284 D5
Somervale ST17 . . . . . . 175 C6
Somerville Ave ST5 . . . . . 56 D3
Somerville Ct B79 . . . . . 249 D6
Somerville Rd DE13 . . . . 201 A2
Somerville Sq ST17 . . . . 174 F6
Somerville Terr 5 WS15 196 E8
Sonning Dr WV9 . . . . . . 239 F2
Sophia Way ST5 . . . . 56 B8
Sopwith Cl ST15 . . . . . . 118 F6
Sorbus B77 . . . . 251 B4
Sorrel Ave ST10 . . . . 92 F3
Sorrel Cl Bucknall ST2 . . . 58 A3
　Featherstone WV10 . . . 241 B7
　Lichfield WS13 . . . . 230 E6
　Uttoxeter ST14 . . . . . . 126 B6
Sorrel Dr ST5 . . . . 251 B5
Sorrento Gr ST3 . . . . 73 E4
Sotherby Ho ST15 . . . . . 285 A3
Souldern Way ST3 . . . . . . 73 D4
Southall Way ST21 . . . . . 58 A1
Southampton St ST1 . . . 282 C4
Southbank St ST13 . . . . . 30 F5
Southbank View DY6 . . . 275 E4
Southborough Cres ST6 . . 42 C4
Southbourne Pl WS11 . . 209 D2
South Broadway St
　DE14 . . . . 185 C8
South Cres WV10 . . . . . 241 C6
South Dr DE11 . . . . 186 F5
Southern Cl DY6 . . . . . . 275 F3

Southern Cross WS14 . . 231 C7
Southern Ct 5 ST4 . . . . . 72 A7
Southerndown Rd DY3 . . 271 B7
Southern Way ST6 . . . . . . 42 D1
Southfield Cl WS9 . . . . . 256 A6
Southfield Gr WV3 . . . . . 265 C7
Southfields Cl ST17 . . . . 174 D5
Southfields Rd ST17 . . . 174 D5
Southfield Way WS6 . . . 226 F2
Southgate Ave ST4 . . . . . 88 C6
Southgate Brewood ST19 223 D7
　Cannock WS11 . . . . 226 B7
Southgate End WS11 . . . 226 B7
South Gn WV4 . . . . 265 D5
South Hill DE13 . . . . 147 D4
Southlands Ave
　Longton ST3 . . . . 284 B1
　Newcastle-u-L ST5 . . . . . 56 C5
Southlands Cl ST13 . . . . . 30 C6
Southlands Ct ST21 . . . . 133 E7
Southlands Rd CW12 . . . . 16 A8
Southlowe Ave ST9 . . . . . 59 E4
Southlowe Rd ST9 . . . . . . 59 E4
South Oak St DE14 . . . . 185 B8
South Oval DY3 . . . . 271 C8
South Pl ST6 . . . . 42 D6
South Rd Bucknall ST2 . . 58 B5
　Coldmeece ST15 . . . . . 118 D6
　Stourbridge DY8 . . . . . 279 E4
　Wolverhampton WV4 . . 266 F4
South Staffordshire Bsns Pk
　WS11 . . . . 226 C4
South St
　Mount Pleasant ST7 . . . . 26 B6
　Stafford ST16 . . . . 285 A3
　Stoke-on-T ST4 . . . . 42 D6
South Terr
　Newcastle-u-L ST5 . . . . . 56 C5
　Stoke-on-T ST4 . . . . 72 A5
South Uxbridge St DE14 185 B8
South View 4 ST8 . . . . . . 27 C8
South View Cl
　Codsall WV8 . . . . 239 B2
　Featherstone WV10 . . . 241 B6
South View DE6 . . . . 81 D6
South View Rd DY3 . . . . 271 C8
South View ST14 . . . . . . 126 B7
South View Wlk ST14 . . . 95 F3
South Walls ST16 . . . . . . 285 B3
Southwark St WS13 . . . . 214 C3
Southway Ct DY6 . . . . . . 275 F4
Southwell Est ST21 . . . . 133 E6
South Wlk ST3 . . . . 74 B1
South Wolfe St ST4 . . . . . 72 B7
Southwood Cl DY6 . . . . . 275 E5
Southwood St ST5 . . . . . . 85 A7
Sovereign Bsns Pk DE14 166 D5
Sovereign Dr
　Burton u T DE14 . . . . . 185 B8
　Dudley DY1 . . . . 271 E2
Sovereign La TF9 . . . . . . 100 C5
Sovereign Works DY1 . . . 271 E2
Sowdley Gn ST19 . . . . . 205 B5
Sowdley La ST19 . . . . . . 205 B4
Sowers Ct B75 . . . . 258 D4
Spalding Pl ST2 . . . . 73 E8
Sparch Ave ST5 . . . . 56 C4
Sparch Gr ST5 . . . . 56 C4
Sparch Hollow ST5 . . . . . 56 C4
Spark St ST4 . . . . 72 A7
Spark Terr ST4 . . . . 72 A7
Sparrowbutts Gr ST7 . . . . 26 C2
Sparrow Cl ST18 . . . . . . 177 D8
Sparrows End La ST19 . . 223 D6
Sparrow St ST5 . . . . 42 D2
Sparrow Terr ST5 . . . . . . 56 B6
Spa St ST6 . . . . 57 C7
Speakman St ST3 . . . . . 284 D2
Spearhill WS14 . . . . 231 E8
Spedding Rd ST4 . . . . 72 F8
Spedding Way ST8 . . . . . 27 F8
Speechly Dr WS15 . . . . . 178 D2
Speedwall St ST3 . . . . . . 73 C5
Speedwell Cl WS9 . . . . . 256 A5
Speedwell Gdns WV10 . . 241 B8
Speedwell Rd ST5 . . . . . . 40 F1
Speedwell Rise ST16 . . . 155 A5
Speedy Cl WS11 . . . . . . 209 E5
Speedymill Cotts WS13 . . 213 F8
Spencer Ave Endon ST9 . . 43 E6
　Leek ST13 . . . . 30 E5
Spencer Cl Dudley DY3 . . 271 A4
　Stretton DE13 . . . . 147 D1
　Uttoxeter ST14 . . . . . . 126 C5
　Weston ST18 . . . . 138 C2
Spencer Dr WS7 . . . . . . 228 E8
Spencer Pl ST5 . . . . 55 E6
Spencer Rd
　Lichfield WS14 . . . . . . 231 B6
　Stoke-on-T ST4 . . . . 72 C8
Spencroft Rd ST5 . . . . . . 56 A5
Spend La Mapleton DE6 . 66 F7
　Thorpe DE6 . . . . 51 E2
Spenser Ave WV6 . . . . . 254 F4
Spenser Cl Stafford ST17 174 C4
　Tamworth B79 . . . . 250 A6
Spens St ST6 . . . . 56 F8
Sperry Cl ST3 . . . . 90 B7
Spey Dr ST7 . . . . 26 C2
Spiceal Mews ST14 . . . . 126 C7
Spicer's Cl WV5 . . . . 267 C8
Spills Mdw DY3 . . . . 271 E5
Spindlewood Cl 1
　WS12 . . . . 210 D1
Spinney
　Burntwood WS7 . . . . . . 212 A1
　Endon ST9 . . . . 43 E8
　Norton Canes WS11 . . . 227 F5

Spinney Cl continued
Polesworth B78 . . . . 262 F8
Stourbridge DY8 . . . . 275 C3
Walsall WS3 . . . . 244 A2
Spinney Dr CW2 . . . . 37 B5
Spinney Farm Rd WS11 . 226 B7
Spinneyfields 2 ST17 . . . 175 D5
Spinney La ST7 . . . . 211 F1
Spinney Lodge DE13 . . . 145 E6
Spinney Rd DE14 . . . . . . 184 F8
Spinney The Biddulph ST8 . 27 C6
Dudley DY3 . . . . 271 C2
Lawton-gate ST7 . . . . 25 E4
Little Aston B74 . . . . 257 B6
Madeley Heath CW3 . . . . . 69 A8
Newcastle-u-L ST5 . . . . . . 71 C2
Wolverhampton WV3 . . . . 255 D1
Spinning School La B79 . 250 B5
Spiral Ct DY3 . . . . 271 D3
Spire Cl ST6 . . . . 42 E3
Spires Croft WV10 . . . . . 225 D1
Spires The WS14 . . . . . . 231 E6
Spitfire Cl ST16 . . . . 136 B1
Spitfire Way ST6 . . . . 41 C4
Splash La WS12 . . . . 210 C3
Spode Ave
Armitage WS15 . . . . 198 C4
Hopton ST18 . . . . 156 B8
Spode Cl Cheadle ST10 . . . 76 C2
Stone ST15 . . . . 119 E5
Spode Gr ST5 . . . . 71 B3
Spode Mus★ ST4 . . . . 72 B7
Spode Pl WS11 . . . . 210 B2
Spode St ST4 . . . . 72 B5
Spoutfield Rd ST4 . . . . . . 56 F1
Spout La ST2 . . . . 43 C1
Spragg House La ST6 . . . . 42 E3
Spratslade Dr ST3 . . . . . 284 B2
Spreadoaks Dr ST17 . . . . 175 D5
Sprengers Cl ST19 . . . . . 193 A1
Springbank Ave ST9 . . . . . 43 E6
Spring Bank Flats ST16 . 155 D6
Spring Bank ST7 . . . . 26 A7
Spring Cl Hagley DY9 . . . 281 F4
Kinver DY7 . . . . 277 F5
Swadlincote DE11 . . . . . . 186 F1
Walsall WS4 . . . . 244 C2
Spring Cres ST6 . . . . 43 C7
Springcroft ST11 . . . . 90 F6
Springcroft Prim Sch
ST11 . . . . 90 F7
Springdale Jun & Inf Schs
WV4 . . . . 265 D5
Springfarm Rd DE15 . . . . 167 A1
Springfield Ave
Newport TF10 . . . . 168 E1
Rugeley WS15 . . . . 196 F7
Sedgley DY3 . . . . 266 C6
Springfield ST11 . . . . 90 E6
Springfield Cl Leek ST13 . . 31 A5
Newcastle-u-L ST5 . . . . . . 55 F6
Springfield Com Specl Sch
ST13 . . . . 31 A5
Springfield Cres ST3 . . . 284 B2
Springfield Ct Leek ST13 . . 31 A6
Stafford ST17 . . . . 174 E5
Wolverhampton WV10 . . . 240 D4
Springfield Dr
Forsbrook ST11 . . . . 91 A8
Leek ST13 . . . . 31 A6
Stafford ST17 . . . . 174 E5
Talke ST7 . . . . 40 E8
Wheaton Aston ST19 . . . . 205 C7
Springfield Gn DY3 . . . . . 266 C6
Springfield Gr
Biddulph ST8 . . . . 27 D7
Sedgley DY3 . . . . 266 D1
Springfield La WV10 . . . . 240 D4
Springfield TF9 . . . . 99 E5
Springfield Mobile Home Pk
4 TF9 . . . . 112 A8
Springfield Prim Sch ST4 . 71 E6
Springfield Rd
Biddulph ST8 . . . . 27 D7
Leek ST13 . . . . 31 A6
Tamworth B77 . . . . 261 D8
Uttoxeter ST14 . . . . 126 B8
Springfield Rise WS12 . . 210 C6
Springfields Fst Sch
ST15 . . . . 118 F1
Springfields Ind Est
TF10 . . . . 168 F1
Springfields TF10 . . . . . . 168 F1
Springfields Rd
Rugeley WS15 . . . . 178 D3
Stoke-on-T ST6 . . . . 71 E6
Springfield Terr DE15 . . 167 A1
Spring Garden Rd ST3 . . 284 B2
Spring Gdns
Forsbrook ST11 . . . . 91 B8
Leek ST13 . . . . 30 C5
Stone ST15 . . . . 120 A5
Springhead Cl ST7 . . . . . . 40 D6
Springhead Prim Sch ST7 40 D6
Springhill Ave WV4 . . . . 265 C4
Springhill Cl WS4 . . . . . . 244 D1
Springhill Gr WV4 . . . . . 265 C4
Springhill La WV4 . . . . . 265 B4
Springhill Pk WV4 . . . . . 265 B3
Springhill Prim Sch
WS7 . . . . 229 B6
Springhill Rd
Brownhills WS8 . . . . 245 A7
Burntwood WS7 . . . . 229 A6
Springhill Terr WS15 . . . 196 F7
Spring Hollow ST21 . . . . 133 E6
Spring La
Bishops Wood ST19 . . . . . 221 E8

Spring La continued
Walsall WS4 . . . . 244 C2
Whittington WS14 . . . . . 232 E6
Spring Leasow ST20 . . . . 151 A4
Springle Styche La WS7 . 212 C1
Spring Mdw WS6 . . . . . . 226 D1
Spring Meadows Cl WV8 239 B4
Springpool ST5 . . . . 70 C6
Spring Rd Lichfield WS13 214 D2
Longton ST3 . . . . 73 E2
Walsall WS4 . . . . 244 D1
Springs Bank ST9 . . . . 44 A2
Springside Pl ST3 . . . . 88 E7
Spring St Cannock WS11 . 226 E8
Stoke-on-T ST5 . . . . 56 D1
Spring Terrace Rd DE15 . 166 F1
Spring Terr WS7 . . . . 228 E5
Springvale Prim Sch
WS11 . . . . 226 E8
Spring Vale Prim Sch
WV4 . . . . 266 E4
Springvale Rise ST16 . . . 155 D8
Spring View ST6 . . . . 43 C7
Springwater Dr CW2 . . . . 37 C1
Springwood Dr ST15 . . . . 120 D7
Springwood Rd ST5 . . . . . 56 C8
Sprinkbank Rd ST6 . . . . . 42 A5
Sprink La CW12 . . . . 6 D5
Sprinkswoods La DE6 . . . 81 E5
Sprinkwood Gr ST3 . . . . . 74 A3
Sproston Rd ST6 . . . . 41 F4
Spruce Rd WS12 . . . . 194 F1
Spruces The DY9 . . . . . . 281 F4
Spruce B77 . . . . 251 B4
Spruce Way
Stafford ST16 . . . . 155 C3
Wolverhampton WV3 . . . . 255 D1
Spruce Wlk WS15 . . . . . . 178 C3
Spur Lea ST18 . . . . 173 C1
Spur St ST1 . . . . 282 C1
Spur Tree Ave WV3 . . . . . 255 A1
Square The Aldridge WS9. 256 B6
Caverswall ST11 . . . . 74 E2
Checkley ST14 . . . . 109 E7
Codsall WV8 . . . . 238 F4
Derrington ST18 . . . . . . 154 D2
Elford B79 . . . . 216 D2
Fazeley B78 . . . . 261 A8
Great Haywood ST18 . . . . 158 B2
Marchington ST14 . . . . . 127 E2
Meir ST3 . . . . 74 B2
Newcastle-u-L ST5 . . . . . . 71 B6
Newport TF10 . . . . 168 F3
Oakamoor ST10 . . . . 78 A6
Pattingham WV6 . . . . . . 253 C2
Whiston ST10 . . . . 62 D3
Wolverhampton WV2 . . . . 266 D8
Woore CW3 . . . . 67 C1
Squires Gate WS7 . . . . . . 229 C8
Squires View ST4 . . . . . . 72 C7
Squirrel Cl
Cannock WS12 . . . . 210 D2
Huntington WS12 . . . . . 209 C6
Squirrel Hayes Ave ST8 . . 27 E6
Squirrel Hayes Cotts ST8. 27 E6
Squirrel Hayes Fst Sch
ST8 . . . . 27 D7
Squirrels Cnr DE13 . . . . . 162 F7
Squirrels Hollow WS7 . . 212 A2
Squirrels The
Lichfield WS14 . . . . 231 C7
Newcastle-u-L ST5 . . . . . . 71 C3
Squirrel Wlk
Little Aston B74 . . . . 257 C5
Stafford ST17 . . . . 174 E4
Wolverhampton WV4 . . . . 266 A5
Stable Ct DY3 . . . . 271 E6
Stableford Bank ST5 . . . . 86 A1
Stableford Cvn Pk ST5 . . 86 B2
Stable La
Market Drayton TF9 . . . . . 97 B1
Shareshill WV10 . . . . . . 225 A7
Wetton DE6 . . . . 35 B1
Stables The
Great Haywood ST18 . . . . 158 B2
Lawton-gate ST7 . . . . 25 C4
Stacey Cl SK17 . . . . 23 B2
Stackhouse Cl WS9 . . . . . 245 A4
Stackhouse Dr WS3 . . . . 244 A4
Stackyard La TF10 . . . . . 168 A4
Stadium Ct ST6 . . . . 57 A6
Stadmorslow La
Harriseahead ST7 . . . . . . 26 F4
Packmoor ST6,ST7 . . . . . 27 A3
Stafford Ave ST9 . . . . 71 C5
Stafford Brook Rd WS15 . 195 F8
Stafford Castle★ ST16 . . . 155 A4
Stafford Cl Stone ST15 . . 120 A7
Walsall WS3 . . . . 243 B2
Stafford Coll ST16 . . . . . 285 A3
Stafford Cres
Newcastle-u-L ST5 . . . . . . 71 C4
Whittington WS14 . . . . . 232 D3
Stafford Ct WV10 . . . . . . 240 D1
Stafford Gram Sch ST18 . 174 C6
Stafford La
Cannock WS12 . . . . 210 B5
Codsall WV8 . . . . 238 C1
Hanley ST1 . . . . 282 B3
Stafford Rd
Brewood WV10 . . . . 224 C5
Cannock WS11 . . . . 209 D1
Coven Heath WV10 . . . . . 240 D4
Eccleshall ST21 . . . . 133 F6
Gnosall ST20 . . . . 171 E6
Huntington WS11,WS12 . 209 C5
Lichfield WS13 . . . . 213 E2
Newport TF10 . . . . 169 A3

Stafford Rd continued
Penkridge ST19 . . . . 192 E2
Stone ST15 . . . . 120 A6
Stone ST15 . . . . 120 A7
Uttoxeter ST14 . . . . 126 A6
Weston ST18 . . . . 138 C3
Staffordshire Ct ST18 . . . 156 D4
Staffordshire Enamels★
ST3 . . . . 73 F3
Staffordshire General Hospl
ST16 . . . . 156 B4
Staffordshire Regiment Mus
The★ WS14 . . . . 232 C2
Staffordshire Tech Pk
ST18 . . . . 156 C5
Staffordshire Univ WS13 231 B7
Staffordshire Univ (Stafford
Campus) ST18 . . . . . . 156 C5
Staffordshire Univ (Stoke
Campus) ST4 . . . . 72 C8
Staffordshire Yeomanry
Mus★ ST16 . . . . 285 B3
Stafford Sta ST16 . . . . . . 285 A2
Stafford St Brewood ST19 223 C6
Burton u T ST18 . . . . 166 D5
Cannock WS12 . . . . 210 E1
Eccleshall ST21 . . . . 133 E7
Hanley ST1 . . . . 282 B3
Market Drayton TF9 . . . . . 97 D1
Newcastle-u-L ST5 . . . . . 283 C2
Newport TF10 . . . . 168 F3
Stafford ST16 . . . . 285 B3
Stagborough Way WS15 . 210 B4
Stag Cl WS15 . . . . 178 B1
Stag Cres WS11 . . . . 228 A6
Stag Dr WS12 . . . . 209 C6
Staines Ct ST15 . . . . 120 C7
Staite Dr DY10 . . . . 280 D5
Staite Terr DY10 . . . . 280 A5
Stakenbridge La DY10 . . . 281 D4
Staley Croft WS12 . . . . . 209 C4
Stalling's La DY6 . . . . . . 275 D8
Stallington Cl ST11 . . . . . 90 D4
Stallington Gdns ST11 . . . 90 F6
Stallington Rd ST11 . . . . . 90 C3
Stamer St ST4 . . . . 72 B6
Stamford Cres WS7 . . . . 229 A8
Stamford St DY8 . . . . . . 279 F7
Stamford Way WS9 . . . . . 245 C1
Stamps Cl DE15 . . . . 167 C3
Standard St ST4 . . . . 72 C6
Standedge B77 . . . . 262 B7
Standersfoot Pl ST6 . . . . . 42 B6
Standhills Rd DY6 . . . . . . 275 E6
Standing Butts Cl DE12 . . 202 D8
Standon Ct ST21 . . . . 101 F4
Stanfield Cres ST10 . . . . . 76 D1
Stanfield Rd ST6 . . . . 42 A1
Stanfield St 4 ST3 . . . . . 73 D6
Stanford Ct ST19 . . . . . . 192 E1
Stanford Rd WV2 . . . . . . 266 C8
Stanhope Gn DE15 . . . . . 167 F1
Stanhope Ho B79 . . . . . . 250 A4
Stanhope St
Burton u T DE15 . . . . . . 167 B3
Hanley ST1 . . . . 282 A1
Stanier St
Newcastle-u-L ST5 . . . . . 283 B3
Stoke-on-T ST4 . . . . 72 A4
Stanley Bank ST9 . . . . 44 A5
Stanley Cl DE12 . . . . 219 F7
Stanley Cres ST14 . . . . . . 111 A2
Stanley Ct WV6 . . . . 254 E4
Stanley Dr
Newcastle-u-L ST5 . . . . . . 40 D1
Swindon DY3 . . . . 269 D1
Stanley Gr
Newcastle-u-L ST5 . . . . . . 56 D2
Stoke-on-T ST3 . . . . 41 E4
Stanley Matthews Sports Ctr
ST4 . . . . 72 C8
Stanley Matthews Way
Stoke-on-T,Hem Heath
ST4 . . . . 88 D7
Stoke-on-T,Hollybush ST4 . 72 C3
Stanley Moss La ST9 . . . . 43 E5
Stanley Moss Rd ST9 . . . . 43 F5
Stanley Rd Biddulph ST8 . 16 C2
Cannock WS12 . . . . 210 A6
Newcastle-u-L ST5 . . . . . . 56 D2
Stoke-on-T,Hartshill ST4 . . 71 E8
Stoke-on-T,Stanley Moor
ST9 . . . . 43 E4
Stourbridge DY8 . . . . . . 279 F3
Wolverhampton WV10 . . . 240 D1
Stanley St Biddulph ST8 . . 27 C8
Burton u T DE14 . . . . 166 C2
Leek ST13 . . . . 30 D5
Stoke-on-T ST6 . . . . 41 E4
Walsall WS3 . . . . 243 D1
Stansgate Pl ST1 . . . . . . 282 A4
Stanshope La DE6 . . . . . . 35 C2
Stansmore Rd ST3 . . . . . . 74 B2
Stanton Ave DY1 . . . . . . 271 F6
Stanton Cl ST5 . . . . 55 F2
Stanton La Ellastone DE6 . 80 C4
Upper Mayfield DE6 . . . . . 66 A2
Stanton Prim Sch DE15 . 186 B5
Stanton Rd
Burton u T DE15 . . . . . . 185 F7
Meir ST3 . . . . 74 A1
Stanway Ave ST6 . . . . 57 C7
Stanway Cl ST14 . . . . 126 A6
Stanway Ct ST15 . . . . 155 F5
Stanways La ST8 . . . . 17 F2
Stapenhill Rd DE15 . . . . . 166 F2
Stapleford Gdns WS7 . . . 229 D6

Stapleford Gr DY8 . . . . . 275 E2
Stapleton Cres ST3 . . . . . 73 A1
Star And Garter Rd ST3 . . 89 E8
Star Bank Cotton ST10 . . . 63 C1
Oakamoor ST10 . . . . 78 C7
Star Cvn Site The WV9 . . 224 B1
Starkey's La ST19 . . . . . . 205 D7
Sterling Pk ST7 . . . . 26 D3
Starling Ct WV10 . . . . . . 240 B3
Star St WV3 . . . . 265 E8
Startley La WS15 . . . . . . 196 F1
Starwood Rd ST3 . . . . 89 E8
Starwood Terr ST10 . . . . . 78 A6
Statfold La Alrewas DE13 . 200 F3
Fradley WS13 . . . . 215 D8
Statham St ST1 . . . . 282 A2
Station App
Lichfield WS13 . . . . 231 F6
Stone ST15 . . . . 104 F1
Sutton Coldfield,Hill Hook
B74 . . . . 257 F6
Station Bridge Rd ST4. . . . 72 E5
Station Cl WV8 . . . . 238 F3
Station Cotts
Sudbury DE6 . . . . 128 C3
Whitmore ST5 . . . . 85 D5
Station Cres ST6 . . . . 42 D2
Station Ct Cannock WS11 . 226 F8
Newport TF10 . . . . 169 A1
Station Dr Armitage WS15 198 B4
Blakedown DY10 . . . . . . 281 C2
Four Ashes WV10 . . . . . . 224 C5
Keele ST5 . . . . 69 D8
Stationfields Park Homes
B79 . . . . 250 C5
Station Gr ST2 . . . . 43 A1
Station Ind Est ST1 . . . . . 57 F3
Station La
Rushton Spencer SK11 . . . . 8 B2
Walton-on-T DE12 . . . . . 184 D1
Station Rd
Albrighton WV7 . . . . 237 B5
Aldridge WS9 . . . . 256 A5
Alton ST10 . . . . 78 E1
Barlaston ST12 . . . . 88 D1
Barton-u-N DE13 . . . . . . 183 E4
Biddulph ST8 . . . . 16 C1
Biddulph ST8 . . . . 27 C8
Cannock WS12 . . . . 210 C6
Cheadle ST10 . . . . 76 D2
Cheddleton ST13 . . . . 45 D6
Codsall WV8 . . . . 238 E3
Coldmeece ST15 . . . . . . 118 C6
Cotes Heath ST21 . . . . . . 102 D3
Draycott in t C DE6 . . . . . 144 B8
Four Ashes WV10 . . . . . . 224 D5
Gnosall ST20 . . . . 171 D6
Great Wyrley WS6 . . . . . 226 F4
Halmer End ST7 . . . . 54 D7
Hammerwich WS7 . . . . . 229 E3
Hatton DE65 . . . . 146 D8
Haughton ST18 . . . . 172 E7
Keele ST5 . . . . 69 D8
Kidsgrove ST7 . . . . 25 F1
Lichfield WS13 . . . . 231 D7
Madeley CW3 . . . . 68 E5
Madeley Heath ST5 . . . . . 69 D8
Mow Cop ST7 . . . . 26 C8
Newcastle-u-L ST5 . . . . . . 55 B2
Newchapel ST7 . . . . 26 C2
Newport TF10 . . . . 168 F1
Norton Bridge ST15 . . . . 118 F1
Onneley CW3 . . . . 68 B2
Penkridge ST19 . . . . 192 E1
Rolleston on D DE13 . . . . 147 C4
Rugeley WS15 . . . . 178 F2
Scholar Green ST7 . . . . . . 26 A8
Shenstone WS14 . . . . . . 246 F6
Stafford ST16 . . . . 285 A3
Stoke-on-T,Endon ST9 . . . 43 F7
Stoke-on-T ST4 . . . . 72 B8
Stone ST15 . . . . 104 F1
Stowe-by-Chartley ST18 . 139 C4
The Bank ST7 . . . . 26 A8
Uttoxeter ST14 . . . . 126 D7
Walsall WS3 . . . . 244 A3
Wombourne WV5 . . . . . . 270 A8
Station St Burslem ST6 . . . 56 D8
Burton u T DE14 . . . . . . 166 D3
Cheslyn Hay WS6 . . . . . . 226 E3
Leek ST13 . . . . 30 D5
Station View ST3 . . . . 74 A1
Station Wlks ST7 . . . . 54 D7
Station Yd ST3 . . . . 201 B2
Staunton Rd WS3 . . . . . . 243 A3
Staveley Ct ST2 . . . . 58 A3
Staveley Pl ST5 . . . . 55 A1
Steadman Cres ST17 . . . . 174 E6
Stedman St ST1 . . . . 282 C4
Steele Ave ST6 . . . . 42 B2
Steele Ct ST13 . . . . 45 D5
Steelhouse La WV2 . . . . . 266 E8
Steel St ST4 . . . . 71 E8
Steenwood La WS15 . . . . 160 A2
Steeple Way ST4 . . . . 72 A5
Steere Ave B79 . . . . 250 C7
Stellar St ST6 . . . . 42 C1
Stenbury Ct WV10 . . . . . . 240 F4
Stephanie Gr B77 . . . . . . 251 A6
Stephen Ave ST10 . . . . . . 61 D2
Stephenson Cl B77 . . . . . 251 A2
Stephenson Dr WV6 . . . . 254 E5
Stephenson Way WS12 . . 210 B5
Stephens Rd DE14 . . . . . 185 B8
Stephens Way ST7 . . . . . . 39 F2
Stephens Wlk WS13 . . . . 214 A2
Stepping Stones
4 Leek ST13 . . . . 30 E5

Stepping Stones continued
Rugeley WS15 . . . . 178 D1
Step Row 12 ST13 . . . . . . 30 E5
Steps Gdns ST18 . . . . . . 172 E6
Sterling Pk B77 . . . . 261 E7
Sterndale Dr Longton ST4 . 73 B6
Newcastle-u-L ST5 . . . . . . 71 B3
Sterndale Moor SK17 . . . . . 5 E6
Sterrymere Gdns DY7 . . . 278 B4
Stevens Dr WS12 . . . . . . 210 D6
Stevens Gate 6 WV2 . . . 266 C8
Stevenson Dr ST17 . . . . . 174 C7
Stevenson Rd Bucknall ST2 58 A4
Doveridge DE6 . . . . 127 B8
Tamworth B79 . . . . 250 A6
Stevenson Wlk WS14 . . . 231 B6
Steventon Pl 18 ST6 . . . . 56 F8
Stewart Cl DE14 . . . . 185 A6
Stewart Ct ST2 . . . . 58 D1
Stewart Rd
Brownhills WS9 . . . . 245 A3
Kingswinford DY6 . . . . . . 275 D4
Stewart St Stoke-on-T ST4 . 72 D6
Wolverhampton WV2 . . . . 266 C8
Stewkins Ct 4 DY8 . . . . . 279 E8
Stewkins ST8 . . . . 279 E8
Stewponey The DY7 . . . . 278 E6
Stickley La DY3 . . . . 271 C4
Stile Cl Biddulph ST8 . . . . . 27 B5
Rugeley WS15 . . . . 196 F6
Stile Cop Rd WS15 . . . . . 196 D4
Stile House La ST13 . . . . . 31 E6
Stirling Bucknall ST2 . . . . . 73 F7
Castle Gresley DE11 . . . . 186 F1
Stirling Pl WS11 . . . . 226 B8
Stirling Rise 7 DE13 . . . . 166 D8
Stirling St 8 ST6 . . . . 57 A8
Stitchings The DE6 . . . . . . 65 C1
Stockbridge Cl WV6 . . . . 254 F2
Stockfield Rd ST3 . . . . 89 F7
Stockford La WS13 . . . . . 216 A3
Stockhay La WS7 . . . . . . 229 D5
Stockholm Gr ST1 . . . . 57 E7
Stocking-Gate La ST18 . . 153 F2
Stocking La ST18 . . . . . . 153 B5
Stockings La
Longdon WS15 . . . . 197 D2
Wheaton Aston ST19 . . . . 205 D5
Stock La ST14 . . . . 143 B8
Stocks La ST14 . . . . 125 C7
Stockton La ST17 . . . . . . 175 E7
Stockwell End WV6 . . . . . 255 D6
Stockwell Gr ST3 . . . . 73 D3
Stockwell Rd WV6 . . . . . 255 D5
Stockwell St ST13 . . . . 30 F6
Stockwood Rd ST5 . . . . . . 71 A3
Stoke Bsns Pk ST4 . . . . . . 72 B6
Stoke Old Rd ST4 . . . . 56 E1
Stoke-on-Trent Coll
(Burslem Campus)
Burslem ST6 . . . . 57 B8
Stoke-on-T ST6 . . . . 42 B1
Stoke-on-Trent Coll
(Cauldon Campus) ST4. . 57 B1
Stoke-on-Trent Sta ST4. . . 72 B8
Stoke Rd ST4 . . . . 57 B1
Stoke Recn Ctr ST4 . . . . . 72 B6
Stokesay Ave WV6 . . . . . 254 F3
Stokesay Dr ST10 . . . . 76 F3
Stokesay Gr ST6 . . . . 57 A7
Stokesay Rise DY1 . . . . . 271 E3
Stoke Ski Ctr ST6 . . . . 56 F5
Stoke's La WS11 . . . . 227 F7
Stoneacre Cl WV3 . . . . . . 255 A1
Stone Bank Rd ST7 . . . . . 41 E8
Stonebridge Rd ST19 . . . 223 D6
Stone Bsns Pk ST15 . . . . 120 B4
Stone Chair La ST7 . . . . . . 25 E7
Stone Cotts Clifton DE6 . . . 81 E8
Congleton CW12 . . . . 6 E2
Weston-Under-Lizard
TF11 . . . . 203 C4
Stonecrop Cl WS8 . . . . . . 244 D6
Stone Cross ST19 . . . . . . 192 E1
Stone Ent Ctr ST15 . . . . . 120 B4
Stonefield Ct 2 ST15 . . . 104 F2
Stonefield Sq ST15 . . . . . 105 A1
Stonehaven Gr ST1 . . . . . 282 C1
Stonehaven B77 . . . . 250 F5
Stonehill Wlk 5 B77 . . . . 261 F6
Stonehouse Cres ST9 . . . . 59 B3
Stonehouse Dr B74 . . . . . 257 C4
Stonehouse Rd
Rugeley WS15 . . . . 178 A1
Werrington ST9 . . . . 59 B3
Stone La DY7 . . . . 278 A4
Stonelea WS9 . . . . 256 B5
Stoneleigh Ct ST18 . . . . . 174 C5
Stoneleigh Gdns WV8 . . . 238 F4
Stoneleigh Rd ST6 . . . . . . 42 A5
Stoneleigh Way DY3 . . . . 271 D6
Stone Pine Cl WS12 . . . . 209 F8
Stonepine Cl ST17 . . . . . . 175 C7
Stonepine Pl DY3 . . . . . . 271 E6
Stonepit B77 . . . . 250 C1
Stone Rd Eccleshall ST21 . 134 B7
Stafford,Parkside ST16 . . 155 C7
Stafford ST16 . . . . 155 D5
Stoke-on-T,Hanford ST4. . . 71 E4
Stoke-on-T,Trent Vale ST4 . 71 F1
Tittensor ST4,ST12 . . . . . 88 A3
Trentham ST4 . . . . 87 F7
Uttoxeter ST14 . . . . 126 B8
Yarlet ST16,ST18 . . . . . . 136 B2

Stone Sta ST15 . . . . 104 F2
Stone St ST4 . . . . 72 A7
Stonewall Ind Est ST5 . . . 55 D2
Stonewall Pl ST5 . . . . 55 D2
Stonewell La SK17 . . . . . . 24 D5
Stonewood Cl ST4 . . . . . . 71 E3
Stoney Brook Leys WV5 . 269 E5
Stoney Croft WS11 . . . . . 209 F1
Stoneycroft ST2 . . . . 43 B2
Stoneydale Cl DE11 . . . . 186 F5
Stoney Dale ST10 . . . . . . 77 E4
Stoneydelph Prim Sch
   B77 . . . . 251 A1
Stoneyfields Ave ST2 . . . 43 B2
Stoneyfields ST8 . . . . 28 B8
Stoneyfields Cl WS11 . 209 F2
Stoneyfields Ct ST5 . . . 283 D4
Stoneyfold La SK17 . . . . . 22 D3
Stoneyford Terr ST14 . . . 126 C6
Stoney La Cauldon ST10 . . 63 D6
   Endon ST9 . . . . 43 E7
   Gratwich ST14 . . . . . . 124 B3
   Stakenbridge DY10 . . . 281 E3
   Stretton ST19 . . . . 206 D3
   Walsall WS3 . . . . 243 D3
   Wolverhampton WV4 . . 266 B5
Stoney Lea Rd WS11 . . . 209 F1
Stoneywell La WS13 . . . . 213 A6
Stonier Dr ST14 . . . . 141 C8
Stonnall Gate WS9 . . . . . 256 C8
Stonnall Rd WS9 . . . . . . 256 C8
Stonor St ST6 . . . . 57 A6
Stonydelph La B77 . . . . . 262 A7
Stony La ST10 . . . . 49 D1
Stormont Cl ST6 . . . . 42 C2
Stourbridge Coll (Longlands
   Ctr) DY8 . . . . 279 E5
Stourbridge Rd
   Hackman's Gate DY9 . . 281 F1
   Kidderminster DY10 . . . 280 D2
   Wombourne WV5,DY9 . . 270 B5
Stour Cl Burntwood WS7 . 229 D6
   Hilton DE65 . . . . 147 E8
Stour B77 . . . . 262 A5
Stourton Cres DY7 . . . . . 278 F7
Stourton Dr WV4 . . . . . . 265 C5
Stowecroft WS13 . . . . . . 214 C2
Stowe Hill Gdns WS13 . . 214 C1
Stowe La ST18 . . . . 139 C2
Stowell Gn ST4 . . . . 71 E8
Stowe Rd WS13 . . . . 231 C8
Stowe St WS13 . . . . 231 C8
Stowford Gr ST4 . . . . 88 B8
Stradbroke Dr ST3 . . . . . 73 A1
Straight Mile WV10 . . . . 225 B6
Straits Gn DY3 . . . . 271 B4
Straits Prim Sch DY3 . . . 271 B5
Straits Rd DY3 . . . . 271 B3
Straits The DY3 . . . . 271 A4
Strand Cl ST2 . . . . 58 C2
Strand Pas ST3 . . . . 284 B4
Strand The ST3 . . . . 284 B3
Strangman St ST13 . . . . . 30 E5
Stranraer Cl ST3 . . . . 74 C4
Stratford Ave ST5 . . . . . . 56 D3
Stratford Cl Dudley DY1 . 271 E2
   Forsbrook ST11 . . . . . . 91 A8
   Stoke-on-T ST6 . . . . . . 42 F1
Stratford Dr WS9 . . . . . . 256 C8
Stratford Way WS11 . . . 209 F5
Stratheden Rd ST6 . . . . . 42 B2
Strathfield Wlk WV3,
   WV4 . . . . 265 C6
Strathmore Cres WV5 . . 265 A1
Strathmore Pl 6 WS11 . 209 F2
Strawberry La WS6 . . . . 242 E8
Strawmoor La WV8 . . . . 238 C3
Stream Mdw WS4 . . . . . 244 D1
Stream Pk DY6 . . . . 275 E4
Stream Rd DY6,DY8 . . . 275 D4
Streamside Cl ST19 . . . . 207 F8
Streather Rd B75 . . . . . . 258 C2
Streetly Cres B74 . . . . . . 257 D3
Streetly Dr B74 . . . . 257 D3
Streetly La B74 . . . . 257 D3
Streetly Wood B74 . . . . . 257 A2
Streets Corner Gdns
   WS9 . . . . 245 A4
Streets La WS6 . . . . 226 F1
Street The ST20 . . . . 150 F5
Streetway Rd WS14 . . . . 247 B7
Stretton Ave
   Newport TF10 . . . . 168 C2
   Stafford ST16 . . . . 155 B6
Stretton Brook Sch
   DE13 . . . . 147 C1
Stretton Gdns WV8 . . . . 238 F4
Stretton Rd Lapley ST19 . 206 A6
   Newcastle-u-L ST5 . . . . 54 F2
   Willenhall WV12 . . . . . 242 D1
Stretton St B77 . . . . 250 E3
Strine Way TF10 . . . . . . 168 F4
Stringer Cl B75 . . . . 258 A4
Stringer Ct 17 ST6 . . . . . 41 D3
Stringers Hill WS12 . . . . 210 D7
Stringer's La DE13 . . . . . 182 D2
Stringer's St 2 ST8 . . . . 27 C8
Strode Ho B79 . . . . 250 A4
Strode Rd WV2 . . . . 266 C6
Stroma Cl 3 ST6 . . . . . . 56 F7
Stross Ave ST6 . . . . 41 F5
Stroud Cl ST3 . . . . 90 B7
Stuart Ave
   Draycott in t M ST11 . . 91 C6

Stuart Ave continued
   Stoke-on-T ST4 . . . . . . 88 A7
Stuart Cl N ST15 . . . . . . 119 F6
Stuart Cl ST15 . . . . 119 F5
Stuart Gr ST5 . . . . 56 C4
Stuart Rd ST1 . . . . 57 E2
Stuart Way TF9 . . . . 97 B2
Stubbers Green Rd WS9 . 256 A7
Stubbs Dr ST15 . . . . 120 D7
Stubbsfield Rd ST5 . . . . 283 C1
Stubbs' Gate ST5 . . . . . 283 C2
Stubbs La Hanley ST1 . . 282 C2
   Stanton DE6 . . . . 65 C2
Stubbs Rd WV3 . . . . 266 A6
Stubbs St ST6 . . . . 56 E8
Stubbs' St ST5 . . . . 283 C2
Stubby La DE6 . . . . 144 B6
Stubwood Hollow ST14 . . 95 D5
Stubwood La ST14 . . . . . 95 D4
Stud Farm Cotts B78 . . . 249 E2
Studley Gate DY8 . . . . . 279 D5
Studley Rd WV3 . . . . . . 265 C8
Sturgeon's Hill WS14 . . . 231 C7
Sturgess St ST4 . . . . 72 A6
Stychbrook Gdns WS13 . 214 B2
Stychfields ST17 . . . . . . 285 C1
Suckling Green La WV8 . 238 F2
Sudbourne Cl ST6 . . . . . 41 E8
Sudbury Hall & Mus of
   Childhood* DE6 . . . . . 128 D5
Sudbury Pk DE6 . . . . . . 128 D7
Sudbury Pl ST5 . . . . 71 B2
Sudbury Prim Sch DE6 . 128 E4
Sudbury Rd DE13 . . . . . 182 A4
Sudeley Gdns DY1 . . . . . 271 D2
Sudeley B77 . . . . 261 C8
Sudlow St ST6 . . . . 57 B7
Suffolk Cl ST5 . . . . 71 D4
Suffolk Gr WS9 . . . . 256 B8
Suffolk Rd
   Burton u T DE15 . . . . . 185 D7
   Stoke-on-T ST3 . . . . . . 89 C8
Suffolk Way B78 . . . . . . 250 A1
Sugar Loaf La DY10 . . . . 281 B7
Sugar St SK11 . . . . 8 C2
Sugnall Bsns Ctr ST21 . . 116 D2
Sullivan Way WS13 . . . . 214 C2
Sullivan Wlk WS13 . . . . . 214 C2
Summerbank Prim Sch
   ST6 . . . . 41 D4
Summercourt Dr DY6 . . 275 C8
Summercourt Sq DY6 . . 275 C5
Summer Dr DY3 . . . . 271 C3
Summerfield Arc 6
   ST15 . . . . 120 A8
Summerfield Ave DY6 . . 275 C7
Summerfield Cl B77 . . . . 250 D4
Summerfield Dr ST14 . . 126 A8
Summerfield ST7 . . . . . . 26 B1
Summerfield Rd
   Burntwood WS7 . . . . . 229 A5
   Tamworth B77 . . . . . . 250 D4
Summerfields ST15 . . . . 118 E6
Summergate DY3 . . . . . 271 C4
Summer Gr WS13 . . . . . 214 D2
Summerhill Dr ST5 . . . . . 40 D1
Summerhill Gdns TF9 . . 112 C8
Summer Hill WS6 . . . . . 275 C6
Summerhill La ST18 . . . . 135 E5
Summerhill Sch The
   DY6 . . . . 275 B6
Summerhill WS14 . . . . . 245 E8
Summerhouse Gr TF10 . 168 F4
Summerhouse La WS13 . 212 E3
Summer La Dudley DY3 . 271 C3
   Walsall WS4 . . . . 244 C2
Summer Row ST3 . . . . . 284 C2
Summerside Ave WS12 . 211 C4
Summer St
   Kingswinford DY6 . . . . 275 D6
   Stoke-on-T ST4 . . . . . . 72 A1
   Stourbridge DY8 . . . . . 279 F5
Summerville Rd ST4 . . . . 71 E3
Summit Pl DY3 . . . . 271 B2
Sunbeam Dr WS6 . . . . . 226 F3
Sunbeam St WV2 . . . . . 266 C7
Sunbeam B77 . . . . 250 E3
Sunbury Ave WS14 . . . . 231 E7
Sunbury Ct ST4 . . . . 88 C6
Sundorne Pl ST2 . . . . . . 58 B2
Sundour Cres WV11 . . . 241 B1
Sundown Dr ST17 . . . . . 174 B7
Sundridge Wlk WV4 . . . 265 C6
Sunfield Rd WS11 . . . . . 209 B1
Suningdale Cl DE13 . . . . 147 C1
Sunley Dr WS12 . . . . . . 210 D7
Sunningdale Ave WV6 . . 254 D5
Sunningdale Cl
   Stoke-on-T ST6 . . . . . . 42 B3
   Stourbridge DY8 . . . . . 279 F2
Sunningdale Dr ST16 . . . 156 C3
Sunningdale Gr ST5 . . . . 55 D8
Sunningdale Rd DY3 . . . 266 B1
Sunningdale Stone ST15 . 120 A7
   Tamworth B77 . . . . . . 251 C5
Sunningdale View ST3 . . 89 E3
Sunningdale Way WS3 . . 243 A3
Sunny Bank WS6 . . . . . . 56 E6
Sunnybank Cl WS9 . . . . 256 E2
Sunnybank Ct ST6 . . . . . 42 A3
Sunnybank Cvn Pk ST19 . 205 E7
Sunny Bank DE6 . . . . . . 81 C7
Sunnybank Rd DY3 . . . . 271 F5
Sunnycroft Ave ST3 . . . . 284 A1
Sunnyfield Oval ST2 . . . 43 C1
Sunny Gdns TF10 . . . . . 168 F5

Sunny Hill Cl WV5 . . . . . 270 B6
Sunnyhills Rd ST13 . . . . 30 D3
Sunny Hollow ST5 . . . . . 56 C3
Sunnymead Rd 1 WS7 . 229 A8
Sunnymede Rd 1 DY6 . 275 F4
Sunnyside Ave ST6 . . . . 41 F4
Sunnyside WS9 . . . . 245 A2
Sunnyside Ct DE11 . . . . 186 F7
Sunny Side ST10 . . . . . . 61 D3
Sunnyside Rd ST14 . . . . 111 B1
Sunnyside DE11 . . . . . . 186 E7
Sunridge Ave WS5 . . . . . 270 A7
Sunridge Cl ST2 . . . . . . 43 B2
Sunrise Hill WS12 . . . . . 210 B6
Sunset Cl WV9 . . . . 224 B3
   Great Wyrley WS6 . . . . 226 F3
   Tamworth B79 . . . . . . 250 A5
Sunset Pl WV4 . . . . 266 F3
Sun St Cheadle ST10 . . . 76 E3
   Hanley ST1 . . . . 282 A2
Sunwell Gdns ST10 . . . . 76 E3
Surrey Cl Cannock WS11 . 226 E8
   Rugeley WS15 . . . . . . 196 D6
Surrey Dr
   Kingswinford DY6 . . . . 275 F3
   Tamworth B78 . . . . . . 250 A1
   Wolverhampton WV3 . . 255 E1
Surrey Ho 2 DY8 . . . . . 279 F8
Surrey Rd Kidsgrove ST7 . 26 A2
   Stafford ST17 . . . . 174 C8
Surrey Wlk WS9 . . . . . . 245 A1
Surtees Gr ST4 . . . . 73 B5
Sussex Ave WS9 . . . . . . 256 A8
Sussex Dr Cannock WS12 . 210 B5
   Kidsgrove ST7 . . . . 25 F2
   Wolverhampton WV3 . . 255 E1
Sussex Pl ST3 . . . . 73 D1
Sussex Rd DE15 . . . . . . 185 E6

Sutherland Ave
   Longton ST3 . . . . 284 B1
   Wolverhampton WV2 . . 266 F8
Sutherland Cres ST11 . . 90 E6
Sutherland Dr
   Newcastle-u-L ST5 . . . . 70 F5
   Wombourne WV5 . . . . 265 A1
Sutherland Gr WV6 . . . . 254 F4
Sutherland Prim Sch ST3 . 72 F1
Sutherland Rd
   Cheslyn Hay WS6 . . . . 226 E2
   Longsdon ST9 . . . . 30 A1
   Longton ST3 . . . . 284 C3
   Stone ST15 . . . . 120 C7
   Tittensor ST12 . . . . . . 88 A1
   Wolverhampton WV4 . . 266 B5
Sutherland St ST4 . . . . . 72 C6
Sutton Ave B78 . . . . 250 A2
Sutton Cl WS15 . . . . 196 F6
Sutton Ct Forton TF10 . . 169 C8
   Wolverhampton WV4 . . 266 E2
Sutton Dr Stafford ST16 . 155 A4
   Stoke-on-T ST4 . . . . . . 71 F4
   Stoke-on-T ST4 . . . . . . 71 F5
Sutton La TF9 . . . . 112 C4
Sutton Pl ST6 . . . . 42 B5
Sutton Rd Aldridge WS9 . 256 A1
   Mile Oak B78 . . . . 260 A7
   Tamworth B78 . . . . . . 249 C1
Sutton St
   Newcastle-u-L ST5 . . . . 55 E6
   Stourbridge DY8 . . . . . 275 F1
Sutton Way TF9 . . . . . . 112 B7
Swadlincote La DE11 . . 186 E2
Swaffham Way ST2 . . . . 58 D2
Swaffield Pk WS11 . . . . 210 B3
Swainsfield Rd DE13 . . . 182 A2
Swainsley Cl 3 ST6 . . . . 57 A7
Swaledale Ave CW12 . . . 6 A5
Swallow Cl
   1 Kidsgrove ST7 . . . . . 26 B2
   Huntington WS12 . . . . 209 C7
   Meir ST3 . . . . 90 A7
   Rugeley WS15 . . . . . . 178 D2
   Uttoxeter ST14 . . . . . . 126 B6
Swallow Croft Leek ST13 . 30 C3
   Lichfield WS13 . . . . . . 214 A1
Swallow Ct Alrewas DE13 . 201 A2
   Wolverhampton WV10 . 240 B3
Swallowdale
   5 Stafford ST17 . . . . . 175 D6
   Brownhills WS9 . . . . . 245 A4
   Wolverhampton WV6 . . 254 F2
Swallowfall Ave DY8 . . . 279 C4
Swallowfields Dr WS12 . 210 B3
Swallowfields Rd DY3 . . 266 C2
Swallowfield B79 . . . . . 249 E6
Swallowmore View ST7 . 40 C8
Swallow Rd 4 ST7 . . . . . 26 F1
Swallows Cl ST3 . . . . . . 244 A5
Swallowsreach WS13 . . 213 F1
Swallow Wlk ST8 . . . . . . 27 D7
Swanage Cl ST3 . . . . . . 90 B7
Swan Bank Talke ST7 . . . 40 D7
   Wolverhampton WV4 . . 265 F4
Swan Cl Blakedown DY10 . 281 B3
   Cheslyn Hay WS6 . . . . 226 D2
   Longdon WS15 . . . . . . 197 F2
   Rugeley WS15 . . . . . . 197 A5
   Stafford ST16 . . . . 155 C2
   Talke ST7 . . . . 40 D8
Swan Corner Sh Ctr
   WS7 . . . . 229 C6
Swancote Dr WV4 . . . . . 265 C6
Swan Cotts WS14 . . . . . 232 E6
Swan Ct Burton u T DE14 . 166 B3
   Church Eaton ST20 . . . 190 B8
Swan Dr WS8 . . . . 244 E7
Swan Farm La CW3 . . . . 67 B1
Swanfield Rd DY8 . . . . . 275 F1

Swanfields WS7 . . . . . . 229 C6
Swan Gr ST6 . . . . 41 D1
Swanholme Way ST5 . . . 85 C4
Swan La WS15 . . . . 161 A6
Swanland Gr ST3 . . . . . . 73 D4
Swan La Penkridge ST18 . 192 F6
   Shareshill WV10 . . . . . 225 C1
   Stoke-on-T ST5 . . . . . . 71 E3
   Stourbridge DY8 . . . . . 275 F2
Swanmere TF10 . . . . . . 168 F5
Swan Mews WS13 . . . . . 231 A8
Swanmore Cl WV3 . . . . . 265 E8
Swanmote B79 . . . . 249 F5
Swannington St DE13 . . 166 B6
Swan Pas ST11 . . . . 90 F7
Swan Pk B77 . . . . 250 C3
Swan Pool Gr WS4 . . . . 244 D1
Swan Rd
   Draycott in t C DE6 . . . 144 D6
   Lichfield WS13 . . . . . . 231 A7
   Whittington WS14 . . . . 232 E6
Swansmoor Dr ST18 . . . 139 C1
Swan Sq ST6 . . . . 56 F8
Swan St Stoke-on-T ST4 . 72 B8
   Stourbridge DY8 . . . . . 279 E5
Swanton Pl ST4 . . . . 87 F7
Swan Wlk DE14 . . . . . . 166 D2
Swarbourn Cl DE13 . . . . 182 A2
Swaythling Gr ST2 . . . . . 58 D1
Sweetbriar Way
   Cannock WS12 . . . . . . 210 D2
   Stafford ST17 . . . . 175 C6
Sweetbrier Dr 4 DY8 . . 275 E1
Sweetman St WV6 . . . . . 255 F4
Sweetplace La ST20 . . . 189 E2
Sweetpool La DY8 . . . . . 281 F5
Swift Cl Kidsgrove ST7 . . 26 B2
   Uttoxeter ST14 . . . . . . 126 B6
Swift Dr ST8 . . . . 27 E8
Swift Pl ST3 . . . . 73 F5
Swift B77 . . . . 250 E3
Swinburne Cl
   Stafford ST17 . . . . 174 C8
   Stoke-on-T ST3 . . . . . . 72 F2
Swindale B77 . . . . 262 B7
Swindon Rd DY6 . . . . . . 275 B6
Swinfen Broun Rd WS13 . 231 A8
Swinford Leys WV5 . . . . 269 D5
Swin Forge Way DY3 . . . 269 C2
Swingle Hill Rd ST3 . . . . 72 F3
Swinscoe Hill DE6 . . . . . 66 B2
Swinson Cl ST14 . . . . . . 96 A3
Swiss Dr DY8 . . . . 275 F2
Swiss Lodge Dr B78 . . . 260 F8
Swithin Cl ST4 . . . . 73 B6
Swynnerton Dr WV11 . . 241 F4
Sycamore Cl Biddulph ST8 . 16 E2
   Burton u T DE15 . . . . . 185 E5
   Meir Heath ST3 . . . . . . 90 A5
   Stourbridge DY8 . . . . . 279 D2
   Talke ST7 . . . . 40 E8
   Uttoxeter ST14 . . . . . . 125 F8
Sycamore Cres WS15 . . 197 A6
Sycamore Dr Hixon ST18 . 158 C8
   Wolverhampton WV3 . . 255 D1
Sycamore Gdns ST6 . . . 56 D8
Sycamore Gn
   Cannock WS11 . . . . . . 209 E6
   Dudley DY1 . . . . 271 E6
Sycamore Green Prim Sch
   DY1 . . . . 271 F5
Sycamore Gr
   Newcastle-u-L ST5 . . . . 56 D3
   Stoke-on-T ST3 . . . . . . 72 C6
Sycamore Hill WS15 . . . 211 F5
Sycamore La ST17 . . . . . 174 B8
Sycamore Pl WS7 . . . . . 228 F7
Sycamore Rd
   Burntwood WS7 . . . . . 228 F5
   Burton u T DE15 . . . . . 185 F6
   Cannock WS12 . . . . . . 210 F4
   Kingswinford DY6 . . . . 275 E6
   Mayfield DE6 . . . . 81 C7
   Stone ST15 . . . . 120 B8
Sycamores The
   Hagley DY9 . . . . 281 F5
   Lichfield WS13 . . . . . . 231 B5
   Sutton Coldfield B74 . . 257 F2
Sycamore B77 . . . . 261 E7
Sycamore Way
   Huntington WS12 . . . . 209 D8
   Market Drayton TF9 . . . 97 B2
Sydenham Pl ST2 . . . . . 73 D8
Sydnall La TF9 . . . . 112 F1
Sydney St
   Burton u T DE14 . . . . . 166 D6
   Newcastle-u-L ST5 . . . . 56 D2
Syerscote La
   Clifton Campville B79 . 218 B1
   Wigginton B79 . . . . . . 234 C2
Sykesmoor B77 . . . . . . 262 B7
Sylvan Gr ST4 . . . . 71 B4
Sylvan Way ST17 . . . . . . 175 C5
Sylvester St ST6 . . . . . . 57 A8
Sytch La WV5 . . . . 270 A5
Sytch Rd ST6 . . . . 43 B7

T

Tack Farm Rd DY8 . . . . . 275 D1
Tadgedale Ave TF9 . . . . 99 D5
Tagg La DE45 . . . . 14 E8
Tag La Cheswardine TF9 . 113 F3
   Chipnall TF9 . . . . 114 A3
Talaton Cl WV9 . . . . 240 A2
Talbot Ave B74 . . . . 257 B3
Talbot Fd TF10 . . . . 168 D1

Talbot Fst Sch ST14 . . . 141 C8
Talbot Rd Rugeley WS15 . 196 F6
   Stafford ST17 . . . . 285 B1
   Wolverhampton WV2 . . 266 C6
Talbotshill La DY10 . . . . 280 C4
Talbot St 5 Leek ST13 . . 30 C5
   Hanley ST1 . . . . 282 C1
   Rugeley WS15 . . . . . . 196 F8
Talbot B77 . . . . 250 E5
Talbot Way TF9 . . . . 97 C2
Talke Rd
   Newcastle-u-L,Red Street
     ST7 . . . . 40 D4
   Newcastle-u-L ST5 . . . . 55 F8
Talland Ave B77 . . . . . . 250 E5
Tall Ash Ave CW12 . . . . 6 A4
Tallis Gr ST1 . . . . 57 F5
Tallpines ST17 . . . . 175 C5
Tall Trees Cl B74 . . . . . . 257 D4
Tally Cl ST2 . . . . 73 D7
Talsarn Gr ST4 . . . . 88 C6
Tamar Gr Cannock WS8 . 228 C2
Tamar Dr DY3 . . . . 271 C4
Tamar Gr Cheadle ST10 . 76 E1
   Perton WV6 . . . . 254 E4
   Stafford ST17 . . . . 174 B8
Tamar Rd Kidsgrove ST7 . 26 B2
   Tamworth B77 . . . . . . 262 A5
Tame Ave WS7 . . . . 229 D6
Tame Cl ST8 . . . . 16 D1
Tame Ct Fazeley B78 . . . 261 B8
   Tamworth B79 . . . . . . 250 A5
Tamedrive B78,B79 . . . . 250 A4
Tame Dr WS3 . . . . 244 A1
Tame Gr WS11 . . . . 226 D8
Tame St ST7 . . . . 250 C3
Tame Valley Bsns Pk
   B77 . . . . 261 E6
Tame Valley Ind Est B77 . 261 E6
Tame Wlk ST3 . . . . 74 A4
Tamworth Bsns Ctr B77 . 251 B3
Tamworth Bsns Pk B77 . 251 B3
Tamworth Castle Mus*
   B79 . . . . 250 B4
Tamworth Castle* B79 . 250 B4
Tamworth Cl WS8 . . . . . 228 C2
Tamworth & Lichfield Coll
   (Tamworth Campus)
   B79 . . . . 250 B6
Tamworth Rd (Amington)
   B77 . . . . 250 F5
Tamworth Rd B78 . . . . . 261 C2
Tamworth Rd (Dosthill)
   B77 . . . . 261 C6
Tamworth Rd Elford B79 . 233 E8
   Lichfield WS14 . . . . . . 231 E1
   Polesworth B78 . . . . . 251 E1
   Sutton Coldfield B75 . . 259 A2
   Tamworth,Mount Pleasant
     B77 . . . . 250 C1
   Tamworth,Two Gates B77 . 261 D8
   Whittington WS14 . . . . 232 B3
   Wood End CV9 . . . . . . 262 C1
Tamworth Sta B79 . . . . . 250 C5
Tamworth St WS13 . . . . 231 B8
Tan Bank TF10 . . . . 168 F3
Tanfield Cl WV6 . . . . . . 255 B3
Tanglewood Gr DY3 . . . 266 C2
Tangmere Cl WV6 . . . . . 254 E5
Tanhill B77 . . . . 262 B7
Tanners Rd ST2 . . . . . . 58 B7
Tannery Cl WS15 . . . . . . 178 F1
Tansey Cl ST2 . . . . 58 A3
Tansey Green Rd DY6 . . 271 A1
Tansley View WV2 . . . . . 266 D7
Tansy Sutton Coldfield B74 . 257 F4
   Tamworth B77 . . . . . . 250 C3
Tanyard WS13 . . . . 231 C8
Tape St ST10 . . . . 76 D3
Taplin Cl ST16 . . . . 155 D7
Taplow Pl WS11 . . . . . . 209 F4
Tapton Cl WS3 . . . . 243 C3
Tara Gr ST2 . . . . 43 A3
Targate Ct WS15 . . . . . . 198 A5
Target Cl ST7 . . . . 40 E6
Tarleton Rd ST1 . . . . . . 57 E4
Tarporley Gr ST4 . . . . . . 71 E5
Tarquin Cl DE13 . . . . . . 147 E2
Tarragona Dr ST17 . . . . 175 A8
Tarragon Dr ST3 . . . . . . 90 A6
Tarrant B77 . . . . 261 F8
Tarvin Gr ST6 . . . . 41 F6
Tasman Dr ST18 . . . . . . 156 C5
Tasman Gr WV6 . . . . . . 254 E5
Tasman Sq ST1 . . . . 57 E5
Tatenhill Comm DE13 . . 164 E1
Tatenhill La
   Burton u T DE14 . . . . . 184 D7
   Rangemore DE13 . . . . 164 C2
   Tatenhill DE13 . . . . . . 184 A8
Tatlowfold La ST10 . . . . 48 F4
Tatton Cl ST13 . . . . 30 B5
Tatton St ST3 . . . . 284 C2
Taunton Ave WV10 . . . . 240 D4
Taunton Pl ST5 . . . . 55 F7
Taunton Way ST2 . . . . . 58 D2
Taurus Gr ST6 . . . . 41 F6
Taverners Cl WV12 . . . . 242 C1
Taverners Dr ST15 . . . . . 120 D6
Tavistock Ave ST17 . . . . 156 D1
Tavistock Cl B79 . . . . . . 250 C7
Tavistock Cres ST4 . . . . 71 A5
Tavistock Pl ST4 . . . . . . 56 E1
Tawney Cl ST7 . . . . 26 B2
Tawny Cres ST3 . . . . . . 90 A6
Tay Cl Biddulph ST8 . . . 16 E1
   Cheadle ST10 . . . . 76 E5
   Longton ST3 . . . . 284 C5

Taylor Ave ST5 ... 56 C4
Taylor Rd Bucknall ST2 ... 58 B6
Wolverhampton WV4 ... 266 F5
Taylors La ST14 ... 95 D4
Taylor's La WS15 ... 178 E1
Taylor St
Newcastle-u-L ST5 ... 56 C4
Stoke-on-T ST6 ... 41 C7
Taylor Wlk ST17 ... 174 C7
Taynton Cl ST6 ... 42 B8
Teal Cl ST5 ... 85 C5
Teal View ST6 ... 42 D2
Tean Cl Burntwood WS7 .. 229 D6
Burton u T DE15 ... 167 A1
Teanhurst Cl ST10 ... 92 F2
Teanhurst Rd ST10 ... 92 F2
Tean Rd ST10 ... 76 D1
Teasel Gr WV10 ... 241 B7
Tebworth Cl WV9 ... 239 F2
Tedder Rd ST16 ... 156 B5
Teddesley Ct WS11 ... 209 E3
Teddesley Rd
Acton Trussell ST19 ... 193 B6
Penkridge ST19 ... 192 F2
Stafford ST17 ... 175 D1
Teddesley Way WS12 ... 209 C6
Teign B77 ... 262 A5
Telegraph St ST17 ... 285 B1
Telford Ave
Albrighton WV7 ... 237 B6
Great Wyrley WS6 ... 226 F3
Telford Cl
Burntwood WS7 ... 229 C8
Congleton CW12 ... 6 B2
Stone ST15 ... 120 C6
Talke ST7 ... 40 E8
Telford Dr ST16 ... 155 F8
Telford Gdns
Brewood ST19 ... 223 C7
Wolverhampton WV3 ... 265 D7
Telford Gr WS12 ... 210 B7
Telford La ST20 ... 171 C5
Telford Rd B79 ... 249 F8
Telford Way ST6 ... 42 A4
Tellwright Gr ST5 ... 56 B7
Tellwright St ST6 ... 42 A1
Telmah Cl DE13 ... 147 D1
Teme Rd DY8 ... 279 F3
Temperance Pl ST6 ... 41 D7
Tempest St B79 ... 250 A5
Templar Cres ST5 ... 56 B6
Templars Way ST19 ... 207 F8
Templar Terr ST5 ... 56 B6
Temple Cl DE14 ... 166 E7
Temple St Dudley DY3 ... 271 D3
Stoke-on-T ST4 ... 72 D6
Templeton Ave ST2 ... 73 C8
Tenacre La DY3 ... 271 E6
Tenbury Cl WS9 ... 256 C8
Tenbury Ct WV4 ... 265 D5
Tenbury Gdns WV4 ... 265 D5
Tenbury Gn ST2 ... 58 C1
Ten Butts Cres ST17 ... 174 F5
Tenby Dr ST16 ... 155 F6
Tenby Gr ST5 ... 55 F7
Tenford La ST10 ... 92 E5
Tennant Pl ST5 ... 56 B7
Tennscore Ave WS6 ... 226 E3
Tennyson Ave
Burntwood WS7 ... 212 A1
Kidsgrove ST7 ... 41 A8
Sutton Coldfield B74 ... 257 F6
Tamworth B79 ... 250 A6
Tennyson Cl Cheadle ST10 . 76 B2
Market Drayton TF9 ... 112 A7
Tennyson Gdns ST3 ... 72 F2
Tennyson Rd
Burton u T DE14 ... 166 D7
Dudley DY3 ... 271 A4
Stafford ST17 ... 174 C8
Wolverhampton WV10 ... 241 A1
Tenterbanks ST16 ... 285 A3
Tercel Gr ST3 ... 90 A7
Terence Wlk ST8 ... 27 B2
Tern Ave ST7 ... 26 C2
Tern Cl Biddulph ST8 ... 27 E8
Wolverhampton WV4 ... 266 D3
Tern Gr TF9 ... 99 E5
Tern Ridge TF9 ... 97 D1
Tern View TF9 ... 112 B7
Terrace The Cheadle ST10 . 76 D3
Wolverhampton WV3 ... 255 C1
Terrington Dr ST5 ... 71 B2
Terry Cl Lichfield WS13 ... 213 F2
Meir ST3 ... 74 B3
Terson Way ST3 ... 73 F4
Tettenhall Arc WV6 ... 255 D5
Tettenhall Coll WV6 ... 255 D4
Tettenhall Rd WV1,WV3,
WV6 ... 255 F4
Tettenhall Wood Sch
WV6 ... 255 B3
Teveray Dr ST19 ... 207 F7
Teviot Gdns WV8 ... 239 A5
Tewe Pl WS13 ... 231 A6
Tewkesbury Gr ST2 ... 58 A4
Tewkesbury Rd WS3 ... 242 E2
Tewnals La WS13 ... 213 E5
Tewson Gn ST6 ... 57 C7
Thackeray Dr Longton ST3 . 73 A2
Tamworth B79 ... 250 A7
Thackeray Wlk ST17 ... 174 C7
Thames Dr Biddulph ST8 ... 27 E8
Cheadle ST10 ... 76 E1
Thames Ho DY3 ... 271 D3
Thames Rd
Newcastle-u-L ST5 ... 71 B4
Walsall WS3 ... 243 E1
Thames Way ST17 ... 174 B8
Thanet Cl DY6 ... 275 C7
Thanet Gr ST3 ... 284 A3
Thatcham Gn ST3 ... 88 F7
Thatcher Gr ST8 ... 27 B8
Thatchers Ct WV5 ... 264 C1
Thatchmoor La DE13 ... 182 C7
Thelma Ave ST6 ... 43 B7
Theodore Rd ST2 ... 58 B3
Theresa Cl ST4 ... 72 A2
Third Ave Branston DE14 . 165 F1
Brownhills WS8 ... 229 A1
Bucknall ST2 ... 58 D4
Kidsgrove ST7 ... 25 F1
Kingswinford DY6 ... 275 F8
Thirlmere Cl
Cannock WS11 ... 209 E1
Wolverhampton WV6 ... 255 D8
Thirlmere Dr WV11 ... 242 A2
Thirlmere Gr Longton ST3 . 73 E3
Perton WV6 ... 254 F4
Thirlmere Pl ST5 ... 71 B5
Thirlmere Rd WV6 ... 255 D8
Thirlmere Way ST17 ... 174 E7
Thirsk Pl ST5 ... 55 A2
Thistleberry Ave ST5 ... 70 F7
Thistle Cl Dudley DY3 ... 271 F6
Rugeley WS15 ... 178 C2
Thistledown Ave WS7 ... 229 A6
Thistle Down Cl B74 ... 257 A2
Thistledown Dr
3 Cannock WS12 ... 210 D1
Featherstone WV10 ... 241 A7
Thistledown Wlk DY3 ... 266 C1
Thistles The ST5 ... 70 F7
Thistley Hough High Sch
ST4 ... 71 E6
Thistley Hough ST4 ... 71 F6
Thistley Nook WS13 ... 214 A1
Thomas Alleyne's High Sch
ST14 ... 126 C8
Thomas Ave
Newcastle-u-L ST5 ... 56 A4
Stafford ST16 ... 155 B3
Stone ST15 ... 120 C6
Thomas Barnes Prim Sch
B78 ... 249 B7
Thomas Greenway
WS13 ... 214 A2
Thomas Hardy Ct B79 ... 250 A7
Thomas Ho WS3 ... 243 D3
Thomas Russell Inf Sch
DE13 ... 183 E1
Thomas Russell Jun Sch
DE13 ... 183 E1
Thomas St Biddulph ST8 ... 16 D1
Leek ST13 ... 30 D6
Packmoor ST7 ... 26 F1
Talke ST7 ... 40 D8
Tamworth B77 ... 250 D4
Wolverhampton WV2 ... 266 C8
Thompson Ave WV2 ... 266 E6
Thompson Cl ST17 ... 174 C7
Thompson Rd WS15 ... 197 B6
Thompstone Ave ST5 ... 55 F3
Thor Cl WS11 ... 210 A5
Thoresby Croft DY1 ... 271 F3
Thoresby B79 ... 249 E6
Thorley Dr ST10 ... 76 F2
Thorley's Hill WS15 ... 212 C6
Thornbridge Gr WS9 ... 244 F3
Thornburrow Dr ST4 ... 71 E8
Thornbury Ct WV6 ... 255 A3
Thornby Ave B77 ... 261 E8
Thorncliffe View ST13 ... 31 B8
Thorncliff Gr ST1 ... 57 F5
Thorncliff Rd ST13 ... 31 C7
Thorn Cl WS15 ... 197 A7
Thorndyke St ST1 ... 282 A1
Thorne Pl ST3 ... 74 B3
Thornescroft Gdns DE14 185 B8
Thornes Croft WS9 ... 245 E4
Thornewill Dr DE13 ... 147 F1
Thorneycroft Ave ST6 ... 42 B2
Thorneyfields La
Stafford ST17 ... 174 A8
Stafford ST17 ... 174 B7
Thorney Lanes
Gorsty Hill DE13 ... 143 B2
Newborough DE13 ... 162 D6
Thorney Rd B74 ... 256 F1
Thornfield Ave ST13 ... 31 B5
Thornfield Cres WS7 ... 229 A8
Thornfield Croft DY3 ... 271 E7
Thornham Cl ST5 ... 71 B2
Thornham Gn ST2 ... 58 C1
Thornhill Cl DE13 ... 183 C2
Thornhill Dr CW3 ... 68 E7
Thornhill Rd Bucknall ST2 . 73 E8
Cannock WS12 ... 209 F7
Leek ST13 ... 30 C4
Little Aston B74 ... 257 B1
Thornleigh DY3 ... 271 D5
Thornley Cl WV11 ... 241 F1
Thornley Croft WS6 ... 226 D1
Thornley Rd
Stoke-on-T ST6 ... 42 A3
Wolverhampton WV11 ... 241 F1
Thornley St DE14 ... 166 D5
Thornton Rd ST4 ... 72 C8
Thornton Way B77 ... 261 C8
Thorn Tree La DE11 ... 186 F8
Thornyedge Rd
Bagnall ST9 ... 44 A1
Bagnall,Tompkin ST9 ... 44 C1
Thornyhurst La WS14 ... 246 A6
Thorny Rd ST15 ... 118 B6
Thorpe Ave WS7 ... 228 D8
Thorpe Cl
Burntwood WS7 ... 228 D8
Burton u T DE15 ... 167 C2
Thorpe Dr WS13 ... 215 E8
Thorpe Gn ST3 ... 88 F7
Thorpe Rise ST10 ... 76 E6
Thorpe St WS7 ... 228 D8
Thorswood La DE6 ... 65 B2
Three Mile La ST5 ... 69 F4
Three Spires Sh Ctr
WS13 ... 231 B7
Three Tuns La WV10 ... 240 D1
Three Tuns Par WV10 ... 240 C2
Thrift Rd DE14 ... 185 B8
Thurlstone Dr WV4 ... 265 F4
Thurlstone Rd WS3 ... 243 B3
Thurlwood Dr ST6 ... 42 F2
Thurne B77 ... 261 F8
Thursfield Ave ST7 ... 26 C3
Thursfield Pl ST6 ... 42 D4
Thursfield Prim Sch ST7 . 26 E3
Thursfield Wlk ST6 ... 42 D5
Thurso B77 ... 250 E5
Thurston Way ST2 ... 73 C8
Thurvaston Rd DE6 ... 96 F1
Thyme Gr ST3 ... 90 B6
Tibberton Cl WV3 ... 265 D7
Tibb St ST7 ... 39 F2
Tiber Dr ST5 ... 55 D5
Tickhill La ST10,ST11 ... 74 F5
Tidebrook Pl ST6 ... 41 E7
Tideswell Gn DE11 ... 186 E5
Tideswell Rd ST3 ... 284 C5
Tierney St ST1 ... 282 C4
Tiffany La WV9 ... 239 F2
Tilbrook Cl ST2 ... 73 C8
Tilbury Cl WV3 ... 265 A8
Tilcon Ave ST18 ... 156 D2
Tildesley Cl ST19 ... 207 E8
Tildesley Ct ST19 ... 207 E8
Tilehurst Pl ST3 ... 72 E1
Tilery La ST3 ... 88 D8
Tilewright Cl ST7 ... 26 B2
Tilia Rd B77 ... 251 B5
Tiller Gr B75 ... 258 D4
Tillett Gn ST3 ... 74 B3
Tilling Dr ST15 ... 120 A6
Tillington Manor Prim Sch
ST16 ... 155 C6
Tillington St ST16 ... 155 D5
Till Wlk ST3 ... 73 D6
Tilson Ave ST4 ... 71 F7
Tilstone Cl ST7 ... 41 A8
Timberfields Rd ST16 ... 155 C4
Timberfields ST15 ... 118 E6
Timber Gr ST19 ... 223 D6
Timber La ST14 ... 126 B6
Timber Pit La ST19 ... 205 B4
Timble Cl ST2 ... 73 C8
Times Sq ST3 ... 284 B4
Timmis St ST1 ... 57 A3
Timor Gr ST4 ... 88 B8
Timothy Cl ST3 ... 73 C6
Tinacre Hill WV6 ... 254 E2
Tinker's Castle Rd WV5 . 263 D1
Tinkers Green Rd B77 ... 261 F6
Tinkers La Ashley TF9 ... 100 A4
Brewood ST19 ... 223 E6
Tinker's La ST14 ... 143 A7
Tinsell Brook DE65 ... 147 E8
Tintagel Cl Perton WV6 .. 254 F3
Stretton DE13 ... 147 E2
Tintagel Dr DY1 ... 271 E2
Tintagel Pl ST2 ... 73 D8
Tintern Cres WS3 ... 242 F2
Tintern Ct WV6 ... 254 E4
Tintern Pl ST5 ... 55 F7
Tintern St ST1 ... 57 E3
Tintern Way WS3 ... 242 F2
Tipping Ave ST3 ... 74 B1
Tipping St ST16 ... 285 B3
Tipton Rd DY3 ... 271 F7
Tipton St DY3 ... 271 E7
Tirley St ST4 ... 72 E5
Tissington Pl ST3 ... 90 C7
Titan Way WS13 ... 231 F8
Titchfield Cl WV10 ... 240 E4
Tithe Barn Ct ST16 ... 156 A4
Tithe Barn La WS13,
WS15 ... 212 C5
Tithebarn Rd WS15 ... 178 E2
Tithe Barn Rd ST16 ... 156 A4
Tittensor CE Fst Sch ST12 88 A1
Tittensor Rd
Barlaston ST12 ... 104 B8
Newcastle-u-L ST5 ... 71 C5
Titterton La ST13 ... 33 B4
Titterton St ST4 ... 72 C6
Tittesworth Ave ST13 ... 31 A7
Tittesworth Est ST13 ... 20 E4
Tiverton Ave ST17 ... 175 D8
Tiverton Cl DY8 ... 275 F3
Tiverton Rd ST2 ... 73 C8
Tixall Ct ST18 ... 157 E3
Tixall Mews ST18 ... 157 D3
Tixall Rd Stafford ST18 ... 156 D3
Tixall ST18 ... 157 B2
Toby's Hill DE6 ... 144 C7
Toft End Rd ST5 ... 41 B1
Tolkien Way ST4 ... 72 A8
Toll Bar Rd ST9 ... 59 D4
Tolldish La ST18 ... 158 C4
Tollgate Ave ST5 ... 85 D5
Tollgate Cl ST7 ... 40 C8
Tollgate Cotts DE6 ... 81 E8
Tollgate Dr ST16 ... 155 F8
Tollgate Ind Est ST16 ... 155 F8
Tollgate La B79 ... 233 E3
Tollgate Rd ST13 ... 29 C6
Tollhouse Way WV5 ... 269 E7
Tolman Dr B77 ... 250 D3
Tolson Ave B78 ... 261 B8
Tolson Cl B77 ... 261 D5
Tolworth Gdns WV2 ... 266 E7
Tom Fields ST7 ... 39 F1
Tomkinson Cl TF10 ... 169 A4
Tom La DY7 ... 268 E5
Tomlinson Bsns Pk DE65 129 F4
Tomlinson St ST6 ... 56 D8
Tommy's La CW12 ... 6 A4
Tompkin Rd ST9 ... 44 B4
Tom Williams Way B77 .. 261 C8
Tonadine Cl WV11 ... 242 A1
Tonbridge Ave ST6 ... 42 B4
Toney Pl ST2 ... 57 F3
Tong Cl ST19 ... 221 E8
Tong Dr TF11 ... 203 F1
Tong Rd ST19 ... 221 F7
Tongue Ave B78 ... 261 A8
Tongue La ST6 ... 27 F1
Tontine Sq ST1 ... 282 B3
Tontines Sh Ctr The ST1 . 282 B3
Tontine St ST1 ... 282 B3
Tony Waddington Pl ST4 . 72 D4
Toothill Rd ST14 ... 126 D4
Top Chapel La ST6 ... 28 B1
Topham Pl ST2 ... 57 F3
Top Heath Row ST6 ... 43 B8
Top La Beech ST4 ... 103 C8
Beech ST4 ... 87 C1
Top Rd
Acton Trussell ST17 ... 175 B1
Biddulph ST8 ... 17 D3
Top Station Rd ST7 ... 26 D7
Torbay B77 ... 250 E5
Torc Ave B77 ... 250 E4
Torc High Sch B77 ... 250 F1
Torfield WV8 ... 239 E2
Torrance Cl DE14 ... 185 A6
Torrance Gr ST14 ... 110 F2
Torres Wlk ST1 ... 57 E5
Torridge Dr ST17 ... 174 B8
Torridge B77 ... 262 A5
Torridon Cl ST4 ... 88 C6
Torridon Rd WV11 ... 242 B1
Torrington Ave ST17 ... 175 E8
Torside B77 ... 262 B7
Tor St ST1 ... 57 D7
Torvale Rd WV6 ... 255 A2
Torville Dr ST8 ... 27 E8
Tor Way WS3 ... 243 F3
Totnes Cl DE13 ... 166 D7
Tower Bsns Pk WS15 ... 197 B5
Tower Cl Biddulph ST8 ... 27 B6
Market Drayton TF9 ... 97 B1
Tower Crane Dr ST10 ... 76 B1
Tower Hill Rd
Biddulph ST8 ... 27 A6
Mow Cop ST7 ... 26 F7
Tower Rd Burton u T DE15 167 B2
Cannock WS12 ... 194 F1
Loggerheads TF9 ... 99 F4
Sutton Coldfield B75 ... 258 B3
Tower Sq ST6 ... 41 D3
Tower St DY3 ... 266 D1
Tower View Prim Sch
DE15 ... 167 C3
Tower View Rd WS6 ... 242 F8
Town End ST10 ... 76 C3
Townend ST11 ... 106 E8
Townend La Swinscoe DE6. 65 E5
Waterhouses ST10 ... 48 F4
Townfield Cl ST7 ... 25 D2
Townfields WS13 ... 231 A7
Townfold WS3 ... 244 A4
Town Head ST10 ... 78 F1
Town Head Farm ST10 ... 78 F1
Town Hill DE13 ... 182 B2
Town Meadows Way
ST14 ... 126 C8
Town Rd ST1 ... 282 B4
Townsend Ave DY3 ... 271 D8
Townsend Cl B79 ... 236 D4
Townsend Ho B79 ... 250 A4
Townsend La ST7 ... 25 A8
Townsend Pl Bucknall ST2 . 58 B3
Kingswinford DY6 ... 275 D6
Town Wells Mews TF10 . 168 F1
Town Yard Ind Est ST13 ... 30 D5
Toy Cl WS15 ... 178 D1
Trade St ST4 ... 72 B7
Trafalgar Cl WS12 ... 210 E4
Trafalgar Ct 6 ST6 ... 57 A7
Trafalgar Ho WS12 ... 210 E4
Trafalgar Rd ST4 ... 71 E8
Trafalgar St ST1 ... 282 B4
Trafford Cl ST13 ... 31 B5
Tramway The DE11 ... 186 F7
Transport La ST3 ... 284 B3
Tranter Cres WS11 ... 210 B3
Tranter Rd ST2 ... 58 B6
Tranwell Cl WV9 ... 239 F2
Travellers Cl WS7 ... 229 A5
Travers Ct ST4 ... 72 D6
Travers St ST6 ... 56 E7
Treasure Cl B77 ... 250 E4
Trecastle Gr ST3 ... 73 E1
Treetops 7 ST17 ... 175 C7
Tree Tops WV5 ... 269 E8
Trefoil B77 ... 251 B5
Tregaron Ct ST2 ... 59 A3
Tregenna Cl 8 ST3 ... 90 A7
Tregew Pl ST5 ... 55 D2
Tregony Rise WS14 ... 231 D6
Tregowan Cl ST6 ... 42 B3
Trenance Cl WS14 ... 231 D7
Trenchard Ave ST16 ... 156 A5
Trent Bridge Cl ST4 ... 88 D7
Trent Bridge Ho DE14 ... 166 F3
Trent Cl Burntwood WS7 .. 229 D6
Cheadle ST10 ... 76 E1
Great Haywood ST18 ... 158 B2
Perton WV6 ... 254 E4
Stafford ST17 ... 174 F6
Stone ST15 ... 119 F8
Trent Ct ST15 ... 119 F8
Trentfield La ST18 ... 137 D5
Trentfields Rd ST2 ... 43 B2
Trent Gr Biddulph ST8 ... 27 D6
Newcastle-u-L ST5 ... 71 A3
Trentham Bsns Ctr ST4 .. 88 D7
Trentham Cl WS11 ... 210 B1
Trentham Ct ST4 ... 87 E7
Trentham Gardens Cl ST4 87 F7
Trentham Gdns* ST4 ... 87 F6
Trentham Gr ST5 ... 56 C4
Trentham High Sch ST4 .. 87 F8
Trentham Rd
Hanchurch ST5 ... 86 E8
Newcastle-u-L ST5 ... 71 A1
Stoke-on-T ST4,ST3 ... 88 E7
Trentham Rise WV2 ... 266 F7
Trent Ho Cannock WS12 .. 210 C5
Dudley DY3 ... 271 E3
Trent Ind Est DE14 ... 166 E4
Trent La
Great Haywood ST18 ... 158 B2
Hixon ST18 ... 157 E8
Newton Solney DE15 ... 167 D8
Trentley Dr ST8 ... 28 B8
Trentley Rd ST4 ... 88 A7
Trentmill Rd ST1 ... 57 E2
Trent Rd
Blythe Bridge ST11 ... 91 A7
Cannock WS11 ... 209 E5
Stone ST15 ... 104 E1
Walsall WS3 ... 244 A1
Trentside Rd ST6 ... 43 A5
Trent St Bucknall ST2 ... 57 F3
Burton u T DE14 ... 166 C1
Trent Terr
Burton u T DE14 ... 166 E3
Stoke-on-T ST6 ... 43 A5
Trent Vale CE Prim Sch
ST4 ... 71 E3
Trent Valley Cotts WS13 . 214 F1
Trent Valley Rd
Lichfield WS13,WS14 ... 231 D8
Stoke-on-T ST4 ... 71 F5
Trent Valley Trad Est
WS15 ... 178 F2
Trent View Cl WS15 ... 197 A7
Trentway Cl ST2 ... 58 A3
Trent Wlk Hanley ST1 ... 282 C1
Ingestre ST18 ... 157 E7
Tresham Rd 2 DY6 ... 275 D8
Trevelyan's Gn ST16 ... 155 C8
Trevelyn Cl DE15 ... 167 C2
Trevithick Cl Bucknall ST2 . 73 D7
Burntwood WS7 ... 229 C8
Trevitt Pl ST19 ... 205 C6
Trevor Ave WS6 ... 227 A3
Trevor Dr ST11 ... 74 D3
Trevor Rd WS3 ... 243 F5
Trevose Cl WS3 ... 242 F3
Trimley Way ST2 ... 58 B2
Trimpley Gdns WV4 ... 265 E3
Trimpos ST10 ... 76 A4
Triner Pl ST6 ... 42 E4
Tring Cl ST2 ... 73 C8
Tring Ct WV6 ... 255 F4
Trinity Cl Cannock WS11 .. 226 E8
Shenstone WS14 ... 246 F6
Stourbridge DY8 ... 275 D2
Trinity Ct Congleton CW12 .. 6 B1
Newcastle-u-L ST5 ... 55 E7
Trinity Dr Stone ST15 ... 104 F1
Tamworth B79 ... 249 D6
Trinity Gorse ST16 ... 155 B8
Trinity Pl Bucknall ST2 ... 58 B4
Congleton CW12 ... 16 B8
Trinity Rd Eccleshall ST21 133 D6
Sutton Coldfield B75 ... 258 C1
Uttoxeter ST14 ... 126 C7
Wood End B78,CV9 ... 262 B3
Trinity Rise ST16 ... 155 B8
Trinity Sq ST14 ... 126 C7
Trinity St ST1 ... 282 B3
Trinity Wlk ST14 ... 126 C7
Tristram Gr DE13 ... 147 E2
Triton Cl WS6 ... 226 F1
Triton Wlk ST6 ... 42 D1
Triumph B77 ... 250 E3
Trojan B77 ... 250 E3
Troon Cl Stretton DE13 ... 147 C1
Walsall WS3 ... 243 A3
Troon Ct WV6 ... 254 D5
Troon Pl DY8 ... 275 C3
Troon B77 ... 251 C4
Troutdale Cl ST4 ... 73 B6
Trowbridge Cres ST2 ... 58 C3
Trubshaw Cl ST18 ... 177 E8
Trubshaw Cross ST6 ... 56 D8
Trubshaw Ct ST7 ... 26 C3
Trubshawe St ST6 ... 56 D8
Trubshaw Pl ST7 ... 26 B3
Truro Cl Congleton CW12 .. 15 E8
Lichfield WS13 ... 214 B3
Rugeley WS15 ... 196 D6
Truro Pl Bucknall ST2 ... 58 B2
Cannock WS12 ... 227 C8

Truro Way ST17 . . . . . 156 D1
Trussel Grange ST17 . . . 175 B1
Trussell Cl ST17 . . . . . 175 A1
Trustley Cl DE14 . . . . . 185 B7
Trysull Gdns WV5 . . . . . 265 D7
Trysull Holloway WV5 . . . 264 C3
Trysull Rd Orton WV5 . . . 264 E1
  Wolverhampton WV3 . . . 265 D7
  Wombourne WV5 . . . . . 269 E8
Tuckers Pl TF10 . . . . . . 168 E3
Tudor Cl Burntwood WS7 . 229 C6
  Cheslyn Hay WS6 . . . . . 226 E3
  Lichfield WS14 . . . . . . 231 F6
  Market Drayton TF9 . . . . 97 B2
  Newport TF10 . . . . 169 A4
  Stoke-on-T ST4 . . . . . . 72 A6
  Stone ST15 . . . . 119 F6
Tudor Cres Tamworth B77 250 F4
  Wolverhampton WV2 . . . 266 B6
Tudor Ct Essington WV11 . 241 E4
  Fulford ST11 . . . . 90 E1
  Newcastle-u-L ST5 . . . . 56 B6
  Sutton Coldfield B74 . . . 258 A2
Tudor Gdns DY8 . . . . . . 279 E5
Tudor Gr ST5 . . . . 56 C4
Tudor Hollow
  2 Burton u T DE13 . . . . . 166 D8
  Fulford ST11 . . . . 90 E1
Tudor Park Ct B74 . . . . . 257 F3
Tudor Park Gdns WS7 . . . 226 E2
Tudor Pl DY3 . . . . 271 E6
Tudor Rd Burntwood WS7 . 229 C6
  Cannock WS14 . . . . . . 209 F8
  Dudley DY3 . . . . 271 E6
Tudor Rise
  Clifton Campville B79 . . 218 E2
  Stafford ST16 . . . . 155 C8
Tudor Rose Ct ST6 . . . . . 42 E2
Tudor Rose Way ST6 . . . . 42 E2
Tudor Row **3** WS13 . . . . 231 B7
Tudors The ST6 . . . . . . 41 E4
Tudor Vale DY3 . . . . . . 271 E6
Tudor Way
  Cheslyn Hay WS6 . . . . . 226 D1
  Stafford ST17 . . . . 155 B1
Tuke Pl WS13 . . . . 213 F1
Tulip Gr ST5 . . . . 283 C4
Tulley Pl ST2 . . . . 58 A3
Tullis Cl ST16 . . . . 155 C2
Tulsa Cl ST2 . . . . 58 A1
Tunbridge Dr ST5 . . . . . 54 F2
Tunley St ST15 . . . . . . 104 F1
Tunnicliffe Cl ST3 . . . . . 73 E3
Tunnicliffe Dr WS15 . . . . 178 D1
Tunnicliffe Way ST14 . . . 110 F2
Tunstall La ST20 . . . . . . 131 F2
Tunstall Rd Biddulph ST8 . 27 C5
  Bosley CW12,SK11 . . . . 7 C7
  Congleton CW12 . . . . . 6 F2
Tunstall Road Ind Est ST8 27 B4
Tuppenhurst La WS15 . . . 198 D3
Turf Cl WS11 . . . . 228 A4
Turf Cotts WV4 . . . . . . 265 F2
Turf Pitts La B75 . . . . . 258 F4
Turin Cl ST3 . . . . 73 E4
Turin Dr ST5 . . . . 70 E6
Turls Hill Rd Sedgley DY3 . 271 E8
  Sedgley WV14 . . . . . . 271 F8
Turls St DY3 . . . . 271 E8
Turnberry Dr ST4 . . . . . 88 A8
Turnberry Gr WV6 . . . . . 254 D5
Turnberry Rd WS3 . . . . . 243 A4
Turnberry B77 . . . . 251 C5
Turnbull Rd WS13 . . . . . 215 C6
Turnbury Cl DE14 . . . . . 185 A7
Turner Ave Audley ST7 . . . 40 A1
  Wolverhampton WV4,
  WV14 . . . . 266 F2
Turner Cl WS11 . . . . . . 210 D2
Turner Cres ST5 . . . . . . 55 E6
Turner Croft WS13 . . . . 215 D8
Turner Gr WV6 . . . . . . 255 A4
Turner's Gr DY3 . . . . . . 271 C4
Turner's Hill Rd DY3 . . . 271 C4
Turners La TF10 . . . . . . 168 A3
Turner St
  Dudley,Gornalwood DY3 . 271 D3
  Hanley ST1 . . . . 57 E5
Turney Gr ST17 . . . . . . 174 C8
Turney Rd DY8 . . . . 279 F6
Turnham Gn WV6 . . . . . 254 E3
Turnhill Cl ST18 . . . . . . 174 C6
Turnhill Gr ST5 . . . . . . 56 B7
Turnhurst Rd ST7 . . . . . 41 F7
Turnlea Cl ST8 . . . . 27 B6
Turnock St ST2 . . . . . . 58 C4
Turnpike Way WV9 . . . . . 224 C1
Turnstone Dr WV10 . . . . 241 B7
Turquoise Gr WS11 . . . . 210 C3
Turton Cl Alrewas DE13 . . 201 A2
  Walsall WS3 . . . . 243 A4
Tuscan Cl ST10 . . . . . . 76 D1
Tuscan Ho ST3 . . . . . . 284 B2
Tuscan St ST3 . . . . 284 C4
Tuscan Way ST5 . . . . . . 55 D6
Tutbury Ave WV6 . . . . . 255 A3
Tutbury Castle★ DE13 . . 146 B7
Tutbury Cl WS11 . . . . . 210 C3
Tutbury Gr ST3 . . . . . . 73 D4
Tutbury & Hatton Sta
  DE65 . . . . 146 D8
Tutbury Rd
  Burton u T DE13 . . . . . 166 B8
  Stretton DE13 . . . . . . 147 A1
Tutbury B77 . . . . 261 C7

Tutehill B77 . . . . 262 B7
Twayblade DE14 . . . . . . 185 B8
Tweed Gr ST5 . . . . 71 A4
Tweed St ST4 . . . . 72 E4
Twemlow Cl ST18 . . . . . 154 D2
Twemlow St ST1 . . . . . . 57 A3
Twentylands DE13 . . . . . 147 D4
Twickenham Ct DY8 . . . . 279 C7
Twigg St ST2 . . . . 58 B2
Twizles La B79 . . . . 218 A1
Two Gates Com Prim Sch
  Tamworth B77 . . . . . . 261 C8
  Tamworth,Mount Pleasant
  B77 . . . . 250 C1
Two Gates Ind Est B77 . . 261 D7
Two Oaks Ave WS7 . . . . 228 D8
Two Trees Cl B78 . . . . . 249 B6
Twyford Cl Aldridge WS9 . 256 B5
  Swadlincote DE11 . . . . 186 F2
Twyning Gn ST3 . . . . . . 88 F7
Tylecote Cres ST18 . . . . 158 B2
Tyler Gr **5** Burslem ST6 . 56 E8
  Stone ST15 . . . . 119 E7
Tyndall Pl ST4 . . . . 71 E7
Tyne Cl WS8 . . . . 228 C2
Tynedale Cres WV4 . . . . 266 E3
Tyneham Gr ST2 . . . . . . 43 A2
Tyne Way ST5 . . . . 71 B4
Tyning Cl WV9 . . . . 240 A2
Tyninghame Ave WV6 . . . 255 D7
Tynings La WS9 . . . . . . 256 A5
Tynsel Parkes CE Fst Sch
  ST14 . . . . 110 F1
Tynwald Grange ST5 . . . . 56 A3
Tyrell Gr ST1 . . . . 57 F8
Tyria Way **3** ST17 . . . . 175 A8
Tyrley Cl WV6 . . . . 255 D7
Tyrley Rd TF9 . . . . 112 F5
Tyrol Cl DY8 . . . . 279 D6
Tyson Gr ST2 . . . . 73 D8
Tythebarn Dr DY6 . . . . . 275 A7

U
Ubberley Gn ST2 . . . . . . 58 C2
Ubberley Rd ST2 . . . . . . 58 C1
Uffington Par ST2 . . . . . 73 C8
Ufton Cl ST3 . . . . 88 F7
Ullswater Ave ST6 . . . . . 56 F7
Ullswater Dr Cheadle ST10. 76 F4
  Stone ST15 . . . . 120 D7
Ullswater Gdns DY6 . . . . 275 D6
Ullswater Ho ST17 . . . . 174 E6
Ullswater Pl WS11 . . . . . 209 E1
Ullswater Rd WV11 . . . . 242 B1
Ullswater B77 . . . . 262 B7
Ulster Cl WS11 . . . . 210 A3
Ulster Dr DY6 . . . . 275 E4
Ulster Terr ST4 . . . . . . 72 A5
Ulverston Rd ST4 . . . . . 88 F7
Umberleigh Rd ST3 . . . . 88 F7
Underhill Cl TF10 . . . . . 168 F3
Underhill La WV10 . . . . . 241 A2
Underhill Prim Sch
  WV10 . . . . 241 B1
Underhill Wlk DE14 . . . . 166 D1
Underley Cl WS6 . . . . . . 275 B7
Under Rainow Rd CW12 . . 6 E1
Under The Hill ST8 . . . . 17 A2
Undertown La DE6 . . . . . 96 D6
Underwood Cl ST16 . . . . 155 D6
Underwood Rd ST5 . . . . 55 A1
Unicorn Ind Est ST5 . . . . 56 B8
Unicorn Pl ST6 . . . . . . 41 F5
Union Ct ST1 . . . . 282 B4
Union La WV5 . . . . 264 D2
Union St Burntwood WS7 . 228 E5
  Burton u T DE14 . . . . . 166 D2
  Cannock WS11 . . . . . . 226 E6
  Hanley ST1 . . . . 282 B4
  Leek ST13 . . . . 30 F6
Unity Ave ST1 . . . . 57 D7
Unity Way ST7 . . . . 40 D8
University Cl ST18 . . . . . 156 C5
University Way CW1 . . . . 37 A8
Univ of Sheffield SK17 . . 4 E1
Univ of Wolverhampton
  Compton Park Campus
  WV6 . . . . 255 D2
Unwin Cres DY8 . . . . . . 279 E5
Unwin St ST6 . . . . 42 B3
Upfield Cotts WS7 . . . . . 229 E7
Upfield Way WS15 . . . . . 178 C2
Uplands Ave
  Stoke-on-T ST6 . . . . . . 41 F6
  Werrington ST9 . . . . . . 59 B3
  Wolverhampton WV3 . . . 265 D8
Uplands Cl
  Cannock Wood WS15 . . . 211 F5
  Penkridge ST19 . . . . . . 192 E2
Uplands Croft ST9 . . . . . 59 A4
Uplands Dr Sedgley DY3 . . 271 D8
  Werrington ST9 . . . . . . 59 A3
  Wolverhampton WV3 . . . 265 D8
  Wombourne WV5 . . . . . 270 A6
Uplands Gn WS15 . . . . . 196 D6
Uplands Jun Sch WV3 . . . 265 D8
Uplands Rd Bucknall ST2 . 58 B7
  Stafford ST17 . . . . 155 B1
Uplands The Biddulph ST8 . 16 E3
  Great Haywood ST18 . . . 158 B2
  Walsall WS3 . . . . 243 D1
Upmeadows Dr ST16 . . . . 155 B1
Upper Ave
  Codsall Wood ST19 . . . . 222 F2
  Coven WV9 . . . . 223 B3
Upper Bar TF10 . . . . . . 168 F2

Upper Belgrave Rd ST3 . . 73 D1
Upper Brook St **2** WS15 196 E8
Upper Cres ST4 . . . . . . 71 E8
Upper Cross Rd WS15 . . . 196 E1
Upper Cross St ST3 . . . . 284 C4
Upper Furlong St ST4 . . . 72 D6
Upper Gn WV6 . . . . 255 D5
Upper Gungate B79 . . . . 250 B6
Upper Hattons Cotts
  WV9 . . . . 239 D5
Upper Hillchurch St ST1 . 282 C3
Upper Huntbach St ST1 . 282 C3
Upper Landywood La
  Cheslyn Hay WS6 . . . . . 226 D1
  Great Wyrley WS6 . . . . 242 D8
Upper Lodge Rd WS15 . . . 197 F4
Upper Market Sq ST1 . . . 282 B3
Upper Marsh ST1 . . . . . 56 D3
Upper Normacot Rd **1**
  ST3 . . . . 73 D2
Upper St John St WS14 . 231 B6
Upper Sneyd Rd WV11 . . 242 B2
Upper St WV6 . . . . 255 D5
Upper Villiers St WV2 . . . 266 C6
Upper Way ST15 . . . . . . 197 B2
Upper Zoar St WV3 . . . . 266 B8
Upton Ct TF9 . . . . 97 D1
Upton Pl WS15 . . . . 178 D2
Urmston Pl ST3 . . . . . . 88 F7
Usam Trad Est WV10 . . . 240 D2
Usulwall Cl ST21 . . . . . 133 D6
Utterby Side ST2 . . . . . 73 C8
Uttoxeter Heritage Ctr★
  ST14 . . . . 126 C7
Uttoxeter Race Course★
  ST14 . . . . 126 E6
Uttoxeter Rd
  Abbots Bromley WS15 . . 160 E6
  Alton ST10 . . . . 94 E8
  Armitage WS15 . . . . . . 198 C4
  Blithbury WS15 . . . . . . 180 A5
  Blythe Bridge ST11 . . . . 90 E7
  Checkley ST10,ST14 . . . . 109 D8
  Foston DE65 . . . . 129 E4
  Foston,HM Detention Ctr
  DE65 . . . . 129 C4
  Fradswell ST18 . . . . . . 123 B6
  Hilderstone ST15 . . . . . 121 D7
  Hill Ridware WS15 . . . . 198 A8
  Longton ST3 . . . . 284 C3
  Meir ST3 . . . . 74 A1
  Milwich ST18 . . . . 122 D5
  Scropton DE65 . . . . . . 129 F3
  Stone ST15 . . . . 120 E7
Uttoxeter Sta ST14 . . . . 126 D7
Uxbridge Cl DY3 . . . . . . 271 D2
Uxbridge Ct
  Burntwood WS7 . . . . . 228 F5
  Cannock WS12 . . . . . . 210 C5
Uxbridge St
  Burton u T DE14 . . . . . 166 C1
  Cannock WS12 . . . . . . 210 C4

V
Vale Ave Aldridge WS9 . . 256 D3
  Dudley DY3 . . . . 271 D6
Vale Cl WS3 . . . . 214 B1
Vale Gdns ST19 . . . . . . 207 E8
Vale Head Dr WV6 . . . . . 255 A2
Valentine Rd ST7 . . . . . 26 A1
Vale Park (Port Vale FC)★
  ST6 . . . . 42 A1
Vale Pleasant ST5 . . . . . 55 C2
Vale Pl ST1 . . . . 282 A4
Vale Rise ST19 . . . . . . 207 F8
Vale Row DY3 . . . . 271 D5
Vale St Dudley DY3 . . . . 271 D5
  Newcastle-u-L,Chesterton
  ST5 . . . . 55 E8
  Newcastle-u-L,Silverdale
  ST5 . . . . 55 B2
  Stoke-on-T ST4 . . . . . . 72 B7
Vale Valve Aldridge WS9 . 256 B4
  Cheddleton ST13 . . . . . 45 D5
  Newcastle-u-L ST5 . . . . 56 D7
Valley Dr ST13 . . . . 30 B5
Valley Gn WS6 . . . . 226 C2
Valley Heritage Ctr★
  WS12 . . . . 210 D6
Valley La Lichfield WS13 . 231 D8
  Tamworth B77 . . . . . . 261 E7
Valley Park Nature Reserve★
  WV6 . . . . 255 D3
Valley Park Way ST3 . . . 72 F3
Valley Prim Sch ST10 . . . 78 A7
Valley Rd
  Cannock,Hazelslade
  WS12 . . . . 211 A6
  Cannock,Hednesford
  WS12 . . . . 210 D6
  Coldmeece ST15 . . . . . 118 B7
  Dudley DY3 . . . . 271 E6
  Meir ST3 . . . . 74 B3
  Stone ST15 . . . . 120 B6
  Walsall WS3 . . . . 243 D1
Valley Side WS3 . . . . . . 243 F2
Valley The WS7 . . . . . . 228 D8
Valley View
  Brownhills WS8 . . . . . . 245 A4
  Market Drayton TF9 . . . 112 A7
Valley View Wlk ST14 . . . 96 A3
Vanbrugh Ct WV6 . . . . . 254 E3

Vancouver Dr DE15 . . . . 167 C3
Van Diemans Rd WV5 . . . 269 F5
Van Gogh Cl WS11 . . . . 210 D2
Vanguard B77 . . . . 261 D6
Vanity Cl ST15 . . . . 105 C4
Vanity La ST15 . . . . 105 C4
Varden Ct WS15 . . . . . . 178 E1
Vardon Cl ST16 . . . . . . 156 C3
Vaughan Ct B77 . . . . . . 257 F6
Vaughan Gdns WV8 . . . . 238 F4
Vaughan's La WS15 . . . . 159 C6
Vaughan Way ST17 . . . . 155 C1
Vauxhall Cres TF10 . . . . 168 E2
Vauxhall Terr TF10 . . . . 168 E3
Venice Ct ST5 . . . . 70 E7
Venn Pl ST1 . . . . 57 E2
Venton Cl ST6 . . . . 42 E4
Ventnor Gr ST3 . . . . . . 88 F6
Ventura Park Rd ST6 . . . 249 E3
Ventura Pk Rd B78 . . . . 250 A3
Ventura B78 . . . . 250 A3
Venture Way ST6 . . . . . 42 C3
Vercourt B77 . . . . 257 B3
Verdi Ct WS13 . . . . 214 C2
Verdon Cl ST19 . . . . . . 208 A7
Verity Wlk DY8 . . . . . . 275 E1
Vermont Gn **4** WS11 . . . 210 A3
Verney Cl ST14 . . . . . . 125 C7
Verney Way ST3 . . . . . . 88 F7
Vernon Ave Audley ST7 . . 39 D2
  Brownhills WS8 . . . . . . 245 A8
  Congleton CW12 . . . . . 15 F8
Vernon Cl Audley ST7 . . . 39 D2
  Essington WV11 . . . . . 241 F4
  Sutton Coldfield B74 . . . 257 E5
Vernon Ho ST14 . . . . . . 126 C7
Vernon Lodge Prep Sch
  ST19 . . . . 206 C3
Vernon Rd ST4 . . . . 72 B8
Vernons Pl WV10 . . . . . 225 D1
Vernon Terr DE14 . . . . . 166 C4
Vernon Way ST3 . . . . . . 88 F7
Verona Gr ST3 . . . . 73 E5
Veronica Ave WV4 . . . . . 266 E5
Verulam Ct ST16 . . . . . 155 E7
Verulam Rd ST16 . . . . . 155 E7
Verwood Cl ST16 . . . . . 156 C4
Vesey Cl B74 . . . . 257 F2
Vessey Terr ST5 . . . . . . 283 C2
Vestry Ct DY8 . . . . 279 E6
Vicarage Bank ST18 . . . . 138 E6
Vicarage Cl
  Brownhills WS8 . . . . . . 245 A7
  Burton u T DE15 . . . . . 167 B4
  Dordon B78 . . . . 262 F5
  Eccleshall ST21 . . . . . . 133 D7
Vicarage Cres
  Caverswall ST11 . . . . . 74 D3
  Newcastle-u-L ST5 . . . . 283 C1
  Tittensor ST12 . . . . . . 88 A1
  Upper Tean ST10 . . . . . 92 E3
Vicarage Croft DE13 . . . 199 D6
Vicarage Ct
  Burntwood WS7 . . . . . 228 F6
  Kinver DY7 . . . . 278 A3
Vicarage Dr Kinver DY7 . . 278 A3
  Stramshall ST14 . . . . . 110 F4
Vicarage Field DE15 . . . . 166 F1
Vicarage Hill B78 . . . . . 260 B1
Vicarage La Barlaston ST12 88 F2
  King's Bromley DE13 . . . 199 D6
  Madeley CW3 . . . . 68 E5
  Stoke-on-T ST4 . . . . . . 71 E4
Vicarage Rd
  Brewood ST19 . . . . . . 223 D6
  Brownhills WS8 . . . . . . 245 A7
  Dudley,Woodsetton DY3 . 271 F5
  Four Ashes WV10 . . . . . 224 F6
  Leek ST13 . . . . 30 F6
  Stoke-on-T ST4 . . . . . . 71 F8
  Stourbridge DY8 . . . . . 279 D7
  Upper Tean ST10 . . . . . 92 E3
  Walsall WS3 . . . . 244 B2
  Wolverhampton,Blakenhall
  WV2 . . . . 266 D8
  Wolverhampton,Penn WV4 265 E3
Vicarage Row WS10 . . . . 78 E1
Vicarage Way Hixon ST18 139 C1
  Stafford ST17 . . . . 285 A1
Vicar's Cl Lichfield WS13 . 231 A8
  Oulton ST15 . . . . 105 C4
Vicars Croft WS15 . . . . . 178 F2
Vicar St DY3 . . . . 271 D8
Vichy Cl ST5 . . . . 70 E7
Vickers Rd ST6 . . . . . . 42 A5
Victoria Ave
  Halmer End ST7 . . . . . . 54 E7
  Hanley ST1 . . . . 282 B1
  Kidsgrove ST7 . . . . . . 25 F2
  Walsall,Wallington Heath
  WS3 . . . . 243 C1
Victoria Cl WS15 . . . . . 55 C1
Victoria Cotts ST10 . . . . 61 A2
Victoria Cres DE14 . . . . 166 C5
Victoria Ct
  8 Kidsgrove ST7 . . . . . 26 A2
  Biddulph ST8 . . . . 27 B4
  Leek ST13 . . . . 30 D5
  Market Drayton TF9 . . . 112 B8
  Newcastle-u-L ST5 . . . . 56 C3
  Norton Canes WS11 . . . 228 B5
  Stoke-on-T ST4 . . . . . . 72 E6
Victoria Dr DE14 . . . . . 261 A8
Victoria Gdns WS13 . . . . 230 F6
Victoria Gr WV5 . . . . . . 270 A8
Victoria Ho **2** ST4 . . . . 71 F8

Victoria Hosp★ WS13 . . . 231 A6
Victoria Ind Complex
  ST4 . . . . 284 A5
Victoria Mdw DE13 . . . . 199 D6
Victoria Park Rd ST6 . . . 41 E4
Victoria Pk TF10 . . . . . 168 F3
Victoria Pl
  Newcastle-u-L,Chesterton
  ST5 . . . . 55 E7
  Newcastle-u-L,Wolstanton
  ST5 . . . . 56 D5
  Stoke-on-T ST4 . . . . . . 72 E6
Victoria Rd
  Burton u T DE14 . . . . . 166 C4
  Market Drayton TF9 . . . 97 B1
  Newcastle-u-L ST5 . . . . 283 C2
  Sedgley DY3 . . . . 271 E8
  Stafford ST16 . . . . 285 A3
  Stoke-on-T ST4 . . . . . . 72 E5
  Tamworth B79 . . . . . . 250 C5
  Walsall WS3 . . . . 244 A3
  Wolverhampton,Penn WV3 265 E7
  Wolverhampton,Tettenhall
  WV6 . . . . 255 C5
Victoria Row ST8 . . . . . 27 C4
Victoria Sq Hanley ST1 . 282 A1
Victoria St
  Broomhill WS11 . . . . . . 209 E4
  Burton u T DE14 . . . . . 166 C4
  Cannock,Bridgtown WS11 226 D8
  Cannock WS12 . . . . . . 210 C6
  Cheadle ST10 . . . . 76 E3
  Kingswinford DY6 . . . . . 270 B1
  Leek ST13 . . . . 31 A6
  Newcastle-u-L,Chesterton
  ST5 . . . . 55 E7
  Newcastle-u-L,Silverdale
  ST5 . . . . 55 C2
  Newcastle-u-L ST5 . . . . 283 C2
  Stafford ST16 . . . . 285 B4
  Stoke-on-T ST4 . . . . . . 56 D1
  Stone ST15 . . . . 105 A1
  Yoxall DE13 . . . . 182 A3
Victoria Terr ST16 . . . . 155 E5
Victoria Way ST17 . . . . 175 E5
Victor St Stone ST15 . . . 104 F1
  Walsall WS3 . . . . 244 A1
Victory Ave WS7 . . . . . 228 F7
Victory Cl WS12 . . . . . . 210 F4
Victory Cres ST10 . . . . . 76 E4
Victory Terr B78 . . . . . 261 B8
Vienna Pl ST5 . . . . 70 F6
Vienna Way ST3 . . . . . . 73 E5
Viewfield Ave WS12 . . . . 209 F7
Viewfield Cres DY3 . . . . 271 D6
Viewlands Dr WV6 . . . . . 255 A2
View St WS12 . . . . 209 F6
Viggars Pl ST5 . . . . 55 F2
Vigo Cl WS9 . . . . 244 F2
Vigo Pl WS9 . . . . 256 A8
Vigo Rd WS9 . . . . 244 F2
Vigo Terr WS9 . . . . 244 F2
Viking Cl DY7 . . . . 261 D7
Villa Cl Biddulph ST8 . . . 27 C7
  Shareshill WV10 . . . . . 225 D1
Village Gdns ST17 . . . . 175 F7
Village Mews The WV6 . . 255 C5
Village The Astbury CW12 . 15 B8
  Endon Bank ST9 . . . . . . 29 A1
  Keele ST5 . . . . 69 F7
  Kingswinford DY6 . . . . . 275 E7
  Walton-on-t-H ST17 . . . 175 F6
Villa Melita ST11 . . . . . 90 D7
Villa Rd ST13 . . . . 45 C8
Villas The Foxt ST10 . . . 62 C5
  Stoke-on-T ST4 . . . . . . 72 A5
  Stoke-on-T ST4 . . . . . . 72 A5
Villiers Ind Est WV2 . . . 266 C6
Villiers St ST3 . . . . 284 B1
Vincent St ST1 . . . . 57 E5
Vine Bank Rd ST7 . . . . . 26 A1
Vinebank St ST4 . . . . . . 72 A6
Vine Cl Hixon ST18 . . . . 158 B8
  Wolverhampton WV10 . . 240 D3
Vinegar Hill ST21 . . . . . 132 C7
Vine La WS11 . . . . 226 D5
Vine Row ST4 . . . . 72 A6
Vine St DY8 . . . . 275 E1
Vineyard Dr TF10 . . . . . 168 F3
Vineyard Rd TF10 . . . . . 168 F3
Violet La DE15 . . . . 185 F8
Violet Lane Inf Sch DE15 185 F8
Violet Way DE15 . . . . . . 186 A8
Virginia Ave ST17 . . . . . 175 A8
Virginia Dr WV4 . . . . . . 265 F4
Virginsalley La DE6 . . . . 81 D2
Viscount Rd WS7 . . . . . 211 E1
Viscount Wlk **6** ST3 . . . 90 A7
Vista The DY3 . . . . 266 D2
Vivian Rd ST4 . . . . 72 F6
Vowchurch Way ST2 . . . . 58 C1
Voyager Dr WS11 . . . . . 226 F6
Vulcan Rd WS13 . . . . . . 214 E1

W
Waddell Cl WV14 . . . . . 266 F2
Wadden La ST18 . . . . . . 138 E4
Wade Ave ST5 . . . . 56 D6
Wadebridge Rd ST2 . . . . 58 B1
Wade Cl Cheadle ST10 . . . 76 D1
  Hill Ridware WS15 . . . . 197 F8
Wade Croft WS15 . . . . . 179 F1
Wade St ST7 . . . . 26 A1
Wade La WS15 . . . . 197 F8
Wadesmill Lawns WV10 . 240 E4

Wad – Wen 331

Wade St Lichfield WS13 231 B7
Stoke-on-T ST6 42 B1
Wadham St ST4 72 A7
Waggon Cotts ST7 38 E1
Waggoner's La B78 259 E8
Waggon La DY10 281 A3
Wain Ave
Newcastle-u-L ST5 70 F8
Stoke-on-T ST6 42 E5
Wain Dr ST4 71 E5
Wainrigg B77 262 B7
Wain St ST6 41 F1
Wainwood Rise ST4 71 F5
Wainwright Cl DY6 275 A8
Wainwright Wlk ST1 282 C3
Wakefield Ave DE13 146 B6
Wakefield Rd ST4 71 F4
Wakelams Fold DY3 271 C3
Wakeley Hill WV4 265 F4
Wakeman Ct WV11 241 F3
Walcot Cl B75 258 B3
Walcot Gr ST2 58 A2
Waldale Cl WV11 242 C1
Walden Ave ST16 155 D6
Walden Gdns WV4 265 E6
Wales La DE13 183 D1
Walford Ave WV3 265 F8
Walford Back La ST21 117 C8
Walford Rd DE13 147 D3
Walhouse CE Jun Sch
WS11 209 C1
Walhouse Dr ST19 207 F7
Walhouse St WS11 226 E8
Walker Dr DY10 280 A1
Walker Rd ST6 41 F4
Walkers Croft WS13 214 C2
Walkersgreen Rd ST5 40 D2
Walkers Rise WS12 210 D8
Walker St Burton u T DE14 166 B1
Stoke-on-T ST6 41 D2
Walkfield Rd DE13 200 F2
Walklate Ave ST5 56 D3
Walk La WV5 270 A6
Walkley Bank TF10 169 C4
Walkmill Bsns Pk
Cannock WS11 226 D5
Market Drayton TF9 112 C7
Walkmill Dr TF9 112 D8
Walkmill La WS11 226 D5
Walkmill Marsh Nature
Reserve* TF9 112 C7
Walkmill Rd TF9 112 C8
Walkmill Way WS11 226 D5
Walks The ST13 30 D5
Walk The DY3 266 D1
Wallace Cl WS11 227 F5
Wallace Ct WS6 226 D1
Wallace Rd WS8 244 E8
Walland Gr ST16 155 B4
Wallash DE6 81 C7
Wallbridge Cl ST13 30 D4
Wallbridge Dr ST13 30 C4
Wallbridge Prec ST13 30 C4
Wallbrook Rd ST18 122 F3
Wall Croft WS9 256 B7
Wall Ditch DE6 35 B2
Wall Dr B74 257 F4
Walley Dr ST6 41 D6
Walley Pl ST6 57 A7
Walley's Dr ST5 56 D2
Walley St Biddulph ST8 27 C8
Burslem ST6 57 A7
Wallfield Cl ST10 92 D4
Wallheath Cres WS14 245 E5
Wallheath La WS14 245 F5
Wallhill Ct ST13 30 E3
Wallington Cl WS3 243 B2
Wallington Heath WS3 243 B2
Wallis Pl ST2 58 B5
Wallis St ST4 72 F6
Wallis Way ST2 43 B2
Wall Lane Terr ST13 45 C6
Wall La WS13,WS14 230 D3
Wall (Letocetvm) Roman Site
(Town)* WS14 230 E2
Wallnut Wlk WS13 230 F6
Wallows Wood DY3 271 A4
Wall Rd DE14 185 A7
Wall Roman Site (Letocetvm)
Mus* WS14 230 D2
Wallshead Way TF10 168 F1
Walls Wood ST5 85 B7
Walmer Mdw WS9 256 B7
Walmer Pl ST4 284 B5
Walmers The WS9 256 B7
Walmsley Ct DY7 278 B3
Walney Gr ST1 282 B4
Walnut Ave WV8 239 B3
Walnut Ct Cannock WS11 209 F3
Newport TF10 168 F1
Walnut Crest ST18 158 C8
Walnut Ct WS15 197 A6
Walnut Dr Cannock WS11 209 F3
Wolverhampton WV3 255 D1
Walnut Gr Lichfield WS14 231 F7
Newcastle-u-L ST5 55 D8
Walnut Tree La TF10 188 B7
Walpole St ST3 284 D5
Walrand Cl B79 234 B1
Walsall Acad WS3 243 C2
Walsall Rd Aldridge WS9 256 A5
Brownhills WS9 244 E2
Cannock WS11 226 E7
Great Wyrley WS6 227 A2
Leamonsley WS13 230 E6
Lichfield,Christ Church
WS13 231 A7
Walsall Rd *continued*
Lichfield,Pipehill WS13,
WS14 230 C5
Norton Canes WS11 227 F4
Stonnall WS14 245 E8
Sutton Coldfield B74 257 D4
Walsall WS3 244 A1
Walsall Wood Rd WS9 256 B7
Walsall Wood Sch WS8 245 A4
Walsingham Gdns ST5 71 B2
Walter St WS3 244 A1
Waltonbury Cl ST17 175 F6
Walton Cres
Stoke-on-T ST4 72 C6
Wolverhampton WV4 266 E5
Walton Cross ST15 120 A7
Walton Gdns WV8 238 F4
Walton Grange ST15 120 A7
Walton Gr ST7 40 C8
Walton Hall ST21 134 B5
Walton Hall Sch ST21 134 B5
Walton Heath WS3 242 F3
Walton High Sch ST17 175 E6
Waltonhurst La ST21 134 C4
Walton Ind Est ST15 120 A6
Walton La ST17 176 B5
Walton Lodge ST17 175 F6
Walton Mead Cl ST17 175 F7
Walton-on-Trent CE Prim
Sch DE12 202 D8
Walton Pl ST5 55 F6
Walton Priory Mid Sch
ST15 119 F6
Walton Rd Aldridge WS9 245 A1
Stoke-on-T ST4 71 F3
Swadlincote DE15 185 D5
Wolverhampton WV4 266 F5
Walton Way Stone ST15 119 F7
Talke ST7 40 C8
Wanderers Ave WV2 266 C6
Wandsbeck B77 261 E8
Wannerton Rd DY10 281 B1
Wansbeck Wlk DY3 271 F6
Warburton Ct 10 ST6 57 A7
Warburton St 7 ST6 57 A7
Ward Cl WS13 215 D6
Ward Gr WV4 266 F5
Wardle Cl B75 258 A4
Wardle Cres ST13 30 E4
Wardle La ST2 43 C1
Wardle Pl WS11 209 E5
Wardles La WS6 226 F2
Wardle St Stoke-on-T ST6 41 E3
Tamworth B79 250 A5
Wardlow Cl WV4 266 B6
Ward Pl ST6 42 B5
Ward Rd Codsall WV8 238 F3
Wolverhampton WV4 266 D5
Wards La CW12 16 C8
Ward St WS12 209 F6
Warings The WV5 269 F4
Warm Croft ST15 120 C7
Warminster Pl ST3 284 A3
Warmson Cl ST3 73 C6
Warner Rd WV8 238 F3
Warner St ST1 282 B2
Warnford Wlk WV4 265 C6
Warren Cl Cannock WS12 211 A5
Lichfield WS14 231 E7
Stretton DE13 147 E1
Warren Croft WS15 198 C4
Warren Ct 5 TF9 97 C1
Warren Dr DY3 266 C1
Warren Gdns DY6 275 C6
Warren Hill DE11 186 E5
Warren La DE14 184 F7
Warren Pl
Brownhills WS8 245 A7
Longton ST3 284 D2
Warren Rd
Burntwood WS7 229 A5
Stoke-on-T ST6 42 B6
Warrens La ST16 155 B6
Warren St ST3 284 D2
Warrilow Cl 1 ST3 90 A7
Warrilow Heath Rd ST5 40 C1
Warrington Dr ST13 30 C5
Warrington Rd ST1 57 D1
Warrington St ST4 72 F6
Warsill Gr ST3 73 D4
Warstone Hill Rd WV6 253 F4
Warstone Rd WS6 242 C7
Warstones Cres WV4 265 D5
Warstones Dr WV4 265 C6
Warstones Gdns WV4 265 C6
Warstones Jun & Inf Sch
WV4 265 E6
Warstones Rd WV4 265 D5
Wartell Bank Ind Est
DY6 275 D7
Wartell Bank DY6 275 D7
Warwick Ave
3 Longton ST3 73 F1
Cheadle ST10 76 C2
Newcastle-u-L ST5 71 C4
Perton WV6 254 F3
Warwick Cl
Burton u T DE14 184 F8
Cannock WS11 226 F8
Kidsgrove ST7 26 A3
Market Drayton TF9 97 D2
Warwick Ct
6 Wolverhampton WV4 266 F4
Dudley DY3 271 D3
Warwick Dr WV8 238 E3
Warwick Gr ST5 56 E3
Warwick Rd
Stafford ST17 175 B8
Warwick Rd *continued*
Stourbridge DY8 275 D1
Tamworth B77 250 E4
Warwick St Biddulph ST8 27 C7
Burton u T DE13 166 C6
Hanley ST1 57 A3
Newcastle-u-L ST5 55 E7
Warwick Way WS9 245 A1
Wasdale Dr DY6 275 E6
Wasdale Rd WS8 244 D6
Washbrook La
Norton Canes WS11 227 D5
Thorpe DE6 51 F4
Wash Dale La ST15 105 A6
Washerwall La ST9 59 A4
Washerwall St ST2 73 D8
Washford Rd DE65 147 E8
Washington Cl ST8 16 C2
Washington Ct WV3 255 D1
Washington Dr ST17 175 A8
Washington St ST6 41 E2
Waste La DE6 79 D4
Wastwater Ct WV6 254 F4
Watchfield Cl ST3 73 F1
Waterbeck Gr ST4 88 C5
Waterbridge La WV5 269 E7
Waterbrook Cl ST19 207 E7
Waterbrook Way WS11 226 E6
Waterdale Gr ST3 73 E3
Water Dale WV3 255 E2
Waterdale WV5 269 E5
Water Eaton La ST19 207 B5
Waterfall La ST10 48 F2
Waterford Dr TF10 168 E1
Waterford Rd DY6 275 D7
Watergate St ST6 41 D3
Water Glades Cl 2 ST1 56 F2
Waterhead Cl WV10 241 A2
Waterhead Dr WV10 241 B2
Waterhead Grange WS8 244 E7
Waterhead Rd ST3 73 F1
Waterhouses CE Prim Sch
ST10 48 F2
Watering Cl ST5 85 C4
Watering Trough Bank
CW3 69 B8
Water La Bobbington DY7 268 D2
Newport TF10 168 F3
Waterlily Cl WS12 210 E3
Water Lily Gr WS8 244 E7
Waterloo Bvd WS12 210 E4
Waterloo Ct ST13 30 D5
Waterloo Gr ST7 26 A2
Waterloo Ho WS15 197 B6
Waterloo Rd
Burslem ST6,ST1 57 A6
Edgmond TF10 168 A6
Waterloo St
Burton u T DE14 166 C4
Hanley ST1 282 C2
Leek ST13 30 D5
Watermeadow Dr WS4 244 D1
Watermeadow Gr 3 ST1 56 F2
Watermeet Gr ST1 56 F3
Watermill Cl WV10 240 D3
Watermint Cl WS12 210 E4
Waterpark Rd DE6 127 B8
Water Rd DY3 271 C2
Waters Dr B74 257 D3
Waters Edge WS15 198 C5
Watersedge Gr 4 ST1 56 F2
Waterside Bsns Pk
WS15 197 A7
Waterside DE15 185 E7
Waterside Cl Madeley CW3 68 E6
Slade Heath WV10 224 E2
Wolverhampton WV2 266 D7
Waterside Com Jun Sch
DE15 185 E7
Waterside Ct
Branston DE14 165 F1
Gnosall ST20 171 C5
Tamworth B77 250 F5
Waterside Dr
Market Drayton TF9 97 E2
Stoke-on-T ST3 88 E7
Waterside Mews TF10 168 E3
Waterside Rd DE15 185 D7
Waterside WS15 196 F6
Waterside Way
Brownhills WS8 228 D2
Wolverhampton WV9 240 A3
Watersmead Cl WS12 210 F4
Watersmeet Ct ST15 120 C6
Watersmeet Ho B78 261 B8
Waters Rd WS15 160 F3
Water St Burntwood WS7 228 E8
Kingswinford DY6 275 D7
Newcastle-u-L,Red Street
ST5 40 D2
Newcastle-u-L ST5 283 C3
Stafford ST16 285 B3
Stoke-on-T ST4 72 A5
Waters View WS3 244 B5
Waterton Cl DE13 148 A1
Waterways Gdns DY8 275 E1
Waterworks Cotts DY6 274 F4
Watery La
Abbots Bromley WS15 160 D4
Astbury CW12 15 C5
Clifton DE6 81 E7
Codsall WV8 239 A5
Ellastone DE6 80 B4
Gentleshaw WS7,WS15 212 B3
Hangingbridge DE6 81 F8
Haughton ST18 172 F5
Kingstone ST14 125 B2
Lichfield WS13 214 C4
Watery La *continued*
Longton ST3 73 D1
Scropton DE65 129 E2
Stourbridge DY8 275 E2
Swadlincote DE11 186 D5
Uttoxeter ST14 110 C6
Watford Gap Rd WS14 258 A7
Watford Gap WS14 258 A7
Watford St ST4 72 C8
Wathan Ave WV14 266 F1
Watkin St ST4 72 D6
Watkiss Dr WS15 178 D1
Watlands Ave ST5 56 C6
Watlands Rd ST7 39 E2
Watlands View ST5 56 B6
Watling St
Blymhill Lawn TF11 204 C2
Brownhills WS8 228 D1
Cannock WS11 226 D6
Dordon B77,B78 262 D6
Hints B78 248 D3
Norton Canes WS11 227 D3
Watling Street Bsns Pk
WS11 228 A2
Watling Street Prim Sch
WS8 228 E1
Watling St
Tamworth,Bonehill B78 249 E1
Tamworth,Two Gates B77 261 D7
Tamworth,Wilnecote B77,
B78 261 E7
Watson Cl Fradley WS13 215 E8
Rugeley WS15 178 D3
Watson Rd Stoke-on-T ST4 71 F4
Wolverhampton,Lanesfield
WV14 266 F2
Wolverhampton,Pendeford
WV10 240 B2
Watson St
Burton u T DE14 166 D1
Stoke-on-T ST4 72 A8
Wattfield Cl WS15 197 A5
Watt Ho DY6 275 F7
Wattles La ST17 175 B2
Watt Pl ST10 76 D3
Watts Cl ST17 174 B8
Wat Tyler Cl WS15 178 D3
Waveney Ave WV6 254 E4
Waveney Ct ST5 71 B4
Waveney Gr
Cannock WS11 209 B1
Newcastle-u-L ST5 71 B4
Waveney B77 261 E8
Waveney Wlk N ST6 42 A4
Waveney Wlk S ST6 42 A4
Wavenham Cl B74 257 E5
Waverley Cres
Wolverhampton,Goldthorn Hill
WV4 266 B6
Wolverhampton,Lanesfield
WV4 266 F3
Waverley Gdns
Rugeley WS15 178 B2
Wombourne WV5 270 B7
Waverley La DE14 166 B4
Waverley Pl ST5 71 B5
Waverley Rd WS3 242 F2
Waverley Wlk WS14 231 B6
Waverton Rd ST2 73 E7
Wavertree Ave ST7 25 E7
Waybutt La CW2 52 D8
Wayfield Dr ST16 155 D8
Wayfield Gr ST4 71 D8
Wayside Acres WV8 238 F2
Wayside Ave ST5 56 C4
Wayside Dr B74 257 C3
Wayside WV8 239 F2
Wayte St ST1 282 A4
Wealden Hatch WV10 240 E4
Wealdstone Dr DY3 271 D2
Weathercock La CW12 6 E3
Weatheroaks WS9 245 B4
Weaver Cl Biddulph ST8 16 D1
Cheadle ST10 76 E5
Weaver Ct 8 B75 258 E3
Weaver Dr ST17 174 B8
Weaverlake Dr DE13 181 F3
Weaver Pl ST5 71 B4
Weaver Rd ST14 111 B2
Weavers La ST15 120 C7
Weaver St ST1 282 B3
Weavers The ST14 95 D6
Weavers Wlk ST15 103 C4
Weaving Gdns 1 WS11 209 E1
Webb Ave WV6 254 E5
Webb Cl WS13 215 C6
Webberley La ST3 284 C3
Webb St ST3 74 B3
Webley Rise WV10 240 F4
Webster Ave ST3 73 E5
Webster St ST5 283 C2
Webster Wlk WS11 210 A4
Wedgewood Ave ST15 119 E6
Wedgewood Cl
Burntwood WS7 229 C7
Burton u T DE15 167 B1
Wedgewood Ct WS4 244 C1
Wedgwood Ave
Audley ST7 40 A1
Newcastle-u-L ST5 71 A7
Wedgwood Cl WV5 269 F7
Wedgwood Ct ST1 57 A3
Wedgwood Dr ST12 88 E4
Wedgwood Halt ST12 88 D3
Wedgwood La
Barlaston ST12 88 E4
Biddulph ST8 16 C2
Biddulph ST8 16 C3
Wedgwood Pl 1 ST6 56 F8
Wedgwood Rd
Cheadle ST10 76 D1
Hopton ST18 156 B8
Stoke-on-T ST4 72 F6
Talke ST7 40 D7
Wedgwood St
4 Burslem ST6 56 F8
Newcastle-u-L ST5 56 D5
Wedgwood Story The*
ST12 88 D4
Weeford Dell 2 B75 258 E3
Weeford Rd B75 258 F3
Weeping Cross ST17 175 D7
Weetman Cl ST6 41 C7
Weighton Gr ST2 58 E1
Weir Bank DE15 185 E6
Weir Gr ST7 26 B2
Weirside DE6 81 D7
Welbeck Pl ST2 58 C5
Welbury Gdns WV6 255 F5
Welby St ST4 72 D5
Welch St ST4 72 B7
Weldon Ave ST3 74 B4
Welford Gr B74 257 F3
Welford Rd B77 261 C5
Welford Rise DE13 166 A6
Welland Cl DE15 167 A5
Welland Gr ST5 71 A3
Welland Rd DE65 147 D8
Wellbury Cl ST4 88 C5
Wellcroft Grange DE6 65 D1
Weller Cl ST11 90 D3
Weller Ct WV3 255 D1
Weller St ST4 71 E8
Wellesbourne Cl WV3 265 B8
Wellesbourne B79 250 C8
Wellesley St ST1 282 A1
Wellfield Cl WS11 226 B7
Wellfield Rd
Aldridge WS9 256 B8
Alrewas DE13 201 A2
Bucknall ST2 58 C1
Wellington Ave WV3 265 F7
Wellington Cl
Kingswinford DY6 275 E4
Stafford ST16 155 E5
Wellington Cres WS13 215 B4
Wellington Ct
2 Leek ST13 30 E5
Hanley ST1 282 C3
Wellington Dr
Cannock WS11 226 B8
Rugeley WS15 196 E8
Wellington Mill 1 ST13 30 E5
Wellington Rd
Albrighton WV7 220 F1
Burton u T,Branston DE14 184 E8
Burton u T DE14 166 A2
Hanley ST1 282 C2
Kidsgrove ST7 26 A2
Newport TF10 168 E1
Wellington St W DE14 166 B3
Wellington St
1 Newcastle-u-L ST5 56 C5
Burton u T DE14 166 B3
Hanley ST1 282 C2
Leek ST13 30 E6
Wellington Terr ST1 282 C2
Well La Biddulph ST8 16 D3
Great Wyrley WS6 227 A1
Walsall WS3 243 E1
Warslow SK17 22 B2
Weston Jones TF10 150 C4
Wells Cl Biddulph ST8 27 D8
Cannock WS11 209 E6
Perton WV6 254 D4
Rugeley WS15 196 C6
Wells Dr ST17 175 E7
Wells La ST18 191 C8
Wells Rd WV4 265 F5
Well St Biddulph ST8 27 D7
Cheadle ST10 76 E3
Forsbrook ST11 91 A8
Hanley ST1 282 C2
Leek ST13 30 F5
Mow Cop ST7 26 D7
Newcastle-u-L ST5 283 C2
Wellyards Cl ST18 138 D2
Welney Gdns WV9 240 A3
Welsh Cl ST3 89 D8
Wembley La WS7 228 D8
Wembury B77 250 E5
Wem Gr ST5 40 E2
Wendell Crest WV10 240 F4
Wendling Cl ST2 58 D1
Wendover Gr ST2 58 C1
Wendover Rd WV4 266 F2
Wendy Cl ST2 58 B1
Wenger Cres ST4 88 A7
Wenham Dr ST3 90 B7
Wenlock Ave WV3 265 E8
Wenlock Cl
Newcastle-u-L ST5 40 E2
Sedgley DY3 271 C7
Stoke-on-T ST6 42 B8
Wenlock Dr TF10 168 E2
Wenlock B77 250 D3
Wensleydale Ave CW12 6 A5
Wensleydale Cl ST1 57 D7
Wentlows Ave ST10 92 D5
Wentlows Rd ST10 92 D5
Wentworth Cl WS7 229 C7
Wentworth Ct B75 258 B1

Wentworth Dr
Kidsgrove ST7 . . . . 26 C3
Lichfield WS14 . . . . 231 D5
Stafford ST16 . . . . 156 C3
Stretton DE13 . . . . 147 D1
Wentworth Gr
Perton WV6 . . . . 254 D5
Stoke-on-T ST1 . . . . 57 F8
Wentworth Rd
Stourbridge DY8 . . . . 279 E7
Walsall WS3 . . . . 242 F3
Wolverhampton WV10 . . . . 240 F3
Werburgh Dr ST4 . . . . 88 A7
Wereton Rd ST7 . . . . 39 D1
Wergs Dr WV6 . . . . 255 A7
Wergs Hall WV8 . . . . 254 F7
Wergs Hall Rd
Codsall WV8 . . . . 254 F8
Wolverhampton WV6,WV8 255 A7
Wergs Rd Codsall WV8 . . . 254 F7
Wolverhampton WV6 . . . . . 255 B6
Werneth Gr WS3 . . . . 243 A4
Werrington Prim Sch ST9 59 B3
Werrington Rd ST2 . . . . . . 58 B4
Wesker Pl ST3 . . . . 73 F4
Wesleyan Ct 5 ST13 . . . . . 30 D6
Wesleyan Rd TF9 . . . . 100 A6
Wesley Ave
Cheslyn Hay WS6 . . . . 226 D3
Codsall WV8 . . . . 239 B2
Wesley Cl Burntwood WS7 211 F1
Wombourne WV5 . . . . 269 F5
Wesley Ct
5 Wolverhampton WV4 . . 266 F4
Betley CW3 . . . . 53 A6
Cannock WS11 . . . . 209 E1
Wesley Dr ST15 . . . . 120 C6
Wesley Gdns 7 ST7 . . . . . . 26 A2
Wesley Pl Cannock WS12 . 210 C7
Halmer End ST7 . . . . 54 D7
Newcastle-u-L ST5 . . . . 70 F8
Wesley Rd WV8 . . . . 239 B2
Wesley St Audley ST7 . . . . . 40 A1
Blythe Bridge ST11 . . . . 91 A7
Stoke-on-T ST6 . . . . 41 D3
Wesley Way B77 . . . . 250 F4
Wessenden B77 . . . . 262 B7
Wessex Cl WS8 . . . . 244 F7
Wessex Ct B79 . . . . 251 F7
Wessex Dr Cannock WS11 209 F2
Stoke-on-T ST4 . . . . 88 A8
Wessex Rd WV2 . . . . 266 F6
Westacre ST1 . . . . 57 F3
Westacre Cres WV3 . . . . . 255 C1
Westacre Dr DE11 . . . . 186 F2
Westacre Inf Sch WV3 . . . 255 C1
West Acres ST14 . . . . 141 C8
West Ave Kidsgrove ST7 . . . 25 C1
Newcastle-u-L ST5 . . . . 56 D2
Stoke-on-T ST4 . . . . 71 F8
Weston CW2 . . . . 37 B5
West Bank ST4 . . . . 72 A6
West Beeches WV9 . . . . . 224 B2
Westbeech Rd WV6 . . . . . 253 D5
Westbook Way WV5 . . . . . 269 F5
Westbourne Ave
Cannock WS11 . . . . 209 D3
Cheslyn Hay WS6 . . . . 226 E3
Westbourne Cl ST13 . . . . . 30 C6
Westbourne Cres WS7 . . 229 B7
Westbourne Dr ST6 . . . . . . 41 E5
Westbourne Rd WV4 . . . 266 A5
Westbourne Villas ST16 . 285 B4
West Brampton ST5 . . . . . 283 B3
Westbrook Ave WS9 . . . . 256 A5
Westbury Cl ST1 . . . . 57 F5
Westbury Hayes ST17 . . . 174 A8
Westbury Rd ST5 . . . . 71 B3
West Butts Rd WS15 . . . . 178 B1
West Cannock Way
WS12 . . . . 195 D1
Westcliffe 3 ST13 . . . . 30 D6
Westcliffe Ave ST5 . . . . . . 71 A3
Westcliffe Hospl ST6 . . . . 41 F7
West Cl Stafford ST16 . . . . 156 A3
Stone ST15 . . . . 119 F7
West Coppice Rd WS8 . . . 244 C8
Westcott Cl DY6 . . . . 275 F3
Westcott La TF9 . . . . 130 A7
West Cres ST1 . . . . 57 E8
Westcroft Ave WV10 . . . . 241 A1
Westcroft Rd
Sedgley DY3 . . . . 266 B2
Wolverhampton WV6 . . . . . 254 F6
Westcroft Sch WV10 . . . . . 241 B2
West Dr Cheddleton ST13 . . 45 C7
Fazeley B78 . . . . 249 E2
West End Ave ST13 . . . . . . 30 D5
Westerby Dr ST9 . . . . 59 A3
Westerham Cl ST4 . . . . 87 F7
Westering Parkway
WV10 . . . . 240 F4
Western Ave DY3 . . . . 271 B8
Western By Pass WS13 . . 213 E1
Western By-Pass WS13 . 230 F8
Western Rd
Cannock WS12 . . . . 210 B6
Stourbridge DY8 . . . . 279 F4
Western Springs Prim Sch
WS15 . . . . 178 D2
Western Springs Rd
WS15 . . . . 178 D2
Westfield Ave ST7 . . . . 39 C2
Westfield Dr
Aldridge WS9 . . . . 256 A6
Westfield Dr *continued*
Wombourne WV5 . . . . 269 F7
Westfield Gr WV3 . . . . 265 C8
Westfield Manor B75 . . . . 258 A4
Westfield Prim Sch WV5 269 F7
Westfield Rd Bucknall ST2 . 58 B3
Burton u T DE13 . . . . 166 B6
Mow Cop ST7 . . . . 26 C7
Sedgley DY3 . . . . 266 E1
Westfields
Cauldon Lowe ST10 . . . . . . 63 E4
Leek ST13 . . . . 30 F5
Westfields Rd WS15 . . . . . 197 F4
Westfields Rise CW3 . . . . 67 C1
Westfields B78 . . . . 262 D8
Westgate Brewood ST19 . . 223 D7
Cannock WS12 . . . . 210 F6
Westgate Cl DY3 . . . . 271 E7
West Gn WV4 . . . . 265 C5
Westhall Cl ST19 . . . . 223 D6
Westhall Gate WS3 . . . . . 243 B2
Westhead Ave ST16 . . . . . 156 A4
Westhead Rd DY10 . . . . . . 280 A4
Westhead Rd N DY10 . . . . 280 A4
Westhead Wlk ST1 . . . . . . 282 A2
West Hill Ave WS12 . . . . . 210 B6
West Hill Prim Sch
WS12 . . . . 210 B6
West Hill ST14 . . . . 126 C6
Westhill WV3 . . . . 255 C2
Westhouse La ST14 . . . . . . 79 F3
Westland Ave WV3 . . . . . . 255 F2
Westland Gdns DY8 . . . . . 279 F7
Westland Rd
Market Drayton TF9 . . . . . . 97 B1
Wolverhampton WV6 . . . . . 255 F2
Westlands ST7 . . . . 39 F2
Westlands Ave ST5 . . . . . . 70 F7
Westlands Prim Sch ST5 . 70 F6
Westlands Rd ST14 . . . . . 126 B6
Westlands The ST14 . . . . . 95 D6
Westland St ST4 . . . . 72 A7
Westlands CW3 . . . . 83 B7
Westleigh Rd WV5 . . . . . . 269 F5
Westley Ct DY10 . . . . 280 C5
Westmarsh Gr ST6 . . . . . . 42 A4
Westmead Rd DE13 . . . . . 183 C1
Westmere Cl CW2 . . . . 37 B5
Westmill St ST1 . . . . 282 C1
Westminster Ave WV4 . . . 266 B5
Westminster Cl ST17 . . . . 175 C8
Westminster Dr
4 Burton u T DE13 . . . . . . 166 D8
Market Drayton TF9 . . . . . . 112 A7
Westminster Pl ST4 . . . . . 72 A1
Westminster Rd
Cannock WS11 . . . . 209 E6
Leek ST13 . . . . 31 A7
Stourbridge DY8 . . . . 275 D2
Westmorland Ave ST7 . . . . 40 F7
Westmorland Cl
Stoke-on-T ST6 . . . . 42 A8
Tamworth B78 . . . . 250 A1
Weston Bank Cl TF11 . . . . 203 E2
Weston Bank
Thurvaston DE6 . . . . 96 F1
Weston ST18 . . . . 138 A2
Weston-Under-Lizard TF11 203 E2
Weston Cl
Bishops Wood ST19 . . . . . . 221 E8
Cannock WS11 . . . . 210 C1
Newcastle-u-L ST5 . . . . 55 F3
Werrington ST2 . . . . 59 A4
Weston Coyney Inf Sch
ST3 . . . . 74 B5
Weston Coyney Jun Sch
ST3 . . . . 74 A3
Weston Coyney Rd
Longton ST3 . . . . 73 E3
Meir ST3 . . . . 74 A4
Weston Cres WS9 . . . . 256 B4
Weston Ct ST3 . . . . 74 A4
Weston Dr
Great Wyrley WS6 . . . . 226 F1
Meir ST3 . . . . 74 A4
Westonfields Dr ST3 . . . . . 73 E3
Weston Ho WV6 . . . . 255 E5
Weston La Bowers ST21 . . 102 A4
Standon ST21 . . . . 101 F6
Weston CW2 . . . . 37 A5
Weston Park Ave DE14 . . . 166 D7
Weston Park★ TF11 . . . . . 203 F1
Weston Rd
Albrighton WV7 . . . . 237 B5
Hopton ST16,ST18 . . . . 156 C4
Lichfield WS13 . . . . 214 A2
Meir ST3 . . . . 74 A3
Stowford CW1 . . . . 37 B8
Weston Road High Sch
ST18 . . . . 156 D5
Weston St Leek ST13 . . . . . 31 A6
Longton ST3 . . . . 73 D6
Westonview Ave ST3 . . . . . 73 D5
Weston Village Prim Sch
CW2 . . . . 37 C5
Westover Dr ST15 . . . . 120 C7
West Par ST4 . . . . 72 C5
Westport Lake Rd ST6 . . . . 41 D1
Westport Rd ST6 . . . . 41 E1
West Prec ST1 . . . . 282 B2
West Rd WV4 . . . . 266 F5
Westridge DY3 . . . . 271 C8
Westsprink Cres ST3 . . . . . 73 E2
West St Biddulph ST8 . . . . . 27 C7
Burton u T DE15 . . . . 167 B3
Cannock WS11 . . . . 226 E6
Leek ST13 . . . . 30 E6
Meir ST3 . . . . 74 B5
West St *continued*
Mount Pleasant ST7 . . . . . . 26 B6
Newcastle-u-L,Porthill ST5 . 56 D7
Newcastle-u-L,Silverdale
ST5 . . . . 55 B1
Newcastle-u-L ST5 . . . . . . 283 C2
Stourbridge DY8 . . . . 279 F5
Tamworth B79 . . . . 250 C5
Tamworth,Kettlebrook B77 250 C3
West Terr ST6 . . . . 42 B6
West View ST14 . . . . 125 C7
Westview Cl ST13 . . . . 30 C6
West View Dr DY6 . . . . . . 275 E5
West View Mayfield DE6 . . . 81 D6
Newcastle-u-L ST5 . . . . 56 B5
Rocester ST14 . . . . 96 A3
Stoke-on-T ST3 . . . . 89 F4
Westward Cl ST14 . . . . . . 111 B1
West Way Gn ST17 . . . . . . 155 C1
Westway Ho WS4 . . . . 244 B1
West Way Stafford ST17 . . 174 C8
Uttoxeter ST14 . . . . 110 F1
Walsall WS4 . . . . 244 B2
Westwick Cl WS9 . . . . 245 E4
West Winds WV10 . . . . . . 241 C7
Westwood Ave DY8 . . . . . 279 D3
Westwood Cl
Cheddleton ST13 . . . . 45 C4
Chorlton CW2 . . . . 37 B1
Westwood Ct
13 Leek ST13 . . . . 30 D6
Hanley ST1 . . . . 282 C3
Westwood Fst Sch ST13 . . 30 C5
Westwood Gr 10 ST13 . . . . 30 D6
Westwood Heath Rd ST13 30 C6
Westwood High Sch ST13 30 B5
Westwood Holdings
WS12 . . . . 209 B6
Westwood Park Ave ST13 30 B5
Westwood Park Dr ST13 . . 30 B5
Westwood Pk DE11 . . . . . . 186 F5
Westwood Rd Leek ST13 . . 30 D5
Meir ST3 . . . . 74 A2
Newcastle-u-L ST5 . . . . 56 D6
Westwoods Hollow WS7 229 B8
Westwood Terr 7 ST13 . . . 30 D6
Westwood View 14 ST13 . 30 D6
Wetherall Cl WS15 . . . . . . 178 D2
Wetherby Cl Cheadle ST10 . 76 E5
Newcastle-u-L ST5 . . . . 55 E7
Wolverhampton WV10 . . . . 240 D5
Wetherby Ct DE14 . . . . . . 184 F7
Wetherby Rd
Stoke-on-T ST4 . . . . 88 B7
Walsall WS3 . . . . 243 A4
Wetherel Rd DE15 . . . . 167 C2
Wetley Ave ST9 . . . . 59 F4
Wetley La ST13 . . . . 33 A2
Wetmore La DE14 . . . . 166 F6
Wetmore Rd
Burton u T DE14 . . . . 166 E5
Burton u T DE14 . . . . 166 E6
Wettenhall Dr ST13 . . . . . . 30 B4
Wetton Rd ST13 . . . . 34 B5
Wexford Cl DY1 . . . . 271 F2
Weybourne Ave ST2 . . . . . . 43 B3
Weyhill Cl WV9 . . . . 239 F2
Weymouth Dr B74 . . . . 257 F4
Weymouth Ho B79 . . . . . . 250 B5
Whalley Ave ST4 . . . . 71 E6
Wharf Cl WS14 . . . . 231 C7
Wharfe Cl ST14 . . . . 126 C8
Wharfedale Cl DY6 . . . . . . 275 B7
Wharfedale Rd CW12 . . . . . . 6 A5
Wharfedale Wlk ST3 . . . . 284 A3
Wharf Hos DE13 . . . . 184 A1
Wharf La Astbury CW12 . . . 15 B3
Burntwood WS8 . . . . 228 F3
Wharf Pl ST4 . . . . 72 C7
Wharf Rd Biddulph ST8 . . . . 27 C8
Burton u T DE14 . . . . 166 E5
Gnosall ST20 . . . . 171 C5
Rugeley WS15 . . . . 196 E7
Wharf Road Ind Est
DE14 . . . . 166 E5
Wharf St ST5 . . . . 283 D3
Wharf Terr CW3 . . . . 69 B8
Wharmadine La
Ashley TF9 . . . . 100 E7
Maer TF9 . . . . 84 F1
Wharwell La WS6 . . . . 227 A1
Whateley La B77,B78 . . . . 261 F4
Whateley Villas CV9 . . . . . 262 A2
Whatmore St ST6 . . . . 42 C1
Wheat Breach Cl DE13 . . 166 B6
Wheatcroft Cl
3 Sutton Coldfield B75 . . 258 E3
Burntwood WS7 . . . . 229 A5
Penkridge ST19 . . . . 207 F8
Wheatfields ST6 . . . . 42 C3
Wheathill Cl WV4 . . . . 265 E3
Wheatland Gr WS9 . . . . . . 256 B4
Wheatlands Cl 1 WS12 . 210 C1
Wheatlands Rd DE15 . . . . 185 E7
Wheatlands The WV6 . . . . 254 D3
Wheatley Ave ST4 . . . . 71 E6
Wheatley Cl B75 . . . . 258 C3
Wheatley Gr WS6 . . . . 227 A2
Wheatley La DE15 . . . . 167 C4
Wheatley St WV2 . . . . 266 F6
Wheatmill Cl DY10 . . . . . . 281 B2
Wheatridge Cl DY6 . . . . . . 275 A8
Wheatsheaf Cl B75 . . . . . . 258 E4
Wheatsheaf Rd WV8 . . . . . 239 E1
Wheatstone Cl DY3 . . . . . . 271 E6
Wheel Ave WV8 . . . . 238 F3
Wheel Ct The WV8 . . . . . . 238 F3
Wheeler Cl WV8 . . . . 238 F4
Wheeler St DY8 . . . . 279 F5
Wheelfield WV8 . . . . 238 F3
Wheelhouse Rd WS15 . . . . 197 B6
Wheel La WS13 . . . . 213 F1
Wheelock Way 2 ST7 . . . . . 26 B2
Wheelwrights La ST21 . . 134 D7
Whetstone Field Prim Sch
WS9 . . . . 256 B4
Whetstone Gn WV10 . . . . . 240 D1
Whetstone La WS9 . . . . . . 256 B4
Whetstone Rd ST8 . . . . 16 C2
Whieldon Cres ST4 . . . . . . 72 C5
Whieldon Ind Est ST4 . . . . 72 C6
Whieldon Rd ST4 . . . . 72 C6
Whilmot Cl WV10 . . . . 241 B6
Whimple Side ST2 . . . . 58 B1
Whimster Sq ST17 . . . . . . 174 A8
Whinberry Rise DY5 . . . . . 271 C1
Whinyates Rise WS11 . . . . 226 F8
Whisper La ST4,ST5 . . . . . . 86 E7
Whiston Cl WV7 . . . . 237 A5
Whiston Eaves La ST10 . . . 62 D2
Whitacre La WS14 . . . . 245 E7
Whitaker Rd ST3 . . . . 72 F3
Whitbread Dr ST8 . . . . 27 E8
Whitburn Cl WV9 . . . . 240 A2
Whitby Cl Stafford ST17 . . 174 C7
Walsall WS3 . . . . 242 F3
Whitby Way WS11 . . . . 226 C8
Whitchurch Gr ST5 . . . . . . 40 E2
Whitcliffe Pl ST3 . . . . 72 F3
Whitcombe Rd ST3 . . . . . . 74 A2
White Bark Cl WS12 . . . . . 210 A8
Whitebeam Cl
Brownhills WS8 . . . . 244 E6
Dudley DY3 . . . . 271 C4
Newcastle-u-L ST5 . . . . 40 D1
Whitebridge Ind Est
ST15 . . . . 104 F2
Whitebridge La ST15 . . . . . 104 E2
Whitebridge Way ST15 . . 104 F2
White Farm Rd B74 . . . . . . 257 E4
Whitefield Cl WV8 . . . . 239 B2
Whitefields La ST10 . . . . . . 49 B2
Whitegates CW12 . . . . 16 D4
Whitehall Ave ST7 . . . . 25 F2
Whitehall Cl ST14 . . . . 141 C8
Whitehall Ct WV3 . . . . 265 F6
Whitehall Rd
Kingswinford DY6 . . . . 275 C6
Wolverhampton WV4 . . . . . 266 B4
White Harte Cvn Pk DY7 . 278 A3
Whitehaven Dr ST1 . . . . . . 282 B4
Whitehead Rd ST6 . . . . 42 B5
Whiteheart Mews DE13 . . 201 A2
White Hill DY7 . . . . 277 F5
Whitehill Rd ST7 . . . . 26 B2
White Hollies WS3 . . . . . . 243 F4
White Horse Rd WS8 . . . . 228 E2
Whitehouse Ave WV3 . . . 265 D8
Whitehouse Cres
Burntwood WS7 . . . . 229 B7
Wolverhampton WV11 . . . . 241 F1
Whitehouse Dr WS13 . . . . 230 F6
White House La DY7 . . . . . 268 F1
Whitehouse La
Codsall WV8 . . . . 238 D7
Sandon ST15 . . . . 121 B7
White House La DY3 . . . . 269 B1
Whitehouse La DY7,DY3 . 269 B1
Whitehouse Rd
Bucknall ST2 . . . . 58 B5
Newcastle-u-L ST5 . . . . 56 B3
Whitehouse Rd N ST5 . . . . 56 B4
Whitehouse Rd B78 . . . . . . 262 F7
White Houses La WV10 . . 241 B5
Whitehurst La ST10 . . . . . . 75 D6
White Ladies Priory★
TF11 . . . . 221 D4
White Lion St ST17 . . . . . . 285 B2
Whitemill La ST15 . . . . 119 F7
White Oak Dr
Kingswinford DY6 . . . . 275 C6
Wolverhampton WV3 . . . . . 255 C1
Whiteoaks Dr ST19 . . . . . . 221 E8
White Oaks ST17 . . . . 175 D5
Whiteridge Rd ST7 . . . . 26 B2
White Row WV5 . . . . 264 C1
Whitesands Cl B77 . . . . . . 250 E5
Whitesands Gr ST3 . . . . 90 B7
White's Dr DY3 . . . . 271 E8
Whites La CW2 . . . . 37 B6
White's Mdw ST18 . . . . . . 153 D4
Whitesmiths Cl DY3 . . . . . 271 D8
Whitestone Rd ST3 . . . . 90 B6
Whites Wood WV5 . . . . 270 A5
Whitesytch La ST15 . . . . . 121 B8
Whitethorn Ave ST12 . . . . . 88 D1
Whitethorn Cl WS12 . . . . . 210 A8
Whitethorn Cres B74 . . . . 256 D1
Whitethorn Rd 2 DY8 . . . . 275 F1
Whitethorn Way ST5 . . . . . . 40 E1
Whitfield Ave ST5 . . . . 283 A1
Whitfield Rd
Cannock WS12 . . . . 210 C7
Kidsgrove ST7 . . . . 26 B2
Stoke-on-T ST6 . . . . 42 D6
Whitfield St ST13 . . . . 30 E4
Whitfield Valley Prim Sch
ST6 . . . . 42 B7
Whitgreave Ave WV10 . . . 241 B7
Whitgreave Ct
Featherstone WV10 . . . . . . 241 B6
Stafford ST16 . . . . 155 D5
Whitgreave La
Great Bridgeford ST18 . . . 135 D3
Rugeley WS15 . . . . 196 E6
Whitgreave ST18 . . . . 136 A4
Whitgreave Prim Sch
WV10 . . . . 241 B7
Whiting B77 . . . . 261 D7
Whitley Ave B77 . . . . 250 E5
Whitley Cl WV6 . . . . 255 B2
Whitley Rd ST6 . . . . 42 D6
Whitmore Ave ST9 . . . . 59 B4
Whitmore Rd
Hanchurch ST4 . . . . 87 D8
Newcastle-u-L ST5 . . . . 70 D4
Stourbridge DY8 . . . . 279 D5
Whitmore ST5 . . . . 86 B8
Whitmore St ST1 . . . . 57 A2
Whitney Ave DY8 . . . . 279 D6
Whitridge Gr ST2 . . . . 73 D8
Whittaker Mews ST14 . . . . 95 F3
Whittaker St WV2 . . . . 266 E6
Whittingham Dr ST17 . . . 174 B8
Whittington Common Rd
WS14 . . . . 232 B5
Whittington Hall La
Kinver DY7 . . . . 278 E2
Stourbridge DY7 . . . . 279 B3
Whittington Ho WS13 . . . 214 E1
Whittington Prim Sch
WS14 . . . . 232 E4
Whittington Rd DY8 . . . . . 279 E3
Whittle Ct ST1 . . . . 282 C4
Whittle Rd ST3 . . . . 90 B8
Whitty La
Blackshaw Moor ST13 . . . . . 20 C6
Upper Hulme ST13 . . . . 20 D6
Whitworth La WS15 . . . . . 178 B1
Whygate Gr ST1 . . . . 57 F6
Whytmore The WS13 . . . . 230 F5
Wickenlow La SK17 . . . . 3 C1
Wickenstones Ct ST8 . . . . . 27 D7
Wicket La DY7 . . . . 274 E1
Wickets The DE15 . . . . 185 F8
Wickstead Row CW3 . . . . . 53 A6
Widecombe Ave ST17 . . . 175 E7
Widecombe Rd ST1 . . . . . . 57 F5
Widgeon Gr WV10 . . . . 241 B7
Widney Ave WS9 . . . . 245 B1
Wigford Rd B77 . . . . 261 C5
Wiggin Ho WS3 . . . . 243 C3
Wigginton Rd B79 . . . . 250 B7
Wightman Cl WS14 . . . . . . 231 E6
Wightwick Bank WV6 . . . . 255 A2
Wightwick Cl WS3 . . . . 243 B1
Wightwick Ct WV6 . . . . . . 255 A2
Wightwick Gr WV6 . . . . . . 255 A2
Wightwick Hall Rd WV6 . 254 E1
Wightwick Hall Sch
WV6 . . . . 254 E2
Wightwick Manor★ WV6 254 F1
Wigley Bank Rd DY7 . . . . 277 D6
Wigmore Pl ST3 . . . . 73 C6
Wignall Rd ST6 . . . . 41 D6
Wilbraham's Wlk ST7 . . . . 39 D2
Wilcox Ave WS12 . . . . 210 B7
Wildacres DY8 . . . . 279 C6
Wildfowl Wlk ST5 . . . . 85 C4
Wild Goose Ave ST7 . . . . . . 26 D3
Wildhay La Stanton DE6 . . . 80 C7
Wootton DE6 . . . . 80 A7
Wilding Rd ST6 . . . . 42 D6
Wildtree Ave WV10 . . . . . 241 A2
Wildwood Dr
Stafford ST17 . . . . 175 C6
Stafford ST17 . . . . 175 C7
Wildwood Gate 2 ST17 . 175 D6
Wildwood Lawns ST17 . . 175 C7
Wildwood Sh Ctr ST17 . . 175 D6
Wileman Pl ST4 . . . . 72 E6
Wileman St ST4 . . . . 72 F6
Wilfred Owen Cl TF9 . . . . 112 A7
Wilfred Pl ST4 . . . . 71 F8
Wilkes Cl WS3 . . . . 243 E3
Wilkes Croft DY3 . . . . 271 D7
Wilkes Rd WV8 . . . . 238 F3
Wilke's Wood ST18 . . . . . . 154 F8
Wilkin Rd WS8 . . . . 228 C2
Wilkins Croft DE13 . . . . . . 200 F2
Wilkins Ho WS3 . . . . 243 A1
Wilkinson Cl WS7 . . . . 229 B8
Wilkinson St ST6 . . . . 41 D2
Wilkinson Wlk 1 TF9 . . . . . 97 C1
Wilks St ST6 . . . . 41 E4
Willatt Pl ST2 . . . . 43 A1
Willcock Rd
Burton u T DE14 . . . . 185 A7
Wolverhampton WV2 . . . . . 266 E7
Willdale Gr ST1 . . . . 57 F5
Willerby Fold WV10 . . . . . 240 F4
Willeton St ST2 . . . . 58 A3
Willett Ave WS7 . . . . 228 E5
Willey La ST20 . . . . 171 C6
Willfield La ST6,ST9 . . . . . . 43 C6
William Allitt Sch DE11 . . 186 E7
William Ave Biddulph ST8 . . 27 D7
Meir ST3 . . . . 90 C8
William Baxter Sch
WS12 . . . . 210 A6
William Birch Ct ST2 . . . . . 58 A1
William Birch Rd ST2 . . . . 58 A1
William Cl ST11 . . . . 91 B7
William Clowes St ST6 . . . . 56 F8
William Coltman Way
ST6 . . . . 41 C5
William Fiske Ct ST4 . . . . . 71 F4
William Hutson Jun Sch
DE13 . . . . 166 B8
William IV Rd DE13 . . . . . 201 A3
William Lunn's Homes 2
WS14 . . . . 231 C8
William MacGregor Prim Sch
B77 . . . . 250 D4

William Mews WV10 .... 225 C2
William Morris Ct WS15 178 D3
William Morris Gr WS11. 209 E4
William Nadin Way DE11 186 E3
William Newton Cl DE65. 148 B5
William Rd ST7 .... 26 A2
William Ruston Rd ST6... 42 D2
Williams Ave WS13 ...... 215 C6
Williams Cl ST16........ 155 B3
Williams Ct ST16........ 155 F7
William Shrewsbury Prim Sch DE13............. 147 F2
Williamson Ave
Prospect Village WS12 ... 211 C4
Stoke-on-T ST6 .... 42 E6
Williamson St ST6 .... 41 E2
William St
Burton u T DE14......... 166 C5
Congleton CW12 .... 6 A4
Stoke-on-T ST4 .... 72 E6
Williams Wlk ST15 ...... 103 C4
William Terr ST6......... 42 B6
William Tolson's Ind Est B78................... 261 A8
William Wiggin Ave
WS3..................... 243 B2
Willington Rd B79 ...... 250 B7
Williscroft Pl WS15 ..... 179 A6
Willmer Cres ST7 .... 26 B6
Willmott Cl B75......... 258 D3
Willmott Rd B75 .... 258 D3
Willotts Hill Rd ST5 ...... 40 D1
Willoughby Cl ST19 ..... 207 F7
Willoughby Ct ST14 ..... 125 C7
Willoughby Rd B79 ...... 249 E7
Willoughby St ST6 .... 41 D7
Willow Ave WS7 .... 229 C6
Willowbank B78 .... 250 B1
Willow Bank WV3........ 255 C1
Willow Bottom La B79 .. 234 B7
Willowbrook ST18 ...... 154 E2
Willowbrook Dr ST6 ..... 42 E1
Willow Cl Coven WV9 .... 224 B2
Fradley WS13 .... 215 E8
Hagley DY9 .... 281 F5
Kidsgrove ST7 .... 41 A7
Newcastle-u-L ST5........ 40 D1
Penkridge ST19.......... 207 F6
Upper Tean ST10......... 92 D5
Walton-on-t-H ST17...... 175 F6
Willowcroft Rise ST11.... 90 D7
Willowcroft Way ST7..... 26 E4
Willowcroft ST20 .... 151 E7
Willow Ct WS14.......... 231 C5
Willowdale Ave ST4....... 72 C5
Willowdale Grange WV6 255 E5
Willow Dale ST15 .... 120 C3
Willow Dr Cheddleton ST13. 45 C8
Codsall WV8 .... 239 B3
Swadlincote DE11 .... 186 F7
Willowfield Ct ST4....... 88 D7
Willowfield Dr ST4....... 88 C7
Willow Gr
Essington WV11......... 242 B3
Stoke-on-T ST3 .... 72 E2
Willowherb Cl WS11 .... 210 C2
Willow Ho WS4 .... 244 D1
Willow La ST3 .... 90 A3
Willowmoor ST17....... 174 E5
Willowood Gr ST3 .... 74 C1
Willow Pl Biddulph ST8.... 17 B1
Burton u T DE15......... 185 E7
Willow Rd
Barton-u-N DE13........ 183 D1
Kinver DY7............. 278 C3
Stone ST15 .... 120 B7
Wolverhampton WV3..... 265 D8
Willow Row ST3 .... 284 B3
Willows Dr ST3 .... 90 A4
Willowsmere Dr WS14 .. 231 F7
Willows Prim Sch WS13 . 214 B2
Willows Prim Sch The ST4.................... 71 F7
Willows The
Burton u T DE14......... 166 D2
Cannock WS11.......... 209 C1
Leek ST13 .... 30 C5
Rugeley WS15 .... 197 A5
Stone ST15 .... 120 B6
Sutton Coldfield,Streetly B74..................... 257 F2
Wombourne WV5........ 269 F5
Wrinehill CW3........... 53 A3
Yarnfield ST15.......... 118 E6
Willowtree Cl WS13..... 214 B2
Willow Tree Gr ST4 ...... 72 E4
Willow Way ST11 .... 91 A8
Willow Wlk WS12 .... 209 D8
Willridding La DE6........ 80 C7
Willsford Ave ST14....... 126 D7
Wilmcote Dr B75 .... 258 B3
Wilmore Ct ST18......... 137 D1
Wilmore Hill La ST18.... 137 D1
Wilmore La DE13 .... 164 B3
Wilmot Cl ST5 .... 55 F3
Wilmot Dr ST5.......... 55 F3
Wilmot Gr ST3........... 73 C6
Wilmott Cl WS13........ 231 A7
Wilnecote High Sch B77 261 F6
Wilnecote Jun Sch B77 . 261 F7
Wilnecote La B77 .... 250 D2
Wilnecote Sta B77 .... 261 D7
Wilner's View WS3...... 243 F5
Wilson Gr WS11 .... 210 C2
Wilson Keys Ct WS15.... 178 F2
Wilson Rd ST4........... 71 F1
Wilson St
Newcastle-u-L ST5....... 283 B3

Wilson St *continued*
Stoke-on-T ST6 .... 42 B2
Wilson Way ST6 .... 41 C6
Wiltell Rd Ind Est WS14 . 231 B7
Wiltell Rd WS14 .... 231 B6
Wilton Ave ST9 .... 59 F4
Wilton Cl DY3 .... 271 E7
Wilton St ST5........... 283 A4
Wiltshire Gr ST5 .... 71 C4
Wiltshire Ho 3 DY8..... 279 F8
Wimberry Dr ST5 .... 40 D1
Wimblebury Rd WS12 ... 210 F2
Wimborne Ave ST3 ...... 88 F7
Wimshurst Mdw WV10 .. 240 F4
Winceby Rd WV6 .... 254 F3
Winchcombe Cl DY1 .... 271 E3
Winchcombe Dr DE15 ... 167 B1
Winchester Ave ST2...... 58 D1
Winchester Cl
Armitage WS15 .... 198 B4
Lichfield WS13.......... 214 C3
Winchester Ct
Stafford ST17 .... 175 D6
Sutton Coldfield B74 ..... 257 F2
Winchester Dr
Burton u T DE14......... 185 C8
Newcastle-u-L ST5........ 70 F4
Winchester Mews WS9.. 256 B4
Winchester Rd
Cannock WS11.......... 210 A3
Tamworth B78........... 249 F3
Wolverhampton WV10.... 240 C3
Wincote Dr WV6 .... 255 C4
Wincote La ST21......... 133 C3
Windemere Way ST10.... 76 F4
Windermere Dr
Aldridge B74 .... 256 F3
Kingswinford DY6 .... 275 D6
Windermere Ho ST16 ... 285 C3
Windermere Pl WS11 ... 209 E1
Windermere Rd
Newcastle-u-L ST5........ 71 B4
Wolverhampton WV6...... 255 D8
Windermere St ST1 ...... 282 A4
Windermere B77 .... 262 A7
Windings The WS13...... 214 A1
Windmill Ave ST7 .... 41 A8
Windmill Bank
Gentleshaw WS15 .... 212 B5
Wombourne WV5........ 270 A7
Windmill Cl
4 Uttoxeter ST14......... 111 B1
Lichfield WS13.......... 214 A2
Stoke-on-T ST3 .... 89 F4
Tamworth B79........... 250 A8
Windmill Cres WV3 ..... 255 A1
Windmill Dr ST14 .... 127 E3
Windmill Gr DY6........ 275 B8
Windmillhill La WS14 ... 232 E5
Windmill Hill ST3 .... 89 F4
Windmill La Croxton ST21 116 A4
Gentleshaw WS15 .... 212 A4
Lichfield WS13.......... 214 A2
Snelston DE6............. 81 E2
Wolverhampton WV3..... 255 A1
Windmill St
Dudley,Gornalwood DY3 .. 271 D5
Hanley ST1 .... 282 C3
Windmill View ST9........ 59 C4
Windrow The WV6 ...... 254 D4
Windrush Cl
Stoke-on-T ST4 .... 88 C5
Walsall WS3 .... 244 A1
Windrush Rd
Cannock WS11.......... 209 E6
Hilton DE65 .... 147 D8
Windsmoor St ST4 .... 72 B5
Windsor Ave
Cannock WS12.......... 210 B6
Longton ST3............ 284 D2
Wolverhampton WV4..... 265 E6
Windsor Cl
Burntwood WS7......... 211 E1
Dudley DY3 .... 271 B2
Rugeley WS15 .... 196 D7
Stone ST15 .... 119 F5
Tamworth B79........... 250 C7
Windsor Cres DY7 ...... 277 F4
Windsor Ct
Cannock WS12.......... 210 B6
Lichfield WS14.......... 231 B6
Windsor Dr
Burton u T DE15......... 166 F1
Leek ST13 .... 31 B7
Market Drayton TF9....... 97 E2
Windsor Gdns
Codsall WV8 .... 238 F3
Wolverhampton WV3..... 265 A8
Windsor Gr
Stourbridge DY8 .... 275 E1
Walsall WS4 .... 244 C2
Windsor Holloway DY7.. 278 C1
Windsor Ho ST7 .... 40 D6
Windsor Ind Est DE14 ... 166 E4
Windsor Park CE Mid Sch ST14................... 126 B8
Windsor Rd
Albrighton WV7......... 237 A6
Cheslyn Hay WS6........ 226 E4
Pattingham WV6 .... 253 C2
Stafford ST17 .... 175 B8
Stoke-on-T ST4 .... 72 A1
Stourbridge DY8 .... 279 E3
Uttoxeter ST14 .... 111 A1
Wolverhampton WV4..... 266 F5
Wombourne WV5........ 269 F6
Windsor St ST5 .... 283 C3
Windy Arbour ST10 ...... 76 E4

Windy Arbour La WV10.. 225 E4
Windycote La ST10....... 60 B2
Windyridge SK17 .... 13 B6
Winford Ave DY6 .... 275 E4
Wingate Ct B74......... 257 E4
Wingate Wlk ST3 .... 88 F7
Winghay Cl ST6.......... 56 C8
Winghay Pl ST6.......... 42 B5
Winghay Rd ST7 .... 26 B2
Winghouse La ST15..... 103 E7
Wingrove Ave 1 ST3.... 73 D1
Winifred Gdns ST3....... 88 E8
Winifred St ST1......... 282 A4
Winnipeg Cl ST4......... 88 B8
Winpenny Rd ST5........ 55 F8
Winrush Cl DY3......... 271 D3
Winscar Croft DY3 ..... 271 D3
Winsford Ave ST3........ 73 E2
Winsford Cres ST17..... 175 E6
Winslow Dr WV6........ 255 E4
Winslow Gn ST2 .... 58 C1
Winsor Ave WS12....... 210 B6
Winstanley Cl WS15..... 178 D2
Winstanley Pl WS15..... 178 D2
Winster Gn DE11........ 186 E5
Winston Pl ST2 .... 58 A3
Winston Rd Cookley DY11. 280 A6
Swindon DY3 .... 269 E2
Winston Terr ST5 .... 56 C6
Winterbourne Gr ST3 .... 73 E3
Winter Cl WS13......... 214 D2
Wintercroft La DE6 ...... 51 E1
Winterfield La ST3....... 74 B7
Winterley Gdns DY3..... 271 E6
Winterside Cl ST5........ 40 D1
Wintonfield St ST4....... 72 C7
Winton Sq ST4........... 72 C8
Winwood Ct DY8........ 279 F4
Wiscombe Ave ST19 .... 193 A1
Wise St ST3 .... 284 C1
Wissage Ct WS13 .... 231 D8
Wissage La WS13 .... 214 D1
Wissage Rd WS13....... 231 D8
Wisteria Dr WS8 .... 228 C2
Wistmans Cl DY1 .... 271 E2
Wistwood Hayes WV10 .. 240 F4
Witchford Cres ST3 ...... 88 F7
Witham Way ST8 .... 16 E1
Withern Way DY3 .... 271 D3
Withers Rd WV8 .... 239 B3
Withies Rd ST4 .... 71 E4
Withington Rd ST6........ 42 A6
Within La ST18 .... 137 D1
Withnell Gn ST6 .... 42 A6
Withymere La WV5 ..... 270 C8
Withystakes Rd ST9...... 59 D4
Withywood Cl WV12..... 242 C1
Witley Dr 1 WS13 ...... 231 E8
Witney Cl B79 .... 249 F7
Witney Gr WV10 .... 240 B3
Witney Rd ST17......... 156 D1
Witney Wlk ST3.......... 88 F7
Witton Rd WV4 .... 266 A6
Witton St DY8 .... 279 F4
Wobaston Ct WV10...... 240 B3
Wobaston Rd
Codsall WV9 .... 239 E4
Wolverhampton WV9, WV10 .... 240 B4
Woburn Cl ST4 .... 88 C5
Woburn Dr CW12 .... 16 B8
Woburn B77............ 250 D3
Wodehouse Cl WV5..... 269 E5
Wodehouse Cotts WV5 . 270 D8
Wodehouse La WV5,DY3 . 270 E8
Woden Cl WV5.......... 269 F7
Wogan St ST16 .... 155 E5
Wold The WV5.......... 267 D7
Wolfe St ST4 .... 72 B6
Wolfscote Dale DE11 .... 186 F2
Wolgarston High Sch ST19.................... 208 A8
Wolgarston Way ST19... 207 F7
Wollaston Ct DY8 .... 279 C6
Wollaston Rd
Stourbridge DY8 .... 279 E8
Stourton DY7 .... 279 C7
Wollery La TF11 .... 204 C2
Wolmer Rd WV11 .... 242 A2
Wolmore La WV5 .... 263 B2
Wolseley Cl ST17 .... 177 E7
Wolseley Ctr The★ ST17 178 A5
Wolseley Ct
Rugeley WS15 .... 197 B6
Stafford ST18 .... 156 D5
Wolseley Rd
Newcastle-u-L ST5........ 56 B5
Rugeley,Cannock Chase Ctry Pk WS15 .... 177 E1
Rugeley WS15 .... 178 E2
Stafford ST16 .... 156 C3
Stoke-on-T ST4 .... 71 F4
Wolseley B77.......... 250 F3
Wolsey Rd WS13........ 213 F2
Wolstanton High Sch ST5 56 C4
Wolstanton Rd ST5 ...... 55 F6
Wolstanton Ret Pk ST5... 56 E4
Wolstern Rd ST3......... 73 D5
Wolverhampton Bsns Airport DY7................... 268 C2
Wolverhampton Coll Wulfrun Campus WV6 .... 255 E3
Wolverhampton Girls' High Sch WV6 .... 255 F3
Wolverhampton Gram Sch WV3 .... 255 F2
Wolverhampton Rd
Cannock WS11.......... 226 D8

Wolverhampton Rd *continued*
Cheslyn Hay WV10,WS6 .. 226 B2
Codsall WV8 .... 239 A3
Cookley DY10........... 280 B3
Essington WV11......... 242 A3
Wolverhampton Rd E
WV4.................... 266 D5
Wolverhampton Rd
Kingswinford DY6 .... 270 C1
Nurton WV6............ 254 A3
Pattingham WV6 .... 253 E3
Penkridge WS11 .... 207 E8
Sedgley DY3............ 266 D2
Stafford ST17 .... 285 B1
Stourton DY7 .... 278 F7
Walsall,Pelsall WS3...... 243 F3
Walsall,Wallington Heath WS3 .... 243 B1
Wedges Mills WS11...... 226 B6
Wolverley Ave
Stourbridge DY8 .... 279 C6
Wolverhampton WV4..... 265 D5
Wolverley Ct WV7 ...... 237 A5
Wolverley Rd DY10...... 280 A2
Wolverson Rd WS9...... 245 A4
Wombourne Cl DY3 ..... 271 C8
Wombourne Ent Pk WV5 .... 269 D5
Wombourne Pk WV5.... 269 F4
Wombourne Rd DY3,WV5 269 F3
Wombrook Dale WV5 ... 269 D6
Wombrook Ind Est WV5 . 269 E6
Woodall St ST1.......... 57 B6
Wood Ave Coven WV9.... 224 B3
Dudley DY3 .... 271 C4
Kingsley ST10 .... 61 D2
Wood Bank La ST19..... 193 B2
Woodbank Rd DY3 ...... 271 C7
Wood Bank Rd WV3 ..... 265 A8
Woodbank St ST6 .... 56 F8
Woodberry Ave ST4 ...... 71 F5
Woodberry Cl
Stafford ST17 .... 174 F4
Stoke-on-T ST4 .... 71 E5
Woodbine Cl DE14 ...... 184 E6
Woodbridge Cl
Walsall,Wallington Heath WS3 .... 243 A3
Walsall WS4 .... 244 D1
Woodbridge Rd ST5...... 71 B2
Woodburn Rd ST6 .... 42 E2
Woodcock Gdns WV10 .. 241 B7
Woodcock La ST7........ 26 C6
Woodcock Rd WS15..... 178 C1
Woodcocks' Well CE Prim Sch ST7................ 26 C6
Wood Common Grange
WS3..................... 243 F4
Woodcote Rd WV6...... 255 C4
Woodcote The 3 ST17.. 175 C7
Wood Cres Stafford ST16 . 155 B6
Stone ST15 .... 119 F5
Woodcroft ST7 .... 40 A1
Woodcroft Ave Leek ST13 . 30 D4
Tamworth B79........... 250 B6
Woodcroft Fst Sch ST13.. 30 C4
Woodcroft Rd ST13 ...... 30 D4
Woodcross La WV14 .... 266 F2
Woodcross St WV14..... 266 F2
Wood Ct DE14 .... 166 C1
Woodcdisse La ST13 ..... 33 E2
Wood Eaton Rd ST20.... 190 A7
Woodedge La ST14 ..... 143 F6
Wood End La
Fradley WS13 .... 215 A5
Lichfield WS13.......... 214 B7
Woodend Pl WV6 .... 255 B4
Wood End Prim Sch CV9 262 C1
Wood End Rd WV11..... 241 C1
Woodend St ST4......... 72 F6
Wood End Way WS9 .... 245 B1
Woodfield Ave WV4...... 265 F6
Woodfield Cl WS11 ..... 227 F7
Woodfield Ct ST13 .... 31 A6
Woodfield Dr WS11 ..... 227 F7
Woodfield Ho WS3...... 244 B3
Woodfield Hts WV6 ..... 255 D4
Woodfield Jun & Inf Schs WV4 .... 265 F6
Woodfield Rd DY3 ...... 271 C4
Woodfields Dr WS14 .... 231 E5
Woodfold Croft WS9.... 256 B7
Woodford Cl WV9........ 239 F2
Woodford Cres WS7 .... 229 B7
Woodford End 1 WS11 .. 209 F4
Woodford La WV5 ...... 269 D8
Woodford Way
Cannock WS12.......... 210 D1
Wombourne WV5........ 269 D6
Woodgate Ave ST7........ 25 A5
Woodgate St ST3 .... 74 A1
Woodgreen WS6......... 226 E5
Woodhall Pl ST5 .... 54 F2
Woodhall Rd
Kidsgrove ST7 .... 26 C3
Wolverhampton WV4..... 265 E5
Woodhaven Walsall WS4 . 244 D1
Wedges Mills WS11...... 226 B5
Woodseaves ST20........ 151 E7
Wood Hayes Croft WV10 241 C2
Wood Hayes Rd WV11... 241 C1
Woodhead Rd ST2 .... 58 C8
Woodhead Yd ST10 ...... 76 E5
Woodheyes Lawns
WS15................... 178 C1
Woodhill Cl WV5........ 269 F6
Wood Hill Dr WV5 ...... 269 F5

Woodhouse High Sch B77.................... 250 F4
Woodhouse La
Albrighton WV7 .... 237 C2
Biddulph Moor ST8 .... 17 A1
Biddulph ST8 .... 16 F2
Brown Edge ST6 .... 42 F6
Foston DE65 .... 129 F7
Haughton ST18 .... 172 D8
Norton in H CW3......... 82 A7
Tamworth B77 .... 251 A5
Woodhouse Mid Sch ST8. 16 E2
Woodhouse Rd N WV6 .. 255 B4
Woodhouse Rd WV6 .... 255 B4
Woodhouses La WS7.... 229 F6
Woodhouses Rd WS7 ... 230 A7
Woodhouse St ST4....... 72 B6
Woodhurst Cl B77 ...... 250 F5
Woodingdean Cl 3 ST3 .. 73 D5
Woodkirk Cl ST6......... 42 A8
Wood La Aldridge B74..... 256 E2
Cannock WS12.......... 210 C4
Cheslyn Hay WS11....... 225 F6
Gratwich ST14.......... 124 D2
Hanbury DE13 .... 144 F3
Maer ST5................ 84 D3
Woodland Ave
Cheddleton ST13 .... 45 B1
Hagley DY8 .... 281 F5
Newcastle-u-L ST5........ 56 C5
Stoke-on-T ST6 .... 42 F4
Wolverhampton WV6..... 255 B3
Woodland Cl
Albrighton WV7 .... 237 A6
Cannock WS12.......... 210 B8
Leek ST13 .... 30 F2
Woodland Cres WV3 .... 265 D7
Woodland Ct
Cannock WS12.......... 209 C4
Shenstone WS14......... 258 A7
Woodland Dr
Cheslyn Hay WS6........ 226 E4
Foston DE65 .... 129 D4
Rocester ST14 .... 95 F3
Woodland Gr Dudley DY3. 271 B3
Kidderminster DY10 ..... 280 C3
Stoke-on-T ST6 .... 42 B2
Woodland Hills CW3 ..... 68 E8
Woodland Rd
Stanton DE15........... 186 B4
Tamworth B77 .... 251 A4
Wolverhampton WV3..... 265 D7
Woodlands Ave
Kidsgrove ST7 .... 25 D1
Stone ST15 .... 119 F8
Woodlands Cl
Stafford ST16 .... 155 C7
Stone ST15 .... 119 E8
Thorpe DE6 .... 51 D1
Woodlands Com Prim Sch The B77 .... 250 E4
Woodlands Cotts WV4 .. 265 F4
Woodlands Cres WS3 ... 243 F5
Woodlands Dr
Chorlton CW2 .... 37 C3
Coven WV9 .... 224 B3
Stone ST15 .... 120 C3
Woodlands Gr ST3....... 90 A4
Woodlands La
Cheslyn Hay WS11....... 225 B8
Forsbrook ST11.......... 91 B6
Woodlands Paddock
WV4.................... 265 E4
Woodlands Rd
Cookley DY10........... 280 A4
Stafford ST16 .... 155 B7
Stoke-on-T ST4 .... 71 E4
Wombourne WV5........ 270 A5
Woodlands Rise DE6.... 144 A7
Woodland St ST8 .... 27 D6
Woodlands The
Coldmeece ST15 .... 118 C6
Kidsgrove ST7 .... 25 E3
Lichfield WS13.......... 231 D8
Stoke-on-T ST4 .... 71 E4
Tatenhill DE13 .... 184 A8
Wood End CV9.......... 262 C1
Woodland St ST6 .... 41 E3
Woodlands Way WS15 .. 198 C4
Woodland View DE12 ... 219 F3
Woodland Views ST14... 127 E2
Woodland View DY3 .... 269 C4
Woodland Way
Burntwood WS7......... 229 A6
Polesworth B78.......... 262 F8
Wood Lane Prim Sch ST7 40 A1
Wood La Shenstone WS14. 246 B2
Stone ST15 .... 119 F5
Stretton ST19 .... 206 C4
Swadlincote DE11 .... 186 F7
Uttoxeter ST14 .... 126 E6
Walsall WS3 .... 243 F4
Wedges Mills WS11...... 226 A6
Woodlawn Gr DY6 ...... 275 D5
Wood La
Wolverhampton WV10.... 240 D2
Yoxall DE13 .... 182 A6
Woodleighton Gr ST14 .. 126 C6
Woodleighton Rd ST14 .. 126 C6
Woodleyes Cres ST17 ... 175 D6
Woodman Gr 5 B75 .... 258 E3
Woodman La WS6 .... 226 E4
Woodman St ST2 .... 43 B1
Woodmill La WS15 ...... 161 B7
Woodpark La ST3........ 89 D7

Woodpecker Dr
Packmoor ST7 . . . . 26 E1
Stoke-on-T ST7 . . . . 41 E8
Woodpecker View TF9 . . . 99 C3
Woodpecker Way WS11 . 210 C3
Wood Pl ST3 . . . . 74 B2
Wood Rd Codsall WV8 . . . . 238 E4
Dudley DY3 . . . . 271 C4
Longsdon ST9 . . . . 45 A8
Wolverhampton WV6 . . . . 255 C3
Wombourne WV5 . . . . . . 270 B7
Woodridge Cl TF10 . . . . . 168 A4
Wood Ridings WS13 . . . . 214 A1
Woodroffe's Cliff ST14 . 143 C5
Woodrow Way
Ashley TF9 . . . . 100 C5
Newcastle-u-L ST5 . . . . . . 40 F1
Woodruff Cl ST7 . . . . 27 A1
Woods Croft WS13 . . . . . 214 A1
Woodseat Gr ST14 . . . . . 96 A4
Woodseaves CE Prim Sch
  ST20 . . . . 151 E7
Woodsetton Sch The
  DY3 . . . . 271 F7
Woodshot Ave WS15 . . . 198 C4
Woodshutt's St ST7 . . . . 25 E1
Woodside Ave
Brown Edge ST6 . . . . 43 B6
Kidsgrove ST7 . . . . 26 A1
Woodside ST5 . . . . 85 C3
Woodside Cl
Colwich ST18 . . . . 177 D8
Wood End CV9 . . . . 262 C1
Woodside Cotts ST10 . . . 77 F7
Woodside Cres ST5 . . . . . 71 C2
Woodside Dr
Little Aston B74 . . . . 257 C5
Meir Heath ST3 . . . . 90 A4
Woodside Gr WV8 . . . . . . 239 B2
Woodside La ST13 . . . . . . 30 C2
Woodside Lawton-gate ST7 25 E4
Madeley CW3 . . . . 68 E7
Woodside Pl
Cannock WS11 . . . . 209 E5
Stoke-on-T ST2 . . . . 43 B1
Woodside B74 . . . . 257 E2
Woodside Villas ST3 . . . 284 D4
Woodside Way WS9 . . . . 256 B5
Woods La
Burton u T DE15 . . . . 167 A1
Burton u T DE15 . . . . 167 B1
Woodsorrel Rd DY1 . . . . 271 F4
Wood St Audley ST7 . . . . . 39 E3
Burton u T DE14 . . . . 166 C1
Woodstile Cl B75 . . . . . . 258 D3
Wood St Leek ST13 . . . . . 30 F5
Longton ST3 . . . . 284 C4
Mow Cop ST7 . . . . 26 D7
Woodstock Cl
Newcastle-u-L ST5 . . . . . . 56 C3
Stourbridge DY8 . . . . 275 C1
Woodstock Dr
Huntington WS12 . . . . . . 209 C7
Stourbridge DY8 . . . . 275 C2
Sutton Coldfield B74 . . . . 257 D4
Woodstock Rd
Kidsgrove ST6 . . . . 41 A7
Stafford ST17 . . . . 156 D1
Woodstock St ST6 . . . . . 41 C8

Woodstone Ave ST9 . . . . . 43 E6
Wood St Stourbridge DY8 . 279 D6
  Wood End CV9 . . . . 262 C1
Wood Terr ST1 . . . . 282 A1
Wood The ST3 . . . . 74 C2
Woodtherne Cl ST19 . . . 207 F7
Woodthorne Cl
Dudley DY1 . . . . 271 D2
Rugeley WS15 . . . . 178 C2
Woodthorne Prim Sch
  WV6 . . . . 255 B4
Woodthorne Rd S WV6 . . 255 A5
Woodthorne Rd WV6 . . . 255 A6
Woodthorne Wlk DY6 . . 275 E8
Woodvale Cres ST9 . . . . . 43 E8
Wood View ST7 . . . . 40 A1
Woodview Rd DE11 . . . . 186 E5
Wood View WS15 . . . . . . 196 F6
Woodville Gdns DY3 . . . 266 F1
Woodville Pl ST3 . . . . 74 A2
Woodville Rd ST3 . . . . . . 74 A2
Woodville Terr ST3 . . . . . 74 B2
Woodward St ST1 . . . . . . 57 D6
Woodyard Dr B79 . . . . . . 217 C5
Woodyard La DE65 . . . . . 129 F5
Woody Bank WS6 . . . . . . 226 E2
Woolliscroft Ave ST5 . . . 56 D3
Woolliscroft Rd ST2 . . . . 58 B3
Woolrich St ST6 . . . . 56 E7
Woolridge Ct ST6 . . . . . . 42 D1
Woolston Ave CW12 . . . . . 6 A2
Woosnam Cl DE14 . . . . . 185 A6
Wootton Cl WS11 . . . . . 210 B3
Wootton Dr ST16 . . . . . . 155 A7
Wootton La
Eccleshall ST21 . . . . 133 E3
Oakamoor ST10 . . . . 78 E4
Wootton Rd WV3 . . . . . . 265 D8
Woottons St WS11 . . . . . 209 F1
Worcester Cl
Cannock WS11 . . . . 226 F8
Lichfield WS13 . . . . 214 C3
Rugeley WS15 . . . . 196 C6
Sutton Coldfield B75 . . . . 258 D3
Talke ST7 . . . . 40 D7
Worcester Ct WV3 . . . . . 266 A6
Worcester Gr WV6 . . . . . 254 C4
Worcester La B75 . . . . . . 258 D4
Worcester Pl ST2 . . . . . . 58 D2
Worcester Rd
Burton u T DE15 . . . . 185 E6
Hagley DY9 . . . . 281 F3
Whittington WS14 . . . . . . 232 C3
Wordsley Ct DY8 . . . . . . 275 E3
Wordsley Green Sh Ctr
  DY8 . . . . 275 D2
Wordsley Hospl DY8 . . . . 275 E3
Wordsley Sch The DY8 . . 275 F3
Wordsworth Ave
Stafford ST17 . . . . 174 C8
Tamworth B79 . . . . 250 A6
Wolverhampton WV4 . . . . 266 F4
Wordsworth Cl
Armitage WS15 . . . . 198 A4
Burton u T DE14 . . . . 166 D6
Cannock WS11 . . . . 209 D4
Cheadle ST10 . . . . 76 C2
Lichfield WS14 . . . . 231 B5
Wordsworth Ct WV6 . . . 254 E4
Wordsworth Dr TF9 . . . . 112 A7
Wordsworth Rd

Burntwood WS7 . . . . 229 A8
Dudley DY3 . . . . 271 B5
Worfield Gdns WV3 . . . . 265 F6
Worsley Dr CW12 . . . . 6 B1
Worston La ST15,ST18 . . 135 B5
Worth Cl ST3 . . . . 73 D4
Worthing Pl ST3 . . . . . . 284 B3
Worthington Rd WS13 . . 215 D6
Worthington Way DE14 . 166 D3
Wragby Cl WV9 . . . . 240 B3
Wraggs La ST8 . . . . 17 B1
Wrekin Ave TF10 . . . . . . 168 E2
Wrekin Ct B74 . . . . 257 F2
Wrekin Dr
Wolverhampton,Penn
  WV3 . . . . 265 E8
Wolverhampton,Tettenhall
  WV6 . . . . 255 A5
Wrekin Gr WV11 . . . . . . 242 B1
Wrekin La WV6 . . . . 255 A5
Wrekin View
Brownhills WS8 . . . . 245 A5
Huntington WS12 . . . . . . 209 C7
Wrekin View Rd DY3 . . . 271 C8
Wren Ave WV6 . . . . 254 D3
Wrenburry Cl ST5 . . . . . . 40 D1
Wrenbury Cres ST2 . . . . . 58 B1
Wren Cl ST8 . . . . 27 E8
Wrens Croft WS11 . . . . . 210 B1
Wrenswood ST17 . . . . . . 175 C6
Wren View
Loggerheads TF9 . . . . 99 C4
Longton ST3 . . . . 284 D2
Wrexham Cl ST8 . . . . 16 D1
Wright Ave ST5 . . . . 55 F7
Wrighton Cl ST2 . . . . 57 F2
Wrighton Dr DY5 . . . . . . 271 C1
Wrighton Gr B78 . . . . . . 261 A8
Wright's Ave WS11 . . . . . 209 F5
Wright St Kidsgrove ST7 . 25 D1
  Stafford ST16 . . . . 155 E5
Wrinehill Rd CW5 . . . . . . 52 A6
Wrottesley Ct WV8 . . . . 254 C8
Wrottesley Park Rd WV6,
  WV8 . . . . 254 D5
Wrottesley Rd WV6 . . . . 255 B5
Wrottesley Rd W
Perton WV6 . . . . 254 F6
Wolverhampton WV6 . . . . 255 A6
Wroxham Way ST5 . . . . . 71 B2
Wulfad Ct ST15 . . . . 120 C7
Wulfric Cl ST19 . . . . 208 A8
Wulfruna Gdns WV3 . . . 255 F1
Wulstan Dr ST5 . . . . 56 C3
Wulstan Rd ST6 . . . . 57 A6
Wyatt St ST6 . . . . 41 C7
Wychall Dr WV10 . . . . . . 240 E4
Wychbold Cl WV12 . . . . 242 D1
Wychbold Way WV12 . . 242 D1
Wychbury Rd WV3 . . . . . 265 C7
Wych Elm Rd WS8 . . . . . 244 E5
Wycherwood Gdns ST17 175 D5
Wychwood Pk
Chorlton CW2 . . . . 37 B2
Gorstyhill CW2 . . . . 37 E2
Wycliffe Rd ST6 . . . . 56 F8
Wye Cl Cheadle ST10 . . . . 76 E1
  Hilton DE65 . . . . 147 D8
  Perton WV6 . . . . 254 F4
Wye Dale DE11 . . . . 186 F2
Wye Ho DY3 . . . . 271 D3
Wye Rd Newcastle-u-L ST5 . 71 A3

Walsall WS3 . . . . 243 E1
Wyggeston St DE13 . . . . 166 C6
Wykeham Gr WV6 . . . . . 254 D3
Wyllie Mews DE14 . . . . . 166 D3
Wymondley Gr ST4 . . . . . 88 B6
Wynbank Cl ST7 . . . . 54 E8
Wynchcombe Ave WV4 . 265 D4
Wyndham Cres DE15 . . . 167 C3
Wyndham Rd ST3 . . . . . . 88 F7
Wyndham Wood Cl
  WS13 . . . . 215 D7
Wyndley Cl B74 . . . . 257 F6
Wyndley Manor B74 . . . 258 A6
Wynd The DY3 . . . . 266 D1
Wynford Pl ST2 . . . . 58 B1
Wynne Cres WV4 . . . . . . 265 C3
Wynn Rd WV4 . . . . 265 F5
Wynstay Ave ST9 . . . . . . 59 A3
Wynstay Ct ST5 . . . . 71 C1
Wynyates B79 . . . . 249 E6
Wyre Cl WS9 . . . . 244 F4
Wyre Rd DY8 . . . . 279 E7
Wyrley Brook Pk WS11 . 226 D5
Wyrley Brook Ret Pk
  WS11 . . . . 226 D6
Wyrley Cl Burntwood WS8 228 F3
  Lichfield WS14 . . . . 231 A5
Wyrley La WS3 . . . . 243 E8
Wyrley Rd B75 . . . . 258 D1
Wyvern Gr WS12 . . . . . . 210 A5
Wyvern B77 . . . . 250 F3
Wyvis Cl WV6 . . . . 255 D6

Y

Yale St ST6 . . . . 56 E7
Yardley Pl ST3 . . . . 88 F6
Yardley St ST6 . . . . 42 F5
Yardley Wlk ST3 . . . . 88 F6
Yarlet Croft ST16 . . . . . 155 D6
Yarlet La ST18 . . . . 136 D5
Yarlet Sch ST18 . . . . 136 C3
Yarmouth Wlk ST3 . . . . 284 D5
Yarnbrook Gr ST6 . . . . . . 42 D3
Yarner Cl DY1 . . . . 271 E2
Yarnfield Cl ST3 . . . . 74 A2
Yarnfield La ST15 . . . . . 119 B8
Yarrow Cl
Burton u T DE15 . . . . 167 D8
Walsall WS3 . . . . 244 A5
Yateley Cl ST2 . . . . 58 B2
Yates Croft B74 . . . . 257 F6
Yates Ind Est WS3 . . . . . 227 F2
Yates St ST1 . . . . 282 A2
Yaxley Ct ST5 . . . . 71 B2
Yaxley Pl ST3 . . . . 88 F6
Yeadon Gdns WV3 . . . . 265 D8
Yeager Ct ST11 . . . . 118 F6
Yeaman St ST4 . . . . 72 B6
Yeatsall Rd WS15 . . . . . 160 E5
Yeldham Pl ST3 . . . . 88 F6
Yelt La DE6 . . . . 127 D8
Yelverton Ave ST17 . . . . 175 D8
Yelverton Cl WS3 . . . . . . 243 B4
Yemscroft WS6 . . . . 243 A8
Yenton Cl B78 . . . . 250 A1
Yeoman Ind Est DE14 . . 166 E5
Yeoman Way WS15 . . . . 198 A4
Yeovil Pl ST3 . . . . 88 F6
Yeovilton B79 . . . . 250 C8
Yerley Hill DE6 . . . . 66 C5

Yew Cl WS15 . . . . 198 B4
Yew Pl ST5 . . . . 55 D8
Yew Tree Ave
Lichfield WS14 . . . . 231 E8
Stoke-on-T ST3 . . . . 72 E2
Yew Tree Cl
Derrington ST18 . . . . 154 E2
Norton Canes WS11 . . . . 228 A5
Stoke-on-T ST2 . . . . 43 D1
Yewtree Cres DE15 . . . . 185 F7
Yew Tree Ct ST17 . . . . . 174 E4
Yew Tree Dr ST19 . . . . . 205 C6
Yew Tree Gdns WV8 . . . 239 A4
Yew Tree La Astbury CW12 15 C3
Bridgemere CW5 . . . . 67 A6
Wolverhampton WV6 . . . . 255 A5
Yew Tree Pl WS3 . . . . . . 243 D3
Yew Tree Rd
Pattingham WV6 . . . . 253 D2
Rugeley WS15 . . . . 196 F6
Yewtree Rd DE11 . . . . . . 186 F7
Yew Tree Rd WS4 . . . . . . 244 B1
Yew Tree Terr ST7 . . . . . 41 A8
York Ave Fulford ST11 . . . . 90 E1
Wolverhampton WV3 . . . . 255 E1
York Cl Biddulph ST8 . . . . 16 C2
Forsbrook ST11 . . . . 91 B8
Lichfield WS13 . . . . 214 C3
Rugeley WS15 . . . . 196 D6
Talke ST7 . . . . 40 D7
York Cres
Stourbridge DY8 . . . . 279 D7
Wolverhampton WV3 . . . . 255 E1
Yorkdale Cl DY3 . . . . 271 D3
York Gdns WV3 . . . . 255 E1
York Pl ST5 . . . . 283 B3
York Rd Cannock WS11 . . 226 F7
  Meir ST3 . . . . 74 B3
  Stafford ST17 . . . . 175 B8
  Wolverhampton WV3 . . . . 265 B8
Yorksand Rd B78 . . . . . . 260 F4
Yorkshire Way WS7 . . . . 229 F8
York St Burton u T DE14 . 166 C4
  Hanley ST1 . . . . 282 B3
  Leek ST13 . . . . 30 F6
  Newcastle-u-L ST5 . . . . . 283 D3
  Stone ST15 . . . . 105 A2
Youlgreave Ave ST2 . . . . 58 B2
Youlton Pl ST2 . . . . 58 B2
Young Ave ST16 . . . . 155 C6
Younger St ST4 . . . . 72 D6
Young St Cheadle ST10 . . 76 B3
  Stoke-on-T ST6 . . . . 41 F6
Yoxall Ave ST4 . . . . 71 F8
Yoxall Rd
King's Bromley DE13 . . . . 199 D7
Newborough DE13 . . . . . 162 E7

Z

Zamenhof Gr ST6 . . . . . . 42 C1
Zennor Gr ST2 . . . . 58 B2
Zetland Pl ST3 . . . . 88 F6
Zetland Wlk ST3 . . . . 88 F6
Zion Cl WS6 . . . . 226 D3
Zion St ST6 . . . . 57 A8
Zoar St DY3 . . . . 271 C3
Zodiac Dr ST6 . . . . 41 E6
Zouche Cl DY8 . . . . 279 E8